2

Better Homes & Gardens

*SEPTEMBER 1946*

# Better Homes & Gardens

*100th Anniversary*

Hot, fragrant, and fresh-baked!

# then — & — now

## A LOOK BACK—AND FORWARD—AT THE TRENDS THAT INFLUENCE OUR COOKING.

**STAYING POWER**
Orange Bowknots, a prizewinning recipe from 1946, have appeared in every edition of our famous *New Cook Book* since.
▼

**BETTER HOMES & GARDENS**
Cook Book

*Every Recipe Tested in Better Homes & Gardens' Testing-Test Kitchen*

▲
**THE RED PLAID**
What began as a 10-cent, 56-page recipe pamphlet has become the go-to cookbook for nearly 40 million home cooks.

Let's make it a
*Casserole supper*

Better Homes & Gardens® magazine is celebrating 100 years! It's not surprising that among the gems in our archives, we unearthed recipes we're happy to leave in the past (so long, hot dog crown roasts). But we also found plenty of familiar ones we'd like to keep. Enjoy this collection of classics we refreshed to fit seamlessly with the ways we are cooking today.

# celebrating our Test Kitchen

Since its inception in 1928 as a "Testing-Tasting Kitchen," the Better Homes & Gardens Test Kitchen has guided home cooks through ever-changing cooking trends.

## 1920s
### IN THE BEGINNING
The Test Kitchen (TK) launched late in the Roaring '20s and was a tiny, bare-bones work space. At that time, electricity was brand-new, so woodstoves were still used for cooking in many kitchens. Testers and tasters developed layered salads that used a new ingredient: colorful gelatin in many flavors. They also offered the fun of a cake recipe contest, which was iced with whorls of reader enthusiasm.

## 1930s
### HELLO, MIXER
The Great Depression of the 1930s also brought innovation to readers' homes. At the same time as shiny, "work saving" washing machines agitated into homes to lighten laundry baskets, our Test Kitchen experts tested another helpful invention: the kitchen mixer. As readers were just starting to purchase this marvelous new tool, TK staff had already created and critiqued recipes like ethereal meringues and chewy peanut butter cookies.

## 1940s
### POSTWAR TIMES
The 1940s brought us chocolate chips and kitchen upgrades. With postwar vigor, modern refrigerators replaced drippy iceboxes. Kitchens grew to make room for big cooking events, such as food preservation days. Home cooks laden with Victory Garden harvests turned to the Test Kitchen for recipes and inspiration. When ration cards limited many ingredients, the TK tested Chiffon Cake, a treat that required less sugar and used oil instead of butter.

## 1950s
### THE BACKYARD BBQ
The decade saw a return to peace and prosperity, and the overall exuberance of the times made its way onto the family table and into the backyard. "Dad's the chef. Sis and brother kibitz, pitch in on tasks their size, and have the time of their lives. No kitchen chores for Mom." That's how editors described barbecuing in 1956. The Test Kitchen developed hundreds of outdoor-cooking recipes through the '50s to help fire up readers' enthusiasm for backyard grilling.

# 1960s

## FUN AT HOME

Forty years before smoothies arrived on the scene, the 1960s showcased turquoise blenders twirling margaritas and malts in paisley, neon kitchens. Cooks shopped for groceries in markets with ample frozen-food space. Casual home entertaining became fashionable, with the Test Kitchen's Swiss Fondue recipe sparking the trend. Words like tempura, Kiev, and cacciatore made their way onto our pages reflecting a newfound love for foods from around the world.

# 1970s

## QUICK & EASY

This decade ushered in earthy kitchen decor—think harvest gold and avocado green. As home food processors debuted, Test Kitchen staffers designed dishes that made the most of the chop-saving device. Brunch, too, had its moment, spurring TK recipes for quiche and crepes. Moms joining the workforce at an accelerated rate, plus a recession, drove the need for quick weeknight and budget-friendly recipes. That birthed another revolutionary kitchen helper: the slow cooker.

# 1980s

## NUTRITION MATTERS

The migration of women from home to careers framed the '80s. As working women themselves, TK staffers educated cooks newly interested in Cajun and Tex-Mex foods as well as "skinny" recipes. Each recipe now included a nutritional analysis as a guide to healthful meals. When the economy stumbled, the TK revamped comfort food favorites, such as pot roast and mashed potatoes.

# 1990s

## CHEF-INSPIRED

Fabulous food was the hallmark of this decade as celebrity chefs inspired and entertained us. Thanks to the internet, lesser-known ingredients (including preserved lemons and red lentils) and kitchen gadgets (such as cherry pitters and pineapple peelers) were easily available. Food became fashionable, and families submitted their "Century's Best Recipe" to the TK in hopes of winning the $10,000 prize.

# 2000s

## GO FRESH

With the new millennium came a redesign of the Test Kitchen that made it more efficient and modern. "Fresh" was the culinary buzzword, which the TK underscored by developing produce-first recipes made from ingredients found at local farmers markets or grown in home gardens. Keeping in step with the latest tech trends, the TK staff coached cooks on how to use newly available small appliances, such as air fryers and multicookers.

# TODAY

## IN OUR KITCHEN

The Test Kitchen team is made up of home cooks with food science and nutrition degrees or culinary arts diplomas. We're well-equipped and eager to navigate the next big-tech appliances and explore new and exciting flavors.

## BY THE NUMBERS

### 13,889
BHG RECIPES IN THE PRINT ARCHIVES

### $157k
SPENT BY TK ON GROCERIES IN 2021

### 13
THOUSAND RECIPES IN THE TEST KITCHEN DATABASE

### 10
KITCHENS FOR TESTING + 8 KITCHENS FOR PHOTOGRAPHY

### 375
FOOD VIDEOS FILMED IN 2021

### 2,285
FOOD PHOTOS TAKEN IN 2021

## 1938
### YEAST ROLLS

Homemade yeast rolls were, well, HOT! Editors in the '30s referred to yeast rolls as "hot breads" since they were served piping hot. Our editors wrote, "It's high fashion to serve hot breads. They're easy, too."

## 1943
### BREAD SHORTAGE

When WWII caused low bread inventory, we enticed readers to bring back baking days for "those homey whiffs of big brown loaves, the crunch of a knife thru tender golden crust, those whoops from the family over *real homemade bread.*"

### PRIZEWINNING YEAST ROLLS

In exchange for a 3-cent stamp, readers were sent a booklet of rollmaking tips and the latest in-fashion hot bread recipes.

## THEN:
# bread on the rise

Take a spin through our wheel of time to see how bread baking has looked on our pages through the past century.

## 1970s
### HOBBY BAKING

Spurred by a back-to-basics mindset, home cooks were into baking with natural ingredients, but their skills were rusty. Their biggest fear? Killing the yeast. This 1976 tip still stands: Try the baby bottle test. A drop or two of liquid on the wrist should feel neither hot nor cold but lukewarm.

## 2018
### SOURDOUGH

We were ahead of our time when we included a deep dive on sourdough in the 17th edition of our cookbook—two years before the pandemic-fueled craze—and it's still trending.

### GOING GLUTEN-FREE

Making a light-textured GF sandwich loaf is harder than you might think, but our Test Kitchen created a never-fail loaf based on our own Gluten-Free Flour Mix. It's still our go-to for GF baking—period. Find the recipe on *page 472.*

## 1993
### BREAD MACHINES

Our bread baking shifted into automated territory when this revolutionary appliance topped the wish lists of newlyweds in the 1990s. In five years our Test Kitchen turned out more than 500 recipes.

# BREAD WORTH SHARING

OUR UPDATED PULL-APART EMBRACES TWO TOPICS AS POPULAR IN THE '50S AS THEY ARE TODAY—BREAD BAKING AND ENTERTAINING. LET THE GATHERING BEGIN.

## CARAMEL-PUMPKIN SNICKERDOODLE MONKEY BREAD

**HANDS ON** 30 minutes  **RISE** 1 hour 30 minutes  **BAKE** 40 minutes at 350°F
**COOL** 30 minutes

| | |
|---|---|
| ¾ | cup milk |
| 1 | pkg. active dry yeast |
| ¾ | cup canned pumpkin |
| ¼ | cup butter, melted |
| ¼ | cup granulated sugar |
| 1 | egg |
| 1 | tsp. salt |
| 4¼ to 4¾ | cups all-purpose flour |
| 1 | recipe Caramel Syrup |
| 1 | cup chopped toasted pecans |
| ¾ | cup granulated sugar |
| 1 | Tbsp. pumpkin pie spice or ground cinnamon |
| ¼ | cup butter, melted |

**1.** In a small saucepan heat milk just until warm (105°F to 115°F). In a large bowl stir together milk and yeast. Let stand about 5 minutes or until foamy.
**2.** Add the next five ingredients (through salt) to yeast mixture. Beat with a mixer on medium until combined. Add 2 cups of the flour; beat on low 30 seconds, scraping bowl constantly. Beat on medium 3 minutes. Stir in as much of the remaining flour as you can.
**3.** Turn dough out onto a lightly floured surface. Knead in enough of the remaining flour to make a soft dough that is smooth and elastic (3 minutes). Shape dough into a ball. Place in a lightly greased bowl, turning to grease surface of dough. Cover; let rise in a warm place until nearly double (45 to 60 minutes).
**4.** Grease and flour a 10-inch nonstick fluted tube pan or angel food cake pan. Prepare Caramel Syrup. Sprinkle ½ cup of the pecans into bottom of prepared pan. Drizzle ½ cup of the Caramel Syrup over pecans. In a small bowl combine the ¾ cup granulated sugar and the pumpkin pie spice. Place the ¼ cup melted butter in another small bowl.
**5.** Turn dough out onto a lightly floured surface. Divide dough into 32 pieces. Roll pieces into balls. Dip balls in melted butter, then roll in sugar mixture to coat. Arrange 16 of the balls over the Caramel Syrup in pan. Sprinkle with the remaining ½ cup pecans; drizzle the remaining ½ cup Caramel Syrup over top. Add remaining coated balls. Cover; let rise in a warm place until nearly double (about 45 minutes).
**6.** Preheat oven to 350°F. Bake 40 to 45 minutes or until golden brown. If needed to prevent overbrowning, cover bread loosely with foil the last 10 minutes. Cool in pan 10 minutes. Invert onto a large serving platter and remove pan. Cool 20 minutes. **Makes 12 servings (about 2½ pieces each).**
**CARAMEL SYRUP** In a medium bowl stir together ¾ cup packed brown sugar, ½ cup melted butter, and ¼ cup light-color corn syrup.
**PER SERVING** *296 cal., 8 g fat (4 g sat. fat), 32 mg chol., 254 mg sodium, 53 g carb., 2 g fiber, 27 g sugars, 5 g pro.*

## THEN:
### WHAT'S IN A NAME?

Monkey bread, pull-apart rolls, jumble bread, or bubble bread—this popular brunch staple has been called many things through the years. In March 1956 we published a shortcut version of the tear-and-share ring using tube biscuits in place of from-scratch dough.

## NOW:
### FALL FLAVORS

The longevity of the PSL (pumpkin spice latte) is a testament to the love for all things pumpkin. With the arrival of fall each year, our readers can't seem to get enough of its hallmark flavors, so we baked them all into this decadent treat. It's worth every minute of prep.

# SO-SOFT MILK BREAD

AFTER OUR LOVE AFFAIR WITH SOURDOUGH BREAD BAKING, WE'RE CRUSHING ON MILK BREAD.
THIS SIMPLE TECHNIQUE CREATES FEATHER-LIGHT BREAD AND ROLLS.

## HONEY MILK BREAD ROLLS

**HANDS ON** 30 minutes   **RISE** 1 hour 45 minutes   **BAKE** 25 minutes at 350°F

⅓   cup plus 1 Tbsp. water
1⅓  cups milk
5¼  cups bread flour
2   pkg. active dry yeast
½   cup honey
¼   cup sugar
½   cup butter, cut up
2   tsp. salt
3   eggs
¼   cup regular rolled oats
¼   cup butter, softened

**1.** In a small saucepan whisk together ⅓ cup of the water, ⅓ cup of the milk, and ¼ cup of the flour. Cook and stir over medium heat until a paste-like consistency. Remove from heat and cool 30 minutes.
**2.** Meanwhile, in a large bowl stir together 2½ cups of the flour and the yeast. In a 2-qt. saucepan combine the remaining 1 cup milk, ¼ cup of the honey, the sugar, cut-up butter, and salt. Cook and stir over medium just until warm (120°F to 130°F) and butter almost melts. Stir milk mixture, cooled paste mixture, and two of the eggs into flour mixture. Stir in as much of the remaining flour as you can.
**3.** Turn dough onto a lightly floured surface. Knead in enough remaining flour to make a dough that is smooth, elastic, and slightly tacky (3 to 5 minutes). Place in a lightly greased bowl, turning to grease surface of dough. Cover; let rise in a warm place until nearly double (1 hour).
**4.** Punch dough down. Let rest 10 minutes. Grease a 13×9-inch baking pan. Shape dough into 20 balls. Arrange balls in prepared pan. Cover lightly with greased plastic wrap and let rise in a warm place until nearly double in size (45 minutes).
**5.** Preheat oven to 350°F. In a small bowl whisk together remaining egg and 1 Tbsp. water. Brush rolls with egg mixture. Sprinkle with oats. Bake about 25 minutes or until golden. Let cool slightly. In a small bowl whisk together remaining ¼ cup honey and the softened butter. Serve rolls warm with honey butter. **Makes 20 rolls.**

**PER ROLL** *253 cal., 9 g fat (5 g sat. fat), 48 mg chol., 307 mg sodium, 38 g carb., 1 g fiber, 10 g sugars, 6 g pro.*

## NOW: ON-THE-RISE MILK BREAD

Japanese milk bread starts with a cooked flour paste (water and milk heated with a small amount of flour) called a tangzhong. Breads made with tangzhong have greater oven spring (the rise that occurs when dough is put in a hot oven), making a light and tender texture. They also stay fresh longer.

# EATING WITH OUR EYES

BEAUTIFUL PHOTOS ARE PART OF BHG'S HISTORY AND ARE MORE IMPORTANT TODAY SO HOME COOKS CAN USE THEM TO SELECT RECIPES—AND SHARE ON SOCIAL MEDIA.

## APRICOT CORNMEAL LOAF WITH HATCH CHILES

**HANDS ON** 45 minutes   **BAKE** 1 hour 5 minutes at 350°F   **COOL** 20 minutes

| | |
|---|---|
| 3 | large hatch or Anaheim peppers (about 12 oz. total) |
| 2 | cups all-purpose flour |
| 1 | cup yellow cornmeal |
| ⅔ | cup sugar |
| 1½ | tsp. baking powder |
| ¾ | tsp. salt |
| 1¼ | cups buttermilk |
| ½ | cup butter, melted |
| ⅓ | cup apricot preserves |
| 2 | eggs |

**1.** Preheat broiler. Arrange peppers on a foil-lined baking sheet. Broil 4 to 6 inches from heat about 10 minutes or until charred all over, turning occasionally. Bring foil up around peppers; fold to enclose. Let stand 15 minutes. Wearing gloves, scrape off and discard skins. Cut a small slit on one side of each pepper, keeping pepper intact. Gently scoop out seeds and remove stems.
**2.** Preheat oven to 350°F. Grease a 9×5-inch loaf pan. Chop two of the peppers and cut the remaining pepper in half lengthwise.
**3.** In a large bowl combine the next five ingredients (through salt). In a medium bowl whisk together buttermilk, butter, apricot preserves, eggs, and chopped peppers. Add to flour mixture; stir just until combined. Spoon batter into pan. Arrange pepper halves over batter.
**4.** Bake 65 to 70 minutes or until top is golden brown and a toothpick comes out clean (a thermometer will register 205°F). Cool in pan on a wire rack 20 minutes. Loosen sides with a knife. Remove from pan; cool completely on wire rack.
**5.** Wrap and store overnight before slicing. Serve with *softened butter* and additional apricot preserves.
**Makes 16 servings (1 slice each).**
**PER SERVING** *211 cal., 7 g fat (4 g sat. fat), 39 mg chol., 244 mg sodium, 33 g carb., 1 g fiber, 12 g sugars, 4 g pro.*

## THEN:
### 1933 CORN MUFFINS

This staple "hot bread" debuted in one of our earliest editions of the *New Cook Book*. Calling for pastry flour and just a touch of sugar, the basic muffins were mildly sweet with a fine crumb.

## NOW:
### CORN BREAD PLUS

In contrast to the 1933 muffins, this corn bread is anything but basic. Buttermilk and apricot preserves give the loaf a sweet, tangy flavor. Broiled Hatch chile peppers (in season August and September) baked on top make a statement. Out of season, use Anaheims or poblanos.

# FRENCH TOAST GROWS UP

SAVORY DESSERTS POPPING UP ON RESTAURANT MENUS SPARKED THE IDEA
FOR THIS NEW TWIST. THINK FRENCH TOAST MEETS STRATA.

## SAUSAGE AND ASPARAGUS FRENCH TOAST BAKE

**HANDS ON** 25 minutes  **CHILL** 2 hours  **BAKE** 50 minutes at 375°F
**STAND** 10 minutes

| | |
|---|---|
| 12 | oz. Texas toast, cut into 1-inch strips (about 10 slices) |
| 8 | oz. bulk pork sausage |
| 8 | oz. mixed fresh mushrooms, such as cremini, oyster, and/or button, sliced |
| 2 | Tbsp. butter |
| 2 | cloves garlic, minced |
| 1 | tsp. caraway seeds, crushed |
| 8 | oz. fresh asparagus, trimmed and cut into 1-inch pieces |
| ½ | of a 15-oz. carton whole milk ricotta cheese |
| 1 | cup shredded Swiss cheese (4 oz.) |
| ¼ | cup chopped fresh herbs, such as flat-leaf parsley, chives, dill, and/or basil |
| ¾ | tsp. salt |
| ½ | tsp. black pepper |
| 4 | eggs |
| 1¾ | cups milk |

**1.** Grease a 2- to 2½-qt. baking dish. Arrange half of the bread strips in bottom of dish, overlapping as needed. For filling, in a 10-inch skillet cook the next five ingredients (through caraway seeds) over medium-high 8 to 10 minutes or until meat and mushrooms are browned. Drain off fat. Stir in asparagus. Spoon evenly over bread in dish. In a medium bowl stir together next five ingredients (through pepper). Spoon over filling. Arrange the remaining bread strips on top.

**2.** In a large bowl whisk together eggs, milk, and an additional ½ tsp. salt and ¼ tsp. pepper. Pour egg mixture over bread, pressing bread down lightly to moisten. Cover; chill 2 to 24 hours.

**3.** Preheat oven to 375°F. Bake, uncovered, 50 to 60 minutes or until center is set (180°F). Let stand 10 minutes before serving. If desired, top with additional herbs. **Makes 8 servings (1 cup each).**

**PER SERVING** 371 cal., 20 g fat (9 g sat. fat), 149 mg chol., 730 mg sodium, 28 g carb., 1 g fiber, 6 g sugars, 20 g pro.

## THEN: SWEET, SAVORY & FANCY

It's not the first time we nudged French toast in a savory direction. In 1949 bread slices took a sweet dip into eggs, orange juice, and milk then were browned on the griddle. Savory steamed asparagus was bundled in a toast ring created with a donut cutter. Now that's fancy.

*French Toast,* orange-flavored, is served here w[...] bine ¼ cup orange juice, 1 teaspoon grated orang[...] eggs, ¼ teaspoon salt, and ¾ cup milk. Dip brea[...] [...]t until golden brown. Cut toast ring[...] and slip o[...]

# BANANA- AND NUT BUTTER-STUFFED FRENCH TOAST

**HANDS ON** 25 minutes  **CHILL** 2 hours  **BAKE** 50 minutes at 375°F
**STAND** 15 minutes

| | |
|---|---|
| 20 | ½-inch-thick slices brioche bread, halved diagonally (12 oz.) |
| ½ | of an 8-oz. carton mascarpone cheese or whipped cream cheese |
| ¼ | cup plus 1 Tbsp. nut butter* |
| ¾ | cup pure maple syrup |
| 4 | bananas |
| 1¾ | cups milk |
| 4 | eggs |
| 2 | tsp. vanilla |
| 1 | tsp. ground cinnamon |
| 2 | Tbsp. butter |

**1.** Grease a 2- to 2½-qt. baking dish. Arrange 10 of the bread slices in the dish, overlapping as needed. For filling, in a small bowl whisk together mascarpone cheese, the ¼ cup nut butter, and ¼ cup of the maple syrup until smooth. Spoon evenly over bread in dish. Slice two of the bananas crosswise. Layer slices over filling. Arrange the remaining bread slices on top.
**2.** In a large bowl whisk together milk, eggs, ¼ cup of the maple syrup, the vanilla, and cinnamon. Pour egg mixture over bread while pressing bread down lightly to moisten. Cover; chill 2 to 24 hours.
**3.** Preheat oven to 375°F. Bake, uncovered, 50 to 65 minutes or until center is set (180°F), covering loosely with foil after 25 minutes. Let stand 15 minutes before serving.
**4.** Meanwhile, bias-slice the remaining two bananas. In a 10-inch skillet heat butter, the remaining ¼ cup maple syrup, and the 1 Tbsp. nut butter over medium heat until bubbly. Add banana slices. Cook 2 minutes or until thickened, stirring occasionally. Spoon over French toast. **Makes 8 servings (1 cup each).**
**\*NOTE** Both no-stir and all-natural varieties of peanut, almond, and cashew butters work in this recipe.
**PER SERVING** *524 cal., 30 g fat (14 g sat. fat), 172 mg chol., 289 mg sodium, 54 g carb., 3 g fiber, 30 g sugars, 12 g pro.*

## NOW: NUT BUTTERS

You can find a nut butter for almost every type of nut on grocery shelves. Our Test Kitchen tried almond, cashew, and peanut butter when testing this recipe. Feel free to use your family's favorite.

## BREAD PICKS

Our Test Kitchen prefers brioche, an egg-rich bread, for making excellent French toast. It's light but firm, which allows it to absorb the egg mixture. Texas toast has similar qualities but tastes less sweet.

## SPICE SWAP

Cinnamon is the primary spice in the sweet French toast casserole, *above.* But if your taste buds need a surprise, substitute five-spice powder. You'll note cinnamon, fennel, star anise, cloves, and Szechwan pepper.

# SWEET + HEAT

FIERY-HOT FOODS ARE IN FASHION RIGHT NOW. THIS SOUTHERN FAVORITE JUST GOT A LITTLE MORE HIP, COURTESY OF HOT HONEY.

## CORN BREAD WAFFLES WITH HOT HONEY-SPICED CHICKEN

**HANDS ON** 30 minutes
**COOK** 10 minutes per batch

### NOW: HOT HONEY

A relative newcomer to the grocery store condiment aisle, spicy and sweet honey is infused with fresh or dried chile peppers. The heat level of hot honey may vary depending on the type of chiles used. To make your own, stir 1 Tbsp. crushed red pepper into ¾ cup honey.

Vegetable oil
2½ cups all-purpose flour
2 tsp. hot paprika
1½ tsp. dried basil or thyme
1 tsp. onion powder
1 tsp. cayenne pepper
½ tsp. garlic powder
½ tsp. black pepper
3 cups buttermilk
6 skinless, boneless chicken thighs
¾ cup hot honey, warmed
¼ cup cornmeal
1 Tbsp. sugar
1 tsp. baking powder
¼ tsp. baking soda
2 eggs, lightly beaten
½ cup vegetable oil
½ cup shredded cheddar cheese (2 oz.) (optional)
1 recipe Cream Cheese-Hot Honey Spread (optional)
Louisiana hot sauce

**1.** Preheat oven to 200°F. In a deep 10-inch skillet heat 1 inch vegetable oil over medium heat to 350°F.

**2.** Meanwhile, in a shallow bowl whisk together 1 cup of the flour, the paprika, basil, 1 tsp. *salt,* the onion powder, cayenne pepper, garlic powder, and black pepper. Place 1 cup of the buttermilk in another shallow bowl. Coat chicken with flour mixture; dip in the buttermilk and coat again with flour mixture.

**3.** Using tongs, carefully add three pieces of chicken to hot oil at a time. (Oil temperature will drop; adjust the heat to maintain temperature at 350°F.) Fry chicken about 10 minutes or until coating is golden and chicken is done (175°F), turning once. Drain briefly on paper towels. Brush each piece with 2 Tbsp. of the hot honey. Place chicken in a shallow baking pan in oven to keep warm.

**4.** For waffles, in a medium bowl stir together the remaining 1½ cups flour, the cornmeal, sugar, baking powder, baking soda, and ¼ tsp. salt. In another bowl whisk together eggs, the remaining 2 cups buttermilk, and the ½ cup oil. Add to flour mixture. Stir just until moistened. Stir in cheese (if using).

**5.** Add batter to a preheated, lightly greased waffle baker according to manufacturer's directions. Close lid quickly; do not open until done.

Bake according to manufacturer's directions until brown and crisp. When done, use a fork to lift waffle off grid. Repeat with remaining batter. Keep waffles warm in oven.

**6.** Spread Cream Cheese-Hot Honey Spread (if using) over waffles; top with chicken. Drizzle additional hot honey and the hot sauce over top. **Makes 6 servings (1 waffle + 1 piece chicken each).**
**PER SERVING** *762 cal., 32 g fat (5 g sat. fat), 135 mg chol., 979 mg sodium, 87 g carb., 2 g fiber, 41 g sugars, 29 g pro.*

**CREAM CHEESE-HOT HONEY SPREAD** In a small bowl stir together 4 oz. softened cream cheese and 2 Tbsp. hot honey.

**TO AIR-FRY CHICKEN** Preheat air fryer to 375°F. Coat air-fryer basket with nonstick cooking spray. Coat chicken pieces as directed in Step 2; coat pieces with cooking spray. Working in batches, place pieces in a single layer in prepared basket. Air-fry 15 to 18 minutes or until coating is golden and chicken is done (175°F), turning once.

**PER SERVING (WITH AIR-FRIED CHICKEN)** *700 cal., 25 g fat (4 g sat. fat), 135 mg chol., 979 mg sodium, 87 g carb., 2 g fiber, 41 g sugars, 29 g pro.*

## TABLESIDE TOAST

**September 1929** Family breakfast was a sit-down event when toasters first appeared. Making toast at the table called for creative ways to run cords to electrical outlets. Our editors wrote, "Skilled electricians can pierce even the finest rugs without injuring them." Gasp.

## SAVORY GRIDDLE CAKES

**February 1935** During the thrifty '30s, savvy homemakers nudged pancakes out of the sweet zone and embraced using the batter as a smart way to finish off the leftovers. Chicken, fish, lamb, ham, veggies—anything in the icebox was fair game. "Have you eaten a mushroom pancake with cream gravy? If not, you haven't really lived!"

## 100 YEARS OF WAFFLES

Over the decades, we've published nearly 100 waffle recipes. We've stirred in nuts, crushed cornflakes, oats, PB&J, and cheese. "Will It Waffle?" The answer was YES to hash browns, brownie batter, corn bread, and shortcakes. **1929** Editors suggested a BYO-Waffle-Iron dinner party. **1947** Chicken à la King Waffles made their debut. And from **1990,** try this clever mix fix-up: 2 cups pancake mix, two 8-oz. lemon yogurts, 2 eggs, ¼ cup oil, and 2 Tbsp. poppy seeds.

## THEN:
# the BHG breakfast menu

Eggs, bacon, pancakes, hash browns, coffee— we've tested and tasted so many versions of these morning starters over the past century. Enjoy a sampling of our favorite highlights.

## DRINK YOUR BREAKFAST

We're not talking mimosas—though we've served up plenty of brunch cocktails on our pages. For nonbreakfast eaters and teens on the go, we offered our first "smoothie" in **October 1960.** The recipe—ripe banana, vanilla ice cream, evaporated milk, and OJ—was decidedly less healthful than the ones we offer today.

## GETTING GLAM

In the '50s entertaining at home got a whole lot more elaborate. Even breakfast was an event, as evidenced by this glamorous French-inspired spread from **March 1958** featuring Eiffel Tower Eggs. The fluffy whipped egg whites were spiked with Tabasco, layered with deviled ham, and piled sky-high into little white ramekins. Also on the menu: from-scratch croissants and easy shortcut blintzes of sliced bread filled with cottage cheese then toasted.

# OH-SO VERSATILE SHEET PAN

THE NEXT EVOLUTION OF THE SHEET-PAN DINNER?
SHEET-PAN BREAKFAST, OF COURSE. THE RIMMED BAKING SHEET
(15×10-INCH PAN) IS THE HARDEST-WORKING PAN IN YOUR KITCHEN.

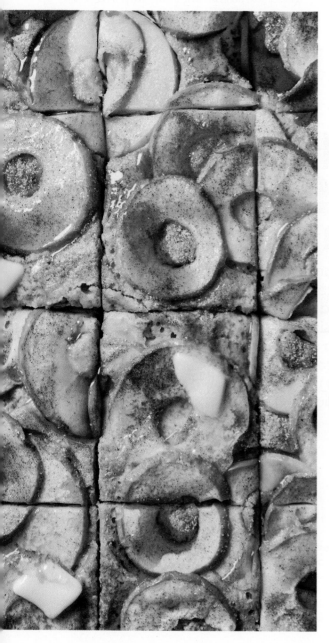

## SHEET PAN APPLE PANCAKE

**PREP** 15 minutes   **BAKE** 25 minutes at 400°F   **STAND** 10 minutes

  Nonstick cooking spray
1½ cups all-purpose flour
1½ cups whole wheat flour
1 Tbsp. baking powder
2¼ tsp. ground cinnamon
½ tsp. salt
1½ cups milk
4 large eggs
¼ cup plus 1 Tbsp. butter, melted
¼ cup pure maple syrup
1 Tbsp. vanilla
4 medium apples, such as Braeburn, Granny Smith, or Pazazz
2 Tbsp. sugar

**1.** Preheat oven to 400°F. Coat a 15×10-inch baking pan with cooking spray. Line bottom of pan with parchment paper.
**2.** In a medium bowl whisk together flours, baking powder, 2 tsp. of the cinnamon, and the salt.
**3.** In a large bowl whisk together milk, eggs, ¼ cup of the melted butter, the maple syrup, and vanilla. Core and coarsely shred two of the apples (measure 2 cups shredded apples). Stir shredded apples into milk mixture.
**4.** Stir flour mixture into milk mixture just until combined. Pour batter into prepared baking pan, spreading evenly.
**5.** Core and thinly slice the remaining two apples and arrange slices on top of batter. Lightly brush apple slices with the 1 Tbsp. melted butter. In a small bowl stir together sugar and the remaining ¼ tsp. cinnamon. Sprinkle over apples.
**6.** Bake about 25 minutes or until edges are golden brown and a toothpick comes out clean. Let stand 10 minutes before serving. Cut into 12 squares and drizzle with additional maple syrup. **Makes 12 servings (1 piece each).**
**PER SERVING** *239 cal., 8 g fat (4 g sat. fat), 77 mg chol., 296 mg sodium, 36 g carb., 4 g fiber, 10 g sugars, 7 g pro.*

## THEN:
## PANCAKE MATH

Through the years, we've published 171 traditional pancake recipes, 107 mentions of "griddle," 10 ideas for camping pancakes, and two suggestions for "husky plaid-shirt breakfasts," described by our editors as a "big, hot, rib-sticking, downright delicious breakfast."

## NOW:
## HANDS-OFF HOSTING

Savvy hosts shied away from serving pancakes for brunch until now. This versatile sheet pan bakes one delicious pancake to serve 12, eliminating hands-on responsibilities at the griddle and leaving more time for enjoying guests.

# MAKE-AHEAD BREAKFAST

WE'RE HAPPY TO REPORT THE FAMILY BREAKFAST TABLE IS BACK. WE ENJOY SITTING DOWN TOGETHER FOR A SATISFYING BREAKFAST BUT STILL NEED EASY MORNING STARTERS. ENTER THE EGG BITE.

## BACON-SPINACH EGG BITES

**PREP** 15 minutes
**BAKE** 35 minutes at 325°F

Nonstick cooking spray
8  eggs
4  slices bacon, crisp-cooked and crumbled
½  cup torn fresh spinach or chopped cooked broccoli (crisp-tender)
½  cup roasted red bell peppers, chopped
½  cup shredded white cheddar, Gouda, Gruyère, or Monterey Jack cheese (2 oz.)
½  tsp. salt
⅛  tsp. black pepper
Crème fraîche, chopped fresh chives, and/or hot sauce (optional)

**1.** Preheat oven to 325°F. Coat six half-pint jars with cooking spray. Place jars in a 13×9-inch baking pan.
**2.** In a large bowl whisk together eggs,* bacon, spinach, roasted peppers, cheese, salt, and black pepper. Divide egg mixture among jars. Place pan on oven rack. Pour enough boiling water into pan to reach halfway up sides of jars. Bake 35 minutes or until eggs are set.
**3.** Remove jars from water; cool slightly.** If desired, top with crème fraîche, chives, and/or hot sauce.
**Makes 6 servings (1 jar each).**
***NOTE** For a fluffier texture, whisk 1 Tbsp. water into the eggs before

adding the other ingredients in Step 2.
****NOTE** Egg bites can be cooled completely, covered, and chilled up to 3 days. To reheat, uncover and microwave in 30-second increments 1 to 1½ minutes or until heated through. Let stand 1 minute before eating.
**PER SERVING** 164 cal., 12 g fat (5 g sat. fat), 262 mg chol., 489 mg sodium, 2 g carb., 0 g fiber, 1 g sugars, 13 g pro.

### MONTE CRISTO EGG BITES

Preheat oven and prepare jars as directed in Step 1. Cut enough day-old French bread into ¾-inch cubes to make 1½ cups. In a 10-inch skillet melt 1 Tbsp. butter. Add bread cubes; cook over medium about 5 minutes or until toasted, tossing frequently. Divide croutons among jars. Continue as directed in Step 2, except substitute ½ cup chopped sliced ham and/or turkey for the bacon, omit spinach and roasted peppers, and use the Gruyère cheese option. Bake as directed. Immediately top each with ½ tsp. raspberry or cherry jam. Cool slightly. Substitute chopped fresh basil for the optional toppings.

### ANDOUILLE-MUSHROOM EGG BITES

Preheat oven and prepare jars as directed in Step 1. In an 8-inch skillet melt 1 Tbsp. butter. Add 2 cups chopped fresh mushrooms; cook about 8 minutes or until tender. Remove from heat. Quarter lengthwise and thinly slice

## NOW: SINGLE SERVING

These egg bites, similar to mini crustless quiches, are inspired by a Starbucks menu item. For at least three reasons, they're what we want for breakfast today. First, they're high in protein (13 g each). Second, they're customizable: Add ingredients you love or clean out your fridge. Third, you can make them ahead. Bake a batch and chill them, then reheat in less time than it takes to brew your morning coffee.

one 3-oz. fully cooked smoked andouille sausage link. Add sausage and ¼ tsp. sweet or smoked paprika to skillet; toss to combine. Remove from heat. Continue as directed in Step 2, except substitute the sausage-mushroom mixture for the bacon, spinach, and roasted peppers; substitute ½ cup shredded Manchego cheese for the cheddar; and add ¼ cup chopped green onions. Bake as directed. Cool slightly. Substitute a sprinkle of additional paprika for the optional toppings.

# NEW WAYS WITH GRAINS

BARLEY, FARRO, AND QUINOA—AMONG OTHER GRAINS—ARE STEPPING OUT OF THEIR SAVORY COMFORT ZONE AND LANDING SQUARELY IN DESSERT TERRITORY.

## GINGER-TURMERIC BARLEY PUDDING

**HANDS ON** 20 minutes   **COOK** 30 minutes

| | |
|---|---|
| 3 | cups whole milk |
| ½ | cup uncooked pearled barley |
| ¼ | cup granulated sugar or honey |
| 2½ | tsp. packed grated fresh ginger |
| 1 | cinnamon stick |
| ¼ | tsp. freshly grated nutmeg |
| | Pinch salt |
| ½ | of a vanilla bean |
| 2 | egg yolks |
| ½ | tsp. ground turmeric |
| ½ | cup packed dark brown sugar |
| ¼ | cup water |
| 1⅓ | cups chopped pitted Medjool dates |
| ¼ | tsp. salt |
| ⅛ | tsp. black pepper |

**1.** In a 3-qt. saucepan combine milk, barley, granulated sugar, 2 tsp. of the ginger, the cinnamon stick, nutmeg, and the pinch salt. Split vanilla bean lengthwise and scrape out seeds. Add seeds and pod to pan. Bring to boiling; reduce heat. Simmer, uncovered, 30 minutes, stirring occasionally.

**2.** In a small bowl whisk together egg yolks and turmeric. Gradually stir in about 1 cup of the hot barley mixture. Stir egg mixture into pan; cook 1 minute or just until mixture thickens and a thermometer registers 195°F. Remove from heat; cool slightly. Remove and discard cinnamon stick and vanilla pod.

**3.** Meanwhile, for date-ginger syrup, in a 1-qt. saucepan stir together brown sugar, the water, and the remaining ½ tsp. ginger. Bring to a simmer over medium-high heat. Simmer, uncovered, about 3 minutes or until syrup is reduced to ½ cup. Remove from heat; stir in dates, the ¼ tsp. salt, and the pepper. If needed, stir in 1 to 2 Tbsp. water to reach drizzling consistency. Use immediately or chill until needed. Serve pudding warm or chilled. Drizzle with date-ginger syrup. **Makes 4 servings (about ⅔ cup each).**

**PER SERVING** *398 cal., 9 g fat (4 g sat. fat), 111 mg chol., 249 mg sodium, 74 g carb., 5 g fiber, 53 g sugars, 10 g pro.*

### THEN: BEST LEFT IN THE PAST

In September 1968 the shortcut Rice Pudding Royale called for stirring together ½ cup cooked rice and creamed cottage cheese, plus a touch of citrus zest and coriander. Maybe we took one shortcut too many!

### NOW: GOOD GRAINS

Compared to traditional rice, barley has more fiber (5 g per serving!), which gives this classic old-timey pudding dessert a chewier, more interesting bite than rice.

### NICE SPICE

Fresh ginger and turmeric are equally delicious and good for you. Both are known for their powerful anti-inflammatory properties.

# KITCHEN TRAVELS

MORE AND MORE, WE COUNT ON RECIPES TO MAGICALLY TRANSPORT US BEYOND
OUR KITCHENS. TAKE A QUICK TRIP TO SPAIN—PASSPORT NOT REQUIRED.

## LEMON BASQUE CHEESECAKE

**HANDS ON** 30 minutes
**BAKE** 50 minutes at 425°F
**COOL** 2 hours

1⅓   cups sugar
2     tsp. lemon zest
3     8-oz. pkg. cream cheese, room temperature
1     8-oz. carton mascarpone cheese, room temperature
6     eggs, room temperature
1¼   cups heavy cream, room temperature
1     Tbsp. limoncello
1     tsp. salt
1     tsp. vanilla
¼    cup all-purpose flour
      Sea salt flakes (optional)

**1.** Preheat oven to 425°F. Line a 9-inch springform pan with two 15-inch square pieces of parchment paper, extending paper 2 to 3 inches over edge of pan. Place prepared pan on a large rimmed baking sheet.
**2.** In a large bowl beat sugar and zest with a mixer on medium until evenly combined. Add cream cheese and mascarpone; beat on medium until smooth and sugar has dissolved, scraping bowl as needed Beat in eggs, one at a time, until combined. Beat in the next four ingredients (through vanilla). Sift flour evenly over cream cheese mixture. Beat on low just until combined, scraping bowl as needed. (Mixture will be thin.)
**3.** Pour into prepared pan. Tap pan on counter a few times to remove any air bubbles. Bake 50 to 55 minutes or until outside edge is set and center is still wobbly when shaken. Cheesecake should be medium to dark brown.
**4.** Cool in pan on a wire rack 15 minutes. Remove sides of pan; cool completely on wire rack. Gently peel off parchment. Serve at room temperature or cover and chill up to 3 days. Let stand at room temperature 30 minutes before serving. If desired, sprinkle with salt flakes. **Makes 12 servings (1 slice each).**
**NOTE** Change up the flavor by omitting the lemon zest and substituting orange-flavor liqueur, kirsch, or raspberry-flavor liqueur for the limoncello.
**PER SERVING** *502 cal., 40 g fat (23 g sat. fat), 203 mg chol., 425 mg sodium, 30 g carb., 0 g fiber, 26 g sugars, 9 g pro.*

## NOW: SPANISH INFLUENCE

Burnt Basque Cheesecake originated in a restaurant in San Sebastian, Spain, when a chef added this custardy cheesecake to the dessert menu. It forgoes the crust and bakes at a high temperature that scorches the surface, caramelizing the sugars and making a scrumptious soft interior.

# FAST AND WHOLESOME FROM SCRATCH

THOUGH CONVENIENCE BAKING MIXES ARE EXCELLENT TIME-SAVERS, HOME COOKS ARE EMBRACING SCRATCH BAKING—EVEN ON THE BUSIEST OF DAYS.

### NOW:
### BUSY-DAY CAKE

Though the basic formula for our updated one-bowl cake is close to its original 1930 predecessor, we added more sugar and two more eggs, swapped in some almond flour for texture, and stirred in yogurt instead of milk. It's richer and more tender but still no-fuss and done in 60.

### THEN:
### YOGURT DEBUT

In April 1951 editors introduced home cooks to yogurt—"the new edition of nature's most perfect food: ... milk transformed to 'yogurt' by adding a special culture. It's smooth as custard, mildly tart, [and] *fresh* tasting. You eat it with a spoon."

## FRENCH YOGURT CAKE
## WITH APRICOT-CHERRY COMPOTE

**HANDS ON** 20 minutes   **BAKE** 40 minutes at 350°F   **COOL** 2 hours

| | |
|---|---|
| 1 | cup all-purpose flour |
| ½ | cup almond flour |
| 2 | tsp. baking powder |
| ¼ | tsp. salt |
| 1 | cup granulated sugar |
| 2 | tsp. lemon zest |
| 1 | 5-oz. jar French-style vanilla yogurt (such as Oui) or ½ cup vanilla Greek yogurt |
| 3 | eggs |
| 1 | tsp. vanilla |
| ½ | cup neutral oil, such as canola Powdered sugar |
| 1 | recipe Apricot-Cherry Compote Crème fraîche (optional) |

**1.** Preheat oven to 350°F. Grease the bottom of an 8-inch round baking pan.* Line bottom with waxed paper; grease pan. In a medium bowl whisk together flours, baking powder, and salt.

**2.** In a large bowl combine granulated sugar and zest. Using fingers, rub zest into sugar until sugar is moist and aromatic. Add yogurt, eggs, and vanilla; whisk until well blended. Gently whisk in flour mixture. Using a large rubber spatula, fold in oil until combined. Spread batter in prepared pan.

**3.** Bake 40 to 45 minutes or until top of cake feels springy and a toothpick comes out clean. Cool cake in pan on a wire rack 15 minutes. Use a knife to loosen edges of cake from pan. Remove cake from pan; peel off waxed paper. Cool on wire rack.

**4.** Dust cake with powdered sugar. Serve with Apricot-Cherry Compote and, if you like, crème fraîche.

**Makes 8 servings (1 slice cake + about ⅓ cup compote each).**

**APRICOT-CHERRY COMPOTE**

In a large saucepan combine ¼ cup each sugar, water, and dry white wine (such as Sauvignon Blanc) or water, and 1 tsp. lemon zest (optional). Cook and stir over medium heat until sugar is dissolved. Stir in 12 oz. (3 to 4) fresh apricots, peaches, or pluots, pitted and sliced, and 8 oz. (1½ cups) fresh sweet cherries, pitted. Bring to boiling; reduce heat. Simmer, uncovered, about 15 minutes or until fruit softens and syrup thickens. Remove from heat; cool slightly. Transfer to a container; cover and chill before serving.

**\*NOTE** You can bake this cake in a 1½- or 2-inch-deep pan. With a 1½-inch-deep pan, it will be more full, and the cake will bake up to the edge of the pan. Bake at least 45 minutes in this pan.

**PER SERVING** *461 cal., 21 g fat (4 g sat. fat), 77 mg chol., 231 mg sodium, 59 g carb., 2 g fiber, 43 g sugars, 8 g pro.*

# BELOVED MASH-UP

FUSING TREASURED CLASSICS ISN'T A NEW TREND (THINK RED VELVET CHEESECAKE AND S'MORES CAKE), BUT IT'S ONE THAT'S HERE TO STAY. ENJOY OUR LATEST.

## STONE FRUIT-PECAN DEEP-DISH PIE

**HANDS ON** 45 minutes
**BAKE** 1 hour at 375°F + 30 minutes at 350°F   **COOL** 2 hours

| | |
|---|---|
| 1 | recipe Pastry for Single-Crust Pie (p. 609) |
| 3 | Tbsp. granulated sugar |
| 1 | Tbsp. cornstarch |
| 2 | cups pitted and sliced fresh nectarines, peaches, or plums (10 oz.) |
| 3 | eggs, lightly beaten |
| 1 | cup dark-color corn syrup |
| ⅔ | cup granulated sugar |
| ⅓ | cup butter, melted |
| 1 | tsp. vanilla |
| 1¼ | cups pecan halves |
| 1 | cup all-purpose flour |
| ½ | cup packed brown sugar |
| ⅓ | cup butter, cut up |
| ½ | cup chopped pecans |
| | Ice cream (optional) |

**1.** Preheat oven to 375°F. Prepare and roll out Pastry for Single-Crust Pie into a 13-inch circle. Line a 9-inch deep-dish pie plate with pastry circle and trim. Crimp edge as desired (pp. 608-609). Chill crust while preparing fillings.
**2.** In a medium bowl combine the 3 Tbsp. granulated sugar and the cornstarch. Add fruit; toss to coat.
**3.** In another medium bowl combine the next five ingredients (through vanilla). Stir in pecan halves.
**4.** For streusel, in a small bowl combine flour and brown sugar. Use your fingers to work butter into flour mixture until it resembles coarse crumbs. Stir in chopped pecans.
**5.** Stir fruit mixture and spoon into pastry. Carefully pour pecan mixture over fruit mixture. Sprinkle streusel over top.
**6.** To prevent overbrowning, cover pie loosely with foil. Bake 1 hour. Remove foil and reduce oven temperature to 350°F.

Bake 30 to 45 minutes more or until filling is puffed, appears set, and reaches 200°F on an instant-read thermometer. (If needed to prevent overbrowning, cover edges with foil the last 15 minutes of baking.) Cool completely on a wire rack. If desired, serve with ice cream. Store leftovers in the refrigerator. **Makes 8 servings (1 slice each).**

**PER SERVING** 800 cal., 43 g fat (15 g sat. fat), 118 mg chol., 383 mg sodium, 102 g carb., 4 g fiber, 71 g sugars, 9 g pro.

## THEN: PIE SKILLS

"Nothing makes a good cook prouder than turning out a perfect pie," we said in the October 1953 issue, which debuted pies and tips from the new Red Plaid.

## NOW: PIE WOW

If you love stone fruit and pecan pie, this two-in-one bakes into separate layers of each pie in the same crust. You'll never have to choose again.

# ONE-DISH DINNER

THE TRADITIONAL DINNER PLATE—MEAT, VEGGIES, AND STARCH—IS CHANGING.
BUSY HOME COOKS FAVOR SINGLE RECIPES THAT INCLUDE EACH ELEMENT IN ONE DISH.

## HERBED MEAT LOAF WITH SCALLOPED POTATO CRUST

**HANDS ON** 30 minutes  **BAKE** 10 minutes at 400°F + 1 hour at 375°F
**STAND** 10 minutes

| | |
|---|---|
| 2 | Tbsp. butter, melted |
| 5 | oz. whole tiny yellow or red potatoes, very thinly sliced |
| 1 | Tbsp. olive oil or canola oil |
| 1 | cup finely chopped onion |
| 2 | cloves garlic, minced |
| ¼ | cup chopped fresh parsley |
| 1 | Tbsp. chopped fresh thyme |
| 1 | Tbsp. chopped fresh sage |
| 1 | lb. ground beef chuck (85% lean) |
| 1 | lb. ground pork |
| 1 | cup riced vegetables, thawed if frozen, any liquid squeezed out |
| ½ | cup panko bread crumbs |
| 1½ | Tbsp. Worcestershire sauce |
| 1 | Tbsp. tomato paste |
| 1 | egg |
| 1 | recipe Tomato-Vinegar-Maple Sauce |

**1.** Preheat oven to 400°F. Brush bottom of a 9×5-inch loaf pan with 1 Tbsp. of the butter. Arrange potato slices in bottom of pan, overlapping as needed. Drizzle with remaining 1 Tbsp. butter and sprinkle with ¼ tsp. each *salt* and *black pepper*.
**2.** Bake about 10 minutes or until edges of potatoes begin to brown. Remove from oven; cool 15 minutes.
**3.** Meanwhile, in a 10-inch skillet heat oil over medium-low heat. Add onion, garlic, 2 Tbsp. of the parsley, 1½ tsp. each of the thyme and sage, and ¼ tsp. each salt and pepper. Cook about 6 minutes or until tender, stirring occasionally. Remove from heat; let cool. Reduce oven temperature to 375°F.

**4.** In a large bowl gently mix beef; pork; riced vegetables; onion mixture; panko; the remaining parsley, thyme, and sage; the Worcestershire sauce; tomato paste; egg; and ½ tsp. each salt and pepper just until combined and uniform. (Don't overwork.)
**5.** Place meat mixture on top of potatoes in pan; pat evenly. Bake about 1 hour or until done (160°F). Let stand 10 minutes.
**6.** Preheat broiler. Invert a foil-lined 15×10-inch baking pan on loaf pan. Carefully hold pans together and invert meat loaf onto baking pan. Remove loaf pan. Tilt baking pan slightly to drain off fat. Brush potatoes and sides of meat loaf with 3 Tbsp. of the Tomato-Vinegar-Maple Sauce. Broil meat loaf 3 inches from heat about 5 minutes or until potatoes are browned. Serve meat loaf with the remaining Tomato-Vinegar-Maple Sauce.
**Makes 6 servings (1 slice each).**
**TOMATO-VINEGAR-MAPLE SAUCE**
In a small bowl whisk together ½ cup plus 2 Tbsp. ketchup, 3 Tbsp. pure maple syrup or packed light brown sugar, 2 Tbsp. red wine vinegar, 1 Tbsp. Worcestershire sauce, ¼ tsp. black pepper, and a dash hot sauce.
**PER SERVING** *528 cal., 33 g fat (13 g sat. fat), 145 mg chol., 888 mg sodium, 27 g carb., 2 g fiber, 14 g sugars, 30 g pro.*

## THEN: THE SHAPE OF MEAT LOAF

In March 1960 editors wrote, "The best recipes may be old-timers, but you can give a loaf a new figure by baking it as a ring or round." Beef, tuna, ham, and chicken loaves were transformed.

## NOW: MEAT LOAF MAKEOVER

We kept the loaf shape, but the similarity to yesteryear's meat loaf ends there. Riced veggies in the meat, a shingled potato topper, and tangy vinegar maple sauce make this version, *above*, thoroughly modern.

# FLAVOR EXPLORATION

FLAVOR IS STILL KING, AND HOME COOKS ARE SEARCHING FOR NEW TASTE EXPERIENCES FROM AROUND THE GLOBE.

## FILIPINO BBQ PORK SKEWERS

**PREP** 20 minutes   **MARINATE** 4 hours   **GRILL** 10 minutes

6    Tbsp. low-sodium soy sauce
½    cup Jufran Banana Sauce*
¼    cup lemon-lime soda
2    Tbsp. packed brown sugar
2    Tbsp. lemon juice
1    large clove garlic, minced
2    fresh Thai chiles, finely
     chopped
¼    tsp. salt
¼    tsp. black pepper
2    lb. pork tenderloin or
     boneless pork loin, trimmed
     and cut into 1-inch pieces
¼    cup cider vinegar
     Hot cooked rice (optional)
     Pickled vegetables (optional)

**1.** In a large bowl stir together ¼ cup of the soy sauce, ¼ cup of the Jufran Banana Sauce, and the next seven ingredients (through black pepper). Add the pork; toss to coat. Cover and chill 4 hours or overnight.

**2.** Meanwhile, in a small bowl stir together the remaining ¼ cup banana sauce and 2 Tbsp. soy sauce and the vinegar. Remove ¼ cup to use during grilling. Reserve the remaining glaze.

**3.** If using wooden skewers, soak them in water 30 minutes before grilling. Let pork stand at room temperature 30 minutes before grilling. Thread pork onto eight 10- to 12-inch skewers.

**4.** Lightly oil grates on grill. Grill skewers, covered, over medium heat about 10 minutes or until done (145°F), turning and brushing with the ¼ cup glaze halfway through grilling. If desired, serve with rice and pickled vegetables. Drizzle with the reserved glaze. **Makes 4 servings (2 skewers each).**

**\*NOTE** Jufran Banana Sauce is a popular Filipino alternative to ketchup that is fruitier and tangier than traditional tomato ketchup. If you can't find it, stir together ¼ cup ketchup, 2 Tbsp. packed brown sugar, 2 Tbsp. lemon juice, and 1 Tbsp. mashed very ripe banana.

**PER SERVING** *297 cal., 4 g fat (1 g sat. fat), 140 mg chol., 1,052 mg sodium, 13 g carb., 0 g fiber, 11 g sugars, 47 g pro.*

**NOW: NEW-TO-YOU SAUCE** Skip the usual BBQ sauce for your kabobs and take a spin through the Philippines to wake up your grilling routine. Banana sauce, a Filipino condiment, acts as the base for the brushing sauce that gives these pork skewers a sweet-sour flavor and caramelized char. Purchase it online or make your own using the recipe, *left.*

**THEN:**
**GRILLING REWIND**

Kabobs claimed the *Better Homes & Gardens* cover in June 1965, celebrating 25 years of BBQ recipes.

**MEATS TO SWEETS**
We skewered every course in June of 1960, but dessert took the cake—grilled pound cake cubes iced with jelly and rolled in coconut.

**KITSCHY KABOBS**
"It's all done in fun ... when food takes to a skewer," such as 1954's themed kabobs: Picnic Piggies, Rancher's Shishkebobs, and Dad's Delight.

**CHEAP EATS**
Kudos to cost cutting, but we think these Mustard-Brushed Bologna Kabobs might be best left in the summer of '71.

# SCROLLING FOR DINNER

HOME COOKS LOOK TO INSTAGRAM, TIKTOK, FACEBOOK, AND PINTEREST TO FIND THE LATEST DELICIOUS CROWD-PLEASERS GONE VIRAL, LIKE MARRY-ME CHICKEN.

## CREAMY TUSCAN CHICKEN

**HANDS ON** 20 minutes   **COOK** 27 minutes

- 4   6- to 8-oz. skinless, boneless chicken breast halves
- ¾   tsp. salt
- ¾   tsp. black pepper
- 1   Tbsp. olive oil
- 1   Tbsp. butter
- 4   cups sliced fresh cremini mushrooms
- 4   cloves garlic, minced
- ¾   cup reduced-sodium chicken broth
- ¾   cup heavy cream
- 1   6-oz. jar quartered marinated artichoke hearts, drained
- 1   Tbsp. chopped fresh oregano or 1 tsp. dried oregano, crushed
- ½   to 1 tsp. crushed red pepper
- ½   cup drained and chopped oil-packed dried tomatoes
- ⅓   cup grated Parmesan cheese
- 4   cups hot cooked gnocchi, angel hair pasta, or mashed potatoes
  Balsamic vinegar (optional)

**1.** Sprinkle chicken with salt and pepper. In a 10-inch cast-iron or nonstick skillet heat oil over medium heat. Cook chicken in hot oil about 8 minutes or until browned, turning once. Transfer to a plate.

**2.** Melt butter in skillet. Add mushrooms; cook about 5 minutes or until mushrooms are browned and liquid evaporates, stirring occasionally. Add garlic; cook and stir 1 minute more. Stir in next five ingredients (through crushed red pepper). Bring to boiling; reduce heat. Simmer, uncovered, 5 minutes. Stir in tomatoes and Parmesan cheese.

**3.** Return chicken to skillet. Spoon sauce over chicken. Simmer, uncovered, 8 to 10 minutes or until done (165°F).

**4.** Serve chicken and mushroom sauce over gnocchi. If desired, top with a drizzle of balsamic vinegar and additional fresh oregano and Parmesan cheese. **Makes 4 servings (1 chicken breast half + ¾ cup mushroom sauce each).**

PER SERVING 729 cal., 26 g fat (8 g sat. fat), 153 mg chol., 1,527 mg sodium, 76 g carb., 7 g fiber, 5 g sugars, 52 g pro.

## THEN: CHICKEN WINS

Chicken was a very popular category in our Prize Tested Recipes contest that originated in 1933. Winners through the decades have included A la King on Noodles ('46), Chicken Party Pie Salad ('54), Crab-Stuffed Chicken Breast ('72), Raspberry Chicken ('85), and Rosemary Chicken and Vegetables ('95).

## NOW: MARRY-ME CHICKEN

Not familiar with Marry-Me Chicken? This viral TikTok recipe sensation is allegedly so delicious that it will elicit a marriage proposal when served to your significant other. Our version of the creamy tomato-sauced chicken is full of mushrooms and marinated artichoke hearts.

# CHICKEN SOUP, OLD SCHOOL

GRANDMA MADE EVERYTHING FROM SCRATCH, AND WE'RE STILL TAKING CUES FROM HER IN THE KITCHEN.

## CHICKEN, ORECCHIETTE, AND ESCAROLE SOUP

**HANDS ON** 30 minutes   **COOK** 1 hour 25 minutes

3   lb. meaty chicken pieces (bone-in breasts, thighs, and/or drumsticks)
1   large onion, cut into thin wedges
2   tsp. salt
1   tsp. dried thyme, crushed
½   tsp. black pepper
4   cloves garlic, sliced
2   bay leaves
8   cups water
10   cups torn escarole and/or frisée
1   cup thinly bias-sliced carrots
1   cup thinly sliced celery
2   cups dried orecchiette pasta
½   cup chopped fresh basil
    Grated Parmesan cheese

**1.** In a 6- to 8-qt. pot combine the first seven ingredients (through bay leaves). Pour the water over all. Bring to boiling; reduce heat. Simmer, covered, 1 hour or until chicken is very tender.

**2.** Remove chicken from broth. When cool enough to handle, remove meat from bones. Discard bones and skin. Cut meat into bite-size pieces. Discard bay leaves. Skim fat from broth.

**3.** Return chicken to broth. Add 8 cups of the escarole, the carrots, and celery. Return to boiling; reduce heat. Simmer, covered, 15 minutes. Stir in pasta. Simmer, covered, 7 to 9 minutes or until pasta is tender. Stir in basil and the remaining escarole. Top servings with grated Parmesan cheese. **Makes 8 servings (about ¾ cup each).**

**PER SERVING** *332 cal., 11 g fat (3 g sat. fat), 79 mg chol., 713 mg sodium, 29 g carb., 4 g fiber, 3 g sugars, 30 g pro.*

### THEN: SOUP FOR BREAKFAST?

November 1954: It's true that "soup is nutritious. When you put together refrigerator soup, the result is not only economical, but so good it's hard to believe it's a package of minerals, vitamins, and proteins. Added to ... breakfast, it brings goodness plus."

### NOW: BROTH FROM SCRATCH

Just ask Grandma: The best chicken soup starts with stewing bone-in chicken pieces in seasonings and herbs, resulting in a rich broth layered with flavor. Our update is a cross between Italian wedding soup (minus the meatballs) and old-fashioned chicken noodle soup.

# PLANT-FORWARD
## DINNERS

FLEXITARIANISM AND REDUCETARIANISM ARE ON THE RISE AS WE'RE MORE OFTEN CHOOSING TO LIMIT MEAT OR SKIP IT IN FAVOR OF PLANT-BASED MEALS.

## SPRING STROGANOFF

**START TO FINISH** 40 minutes

| | |
|---|---|
| 4 | to 6 oz. dried mafalda pasta, broken into 2-inch pieces, or mini lasagna noodles* |
| 1 | bunch (12 oz.) asparagus, trimmed and cut lengthwise into thin strips |
| 1 | cup fresh or frozen peas |
| 8 | oz. beef flank steak or sirloin steak |
| ¾ | tsp. kosher salt |
| 2 | Tbsp. butter |
| 3 | cups sliced mixed fresh mushrooms, such as cremini, shiitake, baby portobello, beech, or hen of the woods |
| ½ | cup sliced green onions |
| 3 | cloves garlic, minced |
| ½ | cup dry white wine, dry sherry, or broth |
| 1½ | cups reduced-sodium beef broth or vegetable broth |
| 1 | 5- to 8-oz. carton plain whole milk Greek yogurt or sour cream |
| 2 | Tbsp. all-purpose flour |
| 1 | tsp. lemon zest |
| ¼ | tsp. black pepper |

**1.** Cook pasta according to package directions, adding asparagus and peas the last 2 minutes of cooking; drain.

**2.** Meanwhile, trim fat from meat. Thinly slice meat across grain into bite-size strips; season with ¼ tsp. of the salt. In a 10-inch skillet melt 1 Tbsp. of the butter. Brown meat, half at a time, turning once. Remove meat from skillet; keep warm.

**3.** In the same skillet melt the remaining 1 Tbsp. butter. Cook mushrooms, green onions, and garlic over medium-high heat 3 minutes, stirring occasionally. Add wine; cook and stir until bubbly, scraping browned bits from bottom of pan. Stir in meat and beef broth.

**4.** In a small bowl stir together yogurt, flour, and zest; stir into meat mixture. Cook and stir until thickened and bubbly. Cook and stir 1 minute more. Season with the remaining ½ tsp. salt and the pepper. Add pasta mixture; toss.

**Makes 4 servings (1½ cups each).**

**\*NOTE** Instead of using noodles, you could serve this over sautéed zucchini noodles or cauliflower rice.

**PER SERVING** *374 cal., 12 g fat (6 g sat. fat), 44 mg chol., 744 mg sodium, 37 g carb., 4 g fiber, 5 g sugars, 24 g pro.*

## NOW:
## MUSHROOMS FOR MEAT

If it's a Meatless Monday, go with 5 cups mixed mushrooms and no beef. If you're into meat in moderation, 8 oz. of flank steak and a hefty helping of mushrooms should satisfy four.

## REDUCE PASTA; ADD VEGGIES

The job of noodles in stroganoff is to capture the yummy sauce—and fill us up. We couldn't skip them, but we did cut the amount by half and tossed in fresh asparagus and peas to make up the difference.

## LIGHT & LEMONY

Fresh lemon zest and Greek yogurt (in place of the sour cream typically used) lighten the sauce. It's still smooth and tangy, and it coats beautifully.

### ▶ ASPARAGUS NOODLES

Thinly slice asparagus stalks lengthwise to create wispy green "noodles."

# THEN: less meat, more veg

**1941** **GARDEN MEALS**
"Zip [vegetables] from garden to table. They'll arrive with all their vitamin goodness and fresh-grown flavor." Some things never change.

**1943** **WARTIME RATIONING**
When popular beef cuts were scarce, we extolled the virtue of ground meat. "A roast's a roast and a steak's a steak. But ground meat becomes anything you wish." And we made it into a lot of things—Beef Roll-Ups, Stuffed Meat Loaves, and Hamburger Pie.

### ▶ CHEF'S SALAD
Our first chef's-style salad appeared in August 1949. We tossed together endive, watercress, lettuce, tomato quarters, chicken, almonds, grapes, and sliced eggs.

**1958** **SALADS MEN GO FOR**
Though we would never phrase it this way now, in the '50s our editors conspired with our housewife readers to serve their spouses main-dish meat-and-veggie salads. "They make a fine summer supper, and go over so big with men they'll often do the concocting."

**1976** **PENNY PINCHING**
This falls in the head-scratcher category. When meat prices hit the roof in the '70s, variety (aka organ) meats got a lot of attention. We apologize for Caper-Sauced Brains and Creamy Beef Heart & Rice Skillet.

**2014** **CENTER-OF-THE-PLATE SWITCH**
Move over, meat. We started giving a lot of vegetables the same treatment as prime cuts of meat in the twenty-teens. We've seared cauliflower steaks, roasted portobello pot roasts, and grilled eggplant burgers.

# FANCY GETS CASUAL

LIKE FASHION, FOOD IS GETTING A LITTLE LESS FUSSY AND A LOT MORE COMFORTABLE. THIS DRESSED-DOWN RUSTIC SOUFFLÉ IS BAKED IN A DISH EVERYONE OWNS.

## THEN:
### SOUFFLÉ SECRETS

May 1956: "Yolks aren't as likely to break if you separate them from the whites while still cold from the refrigerator. If you then let the egg whites warm to room temperature before beating, they'll fluff up better."

## NOW:
### NO PRESSURE TO RISE UP

You don't need to tiptoe around the kitchen as this cheesy potato soufflé bakes. It's loaded with so many yummy ingredients that it won't puff like a traditional soufflé. Simply bring it to the table and let everyone dig in.

## CELERY ROOT AND GOLDEN POTATO SOUFFLÉ
**HANDS ON** 25 minutes **COOK** 40 minutes **COOL** 20 minutes
**BAKE** 40 minutes at 375°F

| | |
|---|---|
| 1 | lb. Yukon gold potatoes, peeled and cut up (about 3 cups) |
| 8 | oz. celeriac or Yukon gold potatoes, peeled and cut up (about 1½ cups) |
| 3 | Tbsp. butter |
| 1 | large sweet onion, halved lengthwise and thinly sliced (2½ cups) |
| 2 | oz. soppressata or other dry salami, finely chopped (½ cup) |
| ¾ | cup half-and-half |
| 6 | oz. Fontina or smoked Gouda cheese, shredded (1½ cups) |
| ½ | cup shredded Pecorino Romano cheese (2 oz.) |
| 1 | Tbsp. chopped fresh flat-leaf parsley |
| 1½ | tsp. chopped fresh sage |
| 1 | tsp. chopped fresh rosemary |
| ½ | tsp. chopped fresh thyme |
| ¼ | tsp. kosher salt |
| ¼ | tsp. black pepper |
| 5 | egg yolks, room temperature |
| 7 | egg whites, room temperature |
| ⅛ | tsp. cream of tartar |

**1.** In a 3-qt. saucepan cook potatoes and celeriac in enough lightly salted boiling water to cover about 20 minutes or until tender; drain. Return to saucepan. Cook over high heat 1 minute while shaking pan to dry out potatoes. Add 2 Tbsp. of the butter. Mash potatoes and celeriac until light and fluffy.* Transfer to a large bowl and let cool 20 minutes or until mixture has reached room temperature.
**2.** Meanwhile, place oven rack in the bottom third of the oven and preheat to 425°F. Butter and flour a 3-qt. rectangular baking dish.
**3.** In a 10-inch skillet melt the remaining 1 Tbsp. of the butter over medium-low heat. Add onion. Cook, covered, 13 to 15 minutes or until onion is tender, stirring occasionally. Uncover; cook and stir over medium-high heat 3 to 5 minutes more or until golden.
**4.** Rinse and dry skillet. Add soppressata. Cook over medium heat 3 minutes or until browned and crisp. Transfer to paper towels.
**5.** Stir caramelized onions, half of the soppressata, and the next nine ingredients (through pepper) into potato mixture. Stir in egg yolks.
**6.** In a large bowl beat egg whites and cream of tartar with a mixer on medium until stiff peaks form (tips stand straight). Stir one-third of the egg whites into potato mixture to lighten. Fold in the remaining whites. Transfer to the prepared dish.
**7.** Place dish in oven and reduce temperature to 375°F. Bake 40 to 45 minutes or until golden brown and center is puffed. Serve immediately. Top with the remaining soppressata. **Makes 10 servings (1 cup each).**
**\*NOTE** If you have one, use a ricer to mash the potatoes and celeriac for fluffier results.
**TO BAKE IN A SOUFFLÉ DISH**
Prepare as directed, except use a 2½- to 3-qt. soufflé or round baking dish with straight sides. Bake 60 to 65 minutes or until puffed and golden brown and the mixture appears set when gently shaken.
**PER SERVING** *252 cal., 16 g fat (9 g sat. fat), 137 mg chol., 477 mg sodium, 14 g carb., 1 g fiber, 4 g sugars, 13 g pro.*

# LIGHT, CRUNCHY SALADS

THE MANDOLINE—THE TOOL THAT CREATES WHISPER-THIN SLICES—IS GIVING SHAVED SALADS A WELL-DESERVED MOMENT.

## SHAVED FENNEL AND FINGERLING POTATO SALAD

**START TO FINISH** 25 minutes

- 1    lb. fingerling potatoes, halved lengthwise
- 1¼  tsp. kosher salt
- 3    Tbsp. white wine vinegar
- 2    tsp. Dijon mustard
- ½    tsp. sugar
       Pinch black pepper
- 3    Tbsp. olive oil
- 1    fennel bulb, cored and halved
- ¾    cup slivered yellow bell pepper
- ½    cup sliced green onions
- ½    cup chopped fresh flat-leaf parsley

**1.** In a 4-qt. saucepan combine potatoes, 1 tsp. of the salt, and enough cold water to cover. Bring to boiling; reduce heat. Simmer, uncovered, about 10 minutes or until potatoes are just tender. Drain; return potatoes to saucepan.
**2.** In a small bowl whisk together the next four ingredients (through black pepper) and the remaining ¼ tsp. salt. Drizzle in oil while whisking. Pour half of the vinaigrette over warm potatoes; toss to coat.
**3.** Using a mandoline or a sharp knife, thinly shave fennel bulb lengthwise. Place in a large bowl with bell pepper, onions, and parsley.
**4.** Add potatoes and the remaining vinaigrette to fennel mixture; toss to coat. **Makes 4 servings (1 cup each).**
**PER SERVING** 207 cal., 10 g fat (1 g sat. fat), 0 mg chol., 217 mg sodium, 26 g carb., 4 g fiber, 6 g sugars, 3 g pro.

*Perfect Potato Salad was easy!*
*Still as true as when we first published the recipe: "To rate tops, a pota-
to salad must have all flavors blended to mellow goodness, be just the
right tartness—like this." There's no dressing to make. And the potatoes are sliced—takes less time than dicing. You sprinkle the cooked
potatoes with vinegar and a bit of sugar, toss with assorted mayonnaise.*

## THEN: POPULAR TATERS

September 1959: In celebration of 30 years, the Test Kitchen voted this potato salad a Top 10 recipe. Potatoes were sprinkled with vinegar and sugar then tossed with mayo. "A potato salad must have all flavors blended to a mellow goodness, and be just the right tartness—like this."

## NOW: POTLUCK PERFECT

This is the potato salad, *above,* we want to tote to any bring-a-dish gathering. The light mustard vinaigrette not only holds well without the safety concerns of a mayo-based dressing, but it also lets the freshness of the shaved fennel, onions, and parsley come through brightly.

# SALAD PIZZA

THERE'S NO SHORTAGE OF INNOVATIVE STRATEGIES FOR EATING MORE VEGGIES, BUT THIS ONE TOPS THEM ALL—LITERALLY.

## POTATO AND LEEK PIZZA WITH ARUGULA

**HANDS ON** 25 minutes   **RISE** 45 minutes   **BAKE** 15 minutes at 450°F

- 2   cups all-purpose flour
- 1   pkg. active dry yeast
- 1   tsp. sugar
- 1   tsp. kosher salt
- 5   Tbsp. olive oil
- ⅔   cup warm water (105°F to 115°F)
- 8   oz. Yukon gold or red potatoes, sliced ⅛ inch thick
- 2   medium leeks, halved and thinly sliced (2 cups)
- ⅓   cup thinly sliced onion
- 1   tsp. chopped fresh rosemary
- ½   tsp. black pepper
      Cornmeal
- 1   tsp. lemon zest
- 1   Tbsp. lemon juice
- ¼   tsp. Dijon mustard
- 1   5-oz. pkg. baby arugula
- ¼   cup grated Parmesan cheese (1 oz.)

**1.** In a food processor combine flour, yeast, sugar, and ½ tsp. of the salt. With food processor running, add 1 Tbsp. of the olive oil and the warm water. Process until dough forms; shape into a ball. Place dough in a lightly greased bowl; turning once to grease surface. Cover; let rise in a warm place until double in size (45 to 60 minutes).
**2.** Meanwhile, in a 10-inch skillet heat 1 Tbsp. of the olive oil over medium-high heat. Add potatoes, leeks, onion, rosemary, and ¼ tsp. each of the salt and pepper. Cook 5 to 6 minutes or until potatoes are light brown and leeks and onion are tender, turning occasionally.
**3.** Preheat oven to 450°F. Lightly grease a baking sheet; sprinkle with cornmeal. On a lightly floured surface, roll and stretch dough into a 12×8-inch rectangle. Place on the prepared baking sheet. Lightly brush with additional olive oil. Top with potato-leek mixture. Sprinkle with additional salt. Bake about 15 minutes or until crust is golden.
**4.** Meanwhile, in a medium bowl whisk together the remaining 3 Tbsp. olive oil, the lemon zest and juice, mustard, and the remaining ¼ tsp. each salt and pepper. Add arugula; toss to coat. Top pizza with salad. Sprinkle with Parmesan and additional pepper. **Makes 4 servings (2 slices each).**
**PER SERVING** *511 cal., 20 g fat (3 g sat. fat), 4 mg chol., 560 mg sodium, 72 g carb., 5 g fiber, 5 g sugars, 12 g pro.*

## THEN: CRUST HACKS

March 1961: "No wonder pizza is already [as] American as apple pie—it fits right into our scheme of easygoing meals." Editors offered convenience options like packaged mixes and purchased dough for quick pizza nights.

## NOW: PIZZA FRIDAY

Everyone knows Tuesday night is taco night. And Friday? Well, that's pizza night. According to a reader survey, 80% consider pizza an end-of-the-week reward. To make our recipe easier, make the dough ahead. Chill up to 2 days or freeze up to 3 months.

# SOMETHING FOR EVERYONE

IT'S EASIER THAN EVER TO MAKE VEGAN- AND VEGETARIAN-FRIENDLY APPETIZERS FOR GATHERINGS—AND NO ONE WILL BE ABLE TO TASTE THE DIFFERENCE.

## CREAMY CASHEW AND SHALLOT DIP

**START TO FINISH** 30 minutes

- 10 oz. raw unsalted cashews
  Boiling water
- 3 Tbsp. neutral oil, such as avocado or grapeseed
- 1 cup thinly sliced shallots
- 3 cloves garlic, sliced
- 1 tsp. fine sea salt
- ½ cup water
- ¼ cup cider vinegar
- 1 tsp. smoked paprika

**1.** Place cashews in a large bowl and cover with boiling water. Let stand 15 minutes.
**2.** Meanwhile, in a 10-inch skillet heat oil over medium-low heat. Add shallots, garlic, and salt. Cook, covered, 10 to 12 minutes or until tender, stirring occasionally. Uncover; increase heat to high. Cook and stir about 3 minutes or until golden brown.
**3.** Drain cashews; transfer to a food processor. Add the water, cider vinegar, and paprika. Process about 5 minutes or until smooth. Fold in half of the shallot mixture. Transfer to a bowl. Top with the remaining shallot mixture. **Makes 9 servings (¼ cup each).**
**PER SERVING** *229 cal., 18 g fat (3 g sat. fat), 0 mg chol., 255 mg sodium, 13 g carb., 2 g fiber, 3 g sugars, 6 g pro.*

## BUTTERMILK-MISO RANCH

**START TO FINISH** 35 minutes

- ⅓ cup buttermilk
- ¼ cup white miso paste
- 1 tsp. white vinegar
- ½ tsp. onion powder
- ½ tsp. garlic powder
- ½ tsp. fine sea salt
- 1 tsp. cracked black pepper
- 1 cup sour cream
- 1 cup mayonnaise
- ¼ cup chopped fresh flat-leaf parsley
- ¼ cup chopped fresh dill
- ¼ cup chopped fresh chives

**1.** In a large bowl whisk together the first seven ingredients (through pepper) until smooth. Stir in sour cream and mayonnaise until combined. Fold in parsley, dill, and chives. **Makes 20 servings (2 Tbsp. each).**
**PER SERVING** *109 cal., 10 g fat (2 g sat. fat), 12 mg chol., 248 mg sodium, 3 g carb., 0 g fiber, 2 g sugars, 1 g pro.*

## THEN: DIP WISDOM

December 1947: "Do you know about dips? They're one of the easiest snacks to fix. And there has never been a guest yet, or a snack-loving kitchen prowler, who hasn't thought the whole idea fun and said so—while fixing another bite to pop into his mouth."

## NOW: CASHEW CREAM

A vegan-friendly substitute for cream, cashew cream is easy to make at home. Soak 1 cup of raw unsalted cashews in boiling water 15 minutes, then drain. In a blender or food processor blend nuts with ½ cup water 5 minutes or until smooth. Store in the refrigerator up to 1 week.

# always in style —forever a classic

In 1930 the foreword in the first edition of our iconic cookbook promised "the cream of thousands of tested and tasted recipes approved by the *Better Homes and Gardens*® Testing-Tasting Kitchen." Each edition of our iconic cookbook receives a cover redesign and a thorough recipe review to ensure we uphold the same promise today.

**1930**

**1937**

**1939**

**1941**

**1951**

**1953**

**1962**

**1968**

**1981**

**1989**

**1996**

**1999**

**2002**

**2006**

**2010**

**2014**

**2018**

# Better Homes & Gardens

## 17TH EDITION

# NEW COOK BOOK

Our seal assures you that every recipe in *Better Homes & Gardens. New Cook Book* has been tested in the Better Homes & Gardens. Test Kitchen. This means that each recipe is practical and reliable and meets our high standards of taste appeal. We guarantee your satisfaction with this book for as long as you own it.

**BETTER HOMES & GARDENS.**
**NEW COOK BOOK**

**Editor** Jessica Saari Christensen

**Design Director** Stephanie Hunter

**Contributing Project Editor** Shelli McConnell

**Contributing Editors** Ellen Boeke; Carrie Boyd; Caitlyn Diimig, RD; Diana McMillen; Annie Peterson; Deb Wagman; Mary Williams; Liz Woolever

**Contributing Illustrator** Edwin Fotheringham

**Contributing Copy Editor and Proofreaders** Gretchen Kauffman, Sheila Mauck, Angela Renkoski

**Test Kitchen Director** Lynn Blanchard

**Senior Test Kitchen Brand Managers** Juli Hale, Colleen Weeden

**Test Kitchen Brand Manager** Sarah Brekke

**Test Kitchen Culinary Specialists** Linda Brewer, RD; Sammy Mila; Emily Nienhaus

**Contributing Photographers** Adam Albright, Marty Baldwin, Joe Crimmings, Jason Donnelly, Carson Downing, Jacob Fox, Andy Lyons, Blaine Moats, Scott Morgan, Brie Passano

**Contributing Stylists** Sue Hoss, Greg Luna, Lauren McAnelly, Kelsey Moylan, Dianna Nolin, Jennifer Peterson, Charlie Worthington

**WATERBURY PUBLICATIONS, INC.**

**Design Director** Ken Carlson

**Editorial Director** Lisa Kingsley

**Associate Design Director** Doug Samuelson

**BETTER HOMES & GARDENS.**

**Vice President, Editor in Chief** Stephen Orr

**Creative Director** Jennifer D. Madara

**Executive Food Editor** Jan Miller

**DOTDASH MEREDITH**

**President, Lifestyle** Alysia Borsa

ISBN 978-1-957317-00-7

This edition published in 2022 by
IPG Publishing
814 N. Franklin Street
Chicago, Illinois 60610

Printed in the United States of America.

# CONTENTS

**THE RED PLAID COOKBOOK MADE NEW!** THE WAY WE COOK AND EAT THESE DAYS CHANGES AS FAST AS IMAGES POP UP ON SOCIAL MEDIA. THAT'S WHY EVERY FEW YEARS WE TAKE THIS BOOK APART, QUESTION EVERY DETAIL, AND PUT IT BACK TOGETHER.

A "new kind of cook book for a new kind of homemaker." That's how the editors described the first edition of *Better Homes & Gardens New Cook Book* in 1930. They were proud to deliver a cookbook that offered the "cream of thousands of recipes officially endorsed by the Tasting-Test Kitchen" and hoped it would "take its rightful place as the 'master' Cook Book for your kitchen."

Obviously, over the past 88 years the role of the homemaker has become anything but a stereotype. And the way we prepare meals and think about our food evolves daily. Regardless of who cooks in your kitchen or who makes up the family seated at your table, this newly revised edition celebrates what home cooking is all about today.

For starters, we've reorganized the table of contents. Abandoning the alphabetical list, we grouped recipes into four sections based on what you want to cook when: Everyday (quick dinners, breakfasts, easy sides, and snacks), Gatherings (entertaining and holiday recipes), Baking, and Preserving (canning, pickling, fermenting, freezing).

To satisfy our ever-expanding global palate, it has more flavorfully diverse dishes (Tandoori Chicken, Butternut Squash Shakshuka, and Tahini Dressing, for example) and on-trend recipes (grain bowls, vegetarian meals, and one-pan dinners). Because we know you will also turn to this book for the classics, we scrutinized each iconic recipe—think Mac and Cheese—to make sure it's the best. And if it's your first holiday dinner, we'll show you how to roast that turkey.

One thing we didn't change. The foundation upon which the cookbook was based: our guarantee that these recipes—the "cream"—are tested and tasted for quality and practicality. We promise you will have success in your kitchen like we've had in ours. Some things never change—and shouldn't.

*Jessica Christensen* *Jan Miller*

**JESSICA CHRISTENSEN & JAN MILLER**
EDITORS, *NEW COOK BOOK* 17TH EDITION

## WHAT'S NEW?

**HELLO, HARDCOVER**
We said goodbye to the ring-bound notebook of past editions. We promise, this book stays open and lies flat no matter what page you're reading.

**TABLE OF CONTENTS**
The book is now organized according to how you cook. Four sections make it easy to find recipes for Everyday, Gatherings, Baking, and Preserving.

**BETTER BASICS**
Two informative visual sections, "How to Cook" and "How to Bake," answer your questions. Plus you'll find the top 5 recipes everyone should know how to cook.

**A PHOTO OF EVERY RECIPE**
For the first time, there's a photo with every recipe! Step-by-step images are where you need them most.

**THE RECIPE MIX**
Look for on-trend flavors, updated classics, customizable favorites, and cooking-class recipes.

# *how to* COOK

TEST KITCHEN

(l to r):
Sarah Brekke,
Sammy Mila,
Kelsey Bulat

# COME IN! THIS IS OUR TEST KITCHEN

## THE BONES

### 8

NUMBER OF GALLEY KITCHENS IN OUR TEST KITCHEN

Each is about the size of many NYC apartment kitchens. You won't find fancy gadgets or restaurant-style ovens; we test with appliances and tools the average home cook might use.
We do, however, have one awesome chandelier that hangs above our sharing table (aka the trough).

**Q:** DO YOU GO HOME AND COOK SUPPER EVERY NIGHT?
(THE #1 QUESTION ASKED OF OUR CULINARY PROFESSIONALS)

**A:** YES, ABSOLUTELY. OUR CULINARY SPECIALISTS ARE HOME COOKS AT HEART—LIKE YOU. SO AT THE END OF THEIR DAY THEY OFTEN STEP RIGHT BACK INTO THEIR KITCHENS AT HOME!

### 84
years of ON-STAFF cooking experience

*We fail in our kitchen so you have success in yours!*

Lynn Blanchard,
Test Kitchen
Director

*Food Science*
+
*Culinary Arts*
+
*Consumer Science*
+
*Dietetics*
=

VARIETY OF COLLEGE DEGREES OUR TEST KITCHEN STAFF HOLDS

# 5 A DAY

**AVERAGE NUMBER OF RECIPES EACH CULINARY PROFESSIONAL TESTS DAILY**

*Juli Hale*

**KITCHEN HELPERS:** The Test Kitchen wouldn't function as efficiently without our kitchen helpers. They move through the galley kitchens wrangling dirty dishes, loading dishwashers, and working to keep things as orderly as possible as the testers are cooking away.

**A SHOPPER:** The only way we can test so many recipes each day is with the help of a very key person: the shopper! She makes one enormous shopping list daily for the next day's testing, then heads out to shop major grocery stores and specialty markets.

Better Homes & Gardens.

TEST KITCHEN

The Test Kitchen seal assures you that every recipe tested in the Better Homes & Gardens® Test Kitchen is practical and reliable and meets our high standards of taste appeal.

## INGREDIENTS BY THE NUMBERS

**1,000** CUPS OF FLOUR

--------

**480** CUPS OF SUGAR

--------

**288** DOZEN EGGS

--------

**240** CUPS OF MILK

--------

**480** POUNDS OF BUTTER

--------

**144** POUNDS OF ONIONS

--------

**50** WOODEN SPOONS

--------

**12** JARS OF CINNAMON

## RECIPE TESTING BASICS

**MEASURING FLOUR:** The way you measure flour can really make a difference! So we're all on the same page: Stir the flour in the container to lighten, then spoon it into a measuring cup. Level the measure.

**EGGS:** We test with large eggs. 1 large egg = 3¼ Tbsp.

**MILK:** We test with 2% milk unless otherwise written.

**VEGETABLE OIL:** If the recipe calls for vegetable oil, we test with neutral oils, such as canola oil and corn oil, unless otherwise written.

**BUTTER:** We use and love butter! If you need to use margarine, that's OK for cooking, but butter bakes better.

*No one person is the boss of a recipe!* We gather editors and Test Kitchen folks around a table or stand at a kitchen counter to chew on things, literally. Flavor, difficulty, ingredients: they're all up for discussion!

Better Homes & Gardens

17TH EDITION

NEW COOK BOOK

**THE RED PLAID COOKBOOK** Since first publishing *Better Homes & Gardens® New Cook Book* in 1930, the Test Kitchen team has been at the heart of its creation. Every kitchen discovery made— including creative techniques, innovative ingredient info, and flavor trends—is added to each new edition.

# MEASURING

HOW YOU MEASURE INGREDIENTS MATTERS. THIS IS ESPECIALLY TRUE IN BAKING, WHERE THERE'S QUITE A BIT OF CHEMISTRY INVOLVED. TAKE THE TIME TO MEASURE EACH INGREDIENT CORRECTLY AND YOU'LL SEE (AND TASTE) THE RESULTS.

### FLOUR
Stir to fluff flour. Lightly spoon it into a dry measuring cup. Level with a table knife. (Don't use the measuring cup as a flour scoop.)

### BROWN SUGAR
Scoop or spoon brown sugar into a dry measuring cup and pack firmly. Add more sugar and pack until level.

### BUTTER, SHORTENING & CREAM CHEESE
Look for tablespoon markings on the wrapper of these ingredients (even shortening and cream cheese have measurements on the wrappers). Straighten wrapper; cut off what you need. Or spoon the ingredient into a dry measuring cup, packing firmly to fill air pockets. Level the top.

### STICKY LIQUIDS
Control the stickiness of syrups and honey. Coat the liquid measure with nonstick cooking spray first. This allows the syrup to settle evenly, and it will slide right out.

### LIQUID MEASURING CUPS
These glass or plastic cups have spouts and measurement markings on the side. For accurate measuring, look at eye level at the liquid in cup.

### DRY MEASURING CUPS
These cups look like scoops and have flat tops. Use a table knife to level dry ingredients. (Resist the urge to shake flour to level—you'll end up with too much.)

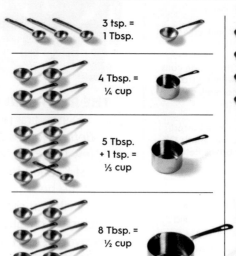

3 tsp. = 1 Tbsp.

4 Tbsp. = ¼ cup

5 Tbsp. + 1 tsp. = ⅓ cup

8 Tbsp. = ½ cup

16 Tbsp. = 1 cup

We did the math so you would know how much to buy when you head to the store.

**1 GAL. =**
4 qt.
8 pt.
16 cups
128 fl. oz.
3.8 L

**1 QT. =**
2 pt.
4 cups
32 fl. oz.
0.95 L

**1 PT. =**
2 cups
16 fl. oz.
480 ml

**1 CUP =**
8 fl. oz.
240 ml

**¼ CUP =**
4 Tbsp.
12 tsp.
2 fl. oz.
60 ml

**1 TBSP. =**
3 tsp.
½ fl. oz.
15 ml

### LEMONS

1 medium lemon =
about 2 tsp. zest

1 large lemon =
about 2½ tsp. zest

1 medium lemon =
about 3 Tbsp. juice

1 large lemon =
about ¼ cup juice

1 medium lemon =
about 3½ oz.

1 large lemon =
about 5 oz.

### LIMES

1 small lime =
1 tsp. zest

1 medium lime =
1½ tsp. zest

1 small lime =
about 1½ Tbsp. juice

1 medium lime =
about 2 Tbsp. juice

1 small lime = about 1½ oz.

1 medium lime = about 2½ oz.

## ODD MEASURES

What is a pinch, a dash, and ⅛ tsp.? Some measuring spoon sets include ⅛ tsp. If yours doesn't, use half of the ¼ tsp. measure. Technically, a dash is about ⅟₁₂ of a tsp., and a pinch is about ⅟₁₆ of a tsp. But it's OK to eyeball these amounts.

**ONIONS**

1 small onion =
½ cup chopped

1 medium onion =
1 cup chopped

1 large onion =
2 cups chopped

**EGGS**

1 medium egg =
3 Tbsp.

1 large egg =
3½ Tbsp.

1 extra-large egg =
¼ cup

**HERBS**

1 tsp. dried herbs =
1 Tbsp. chopped
fresh herbs

# CUTTING

TO KEEP IT CONCISE, OUR RECIPES OFTEN INCLUDE IN THE INGREDIENT LIST THE WAY A FRUIT OR VEGETABLE SHOULD BE CUT (CHOPPED, BIAS-SLICED, ETC.). HERE ARE OUR TIPS FOR PREPPING SOME COMMON FRUITS AND VEGGIES.

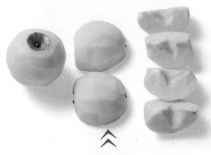

## APPLES

If desired, use a vegetable peeler to peel. Halve, then cut into quarters from stem to end; trim the core and discard seeds, stem, and ends. Cut quarters in half lengthwise for wedges. Cut wedges lengthwise into thin slices.

## CITRUS

To section, cut a thin slice from both ends. Cut off peel and white pith from top to bottom. Working over a bowl to catch juice, remove sections by cutting toward the center between a section and membrane. Cut along the other side of the section to free it.

## POTATO

If desired, use a vegetable peeler to peel. Cut crosswise into slices. For strips, cut slices into desired-size strips. For cubes, cut the strips crosswise into desired-size cubes.

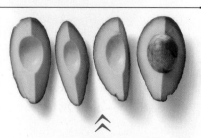

## AVOCADO

Cut in half lengthwise, working around the seed. Separate by twisting halves in opposite directions. Cut half with seed in half again; pluck out seed. Use a spoon to scoop flesh from peels. To slice, cut quarters lengthwise.

## ONION

Peel onion and halve it lengthwise. For slices, place halves flat sides down and cut crosswise. To chop, cut halves into very thin wedges, then cut crosswise into pieces. For wedges, cut halved onion lengthwise, angling toward center.

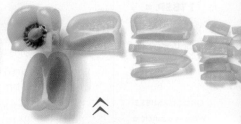

## SWEET PEPPER

Hold the pepper upright; slice off the sides to make four pieces (cut as close to stem as possible). Remove any seeds on sections. For strips, cut sections lengthwise. To chop, cut strips crosswise.

## PINEAPPLE

Remove top and bottom. Cut off peel from top to bottom. Slice off sides to make four pieces (cut close to core). For rings, slice peeled pineapple crosswise. Use a small cutter to remove core from slices.

## CHOPPED
Our Test Kitchen defines "chopped" as ½-inch pieces. It's an estimate, so don't worry about measuring them.

## FINELY CHOPPED
Once you chop your ingredient, use your chef's knife to go a step further to roughly chop into ¼-inch cubes.

## MINCED
Minced is smaller, about ⅛ inch. Keep chopping until the pieces get smaller. Garlic should be very finely minced.

## KNIVES
These are the best basic knives to start your set.

### SERRATED BREAD KNIFE
Use a sawing motion to cut crusty bread, crumbly cake, or even delicate tomatoes.

### CHEF'S KNIFE
Slice, dice, chop, and mince with this all-purpose blade.

## JULIENNE
These matchstick-size strips are about 2¼ inches long. First cut long slices, then stack; cut into ⅛- to ¼-inch-wide strips.

## BIAS-SLICE
This cut is for long vegetables like carrots and green onions. It makes the slices more oval. To cut, slice crosswise at an angle.

### KITCHEN SCISSORS
Open packages, cut chicken, snip herbs, and more.

## WEDGE
Wedges are cut from whole produce like apples and onions. Cut halves, flat sides down, angling toward the center.

## ZEST
Use a Microplane (rasp) grater for citrus zest. Rub peel firmly across grater, rotating fruit as you rub. (Don't grate white pith.)

### PARING KNIFE
Have a few of these small knives for coring, cutting, and slicing small produce like strawberries.

# COOKING & COOKWARE

THESE ARE THE MOST FREQUENTLY USED COOKING TECHNIQUES, PLUS A GUIDE TO THE COOKWARE THAT'S OFTEN USED IN THIS BOOK.

## SAUTÉ

Cook and stir food in a small amount of oil over medium to medium-high heat in a skillet. The goal is crisp-tender veggies with caramelized surfaces.

## STIR-FRY

This fast, medium-high to high heat method is for quick-cooking larger quantities of uniform-size ingredients. Small amounts of oil are used in a wok or extra-large skillet. Stir foods constantly.

## PAN-FRY

This method uses enough oil to lightly coat the bottom of the skillet. The surface of the food browns and, if coated, turns crisp. Thin cuts of fish and chicken cook well this way.

## ROAST

Roasting is a dry-heat cooking method that browns the outside of foods. Place large items, such as turkey and beef roast, on a rack to provide air circulation under the meat. This method is also used to caramelize veggies.

## BROIL

The broiler (i.e., the oven's top heating element) cooks food quickly under intense heat. Arrange food so its top (not the rack) is the specified distance from the broiler. Watch food closely. If you don't have a broiler pan, use a foil-lined baking pan.

## STEAM

Place food in a covered steamer basket set over boiling water. The steam quickly cooks the food, usually vegetables, which retains color and nutrients. Steamed veggies are done when crisp-tender.

# SKILLETS & SAUCEPANS

Good-quality cookware is an investment worth making—if you treat it well, it will last for years. Always check the manufacturer's directions to see if your skillet is oven-safe. All-metal pans—with metal handles—are typically fine for use in the oven. (Skillets with enamel or nonstick coating or plastic handles may be for stove top only.) These cookware materials are readily available.

## ALUMINUM
Aluminum is a good heat conductor—the heavier the pan, the better. Nonstick finishes prevent acidic food reactions, which may discolor the food.

## CAST IRON
These pans are heavy and sturdy. They conduct and retain heat well but require seasoning and careful cleaning. Follow manufacturer's directions.

## CERAMIC
This skillet is aluminum with a nonstick ceramic coating. It conducts heat well, and the coating can withstand higher temperatures than traditional nonstick coatings.

## COPPER
Typically lined with stainless steel, these pans are heavy and sturdy. Copper is the best heat conductor, but it needs occasional polishing (and is pricey).

## STAINLESS STEEL
This metal conducts heat poorly, so it usually has a core of aluminum or copper called tri-ply. Stainless steel doesn't scratch or dent easily or react to acidic foods; it does clean easily.

**MEDIUM SKILLET = 8 INCHES**

**LARGE SKILLET = 10 INCHES**

**EXTRA-LARGE SKILLET = 12 INCHES**

Straight-sided sauté pans with lids work well for browning and simmering.

Sloped sides on a skillet make it easy to toss, flip, and remove foods.

**SMALL SAUCEPAN = 1 or 1½ qt.**

**MEDIUM SAUCEPAN = 2 qt.**

**LARGE SAUCEPAN = 3 or 4 qt.**

## SAUCEPANS
Saucepans have tall, straight sides with tight-fitting lids. Use a small saucepan for melting chocolate and butter. A medium saucepan works well for making sauces and cooking rice. A large saucepan cooks small-batch soups and stews.

**FOR BIG RECIPES,** we often call for a Dutch oven. This stove-to-table pot lets you brown foods and bake in the same vessel. A 4- to 6-qt. size with lid can handle most jobs.

# GRILLING

CONTROLLING THE FIRE IS THE KEY TO PERFECT, FLAME-SEARED MEATS AND VEGGIES.
GET A HANDLE ON THE TERMINOLOGY, TECHNIQUES, AND SAFETY TIPS.
THEN FIRE UP THE GRILL TO GET YOUR BACKYARD PARTY STARTED.

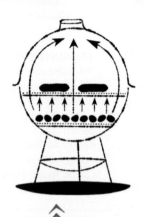

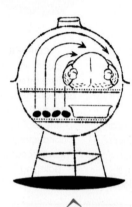

## DIRECT GRILLING

involves placing food directly over an intense heat source with the lid closed. It works best with foods that grill in 30 minutes or less, including tender, thin, and small cuts of food. To cook evenly, turn food once halfway through grilling time.

### FOODS TO DIRECT-GRILL

Burgers ▪ steaks ▪ chops ▪ chicken pieces ▪ brats ▪ hot dogs ▪ vegetables

## INDIRECT GRILLING

is usually done at lower temperatures with food positioned on the grill rack to the side of the heat source with grill cover closed. This slower grilling method works like an oven and is used for foods that take longer to cook. The heat circulates, so turning food isn't necessary.

### FOODS TO INDIRECT-GRILL

Large roasts ▪ ribs ▪ whole chicken and turkey ▪ whole fish

## GAS GRILLS

are clean, convenient, and easy to control. Follow the manufacturer's directions to preheat your gas grill and to use for indirect cooking (*opposite*).

### ADJUSTING HEAT

Adjust burners to higher or lower settings as needed.

## CHARCOAL GRILLS

take more effort but are worth it for the smoky flavor.

### PREP

About 25 to 30 minutes before cooking, remove the grill cover and rack and open all the vents.

### DIRECT COOKING

Use enough briquettes to cover the charcoal grate with one layer. Pile briquettes into a pyramid in the center of the grate for lighting (*opposite*).

### INDIRECT COOKING

The number of briquettes you need to use is based on your grill size (chart, *opposite*).

### ADJUSTING HEAT
If grill is too hot, raise rack, spread coals apart, close air vents halfway, or remove some coals. If grill is too cool, use long-handled tongs to tap ashes off burning coals, move coals closer, add briquettes, lower rack, or open vents.

## CLEANING GRATES

To prevent flare-ups and stuck-on food, clean grates after each grilling session. Particles release easier when the grate is still hot (but let coals die down slightly before scrubbing).

**1**
*Scrub steel grill racks with a long-handled iron-bristle brush and enameled grates with a brass-bristle brush. Wear heat-resistant mitts.*

**2**
*If you don't have a brush, scrub off burned bits of foods with a sturdy long-handled metal spatula. Or grip a ball of foil with tongs and rub grates.*

**3**
*For thorough cleaning, after the grill grate has cooled completely, wash using mild soap and steel wool; rinse well. Let stand to dry.*

## *ABOUT CHARCOAL*

Fire up the coals using a fire starter or an electric starter or place briquettes in a chimney starter. (If you use liquid starter, wait 1 minute before igniting the fire.) Before grilling, let the fire burn 20 to 25 minutes or until the coals are covered with a light coating of gray ash.

| Grill diameter **18½ INCHES** | Grill diameter **22½ INCHES** | Grill diameter **26¾ INCHES** |
|---|---|---|
| Briquettes to start **32** | Briquettes to start **50** | Briquettes to start **60** |
| Briquettes to add for longer grilling **10** | Briquettes to add for longer grilling **16** | Briquettes to add for longer grilling **18** |

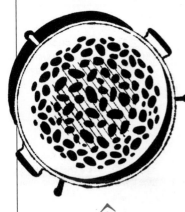

**DIRECT COOKING** Use long-handled tongs to spread hot coals evenly across the bottom of the grill, covering an area 3 inches larger on all sides of the food you are cooking.

**WEATHER & TEMP**
Weather can influence coal temperatures, and not everyone judges temperature alike. So use timings given with each recipe as a guideline and watch foods on the grill. Adjust heat when the temperature isn't right (*opposite*).

**INDIRECT COOKING** Use long-handled tongs to arrange coals around the edge of grill bottom. Place a disposable foil pan in center (drip pan). Or place coals on one side of grill; place drip pan on other side.

**FLARE-UPS**
Fat and meat juices that drip onto coals can cause flare-ups. If this happens, move food away from the flare-up and close the lid. If necessary to put out flame, close vents (or turn off gas). As a last resort, mist with water in a spray bottle.

**HOW HOT IS HOT?**
Check the temperature of the coals using a built-in or separate grill thermometer. Or use the hand test to test the heat level of your grill: Hold your palm above the heat source close to the cooking level and time how long you can comfortably keep it there.

**HOT (HIGH)**
(400°F to 450°F)
2-second or less hand count

**MEDIUM-HIGH**
(375°F to 400°F)
3-second or less hand count

**MEDIUM**
(350°F to 375°F)
4-second or less hand count

**LOW**
(300°F to 350°F)
5-second or less hand count

## *GRILL SAFETY*

**POSITION** grill in a well-ventilated area at least 10 feet away from trees, houses, and combustible materials. Never grill inside a garage, porch, or enclosed area.

**KEEP** children and pets a safe distance from the hot grill.

**USE** heat-resistant mitts and tools with long handles.

**HAVE** a fire extinguisher handy in case of emergency. Do not pour water on a grease fire.

**NEVER LEAVE** a grill unattended or try to move it while it is in use or is still hot.

**PERIODICALLY** test your gas grill for leaks and clean the venturi tubes regularly according to the manufacturer's directions.

**EXTINGUISH COALS** by closing vents and lid. Let ashes cool 24 hours before disposing of them.

**LET** the grill cool completely before covering or storing it.

# KEY INGREDIENTS

THESE COMMON INGREDIENTS APPEAR OFTEN IN OUR RECIPES. HERE ARE THE SPECIFICS ABOUT HOW EACH INGREDIENT IS PREPPED IN OUR TEST KITCHEN DURING TESTING.

## NUTS

Shelled nuts are sold in the supermarket baking aisle or bulk section. They are available whole, chopped (labeled "pieces"), roasted, salted, and sugared.

### APPEARANCE

Look for shelled nuts that are plump and firm (not withered or rubbery) and uniform in color.

### STORAGE

Nuts contain high amounts of oil and turn rancid quickly. Store nuts in tightly closed containers or bags in the freezer up to 8 months or pantry 1 to 2 months. Always taste before using.

**GROUND NUTS**

Use a blender or food processor to get this finer texture, adding 1 Tbsp. of the sugar or flour called for in the recipe for each cup of nuts. This absorbs some oil, keeping the nuts from clumping. Use on/off pulses to prevent overprocessing, which can result in a gooey nut butter.

**TOAST FOR FLAVOR**

Toasting nuts, seeds, and coconut adds depth of flavor. To toast nuts or coconut, spread evenly in a shallow pan and bake in a 350°F oven 5 to 10 minutes, stirring once or twice (watch closely). Toast seeds and finely chopped nuts in a dry skillet over medium heat, stirring often.

**COARSELY CHOPPED**

Use a chef's knife to chop into large irregular pieces more than ¼ inch in size.

**CHOPPED**

Use a chef's knife to chop into medium irregular pieces about ¼ Inch in size.

**FINELY CHOPPED**

Use a chef's knife to chop into pieces about ⅛ inch in size.

## CRUMBS & CUBES

**DRY BREAD CUBES**

Crunchy bread cubes are used in stuffings and bread puddings. To make, stack a few bread slices and cut into ½-inch cubes. Bake cubes in a shallow baking pan in a 300°F oven 10 to 15 minutes or until dry and crisp, stirring twice; cool.

**DRY BREAD CRUMBS**

Fine dry bread crumbs can be purchased, or you can make your own. Use slightly stale dry bread slices or bake slices in a 300°F oven about 10 minutes or until slightly crisp. Use a food processor to make slightly coarse or fine crumbs. One slice yields ¼ cup fine dry crumbs.

**SOFT BREAD CRUMBS**

To create soft bread crumbs, cut fresh bread into cubes and pulse them in a food processor until crumbs form. One slice of bread, cubed and processed, yields ¾ cup crumbs.

**PANKO CRUMBS**

Look for panko bread crumbs at the supermarket with other breadings and coatings. They are light and crisp with a coarse texture. These crumbs work well for toppings, coatings, stir-ins, and any other dish where you would use traditional dry bread crumbs.

**CRACKER CRUMBS**

For 1 cup of cracker crumbs, use 28 saltine crackers, 24 rich round crackers, or 14 graham cracker squares. Pulse them in a food processor to desired fineness or crush them in a resealable plastic bag using a rolling pin.

---

---

## CREAM CHEESE

Unless specified in the recipe, we test with regular cream cheese. However, we found that reduced-fat versions work equally well in most recipes. Avoid using fat-free cream cheese for cooking and baking—this product works best as a spread. To soften cream cheese, let stand at room temperature 30 minutes.

## THICKENERS

Flour and cornstarch are the most common thickeners. To thicken 1 cup sauce to medium thickness, in a jar with a screw-top lid combine 2 Tbsp. flour with ¼ cup cold water or 1 Tbsp. cornstarch with 1 Tbsp. cold water. Shake it in the jar until well mixed (if in a bowl, whisk to combine ingredients). Stir into the sauce; cook and stir the sauce over medium heat until bubbly. To completely cook the starch, cook and stir 2 minutes more.

## EGGS

Recipes in this cookbook were developed and tested using large-size eggs.

Before adding eggs to a recipe, crack them into a separate bowl to make sure eggshells don't end up in the food. To crack an egg, tap it on a flat countertop or on the rim of a bowl. If a piece of shell falls into the raw egg, use a spoon to scoop it out.

### PASTEURIZING EGG WHITES

For food safety, start with purchased pasteurized egg whites when recipes use raw egg whites that are never cooked. Or follow these steps to pasteurize them yourself. In a 1- or 1½-qt. saucepan stir together 2 egg whites, 2 Tbsp. sugar, 1 tsp. water, and ⅛ tsp. cream of tartar just until combined but not foamy. Heat and stir over low heat until mixture registers 160°F. (Don't worry if you notice a few small bits of cooked white in the mixture.) Remove from heat and place saucepan in a large bowl half-filled with ice water. Stir 2 minutes to cool quickly.

## SALT

Unless noted, our recipes are tested with iodized table salt. Here are tips for using specialty salts.

**FLEUR DE SEL** This pricey salt is used to finish a dish, adding a mild but distinct flavor. Sprinkle lightly on salads, rich chocolate or caramel desserts, and before serving meats and fish.

**MALDON** This popular flaked sea salt is made from purified seawater from the shores of Essex, England. It has a pyramid shape and delightfully briny flavor. Sprinkle over delicately flavored food just before serving.

**KOSHER SALT** This salt, a favorite with chefs, usually has no additives (such as iodine). Each grain is large and flat, so kosher salt dissolves quickly and can be added at any stage of the cooking process. Because of its size, 1 tsp. kosher salt contains less sodium than 1 tsp. table salt.

## SUGAR

Most sugar bowls are filled with granulated (white) sugar. The finely textured crystals are easy to measure and dissolve quickly. Powdered sugar is very finely ground, combined with an anticaking agent, and sifted. Other sugars, including blond-color raw turbinado and light and dark brown sugars, give a molasses sweetness to recipes. For information on baking with sugar, see *p. 473.*

## FLOUR

Wheat flour is the most common flour used in cooking. All-purpose wheat flour has a moderate protein content and is available both bleached and unbleached. Bread flour (also wheat), in comparison, has a higher protein content for sturdier foods like crusty breads, rolls, and pizza doughs. For information on flour and for our Gluten-Free Flour Mix, see *p. 472.*

## OATS & OATMEAL

**OAT GROATS**
The least-processed option, groats (hulled, unbroken oat grains) can be cooked and served as a cereal and prepared like rice for a side dish or salad.

**STEEL-CUT OATS**
Also called Irish or Scottish oats, these coarse oats are made by chopping groats into smaller pieces. They require longer cooking than rolled and quick-cooking oats and are chewier.

**ROLLED OATS**
Rolled oats (aka old-fashioned) are whole groats that have been hulled, steamed, and flattened. They cook faster than steel-cut. (To toast, stir in a dry skillet over medium heat until golden brown.)

**QUICK-COOKING ROLLED OATS**
This version is made from groats that have been chopped before undergoing the steaming process. They are flattened more than rolled oats, so they cook faster and are less chewy.

**INSTANT OATS**
Instant oats are precooked (which makes them super soft) and dried before they are flattened with rollers. They cook extra fast for breakfast but don't work well in baked goods.

**OAT FLOUR**
Oat flour is made by grinding gluten-free oats. But contamination can occur during grinding, so it isn't considered a gluten-free substitute for wheat. If you bake with it, experiment by substituting small amounts.

**OAT BRAN**
Bran is the outer coating of the grain and is packed with soluble fiber. You can add it to baked goods to increase the fiber content. Experiment by starting with small amounts.

## MILK

During testing, we always use reduced-fat (2%) dairy milk (unless otherwise noted in the ingredient list). In many recipes, any milk will work—even nondairy milks—but the richness of the product may be affected. Nondairy milks made from soy, almond, rice, coconut, cashew, macadamia, oat, and hemp are located alongside refrigerated dairy milk. Shelf-stable options are also available. Some brands offer unsweetened and sweetened milks along with added flavors, especially vanilla. Use your judgment when swapping (i.e., sweetened vanilla-almond milk is a good choice for a fruit smoothie; unsweetened plain soymilk is better for sauces). Use only dairy milk for custards and puddings.

## BROTH

When the sodium level of a recipe (specifically for soups and stews) gets too high, our Test Kitchen balances it by using reduced-sodium or no-salt-added broth. Stock and bone broth products are also available and work as substitutes for regular broth. Broth bases, granules (bouillon), and concentrates can be used for sauces or soups and as seasoning for rice and boiled potatoes as they cook. Adjust other seasonings as necessary depending on the sodium in the product you use.

## PEANUT BUTTER

The market is filled with peanut butter choices. Most versions rely on shelf-stable oils—such as palm oil—for a smooth, evenly blended consistency that doesn't separate at room temperature. This is the type we use to test all of our recipes. Some peanut butter varieties, labeled as "natural," just use peanuts and peanut oil and require refrigeration. These types tend to separate upon standing and require stirring. It can be difficult to fully blend them for an even consistency, which may affect cooking and baking results.

## *OILS*

These are the most common oils and their uses. (Smoke point: how hot an oil can get before it starts to smoke.)

### CANOLA

*SMOKE POINT 400°F*
A mild flavor and medium smoke point make canola a good all-purpose oil. Use for all baking and cooking tasks.

### COCONUT

*SMOKE POINT 350°F–400°F*
Refined coconut oil has a very mild coconut flavor and a higher smoke point (400°F); unrefined has a stronger coconut taste and lower smoke point (350°F). It is a solid at room temp and below.

### CORN

*SMOKE POINT 450°F*
Its high smoke point and neutral flavor make this oil an excellent choice for frying, baking, and cooking.

### OLIVE

*SMOKE POINT 325°F–410°F*
Unprocessed extra virgin olive oil has a strong olive flavor (almost grassy or fruity) and a lower smoke point (325°F). Use it as a dipping oil or a vinaigrette base. Pure olive oil is a combination of refined and extra virgin oils filtered for light flavor and a higher smoke point (410°F).

### PEANUT

*SMOKE POINT 450°F*
This is the go-to oil for deep-fat frying and stir-frying.

# CHILE PEPPERS

WE LOVE CHILE PEPPERS FOR THE BIG FLAVOR BOOST THEY ADD TO FOODS AND FOR THAT KICK OF SPICY HEAT. LEARN WHICH ONES ARE MILDER AND WHICH ARE FLAMING HOT SO YOU ALWAYS PICK THE RIGHT VARIETY FOR THE JOB.

### HOW TO HANDLE CHILES

Always wear plastic or rubber gloves when working with chile peppers. If the cut chiles touch your skin, the oils (depending on the potency of the chile pepper) create a painful tingle that lasts for hours and can't be washed off. If you do accidentally touch the chiles, wash hands well with soapy water; avoid touching your eyes until the tingle subsides.

### DRIED CHILES

To hydrate dried chiles, cover them in boiling water; let them stand until the skins become soft and pliable (about 30 minutes). Cut the chiles into small pieces, discarding stems and, if desired, membranes and seeds. To use as a fine powder, omit hydrating step and grind dried chiles into a fine powder using a mortar and pestle or spice grinder.

### ROAST FOR FLAVOR

Preheat broiler. Place whole peppers on a foil-lined baking sheet. Broil 4 inches from heat 8 to 10 minutes or until charred on all sides, turning occasionally. Bring foil up around peppers; fold to enclose completely. Let stand 10 minutes. Wearing gloves, scrape off and discard skins. Remove seeds and stems.

## CHILI PASTE

Use this condiment to make marinades, vinaigrettes, sauces, and soups.

### 1
*Place stemmed and seeded dried chiles in an ungreased skillet. Cook a few minutes until fragrant.*

### 2
*Transfer chiles to a bowl; cover with boiling water. Let soak 30 minutes to soften; drain.*

### 3
*Transfer chiles to a food processor or blender. Process until a smooth paste forms.*

## *MEET THE CHILES*

When buying fresh or dried, look for these varieties.

**1. CHILE DE ÁRBOL** Whether fresh or dried, this chile goes by the same name. Its high heat level and full flavor make it a good choice when you want extra-spicy chili.

**2. PASILLA** The long, slender dried pasilla is medium-hot with a deep, smoky flavor. It's often used in mole and adobo sauces and salsas.

**3. ANAHEIM** The mild, green Anaheim is a California chile that grows 6 to 8 inches long. Canned green chiles are preserved Anaheims.

**4. CALIFORNIA** This is the dried ripe red Anaheim chile.

**5. THAI CHILE** Several chiles are labeled "Thai chile." Most of these (such as Thai Bird chiles) are small, red, and very hot.

**6. CHIPOTLE** These smoked jalapeños are canned in a tangy adobo sauce. They are used (in small quantities) in soups, chilies, and sauces.

**7. JALAPEÑO** This pepper is versatile and is readily available in supermarkets. It has a complex sweet flavor; the level of heat varies dramatically from pepper to pepper.

**8. HABANERO &**
**9. DRIED HABANERO** Caution! These chiles are extremely hot; use only if you love the burn. Start small when adding to dishes.

**10. POBLANO** The poblano, Mexico's largest chile, has a complex flavor with mild heat. Stuff it or chop it to use in soups and chilies.

**11. ANCHO** Ancho is the dried poblano. It's the sweetest dried chile, featuring hints of chocolate and plum.

**12. GUAJILLO** With an earthy flavor and medium heat, the dried guajillo is often used for making tamale sauce.

**13. SERRANO** These hot green chiles turn from bright green to red as they ripen. Use care when adding to salsas, marinades, and sauces.

## HEAT LEVELS
In 1912 Wilbur Scoville created a scale for a pharmaceutical company to measure the spicy heat in chiles. Scoville Heat Units (SHU) range from 0 (in sweet peppers) to 2 million (in scorpion chiles [not pictured]). These are the SHU for common types of chiles *(left)*.

**100,000–300,000**
HABANERO

**50,000–100,000**
THAI CHILE

**15,000–30,000**
ÁRBOL & SERRANO

**7,000–15,000**
CHIPOTLE

**3,500–11,000**
JALAPEÑO

**4,000–8,000**
PASILLA

**3,000–6,000**
GUAJILLO

**1,000–2,000**
ANAHEIM & CALIFORNIA

**1,000–1,500**
POBLANO & ANCHO

# GARLIC & SPICES

WE ALL COULD USE MORE SPICE IN OUR LIVES, SO HERE'S THE ULTIMATE GUIDE TO PERKING UP YOURS. KEEP A COLLECTION OF SOME OR ALL OF THESE ESSENTIAL SPICES (PLUS BULBS OF GARLIC) ON HAND TO FLAVOR YOUR RECIPES. (SPICE BLENDS, *PP. 28–29.*)

## GARLIC

Whole bulbs last the longest when stored in a cool, dry, dark place with good air circulation. If garlic sprouts, remove green portion. Discard if cloves are shriveled. To peel, smash a clove with the flat side of a chef's knife to loosen; remove the peel. Mince garlic with a chef's knife or use a garlic press.

**1 garlic bulb = 12 to 15 cloves
1 clove = ½ tsp. minced =
⅛ tsp. garlic powder**

**ROASTED GARLIC** Preheat oven to 400°F. Cut ½ inch off the top of the bulb to expose the ends of the cloves. Leaving bulb whole, remove any loose, papery outer layers. Place bulb, cut end up, on a double thickness of foil on a baking sheet. Drizzle bulb with oil; sprinkle with salt. Bring foil up around the bulb and fold edges. Roast 35 to 40 minutes or until garlic feels soft when squeezed; cool. Remove garlic cloves from paper husks by squeezing bottom of bulb or each clove.

## BLACK PEPPER

**WHOLE PEPPERCORNS** Ground pepper loses flavor quickly, so buy whole peppercorns to grind fresh in a pepper mill. Tricolor varieties are available.

**CRACKED PEPPERCORNS** Cracked whole peppercorns add texture and bite to rubs and marinades. Use a mortar and pestle to crack peppercorns.

**COARSE-GROUND PEPPER** Pepper mills offer settings for grinding. The coarser the grind, the stronger the flavor. This grind is often used for finishing a dish.

**FINELY GROUND PEPPER** Finely ground is better for stirring into a dish. The flavor is more evenly distributed throughout the food with less harshness.

**MARK THE DATE ON THE BOTTOM OF THE SPICE BOTTLE THE DAY IT IS OPENED.** GROUND SPICES START TO LOSE FLAVOR AFTER ONE YEAR. FOR THE MOST INTENSE FLAVOR, BUY WHOLE SPICES AND GRIND THEM AT HOME. STORE SPICES AWAY FROM HEAT AND SUNLIGHT.

# CREATE YOUR SPICE PANTRY

These are the most common spices you'll want to have on hand for cooking and baking.

**1. STAR ANISE**
*licoricelike*
**BEST USES** Asian cuisine, mulled drinks

**2. HOT OR SWEET PAPRIKA**
*peppery*
**BEST USES** meat rubs, soups and stews

**3. SMOKED PAPRIKA**
*smoky pepper*
**BEST USES** meat rubs, soups and stews

**4. GROUND CINNAMON**
*spicy-sweet*
**BEST USES** breads, desserts, meat rubs

**5. CINNAMON STICKS**
*spicy-sweet*
**BEST USES** mulled drinks

**6. FENNEL SEEDS**
*licoricelike*
**BEST USES** Italian dishes, meat rubs, savory breads

**7. GROUND CUMIN**
*earthy, warm*
**BEST USES** chilies, meat rubs, Mexican dishes

**8. CUMIN SEEDS**
*earthy, warm*
**BEST USES** toast and grind; use like ground

**9. GROUND CLOVES**
*sharp, warm*
**BEST USES** pumpkin pie, spice blends

**10. WHOLE CLOVES**
*sharp, warm*
**BEST USES** baked ham, mulled drinks

**11. GROUND NUTMEG**
*sweet*
**BEST USES** baked goods, meatballs, white sauce

**12. WHOLE NUTMEG**
*fresh, sweet*
**BEST USES** Grate on a Microplane (rasp) grater (p. 476); use two times the amount of purchased ground

**13. CHILI POWDER**
*complex spice blend*
**BEST USES** chilies, meat rubs

**14. CAYENNE PEPPER**
*hot, spicy*
**BEST USES** barbecue rubs and sauces, Mexican and Cajun dishes

**15. GROUND CHIPOTLE CHILI POWDER**
*smoky, hot*
**BEST USES** chilies and stews, marinades

**16. GROUND MUSTARD**
*sharp, tangy*
**BEST USES** cheese sauces, salad dressings

**17. MUSTARD SEEDS**
*sharp, tangy*
**BEST USES** pickling recipes

**18. GROUND CARDAMOM**
*citrusy, fragrant*
**BEST USES** baked goods, chai

**19. CARDAMOM PODS**
*citrusy, fragrant*
**BEST USES** grind; use like ground

**20. CURRY POWDER**
*complex spice blend*
**BEST USES** chicken salad, curries, sauces

**21. CRYSTALLIZED GINGER**
*sweet, spicy*
**BEST USES** baked goods

**22. GROUND GINGER**
*pungent, zesty*
**BEST USES** Asian cuisine, baked goods

# HERBS

ALTHOUGH SUMMER HERALDS THE SEASON FOR FRESH HERBS (EITHER FROM YOUR OWN GARDEN OR FROM THE FARMERS MARKET), MOST SUPERMARKETS OFFER A SELECTION IN THE PRODUCE DEPARTMENT YEAR-ROUND. WHEN FRESH ISN'T AVAILABLE, DRIED IS A FLAVORFUL OPTION.

## DRIED HERBS

For the most flavor, crush dried herbs with a mortar and pestle to release the aromatic oils. Or place the dried herb in your palm and crush it with your thumb and fingers.

### SWAPPING DRIED FOR FRESH

In general, we recommend using one-third the amount of dried herb for the amount of fresh in a recipe. When substituting a ground herb for dried leaf herb, use about half the amount dried.

**1 Tbsp. fresh herb =
1 tsp. dried herb =
½ tsp. ground herb**

### STORAGE

Store dried herbs and spices in a cool, dark place 1 to 2 years.

## FRESH HERBS

Pick herbs with plump leaves (avoid herbs that look wilted or shriveled).

### CHOPPING FRESH HERBS

When herbs are stirred into recipes, you can chop the leaves with your chef's knife. If you're sprinkling fresh herbs on a dish to garnish, snip leaves with kitchen scissors so they don't get crushed or bruised.

### STORAGE

Trim ends of stems; stand herbs in a jar with water. Loosely cover with a plastic bag; store in the refrigerator. (Store fresh basil at room temp to prevent discoloration.)

## FREEZING HERBS

**PRESERVE** fresh herbs for months in the freezer. Chop or snip fresh herb leaves and tuck them loosely into the compartments of an ice cube tray.

**POUR** olive oil or water over herbs to cover; use a spoon to gently submerge the herbs.

**PLACE** ice cube trays in the freezer; freeze until firm. If desired, remove frozen cubes from tray and store in a resealable plastic freezer bag. Freeze up to 3 months.

**TO USE,** drop an herb cube into a hot soup or sauce.

## *MEET THE HERBS*

Because heat diminishes the flavor of fresh herbs, stir in chopped or snipped leaves just before serving.

**1. OREGANO**
*pungent, peppery*
**BEST USES** chilies, pizza and marinara sauces, roasted/grilled meat
**SWAP** marjoram

**2. WHOLE BAY LEAVES**
*herbal, slightly bitter*
**BEST USES** braised meats, soups and stews (remove leaves before serving)

**3. ITALIAN PARSLEY**
*bright, grassy*
**BEST USES** multipurpose, grain salads, sauces (p. 30)
**SWAP** curly-leaf parsley

**4. CURLY-LEAF PARSLEY**
*subtle, grassy*
**BEST USES** multipurpose, garnish
**SWAP** Italian parsley

**5. MARJORAM**
*pungent, perfumy*
**BEST USES** beef, lamb, soups, vegetables
**SWAP** oregano

**6. BASIL**
*peppery, licoricelike*
**BEST USES** curries, Basil Pesto (p. 31), tomato dishes and sauces
**SWAP** Italian parsley

**7. DILL**
*grassy, slightly sour*
**BEST USES** egg salad or egg dishes, fish, vegetable salads
**SWAP** chives

**8. TARRAGON**
*slightly bitter, licoricelike*
**BEST USES** chicken, cream and butter sauces, roasted vegetables
**SWAP** basil

**9. CHIVES**
*mild onion*
**BEST USES** dips, fish, savory breads
**SWAP** green onion

**10. SAGE**
*warm, woodsy*
**BEST USES** breakfast sausage, stuffing, turkey
**SWAP** Poultry Seasoning (p. 28)

**11. THYME**
*fragrant, earthy*
**BEST USES** meat rubs, roasted vegetables, soups and stews
**SWAP** oregano or Italian parsley

**12. ROSEMARY**
*piney, floral*
**BEST USES** dipping oils, roasted meats, savory breads
**SWAP** thyme

**13. CILANTRO**
*spicy, slightly citrus*
**BEST USES** curries/Thai dishes, salsa/Mexican dishes
**SWAP** Italian parsley

**14. MINT**
*fresh, icy*
**BEST USES** cocktails, desserts, marinades
**SWAP** depends on use

# SPICE BLENDS

USE DRIED SPICES AND HERBS TO MAKE YOUR OWN MIXTURES. SPRINKLE THEM ON MEAT, POULTRY, AND FISH; STIR INTO SAUCES AND SOUPS; AND BLEND INTO SOFTENED BUTTER FOR A BREAD OR VEGETABLE TOPPERS.

**1. PUMPKIN PIE SPICE**
¼ tsp. ground nutmeg + ½ tsp. ground allspice + ½ tsp. ground ginger + 1 tsp. ground cinnamon

**2. ITALIAN SEASONING**
¼ tsp. crushed red pepper + 1 Tbsp. dried thyme, crushed + 1 Tbsp. dried rosemary, crushed + 1 Tbsp. dried oregano, crushed + 1 Tbsp. dried basil, crushed

**3. GREEK SEASONING**
½ tsp. dried minced garlic + 1 tsp. dried minced onion + 1 tsp. dried marjoram, crushed + 1 tsp. dried basil, crushed + 2 tsp. dried thyme, crushed + 1 Tbsp. dried oregano, crushed

**STORE** SPICE MIXTURES IN SMALL AIRTIGHT CONTAINERS IN A COOL, DARK PLACE UP TO 1 YEAR.

**4. TACO SEASONING**
1 Tbsp. salt + 1 Tbsp. cornstarch + 1 to 2 tsp. black pepper + 3 to 4 tsp. garlic powder + 1 tsp. dried oregano, crushed + 2 Tbsp. ground cumin + ½ to 1 tsp. crushed red pepper + 2 Tbsp. sugar + 3 to 4 Tbsp. chili powder

**5. CHAI SPICE** A dash freshly ground black pepper + 1 tsp. ground cinnamon + 1 tsp. ground ginger + 2 tsp. ground cardamom + 1 tsp. whole cloves, finely ground + 1 tsp. fennel seeds, finely ground

**6. HERBES DE PROVENCE** 1 tsp. fennel seeds, crushed + 1 tsp. dried lavender, crushed + 1 tsp. dried sage, crushed + 1 tsp. dried rosemary, crushed + 1 Tbsp. dried marjoram, crushed + 1 tsp. dried thyme, crushed + 1 tsp. dried basil, crushed

**7. POULTRY SEASONING**
¼ tsp. celery salt + ½ tsp. black pepper + 1 tsp. dried rosemary, crushed + 1 Tbsp. dried marjoram, crushed + 1 Tbsp. dried thyme, crushed + 1 Tbsp. dried sage, crushed

**UP & COMING**
These blends are gaining popularity but are still hard to find in supermarkets.

**MOROCCAN SEASONING (RAS EL HANOUT)**
1 tsp. paprika + ½ tsp. ground cumin + ¼ tsp. ground cinnamon + ¼ tsp. ground coriander + ¼ tsp. ground ginger + ¼ tsp. black pepper + ¼ tsp. ground turmeric + ⅛ tsp. cayenne pepper

**TANDOORI SPICE**
1¼ tsp. curry powder + 1 tsp. garam masala + ½ tsp. ground ginger + ½ tsp. ground cumin + ½ tsp. coriander + ½ tsp. ground cardamom + ¼ tsp. salt + ⅛ tsp. ground cinnamon + ⅛ tsp. black pepper

**ZA'ATAR**
1 Tbsp. ground sumac (info, *p. 288*) + 1 Tbsp. ground dried thyme + 1 tsp. sesame seeds + 1 tsp. salt + 1 tsp. black pepper

PUMPKIN PIE SPICE

ITALIAN SEASONING

GREEK
SEASONING

TACO
SEASONING

CHAI SPICE

HERBES DE
PROVENCE

POULTRY
SEASONING

# SAUCES

CHOP, PUREE, AND PULSE YOUR WAY TO HIGH-FLAVOR SAUCES MADE FROM FRESH INGREDIENTS. WE REFER TO THESE RECIPES THROUGHOUT THE BOOK, BUT YOU CAN ALSO MAKE A BATCH TO FLAVOR FISH, BURGERS, PASTA, VEGGIES, DIPS, AND EGGS.

## HARISSA PASTE

**START TO FINISH** 35 minutes

4   oz. dried guajillo, ancho, pasilla, and/or New Mexico chile peppers*
½   tsp. caraway seeds
½   tsp. coriander seeds
½   tsp. cumin seeds
3   Tbsp. olive oil
2   Tbsp. lemon juice
5   cloves garlic, peeled
1   tsp. kosher salt
3   to 4 Tbsp. water

**1.** In a large bowl combine dried chile peppers and enough boiling water to cover. Let stand 30 minutes.
**2.** In an dry 8-inch skillet heat caraway, coriander, and cumin seeds over medium heat about 2 minutes or until toasted and fragrant, shaking skillet occasionally. Remove seeds from skillet; cool. Grind seeds in a spice grinder.
**3.** Drain peppers; remove stems, seeds, and membranes (tip, p. 22). In a food processor or blender combine ground seeds, hydrated chile peppers, oil, lemon juice, garlic, and salt. Cover and pulse until smooth, adding enough of the water to reach desired consistency. **Makes 1¼ cups.**
***NOTE** The color of your paste will vary depending on the colors of the chile peppers you use.
**EACH 1 TSP.** *12 cal., 1 g fat (0 g sat. fat), 0 mg chol., 34 mg sodium, 1 g carb., 0 g fiber, 0 g sugars, 0 g pro.*

## CHIMICHURRI

**HANDS-ON TIME** 15 minutes
**CHILL** 2 hours

1¼  cups packed fresh Italian parsley leaves
¼   cup olive oil
1   shallot, peeled
2   Tbsp. fresh oregano leaves
2   Tbsp. cider vinegar or red wine vinegar
1   Tbsp. lemon juice
3   to 4 cloves garlic, peeled
½   tsp. salt
¼   to ½ tsp. crushed red pepper

**1.** In a food processor or blender combine all ingredients. Cover; process just until chopped. Transfer to covered container; chill 2 hours.
**Makes ⅔ cup.**
**TO STORE** Refrigerate up to 1 week. Let stand at room temperature before serving.
**EACH 1 TBSP.** *53 cal., 5 g fat (1 g sat. fat), 0 mg chol., 114 mg sodium, 2 g carb., 0 g sugars, 0 g fiber, 0 g pro.*

## GREMOLATA

**START TO FINISH** 10 minutes

½   cup chopped fresh Italian parsley, basil, or cilantro
2   Tbsp. lemon, lime, or orange zest
6   cloves garlic, minced

**1.** In a bowl toss together all ingredients. **Makes ⅔ cup.**
**EACH 1 TSP.** *3 cal., 0 g fat, 0 mg chol., 0 mg sodium, 1 g carb., 0 g fiber, 0 g sugars, 0 g pro.*

## ROMESCO SAUCE

**START TO FINISH** 20 minutes

4   medium roma tomatoes, peeled, seeded, and cut up
1   ¾-inch slice country-style bread (2 oz.), toasted and torn into pieces
⅔   cup roasted red sweet peppers, cut up
½   cup blanched* whole almonds, toasted (tip, p. 18)
¼   cup red wine vinegar
1   Tbsp. chopped fresh Italian parsley
4   cloves garlic, smashed
1   tsp. smoked paprika
½   tsp. ground ancho chile pepper
⅛   tsp. cayenne pepper
¼   to ⅓ cup olive oil
    Salt

**1.** In a food processor or blender combine first 10 ingredients (through cayenne pepper). Cover and pulse until mixed. With processor or blender running, slowly add oil in a steady stream until mixture is combined and finely chopped. Season to taste with salt.
**Makes 2 cups.**
***NOTE** Blanched almonds are almonds with their skins removed.
**TO STORE** Refrigerate up to 1 week. Let stand at room temperature before serving.
**EACH 2 TBSP.** *76 cal., 6 g fat (1 g sat. fat), 0 mg chol., 61 mg sodium, 5 g carb., 1 g fiber, 1 g sugars, 2 g pro.*

| HARISSA PASTE | CHIMICHURRI | GREMOLATA | ROMESCO SAUCE | BASIL PESTO |

**HARISSA PASTE**

- Stir into yogurt or sour cream for a dip.
- Mix with hummus or mayo for a sandwich spread.
- Mix into raw burger meat before cooking.
- Spoon over cooked eggs and meat.

**CHIMICHURRI**

- Serve over cooked meat, poultry, fish, and eggs.
- Spread on warm garlic bread.
- Stir into sour cream for a potato topper.

**GREMOLATA**

- Sprinkle over grilled meat and flatbread.
- Toss with warm pasta.
- Sprinkle on soups and stews.
- Top roasted vegetables.

**ROMESCO SAUCE**

- Serve with meat and seafood.
- Thin sauce to use as a dressing for grain salads.
- Toss with grilled or roasted veggies and warm pasta.

**BASIL PESTO**

- Toss with warm pasta.
- Spoon over cooked eggs and grilled steak.
- Substitute for pizza sauce.
- Whisk into salad dressings.

## BASIL PESTO

**START TO FINISH** 15 minutes

- 1½ cups firmly packed fresh basil leaves
- ½ cup grated Parmesan cheese (2 oz.)
- ½ cup pine nuts, toasted (tip, *p. 18*)
- ⅓ cup olive oil
- 2 to 4 cloves garlic, peeled and halved
- ¼ tsp. kosher salt

**1.** In a food processor combine all ingredients. Cover; process until nearly smooth. Add up to 2 Tbsp. additional oil to reach desired consistency. **Makes 1 cup.**

**TO STORE** Transfer pesto to an airtight container. Cover surface with plastic wrap; cover container. Refrigerate up to 3 days.

**EACH 1 TBSP.** *81 cal., 8 g fat (1 g sat. fat), 2 mg chol., 63 mg sodium, 1 g carb., 0 g fiber, 0 g sugars, 2 g pro.*

### MORE SAUCES

Love sauces? Look for these other favorites in the book.

# MARINADES & RUBS

BEFORE GRILLING OR COOKING, GIVE MEAT AND POULTRY A SLOW SOAK IN A MARINADE OR GENEROUSLY RUB ON A SPICE MIX. THAT EXTRA BOOST OF SAVORY FLAVOR MAKES ALL THE DIFFERENCE.

## MARINADES

Combine the marinade ingredients in a resealable plastic bag; add meat or poultry. Seal bag and turn to coat. Set bag in a shallow dish. Marinate in the refrigerator 4 to 6 hours, turning bag occasionally. Drain and discard marinade. Cook as desired.

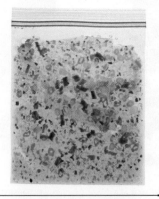

### SWEET CHILI MARINADE

- ⅓ cup Asian sweet chili sauce
- ¼ cup rice vinegar
- 1 Tbsp. chopped green onion
- 1 tsp. ground ginger
- ¼ tsp. crushed red pepper
- ¼ teaspoon salt

### CURRIED YOGURT MARINADE

- ½ cup plain yogurt
- 2 Tbsp. honey
- 2 Tbsp. olive oil or vegetable oil
- 4 tsp. curry powder
- ½ tsp. salt

### TEX-MEX MARINADE

- ¼ cup red wine vinegar
- 2 Tbsp. olive oil
- 1 Tbsp. minced garlic
- 1½ tsp. crushed dried oregano
- 1 tsp. chili powder
- ½ tsp. ground cumin
- ¼ tsp. salt

### MOROCCAN MARINADE

- ½ cup lemon juice
- ½ cup finely chopped onion
- 2 Tbsp. water
- 1 Tbsp. ground cumin
- 1 Tbsp. ground coriander
- 1 Tbsp. honey
- 6 cloves garlic, minced
- 1 tsp. ground turmeric
- ½ tsp. crushed red pepper

### JERK MARINADE

- ¼ cup pineapple juice
- 2 Tbsp. olive oil
- 1 Tbsp. Jamaican jerk seasoning
- 1 Tbsp. minced garlic
- ¼ tsp. salt
- Dash crushed red pepper (optional)

### ASIAN MARINADE

- ½ cup beef broth
- ⅓ cup hoisin sauce
- ¼ cup soy sauce
- ¼ cup sliced green onion
- 3 Tbsp. apple or orange juice
- 1 Tbsp. sugar
- 4 cloves garlic, minced
- 1 tsp. grated fresh ginger

# RUBS

Mix ingredients, then sprinkle over meat, poultry, and fish. Massage rub into meat. Let stand 15 minutes before cooking. (Cooking charts, *pp. 52–67.*)

## CAJUN RUB

- 1 Tbsp. white pepper
- 1 Tbsp. black pepper
- 2 tsp. cayenne pepper
- 2 tsp. crushed dried thyme
- 2 tsp. onion powder
- 2 tsp. garlic powder
- 1 tsp. salt

## MUSTARD-PEPPERCORN RUB

- 2 Tbsp. coarse-ground brown mustard
- 1 Tbsp. cracked black pepper
- 1 Tbsp. chopped fresh tarragon
- 1 Tbsp. olive oil
- 2 tsp. coarse salt

## CHILI RUB

- 2 Tbsp. paprika
- 2 tsp. ground cumin
- 2 tsp. chili powder
- 1 tsp. salt
- 1 tsp. coriander
- 1 tsp. black pepper
- ½ tsp. cayenne pepper

## JAMAICAN JERK RUB

- 1 Tbsp. onion powder
- 1 Tbsp. packed brown sugar
- 1 Tbsp. crushed dried thyme
- 1½ tsp. salt
- 1½ tsp. ground allspice
- 1 tsp. cracked black pepper
- ½ tsp. ground nutmeg
- ½ tsp. ground cinnamon
- ½ tsp. ground cloves
- ¼ tsp. cayenne pepper

## FRESH HERB RUB

- ⅓ cup chopped fresh basil
- 3 Tbsp. chopped fresh thyme
- 1 Tbsp. chopped fresh rosemary
- 1 Tbsp. chopped fresh mint
- 3 cloves garlic, minced
- 3 Tbsp. olive oil
- ½ tsp. salt
- ½ tsp. black pepper

## BBQ RUB

- ¼ cup barbecue seasoning
- 2 Tbsp. garlic powder
- 2 tsp. onion salt
- 1 tsp. ground celery seeds
- ½ teaspoon cayenne pepper

**WET RUBS** Wet rubs contain melted butter or oil (or other liquids). The moisture helps the rub adhere to the meat and keeps the meat moist. Turn a dry rub into a wet rub by stirring in 2 to 3 Tbsp. melted butter or oil. Rub or brush on meat, poultry, and fish before cooking.

# STORAGE & SAFETY

IT'S IMPORTANT WHEN YOU HANDLE AND COOK FOOD AT HOME TO STORE, PREPARE, AND SERVE IT SAFELY.

## GET THE ANSWERS

For the latest information on food safety regulations, recalls, and precautions, go to *foodsafety.gov*. For food storage guidelines, see the FoodKeeper App under Keep Food Safe on the site's menu bar. Download it to your smartphone so it's just a click away.

**COLD**
## 40°F
**HOT**
## 140°F

## TEMPERATURE

You can't always see, taste, or smell the bacteria that cause foodborne illness, so prevent them from growing in the first place. Store cold foods at 40°F or below. Serve hot foods immediately or hold them at 140°F or above. Bacteria grow fastest between these two temps.

## TWO-HOUR LIMIT

Cooked food should stand at room temperature no longer than 2 hours (1 hour if outside temp is 80°F or higher). Refrigerate leftovers immediately.

## HOW COLD IS COLD ENOUGH?

YOUR FRIDGE SHOULD BE 38°F TO 40°F. THE FREEZER SHOULD BE 0°F.

## TEMP CHECK

Always use a food thermometer to ensure food has reached a high enough temperature to destroy harmful bacteria. Here are United States Department of Agriculture (USDA) recommended minimum internal temperatures.

**145°F**
BEEF, LAMB & VEAL STEAKS, CHOPS & ROASTS

**145°F**
PORK CHOPS, RIBS & ROASTS

**160°F**
EGG DISHES

**160°F**
GROUND BEEF, PORK, VEAL & LAMB (BURGERS & MEAT LOAF)

**165°F**
STUFFINGS, POULTRY & CASSEROLES

## FREEZE FOR QUALITY

Freeze the right way so foods maintain the highest quality. Cool foods quickly, portion into shallow freezer-safe containers or bags, label, and arrange in single layers so they freeze quickly. Stack when completely frozen to save space. Cover baking dishes with plastic freezer wrap or heavy-duty foil. Major brands of wide-mouth canning jars are acceptable for freezing. In all containers, leave room for food to expand, but not so much that it dries out, causing "freezer burn."

## FOOD SAFE

Cross-contamination occurs when ready-to-eat foods pick up bacteria from other foods and unclean hands, cutting boards, and utensils. To avoid this, keep raw meat, poultry, eggs, fish, shellfish, and the juices away from other foods. Wash your hands and utensils after working with raw ingredients. Avoid rinsing meat, poultry, and fish before cooking.

### GROCERY STORE

Keep raw meat and poultry separate from other foods in your cart and bags.

### STORAGE

At home, store meat and poultry in sealed containers or on rimmed plates so juices don't drip onto other foods.

### PREPARATION

Designate one cutting board in your cupboard for raw meat, poultry, and seafood. Use a different one for prepping vegetables.

## REHEAT ALL LEFTOVERS TO 165°F.

# FRIDGE/FREEZER STORAGE

These timings are for flavor and quality. Note: Frozen food will be safe longer, but quality suffers.

**BACON, HAM, HOT DOGS & COOKED SAUSAGE** (links and patties)
Refrigerate in original packaging. Overwrap in freezer wrap to freeze.
**FRIDGE** opened package 7 days
**FREEZER** 1 month

**BUTTER**
Refrigerate in original packaging. Overwrap with moistureproof and vaporproof wrap to freeze.
**FRIDGE** 1 to 2 months
**FREEZER** 6 to 9 months

**BUTTERMILK**
Refrigerate in original packaging. To freeze, transfer to freezer container; leave a little headspace.
**FRIDGE** 1 to 2 weeks
**FREEZER** Up to 3 months (use for baking and cooking only)

**CHEESE** (cottage cheese and ricotta)
Refrigerate in original packaging.
**FRIDGE** Use by date on container or within 1 week after opening.
**FREEZER** Not recommended

**CHEESE** (hard and semihard)
Wrap in plastic wrap. Overwrap in freezer wrap to freeze.
**FRIDGE** 3 to 4 weeks
**FREEZER** Up to 6 months (use for cooking only)

**DELI MEAT**
Refrigerate in original packaging.
**FRIDGE** opened package 3 to 5 days; unopened package 2 weeks or until expiration date
**FREEZER** 1 month

**EGGS** (hard-boiled in shells)
**FRIDGE** 7 days
**FREEZER** Not recommended

**EGGS** (whites and yolks)
Refrigerate in tightly covered containers. Transfer to freezer containers to freeze.
**FRIDGE** 2 to 4 days
**FREEZER** 12 months

**EGGS** (whole in shells)
Store in carton in coldest part of fridge. Do not wash or store in the fridge door.
**FRIDGE** 3 to 5 weeks after packing date
**FREEZER** Not recommended

**FISH & SHELLFISH**
Store in moistureproof and vaporproof wrap in coldest part of fridge. Overwrap in freezer wrap to freeze.
**FRIDGE** 1 to 2 days
**FREEZER** 3 months

**MEAT** (roasts, steaks, chops) **& POULTRY** (whole and pieces)
Refrigerate in original wrapping. Overwrap in freezer wrap to freeze.
**FRIDGE** 3 to 5 days
**FREEZER** 4 to 12 months

**MEAT** (uncooked ground) **& POULTRY** (uncooked ground)
Refrigerate in original wrapping. Overwrap in freezer wrap to freeze.
**FRIDGE** 1 to 2 days
**FREEZER** 3 to 4 months

**SOUR CREAM & YOGURT**
Refrigerate in original packaging.
**FRIDGE** Use by date on container or within 5 days of opening.
**FREEZER** Not recommended

## SAFE THAW

Thaw foods in the refrigerator—not at room temp. The exception: Breads and sweets that are OK to store at room temperature can be thawed on the counter. Some foods can be thawed in the microwave; follow manufacturer's directions and cook food immediately after thawing. Also thaw food by placing it in a resealable plastic bag and immersing it in cold tap water in the sink. Change water every 30 minutes to keep it cold.

## NO-FREEZE FOODS

These foods lose their flavor, texture, and overall quality when frozen.

Homemade battered and fried foods

Cooked egg whites and yolks; icings made from egg whites

Cottage and ricotta cheeses

Custard and cream pies and desserts with cream fillings

Soups made with potatoes (which darken and get mushy)

Stews and sauces thickened with cornstarch or flour

Sour cream, mayonnaise, and salad dressings

Stuffed pork chops, lamb chops, and chicken breasts

Whole eggs in the shell, raw or cooked

# ESSENTIAL RECIPES EVERY COOK NEEDS TO MASTER

[GO-TO BASIC RECIPE]

# CHICKEN BREASTS

AT THE TOP OF THE LIST OF ESSENTIAL WEEKNIGHT RECIPES— SKINLESS, BONELESS CHICKEN BREASTS. HERE ARE THREE WAYS TO PREPARE THEM, PLUS FLAVOR IDEAS.

**ADD FLAVOR**
We added sautéed mushrooms and garlic to this version of the pan sauce. Check out additional delicious sauce ideas *(opposite)*.

**DINNER SWAP**
For another meal, omit the pan sauce. Serve cooked chicken slices over salad greens with desired dressing *(pp. 300–301)* or in a sandwich with your choice of sauce *(pp. 30–31)*.

## CHICKEN WITH PAN SAUCE

**START TO FINISH** 35 minutes

| | |
|---|---|
| 2 | skinless, boneless chicken breast halves (6 to 8 oz. each) |
| ¼ | tsp. salt |
| ¼ | tsp. black pepper |
| 1 | Tbsp. olive oil |
| ½ | cup dry white wine or chicken broth |
| ½ | cup chicken broth |
| ¼ | cup finely chopped shallot or onion |
| 2 | Tbsp. heavy cream |
| ¼ | cup cold butter, cut up |

**1.** Cut each chicken breast in half horizontally. Using the flat side of a meat mallet, flatten chicken between two pieces of plastic wrap to ¼ inch thick. Sprinkle chicken with salt and pepper.
**2.** In a 12-inch skillet heat the oil over medium-high heat. Add chicken to skillet. Cook chicken 5 to 6 minutes or until no longer pink, turning once. Transfer chicken to a platter; cover with foil to keep warm. Remove skillet from heat.
**3.** Add wine, broth, and shallot to the hot skillet. Return skillet to heat. Cook and stir to scrape up browned bits from bottom of pan. Bring to boiling. Boil gently, uncovered, about 10 minutes or until liquid is reduced to ¼ cup. Reduce heat to medium-low.
**4.** Stir in cream. Add butter, 1 Tbsp. at a time, stirring until butter melts after each addition. Sauce should be slightly thickened. Season with additional salt and pepper. Serve over chicken.
**Makes 4 servings (1 piece each).**
**EACH SERVING** *287 cal., 20 g fat (10 g sat. fat), 96 mg chol., 458 mg sodium, 3 g carb., 0 g fiber, 1 g sugars, 19 g pro.*

**CHICKEN BREAST SIZE CHECK** Chicken breast halves are big—some are 12 to 16 oz. Whenever you can, use breast halves in the 6- to 8-oz. range. You can cut thicker 12- to 16-oz. chicken breast halves horizontally into thinner portion-appropriate pieces. As you cut, press down lightly on top of breast half. (Do not cut in half crosswise; the pieces will be too thick.) Use a kitchen scale to check the weight of the pieces so cooking times are accurate.

## *ROASTING*

Roasting is an easy way to cook a large batch. Start with skinless, boneless chicken breast halves (about 6 oz. each; tip, *left*). Preheat oven to 400°F. Arrange chicken in a shallow baking pan. Brush with olive oil; sprinkle with desired spice blend (*p. 28*) or rub (*p. 33*). Roast, uncovered, 25 to 30 minutes or until done (165°F).

## *SAUCE CHANGE-UPS*

Spice up the flavor of your pan sauce with these ideas or come up with your own.

### CILANTRO-CHIPOTLE PAN SAUCE

Stir 1 Tbsp. snipped fresh cilantro and ½ tsp. finely chopped chipotle chile pepper in adobo sauce into the finished sauce.

### TOMATO-PARMESAN PAN SAUCE

Add ½ cup quartered grape tomatoes to skillet with shallot. Stir 2 Tbsp. grated Parmesan cheese into the finished sauce.

## *POACHING*

Poaching chicken is a quick way to get cooked chicken for recipes where you won't miss the browning. To poach, bring 1½ to 2 cups chicken broth or water to boiling. Add skinless, boneless chicken breasts and, if desired, fresh herb sprigs. Add water if needed to cover meat. Return to boiling; reduce heat. Cover and simmer 12 to 15 minutes or until chicken is done (165°F). Transfer to a cutting board; let stand until cool enough to chop or shred.

### BACON-LEEK PAN SAUCE

Add ½ cup sliced leek to skillet with shallot. Top with 3 slices crumbled crisp-cooked bacon.

### LEMON-THYME PAN SAUCE

Stir 2 tsp. lemon juice and 2 tsp. snipped fresh thyme into the finished sauce. Top with lemon slices.

# BURGERS

YES, YOU CAN LEARN HOW TO MIX, SHAPE, AND FLIP BURGERS JUST RIGHT! ONCE YOU MASTER THE TECHNIQUE, CUSTOMIZE WITH TOPPINGS, SAUCES, AND SEASONINGS.

## BURGERS

**START TO FINISH** 35 minutes

- 1½  lb. 85%-lean ground beef
- ½  tsp. salt
- ¼  tsp. black pepper
- 4  hamburger buns or rolls, split and toasted (tip, *p. 270*)
  Desired toppings, condiments, and/or Bacon Aïoli (optional)

**1.** In a large bowl combine meat, salt, and pepper; mix well. Shape into four ¾-inch-thick patties (tip, *opposite*).

**2.** Grill burgers, covered, directly over medium heat (tips, *pp. 16–17*) 14 to 18 minutes or until done (160°F to 165°F), turning once halfway through cooking. Serve in toasted buns with desired toppings. **Makes 4 burgers.**

**SKILLET BURGERS** Shape patties as directed. Lightly coat a 10-inch heavy skillet with nonstick cooking spray. Preheat skillet over medium-high heat. Add patties; reduce heat to medium. Cook, uncovered, 12 to 15 minutes or until done (160°F), turning once halfway through cooking.

**EACH BURGER** *463 cal, 25 g fat (9 g sat. fat), 113 mg chol., 615 mg sodium, 22 g carb., 1 g fiber, 3 g sugars, 36 g pro.*

**BACON AÏOLI** Prepare Roasted Garlic (*p. 24*); mash softened cloves. In a 10-inch skillet cook and stir 8 slices thick-sliced bacon, chopped, over medium-high heat about 7 minutes or until crisp; drain bacon on paper towels. In a bowl stir together 1 cup mayonnaise, mashed garlic, and bacon.

**1** For the juiciest burgers, use 85%-lean (15%-fat) ground beef rather than a leaner mix of beef. Much of the fat drips away during cooking but leaves behind moisture and flavor. Extra-lean beef results in dry burgers.

**2** When mixing, work the burger mixture as little as possible (overworking causes tough burgers). To divide the meat into even patties, first gently pat the meat into a square, then cut into fourths. Roll each square into a ball.

**3** Pat each ball into a circle ¾ inch thick. Using your fingers, press lightly in the center of each patty to form a shallow indentation. The "dimple" prevents the burger from shrinking while cooking and results in even cooking.

**LET IT BE**
When cooking burgers, resist the urge to press them with a spatula. Pressing does one thing only: squeezes out juices. To keep your burgers moist, you want those juices on the inside.

**IS IT DONE?** A round meat patty cooked to 160°F is safe regardless of color. Check by inserting an instant-read thermometer through the side of the patty so the point is in the center.

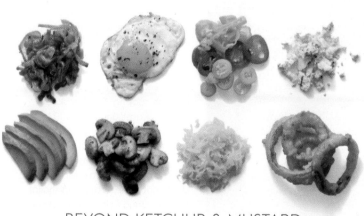

## BEYOND KETCHUP & MUSTARD
Finish your burger with one or more of these delicious toppings.

| | | | |
|---|---|---|---|
| **Caramelized onions** | **Fried egg** | **Sliced pickled peppers** | **Sliced or crumbled cheese** |
| **Avocado slices** | **Sautéed mushrooms** | **Sauerkraut** | **Onion rings** |

## MAYO BOOSTERS
Bump up the flavor of basic mayonnaise with one or two of these stir-ins.

Chopped chipotle in adobo sauce

Diced jalapeño pepper

Dijon mustard

Pickle relish

Peanut sauce

Chopped cooked bacon

Sriracha sauce

Minced fresh garlic

Chopped fresh herb

Lemon, lime, or orange zest

Curry powder

Chutney

**TURN BURGERS INTO SLIDERS** MAKE AS DIRECTED, EXCEPT SHAPE INTO TWELVE ½-INCH-THICK PATTIES (ABOUT ¼ CUP EACH). COOK 8 TO 10 MINUTES OR UNTIL DONE (160°F), TURNING ONCE.

# STEAKS

IN EACH OF US, THERE'S A STEAK MASTER WAITING TO EMERGE—PICK THE CUT, CHOOSE THE
COOKING METHOD, AND PRACTICE COOKING STEAK TO THE PERFECT DONENESS.

½   tsp. freshly ground black pepper
6   Tbsp. cold unsalted butter, sliced
½   cup dry red wine or apple juice
⅓   cup reduced-sodium beef broth
3   Tbsp. finely chopped shallot or
    2 cloves garlic, minced
2   Tbsp. heavy cream (no substitutes)

**1.** Allow steaks to stand at room temperature 30 minutes. Preheat oven to 400°F. Trim fat from steaks. Pat steaks dry with paper towels. Sprinkle salt and pepper over all sides of steaks. Heat a 10-inch oven-going skillet over medium-high heat (tips, *opposite*). Add 2 Tbsp. of the butter to hot skillet; reduce heat to medium. Add steaks; cook about 4 minutes or until browned, turning once halfway through cooking. Transfer skillet to oven. Roast, uncovered, 10 to 13 minutes or until medium rare (145°F). Transfer steaks to a platter. Cover with foil; let stand while preparing sauce.

**2.** For pan sauce, drain fat from skillet. Add wine, broth, and shallot to skillet. Bring to boiling, whisking constantly to scrape up any crusty browned bits from bottom of skillet. Boil gently, uncovered, over medium heat 6 minutes or until liquid is reduced to ¼ cup.

**3.** Whisk in cream. Boil gently 1 to 2 minutes more or until slightly thickened. Whisk in the remaining 4 Tbsp. butter, 1 Tbsp. at a time, until butter is melted and sauce is thickened. Serve steaks with pan sauce. **Makes 4 servings (½ top loin or 1 tenderloin steak each).**

**EACH SERVING** *529 cal., 39 g fat (19 g sat. fat), 173 mg chol., 437 mg sodium, 3 g carb., 0 g fiber, 1 g sugars, 37 g pro.*

## SHOPPING FOR STEAK

Whether you choose ribeye, top loin, or tenderloin steaks, look for well-marbled meat with bright red color and a moist (but not wet) surface. For even cooking, let steaks stand at room temp 30 minutes before searing.

## STEAKS WITH PAN SAUCE

**HANDS-ON TIME** 20 minutes
**STAND** 30 minutes
**ROAST** 10 minutes at 400°F

2   beef top loin or ribeye steaks or 4 beef tenderloin steaks, cut 1 inch thick (1½ to 2 lb. total)
½   tsp. kosher salt

## *STEAKS WITH PAN SAUCE*

**1** Get the pan really hot before you add the steaks. If it's hot enough, the steak browns quickly. If not, it steams in its juices and turns pale gray. After searing in skillet, immediately transfer to oven to finish cooking.

**2** To check doneness, insert a thermometer into the thickest part of a steak at an angle or through the side. Cook steaks to 145°F for medium rare or 160°F for medium. Tent with foil; let stand 5 minutes.

**3** Deglaze the pan by adding wine and broth while the pan is still hot. Scrape the bottom of the skillet to pick up the caramelized browned bits (they add flavor to your sauce).

**PICK A SKILLET**

For best results, don't use a skillet with a nonstick surface. It won't caramelize the steaks well and may not be safe to use in the oven. Cast-iron and stainless-steel skillets tolerate high heat and retain heat well, making either one ideal for this recipe.

**MEDIUM RARE**

# 145°F

**MEDIUM**

# 160°F

**WELL DONE**

# 170°F

## DOWNTIME
BEFORE SERVING, TENT HOT STEAKS WITH FOIL TO LET JUICES REDISTRIBUTE— 10 MINUTES WILL DO THE TRICK.

## FLAVOR ADD-INS
Any of these ingredients will enhance the sauce.

Add 1 tsp. chopped fresh thyme, tarragon, or oregano with the shallot.

Stir 2 tsp. chopped capers into the finished sauce.

Add 1 tsp. Dijon mustard with the shallot.

Stir 1 tsp. balsamic vinegar into the finished sauce.

## *GRILLING*

Instead of skillet-cooking, grill seasoned steaks, covered, directly over medium heat (tips, *pp. 16–17*) 10 to 12 minutes for medium rare (145°F) or 12 to 15 minutes for medium (160°F), turning once halfway through. If desired, top with Flavored Butter (recipes, *p. 45*).

# PORK CHOPS

A BIG BONE-IN PORK CHOP IS IMPRESSIVE—BUT ONLY IF IT'S STILL JUICY ON THE INSIDE. LEAN PORK SHOULD BE SERVED WHEN SLIGHTLY PINK, SO PULL THESE CHOPS WHEN THEY REACH 145°F.

**«**

We brushed these chops with a quick stir-together of bourbon and molasses when they came out of the oven. More ideas, *opposite*.

# BAKED PORK CHOPS

**HANDS-ON TIME** 25 minutes
**BAKE** 14 minutes at 350°F
**STAND** 3 minutes

4   bone-in pork loin or rib chops, cut 1¼ inches thick (about 3 lb. total), or 4 boneless pork loin chops, cut 1¼ inches thick (about 2½ lb. total)
¼   tsp. salt
¼   tsp. black pepper
1   Tbsp. olive oil

**1.** Preheat oven to 350°F. Trim fat from chops; pat dry with paper towels. Sprinkle chops with salt and pepper.
**2.** In a 12-inch skillet heat the oil over medium-high heat. Add 2 bone-in chops or all of the boneless chops. Cook 6 minutes or until browned, turning to brown evenly. Transfer chops to a 15×10-inch baking pan. Repeat with remaining chops if necessary.
**3.** Bake chops, uncovered, 14 to 17 minutes or until done (145°F). Cover and let stand 3 minutes.
**Makes 4 servings (1 chop each).**
**EACH SERVING** *271 cal., 10 g fat (3 g sat. fat), 131 mg chol., 0 g carb., 235 mg sodium, 0 g sugars, 0 g fiber, 41 g pro.*

### BONE-IN & BONELESS
We tested this recipe with both bone-in chops and boneless chops. As long as they're the same thickness, the cooking time is the same for both.

**RIB CHOP**
This slice of loin is connected to a curved rib bone.

**LOIN CHOP**
The T-bone is attached to the loin and tenderloin.

## GRILLING

Grill chops, covered, over medium heat (tips, *pp. 16–17*) 15 to 18 minutes (145°F), turning once.

## BRUSH-ONS

These purchased and easy stir-togethers add extra flavor after baking.

Sweet-and-sour sauce

———

Honey + yellow mustard

———

Olive oil + smoked paprika

———

Bourbon + molasses

———

Orange marmalade

———

Pure maple syrup

## TOPPERS

If you skip the brush-on, mix up one of these toppers to spoon over chops.

**SAVORY STRAWBERRY SALSA**
In a medium bowl combine 2 cups fresh strawberries, coarsely chopped; 1 medium avocado, seeded, peeled, and chopped; ½ cup chopped, seeded cucumber; 2 Tbsp. honey; 1 tsp. lime zest; 2 Tbsp. lime juice; 1 to 2 fresh jalapeño chile peppers, seeded and finely chopped (tip, *p. 22*); and ¼ tsp. cracked black pepper. Cover and chill 1 hour.

**CORN AND PEPPER RELISH**
In a 10-inch skillet cook 2 cups fresh or frozen whole kernel corn; 1 medium red sweet pepper, cut into slivers; ½ cup chopped onion; and 1 clove garlic, minced, in 1 Tbsp. olive oil over medium heat about 5 minutes or until tender, stirring occasionally. Stir in 2 Tbsp. chopped fresh parsley, 1 Tbsp. red wine vinegar, 1 to 2 tsp. chopped fresh thyme, 1 tsp. sugar, ¼ tsp. salt, and ¼ tsp. black pepper.

# FISH

FISH IS A LEAN OPTION FOR PROTEIN, PERFECT FOR WEEKNIGHTS BECAUSE IT COOKS FAST.
HERE ARE FOUR WAYS TO PREPARE IT, PLUS TOPPINGS.

Top with finely grated Parmesan cheese + chopped toasted walnuts + snipped fresh thyme

Top with chopped avocado + fresh salsa

Top with mayo + lemon zest + freshly ground black pepper

Top with prepared coleslaw + toasted sliced almonds

Top with yogurt-marinated cucumbers + snipped fresh dill

## ROASTED FISH
**START TO FINISH** 20 minutes

1   lb. fresh or frozen skinless fish
    fillets, ½ to ¾ inch thick
    Salt and black pepper
    Nonstick cooking spray

**1.** Thaw fish if frozen. Pat dry with paper towels. Cut fish into four serving-size pieces if necessary. Measure thickness of fish. Season with salt and pepper.
**2.** Preheat oven to 450°F. Line a 15×10-inch baking pan with foil; coat with nonstick cooking spray. Arrange fish in pan. Bake 4 to 6 minutes per ½-inch thickness of fish or until fish flakes easily.
**Makes 4 servings (1 piece each).**
**EACH SERVING** *147 cal., 6 g fat (1 g sat. fat), 65 mg chol., 131 mg sodium, 0 g carb., 0 g fiber, 0 g sugars, 22 g pro.*

## FISH CUTS
Know these terms for buying fish.

### PAN-DRESSED
Ready-to-cook whole fish with organs, fins, scales, gills, head, and tail removed.

### STEAK
A ready-to-cook crosscut slice from a large fish (like salmon).

### FILLET
A ready-to-cook boneless piece of fish cut from the side and away from the backbone; it might or might not be skinned.

## CHOOSING

Before you buy seafood, check out the recommendations from Monterey Bay Aquarium's Seafood Watch (download the app at *seafoodwatch.org*). You'll find seafood options that are sustainable and environmentally responsible.

## SHOPPING

Pick the freshest fish possible. Here's what to look for when you're making your selections: clear eyes (in whole fish), firm flesh that springs back when pressed, and fresh and mild scent (not fishy or sour). When you grab a package of frozen fish, it should be frozen solid.

## PREPARING

If frozen, transfer fish to a resealable plastic bag and submerge in cold water to thaw (tip, *p. 35*). Don't thaw fish in unopened Cryovac packages. We recommend not rinsing the fish unless you need to rinse off any scales (do it in cold water). Pat dry with paper towels.

## *BROILING*

To broil, thaw fish if frozen. Pat dry with paper towels. Preheat broiler. Arrange fish on the unheated greased rack of a broiler pan (or an oven-safe rack set over a baking pan). Broil 4 inches from heat 4 to 6 minutes per ½-inch thickness of fish or until fish flakes easily.

## FLAVORED BUTTERS

Roll one of these softened butters into a log, chill, and, just before serving, place a slice on hot fish to melt.

### HERBED GARDEN BUTTER

Add 1 Tbsp. herbed pepper seasoning blend, 1 Tbsp. fresh lemon juice, and 1 Tbsp. desired chopped fresh herbs (such as thyme and dill) to ½ cup softened butter.

### MAPLE-BACON-BLUEBERRY BUTTER

Add 1 slice finely chopped crisp-cooked bacon, 2 Tbsp. maple syrup, and 2 Tbsp. mashed blueberries to ½ cup softened butter.

### GARLICKY TOMATO BUTTER

Add 1 Tbsp. tomato paste, 1 tsp. finely chopped green onion, and 1 tsp. roasted minced garlic to ½ cup softened butter.

### CITRUSY BUTTER

Add 1 Tbsp. orange zest, 1 Tbsp. fresh orange juice, and 1 Tbsp. finely chopped green onion to ½ cup softened butter.

## *POACHING*

To poach fish, start by thawing four 5- to 6-oz. (¾ to 1 inch thick) fish fillets (salmon, cod, or haddock) if frozen. Add 1 cup water to a 10-inch nonstick skillet (if desired, replace some of the water with freshly squeezed orange, lime, or lemon juice). Bring to boiling; add fish. Reduce heat to medium. Simmer, covered, 8 to 12 minutes or until fish flakes easily.

You'll know the fish is done when it starts to flake when tested with a fork. Start checking at the minimum timing to avoid overcooking.

## *SKILLET COOKING*

To pan-sear, thaw fish and pat very dry with paper towels (to prevent splattering). Heat 1 Tbsp. butter and 1 Tbsp. vegetable oil in a 12-inch skillet over medium-high heat until butter melts. Add fish to skillet. Cook 4 to 6 minutes per ½-inch thickness of fish or until fish flakes easily, turning once.

# EGGS

IS IT BREAKFAST OR IS IT DINNER? WE'LL LET YOU CHOOSE. PICK AN EGG-PREP METHOD—
HARD-BOILED, FRIED, SCRAMBLED, POACHED, OR OMELET—FOR ANY OCCASION.

## HARD-BOILED EGGS

**START TO FINISH** 25 minutes

6    large eggs

**1.** Place eggs in a single layer in a 3-qt. saucepan (do not stack eggs). Add enough cold water to cover the eggs by 1 inch. Bring to a rapid boil over high heat (water will have large rapidly breaking bubbles). Remove from heat, cover, and let stand 15 minutes (18 minutes for extra- large eggs); drain. Place in ice water until cool enough to handle; drain.

**2.** To peel eggs, gently tap each egg on the countertop. Roll egg on countertop under the palm of your hand. Peel off eggshell, starting at the large end. **Makes 6 eggs.**

**\*NOTE** For soft-boiled eggs, bring water to boiling. Using a slotted spoon, lower eggs into water. Reduce heat to maintain a gentle boil. Boil 6 minutes for soft-boiled or 8 minutes for jammy (not set) yolk.

**EACH EGG** *78 cal., 5 g fat (2 g sat. fat), 212 mg chol., 62 mg sodium, 1 g carb., 0 g fiber, 0 g sugars, 6 g pro.*

**HARD
YOLK**

# 15

minutes

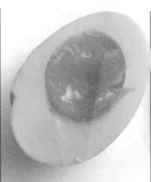

**JAMMY
YOLK**

# 8

minutes

**SOFT
YOLK**

# 6

minutes

### EASY PEELING

There's a secret to peeling eggs. Whenever possible, use eggs that are 7 to 10 days old. As eggs age, the air pocket in the shell grows, making it easier to dislodge the shell after boiling.

### SOFT AND JAMMY YOLKS

Soft and jammy cooked eggs are popping up in more than just breakfast dishes, including ramen noodle bowls, salads, pasta, asparagus, and grain bowls. Follow the timings *above* to get the yolk consistency you desire. In addition to a halved soft-boiled egg, this grain bowl contains cooked tricolor quinoa, a roasted sweet potato half, steamed kale, roasted chickpeas, chopped avocado, snipped fresh chives, and salt and black pepper.

# FRIED EGGS

**START TO FINISH** 10 minutes

2   tsp. butter or nonstick
    cooking spray
4   eggs
    Salt and black pepper

**1.** In a 10-inch skillet melt butter over medium heat. (Or coat an unheated skillet with cooking spray.) Break eggs into skillet. Sprinkle with salt and pepper. Reduce heat to medium-low. For sunny-side-up fried eggs, cook eggs 3 to 4 minutes or until whites are almost completely set and yolks start to thicken.
**2.** For over-easy or over-hard fried eggs, when the whites are completely set and the yolks start to thicken, turn the eggs and cook 30 seconds more (over-easy) or 1 minute more (over-hard). **Makes 4 eggs.**

## STEAM-BASTED FRIED EGGS

Prepare as directed, except when egg edges turn white, add 1 to 2 tsp. water. Cover skillet and cook eggs 3 to 4 minutes or until yolks begin to thicken but are not hard.
**EACH EGG** *88 cal., 7 g fat (3 g sat. fat), 217 mg chol., 84 mg sodium, 0 g carb., 0 g fiber, 0 g sugars, 6 g pro.*

### FIRM-SET YOLK
If you like your fried eggs without runny yolks (but like the sunny-side-up look), break the yolk after adding the egg to the skillet. It will cook in the same time it takes to cook the white.

# SCRAMBLED EGGS

*See p. 89 for more scrambled egg info and ideas.*
**START TO FINISH** 10 minutes

6   eggs
⅓   cup milk or half-and-half
¼   tsp. salt
1   Tbsp. butter

**1.** In a bowl whisk together eggs, milk, salt, and a dash *black pepper*. In a 10-inch skillet melt butter over medium heat; pour in egg mixture. Cook, without stirring, until mixture begins to set on bottom and around edges.
**2.** Using a spatula or large spoon, lift and turn partially cooked egg mixture so that uncooked portion flows underneath *(below)*. Continue cooking 2 to 3 minutes or until egg mixture is cooked through but is still glossy and moist. Immediately remove from heat. **Makes 3 servings (¾ cup each).**
**EACH SERVING** *191 cal., 14 g fat (6 g sat. fat), 384 mg chol., 379 mg sodium, 2 g carb., 0 g fiber, 2 g sugars, 13 g pro.*

Add eggs to hot skillet; let sit 20 to 30 seconds or until ribbons of cooked eggs begin to form before you put your spatula to work. Lift and fold the eggs toward the center of the pan, allowing uncooked eggs to flow under the spatula. Keep lifting and folding eggs until they are just set and still appear slightly wet.

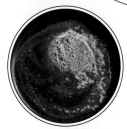

Heat the butter in the pan, swirling to coat bottom. Get the pan fairly hot before adding the eggs so they set quickly and don't run together. Cook eggs in batches to avoid overcrowding the pan.

For over-easy or over-hard eggs, use a pancake turner to carefully flip the eggs when the whites are nearly set. (Be gentle so the yolks don't break.)

To set the tops of the eggs without flipping them, try steam-basting. Instead of turning the eggs, add 1 to 2 Tbsp. water to skillet; cover. Cook until yolks are set but still a little runny.

## POACHED EGGS

**START TO FINISH** 10 minutes

| | |
|---|---|
| 4 | cups water |
| 1 | Tbsp. vinegar |
| 4 | eggs |
| | Salt and black pepper |

**1.** Add water to a 10-inch skillet; add vinegar. Bring to boiling; reduce heat to simmering (bubbles should begin to break the surface of the water).

**2.** Break an egg into a cup and slip egg into simmering water. Repeat with remaining eggs, allowing each egg an equal amount of space in the water.

**3.** Simmer eggs, uncovered, 3 to 5 minutes or until whites are completely set and yolks begin to thicken but are not hard. Remove eggs. Season to taste with salt and pepper. **Makes 4 eggs.**

**TO MAKE AHEAD** Poach eggs as directed. Place cooked eggs in a bowl of cold water. Cover; chill up to 2 hours. To reheat eggs, in a saucepan bring water to simmering. Use a slotted spoon to slip eggs into water; heat 2 minutes. Remove with slotted spoon.

**EACH EGG** *78 cal., 5 g fat (2 g sat. fat), 212 mg chol., 62 mg sodium, 1 g carb., 0 g fiber, 0 g sugars, 6 g pro.*

**VINEGAR SPLASH**
We add a splash of vinegar to the simmering poaching water to help the protein in the egg whites coagulate quickly for a more uniform shape.

Hold the lip of the cup close to the simmering water to slip the whole egg in at once—this prevents the white from spreading and getting stringy.

When the eggs are cooked, use a slotted spoon to remove them from the skillet, letting the water drain away from the eggs.

## *POACHING PAN*

Special pans aren't required for poaching, but they do create a perfectly shaped poached egg. If you use one, follow the manufacturer's directions for cooking (4 to 6 minutes). Run a knife around edges to loosen eggs.

## EASY OMELET

**START TO FINISH** 10 minutes

| | |
|---|---|
| 2 | **eggs** |
| 2 | **Tbsp. water** |
| ⅛ | **tsp. salt** |
| | **Dash black pepper** |
| 1 | **Tbsp. butter** |
| ⅔ | **to 1 cup desired fillings** |
| | **Desired toppers (optional)** |

**1.** In a bowl combine eggs, water, salt, and pepper. Beat with a fork until combined but not frothy.

**2.** Heat an 8-inch nonstick skillet with flared sides over medium-high heat. Melt butter in skillet. Add egg mixture to skillet; reduce heat to medium. With a heatproof spatula, begin stirring gently but continuously until egg mixture turns into small pieces of cooked egg surrounded by liquid egg. Stop stirring. Cook 30 to 60 seconds more or until egg is set and shiny.

**3.** Arrange filling on half of omelet. Lift edge over filling to fold omelet in half. (If making more than one omelet, keep warm while preparing additional omelets.) If desired, add toppers. **Makes 1 omelet.**
**EGG WHITE OMELET** Prepare as directed, except substitute 2 egg whites for one of the whole eggs.

### FILLINGS

**CHEESE** mozzarella, Parmesan, cheddar, feta

**MEATS** cooked bacon, smoked salmon, cooked kielbasa, cooked ham

**VEGETABLES** grape tomatoes, avocado, spinach, sautéed mushrooms, cooked broccoli, caramelized onions, sautéed peppers, steamed asparagus

### TOPPERS

Olive tapenade, sour cream or Greek yogurt, fresh salsa, or Tzatziki Sauce (p. 197); fresh herbs such as basil, oregano, Italian parsley, or dill

« Immediately reduce the heat to medium after adding the egg mixture to the skillet to avoid overbrowning the bottom of the omelet.

« Put the fillings on one half of the egg mixture.

« Use a heatproof spatula (instead of a pancake turner) to fold the other half of the omelet over the top of the filling.

# COOKING
## *charts*

FIND TIMINGS, TECHNIQUES, TIPS, AND
TEMPERATURES IN THESE AT-A-GLANCE CHARTS.

# COOKING POULTRY

FIND THE TECHNIQUES, TIMINGS, AND TEMPERATURES YOU NEED TO KNOW
WHEN COOKING CHICKEN, TURKEY, CORNISH GAME HENS, PHEASANT, GOOSE, AND DUCK.
(LOOK FOR POULTRY RECIPES ON *PP. 36–37, 154–169, AND 437–441.*)

**REFRIGERATE**
Refrigerate raw poultry in a container or on a rimmed tray in the original packaging 3 to 5 days. Freeze before expiration date.

**FREEZE**
Leave raw poultry in its original packaging. Overwrap in heavy-duty freezer foil or plastic wrap. Freeze up to 12 months.

**THAW**
For best results, thaw frozen poultry in the refrigerator overnight in a container. For more tips on freezing and thawing, see *pp. 34–35.*

## DIRECT-GRILLING POULTRY

| TYPE OF BIRD | WEIGHT/ THICKNESS | GRILLING TEMPERATURE | DIRECT-GRILLING TIME* | DONENESS |
|---|---|---|---|---|
| **CHICKEN** | | | | |
| Skinless, boneless breast halves | 6 to 8 oz. | Medium | 15 to 18 minutes | 165°F |
| Skinless, boneless thighs | 4 to 5 oz. | Medium | 12 to 15 minutes | 170°F |
| **TURKEY** | | | | |
| Turkey breast tenderloin | 8 to 10 oz. (¾ to 1 inch thick) | Medium | 16 to 20 minutes | 165°F |
| **UNCOOKED GROUND TURKEY OR CHICKEN** | | | | |
| Patties (turkey and chicken) | ½ inch thick ¾ inch thick | Medium Medium | 10 to 13 minutes 14 to 18 minutes | 165°F 165°F |

*All grilling times are based on poultry removed directly from refrigerator.

### DIRECT-GRILLING POULTRY

**REMOVE SKIN** if desired. Sprinkle with salt and black pepper.

**FOR A CHARCOAL OR GAS GRILL,** grill poultry, skin side(s) down, covered, over medium heat (tips, *pp. 16–17*) for time given *(left)* or until the proper temperature is reached and poultry is done, turning skin side(s) up halfway through grilling.

**DONENESS** should be determined using an instant-read thermometer.

## INDIRECT-GRILLING POULTRY

**REMOVE SKIN** if desired. Sprinkle with salt and black pepper.

**FOR A CHARCOAL OR GAS GRILL,** prepare grill for indirect heat using a drip pan (tips, *pp. 16–17*). Place poultry, skin side(s) down, over drip pan (for whole poultry, place, breast side up, and do not stuff). Grill, covered, over indirect medium heat for the time given *(right)* or until poultry is done and proper temperature is reached. Or, if desired, place whole birds on a rack in a roasting pan and omit the drip pan.

**DONENESS** should be determined using an instant-read thermometer. For whole birds, insert thermometer into center of the inside thigh muscle, away from bone. Poultry sizes vary; use these times as a general guide.

## INDIRECT-GRILLING POULTRY

| TYPE OF BIRD | WEIGHT/THICKNESS | GRILLING TEMPERATURE | INDIRECT-GRILLING TIME* | DONENESS |
|---|---|---|---|---|
| **CHICKEN** | | | | |
| Chicken, broiler-fryer, half | 1½ to 1¾ lb. | Medium | 1 to 1¼ hours | 170°F |
| Chicken, broiler-fryer, quarters | 12 to 14 oz. each | Medium | 50 to 60 minutes | 175°F |
| Chicken, whole | 2½ to 3 lb.<br>3½ to 4 lb.<br>4½ to 5 lb. | Medium<br>Medium<br>Medium | 1 to 1¼ hours<br>1¼ to 1¾ hours<br>1¾ to 2 hours | 170°F<br>170°F<br>170°F |
| Meaty chicken pieces (breast halves, thighs, and drumsticks) | 2½ to 3 lb. total | Medium | 50 to 60 minutes | 170°F (breast halves); 175°F (thighs and drumsticks) |
| **GAME** | | | | |
| Cornish game hen, halved lengthwise | 10 to 12 oz. each | Medium | 40 to 50 minutes | 175°F |
| Cornish game hen, whole | 1¼ to 1½ lb. | Medium | 50 to 60 minutes | 175°F |
| Pheasant, quarters | 8 to 12 oz. each | Medium | 50 to 60 minutes | 180°F |
| Pheasant, whole | 2 to 3 lb. | Medium | 1 to 1½ hours | 180°F |
| Quail, semiboneless | 3 to 4 oz. | Medium | 15 to 20 minutes | 180°F |
| **TURKEY** | | | | |
| Turkey breast, half | 2 to 2½ lb. | Medium | 1¼ to 2 hours | 170°F |
| Turkey breast, whole | 4 to 6 lb.<br>6 to 8 lb. | Medium | 1¾ to 2¼ hours<br>2½ to 3½ hours | 170°F<br>170°F |
| Turkey breast tenderloin | 8 to 10 oz. (or ¾ to 1 inch thick) | Medium | 25 to 30 minutes | 165°F |
| Turkey breast tenderloin steak (to make ½-inch-thick steaks, cut turkey tenderloin in half horizontally) | 4 to 6 oz. | Medium | 15 to 18 minutes | 165°F |
| Turkey drumstick | 8 to 16 oz. | Medium | ¾ to 1¼ hours | 175°F |
| Turkey thigh | 1 to 1½ lb. | Medium | 50 to 60 minutes | 175°F |
| Turkey, whole | 6 to 8 lb.<br>8 to 12 lb.<br>12 to 16 lb. | Medium | 1¾ to 2¼ hours<br>2½ to 3½ hours<br>3 to 4 hours | 175°F<br>175°F<br>175°F |

*All grilling times are based on poultry removed directly from refrigerator.

## BROILING POULTRY

**REMOVE SKIN** if desired. Sprinkle with salt and black pepper.

**TO BROIL,** preheat broiler 5 to 10 minutes. Arrange poultry on the unheated rack of the broiler pan, bone side(s) up. If desired, brush poultry with vegetable oil. Place pan under broiler so surface of the poultry is 4 to 5 inches from the heat (chicken should be 5 to 6 inches from the heat). Turn pieces over when browned on one side, usually halfway through the broiling time. Chicken halves and quarters and meaty pieces should be turned after 15 minutes. Brush again with oil.

**DONENESS** should be determined with an instant-read thermometer. Although all poultry is considered safe when it reaches 165°F, we prefer the texture of these cuts at these temperatures: 175°F for thighs and drumsticks, 170°F for bone-in breast meat, and 165°F for boneless breast meat. If desired, use a clean brush to brush on a sauce the last 5 minutes of broiling.

## SKILLET-COOKING POULTRY

**SELECT A SKILLET** that is heavy and the right size for the amount of poultry being cooked. (If the skillet is too large, pan juices can burn. If it's too small, poultry will steam instead of brown.)

**TO COOK,** lightly coat skillet (if it is not made of a nonstick material) with 2 to 3 tsp. vegetable oil or nonstick cooking spray. Preheat skillet over medium-high heat until hot. Add poultry. Do not add any liquid and do not cover the skillet. Reduce heat to medium; cook for the time given (right) or until done, turning poultry occasionally. (If poultry browns too quickly, reduce heat to medium-low.)

**DONENESS** should be determined with an instant-read thermometer: 165°F for breast meat and at least 175°F for thighs.

## BROILING POULTRY

| TYPE OF BIRD | WEIGHT | BROILING TIME |
|---|---|---|
| **CHICKEN** | | |
| **Kabobs** (boneless breast, cut into 2½-inch strips* and threaded loosely onto skewers) | | 8 to 10 minutes |
| **Meaty pieces** (breast halves, drumsticks, and thighs with bone) | 2½ to 3 lb. | 25 to 35 minutes |
| **Skinless, boneless breast halves** | 6 to 8 oz. | 15 to 18 minutes |
| **GAME** | | |
| **Boneless duck breast, skin removed** | 6 to 8 oz. | 14 to 16 minutes |
| **TURKEY** | | |
| **Breast cutlets*** | 2 oz. | 6 to 8 minutes |
| **Breast tenderloin steaks** (to make ½-inch-thick steaks, cut turkey tenderloin in half horizontally) | 4 to 6 oz. | 8 to 10 minutes |

*Chicken strips and cutlets are too thin to get an accurate doneness temperature. Cook them until no longer pink.

## SKILLET-COOKING POULTRY

| TYPE OF BIRD | WEIGHT | COOKING TIME |
|---|---|---|
| **CHICKEN** | | |
| **Breast tenders*** | 1 to 2 oz. | 6 to 8 minutes |
| **Skinless, boneless breast halves** | 6 to 8 oz. | 15 to 18 minutes |
| **Skinless, boneless thighs** | 3 to 4 oz. | 14 to 18 minutes |
| **TURKEY** | | |
| **Breast tenderloin steaks** (to make ½-inch-thick steaks, cut turkey tenderloin in half horizontally) | 4 to 6 oz. | 15 to 18 minutes |

*Chicken tenders are too thin to get an accurate doneness temperature. Cook them until no longer pink.

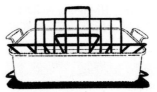

## ROASTING POULTRY

| TYPE OF BIRD | WEIGHT | OVEN TEMPERATURE | ROASTING TIME |
|---|---|---|---|
| **CHICKEN** | | | |
| Capon | 5 to 7 lb. | 325°F | 1¾ to 2½ hours |
| **Meaty pieces** (breast halves, drumsticks, and thighs with bone) | 2½ to 3 lb. | 375°F | 45 to 55 minutes |
| Whole | 2½ to 3 lb.<br>3½ to 4 lb.<br>4½ to 5 lb. | 375°F<br>375°F<br>375°F | 1 to 1¼ hours<br>1¼ to 1½ hours<br>1¾ to 2 hours |
| **GAME** | | | |
| Cornish game hen | 1¼ to 1½ lb. | 375°F | 1 to 1¼ hours |
| Duckling, domestic | 4 to 6 lb. | 350°F | 1¾ to 2½ hours |
| Goose, domestic | 7 to 8 lb.<br>8 to 10 lb. | 350°F<br>350°F | 2 to 2½ hours<br>2½ to 3 hours |
| Pheasant | 2 to 3 lb. | 325°F | 1½ to 2 hours |
| **TURKEY** | | | |
| Breast, boneless whole* | 2½ to 3 lb. | 325°F | 40 to 60 minutes |
| Breast, whole | 4 to 6 lb.<br>6 to 8 lb. | 325°F<br>325°F | 1½ to 2¼ hours<br>2¼ to 3¼ hours |
| Breast, boneless half | 1¼ to 1½ lb. | 325°F | 35 to 40 minutes |
| Breast, half | 2 to 2½ lb. | 325°F | 60 to 70 minutes |
| Drumstick | 1 to 1½ lb. | 325°F | 1¼ to 1¾ hours |
| Thigh | 1½ to 1¾ lb. | 325°F | 1½ to 1¾ hours |
| Whole (unstuffed)** | 8 to 12 lb.<br>12 to 14 lb.<br>14 to 18 lb.<br>18 to 20 lb.<br>20 to 24 lb. | 325°F<br>325°F<br>325°F<br>325°F<br>325°F | 2¾ to 3 hours<br>3 to 3¾ hours<br>3¾ to 4¼ hours<br>4¼ to 4½ hours<br>4½ to 5 hours |

*If you can't find a boneless whole turkey breast, have the butcher remove the bone.
**Stuffed birds generally require 15 to 45 minutes more roasting time than unstuffed birds. Always verify doneness temperatures of poultry and center of stuffing (165°F) with a meat thermometer.

## ROASTING POULTRY

**TIMING** varies based on the size and shape of each bird. Use times as general guides. For stuffed birds, see tip at bottom of chart (left).

**ADD AROMATICS,** if desired, by placing quartered onions and celery in body cavity. Pull neck skin to back and fasten with a skewer. If a band of skin crosses tail, tuck drumsticks under band. If there is no band, tie drumsticks to tail with 100%-cotton kitchen string. Twist wing tips under back. Place bird, breast side up, on a rack in a shallow roasting pan; brush with vegetable oil and, if desired, sprinkle with dried herbs, such as thyme or oregano (crushed). (When cooking a domestic duckling or goose, prick skin generously all over and omit oil.)

**COVER** Cornish game hens, pheasants, and whole turkeys with foil, leaving air space between bird and foil. Lightly press foil at ends of drumsticks and neck to enclose bird. Leave other poultry uncovered.

**MEAT THERMOMETER** (oven-going) may be inserted into the center of an inside thigh muscle of large birds, not touching the bone. (Or, during/after roasting, insert an instant-read thermometer into center of the inside thigh muscle, away from bone, checking temperature in several places.)

**ROAST** in an uncovered pan. Two-thirds of the way through roasting time, cut band of skin or string between drumsticks. Uncover large birds the last 45 minutes of roasting; uncover small birds the last 30 minutes of roasting. Continue roasting until meat thermometer registers 175°F in thigh muscle or until drumsticks move easily in sockets. (For a whole or half turkey breast, bone in, thermometer should register 170°F. For whole boneless breast, thermometer should register 165°F.) Remove bird from oven; cover. Allow whole birds and turkey portions to stand 15 minutes before carving.

# COOKING MEAT

FIND THE TECHNIQUES, TIMINGS, AND TEMPERATURES YOU NEED TO KNOW WHEN COOKING BEEF, LAMB, PORK, AND VEAL. (LOOK FOR MEAT RECIPES ON *PP. 38–43, 130–153,* AND *430–436*.)

## DIRECT-GRILLING MEAT

| CUT | THICKNESS | GRILLING TEMPERATURE | DIRECT-GRILLING TIME* | DONENESS |
|---|---|---|---|---|
| **BEEF** | | | | |
| **Boneless steak** (top loin [strip], ribeye, shoulder top blade [flat iron], shoulder petite tender medallions, shoulder center [ranch], chuck eye, tenderloin) | 1 inch | Medium | 10 to 12 minutes | 145°F medium rare |
| | 1 inch | Medium | 12 to 15 minutes | 160°F medium |
| | 1½ inches | Medium | 15 to 19 minutes | 145°F medium rare |
| | 1½ inches | Medium | 18 to 23 minutes | 160°F medium |
| **Boneless top sirloin steak** | 1 inch | Medium | 14 to 18 minutes | 145°F medium rare |
| | 1 inch | Medium | 18 to 22 minutes | 160°F medium |
| | 1½ inches | Medium | 20 to 24 minutes | 145°F medium rare |
| | 1½ inches | Medium | 24 to 28 minutes | 160°F medium |
| **Boneless tri-tip steak** (bottom sirloin) | ¾ inch | Medium | 9 to 11 minutes | 145°F medium rare |
| | ¾ inch | Medium | 11 to 13 minutes | 160°F medium |
| | 1 inch | Medium | 13 to 15 minutes | 145°F medium rare |
| | 1 inch | Medium | 15 to 17 minutes | 160°F medium |
| **Flank steak** | 1 to 1¼ inches | Medium | 13 to 16 minutes | 145°F medium |
| **Steak with bone** (porterhouse, T-bone, rib) | 1 inch | Medium | 10 to 13 minutes | 145°F medium rare |
| | 1 inch | Medium | 12 to 15 minutes | 160°F medium |
| | 1½ inches | Medium | 18 to 21 minutes | 145°F medium rare |
| | 1½ inches | Medium | 22 to 25 minutes | 160°F medium |
| **Ground meat patties** (beef, lamb, pork, and veal) | ½ inch | Medium | 10 to 13 minutes | 160°F medium |
| | ¾ inch | Medium | 14 to 18 minutes | 160°F medium |
| **LAMB** | | | | |
| **Chop** (loin or rib) | 1 inch | Medium | 12 to 14 minutes | 145°F medium rare |
| | | Medium | 15 to 17 minutes | 160°F medium |
| **Chop** (sirloin) | ¾ to 1 inch | Medium | 14 to 17 minutes | 160°F medium |
| **PORK** | | | | |
| **Chop** (boneless or bone-in loin, sirloin, and rib) | ¾ to 1 inch | Medium | 10 to 12 minutes | 145°F medium |
| | 1¼ to 1½ inches | Medium | 15 to 18 minutes | 145°F medium |
| **VEAL** | | | | |
| **Chop** (loin or rib) | 1 inch | Medium | 12 to 15 minutes | 160°F medium |
| **MISCELLANEOUS** | | | | |
| **Kabobs** (beef or lamb) | 1-inch cubes | Medium | 8 to 12 minutes | 160°F medium |
| **Kabobs** (veal) | 1-inch cubes | Medium | 10 to 14 minutes | 160°F medium |
| **Kabobs** (pork) | 1-inch cubes | Medium | 10 to 14 minutes | 145°F medium |
| **Sausages, cooked** (hot dogs, smoked bratwurst, etc.) | | Medium | 3 to 7 minutes | Heated through |

*All grilling times are based on meat removed directly from refrigerator.

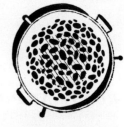

## DIRECT-GRILLING MEAT

**FOR A CHARCOAL OR GAS GRILL,** grill meat, covered, over medium heat (tips, *pp. 16–17*) for the time given *(left)* or to desired doneness, turning once halfway through grilling.

**DONENESS** should be determined using an instant-read thermometer. Tent steaks and chops with foil; let stand at room temperature 5 minutes (beef, lamb, and veal) or 3 minutes (pork) before cutting and serving. The temperature will continue to rise during the time it stands.

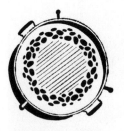

# INDIRECT-GRILLING MEAT

**FOR A CHARCOAL OR GAS GRILL,** prepare grill for indirect heat using a drip pan (tips, *pp. 16–17*). Place meat, fat side(s) up, over drip pan. Grill, covered, over indirect medium heat for the time given (*right*) or to desired temperature.

**DONENESS** should be determined using a meat thermometer (roasts) or an instant-read thermometer (smaller cuts of meat). Thermometer should register temperature listed under "doneness." After grilling, tent meat with foil; let stand 15 minutes (large cuts of meat, such as roasts), 5 minutes (steaks and lamb chops), and 3 minutes (pork chops) before slicing. The meat's temperature will continue to rise during the time it stands.

## INDIRECT-GRILLING MEAT

| CUT | THICKNESS/WEIGHT | INDIRECT-GRILLING TIME* | DONENESS |
|---|---|---|---|
| **BEEF** | | | |
| Boneless top sirloin steak | 1 inch | 22 to 26 minutes | 145°F medium rare |
| | 1 inch | 26 to 30 minutes | 160°F medium |
| | 1½ inches | 32 to 36 minutes | 145°F medium rare |
| | 1½ inches | 36 to 40 minutes | 160°F medium |
| Boneless tri-tip roast (bottom sirloin) | 1½ to 2 lb. | 35 to 40 minutes | 135°F medium rare |
| | 1½ to 2 lb. | 40 to 45 minutes | 150°F medium |
| Rib roast (chine bone removed) (medium-low heat) | 4 to 6 lb. | 2 to 2¾ hours | 135°F medium rare |
| | 4 to 6 lb. | 2½ to 3¼ hours | 150°F medium |
| Ribeye roast (medium-low heat) | 4 to 6 lb. | 1¼ to 1¾ hours | 135°F medium rare |
| | 4 to 6 lb. | 1½ to 2¼ hours | 150°F medium |
| Steak (top loin [strip], ribeye, shoulder top blade [flat iron], whole shoulder petite tender, tenderloin, porterhouse, T-bone, rib [cowboy]) | 1 inch | 16 to 20 minutes | 145°F medium rare |
| | 1 inch | 20 to 24 minutes | 160°F medium |
| | 1½ inches | 22 to 25 minutes | 145°F medium rare |
| | 1½ inches | 25 to 28 minutes | 160°F medium |
| Tenderloin roast (medium-high heat) | 2 to 3 lb. | 45 to 60 minutes | 135°F medium rare |
| | 4 to 5 lb. | 1 to 1¼ hours | 135°F medium rare |
| **LAMB** | | | |
| Boneless leg roast (medium-low heat) | 3 to 4 lb. | 1½ to 2¼ hours | 135°F medium rare |
| | 3 to 4 lb. | 1¾ to 2½ hours | 150°F medium |
| | 4 to 6 lb. | 1¾ to 2½ hours | 135°F medium rare |
| | 4 to 6 lb. | 2 to 2¾ hours | 150°F medium |
| Boneless sirloin roast (medium-low heat) | 1½ to 2 lb. | 1 to 1¼ hours | 135°F medium rare |
| | 1½ to 2 lb. | 1¼ to 1½ hours | 150°F medium |
| Chop (loin and rib) | 1 inch | 16 to 18 minutes | 145°F medium rare |
| | 1 inch | 18 to 20 minutes | 160°F medium |
| Leg of lamb (with bone) (medium-low heat) | 5 to 7 lb. | 1¾ to 2¼ hours | 135°F medium rare |
| | 5 to 7 lb. | 2¼ to 2¾ hours | 150°F medium |
| **PORK** | | | |
| Boneless top loin roast (medium-low heat) | 2 to 3 lb. (single loin) 3 to 5 lb. (double loin, tied) | 1 to 1½ hours | 145°F medium |
| | | 1½ to 2¼ hours | 145°F medium |
| Chop (boneless or bone-in loin, sirloin, and rib) | ¾ to 1 inch | 20 to 24 minutes | 145°F medium |
| | 1¼ to 1½ inches | 30 to 35 minutes | 145°F medium |
| Country-style ribs | | 1½ to 2 hours | 185°F tender |
| Ham, cooked (boneless)** (medium-low heat) | 3 to 5 lb. | 1¼ to 2 hours | 140°F |
| | 6 to 8 lb. | 2 to 2¾ hours | 140°F |
| Ham steak, cooked (medium-high heat) | 1 inch | 20 to 24 minutes | 140°F |
| Loin back ribs or spareribs | | 1½ to 1¾ hours | Tender |
| Loin center rib roast (backbone loosened) (medium-low heat) | 3 to 4 lb. | 1¼ to 2 hours | 145°F medium |
| | 4 to 6 lb. | 2 to 2¾ hours | 145°F medium |
| Sausages, uncooked (bratwurst, Polish, and Italian sausage links) | about 4 per lb. | 20 to 30 minutes | 160°F medium |
| Smoked shoulder picnic (with bone), cooked (medium-low heat) | 4 to 6 lb. | 1½ to 2¼ hours | 140°F heated through |
| Tenderloin (medium-high heat) | ¾ to 1 lb. | 30 to 35 minutes | 145°F medium |
| **VEAL** | | | |
| Chop (loin and rib) | 1 inch | 19 to 23 minutes | 160°F medium |

*All grilling times are approximate and based on meat removed directly from refrigerator.
**If using a natural ham, cooking may require 45 to 60 minutes more to reach temperature.

## BROILING MEAT

**TO BROIL,** place meat on the unheated rack of a broiler pan. Preheat broiler 5 to 10 minutes. For cuts less than 1½ inches thick, broil 3 to 4 inches from the heat. For 1½-inch-thick cuts, broil 4 to 5 inches from the heat. Broil for the time given *(right)* or until done, turning meat over halfway through broiling time. Tent with foil; let stand 5 minutes (beef steaks and lamb or veal chops) and 3 minutes (pork chops) before serving.

## BROILING MEAT

| CUT | THICKNESS/WEIGHT | BROILING TIME* | DONENESS |
|---|---|---|---|
| **BEEF** | | | |
| **Boneless steak** (top loin [strip], ribeye, shoulder top blade [flat iron], shoulder center [ranch], chuck eye, tenderloin) | 1 inch<br>1 inch<br>1½ inches<br>1½ inches | 12 to 14 minutes<br>15 to 18 minutes<br>18 to 21 minutes<br>22 to 27 minutes | 145°F medium rare<br>160°F medium<br>145°F medium rare<br>160°F medium |
| **Boneless top sirloin steak** | 1 inch<br>1 inch<br>1½ inches<br>1½ inches | 15 to 17 minutes<br>20 to 22 minutes<br>25 to 27 minutes<br>30 to 32 minutes | 145°F medium rare<br>160°F medium<br>145°F medium rare<br>160°F medium |
| **Boneless tri-tip steak** (bottom sirloin) | ¾ inch<br>¾ inch<br>1 inch<br>1 inch | 6 to 7 minutes<br>8 to 9 minutes<br>9 to 10 minutes<br>11 to 12 minutes | 145°F medium rare<br>160°F medium<br>145°F medium rare<br>160°F medium |
| **Flank steak** | 1 to 1¼ inches | 13 to 16 minutes | 145°F medium |
| **Steak with bone** (porterhouse, T-bone) | 1 inch<br>1 inch<br>1½ inches<br>1½ inches | 12 to 15 minutes<br>15 to 20 minutes<br>20 to 25 minutes<br>25 to 30 minutes | 145°F medium rare<br>160°F medium<br>145°F medium rare<br>160°F medium |
| **Ground meat patties** (beef, lamb, pork, and veal) | ½ inch<br>¾ inch | 10 to 12 minutes<br>12 to 14 minutes | 160°F medium<br>160°F medium |
| **LAMB** | | | |
| **Chop** (loin or rib) | 1 inch | 10 to 15 minutes | 160°F medium |
| **Chop** (sirloin) | 1 inch | 12 to 15 minutes | 160°F medium |
| **PORK** | | | |
| **Chop** (boneless or bone-in loin, sirloin, and rib) | ¾ to 1 inch<br>1¼ to 1½ inches | 5 to 8 minutes<br>13 to 16 minutes** | 145°F medium<br>145°F medium |
| **Ham steak, cooked** | 1 inch | 12 to 15 minutes | 140°F heated through |
| **SAUSAGES** | | | |
| **Hot dogs and sausage links, cooked** | | 3 to 7 minutes | 140°F heated through |
| **VEAL** | | | |
| **Chop** (loin or rib) | ¾ to 1 inch<br>1½ inches | 14 to 16 minutes<br>21 to 25 minutes | 160°F medium<br>160°F medium |

*All broiling times are based on meat removed directly from refrigerator.
**Turn two or three times during broiling.

## SKILLET-COOKING MEAT

**SELECT A SKILLET** that is heavy and is the right size for the amount of meat you're cooking. (If the skillet is too large, the pan juices can burn.) Lightly coat the skillet with nonstick cooking spray or use a heavy nonstick skillet.

**TO COOK,** preheat skillet over medium-high heat until very hot. Add meat. Do not add any liquid and do not cover the skillet. Reduce heat to medium and cook for the time given (*right*) or until done, turning meat occasionally. If meat browns too quickly, reduce heat to medium-low. Tent with foil and let stand 5 minutes (beef steaks and lamb and veal chops) or 3 minutes (pork chops) before serving.

**STIR-FRYING** works best using lean meats. Always heat the pan and oil before adding the food (for good browning, cook meat in batches so pan doesn't cool down). Adding ingredients to a pan before it has reached medium-high will cause the ingredients to juice out and steam instead of brown.

# SKILLET-COOKING MEAT

| CUT | THICKNESS | COOKING TIME* | DONENESS |
|---|---|---|---|
| **BEEF** | | | |
| **Boneless chuck-eye steak** | ¾ inch<br>1 inch | 9 to 11 minutes<br>12 to 15 minutes | 145°F medium rare to<br>160°F medium |
| **Boneless top sirloin steak or top loin steak** (strip) | ¾ inch<br>1 inch | 10 to 13 minutes<br>15 to 20 minutes | 145°F medium rare to<br>160°F medium |
| **Boneless tri-tip steak** (bottom sirloin) | ¾ inch<br>1 inch | 6 to 9 minutes<br>9 to 12 minutes | 145°F medium rare to<br>160°F medium |
| **Cubed steak** | ½ inch | 5 to 8 minutes | 160°F medium |
| **Porterhouse or T-bone steak** | ¾ inch<br>1 inch | 11 to 13 minutes<br>14 to 17 minutes | 145°F medium rare to<br>160°F medium |
| **Ribeye steak** | ¾ inch<br>1 inch | 8 to 10 minutes<br>12 to 15 minutes | 145°F medium rare to<br>160°F medium |
| **Shoulder center steak** (ranch) | ¾ inch<br>1 inch | 9 to 12 minutes (turn twice)<br>13 to 16 minutes (turn twice) | 145°F medium rare to<br>160°F medium |
| **Shoulder top blade steak** (flat iron) | 6 to 8 oz. | 8 to 15 minutes (turn once<br>or twice) | 145°F medium rare to<br>160°F medium |
| **Tenderloin steak** | ¾ inch<br>1 inch | 7 to 9 minutes<br>10 to 13 minutes | 145°F medium rare to<br>160°F medium |
| **Top loin steak** | ¾ inch<br>1 inch | 10 to 12 minutes<br>12 to 15 minutes | 145°F medium rare to<br>160°F medium |
| **Ground meat patties**<br>(beef, lamb, pork, and veal) | ½ inch<br>¾ inch | 9 to 12 minutes<br>12 to 15 minutes | 160°F medium<br>160°F medium |
| **LAMB** | | | |
| **Chop** (loin or rib) | 1 inch | 9 to 11 minutes | 160°F medium |
| **PORK** | | | |
| **Canadian-style bacon** | ¼ inch | 3 to 4 minutes | Heated through |
| **Chop** (boneless or bone-in loin, sirloin, and rib) | ¾ to 1 inch | 6 to 10 minutes | 145°F medium |
| **Cutlet** | ¼ inch | 3 to 4 minutes | No longer pink |
| **Ham slice, cooked** | ½ inch | 9 to 11 minutes | 140°F heated through |
| **VEAL** | | | |
| **Chop** (loin or rib) | ¾ to 1 inch | 10 to 14 minutes | 160°F medium |
| **Cutlet** | ⅛ inch<br>¼ inch | 2 to 3 minutes<br>4 to 6 minutes | No longer pink<br>No longer pink |

*All cooking times are based on meat removed directly from refrigerator.

# ROASTING MEAT

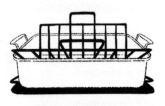

## ROASTING MEAT

**SELECT A PAN** that fits the task of roasting big pieces of meat—a large, sturdy shallow pan with a rack set inside. The pan's sides should be 2 to 3 inches high. This setup keeps the meat above the juices so the heat circulates all around the meat. You can also use a 13×9-inch baking pan with an oven-safe wire rack set inside.

**TO ROAST,** place meat, fat side up, on a rack in a shallow roasting pan. (Bone-in rib roasts do not need a rack.) Insert a meat thermometer in the thickest part of the roast (or check with an instant-read thermometer near the end of cooking time). Do not add water or liquid and do not cover. Roast in a 325°F oven (unless chart says otherwise) for time given *(right)* and until thermometer registers the temperature listed under "Doneness." Remove the meat from the oven. Tent with foil; let stand 15 minutes before carving. The meat's temperature will rise to the standard for medium rare (145°F) and medium (160°F) during the time it stands.

| CUT | WEIGHT | ROASTING TIME* | DONENESS |
|---|---|---|---|
| **BEEF** | | | |
| Boneless tri-tip roast (bottom sirloin) (Roast at 425°F) | 1½ to 2 lb. | 30 to 35 minutes<br>40 to 45 minutes | 135°F medium rare<br>150°F medium |
| Eye round roast (Roasting past medium rare is not recommended) | 2 to 3 lb. | 1½ to 1¾ hours | 135°F medium rare |
| Ribeye roast (Roast at 350°F) | 3 to 4 lb.<br><br>4 to 6 lb.<br><br>6 to 8 lb. | 1½ to 1¾ hours<br>1¾ to 2 hours<br>1¾ to 2 hours<br>2 to 2½ hours<br>2 to 2¼ hours<br>2½ to 2¾ hours | 135°F medium rare<br>150°F medium<br>135°F medium rare<br>150°F medium<br>135°F medium rare<br>150°F medium |
| Rib roast (chine bone removed) (Roast at 350°F) | 4 to 6 lb.<br><br>6 to 8 lb.<br><br>8 to 10 lb.** | 1¾ to 2¼ hours<br>2¼ to 2¾ hours<br>2¼ to 2½ hours<br>2¾ to 3 hours<br>2½ to 3 hours<br>3 to 3½ hours | 135°F medium rare<br>150°F medium<br>135°F medium rare<br>150°F medium<br>135°F medium rare<br>150°F medium |
| Round tip roast | 3 to 4 lb.<br><br>4 to 6 lb.<br><br>6 to 8 lb. | 1¾ to 2 hours<br>2¼ to 2½ hours<br>2 to 2½ hours<br>2½ to 3 hours<br>2½ to 3 hours<br>3 to 3½ hours | 135°F medium rare<br>150°F medium<br>135°F medium rare<br>150°F medium<br>135°F medium rare<br>150°F medium |
| Tenderloin roast (Roast at 425°F) | 2 to 3 lb.<br><br>4 to 5 lb. | 35 to 40 minutes<br>45 to 50 minutes<br>50 to 60 minutes<br>60 to 70 minutes | 135°F medium rare<br>150°F medium<br>135°F medium rare<br>150°F medium |
| Top round roast (Roasting past medium rare is not recommended) | 4 to 6 lb.<br>6 to 8 lb. | 1¾ to 2½ hours<br>2½ to 3 hours | 135°F medium rare<br>135°F medium rare |
| **LAMB** | | | |
| Boneless leg of lamb | 4 to 5 lb.<br><br>5 to 6 lb. | 1¾ to 2¼ hours<br>2 to 2½ hours<br>2 to 2½ hours<br>2½ to 3 hours | 135°F medium rare<br>150°F medium<br>135°F medium rare<br>150°F medium |
| Boneless shoulder roast | 3 to 4 lb.<br><br>4 to 5 lb. | 1½ to 2 hours<br>1¾ to 2¼ hours<br>2 to 2½ hours<br>2¼ to 3 hours | 135°F medium rare<br>150°F medium<br>135°F medium rare<br>150°F medium |
| Boneless sirloin roast | 1½ to 2 lb. | 1 to 1¼ hours<br>1¼ to 1½ hours | 135°F medium rare<br>150°F medium |
| Leg of lamb (with bone) | 5 to 7 lb.<br><br>7 to 8 lb. | 1¾ to 2¼ hours<br>2¼ to 2¾ hours<br>2¼ to 2¾ hours<br>2½ to 3 hours | 135°F medium rare<br>150°F medium<br>135°F medium rare<br>150°F medium |
| Leg of lamb, shank half (with bone) | 3 to 4 lb. | 1¾ to 2¼ hours<br>2 to 2½ hours | 135°F medium rare<br>150°F medium |
| Leg of lamb, sirloin half (with bone) | 3 to 4 lb. | 1½ to 2 hours<br>1¾ to 2¼ hours | 135°F medium rare<br>150°F medium |
| **PORK** | | | |
| Boneless country-style ribs (loin) (Brown in oil before roasting; roast at 350°F) | | 30 minutes | 145°F |
| Boneless country-style ribs (shoulder) (Brown in oil before roasting; roast at 350°F) | | 50 minutes | 185°F tender |
| Boneless sirloin roast | 2 to 2½ lb. | 1¼ to 1¾ hours | 145°F |

| CUT | WEIGHT | ROASTING TIME* | DONENESS |
|---|---|---|---|
| **PORK** | | | |
| **Boneless top loin roast** (single loin) | 2 to 3 lb. | 1 to 1½ hours | 145°F |
| **Crown roast** | 6 to 8 lb. | 1¾ to 2½ hours | 145°F |
| **Ham, cooked** (boneless)*** | 1½ to 3 lb.<br>3 to 5 lb.<br>6 to 8 lb.<br>8 to 10 lb.** | ¾ to 1¼ hours<br>1 to 1¾ hours<br>1¾ to 2½ hours<br>2¼ to 2¾ hours | 140°F<br>140°F<br>140°F<br>140°F |
| **Ham, cooked** (with bone)*** (half or whole) | 6 to 8 lb.<br>14 to 16 lb.** | 1½ to 2¼ hours<br>2¾ to 3¾ hours | 140°F<br>140°F |
| **Ham, cook before eating** (with bone) | 3 to 5 lb.<br>7 to 8 lb.<br>14 to 16 lb.** | 1¾ to 3 hours<br>2½ to 3¼ hours<br>4 to 5¼ hours | 150°F<br>150°F<br>150°F |
| **Loin back ribs or spareribs** | | 1½ to 1¾ hours | tender |
| **Loin center rib roast** (backbone loosened) | 3 to 4 lb.<br>4 to 6 lb. | 1¼ to 1½ hours<br>1½ to 2½ hours | 145°F<br>145°F |
| **Smoked shoulder picnic, cooked** (with bone) | 4 to 6 lb. | 1¼ to 2 hours | 140°F |
| **Tenderloin** (Roast at 425°F) | 1 lb | 30 to 35 minutes | 145°F |
| **VEAL** | | | |
| **Loin roast** (with bone) | 3 to 4 lb. | 1¾ to 2¼ hours | 150°F medium |
| **Rib roast** (chine bone removed) | 4 to 5 lb. | 1½ to 2¼ hours | 150°F medium |

*All roasting times are based on meat removed directly from refrigerator.
**Roasts weighing more than 8 lb. should be loosely covered with foil halfway through roasting.
***If using a natural ham, cooking may require 45 to 60 minutes more to reach temperature.

# MEAT CUTS

BEFORE YOU SHOP, LEARN WHERE EACH CUT OF BEEF, LAMB, AND PORK CAME FROM AND WHAT THE BEST USES ARE FOR EACH.

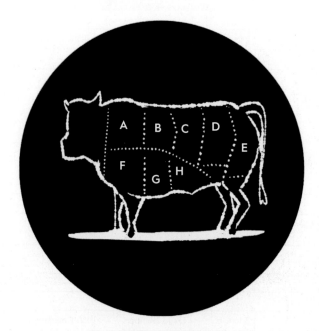

## BEEF CUTS

### (A) CHUCK

**Center steak (Ranch steak)** Broil, grill, skillet-cook

**Chuck eye steak** Broil, grill, skillet-cook, stir-fry

**Roast** Braise (cook in liquid)

**Short ribs** Braise (cook in liquid)

**Shoulder petite tender** Broil, grill, roast

**Shoulder steak (boneless)** Braise (cook in liquid)

**Top blade steak (boneless)** Broil, grill, roast

**Top blade steak (flat iron)** Broil, grill, skillet-cook, stir-fry

### (B) RIB

**Back ribs** Parboil before grilling

**Ribeye and rib roasts** Grill, roast

**Ribeye steak** Broil, grill, skillet-cook

### (C) LOIN

**T-bone and Porterhouse steak** Broil, grill, skillet-cook

**Tenderloin roast** Grill, roast

**Tenderloin steak** Broil, grill, skillet-cook, stir-fry

**Top loin (strip) steak** Broil, grill, skillet-cook, stir-fry

### (D) SIRLOIN

**Tri-tip and top sirloin steaks** Broil, grill, skillet-cook, stir-fry

**Tri-tip roast** Grill, roast

### (E) ROUND

**Bottom round roast** Braise (cook in liquid), roast

**Bottom round steak** Braise (cook in liquid)

**Eye round roast** Braise (cook in liquid), roast

**Eye round steak** Braise (cook in liquid), broil, grill, skillet-cook

**Round tip roast** Roast

**Top round roast** Roast

**Round tip steak** Skillet-cook, stir-fry

### (F) FORESHANK & BRISKET

**Brisket** Braise (cook in liquid)

**Shank crosscut** Braise (cook in liquid)

### (G) SHORT PLATE

**Skirt steak** Broil, grill, stir-fry

### (H) FLANK

**Flank steak** Broil, grill, stir-fry

**NOTE** Beef cut terminology varies among packagers.

### GRADES

Beef is graded by the United States Department of Agriculture (USDA) based on factors that affect tenderness and flavor, such as marbling (percentage of fat in meat), firmness, and color. The grades are prime, choice, and select. Prime (the most expensive and highest quality) is from young cattle, and the meat is well-marbled. Choice is also high quality (with juicy, tender meat) but contains less marbling than prime. Select tends to be leaner (less marbling), which also may make it slightly less tender and less flavorful.

### SELECTING

Look for beef with a fresh pink/red color. Some fat around the exterior of beef cuts is good, but trim any large pieces surrounding the meat.

### SLICING

Make tougher cuts of beef (such as brisket, flank steak, and tri-tip) fork-tender by cutting them thinly across the grain (the long fibers running through meat).

## LAMB CUTS

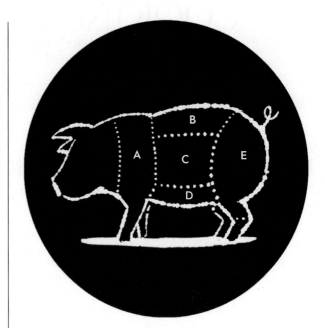

## PORK CUTS

### GRADES

Although lamb has five grades, the two you'll find in the supermarket are prime and choice. Like beef, prime lamb is well-marbled, which makes it exceptionally tender and flavorful. Choice is less well-marbled but is still considered quality in terms of flavor, juiciness, and tenderness. Buy lamb that has a USDA grade on the package to avoid purchasing meat from older animals (mutton).

### (A) SHOULDER

**Arm chop** Braise (cook in liquid), broil, grill, skillet-cook

**Blade chop** Braise (cook in liquid), broil, grill, skillet-cook

**Boneless roast** Braise (cook in liquid), roast

### (B) FORESHANK & BREAST

**Foreshank** Braise (cook in liquid)

### (C) RIB

**Rib chop** Broil, grill, roast, skillet-cook

**Rib roast** Grill, roast

### (D) LOIN

**Loin chop** Broil, grill, skillet-cook

**Loin roast** Grill, roast

### (E) LEG

**Boneless leg of lamb** Grill, roast

**Hind shanks** Braise (cook in liquid)

**Leg center slice** Broil, grill, skillet-cook

**Loin chop** Broil, grill, skillet-cook

**Loin roast** Grill, roast

**Shank half of leg** Grill, roast

**Sirloin chop** Broil, grill, skillet-cook

**Sirloin half leg of lamb** Roast

### (A) SHOULDER

**Blade roast** Braise (cook in liquid), roast

**Blade steak** Braise (cook in liquid), broil, grill, skillet-cook

**Sausage links** Skillet-cook

**Smoked hocks** Braise (cook in liquid)

**Smoked picnic** Cook in liquid, roast

### (B) LOIN

**Boneless sirloin chop** Braise (cook in liquid), broil, roast

**Boneless sirloin roast** Grill, roast

**Boneless top loin roast (single and double)** Grill, roast

**Canadian-style bacon** Braise (cook in liquid), broil, roast

**Center rib roast** Grill, roast

**Chops (top loin, loin, butterfly, rib)** Broil, grill, skillet-cook

**Ribs (loin-back, country-style)** Braise (cook in liquid), broil, roast

**Smoked loin chop** Braise (cook in liquid), broil, roast

**Tenderloin** Grill, roast

### (C) SIDE

**Spareribs** Braise (cook in liquid), broil, roast

### (D) BELLY

**Slab bacon** Slice before baking or skillet-cooking

**Sliced bacon** Bake, broil, skillet-cook

**Pork belly** Roast

### (E) LEG

**Cutlet** Braise (cook in liquid), skillet-cook

**Ham** Grill, roast

**Ham steak** Broil, grill, skillet-cook

### GRADES

Pork is not graded like beef and lamb because all pork comes from younger hogs that have been bred to yield meat that is consistent in tenderness and flavor.

### SELECTING

Look for pork that has minimal fat around the exterior of the cuts and is firm in texture with a pinkish color.

**NOTE** For storing, freezing, and thawing information, see *pp. 34–35.*

# COOKING FISH & SEAFOOD

FIND THE TECHNIQUES, TIMINGS, AND TEMPERATURES YOU NEED TO KNOW WHEN COOKING FISH AND SEAFOOD. (FIND FISH AND SEAFOOD RECIPES ON *PP. 44–45, 170–179,* AND *442–445.*)

## GUIDE TO FISH

| TYPE | MARKET FORM | TEXTURE | FLAVOR | SUBSTITUTIONS |
|------|-------------|---------|--------|---------------|
| **FRESHWATER FISH** | | | | |
| Catfish | Whole, fillets, steaks | Firm | Mild | Grouper, rockfish, sea bass, tilapia |
| **Lake trout** (North American char) | Whole, fillets, steaks | Slightly firm | Moderate | Pike, sea trout, whitefish |
| **Rainbow trout** | Fillets | Slightly firm | Delicate | Salmon, sea trout |
| **Tilapia** | Whole, dressed, fillets | Slightly firm | Delicate | Catfish, flounder, orange roughy |
| **Whitefish** | Whole, fillets | Moderately firm | Delicate | Cod, lake trout, salmon, sea bass |
| **SALTWATER FISH** | | | | |
| **Atlantic ocean perch** (redfish) | Whole, fillets | Slightly firm | Mild | Orange roughy, rockfish, snapper |
| **Cod** | Fillets, steaks | Moderately firm | Delicate | Flounder, haddock, pollock |
| **Flounder** | Whole, fillets | Fine | Delicate to mild | Cod, orange roughy, sea trout, sole, whitefish, whiting |
| **Grouper** | Whole, dressed, fillets | Moderately firm | Mild | Mahi mahi, sea bass |
| **Haddock** | Fillets | Moderately firm | Delicate | Cod, grouper, halibut, lake trout, sole, whitefish, whiting |
| **Halibut** | Fillets, steaks | Firm | Delicate | Cod, grouper, red snapper, sea bass |
| **Mackerel** | Whole | Delicate | Pronounced | Mahi mahi, swordfish, tuna |
| **Mahi mahi** (dolphinfish) | Whole, fillets | Firm | Mild to moderate | Grouper, orange roughy, red snapper |
| **Orange roughy** | Fillets | Moderately firm | Delicate | Cod, flounder, haddock, ocean perch, sea bass, sole |
| **Red snapper** | Whole, fillets | Moderately firm | Mild to moderate | Grouper, lake trout, ocean perch, rockfish, whitefish |
| **Rockfish** | Whole, fillets | Slightly firm | Mild to moderate | Cod, grouper, ocean perch, red snapper |
| **Salmon** | Whole, fillets, steaks | Moderately firm | Mild to moderate | Rainbow trout, swordfish, tuna, arctic char |
| **Shark** (mako) | Fillets, steaks | Firm, dense | Moderate | Swordfish, tuna |
| **Sole** | Fillets | Fine | Delicate | Flounder, haddock, halibut, pollock |
| **Swordfish** | Loins, steaks | Firm, dense | Mild to moderate | Halibut, shark, tuna |
| **Tuna** | Loins, steaks | Firm | Mild to moderate | Mackerel, salmon, shark, swordfish |

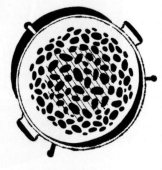

## DIRECT-GRILLING FISH

**PREP** your fish or seafood by thawing if frozen. (Rinse only if necessary.) Pat dry with paper towels. Place fish fillets in a well-greased grill basket. For fish steaks and whole fish, grease grill rack. Thread scallops or shrimp on skewers, leaving a ¼-inch space between pieces.

**FOR A CHARCOAL OR GAS GRILL,** grill fish, covered, over medium heat (tips, *pp. 16–17*) for the time given *(left)* or until fish flakes when tested with a fork (seafood should look opaque), turning once halfway through grilling. If desired, brush with vegetable oil or melted butter after turning.

## INDIRECT-GRILLING FISH

**PREP** your fish as directed *opposite*.

**FOR A CHARCOAL OR GAS GRILL,** prepare grill for indirect cooking using a drip pan (tips, *pp. 16-17*). Place fish over drip pan. Grill, covered, over indirect medium heat for the time given (*right*) or until fish begins to flake when tested with a fork (seafood should look opaque), turning once halfway through grilling if desired. If desired, brush with vegetable oil or melted butter after turning.

## DIRECT-GRILLING FISH

| FORM OF FISH | THICKNESS/WEIGHT | GRILLING TEMPERATURE | DIRECT-GRILLING TIME* | DONENESS |
|---|---|---|---|---|
| **Dressed whole fish** | ½ to 1½ lb. | Medium | 6 to 9 minutes per 8 oz. | Flakes |
| **Fillets, steaks, cubes** (for kabobs) | ½ to 1 inch thick | Medium | 4 to 6 minutes per ½-inch thickness | Flakes |
| **Lobster tails** | 6 to 8 oz. | Medium<br>Medium | 10 to 12 minutes<br>12 to 15 minutes | Opaque<br>Opaque |
| **Sea scallops** (for kabobs) | 12 to 15 per lb. | Medium | 5 to 8 minutes | Opaque |
| **Shrimp** (for kabobs) | 20 per lb.<br>12 to 15 per lb. | Medium<br>Medium | 5 to 8 minutes<br>7 to 9 minutes | Opaque<br>Opaque |

*All cooking times are based on fish or seafood removed directly from refrigerator.*

## INDIRECT-GRILLING FISH

| FORM OF FISH | THICKNESS, WEIGHT, OR SIZE | GRILLING TEMPERATURE | INDIRECT-GRILLING TIME* | DONENESS |
|---|---|---|---|---|
| **Dressed fish** | ½ to 1½ lb. | Medium | 15 to 20 minutes per 8 oz. | Flakes |
| **Fillets, steaks, cubes** (for kabobs) | ½ to 1 inch thick | Medium | 7 to 9 minutes per ½-inch thickness | Flakes |
| **Sea scallops** (for kabobs) | 12 to 15 per lb. | Medium | 11 to 14 minutes | Opaque |
| **Shrimp** (for kabobs) | 20 per lb.<br>12 to 15 per lb. | Medium<br>Medium | 8 to 10 minutes<br>9 to 11 minutes | Opaque<br>Opaque |

*All cooking times are based on fish or seafood removed directly from refrigerator.*

**SELECTING**
Pick fresh fish with firm flesh and a fresh and mild scent (not fishy or sour). Download the app about sustainable fish at *seafoodwatch.org.*

**STORING**
Refrigerate fish in original packaging 1 to 2 days. For more storage info on shellfish, see *p. 178.*

**FREEZING**
Wrap fresh fish in freezer wrap or foil. Freeze 3 to 6 months (never refreeze fish).

**THAWING**
Thaw in a container in the refrigerator overnight. For more storing, freezing, and thawing info, see *pp. 34–35.*

## COOKING FISH

**FISH SKIN** may have a few remaining scales when you purchase it. Before cooking fish with the skin on, scrape away any scales that remain. Or, if desired, remove the skin or have it removed at the market.

**PIN BONES** may occasionally remain in larger fish even if they were deboned at the market. Remove these with a clean pair of needle-nose pliers dedicated for kitchen use only. Pull out the pin bones at a 45-degree angle toward where the head would be.

**TIMING** is everything when it comes to cooking fish. To best estimate the cooking time, weigh dressed fish or use a ruler to measure the thickness of fillets and steaks. Properly cooked fish is opaque, flakes when tested with a fork, and readily comes away from the bones; the juices should be a milky white. If you like, serve with one of the sauces on pp. 30–31.

**DONENESS** is tested by inserting a fork into the fish and gently twisting. If the fish easily flakes, it is done. Check fish at the minimum cooking time to prevent overcooking.

## COOKING FISH

| COOKING METHOD | PREPARATION | FRESH OR THAWED FILLETS OR STEAKS | DRESSED |
|---|---|---|---|
| Bake | Place fish in a single layer in a greased shallow baking pan. For fillets, tuck under any thin edges. Brush with olive oil or melted butter. | Bake, uncovered, in a 450°F oven 4 to 6 minutes per ½-inch thickness of fish. | Bake, uncovered, in a 350°F oven 6 to 9 minutes per 8 oz. of fish. |
| Broil | Preheat broiler. Place fish on greased unheated rack of a broiler pan. For fillets, tuck under any thin edges. Brush with vegetable oil or melted butter. | Broil 4 inches from the heat 4 to 6 minutes per ½-inch thickness of fish. If fish is 1 inch or more thick, turn once halfway through broiling time. | Not recommended. |
| Grill | See Direct-Grilling and Indirect-Grilling Fish charts, p. 65. | | |
| Poach | Add 1½ cups water, broth, or wine to a 10-inch skillet. Bring to boiling. Add the fish. Return to boiling; reduce heat. | Simmer, uncovered, 4 to 6 minutes per ½-inch thickness of fish. | Simmer, covered, 6 to 9 minutes per 8 oz. of fish. |
| Skillet-cook | In a 12-inch skillet melt 1 Tbsp. butter and 1 Tbsp. vegetable oil over medium-high heat. | Add fish and cook 4 to 6 minutes per ½-inch thickness of fish, turning carefully halfway through. | Not recommended. |

# PREPARING & COOKING SHELLFISH

| TYPE | AMOUNT PER SERVING | PREPARATION | COOKING |
|---|---|---|---|
| Clams | 6 in shells (info, *p. 178*) | Scrub live clams under cold running water. For 24 clams in shells, in an 8-qt. pot combine 4 qt. cold water and ⅓ cup salt. Add clams and soak 15 minutes; drain and rinse. Discard water; repeat. | For 24 clams in shells, add ½ inch water to an 8-qt. pot; bring to boiling. Place clams in a steamer basket. Steam, covered, 5 to 7 minutes or until clams open. Discard any that do not open. |
| Crabs, hard-shell | 1 lb. live | Grasp live crabs from behind, firmly holding the back two legs on each side. Rinse under cold running water. | To boil 3 lb. live hard-shell blue crabs, in a 12- to 16-qt. pot bring 8 qt. water and 2 tsp. salt to boiling. Add crabs. Simmer, covered, about 10 minutes or until crabs turn pink; drain. |
| Crawfish | 1 lb. live | Rinse live crawfish under cold running water. For 4 lb. crawfish, in a 12- to 16-qt. pot combine 8 qt. cold water and ⅓ cup salt. Add crawfish and soak 15 minutes; rinse and drain. | For 4 lb. live crawfish, in a 12- to 16-qt. pot bring 8 qt. water and 2 tsp. salt to boiling. Add crawfish. Simmer, covered, 5 to 8 minutes or until shells turn red; drain. |
| Lobster tails (To boil a live lobster, see *p. 442*.) | One 8-oz. frozen | Thaw frozen lobster tails in the refrigerator. | For four 8-oz. lobster tails, in a 3-qt. saucepan bring 6 cups water and 1½ tsp. salt to boiling; add tails. Simmer, uncovered, 8 to 12 minutes or until shells turn bright red and meat is tender; drain. |
| Mussels | 12 in shells (info, *p. 178*) | Scrub live mussels under cold running water. Using your fingers, pull out beards that are visible between the shells. | For 24 mussels, add ½ inch water to an 8-qt. pot; bring to boiling. Place mussels in a steamer basket. Steam, covered, 5 to 7 minutes or until shells open. Discard any that do not open. |
| Oysters | 6 in shells (info, *p. 178*) | Scrub live oysters under cold running water. For easier shucking, chill. To shuck, hold oyster in a heavy towel or mitt. Carefully insert oyster knife tip into hinge between shells. Move blade along inside of upper shell to free the muscle; twist knife to pry shell open. Slide knife under oyster to cut muscle from bottom shell. | For 2 pt. shucked oysters, rinse oysters; pat dry with paper towels. In a 10-inch skillet cook and stir oysters in 1 Tbsp. hot butter over medium heat 3 to 4 minutes or until oyster edges curl; drain. |
| Shrimp | 6 oz. in shells or 3 to 4 oz. peeled, deveined (info, *p. 178*) | To peel, open shell down the underside. Starting at head end, pull back the shell. Gently pull on the tail to remove. Use a sharp knife to remove the black vein that runs along center of back. Rinse under cold running water. | For 1 lb. shrimp, in a 3-qt. saucepan bring 4 cups water and 1 tsp. salt to boiling. Add shrimp. Simmer, uncovered, 1 to 3 minutes or until shrimp turn opaque, stirring occasionally. Rinse under cold running water, drain, and, if desired, chill. |

# COOKING BEANS & GRAINS

FIND THE TECHNIQUES, TIMINGS, AND TIPS YOU NEED TO KNOW WHEN COOKING DRIED LEGUMES (BEANS, LENTILS, AND SPLIT PEAS) AND GRAINS (INCLUDING RICE). (FIND RECIPES AND PHOTOS ON *PP. 180–211.*)

## COOKING DRIED LEGUMES

**RINSE** beans, lentils, and split peas in a sieve or colander to remove any dirt. Remove any pebbles and broken or shriveled beans. Unless noted *(right)*, presoak beans as directed *(below)*.

**PRESOAK BEANS** in a 4- to 6-qt. Dutch oven. Combine 1 lb. beans and 8 cups cold water. Bring to boiling; reduce heat. Simmer 2 minutes. Remove from heat. Cover and let stand 1 hour. (Or omit cooking step and soak beans in cold water overnight in a covered Dutch oven in the refrigerator.) Drain and rinse. In the same Dutch oven combine beans and 8 cups fresh water. Bring to boiling; reduce heat. Simmer, covered, for time given or until beans are tender, stirring occasionally.

**TO PRESSURE-COOK** (info, p. 336), follow the manufacturer's directions. But here's a quick formula: Cook 1 cup unsoaked dried beans, 3 cups water, and 1 Tbsp. oil on high pressure about 25 minutes; use natural-release method for depressurizing.

## COOKING DRIED LEGUMES

| TYPE | AMOUNT | COOKING TIME | YIELD |
|---|---|---|---|
| Black beans | 1 lb. | 1 to 1½ hours | 6 cups |
| Black-eyed peas | 1 lb. | Do not presoak. Simmer, covered, ¾ to 1 hour. | 7 cups |
| Cranberry beans | 1 lb. | ¾ to 1½ hours | 7 cups |
| Fava or broad beans | 1 lb. | Follow these soaking directions instead of ones *left:* Bring beans to boiling; simmer, covered, 15 to 30 minutes to soften skins. Let stand 1 hour. Drain and peel. To cook, combine peeled beans and 8 cups fresh water. Bring to boiling; simmer, covered, 45 to 50 minutes or until tender. | 6 cups |
| Garbanzo beans (chickpeas) | 1 lb. | 1½ to 2 hours | 6¼ cups |
| Great Northern beans | 1 lb. | 1 to 1½ hours | 7 cups |
| Kidney beans, red | 1 lb. | 1 to 1½ hours | 6⅔ cups |
| Lentils, brown, French, red, and yellow | 1 lb. | Do not presoak. Use 5 cups water. Simmer brown, French, and yellow lentils, covered, 25 to 30 minutes; simmer red, covered, 5 to 10 minutes. | 7 cups |
| Lima beans, baby | 1 lb. | ¾ to 1 hour | 6½ cups |
| Lima beans, Christmas (calico) | 1 lb. | ¾ to 1 hour | 6½ cups |
| Lima beans, large (butter beans) | 1 lb. | 1 to 1¼ hours | 6½ cups |
| Navy or pea beans | 1 lb. | 1 to 1½ hours | 6¼ cups |
| Pinto beans | 1 lb. | 1¼ to 1½ hours | 6½ cups |
| Red beans | 1 lb. | 1 to 1½ hours | 6½ cups |
| Soybeans | 1 lb. | 3 to 3½ hours | 7 cups |
| Split peas | 1 lb. | Do not presoak. Use 5 cups water. Simmer, covered, 45 minutes. | 5½ cups |

**3½ TO FOUR 15-OZ. CANS**
= 1 lb. dried beans

**1 LB. DRIED, UNCOOKED BEANS (2¼ TO 2½ CUPS)**
= 6 to 7 cups cooked beans

## COOKING GRAINS

**POUR** the required amount of water *(right)* into a 2-qt. saucepan. Bring the water to a full boil unless the chart specifies otherwise. If desired, add ¼ tsp. salt to the water. Slowly add the grain and return to boiling; reduce heat. Simmer, covered, for the time specified or until most of the water is absorbed and grain is tender.

**QUINOA** requires rinsing before cooking (if it doesn't come prerinsed). Place dry quinoa in a sieve and run it under cold water. This will remove the bitter-tasting natural coating called saponin.

**RICE** should be fluffed with a fork after cooking (not stirred with a spoon). This will keep the rice light and fluffy and prevent clumping.

## COOKING GRAINS

| TYPE | AMOUNT OF GRAIN | AMOUNT OF WATER | COOKING DIRECTIONS | YIELD |
|------|-----------------|-----------------|--------------------|-------|
| Barley, quick-cooking pearl | 1¼ cups | 2 cups | Simmer, covered, 10 to 12 minutes; drain if necessary. | 3 cups |
| Barley, regular pearl | ¾ cup | 3 cups | Simmer, covered, 45 minutes; drain if necessary. | 3 cups |
| Buckwheat groats or kasha | ⅔ cup | 1½ cups | Add to cold water. Bring to boiling. Simmer, covered, 6 to 8 minutes. | 2¼ cups |
| Bulgur | 1 cup | 2 cups | Add to cold water. Bring to boiling. Simmer, covered, 15 minutes. | 3 cups |
| Farina, quick-cooking | ¾ cup | 3½ cups | Simmer, uncovered, 2 to 3 minutes, stirring constantly. | 3½ cups |
| Farro, pearled | 1 cup | 3 cups | Combine farro and water in saucepan. Bring to boiling. Simmer, covered, 25 to 30 minutes; drain if necessary. | 2½ cups |
| Hominy grits, quick-cooking | ¾ cup | 3 cups | Simmer, covered, 5 minutes, stirring occasionally. | 3 cups |
| Millet | ¾ cup | 2 cups | Simmer, covered, 15 to 20 minutes. Let stand, covered, 5 minutes. | 3 cups |
| Oats, rolled, quick-cooking | 1½ cups | 3 cups | Simmer, uncovered, 1 minute. Let stand, covered, 3 minutes. | 3 cups |
| Oats, rolled, regular | 1⅔ cups | 3 cups | Simmer, uncovered, 5 to 7 minutes. Let stand, covered, 3 minutes. | 3 cups |
| Oats, steel-cut | 1⅓ cups | 4 cups | Cook in 4-qt. saucepan. Add ½ tsp. salt. Simmer, covered, 25 to 30 minutes. | 4 cups |
| Quinoa, plain, red | ¾ cup | 1½ cups | Rinse well. Simmer, covered, 15 minutes; drain if necessary. | 1¾ cups |
| Rice, black | 1 cup | 1¾ cups | Combine black rice and water in saucepan. Bring to boiling. Simmer, covered, 30 minutes. | 3 cups |
| Rice, long grain, white | 1 cup | 2 cups | Simmer, covered, about 15 minutes. Let stand, covered, 5 minutes. | 2 cups |
| Rice, red | 1 cup | 1½ cups | Combine red rice and water in saucepan. Bring to boiling. Simmer, covered, 20 minutes. Remove from heat; let stand 10 minutes. | 2½ cups |
| Rice, regular, brown | 1 cup | 2 cups | Simmer, covered, 45 minutes. Let stand, covered, 5 minutes. | 3 cups |
| Rye berries | ¾ cup | 2½ cups | Simmer, covered, 60 minutes; drain. (Or soak berries in 2½ cups water in the refrigerator 6 to 24 hours. Do not drain. Bring to boiling; reduce heat. Simmer, covered, 30 minutes.) | 2 cups |
| Spelt | 1 cup | 3 cups | Simmer, covered, 50 to 60 minutes. | 2½ cups |
| Wheat, cracked | ⅔ cup | 1½ cups | Add to cold water. Bring to boiling. Simmer, covered, 12 to 15 minutes. Let stand, covered, 5 minutes. | 1¾ cups |
| Wheat berries | ¾ cup | 2½ cups | Simmer, covered, 45 to 60 minutes; drain. (Or soak and cook as for rye berries.) | 2 cups |
| Wild rice | 1 cup | 2 cups | Rinse well. Simmer, covered, 40 minutes or until most of the water is absorbed; drain if necessary. | 3 cups |

# FRUITS & VEGETABLES

FIND THE TECHNIQUES, TIMINGS, AND TIPS YOU NEED TO KNOW WHEN SELECTING, COOKING, AND STORING PRODUCE. (FOR COOKING INFO, SEE *PP. 78–81*; FOR RECIPES, SEE *PP. 304–323* AND *448–469*.)

## SELECTING FRESH VEGETABLES

| VEGETABLE | IN SEASON | HOW TO CHOOSE | HOW TO STORE |
|---|---|---|---|
| Asparagus | Available March through June with peak season in April and May; available year-round in some areas. | Choose crisp, firm, straight stalks with good color and compact, closed tips. If possible, select spears that are the same size for even cooking. | Wrap the bases of fresh asparagus spears in wet paper towels and place in a plastic bag in the refrigerator up to 3 days. |
| Beans, green: snap or string | Available April through September; available year-round in some areas. | Select fresh beans that are bright-color and crisp. Avoid those that are bruised, scarred, or rusty with brown spots or streaks. Bulging, leathery beans are old. | Refrigerate beans in a plastic bag in the crisper drawer of the refrigerator up to 1 week. |
| Beets | Available year-round with peak season from June through October. | Select small or medium beets; large beets tend to be pithy, tough, and less sweet. | Trim beet greens, leaving 1 to 2 inches of stem. Do not cut the long root. Store unwashed beets in an open container in the refrigerator up to 1 week. |
| Bok choy | Available year-round. | Look for firm, white, bulblike bases with deep green leaves. Avoid soft spots on bases or wilted, shriveled leaves. | Refrigerate bok choy in a plastic bag and use within 5 days. |
| Broccoli | Available year-round with peak season from October through May. | Look for firm stalks with tightly packed, deep-green or purplish-green heads. Avoid heads that are light green or yellowing. | Keep unwashed broccoli in a plastic bag in the refrigerator up to 4 days. |
| Brussels sprouts | Available year-round with peak season from August through April. | Pick out the smaller sprouts that are vivid green; they will taste the sweetest. Large ones might be bitter. | Refrigerate sprouts in a plastic bag in the crisper drawer of the refrigerator up to 5 days. |
| Cabbage: green, napa, red, and savoy | Available year-round. | The head should feel heavy for its size; leaves should be unwithered, bright-color, and free of brown spots. | Refrigerate cabbage in a plastic bag up to 5 days. |
| Carrots | Available year-round. | Select straight, rigid, bright orange carrots without cracks. | Refrigerate carrots in a plastic bag up to 2 weeks. |
| Cauliflower | Available year-round. | Look for solid, heavy heads with bright-green leaves. Avoid those with brown bruises, yellowed leaves, or speckled appearance. | Refrigerate cauliflower in a plastic bag in the crisper drawer of the refrigerator up to 5 days. Keep away from ethylene-producing fruit, such as apples, mangoes, melons, pears, peaches, and plums. |
| Celery | Available year-round. | Look for crisp celery ribs that are firm, unwilted, and unblemished. | Refrigerate celery in a plastic bag up to 2 weeks. |
| Corn (sweet) | Available summer and fall with peak season from July through September. | Look for corn with plump kernels and green husks (avoid corn with kernels or husks that look dry). | For the sweetest flavor, prepare corn within 1 day of picking. Or refrigerate corn in husks up to 7 days. |
| Cucumbers | Available year-round with peak season from late May through early September. | Select firm cucumbers without shriveled or soft spots. Edible wax sometimes is added to prevent moisture loss. | Keep cucumbers in a plastic bag in refrigerator 3 to 5 days. |
| Eggplant | Available year-round with peak season from August through September. | Look for plump, glossy eggplants that have fresh-looking, mold-free caps. Skip any that are scarred or bruised. | Refrigerate whole eggplants in a perforated plastic bag 2 to 4 days. |
| Fennel | Available October through April; available year-round in some areas. | Look for crisp, clean bulbs without brown spots or blemishes. Tops should be bright green and look fresh. | Refrigerate fennel, tightly wrapped in a plastic bag, up to 5 days. |

| VEGETABLE | IN SEASON | HOW TO CHOOSE | HOW TO STORE |
|---|---|---|---|
| Greens, cooking: beet, chard, collard, kale, mustard, and turnip | Most available year-round with peak season from September through May; peak season for chard is from June through August. | Look for crisp or tender leaves with bright or rich color. Avoid wilted or yellowing leaves. | Cut away center stalk of kale leaves. Refrigerate most greens in a plastic bag up to 5 days; refrigerate mustard greens up to 1 week. |
| Leeks | Available year-round. | Look for leeks that have clean white ends and fresh green tops. | Refrigerate leeks, wrapped loosely in plastic, 10 to 14 days. |
| Mushrooms (all varieties) | Available year-round; morel mushrooms available April through June. | Mushrooms should be firm, fresh, plump, and bruise-free. Size is a matter of preference. Avoid spotted or slimy mushrooms. | Store unwashed mushrooms in the refrigerator up to 2 days in a paper bag. If in original packaging, remove plastic and wrap carton in barely damp paper towels. |
| Okra | Available year-round with peak season from May through September. | Look for small, crisp, bright-color pods without brown spots or blemishes. Avoid shriveled pods. | Refrigerate okra in a paper bag in crisper drawer of the refrigerator up to 3 days. |
| Onions (all varieties) | Variety determines availability. Some varieties, such as white, red, pearl, and boiling onions, are available year-round. Various sweet onion varieties, such as Vidalia and Walla Walla, are available on and off throughout the year. | Select dry bulb onions that are firm, free from blemishes, and not sprouting. They should have papery outer skins and short necks. | Keep onions in a cool, dry, well-ventilated place for several weeks. |
| Peas, Pea pods | Peas: available January through June with peak season from March through May. Pea pods: available February through August. | Select fresh, crisp, bright-color peas, snow peas, or sugar snap peas. Avoid shriveled pods or those with brown spots. | Store peas in a perforated plastic bag in the crisper drawer of the refrigerator 2 to 4 days. |
| Peppers: hot and sweet | Available year-round. | Fresh peppers, whether hot or sweet, should be bright-color and have a good shape for the variety. Avoid shriveled, bruised, or broken peppers. | Refrigerate peppers in a plastic bag up to 5 days. |
| Potatoes | Available year-round. | Look for clean potatoes that have smooth, unblemished skins. They should be firm and have a typical shape for their variety. Avoid those that have green spots or are soft, moldy, or shriveled. | Store potatoes in an open paper bag or basket for several weeks in a dark, well-ventilated, cool place that is slightly humid but not wet. Do not refrigerate; potatoes tend to get sweet at cold temperatures. |
| Root vegetables: parsnips, rutabagas, and turnips | Available year-round. Parsnips: peak season from November through March. Rutabagas: peak season from September through March. Turnips: peak season from October through March. | Choose vegetables that are smooth-skinned and heavy for their size. Sometimes parsnips, rutabagas, and turnips are covered with a wax coating to extend storage; cut off this coating before cooking. | Refrigerate root vegetables in a plastic bag up to 2 weeks. |
| Spinach | Available year-round. | Leaves should be crisp and free of moisture. Avoid spinach with broken or bruised leaves. | Rinse leaves in cold water and thoroughly dry. Place the leaves in a storage container with a paper towel and refrigerate up to 3 days. |
| Squash, winter | Some varieties available year-round with peak season from September through March. | Choose firm squash that are heavy for their size. Avoid those with soft spots. | Store whole squash in a cool, dry place up to 2 months. Refrigerate cut squash, wrapped in plastic, up to 4 days. |
| Sweet potatoes | Available year-round with peak season from October through January. | Choose small to medium smooth-skin sweet potatoes that are firm and free of soft spots. | Store sweet potatoes in an open paper bag or basket in a cool, dry, dark place up to 1 week. |
| Tomatoes | Available year-round with peak season from June through early September. | Pick well-shaped, plump, fairly firm tomatoes. Ripe tomatoes yield to slight pressure and smell like a tomato. | Store tomatoes at room temperature up to 3 days. Do not store tomatoes in the refrigerator; they lose their flavor. |
| Zucchini, summer squash | Some varieties available year-round with peak season from June through September. | It is almost impossible for tender-skin zucchini to be blemish-free, but look for small ones that are firm and free of cuts and soft spots. | Refrigerate squash, tightly wrapped, up to 4 days. |

# RIPENING FRUIT

**PLACE FRUIT** in a small clean paper bag. (Do not use plastic bags; they don't allow air circulation and can cause the fruit to grow mold.)

**LOOSELY CLOSE** the bag and store it at room temperature. To speed up ripening, place an apple or ripe banana in the bag with the underripe fruit.

**CHECK DAILY** and remove fruit that yields to gentle pressure. To check the fruit, cradle it in the palm of your hand and gently squeeze rather than prodding the fruit with your thumb or finger, which can bruise it.

**EAT RIPE FRUIT** immediately or refrigerate it for a couple of days. (Refrigeration slows down further ripening.)

# SELECTING FRESH FRUITS

| FRUIT | IN SEASON | HOW TO CHOOSE | HOW TO STORE |
|---|---|---|---|
| Apples | Available year-round with peak season September through November. | Select firm apples, free from bruises or soft spots. Apples are sold ready for eating. Select variety according to intended use. | Refrigerate up to 6 weeks; store bulk apples in a cool, moist place. Don't store near foods with strong odors that can be absorbed. |
| Apricots | Available May through July. | Look for plump, fairly firm apricots with deep yellow or yellowish orange skin. | Ripen firm fruit as directed (left) until it yields to gentle pressure and is golden in color. Refrigerate ripened fruit up to 2 days. |
| Avocados | Available year-round. | Avoid bruised fruit with gouges or broken skin. Soft avocados can be used immediately (and are especially good for guacamole). | Ripen firm fruit as directed (left) until it yields to gentle pressure in cradled hands. Store ripened fruit in the refrigerator up to 5 days. |
| Bananas | Available year-round. | Choose bananas at any stage of ripeness, from green to yellow. | Ripen at room temperature until they have a bright yellow color. Overripe bananas are brown. |
| Berries | Blackberries: Available June through August. Blueberries: Available late May through October. Boysenberries: Available late June through early August. Raspberries: Available year-round with peak season from May through September. Strawberries: Available year-round with peak season from April through June. | If picking your own, select berries that separate easily from their stems. | Refrigerate berries in a single layer, loosely covered, up to 3 days. Rinse just before using. |
| Cantaloupe | Available year-round with peak season from June through September. | Select cantaloupe that has a delicate, sweet, aromatic scent; look for cream-color netting over rind that is yellowish green or gray. Melon should feel heavy for its size. | Ripen cantaloupe as directed (left). Refrigerate ripened whole melon up to 4 days. Refrigerate cut fruit in a covered container or tightly wrapped up to 3 days. |
| Carambolas (Star fruit) | Available late August through February. | Look for firm, shiny-skin golden fruit. Some brown on the edge of the fins is natural and does not affect the taste. | Ripen fruit as directed (left). Refrigerate ripened fruit in a covered container or tightly wrapped up to 1 week. |
| Cherries | Sweet: Available May through August with peak season in June and July. Tart: Available June through August with peak season in June and July. | Select firm, bright-color fruit. | Refrigerate cherries in a covered container 2 to 3 days. |
| Cranberries | Available October through December with peak season in November. | Fruit is ripe when sold. Avoid soft, shriveled, or bruised cranberries. | Refrigerate cranberries up to 2 weeks or freeze up to 1 year. |
| Figs | Available mid-May through December. | Look for fruit with smooth, dry skin and no blemishes or cracks. Figs will be firm but give slightly to touch. | Use figs as soon as possible. Can refrigerate in a plastic bag up to 3 days. |
| Grapefruit | Available year-round. | Choose bright-color grapefruit with a nicely rounded shape. Juicy grapefruit will be heavy for its size. | Refrigerate grapefruit up to 2 weeks. |
| Grapes | Available year-round. | Look for plump grapes without bruises, soft spots, or mold. Bloom (a frosty white cast) is typical and doesn't affect quality. | Refrigerate grapes in a perforated plastic bag up to 1 week. |

| FRUIT | IN SEASON | HOW TO CHOOSE | HOW TO STORE |
|---|---|---|---|
| Honeydew melon | Available year-round with peak season from June through September. | Choose a melon that is firm and a creamy-yellow color with a sweet, aromatic scent. Avoid wet, dented, bruised, or cracked ones. | Ripen melon as directed (left). Refrigerate ripened whole melons up to 4 days. Refrigerate cut fruit in a covered container or tightly wrapped up to 3 days. |
| Kiwifruits | Available year-round. | Choose fruit that is free of wrinkles, bruises, and soft spots. | Ripen firm fruit as directed (opposite) until skin yields to gentle pressure; refrigerate ripened fruit 3 to 5 days. |
| Lemons, Limes | Available year-round. | Look for firm, well-shaped fruit with smooth, bright-color skin. Avoid fruit with shriveled skin. | Refrigerate citrus fruit up to 2 weeks. |
| Mangoes | Available April through September with peak season from June through July. | Look for fully ripe fruit that smells fruity and feels fairly firm when pressed. | Ripen firm fruit as directed (opposite). Refrigerate ripened fruit up to 3 days. |
| Oranges | Available year-round. | Choose oranges that are firm and heavy for their size. Brown specks or a slight greenish tinge on the rind of an orange will not affect the eating quality. | Refrigerate oranges up to 2 weeks. |
| Papayas | Available year-round. | Choose fruit that is at least half yellow and feels somewhat soft when pressed. The skin should be smooth. | Ripen papayas as directed (opposite) until yellow. Refrigerate ripened fruit, unwrapped, 3 to 5 days. |
| Peaches, Nectarines | Peaches: Available May through September. Nectarines: Available May through September with peak season in July and August. | Look for fruit with a golden-yellow skin and no tinges of green. Ripe fruit should yield slightly to gentle pressure. | Ripen pears as directed (opposite). Refrigerate ripened fruit up to 5 days. |
| Pears | Available year-round. | Skin color is not always an indicator of ripeness because the color of some varieties does not change much as the pears ripen. Look for pears without bruises or cuts. Choose a variety according to intended use. | Ripen as directed (opposite) until skin yields to gentle pressure at the stem end. Refrigerate ripened fruit 5 to 7 days. |
| Persimmons (Fuyu and Hachiya) | Available October through February. | Fuyu persimmons have a bright yellow-orange color and should be firm to the touch. Hachiya persimmons should have a deep solid-orange color with no dark spots. | Ripen as directed (opposite) until soft. Fuyu persimmons will stay firm up to 3 weeks. Hachiya persimmons can be stored up to 1 week at room temperature. |
| Pineapple | Available year-round with peak season from March through July. | Look for a plump pineapple with a sweet, aromatic smell. It should be slightly soft to the touch, heavy for its size, and have deep green leaves. Avoid those with soft spots. | Refrigerate pineapple up to 2 days. Refrigerate cut pineapple in an airtight container up to 3 days. |
| Plums | Available May through October with peak season in June and July. | Find firm, plump, well-shaped fresh plums. Fruit should give slightly when gently pressed. Bloom (light gray cast) on the skin is natural and doesn't affect quality. | Ripen plums as directed (opposite). Refrigerate ripened fruit up to 3 days. |
| Rhubarb | Available February through June with peak season from April through June. | Look for crisp stalks that are firm and tender. Avoid rhubarb that looks wilted or has very thick stalks. | Wrap rhubarb stalks tightly in plastic wrap and refrigerate up to 5 days. |
| Watermelon | Available May through September with peak season from mid-June through late August. | Choose watermelon that has a hard, smooth rind and is heavy for its size. Avoid wet, dented, bruised, or cracked fruit. | Watermelon does not ripen after it is picked. Refrigerate whole melon up to 4 days. Refrigerate cut fruit in a covered container or tightly wrapped up to 3 days. |

THE U.S. DEPARTMENT OF AGRICULTURE RECOMMENDS MOST ADULTS EAT AT LEAST 2 CUPS FRUITS AND 2½ CUPS VEGETABLES A DAY.

**SPRING PRODUCE 1.** Artichoke **2.** Rhubarb **3.** Asparagus **4.** Carrots (purple, white, and orange) **5.** Cauliflower **6.** Kohlrabi (white and purple) **7.** Leek **8.** Green onions (also called scallions) **9.** Snow peas **10.** Sugar snap peas **11.** Broccoli **12.** Broccoli rabe **13.** White button mushrooms **14.** Cremini mushrooms **15.** Oyster mushrooms **16.** Shiitake mushroom **17.** Portobello mushroom

**SUMMER PRODUCE 1.** Tomatillos **2.** Campari tomatoes **3.** Roma tomato **4.** Persian cucumber **5.** English (hot house) cucumber **6.** Cucumber **7.** Zucchini **8.** Yellow summer squash **9.** Eggplant **10.** Heirloom tomato **11.** Grape tomatoes **12.** Cherry tomatoes **13.** Avocado **14.** Swiss chard **15.** Green sweet pepper **16.** Red sweet pepper **17.** Serrano chile peppers **18.** Habanero chile peppers **19.** Green beans **20.** Okra **21.** Jalapeño chile pepper **22.** Anaheim chile pepper **23.** Poblano chile pepper **24.** Corn **25.** Blackberries **26.** Red raspberries **27.** Blueberries **28.** Strawberries **29.** Plum **30.** Peach **31.** Watermelon **32.** Cantaloupe **33.** Honeydew melon

**FALL PRODUCE** 1. Butternut squash 2. Beets (red and golden) 3. Cipollini onions 4. Pearl onions 5. Shallots 6. White onion 7. Red onion 8. Russet potato 9. Round white potato 10. Fingerling potato 11. Purple potato 12. Round red potato 13. Yukon gold potato 14. Yellow onion 15. Spaghetti squash 16. Green cabbage 17. Red cabbage 18. Bok choy 19. Savoy cabbage 20. Napa cabbage 21. Acorn squash 22. Red Delicious apple 23. Braeburn apple 24. Granny Smith apple 25. Golden Delicious apple

**WINTER PRODUCE 1.** Mustard greens **2.** Collard greens **3.** Kale **4.** Sweet potato **5.** Bartlett pear **6.** Anjou pear
**7.** Fennel bulb **8.** Pineapple **9.** Cranberries **10.** Brussels sprouts **11.** Lemon **12.** Lime **13.** Clementine **14.** Grapefruit
**15.** Blood orange **16.** Navel orange **17.** Turnip **18.** Rutabaga **19.** Parsnip

## COOKING FRESH VEGGIES

**AMOUNTS** given *(right and opposite)* each yield enough cooked vegetables for 4 servings (except where noted).

**TO PREPARE** fresh vegetables, wash with cool tap water; scrub firm vegetables with a produce brush.

**TO STEAM** vegetables, place a steamer basket in a saucepan. Add water to just below the bottom of the basket. Bring water to boiling. Add prepped vegetables to steamer basket. Cover and reduce heat. Steam for the time specified in the chart or until veggies reach desired doneness.

**TO MICROWAVE,** use a microwave-safe baking dish or casserole and follow the directions in the chart, keeping in mind that times might vary depending on the oven. Cover with waxed paper or the lid of the baking dish or casserole.

# COOKING FRESH VEGETABLES

| VEGETABLE AND AMOUNT | PREP (YIELD) | CONVENTIONAL COOKING DIRECTIONS | MICROWAVE COOKING DIRECTIONS |
|---|---|---|---|
| **Artichokes** 2 (10 oz. each) (2 servings) | Wash; trim stems. Cut off 1 inch from tops; snip off sharp leaf tips. Brush cut edges with lemon juice. | Cook, covered, in a large amount of boiling salted water 20 to 30 minutes or until a leaf pulls out easily. (Or steam 20 to 25 minutes.) Invert artichokes to drain. | Place in a casserole with 2 Tbsp. water. Microwave, covered, 7 to 9 minutes or until a leaf pulls out easily, rearranging artichokes once. Invert artichokes to drain. |
| **Asparagus** 1 lb. (15 to 24 spears) | Wash and break off woody bases where spears snap easily. Leave spears whole or cut into 1-inch pieces. | Cook, covered, in a small amount of boiling salted water 3 to 5 minutes or until crisp-tender. (Or steam 3 to 5 minutes.) | Place in a baking dish or casserole with 2 Tbsp. water. Microwave, covered, 2 to 4 minutes or until crisp-tender. |
| **Beans: green, French-cut, Italian green, purple, yellow wax** 12 oz. | Wash; remove ends and strings. Leave whole or cut into 1-inch pieces (2½ cups pieces). For French-cut beans, slice lengthwise. | Cook, covered, in a small amount of boiling salted water 10 to 15 minutes for whole or cut beans (5 to 10 minutes for French-cut beans) or until crisp-tender. (Or steam 15 to 18 minutes.) | Place in a casserole with 2 Tbsp. water. Microwave, covered, 8 to 12 minutes for whole or cut beans (7 to 10 minutes for French-cut beans) or until crisp-tender, stirring once. |
| **Beets** 4 medium (1 lb.) | For whole beets, cut off all but 1 inch of stems and roots; wash. Do not peel. Or peel beets; cube or slice (2¾ cups cubes). | Cook, covered, in enough boiling salted water to cover 35 to 45 minutes for whole beets (20 minutes for cubed or sliced beets) or until tender. Slip skins off whole beets. | Place in a casserole with 2 Tbsp. water. Microwave cubed or sliced beets, covered, 9 to 12 minutes or until tender, stirring once. |
| **Broccoli** 1 lb. | Wash; remove outer leaves and tough parts of stalks. Cut lengthwise into spears or into 1-inch florets (3½ cups florets). | Cook, covered, in a small amount of boiling salted water 8 to 10 minutes or until crisp-tender. (Or steam 8 to 10 minutes.) | Place in a baking dish with 2 Tbsp. water. Microwave, covered, 5 to 8 minutes or until crisp-tender, rearranging or stirring once. |
| **Brussels sprouts** 12 oz. | Trim stems and remove any wilted outer leaves; wash. Cut large sprouts in half lengthwise (3 cups). | Cook, covered, in enough boiling salted water to cover 10 to 12 minutes or until crisp-tender. (Or steam 10 to 15 minutes.) | Place in a casserole with ¼ cup water. Microwave, covered, 5 to 7 minutes or until crisp-tender, stirring once. |
| **Cabbage** Half of a 1½-lb. head | Remove wilted outer leaves; wash. Cut into 4 wedges or coarsely chop (3 cups coarsely chopped). | Cook, uncovered, in a small amount of boiling water 2 minutes. Cover; cook 6 to 8 minutes more for wedges (3 to 5 minutes for pieces) or until crisp-tender. (Or steam wedges 10 to 12 minutes.) | Place in a baking dish or casserole with 2 Tbsp. water. Microwave, covered, 9 to 11 minutes for wedges (4 to 6 minutes for pieces) or until crisp-tender, rearranging or stirring once. |
| **Carrots** 1 lb. | Wash, trim, and peel or scrub if necessary. Cut standard-size carrots into ¼-inch slices or into strips (2½ cups slices) or measure 3½ cups packaged peeled baby carrots. | Cook, covered, in a small amount of boiling salted water 7 to 9 minutes for slices (4 to 6 minutes for strips; 8 to 10 minutes for baby carrots) or until crisp-tender. (Or steam slices or baby carrots 8 to 10 minutes or strips 5 to 7 minutes.) | Place in a casserole with 2 Tbsp. water. Microwave, covered, 6 to 9 minutes for slices (5 to 7 minutes for strips; 7 to 9 minutes for baby carrots) or until crisp-tender, stirring once. |
| **Cauliflower** 12 oz. florets or 1½-lb. head | Wash; remove leaves and woody stem. Leave whole or break into florets (3 cups florets). | Cook, covered, in a small amount of boiling salted water 10 to 15 minutes for a head (8 to 10 minutes for florets) or until crisp-tender. (Or steam head or florets 8 to 12 minutes.) | Place in a casserole with 2 Tbsp. water. Microwave, covered, 9 to 11 minutes for a head (7 to 10 minutes for florets) or until crisp-tender, turning or stirring once. |
| **Corn** (sweet) 4 ears | Remove husks. Scrub with a stiff brush to remove silks; rinse. Cut kernels from cob (2 cups). | Cook, covered, in a small amount of boiling salted water 4 minutes. (Or steam 4 to 5 minutes.) | Place in a casserole with 2 Tbsp. water. Microwave, covered, 5 to 6 minutes, stirring once. |
| **Corn on the cob** 1 ear per serving | Remove husks from fresh ears of corn. Scrub with a stiff brush to remove silks; rinse. | Cook, covered, in enough boiling lightly salted water to cover 5 to 7 minutes or until kernels are tender. | Wrap each ear in waxed paper; place on paper towels in microwave. Microwave 3 to 5 minutes for 1 ear, 5 to 7 minutes for 2 ears, or 9 to 12 minutes for 4 ears; rearrange once. |
| **Greens: beet and chard** 12 oz. | Wash in cold water; drain well. Remove stems; trim bruised leaves. Tear into pieces (12 cups). | Cook, covered, in a small amount of boiling salted water 8 to 10 minutes or until tender. | Not recommended. |

| VEGETABLE AND AMOUNT | PREP (YIELD) | CONVENTIONAL COOKING DIRECTIONS | MICROWAVE COOKING DIRECTIONS |
|---|---|---|---|
| Greens: kale, mustard, and turnip 12 oz. | Wash thoroughly in cold water; drain well. Remove stems; trim bruised leaves. Tear into pieces (12 cups torn). | Cook, covered, in a small amount of boiling salted water 15 to 20 minutes or until tender. | Not recommended. |
| Kohlrabi 1 lb. | Cut off leaves; wash. Peel; chop or cut into strips (3 cups strips). | Cook, covered, in a small amount of boiling salted water 4 to 6 minutes or until crisp-tender. (Or steam 6 minutes.) | Place in a casserole with 2 Tbsp. water. Microwave, covered, 5 to 7 minutes or until crisp-tender, stirring once. |
| Mushrooms 1 lb. | Wipe mushrooms with a damp towel or paper towel. Leave whole or slice (6 cups slices). | Cook sliced mushrooms in 2 Tbsp. butter 5 minutes. | Place in a casserole with 2 Tbsp. butter. Microwave, covered, 4 to 6 minutes, stirring twice. |
| Okra 8 oz. | Wash; cut off stems. Cut into ½-inch slices (2 cups slices). | Cook, covered, in a small amount of boiling salted water 8 to 10 minutes or until tender. | Place in a casserole with 2 Tbsp. water. Microwave, covered, 4 to 6 minutes or until tender, stirring once. |
| Onions: boiling and pearl 8 oz. | Peel boiling onions before cooking; peel pearl onions after cooking (2 cups). | Cook, covered, in a small amount of boiling salted water 10 to 12 minutes (boiling onions) or 8 to 10 minutes (pearl onions). (Or steam boiling onions 12 to 15 minutes or pearl onions 10 to 12 minutes.) | Place in a casserole with 2 Tbsp. water. Microwave, covered, 3 to 5 minutes. |
| Parsnips 12 oz. | Wash, trim, and peel or scrub. Cut into ¼-inch slices (2 cups slices). | Cook, covered, in a small amount of boiling salted water 7 to 9 minutes or until tender. (Or steam 8 to 10 minutes.) | Place in a casserole with 2 Tbsp. water. Microwave, covered, 4 to 6 minutes or until tender, stirring once. |
| Peas, green 2 lb. | Shell and wash (3 cups shelled). | Cook, covered, in a small amount of boiling salted water 10 to 12 minutes or until crisp-tender. (Or steam 12 to 15 minutes.) | Place in a casserole with 2 Tbsp. water. Microwave, covered, 6 to 8 minutes or until crisp-tender, stirring once. |
| Peas: snow and sugar snap peas 6 oz. | Remove strings and tips; wash (2 cups). | Cook, covered, in a small amount of boiling salted water 2 to 4 minutes or until crisp-tender. (Or steam 2 to 4 minutes.) | Place in a casserole with 2 Tbsp. water. Microwave, covered, 2 to 4 minutes or until crisp-tender. |
| Potatoes 1 lb. | Wash, peel, and remove eyes, sprouts, or green areas. Cut into quarters or cubes (2¾ cups cubes). | Cook, covered, in enough boiling salted water to cover 20 to 25 minutes for quarters (15 minutes for cubes) or until tender. (Or steam 20 minutes.) | Place in a casserole with 2 Tbsp. water. Microwave, covered, 8 to 10 minutes or until tender, stirring once. |
| Rutabagas 1 lb. | Wash and peel. Cut into ½-inch cubes (3 cups cubes). | Cook, covered, in a small amount of boiling salted water 18 to 20 minutes or until tender. (Or steam 18 to 20 minutes.) | Place in a casserole with 2 Tbsp. water. Microwave, covered, 11 to 13 minutes or until tender, stirring 3 times. |
| Spinach 1 lb. | Wash and drain; remove stems and tear into pieces (12 cups torn). | Cook, covered, in a small amount of boiling salted water 3 to 5 minutes or until tender. (Or steam 3 to 5 minutes.) | Not recommended. |
| Squash: acorn and delicata 1¼ lb. | Wash, halve, and remove seeds. | Place squash halves, cut sides down, in a baking dish. Bake in a 350°F oven 45 to 50 minutes or until tender. | Place, cut sides down, in a baking dish with 2 Tbsp. water. Microwave, covered, 7 to 10 minutes or until tender, rearranging once. Let stand, covered, 5 minutes. |
| Squash: buttercup and butternut 1½ lb. | Wash, halve lengthwise, and remove seeds. | Place squash halves, cut sides down, in a baking dish. Bake in a 350°F oven 45 to 50 minutes or until tender. | Place, cut sides down, in a baking dish with 2 Tbsp. water. Microwave, covered, 9 to 12 minutes or until tender, rearranging once. |
| Squash, spaghetti Half of one 3 lb. or 1½-lb. piece | Wash and remove seeds. | Place, cut sides down, in a baking dish. Bake in a 350°F oven 45 to 50 minutes or until tender. | Place, cut sides down, in a baking dish with ¼ cup water. Microwave, covered, 15 minutes or until tender. |
| Squash: yellow summer, pattypan, and zucchini 12 oz. | Wash; do not peel. Cut off ends. Cut into ¼-inch slices (3 cups slices) or leave pattypan whole. | Cook, covered, in a small amount of boiling salted water 3 to 5 minutes or until crisp-tender. (Or steam 4 to 6 minutes.) | Place in a casserole with 2 Tbsp. water. Microwave, covered, 4 to 5 minutes or until crisp-tender, stirring twice. |
| Sweet potatoes 1 lb. | Wash, peel, and cut off woody portions and ends. Cut into quarters (for microwave) or into cubes. | Cook, covered, in enough boiling salted water to cover 20 to 25 minutes or until tender. (Or steam 20 to 25 minutes.) | Place in a casserole with ½ cup water. Microwave, covered, 10 minutes or until tender, stirring once. |
| Turnips 1 lb. | Wash and peel. Cut into ½-inch cubes or strips (2¾ cups cubes). | Cook, covered, in a small amount of boiling salted water 10 to 12 minutes or until tender. (Or steam 10 to 15 minutes.) | Place in a casserole with 2 Tbsp. water. Microwave, covered, 10 to 12 minutes or until tender, stirring once. |

# DIRECT-GRILLING VEGETABLES

## ASPARAGUS
**PREP** Snap off and discard tough, woody bases from stems.
**PRECOOK** No
**GRILL** 7 to 10 minutes, covered, over medium heat; grill perpendicular to grates so asparagus does not fall through, place on a piece of heavy foil, or use a grill basket.

## CARROTS
**PREP** Cut off carrot tops. Wash and peel carrots.
**PRECOOK** 3 to 5 minutes (tip, *opposite*)
**GRILL** 3 to 5 minutes, covered, over medium heat; grill perpendicular to grates so carrots do not fall through, place on a piece of heavy foil, or use a grill basket.

## CORN ON THE COB
**PREP** Peel back husks and remove silks. Replace husks around corn. Place corn with husks in a bowl or pan. Cover with water. Soak 1 hour; drain. Tie husks at the tops with strips of husk or 100%-cotton kitchen string. Remove husk strips or string and pull down husks to serve.
**PRECOOK** No
**GRILL** 25 to 30 minutes, covered, over medium heat.

## EGGPLANT
**PREP** Cut off tops. If smaller diameter, cut lengthwise into 1-inch-thick slices; if larger, cut crosswise.
**PRECOOK** No
**GRILL** 8 to 12 minutes, covered, over medium heat.

## FENNEL
**PREP** Snip off feathery fronds. Cut off stems and base. Remove core; cut into thick wedges.
**PRECOOK** 5 minutes (tip, *opposite above*).
**GRILL** 8 minutes, covered, over medium heat.

## MUSHROOMS
**PREP** Remove stems and scrape out gills of larger mushrooms, such as portobellos.
**PRECOOK** No
**GRILL** Large: 10 to 12 minutes, covered, over medium heat; small: 6 to 8 minutes, covered, over medium heat on grates, on a piece of heavy foil, or in a grill basket.

## TO PRECOOK VEGETABLES

Some veggies need a jump start so they grill evenly. Bring a small amount of water to boiling in a saucepan, add desired vegetable, and simmer, covered, for the time specified. Drain well. Generously brush vegetables with olive oil or melted butter before grilling to prevent sticking.

### ONIONS (WHITE, YELLOW, AND RED)

**PREP** Peel and cut into 1-inch crosswise slices.

**PRECOOK** No

**GRILL** 10 minutes, covered, over medium heat, turning halfway through grilling.

### POTATOES (BAKING)

**PREP** Scrub potatoes; prick with a fork. Wrap individually in a double thickness of foil.

**PRECOOK** No

**GRILL** 1 to 1½ hours, covered, over medium heat, turning every 15 minutes.

### POTATOES (NEW)

**PREP** Halve large potatoes.

**PRECOOK** 10 minutes or until nearly tender; drain well (tip, *above*).

**GRILL** 10 to 12 minutes, covered, over medium heat on grates, on a piece of heavy foil, or in a grill basket.

### SWEET PEPPERS

**PREP** No prep needed for mini peppers. For regular size, remove stems, halve peppers lengthwise, remove seeds, and cut into 1-inch-wide strips.

**PRECOOK** No

**GRILL** 6 to 8 minutes, covered, over medium heat. If desired, use a grill basket.

### TOMATOES

**PREP** For large tomatoes, remove cores; cut in half crosswise. No prep needed for grape and cherry tomatoes.

**PRECOOK** No

**GRILL** Large tomatoes: 5 minutes, covered, over medium heat; grape and cherry tomatoes: 5 to 7 minutes, covered, in a grill basket (stir once).

### ZUCCHINI OR YELLOW SUMMER SQUASH

**PREP** Cut lengthwise into 4 slices.

**PRECOOK** No

**GRILL** 5 to 6 minutes, covered, over medium heat.

# ADD A SPRINKLE OF FLAVOR

Liven up roasted, sautéed, or grilled vegetables with simple additions of flavor.

**BACON CRUMBLE**
Crisp-cook bacon for a salty, smoky topper.

**CITRUS ZEST**
Orange, lemon, or lime zest adds a burst of bright flavor that enhances plain vegetables.

**GREMOLATA** Make a quick Gremolata or any sauce from *pp. 30–31* to top veggies.

**OLIVE TAPENADE**
Make an easy olive tapenade with chopped assorted olives, minced garlic, olive oil, and chopped fresh parsley. Or top veggies with purchased olive, tomato, or artichoke tapenade.

**FRESH HERBS**
Sprinkle your favorite fresh herbs over veggies after cooking (or mix with a little melted butter). Good options include thyme, chives, Italian parsley, basil, and tarragon.

**CHEESE** Crumble or shred a strong-flavor, high-quality cheese, such as Parmesan, blue, feta, or chèvre, over hot vegetables.

ORANGE ZEST ON BRUSSELS SPROUTS

BACON ON CORN

OLIVE TAPENADE ON TOMATOES

GREMOLATA ON POTATOES

BLUE CHEESE ON FINGERLING POTATOES

FRESH THYME ON BEETS

# FRUIT & VEGETABLE MEASURING EQUIVALENTS

| FOOD | BEGINNING SIZE OR AMOUNT | YIELD AND CUT |
|---|---|---|
| Apple | 1 medium (6 oz.) | 1⅓ cups sliced or 1 cup chopped |
| Apricots | 1 lb. (8 to 12 medium) | 2½ cups sliced or chopped |
| Asparagus | 1 lb. (20 spears) | 2 cups 1-inch pieces |
| Avocado | 1 medium (7 oz.) | ¾ cup cubed or ½ cup mashed |
| Banana | 1 medium (6 oz.) | ½ cup mashed or ¾ cup sliced |
| Beans, green | 1 lb. | 3 to 3½ cups 1-inch pieces |
| Beet | 1 medium (6 oz.) | ¾ cup peeled and grated |
| Blueberries | 1 lb. | 3 cups |
| Broccoli | 1 lb. | 3½ cups florets |
| Cabbage | 1 medium head (2 lb.) | 10 cups shredded or chopped |
| Carrot | 1 medium (2 oz.) | ½ cup sliced, chopped, julienned, or finely shredded |
| Cauliflower | 1 head (1½ lb.) | 5 cups florets or 4 cups rice |
| Celery | 1 stalk (1 oz.) | ½ cup sliced or chopped |
| Cherries | 1 lb. | 3 cups whole or 2½ cups halved |
| Cranberries | 1 lb. | 4 cups |
| Cucumber | 1 medium (10 oz.). | 2½ cups sliced |
| Eggplant | 1 medium (1 lb.) | 6 cups cubed |
| Fennel | 1 medium ( 1 lb.) | 3 cups chopped |
| Garlic | 1 medium clove | 1 tsp. minced |
| Grapes | 1 lb. | 2½ cups |
| Greens, cooking | 12 oz. | 12 cups torn |
| Greens, salad (see p. 302) | | |
| Kale | 1 bunch (10 oz.) | 8 cups chopped |
| Leek | 1 medium (8 oz.) | 1 cup chopped |
| Lemon | 1 medium | 2 tsp. finely shredded zest (1 tsp. packed) or 3 Tbsp. juice |

| FOOD | BEGINNING SIZE OR AMOUNT | YIELD AND CUT |
|---|---|---|
| Lime | 1 medium | 1½ tsp. finely shredded zest (¾ tsp. packed) or 2 Tbsp. juice |
| Mango | 1 medium (12 oz.) | 1 cups cubed |
| Melon (cantaloupe, honeydew) | 1 medium (2½ lb.) | 6 cups cubed or 5½ cups balls |
| Mushrooms | 8 oz. | 3 cups sliced or chopped |
| Nectarine | 1 medium (6 oz.) | 1 cup sliced or chopped |
| Onion | 1 medium (6 oz.) | 1 cup chopped |
| Onion, green | 1 medium | 2 Tbsp. sliced |
| Orange | 1 large (10 oz.) | 1 Tbsp. finely shredded zest (1½ tsp. packed) or ⅓ cup juice or ⅓ cup sections |
| Papaya | 1 medium (1 lb.) | 1¼ cups sliced |
| Parsnip | 1 medium | ½ to ¾ cup sliced or chopped |
| Peach | 1 medium | 1 cup sliced or chopped |
| Pear | 1 medium (8 oz.) | 1½ cups chopped |
| Pepper, sweet | 1 medium | 1¼ cups strips or 1 cup chopped |
| Pineapple | 1 medium (4 lb.) | 4½ cups peeled and cubed |
| Plum | 1 medium (4 oz.) | ½ cup sliced |
| Potatoes | 1 lb. | 3 cups cubed (peeled) |
| Potatoes, sweet | 1 medium (8 oz.) | 1½ cups peeled and cubed |
| Raspberries | 1 lb. | 4½ cups |
| Rhubarb | 1 lb. | 4 cups sliced |
| Shallot | 1 medium | 2 Tbsp. finely chopped |
| Squash, summer (yellow, zucchini) | 1 medium (8 oz.) | 2 cups sliced or 3 cups zoodles |
| Squash, winter (acorn, butternut) | 2 lb. | 6 cups cubed |
| Strawberries | 1 pt. (about 1 lb.) | 3 cups whole or sliced |
| Tomato | 1 medium (6 oz.) | 1 cup chopped |

# *everyday* COOKING

# BREAKFAST

TEST KITCHEN

**MAKE-AHEAD RECIPE**

## COOKING CLASS

LIFT AND TURN; LIFT AND TURN. FOR THE FLUFFIEST, LIGHTEST SCRAMBLED EGGS, THE SECRET IS IN THE WRIST. RESIST THE STIR AND EMBRACE THE LIFT!

**EGG-CELLENT EGGS**
To keep your eggs in tip-top shape, store them in their cartons on an inside shelf of the refrigerator. Eggs are good for up to 5 weeks after the packing date on the carton.

# SCRAMBLED EGGS

**START TO FINISH** 10 minutes

| | |
|---|---|
| 6 | eggs |
| ⅓ | cup milk or half-and-half |
| ¼ | tsp. salt |
| | Dash black pepper |
| 1 | Tbsp. butter |

**1.** In a bowl whisk together eggs, milk, salt, and pepper. In a 10-inch skillet melt butter over medium heat; pour in egg mixture. Cook, without stirring, until mixture begins to set on bottom and around edges.
**2.** Using a spatula or spoon, lift and turn partially cooked egg mixture so that uncooked portion flows underneath. Continue cooking 2 to 3 minutes or until egg mixture is cooked through but is still glossy and moist (photo 3, *below*). Immediately remove from heat.
**Makes 3 servings (¾ cup each).**
**EACH SERVING** *191 cal., 14 g fat (6 g sat. fat), 384 mg chol., 379 mg sodium, 2 g carb., 0 g fiber, 2 g sugars, 13 g pro.*

**CHEESE-AND-ONION SCRAMBLED EGGS** Prepare as directed, except cook 2 Tbsp. sliced green onion in the butter 30 seconds; add egg mixture and continue as directed. After eggs begin to set, fold in ½ cup shredded cheddar, mozzarella, or Monterey Jack cheese with jalapeño chile peppers (2 oz.). If desired, top with crumbled crisp-cooked bacon.

**DENVER SCRAMBLED EGGS**
Prepare as directed, except omit salt and increase butter to 2 Tbsp. In the skillet cook 1 cup sliced fresh mushrooms, ⅓ cup diced cooked ham, ¼ cup chopped onion, and 2 Tbsp. finely chopped green sweet pepper in the butter. Add egg mixture and continue as directed.

**QUICK EGGS IN A CUP** Coat a 10-oz. ramekin or custard cup with nonstick cooking spray. Break 2 eggs into ramekin and beat to break yolks. If desired, sprinkle with salt and black pepper. Microwave 45 seconds; stir. Microwave 20 to 30 seconds more or until eggs are puffed and set.

## *BREAKFAST BURRITOS*

Tuck scrambled eggs into warmed tortillas with shredded or crumbled cheese; sautéed veggies; salsa; chopped fresh cilantro; and/or crumbled crisp-cooked bacon, cooked sausage or chorizo, or chopped cooked ham.

**1** Vigorously whisking the egg mixture incorporates air and helps give the scrambled eggs a light and fluffy texture.

**2** After you pour the eggs into the heated skillet, let them sit 20 to 30 seconds or until the eggs begin to set on the bottom. Let ribbons of cooked egg begin to form before you put your spatula to work.

**3** Lift and turn the cooked egg toward the center, allowing uncooked eggs to flow under the edges. Repeat until eggs are just set and still appear slightly wet. Immediately remove from the heat.

## WHAT IS A FRITTATA? THINK OF A FRITTATA AS A QUICK, CRUSTLESS COUSIN TO THE QUICHE AND A CLEVER WAY TO USE UP LEFTOVER VEGGIES AND MEATS. SAUTÉ INGREDIENTS, ADD EGGS, AND BROIL AS DIRECTED FOR AN EASY, FILLING ANYTIME-OF-DAY DISH.

## FRITTATA WITH TOMATOES
**START TO FINISH** 25 minutes

| | |
|---|---|
| 8 | eggs, lightly beaten |
| ½ | cup milk or half-and-half |
| ½ | cup chopped thinly sliced prosciutto |
| 2 | Tbsp. chopped fresh basil |
| ¼ | tsp. salt |
| ⅛ | tsp. black pepper |
| 2 | Tbsp. olive oil |
| 2 | cups cherry tomatoes |
| ½ | to 1 cup frozen, thawed artichoke hearts |
| ½ | cup chopped red onion |
| ¼ | cup shredded Parmesan cheese (1 oz.) |

**1.** Preheat broiler. In a medium bowl whisk together eggs, milk, prosciutto, 1 Tbsp. of the basil, the salt, and pepper.
**2.** In a 12-inch broilerproof nonstick skillet heat oil over medium heat. Add tomatoes; cook 1 minute, stirring once or twice. Transfer to a bowl and stir in remaining basil. In same skillet cook artichokes and red onion 4 minutes, stirring occasionally.
**3.** Pour egg mixture over artichoke mixture. Cook over medium heat. As mixture sets, run a spatula around edges of skillet, lifting egg mixture so that uncooked portion flows underneath. Continue cooking until mixture is almost set (surface will be moist). Sprinkle with cheese.
**4.** Place skillet under broiler 4 to 5 inches from heat. Broil 1 to 2 minutes or just until top is set. Top with tomato mixture. **Makes 6 servings (1 wedge each).**

**EACH SERVING** *209 cal., 14 g fat (4 g sat. fat), 256 mg chol., 504 mg sodium, 6 g carb., 1 g fiber, 3 g sugars, 15 g pro.*

### CHICKEN FRITTATA WITH CHIMICHURRI

Prepare egg mixture as directed, except omit prosciutto and basil and add 1 Tbsp. chopped fresh cilantro. In the skillet cook one 4-oz. can diced green chile peppers, drained, in 1 Tbsp. olive oil over medium heat 3 minutes. Add 1 cup shredded cooked chicken and ⅔ cup canned red kidney or black beans, rinsed and drained. Pour egg mixture over chicken mixture. Cook frittata as directed, topping with ½ cup shredded Monterey Jack cheese (2 oz.) before broiling.

Meanwhile, for chimichurri, in a food processor or blender combine 1 cup each packed fresh cilantro and parsley; ¼ cup white wine vinegar; 3 cloves garlic; and ½ tsp. each salt, ground cumin, and crushed red pepper. With processor or blender running, slowly add ¼ cup olive oil and blend until smooth. Top frittata with chimichurri and snipped cilantro.

### BACON, POTATO, AND KALE FRITTATA

Prepare egg mixture as directed, except omit milk. In a covered 2-qt. saucepan cook 12 oz. tiny red new potatoes, quartered, in enough boiling water to cover 10 minutes or just until tender; drain. In the skillet cook 6 slices bacon, coarsely chopped, over medium-high heat until starting to crisp. Add 2 cups chopped fresh kale and ½ cup coarsely chopped onion; cook 5 minutes or until onion is tender. Stir in cooked potatoes. Pour egg mixture over potato mixture; cook frittata as directed.

### SMOKED SALMON AND RED PEPPER FRITTATA

In a medium bowl combine 8 lightly beaten eggs; ¾ cup cottage cheese or crumbed feta cheese; 1 tsp. dried herbes de Provence or Italian seasoning, crushed, or ½ tsp. dried dill; and ⅛ tsp. black pepper. In the skillet cook ½ cup chopped red onion and 2 cloves garlic, minced, in 1 Tbsp. olive oil over medium heat 4 minutes or just until onion is tender. Stir in 4 cups fresh baby spinach; cook 1 minute or until wilted. Pour egg mixture over spinach mixture; cook frittata as directed. Top with ½ cup thinly sliced red sweet pepper and 1 oz. thinly sliced smoked salmon (lox-style).

**WHAT ARE CHILAQUILES?** THIS ONE-PAN MEXICAN DISH SIMMERS CRUNCHY TORTILLA STRIPS TO SOFTNESS IN A BOLD SAUCE. TOPPERS VARY, BUT FRIED EGGS PUT OUR VERSION SQUARELY IN BREAKFAST TERRITORY.

## CHEESY HAM CHILAQUILES
**START TO FINISH** 35 minutes

| | |
|---|---|
| 5 | 6-inch corn tortillas, cut into 1-inch strips |
| 3 | cups refrigerated fresh salsa |
| 1 | cup reduced-sodium chicken broth |
| 1½ | cups diced cooked ham |
| | Sliced fresh jalapeño chile peppers (optional) (tip, *p. 22*) |
| 1 | cup shredded cheddar cheese (4 oz.) |
| ¼ | cup sour cream |
| 1 | recipe Fried Eggs (*p. 47*) (optional) |
| | Fresh snipped cilantro |

**1.** Preheat oven to 350°F. Spread tortilla strips in a single layer on a large baking sheet. Bake 15 minutes or until crisp.
**2.** In a 12-inch skillet bring salsa to simmering over medium heat; stir in broth. Return to simmering. Simmer 2 minutes. Stir in ham.
**3.** Set aside a few of the tortilla strips for garnish. Stir remaining tortilla strips into salsa mixture. Simmer 3 minutes more or until tortilla strips are softened and mixture is slightly thickened.
**4.** Sprinkle with reserved tortilla strips and, if desired, jalapeño peppers. Serve with cheese, sour cream, Fried Eggs (if desired), and cilantro. **Makes 6 servings (¾ cup each).**
**EACH SERVING** *226 cal., 12 g fat (6 g sat. fat), 46 mg chol., 657 mg sodium, 19 g carb., 1 g fiber, 5 g sugars, 13 g pro.*

# TOP OFF YOUR TOAST

Spreads, sprinkles, crumbles—toast toppers have come a long way from
butter and jam. Use these ideas as the building blocks for your own versions.

**PEANUT OR ALMOND BUTTER**
**SLICED BANANA**
**SLICED STRAWBERRIES**
**HONEY**
**GRANOLA**

**MASHED AVOCADO**
**SLICED TOMATO**
**SLICED RED ONION**
**CHOPPED HARD-BOILED EGG**
**SALT AND BLACK PEPPER**

**CREAM CHEESE**
**SMOKED SALMON**
**CUCUMBER SLICES**
**EVERYTHING BAGEL SEASONING**

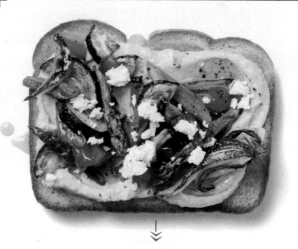

**HUMMUS**
**ROASTED VEGGIES**
**OLIVE OIL**
**CRUMBLED FETA**
**CRACKED BLACK PEPPER**

# BUILD A BREAKFAST SANDWICH

Stack your favorite breakfast ingredients between bread for an easy grab-and-go morning meal. Customize these ideas below however you like.

**TOASTER WAFFLES**
**SCRAMBLED EGG**
**SLICED CHEDDAR CHEESE**
**MAPLE SAUSAGE PATTY**
**MAPLE SYRUP DRIZZLE**

**BUTTERMILK BISCUIT**
**CRISPY HASH BROWNS**
**SLICED CANADIAN BACON OR HAM**
**SLICED SWISS OR CHEDDAR CHEESE**
**FRIED EGG**

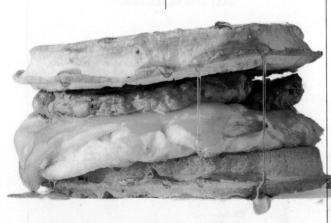

**HEARTY TOAST SLICES**
**MAYONNAISE**
**SLICED TOMATO**
**SLICED HARD-BOILED EGG**
**BACON SLICES**
**ARUGULA OR BABY SPINACH**

**TOASTED BAGEL**
**MASHED AVOCADO**
**SAUTÉED MUSHROOMS, SWEET PEPPERS, AND ONIONS**
**SLICED PEPPER JACK CHEESE**
**OVER-EASY EGG**
**HOT SAUCE**

# ON THE SIDE

A weekend morning calls for the full breakfast spread—side dishes included. Get the scoop on how to fix hash browns and perfectly cooked meats.

## BACON & SAUSAGE

### PORK BACON

TO FRY, place bacon slices in an unheated skillet. Cook over medium heat 8 to 10 minutes, turning occasionally. If bacon browns too quickly, reduce heat. Drain well on paper towels.

TO MICROWAVE, place bacon slices on a microwave-safe rack or plate lined with microwave-safe paper towels. Cover with a paper towel. Microwave to desired doneness, rearranging slices once.

TO BAKE, preheat oven to 400°F. Place bacon slices side by side on a rack in a foil-lined shallow baking pan with sides. Bake 18 to 21 minutes or until bacon is crisp-cooked. Drain well on paper towels.

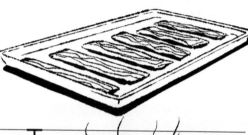

### UNCOOKED SAUSAGE PATTIES

TO FRY, place ½-inch-thick sausage patties in an unheated skillet and cook over medium-low heat about 12 minutes or until centers are no longer pink, turning once. Drain sausage patties on paper towels.

TO BAKE, preheat oven to 400°F. Arrange ½-inch-thick patties on a rack in a shallow baking pan with sides. Bake 18 to 20 minutes or until centers are no longer pink. Drain on paper towels.

### UNCOOKED SAUSAGE LINKS

TO FRY, place sausage links in an unheated skillet; cook over medium-low heat 14 to 16 minutes or until centers are no longer pink, turning frequently to brown evenly. Drain on paper towels.

TO BAKE, preheat oven to 375°F. Place uncooked links in a shallow baking pan with sides. Bake 16 to 18 minutes or until centers are no longer pink, turning once. Drain on paper towels.

## CRISPY HASH BROWNS

To make good hash browns you don't have to shred your own potatoes. Start with a package of frozen or refrigerated shredded or cubed hash browns. Check the label for the most accurate directions, but here's a good rule of thumb to start. In a 12-inch skillet heat 2 Tbsp. vegetable oil over medium-high heat. Carefully add 4 cups hash browns; spread evenly. Cook 5 to 6 minutes. Drizzle top with 1 Tbsp. oil. Turn hash browns. Cook 5 to 7 minutes more until golden brown.

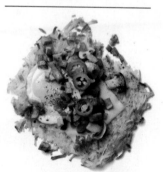

## LOADED HASH BROWNS

Top crispy hash browns with cheese; fried eggs; crumbled bacon; cooked pork or chicken sausage; chopped ham or turkey; sautéed chopped onion, sweet pepper, and/or mushrooms; pickled jalapeño pepper slices; salsa; sour cream; hot sauce; plus salt, black pepper, and/or snipped fresh herbs.

## FRENCH TOAST

**START TO FINISH** 20 minutes

- 4   eggs
- 1   cup milk
- 2   Tbsp. sugar
- 2   tsp. vanilla
- ½   tsp. ground cinnamon (optional)
- ½   tsp. orange zest (optional)
- ¼   tsp. ground nutmeg (optional)
- 8   slices Texas toast or ½-inch slices country Italian bread or rich egg bread (challah or brioche)
- 2   Tbsp. butter
      Maple syrup and/or powdered sugar (optional)

**1.** In a shallow bowl whisk together first seven ingredients (through nutmeg). Dip bread slices into egg mixture, turning to coat (let soak in egg mixture 10 seconds per side). **2.** On a griddle or in a heavy skillet melt 1 Tbsp. of the butter over medium heat. Add half of the bread slices; cook 2 to 3 minutes on each side or until golden. Remove from griddle. Repeat with remaining butter and bread slices. Serve warm. If desired, serve with syrup and/or powdered sugar. **Makes 4 servings (2 slices each).**

**EACH SERVING** *410 cal., 17 g fat (7 g sat. fat), 272 mg chol., 530 mg sodium, 48 g carb., 2 g fiber, 11 g sugars, 16 g pro.*

Pancakes are ready to flip when top surfaces are bubbly and edges look slightly dry.

## BUTTERMILK PANCAKES

**START TO FINISH** 25 minutes

- 1¾  cups all-purpose flour
- 2   Tbsp. sugar
- 2   tsp. baking powder
- ½   tsp. baking soda
- ¼   tsp. salt
- 1   egg, lightly beaten
- 1½  cups buttermilk or sour milk (tip, p. 474)
- 3   Tbsp. vegetable oil
      Butter and/or maple syrup (optional)

**1.** In a large bowl stir together first five ingredients (through salt). In a medium bowl combine egg, buttermilk, and oil. Add egg mixture all at once to flour mixture. Stir just until moistened (batter should be slightly lumpy). If desired, fold in fruit (ideas, *opposite*). **2.** For standard-size pancakes, pour ¼ cup batter onto a hot, lightly greased griddle or heavy skillet. Spread batter if necessary. (For mini pancakes, use 1 Tbsp. batter.) Cook over medium heat 1 to 2 minutes on each side or until pancakes are golden; turn over when surfaces are bubbly and edges are slightly dry. If desired, top with butter and/or syrup. Serve pancakes warm. **Makes 12 standard-size pancakes.**

**PANCAKES** Prepare as directed, except substitute milk for the buttermilk, increase baking powder to 1 Tbsp., and omit baking soda.

**BUCKWHEAT OR WHOLE WHEAT PANCAKES** Prepare as directed, except use ¾ cup all-purpose flour and add 1 cup buckwheat flour or whole wheat flour.

**EACH PANCAKE (ALL VARIATIONS)** *123 cal., 4 g fat (1 g sat. fat), 19 mg chol., 179 mg sodium, 18 g carb., 0 g fiber, 4 g sugars, 3 g pro.*

FRENCH TOAST

## BUTTERMILK WAFFLES

Prepare as directed, except reduce baking powder to 1 tsp. and add ½ tsp. baking soda to flour mixture. Substitute 2 cups buttermilk or sour milk (tip, p. 474) for the milk. If desired, top with strawberries and honey.

## GINGERBREAD WAFFLES

Prepare as directed, except increase flour to 2 cups and omit the sugar. Add ½ tsp. each ground ginger and cinnamon and ¼ tsp. ground cloves to flour mixture. Add 2 Tbsp. molasses to egg mixture. If desired, top with lemon curd and sprinkle with ground cinnamon.

## CHOCOLATE WAFFLES

Prepare as directed, except reduce flour to 1½ cups, increase sugar to ¼ cup, and add ⅓ cup unsweetened cocoa powder to flour mixture. Fold ¼ cup mini semisweet chocolate chips into batter. (Lightly coat the waffle baker with nonstick cooking spray between each waffle to prevent sticking.) If desired, top with chocolate-flavor syrup.

# WAFFLES

**HANDS-ON TIME** 15 minutes
**BAKE** according to manufacturer's directions

| | |
|---|---|
| 1¾ | cups all-purpose flour |
| 2 | Tbsp. sugar |
| 1 | Tbsp. baking powder |
| ¼ | tsp. salt |
| 2 | eggs, lightly beaten |
| 1¾ | cups milk |
| ½ | cup vegetable oil or butter, melted |
| 1 | tsp. vanilla |
| | Butter and/or maple syrup (optional) |

**1.** In a medium bowl stir together flour, sugar, baking powder, and salt. Make a well in center of flour mixture.
**2.** In another bowl combine eggs, milk, oil, and vanilla. Add egg mixture to flour mixture. Stir just until moistened.
**3.** Add batter to a preheated, lightly greased waffle baker according to manufacturer's directions (use a regular or Belgian waffle baker).

Close lid quickly; do not open until done. Bake according to manufacturer's directions. When done, use a fork to lift waffle off grid. Repeat with remaining batter. If desired, top with butter and/or syrup. Serve warm. **Makes twelve 4-inch waffles.**

**EACH WAFFLE** *186 cal., 11 g fat (2 g sat. fat), 34 mg chol., 199 mg sodium, 18 g carb., 0 g fiber, 4 g sugars, 4 g pro.*

## *FRUIT WAFFLES OR PANCAKES*

Stir one of the following into the batter at the end of Step 1 for pancakes and Step 2 for waffles: ½ cup fresh or frozen blueberries or chopped fresh apple, apricot, peach, nectarine, or pear; or ¼ cup snipped dried apple, apricot, pear, raisins, currants, dates, cranberries, blueberries, cherries, or mixed fruit.

BREAKFAST
FRUIT-AND-NUT
COOKIES

BLUEBERRY
CEREAL BARS

## BREAKFAST FRUIT-AND-NUT COOKIES

**HANDS-ON TIME** 25 minutes
**BAKE** 10 minutes at 350°F

4  eggs, lightly beaten
1⅓ cups packed brown sugar
6  Tbsp. butter, melted
2  tsp. vanilla
½  cup finely snipped pitted whole dates or dried golden figs
2  cups all-purpose flour
1  cup whole wheat flour
½  cup oat bran
¼  cup flaxseed meal
1  tsp. baking soda
1  tsp. ground cinnamon
½  cup chopped toasted pecans

**1.** Preheat oven to 350°F. Line two cookie sheets with parchment paper. In a large bowl combine eggs, brown sugar, butter, and vanilla. Stir in dates.
**2.** In a medium bowl combine next six ingredients (through cinnamon). Add flour mixture to date mixture, stirring until moistened. Stir in pecans. For each cookie, drop about ¼ cup dough into mounds 3 inches apart on cookie sheets.

**3.** Bake 10 to 12 minutes or until edges are golden. Cool on cookie sheets 1 minute. Remove; cool on wire racks. **Makes 20 cookies.**
**TO STORE**  Layer cookies between waxed paper in an airtight container. Store at room temperature up to 2 days or freeze up to 3 months.
**EACH COOKIE**  *211 cal., 7 g fat (3 g sat. fat), 46 mg chol., 109 mg sodium, 34 g carb., 2 g fiber, 17 g sugars, 4 g pro.*

## BLUEBERRY CEREAL BARS

**HANDS-ON TIME** 15 minutes
**CHILL** 2 hours

   Nonstick cooking spray
½  cup almond butter
⅓  cup butter, cut up
⅓  cup packed brown sugar
⅓  cup pure maple syrup
1  tsp. vanilla
¼  tsp. salt
3  cups regular rolled oats, toasted (tip, p. 20)
1  cup crisp rice cereal

⅔  cup dried blueberries
½  cup chopped pecans or almonds, toasted
2  Tbsp. chia seeds

**1.** Line a 13×9-inch baking pan with foil, extending foil over edges. Lightly coat foil with cooking spray.
**2.** In a 4-qt. saucepan combine almond butter, butter, brown sugar, and maple syrup. Bring to boiling over medium-high heat, stirring to dissolve sugar. Boil 30 seconds, stirring constantly. Remove from heat. Stir in vanilla and salt. Stir in remaining ingredients.
**3.** Press mixture into prepared baking pan. Cover with waxed paper, set another pan inside, and weight mixture down with cans of food. Chill 2 hours or until firm enough to cut. Remove cans and pan. Using foil, lift out uncut bars. Cut into bars. **Makes 18 bars.**
**TO STORE**  Place bars in a single layer in an airtight container. Store in refrigerator up to 3 days.
**EACH BAR**  *209 cal., 11 g fat (3 g sat. fat), 9 mg chol., 86 mg sodium, 26 g carb., 3 g fiber, 13 g sugars, 4 g pro.*

**CUSTOMIZE IT**

PICK THE INGREDIENTS TO CREATE A RECIPE THAT'S ALL YOUR OWN.

# CRUNCHY GRANOLA

**HANDS-ON TIME** 20 minutes
**BAKE** 20 minutes at 300°F +
15 minutes at 350°F
**COOL** 15 minutes

Nonstick cooking spray
2½ cups regular rolled oats
⅔ cup chopped NUTS
2 Tbsp. SEEDS
¼ cup butter
¼ cup packed brown sugar
 LIQUID SWEETENER
 FLAVORING
½ tsp. salt
½ cup toasted wheat germ
¼ cup oat bran
½ cup DRIED FRUIT
 Fat-free milk or yogurt
 (optional)

**1.** Preheat oven to 300°F. Line a 13×9-inch baking pan with foil, extending foil over edges. Coat foil with cooking spray. Spread oats, NUTS, and SEEDS in baking pan. Bake 20 minutes, stirring twice.
**2.** Meanwhile, in a 1- or 1½-qt. saucepan combine butter, brown sugar, and LIQUID SWEETENER. Cook and stir over medium heat until butter is melted and mixture is smooth. Remove from heat. Stir in FLAVORING and salt.
**3.** Remove baking pan from oven and place on a wire rack. Increase oven temperature to 350°F. Add wheat germ and oat bran to oat mixture. Pour warm brown sugar mixture over oat mixture; stir to coat. Bake 5 minutes. Remove from oven and place on wire rack.
**4.** Using a spatula, press granola in pan, making an even layer. Bake 10 minutes more or until golden. Cool on a wire rack 15 minutes. Using foil, lift out granola. Crumble granola; cool. Stir in DRIED FRUIT.
**5.** Store in an airtight container at room temperature up to 2 weeks. If desired, serve granola with milk.
**Makes 13 servings (½ cup each).**
**EACH SERVING** *216 cal., 10 g fat (3 g sat. fat), 9 mg chol., 131 mg sodium, 29 g carb., 3 g fiber, 14 g sugars, 5 g pro.*

## *IN THE SLOW COOKER*

Lightly coat a 3½- or 4-qt. slow cooker with cooking spray. In prepared cooker stir together oats, NUTS, and SEEDS. Prepare brown sugar mixture as directed in Step 2; stir into mixture in cooker. Cover and cook on high 1 hour, stirring from bottom up every 20 to 30 minutes. Stir in wheat germ, oat bran, and DRIED FRUIT. Cover and cook 30 to 60 minutes more or until golden.

## *OUR FAVORITE COMBOS*

Almonds, flaxseeds, maple syrup, vanilla, dried cherries

Pistachio nuts, sesame seeds, agave syrup, orange zest, dried blueberries

Walnuts, chia seeds, maple syrup, mild-flavor molasses, ginger, dried apples

# MIX & MATCH INGREDIENTS

**NUTS** *(Pick 1)*
- Almonds
- Hazelnuts
- Pecans
- Pistachio nuts
- Walnuts

**SEEDS** *(Pick 1)*
- Chia seeds
- Flaxseeds
- ¼ cup pumpkin seeds (pepitas)
- Sesame seeds
- Raw sunflower kernels

**LIQUID SWEETENER** *(Pick 1)*
- 2 Tbsp. each honey and light-color corn syrup
- ¼ cup maple syrup or agave syrup
- 2 Tbsp. each pure maple syrup and mild-flavor molasses

**FLAVORING** *(Pick 1 or 2)*
- ½ tsp. almond extract
- ½ tsp. ground cinnamon
- ¼ tsp. ground ginger
- ½ tsp. orange zest
- 1 tsp. vanilla

**DRIED FRUIT** *(Pick 1)*
- Apples or pears, snipped
- Apricots, snipped
- Blueberries
- Cherries, snipped
- Cranberries
- Raisins

ALMOND-APRICOT
CEREAL MIX

## COCONUT-CHIA OAT SQUARES

**HANDS-ON TIME** 20 minutes
**BAKE** 18 minutes at 325°F
**COOL** 1 hour

Nonstick cooking spray
1  cup regular rolled oats
½  cup oat bran
½  cup flaked or shredded coconut
⅓  cup packed brown sugar
¼  cup whole wheat flour
3  Tbsp. almond butter or peanut butter
2  Tbsp. water
1  Tbsp. honey
⅛  tsp. baking soda
⅛  tsp. salt
⅛  tsp. coconut extract
2  Tbsp. chia seeds
Milk and desired fruit (optional)

**1.** Preheat oven to 325°F. Coat a 15×10-inch baking pan with cooking spray. In a food processor combine next five ingredients (through flour). Cover and process until finely ground. Add next six ingredients (through coconut extract). Cover and process until combined. Transfer to a large bowl. Stir in chia seeds (mixture will be crumbly).
**2.** Using bottom of a measuring cup, press oat mixture firmly into prepared baking pan. Bake 18 to 20 minutes or until golden. Cool in pan on a wire rack (mixture will crisp as it cools).
**3.** Using a table knife or small metal spatula, release oat mixture from pan. Break into small bite-size pieces. Store at room temperature up to 1 week. If desired, serve with milk and fruit. **Makes 6 servings (½ cup each).**

**EACH SERVING** *296 cal., 10 g fat (3 g sat. fat), 0 mg chol., 116 mg sodium, 48 g carb., 8 g fiber, 18 g sugars, 9 g pro.*

## ALMOND-APRICOT CEREAL MIX

**START TO FINISH** 10 minutes

1  cup regular rolled oats
1  cup quick-cooking barley
1  cup bulgur or cracked wheat
1  cup snipped dried apricots, dried cranberries, and/or raisins
¾  cup sliced almonds, toasted (tip, *p. 18*)
⅓  cup sugar
1  Tbsp. ground cinnamon
¼  tsp. salt

**1.** In an airtight container stir together all ingredients. Store at room temperature up to 2 months or freeze up to 6 months. To prepare each serving, in a 1-qt. bowl combine ¾ cup water and ⅓ cup cereal mix. Microwave on 50% power (medium) 8 to 11 minutes or until cereal reaches desired consistency, stirring once. Stir before serving. If desired, serve with milk. **Makes 13 servings (⅓ cup each).**

**EACH SERVING** *201 cal., 4 g fat (0 g sat. fat), 0 mg chol., 47 mg sodium, 39 g carb., 6 g fiber, 12 g sugars, 6 g pro.*

**CHIA SEEDS**
Fiber-rich chia seeds add texture and heart-healthy, plant-based omega-3 fatty acids. Add them to oatmeal, smoothies, and yogurt parfaits.

COCONUT-CHIA
OAT SQUARES

**MAKE IT AHEAD**
Chill leftover oatmeal in an airtight container up to 3 days. For one serving, microwave ⅔ cup oatmeal, covered, 1 minute or until warm, stirring once. Add milk to desired consistency.

# STEEL-CUT OATMEAL

**HANDS-ON TIME** 10 minutes
**COOK** 25 minutes

4     cups water
½     tsp. salt
1⅓   cups steel-cut oats (tip, p. 20)
       Topper(s) (optional) (below left)

**1.** In a 3- or 4-qt. saucepan bring the water and salt to boiling. Stir in oats. Simmer, covered, 25 to 30 minutes or just until oats are tender and water is nearly absorbed. Serve warm. If desired, top servings with topper(s). **Makes 6 servings (⅔ cup each).**
**EACH SERVING** *142 cal., 3 g fat (0 g sat. fat), 0 mg chol., 199 mg sodium, 24 g carb., 4 g fiber, 0 g sugars, 6 g pro.*

**SLOW COOKER** In a 3½- or 4-qt. slow cooker combine 6 cups water, 2 cups steel-cut oats, and 1 tsp. salt. Cover and cook on low 6 to 7 hours or high 3 to 3½ hours. Serve as directed. **Makes 9 servings (⅔ cup each).**

**PRESSURE COOKER** In a 4- or 6-qt. electric or stove-top pressure cooker (info, p. 336) combine 4 cups water, 1⅓ cups steel-cut oats, and ½ tsp. salt. Lock lid in place. Set electric cooker on high pressure to cook 10 minutes. For stove-top cooker, bring up to pressure over medium-high heat; reduce heat to maintain steady (but not excessive) pressure. Cook 10 minutes. Remove from heat. For both models, let stand 15 minutes to release pressure naturally. Open lid carefully. Serve as directed.

**TOPPERS** Warm oatmeal can be topped with dried fruit, chopped nuts (almonds, pecans, walnuts, hazelnuts), shredded or flaked toasted coconut, brown sugar, maple syrup, and/or milk or half-and-half.

# OVERNIGHT BULGUR

**HANDS-ON TIME** 10 minutes
**CHILL** 12 hours

- ⅔ cup plain low-fat yogurt or whole-milk Greek yogurt
- ¼ cup bulgur
- 3 Tbsp. milk or refrigerated unsweetened coconut milk
- 2 Tbsp. packed brown sugar or honey (optional)

**1.** In a small bowl stir together all of the ingredients. If desired, divide mixture between two ½-pt. jars or small storage containers. Cover and chill overnight (up to 3 days). Stir before serving. **Makes 2 servings (1 cup each).**

**EACH SERVING** *123 cal., 2 g fat (1 g sat. fat), 7 mg chol., 71 mg sodium, 20 g carb., 2 g fiber, 7 g sugars, 7 g pro.*

**RASPBERRY-JAVA OVERNIGHT BULGUR** Prepare as directed, using brown sugar and stirring ½ tsp. instant espresso powder into mixture before dividing into jars. Top with ¼ cup raspberries before chilling.

**EACH SERVING** *185 cal., 2 g fat (1 g sat. fat), 7 mg chol., 75 mg sodium, 36 g carb., 3 g fiber, 21 g sugars, 7 g pro.*

**BLACKBERRY-GINGER OVERNIGHT BULGUR** Prepare as directed, using honey and stirring 1 Tbsp. snipped crystallized ginger or ¼ tsp. ground ginger into mixture before dividing into jars. Top with ¼ cup blackberries before chilling. If desired, top with chopped toasted hazelnuts.

**EACH SERVING** *215 cal., 2 g fat (1 g sat. fat), 7 mg chol., 74 mg sodium, 45 g carb., 3 g fiber, 25 g sugars, 8 g pro.*

RASPBERRY-JAVA OVERNIGHT BULGUR

BLACKBERRY-GINGER OVERNIGHT BULGUR

**BULGUR** These wheat kernels are processed by steaming or boiling, drying, then grinding (aka cracking) into coarse, medium, or fine pieces. It has a tender, chewy texture; an earthy flavor; and lots of fiber. And surprise—as a breakfast cereal, it's just as delicious as oatmeal.

SHORTCUT DONUTS

PEANUT BUTTER-
BANANA OVERNIGHT
OATMEAL

**PEANUT
BUTTER-
BANANA
OVERNIGHT
OATMEAL**
Prepare as
directed, using
honey and
stirring ½ cup
sliced banana
and 1 Tbsp.
peanut butter
into oat mixture
before jarring.
If desired, top
servings with
blueberries
and additional
banana
or honey.

## OVERNIGHT OATMEAL

**HANDS-ON TIME** 10 minutes
**CHILL** 12 hours

1   6-oz. carton plain low-fat
    yogurt or one 5.3-oz. carton
    plain whole-milk Greek yogurt
⅔   cup regular rolled oats
⅔   cup milk
2   Tbsp. honey or maple syrup
1   Tbsp. chia seeds or flaxseed
    meal (optional)

**1.** In a medium bowl stir together
all of the ingredients. If desired,
transfer mixture to three ½-pt.
jars or divide among three small
storage containers. Cover and chill
overnight (up to 3 days). **Makes
3 servings (¾ cup each).**

**EACH SERVING** *172 cal., 3 g fat (1 g sat.
fat), 8 mg chol., 66 mg sodium, 30 g
carb., 2 g fiber, 19 g sugars, 7 g pro.*

## SHORTCUT DONUTS

**HANDS-ON TIME** 20 minutes
**FRY** 2 to 4 minutes per batch

     Vegetable oil for deep-
     fat frying (tip, *p. 21*)
½    cup granulated sugar
1    Tbsp. ground cinnamon
1    17.3-oz. pkg. (2 sheets) frozen
     puff pastry sheets, thawed,
     or two 7.5-oz. pkg. (10 each)
     refrigerated biscuits

**1.** In a 4-qt. saucepan or deep-fat
fryer heat 2 inches of oil to 365°F.
Meanwhile, in a bowl stir together
granulated sugar and cinnamon.
Unfold pastry sheets or separate
biscuits. Using a 2½-inch donut
cutter (or a 2½-inch and 1-inch
round cutter), cut rounds.
**2.** Fry pastry rounds and holes,
two or three at a time, in hot oil 2 to
4 minutes or until golden, turning
once. Remove with a slotted spoon;
drain on paper towels. While warm,
toss donuts in cinnamon-sugar
or, if desired, *powdered sugar.*
**Makes 16 servings (1 donut +
1 hole each).**

**EACH SERVING** *254 cal., 18 g fat (4 g
sat. fat), 0 mg chol., 76 mg sodium, 20 g
carb., 1 g fiber, 7 g sugars, 2 g pro.*

**FILLED DONUTS** Cut puff pastry
into 2½-inch rounds (do not cut
holes in rounds). Fry as directed;
cool slightly. Holding each warm
donut (use tongs if necessary), use a
chopstick to poke a hole in one side
of donut. Pipe chocolate-hazelnut
spread or desired-flavor jam into
opening. Repeat on opposite side.
**ICED DONUTS** Omit sugars and
cinnamon. Prepare Powdered
Sugar Icing or Chocolate Powdered
Sugar Icing as directed on *p. 538.*
Drizzle or spread on warm donuts. If
desired, top with sprinkles, toasted
coconut, finely chopped toasted
nuts, or chopped chocolate-
covered espresso beans.
**CINNAMON ROLL DONUTS**
Prepare as directed, except
omit sugars and cinnamon.
Substitute two 12.4-oz. pkg.
(8 each) refrigerated cinnamon
rolls with icing for the puff pastry.
Separate dough and fry as
directed. Drizzle with icing.
**CRESCENT ROLL DONUTS**
Prepare as directed, except
substitute two 8-oz. pkg. (8 each)
refrigerated crescent rolls for the
puff pastry. Separate dough; shape
into crescents. Fry as directed.

## KIWI-PEACH GREEN SMOOTHIES

**START TO FINISH** 15 minutes

- 2 cups chopped Swiss chard or spinach leaves
- 1½ cups frozen unsweetened peach slices
- 1⅓ cups peeled and chopped kiwifruits
- 1 cup ice cubes
- 1 avocado, halved, seeded, peeled, and chopped
- ½ cup unsweetened pineapple or orange juice
- 2 Tbsp. lime juice (optional)

**1.** In a blender combine all ingredients. Cover and blend until smooth. If desired, top servings with additional kiwifruit pieces. **Makes 4 servings (1 cup each).**

**EACH SERVING** *153 cal., 7 g fat (1 g sat. fat), 0 mg chol., 44 mg sodium, 24 g carb., 6 g fiber, 14 g sugars, 2 g pro.*

## RED STRAWBERRY-VEGGIE SMOOTHIES

**START TO FINISH** 30 minutes

- 1½ cups small cauliflower florets
- 2 cups frozen raspberries
- 1½ cups frozen unsweetened whole strawberries
- 1 to 1¼ cups unsweetened vanilla almond milk
- 1 cup red sweet pepper strips
- 1 5.3- to 6-oz. carton strawberry low-fat Greek yogurt
- 2 Tbsp. strawberry preserves (optional)

**1.** In a 1- or 1½-qt. saucepan cook cauliflower in enough boiling water to cover 10 minutes or until very tender; drain. Rinse with cold water to cool quickly; drain again.
**2.** In a blender combine cauliflower and the remaining ingredients. Cover and blend until smooth. If desired, top servings with additional berries. **Makes 4 servings (1 cup each).**

**EACH SERVING** *123 cal., 3 g fat (1 g sat. fat), 5 mg chol., 72 mg sodium, 22 g carb., 8 g fiber, 12 g sugars, 5 g pro.*

## BERRY-BANANA SMOOTHIES

**START TO FINISH** 10 minutes

- 1½ cups frozen unsweetened pitted dark sweet cherries
- 1¼ cups unsweetened vanilla almond milk
- 1 5.3- to 6-oz. carton blueberry Greek yogurt
- 1 large banana, peeled, sliced, and frozen
- ½ cup frozen blueberries
- ½ cup ice cubes

**1.** In a blender combine all ingredients. Cover and blend until smooth. If desired, top servings with additional banana slices and blueberries. **Makes 4 servings (1 cup each).**

**EACH SERVING** *183 cal., 1 g fat (0 g sat. fat), 1 mg chol., 70 mg sodium, 41 g carb., 4 g fiber, 33 g sugars, 5 g pro.*

**PROTEIN POWER**
Boost the protein in your morning sipper with the addition of one or more of the following:

Dried protein powder, such as whey, pea, or soy

Greek yogurt (plain or flavored)

Almond butter or other nut butters

Seeds such as chia, hemp, or flax

Silken tofu

**MAKE IT AHEAD**
Prep a big batch of smoothies for quick weekday breakfasts. Transfer each serving to an airtight container. Store in the fridge up to 3 days (or freeze up to 6 months; thaw in fridge). Stir before serving.

## CUSTOMIZE IT

PICK THE INGREDIENTS
TO CREATE A RECIPE
THAT'S ALL YOUR OWN.

## MIX & MATCH INGREDIENTS

To turn any smoothie into a Smoothie Bowl, reduce the liquid in the smoothie by
¼ to ½ cup. Because a Smoothie Bowl has a thicker consistency, you can sprinkle
it with any of the toppings, *below,* and scoop everything up with a spoon.

**POWDERS**
- Acai powder
- Cacao powder
- Matcha powder
- Peanut butter powder
- Probiotic powder
- Veggie powder

**SEEDS & NUTS**
- Chia seeds
- Chopped nuts
- Flaxseeds
- Pumpkin seeds (pepitas)
- Raw sunflower kernels

**SWEETENER**
- Agave syrup
- Honey
- Maple syrup

**FRUITS**
- Banana
- Berries
- Kiwifruit
- Mango
- Pineapple
- Pomegranate seeds

**DRIED FRUITS**
- Dried fruits, snipped
- Shredded or flaked coconut

**GRAINS**
- Cereal
- Granola
- Muesli
- Oats

# CASSEROLES

Better Homes
&Gardens.

TEST KITCHEN

**MAKE-AHEAD RECIPE.** See also make-ahead tip, *p. 120.*

# FOUR-CHEESE MACARONI AND CHEESE

**HANDS-ON TIME** 30 minutes
**BAKE** 20 minutes at 350°F

5⅓ cups dried cavatappi or
    corkscrew-shape pasta (16 oz.)
1   recipe Basic White Sauce
    *(opposite)*
2   cups shredded Gouda cheese
    (8 oz.)
1   cup shredded sharp cheddar
    cheese (4 oz.)
1   cup shredded Swiss cheese
    (4 oz.)
½   cup grated Parmesan cheese
½   cup panko bread crumbs
1   Tbsp. butter, melted

**1.** Preheat oven to 350°F. Lightly grease a 2½- to 3-qt. baking dish. Bring a large pot of lightly salted water to boiling. Add pasta and cook according to package directions. Drain and return to the warm pot.
**2.** Meanwhile, prepare Basic White Sauce. Add Gouda, cheddar, Swiss, and ¼ cup of the Parmesan cheese to the sauce, whisking until cheeses melt and sauce is smooth. Add the cheese sauce to cooked pasta; stir to coat. Transfer mixture to prepared dish.
**3.** In a bowl combine the panko, melted butter, and remaining ¼ cup Parmesan cheese. Sprinkle panko mixture over pasta mixture. Bake 20 to 25 minutes or until crumbs are golden. **Makes 6 servings (1¼ cups each).**
**EACH SERVING** *744 cal., 35 g fat (21 g sat. fat), 114 mg chol., 911 mg sodium, 70 g carb., 3 g fiber, 8 g sugars, 35 g pro.*

» **PANKO** is a light and airy bread crumb. When mixed with butter and cheese, it creates a crispy casserole topper. Panko crumbs are easy to find with other bread crumbs in the supermarket.

## COOKING CLASS

THE SECRET TO A SILKY CHEESE SAUCE—BUY A BLOCK OF CHEESE AND SHRED IT YOURSELF BY HAND. WHY? DURING TESTING, WE FOUND PRESHREDDED CHEESE DOESN'T MELT AS SMOOTHLY BECAUSE OF ADDED STARCHES.

**STOVE TOP TO TABLETOP**
If you're short on time (or just want extra-creamy mac and cheese), skip the oven. Omit the baking dish and crumb mixture in Step 3; dive in after stirring everything together.

**CAULIFLOWER MACARONI AND CHEESE** Preheat oven to 400°F. Line a 15×10-inch baking pan with parchment paper. In a bowl toss 4 to 5 cups cauliflower florets with 2 tsp. oil and ¼ tsp. salt; transfer to pan. Roast 30 minutes or until tender and browned, stirring once. Reduce oven to 350°F. Prepare Four-Cheese Macaroni and Cheese as directed, except reduce pasta to 8 oz.; add cauliflower with cheese sauce in Step 2.

**BACON-BLUE CHEESE MACARONI AND CHEESE** Prepare as directed, except stir 3 slices crisp-cooked, drained, and crumbled bacon and ¼ cup crumbled blue cheese (1 oz.) into panko mixture before sprinkling over pasta mixture. If desired, top with additional blue cheese and bacon before serving.

**BUTTERNUT SQUASH MACARONI AND CHEESE** Prepare as directed, except preheat oven to 450°F. Coat a 15×10-inch baking pan with nonstick cooking spray. Toss 1½ lb. butternut squash, peeled, seeded, and cut into 1-inch cubes, with 2 Tbsp. olive oil. Roast, uncovered, 25 minutes or until tender, stirring occasionally. Add squash with cheese sauce in Step 2.

**BÉCHAMEL OR WHITE SAUCE?** Named after its French inventor, Louis de Béchamel, this basic white sauce serves as the base for the mac and cheese sauce and is one of the five French Mother Sauces (the others are Velouté, Espagnole, Sauce Tomat, and Hollandaise), from which most French sauces are derived. Béchamel is made by combining milk with a mixture of butter and flour (called a "roux"), then cooking until thickened. In this book, we use the names White Sauce and Béchamel interchangeably.

## BASIC WHITE SAUCE

In a 3-qt. saucepan melt 3 Tbsp. butter over medium heat. Stir in 3 Tbsp. all-purpose flour, ½ tsp. salt, and ½ tsp. black pepper. Gradually whisk in 2½ cups milk. Cook, whisking constantly, until thickened and bubbly. Cook and whisk 2 minutes more. Remove from heat. Makes about 2⅔ cups.

**1** Whisk the roux—a mixture of equal parts melted butter and flour—until bubbly and just golden. This allows the butter to coat the flour particles, which prevents clumps from forming when the milk is added.

**2** Whisk the cold milk into the roux. Using cold milk allows flour particles to stay suspended—again preventing clumps. Warm milk may cause clumping because the particles warm up before they are able to disperse.

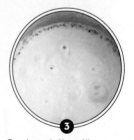

**3** Cook and stir until you see bubbles start to break across the surface. The sauce will thicken as the heat expands the flour particles. Cook 2 minutes more to fully cook the flour.

// CASSEROLES //

# HEARTY CASSOULET THIS TRADITIONAL FRENCH DISH OF WHITE BEANS SIMMERED WITH A MIX OF MEATS AND VEGGIES IN A RICH, SAVORY SAUCE DEFINES COMFORT FOOD. TO KEEP THE SIMMER TIME SHORT, THIS WEEKNIGHT VERSION USES PORK TENDERLOIN.

## PORK CASSOULET

**HANDS-ON TIME** 30 minutes
**BAKE** 25 minutes at 350°F

| | |
|---|---|
| 1 | Tbsp. olive oil |
| ½ | cup chopped onion |
| ½ | cup chopped carrot |
| ½ | cup thinly sliced celery |
| 1 | lb. pork tenderloin, trimmed and cut into 1-inch pieces |
| 6 | oz. smoked turkey sausage, thinly sliced |
| 2 | 15- to 16-oz. cans reduced-sodium Great Northern beans, rinsed and drained |
| ⅔ | cup chopped roma tomatoes |
| ½ | cup reduced-sodium chicken broth |
| 2 | Tbsp. tomato paste |
| 1 | Tbsp. white wine vinegar |
| 1 | tsp. dried Italian seasoning, crushed |
| 2 | Tbsp. snipped fresh parsley |

**1.** Preheat oven to 350°F. In an oven-safe 3- to 4-qt. Dutch oven heat oil over medium heat. Add onion, carrot, and celery; cook 5 minutes, stirring occasionally. Add pork and sausage; cook 5 minutes more or until browned.
**2.** Mash half of the beans. Stir mashed beans, remaining beans, and next five ingredients (through Italian seasoning) into meat mixture.
**3.** Cover; bake 25 minutes or until pork is tender. Sprinkle with parsley. Season with *salt* and *black pepper*.
**Makes 4 servings (1½ cups each).**
EACH SERVING *417 cal, 10 g fat (2 g sat. fat), 96 mg chol, 938 mg sodium, 39 g carb, 10 g fiber, 4 g sugars, 43 g pro.*

**EXTRA, EXTRA!** If you use canned tomato paste, save the remainder of the can by scooping tablespoon-size portions onto a parchment-lined baking sheet. Freeze until firm, then transfer to a freezer bag and use as needed. Or purchase tomato paste in a tube and use just what you need. Refrigerate the remaining paste in the tube.

BEEF
BOURGUIGNONNE
CASSEROLE

BAKED RISOTTO
WITH SAUSAGE AND
ARTICHOKES

# BEEF BOURGUIGNONNE CASSEROLE

**HANDS-ON TIME** 25 minutes
**BAKE** 20 minutes at 375°F

　　Nonstick cooking spray
¼　cup butter
1½　cups coarsely chopped carrots
1½　cups coarsely chopped celery
1　cup frozen small whole onions, thawed and halved
½　tsp. black pepper
3　cups sliced fresh mushrooms (8 oz.)
1　cup Burgundy or dry red wine
1　Tbsp. stone-ground Dijon mustard
4　cloves garlic, minced
2　tsp. finely chopped fresh rosemary
2　tsp. dried thyme, crushed
2　17-oz. pkg. refrigerated cooked beef tips with gravy
1　cup reduced-sodium beef broth
3　croissants, halved lengthwise

**1.** Preheat oven to 375°F. Coat a 3-qt. rectangular baking dish with cooking spray; set aside.
**2.** In a 12-inch skillet melt 3 Tbsp. of the butter over medium heat. Add carrots, celery, onions, and pepper. Cook 7 to 9 minutes or just until tender, stirring occasionally. Remove from heat. Add next six ingredients (through thyme).

Return to heat. Bring to boiling; reduce heat. Simmer, uncovered, 5 minutes. Stir in beef with gravy and broth; heat through. Cover; keep warm.
**3.** Microwave the remaining 1 Tbsp. butter on 70% power (medium-high) about 30 seconds or until melted. Brush cut sides of croissants with melted butter; cube croissants. Transfer meat mixture to prepared baking dish. Top with cubed croissants. Bake, uncovered, 20 to 25 minutes or bubbly and golden.
**Makes 8 servings (1 cup each).**
**EACH SERVING** *330 cal., 16 g fat (8 g sat. fat), 77 mg chol., 885 mg sodium, 21 g carb., 3 g fiber, 8 g sugars, 21 g pro.*

# BAKED RISOTTO WITH SAUSAGE AND ARTICHOKES

**HANDS-ON TIME** 40 minutes
**BAKE** 1 hour 10 minutes at 350°F
**STAND** 5 minutes

1　lb. bulk Italian sausage
1　cup chopped fennel bulb
½　cup chopped onion
2　cloves garlic, minced
¾　cup uncooked Arborio or long grain rice
2　9-oz. pkg. frozen artichoke hearts, thawed, drained, and halved

1　cup coarsely shredded carrots
2　tsp. chopped fresh thyme or ½ tsp. dried thyme, crushed
½　tsp. black pepper
2　cups chicken broth
⅓　cup dry white wine or chicken broth
½　cup panko bread crumbs (tip, p. 108) or soft bread crumbs
¼　cup finely shredded Asiago or Parmesan cheese
1　Tbsp. butter, melted
½　tsp. lemon zest

**1.** Preheat oven to 350°F. In a 12-inch skillet cook and stir sausage, fennel, onion, and garlic over medium-high heat until vegetables are tender but not browned. Drain fat; discard. Add rice; cook and stir 1 minute more.
**2.** Add artichoke hearts, carrots, thyme, and pepper. Stir in broth and wine. Bring just to boiling. Transfer to a 2½-qt. casserole. Bake, covered, about 60 minutes or until rice is tender, stirring once.
**3.** Meanwhile, in a bowl combine panko, cheese, butter, and lemon zest. Uncover casserole and top with crumb mixture. Bake, uncovered, 10 minutes more. Let stand 5 minutes before serving. If desired, top with *fennel fronds*.
**Makes 6 servings (1⅓ cups each).**
**EACH SERVING** *476 cal., 28 g fat (11 g sat. fat), 68 mg chol., 1,038 mg sodium, 36 g carb., 8 g fiber, 3 g sugars, 17 g pro.*

**FROZEN ARTICHOKE HEARTS** can be found in the freezer case of many large supermarkets. If you can't find them, swap for one 14-oz. can artichoke hearts, drained and halved.

# CLASSIC SHEPHERD'S PIE

**HANDS-ON TIME** 25 minutes
**BAKE** 20 minutes at 350°F

- 2¼ lb. russet potatoes, peeled and cut up
- ¼ cup sour cream
- ¼ to ⅓ cup milk
- 2 lb. ground lamb and/or beef
- ½ cup chopped onion
- ½ tsp. dried thyme, crushed
- 3 Tbsp. all-purpose flour
- 3 Tbsp. tomato paste
- 2¼ cups reduced-sodium chicken broth
- 2 tsp. Worcestershire sauce
- 1 16-oz. pkg. frozen mixed vegetables

**1.** Preheat oven to 350°F. In a covered 4-qt. saucepan cook potatoes in enough boiling, lightly salted water to cover 15 to 20 minutes or until tender; drain. Mash potatoes. Stir in sour cream, ½ tsp. *salt*, and enough milk to reach desired consistency.
**2.** Meanwhile, in a 12-inch skillet cook lamb, onion, and thyme over medium-high heat until meat is browned. Drain off excess fat. Add flour. Cook and stir over medium heat 1 minute. Stir in tomato paste. Stir in broth and Worcestershire sauce. Bring to boiling; reduce heat and simmer, uncovered, 5 minutes. Stir in frozen vegetables, ½ tsp. *salt*, and ¼ tsp. *black pepper*.
**3.** Transfer meat mixture to a 3-qt. rectangular baking dish. Spread mashed potatoes over meat mixture. Bake 20 to 25 minutes or until heated through and bubbly around the edges. If desired, sprinkle with *snipped fresh parsley*.
**Makes 6 servings (2 cups each).**
**EACH SERVING** *571 cal., 31 g fat (13 g sat. fat), 109 mg chol., 799 mg sodium, 40 g carb., 6 g fiber, 4 g sugars, 33 g pro.*

**EASY EVERYDAY**
*Skip a step by using two 24-oz. pkg. refrigerated mashed potatoes rather than making your own (omit russet potatoes, sour cream, salt, and milk).*

**GET-TOGETHER**
*Make this casserole company-special by piping on the mashed potato topper using a piping bag fitted with a large open star tip.*

**HEALTHY TWIST**
*By using reduced-sodium ingredients such as chicken broth and adding salt only as needed in a recipe, you can better control how much sodium ends up in your food.*

**CHEESY BARBECUE PORK SHEPHERD'S PIE** Prepare as directed, except add ½ cup shredded cheddar cheese to the potato mixture. Substitute ground pork for the lamb and omit the thyme. Add ½ cup barbecue sauce with tomato paste. Reduce broth to 1¾ cups.

**TURKEY-SWEET POTATO SHEPHERD'S PIE** Prepare as directed, except substitute sweet potatoes for the russet potatoes, omit milk, and substitute ground turkey for the ground lamb.

# SPAGHETTI PIE

**HANDS-ON TIME** 30 minutes
**BAKE** 20 minutes at 350°F

| | |
|---|---|
| 4 | oz. dried spaghetti |
| 1 | Tbsp. butter |
| 1 | egg, beaten |
| ¼ | cup grated Parmesan cheese |
| 8 | oz. lean ground beef or bulk Italian sausage |
| 2 | cups sliced fresh button mushrooms |
| ½ | cup chopped onion |
| ½ | cup chopped green sweet pepper |
| 2 | cloves garlic, minced |
| 1 | 8-oz. can tomato sauce |
| 1 | tsp. dried oregano, crushed |
| | Nonstick cooking spray |
| 1 | cup cottage cheese, drained |
| ½ | cup shredded mozzarella cheese (2 oz.) |

**1.** Preheat oven to 350°F. Cook spaghetti according to package directions; drain. Return spaghetti to warm saucepan. Stir butter into hot pasta until melted. Stir in egg and Parmesan cheese.

**2.** Meanwhile, in a 10-inch skillet cook beef, mushrooms, onion, sweet pepper, and garlic until meat is browned and onion and mushrooms are tender; drain. Stir in tomato sauce and oregano; heat through.

**3.** Coat a 9-inch pie plate with cooking spray. Press spaghetti mixture onto bottom and up sides of pie plate, forming a crust. Spread cottage cheese over bottom and up the crust. Top with meat mixture, then cheese.

**4.** Bake 20 to 25 minutes or until bubbly and heated through. Cut into six wedges. If desired, sprinkle with small fresh *basil leaves*. **Makes 6 servings (1 wedge each).**

**EACH SERVING** *270 cal., 11 g fat (6 g sat. fat), 76 mg chol., 500 mg sodium, 20 g carb., 1 g fiber, 3 g sugars, 21 g pro.*

# CLASSIC BEEF ENCHILADAS

**HANDS-ON TIME** 25 minutes
**BAKE** 30 minutes at 375°F
**STAND** 10 minutes

1    recipe Easy Enchilada Sauce or one 28-oz. can enchilada sauce
1    lb. lean ground beef
2    cloves garlic, minced
1    fresh jalapeño chile pepper, seeded, if desired, and finely chopped (optional) (tip, *p. 22*)
½    tsp. ground cumin
¼    tsp. salt
¼    tsp. black pepper
2    cups shredded Monterey Jack cheese (8 oz.)
½    cup sliced green onions
12   6- to 7-inch corn tortillas

**1.** Preheat oven to 375°F. Lightly grease a 3-qt. rectangular baking dish. Prepare Easy Enchilada Sauce if using.
**2.** For filling, in a 10-inch skillet cook beef until browned; drain. Stir in garlic, jalapeño (if desired), cumin, salt, and black pepper. Cook and stir over medium heat 2 minutes. Transfer to a bowl; cool 5 minutes. Stir in 1 cup of the cheese and the green onions.
**3.** Spoon ⅓ cup filling into each tortilla; roll up. Place filled tortillas, seam sides down, in prepared baking dish. Pour on sauce evenly.
**4.** Bake 25 to 30 minutes or until heated through and bubbly around the edges. Sprinkle with remaining cheese. Bake 5 minutes more or until cheese melts. Let stand 10 minutes before serving. If desired, top with *pico de gallo*. **Makes 6 servings (2 enchiladas each).**

### EASY ENCHILADA SAUCE
In a 2-qt. saucepan heat 2 Tbsp. vegetable oil over medium heat. Stir in 2 Tbsp. all-purpose flour; cook and stir 2 minutes. Add 2 Tbsp. chili powder, ½ tsp. ground cumin, and ½ tsp. garlic powder. Cook and stir 30 seconds more. Add one 15-oz. can tomato sauce and one 14.5-oz. can reduced-sodium chicken broth; whisk until smooth. Cook and stir over medium-high heat until boiling. Reduce heat; simmer 1 minute. Season to taste with salt, black pepper, and, if desired, hot sauce.
**EACH SERVING** *452 cal., 25 g fat (10 g sat. fat), 82 mg chol., 1,051 mg sodium, 29 g carb., 5 g fiber, 5 g sugars, 29 g pro.*

## *A TOUCH OF AUTHENTICITY*

Traditional Mexican enchilada recipes soften the tortillas before filling by lightly frying and dipping them in enchilada sauce. If you have time, the extra steps are worth it.

**1**

Heat 1 to 2 Tbsp. of cooking oil in an 8-inch skillet over medium heat. Fry tortillas, one at a time, until softened, turning once. Drain on paper towels.

**2**

Pour some enchilada sauce on a plate. Using tongs, dip each side of tortillas in the sauce; let excess drip off. Fill and roll as directed.

**ZUCCHINI AND CORN ENCHILADAS** Prepare as directed, except omit beef. For filling, in a 10-inch skillet cook 2 cups chopped zucchini in 1 Tbsp. hot oil over medium-high 3 minutes or until crisp-tender and lightly browned. Stir in 1½ cups frozen whole kernel corn, the garlic, jalapeño (if desired), and the cumin. Cook and stir over medium heat 1 minute. Stir in 1 cup of the cheese, the green onions, salt, and black pepper. Fill and bake as directed.

**CHORIZO-REFRIED BEAN ENCHILADAS** Prepare as directed, except substitute ground uncooked chorizo for the beef. Before filling tortillas, spread each with 1 Tbsp. canned refried beans. Fill and bake as directed.

**CHICKEN ENCHILADAS** Prepare as directed, except omit beef and garlic. In a bowl combine 2 cups shredded cooked chicken and remaining filling ingredients (through green onions). Fill and bake as directed.

**THREE-CHEESE ENCHILADAS** Prepare as directed, except omit beef, garlic, and salt; increase Monterey Jack cheese to 3 cups. In a bowl combine 2 cups of the cheese, 1 cup shredded cheddar cheese, 1 cup crumbled queso fresco, the jalapeño (if desired), cumin, and green onions. Fill and bake as directed.

**BIG CRUNCH**
If you love extra-crispy fries, give them a head start in the oven. Place fries in an even layer on a foil-lined baking sheet. Bake 10 minutes at 400°F; place on casserole. Bake as directed.

**HEALTHY TWIST**

*Cut the sodium in this casserole by using no-salt-added diced canned tomatoes and tomato paste.*

**CHANGE IT UP**

*Try this casserole with different frozen potato options, such as french-fried shoestring or crinkle-cut potatoes, potato crowns, and miniature potato nuggets.*

## CHEESEBURGER AND FRIES CASSEROLE

**HANDS-ON TIME** 25 minutes
**BAKE** 40 minutes at 400°F

1½   lb. lean ground beef
¾    cup chopped green sweet pepper
½    cup chopped onion
2    cloves garlic, minced
1    14.5-oz. can petite diced tomatoes, undrained
½    cup water
1    6-oz. can tomato paste
1    Tbsp. Worcestershire sauce
1    10.75-oz. can condensed cheddar cheese soup
½    cup sour cream
½    of a 28-oz. pkg. frozen french fries with rosemary or regular french fries (about 4 cups)
     Assorted toppers, such as ketchup, pickle slices, yellow mustard, onion, and/or cut-up cherry tomatoes (optional)

**1.** Preheat oven to 400°F. In a 12-inch skillet cook ground beef, sweet pepper, onion, and garlic over medium heat until meat is browned and vegetables are tender. Drain fat; discard. Stir undrained tomatoes, the water, tomato paste, and Worcestershire sauce into beef mixture. Bring to boiling; remove from heat.
**2.** Spoon beef mixture into the bottom of an ungreased 3-qt. rectangular baking dish. In a medium bowl stir together soup and sour cream; spread over meat mixture in baking dish. Place fries over top of soup mixture.
**3.** Bake, uncovered, 40 minutes or until heated through and potatoes are lightly browned and beginning to crisp. If desired, serve with assorted toppers.
**Makes 6 servings (1 cup each).**
**EACH SERVING** *420 cal., 20 g fat (8 g sat. fat), 85 mg chol., 978 mg sodium, 33 g carb., 4 g fiber, 8 g sugars, 28 g pro.*

### MAKE IT A MEAL

Toss together a side salad of romaine lettuce, cherry tomatoes, sliced olives, pickled whole pepperoncini peppers, sliced red onion, and shredded cheese. Prepare Fresh Herb Vinaigrette using red wine vinegar (p. 299). Drizzle over salad.

## UPSIDE-DOWN PIZZA CASSEROLE

**HANDS-ON TIME** 20 minutes
**BAKE** 20 minutes at 400°F

1    lb. lean ground beef or bulk Italian sausage
1    5-oz. pkg. miniature pepperoni slices or one 6-oz. pkg. chopped pepperoni
1½   cups sliced fresh mushrooms
¾    cup chopped green sweet pepper
1    15-oz. can tomato sauce with Italian seasonings
1    2.25-oz. can sliced pitted ripe olives, drained
1½   cups shredded mozzarella cheese or shredded Italian-blend cheeses (6 oz.)
1    7.75- to 10-oz. pkg. refrigerated biscuits (10 biscuits)

**1.** Preheat oven to 400°F. In a 10-inch skillet cook beef, pepperoni slices, mushrooms, and sweet pepper until beef is browned. Drain fat; discard. Stir in tomato sauce and olives. Heat through. Stir in 1 cup of the cheese. Transfer meat mixture to a 2-qt. baking dish.

**2.** Cut biscuits into wedges. Arrange biscuits around the edges of the baking dish. Sprinkle with remaining ½ cup cheese. Bake about 20 minutes or until biscuits are light brown, covering with foil the last 5 minutes to prevent overbrowning.
**Makes 6 servings (1 cup each).**
**EACH SERVING** *456 cal., 27 g fat (12 g sat. fat), 96 mg chol., 1,442 mg sodium, 23 g carb., 2 g fiber, 4 g sugars, 30 g pro.*

» **GARLIC ROLL UPSIDE-DOWN PIZZA CASSEROLE** Prepare as directed, except omit biscuits. Thaw 6 frozen roll dough balls, snip into quarters, and toss in 2 Tbsp. melted butter. Add 2 Tbsp. grated Parmesan cheese and ¼ tsp. garlic powder; toss to coat. Scatter over mixture. Bake as directed.

» **BREADSTICK UPSIDE-DOWN PIZZA CASSEROLE** Prepare as directed, except omit biscuits. Unroll one 11-oz. pkg. refrigerated breadsticks. Brush with 2 Tbsp. melted butter and sprinkle with 1 tsp. dried oregano. Separate, twist, and arrange over hot mixture in dish. Bake as directed.

» **CRISPY CRUST UPSIDE-DOWN PIZZA CASSEROLE** Prepare as directed, except omit biscuits. Unroll one 13.8-oz. pkg. refrigerated pizza crust. Arrange crust over hot mixture in dish. Fold edges under and pinch to seal along edge of baking dish. Cut 1-inch slits in the crust. Brush with milk; top with Parmesan cheese. Bake as directed.

USE IT UP!
Give leftover pesto a purpose by whisking it into vinaigrette salad dressing, spreading it onto a panini or grilled cheese sandwich, or adding it to pasta sauce.

CHICKEN-
TORTELLINI
CASSEROLE

# CHICKEN-TORTELLINI CASSEROLE

**HANDS-ON TIME** 30 minutes
**BAKE** 25 minutes at 350°F

2   9-oz. pkg. refrigerated whole wheat cheese-filled tortellini
8   oz. fresh haricots verts or green beans, trimmed and halved crosswise
8   oz. fresh cremini or button mushrooms, thinly sliced
1   medium onion, thinly sliced
2   Tbsp. olive oil
3   cups coarsely shredded cooked chicken breast (about 1 lb.)
1   12-oz. jar roasted red sweet peppers, undrained
¾   cup dried tomato pesto
¼   tsp. crushed red pepper
½   cup finely shredded Parmesan cheese
½   cup shredded fresh basil

**1.** Preheat oven to 350°F. In a 4-qt. Dutch oven cook tortellini according to package directions, adding haricots verts the last 4 minutes of cooking. Drain and return to pan.
**2.** Meanwhile, in a 10-inch skillet cook mushrooms and onion in hot oil over medium heat 6 to 8 minutes or until tender and lightly browned, stirring occasionally.
**3.** Add mushroom mixture and chicken to pasta mixture. Toss to coat. Place peppers in a blender. Cover and blend until smooth. Stir in pesto and crushed red pepper. Add to pasta mixture; toss to coat. Spread mixture in a 3-qt. rectangular baking dish.
**4.** Cover and bake 20 minutes. Uncover; top with cheese. Bake, uncovered, about 5 minutes more or until cheese is melted. Top with basil just before serving. **Makes 8 servings (1⅓ cups each).**

**EACH SERVING** *387 cal., 15 g fat (4 g sat. fat), 80 mg chol., 649 mg sodium, 37 g carb., 7 g fiber, 6 g sugars, 26 g pro.*

CHICKEN ENCHILADA VERDE CASSEROLE

## SIZE CHECK
Use the recommended-size baking dish to prevent bubbling over. Check a dish's capacity by filling it with water, a quart at a time. Right-size dish not available? Opt for a dish with larger volume.

# CHICKEN ENCHILADA VERDE CASSEROLE

**HANDS-ON TIME** 30 minutes
**BAKE** 45 minutes at 375°F
**STAND** 10 minutes

3   cups shredded cooked chicken
1   8-oz. pkg. cream cheese, cut up and softened
1   4-oz. can chopped green chiles, undrained
½   cup chopped green onions
1   recipe Verde Sauce or one 28-oz. can green enchilada sauce
16  6-inch corn tortillas, halved
2   cups frozen whole kernel corn, thawed
2   15-oz. cans no-salt-added black beans, rinsed and drained
2   cups shredded Colby and Monterey Jack cheese or cheddar cheese (8 oz.)
2   avocados, halved, seeded, peeled, and chopped
    Chopped fresh cilantro

**1.** Preheat oven to 375°F. Lightly grease a 3-qt. rectangular baking dish. In a large bowl combine the chicken, cream cheese, green chiles, and green onions.
**2.** Spread about ⅔ cup Verde Sauce in the prepared baking dish. Arrange 8 tortilla halves over sauce. Sprinkle with about one-third of the corn and one-third of the black beans. Spoon about one-third of the chicken mixture evenly over layers. Top with ⅔ cup of the sauce and ½ cup of the cheese. Repeat layers two more times. Top with remaining tortillas. Top with remaining sauce.
**3.** Cover with foil and bake about 35 minutes or until bubbly around the edges. Top with the remaining cheese. Bake, uncovered, 10 minutes more or until cheese is melted. Let stand 10 minutes. Top with avocados and chopped fresh cilantro. **Makes 12 servings (1 cup each).**

**VERDE SAUCE** In a blender combine two 15- to 16-oz. jars salsa verde; ¾ cup loosely packed fresh cilantro; 2 cloves garlic, peeled and halved; 4 green onions, cut up; and ½ tsp. ground cumin. Pulse until combined and nearly smooth.

**EACH SERVING** *415 cal., 21 g fat (8 g sat. fat), 67 mg chol., 673 mg sodium, 37 g carb., 9 g fiber, 6 g sugars, 23 g pro.*

INDIVIDUAL CHICKEN AND WILD RICE CASSEROLES

## *MAKE IT, THEN FREEZE IT*

*Most casseroles are freezer-friendly, but steer clear of baked egg dishes and casseroles with flour- or cornstarch-thickened sauces. And do not use foil or foil pans with tomato-base casseroles.*

### 1
**PAN PREP**
Line a baking dish that is both oven- and freezer-safe with foil or parchment paper (for easy lining tips, see *p. 478*).

### 2
**PUT IT TOGETHER**
Assemble the casserole in the prepped dish, but don't bake. Cover with foil; freeze overnight. Once frozen, lift casserole and foil lining out of dish; place in a freezer bag. Freeze up to 3 months.

### 3
**SHOWTIME!**
Remember that thawing takes 24 hours or longer. To thaw, remove foil lining from casserole; place in original baking dish. Cover; thaw in the fridge up to 2 days; bake as directed. Or cover and bake the frozen casserole at 325°F for twice its normal baking time or until 160°F.

CHICKEN
TETRAZZINI

> **POTLUCK**
> Get your hot casserole road-ready by covering the baking dish tightly with foil or a lid. Fold a thick layer of newspapers or heavy towels around the casserole or place it in an insulated casserole carrier.

## CHICKEN AND WILD RICE CASSEROLE

**HANDS-ON TIME** 20 minutes
**BAKE** 35 minutes at 350°F

| | |
|---|---|
| 2 | stalks celery, sliced |
| 1 | small onion, chopped |
| 2 | Tbsp. butter |
| 1 | 10.75-oz. can reduced-fat and reduced-sodium condensed cream of chicken soup |
| ½ | cup sour cream |
| ⅓ | cup dry white wine or chicken broth |
| ½ | tsp. dried basil, crushed |
| 2 | cups shredded cooked chicken or turkey |
| 2 | 8.8-oz. pouches cooked long grain and wild rice |
| 1 | cup vegetables, such as packaged shredded carrots and/or frozen whole kernel corn |
| ⅓ | cup finely shredded Parmesan cheese |

**1.** Preheat oven to 350°F. In a 10-inch skillet cook celery and onion in hot butter over medium heat 5 minutes or until tender. Stir in soup, sour cream, wine, and basil. Stir in chicken, rice, and vegetables.
**2.** Transfer mixture to an ungreased 2-qt. rectangular baking dish. Sprinkle with cheese. Bake, uncovered, about 35 minutes or until heated through. **Makes 6 servings (1 cup each).**

**INDIVIDUAL CASSEROLES**
If desired, spoon mixture into six 10-oz. small casserole dishes or ramekins. Bake 25 to 30 minutes or until heated through. Or, if desired, wrap, label, and freeze up to 3 months. Thaw overnight in the refrigerator. Bake as directed.
**EACH SERVING** *345 cal., 14 g fat (6 g sat. fat), 67 mg chol., 827 mg sodium, 32 g carb., 2 g fiber, 5 g sugars, 19 g pro.*

## CHICKEN TETRAZZINI

**HANDS-ON TIME** 30 minutes
**BAKE** 15 minutes at 350°F

| | |
|---|---|
| 8 | oz. dried spaghetti or linguine |
| 2 | cups sliced fresh mushrooms |
| ½ | cup sliced green onions |
| 2 | Tbsp. butter |
| ¼ | cup all-purpose flour |
| ⅛ | tsp. black pepper |
| ⅛ | tsp. ground nutmeg |
| 1¼ | cups chicken broth |
| 1¼ | cups half-and-half or milk |
| 2 | cups chopped cooked chicken or cooked turkey |
| 2 | Tbsp. dry sherry or milk |
| ¼ | cup grated Parmesan cheese |
| ¼ | cup sliced almonds, toasted (tip, *p. 18*) |
| 2 | Tbsp. fresh parsley leaves (optional) |

**1.** Preheat oven to 350°F. Cook spaghetti according to package directions; drain.
**2.** Meanwhile, in a 4-qt. saucepan cook mushrooms and green onions in hot butter over medium heat until tender. Stir in flour, pepper, and nutmeg. Add broth and half-and-half all at once. Cook and stir until thickened and bubbly. Stir in chicken, sherry, and half of the Parmesan cheese. Add cooked spaghetti; stir gently to coat.
**3.** Transfer pasta mixture to a 2-qt. baking dish. Sprinkle with remaining Parmesan cheese and the almonds. Bake, uncovered, about 15 minutes or until heated through. If desired, sprinkle with parsley leaves before serving.
**Makes 6 servings (1 cup each).**
**CHICKEN AND VEGETABLE TETRAZZINI** Prepare as directed, except add 8 oz. fresh asparagus, trimmed and cut into 1-inch pieces, or 1½ cups small fresh broccoli florets to the pasta water during the last minute of cooking.
**EACH SERVING** *421 cal., 21 g fat (9 g sat. fat), 82 mg chol., 630 mg sodium, 38 g carb., 2 g fiber, 3 g sugars, 21 g pro.*

**BROWN FIRST!**
To get the best browning (which equals flavor) from the mushrooms, place them in a single layer in the pan while cooking in the hot butter and avoid stirring too often. If the pan is too full, the mushrooms will steam and water out instead of browning.

// CASSEROLES //

**PERFECT
ON TOP**
If your casserole topping
gets good and golden before
the center reaches 160°F, cover
the dish loosely with foil for
remaining baking time to
prevent overbrowning
or burning.

**SKILLET LOVE** TURN YOUR POT PIE INTO A ONE-DISH WONDER BY COOKING THE FILLING IN A LARGE CAST-IRON OR OTHER OVEN-GOING SKILLET. JUST ADD THE TOPPING DIRECTLY TO THE FILLING IN THE SKILLET AND BAKE AS INSTRUCTED.

CUSTOMIZE IT

PICK THE INGREDIENTS
TO CREATE A RECIPE
THAT'S ALL YOUR OWN.

## POT PIE

**HANDS-ON TIME** 25 minutes
**BAKE** 22 minutes at 400°F
**STAND** 20 minutes

1   lb. GROUND MEAT or 2 cups
    COOKED MEAT
1   9- to 10-oz. pkg. FROZEN
    VEGETABLES (about 2 cups)
    BASE
1   tsp. SEASONING
½   cup water (optional)
½   cup CHEESE (optional)
    TOPPER
    Milk
    Grated Parmesan cheese
    (optional)

**1.** Preheat oven to 400°F. If using
GROUND MEAT: In a 10-inch
skillet cook MEAT until no longer
pink. Drain fat; discard. Stir in
FROZEN VEGETABLES, BASE,
and SEASONING. (If using
COOKED MEAT option: In a
10-inch skillet combine MEAT,
FROZEN VEGETABLES, BASE,
and SEASONING.) Bring meat
and vegetable mixture to boiling.
Add water if needed for desired
consistency. If desired, stir
in CHEESE.
**2.** Transfer meat and vegetable
mixture to a 2-qt. round casserole
or baking dish. For TOPPER, unfold
pastry sheet or unroll piecrust if
using. On a lightly floured surface
roll pastry sheet or piecrust to
1 inch beyond the edges of the
casserole. Place pastry on top
of casserole. Trim evenly with
casserole edges or trim, leaving
1 inch excess. Fold excess under,
even with the casserole edges.
Press pastry along edges to seal.
If using biscuits, quarter individual
pieces and arrange over filling. If
using breadsticks, unroll and loosely
weave over filling.
**3.** Brush TOPPER lightly with
milk and, if desired, sprinkle
with additional SEASONING or
grated Parmesan cheese. Bake,
uncovered, 22 to 25 minutes or until
golden brown and bubbly (bake
30 minutes if using piecrust). Let
stand 20 minutes before serving.
**Makes 6 servings (1 cup each).**

# MIX & MATCH INGREDIENTS

**GROUND OR COOKED MEAT**
- Ground beef
- Ground pork, bulk pork sausage, or Italian sausage
- Cooked chicken
- Cooked turkey

**FROZEN VEGETABLES**
- Baby mixed beans and carrots
- Mixed vegetables
- Peas and carrots
- Peas and pearl onions
- Stew vegetables

**BASE** (Pick 1)
- One 10.5- to 10.75-oz. can condensed soup
- 1¼ cups canned or jarred gravy
- 1¼ cups Alfredo pasta sauce

**SEASONING** (Pick 1)
- Chili powder
- Curry powder
- Dried dill
- Dried tarragon, crushed
- Dried thyme, crushed
- Italian seasoning, crushed

**CHEESE** (Pick 1)
- Cheddar cheese
- Monterey Jack cheese
- Mozzarella cheese

**TOPPER** (Pick 1)
- ½ of a 17.3-oz. pkg. frozen puff pastry sheets (1 sheet)
- ½ of a 15-oz. pkg. rolled refrigerated unbaked piecrust (1 crust)
- One 7.5-oz. pkg. refrigerated biscuits (10)
- One 11-oz. pkg. refrigerated breadsticks (12)

# CHICKEN-BACON ALFREDO POTATO CASSEROLE

**HANDS-ON TIME** 15 minutes
**BAKE** 50 minutes at 350°F
**STAND** 15 minutes

Nonstick cooking spray
6   slices bacon, chopped
2   14.5- to 15-oz. jars light Alfredo sauce
½   cup sliced green onions
¼   cup chopped fresh parsley
1   tsp. dry mustard
2   cloves garlic, minced
1   32-oz. pkg. frozen fried potato nuggets
3   cups chopped cooked chicken
½   cup finely shredded Parmesan cheese
1   cup grape tomatoes, halved

**1.** Preheat oven to 350°F. Coat a 3-qt. rectangular baking dish with cooking spray. In a 10-inch skillet cook bacon over medium heat until crisp; drain.
**2.** In an extra-large bowl combine Alfredo sauce, green onions, parsley, mustard, and garlic. Stir in bacon, potato nuggets, and chicken. Spoon into prepared baking dish. Sprinkle with cheese.
**3.** Bake, uncovered, about 50 minutes or until golden and bubbly. Let stand 15 minutes. Top with tomatoes and additional green onions. **Makes 8 servings (1¼ cups each).**

**EACH SERVING** *472 cal., 27 g fat (10 g sat. fat), 99 mg chol., 1,352 mg sodium, 34 g carb., 3 g fiber, 4 g sugars, 24 g pro.*

**CASSEROLE-READY CHICKEN** Any cooked chicken works here—it's a way to give leftover chicken new purpose. Or you can buy refrigerated grilled chicken strips or a rotisserie chicken from your supermarket. (One rotisserie chicken will yield about 3 cups chopped meat.) Or see how to easily poach chicken on *p. 37*.

»

**TANDOORI SPICE** is a traditional Indian seasoning blend of aromatic curry-style spices. The blend is most commonly put to use in classic Tandoori Chicken, a spiced yogurt sauce chicken dish baked in a clay oven, or tandoor (this casserole plays on the flavors of the original). If you can't find it in the store, make your own (above right).

# TANDOORI-SPICED CHICKEN AND RICE BAKE

**HANDS-ON TIME** 25 minutes
**COOK** 15 minutes
**BAKE** 20 minutes at 350°F

　 Nonstick cooking spray
1 recipe Tandoori Spice Mixture
12 oz. skinless, boneless chicken breast halves, cut into thin strips
2 Tbsp. vegetable oil
⅔ cup coarsely chopped green onions or white onion
½ cup chopped red sweet pepper
1 fresh serrano chile pepper, seeded and chopped (tip, p. 22)
3 cloves garlic, thinly sliced
1 14.5-oz. can reduced-sodium chicken broth
1 14-oz. can unsweetened light coconut milk
¾ cup uncooked long grain rice
¼ cup tomato paste
　 Fresh sprigs cilantro (optional)
　 Lemon wedges (optional)

**1.** Preheat oven to 350°F. Lightly coat a 2-qt. rectangular baking dish with cooking spray.
**2.** In a bowl stir 2 tsp. of the Tandoori Spice Mixture into chicken to coat. In a 12-inch skillet heat 1 Tbsp. of the oil over medium-high heat. Add chicken; cook and stir 3 minutes or until chicken is cooked through. Remove from skillet.
**3.** In the same skillet heat the remaining 1 Tbsp. oil over medium heat. Add onions, sweet pepper, serrano pepper, and garlic; cook and stir 2 minutes. Stir in broth, coconut milk, rice, tomato paste, and the remaining Tandoori Spice Mixture. Bring to boiling; reduce heat. Simmer, covered, 10 minutes.

Uncover; simmer 5 minutes more or until slightly thickened. Stir in chicken.
**4.** Transfer chicken mixture to prepared baking dish. Bake, covered, about 20 minutes or until heated through and rice is tender. If desired, top with cilantro and/or lemon wedges before serving.
**Makes 4 servings (1¼ cups each).**
**EACH SERVING** 414 cal., 16 g fat (8 g sat. fat), 62 mg chol., 850 mg sodium, 39 g carb., 3 g fiber, 4 g sugars, 26 g pro.

## TANDOORI SPICE MIXTURE

In a small bowl combine 1¼ tsp. curry powder, 1 tsp. garam masala, ½ tsp. ground ginger, ½ tsp. ground cumin, ½ tsp. ground coriander, ½ tsp. ground cardamom, ¼ tsp. salt, ⅛ tsp. ground cinnamon, and ⅛ tsp. black pepper. Makes 4½ tsp.

# TUNA NOODLE CASSEROLE

**HANDS-ON TIME** 30 minutes
**BAKE** 25 minutes at 375°F
**STAND** 5 minutes

3   cups dried wide egg noodles (about 5 oz.)
1   cup chopped celery
¾   cup chopped red sweet pepper
¼   cup chopped onion
¼   cup butter
¼   cup all-purpose flour
½   tsp. salt
¼   tsp. black pepper
2¼  cups milk
1   to 2 Tbsp. Dijon mustard
1   12-oz. can chunk water-pack white tuna, drained and broken into chunks, or two 5-oz. pouches chunk light tuna in water
½   cup panko bread crumbs (tip, *p. 108*) or soft bread crumbs
¼   cup grated Parmesan cheese
1   Tbsp. chopped fresh parsley
1   Tbsp. butter, melted

**1.** Preheat oven to 375°F. Lightly grease a 1½-qt. casserole. In a 3- or 4-qt. saucepan cook noodles according to package directions. Drain; return noodles to pan.
**2.** Meanwhile, for sauce, in a 2-qt. saucepan cook celery, sweet pepper, and onion in ¼ cup hot butter over medium heat 8 to 10 minutes or until tender. Stir in flour, salt, and black pepper. Add milk; cook and stir until thickened and bubbly. Stir in mustard. Gently fold sauce and tuna into cooked noodles. Transfer noodle mixture to prepared casserole.
**3.** In a bowl combine panko, cheese, parsley, and 1 Tbsp. melted butter; sprinkle over noodle mixture. Bake, uncovered, 25 to 30 minutes or until heated through. Let stand 5 minutes before serving. **Makes 4 servings (1½ cups each).**
**EACH SERVING** *495 cal., 23 g fat (12 g sat. fat), 115 mg chol., 1,040 mg sodium, 42 g carb., 3 g fiber, 10 g sugars, 33 g pro.*

**SAY CHEESE!**
It's easy to make a cheesy version of this classic casserole. Just add 1 cup cheddar cheese cubes (4 oz.) with the tuna.

## DISH IT OUT

Most of these recipes call for a baking dish, which means a dish made out of glass or ceramic (baking *pans* are made of metal). In contrast, a *casserole* dish refers to a dish that is round and deep. The most important thing is the capacity of your dish (check capacity using tip, *p. 119*). If the dish is too small, you can divide your casserole mixture between two dishes. If your dish is too large, reduce the cook time by 5 minutes.

## SHRIMP FONDUE CASSEROLE

**HANDS-ON TIME** 30 minutes
**BAKE** 35 minutes at 350°F

>> MACARONI is just one choice for the pasta. Look through your cupboards and sub any shape of medium-size pasta you have on hand.

Nonstick cooking spray
3 cups dried elbow macaroni (12 oz.)
3 cups shredded Swiss cheese (12 oz.)
2½ cups shredded Gruyère cheese (10 oz.)
5 Tbsp. all-purpose flour
3 cloves garlic, minced
2 cups chicken broth
¾ cup dry white wine
12 oz. fresh or frozen peeled, deveined uncooked small shrimp, halved lengthwise or chopped
1½ tsp. seafood seasoning
8 oz. Swiss cheese, cubed
¾ cups crushed saltine crackers
3 Tbsp. butter, cut up
½ cup sliced green onions

**1.** Preheat oven to 350°F. Coat a 3-qt. casserole dish with cooking spray. Cook macaroni according to package directions; drain. Return to pan; cover.

**2.** Meanwhile, in a large bowl combine shredded Swiss cheese, Gruyère cheese, flour, and garlic. Toss to combine. In a 4-qt. saucepan heat broth and wine over medium heat just until bubbles form around edges of pan. Add cheese mixture, 1 cup at a time, whisking constantly after each addition until cheese melts. (Mixture may not be completely smooth at this point.) Do not boil. Remove from heat. Stir in shrimp and seafood seasoning.

**3.** Pour cheese mixture over macaroni; stir gently. Fold in cubed Swiss cheese; spoon into prepared casserole. Sprinkle with crushed crackers; dot with butter.

**4.** Bake, uncovered, 35 to 40 minutes or until bubbly. Sprinkle with green onions.
**Makes 10 servings (1 cup each).**
**EACH SERVING** *607 cal., 31 g fat (18 g sat. fat), 145 mg chol., 596 mg sodium, 41 g carb., 2 g fiber, 2 g sugars, 37 g pro.*

**CHEESE FONDUE CASSEROLE**
Prepare as directed, except omit shrimp, seafood seasoning, and green onions. Season to taste with *salt* and *black pepper* in Step 2.
**EACH SERVING** *568 cal., 30 g fat (18 g sat. fat), 93 mg chol., 603 mg sodium, 41 g carb., 2 g fiber, 2 g sugars, 30 g pro.*

# MEAT, FISH & POULTRY

**MAKE-AHEAD RECIPE.** See also "Main Dishes," *pp. 428–447;* cooking charts, *pp. 52–67.*

PANKO BEEF ROAST
WITH ZUCCHINI

## PANKO BEEF ROAST WITH ZUCCHINI

**HANDS-ON TIME** 25 minutes
**ROAST** 1 hour 45 minutes at 325°F
**STAND** 15 minutes

1    3-lb. boneless beef round
     tip roast, trimmed
3    Tbsp. Dijon mustard
2    to 3 tsp. fennel seeds, crushed
2    Tbsp. panko bread crumbs
1½   lb. tiny yellow potatoes
4    Tbsp. olive oil
¾    tsp. garlic powder
½    cup grated Parmesan cheese
1    tsp. chopped fresh oregano
¼    tsp. black pepper
4    small or 2 large zucchini
1    recipe Mustard Sauce

**1.** Preheat oven to 325°F. Sprinkle meat with ½ tsp. *sea salt*. Brush with mustard; sprinkle with fennel seeds. Press panko onto meat.
**2.** Place meat on a rack in a shallow roasting pan. Roast 1¾ to 2 hours for medium rare (135°F) or 2¼ to 2½ hours for medium (150°F).
**3.** Halve any large potatoes. Toss with 2 Tbsp. of the oil, ¼ tsp. of the garlic powder, and ¼ tsp. *sea salt*. Add potatoes to one side of pan the last 1 hour of roasting.
**4.** Combine Parmesan, oregano, pepper, ¼ tsp. *sea salt*, and the remaining ½ tsp. garlic powder. Make cuts in zucchini crosswise every ½ inch, cutting almost to other side. Stuff cheese mixture in slices. Drizzle with remaining 2 Tbsp. oil. Add zucchini to pan the last 30 minutes of roasting.
**5.** Remove from oven. Cover meat with foil and let stand 15 minutes. (The temperature of the meat will rise 5°F to 10°F during standing.) Slice meat. Serve with veggies and Mustard Sauce. **Makes 10 servings (4 oz. meat + 3 potatoes + ⅓ small zucchini +1½ Tbsp. sauce each).**
**EACH SERVING** *322 cal, 15 g fat (4 g sat. fat), 84 mg chol., 804 mg sodium, 14 g carb., 2 g fiber, 2 g sugars, 32 g pro.*

**CUTTING ZUCCHINI**
To prevent slicing all the way through, arrange chopsticks or wooden spoons lengthwise on opposite sides of zucchini. Cut into zucchini, stopping when the knife reaches the chopsticks.

## *MUSTARD SAUCE*

In a small bowl combine ½ cup each Dijon mustard and light sour cream and 1 Tbsp. olive oil. Season to taste with salt and black pepper.

## GREEK FLAT IRON STEAKS

**START TO FINISH** 25 minutes

1    lemon
2    6- to 8-oz. boneless beef
     shoulder flat iron steaks
1    tsp. dried rosemary, crushed
4    tsp. olive oil
2    cups grape tomatoes
2    cloves garlic, minced
⅓    cup pitted green olives, halved
¼    cup crumbled feta cheese

**1.** Remove 1 tsp. zest from the lemon. Cut the lemon into wedges. Trim fat from steaks. Cut each steak in half and generously season both sides with *salt* and *black pepper*. Rub rosemary over both sides of steaks.
**2.** In a 10-inch nonstick skillet heat 2 tsp. of the oil over medium-high heat. Add steaks; cook 8 to 10 minutes for medium rare (145°F) or 12 to 15 minutes for medium (160°F), turning once. Remove steaks from skillet; cover and keep warm.
**3.** Add the remaining 2 tsp. oil, the tomatoes, and garlic to skillet. Cook over medium-high heat about 3 minutes or until tomatoes start to soften. Stir in olives and lemon zest.
**4.** Serve steaks with tomato mixture and lemon wedges. Sprinkle with cheese. **Makes 4 servings (3 oz. meat + ½ cup tomatoes each).**
**EACH SERVING** *220 cal., 13 g fat (4 g sat. fat), 56 mg chol., 467 mg sodium, 6 g carb., 2 g fiber, 3 g sugars, 20 g pro.*

GREEK FLAT IRON STEAKS

BULGOGI BEEF AND
VEGETABLE BOWLS

SOUTHWESTERN
BEEF KABOBS
WITH ORZO SALAD

## BULGOGI BEEF AND VEGETABLE BOWLS

**HANDS-ON TIME** 35 minutes
**MARINATE** 4 hours

»

STEAK slices much easier when partially frozen. Pop your steak in the freezer for 30 to 45 minutes before you start cutting it.

**BULGOGI**
This traditional Korean dish consists of marinated, grilled strips of meat. We serve it as a one-bowl meal with fresh veggies, rice, and a homemade spicy sriracha dressing.

| | |
|---|---|
| 1 | lb. boneless beef sirloin steak, cut 1 inch thick |
| ½ | cup coarsely chopped onion |
| ¼ | cup honey |
| ¼ | cup water |
| 2 | Tbsp. reduced-sodium soy sauce |
| 2 | Tbsp. toasted sesame oil (tip, p. 186) |
| 1 | Tbsp. finely chopped fresh ginger |
| 4 | cloves garlic, halved |
| | Nonstick cooking spray |
| 1⅓ | cups cooked brown rice |
| 1 | cup coarsely shredded carrots |
| 1 | cup finely shredded red cabbage |
| ¾ | cup cooked small broccoli florets |
| ½ | cup coarsely shredded cucumber |
| ¼ | cup chopped fresh cilantro or mint |
| 1 | to 2 tsp. sriracha sauce |
| ½ | cup kimchi (optional) |

### *COOKING RICE*

For 1⅓ cups cooked rice, in a 2-qt. saucepan bring ⅔ cup water and ⅓ cup uncooked long grain brown rice to boiling; reduce heat. Simmer, covered, 35 to 45 minutes or until rice is tender and liquid is absorbed.

**1.** Trim fat from meat. Cut meat across the grain into very thin slices. Place meat in a resealable plastic bag set in a shallow dish. For marinade, in a blender or food processor combine onion, 2 Tbsp. each of the honey and the water, the soy sauce, 1 Tbsp. of the sesame oil, the ginger, and garlic. Cover and blend or process until smooth. Pour over meat. Seal bag; turn to coat meat. Marinate in the refrigerator 4 to 6 hours, turning bag occasionally.
**2.** Drain meat, discarding marinade. Coat a 10-inch grill pan or nonstick skillet with cooking spray; heat over medium-high heat. Working in batches, add meat; cook and stir 40 to 60 seconds or just until slightly pink in center.
**3.** To assemble, divide meat and next five ingredients (through cucumber) among shallow bowls, keeping ingredients in separate piles. In a small bowl combine the remaining 2 Tbsp. honey, 2 Tbsp. water, and 1 Tbsp. sesame oil; the cilantro; and sriracha sauce. Top bowls with honey mixture and, if desired, kimchi and additional cilantro or mint. **Makes 4 servings (1 bowl each).**
**EACH SERVING** *397 cal., 13 g fat (3 g sat. fat), 77 mg chol., 435 mg sodium, 43 g carb., 3 g fiber, 23 g sugars, 30 g pro.*

## SOUTHWESTERN BEEF KABOBS WITH ORZO SALAD

**HANDS-ON TIME** 40 minutes
**GRILL** 8 minutes

| | |
|---|---|
| 4 | tsp. chili powder |
| 2 | tsp. garlic salt |
| 1 | tsp. ground cumin |
| 1 | tsp. ground oregano |
| 2 | lb. boneless beef sirloin, cut into 1-inch cubes |
| 1 | recipe Orzo Salad |
| | Lime slices (optional) |
| | Cilantro sprigs (optional) |

**1.** If using wooden skewers, soak in water 30 minutes. In a resealable plastic bag combine chili powder, garlic salt, cumin, and oregano. Seal bag and shake to mix. Add beef cubes to bag. Seal bag and shake to coat. On eight 10-inch skewers thread meat, leaving a ¼-inch space between pieces.
**2.** Grill kabobs, covered, over medium heat 8 to 12 minutes or until desired doneness, turning once or twice (grilling tips, *pp. 16–17*).
**3.** Serve beef kabobs with Orzo Salad. If desired, serve with lime slices and cilantro sprigs. **Makes 8 servings (1 kabob + 1 cup salad each).**
**ORZO SALAD** Cook ⅔ cup dried orzo pasta according to package directions, adding 2 cups fresh corn kernels (4 ears) for the last minute

of cooking. Drain orzo and corn in a colander; rinse with cold water. In a bowl combine orzo; corn; ¾ cup chopped orange or red sweet pepper; ⅔ cup grape tomatoes, halved; one 15- to 16-oz. can kidney beans, rinsed and drained; ½ cup thinly sliced red onion; and 1 small zucchini, halved lengthwise and sliced. For dressing, in a screw-top jar combine 1 tsp. lime zest; ¼ cup lime juice; 1 fresh jalapeño chile pepper, seeded and finely chopped (tip, p. 22); 2 Tbsp. each chopped fresh cilantro, olive oil, and honey; 3 cloves garlic, minced; and ½ tsp. salt. Cover and shake well. Pour dressing over orzo mixture; stir.

**EACH SERVING** *413 cal., 19 g fat (6 g sat. fat), 82 mg chol., 537 mg sodium, 34 g carb., 5 g fiber, 9 g sugars, 29 g pro.*

## SPICE-RUBBED FLANK STEAK

**HANDS-ON TIME** 10 minutes
**CHILL** 1 hour
**GRILL** 13 minutes
**STAND** 10 minutes

| | |
|---|---|
| 1 | Tbsp. packed brown sugar |
| 2 | tsp. ground cumin |
| 2 | tsp. garlic powder |
| 2 | tsp. chili powder |
| 1 | tsp. onion powder |
| ½ | tsp. salt |
| ¼ | tsp. black pepper |
| 2 | 1- lb. beef flank steaks, 1 to 1¼ inch thick |
| 1 | recipe Chimichurri (p. 30) (optional) Toasted rolls (optional) |

**1.** In a bowl stir together first seven ingredients (through pepper). Rub mixture on both sides of steaks. Wrap in plastic wrap; chill 1 to 24 hours.
**2.** Grill steaks, covered, over medium heat 13 to 16 minutes or until desired doneness (145°F for medium), turning once (grilling tips, *pp. 16–17*).

**3.** Transfer steaks to a cutting board; tent with foil. Let stand 10 minutes. Thinly bias-slice across the grain. If desired, serve with Chimichurri on toasted rolls. **Makes 6 servings (4 oz. meat each). TO BROIL** Preheat broiler. Place meat on an unheated greased rack of a broiler pan. Broil 4 to 6 inches from heat 9 to 12 minutes or until desired doneness (145°F for medium), turning once.

**EACH SERVING** *244 cal., 10 g fat (4 g sat. fat), 104 mg chol., 308 mg sodium, 4 g carb., 1 g fiber, 2 g sugars, 33 g pro.*

SPICE-RUBBED FLANK STEAK

**FAJITA BAR** Make it a party! When you're serving a crowd, mix and match beef, chicken, and shrimp fajitas. Cook skinless, boneless chicken breast until no longer pink; cook peeled and deveined shrimp until opaque. Serve with toppings, salsas, and guacamole so diners can make their own. Serve fajita mixture still sizzling in a preheated cast-iron skillet or grill pan.

## FAJITAS

**HANDS-ON TIME** 25 minutes
**CHILL** 30 minutes

**BEEF SKIRT STEAK**
is the typical
choice for beef
fajitas; it's often
only available at
Mexican markets
and specialty
food stores. It
has a coarser
grain than flank
steak and is more
marbled. Both cuts
should be thinly
sliced across the
grain (against
the meat fibers)
for maximum
tenderness; cook
over medium-
high heat to get a
good sear without
overcooking.

**BEEF SKIRT STEAK**

**FLANK STEAK**

12  oz. beef skirt or flank steak,
    cut into thin bite-size strips
1   recipe Fajita Seasoning
1   medium red or green sweet
    pepper, cut into thin strips
1   medium onion, thinly sliced and
    separated into rings
2   Tbsp. vegetable oil
¾   cup chopped tomato
1   Tbsp. lime juice
4   8-inch flour tortillas, warmed
    Toppers, such as salsa,
    Guacamole (p. 387), sour
    cream, and/or lime wedges

**1.** Sprinkle beef with 2 tsp. of the
Fajita Seasoning; toss to coat.
Cover and chill 30 minutes.
**2.** In a 12-inch skillet cook sweet
pepper, onion, and the remaining
seasoning in 1 Tbsp. of the oil over
medium-high heat until pepper and
onion are crisp-tender. Remove
pepper mixture from skillet. Add
the remaining 1 Tbsp. oil and the
meat to the skillet. Cook and stir 2 to
3 minutes or until browned. Return
pepper mixture to skillet. Stir in
tomato. Cook until heated through.
Remove from heat; stir in lime juice.
**3.** Fill warm tortillas with beef
mixture. If desired, serve with salsa,
Guacamole, sour cream, and/or
lime wedges. **Makes 4 servings
(1 fajita each).**

**EACH SERVING** *356 cal., 21 g fat (6 g
sat. fat), 51 mg chol., 326 mg sodium,
21 g carb., 2 g fiber, 4 g sugars,
20 g pro.*

## *FAJITA SEASONING*

In a bowl combine 1½ tsp. ground
cumin; ½ tsp. dried oregano,
crushed; ¼ tsp. each salt, cayenne
pepper, and black pepper; and
⅛ tsp. each garlic powder and
onion powder.

**BEEF AND NOODLES**

## BEEF AND NOODLES

**HANDS-ON TIME** 25 minutes
**COOK** 1 hour 20 minutes

1   lb. beef stew meat, trimmed
    and cut into ¾-inch cubes
¼   cup all-purpose flour
1   Tbsp. vegetable oil
½   cup chopped onion
2   cloves garlic, minced
3   cups beef broth
1   tsp. dried thyme or basil,
    crushed
¼   tsp. black pepper
½   of a recipe Egg Noodles (p. 214)
    or half of a 16-oz. pkg. frozen
    egg noodles
    Snipped fresh Italian parsley

**1.** In a large bowl toss meat with
flour to coat. In a 3- or 4-qt.
saucepan heat oil over medium-
high heat. Add half of the meat
to the hot oil in pan; cook and stir
until browned. Remove meat from
pan. Add the remaining meat, the
onion, and garlic. Cook and stir
until meat is browned and onion is
tender, adding more oil if necessary.
Drain off fat. Return all meat to
the saucepan.
**2.** Stir in the 3 cups broth, the
thyme, and pepper. Bring to
boiling; reduce heat. Simmer,
covered, 1¼ to 1½ hours or until
meat is tender.
**3.** Stir noodles into broth mixture.
Bring to boiling; reduce heat. Cook,
uncovered, about 5 minutes or
until noodles are tender, stirring
occasionally. (If using frozen egg
noodles, cook, uncovered, about
25 minutes or until noodles are
tender, stirring occasionally.) Add
additional broth to the noodle
mixture as needed to reach
desired consistency. Serve in
bowls; sprinkle with parsley. **Makes
4 servings (1½ cups each).**

**EACH SERVING** *411 cal., 14 g fat
(4 g sat. fat), 131 mg chol., 834 mg
sodium, 37 g carb., 2 g fiber,
2 g sugars, 32 g pro.*

## BEEF POT ROAST

**HANDS-ON TIME** 25 minutes
**COOK** 1 hour 45 minutes

1  2½- to 3-lb. beef chuck arm pot roast, beef chuck shoulder pot roast, or beef chuck 7-bone pot roast
1  tsp. steak seasoning
2  Tbsp. vegetable oil
¾  cup beef broth
1  Tbsp. Worcestershire sauce
1  tsp. dried thyme, crushed
¼  tsp. salt
1  lb. whole tiny new red potatoes or large potatoes halved or quartered
1  lb. carrots and/or parsnips, peeled and cut into 1- to 2-inch pieces
1  medium onion, cut into thin wedges (1½ cups)
½  cup cold water
3  Tbsp. all-purpose flour
   Salt and black pepper

**1.** Trim fat from meat. Sprinkle meat with steak seasoning. In a 5- to 6-qt. Dutch oven brown roast on all sides in hot oil. Combine broth, Worcestershire sauce, thyme, and salt. Pour over roast. Bring to boiling; reduce heat. Simmer, covered, 1 hour.
**2.** Add potatoes, carrots and/or parsnips, and onion to Dutch oven with meat. Stir into liquid. Return to boiling; reduce heat. Simmer, covered, 45 minutes more or until meat and vegetables are tender. Using a slotted spoon, transfer meat and vegetables to a platter. Reserve juices in Dutch oven; keep warm.
**3.** For gravy, skim fat from cooking juices; measure 1½ cups liquid. If necessary, add enough water to juices to equal 1½ cups. Return to Dutch oven. In a small bowl stir together the cold water and flour until smooth. Stir into juices in pan. Cook and stir over medium heat until thickened and bubbly. Cook and stir 1 minute more. Season to taste with salt and pepper. Serve gravy with meat and vegetables.
**Makes 6 servings (3 oz. meat + 1 cup vegetables + ⅓ cup gravy each).**
**EACH SERVING** *408 cal., 13 g fat (4 g sat. fat), 123 mg chol., 652 mg sodium, 27 g carb., 5 g fiber, 7 g sugars, 45 g pro.*

## IN THE OVEN

Preheat oven to 325°F. Prepare any variation as directed through Step 1, except bake, covered, 1 hour. Add potatoes and vegetables to Dutch oven with meat. Cover and bake 1½ to 2 hours more or until meat and vegetables are tender. Remove meat and vegetables from Dutch oven and prepare gravy as directed in Step 3.

## IN THE SLOW COOKER

Trim fat from meat. Sprinkle meat with steak seasoning. Brown roast for any variation as directed in Step 1. Place potatoes and vegetables in a 5- to 6-qt. slow cooker. Place roast on top of vegetables. Combine the broth, Worcestershire sauce, thyme, and salt. Pour over roast in cooker. Cover and cook on low 10 to 11 hours or on high 5 to 5½ hours. Prepare gravy in a saucepan as directed in Step 3.

>> **FENNEL POT ROAST** Prepare as directed, except substitute ½ tsp. each salt and black pepper for the steak seasoning; ¼ cup dry red wine for ¼ cup of the beef broth; dried Italian seasoning for the thyme; 1 fennel bulb, trimmed, cored, and cut into wedges; and 8 oz. cremini mushrooms, quartered, for the carrots and/or parsnips. Add 1 Tbsp. Dijon mustard and 2 cloves garlic, minced, to the broth in Step 1.

>> **CIDER AND SQUASH POT ROAST** Prepare as directed, except substitute ½ tsp. each salt and black pepper for the steak seasoning and ½ to ¾ cup apple cider for the beef broth. Use yellow potatoes and 1 lb. butternut squash, cut into 2-inch cubes, for the carrots and/or parsnips. Add 2 Tbsp. coarse-ground mustard and 2 cloves garlic, minced, to the broth in Step 1.

# MEAT LOAF

**HANDS-ON TIME** 25 minutes
**BAKE** 1 hour at 350°F
**STAND** 10 minutes

GROUND BEEF CHUCK (85% lean, 15% fat) and ground sirloin (90% lean, 10% fat) are the best combo for meat loaf. The higher fat content of ground chuck adds flavor and moisture to the loaf; lean sirloin adds good structure.

1    Tbsp. vegetable oil
½    cup finely chopped fresh mushrooms
½    cup shredded carrot
⅓    cup finely chopped onion
2    cloves garlic, minced
2    eggs, lightly beaten
¼    cup milk
3    Tbsp. ketchup
1    Tbsp. Dijon mustard
1    Tbsp. Worcestershire sauce
½    tsp. kosher salt
1    cup soft bread crumbs
1    lb. ground beef chuck (85% lean)
1    lb. ground beef sirloin (90% lean)
½    cup ketchup
¼    cup packed brown sugar
2    tsp. Dijon mustard

**1.** Preheat oven to 350°F. In a 10-inch skillet heat oil over medium-high heat. Add mushrooms, carrot, onion, and garlic; cook and stir 4 to 5 minutes or until tender. In a large bowl combine next six ingredients (through kosher salt). Add vegetable mixture and bread crumbs, stirring until evenly moistened.
**2.** Add ground beef; using clean hands, mix lightly until combined. Line a 3-qt. rectangular baking dish with foil. Lightly pat the mixture into a 9×5-inch loaf in the prepared dish.
**3.** For glaze, in a small bowl combine the ½ cup ketchup, the brown sugar, and 2 tsp. mustard. (Or substitute one of the glaze options *[right]* for the ketchup-brown sugar glaze.)
**4.** Bake about 1 hour or until done (160°F), spooning glaze over meat loaf the last 25 minutes of baking.
**5.** Let meat loaf stand 10 minutes. Using two spatulas, transfer loaf to a platter; cut into eight slices.
**Makes 8 servings (1 slice each).**
**EACH SERVING** *372 cal., 18 g fat (6 g sat. fat), 123 mg chol., 606 mg sodium, 24 g carb., 1 g fiber, 13 g sugars, 26 g pro.*

**》 APRICOT-MUSTARD GLAZE**
Stir together ½ cup apricot preserves and 2 Tbsp. Dijon mustard.

**》 PEACH-CHILE GLAZE**
Stir together ½ cup peach preserves and 2 tsp. each Asian chili sauce with garlic and grated fresh ginger.

**》 CRANBERRY GLAZE**
Stir together ½ cup ketchup and ¼ cup whole cranberry sauce.

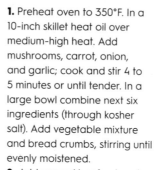

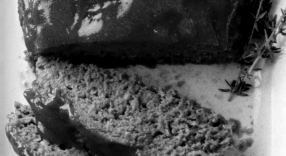

## MEAT COMBOS

Instead of using all beef, we also like these combos (1 lb. of each). If the meat mixture is on the lean side, cover the meat loaf with foil for the first 35 minutes of baking to keep it from drying out.

| GROUND BEEF + BULK SWEET ITALIAN SAUSAGE | GROUND TURKEY BREAST + GROUND PORK | GROUND BEEF CHUCK + GROUND VEAL |
|---|---|---|

GETTING A GOOD SEAR (CARAMELIZED CRUST) ON YOUR RIBS IS WHERE THE REAL FLAVOR COMES FROM. GET THE PAN REALLY HOT AND DON'T OVERCROWD RIBS.

**1.** Start by searing the ribs in hot oil to caramelize the surface of the meat (think flavor and color). Cook them in batches—if you try to brown all of them at once, the pan will cool down, the meat will release liquid, and ribs will steam instead of brown. Be patient.

**2.** To test the doneness of short ribs, insert a fork into the thickest part. They are done when the fork twists easily and the meat pulls apart with no resistance.

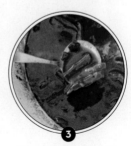

**3.** Here's another key to flavor: Simmering and reducing the sauce concentrate the flavor and thicken the sauce so it coats the ribs.

## ASIAN SHORT RIBS

**HANDS-ON TIME** 30 minutes
**BAKE** 2 hours 45 minutes at 350°F

2½ cups reduced-sodium beef broth
¾ cup hoisin sauce
3 Tbsp. reduced-sodium soy sauce
2 tsp. toasted sesame oil
1½ tsp. five-spice powder
⅛ tsp. cayenne pepper (optional)
3½ to 4 lb. beef short ribs (about 8 to 10 ribs), cut into serving-size pieces
¼ tsp. black pepper
1 Tbsp. vegetable oil
½ cup chopped onion
1 tsp. grated fresh ginger
3 to 4 cloves garlic, minced
1½ cups sliced fresh shiitake mushrooms (stems removed) or button mushrooms
2 to 3 cups hot cooked rice or rice noodles (optional)
Green onions, bias-sliced (optional)

**1.** Preheat oven to 350°F. In a bowl stir together the first six ingredients (through cayenne pepper). Trim fat from ribs. Sprinkle ribs with the black pepper. In a 4- to 5-qt. Dutch oven heat oil over medium-high heat. Cook ribs, half at a time, in hot oil until browned on all sides. Transfer ribs to a large bowl or plate. Add onion, ginger, and garlic to Dutch oven. Cook and stir 1 to 2 minutes or until onion is lightly browned.

**2.** Return ribs to Dutch oven. Add broth mixture. Bring to boiling. Cover Dutch oven; transfer to oven. Bake, covered, 2 hours, stirring once or twice. Stir in mushrooms. Bake, covered, about 45 minutes more or until ribs are tender.

**3.** Transfer ribs to a deep platter; cover to keep warm. Transfer cooking liquid to a large glass measure. Skim fat from cooking liquid. For sauce, return cooking liquid to Dutch oven; bring to boiling. Cook, uncovered, 2 to 3 minutes or until thickened. Pour some of the sauce over ribs. Pass the remaining sauce. If desired, serve with rice and sprinkle with green onions. **Makes 4 servings (2 ribs + ½ cup sauce each).**

**EACH SERVING** *474 cal., 24 g fat (8 g sat. fat), 97 mg chol., 1,565 mg sodium, 26 g carb., 2 g fiber, 15 g sugars, 37 g pro.*

### SHIITAKE PREP

Since shiitake mushroom stems are very tough, remove them before slicing and adding the mushrooms to the dish. We like to save the stems to simmer in Bone Broth *(p. 362).* Freeze stems in a resealable plastic bag until you're ready to use.

**BEEF SHORT RIBS** are cut two ways. English-style, with ribs cut crosswise *(below),* are more commonly available. Ribs cut lengthwise, called flanken-style, are available in Asian markets and specialty grocery stores.

**ASIAN SHORT RIBS** LONG, SLOW BRAISING (MOIST-HEAT COOKING) IS THE SECRET TO SOFTENING THE MEAT FIBERS IN RIBS TO GIVE THEM THAT MELTINGLY TENDER TEXTURE.

# WHAT IS NEW ENGLAND BOILED DINNER? THIS ONE-POT SIMMER IS AN IRISH-AMERICAN TRADITION DISHED UP DURING THE CHILLY MONTH OF MARCH TO CELEBRATE ST. PATRICK'S DAY.

## NEW ENGLAND BOILED DINNER

**HANDS-ON TIME** 20 minutes
**COOK** 2 hours 30 minutes

| | |
|---|---|
| 1 | 2- to 2½-lb. corned beef brisket |
| 1 | tsp. whole black peppercorns |
| 2 | bay leaves |
| 12 | oz. whole tiny new potatoes, halved if large |
| 6 | medium carrots and/or parsnips, peeled and quartered |
| 1 | medium onion, cut into 6 wedges |
| 1 | small cabbage, cut into 6 wedges |
| | Salt and black pepper (optional) |
| 1 | recipe Horseradish-Chive Sauce (optional) |

**»** PEPPERCORNS AND BAY LEAVES can be omitted if your corned beef comes with its own seasoning packet.

**1.** Trim fat from meat. Place meat in a 5- to 6-qt. Dutch oven; add juices from package of corned beef. Add enough water to cover meat. Bring to boiling; reduce heat. Simmer, covered, about 2 hours or until almost tender.

**2.** Add potatoes, carrots and/or parsnips, and onion to meat in Dutch oven. Return to boiling; reduce heat. Simmer, covered, 10 minutes. Add cabbage. Cook, covered, about 20 minutes more or until tender. Discard bay leaves (if using).

**3.** Transfer meat to a cutting board. Thinly slice meat across the grain; arrange on a platter. Using a slotted spoon, remove vegetables from Dutch oven and arrange on platter with meat. Discard cooking liquid. If desired, season meat and vegetables with salt and black pepper and serve with Horseradish-Chive Sauce. **Makes 6 servings (3 to 4 oz. meat + 1 cup vegetables each).**

**EACH SERVING** *357 cal., 18 g fat (5 g sat. fat), 76 mg chol., 1,066 mg sodium, 24 g carb., 6 g fiber, 8 g sugars, 25 g pro.*

> **GET-TOGETHER**
> *Make this a St. Patrick's Day celebration meal by adding hearty rye bread, coarse-grain mustard, and Guinness beer.*

## USE IT UP

### CORNED BEEF HASH
Cut leftover corned beef into small cubes or shred it; cut the potatoes into cubes. Cook the corned beef and cubed cooked potatoes in hot oil until meat is browned and potatoes are a little crispy. Serve with fried eggs for a hearty breakfast or quick dinner.

## HORSERADISH-CHIVE SAUCE

In a bowl stir together 1 cup sour cream, ¼ cup prepared horseradish, 1 Tbsp. each chopped fresh chives and Dijon mustard, 2 tsp. Worcestershire sauce, and ⅛ tsp. cayenne pepper.

// MEAT, FISH & POULTRY //

FLAT CUT          POINT CUT

**KNOW YOUR BRISKET** Beef brisket is cut from the chest of cattle just below the chuck. It consists of two distinct areas separated by a layer of fat. The *point* (also called the deckle) is a well-marbled, fatty cut on top of the *flat*, a bigger, leaner section. A trimmed flat cut is more commonly available in supermarkets since it is the better corned beef option; it is more attractive and slices nicely. The point cut produces juicier cooked meat, thanks to all that fat, and is better for shredding. When the entire brisket is intact (including both cuts), it is sold as an 8- to 12-lb. piece known as a Texas brisket or packer cut.

HERBED PORK ROAST

PORK CHOPS WITH APPLES AND CREAM

## HERBED PORK ROAST

**HANDS-ON TIME** 20 minutes
**ROAST** 20 minutes at 450°F +
40 minutes at 350°F
**STAND** 10 minutes

**TAKE A BREAK**
Your pork loin needs its rest, too. After removing it from the oven, loosely place a piece of foil over the loin; let it stand for 10 minutes. During this time, the internal temperature continues to rise (carryover cooking).

¼   cup olive oil
2    Tbsp. chopped fresh rosemary
2    Tbsp. chopped fresh thyme
6    cloves garlic, minced
1    tsp. salt
½    tsp. black pepper
1    lb. tiny new potatoes, halved
½    of a 1½-lb. butternut squash, peeled, seeded, and cut into 1½-inch pieces
3    carrots and/or parsnips, peeled, halved lengthwise, and cut into 2-inch pieces
1    large onion, cut into wedges
1    2- to 2½-lb. boneless pork top loin roast (single loin), trimmed of fat

**1.** Preheat oven to 450°F. In a small bowl combine first six ingredients (through pepper). Place potatoes, squash, carrots, and onion in a large roasting pan. Drizzle with half of the oil mixture; toss to coat. Push the vegetables to edges of pan.

**2.** Place roast in center of pan; spread with remaining oil mixture. Roast 20 to 25 minutes or until meat is beginning to brown.

**3.** Reduce oven temperature to 350°F. Roast 40 to 45 minutes more or until meat registers 145°F and vegetables are tender, stirring vegetables occasionally. Cover meat and vegetables with foil; let stand 10 minutes before serving.

**Makes 8 servings (4 oz. meat + ¾ cup vegetables each).**

**EACH SERVING** *285 cal., 11 g fat (2 g sat. fat), 71 mg chol., 363 mg sodium, 18 g carb., 3 g fiber, 3 g sugars, 27 g pro.*

## PORK CHOPS WITH APPLES AND CREAM

**START TO FINISH** 35 minutes

4    bone-in rib pork chops, cut 1 inch thick (1¾ to 2 lb. total) Kosher salt and black pepper
1    Tbsp. canola or corn oil
2    cooking apples, such as Gala, cored, cut into ½-inch wedges
1    Tbsp. unsalted butter
⅔    cup finely chopped shallots
4    large garlic cloves, minced
2    sprigs fresh sage
2    Tbsp. + ½ tsp. sherry vinegar
1    cup apple cider
3    Tbsp. heavy cream
1    Tbsp. Dijon mustard
1    tsp. finely chopped fresh sage

**1.** Season pork with salt and pepper. In a 12-inch skillet cook pork chops in hot oil over medium-high heat 2 minutes, turning once. Transfer pork to a plate. Add apples to skillet. Cook 3 to 4 minutes or until golden brown. Season with salt. Transfer to plate with pork.

**2.** Reduce heat to medium. Add butter and shallots to skillet; cook 3 minutes. Add garlic and sage sprigs; cook 30 seconds. Add 2 Tbsp. of the vinegar, stirring to loosen browned bits from the bottom of the pan. Add cider; bring to a simmer. Return pork chops and their juices to pan; reduce heat to low. Cover and gently simmer about 10 minutes or until pork is done (145°F), adding the apples the last 5 minutes of cooking. Transfer pork and apples to a plate.

**3.** Increase heat to medium-high. Simmer about 5 minutes or until liquid is reduced by about half. Whisk in cream, mustard, chopped sage, and ½ tsp. vinegar. Simmer 1 to 2 minutes more or until slightly thickened. Return pork and apples to skillet to coat. **Makes 4 servings (1 chop + ½ cup apples each).**

EACH SERVING *348 cal., 16 g fat (7 g sat. fat), 87 mg chol., 241 mg sodium, 24 g carb., 3 g fiber, 18 g sugars, 27 g pro.*

# GINGER CHOPS WITH WALNUTS

**START TO FINISH** 40 minutes

**GINGER CHOPS WITH WALNUTS**

- 2 Tbsp. vegetable oil
- 1 cup walnuts
- ½ tsp. curry powder
- ⅛ tsp. cayenne pepper
- 4 bone-in pork loin chops, cut ½ inch thick (about 7 oz. each)
- 1 small red onion, cut into thin wedges
- 1 orange
- ¼ cup reduced-sodium soy sauce
- 1 Tbsp. honey
- 1 Tbsp. grated fresh ginger
- 8 oz. butternut squash, peeled, sliced, and steamed or roasted (chart, p. 314)

**1.** In a 12-inch skillet heat 1 Tbsp. of the vegetable oil over medium heat. Add walnuts, curry powder, and cayenne. Cook and stir 5 minutes; remove from skillet.
**2.** Add the remaining 1 Tbsp. oil to skillet. Add pork chops and red onion. Cook about 7 minutes or until pork is done (145°F), turning once.
**3.** Remove zest and squeeze juice from orange. In a bowl stir together zest and juice, soy sauce, honey, and ginger. Add to skillet along with squash. Bring to boiling; heat through. Top chops and squash with the walnut mixture.

**Makes 4 servings (1 chop + ¾ cup vegetables + ¼ cup nuts each).**
EACH SERVING *508 cal., 30 g fat (4 g sat. fat), 79 mg chol., 678 mg sodium, 22 g carb., 5 g fiber, 12 g sugars, 41 g pro.*

**CHANGE IT UP**

*Baked or oven-roasted sweet potatoes make a delicious stand-in for squash. Add a creamy accent with a sprinkle of crumbled blue cheese.*

CRISP-COATED
BAKED PORK CHOPS

**BACON-WRAPPED PORK TENDERLOIN**

## CRISP-COATED BAKED PORK CHOPS

**HANDS-ON TIME** 20 minutes
**BAKE** 20 minutes at 425°F

STUFFING MIX is just one coating option. Swap in crushed cornflakes cereal or panko bread crumbs instead.

»

»

BUTTER AND COOKING SPRAY are both used here. The drizzle of butter adds extra flavor but doesn't provide an even coating. Cooking spray covers evenly so the coating doesn't dry out.

4 boneless pork loin chops, cut ¾ inch thick (1½ to 1¾ lb. total)
¼ tsp. salt
1 egg, lightly beaten
2 Tbsp. milk
¼ tsp. black pepper
1 cup herb-seasoned stuffing mix, finely crushed
2 Tbsp. butter, melted
  Nonstick cooking spray

**1.** Preheat oven to 425°F. Line a 15×10-inch baking pan with foil. Trim fat from chops. Sprinkle chops with salt. In a shallow dish combine egg, milk, and pepper. Place stuffing mix in another shallow dish. Dip chops into egg mixture, then into stuffing mix, turning to coat. Place chops in the prepared baking pan. Drizzle chops with butter and coat with cooking spray.

**2.** Bake, uncovered, 20 to 25 minutes or until juices run clear (145°F). **Makes 4 servings (1 chop each).**

**EACH SERVING** *347 cal., 12 g fat (6 g sat. fat), 143 mg chol., 912 mg sodium, 17 g carb., 2 g fiber, 1 g sugars, 41 g pro.*

## BACON-WRAPPED PORK TENDERLOIN

**HANDS-ON TIME** 20 minutes
**ROAST** 25 minutes at 425°F
**STAND** 3 minutes

⅓ cup apricot or cherry preserves, large pieces chopped
1 tsp. red wine vinegar
10 slices bacon
1 1-lb. pork tenderloin, trimmed
1 Tbsp. olive oil
8 oz. green beans, trimmed if desired
¼ cup reduced-sodium chicken broth
2 Tbsp. honey
¼ tsp. salt
¼ cup sliced almonds, toasted

**1.** Preheat oven to 425°F. Line a shallow roasting pan with foil. Place a rack in pan. In a bowl stir together apricot preserves and vinegar.

**2.** Lay bacon side by side on work surface, overlapping slightly. Place tenderloin crosswise on bacon; roll up, wrapping bacon around tenderloin. Place tenderloin, bacon ends down, on rack in pan. Roast 20 minutes. Brush top of tenderloin with preserves. Roast 5 to 10 minutes more or until bacon is crisp and pork is done (145°F). Remove from oven; let stand 3 minutes.

**3.** Meanwhile, in a 10-inch skillet heat oil over medium-high heat. Add green beans; cook and stir 3 to 5 minutes or just until crisp-tender. Add broth, honey, and salt. Cook and stir about 3 minutes more or until liquid is nearly evaporated. Stir in almonds. Serve green beans with sliced tenderloin. **Makes 4 servings (3 oz. meat + ½ cup beans each).**

**EACH SERVING** *392 cal., 15 g fat (4 g sat. fat), 93 mg chol., 575 mg sodium, 31 g carb., 2 g fiber, 22 g sugars, 33 g pro.*

COCONUT-CRUSTED
PORK TENDERLOIN

## COCONUT-CRUSTED PORK TENDERLOIN

**HANDS-ON TIME** 35 minutes
**MARINATE** 2 hours

1    1½-lb. pork tenderloin, trimmed and cut into 8 slices
¾    cup canned unsweetened coconut milk
2    Tbsp. finely chopped fresh ginger
4    cloves garlic, minced
½    tsp. sea salt
¼    to ½ tsp. cayenne pepper
2    eggs
¼    cup chopped raw macadamia nuts
¼    cup unsweetened shredded coconut
1    to 2 Tbsp. coconut oil
1    recipe Mango Salsa

**1.** Using the flat side of a meat mallet, flatten meat between two pieces of plastic wrap to ½ inch thick. For marinade, in a bowl combine next five ingredients (through cayenne pepper). Add meat; turn to coat. Cover and marinate in the refrigerator 2 to 3 hours, turning meat occasionally. Drain meat, discarding marinade.

**2.** In a shallow dish beat eggs with a fork. In a food processor cover and pulse nuts and shredded coconut just until finely chopped. Dip meat slices in egg, turning to coat. Lightly sprinkle both sides with nut mixture.

**3.** In a 10-inch heavy skillet heat 1 Tbsp. of the oil over medium-high heat. Add meat, half at a time, and cook 4 to 6 minutes or until slightly pink in center, turning once and adding the remaining 1 Tbsp. oil if needed. Serve with Mango Salsa. **Makes 4 servings (4 oz. meat + ½ cup salsa each).**

**EACH SERVING** *447 cal., 29 g fat (18 g sat. fat), 204 mg chol., 443 mg sodium, 5 g carb., 1 g fiber, 1 g sugars, 40 g pro.*

### *MANGO SALSA*

Remove ½ tsp. zest and squeeze 2 Tbsp. juice from 1 lime. In a medium bowl combine lime zest and juice; 1½ cups chopped mango; ¾ cup finely chopped red sweet pepper; ¼ cup thinly sliced green onions; 2 Tbsp. coconut oil; 1 fresh Scotch bonnet or serrano chile pepper, seeded and finely chopped (tip, *p. 22*); and ¼ tsp. each salt and black pepper.

COOK tenderloin slices half at a time so your pan and the oil stay hot. Keep the first batch warm in a 300°F oven. Add additional oil to pan if needed.

## BREADED PORK TENDERLOINS

**START TO FINISH** 25 minutes

1    lb. pork tenderloin
¼    cup all-purpose flour
¼    tsp. garlic salt
¼    tsp. black pepper
1    egg
1    Tbsp. milk
½    cup seasoned fine dry bread crumbs
2    Tbsp. vegetable oil

**1.** Trim fat from meat. Cut meat crosswise into four pieces. Using the flat side of a meat mallet, flatten pork between two pieces of plastic wrap to about ¼ inch thick (*opposite*).

**2.** In a shallow bowl combine flour, garlic salt, and pepper. In another shallow bowl whisk together egg and milk. In a third bowl place bread crumbs. Dip meat into flour mixture to coat. Dip into egg mixture, then into bread crumbs, turning to coat.

**3.** In a 10-inch heavy skillet cook meat in hot oil over medium heat 6 to 8 minutes or until coating is browned and meat is slightly pink in center, turning once. **Makes 4 servings (1 tenderloin each).**

**EACH SERVING** *284 cal., 11 g fat (2 g sat. fat), 120 mg chol., 398 mg sodium, 16 g carb., 1 g fiber, 1 g sugars, 28 g pro.*

### MAKE IT A SANDWICH

In restaurants, breaded tenderloins are often sandwiched between large toasted buns. Customize with all the condiments and toppings you like.

**BREADED PORK TENDERLOINS**

**WHAT IS "NATURAL" PORK?**
The U.S. Department of Agriculture states that pork labeled as "natural" undergoes minimal processing and cannot contain artificial ingredients or added color (but this is not the same as organic).

**①**

Cut a whole pork tenderloin crosswise into four equal pieces.

**②**

For the right thickness and shape, use the flat side of the meat mallet to pound meat pieces to an even ¼-inch thickness. For nice round pieces, fold in any long edges toward the center and pound again until even.

**CLASSIC BARBECUE SAUCE** and Asian Barbecue Sauce can be stored in the fridge up to 1 week.

## ON THE GRILL

When you want smoky grilled flavor, start the Saucy Ribs in the oven and finish on the grill. To finish on the grill, prepare and bake as directed 2 to 2½ hours. For a charcoal grill, sprinkle 2 cups soaked hickory wood chips over the coals. (Soak chips for 1 hour in water before using; drain.) Grill ribs, covered, over medium heat 10 to 15 minutes or until ribs are browned, turning once and brushing with sauce. (For a gas grill, add wood chips according to manufacturer's directions.) Serve ribs with remaining sauce. (Get a head start by baking them the day before and refrigerating overnight.)

A RIB RACK has a thin membrane that covers the bones and needs to be removed. (It shrinks during cooking, causing the rack to curl.) To remove, slip the tip of a knife under the membrane to loosen it. Use a paper towel to grip and pull it away from the bones.

## *COOKING CLASS*

WHEN COVERED TIGHTLY WITH FOIL, THIS LOW AND SLOW BAKING METHOD CREATES STEAM TO KEEP THE RIBS MOIST AND TENDER WHILE THEY COOK. TAKE THEM A STEP FURTHER WITH A 10-MINUTE FLIP ON THE GRILL FOR A CRISPY BROWN CRUST AND SMOKY FLAVOR.

## SAUCY RIBS

**HANDS-ON TIME** 25 minutes
**BAKE** 2 hours 15 minutes at 350°F

4    to 5 lb. pork loin back ribs
1    Tbsp. packed brown sugar
1    Tbsp. paprika
1    tsp. garlic powder
1    tsp. celery salt
½    tsp. dry mustard
½    tsp. black pepper
¼    tsp. cayenne pepper
1    recipe Classic Barbecue Sauce, Asian Barbecue Sauce, or Beer Barbecue Sauce (p. 160)

**1.** Preheat oven to 350°F. Trim fat from ribs. Place ribs in a shallow roasting pan. For rub, in a bowl stir together next seven ingredients (through cayenne pepper). Sprinkle rub over both sides of ribs; rub in with your fingers. Place ribs bone side down. Cover pan with foil.
**2.** Bake ribs 2 to 2½ hours or until very tender. Carefully drain fat from roasting pan. Meanwhile, prepare desired sauce. Brush some sauce over both sides of ribs, returning ribs to bone side down. Bake, uncovered, 15 minutes more, basting once with sauce. Pass remaining sauce with ribs. **Makes 6 servings (⅙ of ribs + ¼ cup sauce each).**
**EACH SERVING** *419 cal., 28 g fat (10 g sat. fat), 123 mg chol., 415 mg sodium, 3 g carb., 1 g fiber, 2 g sugars, 37 g pro.*

**CLASSIC BARBECUE SAUCE** In a 2-qt. saucepan melt ¼ cup butter over low heat. Add ½ cup finely chopped onion; 3 cloves garlic, minced; and 1 tsp. kosher salt; cook until onion is tender. Stir in 1½ tsp. each paprika and chili powder, ½ tsp. crushed red pepper, and ¼ tsp. black pepper; cook and stir 1 minute. Stir in 1 cup cold water, ⅔ cup cider vinegar, ½ cup packed brown sugar, and 1 Tbsp. Worcestershire sauce; bring to a simmer. Whisk in ½ cup tomato paste and 2 Tbsp. molasses. Bring to a simmer; cook, uncovered, 10 to 15 minutes or until thickened, stirring occasionally. Add additional salt if needed.

**ASIAN BARBECUE SAUCE** Place ½ cup apricot preserves in a bowl; chop any large pieces of fruit. Stir in ⅔ cup ketchup, ¼ cup reduced-sodium soy sauce, 2 tsp. grated fresh ginger or ½ tsp. ground ginger, and 2 cloves garlic, minced.

## *DONENESS CUES*

**BONE TIPS** When the ribs are close to being done, the meat will begin to retract, exposing the rib tips.

**U SHAPE** Hold the ribs in the middle with tongs. When they are ready, the rack will sag in a reversed U shape. The meat may crack, too, which is a good sign.

**RIB TWIST** Grab an exposed bone tip with your tongs and gently twist. If the bone turns easily, the ribs are done.

**TOOTHPICK TEST** The meat is tender when a toothpick easily penetrates the meat between the ribs.

GLAZED HAM BALLS

## APPLE BUTTER-GLAZED HAM

**HANDS-ON TIME** 20 minutes
**ROAST** 20 minutes at 425°F

Nonstick cooking spray
2 medium sweet potatoes, peeled and cut into 1-inch cubes (1 lb.)
12 oz. Brussels sprouts, trimmed and halved
2 Tbsp. vegetable oil
½ tsp. kosher salt
¼ tsp. black pepper
¼ cup apple butter
¼ cup cider vinegar
1 to 1¼ lb. center-cut ham slice, about 1 inch thick
Toasted baguette slices (optional)

**1.** Preheat oven to 425°F. Line a 15×10-inch baking pan with foil; lightly coat with cooking spray. In a large bowl combine sweet potatoes and Brussels sprouts. Add 1 Tbsp. of the oil, the salt, and pepper; toss to coat. Spread vegetables in a single layer in prepared pan. Roast, uncovered, about 20 minutes or until tender and browned, stirring once.
**2.** Meanwhile, for glaze, in a screw-top jar combine apple butter, vinegar, and the remaining 1 Tbsp. oil. Cover and shake well. Set aside 2 Tbsp. of the glaze. Toss the remaining glaze with roasted vegetables; cover to keep warm.
**3.** Heat a grill pan over medium-high heat. Add ham slice; cook about 8 minutes or until browned and heated through, turning once. Drizzle the 2 Tbsp. reserved glaze over ham. Serve with vegetables and, if desired, baguette slices.
**Makes 4 servings (4 oz. ham + 1 cup vegetables each).**
**EACH SERVING** *396 cal., 11 g fat (2 g sat. fat), 65 mg chol., 1,640 mg sodium, 48 g carb., 7 g fiber, 25 g sugars, 28 g pro.*

## GLAZED HAM BALLS

**HANDS-ON TIME** 25 minutes
**BAKE** 40 minutes at 350°F

2 eggs, lightly beaten
1½ cups soft bread crumbs
½ cup finely chopped onion
2 Tbsp. milk
¼ tsp. black pepper
2 tsp. dry mustard
12 oz. ground cooked ham
12 oz. ground pork
¾ cup packed brown sugar
½ cup ketchup
2 Tbsp. vinegar

»

**GROUND HAM** and **PORK** are sold as a premixed combo in some supermarkets. It may be labeled "ham loaf." You can use 1½ lb. of the mixture as a convenient shortcut.

**1.** Preheat oven to 350°F. Lightly grease a 2-qt. rectangular baking dish. In a large bowl combine first five ingredients (through pepper); stir in 1 tsp. of the mustard. Add ham and pork; mix well. Shape mixture into 12 balls, using about ¼ cup mixture for each. Arrange ham balls in prepared baking dish.
**2.** For sauce, in a bowl stir together the remaining 1 tsp. mustard and remaining ingredients; pour over ham balls. Bake, uncovered, about 40 minutes or until done (160°F).
**Makes 6 servings (2 balls each).**
**EACH SERVING** *375 cal., 13 g fat (4 g sat. fat), 136 mg chol., 830 mg sodium, 40 g carb., 1 g fiber, 33 g sugars, 25 g pro.*

» **SWEET-AND-SOUR GLAZED HAM BALLS** Prepare as directed, except omit 1 tsp. mustard, brown sugar, ketchup, and vinegar. In a 1- or 1½-qt. saucepan stir together ½ cup packed brown sugar and 4 tsp. cornstarch. Stir in ⅓ cup each chicken broth and red wine vinegar; ¼ cup finely chopped green sweet pepper; 2 Tbsp. each chopped pimientos or roasted red sweet pepper and reduced-sodium soy sauce; 1½ tsp. minced fresh ginger; 1 clove garlic, minced; and ⅛ to ¼ tsp. crushed red pepper. Cook and stir until thickened and bubbly. Cook and stir 2 minutes more. Pour over ham balls in Step 2.

» **PARTY-SIZE HAM BALLS**
To make 24 smaller ham balls, shape meat mixture into a 12×8-inch rectangle on a cutting board. Cut the rectangle into twenty-four 2-inch squares (tip, p. 221). Roll each square into a ball. Arrange balls in a 3-qt. baking dish. Bake glazed ham balls about 25 minutes.

APPLE BUTTER-
GLAZED HAM

>>

BISON MEAT is
a lean protein,
lower in fat and
calories than beef,
pork, and chicken.
Look for ground
bison in large
supermarkets,
natural food
stores, and local
butcher shops.
Visit the National
Bison Association
(*bisoncentral.com*)
for more
information.

BISON BURGERS

## BISON BURGERS

**HANDS-ON TIME** 45 minutes
**GRILL** 13 minutes

| | |
|---|---|
| 3 | Tbsp. olive oil |
| 1 | large sweet onion, halved and thinly sliced |
| ½ | tsp. salt |
| ¼ | tsp. black pepper |
| 1 | egg, lightly beaten |
| 2 | tsp. salt-free all-purpose seasoning |
| 1½ | lb. ground bison (buffalo) or ground beef |
| 4 | brioche or kaiser rolls, split |
| ¼ | cup Spicy Mayo Tomato slices and/or fresh basil or leaf lettuce |

**1.** In a 10-inch skillet heat 1 Tbsp. of the olive oil over medium-low heat. Add onion, ¼ tsp. of the salt, and the black pepper. Cook, covered, 13 to 15 minutes or until onion is tender, stirring occasionally. Cook, uncovered, over medium-high heat 3 to 5 minutes more or until golden, stirring constantly.
**2.** In a large bowl combine egg, salt-free seasoning, and the remaining 2 Tbsp. oil and ¼ tsp. salt. Add ground bison; mix well. Shape into four ¾-inch-thick patties; lightly press centers to make dimples.
**3.** Grill patties, covered, over medium heat 13 to 15 minutes or until done (160°F), turning once (grilling tips, *pp. 16–17*).
**4.** Serve burgers in rolls with Spicy Mayo, caramelized onions, tomato, and/or basil or lettuce. **Makes 4 sandwiches.**

**EACH SANDWICH** *781 cal., 53 g fat (16 g sat. fat), 201 mg chol., 754 mg sodium, 35 g carb., 4 g fiber, 10 g sugars, 40 g pro.*

### *SPICY MAYO*

In a bowl stir together ¼ cup mayonnaise, ½ tsp. each ground ancho or chipotle chile pepper and lime juice, and 1 small clove garlic, minced.

// **MEAT, FISH & POULTRY** //

ORANGE-TEQUILA
LAMB SHANKS

1. Preheat oven to 350°F. Remove 1 tsp. zest and squeeze ½ cup juice from oranges. In a 4-qt. oven-going Dutch oven heat oil over medium-high heat. Cook lamb shanks in hot oil until browned on all sides. Remove from Dutch oven.
2. For sauce, add onion, jalapeño pepper, and garlic to drippings in Dutch oven. Cook about 5 minutes or until onion is tender, stirring occasionally. Carefully add tequila; cook 4 minutes or until nearly gone, stirring to scrape up browned bits.
3. Stir in orange zest and juice and next five ingredients (through salt). Bring to boiling. Return lamb shanks to Dutch oven; cover. Bake 2 to 2½ hours or until meat is tender.
4. Serve lamb shanks with Polenta. Skim and discard fat from sauce. Spoon sauce over shanks and polenta. If desired, sprinkle with additional orange zest and chopped fresh rosemary. **Makes 4 servings (1 shank + ¾ cup polenta + ¾ cup sauce each).**
EACH SERVING  *535 cal., 12 g fat (3 g sat. fat), 148 mg chol., 1,242 mg sodium, 35 g carb., 7 g fiber, 7 g sugars, 53 g pro.*

## ORANGE-TEQUILA LAMB SHANKS

HANDS-ON TIME 40 minutes
BAKE 2 hours at 350°F

»

LAMB SHANK recipes may require thinking ahead. Double-check with your supermarket's meat counter or local butcher shop to see if shanks need to be special-ordered.

| | |
|---|---|
| 2 | oranges |
| 1 | Tbsp. vegetable oil |
| 4 | meaty lamb shanks (3 to 4 lb.) |
| 1 | large onion, sliced and separated into rings |
| 1 | fresh jalapeño chile pepper, seeded and finely chopped (tip, p. 22) |
| 3 | cloves garlic, minced |
| ⅓ | cup tequila |
| 1½ | cups reduced-sodium chicken broth |
| 1 | cup chopped tomato |
| ½ | cup fruity red wine, such as Pinot Noir |
| 1½ | tsp. chopped fresh rosemary |
| ½ | tsp. salt |
| 1 | recipe Polenta (p. 323) or 3 cups hot cooked polenta |

## LAMB AND ZUCCHINI KABOBS

HANDS-ON TIME 25 minutes
MARINATE 1 hour
GRILL 12 minutes

| | |
|---|---|
| ¼ | cup packed fresh Italian parsley |
| ¼ | cup packed fresh mint leaves |
| 3 | Tbsp. slivered almonds, toasted |
| 2 | Tbsp. shredded Parmesan cheese |
| 2 | cloves garlic, halved |
| 3 | Tbsp. lemon juice |
| 2 | Tbsp. water |
| 2 | Tbsp. olive oil |
| ⅛ | tsp. kosher salt |
| 2 | Tbsp. balsamic vinegar |
| ¼ | tsp. kosher salt |
| ⅛ | tsp. black pepper |
| 1 | lb. boneless leg of lamb, trimmed of fat and cut into 1½-inch pieces |
| 8 | oz. zucchini, cut into 1-inch pieces |
| 8 | oz. yellow summer squash, cut into 1-inch pieces |

1. For pesto, in a blender or small food processor combine first five ingredients (through garlic). Pulse until coarsely chopped. Add 1 Tbsp. of lemon juice, the water, 2 tsp. of the olive oil, and ⅛ tsp. salt. Process until very finely chopped and fully combined. Cover and refrigerate.
2. For marinade, in a small bowl whisk together the remaining 2 Tbsp. lemon juice, the vinegar, 2 tsp. of the olive oil, ¼ tsp. salt, and the black pepper. Place lamb in a large resealable plastic bag set in a shallow dish. Add marinade to lamb in bag. Seal bag; turn to coat. Marinate in the refrigerator 1 to 4 hours, turning occasionally.
3. If using wooden skewers, soak in water 30 minutes. Drain lamb; discard marinade. Thread meat on four 8- to 10-inch skewers, leaving a ¼-inch space between pieces.
4. Thread vegetables onto another four skewers, alternating zucchini and yellow squash, leaving a ¼-inch space between pieces. Brush vegetables with the remaining 2 tsp. of the olive oil.
5. Grill kabobs, covered, over medium heat 12 to 14 minutes or until lamb is desired doneness and vegetables are tender, turning occasionally (grilling tips, pp. 16–17). Serve with pesto. **Makes 4 servings (1 lamb kabob + 1 vegetable kabob + 4 tsp. pesto each).**
EACH SERVING  *272 cal., 15 g fat (3 g sat. fat), 74 mg chol., 291 mg sodium, 8 g carb., 2 g fiber, 4 g sugars, 27 g pro.*

LAMB AND
ZUCCHINI KABOBS

# HERB ROASTED CHICKEN

**HANDS-ON TIME** 20 minutes
**ROAST** 1 hour 30 minutes at 375°F
**STAND** 10 minutes

| | |
|---|---|
| 1 | 4- to 5-lb. whole broiler-fryer chicken |
| 2 | Tbsp. butter, softened |
| 2 | cloves garlic, minced |
| 1 | tsp. dried basil, crushed |
| 1 | tsp. dried sage, crushed |
| ½ | tsp. dried thyme, crushed |
| ¼ | tsp. salt |
| ¼ | tsp. black pepper |

**1.** Preheat oven to 375°F. Skewer neck skin of chicken to back; tie legs to tail. Twist wing tips under back. Place chicken, breast side up, on a rack in a shallow roasting pan.
**2.** Combine butter and garlic; spread over chicken. In a small bowl stir together remaining ingredients; sprinkle over chicken.
**3.** Roast 1½ to 1¾ hours or until chicken is done (at least 170°F in thigh) and drumsticks move easily in sockets, cutting string and covering with foil to prevent overbrowning after 1 hour. Remove from oven. Cover and let stand 10 minutes before carving. **Makes 4 servings (4 oz. chicken each).**
**EACH SERVING** *701 cal., 50 g fat (16 g sat. fat), 245 mg chol., 364 mg sodium, 1 g carb., 0 g fiber, 0 g sugars, 58 g pro.*

**CITRUS-HERB ROASTED CHICKEN** Prepare chicken as directed, except in a food processor combine ½ cup fresh basil leaves, ¼ cup each fresh Italian parsley leaves and coarsely chopped onion, 1 Tbsp. fresh mint leaves, 2 tsp. chopped fresh sage, 1 tsp. each salt and lemon zest, and ½ tsp. each cracked black pepper and orange zest. Cover and pulse until finely chopped. With processor running, slowly add 2 Tbsp. olive oil in a steady stream until nearly smooth. Loosen skin on chicken breast and legs and spread herb mixture under the skin on meat. Cover chicken tightly with plastic wrap and chill overnight. Spread chicken with butter mixture and sprinkle with salt and black pepper(omit basil, sage, and thyme). Roast as directed in Step 3.

**MOROCCAN-SPICED ROASTED CHICKEN** Prepare as directed, except in a food processor combine ¼ cup each toasted slivered almonds, fresh Italian parsley leaves, and coarsely chopped onion; 2 Tbsp. packed brown sugar; 2 tsp. orange zest and 2 Tbsp. orange juice; 2 tsp. ground cumin; 1½ tsp. ground turmeric; 1 tsp. each salt and ground coriander; ½ tsp. ground cinnamon; ¼ tsp. ground cloves; and ⅛ tsp. cayenne pepper. Cover and process until nearly smooth. Loosen skin on chicken breast and legs and spread spice mixture under the skin on meat. Cover chicken tightly with plastic wrap and chill overnight. Spread chicken with butter mixture and sprinkle with salt and black pepper (omit basil, sage, and thyme). Roast as directed in Step 3.

**TOMATO-BASIL ROASTED CHICKEN** Prepare as directed, except in a food processor combine ½ cup each fresh basil leaves and chopped oil-packed dried tomatoes; ¼ cup cut-up fresh chives; 1 Tbsp. balsamic vinegar; 2 tsp. dried oregano; 1 tsp. salt; and ½ tsp. black pepper. Cover and pulse until finely chopped. With processor running, slowly add 2 Tbsp. olive oil in a steady stream until nearly smooth. Loosen skin on chicken breast and legs and spread herb mixture under the skin on meat. Cover chicken tightly with plastic wrap and chill overnight. Spread chicken with butter mixture and sprinkle with salt and black pepper (omit basil, sage, and thyme). Roast as directed in Step 3.

## *SHOULD YOU RINSE?*

In the past, recipes recommended rinsing pieces of chicken or turkey, or the cavity of a whole bird, with water and patting it dry with paper towels. The U.S. Department of Agriculture has changed its stance on this practice. Research shows rinsing poultry can spread bacteria by splashing contaminated water onto surrounding areas. Instead, move poultry straight from package to pan; cooking will kill any bacteria. If any moisture is present on poultry when it is removed from the packaging, gently pat it dry with paper towels (discard the towels immediately).

### TEMP IT RIGHT
For an accurate read, stick a meat thermometer in the thigh before you start roasting (it stays in the whole time) or use an instant-read thermometer to check after roasting time is up.

## CHICKEN CACCIATORE

**HANDS-ON TIME** 30 minutes
**COOK** 20 minutes

8   small bone-in chicken thighs (about 2 lb. total), skinned (tip, p. 158)
    Salt and black pepper
1   Tbsp. olive oil
3   cups sliced fresh cremini mushrooms
1   large green sweet pepper, seeded and cut into bite-size strips
⅓   cup finely chopped carrot
3   cloves garlic, minced
½   cup dry white wine or chicken broth
1   28-oz. can diced tomatoes, undrained
1½  cups frozen small whole onions
1   tsp. dried oregano, crushed
1   tsp. coarsely ground black pepper
2   Tbsp. balsamic vinegar
    Hot cooked broken lasagna noodles or desired pasta
    Toppers such as Kalamata olives and/or snipped fresh Italian parsley (optional)

**1.** Sprinkle chicken lightly with salt and black pepper. In a 10-inch skillet heat oil over medium heat. Add chicken; cook just until browned, turning once. Remove from skillet.
**2.** Add mushrooms, sweet pepper, carrot, and garlic to the skillet. Cook over medium heat 4 minutes, stirring occasionally. Carefully add wine. Simmer, uncovered, until wine is nearly evaporated. Stir in tomatoes, onions, oregano, and the 1 tsp. coarsely ground pepper.
**3.** Return chicken to skillet. Simmer, covered, about 20 minutes or until chicken is no longer pink (at least 175°F). Stir in vinegar. Season to taste with additional salt. Serve with hot cooked lasagna noodles. If desired, sprinkle with toppers. **Makes 4 servings (2 thighs + 1 cup vegetables each).**

**EACH SERVING** *380 cal., 8 g fat (2 g sat. fat), 80 mg chol., 744 mg sodium, 44 g carb., 7 g fiber, 12 g sugars, 28 g pro.*

## CHICKEN AND NOODLES

**HANDS-ON TIME** 30 minutes
**COOK** 1 hour 5 minutes

1   3½- to 4-lb. broiler-fryer chicken
5   cups reduced-sodium chicken broth
½   tsp. salt
¼   tsp. black pepper
1   recipe Egg Noodles (p. 214) or one 12-oz. pkg. frozen noodles
2   Tbsp. all-purpose flour

**1.** In a 4- to 5-qt. pot combine chicken, 4 cups of the broth, salt, and pepper. Bring to boiling; reduce heat. Simmer, covered, 45 to 60 minutes or until chicken is tender. Remove chicken from pot; cool. Remove meat from bones; discard skin and bones. Chop chicken. Strain broth; return broth to pot. Skim fat.
**2.** Bring broth to boiling. Add Egg Noodles; boil gently, uncovered, 15 minutes, stirring occasionally. In a screw-top jar combine the remaining 1 cup broth and the flour; cover and shake until smooth. Stir into noodle mixture. Cook and stir until thickened and bubbly. Stir in chicken. Cook 5 minutes more, stirring occasionally. Stir in additional broth to make desired consistency. If desired, serve with *Mashed Potatoes (p. 306)*. **Makes 6 servings (1 cup each).**

**EACH SERVING** *381 cal., 7 g fat (2 g sat. fat), 181 mg chol., 944 mg sodium, 39 g carb., 1 g fiber, 1 g sugars, 37 g pro.*

**CHICKEN CACCIATORE**

# CHICKEN AND DUMPLINGS

**HANDS-ON TIME** 30 minutes
**COOK** 1 hour 10 minutes

| | |
|---|---|
| 1 | 3½- to 4-lb. broiler-fryer chicken |
| 4 | cups reduced-sodium chicken broth |
| 1 | cup chopped onions |
| 1 | cup sliced celery |
| 1 | cup thinly sliced carrots |
| 1 | cup sliced fresh mushrooms |
| ½ | tsp. dried sage, crushed |
| 1 | bay leaf |
| ½ | cup water |
| 3 | Tbsp. all-purpose flour |
| 1 | recipe Dumplings |

**1.** In a 4- to 5-qt. pot combine chicken, broth, ½ tsp. *salt*, and ¼ tsp. *black pepper*. Bring to boiling; reduce heat. Simmer, covered, 45 to 60 minutes or until chicken is tender. Remove chicken from pot; cool. Remove meat from bones; discard skin and bones. Chop chicken. Strain broth; return 5 cups broth to pot. Skim fat.

**2.** Add next six ingredients (through bay leaf). Bring to boiling; cover. Simmer 10 minutes. In a screw-top jar combine water and flour; cover and shake until smooth. Stir into vegetable mixture. Cook and stir until thickened and bubbly. Stir in chicken; discard bay leaf. Bring to simmering; spoon Dumplings batter in six mounds on top. Simmer, covered (do not lift lid), 12 to 15 minutes or until toothpick inserted in dumplings comes out clean.
**Makes 6 servings (1 cup each).**
**EACH SERVING** *327 cal., 9 g fat (2 g sat. fat), 90 mg chol., 1,061 mg sodium, 26 g carb., 2 g fiber, 4 g sugars, 34 g pro.*

CHICKEN AND NOODLES

## *DUMPLINGS*

In a medium bowl combine 1 cup all-purpose flour, 1 tsp. baking powder, and ½ tsp. salt. Cut in 2 Tbsp. shortening until mixture resembles coarse crumbs. Add ½ cup buttermilk to flour mixture. Stir just until moistened.

**CHICKEN IN CREAMY MUSHROOM SAUCE**

**CHICKEN SKIN** is slippery, so use a paper towel to grip it. Pull the skin away from the meat, starting at the meaty end and pulling toward the knuckle. Snip skin where attached if necessary.

## CHICKEN IN CREAMY MUSHROOM SAUCE

**HANDS-ON TIME** 20 minutes
**BAKE** 35 minutes at 350°F

2   Tbsp. butter, melted
2   8-oz. pkg. fresh cremini or button mushrooms, sliced
3   cloves garlic, minced
3   8- to 10-oz. skinless, boneless chicken breast halves, halved horizontally
1   10.75-oz. can condensed golden mushroom soup
½   cup dry white wine or chicken broth
½   of an 8-oz. tub cream cheese spread with chives and onion
1   0.7-oz. envelope Italian dry salad dressing mix
    Hot mashed potatoes, cooked rice, or angel hair pasta

**1.** Preheat oven to 350°F. In a 12-inch skillet melt butter over medium heat. Add mushrooms and garlic. Cook, stirring occasionally, about 5 minutes or until mushrooms are browned and liquid evaporates.
**2.** Place chicken pieces in a single layer in a 3-qt. rectangular baking dish. Spoon mushroom mixture over the chicken. In a medium bowl whisk together the next four ingredients (through dressing mix) until combined; spoon over chicken.
**3.** Bake, uncovered, 35 to 40 minutes or until chicken is done (165°F). Serve with hot mashed potatoes. **Makes 6 servings (1 breast half + ⅓ cup sauce each).**
**EACH SERVING** *411 cal., 17 g fat (9 g sat. fat), 117 mg chol., 1,199 mg sodium, 28 g carb., 3 g fiber, 5 g sugars, 32 g pro.*

## CURRIED CHICKEN DRUMSTICKS

**HANDS-ON TIME** 20 minutes
**MARINATE** 4 hours
**ROAST** 40 minutes at 450°F
**REST** 10 minutes

1   cup plain low-fat yogurt (not Greek)
3   Tbsp. canola or corn oil
2   Tbsp. lemon juice
2   Tbsp. grated fresh ginger
2   Tbsp. minced garlic
4   tsp. ground cumin
1   Tbsp. kosher salt
1   Tbsp. ground turmeric
2   tsp. ground coriander
2   tsp. garam masala
⅛   tsp. cayenne pepper (or more to taste)
12  chicken drumsticks (3½ to 4 lb.), skinned
4   Tbsp. unsalted butter, melted
2   large red onions, peeled and cut in 8 wedges each through root end
¼   tsp. kosher salt
¼   tsp. black pepper
    Lemon wedges

**1.** For marinade, in a bowl stir together yogurt, 2 Tbsp. of the oil, and the next nine ingredients (through cayenne pepper).
**2.** Make three or four slashes in meaty part of each drumstick. Place chicken in large resealable plastic bag set in a shallow dish. Add marinade, seal bag, and rub marinade over chicken and into slashes. Refrigerate 4 to 6 hours (not longer).
**3.** Preheat oven to 450°F. Line a 15×10-inch baking pan with foil; place a rack over foil and lightly grease the rack. Shake excess marinade from chicken and arrange chicken on rack. Brush chicken with half of the butter; roast 20 minutes.
**4.** While chicken is roasting, gently toss onion wedges with the remaining 1 Tbsp. oil. Arrange on a foil-lined 15×10-inch baking pan. Season with the ¼ tsp. salt and the black pepper.
**5.** Turn chicken, brush with the remaining butter, and return to oven with the pan of onions. Roast 20 to 30 minutes or until chicken is done (at least 175°F) and onions are charred and crisp-tender. Let chicken rest 10 minutes. Serve with onions and lemon wedges. **Makes 6 servings (2 drumsticks + ½ cup onions each).**
**EACH SERVING** *323 cal., 21 g fat (8 g sat. fat), 104 mg chol., 614 mg sodium, 15 g carb., 3 g fiber, 7 g sugars, 19 g pro.*

CURRIED
CHICKEN
DRUMSTICKS

## HANDLING POULTRY

**STORING** Store raw poultry in its original package in the coldest part of the refrigerator; cook within 2 days of purchase. For longer storage, freeze poultry in its original package wrapped tightly in heavy-duty foil. Or freeze individual portions in plastic wrap, freezer wrap, heavy-duty foil, and/or resealable freezer bags. Whole poultry will keep up to a year and pieces up to 9 months. Never freeze stuffed poultry.

**THAWING** Never thaw poultry at room temperature. Thaw in the refrigerator in a dish or pan to catch any juices. Allow at least 24 hours for poultry parts and per every 3½ to 4 lb. for whole birds.

**QUICK THAWING** To quick-thaw, you can microwave poultry on the defrost setting, but it must be cooked right away after thawing. For a whole bird, place it in a resealable plastic bag in a sink full of cold water. Allow 30 minutes per pound, changing the water every 30 minutes.

// MEAT, FISH & POULTRY //

## OVEN-BARBECUED CHICKEN

**HANDS-ON TIME** 10 minutes
**BAKE** 45 minutes at 375°F

»

IF BREAST HALVES are extra large, use a chef's knife to cut in half crosswise after removing skin for more even cooking.

4    lb. meaty chicken pieces (breast halves, thighs, and drumsticks), skinned (tip, *p. 158*)
1    recipe Beer Barbecue Sauce, Classic Barbecue Sauce (*p. 149*), or Asian Barbecue Sauce (*p. 149*)

**1.** Preheat oven to 375°F. Line a 15×10-inch baking pan with foil.

Arrange chicken, bone sides up, in the prepared pan. Bake 35 minutes.
**2.** Turn chicken bone sides down. Brush about 1 cup of the sauce over chicken. Bake 10 to 20 minutes more or until chicken is no longer pink (170°F for breasts; at least 175°F for thighs and drumsticks). Pass remaining sauce with chicken.
**Makes 6 servings (4 oz. chicken + ¼ cup sauce each).**

**EACH SERVING** *603 cal., 30 g fat (9 g sat. fat), 153 mg chol., 498 mg sodium, 41 g carb., 0 g fiber, 36 g sugars, 39 g pro.*

## *TO GRILL*

Prepare grill for indirect heat using a drip pan (tips, *pp. 16–17*). Place chicken, bone sides up, on greased rack over drip pan. Grill, covered, over indirect medium heat 50 to 60 minutes or until done (170°F for breast halves; at least 175°F for thighs and drumsticks), turning once halfway through grilling and brushing with 1 cup of desired sauce the last 15 minutes of grilling. (Heat and pass remaining sauce with chicken.)

# BUTTERMILK FRIED CHICKEN

**HANDS-ON TIME** 30 minutes
**CHILL** 2 hours
**FRY** 5 minutes
**BAKE** 15 minutes at 350°F

3       cups buttermilk
⅓       cup kosher salt
2       Tbsp. sugar
2½ to 3 lb. meaty chicken pieces
        (breast halves, thighs, and
        drumsticks)
2       cups all-purpose flour
¼       tsp. salt
¼       tsp. black pepper
¾       cup buttermilk
        Vegetable oil

**1.** For brine, in a resealable plastic bag set in a bowl combine the 3 cups buttermilk, the kosher salt, and sugar. Using a chef's knife, cut chicken breast halves in half crosswise. Add all chicken pieces to the brine; seal bag. Turn bag to coat chicken. Chill 2 to 4 hours; remove chicken from brine. Drain chicken; pat dry with paper towels. Discard brine.

**2.** Preheat oven to 350°F. Line a 15×10-inch baking pan with foil; if desired, place a wire rack over the foil. In a large bowl combine flour, the ¼ tsp. salt, and the pepper. Place the ¾ cup buttermilk in a shallow dish. Coat chicken with flour mixture; dip in the buttermilk and coat again with flour mixture.

**3.** Meanwhile, in a deep heavy pot or a deep-fat fryer, heat 1½ inches oil to 350°F. Using tongs, carefully add two or three pieces of chicken to hot oil at a time. (Oil temperature will drop; adjust the heat to maintain temperature at 350°F.) Fry chicken 5 to 6 minutes or until coating on chicken is golden brown, turning once. Drain briefly on paper towels. Place chicken in prepared pan. Bake 15 to 20 minutes or until chicken reaches 170°F for breasts and at least 175°F for thighs and drumsticks. **Makes 6 servings (1 piece each).**

**EACH SERVING** *730 cal., 45 g fat (10 g sat. fat), 135 mg chol., 1,382 mg sodium, 41 g carb., 1 g fiber, 9 g sugars, 39 g pro.*

## QUICK PREP

To save time, omit brining the chicken in Step 1; omit the 3 cups buttermilk, the kosher salt, and sugar. Cut chicken breasts in half as directed in Step 1 and continue as directed in Step 2.

## TEMPERATURE MATTERS

All poultry is safe to eat at 165°F, but we found different cuts taste better at different temps. Test doneness by inserting a thermometer into thickest part of meat without touching bone.

| WHOLE BIRD at least **175°F** in thigh | BONE-IN THIGH & DRUMSTICK at least **175°F** | BONELESS THIGH **175°F** | BONE-IN BREAST **170°F** | BONELESS BREAST/ TENDERS **165°F** |
| --- | --- | --- | --- | --- |

CHICKEN
TENDERS are
the tenderloin
portion of the
chicken breast.
You can make
your own by
cutting skinless,
boneless
chicken breasts
lengthwise into
¾-inch strips.

»

## OVEN-BAKED CHICKEN STRIPS

**HANDS-ON TIME** 30 minutes
**BAKE** 12 minutes at 450°F

Nonstick cooking spray
½ cup all-purpose flour
5 tsp. ranch dry salad dressing mix
3 eggs
2 cups panko bread crumbs
(tip, *p. 108*)
2 Tbsp. butter, melted
1 tsp. dry mustard
½ tsp. black pepper
1½ lb. chicken tenders

**1.** Preheat oven to 450°F. Line a
large baking sheet with foil. Coat
foil with cooking spray.
**2.** In a shallow dish combine flour
and dressing mix. Put the eggs in a
separate shallow dish; lightly beat
eggs with a fork. In a third shallow
dish stir together the bread crumbs,
butter, dry mustard, and pepper.
**3.** Dip chicken tenders in flour
mixture, then eggs, then bread
crumb mixture to coat, turning and
pressing to stick coating to chicken.
Place chicken on prepared baking
sheet. Lightly coat top of chicken
with additional cooking spray.
**4.** Bake about 12 minutes or until
golden and chicken is no longer
pink. **Makes 6 servings (3 oz.
chicken each).**

**EACH SERVING** *299 cal., 9 g fat
(4 g sat. fat), 185 mg chol., 346 mg
sodium, 19 g carb., 1 g fiber, 1 g sugars,
31 g pro.*

## HONEY-MUSTARD DIPPING SAUCE
Stir together ½ cup
mayonnaise, 1 Tbsp.
honey, and 1 Tbsp. Dijon
mustard or yellow
mustard.

## BAKED CHICKEN CHILES RELLENOS

**HANDS-ON TIME** 45 minutes
**BAKE** 30 minutes at 375°F

6 skinless, boneless chicken
breast halves
⅓ cup all-purpose flour
3 Tbsp. cornmeal
¼ tsp. salt
¼ tsp. cayenne pepper
1 egg, lightly beaten
1 Tbsp. water
1 4-oz. can whole green chile
peppers, rinsed, stemmed,
seeded, and halved lengthwise
(6 pieces total)
2 oz. Monterey Jack cheese,
cut into six 2×½-inch sticks
2 Tbsp. chopped fresh cilantro or
fresh parsley
¼ tsp. black pepper
2 Tbsp. butter, melted
1 8-oz. jar salsa verde or
tomato salsa

**1.** Using the flat side of a meat
mallet, flatten chicken between two
pieces of plastic wrap to rectangles
¼ to ½ inch thick.
**2.** Preheat oven to 375°F. Line a
shallow baking pan with foil. In a
shallow bowl stir together flour,
cornmeal, salt, and cayenne
pepper. In a second shallow bowl
combine egg and water.
**3.** Place a chile pepper half on each
chicken piece near an edge. Place
a stick of cheese on each chile
pepper. Sprinkle with cilantro and
black pepper. Fold in side edges;
roll up from edge with cheese
and chile pepper. Secure with
wooden toothpicks.
**4.** Dip chicken rolls into egg
mixture to coat; coat all sides with
cornmeal mixture. Place rolls, seam
sides down, in prepared baking
pan. Brush rolls with melted butter.
**5.** Bake, uncovered, 30 to
35 minutes or until done (165°F).
Remove toothpicks. Meanwhile,
heat salsa; serve over chicken.
**Makes 6 servings (1 roll each).**
**EACH SERVING** *299 cal., 10 g fat
(5 g sat. fat), 141 mg chol., 396 mg
sodium, 11 g carb., 1 g fiber, 0 g sugars,
40 g pro.*

The chicken is wrapped around the filling, so it needs to be thin. Use the flat side of a meat mallet to gently pound chicken pieces to an even thickness of ¼ to ½ inch.

Layer chiles and cheese sticks near one long edge of pounded chicken pieces. Fold in the short sides to enclose the cheese; roll up chicken starting with the edge with the cheese. Use two or three toothpicks to secure.

BAKED CHICKEN
CHILES RELLENOS

# WHAT ARE CHILES RELLENOS? TRADITIONALLY, THEY'RE STUFFED, FRIED CHILE PEPPERS. WE TUCKED THE SAME FLAVORS INTO THE CHICKEN BEFORE COATING AND BAKING.

CHICKEN PICCATA

CHICKEN PARMESAN

EASY BALSAMIC CHICKEN

## CHICKEN PICCATA

**START TO FINISH** 35 minutes

⅓ cup all-purpose flour
½ tsp. salt
¼ tsp. black pepper
4 small skinless, boneless chicken breast halves (4 to 5 oz. each)
2 Tbsp. olive oil
¾ cup dry white wine or chicken broth
⅓ cup chicken broth
3 Tbsp. lemon juice
3 Tbsp. butter
2 Tbsp. drained capers
1 lemon, thinly sliced
2 Tbsp. chopped fresh Italian parsley

>> CHICKEN BREASTS can be swapped for veal cutlets (thinly sliced boneless veal). Cut veal into eight serving-size pieces. If necessary, flatten veal to ⅛-inch-thick pieces.

**1.** In a shallow dish combine flour, salt, and pepper. Cut each chicken breast half in half crosswise. Using the flat side of a meat mallet, flatten chicken between two pieces of plastic wrap to about ⅛ inch thick. Coat chicken with flour mixture.
**2.** In a 12-inch skillet heat oil over medium-high heat. Add chicken pieces, half at a time, to skillet. Cook about 4 minutes or until no longer pink, turning once. Transfer to platter; cover to keep warm.
**3.** For sauce, remove skillet from heat. Add wine and broth. Return skillet to heat. Bring to boiling; reduce heat. Simmer, uncovered, 6 minutes. Add lemon juice, butter, and capers, stirring until butter is melted. Return chicken to skillet with lemon slices; heat through. Transfer chicken and lemon to platter. Spoon sauce over chicken and lemon; sprinkle with parsley. If desired, serve with *hot cooked spaghetti.* **Makes 4 servings (3 oz. chicken + 3 Tbsp. sauce each).**
EACH SERVING *349 cal., 18 g fat (7 g sat. fat), 96 mg chol., 667 mg sodium, 12 g carb., 1 g fiber, 1 g sugars, 26 g pro.*

## CHICKEN PARMESAN

**HANDS-ON TIME** 25 minutes
**COOK** 25 minutes

1 Tbsp. butter
⅓ cup chopped onion
1 clove garlic, minced
1 14.5-oz. can diced tomatoes, undrained
½ tsp. sugar
⅛ tsp. salt
 Dash black pepper
¼ cup chopped fresh basil
4 skinless, boneless chicken breast halves (6 to 8 oz. each)
⅓ cup seasoned fine dry bread crumbs
4 Tbsp. grated Parmesan cheese
½ tsp. dried oregano, crushed
1 egg, lightly beaten
2 Tbsp. milk
3 Tbsp. olive oil or vegetable oil
¼ cup shredded mozzarella cheese (1 oz.)

**1.** For sauce, in a 2-qt. saucepan melt butter over medium heat. Add onion and garlic; cook until tender. Stir in tomatoes, sugar, salt, and pepper. Bring to boiling; reduce heat. Simmer about 10 minutes or until desired consistency, stirring occasionally. Stir in basil.
**2.** Meanwhile, using the flat side of a meat mallet, flatten chicken between two pieces of plastic wrap to about ¼ inch thick.
**3.** In a shallow bowl stir together bread crumbs, 3 Tbsp. of the Parmesan cheese, and the oregano. In a second bowl stir together egg and milk. Dip chicken into egg mixture; coat evenly with crumb mixture.
**4.** In a 12-inch skillet cook chicken in oil over medium heat 4 to 6 minutes or until golden, turning once.
**5.** Spoon sauce over chicken. Top with mozzarella and the remaining 1 Tbsp. Parmesan. Let stand 2 minutes. If desired, serve with *hot cooked pasta.* **Makes 4 servings (3 oz. chicken + ⅓ cup sauce each).**
EACH SERVING *398 cal., 19 g fat (6 g sat. fat), 151 mg chol., 761 mg sodium, 15 g carb., 2 g fiber, 5 g sugars, 41 g pro.*

## EASY BALSAMIC CHICKEN

**HANDS-ON TIME** 10 minutes
**MARINATE** 1 hour
**GRILL** 10 minutes

4 small skinless, boneless chicken breast halves (4 to 5 oz. each)
¼ cup balsamic vinegar
¼ cup olive oil
3 cloves garlic, minced
¼ tsp. salt
¼ tsp. crushed red pepper

**1.** Using the flat side of a meat mallet, flatten chicken between two pieces of plastic wrap to about ½ inch thick.
**2.** Place chicken in a shallow dish. In a bowl stir together the remaining ingredients. Pour over chicken, turning to coat. Cover and marinate in the refrigerator 1 to 4 hours.
**3.** Grill chicken, uncovered, over medium heat 10 to 12 minutes or until done (165°F) (grilling tips, *pp. 16–17*), turning and brushing with marinade once. Discard extra marinade. **Makes 4 servings (3 oz. chicken each).**
EACH SERVING *172 cal., 6 g fat (1 g sat. fat), 66 mg chol., 123 mg sodium, 1 g carb., 0 g fiber, 1 g sugars, 26 g pro.*

// MEAT, FISH & POULTRY //

## CHILI-GARLIC CHICKEN STIR-FRY

**START TO FINISH** 45 minutes

- 1  recipe Quick-Pickled Vegetables
- 2  Tbsp. reduced-sodium soy sauce
- 2  Tbsp. rice vinegar
- 1  Tbsp. Asian chili-garlic sauce
- 1  Tbsp. finely chopped fresh ginger
- 3  cloves garlic, minced
- 1  lb. skinless, boneless chicken breast halves, cut into 1-inch pieces
- 3  Tbsp. honey or packed brown sugar
- 2  tsp. cornstarch
- 8  oz. fresh green beans, trimmed
- 1  Tbsp. toasted sesame oil
- 1  Tbsp. canola oil
- ½  cup chopped onion
- ¾  cup chopped red sweet pepper
- 2  tsp. white and/or black sesame seeds, toasted

**1.** Prepare Quick-Pickled Vegetables; let stand. In a bowl combine the next five ingredients (through garlic). Transfer half of the mixture to a small bowl. Add chicken to the remaining mixture in a medium bowl. Toss to coat.

»

ASIAN CHILI-GARLIC SAUCE is a cousin to sriracha sauce—it's full of chopped chiles and lots of garlic. Look for it in jars in the Asian section of your supermarket.

Add honey and cornstarch to soy sauce mixture in the small bowl, stirring to dissolve cornstarch.
**2.** In a large wok cook beans in just enough boiling water to cover about 4 minutes or just until crisp-tender; drain beans in colander. Carefully wipe wok dry.
**3.** In the same wok heat sesame and canola oils over medium-high heat. Add onion and sweet pepper; cook and stir 4 to 5 minutes or until crisp-tender. Remove vegetables from the wok. Add half of the chicken to wok; cook and stir over medium-high heat 3 to 4 minutes or until chicken is no longer pink. Remove chicken from wok. Repeat with remaining chicken. Return chicken, green beans, onion, and sweet pepper to wok. Stir sauce well. Add to wok; cook and stir until thickened and bubbly.
**4.** Drain Quick-Pickled Vegetables. Top individual servings of chicken mixture with vegetables. Sprinkle with sesame seeds.
**Makes 4 servings (1⅓ cups chicken mixture + ⅓ cup vegetables each).**
**EACH SERVING** *344 cal., 11 g fat (2 g sat. fat), 83 mg chol., 564 mg sodium, 32 g carb., 4 g fiber, 24 g sugars, 29 g pro.*

### QUICK-PICKLED VEGETABLES

In a 1-qt. saucepan combine ½ cup each water and rice vinegar, ¼ cup sugar, ½ tsp. salt, and ⅛ tsp. crushed red pepper. Bring to boiling; reduce heat. Simmer, uncovered, 2 minutes. Remove from heat. Add 1 cup coarsely shredded napa cabbage, ½ cup each shredded carrots and thinly sliced red onion, and 1 tsp. finely chopped fresh ginger; stir until well combined. Cover and let stand at room temperature 30 to 60 minutes. Drain before serving.

## BUFFALO CHICKEN BURGERS

**START TO FINISH** 35 minutes

- 1½  lb. uncooked ground chicken
- 3  Tbsp. Buffalo wing sauce
- 1  Tbsp. vegetable oil
- 1  Tbsp. butter, melted
- ¼  cup light sour cream
- 2  Tbsp. mayonnaise
- 3  Tbsp. crumbled blue cheese
- 1  Tbsp. sliced green onion
- 4  ciabatta buns or hamburger buns, split and toasted (tip, p. 270)
- 4  1-oz. slices cheddar cheese (optional)
     Green leaf lettuce leaves
     Sliced tomato

**1.** In a bowl combine ground chicken and 2 Tbsp. of the Buffalo wing sauce; mix well. Shape mixture into four ¾-inch-thick patties.
**2.** In a 12-inch nonstick skillet heat oil over medium heat. Cook patties in hot oil 12 to 15 minutes or until done (165°F), turning once.
**3.** In a bowl combine melted butter and the remaining 1 Tbsp. Buffalo wing sauce. Brush butter mixture on both sides of patties.
**4.** Meanwhile, for blue cheese dressing, in a bowl stir together sour cream, mayonnaise, blue cheese, and green onion.
**5.** Serve patties in buns with cheddar cheese (if desired). Top with lettuce, tomato, and blue cheese dressing. **Makes 4 sandwiches.**
**EACH SANDWICH** *492 cal., 29 g fat (9 g sat. fat), 166 mg chol., 1,037 mg sodium, 24 g carb., 5 g fiber, 3 g sugars, 34 g pro.*

CHILI-GARLIC CHICKEN STIR-FRY

BUFFALO CHICKEN
BURGERS

BURRITO BOWLS

# BURRITO BOWLS

**START TO FINISH** 35 minutes

- 2 cups water
- 1 cup long grain white rice
- ½ tsp. salt
- 1 lb. skinless, boneless chicken breast halves or boneless pork loin, cut into thin bite-size strips
- 1 Tbsp. taco seasoning mix
  Nonstick cooking spray
- 1 fresh poblano chile pepper, cut into thin strips (tip, *p. 22*)
- 2 cups frozen whole kernel corn, thawed
- 1 cup canned black beans, rinsed and drained
- 1 lime
- 1 medium avocado, halved, seeded, and peeled
- 2 Tbsp. vegetable oil
- 5 cups shredded romaine lettuce
- 1 cup refrigerated pico de gallo
- ¼ cup shredded Mexican-style four-cheese blend (1 oz.)
  Lime wedges and/or chopped fresh cilantro (optional)

**1.** In a 2-qt. saucepan combine the water, rice, and ¼ tsp. of the salt. Bring to boiling; reduce heat. Cover; simmer 15 minutes. Do not lift cover. Remove from heat. Let stand, covered, 10 minutes. Fluff rice with a fork.

**2.** Meanwhile, in a bowl toss together chicken strips, 2 tsp. of the taco seasoning, and the remaining ¼ tsp. salt. Coat a 12-inch nonstick skillet with cooking spray; heat over medium-high heat. Cook chicken and poblano pepper in hot skillet 4 to 6 minutes or until chicken is no longer pink, stirring occasionally.

Reduce heat to medium-low. Add corn and beans; cook about 2 minutes or until heated.

**3.** Remove ½ tsp. zest and squeeze 3 Tbsp. juice from lime. In a bowl mash together avocado and lime zest. In another bowl whisk together oil, the remaining 1 tsp. taco seasoning, and the lime juice.

**4.** Divide lettuce among six bowls. Add rice and chicken mixture. Spoon avocado mixture into centers of bowls. Top with pico de gallo and cheese. Drizzle with lime juice mixture. If desired, serve with lime wedges and/or cilantro.

**Makes 6 servings (1 bowl each).**

**EACH SERVING** *415 cal., 12 g fat (3 g sat. fat), 59 mg chol., 662 mg sodium, 51 g carb., 5 g fiber, 4 g sugars, 25 g pro.*

**WHAT ARE SHEET-PAN DINNERS?** THESE ONE-PAN MEALS START WITH THE ALL-PURPOSE SHEET PAN (A SHALLOW-RIMMED 15×10-INCH BAKING PAN). THE MEAT AND VEGGIES ARE ROASTED TOGETHER, AND CLEANUP IS EXTRA EASY (ESPECIALLY IF YOU LINE THE PAN WITH FOIL).

## ROAST TURKEY SHEET-PAN DINNER

**HANDS-ON TIME** 15 minutes
**ROAST** 35 minutes at 400°F

|   | Nonstick cooking spray |
|---|---|
| ½ | tsp. onion powder |
| ½ | tsp. garlic powder |
| ½ | tsp. black pepper |
| ½ | tsp. salt |
| 2 | turkey breast tenderloins (1½ lb. total) |
| 3 | carrots, peeled and cut into bite-size pieces |
| 2 | tsp. olive oil |
| ½ | cup orange marmalade |
| 1 | Tbsp. grated fresh ginger |
| 1 | lb. fresh Brussels sprouts, trimmed and halved |

**1.** Preheat oven to 400°F. Lightly coat 15×10-inch baking pan with cooking spray. For rub, in a bowl stir together onion powder, garlic powder, pepper, and ¼ tsp. of the salt. Sprinkle over turkey; rub in with your fingers. Place tenderloins in one side of the prepared pan.
**2.** In a bowl toss carrots with olive oil to coat. Place carrots in opposite side of baking pan. Roast, uncovered, 15 minutes.
**3.** Meanwhile, in a 2-qt. saucepan combine orange marmalade, ginger, and the remaining ¼ tsp. salt. Heat and stir over low heat until melted. Reserve 2 Tbsp. of the marmalade mixture. Add Brussels sprouts to the saucepan; stir to coat. Add Brussels sprouts to carrots in baking pan after

15 minutes of roasting; stir to combine. Brush turkey with the reserved marmalade mixture.

**4.** Roast, uncovered, 20 to 25 minutes more or until turkey is done (165°F) and vegetables are tender, stirring vegetables once. Slice turkey; serve with vegetables. **Makes 6 servings (3 oz. turkey + 1 cup vegetables each).**

EACH SERVING *260 cal., 3 g fat (1 g sat. fat), 51 mg chol., 325 mg sodium, 31 g carb., 5 g fiber, 21 g sugars, 30 g pro.*

# TURKEY SKEWERS WITH NECTARINE SALSA

**HANDS-ON TIME** 40 minutes
**MARINATE** 30 minutes
**GRILL** 16 minutes

¼  cup fresh lime juice
2  tsp. olive oil
1  tsp. dried oregano, crushed
1  tsp. ground cumin
½  tsp. cayenne pepper
¼  tsp. salt
1¼  lb. turkey breast tenderloins, cut crosswise into eight 1½-inch-thick slices
1  recipe Nectarine Salsa
1  large red onion, cut into 8 wedges

**1.** For marinade, in a large resealable plastic bag set in a shallow dish combine the first six ingredients (through salt). Add turkey pieces; seal bag. Turn to coat. Marinate in the refrigerator 30 minutes to 8 hours, turning bag occasionally.

**2.** If using wooden skewers, soak in water 30 minutes. Just before grilling, prepare Nectarine Salsa. Coat onion wedges with *nonstick cooking spray.* On eight 6-inch skewers thread onions and turkey pieces.

**3.** Grill skewers, covered, over medium heat 16 to 20 minutes or until turkey is done (170°F), turning occasionally (grilling tips, *pp. 16–17*). Serve turkey skewers with Nectarine Salsa. **Makes 4 servings (2 slices turkey + 2 onion wedges + ⅓ cup salsa each).**

EACH SERVING *230 cal., 4 g fat (1 g sat. fat), 63 mg chol., 705 mg sodium, 21 g carb., 2 g fiber, 13 g sugars, 27 g pro.*

**CHANGE IT UP**

*Turn this knife-and-fork meal into a sandwich. Wrap the turkey, onion wedges, and salsa in soft pitas and add a sprinkle of queso fresco.*

### *NECTARINE SALSA*

In a medium bowl combine 2 Tbsp. each peach or apricot preserves and lime juice, 1 Tbsp. chopped fresh cilantro, and ⅛ tsp. each salt and cayenne pepper. Stir in 1 cup chopped nectarines and ¼ cup each finely chopped red onion and finely chopped green sweet pepper.

# FISH AND CHIPS

**START TO FINISH** 1 hour

| | |
|---|---|
| 1 | lb. fresh or frozen skinless fish fillets, about ½ inch thick |
| 1¼ | lb. medium potatoes (about 4) |
| | Vegetable oil or shortening for deep-fat frying |
| 1 | cup all-purpose flour |
| ½ | cup beer |
| 1 | egg |
| ¼ | tsp. baking powder |
| ¼ | tsp. salt |
| ¼ | tsp. black pepper |
| | Coarse salt |
| | Serve-alongs, such as Tartar Sauce (*opposite*), malt vinegar or cider vinegar, and/or lemon wedges (optional) |

**1.** Thaw fish if frozen (tip, *p. 172*). Preheat oven to 300°F. Cut fish into 3×2-inch pieces. Cover and chill until needed.
**2.** For chips, cut the potatoes lengthwise into ½-inch-wide wedges. Pat dry with paper towels. In a 3-qt. saucepan or deep-fat fryer heat 2 inches vegetable oil to 375°F. Fry potatoes, one-fourth at a time, 4 to 6 minutes or until tender and light brown. Remove potatoes; drain on paper towels. Transfer potatoes to a wire rack set on a baking sheet, arranging them in a single layer. Keep warm in oven.
**3.** Meanwhile, place ½ cup of the flour in a shallow dish. For batter, in a bowl whisk together the remaining ½ cup flour and the next five ingredients (through pepper) until smooth. Coat fish with flour; shake off excess. Dip into batter to coat.
**4.** Fry fish, two or three pieces at a time, in the hot (375°F) oil 4 to 6 minutes or until coating is golden brown and fish flakes easily, turning once. Drain fish on paper towels. Transfer fish to a second baking sheet; keep warm in oven while frying remaining fish. Sprinkle

fish and chips with coarse salt. If desired, serve with serve-alongs.
**Makes 4 servings (3 oz. fish + 8 potato wedges each).**

EACH SERVING 552 cal., 29 g fat (4 g sat. fat), 101 mg chol., 449 mg sodium, 43 g carb., 4 g fiber, 1 g sugars, 27 g pro.

# PAN-FRIED FISH

**START TO FINISH** 20 minutes

1  lb. fresh or frozen skinless fish fillets, ½ to ¾ inch thick
1  egg, lightly beaten
2  Tbsp. water
⅔  cup cornmeal or fine dry bread crumbs
½  tsp. salt
   Dash black pepper
   Vegetable oil or shortening for frying
1  recipe Tartar Sauce (optional)

**1.** Thaw fish if frozen (tip, p. 172). Cut into four serving-size pieces. In a shallow dish combine egg and the water. In another shallow dish combine cornmeal, salt, and pepper. Dip fish into egg mixture; coat with cornmeal mixture.
**2.** Preheat oven to 300°F. In a 10-inch skillet heat ¼ inch vegetable oil. Add half of the fish in a single layer; fry on one side until golden. Turn carefully. Fry until second side is golden and fish flakes easily. Allow 3 to 4 minutes per side. Drain on paper towels. Keep warm in oven while frying remaining fish. If desired, serve with Tartar Sauce and/or *lemon wedges* and/or *fresh dill*. **Makes 4 servings (1 piece each).**

EACH SERVING 255 cal., 13 g fat (2 g sat. fat), 101 mg chol., 230 mg sodium, 12 g carb., 1 g fiber, 0 g sugars, 23 g pro.

Gently press each egg-coated fish piece in the cornmeal mixture to coat the fish; turn the piece over to coat the other side.

When the first side of the fish is golden, flip each portion over using a large spatula and a fork to steady the piece. When turning the fish, be careful to avoid splattering oil. Cook until the second side is golden.

To test for doneness, insert the tines of a fork into the fish and gently twist. It should easily flake when done. Check it at the minimum cooking time.

PAN-FRIED FISH

## TARTAR SAUCE

In a bowl stir together ¾ cup mayonnaise, ¼ cup sweet or dill pickle relish, 2 Tbsp. finely chopped onion, 1 Tbsp. chopped fresh dill or 1 tsp. dried dill, 1 tsp. lemon juice, and, if desired, 2 tsp. capers, drained. Cover and chill at least 2 hours and up to 1 week.

**POTATO CHIP PAN-FRIED FISH** Prepare as directed, except substitute 1⅓ cups finely crushed potato chips (about 4 cups chips) or saltine crackers for the cornmeal and omit salt.

**SPICY-HOT PAN-FRIED FISH** Prepare as directed, except omit black pepper. Reduce cornmeal to ¼ cup and combine with ¼ cup all-purpose flour, ¾ tsp. cayenne pepper, and ½ tsp. each chili powder, garlic powder, and paprika.

## BROILED FISH WITH ROSEMARY

**START TO FINISH** 20 minutes

**THAWING FISH**
The best way to thaw fish is to let it gradually in the fridge overnight. If you must thaw fish quickly, place it in a resealable plastic bag and immerse in cold water. If it will be cooked immediately after thawing, you can microwave it on the defrost setting, stopping when fish is still icy but pliable.

4    4- to 6-oz. fresh or frozen skinless halibut or salmon fillets, cut ½ to 1 inch thick
2    tsp. olive oil
2    tsp. lemon juice
⅛    tsp. salt
⅛    tsp. black pepper
2    cloves garlic, minced
1    Tbsp. capers, rinsed and drained
1    tsp. finely chopped fresh rosemary or parsley

**1.** Thaw fish if frozen (tip, *left*). Preheat broiler. Measure thickness of fish. Brush fish with oil and lemon juice; sprinkle with salt and pepper. Sprinkle garlic on fish; rub in with your fingers.
**2.** Place fish on the greased unheated rack of a broiler pan. Broil 4 to 5 inches from heat or until fish flakes easily. Allow 4 to 6 minutes per ½-inch thickness of fish, turning once if fish is 1 inch thick or more. Before serving, top fish with capers and rosemary. **Makes 4 servings (1 fillet each).**

**EACH SERVING** *127 cal., 4 g fat (1 g sat. fat), 56 mg chol., 201 mg sodium, 1 g carb., 0 g fiber, 0 g sugars, 21 g pro.*

BROILED FISH WITH ROSEMARY

TILAPIA VERACRUZ

**BROILER PAN** The broiler pan is a special two-piece slotted pan that allows fat and juices to drip away (similar to a grill). For easy cleanup, you can line both parts of the pan with foil; just cut slits in the foil on the slotted part. If you don't have a broiler pan, use a foil-lined shallow-rimmed baking pan.

## TILAPIA VERACRUZ

**START TO FINISH** 25 minutes

»

THE FISH
FILLETS can
be replaced
with 1 lb.
cooked peeled
and deveined
shrimp. Add
to skillet in
Step 3 and
heat through.

4   6- to 8-oz. fresh or frozen
    skinless tilapia, red snapper,
    mahi mahi, or other fish fillets,
    1 inch thick
1   Tbsp. olive oil
1   small onion, cut into thin
    wedges
1   fresh jalapeño chile pepper,
    seeded and finely chopped
    (tip, *p. 22*) (optional)
1   clove garlic, minced
1   14.5-oz. can diced tomatoes,
    undrained
1   cup sliced fresh cremini or
    button mushrooms
¾   cup pimiento-stuffed olives,
    coarsely chopped
1   Tbsp. chopped fresh oregano
    or ½ tsp. dried oregano,
    crushed
¼   tsp. salt
⅛   tsp. black pepper
2   cups hot cooked rice

**1.** Thaw fish if frozen (tip, *opposite*).
**2.** For sauce, in a 12-inch skillet heat
olive oil over medium heat. Add
onion, chile pepper (if desired), and
garlic; cook and stir 2 to 3 minutes
or until onion is tender. Add the
next six ingredients (through black
pepper). Bring to boiling.
**3.** Place fish in skillet, spooning
sauce over fish. Return to boiling;
reduce heat. Simmer, covered, 8 to
10 minutes or just until fish flakes.
Carefully lift fish from skillet to a
serving dish. Spoon sauce over fish.
Serve with hot cooked rice. **Makes
4 servings (1 fillet + ½ cup sauce +
½ cup rice each).**
**EACH SERVING** *363 cal., 10 g fat (2 g
sat. fat), 84 mg chol., 1,111 mg sodium,
31 g carb., 3 g fiber, 5 g sugars,
38 g pro.*

## PARMESAN-CRUSTED COD

**HANDS-ON TIME** 20 minutes
**BAKE** 15 minutes at 400°F

4   5- to 6-oz. fresh or frozen
    skinless cod fillets, 1 inch thick
2   medium zucchini and/or yellow
    summer squash, cut into
    ¾-inch pieces (about 3 cups)
2   cloves garlic, minced
¼   cup olive oil
¼   tsp. black pepper
¼   cup panko bread crumbs
    (tip, *p. 108*)
¼   cup grated Parmesan cheese
2   Tbsp. chopped fresh parsley
⅛   tsp. salt

**1.** Thaw fish if frozen (tip, *opposite*).
Preheat oven to 400°F. In a
15×10-inch baking pan combine
squash and garlic. Drizzle with
2 Tbsp. of the oil; toss to coat. Place
fish in pan with squash in a single
layer. Sprinkle fish and squash with
pepper. In a bowl combine panko,
Parmesan cheese, parsley, and salt.
Drizzle with the remaining 2 Tbsp.
oil; toss to coat. Sprinkle Parmesan
mixture on top of fish; press lightly
to adhere.
**2.** Bake about 15 minutes or until
fish flakes easily and crumbs are
golden. If desired, sprinkle with
additional chopped fresh parsley.
**Makes 4 servings (1 fillet + ½ cup
vegetables each).**
**EACH SERVING** *289 cal., 16 g fat
(3 g sat. fat), 65 mg chol., 260 mg
sodium, 7 g carb., 1 g fiber, 3 g sugars,
28 g pro.*

PARMESAN-CRUSTED COD

**3.** Fold parchment over fish and vegetables; fold open edges of parchment several times to secure. Place packets in two shallow baking pans. Place pans on separate oven racks. Bake about 20 minutes or until fish flakes easily. Carefully open packets. If desired, sprinkle with additional snipped fresh oregano. **Makes 4 servings (1 packet each). EACH SERVING** *417 cal., 14 g fat (2 g sat. fat), 71 mg chol., 654 mg sodium, 38 g carb., 3 g fiber, 4 g sugars, 35 g pro.*

## FISH TACOS WITH LIME SAUCE

**START TO FINISH** 30 minutes

| | |
|---|---|
| 1 | lb. fresh or frozen catfish or other whitefish fillets |
| 3 | limes |
| ½ | cup mayonnaise |
| 1 | tsp. chili powder |
| ⅓ | cup all-purpose flour |
| ½ | tsp. salt |
| 2 | Tbsp. vegetable oil |
| 8 | taco shells or 6-inch flour tortillas, warmed |
| 1 | cup shredded cabbage |
| ½ | cup shredded carrot |
| 1 | fresh jalapeño or serrano chile pepper, thinly sliced (tip, p. 22) |

**1.** Thaw fish if frozen (tip, p. 172). Cut fish into 1-inch pieces.
**2.** For sauce, squeeze the juice from two of the limes into a bowl; stir in mayonnaise and chili powder. Cut the remaining lime into wedges. Transfer ⅓ cup of the sauce to a medium bowl. Add fish; toss gently to coat.
**3.** In a shallow dish stir together flour and salt. Add fish pieces, a few at a time, tossing to coat. In a 10-inch skillet heat oil over medium heat.

## SPANISH COD AND ORZO PACKETS

**HANDS-ON TIME** 20 minutes
**BAKE** 20 minutes at 350°F

| | |
|---|---|
| 4 | 4- to 6-oz. fresh or frozen cod or other whitefish fillets |
| 1 | cup dried orzo |
| 1 | Tbsp. chopped fresh oregano |
| 1 | cup red and/or yellow cherry or grape tomatoes, halved |
| ¾ | cup halved pimiento-stuffed green and/or Kalamata olives |
| 1 | small onion, cut into very thin wedges |
| 4 | cloves garlic, thinly sliced |
| 2 | Tbsp. olive oil |
| 2 | Tbsp. lemon juice |
| ¼ | tsp. salt |
| ¼ | tsp. black pepper |
| 1 | lemon, thinly sliced |

**1.** Thaw fish if frozen (tip, p. 172). Preheat oven to 350°F. Cut four 15-inch squares of parchment paper. Cook orzo according to package directions. Stir oregano into cooked orzo. Spoon orzo onto one side of each sheet of parchment. Layer the next four ingredients (through garlic) next to orzo. Top with fish fillets.
**2.** Stir together the olive oil, lemon juice, salt, and pepper. Drizzle over fish and vegetables. Top with lemon slices.

Add fish, about one-third at a time, and cook 2 to 4 minutes or just until fish flakes, turning to brown evenly and adding more oil as needed during cooking. Remove with a slotted spoon and drain on paper towels.

**4.** Fill taco shells (if using) with fish, cabbage, carrot, and jalapeño pepper. (If using tortillas, lay each tortilla on a flat surface; layer ingredients down center. Fold sides over filling.) Serve with the remaining sauce and reserved lime wedges. **Makes 4 servings (2 tacos each).**

EACH SERVING *652 cal., 39 g fat (5 g sat. fat), 67 mg chol., 557 mg sodium, 41 g carb., 2 g fiber, 2 g sugars, 31 g pro.*

# SALMON WITH TOMATOES AND OLIVES

**START TO FINISH** 30 minutes

| | |
|---|---|
| 4 | **4-oz. fresh or frozen skinless salmon fillets** |
| | **Salt and black pepper** |
| 1 | **Tbsp. olive oil** |
| ¼ | **cup sliced shallots** |
| 2 | **cloves garlic, minced** |
| 2 | **cups red and/or yellow grape or cherry tomatoes, halved if large** |
| ½ | **cup halved pitted Kalamata olives** |
| | **Zest of 1 small orange, cut into strips** |
| | **Small fresh oregano leaves** |

**1.** Thaw salmon if frozen (tip, *p. 172*). Season with salt and pepper. In a 12-inch nonstick skillet heat oil over medium-high heat. Add salmon and cook 6 to 8 minutes or just until fish flakes, turning once. Remove fish from skillet; cover to keep warm.

**2.** In the same skillet cook shallots and garlic over medium heat 2 to 3 minutes or until tender. Add tomatoes; cook 2 to 3 minutes or until tomatoes soften and begin to juice. Stir in olives and orange zest.

**3.** Return salmon to skillet. Sprinkle with oregano. **Makes 4 servings (1 fillet + ½ cup tomatoes each).**

EACH SERVING *257 cal., 13 g fat (2 g sat. fat), 62 mg chol., 316 mg sodium, 11 g carb., 3 g fiber, 5 g sugars, 24 g pro.*

FISH TACOS WITH LIME SAUCE

SALMON WITH TOMATOES AND OLIVES

# PLANK-SMOKED SALMON

**HANDS-ON TIME** 25 minutes
**SOAK** 1 hour
**MARINATE** 1 hour
**GRILL** 30 minutes

1   2-lb. fresh or frozen salmon fillet with skin
1   grilling plank (15×6½×⅜-inch) (tip, *below*)
¼   cup reduced-sodium soy sauce
¼   cup balsamic vinegar
3   Tbsp. honey
1   Tbsp. grated fresh ginger
½   tsp. crushed red pepper
3   red, yellow, and/or orange sweet peppers
3   Tbsp. thinly sliced fresh basil
2   Tbsp. chopped pitted Kalamata olives
2   tsp. olive oil
2   tsp. balsamic vinegar
¼   tsp. salt
¼   tsp. black pepper
¼   cup bias-sliced green onions

**1.** Thaw salmon if frozen. (tip, *p. 172*). Soak grilling plank in enough water to cover at least 1 hour before grilling.
**2.** For marinade, in a bowl stir together the next five ingredients (through crushed red pepper). Place salmon in a large resealable plastic bag set in a shallow dish. Pour marinade over salmon. Seal bag; turn to coat salmon. Marinate in the refrigerator 1 hour, turning occasionally. (Marinating longer will affect the flavor and texture of the fish.) Remove salmon from marinade; discard marinade.

**GRILLING PLANKS** Made out of wood, grilling planks provide a level surface for delicate foods—like fish—to sit on while imparting a light, smoky flavor to the food. Cedar and alder are most common woods used for this purpose. To get a good level of smoke (and avoid a fire), soak the planks in water for 1 hour before using. Fill a large shallow pan with water and weight the plank down under a bowl of water or filled jar. Look for planks in the grilling section of hardware and home supply stores.

BAJA MUSSELS

**3.** Grill sweet peppers, covered, over medium heat 10 to 12 minutes or until blistered and charred, turning occasionally (grilling tips, *pp. 16–17*). Wrap peppers in foil, folding edges together to enclose peppers; let stand 15 minutes. Using a knife, loosen edges of skins; gently pull off skins in strips and discard. Chop peppers into ½-inch pieces, discarding stems, seeds, and membranes.
**4.** While peppers are standing, grill the plank, uncovered, over medium heat 3 to 5 minutes or until plank begins to crackle and smoke. Place salmon fillet, skin side down, on plank. Grill, covered, 18 to 22 minutes or just until fish flakes.
**5.** In a medium bowl stir together the chopped sweet peppers and the next six ingredients (through black pepper). Sprinkle salmon with green onions and serve with sweet pepper mixture. **Makes 8 servings (4 oz. salmon + 3 Tbsp. sweet pepper mixture each).**
EACH SERVING *196 cal., 9 g fat (1 g sat. fat), 62 mg chol., 197 mg sodium, 5 g carb., 1 g fiber, 3 g sugars, 23 g pro.*

**SALMON CAKES** If you are only serving Plank-Smoked Salmon to four people, save the other half of the prepared Plank-Smoked Salmon (chill up to 3 days) for Salmon Cakes. In a large bowl beat 1 egg with a fork. Stir in ¾ cup soft bread crumbs, ¼ cup thinly sliced green onions, and 1 Tbsp. chopped fresh basil or cilantro. Using two forks, flake the chilled leftover salmon (about 15 oz.) into small pieces. Add salmon to bread crumb mixture; stir to combine. Using your hands, shape mixture into four ¾-inch-thick cakes. In a 12-inch skillet heat 1 Tbsp. each butter and olive oil over medium heat. Add salmon cakes in a single layer in skillet. Cook about 8 minutes or until done (160°F) and lightly browned, turning once. For topping, in a small bowl stir together ¼ cup each mayonnaise and sour cream, 1 Tbsp. chopped fresh cilantro, 1 tsp. lime zest, and 1 Tbsp. lime juice. Serve with salmon cakes and, if desired, *lime wedges* and *fresh cilantro sprigs.*

MUSSELS are perfect for special occasions—especially as an appetizer. For more tips on buying, storing, and preparing them, see *p. 178.*

## BAJA MUSSELS
**START TO FINISH** 30 minutes

1    lb. fresh mussels
2    Tbsp. butter
½    cup chopped onion
1    fresh jalapeño chile pepper, seeded and finely chopped (tip, *p. 22*)
4    cloves garlic, sliced
1    cup chopped tomato
½    cup dry white wine
     Serve-alongs, such as toasted pine nuts, chopped fresh cilantro, lime wedges, and/or toasted baguette slices (optional)

**1.** Scrub mussels under cold running water. If present, remove beards (tip, *p. 178*).
**2.** In a 12-inch deep skillet melt butter over medium heat. Add onion, jalapeño pepper, and garlic; cook about 5 minutes or until tender, stirring occasionally. Stir in tomato and wine; add mussels.
**3.** Bring to boiling; reduce heat. Simmer, covered, 3 to 4 minutes or until shells open. Discard mussels that do not open. Add desired serve-alongs. **Makes 4 servings (10 mussels + ⅓ cup broth each).**
EACH SERVING *269 cal., 19 g fat (6 g sat. fat), 61 mg chol., 287 mg sodium, 14 g carb., 1 g fiber, 3 g sugars, 7 g pro.*

// MEAT, FISH & POULTRY //

## KNOW YOUR SHELLFISH

**SHRIMP** are available as farmed or wild-caught. The size of shrimp can vary from miniature to colossal, so double-check what your recipe calls for to maintain accurate cooking times.

Shrimp are crustaceans with flexible outer shells that need to be removed. If you buy them with the shell on, here's an easy way to remove: From the back, pinch off and pull the shell away from the shrimp, then pinch off the tail. To devein the shrimp, make a shallow cut next to the dark intestinal vein that runs down the back of the shrimp. Use the tip of the knife to pull it out of the shrimp. If necessary to rinse away any residue, wash the shrimp under running water.

**SCALLOPS** are the adductor muscle of the bivalve scallop mollusk. Look for scallops that are creamy beige to light pink in color. Scallops vary widely in size, but small ones are often more tender and sweet than large ones. Buy the size recommended in the recipe so the cooking times are accurate.

**CLAMS\*** are bivalve mollusks found in varying sizes and varieties in coastal regions of the United States. Like mussels, the shells need to be scrubbed before preparation.

**MUSSELS\*** have dark, elongated shells. Choose smaller mussels when available—the meat will be more tender. When harvested, mussels have fibers called beards or byssal threads extending from their shells. These filaments allow the mussels to attach themselves to surfaces in the sea. The beards are usually removed before you purchase them. If you discover a beard still attached, remove it by grasping it between your thumb and forefinger. Wriggle it back and forth while pulling out. Before cooking the mussels, scrub the shells with a food brush to remove any debris.

**\*NOTE** To guarantee freshness, clams, mussels, and oysters are sold live with tightly closed shells. Check each one while you're scrubbing—the shell should be free from cracks and tightly closed. If the shell is gaping slightly, tap it gently on the counter. The mollusk should react by shutting its shell. If it doesn't (which means it has already died and is possibly spoiled), throw it away. Refrigerate live clams and mussels, covered with a moist cloth, in an open container up to 2 days.

## GRILLED MARGARITA SHRIMP AND SCALLOP SKEWERS

**HANDS-ON TIME** 40 minutes
**GRILL** 8 minutes

| | |
|---|---|
| 20 | large fresh or frozen sea scallops (about 1¾ lb. total) |
| 20 | large fresh or frozen shrimp (about 12 oz. total) |
| ¼ | cup tequila |
| ¼ | cup lime juice |
| ¼ | cup olive oil |
| 2 | Tbsp. chopped fresh oregano |
| 2 | tsp. sugar |
| 2 | tsp. salt |
| 4 | cloves garlic, sliced |
| ½ | tsp. paprika |
| 1 | 1- to 1¼-lb. jicama, peeled and cut into bite-size strips (4 cups) |
| 1 | medium avocado, halved, seeded, peeled, and thinly sliced |
| ½ | cup fresh cilantro leaves |
| | Black pepper |

**1.** Thaw scallops and shrimp if frozen. If using wooden skewers, soak in water 30 minutes. Peel and devein shrimp. Place scallops and shrimp in a large resealable plastic bag set in a shallow dish.

**2.** In a small bowl stir together next eight ingredients (through paprika).

Set aside ½ cup of the tequila mixture to use in the jicama slaw. Pour the remaining tequila mixture over the scallops and shrimp. Seal bag; turn to coat scallops and shrimp. Marinate at room temperature 15 minutes, turning bag occasionally.

**3.** Meanwhile, for the jicama slaw, in a bowl combine jicama, avocado, and cilantro. Pour the reserved ½ cup tequila mixture over jicama mixture. Toss to combine. Season to taste with pepper. Cover and chill until ready to serve.

**4.** Drain scallops and shrimp; discard marinade. On six long skewers alternately thread scallops and shrimp, leaving ¼ inch between pieces. Grill skewers, covered, over medium-high heat 8 to 10 minutes or until scallops and shrimp are opaque, turning once (grilling tips, *pp. 16–17*). Serve skewers with jicama slaw and, if desired, *lime wedges*. **Makes 6 servings (1 skewer + ⅔ cup slaw each).**

**EACH SERVING** *297 cal., 10 g fat (1 g sat. fat), 123 mg chol., 762 mg sodium, 14 g carb., 6 g fiber, 1 g sugars, 33 g pro.*

GRILLED MARGARITA SHRIMP AND SCALLOP SKEWERS

THAI GREEN CURRY SEAFOOD

# THAI GREEN CURRY SEAFOOD

**START TO FINISH** 35 minutes

COCONUT MILK separates in the can, so before measuring, give it a good stir.

»

»

FISH SAUCE and CURRY PASTE are widely available and can be found in the Asian food aisle of most supermarkets. (Same goes for jasmine rice.)

1 lb. medium shrimp in shells, peeled and deveined, and/or sea scallops
1 Tbsp. canola oil
3 cloves garlic, minced
1 cup canned unsweetened coconut milk
⅓ cup reduced-sodium chicken broth
1 Tbsp. fish sauce
2 tsp. packed brown sugar
2 Tbsp. green or yellow curry paste or 3 Tbsp. red curry paste
1 medium red or yellow sweet pepper, seeded and cut into thin bite-size strips
½ of a small eggplant, peeled if desired, cut into bite-size pieces (2 cups)
¼ cup thinly sliced fresh basil leaves
1 tsp. lime zest
2 cups Hot Cooked Jasmine Rice

**1.** Thaw shrimp and/or scallops if frozen. In a wok or 10-inch nonstick skillet heat oil over medium-high heat. Add garlic; cook 30 seconds.
**2.** Stir in coconut milk, broth, fish sauce, and brown sugar. Whisk in curry paste. Bring mixture to boiling. Boil gently, uncovered, 5 minutes, stirring occasionally. Stir in the seafood, sweet pepper, and eggplant. Boil gently about 5 minutes more or until seafood turns opaque, vegetables are just tender, and sauce has thickened slightly, stirring occasionally.
**3.** Remove from heat. Stir the ¼ cup thinly sliced basil leaves and the lime zest into seafood mixture. Serve over hot cooked rice. If desired, top with additional fresh basil and serve with *lime wedges*.

Makes 4 servings (1 cup seafood mixture + ½ cup rice each).
**EACH SERVING** *368 cal., 16 g fat (11 g sat. fat), 137 mg chol., 887 mg sodium, 34 g carb., 4 g fiber, 5 g sugars, 22 g pro.*

## *HOT COOKED JASMINE RICE*

Pour any remaining canned coconut milk into a measuring cup; add enough water to equal 2¼ cups. In a 2-qt. saucepan combine coconut milk mixture and 1 cup uncooked jasmine rice. Bring to boiling; reduce heat. Simmer, covered, 20 minutes or until the liquid is absorbed and rice is tender.

**CHANGE IT UP**

*Substitute 12 oz. skinless, boneless chicken thighs, cut into 1-inch strips, for the seafood. Add after whisking in curry paste in Step 2.*

// MEAT, FISH & POULTRY //

**CURRY PASTE** Because each type of curry paste is made with different chiles, aromatic herbs, and spices, the flavor of your dish will change based on which variety you use. Turmeric is added to yellow curry paste along with red chiles to deepen the color. Red curry paste is made with red chiles and often includes chili powder for richer flavor. Green curry paste is made with green chiles and may include some coriander, basil, and/or kaffir lime leaves. They're all spicy (green and yellow slightly more so than red), so if you're nervous, start with less. You can always add more after the 5-minute simmering time.

# MEATLESS

TEST KITCHEN

**MAKE-AHEAD RECIPE.** See also cooking charts, *pp. 68–69.*

WALNUT-LENTIL BURGERS

**FRESH ON TOP**
We love toppings! Pile the patties with fresh, vibrant ingredients such as basil or other herbs, sautéed red sweet peppers, and a little mayonnaise for richness.

**FIERY QUINOA PATTIES**

# FIERY QUINOA PATTIES

**START TO FINISH** 35 minutes

⅓ cup shredded carrot
⅓ cup shredded broccoli slaw mix
⅓ cup thinly sliced green onions
1 lime
2 eggs
2 Tbsp. reduced-sodium soy sauce
¼ tsp. salt
¼ tsp. cayenne pepper
1 cup cooked quinoa, cooled
1 cup canned cannellini (white kidney) beans, rinsed, drained, and coarsely mashed
½ cup fine dry bread crumbs
2 Tbsp. canola oil
¼ cup chopped roasted peanuts
¼ cup chopped fresh cilantro
8 Bibb lettuce leaves

**1.** In a food processor combine carrot, broccoli slaw, and ¼ cup of the green onions. Cover; pulse until finely chopped.
**2.** Remove 1 tsp. zest and squeeze 2 Tbsp. juice from lime. In a bowl whisk together lime juice and next four ingredients (through cayenne pepper). Add carrot mixture, quinoa, beans, and bread crumbs; mix well. Using damp hands, shape into eight ¾-inch-thick patties.
**3.** In a 10-inch nonstick skillet heat 1 Tbsp. of the oil over medium heat. Add four patties; cook 6 to 8 minutes or until golden and heated through, turning once. Remove from skillet. Repeat with remaining oil and patties.
**4.** In a bowl combine remaining green onions, lime zest, peanuts, and cilantro. Serve patties with peanut mixture, lettuce, and *lime wedges*. **Makes 4 servings (2 patties each).**

**EACH SERVING** *326 cal., 15 g fat (2 g sat. fat), 93 mg chol., 751 mg sodium, 35 g carb., 6 g fiber, 4 g sugars, 14 g pro.*

》

**COOKED QUINOA** can be made up to 3 days ahead and chilled. In a 1- or 1½-qt. saucepan combine ¾ cup reduced-sodium chicken broth and ¼ cup rinsed and drained quinoa. Bring to boiling; reduce heat. Simmer, covered, 15 minutes or until quinoa is tender.

# WALNUT-LENTIL BURGERS

**START TO FINISH** 1 hour

3 Tbsp. olive oil
6 oz. fresh mushrooms, finely chopped (2¼ cups)
2 cups cooked brown lentils
1 cup walnut pieces
1 tsp. dried herbes de Provence
1 egg, lightly beaten
½ cup fine dry bread crumbs
4 sourdough hamburger buns, split and toasted (optional) Toppings (optional) *(opposite)*

**1.** In a 12-inch skillet heat 1 Tbsp. of the oil over medium heat. Add mushrooms; cook and stir 6 minutes or until tender and liquid is evaporated.
**2.** In a food processor combine mushrooms, 1 cup of the lentils, ½ cup of the walnut pieces, the herbes de Provence, ½ tsp. *salt*, and ½ tsp. *black pepper*. Cover; pulse until nearly smooth. In a large bowl combine egg and bread crumbs; stir in mushroom mixture and remaining 1 cup lentils. Shape into four ½-inch-thick patties. Coat with remaining ½ cup walnuts, pressing to adhere.
**3.** In same skillet heat remaining 2 Tbsp. oil over medium heat. Add patties; cook about 6 minutes or until heated through, turning once. If desired, serve burgers in buns with toppings. **Makes 4 servings (1 patty each).**

**EACH SERVING** *448 cal., 32 g fat (4 g sat. fat), 47 mg chol., 425 mg sodium, 31 g carb., 6 g fiber, 3 g sugars, 15 g pro.*

**LENTILS** The many varieties and colors of lentils *(p. 192)* are easy to find in supermarkets, but brown lentils work especially well in this recipe. They maintain some of their shape when cooked; red and yellow lentils cook faster and break down more. French lentils have a stronger flavor and firmer texture that are best in salads.

# VEGGIE-FULL BURGERS

Pass on the red meat for one of these vegetarian burger ideas.

FRESH SPINACH
GRILLED PORTOBELLO MUSHROOM
RED ONION SLICES
DIJON MUSTARD

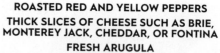

ROASTED RED AND YELLOW PEPPERS
THICK SLICES OF CHEESE SUCH AS BRIE,
MONTEREY JACK, CHEDDAR, OR FONTINA
FRESH ARUGULA

BUTTERHEAD LETTUCE
FRIED AVOCADO (DIP SLICES INTO BEATEN EGG
AND PANKO; FRY IN ½ INCH HOT OIL UNTIL CRISP)
YELLOW TOMATO SLICES
FRIED EGG

GREEK YOGURT WITH CHOPPED PARSLEY AND CAPERS
CAJUN-SEASONED SAUTÉED CAULIFLOWER STEAKS
LETTUCE LEAVES

**FROZEN SPINACH** releases a lot of liquid when thawed. After draining it in a sieve, use your hands to give the spinach a good squeeze before chopping.

# GREEK SPINACH BURGERS

**START TO FINISH** 30 minutes

2  Tbsp. olive oil
1  clove garlic, minced
1  tsp. dried oregano, crushed
1  tsp. dried dill (optional)
¼  tsp. black pepper
1  cup herb stuffing mix or toasted bread cubes (tip, p. 18)
2  eggs, lightly beaten
1  10-oz. pkg. frozen spinach, thawed, drained, and chopped

½  cup crumbled feta cheese (2 oz.)
4  whole wheat hamburger buns or rolls, split and toasted

**1.** In a large bowl combine first five ingredients (through pepper). Add stuffing mix, stirring to coat. Stir in eggs, spinach, and feta cheese. Shape into four ½-inch-thick patties.
**2.** Heat a griddle or 10-inch nonstick skillet over medium heat. Add patties; cook 10 to 12 minutes

or until browned and heated, turning once. Serve in buns.
**Makes 4 sandwiches.**

**EACH SANDWICH** *311 cal., 15 g fat (5 g sat. fat), 110 mg chol., 673 mg sodium, 29 g carb., 8 g fiber, 4 g sugars, 13 g pro.*

**CHANGE IT UP**

*Customize your burger by topping it with crumbled feta, thinly sliced cucumber or red onion, plain Greek yogurt, and/or roasted red peppers.*

## FRIED RICE
**START TO FINISH** 30 minutes

**»**

TOASTED
SESAME OIL
has a strong,
nutty fragrance
and flavor—a
little goes a
long way. Keep
yours chilled
in the fridge
to keep it from
getting old and
tasting rancid.

2   eggs, lightly beaten
1   tsp. soy sauce
1   tsp. toasted sesame oil or vegetable oil
1   small clove garlic, minced
1   Tbsp. vegetable oil
½   cup thinly bias-sliced celery
¾   cup sliced fresh mushrooms
2   cups chilled cooked white rice or one 8.8-oz. pouch cooked white rice
½   cup packaged fresh julienned carrot
½   cup frozen peas
2   Tbsp. soy sauce
¼   cup sliced green onions

**1.** In a small bowl combine eggs and the 1 tsp. soy sauce.
**2.** In a wok or 10-inch skillet heat sesame oil over medium heat. Add garlic; cook and stir 30 seconds. Add egg mixture and cook, without stirring, until set. Turn egg and cook just until set. Turn egg out onto a cutting board, roll it up, and cut into thin slices.
**3.** Pour vegetable oil into wok (add more oil as needed during cooking). Heat over medium-high heat. Add celery; cook and stir 1 minute. Add mushrooms; cook and stir 1 minute or until crisp-tender.
**4.** Add rice, carrot, peas, and the 2 Tbsp. soy sauce to wok. Cook and stir 4 to 6 minutes or until heated through. Add sliced eggs and green onions; cook and stir 1 minute more or until heated through.
**Makes 3 servings (1 cup each).**
**EACH SERVING** *284 cal., 10 g fat (2 g sat. fat), 124 mg chol., 874 mg sodium, 38 g carb., 3 g fiber, 3 g sugars, 11 g pro.*

**BUMP UP THE PROTEIN**
Stir in 8 oz. extra-firm tofu, cut into ¾-inch cubes, or 1 cup thawed frozen edamame when adding the rice.

FRIED RICE

**CHILLED RICE**
Cold is key! When you chill the rice before stir-frying, the starch in each grain has firmed up and separates more easily than warm rice.

## QUINOA CAPRESE CASSEROLE
**HANDS-ON TIME** 35 minutes
**BAKE** 30 minutes at 350°F

Nonstick cooking spray
2   cups water
1   cup quinoa, rinsed and drained
1½  cups marinara sauce
2   Tbsp. tomato paste
⅔   cup finely shredded Parmesan cheese
⅓   cup heavy cream
½   tsp. crushed red pepper
1½  cups grape tomatoes, halved
1   cup shredded mozzarella cheese (4 oz.)

MEDITERRANEAN
FRIED QUINOA

QUINOA
CAPRESE
CASSEROLE

¾ cup thinly sliced fresh basil
6 oz. fresh mozzarella, cut into
½-inch cubes

**1.** Preheat oven to 350°F. Lightly
coat a 2-qt. baking dish with
cooking spray. In a 2-qt. saucepan
combine the water, quinoa, and
½ tsp. *salt.* Bring to boiling; reduce
heat. Simmer, covered, 15 minutes
or until water is absorbed. Remove
from heat. Let stand 5 minutes; fluff.
**2.** Meanwhile, in a 3- to 4-qt.
saucepan combine marinara sauce
and tomato paste. Cook and stir
over low heat until smooth. Stir in
Parmesan, cream, crushed red
pepper, and ¼ tsp. *black pepper.*
Bring to boiling; remove from heat.
Stir in cooked quinoa. Fold in ¾ cup
tomatoes, the shredded mozzarella
cheese, and ¼ cup basil. Spread
mixture into prepared baking dish.
Top with mozzarella cubes.
**3.** Bake 30 minutes or until heated
through. Top with remaining ¾ cup

tomatoes and ½ cup basil and, if
desired, sprinkle with additional
crushed red pepper. **Makes
5 servings (1 cup each).**
**EACH SERVING** *433 cal., 23 g fat
(13 g sat. fat), 70 mg chol., 1,040 mg
sodium, 33 g carb., 5 g fiber, 7 g
sugars, 23 g pro.*

# MEDITERRANEAN FRIED QUINOA

**START TO FINISH** 30 minutes

2 cups reduced-sodium chicken
broth
1 cup red quinoa, rinsed and
drained
1 Tbsp. olive oil
3 cups ½-inch pieces eggplant
¾ cup coarsely chopped onion
2 cloves garlic, minced
½ tsp. coarse-ground black pepper
1 cup grape tomatoes
4 cups fresh baby spinach
¼ cup pitted Kalamata olives,
halved

1 Tbsp. chopped fresh oregano
¼ cup crumbled feta cheese (1 oz.)

**1.** In a 2-qt. saucepan bring broth
to boiling; stir in quinoa. Return
to boiling; reduce heat. Simmer,
covered, 15 minutes or until quinoa
is tender; drain; Return quinoa to
saucepan. Cook and stir over low
heat to dry out any moisture.
**2.** In a 12-inch wok or skillet heat
oil over medium-high heat. Add
quinoa; cook and stir 2 to 4 minutes
or until quinoa starts to brown.
Add eggplant, onion, garlic, and
pepper; cook and stir 3 minutes.
Add tomatoes; cook 2 minutes
or until tomatoes start to burst.
Remove from heat. Add spinach,
olives, and oregano; toss to
combine. Sprinkle with feta
and serve with *lemon wedges.*
**Makes 4 servings (1½ cups each).**
**EACH SERVING** *291 cal., 10 g fat (2 g
sat. fat), 8 mg chol., 593 mg sodium,
41 g carb., 8 g fiber, 6 g sugars, 11 g pro.*

**GOING WITH THE GRAIN**
If you're out of the specific grain called for in a recipe, swap for something else. For this one, try couscous or brown rice in place of farro.

## CREAMY FARRO PORTOBELLOS

**START TO FINISH** 40 minutes

》》 FARRO is an ancient grain with a toothsome texture and nutty flavor (p. 190). You can find whole grain, semipearled, and pearled varieties.

3 cups vegetable broth
1 cup uncooked farro
6 5-inch fresh portobello mushrooms, stems and gills removed
Nonstick cooking spray
2 cups coarsely chopped fresh Swiss chard leaves
¼ cup chopped dried tomatoes (not oil-packed)
2 tsp. chopped fresh thyme or ½ tsp. dried thyme, crushed

4 oz. soft goat cheese (chèvre), cut up
¼ cup shredded Parmesan cheese (1 oz.)
¼ cup sliced green onions

**1.** For filling, in a 2-qt. saucepan bring broth to boiling; stir in farro. Return to boiling; reduce heat. Simmer, covered, 15 minutes.
**2.** Meanwhile, lightly coat both sides of mushrooms with cooking spray. Preheat a grill pan over medium heat. Working in batches, cook mushrooms 8 to 10 minutes or until tender, turning once.

**3.** Stir Swiss chard, dried tomatoes, and thyme into farro. Cook, covered, 5 to 10 minutes more or until farro is tender. Remove from heat. Stir in goat cheese.
**4.** To serve, place mushrooms, stemmed sides up, on a platter. Spoon farro mixture into mushrooms. Sprinkle with cheese, green onions, and *black pepper*.
**Makes 6 servings (1 stuffed mushroom each).**

**EACH SERVING** *227 cal., 6 g fat (3 g sat. fat), 11 mg chol., 605 mg sodium, 31 g carb., 4 g fiber, 6 g sugars, 13 g pro.*

**BLACK BEAN AND SALSA PORTOBELLOS** Prepare as directed, except for filling, in a 2-qt. saucepan combine one 15-oz. can black beans, rinsed and drained; 1 cup salsa; 1 fresh jalapeño, seeded and chopped, (tip, *p. 22*); and salt and black pepper to taste. Heat through. Spoon into mushrooms. Top with ½ cup crumbled queso fresco, fresh cilantro, and cayenne pepper. Serve with lime wedges.

**RISOTTO PORTOBELLOS** Prepare as directed, except for filling, in a 10-inch skillet heat 2 Tbsp. oil over medium heat. Add ¼ cup chopped shallots; cook 2 minutes. Add 8 oz. asparagus, trimmed and cut into ½-inch pieces; cook and stir 3 minutes. Stir in ½ cup dry white wine; season with salt and pepper. Stir in ½ cup uncooked Arborio rice and ½ cup water; bring to boiling. Reduce heat; cook and stir until liquid is absorbed. Continue adding ½ cup water at a time, stirring after each until water is absorbed (use 2 cups water total; cook 30 minutes or until rice is tender). Stir in ½ cup grated Parmesan cheese and 2 tsp. lemon zest. Spoon into mushrooms; top with snipped fresh tarragon.

**»**

FREEKEH is a whole grain wheat (*p. 190*) that has been harvested for centuries (a true "ancient" grain) but has recently gained popularity. The grains go through a process of fire-roasting and sun-drying, which creates smoky, nutty flavors.

# CHICKPEA AND FREEKEH SALAD
**START TO FINISH** 40 minutes

2¾ cups water
½ cup uncooked freekeh
1 15- to 16-oz. can garbanzo beans (chickpeas), rinsed and drained
1 avocado, halved, seeded, peeled, and cubed
3 oz. feta cheese, cubed
¼ cup chopped drained roasted red pepper
½ cup chopped fresh mint
½ cup chopped fresh Italian parsley
1 clove garlic, minced
1 Tbsp. olive oil

**1.** In a 2-qt. saucepan bring the water to boiling; stir in freekeh. Return to boiling; reduce heat. Cook, covered, 20 minutes or until freekeh is tender and most of the liquid is absorbed. Drain any excess liquid. Rinse under cold water to cool quickly; drain again.
**2.** Meanwhile, in a large bowl combine next seven ingredients (through garlic). Drizzle with oil; toss.
**3.** Stir freekeh into bean mixture. Season to taste with *salt* and *black pepper*. If desired, top with sliced *pickled pepperoncini peppers* and *cherry tomatoes*. **Makes 4 servings (1¼ cups each).**

EACH SERVING *318 cal., 15 g fat (5 g sat. fat), 19 mg chol., 370 mg sodium, 36 g carb., 11 g fiber, 4 g sugars, 12 g pro.*

CHICKPEA AND FREEKEH SALAD

**GRAINS** **1.** Basmati rice **2.** Jasmine rice **3.** Arborio rice **4.** Brown rice **5.** White long grain rice **6.** Instant rice **7.** Wild rice **8.** Red rice **9.** Black rice **10.** Jade pearl rice **11.** Quick barley **12.** Pearl barley **13.** Barley (hull-less) **14.** Buckwheat groats **15.** Bulgur **16.** Wheat berries **17.** Wheat bran **18.** Wheat germ **19.** Amaranth **20.** Farro **21.** Freekeh **22.** Spelt **23.** Teff **24.** Millet **25.** Sorghum **26.** Kamut **27.** Groat oats **28.** Steel-cut oats **29.** Old-fashioned oats **30.** Quick-cooking rolled oats **31.** Hemp-seed hearts **32.** Polenta **33.** Hominy grits **34.** White quinoa **35.** Tricolor quinoa **36.** Chia seeds

**BROWN OR GREEN LENTILS** can be used in place of the red or yellow lentils. Simply increase the cooking time to 25 minutes.

# VEGETABLE DAL
**START TO FINISH** 30 minutes

1   tsp. cumin seeds
1   tsp. mustard seeds
¼   tsp. fennel seeds
¼   tsp. black pepper
3   cups water
1   cup red or yellow lentils, rinsed and drained
2   bay leaves
½   cup chopped onion
2   Tbsp. olive oil
1   fresh jalapeño chile pepper, seeded and finely chopped (tip, *p. 22*)
1   Tbsp. grated fresh ginger
2   cloves garlic, minced
1   15-oz. can crushed tomatoes
1   tsp. garam masala
½   tsp. salt

**1.** In a 6-inch skillet toast cumin, mustard, and fennel seeds and black pepper 30 seconds over medium heat or just until fragrant. Transfer to a bowl; cool. Finely grind in a spice grinder.
**2.** In a 2-qt. saucepan bring the water to boiling. Stir in lentils and bay leaves. Return to boiling; reduce heat. Simmer, covered, 12 minutes for red lentils, 20 to 25 minutes for yellow lentils, or until very soft. Remove; discard bay leaves.
**3.** Meanwhile, in a 3-qt. saucepan cook and stir onion in hot oil over medium-high heat 5 minutes. Add jalapeño, ginger, and garlic; cook and stir 3 minutes. Stir in tomatoes and cumin mixture. Bring to boiling; reduce heat. Simmer, uncovered, 5 minutes, stirring occasionally.
**4.** Stir lentils, garam masala, and salt into tomato mixture. If desired, serve with *cooked rice* and/or *naan*; top with *plain yogurt, fresh cilantro,* and additional jalapeños.
**Makes 4 servings (1¼ cups each).**
**EACH SERVING** *590 cal., 13 g fat (2 g sat. fat), 5 mg chol., 998 mg sodium, 88 g carb., 19 g fiber, 10 g sugars, 31 g pro.*

// **MEATLESS** //

**BEANS & LEGUMES 1.** Black beans **2.** Red beans **3.** Kidney beans **4.** Pinto beans **5.** Pink beans **6.** Cranberry beans **7.** Cannellini (white kidney) beans **8.** Navy beans **9.** Great Northern beans **10.** Gigante beans **11.** Fava beans **12.** Mayocoba beans **13.** Baby lima beans **14.** Christmas lima beans **15.** Large lima (butter) beans **16.** Black-eyed peas **17.** Garbanzo beans (chickpeas) **18.** Soybeans **19.** Split green peas **20.** Split yellow peas **21.** French lentils **22.** Black lentils **23.** Brown lentils **24.** Red lentils

## WHAT'S A BUDDHA BOWL?

IT'S A VEGETARIAN OR VEGAN ONE-BOWL DISH PACKED WITH NUTRITIOUS VEGGIES, BEANS, NUTS, AND GRAINS.

## BUDDHA BOWL

**START TO FINISH** 30 minutes

½   cup COOKED GRAIN
½   cup ROASTED VEGETABLE
½   cup RAW VEGETABLE
⅓   cup PROTEIN
2   Tbsp. CRUNCHY TOPPING
¼   cup DRESSING

**1.** In a bowl arrange COOKED GRAIN, ROASTED and RAW VEGETABLES, and PROTEIN. Top with the CRUNCHY TOPPING. Serve with DRESSING. **Makes 1 serving.**

---

## MIX & MATCH INGREDIENTS

### COOKED GRAIN
*(cooked according to package directions)*

- Bulgur
- Farro
- Kamut
- Quinoa

### ROASTED VEGETABLE
*(see Roasting Vegetables chart, p. 314)*

- Butternut squash
- Broccoli florets
- Cherry tomatoes
- Mushrooms

### RAW VEGETABLE

- Sliced avocado or cucumber
- Shredded carrot
- Riced cauliflower or small cauliflower florets
- Leafy greens, such as baby spinach, curly kale, parsley or mint leaves, or arugula

### PROTEIN

- Canned black or red kidney beans
- Canned garbanzo beans (chickpeas)
- Cooked edamame or lentils
- Sautéed, sliced tofu

### CRUNCHY TOPPING

- Shredded carrot or red cabbage, or sliced radishes
- Toasted spiced chickpeas, fried onion salad topper, or croutons
- Toasted nuts such as pepitas, walnuts, almonds, pecans, or cashews

### DRESSING

- Basil Pesto (p. 31)
- Cashew Cream (p. 194)
- Romesco Sauce (p. 30)
- Sesame-Ginger Dressing (p. 300)
- Tahini-Honey Dressing (p. 300)

// MEATLESS //

**MAKE IT AHEAD**
Burrito bowls can be assembled in airtight containers and stored in the refrigerator up to 3 days. You can tote a bowl to work and eat it chilled or at room temperature (let it stand 30 minutes).

CASHEW CREAM—a thick sauce made from blended cashews—can be doubled and the extra drizzled on basically everything. Use it as a dipper for veggies or sauce for pasta.

## CASHEW CREAM

In a small bowl combine 1 cup raw cashews and enough boiling water to cover. Let stand, covered, 30 minutes; drain. In a food processor combine cashews; ½ cup water; 2 tsp. cider vinegar; 1 tsp. lime juice; 1 small clove garlic, minced; and ⅛ tsp. salt. Cover; process until smooth, adding water as needed to reach desired consistency.

## SWEET POTATO BURRITO BOWLS

**HANDS-ON TIME** 10 minutes
**COOK** 45 minutes
**ROAST** 30 minutes at 425°F

- 1½  cups no-salt-added vegetable stock or water
- ⅔  cup uncooked regular brown rice
- ¼  cup chopped fresh cilantro
- 2  Tbsp. sliced green onion
- 3  cups ¾-inch cubes peeled sweet potatoes
- 1  cup coarsely chopped red sweet pepper
- 1  Tbsp. olive oil
- 1  tsp. chili powder
- ¼  tsp. salt
- 1  15- to 16-oz. can pinto beans, rinsed and drained
- ¼  cup salsa
- ¼  cup Cashew Cream or sour cream
  Toppings such as toasted pepitas, chopped avocado, salsa, crumbled queso fresco, and/or additional cilantro, green onions, or chili powder (optional)

**1.** Preheat oven to 425°F. In a 2-qt. saucepan bring stock to boiling. Stir in rice. Return to boiling; reduce heat. Simmer, covered, 45 minutes or until rice is tender and broth is absorbed. Fluff rice with fork; stir in cilantro and green onion.

**2.** Meanwhile, line a 15×10-inch baking pan with foil. In prepared pan combine next five ingredients (through salt); toss to coat. Roast 30 minutes or until light brown and tender, stirring once. In a bowl stir together beans and salsa.

**3.** Divide rice among bowls. Top with sweet potato mixture and bean mixture; drizzle with Cashew Cream. If desired, sprinkle with toppings and serve with *lime wedges.* **Makes 4 servings (1½ cups each).**

**EACH SERVING** *369 cal., 7 g fat (1 g sat. fat), 0 mg chol., 764 mg sodium, 66 g carb., 11 g fiber, 9 g sugars, 10 g pro.*

## CHEESY ITALIAN BAKED BEANS

**HANDS-ON TIME** 20 minutes
**BAKE** 15 minutes at 400°F

- 2 Tbsp. olive oil
- ½ cup coarsely chopped yellow onion
- 3 cloves garlic, sliced
- ⅛ tsp. salt
- 1 28-oz. can fire-roasted crushed tomatoes
- ¼ cup fresh rosemary leaves, coarsely chopped
- 3 15- to 16-oz. cans cannellini (white kidney) beans, rinsed and drained
- ¾ cup shredded Parmesan cheese(3 oz.)
  Coarse salt
  Crushed red pepper
  Freshly ground black pepper
- ½ cup shredded Fontina cheese

**1.** Preheat oven to 400°F. In a 10-inch skillet heat oil over medium-high heat. Add onion, garlic, and ⅛ tsp. salt; cook and stir 5 minutes or until onion is tender. Stir in tomatoes and rosemary. Bring to boiling; reduce heat. Boil gently, uncovered, 5 minutes or until slightly thickened.

**2.** Stir in beans and half of the Parmesan. Season to taste with salt, crushed red pepper, and black pepper. Transfer mixture to a 2-qt. rectangular baking dish. Top with Fontina and remaining Parmesan.

**3.** Bake 15 to 20 minutes or until edges begin to brown. If desired, sprinkle with additional rosemary.

**Makes 6 servings (1 cup each).**

**EACH SERVING** *329 cal., 10 g fat (4 g sat. fat), 18 mg chol., 899 mg sodium, 41 g carb., 12 g fiber, 7 g sugars, 18 g pro.*

// MEATLESS //

CHEESY TACO-STUFFED PEPPERS

EDAMAME AND CORN ENCHILADAS

# CHEESY TACO-STUFFED PEPPERS

**HANDS-ON TIME** 15 minutes
**BAKE** 30 minutes at 425°F

CANNED BEANS need to be drained and rinsed well under running water. This washes off the salt and starch found in the canned water that can affect the flavor and texture of the finished dish.

- 3 red and/or green sweet peppers, halved lengthwise and seeded
- 1 8.8-oz. pouch cooked white or whole grain brown rice
- 1 cup canned black beans, rinsed and drained
- ½ cup sliced green onions
- ½ cup seeded and chopped roma tomatoes
- ½ cup frozen corn
- ¼ cup chopped fresh cilantro
- 1 Tbsp. taco seasoning mix
- 1¼ cups shredded Mexican cheese blend (5 oz.)
- 2 tsp. hot pepper sauce (optional)

**1.** Preheat oven to 425°F. Place pepper halves, cut sides down, in a 15×10-inch baking pan. Bake 10 minutes.
**2.** Meanwhile, in a medium bowl combine next seven ingredients (through seasoning mix). Stir in ½ cup of the cheese and, if desired, hot sauce.
**3.** Turn over pepper halves. Fill with rice mixture. Cover loosely with foil and bake 25 minutes; remove foil. Sprinkle peppers with remaining ¾ cup cheese. Bake 5 minutes more or until cheese is melted. If desired, serve with additional green onions, tomatoes, cilantro, and hot sauce. **Makes 6 servings (1 stuffed pepper half each).**

**EACH SERVING** *217 cal., 8 g fat (4 g sat. fat), 22 mg chol., 342 mg sodium, 26 g carb., 4 g fiber, 4 g sugars, 10 g pro.*

# EDAMAME AND CORN ENCHILADAS

**HANDS-ON TIME** 20 minutes
**BAKE** 35 minutes at 350°F

- Nonstick cooking spray
- 1 cup frozen edamame, thawed
- 1 cup frozen whole kernel corn, thawed
- 2 tsp. fajita seasoning mix
- 2 cups shredded Monterey Jack cheese (8 oz.)
- 10 7- to 8-inch whole wheat flour tortillas
- 1 15-oz. can tomato sauce
- 1 14.5-oz. can fire-roasted or regular diced tomatoes, undrained
- 1½ to 2 tsp. chili powder
- Chopped fresh cilantro

**1.** Preheat oven to 350°F. Coat a 3-qt. rectangular baking dish with cooking spray. In a medium bowl combine edamame, corn, and fajita seasoning. Stir in 1½ cups of the cheese. Spoon about ⅓ cup of the mixture onto each tortilla; roll up. Place, seam sides down, in prepared dish.
**2.** In same bowl combine tomato sauce, tomatoes, and chili powder; pour over filled tortillas.
**3.** Bake, covered, 20 minutes. Bake, uncovered, 15 to 20 minutes more or until heated through, sprinkling with remaining ½ cup cheese the last 5 minutes. Top with cilantro and, if desired, additional chili powder. **Makes 10 servings (1 enchilada each).**

**EACH SERVING** *269 cal., 11 g fat (5 g sat. fat), 20 mg chol., 759 mg sodium, 32 g carb., 5 g fiber, 6 g sugars, 13 g pro.*

**CHANGE IT UP**
*Canned beans are a quick way to change the flavor and texture of the enchiladas: Swap for an equal amount of rinsed and drained black beans or kidney beans in place of the edamame.*

FALAFEL

LENTIL SLOPPY JOES

# FALAFEL

**START TO FINISH** 25 minutes

1   15-oz. can garbanzo beans
    (chickpeas), rinsed and drained
¼   cup coarsely shredded carrot
2   Tbsp. all-purpose flour
2   Tbsp. chopped fresh parsley
1   Tbsp. olive oil
3   cloves garlic, halved
1   tsp. ground coriander
½   tsp. salt
½   tsp. ground cumin
⅛   tsp. black pepper
2   Tbsp. olive oil
½   cup mayonnaise
1   clove garlic, minced
¼   tsp. cayenne pepper
4   pita bread rounds or tortillas
    Tzatziki Sauce (optional)

**1.** In a food processor combine
first 10 ingredients (through black
pepper). Process until finely
chopped and mixture holds
together (you should have some
visible pieces of beans and carrots
remaining).
**2.** Shape into eight 3-inch patties.
In a 10-inch skillet heat 2 Tbsp.
oil over medium-high heat. Add
patties; cook 4 to 6 minutes or until
browned and heated through,
turning once.

**3.** Meanwhile, in a small bowl stir
together mayonnaise, minced
garlic, and cayenne pepper.
Serve patties with mayonnaise
mixture and pita bread, *mint,
spinach, cucumber slices, onion
slices,* and/or *lemon wedges.*
If desired, swap Tzatziki Sauce
for mayonnaise mixture. **Makes
4 servings (2 patties each).**
**EACH SERVING** *557 cal., 33 g fat (5 g
sat. fat), 12 mg chol., 924 mg sodium,
54 g carb., 6 g fiber, 4 g sugars,
11 g pro.*

## *TZATZIKI SAUCE*

In a bowl combine one 6-oz.
carton plain Greek yogurt; 1 cup
shredded, seeded cucumber;
1 Tbsp. lemon juice; 1 Tbsp. olive oil;
1 Tbsp. snipped mint, 1 clove
garlic, minced; and ¼ tsp. salt.

# LENTIL SLOPPY JOES

**HANDS-ON TIME** 15 minutes
**SLOW COOK** 8 to 10 hours (low) or
4 to 5 hours (high)

3   cups water
2   cups brown lentils, rinsed
    and drained
1¼  cups chopped green
    sweet pepper
1   cup shredded carrots
¾   cup chopped onion
1   cup reduced-sodium hot-style
    vegetable juice
¼   cup no-salt-added tomato
    paste
1   4-oz. can diced green chile
    peppers, undrained
1   Tbsp. reduced-sodium
    Worcestershire sauce
2   tsp. chili powder
1   tsp. cider vinegar
2   cloves garlic, minced
½   cup ketchup
2   Tbsp. packed brown sugar
16  whole wheat hamburger buns,
    split and toasted (tip, *p. 270*)

**1.** In a 3½- or 4-qt. slow cooker
combine first 12 ingredients
(through garlic). Cover; cook on low
8 to 10 hours or high 4 to 5 hours.
**2.** Before serving, stir in ketchup
and brown sugar. Serve lentil
mixture on toasted buns and,
if desired, top with *red onion slices*
and additional shredded carrots.
**Makes 16 sandwiches.**
**EACH SANDWICH** *278 cal., 3 g fat
(1 g sat. fat), 0 mg chol., 465 mg
sodium, 54 g carb., 11 g fiber,
9 g sugars, 14 g pro.*

// MEATLESS //

CHICKPEA ALFREDO
WITH VEGGIES

to coat. Sprinkle with additional pepper and, if desired, cheese. **Makes 6 servings (1 cup each).**

EACH SERVING *290 cal., 7 g fat (1 g sat. fat), 0 mg chol., 190 mg sodium, 49 g carb., 8 g fiber, 4 g sugars, 11 g pro.*

## TEMPEH-WALNUT TACOS

START TO FINISH 30 minutes

Nonstick cooking spray
1   medium fresh poblano chile pepper, seeded and chopped (tip, *p. 22*)
½   cup chopped onion
1   8-oz. pkg. tempeh (fermented soybean cake), crumbled (info, *p. 203*)
2   tsp. Mexican seasoning blend
2   cloves garlic, minced
¼   tsp. salt
¼   cup chopped walnuts, toasted
8   6-inch corn tortillas, warmed Guacamole (*p. 387*)
    Shredded lettuce, cilantro, and/or crumbled Cotija cheese

**1.** Coat a 10-inch nonstick skillet with cooking spray; heat over medium heat. Add poblano pepper and onion; cook 3 to 5 minutes or until crisp-tender, stirring occasionally. Add tempeh, Mexican seasoning blend, garlic, and salt. Cook 6 to 8 minutes or until heated through and tempeh is lightly browned, stirring occasionally. Remove from heat; stir in walnuts.
**2.** Spread tortillas with Guacamole; top with tempeh mixture and toppings. **Makes 4 servings (2 tacos each).**

EACH SERVING *429 cal., 21 g fat (5 g sat. fat), 15 mg chol., 668 mg sodium, 41 g carb., 9 g fiber, 6 g sugars, 20 g pro.*

## CHICKPEA ALFREDO WITH VEGGIES

START TO FINISH 45 minutes

⅓   cup unsalted raw cashews
12   oz. dried whole grain or brown rice fettuccine
1   cup chopped fresh asparagus
2   cups lightly packed fresh spinach or arugula
½   cup frozen peas, thawed
1¼   cups water
¼   cup chickpea (garbanzo bean) flour or all-purpose flour
1   Tbsp. lemon juice
2   tsp. olive oil
2   cloves garlic, minced
½   tsp. kosher salt
½   tsp. black pepper
2   Tbsp. chopped fresh basil and/or parsley (optional)
    Shaved Parmesan cheese (optional)

**1.** In a small bowl combine cashews and enough boiling water to cover. Let stand, covered, 30 minutes; drain. Rinse and drain again.
**2.** Meanwhile, cook pasta according to package directions, adding asparagus the last 3 minutes and spinach and peas the last 1 minute; drain.
**3.** In a 1- or 1½ qt. saucepan whisk together the water and flour until smooth (mixture may be a bit foamy). Cook and stir over medium heat just until bubbly.
**4.** For sauce, in a blender combine soaked cashews, flour mixture, and next five ingredients (through pepper). Cover and pulse several times. Blend 5 minutes or until smooth. If desired, stir in basil and/or parsley.
**5.** Transfer pasta mixture to a dish. Drizzle pasta with sauce; toss

**COTIJA CHEESE**
This firm, salty cheese originated in Mexico. The aged version is known as "queso añejo." If you can't find either, swap in any Mexican-style cheese blend.

TEMPEH-WALNUT TACOS

**DINNER'S ON**
For a quick side, microwave one or two 8-oz. pouches of white or brown ready-to-eat rice. You can also serve with hot cooked rice noodles or other Asian noodles (p. 230).

THAI BASIL is spicier than most sweet basil. If using sweet basil (or you just like a spicier stir-fry), stir in some chili paste (such as sambal oelek) or crushed red pepper to kick up the heat.

# CARAMELIZED TOFU AND THAI BASIL STIR-FRY
**START TO FINISH** *40 minutes*

1  16-oz. pkg. water-packed extra-firm refrigerated tofu
2  Tbsp. vegetable oil
5  Tbsp. water
4  Tbsp. reduced-sodium soy sauce
1  Tbsp. packed brown sugar
3  Tbsp. rice wine vinegar
1  Tbsp. cornstarch
1  medium red onion, halved crosswise and cut into thin wedges
2  cups red and/or orange sweet pepper strips
1½  cups thinly sliced, stemmed fresh shiitake mushrooms
¼  cup thinly sliced fresh Thai basil or sweet basil leaves
   Sriracha sauce (optional)

**1.** Drain tofu; pat dry. Cut tofu into bite-size cubes. In a large wok or 12-inch nonstick skillet heat 1 Tbsp. of the oil over medium-high heat. Add tofu; cook 15 minutes or until crisp and golden, stirring occasionally.
**2.** In a small bowl combine 2 Tbsp. of the water, 1 Tbsp. of the soy sauce, and the brown sugar. Pour over tofu; cook over medium heat until tofu is coated and liquid is syrupy, gently stirring frequently. Remove from skillet.
**3.** Meanwhile, for sauce, in a bowl combine remaining 3 Tbsp. water and 3 Tbsp. soy sauce, the vinegar, and cornstarch.
**4.** Add remaining 1 Tbsp. oil to skillet. Add red onion; cook and stir 1 minute. Add sweet peppers; cook and stir 2 to 3 minutes. Add mushrooms; cook and stir 2 minutes more or until onion and peppers are crisp-tender. Make a well in center for sauce.

**WOK THIS WAY** The wok's sloping extra-high sides are perfect for keeping large quantities of veggies contained while you toss and stir. Stove-top models are made from a variety of metals—we prefer those made from cast iron or carbon steel because they conduct heat well. In a pinch, a large skillet with sloped sides will work.

**5.** Stir sauce; add to skillet. Cook and stir until thickened and bubbly. Cook and stir 2 minutes more. Gently stir in tofu and basil. If desired, serve with sriracha sauce and sprinkle with additional basil. **Makes 4 servings (1½ cups each).**

EACH SERVING *239 cal., 12 g fat (2 g sat. fat), 0 mg chol., 573 mg sodium, 21 g carb., 4 g fiber, 12 g sugars, 13 g pro.*

spread sides down; cook 4 to 6 minutes or until golden, turning once. Remove from heat. Drizzle tofu with lime juice.

**4.** Spread bottoms of rolls with remaining mayonnaise mixture. Fill rolls with tofu, pickled vegetables, and cilantro. **Makes 4 sandwiches.**

EACH SANDWICH *401 cal., 17 g fat (3 g sat. fat), 6 mg chol., 648 mg sodium, 45 g carb., 4 g fiber, 6 g sugars, 19 g pro.*

## *MAKE IT A MEAL*

Make your own sweet potato chips. Use a mandoline to thinly slice sweet potatoes over a sheet pan lined with foil. Drizzle with olive oil and sprinkle with kosher salt and black pepper. Roast in a 425°F oven for 20 minutes or until desired doneness, turning chips as necessary.

## TOFU AND PICKLED VEGETABLE SANDWICHES

**START TO FINISH** 45 minutes

- 3 cups thinly sliced cucumbers, radishes, and/or carrots
- ¼ cup rice vinegar or cider vinegar
- 2 Tbsp. very thinly sliced shallot
- ½ tsp. sugar
- ¼ tsp. salt
- 1 16-oz. pkg. water-packed extra-firm refrigerated tofu, drained and cut crosswise into 8 slices
- ¼ cup mayonnaise
- 2 tsp. sriracha sauce
- 1 Tbsp. lime juice
- 4 hoagie rolls, split and toasted (tip, *p. 270*)
- ½ cup fresh cilantro leaves

**1.** For pickled vegetables, in a medium bowl combine first five ingredients (through salt). Let stand at least 10 minutes; drain.

**2.** Meanwhile, press tofu slices between paper towels to squeeze out excess moisture. In a small bowl stir together mayonnaise and sriracha sauce. Thinly spread tofu with half of the mayonnaise mixture.

**3.** Heat a 12-inch nonstick skillet over medium-high heat. Add tofu,

TOFU AND PICKLED VEGETABLE SANDWICHES

# WHAT IS BULGOGI? THIS KOREAN BBQ DISH USUALLY IS THIN STRIPS OF GRILLED, MARINATED BEEF SERVED WITH RICE OR LETTUCE LEAVES. FOR A VEGETARIAN TWIST, WE USED A SIMILAR MARINADE ON MEATLESS SEITAN, THEN SEARED IT IN A SKILLET.

## SPICY SEITAN BULGOGI

**HANDS-ON TIME** 30 minutes
**MARINATE** 2 hours

GOCHUJANG PASTE is a trendy Korean condiment made of chiles, rice, fermented soybeans, and salt. Look for it in the Asian section of the supermarket.

| | |
|---|---|
| 1 | lb. seitan (wheat gluten) or tempeh, cut into ½-inch cubes or strips |
| ½ | cup chopped pear |
| ¼ | cup reduced-sodium soy sauce |
| 2 | Tbsp. packed brown sugar |
| 2 | Tbsp. sliced green onion |
| 2 | Tbsp. water |
| 1 | to 2 Tbsp. gochujang paste or sriracha sauce |
| 1 | Tbsp. rice vinegar |
| 1 | Tbsp. grated fresh ginger |
| 3 | cloves garlic, halved |
| 1 | tsp. cracked black pepper |
| 1 | tsp. toasted sesame oil |
| 2 | Tbsp. vegetable oil |
| | Hot cooked rice |
| | Kimchi (optional) |
| | Toasted sesame seeds |

**1.** Place seitan in a resealable plastic bag set in a shallow dish. For marinade, in a blender combine next 11 ingredients (through sesame oil). Cover and blend until smooth. Pour marinade over seitan. Seal bag and turn to coat seitan. Marinate in the refrigerator 2 to 4 hours. Drain the seitan, reserving marinade.

**2.** In a 12-inch skillet heat vegetable oil over medium heat. Add seitan; cook 8 to 12 minutes or until light brown, turning once.

**3.** Meanwhile, for sauce, in a 1- or 1½-qt. saucepan heat reserved marinade over medium heat, adding enough water to reach drizzling consistency.

**4.** Serve seitan with rice and, if desired, kimchi. Drizzle with sauce; sprinkle with sesame seeds and additional sliced green onion.

**Makes 4 servings (1 cup each).**

**EACH SERVING** *371 cal., 9 g fat (1 g sat. fat), 0 mg chol., 977 mg sodium, 50 g carb., 3 g fiber, 14 g sugars, 24 g pro.*

## MEATLESS PROTEIN

**TOFU** This product is made from curdling soymilk (similar to making cheese from milk). Firm and extra-firm varieties are packed in water and refrigerated. These types of tofu hold their shape well and can be sliced or cubed for frying or stir-frying. Drain well and pat dry with paper towels. Soft and silken tofu varieties are sold in aseptic (sterile) packages that are shelf-stable. These types have delicate texture and are used for stirring into dips, purees, and dressings. Silken tofu is available in soft, firm, and extra-firm textures (but none of these should be used for stir-frying). You can also purchase smoked or marinated/baked tofu.

**SEITAN** Americans are just now embracing this chewy, firm-texture meat substitute. It looks somewhat similar to meat and is known as mock duck in Chinese restaurants. Seitan is made from wheat protein (gluten) and comes whole or precut. Sautéed, roasted, or grilled seitan makes a great substitute for beef or pork in soups, stir-fries, and other combination dishes.

**TEMPEH** Like tofu, tempeh is a soy product that easily takes on other flavors. Tempeh starts as whole soybeans that are fermented for easier digestion; it is shaped into a dense cake that may include beans or whole grains. Tempeh has a nutty flavor and a firm, chewy texture; it can be sliced like chicken or crumbled and sautéed like ground meat. Tempeh comes refrigerated or frozen.

**MYCOPROTEIN** Known as Quorn in the United States, mycoprotein is made from fungi that are grown and fermented in vats. Mycoprotein has a very similar texture and flavor to chicken; some varieties are seasoned to taste more like meat. Mycoprotein contains eggs, so it is not vegan. Look for prepared mycoprotein products, including nuggets, meatball-style balls, burgers, tenders, turkey-style roasts, and barbecue-flavor products.

**MOCK MEATS** Mock meats, such as vegan bacon, meatless crumbles, sausages, veggie patties, and strips, are typically made of compressed soy, pea, and/or wheat proteins. They come in a variety of flavors, such as chicken or beef, and have a texture similar to cooked meat. Add mock meat to chili or chowder as an inexpensive substitute for some or all of the meat.

**TOFU 1.** Soft **2.** Firm **3.** Baked ■ **SEITAN** ■ **TEMPEH**
■ **MYCOPROTEIN** ■ **MOCK MEATS 1.** Bacon **2.** Crumbles **3.** Hot dogs
**4.** Veggie patties **5.** Chicken-style strips

CRANK UP THE HEAT TO GET THE CRISPIEST CRUST. BECAUSE OF THE MOISTURE FROM THE CAULIFLOWER, A PIZZA STONE IS YOUR BEST BET FOR EVEN BROWNING—IT RETAINS AND DISTRIBUTES HEAT WELL. BUT IF YOU DON'T HAVE ONE, SUBSTITUTE A PREHEATED BAKING SHEET.

Removing all the liquid from the cauliflower after microwaving is crucial to getting that crisp, browned crust. Twisting the cauliflower in a towel is the most efficient way to get the job done.

## CAULIFLOWER-CRUSTED PIZZA

**HANDS-ON TIME** 30 minutes
**BAKE** 17 minutes at 425°F

CAULIFLOWER RICE is now widely available at large supermarkets in either the produce section or the freezer aisle. Use about 3 cups riced cauliflower in place of the 4 cups florets.

- 4 cups cauliflower florets
- 2 Tbsp. water
- 1 egg, lightly beaten
- ¼ cup shredded Italian cheese blend (1 oz.)
- ¼ cup grated Parmesan cheese
- ¼ cup panko bread crumbs (tip, p. 108)
- ½ tsp. dried Italian seasoning, crushed
- ¼ tsp. salt
- 1 tsp. olive oil
- 2 cups sliced fresh mushrooms
- 1 cup yellow or green sweet pepper strips
- 1 small red onion, cut into thin wedges
- ¾ cup Fast Pizza Sauce or canned pizza sauce
- 1 cup shredded Italian cheese blend (4 oz.)
  Snipped fresh basil, oregano, and/or parsley

**1.** Place cauliflower in a food processor. Cover and pulse four to six times or until crumbly and mixture resembles couscous.
**2.** Place a pizza stone or baking sheet in the oven. Preheat to 425°F. In a casserole combine cauliflower and the water. Microwave, covered, 3 to 4 minutes or until tender, stirring once or twice; cool. With a slotted spoon, transfer cauliflower to a 100%-cotton flour-sack towel. Wrap towel around cauliflower and squeeze until there is no more liquid (this step is critical).
**3.** For crust, in a medium bowl stir together cauliflower and next six ingredients (through salt). On a piece of parchment paper pat mixture into a 12-inch circle. Transfer on the paper to preheated pizza stone. Bake 12 to 15 minutes or until crisp and golden brown.
**4.** Meanwhile, in a 10-inch skillet heat oil over medium-high heat. Add mushrooms, sweet pepper, and onion; cook 4 to 6 minutes or until crisp-tender, stirring occasionally.
**5.** Spread Fast Pizza Sauce over baked crust. Top with mushroom mixture and sprinkle with 1 cup Italian cheese blend. Bake 5 to 10 minutes more or until heated through and cheese is melted. If desired, sprinkle with fresh herbs. **Makes 4 servings (2 slices each).**

**EACH SERVING** *266 cal., 14 g fat (7 g sat. fat), 75 mg chol., 813 mg sodium, 19 g carb., 5 g fiber, 7 g sugars, 17 g pro.*

Baking on parchment paper makes it easy to remove from the pan.

## *FAST PIZZA SAUCE*

In a 1- or 1½-qt. saucepan cook ½ cup chopped onion and 2 cloves garlic, minced, in 1 Tbsp. hot olive oil over medium heat about 5 minutes or until onion is tender, stirring occasionally. Stir in one 8-oz. can tomato sauce, ½ tsp. crushed dried oregano, ½ tsp. crushed dried basil, ¼ tsp. salt, and ¼ tsp. crushed red pepper. Bring to boiling; reduce heat. Simmer, uncovered, about 5 minutes or until sauce reaches desired consistency. Makes 1 cup.

**BUTTERNUT-KALE** Prepare crust as directed through Step 3. Omit sauce and fresh herb toppers. For topping, in a 10-inch skillet heat 2 Tbsp. hot olive oil over medium heat. Add 2 cups sliced fresh mushrooms, 1½ cups ½-inch cubes butternut squash, and 1 medium onion, cut into thin wedges; cook 10 minutes or until squash is just tender, stirring frequently. Add 2 cups shredded kale; cook and stir 1 minute more. Spread ½ cup Alfredo pasta sauce over crust. Top with squash mixture and sprinkle with 1 cup shredded Italian cheese blend. Bake 5 minutes more or until cheese is melted and golden.

**BROCCOLI-POTATO** Prepare crust as directed through Step 3. Omit sauce and fresh herb toppers. For topping, in a large bowl toss together 4 oz. ¼-inch slices Yukon gold potatoes, 1 cup small broccoli florets, 2 Tbsp. olive oil, 2 tsp. chopped fresh thyme, and 1 tsp. chopped fresh rosemary. Spread vegetables over crust. Bake 20 minutes more or until vegetables are tender and crust is crisp and deeply browned around edges. Top with ½ cup shredded Italian cheese blend; bake 5 minutes more or until cheese is melted and golden.

# BASIL-TOMATO TART

**HANDS-ON TIME** 30 minutes
**BAKE** 12 minutes at 450°F +
35 minutes at 375°F

BASIL-TOMATO TART

- ½ of a 14.1-oz. pkg. (1 crust) rolled refrigerated unbaked piecrust
- 1½ cups shredded mozzarella cheese (6 oz.)
- 5 roma tomatoes or 4 medium tomatoes
- 1 cup loosely packed fresh basil leaves
- 4 cloves garlic, halved
- ½ cup mayonnaise
- ¼ cup grated Parmesan cheese
- ⅛ tsp. white pepper

**1.** Preheat oven to 450°F. Let piecrust stand according to package directions. Place in a 9-inch quiche dish or pie plate. Crimp edge as desired. Line unpricked pastry with a double thickness of foil. Bake 8 minutes; remove foil. Bake 4 to 5 minutes more or until set and dry. Remove from oven. Reduce temperature to 375°F. Sprinkle crust with ½ cup of the mozzarella cheese. Cool slightly on a wire rack.
**2.** Cut tomatoes into wedges; drain on paper towels. Arrange tomato wedges over cheese in crust. In a food processor combine basil and garlic; cover and process until coarsely chopped. Sprinkle over tomatoes.
**3.** In a medium bowl combine remaining 1 cup mozzarella cheese, mayonnaise, Parmesan cheese, and white pepper. Spread cheese mixture over basil mixture.
**4.** Bake 35 to 40 minutes or until golden and bubbly. Serve warm. If desired, top with additional basil and Parmesan cheese. **Makes 8 servings (1 slice each).**
**TO MAKE AHEAD** Bake pastry crust as directed in Step 1; cover and let stand at room temperature up to 2 hours. Drain tomato wedges; let stand at room temperature up to 2 hours. Prepare cheese mixture. Cover and chill up to 2 hours. Assemble and bake as directed.
**EACH SERVING** *275 cal., 21 g fat (6 g sat. fat), 24 mg chol., 369 mg sodium, 17 g carb., 1 g fiber, 1 g sugars, 8 g pro.*

# SHAKSHUKA

**HANDS-ON TIME** 25 minutes
**COOK** 15 minutes

- 2 Tbsp. olive oil
- 1 cup chopped onion
- 1¼ cups chopped red sweet pepper
- 1 fresh jalapeño chile pepper, seeded and chopped (tip, *p. 22*)
- 3 cloves garlic, sliced
- 1 tsp. ground cumin
- 1 tsp. sweet paprika
- 1 tsp. ground turmeric
- ½ tsp. kosher salt
- ¼ tsp. black pepper
- 1 28-oz. can whole plum tomatoes, undrained and coarsely chopped
- 6 eggs
  Crumbled feta cheese
  Fresh cilantro and/or oregano

**1.** In a 10-inch deep skillet heat oil over medium heat. Add next nine ingredients (through black pepper). Cook and stir 10 minutes or until vegetables are softened. Stir in tomatoes. Bring to boiling; reduce heat. Simmer, uncovered, 10 minutes or until slightly thickened, stirring occasionally.
**2.** Break eggs, one at a time, into a small dish and slip eggs into tomato mixture. Reduce heat. Cook, covered, 5 to 10 minutes or until whites are set and yolks are desired doneness. Top with cheese and herbs. **Makes 6 servings (1 egg + ⅔ cup mixture each).**
**EACH SERVING** *174 cal., 11 g fat (3 g sat. fat), 192 mg chol., 478 mg sodium, 11 g carb., 4 g fiber, 6 g sugars, 9 g pro.*

**WHAT IS SHAKSHUKA?** THIS AFRICAN-MIDDLE EASTERN SPECIALTY FEATURES EGGS POACHED IN A SIMMERING TOMATO-BASED SAUCE.

## ZUCCHINI RIBBONS, PASTA, AND ARUGULA

**START TO FINISH** 30 minutes

- 6   oz. dried fettuccine
- 2   medium zucchini or yellow summer squash, cut into ribbons
- 1   lemon
- ¼   cup sliced pepperoncini salad peppers
- 2   Tbsp. olive oil
- 1½  tsp. chopped fresh oregano
- 1   clove garlic, minced
- 3   cups arugula
       Salt and black pepper
       Chopped toasted almonds

**1.** Cook fettuccine in boiling salted water according to package directions. Place zucchini ribbons in a colander; drain fettuccine over zucchini. Rinse under cold water to cool; drain again. Transfer fettuccine mixture to a large bowl. **2.** Remove 1 tsp. zest and squeeze 1 Tbsp. juice from lemon. Stir lemon zest and juice, salad peppers, oil, oregano, and garlic into fettuccine mixture. Add arugula; toss to combine. Season to taste with salt and black pepper. Top with almonds. **Makes 4 servings (2 cups each).**

**EACH SERVING** *282 cal., 11 g fat (1 g sat. fat), 0 mg chol., 453 mg sodium, 37 g carb., 4 g fiber, 5 g sugars, 8 g pro.*

**EASY RIBBONS**
Use a vegetable peeler to slice zucchini lengthwise into thin ribbons. Trim ends, then peel from one end of the zucchini to the other, keeping fingers out of the way.

## ZOODLE PIZZA CASSEROLE

**HANDS-ON TIME** 15 minutes
**STAND** 15 minutes
**BAKE** 25 minutes at 400°F

Nonstick cooking spray
3 10- to 12-oz. zucchini
1½ tsp. kosher salt
2 eggs, lightly beaten
2 cups shredded mozzarella cheese (8 oz.)
¼ cup grated Parmesan cheese
¼ cup all-purpose flour
2 Tbsp. cornmeal
1 8-oz. can pizza sauce
⅓ cup sliced fresh mushrooms
¼ cup chopped green sweet pepper
¼ cup sliced pitted black olives

**1.** Preheat oven to 400°F. Coat a 3-qt. baking dish with cooking spray. Using a vegetable spiralizer, cut zucchini into long, thin noodles (zoodles). Place in a colander and sprinkle with salt; toss gently. Let stand 15 to 20 minutes. Pat dry with paper towels.
**2.** In a large bowl combine eggs, ½ cup of the mozzarella cheese, the Parmesan cheese, flour, and cornmeal. Stir in zoodles. Transfer to prepared dish. Bake 10 minutes or until set and no excess liquid remains.
**3.** Spread with pizza sauce. Top with remaining 1½ cups mozzarella cheese, mushrooms, green sweet pepper, and olives. Bake 15 to 20 minutes more or until cheese is light brown. **Makes 8 servings.**
**EACH SERVING** *163 cal., 8 g fat (4 g sat. fat), 67 mg chol., 585 mg sodium, 12 g carb., 2 g fiber, 4 g sugars, 12 g pro.*

**ZOODLES** are easiest to crank out with a spiralizer, but if you don't have one, you can use a mandoline to thinly slice zucchini or a box grater to coarsely shred it.

**SPIRALIZER** Now available in handheld and countertop models, spiralizers have different blades for varying the thickness and cut (such as fettuccine-style or flat ribbons). You can experiment with what shape you like best.

**EASY EVERYDAY**
*Six cups of purchased zucchini noodles can be substituted for the 3 zucchini as a shortcut to a weeknight meal.*

// MEATLESS //

# EASY PUMPKIN MAC AND CHEESE

**HANDS-ON TIME** 25 minutes
**BAKE** 30 minutes at 375°F
**STAND** 5 minutes

1   14.5-oz. pkg. dried protein-enriched multigrain rotini or penne pasta
1   15- to 16-oz. jar Alfredo pasta sauce
1   15-oz. can pumpkin
½   cup chopped roasted red sweet peppers, drained
½   cup water
¼   tsp. salt
⅛   tsp. cracked black pepper
1½  cups shredded Fontina cheese (6 oz.)

**1.** Preheat oven to 375°F. Grease a 3-qt. rectangular baking dish.
**2.** In a 4- to 6-qt. pot cook pasta in boiling salted water according to package directions; drain. Return to pot. Stir in next six ingredients (through black pepper). Stir in ½ cup of the cheese. Transfer to prepared dish.
**3.** Bake, covered, 25 minutes. Sprinkle with remaining 1 cup cheese. Bake, uncovered, 5 minutes more or until heated through and cheese is melted. Let stand 5 minutes before serving. **Makes 6 servings (1⅓ cups each).**
**EACH SERVING** *511 cal., 22 g fat (11 g sat. fat), 92 mg chol., 894 mg sodium, 56 g carb., 7 g fiber, 7 g sugars, 23 g pro.*

**HEALTHY TWIST**
*For a lower-sodium dish, omit the salt and top the casserole with ¼ cup cheese instead of 1 cup.*

ROSEMARY AND CARROT
RIBBON PAPPARDELLE

# MUSHROOM SOURDOUGH TOASTS

**START TO FINISH** 30 minutes

2    Tbsp. olive oil
1    Tbsp. butter
6    cups sliced assorted fresh
     mushrooms
2    cloves garlic, minced
1    Tbsp. chopped fresh thyme
     Coarse salt and freshly ground
     black pepper
1    tsp. olive oil
4    eggs
4    ½-inch slices rustic sourdough
     bread
8    oz. sliced semisoft cheese,
     such as Fontina
     Mixed fresh herbs or
     microgreens

**1.** Preheat broiler. In a 10-inch
skillet heat 2 Tbsp. oil and butter
over medium-high heat. Add
mushrooms and garlic; cook about
6 minutes or until mushrooms
are tender and browned, stirring
occasionally. Remove from heat.
Sprinkle with thyme; season to taste
with salt and pepper. Transfer
to a bowl.
**2.** In same skillet heat 1 tsp. oil over
medium heat. Break eggs into
skillet. Reduce heat to low; cook
eggs 3 to 4 minutes or until whites
are set and yolks start to thicken.
**3.** Meanwhile, arrange bread slices
on a baking sheet. Broil 4 inches
from heat 2 minutes on each side
or until toasted. Top bread with
cheese; broil 1 minute more or until
cheese melts and starts to bubble.
Remove from broiler. Top cheese
with mushroom mixture and eggs.
Sprinkle with mixed herbs. **Makes
4 toasts.**

**EACH TOAST** *482 cal., 33 g fat
(15 g sat. fat), 259 mg chol., 759 mg
sodium, 20 g carb., 2 g fiber,
5 g sugars, 28 g pro.*

# ROSEMARY AND CARROT RIBBON PAPPARDELLE

**START TO FINISH** 30 minutes

1    lb. carrots, peeled
8    oz. dried pappardelle pasta
½    cup chopped, toasted
     hazelnuts
2    Tbsp. butter
2    Tbsp. chopped fresh rosemary
½    tsp. salt
4    oz. goat cheese (chèvre), cut up

**1.** Using a vegetable peeler, cut
carrots lengthwise into thin ribbons.
Transfer to a large colander.
**2.** Cook pasta in boiling lightly
salted water according to package
directions. Drain in same colander
as carrots, reserving 1 cup of the
pasta cooking water.
**3.** In a 10-inch skillet combine
hazelnuts, butter, rosemary, and
salt. Heat over medium heat until
butter is bubbling. Add cheese and
half of the reserved pasta cooking
water, whisking until combined.
Add pasta mixture, tossing to
coat and thinning with additional
remaining pasta cooking water
as needed. If desired, sprinkle
with additional toasted hazelnuts.
**Makes 4 servings (1¾ cups each).**

**EACH SERVING** *508 cal., 26 g fat
(11 g sat. fat), 45 mg chol., 453 mg
sodium, 52 g carb., 5 g fiber,
6 g sugars, 19 g pro.*

MUSHROOM
SOURDOUGH TOASTS

// MEATLESS //

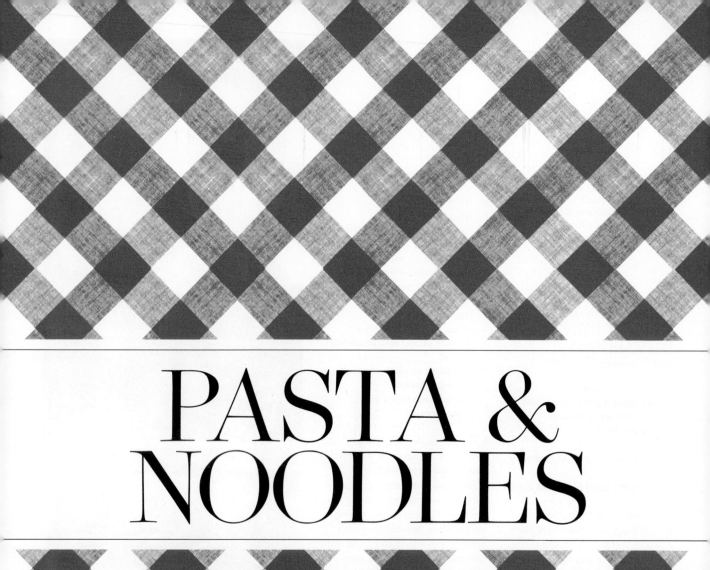

# PASTA & NOODLES

**MAKE-AHEAD RECIPE**

FOUR BASIC INGREDIENTS AND ABOUT AN HOUR (AND NO SPECIAL EQUIPMENT NEEDED)—THAT'S ALL IT TAKES TO MAKE FRESH PASTA. JUST KNEAD, ROLL, AND HAND-CUT THE NOODLES TO BOIL NOW OR FREEZE FOR LATER.

---

## HOMEMADE PASTA

**HANDS-ON TIME** 40 minutes
**STAND** 20 minutes

2⅓ cups all-purpose flour
½  tsp. salt
2   eggs, lightly beaten
⅓  cup water
1   tsp. olive oil

**1.** In a large bowl stir together 2 cups of the flour and the salt; make a well in the center. In a bowl combine eggs, water, and oil; add to flour mixture. Stir to combine.
**2.** Sprinkle a kneading surface with remaining ⅓ cup flour. Knead dough until smooth and elastic (8 to 10 minutes total). Cover dough; let rest 10 minutes. Divide the dough into four equal portions. (Or to freeze the dough, wrap in plastic wrap. Freeze in an airtight container up to 3 months. Thaw completely in the refrigerator; continue with Step 3.)
**3.** On a lightly floured surface, roll each portion into a 12-inch square about ⅟₁₆ inch thick (dough is thin enough when you can start to see through it). Lightly dust with flour. Let stand, uncovered, 20 minutes; cut as desired (tips, *opposite*). (If using a pasta machine, pass each portion through machine according to manufacturer's directions until dough is ⅟₁₆ inch thick. Let stand 20 minutes; cut as desired.)
**4.** To serve pasta immediately, cook in a large pot of boiling, salted water 2 to 3 minutes or until tender; drain.
**5.** To store cut pasta, spread it on a wire cooling rack or hang it from a pasta-drying rack. Let dry 2 hours. Place in an airtight container and chill up to 3 days. Or dry the pasta at least 1 hour; place in a freezer bag or freezer container and freeze up to 8 months (add 1 or 2 minutes to cooking time for frozen pasta).
**Makes 5 servings (1 cup each).**
**EACH SERVING** *255 cal., 3 g fat (1 g sat. fat), 85 mg chol, 262 mg sodium, 46 g carb., 2 g fiber, 0 g sugars, 8 g pro.*

**EGG NOODLES**
Prepare as directed, except start with 1¾ cups flour in Step 1 and substitute 1 egg + 2 egg yolks for the 2 eggs. Sprinkle ¼ cup flour on surface, then knead, roll, cut, and cook as directed.

**FOOD PROCESSOR METHOD**
Place the steel blade in the food processor. Add all of the flour, salt, and eggs to food processor. Cover; process until mixture forms fine crumbs. With the food processor running, slowly pour the water and oil through feed tube. Continue processing until the dough forms a ball. Transfer dough to a lightly floured surface. Cover; let dough rest 10 minutes. Divide the dough into four equal portions. Continue as directed in Step 3.

## LONG PASTA

**1** Knead the dough, adding flour as necessary to keep it from sticking, about 10 minutes or until dough is nice and smooth. This creates a gluten structure that binds the dough and gives the noodles their chewy texture.

**2** Using a long rolling pin, roll dough away from you, pushing down and stretching the dough as you roll. If the dough snaps back into place, let it rest a bit longer. Rotate and flip it over once or twice, dusting with flour as necessary.

**3** Loosely roll each dough portion into a spiral. Use a sharp knife to cut pasta into desired-size strips. Unroll the ribbons. If desired, cut into shorter lengths. Cook or dry and store as directed in recipe.

## TRADITIONAL SEMOLINA PASTA

*Semolina—a coarse wheat flour—is commonly used in fresh Italian pasta, giving it a more granular texture. Most large supermarkets carry semolina near other flours.*

In a bowl combine 1 cup all-purpose flour and ¼ cup semolina flour; create a well in the center. Add 2 eggs. Using a fork, gently beat eggs, mixing in flour with each stroke. Stir as dough thickens. When it can no longer be stirred, knead in remaining flour until firm and elastic. Cover; let rest 20 minutes. On a lightly floured surface roll dough into an 18-inch circle about ¹⁄₁₆ inch thick. Lightly flour surface of the dough. Cut as directed *above right.* Let stand 1 hour. Cook as directed in Step 4 *(opposite).* **Makes 4 servings (about 1 cup each).**

**EACH SERVING** *187 cal., 3 g fat (1 g sat. fat), 93 mg chol., 36 mg sodium, 32 g carb., 1 g fiber, 0 g sugars, 8 g pro.*

## MEAT-FILLED RAVIOLI

**For filling,** in an 8-inch skillet cook 6 oz. ground beef or bulk Italian sausage until no longer pink; drain. In a small bowl stir together ⅓ cup ricotta cheese, ⅓ cup shredded mozzarella cheese, 3 Tbsp. grated Parmesan cheese, and ½ tsp. Italian seasoning. Stir in meat mixture.

**To shape ravioli,** cut rolled dough into 2-inch-wide strips. Leaving a ½-inch margin around the edges, place about 1 tsp. desired filling at 1-inch intervals on one strip of the dough.

**Using your finger,** moisten the dough with water around the mounds of filling. Lay a second strip of dough over the first. Press pasta around each mound of filling so that the two strips of dough stick together.

**With a sharp knife,** trim edges and cut pasta between the mounds of filling to separate into uniform-size individual ravioli. Let stand 10 minutes before cooking.

**Cook ravioli** in a large pot of boiling water 6 to 8 minutes or until tender. **Makes about 48 ravioli.**

**PER 6 RAVIOLI** *247 cal., 9 g fat (4 g sat. fat), 71 mg chol., 245 mg sodium, 29 g carb., 1 g fiber, 0 g sugars, 12 g pro.*

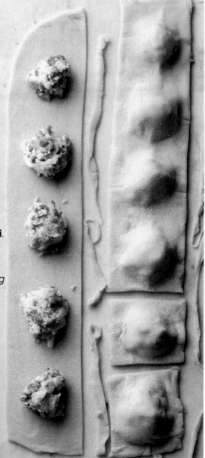

GNOCCHI (NYOH-KEE), WHICH TRANSLATES TO "LUMPS" IN ITALIAN, ARE SMALL, SLIGHTLY CHEWY POTATO PASTA DUMPLINGS. THE SIGNATURE AIRY BUT TOOTHSOME TEXTURE RELIES ON THE RUSSET POTATO AND A LIGHT HAND WITH THE FLOUR AND KNEADING.

## POTATO GNOCCHI WITH BROWNED BUTTER SAUCE

**HANDS-ON TIME** 1 hour 5 minutes
**BAKE** 45 minutes at 425°F

1½  lb. russet potatoes
2    egg yolks
½    tsp. salt
⅛    tsp. black or white pepper
¾    to 1 cup all-purpose flour
¼    cup butter
2    Tbsp. chopped fresh parsley
½    cup finely shredded Parmesan cheese (2 oz.)
     Lemon wedges

**RUSSET DOES BEST**
Starchy, mealy-textured russet potatoes give gnocchi that light and tender bite. Waxier potatoes, such as Yukon golds, tend to give gnocchi a gummier texture.

### THE LIGHTEST TOUCH

To avoid overdeveloping the gluten in the flour—which results in dense, heavy gnocchi—knead the dough just until smooth.

**1.** Preheat oven to 425°F. Prick potatoes with a fork. Bake 45 to 60 minutes or until tender and fork inserts easily. Holding each potato with an oven mitt or towel, peel quickly.

**2.** Press the peeled hot potatoes through a ricer or food mill into a large bowl.

**3.** In a bowl whisk together egg yolks, salt, and pepper. Make a well in the center of the potatoes; add egg mixture. Stir to combine. Add ¾ cup of the flour, stirring just until combined (use your hands if necessary). On a lightly floured surface, knead in just enough of the remaining flour (may not need any) to make a smooth, fairly soft dough that is still slightly sticky. Do not overknead or add too much flour.

**NO RICER OR FOOD MILL?**
Shred the cooked potatoes using a box grater (tip, *opposite, top right*).

**4.** Divide dough into four portions. Roll each portion into a long, thin rope ¾ to 1 inch thick. Cut ropes into ½-inch pieces. Roll each piece into a little ball, adding more flour to the work surface as needed. Roll balls over a lightly floured gnocchi paddle or on a fork to create patterned ridges (tip, *opposite, top right*). Place gnocchi on a baking sheet lightly dusted with flour. Set aside until ready to cook. (Or place in freezer and freeze until firm. Transfer frozen gnocchi to a freezer bag; freeze up to 3 months.)

**5.** Place butter in a 10-inch skillet. Heat over medium-low heat 15 to 17 minutes or until butter turns light brown (watch so it doesn't burn).

**6.** In a large pot or Dutch oven bring a large amount of lightly salted water to boiling; reduce heat to a slow simmer. Add half of the gnocchi, stirring to prevent them from sticking together. Cook 2 to 3 minutes for frozen gnocchi or until gnocchi rise to the top. Using a slotted spoon, transfer gnocchi to a tray or shallow baking pan. Repeat with the remaining gnocchi.

**7.** Return browned butter to medium heat. Stir all of the gnocchi and parsley into browned butter and toss gently until well coated. Cook and stir gently 1 to 2 minutes or until heated through. Transfer to a serving dish. Top with Parmesan cheese. Serve with lemon wedges.
**Makes 6 servings (15 gnocchi each).**
**EACH SERVING** *249 cal., 12 g fat (7 g sat. fat), 89 mg chol., 431 mg sodium, 28 g carb., 2 g fiber, 1 g sugars, 8 g pro.*

**1.** Quickly peel the hot potatoes, then press the pulp through a ricer. This is the easiest method to achieve a smooth texture.

**2.** If you don't have a potato ricer, use a box grater to finely shred the potatoes. (To protect your hand, use a kitchen towel to hold the hot potato as you shred.)

**3.** On a lightly floured surface, use your hands to gently roll each dough portion into a ¾- to 1-inch-thick rope. Use a table knife to cut each rope into 20 to 22 pieces, about ½ inch in size.

**4.** Roll each piece into a ball. Place one ball on a floured fork (or gnocchi paddle) and press with your fingers, rolling dough to make ridges. You will end up with ridges on one side and an indentation on the other side.

## BROWNING BUTTER

Cook the butter until it turns light brown and has a nutty aroma. Pay attention—the butter can quickly go from golden to burned.

**EGG NOODLES 1.** Fine **2.** Medium **3.** Wide/Extra Wide ■ **TUBE PASTA 1.** Manicotti **2.** Long ziti **3.** Bucatini **4.** Campanelle
**5.** Ziti **6.** Ditalini **7.** Mostaccioli **8.** Elbow **9.** Cavatappi **10.** Rigatoni **11.** Penne ■ **FILLED PASTA 1.** Tortellini **2.** Ravioli
■ **LONG PASTA 1.** Nested angel hair **2.** Lasagna **3.** Mafalda **4.** Fettuccine **5.** Linguine **6.** Spaghetti **7.** Vermicelli **8.** Cappellini
■ **SHAPE PASTA 1.** Wagon wheel **2.** Farfalle **3.** Farfallini **4.** Gnocchi shells **5.** Rotini **6.** Tiny shells **7.** Medium shells **8.** Orecchiette
**9.** Radiatore **10.** Gemelli **11.** Cavatelli **12.** Jumbo shells ■ **TINY PASTA 1.** Orzo **2.** Couscous **3.** Israeli couscous **4.** Acini de pepe

## PAIRING PASTA

Pasta comes in all lengths, shapes, and thicknesses. It's hard to go wrong when matching pasta with sauces and soups, but here are some recommendations to start with.

**SOUP PASTAS** Fine egg noodles, ditalini, orzo, acini de pepe, small tortellini, small ravioli

**PASTA FOR CHUNKY, THICK SAUCES** Wide egg noodles, farfalle, rotini, rigatoni, campanelle, spaghetti, fettuccine

**PASTA FOR LIGHT SAUCES** Angel hair, linguine, tortellini, ravioli, ziti

**PASTA FOR STUFFING** Manicotti, jumbo shells

**PASTA FOR SALADS** Farfalle, wagon wheel, radiatore, ziti, elbow, gemelli, tortellini

## SPECIAL PASTAS

The pasta aisle is full of alternatives to traditional pastas. They offer different textures and nutritional benefits.

**GLUTEN-FREE** This type of pasta is made using a combination of rice, corn, potatoes, quinoa, and other gluten-free starches. Because brands of this product vary greatly, you might need to try a few before finding one you like.

**MULTIGRAIN** Made from a mixture of grains, seeds, and sometimes legumes, multigrain pasta has a high fiber and protein content and is often enriched with omega-3 fatty acids and other essential nutrients.

**VEGETABLE-BASE** Made with pureed vegetables, such as spinach, tomatoes, beets, and zucchini, these types of pasta often boast a full serving of vegetables in each serving.

**WHITE FIBER** This product contains similar amounts of fiber and protein as whole wheat pasta, but it has the texture and appearance of regular pasta.

**WHOLE WHEAT** This pasta offers a rich, nutty flavor and higher protein and fiber content than traditional white flour-based pasta.

## CREAMY BAKED ZITI

**HANDS-ON TIME** 30 minutes
**BAKE** 30 minutes at 425°F

- 4 cups dried ziti or penne pasta (12 oz.)
- 1 14.5-oz. can fire-roasted diced tomatoes, undrained
- 1 cup chopped onion
- 12 cloves garlic, minced (2 Tbsp.)
- 2 Tbsp. olive oil
- ½ cup dry white wine
- 2 cups heavy cream
- 1 cup finely shredded Parmesan cheese
- ¾ cup crumbled Gorgonzola or other blue cheese (3 oz.)
- ½ cup shredded Fontina cheese (2 oz.)
- ½ tsp. salt
- ¼ tsp. black pepper
  Snipped fresh Italian parsley (optional)

**1.** Preheat oven to 425°F. In a 6-qt. pot cook pasta according to package directions; drain. Place in an ungreased 3-qt. rectangular baking dish; stir in undrained tomatoes.

**2.** Meanwhile, in a 3-qt. saucepan cook onion and garlic in hot oil over medium heat just until tender. Carefully stir in wine and cook about 3 minutes or until liquid reduces by half. Add cream; heat to boiling. Boil gently, uncovered, about 5 minutes or until mixture thickens slightly, stirring frequently. Remove from heat. Stir in cheeses, salt, and pepper.

**3.** Pour cheese sauce over pasta. Bake, covered, 30 to 35 minutes or until sauce is bubbly. Stir pasta to coat. If desired, top with parsley.

**Makes 6 servings.**

**EACH SERVING** *717 cal., 46 g fat (26 g sat. fat), 141 mg chol., 883 mg sodium, 54 g carb., 3 g fiber, 5 g sugars, 21 g pro.*

**THE PERFECT SERVING**

Typically, a serving is 1½ to 2 oz. dried pasta—any shape or size. Cook pasta in a large pot of salted, boiling water according to package directions.

## MARINARA SAUCE

**HANDS-ON TIME** 15 minutes
**COOK** 30 minutes

**WHOLE TOMATOES** can be cut with kitchen scissors while they're still in the can to contain any mess.

| | |
|---|---|
| 1 | Tbsp. olive oil |
| 1 | cup finely chopped onion |
| 2 | Tbsp. minced garlic |
| 2 | 28-oz. cans San Marzano tomatoes, undrained and snipped |
| 2 | 28-oz. cans crushed tomatoes |
| 2 | tsp. sugar (optional) |
| 1 | tsp. salt |
| ½ | tsp. black pepper |

**1.** In an 8-qt. pot heat oil over medium heat. Add onion and garlic; cook 3 to 5 minutes or until onion is tender, stirring occasionally.

**2.** Stir in remaining ingredients. Bring to boiling; reduce heat. Simmer, uncovered, 30 minutes or until slightly thickened, stirring occasionally.

**Makes 24 servings (½ cup each).**

**TO STORE** Transfer sauce to an airtight container(s). Cover; chill up to 3 days or freeze up to 3 months.

**EACH SERVING** *44 cal., 1 g fat (0 g sat. fat), 0 mg chol., 272 mg sodium, 9 g carb., 2 g fiber, 6 g sugars, 2 g pro.*

### MAKE IT A MEAL

What's on the side? Make a quick grilled romaine salad. Halve 1 medium heart of romaine lettuce; brush cut sides with olive oil. Grill, covered, 1 to 3 minutes or until grill marks develop on the romaine and the romaine is slightly wilted. Drizzle with Fresh Herb Vinaigrette (p. 299) or purchased vinaigrette.

**SAN MARZANO TOMATOES** are imported from Italy, where they are grown in the nutrient-rich volcanic soils near Mt. Vesuvius—only tomatoes from there can legally go by the name San Marzano. Their deep red color, dense flesh, and sweet flavor make them ideal for sauces. Look for canned San Marzano tomatoes at large supermarkets and specialty food stores. If you can't find them, any canned whole peeled tomatoes work.

### CREAMY VODKA SAUCE

Prepare as directed, except stir in ¼ cup vodka with the tomatoes in Step 2. Simmer as directed. Before serving or storing, stir in ¾ cup heavy cream.

### GARDEN VEGETABLE SAUCE

Prepare as directed, except increase olive oil to 2 Tbsp. Add 1 cup chopped green sweet pepper, 1 cup quartered canned artichoke hearts, 1 cup sliced fresh mushrooms, and 1 cup chopped zucchini or eggplant with the onion in Step 1. Continue as directed.

### PUTTANESCA SAUCE

Prepare as directed, except mash 3 or 4 anchovy fillets into onion mixture in Step 1; cook 30 seconds more. Stir ½ cup sliced pitted ripe olives and 2 Tbsp. drained capers into sauce. If desired, stir in ½ cup chopped fresh parsley and ¼ tsp. crushed red pepper.

### MARINARA SAUCE WITH MEATBALLS

Prepare as directed through Step 2. For meatballs, preheat oven to 375°F. In a large bowl combine 2 eggs; ½ cup each fine dry bread crumbs and finely chopped onion; ¼ cup each milk and chopped fresh parsley; 1 clove garlic, minced; ½ tsp. each salt and black pepper; and ¼ tsp. crushed red pepper. Add 1 lb. each bulk pork sausage and ground beef; mix well. Shape mixture into 16 meatballs; place in a shallow baking pan. Bake about 25 minutes or until meatballs are cooked through (160°F), turning occasionally. Use tongs to transfer meatballs to sauce. **Makes 16 meatballs.**

PER MEATBALL *168 cal., 12 g fat (4 g sat. fat), 62 mg chol., 287 mg sodium, 4 g carb., 0 g fiber, 1 g sugars, 11 g pro.*

**SHAPING MEATBALLS**
For 16 equal-size meatballs, shape the meat mixture into an 8-inch square on a cutting board. Cut the square into sixteen 2-inch squares. Roll each square into a ball.

### *FREEZING MEATBALLS*

Make a double batch of meatballs and freeze some for later meals.

**TO FREEZE,** place cooked meatballs in a single layer on a baking sheet. Freeze them overnight and repack in resealable freezer bags. Label with the date and return to the freezer. Use within 2 months.

**TO USE,** thaw meatballs in the refrigerator or microwave. Serve meatballs whole in soups and sandwiches or sliced on top of pizza. Or add them to your favorite sauce, heat through, and serve over pasta.

# WHAT IS BOLOGNESE (BOH-LUHN-YAYZ)?

THIS RICH TOMATO-MEAT SAUCE IS A SPECIALTY OF THE BOLOGNA REGION OF ITALY. IT STANDS OUT FROM OTHER SAUCES WITH A HEAVY-HANDED POUR OF BOTH WINE AND WHOLE MILK.

## GO FOR AL DENTE

To bring out pasta's full, nutty flavor, cook it just until it has the firm, slightly chewy texture known as al dente (Italian for "to the tooth"). Test near the end of cooking time by giving it a taste. When done, drain the cooked pasta in a colander; shake well to remove. Do not rinse unless specified.

## BOLOGNESE

**HANDS-ON TIME** 50 minutes
**COOK** 3 hours 10 minutes

| | |
|---|---|
| 2 | Tbsp. butter |
| 1 | Tbsp. olive oil |
| 4 | oz. pancetta, chopped |
| 1 | cup chopped onion |
| 1 | cup chopped carrots |
| 1 | cup chopped fennel stems (not the bulb)* |
| 2 | lb. ground beef |
| 1 | lb. ground pork |
| ½ | tsp. kosher salt |
| ½ | tsp. black pepper |
| 2 | cups dry white wine |
| 1½ | cups whole milk |
| ⅛ | tsp. ground nutmeg |
| 1 | 28-oz. can whole tomatoes, undrained and cut up |
| 1 | Parmesan cheese rind (tip, *opposite*) |
| | Hot cooked pasta |

**1.** In a 4-qt. Dutch oven heat butter and oil over medium-high heat. Add pancetta; cook and stir about 8 minutes or until starting to brown, stirring occasionally. Reduce heat to medium. Add onion. Cook and stir about 5 minutes or until translucent. Add carrots and fennel. Cook 2 minutes more.
**2.** Add the beef and pork to Dutch oven. Season with salt and pepper. Using a wooden spoon, break up meat (you want to retain some larger pieces for texture). Cook until browned. Add the wine. Scrape up the browned bits from the bottom of the Dutch oven. Simmer, uncovered, until the wine has evaporated, about 40 minutes.
**3.** Add the milk and nutmeg. Simmer, uncovered, about 20 minutes or until the milk has evaporated, stirring frequently. Once the milk has evaporated, add the tomatoes; stir to combine. When the tomatoes just start to bubble, reduce heat to low and add the Parmesan rind. Cook, uncovered, 2½ to 3 hours, stirring occasionally. As the sauce cooks, liquid will evaporate and the sauce will start to look dry. Add ½ cup water at a time (2 to 3 cups water total) and continue to simmer as liquid evaporates. Serve over hot cooked pasta. **Makes 12 servings (¾ cup sauce each).**
**\*NOTE** Save the fennel bulb for another use.
**TO STORE** Transfer mixture to an airtight storage container(s). Cover and chill up to 3 days or freeze up to 3 months.
**EACH SERVING** *408 cal., 28 g fat (11 g sat. fat), 94 mg chol., 444 mg sodium, 8 g carb., 2 g fiber, 5 g sugars, 23 g pro.*

Browning the meat is the first step to creating layers of flavor in this sauce. Take your time. Deep caramelizing on the veggies and meat adds to the richness.

When you add the wine, the liquid helps release those flavorful browned bits at the bottom of the Dutch oven. A wooden spoon is the best tool for scraping them up.

It might seem like an odd stage to add milk, but cooking away the liquid before adding the tomatoes makes the meat even richer and sweet without making the sauce overly creamy.

Keep the heat as low as possible. You want the slightest bubbling for ultratender meat. Add a little water to keep the sauce from sticking to the bottom of the pot.

**THE RIND** is the outer layer of Parmesan cheese wedges (available at cheese counters). After grating the cheese from the wedge, simmer the rind in your sauce for a deliciously rich flavor.

## SPAGHETTI ALLA CARBONARA
**START TO FINISH** 40 minutes

12   oz. dried spaghetti
6   oz. pancetta or bacon, finely chopped
½   cup chopped onion
2   cloves garlic, minced
¼   cup dry white wine
2   pasteurized egg yolks or ¼ cup refrigerated or frozen egg product, thawed
¼   cup heavy cream
1   cup finely shredded Parmigiano-Reggiano or Parmesan cheese (4 oz.)
½   tsp. black pepper

**WHOLE PASTEURIZED EGGS**—which have been heated just enough to kill bacteria like salmonella—can often be found in the egg case in large supermarkets. You can also use refrigerated egg product from cartons, which is also pasteurized and is easy to find.

**1.** In a 6-qt. pot cook pasta according to package directions; drain, reserving ½ cup pasta water. Return pasta to pot; keep warm.
**2.** Meanwhile, in a 12-inch skillet cook and stir pancetta over medium heat until crisp. Using a slotted spoon, transfer pancetta to a paper towel-lined plate. Drain all but 2 Tbsp. drippings from the skillet.
**3.** Add onion and garlic to hot drippings in skillet; cook and stir over medium heat about 5 minutes or until onion is tender. Remove skillet from heat; carefully add wine. Return skillet to heat. Bring wine to boiling; reduce heat. Simmer, uncovered, about 3 minutes or until most of the wine evaporates.
**4.** In a small bowl combine egg yolks or product and cream. Stir in cheese and pepper. Add spaghetti to onion mixture in skillet; toss gently over medium heat 1 to 2 minutes to coat. Remove from heat; add egg mixture, reserved pancetta, and ¼ cup of the pasta water. Toss well to coat. Serve immediately. Add additional pasta water, if needed, to maintain creamy consistency. **Makes 6 servings (1 cup each).**
**EACH SERVING** *460 cal., 22 g fat (10 g sat. fat), 41 mg chol., 569 mg sodium, 45 g carb., 2 g fiber, 3 g sugars, 18 g pro.*

## *CLASSIC CARBONARA*

Authentic Italian carbonara sauce is a combination of raw egg, pasta cooking water, and cheese—but getting it to the right consistency is a little tricky. Instead, our weeknight version uses cream for similar richness and body, and wine for luscious flavor.

## FETTUCCINE ALFREDO

**START TO FINISH** 35 minutes

8    oz. dried fettuccine
2    cloves garlic, minced
2    Tbsp. butter
1    cup heavy cream
½    tsp. salt
⅛    tsp. black pepper
½    cup grated Parmesan cheese (2 oz.)

PREGROUND PEPPER works in a pinch, but using a pepper grinder to grind your own peppercorns makes a big difference in flavor.

**1.** Cook pasta according to package directions; drain.
**2.** In a 3-qt. saucepan cook garlic in hot butter over medium-high heat 1 minute. Add cream, salt, and pepper. Bring to boiling; reduce heat. Boil gently, uncovered, 3 minutes or until beginning to thicken. Remove from heat; stir in Parmesan cheese. Add pasta; toss to coat. If desired, top with additional Parmesan cheese.
**Makes 4 servings (1¼ cups each).**
**EACH SERVING** *514 cal., 32 g fat (19 g sat. fat), 107 mg chol., 511 mg sodium, 45 g carb., 2 g fiber, 2 g sugars, 13 g pro.*

## TORTELLINI EMILIA

**HANDS-ON TIME** 30 minutes
**BAKE** 20 minutes at 400°F
**STAND** 10 minutes

2    8-oz. pkg. dried cheese-filled tortellini
3    Tbsp. finely chopped red onion
2    Tbsp. finely chopped shallots
1    Tbsp. butter
2    cups half-and-half
½    cup milk
2    egg yolks
¼    cup grated Parmesan cheese (1 oz.)
1    Tbsp. chopped fresh sage or 1 tsp. dried sage, crushed
¼    tsp. black pepper
½    cup shredded Gruyère or Swiss cheese (2 oz.)
½    cup walnut pieces
2    oz. prosciutto or cooked ham, finely chopped

**1.** Preheat oven to 400°F. Cook tortellini according to package directions; drain.
**2.** For sauce, in a 2-qt. saucepan cook onion and shallots in hot butter over medium heat until tender. Stir in half-and-half and milk. Bring just to boiling; remove from heat. In a bowl lightly beat egg yolks. Slowly add about 1 cup of the hot milk mixture to the beaten yolks, beating until combined. Return all of the egg yolk mixture to saucepan. Cook and stir over medium-low heat about 10 minutes or until slightly thickened and just bubbly. Stir in Parmesan, sage, and pepper.
**3.** Transfer half of the cooked tortellini to a 2-qt. rectangular or oval baking dish. Sprinkle with the Gruyère cheese. Pour half of the sauce over tortellini. Top with the remaining cooked tortellini, the walnuts, the prosciutto, and the remaining sauce.
**4.** Bake, uncovered, 20 minutes or until top is lightly browned and bubbly. Let stand 10 minutes. If desired, top with fresh sage.
**Makes 8 servings (1 cup each).**
**EACH SERVING** *457 cal., 27 g fat (11 g sat. fat), 127 mg chol., 790 mg sodium, 38 g carb., 4 g fiber, 4 g sugars, 18 g pro.*

## GRATE PASTA CHEESES

Your pasta deserves special treatment. Hand-grate blocks of these classic Italian cheeses over pasta and into sauces.

### PARMIGIANO-REGGIANO

A granular texture and bold, snappy flavor are hallmarks of this time-honored cheese. Also try it thinly shaved in salads.

### PECORINO ROMANO

This gratable sheep's milk cheese brings a sharp, peppery flavor to dishes.

### AGED ASIAGO

Choose this one for its nutty, pleasantly salty flavor.

### GRANA PADANO

This cheese has a fine texture and sweet, mild, fragrant flavor.

### THE RINSING QUESTION

Rinsing removes a light coating of starch that helps the sauce and seasonings cling. So we recommend not rinsing pasta unless it will be baked or served cool in a salad.

# PASTA WITH WHITE CLAM SAUCE

**START TO FINISH** 30 minutes

| | |
|---|---|
| 10 | oz. dried linguine or fettuccine |
| 2 | 6.5-oz. cans chopped or minced clams |
| 2 | cups half-and-half or whole milk |
| ½ | cup chopped onion |
| 2 | cloves garlic, minced |
| 2 | Tbsp. butter |
| ¼ | cup all-purpose flour |
| 2 | tsp. chopped fresh oregano or ½ tsp. dried oregano, crushed |
| ¼ | tsp. salt |
| ⅛ | tsp. black pepper |
| ¼ | cup chopped fresh parsley |
| ¼ | cup dry white wine or chicken broth |
| ¼ | cup finely shredded or grated Parmesan cheese (1 oz.) |

**1.** In a 4-qt. saucepan cook pasta according to package directions; drain and keep warm. Meanwhile, drain canned clams, reserving the juice from one of the cans (you should have about ½ cup). Add enough half-and-half to reserved clam juice to equal 2½ cups liquid.
**2.** In a 2-qt. saucepan cook onion and garlic in hot butter over medium heat until tender but not brown. Stir in flour, dried oregano (if using), salt, and pepper. Add clam juice mixture all at once. Cook and stir until thickened and bubbly. Cook and stir 1 minute more. Stir in drained clams, fresh oregano (if using), parsley, and wine. Heat through. Serve over hot pasta. Sprinkle with Parmesan cheese.
**Makes 4 servings (1½ cups each).**
EACH SERVING *680 cal., 24 g fat (14 g sat. fat), 125 mg chol., 430 mg sodium, 72 g carb., 3 g fiber, 3 g sugars, 40 g pro.*

# SHRIMP SCAMPI

**START TO FINISH** 30 minutes

- 12 oz. fresh or frozen peeled and deveined medium shrimp
- 1 oz. prosciutto, cut into strips
- 1 Tbsp. butter
- 1 Tbsp. olive oil
- 1 Tbsp. minced garlic
- ¼ cup finely chopped shallots
- 1½ cups dry white wine
- 2 Tbsp. lemon juice
- ¼ tsp. salt
- 1 roma tomato, seeded and finely chopped
- 1 Tbsp. finely chopped Italian parsley
- 1 tsp. chopped fresh thyme
- 8 oz. dried angel hair pasta
  Lemon wedges (optional)

**1.** Thaw shrimp if frozen; set aside. In a 10-inch skillet cook prosciutto over medium heat until crisp. Drain on paper towels.
**2.** To the same skillet add butter and olive oil. Heat over medium heat.

Add garlic; cook and stir 30 seconds. Add shallots; cook and stir about 1 minute or until tender. Add shrimp, wine, lemon juice, and salt; bring to boiling. Reduce heat and simmer, uncovered, 2 to 3 minutes or until shrimp turn opaque, stirring occasionally. Remove shrimp with a slotted spoon; cover and keep warm.
**3.** Continue to gently boil liquid in skillet, uncovered, about 10 minutes or until thickened and reduced to about 1 cup. Stir in tomato, parsley,

and thyme. Cook 1 minute. Return shrimp to skillet; toss gently to coat.
**4.** Meanwhile, cook pasta according to package directions; drain. Top pasta with shrimp mixture; sprinkle with crisp prosciutto. If desired, serve with lemon wedges. **Makes 4 servings (1½ cups each).**

**EACH SERVING** *434 cal., 9 g fat (3 g sat. fat), 147 mg chol., 420 mg sodium, 48 g carb., 3 g fiber, 4 g sugars, 27 g pro.*

---

## *KEEPING PASTA WARM*

*Pasta has its best flavor and texture immediately after cooking. But if it needs to sit for a bit while you prep the rest of the meal, here's what to do.*

### 1
**RETURN TO THE PAN**
Return the drained cooked pasta to the warm cooking pan. Stir in a little olive oil to help prevent the noodles from sticking together. Cover and let the pasta stand no more than 15 minutes.

### 2
**HEAT & SERVE**
Fill a serving bowl with hot water and let it stand for a few minutes. Empty and dry the bowl. Add the hot pasta and cover; serve the pasta within 5 minutes.

---

## *MAKE IT A MEAL*

We love serving vibrant scampi with bread to soak up any extra sauce. To make garlicky baguette toasts, rub lightly toasted baguette slices with a halved garlic clove while still warm. Add some extra color to your plate with steamed peas or wilted spinach topped with crumbled crisp-cooked bacon.

**MAKE IT AHEAD**
Lasagna is a classic prep-ahead dish. Prepare it through Step 3, then cover with plastic wrap. Refrigerate up to 24 hours. Uncover and bake in a 375°F oven 45 to 50 minutes or until hot in the center (160°F).

## MEAT SAUCE

In a 12-inch skillet or saucepan cook 8 oz. ground beef; 8 oz. bulk Italian sausage or ground beef; 1 cup chopped onion; and 3 cloves garlic, minced, over medium-high heat until meat is browned, using a wooden spoon to break up meat as it cooks. Drain fat. Stir in ¼ to ⅓ cup dry red wine; bring to boiling. Stir in one 28-oz. can crushed tomatoes; two 8-oz. cans tomato sauce; 1 Tbsp. dried Italian seasoning, crushed; 1 tsp. fennel seeds, crushed; and ¼ tsp. black pepper. Bring to boiling; reduce heat. Cover and simmer 15 minutes, stirring occasionally.

»
**GROUND TURKEY OR BULK TURKEY ITALIAN SAUSAGE** can be substituted for the ground beef and Italian sausage in the Meat Sauce.

# CLASSIC LASAGNA

**HANDS-ON TIME** 45 minutes
**BAKE** 35 minutes at 375°F
**STAND** 15 minutes

1   recipe Meat Sauce
12  dried lasagna noodles
1   egg, lightly beaten
1   15-oz. container whole milk ricotta cheese or 2 cups cottage cheese, drained
¼   cup grated Parmesan cheese
3   cups shredded mozzarella cheese (12 oz.)
    Grated Parmesan cheese (optional)
    Snipped fresh basil (optional)

**1.** Prepare Meat Sauce. Preheat oven to 375°F. Cook lasagna noodles according to package directions; drain. Rinse with cold water; drain again.
**2.** For filling, in a medium bowl combine egg, ricotta cheese, and the ¼ cup Parmesan cheese.
**3.** Spread ¼ cup of the sauce into an ungreased 3-qt. rectangular baking dish. Arrange three of the cooked noodles lengthwise over sauce. Spoon one-fourth of the filling over noodles. Top with one-fourth of the remaining sauce and one-fourth of the mozzarella cheese. Repeat layers three more times, starting with noodles and ending with mozzarella cheese (cover top layer of noodles evenly with sauce). If desired, top with additional Parmesan cheese.
**4.** Bake, uncovered, 35 to 40 minutes or until hot in the center (160°F). Let stand 15 minutes before serving. If desired, garnish with basil.
**Makes 12 servings.**

**EACH SERVING** *432 cal., 20 g fat (10 g sat. fat), 81 mg chol., 695 mg sodium, 37 g carb., 3 g fiber, 6 g sugars, 24 g pro.*

» **LASAGNA WITH BÉCHAMEL** For Béchamel Sauce, prepare Basic White Sauce *(p. 109)* as directed, except add 3 cloves garlic, minced, to the melted butter; cook and stir 1 minute before adding the flour, salt, and pepper. Stir ¼ cup grated Parmesan cheese into finished sauce. Prepare Meat Sauce as directed, except substitute one 15-oz. can crushed tomatoes for the 28-oz. can crushed tomatoes, omit one of the 8-oz. cans tomato sauce, and omit the red wine. Add one-fourth of the Béchamel sauce to each layer over the lasagna filling. Bake as directed.

» **VEGETABLE LASAGNA** Prepare as directed in Steps 1 and 2, except omit beef and sausage in Meat Sauce. Cook 1 lb. fresh cremini mushrooms, quartered, and 1 yellow or red sweet pepper, cut into strips, with the onion and garlic in 2 Tbsp. olive oil over medium-high heat 5 minutes. Stir in 1½ cups coarsely chopped zucchini; cook 3 to 5 minutes more or until vegetables are tender and most of the excess liquid has evaporated. Add wine, tomatoes, and seasoning as directed for sauce. Continue as directed in Steps 3 and 4.

**STUFFED SHELLS** Prepare as directed, except mound the filling into 12 to 15 cooked jumbo shell macaroni.

# STUFFED MANICOTTI

**HANDS-ON TIME** 25 minutes
**BAKE** 40 minutes at 350°F

1  recipe Cheesy Ricotta Filling or Spinach-Pancetta Filling
1  recipe Manicotti Meat Sauce or Creamy Parmesan Sauce
12  dried manicotti or 12 to 15 dried jumbo shells
1  cup shredded mozzarella cheese (4 oz.)

**1.** Preheat oven to 350°F. Prepare desired filling and sauce. Cook manicotti according to package directions; drain. Place manicotti in a single layer on greased foil.
**2.** Using a small spoon, fill manicotti with desired filling; arrange in an ungreased 2-qt. rectangular baking dish. Pour sauce over pasta.
**3.** Bake, covered, 30 minutes. Uncover; top with the 1 cup mozzarella. Bake about 10 minutes more or until mixture heats through and cheese melts. (If using Creamy Parmesan Sauce, bake, covered, 35 to 40 minutes or until heated

through. Top with cheese, then let stand until cheese melts.) **Makes 6 servings (2 manicotti each).**
**EACH SERVING** *515 cal., 25 g fat (13 g sat. fat), 147 mg chol., 886 mg sodium, 41 g carb., 4 g fiber, 9 g sugars, 33 g pro.*

## *CHOOSE A FILLING*

### CHEESY RICOTTA FILLING
Combine one 15-oz. container whole milk ricotta cheese; 2 eggs, lightly beaten; 1 cup shredded mozzarella cheese (4 oz.); ½ cup finely shredded Parmesan cheese (2 oz.); and 1 tsp. dried Italian seasoning, crushed.

### SPINACH-PANCETTA FILLING
Prepare Cheesy Ricotta Filling as directed, except thaw and squeeze liquid from half of a 10-oz. pkg. frozen chopped spinach. Crisp-cook 4 oz. chopped pancetta or bacon; drain. Stir pancetta and spinach into ricotta mixture and reduce mozzarella to ½ cup in ricotta mixture.

## *CHOOSE A SAUCE*

### MANICOTTI MEAT SAUCE
In a 10-inch skillet cook 8 oz. ground beef and/or Italian sausage, ½ cup onion, and 3 cloves garlic, minced, over medium-high heat until meat is browned, stirring to break up meat as it cooks; drain fat. Carefully stir in ¼ cup wine or chicken broth; bring to boiling. Stir in one 15-oz. can crushed tomatoes; one 15-oz. can tomato sauce; 2 tsp. Italian seasoning, crushed; 1 tsp. fennel seeds; and ¼ tsp. black pepper. Bring to boiling; reduce heat. Cover and simmer 15 minutes, stirring occasionally.

### CREAMY PARMESAN SAUCE
Prepare Basic White Sauce (*p. 109*) as directed, except cook and stir 3 cloves garlic, minced, in the melted butter for 1 minute before adding the flour, salt, and pepper. Stir ¼ cup grated Parmesan cheese into the finished sauce.

ASIAN NOODLES **1. Lo mein** These classic Chinese noodles are egg- and wheat-flour-based and have a medium thickness. ■ **2. Udon** Wheat-based udon are thick and chewy Japanese noodles. They're available in refrigerated and dried varieties. ■ **3. Ramen** Wheat-flour-based, these long, thin noodles contain an alkalized water, called *kansui*, that gives them their distinct flavor and chewy texture. ■ **4. Vermicelli** Also called cellophane or glass noodles, these extremely thin noodles are made from either mung beans *(left)* or rice *(right)*. ■ **5. Soba** These buckwheat noodles have a nutty flavor. ■ **6. Rice noodles** This Asian staple varies greatly in thickness, from skinny and stringlike to flat and wide.

**ASIAN CHILI SAUCES** Asian chili sauces run the gamut from sweet to hot. For Pad Thai, go for a sweet Asian chili sauce with garlic (found with the Asian foods in large supermarkets). If you use a chili sauce like sriracha or sambal oelek, the heat level will jump and the flavor profiles will be somewhat different.

## CHICKEN PAD THAI
**START TO FINISH** *45 minutes*

| | |
|---|---|
| 8 | oz. dried linguine-style rice noodles |
| ¼ | cup salted peanuts, finely chopped |
| ½ | tsp. lime zest |
| ¼ | cup fish sauce |
| 2 | Tbsp. packed brown sugar |
| 2 | Tbsp. lime juice |
| 2 | Tbsp. rice vinegar |
| 1 | Tbsp. water |
| 1 | Tbsp. Asian chili sauce with garlic |
| 3 | Tbsp. vegetable oil |
| 1 | lb. skinless, boneless chicken breast halves, patted dry and cut into bite-size strips |
| 6 | cloves garlic, minced |
| 1 | egg, lightly beaten |
| 1 | cup fresh bean sprouts, rinsed and drained |
| ⅓ | cup sliced green onions |
| 2 | Tbsp. fresh cilantro leaves Lime wedges (optional) |

**1.** Place rice noodles in a large bowl. Add enough boiling water to cover; let stand 10 to 15 minutes or until softened but still slightly chewy (al dente), stirring occasionally. Drain well.

**2.** Meanwhile, for peanut topping, in a bowl combine peanuts and lime zest. In another bowl whisk together the next six ingredients (through chili sauce).

**3.** In a 12-inch nonstick skillet heat 1 Tbsp. of the oil over medium-high heat. Add chicken and garlic to skillet; cook and stir about 6 minutes or until chicken is tender and no pink remains. Remove chicken from skillet.

**4.** Add egg to the hot skillet, tilting skillet to spread egg in an even layer (egg might not fill bottom of skillet); cook, without stirring, 30 seconds. Using a wide spatula, carefully turn egg round over; cook 30 to 60 seconds more or just until set. Transfer egg round to a plate. Cut egg round into bite-size strips.

**5.** In same skillet heat the remaining 2 Tbsp. oil over medium-high heat 30 seconds. Add sprouts; cook and stir 2 minutes. Add chicken and drained noodles (the noodles may clump together a bit, but they will separate). Stir in fish sauce mixture; cook 1 to 2 minutes more or until heated through. Transfer noodle mixture to individual plates. Top with egg strips, peanut topping, green onions, and cilantro. If desired, serve with lime wedges.

**Makes 4 servings (1¼ cups each).**

EACH SERVING *551 cal., 19 g fat (3 g sat. fat), 119 mg chol., 1,790 mg sodium, 61 g carb., 2 g fiber, 10 g sugars, 32 g pro.*

## LO MEIN
**START TO FINISH 50** minutes

12 oz. skinless, boneless chicken breast halves
6 Tbsp. reduced-sodium soy sauce
1 Tbsp. rice vinegar
4 tsp. sugar
10 oz. dried Chinese lo mein noodles or linguine
⅓ cup reduced-sodium chicken broth
2 tsp. cornstarch
1 Tbsp. vegetable oil
1 Tbsp. toasted sesame oil (tip, *p. 186*)
4 cloves garlic, minced
½ cup shredded carrot
1 cup chopped bok choy
4 green onions, cut into 2-inch thin strips

**1.** Cut chicken into bite-size strips. In a medium bowl combine 2 Tbsp. of the soy sauce, the rice vinegar, and 2 tsp. of the sugar. Add chicken; toss to coat. Let stand at room temperature 20 minutes or cover and chill 1 hour. Meanwhile, cook noodles according to package directions; drain. Rinse with cold water; drain well. For sauce, in a small bowl stir together chicken broth, the remaining 4 Tbsp. soy sauce, the remaining 2 tsp. sugar, and the cornstarch.

**2.** Pour vegetable oil and sesame oil into a wok or 10-inch nonstick skillet. Heat over medium-high heat. Add garlic; cook and stir 30 seconds. Add carrot; cook and stir 2 minutes. Add bok choy and green onions; cook and stir 2 minutes more. Remove vegetables from wok.

**3.** Drain chicken; discard marinade. Add chicken to wok (add more oil if necessary); cook and stir 3 to 4 minutes or until no longer pink. Push chicken from center of wok. Stir sauce and add to center of wok. Cook and stir until thickened and bubbly. Add the cooked noodles and vegetables. Lightly toss the mixture until combined and heated through. Transfer to a platter. If desired, sprinkle with *sesame seeds.* Serve immediately.

**Makes 6 servings (1⅓ cups each).**

EACH SERVING *326 cal., 7 g fat (1 g sat. fat), 73 mg chol., 615 mg sodium, 42 g carb., 2 g fiber, 7 g sugars, 22 g pro.*

**CHICKEN** can be swapped for beef or pork. Just substitute 12 oz. beef sirloin steak or lean boneless pork for the chicken in either the pad Thai or lo mein. Or go vegetarian by using tofu in place of the chicken.

CHICKEN PAD THAI

LO MEIN

**MAKE IT PERSONAL** BRING THE OPTIONAL TOPPERS TO THE TABLE AND LET YOUR FAMILY CHOOSE HOW THEY WANT TO TOP THEIR NOODLE BOWLS.

## CUSTOMIZE IT
PICK THE INGREDIENTS TO CREATE A RECIPE THAT'S ALL YOUR OWN.

## NOODLE BOWL

**START TO FINISH** 45 minutes

| | |
|---|---|
| 6 | oz. NOODLES |
| 2 | Tbsp. vegetable oil |
| | PROTEIN |
| | Salt and black pepper |
| ½ | cup sliced shallot, onion, or green onion |
| 2 | Tbsp. minced ginger |
| 1 | Tbsp. minced garlic |
| 3 | cups VEGETABLES |
| 1 | 32-oz. carton reduced-sodium chicken, beef, or vegetable broth |
| 2 | Tbsp. reduced-sodium soy sauce |
| 2 | Tbsp. rice vinegar |
| 1 | Tbsp. sriracha sauce (optional) |
| | FLAVORING |
| | TOPPERS |

**1.** Cook NOODLES according to package directions; drain and rinse with cold water to cool completely.
**2.** Meanwhile, in a 6-qt. Dutch oven heat 1 Tbsp. of the oil over medium-high heat. Pat PROTEIN dry with paper towels. Sprinkle with salt and pepper. Cook PROTEIN in hot oil 2 to 4 minutes or until just cooked through and lightly browned. Remove from pot. Add the remaining 1 Tbsp. oil, the shallot, ginger, and garlic. Cook and stir over medium heat 1 minute. Add VEGETABLES. Cook and stir over medium heat about 3 minutes or until crisp-tender.
**3.** Stir in broth, soy sauce, rice vinegar, and, if desired, sriracha sauce. Whisk in FLAVORING. Bring just to boiling. Stir in NOODLES and PROTEIN. Heat through. Remove from heat. Serve with desired TOPPERS. **Makes 4 servings (2 cups each).**

**ASIAN MUSHROOMS**
Branch out from standard button mushrooms with one of these easy-to-find Asian mushrooms.

**SHIITAKE** The meaty texture and woodsy flavor of these mushrooms is delicious in soups, stir-fries, and noodle dishes. The stems are too tough to eat, so always remove them.

**OYSTER** Tender and delicate oyster mushrooms are best served in lightly seasoned dishes (like this brothy noodle bowl) where their flavor can shine through.

**ENOKI** They may look like they'd be more at home in the ocean, but creamy-white enoki are definitely land dwellers. Their appearance makes them a unique addition to Asian-style dishes.

# MIX & MATCH INGREDIENTS

**NOODLES** *(Pick 1)*
- Angel hair pasta
- Cellophane noodles
- Ramen noodles
- Rice noodles
- Soba noodles
- Udon noodles

**PROTEIN** *(Pick 1)*
- One 12- to 14-oz. container firm tofu, cut into strips and chopped
- 1 lb. beef sirloin, cut into bite-size strips
- 1 lb. chicken breast, cut into bite-size strips
- 1 lb. pork tenderloin, cut into bite-size strips
- 1 lb. peeled and deveined shrimp

**VEGETABLES** *(Pick 1–3)*
- Asparagus, trimmed and cut into 1-inch pieces
- Baby bok choy, chopped
- Broccoli florets
- Carrots, thinly sliced
- Shiitake or oyster mushrooms, stemmed and sliced
- Snow pea pods, trimmed and bias- sliced

**FLAVORING** *(Pick 1)*
- ¼ cup ketchup + 1 Tbsp. honey + 2–3 tsp. sambal oelek (chili paste)
- 2 Tbsp. miso paste + ½ cup water
- 2 Tbsp. red curry paste + 1 Tbsp. fish sauce + juice and zest of 1 lime

**TOPPERS** *(Pick 1 or 2)*
- Finely chopped peanuts or cashews
- Hard-boiled eggs, peeled and halved
- Sliced green onions
- Snipped fresh cilantro and/or Thai basil
- Toasted sesame seeds

KOREAN-STYLE STEAK
AND NOODLES

**GET THE KIMCHI** This Korean condiment is a pungent, flavorful mixture of
fermented Asian cabbage, carrots, and/or other vegetables. Because it's fermented, kimchi is
packed with probiotics (good for gut health). We'll show you how to make your own
(*p. 666*) or look for it in the refrigerated section of large supermarkets.

TOFU-CELLOPHANE
NOODLE STIR-FRY

# KOREAN-STYLE STEAK AND NOODLES

**HANDS-ON TIME** 20 minutes
**MARINATE** 30 minutes

¼ cup reduced-sodium soy sauce
2 Tbsp. rice vinegar
2 Tbsp. packed brown sugar
1 Tbsp. toasted sesame oil
1 Tbsp. gochujang paste (tip, *p. 202*) or 1 tsp. sriracha sauce
1 lb. flank steak or skirt steak
8 oz. rice noodles or soba noodles
2 Tbsp. vegetable oil
8 oz. fresh shiitake mushrooms, stemmed and sliced
1 cup packaged julienned carrots
6 green onions, cut into 1-inch pieces (white and green parts)
2 cups fresh baby spinach
1 cup kimchi (tip, *opposite*), coarsely chopped

**1.** In a medium bowl combine the first five ingredients (through gochujang). Transfer 3 Tbsp. of the sauce mixture to a small bowl; cover and reserve for later. Slice steak against the grain into very thin slices.* Add steak to the remaining sauce in the medium bowl; stir to combine. Cover and refrigerate 30 minutes.

**2.** Meanwhile, soak or cook noodles according to package directions. Drain well.
**3.** Heat a large wok or 12-inch skillet over high heat. Add 1 Tbsp. of the vegetable oil. Drain meat; discard marinade. Add the meat to the hot oil. Cook and stir 1 to 2 minutes or until meat is just cooked through. Remove meat from wok.
**4.** Add remaining 1 Tbsp. vegetable oil to the wok. Place over high heat. Add mushrooms, carrots, and green onions. Cook and stir 3 to 4 minutes or just until crisp-tender. Add the noodles, reserved steak, spinach, and kimchi. Cook and stir 1 minute more or until spinach is wilted and mixture is heated through. Stir in the remaining soy sauce mixture; heat through. If desired, serve with additional kimchi. **Makes 4 servings (1½ cups each).**
**\*NOTE** For easier slicing, wrap and freeze steak for 30 to 45 minutes before cutting it.
**EACH SERVING** *522 cal., 16 g fat (4 g sat. fat), 78 mg chol., 737 mg sodium, 62 g carb., 4 g fiber, 8 g sugars, 31 g pro.*

# TOFU-CELLOPHANE NOODLE STIR-FRY

**START TO FINISH** 35 minutes

1 12- to 14-oz. pkg. extra-firm tofu
4 oz. cellophane noodles (bean threads) (noodle ID, *p. 230*)
2 Tbsp. reduced-sodium soy sauce
2 Tbsp. rice vinegar
1 to 2 tsp. Asian chili paste (sambal oelek) (tip, *p. 230*)
1 tsp. toasted sesame oil
2 Tbsp. canola oil
4 oz. shiitake mushrooms, stemmed and sliced ½ inch thick (1½ cups)
2 cloves garlic, thinly sliced

5 oz. yu choy, cut into 2-inch pieces (3 cups)
3 green onions, cut into 1½-inch pieces (white and green parts)
¼ cup water
3 Tbsp. hoisin sauce
2 tsp. grated fresh ginger
¼ tsp. ground cinnamon
   Dash ground cloves
   Lime wedges
¼ cup dry-roasted peanuts, chopped

**1.** Drain tofu. Pat dry with paper towels and place on a paper towel-lined plate. Cut into ¾-inch pieces.
**2.** Fill a 4-qt. saucepan with water and bring to boiling. Add cellophane noodles; remove from heat. Let stand 2 to 3 minutes or until noodles are softened. Drain; rinse with cool water and return to saucepan. Stir in soy sauce, vinegar, chili paste, and sesame oil.
**3.** In a 10-inch nonstick skillet heat 1 Tbsp. of the canola oil over medium heat. Add tofu; cook 5 to 7 minutes until lightly browned, tossing occasionally. Transfer to saucepan with noodles; gently toss.
**4.** Add remaining 1 Tbsp. canola oil to skillet. Add mushrooms; cook and stir 3 minutes. Add garlic; cook and stir 1 minute. Add yu choy and green onions; cook and stir 2 minutes or just until wilted. Add the next five ingredients (through cloves); cook and stir 1 minute. Add noodle mixture and cook until heated through, stirring occasionally.
**5.** Serve with lime wedges and peanuts. **Makes 4 servings (1 cup each).**
**EACH SERVING** *361 cal., 18 g fat (2 g sat. fat), 0 mg chol., 548 mg sodium, 40 g carb., 4 g fiber, 7 g sugars, 13 g pro.*

**YU CHOY**
This sweet-tasting leafy Asian vegetable is sometimes called choy sum and can be found in Asian markets. You can easily swap for an equal amount of baby bok choy or broccoli florets.

# QUICK DINNERS

**TEST KITCHEN**

Quick Dinners make-ahead info and tips, *p. 253.*

# SEARED STEAK WITH JALAPEÑO CHIMICHURRI

**START TO FINISH** 40 minutes

» **BEEF FLANK STEAK** should be sliced against the meat grain for max tenderness. (This means to cut across the meat fibers instead of cutting along them.)

1½ to 1¾ lb. beef flank steak
Salt and black pepper
2 Tbsp. + 2 tsp. olive oil
2 fresh poblano chile peppers, seeded and cut lengthwise into ¾-inch-wide strips (tip, *p. 22*)
1 large red onion, cut into ½-inch wedges
1 medium yellow sweet pepper, cut lengthwise into ¾-inch-wide strips
1 cup loosely packed cilantro leaves, coarsely chopped
1 fresh jalapeño chile pepper, seeded and chopped (tip, *p. 22*)
2 Tbsp. lime juice
1 tsp. dried oregano, crushed
1 clove garlic, minced

» **SKILLET COOKING** is just one option. If you like to grill, this recipe adapts deliciously—grill flank steak, covered, over medium heat 17 to 21 minutes for medium rare, turning once. Give your veggies a little sizzle by cooking them alongside the meat in a cast-iron skillet or grill wok.

**1.** Season steak with salt and black pepper. Heat a heavy 12-inch skillet over medium-high heat. Add 1 Tbsp. of the oil. Add poblano peppers, onion, sweet pepper, and a large pinch of *salt*. Cook 5 minutes without stirring. Cook about 5 minutes more or until vegetables are lightly charred and tender, stirring once. Remove from skillet; keep warm.
**2.** Add the remaining 1 Tbsp. oil to the skillet. Add steak. Cook 12 to 15 minutes or until medium rare (145°F), turning once. Transfer steak to a cutting board. Cover; let stand 5 minutes.
**3.** Meanwhile, for chimichurri, in a small bowl combine the remaining ingredients and a small pinch of *salt*. Stir in the 2 tsp. oil. Slice steak; serve with vegetables and chimichurri. **Makes 4 servings (4 oz. meat + ¾ cup vegetables + 2 Tbsp. chimichurri each).**
**EACH SERVING** *402 cal., 22 g fat (6 g sat. fat), 111 mg chol., 312 mg sodium, 13 g carb., 2 g fiber, 3 g sugars, 38 g pro.*

## STEAK AND TOMATOES ON CIABATTA

**START TO FINISH** 35 minutes

2    Tbsp. butter, softened
2    Tbsp. olive oil
1    Tbsp. chopped fresh oregano
1    Tbsp. chopped fresh rosemary
2    cloves garlic, minced
1    tsp. smoked paprika
½    tsp. salt
½    tsp. cracked black pepper
1    1-lb. ciabatta loaf
1½   lb. beef flank steak
3    cups cherry tomatoes
     Sliced red onion (optional)

**1.** In a small bowl combine the first eight ingredients (through cracked black pepper). Cut ciabatta loaf in half horizontally; cut each half crosswise into thirds to make 6 pieces. Very lightly brush cut sides of bread with some of the herb mixture.

**2.** Score flank steak on both sides, making shallow cuts at 1-inch intervals diagonally across steak in a diamond pattern. Heat a heavy 12-inch skillet over medium-high heat until very hot. Sprinkle both sides of steak with additional salt and cracked black pepper. Cook steak in hot skillet 12 to 15 minutes or until medium rare (145°F), turning once. Transfer steak to a plate. Cover; let stand 5 minutes.

**3.** Meanwhile, place half of the bread, cut sides down, in skillet; cook about 1 minute or until toasted. Remove from skillet. Repeat with remaining bread.

**4.** Add the remaining herb mixture to skillet. When mixture begins to bubble, add tomatoes. Cook and stir about 4 minutes or until skins split. Remove from heat.

**5.** Meanwhile, thinly slice steak across the grain. Arrange sliced steak on toasted bread; top with tomatoes and, if desired, onion slices. Serve immediately.

**Makes 6 open-face sandwiches.**

**EACH SANDWICH** *417 cal., 15 g fat (6 g sat. fat), 88 mg chol., 723 mg sodium, 36 g carb., 3 g fiber, 2 g sugars, 32 g pro.*

**FLANK STEAK** Most whole flank steaks—which come from the belly area of cattle—weigh about 2 pounds (info, *p. 62*). Ask at the meat counter for a smaller portion or cut your own steak to the size needed and freeze the extra for later. Thinly slice the extra to use in stir-fries.

RAVIOLI SKILLET
LASAGNA

# RAVIOLI SKILLET LASAGNA

**START TO FINISH** 25 minutes

- 2 cups chunky-style pasta sauce
- ½ cup water
- 4 cups fresh baby kale or spinach
- 16 oz. frozen meat or cheese-filled ravioli (4½ cups)
- ¼ cup grated Romano or Parmesan cheese
- ½ of a 15-oz. carton ricotta cheese
- 2 Tbsp. chopped fresh parsley (optional)

**1.** In a 10-inch skillet combine pasta sauce and the water. Bring to boiling. Stir in kale until it wilts. Stir in ravioli. Return to boiling; reduce heat to medium. Cover and cook 5 minutes, stirring once to prevent sticking.
**2.** Sprinkle with Romano cheese. Cover; cook over medium-low heat about 10 minutes more or until pasta is just tender. Meanwhile, in a bowl stir together the ricotta cheese and parsley (if using). Smear a spoonful of ricotta mixture in bowls. Top with ravioli mixture; serve immediately. **Makes 4 servings (1¾ cups each).**
**EACH SERVING** *310 cal., 8 g fat (3g sat. fat), 41 mg chol., 1,032 mg sodium, 43 g carb., 5 g fiber, 8 g sugars, 16 g pro.*

INDONESIAN-STYLE
BEEF AND RICE
BOWLS

# INDONESIAN-STYLE BEEF AND RICE BOWLS

**HANDS-ON TIME** 15 minutes
**COOK** 30 minutes

- 3 Tbsp. red curry paste
- 1 13.5- to 14-oz. can unsweetened coconut milk
- 1 cinnamon stick
- ¼ tsp. freshly grated nutmeg
- ⅛ tsp. ground cloves
- 1 lb. lean ground beef
- 2 cups hot cooked rice
- 1 small cucumber, thinly sliced
- ¼ of a head green cabbage, thinly sliced
- 1 shallot, thinly sliced
- 1 fresh orange or red chile pepper, thinly sliced (optional) (tip, p. 22)
  Fresh cilantro sprigs
- 2 limes, halved

**1.** In a 10-inch skillet heat curry paste over medium-high heat, stirring a few seconds or until fragrant. Stir in coconut milk, cinnamon stick, nutmeg, and cloves. Add beef; stir to combine. Bring to boiling. Cook 5 to 7 minutes or until beef is browned, stirring occasionally. Reduce heat. Simmer, uncovered, 30 minutes, stirring occasionally. Remove from heat; discard cinnamon stick.
**2.** Spoon rice into bowls. Top with meat mixture, cucumber slices, cabbage, shallot, chile pepper (if using), and cilantro; squeeze lime over top. **Makes 4 servings (1 bowl each).**
**EACH SERVING** *497 cal., 27 g fat (18 g sat. fat), 72 mg chol., 399 mg sodium, 33 g carb., 3 g fiber, 4 g sugars, 27 g pro.*

# BEEF STROGANOFF

**START TO FINISH** 35 minutes

- 1¼ lb. boneless beef sirloin, thinly sliced*
  Salt and black pepper
- 6 tsp. vegetable oil
- 3 cups sliced fresh button or cremini mushrooms (8 oz.)
- 1 medium onion, cut into thin wedges (1⅓ cups)
- 2 cloves garlic, minced
- 1 14.5-oz. can reduced-sodium beef broth

**BEEF STROGANOFF**

1 Tbsp. Worcestershire sauce
1 Tbsp. chopped fresh thyme
leaves or 1 tsp. dried thyme,
crushed
1 8-oz. carton sour cream
3 Tbsp. all-purpose flour
2 tsp. Dijon mustard
Hot cooked egg noodles

**1.** Season beef with salt and pepper.
In a 12-inch nonstick skillet cook
half of the meat in 2 tsp. of the oil
over medium-high heat about
1 minute or until browned. Remove
meat from skillet. Repeat with the
remaining meat and 2 tsp. of the oil.
Remove from skillet.
**2.** In the same skillet cook
mushrooms, onion, and garlic
in the remaining 2 tsp. oil over
medium-high heat until mushrooms

and onion are softened and
beginning to brown.
**3.** Stir in 1½ cups of the broth, the
Worcestershire sauce, and thyme,
scraping up any browned bits in
skillet. Bring to boiling; reduce heat.
Gently simmer 5 minutes.
**4.** Meanwhile, in a medium bowl
stir together sour cream, flour, and
the remaining ¼ cup broth until
smooth. Gradually stir about 1 cup
of the hot broth from the skillet
into sour cream mixture. Pour sour
cream mixture into skillet, stirring
constantly. Cook and stir until
thickened and bubbly. Stir in
cooked beef and the mustard.
Cook and stir 1 to 2 minutes more
or until beef is just heated through.
Season to taste with additional

salt and pepper. Serve over
noodles and, if desired, sprinkle
with additional fresh thyme. **Makes
6 servings (1 cup each).**
*NOTE For easier slicing, partially
freeze the beef 30 to 45 minutes
before slicing.
**EACH SERVING** *394 cal., 18 g fat
(6 g sat. fat), 111 mg chol., 486 mg
sodium, 31 g carb., 2 g fiber, 5 g sugars,
29 g pro.*

**GET-TOGETHER**

*Rich and creamy stroganoff
is an easy, companyworthy dish.
Make it extra special by
adding ¼ cup dry white
or red wine in Step 3.
(Bonus: Serve the rest of the
bottle of wine with dinner.)*

## BLISTERED BEAN AND BEEF STIR-FRY
**START TO FINISH** 35 minutes

2   Tbsp. cider vinegar
3   Tbsp. reduced-sodium soy sauce
1   Tbsp. packed brown sugar
¼   tsp. crushed red pepper
8   oz. boneless beef sirloin
6   tsp. canola oil
2   cloves garlic, minced
1   lb. fresh thin green beans, trimmed
2   cups sliced stemmed fresh shiitake mushrooms
½   cup sliced red onion
    Hot cooked rice noodles or rice (optional)
1   recipe Pickled Radishes (optional)

**1.** For sauce, in a bowl stir together the first four ingredients (through crushed red pepper). Trim fat from meat. Thinly slice across the grain into bite-size strips.
**2.** In a 12-inch wok or skillet heat 2 tsp. of the oil over medium-high heat. Add garlic; cook and stir 30 seconds. Add beef; cook and stir 2 minutes. Remove from wok.
**3.** Heat 2 tsp. of the oil in wok over medium-high heat. Add half of the beans; cook and stir 3 minutes. Remove from skillet. Add remaining 2 tsp. oil and remaining beans; cook and stir 3 minutes. Return all beans to skillet. Add mushrooms and onion; cook and stir 2 to 3 minutes or until beans are blistered and onion is crisp-tender. Return beef and any accumulated juices to skillet. Add sauce; stir to coat. If desired, serve over rice noodles. If desired, serve with Pickled Radishes. **Makes 4 servings (1¼ cups each).**

**EACH SERVING** *218 cal., 10 g fat (1 g sat. fat), 34 mg chol., 534 mg sodium, 17 g carb., 4 g fiber, 11 g sugars, 17 g pro.*

### PICKLED RADISHES
In a bowl whisk together ¼ cup cider vinegar, 2 Tbsp. packed brown sugar, and ½ tsp. salt until sugar is dissolved. Stir in ½ cup very thinly sliced radishes. Let stand 30 minutes. Drain before using.

## CUSTOMIZE IT

PICK THE INGREDIENTS TO CREATE A RECIPE THAT'S ALL YOUR OWN.

## CLASSIC STIR-FRY

**START TO FINISH** 30 minutes

| | |
|---|---|
| 2 | Tbsp. vegetable oil |
| 3 | cups VEGETABLES 1 |
| 2 | cloves garlic, minced |
| 3 | cups VEGETABLES 2 |
| 1 | lb. PROTEIN |
| | SAUCE |
| | Hot cooked rice |
| | TOPPERS |
| | SPLASH-ONS |

**1.** In an extra-large wok or 12-inch skillet heat 1 Tbsp. of the oil over medium-high heat.

Add VEGETABLES 1 and garlic. Cook and stir 3 minutes. Add VEGETABLES 2. Cook and stir 3 to 5 minutes more or until vegetables are crisp-tender. Transfer vegetables to a bowl.

**2.** In the same skillet heat the remaining 1 Tbsp. oil over medium-high heat. Add PROTEIN. Cook and stir until desired doneness (chicken is no longer pink, beef and pork are just browned, shrimp are opaque, or tofu is lightly browned). Move Protein to edge of skillet.

**3.** Add desired SAUCE to center of skillet; bring to boiling. Cook and

stir until slightly thickened. Return vegetable mixture to skillet. Toss to coat; heat through. Serve over rice. Add desired TOPPERS and SPLASH-ONS. **Makes 4 servings (1¾ cups each).**

**BASIC SAUCE** Stir together ½ cup reduced-sodium soy sauce, 2 Tbsp. each packed brown sugar and rice vinegar, 2 tsp. ground ginger, and ¼ to ½ tsp. crushed red pepper.

**ORANGE SAUCE** Stir together ⅔ cup orange juice, ¼ cup orange marmalade, 2 Tbsp. reduced-sodium soy sauce, and 2 tsp. grated fresh ginger.

---

# MIX & MATCH INGREDIENTS

| **VEGETABLES 1** *(Pick 1–3)* | **VEGETABLES 2** *(Pick 1–3)* | **PROTEIN** *(Pick 1)* | **SAUCE** *(Pick 1)* | **TOPPERS** *(Pick 1 or 2)* | **SPLASH-ONS** *(Pick 1 or 2)* |
|---|---|---|---|---|---|
| ■ Butternut squash, ½-inch cubes (cooked 1 minute in microwave) | ■ Asparagus, 1-inch pieces | ■ Beef flank or sirloin tip steak, cut into bite-size strips | ■ Basic Sauce *(above)* | ■ Chopped peanuts, toasted almonds or hazelnuts, or roasted cashews | ■ Asian chili sauce (sriracha sauce) |
| ■ Carrots, thinly bias-sliced | ■ Broccoli florets (small) | ■ Skinless, boneless chicken breast or thighs, cut into 1-inch pieces | ■ Orange Sauce *(above)* | ■ Chow mein noodles | ■ Chili garlic paste |
| ■ Cauliflower florets (small) | ■ Snow pea pods, halved crosswise | | ■ ⅔ cup sweet-and-sour sauce | ■ Sesame seeds | ■ Fish sauce |
| ■ Celery, thinly bias-sliced | ■ Sweet peppers (any color), cut into bite-size strips | ■ Pork tenderloin, cut into bite-size strips | ■ ⅔ cup stir-fry sauce, teriyaki sauce, or peanut sauce | ■ Snipped fresh cilantro | ■ Reduced-sodium soy sauce |
| ■ Green beans, 1-inch pieces | ■ Zucchini or yellow summer squash, sliced | ■ Shrimp, peeled and deveined | | | ■ Toasted sesame oil |
| ■ Mushrooms, quartered | | ■ Extra-firm tofu, cut into ½-inch cubes (use 14 to 16 oz.) | | | |
| ■ Onion wedges | | | | | |
| ■ Sweet potatoes, ½-inch cubes | | | | | |

EASY BAKED
CAVATELLI

**WHAT IS CAVATELLI?** CAVATELLI IS A SMALL CURLED PASTA
THAT LOOKS LIKE A TINY SHELL AND IS SLIGHTLY CHEWY
WHEN COOKED. SWAP IN ANY SMALL, CURLED PASTA, SUCH
AS GEMELLI, CAMPANELLE, OR CASARECCE.

## EASY BAKED CAVATELLI

**HANDS-ON TIME** 10 minutes
**COOK** 15 minutes
**BAKE** 10 minutes

8   oz. bulk Italian sausage, lean ground beef, or ground turkey
12  oz. dried cavatelli or gemelli pasta (about 3½ cups)
2   14.5-oz. cans diced tomatoes with Italian herbs, undrained
1   14.5-oz. can reduced-sodium chicken or vegetable broth
½   cup fresh basil leaves or spinach leaves, torn (optional)
⅓   cup water
2   Tbsp. olive oil
6   cloves garlic, minced
¼   tsp. kosher salt
¼   to ½ tsp. crushed red pepper
8   oz. shredded mozzarella cheese (2 cups)

**1.** In a deep 10-inch oven-safe skillet or a shallow Dutch oven cook and stir sausage over medium-high heat until browned; drain fat. Add the next nine ingredients (through crushed red pepper). Bring to boiling; reduce heat. Simmer, covered, 15 minutes, stirring occasionally (pasta will not be tender).

**2.** Meanwhile, preheat oven to 400°F. Remove lid from skillet and top pasta mixture with cheese. Bake 10 to 15 minutes or until pasta is tender and cheese is golden brown. If desired, sprinkle with additional fresh basil. Let stand 5 minutes before serving. **Makes 6 servings (1¼ cups each).**
**EACH SERVING** *513 cal., 23 g fat (9 g sat. fat), 53 mg chol., 1,088 mg sodium, 51 g carb., 3 g fiber, 6 g sugars, 24 g pro.*

## KOREAN BARBECUED PORK STIR-FRY

**START TO FINISH** 35 minutes

¼   cup hoisin sauce
3   Tbsp. reduced-sodium soy sauce
2   Tbsp. rice vinegar
1   Tbsp. packed brown sugar
2   tsp. sriracha sauce
1   tsp. toasted sesame oil
1   tsp. grated fresh ginger
2   cloves garlic, minced
2   Tbsp. canola oil
12  oz. pork tenderloin or lean boneless pork, cut into bite-size strips
1   cup thinly bias-sliced carrots
1   medium red sweet pepper, cut into bite-size strips (¾ cup)
1   fresh Asian pear or apple, cored and sliced
6   cups shredded napa cabbage
    Thinly bias-sliced green onions

»

**NAPA CABBAGE,** also called Chinese cabbage, is available in the produce aisle of most large supermarkets. Start by cutting off and discarding the stem end. Rinse leaves and shake dry. Cut the cabbage leaves—including the thick ribs—crosswise into thin strips.

**1.** For the sauce, in a bowl stir together the first eight ingredients (through garlic).

**2.** In an extra-large wok or 12-inch skillet heat 1 Tbsp. of the oil over medium-high heat. Add pork; cook and stir about 4 minutes or until strips are just pink in the center. Remove pork from wok.

**3.** Add the remaining 1 Tbsp. oil to wok. Add carrots; cook and stir 1 minute. Add sweet pepper; cook and stir about 2 minutes or until just crisp-tender. Return pork to wok. Add sauce and Asian pear; cook and stir until heated through. Serve pork mixture over cabbage and top with green onions. **Makes 4 servings (¾ cup pork mixture + 1½ cups cabbage each).**
**EACH SERVING** *303 cal., 12 g fat (2 g sat. fat), 56 mg chol., 791 mg sodium, 28 g carb., 5 g fiber, 18 g sugars, 21 g pro.*

KOREAN BARBECUED PORK STIR-FRY

CHORIZO
AND SQUASH
QUESADILLAS

## CHORIZO AND SQUASH QUESADILLAS

**START TO FINISH** 35 minutes

- 1 medium red onion, halved and very thinly sliced (½ cup)
- 2 Tbsp. fresh lime juice
  Pinch kosher salt
- 2 dried smoked chorizo sausage links (3¼ oz. total), thinly sliced
- 8 6-inch corn tortillas
- 2 cups shredded Monterey Jack cheese or mild cheddar cheese (8 oz.)
- 2 cups thinly sliced small summer squash and/or zucchini
- 1 to 2 Tbsp. olive oil
- 1 cup loosely packed fresh cilantro leaves

**1.** Preheat oven to 250°F. Place a baking sheet in oven. In a bowl toss together onion, lime juice, and salt.
**2.** Meanwhile, heat a 12-inch skillet over medium heat. Add chorizo. Cook 5 minutes, stirring occasionally. Transfer chorizo to a paper towel-lined plate. Wipe out skillet.
**3.** Top four of the tortillas with half of the cheese. Arrange chorizo

and squash on each; top with remaining cheese and remaining tortillas. Heat 1 Tbsp. of the oil in the skillet over medium heat. Place two quesadillas in skillet. Cook about 2 minutes per side or until browned and cheese is melted. Transfer to baking sheet in oven. Repeat with remaining quesadillas, adding more oil to skillet if needed.
**4.** Stir cilantro into onion mixture. Serve with quesadillas. If desired, sauté additional sliced squash in hot olive oil to serve on the side. **Makes 4 servings (1 quesadilla each).**
**EACH SERVING** *427 cal., 27 g fat (13 g sat. fat), 63 mg chol., 725 mg sodium, 26 g carb., 4 g fiber, 6 g sugars, 22 g pro.*

## BLT SALAD WITH CREAMY CHIVE DRESSING

**START TO FINISH** 20 minutes

- 14 slices smoked bacon (12 oz.)
- 2 Tbsp. cider vinegar
- 1 clove garlic, minced
  Pinch salt
- ¾ cup sour cream
- ¼ cup chopped fresh chives

- 2 Tbsp. olive oil
- 1 to 2 Tbsp. milk
- 3 large ripe tomatoes, cut into wedges
- 2 large croissants or one 8-oz. baguette, sliced and toasted
- 1 head green leaf or Bibb lettuce, broken into leaves
  Salt and black pepper

**1.** In a 12-inch skillet cook bacon until crisp; drain bacon on paper towels. Meanwhile, for dressing, in a bowl combine vinegar, garlic, and salt; let stand 10 minutes. Whisk in sour cream, chives, and olive oil. Stir in milk until desired consistency.
**2.** On a platter arrange tomatoes, croissant slices, lettuce, and bacon. Season to taste with salt and pepper; drizzle with dressing. **Makes 4 servings (about 1 cup each).**
**EACH SERVING** *428 cal., 24 g fat (8 g sat. fat), 49 mg chol., 890 mg sodium, 35 g carb., 2 g fiber, 5 g sugars, 16 g pro.*

**HEALTHY TWIST**

*Cut fat and sodium significantly by replacing the bacon with lower-sodium, less-fat bacon. You can also use light sour cream in the dressing.*

# BACON AND PEAR AUTUMN SALAD

**START TO FINISH** 25 minutes

- 8  slices smoked peppered bacon
- 1  Tbsp. olive oil
- 2  shallots, thinly sliced Pinch salt
- 2  Tbsp. red wine vinegar
- 6  cups torn fresh kale, Swiss chard, and/or beet greens
- 1  cup cooled cooked grain, such as barley or farro
- 2  Bosc pears, cored and thinly sliced
- 4  oz. Gouda cheese, cubed Freshly ground black pepper

**1.** In a 10-inch skillet cook bacon until crisp; drain bacon on paper towels. Reserve 1 Tbsp. drippings in skillet. Add olive oil to drippings; add shallots and salt to skillet. Cook over medium heat 3 to 4 minutes or until shallots are tender and golden brown, stirring occasionally. Stir in vinegar; remove from heat. Scrape up any browned bits from bottom of skillet.

**2.** Cut bacon into 1-inch pieces. Arrange bacon, greens, cooked grain, and pears on plates or in bowls. Spoon shallot mixture over salads. Top with cheese. Season to taste with salt and pepper. **Makes 6 servings (1½ cups each).**

**EACH SERVING** *257 cal., 14 g fat (6 g sat. fat), 34 mg chol., 421 mg sodium, 23 g carb., 5 g fiber, 8 g sugars, 12 g pro.*

## CHICKEN AND WINTER GREENS SALAD

**START TO FINISH** 30 minutes

½  of a large head radicchio, halved, cored, and sliced (3 cups)
2  heads Belgian endive, sliced crosswise (3 cups)
3  cups baby kale or spinach
1  large clove garlic, minced
1  Tbsp. balsamic vinegar
½  tsp. Dijon mustard
½  tsp. kosher salt
¼  tsp. black pepper
5  Tbsp. olive oil
2  skinless, boneless chicken breast halves, halved horizontally
1  lemon, quartered
2  oz. Parmesan cheese, shaved

**1.** On a platter combine radicchio, endive, and kale. In a bowl combine garlic, vinegar, mustard, salt, and pepper. Slowly drizzle in ¼ cup of the oil, whisking constantly.

**2.** Season chicken on both sides with additional salt and pepper. In a 10-inch skillet heat the remaining 1 Tbsp. oil over medium-high heat. Add chicken; cook 2 to 3 minutes per side or until done (165°F). Place chicken on greens. Squeeze lemon over and drizzle with dressing. Sprinkle with Parmesan. **Makes 4 servings (1 piece chicken + 2¼ cups salad each).**

**EACH SERVING** *429 cal., 25 g fat (6 g sat. fat), 114 mg chol., 557 mg sodium, 11 g carb., 4 g fiber, 2 g sugars, 41 g pro.*

**KALE**—both baby and mature types—has been given superfood status. Baby kale is more tender and has a milder flavor than mature kale. It also requires less prep as the stems are tender enough to eat (rather than having to be removed). If you can't find baby kale, use 3 cups chopped, stemmed mature kale and massage it gently as directed on *p. 297* before adding to the other greens.

QUICK TANDOORI-STYLE CHICKEN

MOROCCAN CHICKEN AND PEPPERS

# WHAT IS TANDOORI? IT'S A CURRY-SPICED YOGURT-MARINATED MEAT DISH COOKED IN A CLAY OVEN—A TANDOOR. THIS VERSION IS COOKED ON A GRILL.

## QUICK TANDOORI-STYLE CHICKEN

**HANDS-ON TIME** 10 minutes
**STAND** 15 minutes
**GRILL** 8 minutes

½  cup plain Greek yogurt
1   Tbsp. cider vinegar
2   tsp. Madras (hot) curry powder
1   clove garlic, minced
¼   tsp. kosher salt
1½  lb. skinless, boneless chicken thighs, cut into 1- to 1½-inch pieces
    Basmati rice (optional)
    Mango chutney (optional)
    Snipped fresh mint leaves

**1.** In an extra-large bowl whisk together yogurt, vinegar, curry powder, garlic, and salt. Add chicken; toss to coat. Let stand 15 minutes (or cover and chill up to 24 hours).

**2.** Thread chicken onto 6-inch skewers, leaving ¼ inch between pieces. Grill skewers on a greased rack, covered, over medium-high heat 8 to 10 minutes or until done (170°F), turning to brown evenly. If desired, serve over basmati rice with mango chutney. Sprinkle with mint. **Makes 4 servings (4 oz. chicken each).**

**EACH SERVING** *232 cal., 8 g fat (2 g sat. fat), 162 mg chol., 295 mg sodium, 2 g carb., 1 g fiber, 1 g sugars, 37 g pro.*

## MOROCCAN CHICKEN AND PEPPERS

**START TO FINISH** 35 minutes

1   tsp. coriander seeds
1   tsp. cumin seeds
1   to 2 small dried red chiles (such as chile de árbol), torn into pieces (tip, *p. 22*)
½   tsp. kosher salt
¼   tsp. ground cinnamon
8   skinless, boneless chicken thighs
2   Tbsp. olive oil
6   cups coarsely chopped red and/or yellow sweet peppers
1   Meyer lemon, sliced
    Harissa Paste (*p. 30*) (optional)

**1.** In a spice grinder (tip, *right*) grind coriander, cumin, and chiles; stir in salt and cinnamon. Sprinkle mixture over chicken.

**2.** In a 12-inch skillet heat olive oil over medium-high heat. Cook chicken 15 to 17 minutes or until done (170°F). Transfer chicken to a platter; cover to keep warm. Add peppers and lemon to skillet. Cook 6 to 8 minutes or until tender, stirring occasionally. Serve chicken with peppers and, if desired, Harissa Paste. **Makes 4 servings (2 thighs + 1 cup peppers each).**

**EACH SERVING** *443 cal., 19 g fat (4 g sat. fat), 266 mg chol., 569 mg sodium, 7 g carb., 3 g fiber, 4 g sugars, 57 g pro.*

**GRIND IT**
If you don't grind a lot of whole spices, you can use a mortar and pestle to pulverize the coriander and cumin seeds. If you do, a spice grinder is a smart investment. Or place the whole spices in a resealable plastic freezer bag; seal the bag and roll over spices with a rolling pin or pound lightly with a meat mallet or heavy skillet.

## SWEET POTATOES AND BOK CHOY WITH MISO

**START TO FINISH** 30 minutes

1½  lb. assorted sweet potatoes, peeled and cut into 1-inch chunks
6   heads baby bok choy, halved lengthwise
¼   cup minced fresh ginger
2   Tbsp. red or brown miso paste
2   Tbsp. lime juice
2   Tbsp. cider vinegar
2   tsp. maple syrup
2   cloves garlic, minced
6   Tbsp. canola oil
12  oz. cooked chicken breast (tip, p. 37) (optional)
2   cups hot cooked red or white quinoa
    Sesame seeds (optional)

»

**MISO PASTE** is a Japanese condiment made from fermented mashed soybeans. Varieties range in color from light to dark, with the darker colors having a richer flavor. Look for it in the refrigerated section of large supermarkets.

**1.** Place a steamer basket in a 10-inch skillet or large pot. Add water to just below the basket. Bring to boiling; reduce heat. Add sweet potatoes to basket; cover. Steam 10 minutes.

Add bok choy; cover. Steam about 5 minutes more or until tender.
**2.** Meanwhile, for dressing, in a bowl whisk together the next six ingredients (through garlic). Drizzle in canola oil, whisking constantly to blend.
**3.** Serve sweet potatoes, bok choy, and, if desired, chicken, over quinoa; drizzle with dressing. If desired, sprinkle with sesame seeds. **Makes 4 servings (1 cup potatoes + 3 bok choy halves + ½ cup quinoa each).**
**EACH SERVING** *492 cal., 23 g fat (2 g sat. fat), 0 mg chol., 515 mg sodium, 64 g carb., 10 g fiber, 12 g sugars, 10 g pro.*

## SLOPPY TURKEY AND CHILI JOES

**HANDS-ON TIME** 10 minutes
**COOK** 15 minutes

16  to 20 oz. ground turkey breast
½   cup chopped onion
1   medium fresh poblano pepper, seeded and chopped (tip, p. 22)
1   15-oz. can tomato sauce
2   Tbsp. packed brown sugar
1   Tbsp. Worcestershire sauce
2   tsp. chili powder
½   tsp. garlic powder
    Salt and black pepper
4   kaiser rolls, split and toasted
½   medium red onion, sliced

**1.** In a 10-inch nonstick skillet cook turkey, onion, and poblano pepper until turkey is no longer pink, stirring occasionally. Stir in the next five ingredients (through garlic powder). Bring to boiling; reduce heat. Cover and simmer 15 minutes, stirring occasionally. Season to taste with salt and black pepper.
**2.** Fill kaiser rolls with turkey mixture. Top with sliced onion. **Makes 4 sandwiches.**
**EACH SANDWICH** *373 cal., 4 g fat (0 g sat. fat), 70 mg chol., 1,098 mg sodium, 50 g carb., 4 g fiber, 13 g sugars, 36 g pro.*

**SWEET POTATOES AND BOK CHOY WITH MISO**

**SLOPPY TURKEY AND CHILI JOES**

## MEDITERRANEAN TUNA SALAD

**START TO FINISH** 25 minutes

8　oz. fresh green beans, trimmed
2　lemons
3　Tbsp. olive oil
4　tsp. capers, rinsed
2　tsp. Dijon mustard
　　Pinch salt
½　of a head romaine lettuce, thick stem removed and cut crosswise into ribbons (4 cups)
2　5-oz. cans olive oil-packed tuna, drained

1　yellow or red sweet pepper, cut into strips
½　cup pitted green olives
½　cup sliced radishes
　　Freshly ground black pepper

**1.** Place steamer basket in a 3-qt. saucepan. Add water to just below bottom of basket. Bring to boiling. Add beans. Cover; reduce heat. Steam about 10 minutes or until crisp-tender. Transfer beans to a bowl of ice water to cool; drain well.
**2.** Meanwhile, for dressing, remove 1 Tbsp. zest and squeeze 6 Tbsp. juice from lemons. In a bowl whisk together lemon zest and juice, olive oil, capers, mustard, and salt.
**3.** Arrange lettuce on a platter. Top with beans, tuna, sweet pepper, olives, and radishes. Drizzle with some of the dressing. Sprinkle with black pepper. Pass remaining dressing. **Makes 4 servings (¼ of the salad each).**
**EACH SERVING** 265 cal., 18 g fat (3 g sat. fat), 18 mg chol., 686 mg sodium, 10 g carb., 4 g fiber, 5 g sugars, 17 g pro.

**OLIVE LOVE**
Many supermarket delis now have olive bars, where you can choose from an assortment of specialty olives. All varieties work for this salad, but make sure they are pitted.

## STRIPED BASS IN WINE

**START TO FINISH** 25 minutes

- ½ cup dry white wine
- ¼ cup water
- ¼ cup olive oil
- 2 medium tomatoes, sliced
- 2 shallots, sliced ¼ inch thick
- 6 fresh thyme sprigs
- ¼ tsp. kosher salt
- 1 lb. skinless striped bass, red snapper, or halibut fillets, cut into 4 pieces

**1.** In a 10-inch skillet combine wine, water, and the oil. Add tomatoes, shallots, thyme, and salt. Bring to boiling; reduce heat. Simmer, uncovered, 3 to 5 minutes or until tomatoes soften.

**2.** Place fish in skillet; spoon broth over fish. Reduce heat to medium-low. Cook, covered, 8 to 10 minutes or until fish flakes easily. Transfer fish and tomatoes to bowls. Discard thyme sprigs. Ladle broth mixture into bowls. Add additional fresh thyme. **Makes 4 servings (1 piece fish + ½ cup broth mixture each).**
**EACH SERVING** *272 cal., 16 g fat (2 g sat. fat), 91 mg chol., 155 mg sodium, 5 g carb., 1 g fiber, 3 g sugars, 21 g pro.*

### MAKE IT A MEAL

Crusty Italian bread is a given for soaking up broth. Add crunch with a leafy salad topped with green beans, red onion, and herb vinaigrette.

## GRILLED SALMON AND LEEKS

**START TO FINISH** 30 minutes

4    thin leeks (about 1½ lb.)
2    Tbsp. olive oil
½    tsp. salt
½    tsp. black pepper
1    sprig fresh rosemary
4    4- to 6-oz. skin-on salmon
     fillets, ¾ to 1 inch thick
¼    cup unsalted butter,
     softened
2    tsp. Dijon mustard

**1.** Trim dark green tops and root ends from leeks, leaving ends intact. Cut leeks in half lengthwise; peel off tough outer leaves. Wash leeks; pat dry. (Keep leeks a little wet to prevent them from burning on the grill.) Brush leeks with 1 Tbsp. of the oil; season with ¼ tsp. each of the salt and pepper.

**2.** On a grill or in a grill pan grill rosemary sprig, uncovered, over medium-high heat 1 to 2 minutes or until lightly charred; remove. Grill leeks, uncovered, 5 to 7 minutes or until tender, turning occasionally. Remove from grill; cover.

**3.** Brush salmon with the remaining 1 Tbsp. oil; season with the remaining ¼ tsp. each salt and pepper. Grill, skin sides up, 4 minutes; turn salmon over. Grill about 2 minutes or until fish flakes easily. Remove from grill.

**4.** Strip rosemary leaves from stem; chop leaves. In a bowl stir together butter, mustard, and 1 tsp. of the chopped rosemary. Spread butter on fish and leeks; sprinkle with the remaining chopped rosemary. **Makes 4 servings (1 fillet + 1 leek each).**

**EACH SERVING** *369 cal., 26 g fat (9 g sat. fat), 93 mg chol, 415 mg sodium, 11 g carb., 1 g fiber, 3 g sugars, 24 g pro.*

## GET DINNER DONE FAST

**1**

**THINK AHEAD**
Plan your week of meals and make a list so you can get all your grocery shopping done at once.

**2**

**BUY PREPPED OR QUICK FOODS**
Purchase preshredded cheese, cut-up veggies, portioned skinless fish fillets, peeled and deveined shrimp, rotisserie chicken, quick-cooking grains, ready-to-microwave vegetables, and prewashed bagged salad mixes.

**3**

**PREP VEGGIES**
Set aside time (like when you get home from the store on the weekend) to clean, cut up, and organize veggies for the week, then store them in containers in the fridge.

**4**

**MAKE EXTRA**
Make a double or triple batch of rice, pasta, roasted vegetables, and cooked meat or chicken to store in the fridge. Use the extras as quick side dishes or as the base for a completely different meal (such as soups, stir-fries, and enchiladas). Freeze a large batch of lasagna, soup, or chili in individual portions for easy lunches and dinners.

**5**

**FASTER CLEANUP**
Line baking pans with foil or parchment to save on scrubbing and soaking when cleaning up. Clean as you go, too, so there's less to do after the meal.

CRISPY SHRIMP
SANDWICHES

CREAMY SPRING
VEGETABLES AND
SMOKED TROUT

## CRISPY SHRIMP SANDWICHES

START TO FINISH 30 minutes

**KEEP IT HOT**
The oil must
be very hot
(365°F) before
adding the
first batch
of shrimp.
Let the oil get
back up to
temperature
between
batches.
Since the
shrimp cook
for only a
short time,
you want the
coating to get
as crisp
as possible.

20  large shrimp (1 lb.), peeled and deveined
½  cup milk
½  cup cornmeal
¼  cup all-purpose flour
½  tsp. smoked paprika
½  tsp. coarse salt
    Vegetable oil for frying (tip, p. 21)
4   5-inch portions French-style baguettes, split and hollowed out
⅔  cup sliced pickled hot cherry peppers
4   green onions, thinly sliced
4   butter lettuce leaves
¼  cup mayonnaise

**1.** Place shrimp in a shallow bowl. Add milk, turning to coat shrimp. In a shallow dish stir together cornmeal, flour, paprika, and salt. Place half the shrimp in flour mixture; toss to coat. Transfer to a tray. Repeat with remaining shrimp.
**2.** In a 10-inch skillet heat ¼ inch of the oil (about 2 cups) over medium heat. Carefully place shrimp, half at a time, in pan. Cook about

2 minutes or until golden brown on one side. Turn and cook about 1 minute more or until shrimp turn opaque. Transfer to a paper towel-lined tray.
**3.** Arrange shrimp on bread portion bottoms. Top with peppers, onions, and lettuce. Spread mayonnaise on bread portion tops; add to sandwiches. **Makes 4 sandwiches.**
EACH SANDWICH *553 cal., 25 g fat (4 g sat. fat), 167 mg chol., 896 mg sodium, 51 g carb., 1 g fiber, 2 g sugars, 27 g pro.*

## CREAMY SPRING VEGETABLES AND SMOKED TROUT

START TO FINISH 20 minutes

1   Tbsp. olive oil
1   Tbsp. unsalted butter
8   oz. cremini or other mushrooms, sliced
3   medium carrots, thinly bias-sliced
⅔  cup fresh shelled or frozen peas
½  cup heavy cream
¼  cup water
¼  tsp. kosher salt
¼  tsp. black pepper

8   oz. smoked trout, skin removed
2   Tbsp. chopped fresh chives
1   large bunch watercress, tough stalks removed

**1.** In a 10-inch skillet heat olive oil and butter over medium heat. Add mushrooms; cook about 2 minutes or until they release their liquid. Stir in carrots; cover. Cook 3 minutes; uncover. Add peas, cream, the water, salt, and pepper. Bring to boiling; reduce heat. Simmer, uncovered, about 4 minutes or until peas are tender, stirring occasionally.
**2.** Break trout into pieces; gently stir into skillet and heat through. Stir in chives. Top with watercress. **Makes 4 servings (1 cup each).**
EACH SERVING *294 cal., 21 g fat (10 g sat. fat), 84 mg chol., 755 mg sodium, 11 g carb., 3 g fiber, 6 g sugars, 17 g pro.*

**CHANGE IT UP**

*Smoked trout has an intense, salty flavor and flaky texture. If it's not available, replace the trout with smoked salmon (not lox-style) or even high-quality tuna.*

**LEMON-DILL SALMON CAKES**

**CHICKPEA, LEEK, AND SPINACH SOUP**

## LEMON-DILL SALMON CAKES

**START TO FINISH** 40 minutes

| | |
|---|---|
| 1 | egg, lightly beaten |
| 2 | 5- to 6-oz. cans skinless, boneless salmon, drained |
| 1¼ | cups panko bread crumbs (tip, *p. 108*) |
| 1 | Meyer lemon, halved (one half finely chopped, one half juiced) |
| 2 | Tbsp. water |
| 2 | Tbsp. chopped fresh dill |
| ¼ | tsp. salt |
| ¼ | tsp. black pepper |
| 3 | Tbsp. vegetable oil |
| 2 | cups torn mixed greens Olive oil |

**1.** In a bowl stir together egg, salmon, ¾ cup of the panko, the chopped lemon half, and the next four ingredients (through pepper).
**2.** Place the remaining ½ cup panko in a another bowl. For each of eight cakes, shape ¼ cup salmon mixture into a ball. Roll in panko to coat; press until ½ inch thick.
**3.** In a 10-inch skillet heat 2 Tbsp. of the vegetable oil over medium-high heat; add four salmon cakes. Cook 5 to 7 minutes or until browned, turning once. (If necessary, reduce heat to prevent overbrowning.) Remove from skillet; cover. Repeat with remaining vegetable oil and salmon cakes.
**4.** For salad, in a bowl toss greens with lemon juice and a drizzle of olive oil. Serve with salmon cakes; top with additional dill. **Makes 4 servings (2 cakes + ¾ cup salad each).**

**EACH SERVING** *270 cal., 16 g fat (2 g sat. fat), 67 mg chol., 404 mg sodium, 16 g carb., 2 g fiber, 1 g sugars, 17 g pro.*

## CHICKPEA, LEEK, AND SPINACH SOUP

**START TO FINISH** 25 minutes

| | |
|---|---|
| 2 | medium leeks, white and light green parts only, thinly sliced, washed, and drained |
| 2 | Tbsp. olive oil |
| 2 | 15- to 16-oz. cans chickpeas (garbanzo beans), rinsed and drained |
| 2 | cloves garlic, thinly sliced |
| 4 | cups reduced-sodium vegetable or chicken broth |
| 1 | cup water |
| 3 | Tbsp. lemon juice |
| 2 | 5-oz. pkg. baby spinach |
| 1 | Tbsp. chopped fresh thyme Salt and black pepper |

**1.** In a 4-qt. Dutch oven cook leeks in hot oil over medium heat 5 to 7 minutes or until very tender but not browned, stirring occasionally. (Reduce heat if leeks begin to brown.) Stir in chickpeas and garlic. Cook 2 minutes, stirring occasionally.
**2.** Add broth and the water. Bring to boiling; reduce heat. Add lemon juice. Simmer, uncovered, 5 minutes. Gradually stir in spinach and thyme. Cook about 1 minute or until spinach is wilted. Season to taste with salt and pepper. Serve immediately. **Makes 4 servings (2 cups each).**

**EACH SERVING** *268 cal., 10 g fat (1 g sat. fat), 0 mg chol., 978 mg sodium, 36 g carb., 9 g fiber, 8 g sugars, 10 g pro.*

»

**MEYER LEMONS**—a cross between regular lemons and mandarin oranges—are sweet enough to use both the chopped rind and flesh. To use a regular lemon instead, add 1 tsp. lemon zest and 1 Tbsp. lemon juice to the salmon mixture. Toss the greens with an additional 2 Tbsp. lemon juice.

TOMATO AND
ARTICHOKE PASTA

GRILLED BROCCOLI AND ORZO

## TOMATO AND ARTICHOKE PASTA

**START TO FINISH** 25 minutes

| | |
|---|---|
| 8 | oz. dried campanelle or penne pasta |
| ¼ | cup olive oil |
| 1 | 6.5- to 7.5-oz. jar quartered marinated artichoke hearts, drained |
| 10 | to 12 oz. red and/or yellow cherry tomatoes |
| ½ | cup pitted Kalamata olives, drained |
| 6 | sprigs fresh thyme |
| 6 | sprigs fresh oregano |
| ½ | tsp. crushed red pepper (optional) |

**1.** Preheat oven to 400°F. Cook pasta according to package directions; drain. Return pasta to pot. Add 1 Tbsp. of the olive oil; toss to coat.
**2.** In a shallow baking pan toss the remaining ingredients with the remaining 3 Tbsp. oil. Roast 5 to 7 minutes or until tomatoes are sizzling and beginning to burst, stirring once. Add to pasta; toss to combine. **Makes 4 servings (1½ cups each).**

**EACH SERVING** *403 cal., 21 g fat (2 g sat. fat), 0 mg chol., 876 mg sodium, 47 g carb., 3 g fiber, 5 g sugars, 8 g pro.*

**ROASTING BROCCOLI**
Another time, roast broccoli instead of grilling. After tossing broccoli with oil and salt, place spears on a baking sheet. Roast in a 425°F oven 10 to 15 minutes until crisp-tender, turning once.

## GRILLED BROCCOLI AND ORZO

**START TO FINISH** 35 minutes

| | |
|---|---|
| 2 | oranges |
| 1 | large head broccoli (1½ to 2 lb.), trimmed |
| 2 | Tbsp. olive oil |
| ¾ | tsp. kosher salt |
| 1⅓ | cups dried orzo pasta (8 oz.) |
| 1 | clove garlic, minced |
| ⅓ | cup pine nuts, toasted |
| ¼ | cup freshly grated Parmesan cheese |
| | Small fresh basil leaves |
| | Freshly ground black pepper |

BROCCOLI is easy to cut into spears. Cut broccoli head lengthwise through the stem. Continue cutting each half in half to get eight spears.

**1.** Remove 1 tsp. zest and squeeze 3 Tbsp. juice from one of the oranges. Cut remaining orange into slices or wedges.
**2.** Cut broccoli into eight spears. In a large bowl toss broccoli with 1 Tbsp. of the oil and ½ tsp. of the salt. Grill broccoli, covered, over medium heat 7 to 9 minutes or until lightly charred and crisp-tender.
**3.** Meanwhile, cook orzo in a 4-qt. saucepan of lightly salted boiling water about 7 minutes or until al dente; drain. Transfer to a bowl.
**4.** In an 8-inch skillet heat the remaining 1 Tbsp. oil over low heat. Add garlic; cook 1 minute. Stir in orange zest and juice and the remaining ¼ tsp. salt. Add orzo; stir to combine. Top orzo mixture with broccoli, pine nuts, Parmesan, and basil. Season to taste with pepper. Serve with orange slices. **Makes 4 servings (2 broccoli spears + ¾ cup orzo each).**

**EACH SERVING** *449 cal., 18 g fat (2 g sat. fat), 4 mg chol., 519 mg sodium, 61 g carb., 8 g fiber, 9 g sugars, 16 g pro.*

# SANDWICHES & PIZZAS

TEST KITCHEN

**MAKE AHEAD RECIPE**

**WHAT'S ON TOP?**
To top each pizza, use about 3 to 4 Tbsp. sauce or spread, 1½ to 1¾ cups toppings total, and 1 to 1¼ cups cheese.

**CHICKEN ALFREDO** Spread purchased Alfredo sauce on crust. Top with chopped cooked chicken, chopped baby spinach, crumbled crisp-cooked bacon, and chopped cooked artichoke hearts. Sprinkle with mozzarella and Parmesan cheeses.

**BARBECUE CHICKEN** Spread barbecue sauce on crust. Top with chopped cooked chicken, sliced red onion, crumbled crisp-cooked bacon, and chopped tomato. Sprinkle with cheddar and mozzarella cheese blend.

**PHILLY CHEESESTEAK** Mix 8 oz. softened cream cheese and 3 Tbsp. prepared horseradish; spread on crust. Top with chopped deli-style sliced roast beef, sweet pepper strips, chopped onion, and Monterey Jack cheese.

**SUPREME** Spread crust with pizza sauce. Top with cooked pork or Italian sausage, sliced pepperoni, sliced mushrooms, sweet pepper and onion strips, black olives, pickled pepperoncini peppers, and Fontina, mozzarella, or Asiago cheese.

**BREAKFAST** Before baking, sprinkle crust with cheddar or mozzarella; bake 5 minutes. Top with scrambled eggs, cooked sausage, sautéed mushrooms and sweet pepper, and additional cheese. Bake 2 minutes.

**TACO** Spread crust with salsa. Top with cooked ground beef mixed with additional salsa and/or taco seasoning mix. Sprinkle with cheddar cheese. Top baked pizza with shredded lettuce, sliced black olives, and crushed tortilla chips.

## COOKING CLASS

FOR THE CHEWIEST, CRISPIEST CRUST, TWO THINGS ARE KEY: A HOT OVEN AND A HOT BAKING STONE. IF YOU DON'T HAVE A STONE IN YOUR KITCHEN, PREHEAT A BAKING SHEET AND DUST IT LIGHTLY WITH CORNMEAL.

### STONE = CRISPY
Baking stones get really hot—the secret to a crispy outer crust that's chewy in the middle. Place the stone in the oven while it preheats and be careful when transferring the pizza to the stone.

**1** Yeast may seem like a finicky ingredient—after all, it's alive! But if you use a thermometer, your water will be the perfect temp to activate the yeast without scorching it. The success of your crust relies on your yeast's happiness.

**2** To get your dough uniformly mixed, you're going to have to get your hands a little sticky. Once most of the dough has come together through stirring, use your hands to form a ball and start kneading.

**3** Generously dust a baking sheet with cornmeal. Gently transfer one dough circle to the sheet. If you have enough cornmeal on the sheet, the dough will easily transfer onto the hot stone.

**4** Because the stone will be very hot, use the baking sheet to shimmy and shake the topped pizza dough onto the stone, gently pulling the baking sheet back toward you as the pizza settles on the stone.

## HOMEMADE PIZZA

**HANDS-ON TIME** 20 minutes
**RISE** 2 hours
**REST** 10 minutes
**BAKE** 7 minutes at 500°F

**BREAD FLOUR** has a higher protein content than all-purpose flour, so it will give your crust a tuggy, chewy texture. If you don't have it in your pantry, use all-purpose flour.

5 cups bread flour
1 Tbsp. sugar
1½ tsp. salt
1 tsp. active dry yeast
1¾ cups warm water (120°F to 130°F)
2 Tbsp. olive oil
Cornmeal

**1.** In an extra-large bowl stir together flour, sugar, salt, and yeast. Stir in water and oil until combined and all the flour is moistened.

**2.** Turn dough out onto a lightly floured surface. Knead dough until smooth and elastic (3 to 4 minutes).

Place in a lightly greased bowl, turning once to grease surface of dough. Cover; let rise at room temperature until double in size (2 hours).

**3.** Remove dough from bowl (do not punch down). Divide dough into four portions. Gently shape each portion into a ball. Cover; let rest 10 minutes.

**4.** Preheat oven to 500°F. Place a pizza stone, if using, in the oven while it preheats. On a lightly floured surface roll or stretch each dough portion into a 10- to 11-inch circle. Transfer dough circle to a baking sheet that has been sprinkled generously with cornmeal. Add desired toppings (opposite).

**5.** Gently slide one pizza at a time to the heated pizza stone, place the baking sheet in the oven. Bake about 7 minutes for pizza stone or about 10 minutes for the baking sheet, or until crust is golden.

**Makes 8 servings (½ crust each).**
**TO MAKE AHEAD** Prepare as directed through Step 2, cover with plastic wrap coated with nonstick cooking spray, and chill up to 24 hours. Let dough stand at room temperature 30 minutes before rolling. To freeze dough, prepare as directed through Step 2, wrap in plastic wrap, place in airtight containers, and freeze up to 3 months. Thaw in refrigerator before using. Let dough portions stand at room temperature 30 minutes before rolling.

**EACH ½ CRUST** 363 cal., 5 g fat (1 g sat. fat), 0 mg chol., 440 mg sodium, 67 g carb., 2 g fiber, 2 g sugars, 11 g pro.

# EASY FLATBREAD

**HANDS-ON TIME** 15 minutes
**RISE** 45 minutes
**BAKE** 15 minutes at 450°F

　　　Olive oil or nonstick cooking
　　　spray
2　　cups all-purpose flour
1　　pkg. active dry yeast
1　　tsp. sugar
½　　tsp. kosher salt
1　　Tbsp. olive oil
⅔　　cup warm water (120°F to 130°F)
　　　Cornmeal

**1.** Coat a medium bowl with oil. In a food processor combine the next four ingredients (through salt). With the food processor running, add 1 Tbsp. olive oil and the warm water. Process until dough forms. Remove and shape into a smooth ball. Place dough in the prepared bowl; turn once to coat dough surface. Cover bowl with plastic wrap. Let stand in a warm place until double in size (45 to 60 minutes).

**2.** Preheat oven to 450°F. Lightly grease a baking sheet; sprinkle with cornmeal. On a lightly floured surface roll and stretch the dough into a 12×8-inch rectangle or oval. Place dough on prepared baking sheet. Lightly brush with olive oil. Add desired toppings as directed. If desired, drizzle with additional olive oil and sprinkle with salt.

**3.** Bake about 15 minutes or until crust is golden. **Makes 6 servings (1 square each).**

**EACH SERVING** *211 cal., 3 g fat (0 g sat. fat), 0 mg chol., 96 mg sodium, 40 g carb., 2 g fiber, 1 g sugars, 5 g pro.*

**GREEK** Spread artichoke tapenade over flatbread. Sprinkle with Fontina cheese and top with halved grape or cherry tomatoes, halved pitted olives, and chopped red onion. Bake as directed. Sprinkle with snipped fresh parsley.

**PROSCIUTTO AND ARUGULA** Spread dried-tomato pesto over flatbread. Top with crisp-cooked prosciutto (cut into bite-size pieces) and sprinkle with shredded provolone cheese. Bake as directed. Top with fresh arugula and a squeeze of fresh lemon juice.

**QUICK TIP**
Save time by using purchased flatbread. (Bonus: It comes in assorted flavors such as herbed and tomato.) If using a purchased flatbread, reduce the baking time to 5 minutes after adding the toppings.

**MARGHERITA** Top flatbread with halved grape tomatoes, halved small fresh mozzarella balls, and minced fresh garlic. Bake as directed. Top with torn fresh basil.

**CHICKEN CAESAR** Mix equal amounts Caesar dressing and sour cream; spread over flatbread. Top with shredded cooked chicken and shredded mozzarella. Bake as directed. Top with lettuce, cherry tomatoes, Parmesan, and crumbled cooked bacon.

### MAKE A CALZONE

Start with one recipe Easy Flatbread dough (*opposite*), half a recipe Homemade Pizza dough (*p. 261*), or 1 lb. thawed purchased frozen pizza dough for the crust. Let dough stand at room temperature 15 minutes.

Meanwhile, preheat oven to 375°F and line a large baking sheet with parchment paper or foil. Divide the dough into thirds. On a lightly floured surface roll each portion into an 8-inch circle.

Using toppings for the Easy Flatbread or Homemade Pizza (*p. 261*) as a guide, spoon ¾ cup meat and/ or vegetables and ¼ cup shredded cheese onto half of each round.

Mix together 1 egg and 1 Tbsp. water and brush over edges of circles. Fold dough over filling and crimp edges to seal. Cut a few slits in the tops to allow steam to escape.

Place calzones on the prepared baking sheet and brush with remaining egg mixture. Bake 30 to 35 minutes or until golden. Cool slightly on baking sheets before serving with warm marinara sauce and Parmesan cheese.

# DEEP-DISH PIZZA

**HANDS-ON TIME** 40 minutes
**RISE** 1 hour 20 minutes
**STAND** 10 minutes
**BAKE** 55 minutes at 400°F
**COOL** 10 minutes

Olive oil or vegetable oil
Cornmeal
1 cup warm water (120°F to 130°F)
1 pkg. active dry yeast
2¾ to 3¼ cups all-purpose flour
⅓ cup vegetable oil
½ tsp. salt
6 oz. bulk sweet Italian sausage
1 14.5-oz. can diced tomatoes, drained
1 Tbsp. chopped fresh oregano
1 Tbsp. chopped fresh basil
12 oz. sliced mozzarella cheese
¼ cup grated Parmesan cheese

**1.** Brush a 10×2-inch round cake pan or 10-inch springform pan with oil. Sprinkle bottom of pan with cornmeal. In a large bowl combine warm water and yeast, stirring to dissolve yeast. Let stand 5 minutes. Stir in 2½ cups of the flour, ⅓ cup oil, and salt.

**2.** Turn dough out onto a lightly floured surface. Knead in enough remaining flour to make a moderately stiff dough that is smooth and elastic (about 5 minutes). Shape dough into a ball. Place in a lightly greased bowl; turn once to grease surface. Cover and let rise in a warm place until double (50 to 60 minutes). Punch dough down. Cover; let rest 5 minutes.

**3.** Place dough in prepared pan. Using oiled hands, press over bottom and 1½ inches up sides of pan. Cover; let rise in a warm place until double (30 to 35 minutes).

**4.** Preheat oven to 400°F. For filling, in an 8-inch skillet cook sausage until browned; drain fat. Using paper towels, pat sausage and wipe out skillet. Stir in tomatoes, oregano, and basil. Cook and stir until heated through.

**5.** Arrange half of mozzarella over dough. Spoon filling over cheese; top with remaining mozzarella and the Parmesan cheese.

**6.** Bake 55 to 60 minutes or until edge of crust is crisp and golden brown and filling is heated through. If necessary, cover crust loosely with foil the last 10 minutes of baking to prevent overbrowning. Cool on a wire rack 10 minutes. (If using a springform pan, remove the pan ring.) If desired, sprinkle with additional Parmesan cheese and basil. Cut into wedges. **Makes 6 servings (1 wedge each).**

**13×9-INCH PAN PIZZA** Prepare as directed through Step 3, except on a floured surface roll dough to a 14×10-inch rectangle. Brush oil on bottom and sides of a 13×9-inch baking pan. Sprinkle bottom of pan with cornmeal. Place dough in pan, pressing ½ inch up sides. Cover; let rise in a warm place until nearly double in size (30 to 35 minutes). Prepare filling and assemble as directed in Steps 4 and 5. Continue as directed, except reduce baking time to 25 to 30 minutes.

**EACH SERVING** 646 cal., 35 g fat (12 g sat. fat), 51 mg chol., 956 mg sodium, 55 g carb., 3 g fiber, 2 g sugars, 26 g pro.

## HOT HAM AND CHEESE SLIDERS

**HANDS-ON TIME** 30 minutes
**BAKE** 25 minutes at 350°F

- 12    Hawaiian sweet rolls, split
- 12    oz. deli-style thinly sliced Black Forest ham
- 6    oz. thinly sliced white cheddar cheese
- 1    5.2-oz. container semisoft cheese with garlic and fine herbs
- 6    Tbsp. butter, melted
- 2    tsp. finely chopped shallot
- 1    Tbsp. chopped fresh parsley
- 1    tsp. Dijon mustard
- 1    clove garlic, minced

**1.** Preheat oven to 350°F. Arrange bottoms of rolls in a 13×9-inch baking pan or 3-qt. rectangular baking dish. Layer ham and cheddar cheese on rolls in pan. Spread cut sides of roll tops with semisoft cheese and place on cheddar layer. For drizzle, in a bowl combine remaining ingredients and spoon over sandwiches.

**2.** Cover pan with foil. Bake 15 minutes. Remove foil; bake 10 to 15 minutes more or until cheese is melted and roll tops are light brown. **Makes 12 sliders.**

**EACH SLIDER** *298 cal., 19 fat (12 g sat. fat) 72 mg chol., 614 mg sodium, 20 g carb., 1 g fiber, 8 g sugars, 13 g pro.*

### ROAST BEEF SLIDERS

Prepare as directed, except use 3-inch sourdough rolls. Layer roll bottoms with 12 oz. deli-style roast beef and 1½ cups chopped pickled mixed vegetables. Top with 6 oz. thinly sliced provolone cheese. Spread cut sides of roll tops with one 8-oz. tub cream cheese spread with garden vegetables. For drizzle, combine ¼ cup olive oil; 2 cloves garlic, minced; 1 tsp. dried Italian seasoning, crushed; and ½ tsp. crushed red pepper. Bake as directed.

### BARBECUE CHICKEN SLIDERS

Prepare as directed, except use 3-inch sandwich rolls. Cook 1½ lb. skinless, boneless chicken breast; shred. In a bowl combine chicken; 1 cup chopped pineapple, well drained; ⅔ cup barbecue sauce; and ¼ cup chopped pickled jalapeño peppers; spoon onto roll bottoms. Top with 1½ cups shredded Monterey Jack cheese. For drizzle, combine 6 Tbsp. melted butter, 2 Tbsp. honey, 1 Tbsp. Worcestershire sauce, and ½ tsp. black pepper. Bake as directed.

**WHAT IS NIÇOISE SALAD?** THIS SPECIALTY FROM NICE, FRANCE, IS A LAYERED SALAD WITH GREEN BEANS, TUNA, TOMATOES, OLIVES, AND HARD-BOILED EGGS. WE TURNED THE CLASSIC INTO A TO-GO LUNCH BY PACKING THE INGREDIENTS INTO SOFT, FLUFFY PITA BREAD.

## PARSLEY GREMOLATA VINAIGRETTE

In a screw-top jar combine ¼ cup white wine vinegar; ¼ cup olive oil; 2 Tbsp. chopped fresh parsley; 2 tsp. Dijon mustard; 2 cloves garlic, minced; ½ tsp. lemon zest; ¼ tsp. salt; and ¼ tsp. cracked black pepper. Cover and shake well to combine.

## NIÇOISE SALAD SANDWICHES

**START TO FINISH** 20 minutes

- ½ cup fresh thin green beans, trimmed
- 4 leaves butterhead (Boston or Bibb) lettuce
- 4 whole wheat or plain pita bread rounds
- 2 5-oz. cans solid light tuna packed in oil, drained
- 1 medium tomato, thinly sliced
- ½ of a medium red onion, thinly sliced
- 2 Hard-Boiled Eggs (p. 46), sliced (optional)
- 1 recipe Parsley Gremolata Vinaigrette or purchased Greek vinaigrette

**1.** Steam green beans or cook in boiling water 4 to 5 minutes or just until crisp-tender. Plunge into ice water; drain.

**2.** Place a lettuce leaf on each pita round. Arrange green beans on lettuce. Top with tuna, tomato, onion, and, if desired, egg slices. Drizzle with Parsley Gremolata Vinaigrette. Fold over to serve. **Makes 4 sandwiches.**

**TO MAKE AHEAD** Prepare as directed, except place vinaigrette in a container with a tight-fitting lid. Wrap sandwiches in plastic wrap. Refrigerate dressing and sandwiches up to 24 hours. To serve, drizzle vinaigrette over filling.

**EACH SANDWICH** *411 cal., 19 g fat (3 g sat. fat), 9 mg chol., 752 mg sodium, 40 g carb., 5 g fiber, 4 g sugars, 22 g pro.*

SANTA FE
TURKEY WRAPS

**MAKE-AHEAD
WRAPS**
For lunch tomorrow, make
your wrap up to 24 hours
ahead of time. Wrap each
sandwich tightly with plastic
wrap and refrigerate until
you're ready to tote.

CHICKEN
COBB WRAPS

## CHICKEN COBB WRAPS

**START TO FINISH** 30 minutes

| | |
|---|---|
| 1 | recipe Green Onion Aïoli |
| 4 | 10-inch spinach-flavor flour tortillas |
| 2 | cups shredded deli-roasted chicken |
| 2 | cups shredded leaf lettuce |
| 8 | strips bacon, crisp-cooked |
| 2 | Hard-Boiled Eggs (*p. 46*), sliced |
| 1 | avocado, halved, seeded, peeled, and sliced |
| ¾ | cup quartered grape tomatoes |
| ½ | cup crumbled blue cheese (2 oz.) |

**1.** Spread 2 Tbsp. of the Green
Onion Aïoli over each tortilla to
within ½ inch of edges. On bottom
halves of tortillas layer chicken,
lettuce, bacon, eggs, avocado,
tomatoes, and blue cheese. Fold
in sides of tortillas to enclose filling
and roll up. Cut each in half. Serve
with remaining aïoli for dipping.
**Makes 8 servings (½ wrap each).**
**EACH SERVING** *475 cal., 35 g fat (8 g
sat. fat), 112 mg chol., 792 mg sodium,
22 g carb., 3 g fiber, 2 g sugars, 20 g pro.*

## *GREEN ONION AÏOLI*

In a small bowl stir together
1 cup mayonnaise, 6 Tbsp. chopped
green onions; 4 tsp. lemon juice;
2 cloves garlic, minced; and ½ tsp.
cracked black pepper.

## SANTA FE TURKEY WRAPS

**START TO FINISH** 25 minutes

| | |
|---|---|
| ½ | cup cream cheese spread with jalapeño |
| 4 | 10-inch tomato-flavor flour tortillas |
| ¾ | cup frozen roasted or whole kernel corn, thawed |
| 3 | cups chopped cooked turkey breast |
| 1 | avocado, halved, seeded, peeled, and sliced |
| ½ | of a medium red onion, thinly sliced |
| 2 | roma tomatoes, halved lengthwise and thinly sliced |
| 3 | cups shredded romaine lettuce Lime wedges (optional) Southwest chipotle-flavor or plain ranch salad dressing |

**1.** Spread cream cheese on tortillas
to within ½ inch of edges. On bottom
halves of tortillas layer corn, turkey,
avocado, onion, tomatoes, and
lettuce. If desired, squeeze a lime
wedge over each. Fold in sides of
tortillas to enclose filling and roll up.
Cut each in half. Serve with dressing.
**Makes 8 servings (½ wrap each).**
**EACH SERVING** *395 cal., 24 g fat
(5 g sat. fat), 57 mg chol., 580 mg
sodium, 26 g carb., 5 g fiber,
5 g sugars, 21 g pro.*

## BURRITOS

**HANDS-ON TIME** 40 minutes
**BAKE** 15 minutes at 350°F

4   to 6 cups FILLINGS
1½  cups CHEESE
8   10-inch flour or desired-flavor flour tortillas, warmed
    Desired SALSAS

**1.** Preheat oven to 350°F. Select desired FILLINGS. Sprinkle CHEESE on each tortilla just below center. Spoon ½ to ¾ cup total filling onto each tortilla over cheese. Fold bottom edges of tortillas over filling. Fold in sides and roll up from the bottom.
**2.** Arrange burritos, seam sides down, on a baking sheet. Bake 15 to 20 minutes or until heated through. Serve with desired SALSAS. **Makes 8 burritos.**

## FILLINGS

### MEAT FILLINGS
- Cooked bacon
- Cooked ground beef
- Cooked pork sausage or Italian sausage
- Cooked turkey
- Scrambled eggs
- Sliced or shredded cooked beef, chicken, or pork

### RICE & BEAN FILLINGS
- Cooked black beans or pinto beans
- Cooked white rice
- Mexican Red Rice (p. 320)
- Refried beans

### FRESH FILLINGS
- Avocado, sliced
- Cooked sweet potato cubes or butternut squash cubes

- Pickled jalapeño pepper slices
- Red, white, or green onion, sliced and sautéed
- Sweet peppers, sliced and sautéed
- Thawed frozen corn kernels or canned yellow hominy, drained
- Tomato, chopped and seeded

## CHEESE

Choose from shredded cheddar, Mexican-style four-cheese blend, Monterey Jack, or crumbled Cotija or queso fresco.

## SALSAS

**CORN AND BLACK BEAN SALSA** In a bowl combine 1 cup halved or quartered cherry tomatoes; 1 cup canned black beans, rinsed and drained; ¾ cup frozen whole kernel corn, thawed; 2 Tbsp. chopped onion; 1 to 2 Tbsp. chopped fresh cilantro; 1 Tbsp. lime juice; ¼ tsp. salt; and ⅛ tsp. black pepper. Cover; chill at least 2 hours. Store in a covered container in refrigerator up to 3 days. **Makes 3 cups.**

**PICO DE GALLO** Remove ½ tsp. zest and squeeze 1 Tbsp. juice from 1 lime. In a bowl combine zest and juice; 1¾ cups finely chopped tomatoes; 2 Tbsp. finely chopped onion; 1 to 2 small fresh jalapeño peppers, seeded and finely chopped (tip, p. 22); 2 Tbsp. chopped fresh cilantro; 1 clove garlic, minced; and ¼ tsp. salt. Serve immediately or cover and chill up to 4 hours. **Makes 2 cups.**

**AVOCADO SALSA VERDE** In a blender combine one 16-oz. jar salsa verde; 1 small ripe avocado, halved, seeded, peeled, and chopped; and 3 Tbsp. chopped fresh cilantro. Cover and blend until smooth. Transfer to a bowl, cover, and chill up to 24 hours. **Makes 2½ cups.**

### *WRAP IT RIGHT*

Spread the filling on a warmed tortilla so it's just below the center. Fold bottom of tortilla up and over filling. Fold sides of tortilla in and over filling. Roll up from bottom, completely enclosing filling.

## MAKE A QUESADILLA

Sprinkle ½ cup shredded cheese (use cheddar, Chihuahua, Monterey Jack, Colby-Monterey Jack, or Mexican-style four-cheese blend) over half of two 8- to 10-inch flour tortillas. If you like, add cooked chicken, ham, or sausage; sliced avocado; chopped tomato; and/or thinly sliced jalapeño (tip, *p. 22*) or sweet peppers. Fold tortillas in half over cheese and filling. Coat a 12-inch skillet with nonstick cooking spray. Heat over medium heat. Add tortillas to skillet and cook 4 to 6 minutes or until golden brown, turning once.

### BURRITO BAR

Burritos are a fun setup for casual get-togethers. Prepare two or three meat fillings and offer an assortment of rice, beans, and veggies. Add a couple salsas and one or two cheese options.

**TOASTING BUNS**
Toast rolls and hoagie buns in a toaster oven or use your broiler. For the broiler, place rolls, cut sides up, on a baking sheet; broil 4 to 5 inches from heat 1 to 2 minutes or until golden.

## SLOPPY JOES
**START TO FINISH** 25 minutes

1½  lb. ground beef, pork, turkey, or chicken
½  cup chopped green sweet pepper
½  cup chopped onion
1  8-oz. can tomato sauce
2  Tbsp. water
2  tsp. chili powder
6  hamburger or pretzel buns or kaiser rolls, split and toasted
   Mustard, chopped onion, pickles, and/or sliced pepperoncini peppers

**1.** In a 10-inch skillet cook first three ingredients (through ½ cup onion) until meat is browned; drain. Stir in tomato sauce, the water, and chili powder. Simmer, uncovered, 5 minutes. Serve on buns with mustard, onion, pickles, and/or peppers. **Makes 6 sandwiches.**
EACH SANDWICH *412 cal., 22 fat (8 g sat. fat), 78 mg chol., 627 mg sodium, 27 g carb., 2 g fiber, 6 g sugars, 25 g pro.*

AVOCADO BLT
CLUB SANDWICHES

BANH MI
SANDWICHES

# AVOCADO BLT SANDWICHES

START TO FINISH 25 minutes

| | |
|---|---|
| 1 | ripe avocado |
| 2 | Tbsp. light mayonnaise |
| 1 | tsp. lemon juice |
| 1 | clove garlic, minced |
| 4 | slices bacon, crisp-cooked and halved crosswise |
| 4 | leaves romaine lettuce |
| 1 | tomato, thinly sliced |
| 8 | slices whole wheat bread, toasted |

**1.** Halve, seed, and peel avocado. In a bowl mash one of the avocado halves with a wooden spoon. Stir in mayonnaise, lemon juice, and garlic. Thinly slice the remaining avocado half.

**2.** Arrange avocado slices, bacon, lettuce, and tomato on four of the bread slices. Spread mashed avocado mixture over remaining four bread slices; place on sandwiches, spread sides down. **Makes 4 sandwiches.**

EACH SANDWICH *272 cal., 12 g fat (2 g sat. fat), 9 mg chol., 482 mg sodium, 31 g carb., 7 g fiber, 4 g sugars, 12 g pro.*

**AVOCADO BLT CLUB SANDWICHES** Prepare as directed, except add 4 oz. each deli-style thinly sliced cooked ham and turkey or chicken.

EACH SANDWICH *311 cal., 13 g fat (3 g sat. fat), 34 mg chol., 953 mg sodium, 29 g carb., 7 g fiber, 6 g sugars, 20 g pro.*

# BANH MI SANDWICHES

START TO FINISH 30 minutes

| | |
|---|---|
| ⅓ | cup mayonnaise |
| 5 | tsp. sriracha sauce |
| 12 | oz. pork tenderloin |
| 1 | Tbsp. reduced-sodium soy sauce |
| 1 | small cucumber, seeded and cut into thin strips |
| 1 | small red sweet pepper, cut into thin strips |
| ½ | cup shredded carrot |
| ¼ | cup chopped green onions |
| 1 | 10-oz. loaf baguette-style French bread, split horizontally |
| ¼ | cup fresh cilantro leaves |
| 1 | fresh jalapeño pepper, thinly sliced and, if desired, seeded (tip, *p. 22*) |

**1.** For sriracha mayonnaise, in a bowl stir together mayonnaise and 3 tsp. of the sriracha sauce.

**2.** Trim fat from meat. Cut meat crosswise into ½-inch slices. Press each piece with the palm of your hand to make an even thickness. In a bowl combine the remaining 2 tsp. sriracha sauce and the soy sauce. Brush sauce mixture over pork slices. In a greased grill pan or 12-inch skillet cook meat over medium-high heat 4 to 6 minutes or until slightly pink in center and juices run clear, turning once.

**3.** In a bowl combine cucumber, sweet pepper, carrot, and green onions.

**4.** Spread bread with sriracha mayonnaise. Place meat on the bottom half of the baguette. Top with vegetable mixture, cilantro, jalapeño slices, and top half of baguette. Slice into six portions. **Makes 6 servings (1 portion each).**

EACH SERVING *277 cal., 11 g fat (2 g sat. fat), 42 mg chol., 571 mg sodium, 27 g carb., 1 g fiber, 3 g sugars, 16 g pro.*

**WHAT IS BANH MI?** THINLY SLICED PORK, FRESH VEGGIES, AND CILANTRO ARE PILED HIGH ON A BAGUETTE TO CREATE THIS VIETNAMESE-STYLE SANDWICH. IF YOU LIKE IT SPICY, ADD EXTRA SRIRACHA SAUCE TO THE MAYO.

## GRILLED CHEESE SANDWICHES

**START TO FINISH** 20 minutes

- 12 slices white or wheat bread
- 12 1¼-oz. slices CHEESE
   ADD-ONS (optional)
- 3 Tbsp. butter, softened;
   mayonnaise; or olive oil

**1.** Top six bread slices with CHEESE. If desired, top with ADD-ONS. Add remaining bread slices. Spread or brush both sides of each sandwich with butter, mayonnaise, or oil.

**2.** Heat a 12-inch skillet or griddle over medium heat. Add three sandwiches to skillet. Cook 2 minutes or until bottoms are golden. Turn sandwiches over; cook 2 to 3 minutes more or until bottoms are golden and cheese melts. (Adjust heat as necessary to prevent overbrowning.) Repeat with remaining sandwiches.
**Makes 6 sandwiches.**

**EACH SANDWICH** *356 cal., 22 g fat (12 g sat. fat), 57 mg chol., 568 mg sodium, 26 g carb., 1 g fiber, 3 g sugars, 14 g pro.*

## CHEESE

Choose one or two (or more!) cheeses for each sandwich. Good choices are American, Brie, cheddar, Gouda, Havarti, Monterey Jack, mozzarella, Muenster, provolone, smoked cheddar, Swiss, and white cheddar.

## ADD-ONS

### SWEET

- Apple or pear slices
- Caramelized onions
- Chutney
- Cranberry sauce
- Jam

### MEATS

- Chicken, ham, or tuna salad *(p. 276)*
- Crisp-cooked bacon or pancetta
- Shredded barbecue chicken or pork
- Sliced deli meat
- Sliced pepperoni

### SAVORY

- Pepperoncini slices
- Pesto
- Roasted red peppers, squeezed dry
- Sautéed sliced mushrooms
- Sun-dried tomatoes

# PANINI

**START TO FINISH** 20 minutes

    Filling *(below)*
8  slices French, sourdough, or Italian bread, sliced ¾ inch thick
2  Tbsp. olive oil or softened butter

**1.** Preheat a covered indoor grill or panini press. Layer desired amount of Filling ingredients on four slices of bread. Top with the remaining bread slices. Brush outsides of sandwiches with oil or spread with butter.
**2.** Place sandwiches (half at a time if necessary) in indoor grill or panini press. Cover and cook 6 minutes or until cheese melts (or until heated through) and bread is crisp. **Makes 4 sandwiches.**

### HAM & APPLE
Our picks for the sandwich shown: thinly sliced cooked ham, sliced Taleggio or Brie cheese, thinly sliced apple, and mango chutney.

## NO PANINI PRESS? NO PROBLEM.

Make your own panini press with pans and cans you already have on hand.

Heat a 10-inch skillet or grill pan over medium heat. Assemble and oil the sandwiches as directed; place in heated skillet. Weight the sandwiches down by placing a second skillet on top of the sandwiches; add a few unopened cans of food to the top skillet. (If you use a heavy cast-iron skillet, you might not need to use the cans for weight.) Cook about 2 minutes; turn sandwiches. Replace skillet and weights; cook 2 minutes more or until sandwiches are golden and heated through.

**BACON-CHEDDAR CHICKEN**
Shredded chicken, crisp-cooked bacon, sliced tomato, spinach, sliced cheddar, ranch dressing

**REUBEN** Sliced corned beef, sauerkraut, sliced Swiss cheese, Thousand Island salad dressing

**CAPRESE** Sliced roma tomatoes, sliced fresh mozzarella; shredded basil; balsamic vinegar

## BEER-BRAISED BRATS

**HANDS-ON TIME** 20 minutes
**COOK** 10 minutes
**GRILL** 10 minutes

2    medium onions, cut into thin wedges (2 cups)
¼    cup butter
1    12-oz. bottle dark German beer
1    Tbsp. packed brown sugar
1    Tbsp. cider vinegar
1    tsp. Worcestershire sauce
½    tsp. caraway seeds
½    tsp. dried thyme, crushed
5    uncooked bratwurst links (1¼ lb. total)
5    hoagie or bratwurst buns or crusty rolls, split and toasted (tip, p. 270)
     Stone-ground mustard

**1.** In a 3-qt. saucepan cook and stir onion in butter over medium heat 8 to 10 minutes or until beginning to brown. Add the next six ingredients (through thyme). Bring to boiling; reduce heat. Add brats. Cover; simmer 10 minutes. Remove brats from cooking liquid; keep liquid warm.

**2.** Grill brats, covered, over medium heat 10 to 15 minutes or until an instant-read thermometer inserted into brats registers 160°F, turning occasionally. If desired, return brats to cooking liquid to keep warm until serving time.

**3.** To serve, place grilled brats in buns. Strain onions from liquid; discard liquid. Top brats with onions and serve with mustard.

**Makes 5 sandwiches.**

**EACH SANDWICH** *598 cal., 34 g fat (13 g sat. fat), 88 mg chol., 1,309 mg sodium, 44 g carb., 3 g fiber, 9 g sugars, 27 g pro.*

LINK-STYLE BRATS come in several fun flavors like beer, cheese, chipotle, and jalapeño. Any of these work here. For a healthier option, use turkey brats.

### GET-TOGETHER

*Double your batch of grinders for a crowd. Instead of placing the sandwiches under the broiler, wrap each sandwich in foil and pop them all into a 300°F oven 15 minutes; reduce heat to keep-warm setting. The sandwich bundles will stay toasty warm until you're ready to serve them.*

## ITALIAN SAUSAGE GRINDERS

**HANDS-ON TIME** 25 minutes
**COOK** 30 minutes

1    lb. bulk hot or sweet Italian sausage
1    14.5-oz. can fire-roasted diced tomatoes, undrained
1    14.5-oz. can crushed tomatoes
2    cloves garlic, minced
1    tsp. balsamic vinegar
1½   tsp. dried Italian seasoning, crushed
¼    tsp. salt
¼    tsp. crushed red pepper
1    small yellow onion, sliced
1    small green sweet pepper, seeded and cut into strips
2    Tbsp. olive oil
4    French-style rolls or hoagie buns, split
4    slices provolone cheese

**1.** In a 3-qt. saucepan cook sausage over medium heat until no longer pink; drain fat. Stir in the next seven ingredients (through crushed red pepper). Bring to boiling; reduce heat. Simmer, uncovered, 30 minutes or until thickened, stirring occasionally.

**2.** Meanwhile, in a 10-inch skillet cook onion and sweet pepper in hot oil over medium heat until tender. Keep warm.

**3.** Preheat broiler. Place split rolls on a baking sheet. If desired, toast rolls under broiler. Spoon the meat mixture evenly on the bottom halves of rolls. Top with onion mixture and cheese slices. Broil 4 to 5 inches from heat 2 to 3 minutes or until cheese melts and bubbles. If desired, sprinkle with additional Italian seasoning.

**Makes 4 sandwiches.**

**EACH SANDWICH** *710 cal., 50 g fat (18 g sat. fat), 101 mg chol., 1,765 mg sodium, 36 g carb., 4 g fiber, 6 g sugars, 28 g pro.*

BEER-BRAISED BRATS

ITALIAN
SAUSAGE
GRINDERS

## EGG SALAD SANDWICHES

**START TO FINISH** 15 minutes

- 8 Hard-Boiled Eggs *(p. 46),* chopped
- ¼ cup finely chopped green onions
- ¼ cup mayonnaise
- 1 Tbsp. yellow mustard
- 1 Tbsp. pickle relish (optional)
- 1 tsp. chopped fresh dill, tarragon, or chives (optional)
- ¼ tsp. salt
- ⅛ tsp. black pepper
- 8 slices bread or 4 small croissants, split
  Lettuce leaves

**1.** In a large bowl combine eggs and green onions. Stir in the next six ingredients (through pepper). Spread egg salad on four of the bread slices. Top with lettuce and remaining bread slices. **Makes 4 sandwiches.**

**EACH SANDWICH** *394 cal., 23 g fat (6 g sat. fat), 429 mg chol., 729 mg sodium, 27 g carb., 2 g fiber, 4 g sugars, 17 g pro.*

EGG SALAD SANDWICHES

## CHICKEN (OR HAM OR TUNA) SALAD SANDWICHES

**HANDS-ON TIME** 15 minutes
**CHILL** 1 hour

- 2½ cups cubed cooked chicken or ham (1 lb.) or four 4-oz. cans water-pack tuna, drained and broken into chunks
- ½ to 1 cup mayonnaise
- ½ cup finely chopped celery
- ¼ cup thinly sliced green onions
- ¼ tsp. salt*
- 12 slices bread
  Lettuce leaves

**1.** For chicken or ham salad, in a food processor combine meat, ½ cup mayonnaise, the celery, green onions, and salt. Cover and pulse until creamy and finely chopped. (For tuna salad, do not process; in a bowl stir together tuna, ½ cup mayonnaise, the celery, green onions, and salt.) Transfer ham or chicken salad to a bowl. If needed, stir in additional mayonnaise. Cover and chill all salads 1 to 4 hours. Spread on six slices of bread. Top with lettuce and remaining bread slices. **Makes 6 sandwiches.**
**\*NOTE** If using ham, omit salt.
**EACH SANDWICH** *404 cal., 21 g fat (4 g sat. fat), 75 mg chol., 531 mg sodium, 25 g carb., 2 g fiber, 3 g sugars , 27 g pro.*

**HEALTHY TWIST**
Whether you're cutting carbs or going gluten-free, lettuce makes a crunchy substitute for bread. Top large leaves of romaine, butterhead (Boston or Bibb), or iceberg lettuce with up to ⅓ cup chicken, ham, tuna, or egg salad per wrap and fold up like a burrito (tip, *p. 268*).

TUNA SALAD

HAM SALAD

CHICKEN SALAD

**SALADS FOR A CROWD**
If you're hosting a lunch, make all three of these salads to serve with an assortment of breads— whole grain, challah, croissants, and/or ciabatta rolls.

# SANDWICH FLAVOR BOOSTERS

Change up your chicken, ham, or tuna salad with one of these combos.

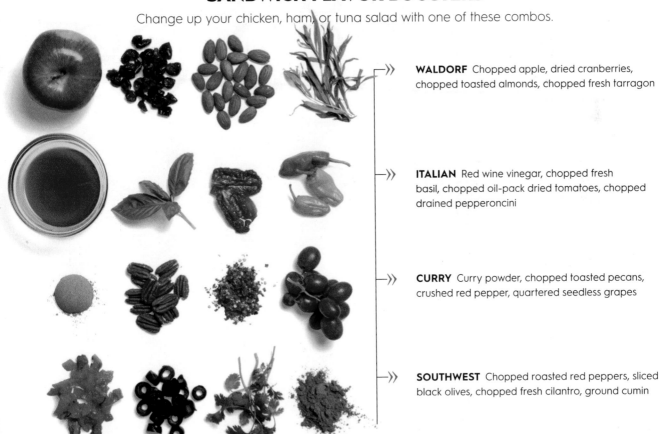

**WALDORF** Chopped apple, dried cranberries, chopped toasted almonds, chopped fresh tarragon

**ITALIAN** Red wine vinegar, chopped fresh basil, chopped oil-pack dried tomatoes, chopped drained pepperoncini

**CURRY** Curry powder, chopped toasted pecans, crushed red pepper, quartered seedless grapes

**SOUTHWEST** Chopped roasted red peppers, sliced black olives, chopped fresh cilantro, ground cumin

# SALADS & DRESSINGS

## CHICKEN SALADS

**248** CHICKEN AND WINTER GREENS SALAD

**280** CHICKEN CAESAR SALAD

## DRESSINGS

**301** BLUE CHEESE DRESSING

**283** BUTTERMILK-AVOCADO DRESSING

**301** BUTTERMILK RANCH DRESSING

**300** CREAMY FRENCH DRESSING

**301** CREAMY ITALIAN DRESSING

**300** CREAMY PARMESAN DRESSING

**299** FRESH HERB VINAIGRETTE

**301** HONEY-MUSTARD DRESSING

**290** RED WINE VINAIGRETTE

**300** SESAME-GINGER DRESSING

**301** STRAWBERRY BALSAMIC VINAIGRETTE

**300** TAHINI-HONEY DRESSING

**300** THOUSAND ISLAND DRESSING

## FISH SALAD

**251** MEDITERRANEAN TUNA SALAD

## FRUIT SALADS

**295** FLUFFY WALDORF SALAD

**295** WALDORF SALAD

## GRAIN SALADS

**289** TABBOULEH

**289** WHEAT BERRY TABBOULEH

## GREENS SALADS

**280** CAESAR SALAD

**280** CHICKEN CAESAR SALAD

**281** ROASTED ROOTS AND WILTED ROMAINE SALAD

**283** TACO SALAD

**296** WARM SPINACH SALAD

## MEAT SALADS

**247** BACON AND PEAR AUTUMN SALAD

**246** BLT SALAD WITH CREAMY CHIVE DRESSING

**292** BROCCOLI-BACON SALAD

**283** TACO SALAD

## PASTA SALADS

**287** DEVILED EGG-MACARONI SALAD

**290** SUMMER PASTA SALAD AND VARIATIONS

## POTATO SALAD

**286** CLASSIC POTATO SALAD AND VARIATIONS

## SALAD TOPPERS

**288** BAKED PITA PIECES

**280** PARMESAN CROUTONS

**283** TORTILLA CHIPS

## SLAWS

**294** CREAMY COLESLAW AND VARIATIONS

**297** WINTER KALE SLAW

## VEGETABLE SALADS

**292** BROCCOLI-BACON SALAD

**284** CAPRESE-STYLE SALAD

**284** CORN SALAD WITH QUESO FRESCO

**293** CUCUMBER SALAD AND VARIATIONS

**288** FATTOUSH SALAD

**281** ROASTED ROOTS AND WILTED ROMAINE SALAD

**285** SOUTHERN-STYLE LAYERED SALAD

**283** SUCCOTASH SALAD

**292** SWEET AND TANGY FOUR-BEAN SALAD

**MAKE-AHEAD RECIPE**

# CAESAR SALAD
**START TO FINISH** 30 minutes

- 3 cloves garlic
- 3 anchovy fillets
- 2 Tbsp. lemon juice
- ¼ cup olive oil
- 1 tsp. Dijon mustard
- ½ tsp. sugar
- 1 Hard-Boiled Egg yolk (p. 46)
- 10 cups torn romaine lettuce
- ¼ cup grated Parmesan cheese (1 oz.) or ½ cup Parmesan curls
- 1 recipe Parmesan Croutons or 2 cups purchased croutons
  Freshly ground black pepper
- 1 lemon, halved or cut into wedges (optional)

**1.** For dressing, in a blender combine garlic cloves, anchovy fillets, and lemon juice. Cover and blend until mixture is nearly smooth, stopping to scrape down sides as needed. Add oil, mustard, sugar, and cooked egg yolk. Cover and blend until smooth. Use immediately or cover and chill up to 24 hours.

**2.** Place romaine in a large bowl. Drizzle dressing over lettuce; toss lightly to coat. Sprinkle Parmesan cheese over top; toss gently. Top with Parmesan Croutons and pepper. If desired, sprinkle with additional Parmesan cheese and serve with lemon halves. **Makes 6 servings (½ cup each).**

**EACH SERVING** *261 cal., 20 g fat (8 g sat. fat), 62 mg chol., 362 mg sodium, 15 g carb., 2 g fiber, 2 g sugars, 6 g pro.*

## CHICKEN CAESAR SALAD
Prepare as directed, except add 2 cups chopped cooked chicken on the romaine. **Makes 6 servings (1 cup each).**

**EACH SERVING** *350 cal., 15 g fat (9 g sat. fat), 104 mg chol., 402 mg sodium, 15 g carb., 2 g fiber, 2 g sugars, 20 g pro.*

## *PARMESAN CROUTONS*

Preheat oven to 300°F. Cut four ¾-inch-thick slices Italian bread or French bread into 1-inch pieces (you should have about 3½ cups bread pieces). In a 1- or 1½-qt. saucepan melt ¼ cup butter over medium heat. Transfer to a large bowl. Stir in 3 Tbsp. grated Parmesan cheese and 2 cloves garlic, minced. Add bread pieces; stir to coat. Spread bread pieces in a single layer in a shallow baking pan. Bake about 20 minutes or until croutons are golden brown, stirring once. Cool completely (croutons will get crisp on standing). If desired, store in an airtight container at room temperature up to 24 hours.

## ROASTED ROOTS AND WILTED ROMAINE SALAD

**HANDS-ON TIME** 20 minutes
**BAKE** 1 hour at 375°F

1    medium fresh beet (about 6 oz.)
4    tsp. olive oil
½    tsp. salt
     Black pepper
1    lb. carrots, turnips, and/or parsnips
2    medium shallots, peeled and quartered
2    Tbsp. olive oil
2    Tbsp. white wine vinegar
1½   tsp. chopped fresh thyme
½    tsp. Dijon mustard
½    tsp. honey
1    clove garlic, minced
4    cups torn romaine lettuce
¼    cup coarsely chopped pecans, toasted
2    Tbsp. snipped fresh Italian parsley

**1.** Preheat oven to 375°F. Wash and peel beet; cut into 1½-inch pieces. Place in a 2-qt. baking dish. Toss with 2 tsp. of the olive oil, ¼ tsp. of the salt, and pepper to taste. Cover dish tightly with foil; bake 30 minutes.
**2.** Meanwhile, peel carrots, turnips, and/or parsnips; cut into irregular-shape 1-inch pieces. Place in a 15×10-inch baking pan. Add shallots. Toss with remaining 2 tsp. of the oil. Sprinkle with ⅛ tsp. salt and pepper to taste.
**3.** Remove foil from dish with beets; stir beets gently. Return beets to oven; place pan with carrot mixture alongside beets. Roast both, uncovered, about 30 minutes or until vegetables are tender.
**4.** Meanwhile, for dressing, in a screw-top jar combine the next six ingredients (through garlic), the remaining ⅛ tsp. salt, and pepper to taste. Cover and shake well.
**5.** In a bowl toss lettuce with dressing to coat. Transfer to a platter. Top with hot roasted vegetables. Sprinkle with pecans and parsley. Serve immediately.
**Makes 12 servings (½ cup each).**
**TO MAKE AHEAD** Prepare dressing; store in the refrigerator up to 3 days. Before serving, bring dressing to room temperature; shake well.
**EACH SERVING** 80 cal., 6 g fat (1 g sat. fat), 0 mg chol., 131 mg sodium, 7 g carb., 2 g fiber, 3 g sugars, 1 g pro.

**BRIGHT RED BEETS** are notorious for staining hands, cutting boards, clothes, you name it. They'll even stain the other veggies in this recipe. To avoid this, we recommend roasting beets in a separate baking dish. The beets also get a jump-start on the other veggies since they take longer to cook. Covering with foil during the first baking round lets them steam a little so they get evenly tender.

TACO SALAD

SUCCOTASH SALAD

## TACO SALAD

**HANDS-ON TIME** 30 minutes
**COOK** 10 minutes

1    recipe Tortilla Chips
8    oz. lean ground beef or uncooked ground turkey
3    cloves garlic, minced
1    15-oz. can dark red kidney beans or black beans, rinsed and drained
1    cup salsa
¾    cup frozen whole kernel corn, thawed (optional)
6    cups shredded leaf or iceberg lettuce
1    cup chopped tomatoes
1    cup chopped green sweet pepper
½    cup thinly sliced green onions
1    cup chopped avocado (optional)
¾    cup shredded sharp cheddar cheese (3 oz.)

**1.** Prepare Tortilla Chips. In a 2-qt. saucepan cook ground beef and garlic until beef is browned. Drain fat. Stir in kidney beans, salsa, and, if desired, thawed corn. Bring to boiling; reduce heat. Simmer, covered, 10 minutes.

**2.** Arrange lettuce on a platter or in dishes. Top with hot meat mixture, tomatoes, sweet pepper, and green onions. If desired, top with avocado. Sprinkle with cheese and serve Tortilla Chips with salad. If desired, serve with *sour cream* and additional *salsa*. **Makes 6 servings (2 cups salad + 1 tortilla each).**

**EACH SERVING** *356 cal., 12 g fat (6 g sat. fat), 38 mg chol., 1,065 mg sodium, 43 g carb., 7 g fiber, 6 g sugars, 20 g pro.*

》》

**FRESH LIMA BEANS** are often available at farmers markets during the spring and summer. When fresh isn't an option, use frozen lima beans or edamame and cook as directed.

## SUCCOTASH SALAD

**HANDS-ON TIME** 25 minutes
**COOK** 20 minutes

2    ears fresh sweet corn
1    cup fresh lima beans
1    large head butterhead (Boston or Bibb) lettuce, torn
2    cups sliced grilled chicken breast (chart, *p. 52*)
6    slices bacon, crisp-cooked and crumbled
½    cup finely chopped red onion
½    cup crumbled blue cheese or feta cheese (2 oz.)
1    recipe Buttermilk-Avocado Dressing

**1.** Cut corn kernels from cobs. In a 1- or 1½-qt. saucepan bring 1 cup water to boiling. Add lima beans; simmer about 15 minutes or until tender. Remove beans with a slotted spoon. Add corn to water. Simmer 3 minutes or until tender; drain.

**2.** Arrange lettuce on a large platter. Arrange the next four ingredients (through blue cheese) and the corn and lima beans on lettuce. Serve with Buttermilk-Avocado Dressing. **Makes 4 servings (1¾ cups salad + about 3 Tbsp. dressing each).**

**EACH SERVING** *365 cal., 15 fat (6 g. sat. fat), 89 mg chol., 711 mg sodium, 24 g carb., 5 g fiber, 7 g sugars, 34 g pro.*

### *BUTTERMILK-AVOCADO DRESSING*

In a blender combine ¾ cup buttermilk; half of an avocado, peeled and seeded; 1 Tbsp. chopped fresh Italian parsley; ¼ tsp. each onion powder, dry mustard, salt, and black pepper; and 1 clove garlic, minced. Cover and blend until smooth. Serve immediately.

## TORTILLA CHIPS

Cut six 7- to 8-inch flour or corn tortillas into wedges. To bake, preheat oven to 350°F (425°F for corn). Lightly coat tortillas with nonstick cooking spray; sprinkle with salt. Arrange on baking sheets. Bake 8 to 10 minutes or until golden; cool in pans. To fry, in a heavy deep skillet heat ½ inch vegetable oil to 375°F. Fry wedges in batches until golden, turning once. Transfer to paper towels with a slotted spoon. While warm, sprinkle with salt.

## CAPRESE-STYLE SALAD

**START TO FINISH** 20 minutes

>>

TOMATOES come in many varieties, sizes, and colors, so mix it up here. If you find the extra-large, juicy heirloom tomatoes at the farmers market (or in your garden), just use fewer tomatoes than we call for here. Since heirloom tomatoes are so juicy, plate the tomatoes right before you are ready to serve.

5   small ripe tomatoes, sliced
½   cup 1-inch fresh mozzarella balls, quartered, or tiny fresh mozzarella balls
¼   cup sliced pitted olives (Kalamata, pimiento-stuffed, or ripe black)
3   Tbsp. olive oil
3   Tbsp. white wine vinegar
2   cloves garlic, minced
¼   tsp. salt
⅛   tsp. black pepper
2   Tbsp. snipped fresh basil

**1.** Arrange tomato slices on a plate or platter. Scatter mozzarella and olives over tomatoes.
**2.** For dressing, in a screw-top jar combine oil, vinegar, garlic, salt, and pepper. Cover and shake well. Drizzle dressing over salad. Sprinkle basil over top. **Makes 6 servings (⅔ cup each).**
EACH SERVING *113 cal., 10 g fat (2 g sat. fat), 7 mg chol., 242 mg sodium, 4 g carb., 1 g fiber, 2 g sugars, 3 g pro.*

## CORN SALAD WITH QUESO FRESCO

**HANDS-ON TIME** 25 minutes
**CHILL** 2 hours

8   ears sweet corn or 4 cups frozen whole kernel corn
2   cups crumbled queso fresco (8 oz.)
1   cup finely chopped red sweet pepper
½   cup finely chopped red onion
1   fresh jalapeño chile pepper, seeded and finely chopped (tip, *p. 22*) (optional)
¼   cup olive oil
¼   cup lime juice
2   Tbsp. chopped fresh cilantro
½   tsp. salt
¼   tsp. black pepper

CAPRESE-STYLE SALAD

**1.** Cut corn from cobs if using. In a 4-qt. saucepan bring about ½ inch water to boiling. Place a steamer basket in the saucepan, not touching the water. Add corn to basket; cover. Steam 2 to 4 minutes or until corn is crisp-tender.
**2.** In a large bowl combine corn and the next four ingredients (through jalapeño if using).
**3.** For dressing, in a screw-top jar combine the next five ingredients (through black pepper). Cover and shake well. Add to corn mixture; toss gently to coat. Chill 2 hours.
**Makes 10 servings (⅔ cup each).**
EACH SERVING *164 cal., 7 g fat (1 g sat. fat), 0 mg chol., 129 mg sodium, 18 g carb., 2 g fiber, 4 g sugars, 8 g pro.*

## SOUTHERN-STYLE LAYERED SALAD

**HANDS-ON TIME** 30 minutes
**COOL** 1 hr.
**CHILL** Overnight

| | |
|---|---|
| 1 | 8.5-oz. pkg. corn muffin mix |
| 1 | cup mayonnaise |
| 1 | 8-oz. carton sour cream |
| 1 | 1-oz. envelope ranch dry salad dressing mix |
| 2 | cups shredded cheddar cheese (8 oz.) |
| 2 | 15-oz. cans pinto beans, rinsed and drained |
| 2 | 15.25-oz. cans whole kernel corn, drained |
| 10 | slices bacon, crisp-cooked, drained, and crumbled |
| 3 | cups coarsely chopped tomatoes |
| 1 | cup chopped green and/or red sweet pepper |
| ½ | cup sliced green onions |

**1.** Prepare corn muffin mix according to package directions for corn bread. Cool and crumble (should have about 5 cups).*
**2.** For dressing, in a small bowl whisk together mayonnaise, sour cream, and salad dressing mix.

**3.** In a 3- to 4-qt. glass bowl or 3-qt. rectangular baking dish layer crumbled corn bread and 1 cup of the cheese. Spread with half of the dressing. In the following order, layer beans, corn, the remaining 1 cup cheese, bacon, tomatoes, sweet pepper, and the remaining dressing. Cover and chill overnight. Before serving, sprinkle salad with green onions. **Makes 18 servings (¾ cup each).**
*NOTE If desired, toast the crumbled corn bread so it has more structure. Preheat oven to 350°F. Spread the corn bread in a 15×10-inch baking pan. Bake about 10 minutes or until crisp; cool.
EACH SERVING *342 cal., 21 g fat (7 g sat. fat), 38 mg chol., 779 mg sodium, 30 g carb., 4 g fiber, 3 g sugars, 11 g pro.*

SOUTHERN-STYLE LAYERED SALAD

CORN SALAD WITH QUESO FRESCO

# CLASSIC POTATO SALAD

**HANDS-ON TIME** 40 minutes
**CHILL** 6 hours

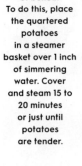

POTATO PEELS contribute color, texture, and added nutrients to potato salad, so we always leave the peels on. (Plus, the skins on new potatoes are super thin.) But if you're not a fan, you can peel your potatoes before cooking them.

POTATOES can also be steamed instead of boiled. To do this, place the quartered potatoes in a steamer basket over 1 inch of simmering water. Cover and steam 15 to 20 minutes or just until potatoes are tender.

| | |
|---|---|
| 2 | lb. red and/or yellow new potatoes, quartered |
| ¾ | tsp. salt |
| 1¼ | cups mayonnaise |
| 1 | Tbsp. yellow mustard |
| ¼ | tsp. black pepper |
| 1 | cup thinly sliced celery |
| ⅓ | cup chopped onion |
| ½ | cup chopped sweet or dill pickles or sweet or dill pickle relish |
| 6 | Hard-Boiled Eggs (p. 46), coarsely chopped Hard-Boiled Eggs, sliced (optional) Paprika (optional) |

**1.** In a 4-qt. saucepan combine potatoes, ¼ tsp. of the salt, and enough cold water to cover. Bring to boiling; reduce heat. Simmer, covered, about 15 minutes or just until potatoes are tender. Drain well; cool slightly.

**2.** Meanwhile, for dressing, in a large bowl stir together mayonnaise, mustard, the remaining ½ tsp. salt, and the pepper. Stir in celery, onion, and pickles. Add the potatoes and chopped eggs; stir gently to coat. Cover and chill at least 6 hours or up to 24 hours.

**3.** Transfer potato salad to a serving bowl. If desired, top with additional sliced eggs and/ or sprinkle with paprika. **Makes 12 servings (¾ cup each).**

**EACH SERVING** *259 cal, 20 g fat (4 g sat. fat), 103 mg chol, 389 mg sodium, 15 g carb., 2 g fiber, 3 g sugars, 5 g pro.*

**BLT POTATO SALAD** Prepare as directed, except use ½ cup sliced green onions instead of the ⅓ cup chopped onion. In a 10-inch skillet cook 6 slices bacon over medium heat until crisp. Remove bacon and drain on paper towels, reserving 1 Tbsp. drippings in skillet. Crumble bacon. Add 1 clove garlic, minced, to the reserved drippings; cook and stir 30 seconds. Stir garlic mixture into dressing. Stir bacon and 1 cup chopped tomato into salad with the potatoes. Serve over shredded romaine lettuce.

**TEX-MEX POTATO SALAD** Prepare as directed, except reduce mayonnaise to ¾ cup and omit yellow mustard, black pepper, and pickles. Stir ¾ cup ranch salad dressing and 1 canned chipotle chile pepper in adobo sauce, finely chopped (tip, p. 22), into dressing. Stir 1 cup rinsed and drained canned black beans and 1 cup frozen corn into salad with the potatoes. Just before serving, top salad with tortilla chips and, if desired, chili powder.

**PICK THE RIGHT POTATO** The flesh of waxy potatoes—such as round red or yellow potatoes or slender fingerlings—has a lower starch content (than, say, russet potatoes) and holds its shape even after boiling, making them perfect for potato salad. For some serious color appeal, you can use waxy purple fingerlings.

**KEEP IT CREAMY**
During storage, the pasta may soak up some liquid in the dressing. Revive the creaminess by stirring in a little extra milk before serving.

# DEVILED EGG-MACARONI SALAD
**START TO FINISH** 30 minutes

2    cups dried elbow macaroni (8 oz.)
½    of a recipe Pickled Red Onion + 1 Tbsp. pickling liquid
½    cup mayonnaise
3    Tbsp. country-style Dijon mustard
¼    tsp. salt
½    tsp. smoked paprika
¼    tsp. cracked black pepper
1½   cups very thinly sliced celery
½    cup chopped sweet pickles
1    recipe Deviled Eggs (p. 375)

**1.** Cook macaroni according to package directions; drain. Rinse with cold water; drain again.
**2.** For dressing, in a bowl stir together the 1 Tbsp. pickling liquid and the next five ingredients (through pepper).
**3.** In a large bowl combine macaroni, celery, and pickles. Add dressing; toss gently to coat. Top with Pickled Red Onion and Deviled Eggs. Sprinkle with additional smoked paprika and/or cracked black pepper. Serve immediately or cover and chill salad, Pickled Red Onion, and eggs separately up to 6 hours.
**Makes 6 servings (1 cup each).**
**EACH SERVING** *447 cal., 27 g fat (5 g sat. fat), 199 mg chol., 616 mg sodium, 35 g carb., 2 g fiber, 6 g sugars, 12 g pro.*

## *PICKLED RED ONION*

In a 1- or 1½-qt. saucepan combine 1 cup thinly sliced red onion, ½ cup cider vinegar, and 2 tsp. sugar. Bring to simmering, stirring occasionally. Remove from heat; let cool. Drain and store, covered, in the refrigerator up to 3 days.

## WHAT IS FATTOUSH (FAAH-TOOSH)? A FRESH MIX OF VEGGIES AND TOASTED PITA BREAD CROUTONS ARE THE BUILDING BLOCKS OF THIS CLASSIC MIDDLE EASTERN SALAD. MAKE IT YOUR OWN BY TOSSING IN GRILLED CHICKEN OR LAMB OR ROASTED EGGPLANT OR ZUCCHINI.

SUMAC is a sour spice made from the bright red berries of a Middle Eastern bush. Look for sumac at specialty stores (or substitute a pinch of lemon zest in its place).

RICOTTA SALATA cheese is an Italian sheep's milk cheese with a salty taste and firm, crumbly texture. Although slightly more moist, feta is a good swap for ricotta salata.

### FATTOUSH SALAD
**START TO FINISH** 30 minutes

2   Tbsp. vegetable oil
2   pita bread rounds, torn into bite-size pieces
¼   cup olive oil
¼   cup lemon juice
2   cloves garlic, minced
½   tsp. ground sumac (optional)
¼   tsp. kosher salt
¼   tsp. black pepper
4   cups torn romaine lettuce
½   of a medium cucumber, seeded and coarsely chopped
½   cup sliced radishes
½   cup sliced green onions
¼   cup chopped fresh mint and/or Italian parsley
½   cup crumbled ricotta salata cheese

**1.** In a 10-inch skillet heat 1 Tbsp. of the vegetable oil over medium-high heat. Add half of the pita pieces. Cook 2 to 3 minutes or until toasted, stirring occasionally. Transfer pita pieces to paper towels to drain. Repeat with the remaining 1 Tbsp. vegetable oil and pita pieces.
**2.** For dressing, in an extra-large bowl whisk together the next six ingredients (through pepper).
**3.** Add the next five ingredients (through mint) to bowl; toss to coat. Add pita pieces and cheese; toss to combine. **Makes 4 servings (2 cups each).**
**EACH SERVING** *331 cal., 24 g fat (5 g sat. fat), 13 mg chol., 486 mg sodium, 24 g carb., 3 g fiber, 3 g sugars, 6 g pro.*

### *BAKE INSTEAD*

For a lighter option, you can bake the pita instead of frying. Preheat oven to 350°F. Omit vegetable oil. Lightly coat torn pita bread with nonstick cooking spray. Arrange pita pieces evenly in a 15×10-inch baking pan. Bake 10 to 15 minutes or until golden and crisp. Continue as directed in Step 2.

# TABBOULEH

**HANDS-ON TIME** 25 minutes
**CHILL** 4 hours

- ¾ cup bulgur
- ¾ cup chopped cucumber
- ½ cup chopped fresh parsley
- ¼ cup thinly sliced green onions
- 1 Tbsp. chopped fresh mint
- 2 Tbsp. water
- 3 Tbsp. vegetable oil
- 3 Tbsp. lemon juice
- ¼ tsp. salt
- ¾ cup chopped tomato
- 4 lettuce leaves
  Lemon wedges and/or mint sprigs (optional)

**1.** Place bulgur in a colander; rinse with cold water. In a large bowl combine bulgur and the next four ingredients (through mint).

**2.** For dressing, in a screw-top jar combine water, oil, lemon juice, and salt. Cover and shake well. Drizzle dressing over bulgur mixture; toss to coat. Cover and chill 4 to 24 hours. Just before serving, stir tomato into bulgur mixture. Serve in a lettuce-lined bowl with lemon wedges (if desired).
**Makes 5 servings (1 cup each).**

**WHEAT BERRY TABBOULEH**
Prepare as directed, except omit bulgur. In a 1- or 1½-qt. saucepan bring one 14-oz. can chicken broth and ¼ cup water to boiling. Add 1 cup wheat berries. Return to boiling; reduce heat. Simmer, covered, 45 to 60 minutes or until tender; drain. Cover and chill up to 3 days. In a large bowl combine 2⅔ cups of the cooked wheat berries, the tomato, cucumber, parsley, green onions, and mint. Prepare dressing as directed, except omit the 2 Tbsp. water. Serve immediately or chill up to 4 hours. Serve as directed.
**EACH SERVING (PLAIN OR WHEAT BERRY VARIATION)** *161 cal, 9 g fat (1 g sat. fat), 0 mg chol, 128 mg sodium, 20 g carb, 5 g fiber, 2 g sugars, 3 g pro.*

**CHANGE IT UP**

*Turn your Tabbouleh into a grab-and-go sandwich. Tuck a layer of lettuce leaves in a halved pita bread pocket and spoon ½ cup of the Tabbouleh into each pocket.*

## SUMMER PASTA SALAD

**HANDS-ON TIME** 40 minutes
**CHILL** 12 hours

8   oz. dried lasagna noodles, broken into 3-inch pieces, or 3 cups dried farfalle or penne pasta
2   Tbsp. olive oil
1   Tbsp. lemon juice
1   tsp. salt
1   clove garlic, minced
1½  cups fresh green beans, trimmed
8   oz. tiny fresh mozzarella balls or cubed fresh mozzarella cheese
1½  cups thinly sliced yellow summer squash and/or zucchini
1   cup chopped tomato, halved cherry tomatoes, and/or halved grape tomatoes
2   oz. thinly sliced prosciutto, torn into bite-size pieces, or salami, halved and sliced (optional)
1   cup arugula or fresh baby spinach
½   cup thinly sliced, halved red onion or sliced green onions
½   cup pitted ripe olives, halved pitted Kalamata olives, or sliced pimiento-stuffed green olives (optional)
2   to 3 Tbsp. slivered fresh basil
1   recipe Red Wine Vinaigrette

**1.** Cook pasta according to package directions; drain. Rinse with cold water; drain again. In an extra-large bowl whisk together olive oil, lemon juice, salt, and garlic. Add pasta; toss to coat. Cover and chill at least 8 hours or up to 24 hours.
**2.** In a 4-qt. saucepan cook green beans in a large amount of boiling water 5 minutes; drain and let cool. Add green beans and the next eight ingredients (through basil) to pasta. Add Red Wine Vinaigrette; toss to coat. Cover and chill at least 4 hours or up to 24 hours. **Makes 16 servings (⅔ cup each).**
**EACH SERVING** *245 cal., 19 g fat (4 g sat. fat), 10 mg chol., 290 mg sodium, 14 g carb., 1 g fiber, 2 g sugars, 5 g pro.*

**PROSCIUTTO** is a deliciously salty cured Italian ham that comes in very thin slices. Store remaining slices of prosciutto, tightly covered, in the refrigerator up to 3 weeks (or freeze up to 3 months). We love it wrapped around asparagus, melon, and fresh mozzarella, but it's also delicious chopped and crisp-cooked in salads and on homemade pizza.

### RED WINE VINAIGRETTE

In a screw-top jar combine 1 cup olive oil; ⅓ cup red wine vinegar, white wine vinegar, rice vinegar, or cider vinegar; ¼ cup finely chopped shallots; 2 Tbsp. chopped fresh oregano, thyme, or basil, or 1 tsp. dried oregano, thyme, or basil, crushed; 1 Tbsp. Dijon mustard or ½ tsp. dry mustard; 2 tsp. sugar; 2 cloves garlic, minced; and ¼ tsp. each salt and pepper. Cover and shake well.

### *ROASTING SQUASH*

Preheat oven to 425°F. Halve, seed, and peel half of a butternut squash; cut into 1-inch cubes. Toss squash cubes with 1 Tbsp. vegetable oil. Place cubes in a shallow baking pan. Sprinkle with salt and black pepper. Roast 15 to 20 minutes or until squash is tender and brown.

**WINTER PASTA SALAD**
Prepare as directed, except substitute 1½ cups fresh broccoli florets and 1½ cups cauliflower florets for the green beans and summer squash. Substitute Monterey Jack cheese for the mozzarella. Substitute chopped fresh oregano or dill for the basil. Add ½ cup roasted red sweet peppers, chopped, and ¼ cup oil-pack dried tomatoes, drained and chopped. Use the sliced green olives option.

**FALL PASTA SALAD** Prepare as directed, except substitute 2 cups cubed roasted butternut squash (*below left*), 1 cup fresh whole kernel corn or broccoli florets, and 1 cup bite-size strips red, green, and/or yellow sweet peppers for the green beans and summer squash. Substitute cheddar, smoked cheddar, or Gouda cheese for the mozzarella. Substitute 1 cup torn kale for the arugula. Use the salami option. Substitute 1 Tbsp. chopped fresh thyme for the basil. Use Fresh Herb Vinaigrette (*p. 299*) for dressing, using cider vinegar for the vinegar and a combination of hazelnut oil and olive oil.

SUMMER PASTA
SALAD

**PASTA PRESOAK**
An overnight soak in
lemon juice and oil keeps
the pasta moist. This presoak
keeps the pasta from
later absorbing
the dressing, which would
dry out the salad.

## BROCCOLI-BACON SALAD

**HANDS-ON TIME** 20 minutes
**CHILL** 2 hours

1    cup mayonnaise
½    cup raisins
¼    cup finely chopped red onion
3    Tbsp. sugar
2    Tbsp. vinegar
7    cups chopped fresh broccoli florets
½    cup shelled sunflower kernels
8    slices bacon, crisp-cooked, drained, and crumbled

**1.** In a large bowl stir together mayonnaise, raisins, onion, sugar, and vinegar. Add broccoli and stir to coat. Cover and chill 2 to 24 hours. Before serving, stir in sunflower kernels and bacon. **Makes 12 servings (½ cup each).**
**EACH SERVING** *247 cal., 20 g fat (4 g sat. fat), 13 mg chol., 242 mg sodium, 13 g carb., 2 g fiber, 8 g sugars, 5 g pro.*

BROCCOLI-BACON SALAD

## SWEET AND TANGY FOUR-BEAN SALAD

**HANDS-ON TIME** 30 minutes
**CHILL** 4 hours

8    oz. fresh green beans, trimmed
1    12-oz. pkg. frozen shelled edamame
¾    cup cider vinegar
⅔    cup tomato juice
½    cup sugar
¼    cup vegetable oil
3    Tbsp. dry red wine or apple juice
2    tsp. Worcestershire sauce
2    tsp. Dijon mustard
1    clove garlic, minced
1    15-oz. can red kidney beans, rinsed and drained
1    14.5-oz. can cut wax beans, rinsed and drained
2    cups coarsely shredded carrots
½    cup finely chopped green onions

**1.** In a 3- or 4-qt. saucepan cook green beans in boiling, lightly salted water 4 minutes. Add edamame; cook about 6 minutes more or just until tender. Drain and rinse with cold water.
**2.** In an extra-large bowl whisk together the next eight ingredients (through garlic). Stir in cooked bean mixture, canned beans, carrots, and green onions. Cover and chill 4 to 48 hours. Serve with a slotted spoon. **Makes 18 servings (½ cup each).**
**TO MAKE AHEAD** If chilling the salad overnight or up to 48 hours, the fresh green beans will lose some color as they marinate in the dressing. For bright-color green beans, prepare as directed but do not add to salad. Cover and refrigerate separately; toss with the salad just before serving.
**EACH SERVING** *58 cal., 1 g fat (0 g sat. fat), 0 mg chol., 100 mg sodium, 9 g carb., 3 g fiber, 3 g sugars, 4 g pro.*

**SWEET AND TANGY FOUR-BEAN SALAD**

### BEAN SWAP
If you don't have all four beans called for in this recipe, make a trade. Use limas or black beans for edamame or red kidneys. Or make it a three-bean salad by doubling the green or wax beans.

# CUCUMBER SALAD

**HANDS-ON TIME** 15 minutes
**CHILL** 1 to 24 hours

1 recipe Sweet-and-Sour Dressing, Sour Cream-Dill Dressing, or Quick Pickle Dressing

2 large cucumbers, peeled (if desired), halved lengthwise, and thinly sliced (5 cups)
½ cup thinly sliced onion

**1.** In a medium bowl prepare desired dressing. Add cucumbers and onion; stir to coat. Serve Sour-Cream Dill cucumbers immediately or chill up to 2 hours. Cover and chill Sweet-and-Sour and Quick Pickle cucumbers at least 1 hour or up to 24 hours, stirring occasionally. Serve with a slotted spoon. **Makes 8 servings (½ cup each).**

**EACH SERVING** *60 cal., 0 g fat, 0 mg chol., 151 mg sodium, 14 g carb., 1 g fiber, 12 g sugars, 1 g pro.*

### SWEET-AND-SOUR DRESSING

In the bowl stir together ⅓ cup each packed brown sugar, rice vinegar, and apple juice or sweet rice wine (mirin); 1 Tbsp. grated fresh ginger (if desired); and ½ tsp. salt.

### SOUR CREAM-DILL DRESSING

In the bowl whisk together ⅔ cup sour cream or plain yogurt, 2 Tbsp. vinegar, ½ tsp. salt, and ¼ tsp. each dried dill and black pepper.

### QUICK PICKLE DRESSING

In the bowl stir together ½ cup cider vinegar, 2 to 3 tsp. sugar, and ½ tsp. salt.

## THAI GREEN BEAN-RAMEN SLAW

Prepare as directed, except omit mayonnaise, vinegar, celery seeds, and salt. For dressing, increase sugar to 3 Tbsp. and stir together with ¼ cup lime juice; 3 Tbsp. fish sauce; and 2 cloves garlic, minced. Add 2 cups cut-up steamed thin green beans and ½ cup chopped fresh cilantro to cabbage mixture. Before serving, break one 3-oz. pkg. any-flavor ramen noodles (discard seasoning packet) into small pieces. Add to salad; toss to combine.

# CREAMY COLESLAW

**HANDS-ON TIME** 20 minutes
**CHILL** 2 hours

| | |
|---|---|
| ½ | cup mayonnaise |
| 1 | to 2 Tbsp. sugar |
| 1 | Tbsp. cider vinegar |
| 1 | Tbsp. lemon juice |
| ½ | tsp. celery seeds |
| ½ | tsp. salt |
| 4 | cups shredded green and/or red cabbage* |
| 1 | cup shredded carrots* |
| ¼ | cup thinly sliced green onions |

**1.** For dressing, in a large bowl stir together the first six ingredients (through salt).

**2.** Add cabbage, carrots, and onions. Stir lightly to coat. Cover and chill 2 to 24 hours. Stir before serving. **Makes 6 servings (⅔ cup each).**

**\*NOTE** If desired, substitute 5 cups packaged shredded cabbage with carrot (coleslaw mix) for cabbage and carrots.

**EACH SERVING** 156 cal., 14 g fat (2 g sat. fat), 8 mg chol., 334 mg sodium, 7 g carb., 2 g fiber, 5 g sugars, 1 g pro.

## TEX-MEX COLESLAW

Prepare as directed, except omit sugar, vinegar, lemon juice, and celery seeds. For dressing, increase mayonnaise to ⅔ cup and whisk together with ⅓ cup salsa and ¼ cup chopped fresh cilantro. Substitute bite-size strips of red sweet pepper for the carrots and add 1 cup frozen roasted corn, thawed. Serve with hot pepper sauce and lime wedges.

## VINAIGRETTE COLESLAW

Prepare as directed, except omit the first six ingredients (through salt). For vinaigrette, stir together ¼ cup cider vinegar, 2 Tbsp. each sugar and canola oil, ½ tsp. salt, and ¼ tsp. each dry mustard and black pepper.

## WALDORF SALAD

**HANDS-ON TIME** 20 minutes
**CHILL** 8 hours

- 4 cups chopped apples and/or pears
- 4 tsp. lemon juice
- ½ cup chopped celery
- ½ cup chopped walnuts or pecans, toasted (tip, *p. 18*)
- ½ cup raisins, chopped pitted whole dates, or dried tart cherries
- ½ cup seedless green grapes, halved
- ⅔ cup mayonnaise

**1.** In a bowl toss apples and/or pears with lemon juice. Stir in celery, nuts, raisins, and grapes. Stir in mayonnaise until combined. Serve immediately or cover and chill up to 8 hours. **Makes 8 servings (½ cup each).**
**EACH SERVING** *245 cal., 20 g fat (3 g sat. fat), 7 mg chol., 107 mg sodium, 18 g carb., 2 g fiber, 13 g sugars, 2 g pro.*

**FLUFFY WALDORF SALAD**
Prepare as directed, except substitute 1½ cups frozen whipped dessert topping, thawed, for the mayonnaise. If necessary, stir in a little milk to make creamy. Stir in 1 cup tiny marshmallows. Serve immediately or cover and chill up to 8 hours.

## WHAT IS WALDORF SALAD? NEW YORK'S WALDORF HOTEL WAS THE BIRTHPLACE OF THIS FAMOUS CREAMY APPLE-WALNUT SALAD.

## WARM SPINACH SALAD

**START TO FINISH** 20 minutes

SPINACH is traditional in this salad, but swap arugula for some (or all) of the spinach to add a peppery punch of flavor.

6    cups fresh baby spinach or torn spinach
¼    cup thinly sliced green onions
     Dash black pepper
4    slices bacon
     Vegetable oil (optional)
⅓    cup cider vinegar
1    Tbsp. sugar
2    tsp. Dijon mustard or 1 tsp. dry mustard
½    cup pecan halves

½    cup dried cherries
1    Hard-Boiled Egg (p. 46), chopped
     Blue cheese wedges (optional)

**1.** In a large bowl combine the spinach and green onions. Sprinkle with pepper.

**2.** In a 10-inch skillet cook bacon until crisp. Drain bacon on paper towels, reserving 2 Tbsp. drippings in skillet (add vegetable oil if necessary). Slice or crumble bacon. Stir vinegar, sugar, and mustard into drippings in skillet. Bring to boiling;

remove from heat and immediately pour over spinach mixture. Toss until spinach is completely coated and just beginning to wilt. Add bacon, pecans, and dried cherries. Toss to combine.

**3.** Transfer spinach mixture to plates. Top with chopped egg and, if desired, blue cheese wedges. Serve immediately.

**Makes 4 servings (1½ cups each).**

**EACH SERVING** *293 cal., 20 g fat (5 g sat. fat), 61 mg chol., 247 mg sodium, 23 g carb., 3 g fiber, 17 g sugars, 7 g pro.*

# WINTER KALE SLAW

**START TO FINISH** 25 minutes

- 4 cups shredded, stemmed kale
- 1 Tbsp. olive oil
- 1 tsp. salt
- 4 cups shredded savoy or green cabbage
- 1 cup shredded red cabbage
- 1 cup shredded carrots
- ¾ cup packed chopped Italian parsley
- ⅓ cup mayonnaise
- 3 Tbsp. sour cream
- 2 Tbsp. sliced green onion
- 1 Tbsp. white wine vinegar
- 1 Tbsp. chopped fresh tarragon or ¼ tsp. dried tarragon, crushed
- 1 tsp. sugar
- 1 clove garlic, minced
- ½ cup pepitas (pumpkin seeds), toasted

**1.** In an extra-large bowl combine kale, olive oil, and salt. Using your fingers, rub the kale to help soften it and brighten its color. Rinse the kale in a colander under cool running water; drain well and return to the bowl. Add the cabbages and carrots; toss to combine.

**2.** For dressing, in a food processor or blender combine the next eight ingredients (through garlic). Cover and process or blend to combine.

**3.** Add dressing to kale mixture; toss to coat. Sprinkle with pepitas. **Makes 10 servings (¾ cup each). TO MAKE AHEAD** Prepare salad as directed. Cover and chill up to 24 hours.

**EACH SERVING** *159 cal., 13 g fat (2 g sat. fat), 5 mg chol., 310 mg sodium, 7 g carb., 3 g fiber, 3 g sugars, 5 g pro.*

**1** Kale has very tough stems that need to be removed. Grip the stem while stripping the leaves. You can tear the leaves into bite-size pieces or shred them.

**2** Because kale has firm, sturdy leaves, we like to give it a little massage to soften the fibers. Use your fingers to rub olive oil and salt into the leaves until they are tender and glossy.

CLASSIC VINAIGRETTE USES A 3:1 RATIO OF
OIL TO VINEGAR (FOR EXAMPLE, 3 TBSP. OF OIL
TO 1 TBSP. VINEGAR). IF YOU LIKE EXTRA TANG,
CHANGE THE RATIO TO FIT YOUR TASTES.

**THE HEAVY LIFTER**
Oil plays a major role
in vinaigrette by
carrying the flavor and
coating the greens.
Flavorful olive oil is
often the first choice,
but light safflower oil,
canola oil, avocado
oil, and vegetable oil
are good, too. You can
substitute up to half the
oil with a nut oil, such as
hazelnut or walnut.

**A LITTLE TANGINESS**
A vinaigrette by name
needs that edgy, acidic
bite. Red or white
wine vinegar is most
commonly used, but
balsamic, rice, cider,
and flavored vinegars
are also good choices.
Citrus juices, such as
lemon and grapefruit,
are excellent stand-ins.

**MUST-HAVE MUSTARD**
Mustard is the secret
ingredient—the one
that makes everyone
get along, bind
together, and stay
suspended (emulsified).
If Dijon isn't your first
choice, dry mustard or
a whole grain variety
also works.

**FRESH FLAVOR**
Herbs are the
backbone of any
flavor highlights in a
vinaigrette. Chop
a combo of fresh herbs
or use just one. If you
don't have fresh,
opt for dried herbs.
The general rule
is 1 tsp. dried herbs
for every 1 Tbsp.
fresh herbs.

**ESSENTIAL ONION**
Finely chopped
shallots give dressings
a mild onion flavor.
Use yellow, white,
sweet, and green
onions as alternatives.

**THE EXTRAS** Once
you get the basics
down, you can make a
different vinaigrette
every day of the year
with add-ins. A little
sugar or honey can
balance any excessive
acidity. Toss in minced
garlic, finely chopped
dried tomatoes,
grated fresh ginger,
finely shredded
Parmesan cheese,
crumbled feta or blue
cheese, chopped
crisp-cooked bacon,
or hot pepper sauce.

# FRESH HERB VINAIGRETTE

**START TO FINISH** 10 minutes

1 cup olive oil or vegetable oil
⅓ cup red wine vinegar, white wine vinegar, rice vinegar, or cider vinegar
¼ cup finely chopped shallots
2 Tbsp. chopped fresh oregano, thyme, or basil or 1 tsp. dried oregano, thyme, or basil, crushed
1 Tbsp. Dijon mustard or ½ tsp. dry mustard
2 to 3 tsp. sugar
2 cloves garlic, minced
¼ tsp. salt
¼ tsp. black pepper

**1.** In a screw-top jar combine all ingredients. Cover and shake well. Serve immediately. **Makes 14 servings (2 Tbsp. each).**
**TO STORE** If using fresh herbs, cover and chill up to 3 days. If using dried herbs, cover and chill up to 1 week. The olive oil will solidify when chilled, so let vinaigrette stand at room temperature 1 hour before using. Shake well.
**EACH SERVING** *144 cal., 16 g fat (2 g sat. fat), 0 mg chol., 68 mg sodium, 2 g carb., 0 g fiber, 0 g sugars, 0 g pro.*

## *PICK AN OIL*

Oils have strong flavors (like extra virgin olive oil) or very mellow (like canola oil). You can also mix different oils to get the best of both worlds.

**OLIVE OIL** Extra virgin olive oil is the highest-quality olive oil available. It has a golden to deep greenish color and offers a rich flavor with a slightly tingly finish (sometimes described as a burn). Olive oils labeled as "light" are more highly processed and are a blend of refined and virgin olive oils. Olive oil will solidify in the refrigerator, so let chilled dressings stand at room temperature before serving.

**VEGETABLE OIL** With a mild, neutral taste, vegetable oil, such as canola, corn, soybean, and safflower, brings body to dressings without overwhelming the flavor of the other ingredients.

**NUT OILS** Hazelnut, walnut, macadamia nut, as well as other nut oils, bring rich flavor to dressings, but they are more expensive than other oils. Use them to replace a portion of the oil in dressings rather than the whole amount. They are highly perishable, so store in the fridge after opening.

## *A TOUCH OF ACIDITY*

Vinegar and other acidic ingredients give your dressing its attitude and vibrancy. Play around with different options until you find what you like.

**WINE VINEGARS** This is the most common choice for vinaigrettes and includes white or red wine, champagne, sherry, and light or dark balsamic vinegars. Each lends its own distinct flavor and color to dressings.

**CIDER VINEGARS** This tartly acidic vinegar is often used for dressing cabbage and other hearty vegetables, but its complex flavor also works with greens.

**RICE VINEGAR** Made from fermented rice, this vinegar has a mild flavor and subtle sweetness that adds contrast to spicy or bitter greens.

**FLAVORED VINEGARS** You can find vinegars infused with herbs (tarragon, basil), fruit (fig, berries, orange), and even chocolate. When using them, keep the vinaigrette simple so their subtle flavors shine through.

**CITRUS JUICE** Freshly squeezed lemon and lime juices can also be used in place of vinegar for bright, fresh flavor.

## CREAMY FRENCH DRESSING

**START TO FINISH**
15 minutes

In a blender combine ⅓ cup each water and vinegar; 2 Tbsp. sugar; 1 Tbsp. lemon juice; 2 tsp. paprika; 1 tsp. each salt, dry mustard, black pepper, and Worcestershire sauce; and 1 clove garlic, minced. Cover; blend until combined. With blender running, add 1⅓ cups vegetable oil in a thin, steady stream. Serve immediately or cover and chill up to 2 weeks. Stir before using. **Makes 16 servings (2 Tbsp. each).**

**EACH SERVING** *170 cal., 18 g fat (2 g sat. fat), 0 mg chol., 150 mg sodium, 2 g carb., 0 g fiber, 2 g sugars, 0 g pro.*

## SESAME-GINGER DRESSING

**HANDS-ON TIME**
15 minutes
**CHILL** 1 hour

In a blender combine ¼ cup cider vinegar; 1 Tbsp. grated fresh ginger; 2 tsp. honey; 1 tsp. toasted sesame oil; 1 clove garlic, minced; ¼ tsp. salt; and ⅛ tsp. crushed red pepper. Cover; blend on low. With blender running, add ½ cup vegetable oil in a thin stream. Transfer to a container. Add 2 tsp. toasted sesame seeds. Cover; chill 1 hour. Stir before using. **Makes 8 servings (2 Tbsp. each).**

**EACH SERVING** *137 cal., 14 g fat (2 g sat. fat), 0 mg chol., 74 mg sodium, 2 g carb., 0 g fiber, 1 g sugars, 0 g pro.*

## THOUSAND ISLAND DRESSING

**START TO FINISH**
15 minutes

In a small bowl stir together 1 cup mayonnaise and ¼ cup bottled chili sauce. Stir in 2 Tbsp. each sweet pickle relish, finely chopped green sweet pepper, and finely chopped onion; and 1 tsp. Worcestershire sauce or prepared horseradish. Serve immediately or cover and chill up to 1 week. If needed, stir in milk to reach desired consistency. **Makes 12 servings (2 Tbsp. each).**

**EACH SERVING** *142 cal., 14 g fat (2 g sat. fat), 6 mg chol., 186 mg sodium, 2 g carb., 0 g fiber, 2 g sugars, 0 g pro.*

## CREAMY PARMESAN DRESSING

**START TO FINISH**
10 minutes

In a small bowl whisk together ½ cup mayonnaise; ¼ cup each grated Parmesan cheese and buttermilk; 1 clove garlic, minced; and 1 Tbsp. chopped fresh Italian parsley. Cover and chill up to 1 week. Stir before using. If needed, stir in additional buttermilk until dressing reaches desired consistency. **Makes 8 servings (2 Tbsp. each).**

**EACH SERVING** *116 cal., 12 g fat (2 g sat. fat), 8 mg chol., 122 mg sodium, 0 g carb., 0 g fiber, 0 g sugars, 2 g pro.*

## TAHINI-HONEY DRESSING

**START TO FINISH**
10 minutes

In a small bowl whisk together the ½ cup tahini (sesame seed paste) (tip, p. 379); ⅓ cup lemon juice; 2 Tbsp. honey; 2 cloves garlic, minced; ½ tsp. ground cumin; ¼ tsp. salt; and ⅛ tsp. cayenne pepper. Gradually whisk in ¼ cup water. Stir in 2 Tbsp. chopped fresh cilantro. Serve or cover and chill up to 3 days. If needed, stir in water to reach desired consistency. **Makes 8 servings (2 Tbsp. each).**

**EACH SERVING** *109 cal., 8 g fat (1 g sat. fat), 0 mg chol., 79 mg sodium, 9 g carb., 1 g fiber, 5 g sugars, 3 g pro.*

## STRAWBERRY BALSAMIC VINAIGRETTE

**START TO FINISH**
15 minutes

In a blender combine 2 cups chopped fresh or frozen strawberries, thawed; ⅓ cup olive oil; 2 Tbsp. white balsamic vinegar or balsamic vinegar; 1 Tbsp. packed brown sugar;* ¾ tsp. black pepper; and ¼ tsp. kosher salt. Cover; blend until smooth. Transfer to a container; chill up to 3 days. Whisk well before using.

**Makes 14 servings (2 Tbsp. each).**

**\*NOTE** If strawberries are sweet, sugar may not be needed.

**EACH SERVING** *60 cal., 5 g fat (1 g sat. fat), 0 mg chol., 36 mg sodium, 4 g carb., 0 g fiber, 3 g sugars, 0 g pro.*

## HONEY-MUSTARD DRESSING

**START TO FINISH**
10 minutes

In a screw-top jar combine ¼ cup each coarse-ground mustard, olive oil or vegetable oil, lemon juice, and honey; and 2 cloves garlic, minced. Cover and shake well. Serve immediately or chill up to 1 week. Shake well before using.

**Makes 8 servings (2 Tbsp. each).**

**EACH SERVING** *102 cal., 8 g fat (0 g sat. fat), 0 mg chol., 102 mg sodium, 10 g carb., 0 g fiber, 8 g sugars, 0 g pro.*

## BUTTERMILK RANCH DRESSING

**HANDS-ON TIME**
10 minutes
**CHILL** 30 minutes

In a bowl stir together ¾ cup buttermilk; ½ cup mayonnaise; 1 Tbsp. chopped fresh parsley; ¼ tsp. each onion powder, dry mustard, and black pepper; and 1 clove garlic, minced. If needed, stir in additional buttermilk to reach desired consistency. Cover and chill 30 minutes or up to 1 week. Stir before using.

**Makes 10 servings (2 Tbsp. each).**

**EACH SERVING** *88 cal., 8 g fat (2 g sat. fat), 4 mg chol., 80 mg sodium, 2 g carb., 0 g fiber, 0 g sugars, 0 g pro.*

## BLUE CHEESE DRESSING

**START TO FINISH**
10 minutes

In a blender or food processor combine ½ cup plain yogurt or sour cream; ¼ cup each cottage cheese, mayonnaise, and crumbled blue cheese; and ¼ tsp. each salt and pepper. Cover and blend or process until smooth. Stir in ½ to ¾ cup more crumbled blue cheese. If needed, stir in milk to reach desired consistency. Serve immediately or cover and chill up to 2 weeks. Stir before using.

**Makes 10 servings (2 Tbsp. each).**

**EACH SERVING** *88 cal., 8 g fat (4 g sat. fat), 12 mg chol., 254 mg sodium, 2 g carb., 0 g fiber, 0 g sugars, 4 g pro.*

## CREAMY ITALIAN DRESSING

**START TO FINISH**
15 minutes

In a small bowl stir together ¾ cup mayonnaise; ¼ cup sour cream; 2 tsp. white wine vinegar or white vinegar; 1 clove garlic, minced; ½ tsp. dried Italian seasoning, crushed; ¼ tsp. dry mustard; and ⅛ tsp. salt. Serve immediately or cover and chill up to 1 week. If needed, stir in milk to reach desired consistency.

**Makes 8 servings (2 Tbsp. each).**

**EACH SERVING** *164 cal., 18 g fat (4 g sat. fat), 10 mg chol., 154 mg sodium, 0 g carb., 0 g fiber, 0 g sugars, 0 g pro.*

**SALAD GREENS 1.** Romaine **2.** Spinach **3.** Watercress **4.** Endive **5.** Mesclun **6.** Arugula **7.** Frisée **8.** Kale
**9.** Savoy cabbage **10.** Butterhead (Bibb or Boston) **11.** Iceberg **12.** Radicchio **13.** Red cabbage **14.** Red-tipped butterhead
**15.** Escarole **16.** Napa cabbage **17.** Red-tipped leaf **18.** Green leaf **19.** Curly endive **20.** Green cabbage

## RINSING

Always rinse your greens to remove soil and other contaminants. Wash greens well under cool running water or swish them around in a sinkful of cool water. Gently shake off excess water.

## TO TEAR OR CUT

Using a knife to cut greens can cause oxidation, resulting in edges that brown upon storing. Tearing greens is a better option if you need to store them for any amount of time. If you are serving them right away, either method works.

## SPIN CYCLE

Dressing clings to dry leaves best (plus, wet greens dilute the dressing). Tear freshly washed greens into bite-size pieces, then give them a whirl in a salad spinner to remove excess water. If necessary, pat the leaves dry with paper towels.

### SO HAPPY TOGETHER

Salad greens vary in texture, so we like to pair our dressings accordingly. Thick, heavy dressings go with sturdy greens; vinaigrettes pair nicely with delicate leaves.

**GREENS**
Iceberg lettuce wedges

**DRESSING**
Blue Cheese Dressing (*p. 301*)

**GREENS**
Kale + Endive + Shredded red cabbage

**DRESSING**
Tahini-Honey Dressing (*p. 300*)

**GREENS**
Red-tipped leaf + Green leaf

**DRESSING**
Fresh Herb Vinaigrette (*p. 299*)

**GREENS**
Mesclun + Arugula

**DRESSING**
Strawberry Balsamic Vinaigrette (*p. 301*)

// SALADS & DRESSINGS //

# EVERYDAY SIDES

**TEST KITCHEN**

**MAKE-AHEAD RECIPE.** See also "Sides," *pp. 448–469; cooking charts, pp. 70–83.*

THERE'S A SCIENCE TO MASHING POTATOES. WHILE HOT, MASH THEM JUST UNTIL THEY'RE FLUFFY. IF YOU OVERWORK THE POTATOES, THE STARCH CELLS WILL BREAK DOWN AND RESULT IN A GLUEY, STICKY TEXTURE.

## MASHED POTATOES

**HANDS-ON TIME** 15 minutes
**COOK** 20 minutes

| | |
|---|---|
| 3 | lb. potatoes (tips, *opposite left*), peeled if desired, cut into 2-inch pieces |
| ¼ | cup butter |
| ½ | to ¾ cup milk, heavy cream, or half-and-half |
| 1 | tsp. salt |
| ½ | tsp. black pepper |

**1.** In a 4- to 5-qt. Dutch oven cook potatoes, covered, in enough lightly salted boiling water to cover 20 to 25 minutes or until tender; drain. Return potatoes to the hot Dutch oven. Add the ¼ cup butter.* Let stand, uncovered, 2 to 3 minutes. Meanwhile, in a 1- or 1½-qt. saucepan, heat the milk over low heat until very warm.
**2.** Mash potatoes until light and fluffy. Stir in milk, salt, and pepper. Stir in additional milk as desired. If desired, top with additional butter and snipped *chives*. **Makes 10 servings (⅔ cup each).**
***NOTE** If using a ricer (tip, *opposite right*), stir in melted butter after pressing through ricer.
**EACH SERVING** *126 cal., 5 g fat (3 g sat. fat), 13 mg chol., 281 mg sodium, 19 g carb., 2 g fiber, 1 g sugars, 3 g pro.*
**TO MAKE AHEAD** Prepare Mashed Potatoes as directed. Place potato mixture in a greased 2-qt. rectangular baking dish; cool. Cover tightly and chill up to 48 hours. To serve, preheat oven to 350°F. Bake, covered with foil, 45 minutes. Uncover; bake 10 to 15 minutes more or until heated through.

## IN THE SLOW COOKER

In a 4-qt. slow cooker combine 3 lb. potatoes and 1¼ cups reduced-sodium chicken broth (if using sweet potatoes, use only ¾ cup broth). Cover and cook on low 6 to 8 hours or on high 3 to 4 hours. Add the butter, milk, salt, and pepper. Mash until potatoes are smooth. Serve immediately or keep warm, covered, on warm or low up to 2 hours.

### ROASTED GARLIC MASHED POTATOES
Roast 2 bulbs of garlic as directed on *p. 24*. Remove cloves and mash. Prepare potatoes as directed, except beat in roasted garlic and 4 oz. cream cheese, cut into small cubes, with the potatoes and butter. If desired, stir in ⅓ cup roasted red peppers, drained and chopped, and ⅓ cup chopped green onions.

### BACON AND ONION MASHED POTATOES
In a 12-inch skillet crisp-cook 6 slices thick-sliced bacon. Transfer bacon to paper towels. Drain all but 1 Tbsp. drippings from skillet; add 2 cups chopped onions. Cook, covered, over medium-low heat 13 to 15 minutes or until onion is tender, stirring occasionally. Uncover; cook and stir over medium-high heat 3 to 5 minutes or until onion is golden. Crumble bacon. Prepare potatoes as directed, except reduce milk to ¼ cup. Add 1 cup sour cream with the milk. Fold in bacon and onions.

### CHEESY HERBED MASHED POTATOES
Prepare potatoes as directed, then stir in 1½ cups shredded cheese, such as cheddar, Fontina, or smoked cheddar, or ½ cup Gouda, Asiago, Parmesan, or Romano; ½ cup chopped fresh parsley and/or basil; and 2 Tbsp. chopped fresh thyme, rosemary, and/or oregano.

### MASHED SWEET POTATOES
Prepare potatoes as directed, using 3 lb. sweet potatoes, peeled, for the potatoes.

**EXTRA FLAVOR**

Add savory richness by cooking the potatoes in chicken broth or vegetable broth instead of lightly salted water. You can reserve and mix some of the cooking liquid into the mashed potatoes to replace some of the milk.

Heating the milk before adding it to the potatoes keeps the potatoes hot until they get to the table. Start by adding the least amount of milk in the range. Add additional milk gradually until the potatoes reach your desired creaminess.

## MASHING METHODS

**RICE 'EM** A ricer is a specialty tool made just for mashing potatoes. It produces very smooth, light, extra-fluffy potatoes. Press cooked, peeled potatoes through the ricer into a bowl. To maintain their lightness, be gentle when stirring additional ingredients into riced potatoes.

**MASH 'EM** A hand masher is the simplest tool for mashing potatoes, and you can mash them directly in the pan. It produces a coarse-texture mashed potato with a homemade appearance. Mashers with the grid plate (not the traditional wavy wire) produce an even texture.

**MIX 'EM** Use this method only with peeled potatoes. A hand mixer requires less muscle than a masher and minimizes lumps. Beat on low speed just until light and fluffy. (Do not overbeat!)

**TATERS FOR MASHING** ■ **YUKON GOLD** These waxy-texture potatoes with golden-yellow skin and flesh are great mashers. They have a rich, almost sweet flavor, and they mash to a creamy consistency. The skins are thin, so peeling is optional. ■ **RED** These fine-texture, white-flesh potatoes possess a mild flavor and creamy waxiness; peeling is optional. ■ **RUSSET** These potatoes contain more starch than the other two, so they create fluffier potatoes. The skin is thick—peeling is recommended.

**SMASH IT**
A potato masher, drinking glass, or measuring cup works perfectly for flattening the potato rounds before roasting them.

## ROASTED SMASHED POTATOES

**HANDS-ON TIME** 15 minutes
**COOK** 25 minutes
**COOL** 10 minutes
**BAKE** 22 minutes at 450°F

12  to 16 small red potatoes (1½ to 2 inches in diameter, 1½ to 2 lb. total)
1  tsp. salt
¼  cup olive oil
¾  tsp. salt
½  tsp. black pepper
¾  cup finely shredded Parmesan cheese
2  Tbsp. finely chopped fresh Italian parsley

**1.** Place potatoes in a 3-qt. saucepan and cover with at least 1 inch of water. Add the 1 tsp. salt. Bring to boiling; reduce heat. Cover and simmer 25 to 30 minutes or until potatoes are very tender; drain.
**2.** Preheat oven to 450°F. Transfer potatoes to a foil-lined 15×10-inch baking pan. Cool 10 minutes. Lightly press down on each potato to smash to about a ½-inch thickness, keeping each potato in one piece.
**3.** Brush half of the olive oil on potatoes. Sprinkle half of the ¾ tsp. salt and ¼ tsp. of the pepper on potatoes. Bake, uncovered, 10 to 15 minutes or until bottoms are lightly browned and crisp. Turn

potatoes; brush with the remaining olive oil and sprinkle with the remaining salt and pepper. Bake 10 to 15 minutes more or until potatoes are lightly browned and crisp. In a bowl combine cheese and parsley. Sprinkle on potatoes. Bake 2 to 3 minutes more or until cheese melts. **Makes 12 servings (1 potato each).**

**EACH SERVING** *101 cal., 6 g fat (2 g sat. fat), 4 mg chol., 257 mg sodium, 9 g carb., 1 g fiber, 1 g sugars, 3 g pro.*

FRENCH
FRIES

SWEET
POTATO
FRIES

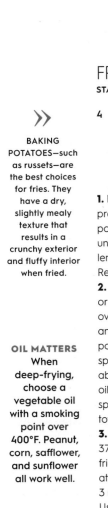

**»**

BAKING
POTATOES—such
as russets—are
the best choices
for fries. They
have a dry,
slightly mealy
texture that
results in a
crunchy exterior
and fluffy interior
when fried.

**OIL MATTERS**
When
deep-frying,
choose a
vegetable oil
with a smoking
point over
400°F. Peanut,
corn, safflower,
and sunflower
all work well.

## FRENCH FRIES
**START TO FINISH** 45 minutes

4   medium baking potatoes
    (6 to 8 oz. each)
    Peanut or vegetable oil for
    deep-fat frying
    Salt or seasoned salt (optional)

**1.** If desired, peel potatoes. To
prevent darkening, immerse peeled
potatoes in a bowl of ice water
until ready to cut. Cut potatoes
lengthwise into ½-inch-wide strips.
Return potato strips to ice water.
**2.** In a heavy, deep 3-qt. saucepan
or deep-fat fryer heat oil to 325°F
over medium heat. Drain potatoes
and place on paper towels; pat
potatoes dry. Using a slotted
spoon, carefully add potato strips,
about one-eighth at a time, to hot
oil. Fry 2 minutes. Using a slotted
spoon, transfer potatoes to paper
towels to drain.
**3.** Preheat oven to 300°F. Heat oil to
375°F over medium-high heat. Add
fried potatoes, about one-eighth
at a time, to hot oil and fry 2 to
3 minutes or until crisp and golden.
Using a slotted spoon, transfer
potatoes to paper towels to drain.
If desired, sprinkle with salt and/or
*fresh rosemary* or *sage*. Keep fries
warm in a baking pan in oven while
frying remaining potatoes. **Makes
6 servings (1 cup each).**
**EACH SERVING** *487 cal., 45 g fat
(8 g sat. fat), 0 mg chol., 6 mg sodium,
20 g carb., 1 g fiber, 1 g sugars, 2 g pro.*

**CHANGE IT UP**
*To make sweet potato fries,
prepare as directed, except
use 4 medium sweet potatoes,
peeled. If desired, sprinkle
with cinnamon-sugar.*

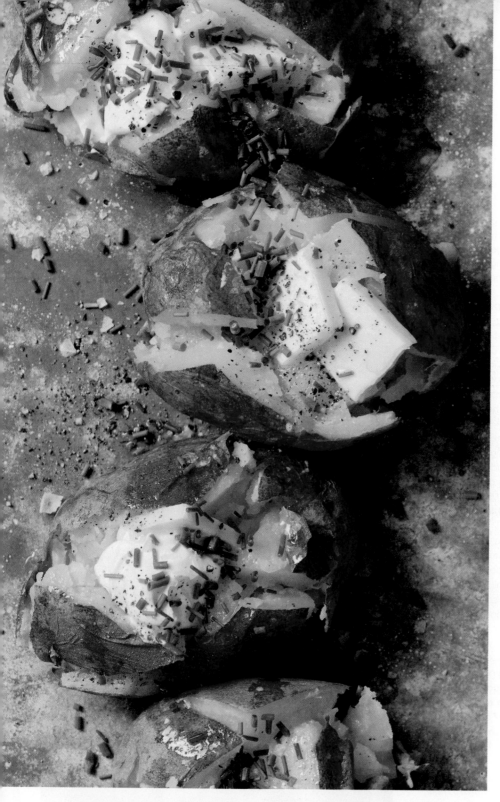

# BAKED POTATOES

**HANDS-ON TIME** 5 minutes
**BAKE** 40 minutes at 425°F

4    medium baking potatoes
     (6 to 8 oz. each)
     Butter (optional)

**1.** Preheat oven to 425°F. Scrub potatoes thoroughly with a vegetable brush; pat dry. Prick potatoes with a fork. (If desired, for soft skins, rub potatoes with butter or wrap each potato in foil.)
**2.** Bake 40 to 60 minutes or until tender. To serve, roll each potato gently under a towel. Using a knife, cut an "X" in top of each potato. Press in and up on the ends of each potato. **Makes 4 potatoes.**
**BAKED SWEET POTATOES**
Prepare as directed, except substitute sweet potatoes for the baking potatoes. If desired, serve sweet potatoes with butter and brown sugar or cinnamon-sugar.
**EACH POTATO** *131 cal., 0 fat, 0 mg chol., 10 mg sodium, 30 g carb., 4 g fiber, 1 g sugars, 3 g pro.*

## *IN THE SLOW COOKER*

Rub scrubbed potatoes lightly with olive oil. Place potatoes in a 4- or 6-qt. slow cooker (4 potatoes in a 4-qt. or 8 potatoes in a 6-qt.). Cover; cook on low 8 hours or high 4 hours or until potatoes are tender.

**POTATO PARTY** A baked potato bar with assorted toppings makes great party food. Keep the Baked Potatoes warm in a slow cooker and offer favorite toppings such as butter, chili, chopped chives, cooked broccoli or cauliflower, crisp-cooked bacon, salsa, shredded or crumbled cheeses, sliced green onions, and/or sour cream.

## TWICE-BAKED POTATOES

**HANDS-ON TIME** 20 minutes
**STAND** 10 minutes
**BAKE** 22 minutes at 425°F

- 1 recipe Baked Potatoes (*opposite*)
- ½ cup sour cream or plain yogurt
- ¼ tsp. garlic salt
- ⅛ tsp. black pepper
  Milk (optional)
- ¾ cup finely shredded cheddar cheese (3 oz.)
- 1 Tbsp. chopped fresh chives (optional)

**1.** Bake potatoes as directed in Step 2 (*opposite*); let stand about 10 minutes. Cut a lengthwise slice off the top of each baked potato; discard skin from slices and place pulp in a bowl. Scoop out potato pulp; add to the bowl.
**2.** Preheat oven to 425°F. Mash the potato pulp with a potato masher or an electric mixer on low speed. Add sour cream, garlic salt, and pepper; beat until smooth. (If necessary, stir in 1 to 2 Tbsp. milk to reach desired consistency.) Season to taste with *salt* and additional pepper. Stir in ½ cup of

the cheddar cheese and, if desired, chives. Spoon the mashed potato mixture into the potato shells. Place in a 2-qt. baking dish.
**3.** Bake, uncovered, 20 to 25 minutes or until light brown. Sprinkle with remaining ¼ cup cheese. Bake 2 minutes or until cheese melts. **Makes 4 potatoes.**
**EACH POTATO** *268 cal., 12 g fat (7 g sat. fat), 35 mg chol., 221 mg sodium, 21 g carb., 2 g fiber, 2 g sugars, 10 g pro.*

Using a spoon, gently scoop out the cooked potato flesh, leaving ¼ inch of flesh in the shells. Avoid scooping out too much— you want a shell that's thick enough to stay open by itself without collapsing.

### ROASTED POBLANO
Prepare as directed, except roast 2 poblano chile peppers (tip, p. 22). Peel and chop the peppers and stir into mashed potato mixture with the cheese. Substitute chopped fresh cilantro for the chives. If desired, garnish with additional cilantro.

### BROCCOLI-CHEESE
Prepare as directed, except stir 1 cup chopped cooked broccoli into the mashed potato mixture with the cheese. Substitute chopped fresh dill for the chives.

### SOUTHWESTERN
Prepare as directed, except in Step 2, substitute Monterey Jack cheese with jalapeños for the cheddar cheese and chopped fresh cilantro for the chives. Serve with purchased salsa.

### MUSHROOM-SWISS
Prepare as directed, except in a 10-inch skillet cook and stir 2 cups sliced fresh mushrooms and 1 clove garlic, minced, in 1 Tbsp. butter 5 to 6 minutes or until tender and browned. Stir into mashed potato mixture. Substitute Swiss cheese for the cheddar cheese and chopped fresh Italian parsley for the chives.

## CURRIED AÏOLI

In a bowl stir together ½ cup mayonnaise; 2 cloves garlic, minced; 1 tsp. lemon juice; and ½ tsp. curry powder. Slowly drizzle ⅓ cup olive oil in a thin stream into the mixture, whisking constantly. Cover; chill up to 3 days.

# ONION RINGS

**START TO FINISH** 45 minutes

- ¾ cup all-purpose flour
- ⅔ cup milk
- 1 egg
- 1 Tbsp. vegetable oil
- ¼ tsp. salt
  Peanut or vegetable oil for deep-fat frying (tip, *p. 309*)
- 4 medium mild yellow or white onions, sliced ¼ inch thick and separated into rings (1¼ lb.)
- 1 recipe Curried Aïoli and/or Chipotle Ketchup

**1.** For batter, in a medium bowl combine flour, milk, egg, 1 Tbsp. oil, and ¼ tsp. salt. Using a whisk, beat just until smooth.

**2.** In a deep-fat fryer or 12-inch deep skillet heat 1 inch oil to 365°F. Using a fork, dip onion rings into batter; drain off excess batter.* Fry onion rings, a few at a time, in hot oil for 2 to 3 minutes or until golden, stirring once or twice with a fork to separate rings. Remove rings from oil; drain on paper towels. Sprinkle with additional salt. Serve with Curried Aïoli and/or Chipotle Ketchup. **Makes 6 servings.**

**\*NOTE** You might need to stir the last few onion rings into batter to coat them well.

**EACH SERVING** *300 cal., 22 g fat (3 g sat. fat), 33 mg chol., 222 mg sodium, 22 g carb., 2 g fiber, 5 g sugars, 5 g pro.*

## CHIPOTLE KETCHUP

In a small bowl stir together 1 cup ketchup and 2 tsp. finely chopped chipotle chile peppers in adobo sauce. Cover and chill up to 3 days.

## *EVERYTHING FRIED*

You can use the same batter mix to fry up other favorites. Prepare batter as directed. In place of the onion rings, use zucchini slices, button mushrooms (*far left*), cauliflower florets, or cocktail sausages. For baby dill pickles (*near left*), pickled okra, or stuffed queen olives, first pat dry with paper towels and dip in all-purpose flour before adding to batter.

# OVEN-FRIED VEGGIES

**HANDS-ON TIME** 25 minutes
**BAKE** 20 minutes at 400°F

1    cup panko bread crumbs
     (tip, *p. 108*)
½    cup grated Parmesan cheese
1    tsp. dried oregano, basil, or
     thyme, crushed
½    tsp. garlic powder
½    tsp. black pepper
1    egg, lightly beaten
1    Tbsp. milk
4    cups cauliflower florets,
     broccoli florets, whole fresh
     button mushrooms, sliced
     zucchini, and/or packaged
     peeled baby carrots
¼    cup butter, melted
     Curried Aïoli *(opposite)* or
     ranch dressing (optional)

VEGGIES need to
be cut in uniform-
size pieces to
bake at the same
rate. You may
need to halve or
quarter large
mushrooms.

**1.** Preheat oven to 400°F. Lightly
grease a 15×10-inch baking pan. In
a resealable plastic bag combine
first five ingredients (through
pepper). In a small bowl combine
egg and milk.
**2.** Toss 1 cup of the vegetables in
the egg mixture. Using a slotted
spoon, transfer vegetables to the
plastic bag. Close bag and shake
to coat with panko mixture. Place
coated vegetables in the prepared
baking pan. Repeat with remaining
vegetables, egg mixture, and
panko mixture. Drizzle melted
butter over vegetables.
**3.** Bake 20 to 25 minutes or until
golden, stirring twice. If desired,
serve with Curried Aïoli. **Makes
6 servings (⅔ cup each).**
**EACH SERVING** *169 cal., 11 g fat
(6 g sat. fat), 62 mg chol., 222 mg
sodium, 12 g carb., 2 g fiber, 3 g sugars,
7 g pro.*

# ROASTING VEGETABLES

Preheat oven to 425°F. Place vegetables in a single layer on a large baking sheet or shallow baking pan. Drizzle with olive oil and season to taste with salt and black pepper (or other desired seasoning); toss gently to coat. Roast until vegetables are lightly browned and desired tenderness is reached, stirring or turning once during baking time. Use timings below as a guide.

| VEGETABLES | PREP | ROAST |
| --- | --- | --- |
| ACORN SQUASH | halved, seeded, and cut into ¾-inch-thick slices | 20 to 25 minutes |
| ASPARAGUS | trimmed | 10 to 12 minutes |
| BEETS | peeled and cut into small wedges; cover pan with foil | 40 to 45 minutes |
| BROCCOLI | stemmed and cut into florets | 10 to 15 minutes |
| BRUSSELS SPROUTS | trimmed and halved if large | 15 to 20 minutes |
| BUTTERNUT SQUASH | peeled, seeded, and cut into 1-inch pieces | 25 to 30 minutes |
| CABBAGE | trimmed and cut into wedges or ½-inch slices | 35 to 40 minutes |
| CARROTS | coarsely chopped or cut into sticks (or baby carrots) | 25 to 30 minutes |
| CAULIFLOWER | cored and cut into florets | 20 to 25 minutes |
| CHERRY/GRAPE TOMATOES | leave whole | 10 to 12 minutes |
| CORN | husked and kernels cut off cob | 15 to 20 minutes |
| DELICATA SQUASH | halved, seeded, and cut into ½-inch-thick slices | 25 to 30 minutes |
| FENNEL | trimmed and cut into wedges | 25 to 30 minutes |
| NEW POTATOES | halved or quartered if large | 20 to 25 minutes |
| OKRA | trimmed | 15 to 20 minutes |
| PARSNIPS | peeled and coarsely chopped | 25 to 30 minutes |
| RADISHES | trimmed and halved if large | 30 to 35 minutes |
| RUTABAGAS | peeled and coarsely chopped | 25 to 30 minutes |
| SUGAR SNAP PEAS | trimmed | 10 to 15 minutes |
| SUMMER SQUASH | coarsely chopped | 15 to 20 minutes |
| SWEET POTATOES | coarsely chopped or cut into ½-inch wedges | 20 to 25 minutes |
| ZUCCHINI | sliced | 15 to 20 minutes |

## *DRIZZLES & SPRINKLES*
### CUSTOMIZE YOUR VEGGIES WITH MORE FLAVOR.

**BACON** Crumble crisp-cooked bacon for a salty, smoky topper.

**CHEESE** Crumble or shred a strong-flavor, high-quality cheese, such as Parmesan, blue, feta, or chèvre, over hot vegetables.

**CITRUS JUICE** Squeeze a wedge of orange, lemon, or lime over steamed or roasted veggies.

**CITRUS ZEST** Orange, lemon, or lime zest adds a burst of bright flavor to plain vegetables.

**SLICED GARLIC** Sauté sliced garlic briefly in olive oil to toast lightly before using as a topper.

**GREMOLATA** Combine lemon zest, fresh parsley, and minced garlic for a powerhouse topping.

**FRESH HERBS** Toss chopped herbs with hot vegetables.

**HONEY OR MAPLE SYRUP** These natural glazes enhance the sweet flavor of roasted vegetables.

**MUSTARD** Whisk together desired mustard and sour cream, then thin with milk for an easy sauce to drizzle over hot or cold veggies.

**TOASTED NUTS** Chopped toasted nuts or nuts sautéed in oil with a little salt, black pepper, and spice (such as cumin, chili powder, five-spice powder, cinnamon, or ginger) add texture and flavor. Or use toasted sesame seeds, sunflower kernels, or pepitas (pumpkin seeds).

**TOASTED SESAME OIL** A little goes a long way with this intensely nutty oil (tip, *p. 186*).

**SOY SAUCE** Add a hint of umami to any stir-fry vegetables.

**SRIRACHA SAUCE** A squirt or more of this bright and spicy Asian sauce adds a little—or a lot—of heat to cooked vegetables.

**VINEGAR** Drizzle any vinegar variety (balsamic, white or red wine, rice, sherry, herb-flavor) over vegetables and greens.

**PLAIN YOGURT** A dollop of yogurt and sprinkle of spice add wholesome tang to baked and roasted root vegetables.

# 12 EASY SIDES

## CABBAGE AND FARRO

In a 12-inch skillet cook 3 cups shredded cabbage; 1 apple, chopped; ½ cup chopped onion; and 3 strips bacon, chopped, over medium heat until tender, stirring occasionally. Add 2 cups cooked farro. Stir in 2 Tbsp. cider vinegar and 1 tsp. each honey and Dijon mustard. Add salt and pepper to taste. Makes 6 servings.

## QUINOA PILAF

In a 10-inch skillet cook 2 cups sliced cremini mushrooms, 1 cup sliced zucchini, and ½ cup chopped onion in 2 Tbsp. olive oil over medium-high heat 5 minutes or until lightly browned, stirring often. Stir in 2 cups fresh baby kale; 1 cup halved grape tomatoes; ½ tsp. herbes de Provence, crushed; and ½ tsp. salt and ¼ tsp. pepper until kale wilts. Stir in 2 cups hot cooked quinoa. Makes 6 servings.

## PESTO SQUASH

Microwave 1 halved and seeded spaghetti squash with ¼ cup water, covered, about 15 minutes or until tender. Scrape squash strands into a bowl. Add ¼ cup basil pesto, 2 Tbsp. shredded Parmesan cheese, ½ tsp. lemon juice, and ¼ tsp. crushed red pepper; toss to coat. If desired, top with additional Parmesan cheese and crushed red pepper. Makes 4 servings.

## CHEESY ORZO

In a 10-inch skillet cook ½ cup chopped onion in 1 Tbsp. oil 4 minutes over medium heat. Stir in ½ cup dried orzo pasta. Add one 14.5-oz. can vegetable broth; ½ tsp. dried thyme, crushed; and ¼ tsp. pepper. Simmer, covered, 5 minutes. Stir in 3 cups broccoli florets. Cover; simmer 5 minutes. Stir in ½ cup shredded white cheddar cheese. Let stand 5 minutes. Serve with lemon wedges. Makes 4 servings.

## MARINATED SUMMER SQUASH

Using a vegetable peeler, cut 2 medium zucchini and/or yellow summer squash lengthwise into ribbons. In a large bowl whisk together 2 Tbsp. olive oil, 1 tsp. lemon zest, 1 Tbsp. lemon juice, and ¼ tsp. each salt and pepper. Add squash ribbons; toss to coat. Let stand 30 minutes. Top with ¼ cup crumbled goat cheese and 2 Tbsp. snipped fresh basil. Makes 6 servings.

## PAN-ROASTED PEPPERS

Cut 3 sweet peppers lengthwise into 1-inch-wide strips, 1 medium sweet onion into thin wedges, and 2 cloves garlic into thin slices. In a 12-inch skillet cook vegetables in 1 Tbsp. olive oil over medium-high heat about 5 minutes or until tender. Toss in 1 Tbsp. each chopped fresh herbs and balsamic vinegar. Add salt and pepper to taste. Makes 6 servings.

## HOISIN VEGGIES

In a double-thick 18-inch square of heavy foil place 1½ cups thinly sliced carrots; 1½ cups snow pea pods, trimmed and halved; and 4 green onions, cut into 1-inch pieces. Top with 2 Tbsp. hoisin sauce. Fold foil into a packet. Grill, covered, over direct medium heat until veggies are crisp-tender, turning twice. Sprinkle with toasted sesame seeds and crushed red pepper. Makes 4 servings.

## PANKO PEAS AND ONIONS

In a 10-inch skillet heat 1 Tbsp. each butter and olive oil over medium-high heat. Add ½ cup panko bread crumbs (tip, *p. 108*). Cook and stir 1 minute until golden. Add one 16-oz. pkg. frozen peas; ⅓ cup slivered onion; 1 clove garlic, minced; and ½ tsp. dried Italian seasoning, crushed. Cook 5 minutes, stirring occasionally. Season with salt and pepper. Makes 6 servings.

## CORN ON THE COB

Remove husks and silks from 8 ears of corn. Cook, covered, in enough boiling lightly salted water to cover 5 to 7 minutes or until tender. Spread with butter, mayonnaise, pesto, or creamy herbed cheese. If desired, sprinkle with salt and pepper, grated Cotija cheese, finely shredded Parmesan cheese, seafood seasoning, or chopped fresh herbs. Makes 8 ears.

## SKILLET SUCCOTASH

In a 10-inch skillet cook 2 or 3 strips bacon, chopped, with ½ cup chopped onion and 1 clove garlic, minced, over medium heat until bacon is crisp, stirring occasionally. Add 2 cups fresh or frozen corn kernels and 1 cup frozen edamame; cook and stir 5 minutes or until tender. Add 1 cup halved cherry tomatoes, 1 Tbsp. chopped fresh dill, and salt and pepper to taste; heat through. Makes 6 servings.

## COMPOUND BUTTER FOR VEGGIES

Combine ½ cup softened butter with 2 tsp. each chopped fresh thyme and oregano OR 1 tsp. lime zest, ½ tsp. salt, and ¼ tsp. ground chipotle chile pepper OR 2 tsp. chopped fresh chives and 1½ to 2 tsp. Roasted Garlic (*p. 24*) until combined. Spoon onto a sheet of plastic wrap. Wrap butter and twist ends to make a log. Chill 1 to 24 hours. Toss with steamed vegetables. Makes ½ cup butter.

## WALNUT-ONION GREEN BEANS

In a 10-inch skillet cook 3 cups fresh green beans, trimmed and cut into 1- to 2-inch pieces; 1½ cups chopped sweet onion; ⅓ cup broken walnuts; ½ tsp. salt; and ¼ tsp. black pepper in 1 Tbsp. each olive oil and butter over medium heat 15 minutes or until beans are crisp-tender, stirring occasionally. Makes 6 servings.

## RISOTTO

**START TO FINISH** 40 minutes

½ cup chopped onion
2 cloves garlic, minced
2 Tbsp. olive oil
1 cup uncooked Arborio rice
2 14.5-oz. cans reduced-sodium chicken broth (3½ cups)
¼ cup grated Parmesan cheese (1 oz.)
Lemon zest (optional)

**SUBSTITUTE ½ CUP WHITE WINE** for ½ cup of the chicken broth. Gently heat the wine separately and stir it into the rice as the first ½ cup of liquid.

**TOASTING = CREAMY**
Cook the rice in the oil with the onion and garlic in saucepan until rice is lightly browned. Toasted rice absorbs broth more evenly as it's cooked and stirred than untoasted rice, resulting in the creamiest risotto.

**1.** In a 3-qt. saucepan cook onion and garlic in hot oil over medium heat 3 to 5 minutes or until onion is tender, stirring occasionally. Add the rice; cook 3 to 5 minutes or until rice is golden brown, stirring often.
**2.** Meanwhile, in a 1½-qt. saucepan bring broth to boiling; reduce heat. Cover and keep broth simmering. Carefully stir ½ cup of the broth into the rice mixture. Cook over medium heat until liquid is absorbed, stirring frequently. Continue adding broth, ½ cup at a time, stirring frequently until the broth is absorbed. Rice should be tender and creamy. (This should take 20 to 25 minutes total.)
**3.** Stir in cheese; heat through. If desired, sprinkle with lemon zest. Serve immediately. **Makes 6 servings (½ cup each).**

**EACH SERVING** *171 cal., 5 g fat (1 g sat. fat), 3 mg chol., 368 mg sodium, 26 g carb., 1 g fiber, 0 g sugars, 5 g pro.*

CUSTOMIZE IT

PICK THE INGREDIENTS
TO CREATE A RECIPE
THAT'S ALL YOUR OWN.

## RICE PILAF

**HANDS-ON TIME** 15 minutes
**COOK** 15 minutes

RICE or GRAIN
2   cloves garlic, minced
2   Tbsp. butter
1   14.5-oz. can reduced-sodium
    chicken broth
¼   cup DRIED FRUIT (optional)
¼   cup CHOPPED VEGETABLE
¼   cup LIQUID
1   to 2 tsp. FRESH HERB or
    ¼ tsp. DRIED HERB
½   cup STIR-IN

**1.** In a 2-qt. saucepan cook and
stir the uncooked desired RICE
or GRAIN and garlic in hot butter
3 minutes. Carefully stir in chicken
broth, DRIED FRUIT (if desired),
CHOPPED VEGETABLE, LIQUID,
and DRIED HERB (if using). Bring
mixture to boiling; reduce heat.
Simmer, covered, for specified time
*(below)* or until rice is tender and
liquid is absorbed. Add STIR-IN
and FRESH HERB (if using). **Makes
4 servings (about ⅔ cup each).**

# MIX & MATCH INGREDIENTS

**RICE OR GRAIN**
*(Pick 1)*
- ¾ cup long grain
  rice or basmati
  rice (Cook 15 to
  20 minutes.)
- ½ cup wild rice
  + ⅓ cup regular
  barley (Cook
  45 to 50 minutes.)

**DRIED FRUIT** *(Pick 1)*
- Chopped
  apricots
- Cherries
- Cranberries
- Raisins

**CHOPPED
VEGETABLE** *(Pick 1)*
- Carrots
- Celery
- Mushrooms
- Sweet peppers
- Zucchini

**LIQUID** *(Pick 1)*
- Apple juice
- Dry white wine
- Water

**FRESH OR
DRIED HERB** *(Pick 1)*
- Basil
- Oregano
- Thyme

**STIR-IN** *(Pick 1 or 2)*
- Crumbled crisp-
  cooked bacon
- Sliced green
  onions
- Toasted chopped
  almonds
- Toasted chopped
  pecans
- Toasted pine nuts
- Toasted chopped
  walnuts

// EVERYDAY SIDES //

MEXICAN GREEN RICE

MEXICAN RED RICE

## MEXICAN RED RICE

**HANDS-ON TIME** 25 minutes
**COOK** 20 minutes

1   Tbsp. vegetable oil
½   cup chopped onion
2   cloves garlic, minced
1   tsp. ground ancho chile pepper
¼   tsp. kosher salt
1   cup uncooked long grain rice
1   14.5-oz. can reduced-sodium chicken broth or vegetable broth
¾   cup Roasted Salsa Roja or purchased red salsa
¼   cup water
½   cup finely chopped fresh cilantro

**1.** In a 2-qt. saucepan heat oil over medium-high heat. Add onion, garlic, ancho chile pepper, and salt; cook 2 minutes. Stir in rice;

cook and stir 1 minute. Add broth, Roasted Salsa Roja, and the water. Bring to boiling; reduce heat. Simmer, covered, about 20 minutes or until rice is tender.

**2.** Remove pan from heat. Remove lid. Cover pan with a clean kitchen towel; replace lid. Let stand 5 minutes. Remove lid and towel. Add cilantro; fluff rice with a fork.

**Makes 6 servings (⅔ cup each).**
**EACH SERVING** *166 cal., 4 g fat (0 g sat. fat), 0 mg chol., 323 mg sodium, 29 g carb., 1 g fiber, 2 g sugars, 4 g pro.*

**ROASTED SALSA ROJA** Preheat broiler. In a 15×10-inch baking pan combine 3 tomatoes (about 1½ lb.), quartered and cored; ⅓ cup chopped onion; 5 cloves garlic, peeled; and 1 jalapeño

chile pepper, stemmed, halved, and seeded (tip, p. 22). Toss with 2 to 3 Tbsp. vegetable oil; spread in pan. Broil 5 to 6 inches from heat 14 minutes or until vegetables char slightly, turning once halfway through broiling. Cool 10 minutes. Transfer to food processor; pulse until coarsely chopped. Add 1 cup chopped fresh cilantro, ¼ cup lime juice, and ½ tsp. sugar; pulse until desired consistency. Season to taste with salt. Serve immediately or cover and chill up to 3 days.

**CHANGE IT UP**
*Turn Mexican Red Rice green. Substitute purchased green salsa for Roasted Salsa Roja.*

# REFRIED BEANS

**HANDS-ON TIME** 20 minutes
**STAND** 1 hour
**COOK** 2 hours 40 minutes

- 8 oz. dried pinto beans (about 1¼ cups)
- 8 cups water
- ½ tsp. salt
- 2 Tbsp. bacon drippings or olive oil
- 2 cloves garlic, minced
  Black pepper

**1.** Rinse beans. In a 3- or 4-qt. saucepan combine beans and 4 cups of the water. Bring to boiling; reduce heat. Simmer, covered, 2 minutes. Remove from heat. Cover and let stand 1 hour. (Or place beans in water in pan. Cover and let soak in a cool place overnight.) Drain and rinse beans.
**2.** In the same saucepan combine beans, remaining 4 cups fresh water, and the salt. Bring to boiling; reduce heat. Simmer, covered, 2½ to 3 hours or until beans are very tender. Drain beans, reserving liquid.

**3.** In a 10-inch heavy skillet heat bacon drippings. Stir in garlic. Add beans; mash thoroughly with a potato masher. Stir in enough of the cooking liquid (about ¼ cup) to make a pastelike mixture. Cook, uncovered, over low heat 8 to 10 minutes or until thick, stirring often. Season to taste with additional salt and the pepper.
**Makes 4 servings (½ cup each).**
**EACH SERVING** *257 cal., 7 g fat (3 g sat. fat), 6 mg chol., 321 mg sodium, 36 g carb., 9 g fiber, 1 g sugars, 12 g pro.*

COLLARD GREENS WITH BACON

## COLLARD GREENS WITH BACON

**HANDS-ON TIME** 30 minutes
**COOK** 1 hour

1   lb. collard greens
3   slices bacon, chopped
2   cups water
1   8- to 10-oz. smoked pork hock
½   cup chopped onion
½   cup chopped green sweet pepper
1   tsp. sugar
¼   tsp. salt
⅛   tsp. cayenne pepper
4   cloves garlic, minced
    Red wine vinegar (optional)
    Crushed red pepper (optional)

**1.** Wash greens in cold water; drain well. Remove and discard stems. Coarsely chop leaves to measure 6 cups lightly packed leaves.
**2.** In a 3-qt. saucepan cook bacon until crisp. Remove bacon, reserving drippings in saucepan. Drain bacon on paper towels. Add next eight ingredients (through garlic) to saucepan. Bring to boiling; add greens. Reduce heat. Simmer, covered, 1 hour to 1¼ hours or until greens are tender. Remove from heat. Remove pork hock. Cover greens; keep warm.
**3.** When cool enough to handle, cut meat off pork hock. Chop or shred meat; discard bone and fat. Return meat to greens mixture along with cooked bacon; heat through. Serve with a slotted spoon. If desired, drizzle each serving with a little vinegar and/or sprinkle with crushed red pepper. **Makes 6 servings (⅔ cup each).**
**EACH SERVING** 176 cal., 13 g fat (4 g sat. fat), 34 mg chol., 312 mg sodium, 6 g carb., 2 g fiber, 2 g sugars, 9 g pro.

SESAME GREEN BEANS WITH TERIYAKI GLAZE

## SESAME GREEN BEANS WITH TERIYAKI GLAZE

**START TO FINISH** 30 minutes

1½  lb. green beans, trimmed
1   cup julienned carrots (info, p. 13) or packaged fresh julienned carrots
¾   cup chicken broth
¼   cup soy sauce
¼   cup hoisin sauce
1   Tbsp. cornstarch
1   Tbsp. toasted sesame oil (tip, p. 186)
3   Tbsp. canola oil
2   cups sliced stemmed fresh shiitake mushrooms
1   Tbsp. grated fresh ginger
4   cloves garlic, minced
2   Tbsp. chopped fresh basil
1   Tbsp. toasted sesame seeds

**1.** Bring a large pot of salted water to boiling. Add green beans; return to boiling. Boil 4 minutes. Add carrots; boil 1 minute more. Drain well.
**2.** In a small bowl stir together next five ingredients (through sesame oil).
**3.** In a large wok or 12-inch nonstick skillet heat canola oil over medium-high heat. Add mushrooms, ginger, and garlic; cook and stir about 3 minutes or until mushrooms are tender. Stir broth mixture and add to skillet; cook and stir about 1 minute or until just thickened and bubbly. Stir in green beans and carrots and the 2 Tbsp. basil; heat through.
**4.** To serve, sprinkle with toasted sesame seeds and garnish with additional fresh basil. **Makes 8 servings (about 1 cup each).**
**EACH SERVING** 131 cal., 8 g fat (1 g sat. fat), 1 mg chol., 741 mg sodium, 14 g carb., 3 g fiber, 7 g sugars, 3 g pro.

**SIDECAR**
Creamy polenta as
a side dish pairs well with
roasts, braised meats,
and roasted vegetables.
Or spoon meaty sauces,
such as Bolognese
(p. 222), over top.

POLENTA

## POLENTA

**HANDS-ON TIME** 15 minutes
**COOK** 25 minutes

1   cup coarse-ground yellow
    cornmeal*
1   cup cold water
1   tsp. salt

»

THE WATER
and salt can be
replaced with
chicken broth for
extra richness.

**1.** In a 3-qt. saucepan bring
2½ cups water* to boiling.
Meanwhile, in a bowl stir together
cornmeal, the 1 cup cold water, and
the salt.
**2.** Slowly add cornmeal mixture to
boiling water, stirring constantly.
Cook and stir until mixture returns
to boiling. Reduce heat to medium-
low. Cook 25 to 30 minutes or until
mixture is very thick and tender,
stirring frequently and adjusting
heat as needed to maintain a slow
boil. Spoon soft polenta into bowls.
**Makes 6 servings (½ cup each).**
**\*NOTE** To use regular cornmeal,
increase water in saucepan
to 2¾ cups; cook and stir 10 to
15 minutes after mixture boils in
Step 2.
**EACH SERVING** 85 cal., 0 g fat,
0 mg chol., 390 mg sodium, 18 g carb.,
1 g fiber, 0 g sugars, 2 g pro.

### GET-TOGETHER

*Make polenta a company dish
by stirring in ½ cup shredded
Fontina cheese and 2 Tbsp.
chopped fresh basil or parsley.*

## BAKED CHEESE GRITS

**HANDS-ON TIME** 20 minutes
**BAKE** 25 minutes at 325°F
**STAND** 5 minutes

2   cups chicken broth
½   cup quick-cooking grits
1   egg, lightly beaten
1   cup shredded cheddar cheese
    (4 oz.)
2   Tbsp. sliced green onion
1   Tbsp. butter
½   cup chopped fresh tomato or
    halved cherry tomatoes
    (optional)

**1.** Preheat oven to 325°F. In a 2-qt.
saucepan bring broth to boiling.
Slowly add grits, stirring constantly.
Gradually stir about ½ cup of the
hot mixture into the egg. Return
egg mixture to saucepan and stir
to combine. Remove saucepan
from heat. Stir in cheese, green
onion, and butter until cheese and
butter melt.
**2.** Pour grits mixture into an
ungreased 1-qt. casserole dish.
If desired, top with additional
cheese. Bake, uncovered, 25 to
30 minutes or until a knife inserted
near the center comes out clean.
Let stand 5 minutes before serving.
If desired, top with tomato and
additional sliced green onion.
**Makes 4 servings (⅔ cup each).**
**EACH SERVING** 238 cal., 14 g fat
(8 g sat. fat), 91 mg chol., 694 mg
sodium, 17 g carb., 0 g fiber,
1 g sugars, 11 g pro.

BAKED
CHEESE
GRITS

# SLOW COOKER

**TEST KITCHEN**

**MAKE-AHEAD RECIPE**

SWEDISH
MEATBALL
PASTA POT

CABBAGE
ROLL
SOUP

## SWEDISH MEATBALL PASTA POT

**HANDS-ON TIME** 20 minutes
**SLOW COOK** 6 to 7 hours (low) or 3 to 3½ hours (high) + 20 minutes (high)

1    32-oz. carton reduced-sodium beef broth
1    Tbsp. Worcestershire sauce
¼    tsp. ground nutmeg
¼    tsp. ground allspice
½    recipe Beef-Pork Meatballs*
3    Tbsp. all-purpose flour
3    Tbsp. butter, softened
2    cups dried mini farfalle pasta
½    cup sour cream
      Salt and black pepper
      Snipped fresh dill

**1.** In a 3½- or 4-qt. slow cooker stir together the first four ingredients (through allspice). Add meatballs. Cover and cook on low 6 to 7 hours or on high 3 to 3½ hours.
**2.** In a bowl stir together flour and butter to make a paste; stir into broth mixture in cooker. Stir in pasta. If using low, turn cooker to high. Cover and cook 20 to 30 minutes or until pasta is tender. Stir in sour cream. Season to taste with salt and pepper. Sprinkle with dill. **Makes 6 servings (1¼ cups each).**
**BEEF-PORK MEATBALLS**
Preheat oven to 375°F. Lightly coat two 15×10-inch baking pans with nonstick cooking spray. In a bowl lightly beat 2 eggs. Stir in ½ cup each fine dry bread crumbs and finely chopped onion, ¼ cup milk, and ½ tsp. each salt and black pepper. Add 1 lb. each ground beef and ground pork; mix well. Shape mixture into 1-inch meatballs. Place in the prepared pans. Bake 12 to 15 minutes or until done (160°F). Drain fat.
**\*NOTE** Freeze leftover meatballs for later use (tip, p. 221).
**EACH SERVING** *464 cal., 24 g fat (11 g sat. fat), 108 mg chol., 728 mg sodium, 37 g carb., 2 g fiber, 3 g sugars, 23 g pro.*

## CABBAGE ROLL SOUP

**HANDS-ON TIME** 20 minutes
**SLOW COOK** 7 to 8 hours (low) or 3½ to 4 hours (high) + 30 minutes

4    cups ½-inch slices cabbage
12   oz. lean ground beef
1    14.5-oz. can reduced-sodium beef broth
1    cup chopped onion
2    Tbsp. Worcestershire sauce
2    cloves garlic, minced
½    tsp. salt
¼    tsp. ground allspice
1    8.8-oz. pouch cooked white or brown rice
1    14.5-oz. can fire-roasted diced tomatoes, undrained
1    cup hot-style vegetable juice
2    Tbsp. tomato paste

**1.** In a 3½- or 4-qt. slow cooker combine the first eight ingredients (through allspice), stirring to break up meat. Cover and cook on low 7 to 8 hours or high 3½ to 4 hours.
**2.** Knead rice pouch to break up rice. Stir rice and the remaining ingredients into cabbage mixture. Cover and cook 30 minutes more. **Makes 6 servings (1½ cups each).**
**EACH SERVING** *218 cal., 7 g fat (2 g sat. fat), 37 mg chol., 690 mg sodium, 25 g carb., 3 g fiber, 8 g sugars, 15 g pro.*

## KNOW YOUR COOKER

**SIZE IT RIGHT** Use the correct-size cooker for each recipe. (If you're not sure of size, fill your cooker with water, 1 qt. at a time, to determine how much it can hold.) Underfilled or overfilled cookers throw off cooking times. Because of the location of the heating elements, the slow cooker should be at least half full to cook correctly. Stick to the cook times, follow doneness cues, and resist the urge to pop the lid for a peek (tip, *p. 328*).

**PREP TIPS** To make your mornings easier, cut up veggies and do other prep work the night before; refrigerate in separate containers. Browning the meat before slow cooking makes all the difference in flavor and texture—but for food safety reasons, that's one task you shouldn't do the night before. (Many new slow cookers now have a brown-sauté setting, so you can bypass stove-top browning.) When filling the cooker, layer the ingredients as directed so each item cooks at the correct rate.

## PEPPERY ITALIAN BEEF SANDWICHES

**HANDS-ON TIME** 30 minutes
**SLOW COOK** 10 to 12 hours (low) or 5 to 6 hours (high)

1   2½- to 3-lb. boneless beef chuck pot roast, trimmed of fat
1   tsp. garlic-pepper seasoning
1   Tbsp. vegetable oil
1   14.5-oz. can reduced-sodium beef broth
1   0.5 to 0.75-oz. envelope Italian dry salad dressing mix
2   tsp. dried Italian seasoning
1   12- to 16-oz. jar pepperoncini salad peppers, drained and stems removed
8   hoagie buns or kaiser rolls, split and toasted
2   cups shredded mozzarella cheese (8 oz.)
    Chopped red sweet pepper (optional)

**1.** If necessary, cut meat to fit into a 3½- or 4-qt. slow cooker. Sprinkle meat with garlic-pepper seasoning; rub in with your fingers. In a 4-qt. Dutch oven heat oil over medium heat. Cook meat in hot oil until browned on all sides.
**2.** Place meat in slow cooker. In a bowl whisk together broth, salad dressing mix, and Italian seasoning. Pour over meat. Top with pepperoncini peppers.

Cover; cook on low 10 to 12 hours or high 5 to 6 hours.
**3.** Transfer meat to a cutting board. Shred beef using two forks. Strain cooking liquid, reserving peppers. Skim fat from cooking liquid. Return beef and peppers to slow cooker. Add enough cooking liquid to moisten meat.
**4.** Use a slotted spoon to spoon shredded meat and peppers into buns; top with cheese and, if desired, sweet pepper. **Makes 8 sandwiches.**

**EACH SANDWICH** *480 cal., 14 g fat (5 g sat. fat), 110 mg chol., 1,308 mg sodium, 39 g carb., 2 g fiber, 3 g sugars, 47 g pro.*

## KEEP A LID ON IT

That slow cooker lid is there for a reason—it maintains the necessary heat level to evenly cook food in the recommended time range. When you pop the top to look at your food, the heat escapes. You may need to add more time to the total if you open the lid frequently. So until you need to check doneness, keep that lid in place.

## CARNITAS TACOS

**HANDS-ON TIME** 20 minutes
**SLOW COOK** 8 to 10 hours (low) or
4 to 5 hours (high)

| | |
|---|---|
| 1 | 2½- to 3-lb. boneless pork shoulder roast, trimmed of fat |
| 1 | Tbsp. ground cumin |
| 1½ | tsp. kosher salt |
| 1 | tsp. dried Mexican oregano or regular oregano, crushed |
| ¼ | to ½ tsp. cayenne pepper |
| ½ | cup chopped white onion |
| 1 | orange, quartered |
| 2 | Tbsp. vegetable oil |
| 18 | 6-inch corn tortillas, warmed |

Toppers: lime wedges, pickled jalapeños, pico de gallo, pineapple bits, shredded cabbage, sliced radishes

**1.** Cut meat into three pieces and place in a 3½- or 4-qt. slow cooker. Sprinkle with cumin, salt, oregano, and cayenne; toss to coat. Add onion. Squeeze orange pieces over top; add orange pieces to cooker.
**2.** Cover and cook on low 8 to 10 hours or high 4 to 5 hours. Transfer meat to a cutting board. Shred meat using two forks.
**3.** In a 12-inch skillet heat oil over medium-high heat. Add half of the meat, pressing it into an even layer. Cook about 1 minute or until crisp and browned. Turn meat and brown 1 minute on the other side; remove from skillet. Repeat with the remaining meat. Serve carnitas on tortillas with desired toppers. **Makes 9 servings (2 tacos each).**
**EACH SERVING** *284 cal., 11 g fat (3 g sat. fat), 75 mg chol., 417 mg sodium, 19 g carb., 3 g fiber, 4 g sugars, 26 g pro.*

**FRYING**
the cooked meat is a traditional step. Slow-roasted pork pieces are crisp-cooked in a skillet in oil or lard to give each piece a well-browned crust. This adds exceptional flavor and texture.

# SLOW-SIMMERED SPAGHETTI SAUCE

**HANDS-ON TIME** 25 minutes
**SLOW COOK** 6 to 8 hours (low) or
3 to 4 hours (high)

- 1   lb. bulk Italian sausage or ground beef
- 1   cup chopped onion
- 2   cloves garlic, minced
- 2   14.5-oz. cans petite diced tomatoes, undrained
- 3   cups sliced fresh mushrooms
- 1   cup chopped green sweet pepper
- 1   6-oz. can tomato paste
- 1   bay leaf
- 2   tsp. dried Italian seasoning, crushed
- ¼   tsp. black pepper
- 16  oz. dried spaghetti, cooked and drained
     Parmesan cheese (optional)

**1.** In a 10-inch skillet cook the sausage, onion, and garlic over medium heat until meat is browned and onion is tender. Drain off fat.

**2.** In a 3½- or 4-qt. slow cooker stir together the next seven ingredients (through black pepper). Stir in meat mixture. Cover and cook on low 6 to 8 hours or high 3 to 4 hours.

**3.** Discard bay leaf. Season to taste with *salt* and additional black pepper. Serve meat mixture over hot cooked spaghetti. If desired, sprinkle with Parmesan cheese.

**Makes 8 servings (¾ cup sauce + 1 cup spaghetti each).**

**EACH SERVING** *456 cal., 10 g fat (6 g sat. fat), 43 mg chol., 824 mg sodium, 57 g carb., 5 g fiber, 9 g sugars, 18 g pro.*

**EXTRA RICHNESS**
For a luscious creamy sauce—similar to Bolognese *(p. 222)*—stir ½ cup heavy cream into the sauce just before serving.

# BUTTERNUT SQUASH SHAKSHUKA

**SHAKSHUKA,** a Tunisian and Israeli specialty, features a tomato-based sauce with soft-poached eggs nestled on top. Our version adds a hint of sweetness with cubed butternut squash and savory saltiness with the feta and parsley topping.

**HANDS-ON TIME** 25 minutes
**SLOW COOK** 11 to 12 hours (low) or 5½ to 6 hours (high) + 25 to 35 minutes (high)

¾ cup chopped red sweet pepper
1 small onion, halved and thinly sliced
1 medium fresh jalapeño chile pepper, seeded and finely chopped (tip, p. 22)
2 cloves garlic, minced
1 tsp. dried oregano, crushed
1 tsp. ground cumin
½ tsp. salt
½ tsp. black pepper
1 2-lb. butternut squash, peeled, seeded, and chopped (6 cups)
1 15-oz. can or ½ of a 28-oz. can crushed tomatoes
1 8-oz. can tomato sauce
6 eggs
¾ cup crumbled feta cheese (3 oz.)
2 Tbsp. snipped fresh parsley
 Pita bread rounds, warmed

**1.** In a 3½- or 4-qt. slow cooker combine first eight ingredients (through black pepper). Stir in squash, crushed tomatoes, and tomato sauce.

**2.** Cover and cook on low 11 to 12 hours or high 5½ to 6 hours. If using low heat, turn to high. Make an indentation in squash mixture and slip an egg into indentation. Repeat with remaining eggs. Cover and cook 25 to 35 minutes more or until eggs are cooked to desired doneness.
**3.** Top with cheese and parsley. Serve with pita bread. **Makes 6 servings (1 cup squash mixture + 1 egg each).**
**PER SERVING** *315 cal., 10 g fat (5 g sat. fat), 203 mg chol., 917 mg sodium, 45 g carb., 6 g fiber, 10 g sugars, 15 g pro.*

BARBECUE PORK RIBS

SPEED IT UP
For even quicker prep, omit the last 10 ingredients and pour 1¼ cups bottled barbecue sauce over ribs in cooker. Warm 1 cup additional sauce to serve with cooked ribs.

# BARBECUE PORK RIBS

**HANDS-ON TIME** 15 minutes
**SLOW COOK** 7 to 8 hours (low) or 3½ to 4 hours (high)

2 large onions, sliced and separated into rings
2½ to 3 lb. boneless pork country-style ribs
 Salt and black pepper
1½ cups vegetable juice
⅓ cup tomato paste
¼ cup molasses
3 Tbsp. cider vinegar
1 Tbsp. Worcestershire sauce
1 tsp. dry mustard
½ tsp. dried thyme, crushed
½ tsp. dried rosemary, crushed
¼ tsp. salt
¼ tsp. black pepper

**1.** Place onions in a 3½- or 4-qt. slow cooker. Trim fat from meat. Place ribs on top of onions. Sprinkle lightly with salt and pepper. In a bowl stir together the remaining ingredients. Reserve 1 cup of the juice mixture; cover and chill. Pour remaining juice mixture over ribs. Cover and cook on low 7 to 8 hours or high 3½ to 4 hours.
**2.** Before serving, for sauce, in a 1- or 1½- saucepan bring reserved juice mixture to boiling; reduce heat. Simmer, uncovered, about 10 minutes or until desired thickness.
**3.** Using a slotted spoon, transfer ribs and onions to a platter; discard cooking liquid. Serve with sauce. **Makes 6 servings (5 to 6 oz. cooked meat each).**
**EACH SERVING** *439 cal., 21 g fat (4 g sat. fat), 139 mg chol., 462 mg sodium, 21 g carb., 2 g fiber, 13 g sugars, 39 g pro.*

BUTTERNUT SQUASH SHAKSHUKA

## CUSTOMIZE IT

PICK THE INGREDIENTS TO CREATE A RECIPE THAT'S ALL YOUR OWN.

## FIRESIDE BEEF STEW

**HANDS-ON TIME** 25 minutes
**SLOW COOK** 8 to 10 hours (low) or 4 to 5 hours (high) + 15 minutes (high)

1½  lb. MEAT
2½  cups ROOT VEGETABLES
1    cup ONIONS
2    cloves garlic, minced
1    14.5-oz. can reduced-sodium beef broth
1    8-oz. can tomato sauce
2    Tbsp. Worcestershire sauce
1    tsp. dry mustard
     PEPPER
     OTHER SEASONING
2    Tbsp. cold water
4    tsp. cornstarch
1½  cups FROZEN VEGETABLES

**1.** Trim fat from MEAT. Cut meat into 1-inch pieces. Place meat in a 3½- or 4-qt. slow cooker. Add ROOT VEGETABLES, ONIONS, and garlic. Stir in the next six ingredients (through OTHER SEASONING).
**2.** Cover and cook on low 8 to 10 hours or high 4 to 5 hours.
**3.** If using low, turn to high. In a small bowl stir together cold water and cornstarch. Stir cornstarch mixture and FROZEN VEGETABLES into mixture in cooker. Cover and cook about 15 minutes more or until thickened. **Makes 6 servings (1⅓ cups each).**

## MIX & MATCH INGREDIENTS

**MEAT** (Pick 1)
- Boneless beef chuck pot roast
- Beef stew meat
- Boneless pork shoulder roast
- Lean boneless lamb

**ROOT VEGETABLES** (Pick 1–3)
- Butternut squash, peeled and cut into 1½-inch pieces
- Red-skin or russet potatoes, cut into 1-inch pieces
- Peeled parsnips or carrots, cut into 1-inch pieces
- Peeled turnips, cut into 1-inch pieces

**ONION** (Pick 1)
- Small onions, cut into wedges
- Frozen small whole onions
- Shallot wedges
- Sliced leeks
- Sliced fennel

**PEPPER** (Pick 1)
- ¼ tsp. black pepper
- 1 tsp. lemon-pepper seasoning
- 1 to 2 tsp. Montreal steak seasoning
- ⅛ tsp. crushed red pepper or cayenne pepper

**OTHER SEASONING** (Pick 1)
- ⅛ tsp. ground allspice
- ⅛ tsp. ground cinnamon
- ½ tsp. ground coriander
- ½ to 1 tsp. ground cumin or garlic powder
- 1 to 2 tsp. dried Italian seasoning

**FROZEN VEGETABLES** (Pick 1)
- Frozen cut green beans or one 9-oz. pkg. frozen Italian green beans
- Frozen whole kernel corn
- Frozen mixed vegetables
- Frozen sweet pepper and onion stir-fry vegetables

# MAKE-AND-FREEZE SIMMER SAUCES—BALSAMIC BBQ, RED CURRY, AND TACO VERDE—YIELD THREE PORTIONS TO TUCK AWAY AND PULL OUT ON BUSY DAYS. JUST TOSS THE SAUCE IN THE SLOW COOKER WITH MEAT OR VEGGIES FOR DELICIOUS DINNER POSSIBILITIES.

**BALSAMIC BBQ PULLED PORK**

**BALSAMIC BBQ PULLED BEEF**

**RED CURRY CHICKEN**

## BALSAMIC BBQ SIMMER SAUCE

**HANDS-ON TIME** 15 minutes

3   cups ketchup
1½  cups apple cider
½   cup balsamic vinegar
½   cup molasses
¼   cup honey
4   tsp. onion powder
4   tsp. chili powder
2   tsp. garlic powder
1   tsp. black pepper

**1.** In a bowl whisk together all ingredients. Divide sauce into three 1¾-cup portions; place in airtight containers. Refrigerate up to 3 days or freeze up to 2 months. To use frozen portions, thaw in refrigerator overnight. **Makes about 5 cups.**

**PER 2 TBSP.** *43 cal., 0 g fat, 0 mg chol., 166 mg sodium, 11 g carb., 0 g fiber, 10 g sugars, 0 g pro.*

### BALSAMIC BBQ PULLED PORK

Trim fat from one 2- to 2½-lb. boneless pork shoulder roast. Place meat in a 3½- or 4-qt. slow cooker, cutting to fit if necessary. Add one portion Balsamic BBQ Simmer Sauce. Cover; cook on low 8 to 10 hours or high 4 to 5 hours. Remove meat; shred using two forks. Skim fat from sauce; stir in meat. If desired, serve on hot french fries with shredded cheese and snipped chives. **Makes 8 servings (½ cup each).**

**PER SERVING** *223 cal., 6 g fat (2 g sat. fat), 68 mg chol., 364 mg sodium, 20 g carb., 0 g fiber, 17 g sugars, 22 g pro.*

### BALSAMIC BBQ PULLED BEEF

Trim fat from one 2- to 2½-lb. boneless beef chuck pot roast. Place meat in a 3½- or 4-qt. slow cooker, cutting to fit if necessary. Add one portion Balsamic BBQ Simmer Sauce. Cover and cook on low 8 to 10 hours or high 4 to 5 hours. Remove meat; shred using two forks. Skim fat from sauce; stir in meat. If desired, serve on buns or rolls with desired condiments. **Makes 10 servings (½ cup each).**

**PER SERVING** *181 cal., 4 g fat (1 g sat. fat), 59 mg chol., 299 mg sodium, 16 g carb., 0 g fiber, 13 g sugars, 20 g pro.*

## RED CURRY SIMMER SAUCE

**HANDS-ON TIME** 20 minutes

2   14-oz. cans unsweetened coconut milk (not light)
1   cup chicken broth
¼   cup packed brown sugar
¼   cup peanut butter
¼   cup red curry paste (tip, p. 179)
¼   cup lime juice
3   Tbsp. quick-cooking tapioca, finely crushed
2   Tbsp. minced fresh ginger
6   cloves garlic, minced
½   tsp. salt

**1.** In a bowl whisk together all ingredients. Divide mixture into three 1¾-cup portions; place in airtight containers. Refrigerate up to 3 days or freeze up to 2 months. To use frozen portions, thaw in refrigerator overnight. **Makes about 5 cups.**

**PER 2 TBSP.** *52 cal., 4 g fat (3 g sat. fat), 0 mg chol., 98 mg sodium, 3 g carb., 0 g fiber, 2 g sugars, 1 g pro.*

VEGETARIAN RED CURRY    STEAK TACO VERDE    CHICKEN TACO VERDE

**RED CURRY CHICKEN** In a 3¹/₂- or 4-qt. slow cooker combine 1¹/₂ lb. chicken breast, cubed; 1¹/₂ cups strips red sweet peppers; and 1 cup chopped onion. Stir in one portion Red Curry Simmer Sauce. Cover; cook on low 3 hours or high 1¹/₂ hours. If desired, serve with rice noodles, fresh basil, and limes. **Makes 6 servings (1 cup each).**
**PER SERVING** *281 cal., 12 g fat (8 g sat. fat), 83 mg chol., 282 mg sodium, 13 g carb., 2 g fiber, 7 g sugars, 28 g pro.*

**VEGETARIAN RED CURRY** In a 3¹/₂- or 4-qt. slow cooker combine 5 cups cubed butternut squash; one 15-oz. can garbanzo beans (chickpeas), rinsed and drained; 1¹/₂ cups chopped red sweet peppers; and 1 cup chopped onion. Stir in one portion Red Curry Simmer Sauce. Cover; cook on low 6 to 7 hours or high 3 to 3¹/₂ hours. If desired, serve with rice, naan, and cilantro. **Makes 6 servings (1 cup each).**
**PER SERVING** *250 cal., 10 g fat (7 g sat. fat), 0 mg chol., 317 mg sodium, 35 g carb., 7 g fiber, 11 g sugars, 6 g pro.*

# TACO VERDE SIMMER SAUCE
**HANDS-ON TIME** 20 minutes

4    11-oz. cans tomatillos, drained
4    fresh poblano chile peppers, seeded and coarsely chopped (tip, *p. 22*)
2    small onions, quartered
4    tsp. ground cumin
2    tsp. ground coriander
4    cloves garlic, minced
¼    tsp. black pepper

**1.** In a food processor combine all ingredients. Cover; process until smooth. Divide mixture into three 2-cup portions; place in airtight containers. Refrigerate up to 5 days or freeze up to 2 months. To use frozen portions, thaw in refrigerator overnight. Stir well (mixture may appear separated). **Makes 6 cups.**
**PER 2 TBSP.** *10 cal., 0 g fat, 0 mg chol., 24 mg sodium, 2 g carb., 0 g fiber, 0 g sugars, 0 g pro.*

**STEAK TACO VERDE** Sprinkle a 1¹/₂- to 2-lb. beef flank steak with ¹/₂ tsp salt. Place meat in a 3¹/₂- or 4-qt. slow cooker. Add one portion Taco Verde Simmer Sauce. Cover; cook on low 7 to 8 hours or high 3¹/₂ to 4 hours. Remove meat; thinly slice. Stir meat into sauce. Stir in ¹/₂ cup chopped fresh cilantro. If desired, serve on chips with sliced radishes and queso fresco. **Makes 12 servings (¹/₂ cup each).**
**PER SERVING** *104 cal., 5 g fat (2 g sat. fat), 38 mg chol., 160 mg sodium, 2 g carb., 1 g fiber, 0 g sugars, 13 g pro.*

**CHICKEN TACO VERDE** Place 2 lb. skinless, boneless chicken thighs in a 3¹/₂- or 4-qt. slow cooker. Add one portion Taco Verde Simmer Sauce. Cover; cook on low 3¹/₂ to 4 hours or high 2¹/₄ hours. Remove chicken; shred using two forks. Stir chicken into sauce. Stir in ¹/₂ cup chopped fresh cilantro. If desired, serve in tortillas with sour cream, jalapeños, and onion. **Makes 12 servings (¹/₂ cup each).**
**PER SERVING** *105 cal., 4 g fat (1 g sat. fat), 71 mg chol., 104 mg sodium, 2 g carb., 1 g fiber, 0 g sugars, 15 g pro.*

**FREEZE IT RIGHT**

**STORE SAUCE** in freezer-safe containers that seal easily, resist cracking at low temps, and lock out moisture and vapors.

**CHOOSE THE RIGHT-SIZE** containers. If they are too big, excess air around the food can lead to freezer burn.

**USE EXPANDABLE** containers or leave headspace (about ¹/₂ inch) to allow for expansion.

## CHICKEN AND MUSHROOM PHO

**HANDS-ON TIME** 40 minutes
**SLOW COOK** 7 to 8 hours (low) or
3½ to 4 hours (high)

- 6 oz. fresh shiitake mushrooms
- 2 lb. bone-in chicken thighs, skinned
- 1 32-oz. carton reduced-sodium chicken broth
- 4 cups water
- 1 cup sliced onion
- ¼ oz. dried porcini mushrooms, rinsed
- 1 3-inch piece fresh ginger, peeled and sliced
- 2 Tbsp. fish sauce
- 1 Tbsp. packed brown sugar
- 1 Tbsp. coriander seeds, toasted
- 4 cloves garlic, sliced
- 4 whole cloves
- 5 oz. dried rice noodles
  Toppers: fresh cilantro, basil, and mint leaves; slivered red onion; thin carrot strips; thin red or yellow sweet pepper strips; thinly sliced fresh red or green chile peppers (tip, p. 22); and/or sriracha sauce
  Lime wedges (optional)

CHICKEN AND
MUSHROOM PHO

**THE PHO TRADITION** Pho (pronounced *fuh*) is Vietnamese comfort food—a noodle soup with a richly flavored broth and a heap of fresh herbs and veggies on top. We made the prep on our version easier, letting the slow cooker develop the broth's flavor low and slow. The squeeze of fresh lime juice before serving brings out all the complex flavors.

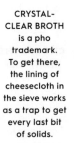

**CRYSTAL-CLEAR BROTH** is a pho trademark. To get there, the lining of cheesecloth in the sieve works as a trap to get every last bit of solids.

**1.** Remove and reserve shiitake stems. Thinly slice caps; cover and chill until needed.
**2.** In a 5- to 6-qt. slow cooker combine shiitake stems and the next 11 ingredients (through cloves). Cover and cook on low 7 to 8 hours or high 3½ to 4 hours.
**3.** Remove chicken from cooker. Strain broth mixture through a fine-mesh sieve lined with 100%-cotton cheesecloth; discard solids. Transfer broth to a 3- or 4-qt. saucepan. Bring to boiling. Stir in noodles and shiitake caps; cook 3 to 5 minutes or just until noodles are softened. Meanwhile, remove chicken from bones; discard bones. Coarsely shred chicken using two forks.
**4.** Ladle broth and noodle mixture into shallow bowls. Top with piles of

chicken. Serve with toppers on the side and, if desired, lime wedges.
**Makes 6 servings (1⅔ cups each).**
**EACH SERVING** *248 cal., 4 g fat (1 g sat. fat), 85 mg chol., 943 mg sodium, 29 g carb., 2 g fiber, 5 g sugars, 23 g pro.*

## CHEESY CAJUN CHICKEN AND PASTA

**HANDS-ON TIME** 20 minutes
**SLOW COOK** 6 hours (low) or 3 hours (high) + 20 minutes (high)
**STAND** 5 minutes

- 8 oz. skinless, boneless chicken thighs, cut into 1-inch pieces
- 1 tsp. Cajun seasoning
- ½ tsp. Louisiana hot sauce
- 8 oz. cooked andouille or other spicy sausage links, halved lengthwise and sliced
- 2½ cups water
- 1 medium red or yellow sweet pepper, cut into 1-inch pieces
- ½ cup chopped onion
- 4¾ cups dried farfalle pasta
- 6 oz. sliced American cheese, torn into bite-size pieces
- ½ cup shredded smoked Gouda or cheddar cheese (2 oz.)
- ¼ to ½ cup milk

**1.** In a 3½- or 4-qt. slow cooker combine chicken, Cajun seasoning, and hot sauce; toss to coat. Stir in the next four ingredients (through onion).
**2.** Cover and cook on low 6 hours or high 3 hours. If using low heat, turn

CHEESY CAJUN
CHICKEN AND PASTA

CHICKEN AND
SHRIMP JAMBALAYA

to high. Stir in pasta. Cover
and cook 10 minutes; stir. Cover
and cook 10 minutes more; stir
mixture again.

**3.** Turn off cooker. If possible,
remove crockery liner from cooker.
Top mixture with cheeses (do not
stir). Cover and let stand 5 minutes.
Stir in enough of the milk to reach
desired consistency.* **Makes
8 servings (1 cup each).**

**\*NOTE** If your slow cooker has
a warm setting, you can hold the
chicken and pasta up to 2 hours on
warm. If mixture begins to look dry,
stir in up to 1/2 cup additional milk to
reach desired consistency.

**PER SERVING** *382 cal., 16 g fat (7 g sat.
fat), 68 mg chol., 627 mg sodium, 37 g
carb., 2 g fiber, 5 g sugars, 21 g pro.*

# CHICKEN AND
# SHRIMP JAMBALAYA

**HANDS-ON TIME** 20 minutes
**SLOW COOK** 5 to 6 hours (low)
or 2½ to 3 hours (high) +
30 minutes (high)

1   lb. skinless, boneless chicken
    thighs, cut into 1-inch pieces
2   cups chopped onions
1   14.5-oz. can diced tomatoes,
    undrained
1   14.5-oz. can reduced-sodium
    chicken broth
1   cup thinly sliced celery
⅓   cup tomato paste
2   tsp. Cajun seasoning
2   cloves garlic, minced
2   8.8-oz. pkg. cooked rice
¾   cup chopped green, red, or
    yellow sweet pepper

8   oz. fresh or frozen peeled and
    deveined cooked shrimp (tails
    on if desired), thawed if frozen
2   Tbsp. chopped fresh parsley

**1.** In a 3½- or 4-qt. slow cooker
combine the first eight ingredients
(through garlic). Cover and cook
on low 5 to 6 hours or high 2½ to
3 hours.

**2.** If using low, turn to high. Stir
in rice and sweet pepper. Cover
and cook 30 minutes more or until
sweet pepper is tender.

**3.** Stir cooked shrimp and parsley
into chicken mixture. Season to
taste with *salt.* **Makes 8 servings
(1⅓ cups each).**

**EACH SERVING** *229 cal., 4 g fat (1 g
sat. fat), 99 mg chol., 572 mg sodium,
28 g carb., 3 g fiber, 5 g sugars, 21 g pro.*

# PRESSURE COOKERS

Pressure cookers cook food quicker and more evenly than any other method. This happens thanks to an airtight gasket seal that traps steam, creating intense pressure and heat inside the cooker. There are two main types of pressure cookers: **ELECTRIC** and **STOVE TOP**. You can also find electric multifunction cookers, such as Instant Pot, that cook both fast and slow.

## KNOW THE PIECES AND PARTS

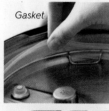

*Gasket*

*Pressure valve*

*Programmable settings*

*Removable pot liner*

## ELECTRIC

These models look like slow cookers (and often have that function as well). They are easy to set and require no further supervision. A timer tracks how long it takes to get up to pressure, cook the food, and depressurize.

**CHECK IT OFF** Take a quick look at all the parts of your pressure cooker. Make sure the gasket is soft, flexible, and crack-free. Snap it into place as directed in the manual. Make sure the pressure valve is free of debris and is in place.

**BROWNING = FLAVOR** Most models have a browning function. Add oil, set the browning function, and allow the pot to heat up. Brown the meat in batches to prevent the pot from cooling down and steaming the meat instead of browning it.

**EVERYTHING IN** Once the meat is browned, add the remaining ingredients (or as directed in your recipe). Lock the lid in place and adjust the pressure valve to the closed position. Select the setting and time. The digital display will indicate when the cooker has gotten up to pressure (usually about 15 or 20 minutes) and the actual cooking time has started to count down.

**LETTING OFF STEAM** When the cooking time is done, the cooker will automatically begin to depressurize, which is called "natural release." This takes about 15 minutes ("quick release" happens when you open the pressure valve to let the steam rush out—not recommended for liquid recipes such as soup). When the pressure has dropped,

the indicator will sink down and you will be able to open the lid. (Until then, the lid stays locked.) After 15 minutes of depressurizing, if the lid is still locked, you can open the pressure valve to let out any remaining steam.

**OPEN SESAME!** The food inside is still extremely hot, so steam will come out when you open the lid. Be careful—protect your arms and face so you don't get burned.

**CLEANING UP** After cooking, clean the removable parts in hot, soapy water, including the pot liner, lid, steam catcher, gasket, and any removable parts on the lid as described in the user's manual.

## STOVE TOP

This cooker looks like a 4-qt. saucepan with a lid that locks tight for safety. It is heated on the stove burner and requires that you monitor the pressure regulator during the cooking process.

**USE IT RIGHT** After browning the meat, adding the remaining ingredients, and locking the lid in place, set the pressure valve per the user's manual. Bring it up to pressure over medium-high heat (you'll know it's been reached when steam comes out of the valve). Reduce the heat to maintain a steady pressure (this will keep the pressure indicator up) for the full cooking time. Remove the cooker from the stove and let the pressure come down naturally (watch for the pressure indicator to drop).

# PAPRIKA SHORT RIBS

**HANDS-ON TIME** 30 minutes
**SLOW COOK** 10 to 12 hours (low) or
5 to 6 hours (high)
**OR**
**PRESSURE COOK** 30 minutes
**PRESSURE RELEASE** 15 minutes

| | |
|---|---|
| 8 | bone-in beef short ribs (3¾ to 4½ lb. total), trimmed |
| 1 | Tbsp. paprika |
| 2 | tsp. kosher salt |
| ¼ | tsp. black pepper |
| 2 | Tbsp. olive oil |
| ½ | cup reduced-sodium beef broth |
| ½ | cup dry red wine |
| 2 | Tbsp. soy sauce |
| 4 | cloves garlic, minced |
| 1 | tsp. dried thyme, crushed |
| 2 | Tbsp. tomato paste |
| 2 | Tbsp. prepared horseradish |
| 4 | cups hot cooked noodles |

## SLOW COOKER

**1.** Season ribs with paprika, salt, and pepper. In a 12-inch skillet brown meat in hot oil over medium-high heat or until well browned, turning occasionally (or use slow cooker browning function). Transfer to 6-qt. slow cooker. Add the next five ingredients (through dried thyme). Cover; cook on low 10 to 12 hours or high 5 to 6 hours.
**2.** Transfer ribs to a serving dish. Skim fat from cooking liquid. Whisk in tomato paste and horseradish. Serve with ribs and noodles. If desired, serve with *sour cream*.

## PRESSURE COOKER

**1.** Season the ribs with paprika, salt, and pepper. For a 6-qt. electric cooker, use sauté setting to brown ribs, half at a time, in hot oil. For a 6-qt. stove-top cooker, brown meat, half at a time, in hot oil in cooker. Return all meat to cooker. Add the next five ingredients (through dried thyme). Lock lid.

**2.** Set electric cooker on high pressure to cook 30 minutes. For stove-top cooker, bring up to pressure over medium-high heat according to manufacturer's directions; reduce heat enough to maintain steady (but not excessive) pressure. Cook 30 minutes. Remove from heat. Let stand to release pressure naturally, at least 15 minutes. Open lid carefully.
**3.** Continue as directed in Step 2 of Slow Cooker directions. **Makes 8 servings (1 short rib + ½ cup noodles + ¼ cup sauce each).**
**EACH SERVING** *631 cal., 41 g fat (17 g sat. fat), 172 mg chol., 760 mg sodium, 23 g carb., 2 g fiber, 1 g sugars, 39 g pro.*

## SEARING FOR FLAVOR

Searing (or browning) means quickly cooking all sides of the meat in a very hot skillet until the surface is a deep brown. This simple process, known as the Maillard reaction, transforms proteins and sugars on the meat's surface, resulting in deliciously complex flavor.

CHICKEN SHAWARMA

RED WINE AND ROOT VEGETABLE POT ROAST

directions; reduce heat enough to maintain steady (but not excessive) pressure. Cook 15 minutes. Remove from heat. Let stand to release pressure naturally, at least 15 minutes. Open lid carefully. Remove and slice chicken

**3.** Divide chicken among pitas. Using a slotted spoon, top chicken with pickled vegetables. Serve with lemon-yogurt sauce. **Makes 4 servings (1 filled pita each).**

**EACH SERVING** *485 cal., 18 g fat (3 g sat. fat), 135 mg chol., 776 mg sodium, 43 g carb., 2 g fiber , 8 g sugars, 36 g pro.*

# SHAWARMA IS A MIDDLE EASTERN DELICACY OF HEAVILY SPICED MEAT ROASTED ON A SPIT AND TUCKED INTO A WRAP OR SANDWICH. WE REWORKED THIS VERSION FOR THE SLOW COOKER.

## CHICKEN SHAWARMA

**HANDS-ON TIME** 25 minutes
**SLOW COOK** 2 hours (high)
**OR**
**PRESSURE COOK** 15 minutes
**PRESSURE RELEASE** 15 minutes

RAS EL HANOUT can be found in specialty spice stores. To make your own, in a bowl combine 1 tsp. paprika; ½ tsp. ground cumin; ¼ tsp. each ground cinnamon, ground coriander, ground ginger, black pepper, and ground turmeric; and ⅛ tsp. cayenne pepper.

»

| | |
|---|---|
| 1 | cup shredded carrots |
| ¼ | cup finely chopped red onion |
| ¼ | cup unseasoned rice vinegar |
| 2 | tsp. sugar |
| ½ | cup plain yogurt |
| 1 | Tbsp. lemon juice |
| ½ | tsp. dried dill |
| ½ | tsp. honey |
| 1¼ | lb. skinless, boneless chicken thighs |
| 1 | Tbsp. ras el hanout spice blend |
| 3 | Tbsp. olive oil |
| 1 | cup reduced-sodium chicken broth |
| 4 | pita bread rounds, warmed |

### SLOW COOKER

**1.** In a bowl combine the first four ingredients (through sugar). If desired, season with *salt* and *black pepper.* Cover and refrigerate. In a bowl whisk together yogurt, lemon juice, dill, and honey until smooth. Cover and refrigerate.

**2.** Rub chicken thighs with ras el hanout. If desired, season with *salt* and *black pepper.* In a 10-inch nonstick skillet heat oil over medium-high heat. Add chicken; cook 3 to 4 minutes or until browned. Turn; cook 2 minutes more. Place chicken in a 3½- or 4-qt. slow cooker. Add broth. Cover; cook on high 2 hours or until done (170°F). Remove; slice chicken. Divide chicken among pitas. Using a slotted spoon, top chicken with pickled vegetables. Serve with yogurt mixture.

### PRESSURE COOKER

**1.** Prepare as directed in Step 1 of Slow Cooker directions. Season chicken as directed in Step 2. For a 6-qt. electric cooker, use sauté setting to heat oil. Add chicken; cook 3 to 4 minutes or until browned. Turn; cook 2 minutes more. For stove-top cooker, brown chicken as directed using cooker in place of skillet. Add broth. Lock lid.

**2.** Set electric cooker on high pressure to cook 15 minutes. For a stove-top cooker, bring up to pressure over medium-high heat according to manufacturer's

# RED WINE AND ROOT VEGETABLE POT ROAST

**HANDS-ON TIME** 30 minutes
**SLOW COOK** 10 to 11 hours (low) or 5 to 5½ hours (high)
**OR**
**PRESSURE COOK** 40 minutes
**PRESSURE RELEASE** 15 minutes

| | |
|---|---|
| 2 | Tbsp. olive oil |
| 1 | 2- to 2½-lb. boneless beef chuck pot roast, trimmed |
| 2 | cloves garlic, minced |
| ¾ | cup dry red wine |
| 1 | lb. tiny new red potatoes |
| 4 | large carrots, cut into 1½-inch pieces |
| 2 | cups 1-inch pieces peeled rutabaga |
| 1 | cup 1-inch pieces celery |
| 2 | Tbsp. tomato paste |
| ¾ | cup reduced-sodium beef broth |
| 2 | Tbsp. quick-cooking tapioca, crushed |
| 1 | tsp. dried thyme, crushed |
| ½ | tsp. salt |
| ½ | tsp. black pepper |

### SLOW COOKER

**1.** In a 10-inch skillet heat oil over medium-high heat. Add meat; cook until browned on both sides. Transfer meat to a 6-qt. slow cooker. Add garlic to hot pan; cook and stir 1 minute. Add wine to the pan, stirring to scrape up any browned bits. Add wine mixture and the remaining ingredients to slow cooker. **2.** Cover and cook on low 10 to 11 hours or high 5 to 5½ hours. Using a slotted spoon, transfer meat and vegetables to a platter. Skim fat from cooking liquid. Season to taste with additional salt and pepper. Serve meat and vegetables with cooking liquid.

**PRESSURE COOKER**

**1.** If necessary, cut meat to fit into cooker. Omit tapioca. For a 6-qt. electric cooker, use sauté setting to heat oil. Add meat; cook until browned on both sides. Add the remaining ingredients (except tapioca). For a 6-qt. stove-top cooker, prepare as directed, using cooker in place of skillet. Lock lid. **2.** Set electric cooker on high pressure to cook 40 minutes. For stove-top cooker, bring up to pressure over medium-high heat according to manufacturer's directions; reduce heat enough to maintain steady (but not excessive) pressure. Cook 40 minutes. Remove from heat. Let stand to release pressure naturally, at least 15 minutes. Open lid carefully. **3.** Using a slotted spoon, transfer meat and vegetables to a platter. Skim fat from cooking liquid. Combine 2 Tbsp. each *cornstarch* and *cold water*; stir into cooking liquid. For electric cooker, heat to simmering on sauté setting; for stove-top cooker, bring to simmering over medium heat. Cook and stir until thickened and bubbly. Season to taste with additional salt and pepper. Serve meat and vegetables with thickened cooking liquid. **Makes 6 servings (3½ oz. cooked meat + 1 cup vegetables + ⅓ cup sauce each).**

**EACH SERVING** *382 cal., 11 g fat (3 g sat. fat), 98 mg chol., 471 mg sodium, 27 g carb., 5 g fiber, 7 g sugars, 37 g pro.*

# SOUTHERN TOT CASSEROLE

**HANDS-ON TIME** 15 minutes
**SLOW COOK** 2¾ to 3 hours (high)
**OR**
**PRESSURE COOK** 30 minutes
**PRESSURE RELEASE** 15 minutes

8   oz. cooked pork breakfast sausage links
1   Tbsp. vegetable oil
6   eggs, lightly beaten
1   cup heavy cream
1   4-oz. jar diced pimiento, drained
¼   tsp. ground mustard
¼   cup finely chopped onion
2   cups shredded cheddar cheese (8 oz.)
1   28-oz. bag frozen miniature fried potato nuggets
¼   cup sliced green onions
    Hot pepper sauce

**SLOW COOKER**

**1.** In an 8-inch skillet cook sausage in hot oil over medium-high heat about 5 minutes or until browned. Cut links into ¼-inch slices. In a 6-qt. slow cooker whisk together the next five ingredients (through onion) and 1 cup of the cheese. Stir in potato nuggets and sausage. **2.** Cover and cook on high 2¾ to 3 hours or until eggs are set, turning cooker insert halfway through cooking. Sprinkle with the remaining 1 cup cheese and the green onions. Pass hot sauce.

**PRESSURE COOKER**

**1.** For a 6-qt. electric cooker, use the sauté setting to cook sausage in oil about 5 minutes or until browned. For a 6-qt. stove-top cooker, cook sausage links in cooker as directed in Step 1 of Slow Cooker directions. Cut links into ¼-inch slices; return to pot. Add the next five ingredients (through onion) and 1 cup of the cheese to cooker; stir well. Add frozen potato nuggets; stir. Lock lid. **2.** Set electric cooker on high pressure to cook 30 minutes. For stove-top cooker, bring up to pressure over medium-high heat; reduce heat enough to maintain steady (but not excessive) pressure. Cook 30 minutes. Remove from heat. Let stand to release pressure naturally, at least 15 minutes. Open lid carefully. Sprinkle with the remaining 1 cup cheese and the green onions. Pass hot sauce. **Makes 8 servings (1½ cups each).**

**EACH SERVING** *593 cal., 46 g fat (18 g sat. fat), 222 mg chol., 1,027 mg sodium, 30 g carb., 3 g fiber, 3 g sugars, 19 g pro.*

SOUTHERN TOT CASSEROLE

# SOUPS & STEWS

Better Homes
& Gardens.

TEST KITCHEN

**MAKE-AHEAD RECIPE.** See also storage/freezing tip, *p. 345.*

## CLASSIC BEEF STEW

**HANDS-ON TIME** 20 minutes
**COOK** 1 hour 30 minutes

¼   cup all-purpose flour
¼   tsp. black pepper
2   lb. beef stew meat or beef
    chuck pot roast, trimmed and
    cut into ¾-inch pieces
3   Tbsp. vegetable oil
3   cups vegetable juice
3   cups reduced-sodium
    beef broth
2   medium onions, cut into
    thin wedges
1   cup thinly sliced celery

2   Tbsp. Worcestershire sauce
1   tsp. dried thyme, crushed
1   bay leaf
4   red potatoes, cut into 1-inch
    cubes
4   carrots, bias-sliced ¼ inch thick
1½  cups frozen peas

**1.** In a large resealable plastic bag combine flour and pepper. Add meat to bag; shake until coated. In a 5- to 6-qt. pot brown half the meat in half of the oil over medium-high heat; remove meat from pot. Repeat with remaining meat and oil. Return all meat to pot. Stir in the next seven ingredients (through bay leaf). Bring to boiling; reduce heat. Simmer, covered, 1 hour.

**2.** Stir potatoes and carrots into stew. Return to boiling; reduce heat. Simmer, covered, 30 to 40 minutes more or until meat and vegetables are tender. Stir in peas. Heat through. Discard bay leaf. **Makes 8 servings (1¾ cups each).**

**EACH SERVING** *328 cal., 10 g fat (2 g sat. fat), 74 mg chol., 505 mg sodium, 28 g carb., 5 g fiber, 9 g sugars, 30 g pro.*

### IN A SLOW COOKER

Prepare and brown meat as directed. In a 4- to 6-qt. slow cooker layer meat, onions, celery, potatoes, and carrots. Reduce vegetable juice to 2 cups and combine with broth, Worcestershire, thyme, and bay leaf. Add to cooker. Cover; cook on low 10 to 12 hours or high 5 to 6 hours. Add peas; heat through.

**TOUGH TO TENDER**
Since stew simmers for hours, we recommend tough cuts of meat—such as chuck steak or chuck roast or a bottom round roast. These tough cuts get perfectly tender during slow cooking. You can purchase precut beef stew meat or buy a larger piece of meat and cut it into bite-size pieces yourself, trimming away any large pieces of fat.

## OLD-FASHIONED CHICKEN NOODLE SOUP

**HANDS-ON TIME** 25 minutes
**COOK** 1 hour 40 minutes

1  3½- to 4-lb. broiler-fryer chicken, cut up, or 3 lb. meaty chicken pieces (breast halves, thighs, and/or drumsticks)
½  cup chopped onion
2  tsp. salt
1  tsp. dried thyme, sage, or basil, crushed
¼  tsp. black pepper
2  cloves garlic, peeled and halved
2  bay leaves
8  cups water
1  cup chopped carrots
1  cup chopped celery
2  cups Homemade Pasta (p. 214)
1  Tbsp. chopped fresh thyme, sage, or basil (optional)

**1.** In a 6- to 8-qt. pot combine the first seven ingredients (through bay leaves). Pour the water over all. Bring to boiling; reduce heat. Simmer, covered, 1½ hours or until chicken is very tender.

**2.** Remove chicken from broth. When cool enough to handle, remove meat from bones. Discard bones and skin. Cut meat into bite-size pieces. Discard bay leaves. Skim fat from broth.

**3.** Bring broth to boiling. Stir in carrots and celery. Return to boiling; reduce heat. Simmer, covered, 7 minutes. Add Homemade Pasta, stirring to combine. Simmer, covered, 3 to 5 minutes more or until noodles are tender. Stir in chicken and, if desired, fresh herb; heat through.

**Makes 8 servings (1⅓ cups each).**

**EACH SERVING** *275 cal., 6 g fat (1 g sat. fat), 136 mg chol., 826 mg sodium, 29 g carb., 2 g fiber, 2 g sugars, 26 g pro.*

### EASY EVERYDAY

*The homemade pasta makes this soup extra special. But if time is short, use 6 oz. dried egg noodles instead.*

**JUST FOR FUN**
Classic lasagna always has a layer of creamy ricotta cheese. To keep the traditional flavor, we smeared a spoonful in each bowl before adding the soup.

# LASAGNA SOUP

**HANDS-ON TIME** 20 minutes
**COOK** 20 minutes

6   to 8 cups reduced-sodium chicken broth
1   14.5-oz. can no-salt-added diced tomatoes, undrained
2   8-oz. cans no-salt-added tomato sauce
½   cup chopped onion
½   cup chopped green sweet pepper
2   tsp. dried Italian seasoning, crushed
3   cloves garlic, minced
1   lb. uncooked bulk Italian turkey sausage or ground turkey
10  oz. lasagna noodles, broken into bite-size pieces

**1.** In a 5- to 6-qt. pot combine 6 cups broth and the next six ingredients (through garlic). Bring to boiling; reduce heat.
**2.** Drop sausage by teaspoonfuls into broth mixture. Add noodles. Simmer gently, covered, 20 minutes or until noodles are tender, stirring occasionally. Add additional broth if needed to reach desired consistency. If desired, top servings with shredded *Parmesan cheese* and snipped *fresh basil.*
**Makes 6 servings (1¾ cups each).**
**EACH SERVING** *342 cal., 8 g fat (2 g sat. fat), 42 mg chol., 1,075 mg sodium, 47 g carb., 8 g fiber, 9 g sugars, 23 g pro.*

**HEALTHY TWIST**
*Whole wheat lasagna noodles can be substituted for an extra boost of fiber and whole grain.*

## SUPREME PIZZA SOUP

**HANDS-ON TIME** 40 minutes
**COOK** 20 minutes

1   lb. bulk Italian sausage or lean ground beef
1   3.5-oz. pkg. sliced pepperoni
2   8-oz. pkg. fresh mushrooms, coarsely chopped
1   cup chopped onion
1½  cups chopped red and/or green sweet peppers
2   Tbsp. olive oil
2   Tbsp. minced garlic
1   tsp. crushed red pepper
3   28-oz. cans diced tomatoes, undrained
2   14.5-oz. cans reduced-sodium chicken broth
½   cup pitted black olives, halved
1   Tbsp. dried Italian seasoning, crushed
    Grated Parmesan cheese

**1.** In a 10-inch skillet cook sausage over medium heat 10 minutes or until browned. Drain on paper towels. If desired, halve pepperoni slices. In the same skillet cook pepperoni over medium heat 5 minutes or until slices start to crisp, stirring often. Drain on paper towels.
**2.** Meanwhile, in an 8- to 10-qt. pot cook mushrooms, onion, and sweet peppers in 1 Tbsp. oil over medium-low heat 10 minutes or until crisp-tender, stirring occasionally. Push vegetables aside and add the remaining 1 Tbsp. oil. Cook and stir garlic and crushed red pepper in the oil 30 seconds or until aromatic.
**3.** Add meats, tomatoes, broth, olives, and Italian seasoning. Simmer, uncovered, 20 minutes, stirring occasionally. Serve with cheese. **Makes 12 servings (1½ cups each).**

**EACH SERVING** *372 cal., 25 g fat (9 g sat. fat), 55 mg chol., 1,207 mg sodium, 21 g carb., 3 g fiber, 7 g sugars, 15 g pro.*

**GO SMALL**
Try swapping miniature pepperoni for the larger slices. They come in a bigger package (about 5 oz.), but you can add it all (just know that the calories and sodium will increase slightly).

### SAVING SOUPS

The interesting truth about soups and stews—we've found they actually taste better the day after they're made (flavors develop as they chill). Here are some tips to prep them for storage.

**COOL** the soup quickly after it's done cooking by placing the pot in a sink filled with several inches of ice water; stir soup occasionally and add ice as necessary.

**FOR THE FRIDGE,** ladle the cooled soup into a large bowl or individual containers. Cover and store in the refrigerator up to 3 days.

**FOR THE FREEZER,** divide cooled soup among shallow freezer-safe containers. Leave ½ to 1 inch space between the top of the soup and the container rim. This gives the soup room to expand when it freezes. Freeze up to 3 months.

**AVOID FREEZING** soups and stews that are milk- or cream-based and those thickened with cornstarch or flour. Soups with chunks of potatoes should also be avoided (potatoes tend to get mealy when frozen and thawed).

**THE MIGHTY POBLANO** This elongated, dark green pepper has a mild heat level perfect for when you want a little heat without the burn. (When dried, the poblano is called an ancho chile pepper.) Even though poblanos are more mild, you'll still want to wear gloves when cutting them up (tip, *p. 22*).

# WHITE CHICKEN CHILI

**HANDS-ON TIME** 35 minutes
**ROAST** 20 minutes at 425°F

2   fresh poblano chile peppers* (tip, *p. 22*)
1   large onion, cut into thin wedges
4   cloves garlic, unpeeled
2   Tbsp. olive oil
2   tsp. ground cumin
1   tsp. dried oregano, crushed
½   tsp. ground coriander
¼   tsp. cayenne pepper
3   15-oz. cans cannellini (white kidney) beans, rinsed, and drained
1   32-oz. carton reduced-sodium chicken broth
2   cups frozen whole kernel corn
4   cups chopped cooked chicken
1   8-oz. carton sour cream
    Salt and black pepper
    Lime wedges, crackers, roasted pumpkin seeds (pepitas), and/or fresh cilantro

**1.** Preheat oven to 425°F. Halve poblanos lengthwise; remove stems, seeds, and membranes. Place peppers (cut sides down), the onion, and garlic on a foil-lined baking sheet. Drizzle with 1 Tbsp. of the oil. Roast 20 to 25 minutes or until peppers are charred and very tender. Bring up foil around pepper mixture to enclose. Let stand 15 minutes or until cool enough to handle. Use a sharp knife to loosen the edges of pepper skins; gently pull off skins and discard. Peel garlic. Chop peppers, onion, and garlic.*
**2.** In a 5- to 6-qt. pot heat the remaining 1 Tbsp. oil over medium heat. Add roasted peppers, onions, and garlic and next four ingredients (through cayenne). Cook and stir 2 minutes.
**3.** Stir in beans and broth. Mash beans until chili is slightly thickened. Add corn. Bring to boiling; reduce heat. Simmer, uncovered, 5 minutes. Stir in chicken and sour cream; heat through. Season to taste with *salt* and *black pepper*. Serve with lime wedges, crackers, pumpkin seeds, and/or cilantro. **Makes 8 servings (1½ cups each).**
*****NOTE** To save time, substitute two 4-oz. cans undrained fire-roasted or regular diced green chiles for poblanos. Omit Step 1. Chop onion and garlic. In Step 2 increase cooking time to 5 to 7 minutes. Continue as directed.
**EACH SERVING** *399 cal., 15 g fat (5 g sat. fat), 77 mg chol., 561 mg sodium, 35 g carb., 9 g fiber, 4 g sugars, 31 g pro.*

# BEEFY TEXAS CHILI

**HANDS-ON TIME** 35 minutes
**COOK** 2 hours

2½ to 3 lb. boneless beef chuck pot
    roast, trimmed and cut into
    ½-inch cubes*
    Black pepper
3   Tbsp. vegetable oil
1½ cups chopped onions
4   cloves garlic, minced
1   Tbsp. ground cumin
1½ to 2 tsp. ground ancho chile
    pepper
1   32-oz. carton reduced-sodium
    beef broth
1   14.5-oz. can diced tomatoes,
    undrained
1   8-oz. can tomato sauce
1   to 2 canned chipotle peppers in
    adobo sauce, finely chopped
    (tip, *p. 22*)
3   Tbsp. very finely crushed
    tortilla chips or masa harina

**1.** Sprinkle meat with black pepper. In a 4- to 5-qt. pot brown one-third of the meat in 1 Tbsp. oil over medium-high heat. Remove meat from pot, draining off liquid. Repeat twice with remaining oil and meat.
**2.** Add onions and garlic to pot (add additional oil if needed). Cook until tender. Add cumin and ground ancho chile; cook 1 minute more.
**3.** Return meat to pot. Add the next four ingredients (through chipotle peppers). Bring to boiling; reduce heat. Simmer, covered, 1 hour, stirring occasionally. Uncover; simmer 1 hour more or until beef is tender, stirring occasionally.
**4.** Slowly add chips to chili, stirring constantly to mix. Simmer 5 minutes.
**Makes 6 servings (1 cup each).**
**\*NOTE** To use ground beef instead of roast, omit oil and cook beef with onions. Drain and add cumin and ancho chile powder; cook 1 minute more. Continue with Step 3.
**EACH SERVING** *378 cal., 16 g fat (4 g sat. fat), 123 mg chol., 782 mg sodium, 13 g carb., 3 g fiber, 5 g sugars, 45 g pro.*

**BEEF AND BEAN CHILI** Prepare as directed, except reduce oil to 2 Tbsp. and meat (cubes or ground) to 2 lb. total; cook meat in oil half at a time. Cook and stir in 1 chopped green or red sweet pepper or poblano pepper (tip, *p. 22*) with the onions. Substitute 1 Tbsp. chili powder for ancho chile pepper and chipotle chiles. Stir in two 15-oz. cans beans (such as black, kidney, pinto, and/or black-eyed peas), rinsed and drained, with the tomatoes.

**CINCINNATI CHILI** Prepare as directed, except use 2 lb. ground beef for meat and omit cumin, ancho chile pepper, diced tomatoes, chipotles, and chips. In Step 3, increase tomato sauce to one 15-oz. can and stir in one 15-oz. can red kidney beans, rinsed and drained; 1 tsp. ground cinnamon; a dash ground allspice; and 1 Tbsp. Worcestershire sauce. Continue as directed, cooking chili, uncovered, 40 minutes. Before serving, if desired, stir in ½ oz. chopped unsweetened chocolate until melted. Serve over spaghetti and top with chopped onions and shredded cheddar cheese.

**A LITTLE ON TOP** Customize your chili with toppers such as sour cream, snipped fresh cilantro, sliced fresh or pickled jalapeño pepper, sliced avocado, chopped onion, and shredded cheddar cheese.

SPLIT PEA SOUP

VEGETABLE-PORK OVEN STEW

**SOUP BONE** The ham hock, which is the smoked and cured knuckle of a hog leg, is slow-simmered in soups to impart a smoky, salty flavor. Ham hocks are skimpy on meat, with rind and fat attached to the bone. For one smoked ham hock, you can substitute 4 oz. chopped smoked bacon, smoked ham, smoked sausage, or smoked turkey; 2 oz. chopped salted pork; or one ham bone.

## SPLIT PEA SOUP

**HANDS-ON TIME** 20 minutes
**COOK** 1 hour 20 minutes

2¾ cups water
1½ cups dried split peas, rinsed and drained
1 14.5-oz. can reduced-sodium chicken broth
1 to 1½ lb. meaty smoked pork hocks or one 1- to 1½-lb. meaty ham bone
¼ tsp. dried marjoram, crushed Dash black pepper
1 bay leaf
½ cup chopped carrot
½ cup chopped celery
½ cup chopped onion

**1.** In a 3-qt. saucepan bring first seven ingredients (through bay leaf) to boiling; reduce heat. Simmer, covered, 1 hour, stirring occasionally. **2.** Remove pork hocks. When cool enough to handle, cut meat off bones and chop. Return meat to pan. Stir in remaining ingredients. Return to boiling; reduce heat. Simmer, covered, 20 to 30 minutes more or until vegetables are tender. Discard bay leaf. **Makes 4 servings (1½ cups each).**

**SLOW COOK** In a 3½- or 4-qt. slow cooker combine split peas, pork hocks, marjoram, pepper, bay leaf, carrot, celery, and onion. Pour the water and chicken broth over all. Cover and cook on low 8 to 10 hours or on high 4 to 5 hours. Discard bay leaf. Remove hocks, cut off meat, and stir meat into soup.

**EACH SERVING** *374 cal., 9 g fat (3 g sat. fat), 29 mg chol., 620 mg sodium, 49 g carb., 19 g fiber, 8 g sugars, 25 g pro.*

## VEGETABLE-PORK OVEN STEW

**HANDS-ON TIME** 20 minutes
**BAKE** 2 hours at 325°F

1½ lb. boneless pork shoulder, trimmed and cut into ¾-inch cubes
1 Tbsp. vegetable oil
1½ cups coarsely chopped onion
2 14.5-oz. cans reduced-sodium chicken broth or vegetable broth
1 tsp. dried thyme, crushed
1 tsp. dried oregano, crushed
1 tsp. lemon-pepper seasoning
½ tsp. salt
¼ cup all-purpose flour
1 16-oz. pkg. frozen whole kernel corn
1 lb. tiny new potatoes, halved
2 cups fresh green beans, cut into 2-inch pieces, or frozen cut green beans

**1.** Preheat oven to 325°F. In an oven-safe 4-qt. pot brown half of the meat in hot oil. Remove meat from pot. Brown remaining meat and the onion. Return all meat to pot. Set aside ½ cup of the broth. Add the remaining broth and the next four ingredients (through salt). Bring to boiling; remove from heat. Cover tightly and bake 1 hour. **2.** In a small bowl whisk together flour and the ½ cup reserved broth; stir into stew. Stir in corn, potatoes, and beans. Bake, covered, 1 hour more or until meat and vegetables are tender and broth is thickened. **Makes 6 servings (1½ cups each).**

**EACH SERVING** *308 cal., 8 g fat (2 g sat. fat), 46 mg chol., 625 mg sodium, 41 g carb., 6 g fiber, 0 g sugars, 20 g pro.*

# BEAN AND BACON SOUP

**HANDS-ON TIME** 25 minutes
**STAND** 1 hour
**COOK** 1 hour 10 minutes

| | |
|---|---|
| 1 | 16-oz. pkg. dried Great Northern beans or cannellini (white kidney) beans |
| 8 | oz. sliced bacon, chopped |
| 1 | cup chopped onion |
| 1 | cup chopped carrots |
| ½ | cup chopped celery |
| 3 | cloves garlic, minced |
| 2 | 32-oz. cartons reduced-sodium chicken broth |
| ½ | tsp. dried oregano, crushed |
| ½ | tsp. black pepper |
| 3 | Tbsp. tomato paste |

**1.** Rinse and drain beans. In a 4- to 5-qt. pot combine beans and enough water to cover by 1 inch. Bring to boiling. Cook, uncovered, 2 minutes; remove from heat. Cover and let stand 1 hour. Drain beans; rinse and drain again.

**2.** In the same pot cook and stir bacon over medium heat until browned and crisp. Remove bacon, reserving drippings in pot. Drain bacon on paper towels. Add onion, carrots, celery, and garlic to drippings in pot. Cook and stir over medium heat 4 minutes or until vegetables are tender.

**3.** Add the beans, broth, oregano, and pepper to pot. Bring to boiling; reduce heat. Simmer, covered, 1 hour or until beans are tender. Mash beans slightly with a potato masher. Stir in tomato paste; simmer, uncovered, 10 minutes. Stir in bacon and season with *salt* and pepper.
**Makes 8 servings (1 cup each).**

**EACH SERVING** *349 cal., 12 g fat (4 g sat. fat), 19 mg chol., 785 mg sodium, 42 g carb., 13 g fiber, 4 g sugars, 20 g pro.*

CUSTOMIZE IT

PICK THE INGREDIENTS TO
CREATE A RECIPE THAT'S
ALL YOUR OWN.

## HOMEMADE CUP OF NOODLES

**HANDS-ON TIME** 20 minutes
**STAND** 15 minutes

3   tsp. STOCK BASE
    FLAVOR BOOST
    PROTEIN
1½  cups COOKED NOODLES
    (about 4 oz. uncooked)
1½  cups VEGETABLES

**1.** Divide STOCK BASE and FLAVOR BOOST among three microwavable pint-size jars with lids. Layer with PROTEIN, NOODLES, and VEGETABLES in that order. Place lids on jars. Store in the refrigerator 3 to 5 days.
**2.** Tote in a lunch bag with a freezer pack. Before heating, let stand at room temperature 10 minutes or run warm water over the jar for a minute or so to warm slightly.

Nearly fill the jar with water (about 1¼ cups water) and microwave, uncovered, 2 minutes. Let stand 5 minutes. Stir to combine.
**Makes 3 servings (2 cups each).**

### TO COOK NOODLES
Cook noodles 1 minute less than package directions; drain. Immediately rinse in cold running water to stop cooking. Drain and toss noodles in vegetable oil to coat. Cut long noodles into shorter lengths.

## *COMBOS TO TRY*

**❶ TERIYAKI**
beef stock base, teriyaki sauce, ginger, garlic, chicken, ramen noodles, bok choy, carrots

**❷ EDAMAME-MUSHROOM**
chicken stock base, miso paste, garlic, ginger, soy sauce, edamame, rice noodles, snow peas, shiitake mushrooms

**❸ CAJUN SAUSAGE**
chicken stock base, Cajun seasoning, cooked sausage, farfalle, corn, broccoli slaw, green onions

**❹ SHRIMP BOWL**
vegetable stock base, Old Bay seasoning, shrimp, angel hair pasta, broccoli slaw, mushrooms

# MIX & MATCH INGREDIENTS

**STOCK BASE** *(Pick 1)*
- Beef stock base
- Chicken stock base
- Vegetable stock base

**FLAVOR BOOST**
*(Pick 1 or 2)*
- 2 cloves garlic, minced
- 1 Tbsp. chopped fresh herbs (dill, cilantro, chives, sage, parsley)
- 1½ tsp. lime, lemon, or orange zest
- ¾ tsp. chili powder

- ¾ tsp. Cajun seasoning
- ¾ tsp. lemon-pepper seasoning
- ¾ tsp. Old Bay seasoning
- 1 Tbsp. soy sauce
- 3 Tbsp. teriyaki sauce
- 2 Tbsp. white miso paste
- 2 Tbsp. rice vinegar
- 1 Tbsp. grated fresh ginger

**PROTEIN** *(Pick 1)*
- 7 oz. cooked shredded chicken, beef, or pork
- 7 oz. cooked meatballs (quartered)
- 7 oz. cooked smoked sausage
- 2 oz. smoked salmon
- 7 oz. cooked peeled shrimp
- 3 sliced hard-boiled eggs
- 1 cup canned beans or frozen edamame

**COOKED NOODLES**
*(Pick 1)*
- Angel hair pasta
- Elbow pasta
- Mini farfalle
- Linguine
- Ramen noodles
- Rice noodles
- Shell pasta
- Spaghetti

**VEGETABLES**
*(Pick 2–3)*
- Bok choy, chopped
- Broccoli slaw
- Carrots, julienned

- Corn, frozen
- Green onions, sliced
- Mushrooms, button or stemmed shiitake, sliced
- Peas, frozen
- Peas and carrots, frozen
- Snow pea pods, sliced
- Spinach, fresh baby, sliced
- Zucchini, finely chopped

## EGG DROP SOUP

**START TO FINISH** 25 minutes

½ cup finely chopped green
   onions
2 cloves garlic, minced
1 Tbsp. vegetable oil
6 cups reduced-sodium chicken
   broth
2 eggs, lightly beaten
¼ cup cornstarch
   Crushed red pepper (optional)

**1.** In a 3-qt. saucepan cook green onions and garlic in hot oil over medium heat 2 to 3 minutes or until tender. Add 5 cups of the broth. Bring to a simmer; reduce heat.
**2.** Slowly pour the lightly beaten eggs into the soup in a steady stream* while gently stirring to create strands (faster stirring creates thin strands; slower stirring creates thicker strands). Heat just to boiling.
**3.** In a bowl whisk together the remaining 1 cup broth and the cornstarch. Add to soup. Cook and stir just until thickened. Top servings with additional green onions and, if desired, crushed red pepper. **Makes 6 servings (1 cup each).**
**\*NOTE** You will want to add the eggs slowly in a thin stream to the soup while it is simmering but not boiling. If the soup is boiling, the egg strands become foamy.
**EACH SERVING** *86 cal., 4 g fat (1 g sat. fat), 62 mg chol., 580 mg sodium, 7 g carb., 0 g fiber, 1 g sugars, 6 g pro.*

**WONTON SOUP** Omit eggs and cornstarch. Cook 4 oz. stemmed and sliced shiitake or button mushrooms and ¾ cup shredded carrots with the green onions. Add all of the broth, 2 Tbsp. reduced-sodium soy sauce, and 1 tsp. grated fresh ginger. Bring to boiling. Add one 9- to 10-oz. pkg. frozen pot stickers (discard any sauce). Simmer, covered, 10 minutes.

**FLAVOR BOOST**
Stir in 2 Tbsp. prepared basil pesto and 2 Tbsp. freshly grated Parmesan cheese before serving. Add a side of grilled cheese sandwiches.

FRESH TOMATO SOUP

MEXICAN TORTILLA SOUP

≫

**FRESH TOMATOES** are best in the summer months. If they're out of season, substitute two 14.5-oz. cans whole tomatoes with juices for the fresh tomatoes.

## FRESH TOMATO SOUP

**START TO FINISH** 30 minutes

2    lb. tomatoes, cored and seeded
2    medium red sweet peppers, seeded and coarsely chopped
½    of a sweet onion (such as Vidalia or Maui), chopped
2    tsp. chopped fresh thyme
1    cup vegetable or chicken broth
2    Tbsp. heavy cream
1    Tbsp. honey
     Olive oil (optional)

**1.** In a food processor combine half of the tomatoes, half of the sweet peppers, half of the onion, half of the thyme, and half of the broth. Cover and process until smooth. Transfer to a 3- to 4-qt. saucepan. Repeat with remaining tomatoes, peppers, onion, thyme, and broth. Cook over medium heat 5 to 6 minutes or until hot. Stir in cream and honey. If desired, drizzle with oil and sprinkle with *black pepper.*
**Makes 6 servings (1 cup each).**
**EACH SERVING** *80 cal., 2 g fat (1 g sat. fat), 6 mg chol., 145 mg sodium, 14 g carb., 3 g fiber, 10 g sugars, 2 g pro.*

## MEXICAN TORTILLA SOUP

**HANDS-ON TIME** 25 minutes
**COOK** 20 minutes
**BAKE** 10 minutes at 375°F

½    cup chopped onion
1    fresh poblano or 2 jalapeño chile peppers, stemmed, seeded, and chopped (tip, *p. 22*)
1    clove garlic, minced
½    tsp. ground cumin
1    Tbsp. vegetable oil
3½    cups reduced-sodium chicken broth
1    14.5-oz. can fire-roasted diced tomatoes, undrained
1    8-oz. can tomato sauce
¼    cup chopped fresh cilantro
1    Tbsp. chopped fresh oregano or 1 tsp. dried oregano, crushed
2    cups shredded cooked chicken
1    15-oz. can black beans, rinsed and drained
1    cup frozen fire-roasted or plain whole kernel corn

4    6-inch corn tortillas
     Toppers, such as shredded cheddar cheese, cilantro, chopped avocado, sour cream, and/or lime wedges

**1.** In a 3-qt. saucepan cook onion, chile pepper, garlic, and cumin in hot oil 3 to 4 minutes or until onion is tender, stirring occasionally. Stir in next five ingredients (through oregano). Bring to boiling; reduce heat. Simmer, covered, 20 minutes. Stir in chicken, beans, and corn; heat through.
**2.** Meanwhile, preheat oven to 375°F. Cut tortillas in half. Cut halves crosswise into ½-inch-wide strips. Place strips on a baking sheet. Bake 10 to 12 minutes or until crisp. Serve soup with tortilla strips and toppers.
**Makes 6 servings (1¼ cups each).**
**EACH SERVING** *263 cal., 7 g fat (1 g sat. fat), 42 mg chol., 947 mg sodium, 30 g carb., 5 g fiber, 6 g sugars, 21 g pro.*

## ANDOUILLE AND SHRIMP GUMBO

**HANDS-ON TIME** 35 minutes
**COOK** 15 minutes

**FRENCH ANDOUILLE SAUSAGE** is a spicy smoked sausage popular in Cajun dishes like gumbo and jambalaya. Look for pork or chicken andouille. Or use any type of sausage you like.

**FILÉ POWDER** thickens and flavors gumbo. To let it work its magic, stir it in after cooking.

- ⅓ cup all-purpose flour
- ⅓ cup vegetable oil
- 1 cup chopped onion
- ½ cup chopped celery
- 1 cup chopped green and/or red sweet pepper
- 12 cloves garlic, minced
- 3 cups reduced-sodium chicken broth
- 2 cups sliced okra or one 10-oz. pkg. frozen sliced okra
- ¼ tsp. black pepper
- ⅛ tsp. cayenne pepper
- 12 oz. cooked andouille sausage or smoked sausage, sliced
- 1 lb. fresh peeled and deveined medium shrimp (tip, p. 178)
- ¼ cup chopped green onions
- 1 to 2 tsp. filé powder (optional)
  Hot cooked rice

**1.** For roux, in a heavy 4-qt. pot stir together flour and oil until smooth. Cook and stir over medium-high heat until bubbly. Reduce heat to medium. Cook and stir about 5 minutes more or until roux is dark reddish brown.

**2.** Stir in the next four ingredients (through garlic). Cook 5 minutes or until vegetables are tender, stirring frequently. Add broth, okra, black pepper, and cayenne. Bring to boiling; reduce heat. Simmer, covered, 15 minutes, stirring occasionally.

**3.** Stir in sausage; heat. Add shrimp and green onions; cook 2 to 4 minutes until shrimp are opaque, stirring frequently. If desired, stir in filé powder. Serve over rice. **Makes 6 servings (1⅓ cups each).**

**EACH SERVING** *510 cal., 28 g fat (7 g sat. fat), 157 mg chol., 910 mg sodium, 36 g carb., 3 g fiber, 3 g sugars, 28 g pro.*

**OKRA** The texture of cooked okra can be polarizing, but that viscous liquid actually thickens gumbo and gives it body. Either fresh or frozen okra will work here. To prepare fresh okra, rinse it well and cut off the tips and stem ends before slicing.

### MAKING A DARK ROUX

**1**

**COMBINE THE OIL AND FLOUR** in the pot. Cook over medium-high heat, stirring until bubbly.

**2**

**REDUCE THE HEAT** to medium and continue to cook and stir until the roux is the color of a penny (this takes 5 to 10 minutes). Constant stirring and a close watch will prevent scorching.

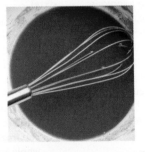

# NEW ENGLAND CLAM CHOWDER

**START TO FINISH** 30 minutes

- 2 pints shucked clams or four 6.5-oz. cans chopped clams, undrained
- 1 8-oz. bottle clam juice
- 6 slices bacon, cut up
- 1 cup chopped onion
- ½ cup chopped celery
- 4 cups chopped, peeled potatoes
- 1 tsp. chopped fresh thyme
- ½ tsp. salt
- ¼ tsp. black pepper
- 2 cups half-and-half

**1.** Chop fresh clams (if using), reserving juice. Strain fresh clam juice to remove bits of shell. (Or drain canned clams, reserving juice.) Add enough bottled clam juice to the reserved clam juice to measure 3 cups.
**2.** In a 4- to 6-qt. pot cook bacon over medium heat until crisp. Drain bacon on paper towels, reserving 1 Tbsp. drippings in pot. Add onion and celery to the reserved drippings. Cook 5 minutes or until soft, stirring occasionally.
**3.** Add the 3 cups clam juice, the potatoes, thyme, salt, and pepper. Bring to boiling; reduce heat. Simmer, uncovered, 10 to 15 minutes or until potatoes are tender, stirring occasionally. Using a potato masher, mash potatoes and solids just until soup is slightly thick and chunky.
**4.** Add clams. Return to boiling; reduce heat and cook 1 minute. Stir in half-and-half; heat through. Sprinkle with bacon and, if desired, additional chopped thyme.
**Makes 6 servings (1⅓ cups each).**
**EACH SERVING** *375 cal., 15 g fat (8 g sat. fat), 83 mg chol., 1,365 mg sodium, 30 g carb., 2 g fiber, 5 g sugars, 30 g pro.*

# OYSTER STEW

**START TO FINISH** 25 minutes

- 1 pint (about 3 dozen) shucked oysters, undrained (about 1 lb.)
- 1 cup finely chopped onion
- ½ cup finely chopped celery
- ½ tsp. salt
- ¼ cup butter
- 2 Tbsp. all-purpose flour
- ¼ tsp. black pepper
- ⅛ tsp. cayenne pepper
- 2 cups whole milk
- 2 cups half-and-half
- 2 Tbsp. cream sherry
  Freshly ground nutmeg (optional)
  Snipped fresh Italian parsley (optional)

**1.** Drain oysters, reserving liquor. Remove any shell pieces.
**2.** In a 3-qt. saucepan cook onion, celery, and salt in butter over medium heat 10 minutes or until tender. Stir in flour, black pepper, and cayenne pepper. Cook and stir 2 minutes more. Slowly whisk in milk and half-and-half. Bring to a simmer over medium heat, stirring slowly.
**3.** Stir in the drained oysters. Cook 3 to 5 minutes or until oysters curl around the edges. Stir in oyster liquor and sherry; heat through. If desired, add additional sherry to taste. Top servings with ground nutmeg and/or parsley.
**Makes 6 servings (¾ cup each).**
**EACH SERVING** *300 cal., 21 g fat (12 g sat. fat), 95 mg chol., 427 mg sodium, 16 g carb., 1 g fiber, 9 g sugars, 13 g pro.*

OYSTER STEW

NEW ENGLAND CLAM CHOWDER

## MINESTRONE

**START TO FINISH** 30 minutes

| | |
|---|---|
| 2 | Tbsp. vegetable oil |
| 8 | oz. MEAT |
| 3 | cups VEGETABLES |
| 1 | 32-oz. carton beef or chicken broth |
| ½ | of a 6-oz. can tomato paste (⅓ cup) |
| 1 | 1-oz. envelope dry onion soup mix |
| | SEASONING |
| 1 | cup STARCH |
| | Salt and black pepper |

**1.** In a 4- or 5-qt. pot heat 1 Tbsp. oil over medium-high heat. Add MEAT; cook and stir until cooked through. If necessary, drain fat. Remove MEAT to a bowl.

**2.** In same pot heat remaining 1 Tbsp. oil over medium-high heat. Add VEGETABLES; cook and stir 3 to 5 minutes or until crisp-tender. Return MEAT to pot.

**3.** Stir in broth, tomato paste, onion soup mix, and SEASONING. Bring to boiling; reduce heat. Simmer, covered, 15 minutes. Stir in STARCH. Season with salt and pepper. **Makes 4 servings (1½ cups each).**

# MIX & MATCH INGREDIENTS

**MEAT**
- Boneless chicken, turkey, beef steak, or lean pork, cut into 1-inch cubes
- Ground beef, ground turkey, ground chicken, or sausage

**VEGETABLES** (Pick 1)
- Small broccoli florets, chopped
- Carrots, chopped
- Celery, chopped
- Onion, chopped
- Peas or corn
- Potatoes, chopped
- Tomatoes, seeded and chopped
- Zucchini, chopped

**SEASONING** (Pick 1)
- ½ tsp. dried basil
- ½ tsp. dried Italian seasoning
- ½ tsp. dried oregano
- ¼ tsp. crushed red pepper
- ½ tsp. dried rosemary
- ¼ tsp. dried thyme

**STARCH** (Pick 1)
- Cooked barley
- Canned beans (kidney, navy, cannellini, or black)
- Cooked noodles
- Cooked pasta
- Cooked rice

## MAC-AND-CHEESE SOUP

**START TO FINISH** 30 minutes

- 2 Tbsp. butter
- ¾ cup chopped onion
- 3 cloves garlic, minced
- 3 cups reduced-sodium chicken broth
- ½ tsp. dry mustard or 1 Tbsp. Dijon mustard
- 1 8-oz. pkg. cream cheese, cubed and softened
- 2 cups half-and-half
- 1 8-oz. pkg. shredded cheddar cheese or three-cheese blend (cheddar, Colby, and Monterey Jack) (2 cups)
- 2 cups cooked elbow macaroni
- 4 oz. cooked ham, cubed
- ½ cup frozen peas

**1.** In a 3-qt. saucepan melt butter over medium heat. Add onion and garlic; cook 4 to 5 minutes or until onion is tender. Stir in broth and mustard. Bring to boiling; reduce heat to maintain simmer. Stir in cream cheese until smooth. Stir in half-and half. Reduce heat to low.

**2.** Add the shredded cheese a little at a time, whisking until cheese is melted before adding more cheese. Stir in macaroni, ham, and peas. Heat through. **Makes 6 servings (1½ cups each).**

**EACH SERVING** *618 cal., 40 g fat (24 g sat. fat), 125 mg chol., 954 mg sodium, 41 g carb., 2 g fiber, 8 g sugars, 24 g pro.*

MEXICAN-STYLE
GAZPACHO

**HEAVY ON THE
TOMATOES**
For a deeper color
and a richer tomato
flavor, replace 1 cup of
the water with 1 cup canned
tomato puree in
this gazpacho.

**WHAT IS GAZPACHO?** THIS CLASSIC SPANISH SOUP
IS ONE OF THE MOST EFFICIENT WAYS TO USE UP
YOUR GARDEN PRODUCE—CUCUMBERS, TOMATOES,
AND PEPPERS. BECAUSE IT'S SERVED COLD, IT'S A
REFRESHING SIPPER IN HOT SUMMER MONTHS.

## MEXICAN-STYLE GAZPACHO

**HANDS-ON TIME** 20 minutes
**CHILL** 1 hour

»

**PEPPER VARIETIES** are vast and numerous. If you want your soup mild, choose a sweet pepper or a Cubanelle pepper. If you want a little heat, pick a spicier chile pepper like poblano (tip, *p. 22*) or Hungarian wax peppers.

3   large tomatoes (about 2 lb.)
1   large cucumber (about 1 lb.)
1   large or 2 to 3 small sweet peppers (about 8 oz.)
2   cups water
1   cup coarsely chopped onion
3   Tbsp. olive oil
2   Tbsp. white wine vinegar or sherry vinegar
1   to 2 tsp. salt
2   fresh serrano or jalapeño chile peppers, seeded and thinly sliced (tip, *p. 22*)
    Watercress (optional)

**1.** Quarter and seed tomatoes. Halve cucumber and peppers lengthwise; scoop out seeds. Chop coarsely.
**2.** In a food processor or blender process tomatoes, cucumber, peppers, the water, and onion in batches. Remove each batch of puree to a bowl, reserving 2 cups to process the next batch.
**3.** Whisk in olive oil, vinegar, and salt. Cover and chill 1 hour. Serve topped with serrano peppers and, if desired, watercress.
**Makes 4 servings (2 cups each).**
**EACH SERVING** *173 cal., 11 g fat (2 g sat. fat), 0 mg chol., 599 mg sodium, 18 g carb., 5 g fiber, 10 g sugars, 4 g pro.*

## FRENCH ONION SOUP

**START TO FINISH** 30 minutes

2   Tbsp. butter
2   cups thinly sliced yellow onions
1   32-oz. carton reduced-sodium beef broth
2   Tbsp. dry sherry or dry white wine (optional)
1   tsp. Worcestershire sauce
    Dash black pepper
4   slices French or Italian bread, toasted
¾   cup shredded Swiss, Gruyère, or Jarlsberg cheese (3 oz.)

**1.** In a 3-qt. saucepan melt butter; add onions. Cook, covered, over medium-low heat 8 to 10 minutes or until tender and golden, stirring occasionally.
**2.** Add broth, sherry (if using), Worcestershire sauce, and pepper to onions in saucepan. Bring to boiling; reduce heat. Simmer, covered, 10 minutes.
**3.** Meanwhile, preheat broiler. Arrange toasted bread on a foil-lined baking sheet; sprinkle with cheese. Broil 3 to 4 inches from the heat about 1 minute or until cheese melts and is lightly browned. Top servings with toasted bread slices.
**Makes 4 servings (1¼ cups each).**
**EACH SERVING** *251 cal., 13 g fat (8 g sat. fat), 35 mg chol., 776 mg sodium, 22 g carb., 2 g fiber, 5 g sugars, 12 g pro.*

### MAKE IT A MEAL

On a platter arrange baby spinach, sliced pears, slivered red onion, and chopped toasted hazelnuts. Drizzle with vinaigrette (tips, *p. 298*) or bottled balsamic vinaigrette.

FRENCH ONION SOUP

CREAM OF BROCCOLI AND CHEESE SOUP

# CREAM OF BROCCOLI AND CHEESE SOUP

**START TO FINISH** 25 minutes

4   cups chopped fresh broccoli
1½  cups reduced-sodium chicken broth or vegetable broth
1   Tbsp. butter
1   Tbsp. all-purpose flour
½   tsp. lemon zest
¼   tsp. salt
    Dash black pepper
1   cup milk or half-and-half
2   oz. American cheese slices, torn

**1.** In a 2-qt. saucepan cook broccoli, covered, in a large amount of boiling water 8 to 10 minutes or until tender. Drain well. Set aside 1 cup cooked broccoli.

**2.** In a food processor or blender combine the remaining cooked broccoli and ¾ cup of the broth. Cover and process until smooth.

**3.** In the same saucepan melt butter. Stir in flour, lemon zest, salt, and pepper. Add milk all at once. Cook and stir until slightly thickened and bubbly. Cook and stir 1 minute more.

**4.** Stir in the reserved 1 cup cooked broccoli, blended broccoli mixture, and the remaining ¾ cup broth. Cook and stir until heated through. Stir in the cheese. If necessary, stir in additional milk to reach desired consistency. Season to taste with additional salt and pepper. **Makes 4 servings (1 cup each).**

**EACH SERVING** *165 cal, 10 g fat (6 g sat. fat), 30 mg chol., 727 mg sodium, 12 g carb., 2 g fiber, 5 g sugars, 9 g pro.*

**CREAM OF POTATO SOUP** Omit broccoli, lemon zest, and cheese. Cook 5 medium potatoes, peeled and cubed (5 cups), and ½ cup chopped onion as directed in Step 1 for 15 minutes or until tender. Set aside 1 cup potato mixture. Blend remaining mixture as directed in Step 2, except use all of the broth. Add ¼ tsp. dried basil, crushed, or dried dill in Step 3.

**CREAM OF MUSHROOM SOUP** Omit broccoli, lemon zest, and cheese. In a 12-inch skillet cook 1 cup each chopped onion and celery in 1 Tbsp. butter. Transfer to food processor. In same skillet cook 1 lb. thinly sliced assorted fresh mushrooms in 2 Tbsp. butter until tender. Blend onion, celery, and half of the mushrooms as directed in Step 2. Add remaining mushrooms and 1 tsp. chopped fresh thyme in Step 3.

**CREAM OF CORN SOUP** Omit broccoli, lemon zest, and cheese. Thaw a 12- to 14-oz. pkg. frozen gold and white baby corn. Cook 1 cup thinly sliced leeks; 1 cup cubed, peeled russet potato; and 2 cloves garlic, minced, as directed in Step 1 until tender. Blend mixture and 1 cup corn as directed in Step 2. Add remaining corn, 2 oz. softened cream cheese, ¼ cup chopped parsley, and ⅛ tsp. cayenne in Step 4.

**CREAM OF ROASTED ASPARAGUS SOUP** Omit broccoli, lemon zest, and cheese. Lightly coat 1 lb. trimmed fresh asparagus with olive oil. Place in a single layer on a foil-lined baking sheet. Roast in a 400°F oven 15 to 20 minutes or until tender. Cut off asparagus tips. Cut stems into 1-inch pieces. Blend stems as directed in Step 2. Stir in ¼ tsp. freshly grated nutmeg in Step 3. Top servings with asparagus tips.

WHEN IT COMES TO HOMEMADE BROTH, BONES CONTRIBUTE RICH FLAVOR (THAT LATER ENDS UP IN YOUR SOUP). PLUS, IT'S A WAY TO USE UP LEFTOVER BONES FROM ROAST CHICKENS AND BIG CUTS OF MEAT.

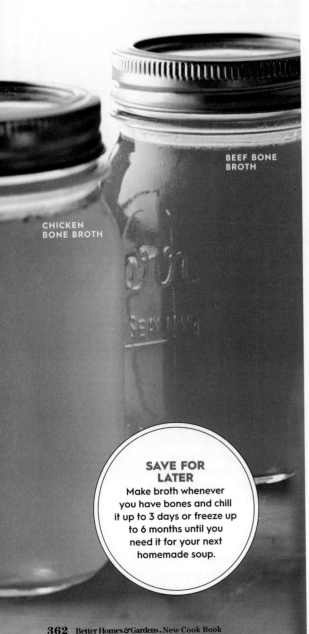

CHICKEN BONE BROTH

BEEF BONE BROTH

**SAVE FOR LATER**
Make broth whenever you have bones and chill it up to 3 days or freeze up to 6 months until you need it for your next homemade soup.

## BEEF BONE BROTH

**HANDS-ON TIME** 30 minutes
**ROAST** 45 minutes at 450°F
**COOK** 8 hours

3   lb. beef soup bones (marrow, knuckle, and/or neck bones)
1   cup water
4   medium carrots, cut up
3   medium onions, unpeeled and cut up
6   stalks celery with leaves, cut up
2   Tbsp. dried basil or thyme, crushed
1   Tbsp. salt
20  whole black peppercorns
16  sprigs fresh parsley
4   bay leaves
6   cloves garlic, unpeeled and halved
18  cups cold water
2   Tbsp. cider vinegar

**1.** Preheat oven to 450°F. Place soup bones in a large shallow roasting pan. Roast about 45 minutes or until browned, turning once.
**2.** Place soup bones in a 10- to 12-qt. pot. Pour the 1 cup water into roasting pan and scrape up browned bits; add bits and water to pot. Add remaining ingredients. Bring to boiling; reduce heat. Gently simmer, covered, 8 to 12 hours. (For a gentle simmer, you should see tiny bubbles rising to the surface; monitor cooking so it does not boil. Gently cooking helps develop the flavor of the broth.)
**3.** Remove soup bones from broth. Scoop out as many vegetables as you can with a slotted spoon.

Strain broth through four layers of 100%-cotton cheesecloth placed in a colander. Discard vegetables and seasonings.
**4.** If using broth while hot, skim off fat. Or chill broth in a bowl at least 6 hours; lift off fat with a spoon. Use in any recipe that calls for broth.
**5.** If desired, when bones are cool enough to handle, remove meat. Chop meat to use as desired; discard bones. **Makes 16 cups.**
**EACH CUP** *36 cal., 1 g fat (0 g sat. fat), 11 mg chol., 170 mg sodium, 2 g carb., 0 g fiber, 0 g sugars, 5 g pro.*

## CHICKEN BONE BROTH

**HANDS-ON TIME** 25 minutes
**COOK** 8 hours

5   lb. bony chicken pieces (wings, backs, and/or necks) or leftover bones from roasted chickens
6   stalks celery with leaves, cut up
4   medium carrots, unpeeled and cut up
3   medium onions, unpeeled and cut up
8   sprigs fresh parsley
4   bay leaves
6   cloves garlic, unpeeled and halved
2   tsp. salt
2   tsp. dried thyme, sage, or basil, crushed
1   tsp. whole black peppercorns or ¼ tsp. ground black pepper
15  cups cold water
2   Tbsp. cider vinegar

**BARE BONES**
Save leftover bones from roasts, steaks (think T-bone), and roasted chickens and turkeys. Pack the bones in resealable plastic freezer bags; freeze up to 3 months. Or buy beef bones—such as marrow, knuckle, and neck bones—from stores that cut their own meat. Call ahead to ask the butcher to save some for you.

**1** Roasting the bones adds color and flavor to the finished broth. If there are any crusty bits stuck to the pan, add some water and scrape them up with a wooden spoon. Add to the broth with the bones.

**2** Cool broth slightly and strain through a sieve or colander lined with cheesecloth, which will trap all the small particles.

**3** The easiest way to remove the fat from the broth is to chill the broth first. Once the fat hardens on the surface, it is easy to scoop off and discard.

**1.** If using wings, cut each wing at joints into three pieces. Place chicken pieces in a 10- to 12-qt. pot. Add remaining ingredients. Bring to boiling; reduce heat. Gently simmer, covered, 8 to 10 hours. (For a gentle simmer, you should see tiny bubbles rising to the surface; monitor cooking so it does not boil. Gently cooking helps develop the flavor of the broth.)
**2.** Remove chicken from pot. Use a slotted spoon to remove as many vegetables as possible.
**3.** Strain broth into a large bowl through four layers of 100%-cotton cheesecloth placed in a colander. Discard vegetables and seasonings.
**4.** If using broth while hot, skim off fat. Or chill broth in a bowl at least 6 hours; lift off fat with a spoon. If desired, cool chicken; remove meat from bones, discarding bones and skin. Place broth and chicken in separate airtight storage containers. Cover and chill up to 3 days or freeze up to 6 months.
**Makes 18 cups.**

**EACH CUP** *38 cal., 1 g fat (0 g sat. fat), 17 mg chol., 294 mg sodium, 2 g carb., 1 g fiber, 1 g sugars, 5 g pro.*

## IN A PRESSURE COOKER

Prepare Broths as directed, except reduce ingredients by half and combine in a 6-qt. stove-top or electric pressure cooker (info, p. 336). Lock lid in place. Set electric cooker on high pressure to cook 1½ hours. For stove-top cooker, bring up to pressure over medium-high heat according to manufacturer's directions; reduce heat to maintain steady (but not excessive) pressure. Cook 1½ hours. Remove from heat. Let stand to release pressure naturally for at least 15 minutes or according to manufacturer's directions. If necessary, carefully open steam vent to release any remaining pressure. Open lid carefully. Continue as directed.

## IN A SLOW COOKER

Prepare Beef Bone Broth or Chicken Bone Broth as directed, except reduce all ingredients by half. Combine all ingredients in a 6-qt. slow cooker. Cover and cook on low 10 to 12 hours. Continue as directed for straining and storing broth.

**VEGETABLE BROTH** In a 10-qt. pot place 8 unpeeled onions, cut into wedges; 12 unpeeled carrots, cut up; 8 stalks celery with leaves, cut up; 4 unpeeled potatoes, cut up; 2 unpeeled sweet potatoes, cut up; and 2 lb. mushrooms. Add 16 cups water; 1 Tbsp. salt; 2 tsp. dried thyme, basil, or marjoram; and 1 tsp. peppercorns. Simmer, covered, 2 hours. Strain through two layers of 100%-cotton cheesecloth placed in a colander. Discard vegetables. Pour broth into storage containers. Cover and chill up to 3 days or freeze up to 6 months.
**Makes 12 cups.**

**EACH CUP** *12 cal., 0 g fat, 0 mg chol., 599 mg sodium, 3 g carb., 1 g fiber, 1 g sugars, 5 g pro.*

# EASY SNACKS

WORK SNACKS, SCHOOL SNACKS, LATE-NIGHT SNACKS—THESE SIMPLE TOSS-TOGETHER IDEAS ARE DESIGNED TO FILL YOU UP WITHOUT WEIGHING YOU DOWN. CHOOSE FROM ANY OF THESE CATEGORIES— POPCORN, FRUITY, CRUNCHY, FROZEN, VEGGIE, OR PROTEIN.

## POPCORN SNACKS

### CURRIED POPCORN TOSS

In a bowl combine 2 Tbsp. melted butter, 1 tsp. curry powder, and, if desired, a dash cayenne pepper. Place 4 cups hot popped popcorn in a bowl; drizzle with butter mixture and toss to coat. Add ¼ cup each golden raisins, snipped dried apricots, and Marcona almonds; toss to combine. Makes about 5 cups.

### ITALIAN POPCORN

Place 4 cups hot popped popcorn in a bowl and drizzle with 1 to 2 Tbsp. melted butter. Add ¼ cup grated Parmesan cheese and 1 tsp. Italian seasoning; toss to combine. Makes 4 cups.

### TROPICAL POPCORN

In a bowl toss together 4 cups hot popped popcorn, ½ cup snipped dried pineapple, and ¼ cup toasted unsweetened large coconut flakes or chips. If desired, drizzle with 1 to 2 Tbsp. melted butter. Toss to combine. Makes 4½ cups.

# FRUITY SNACKS

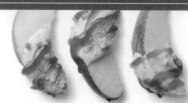

## *WATERMELON WEDGES*

In a bowl combine ½ cup plain Greek yogurt, 2 tsp. honey, and ½ tsp. lime zest. Spoon over four 1-inch-thick watermelon wedges. Sprinkle with toasted shredded coconut, chopped pistachio nuts, and small mint leaves. Serve immediately. Makes 4 wedges.

## *STRAWBERRY- SHORTBREAD APPLE DIPPERS*

Core and cut 1 apple into 12 slices. Dip apple slices halfway into 3 oz. melted white chocolate. Sprinkle with crushed shortbread cookies to coat. Place on a waxed paper-lined tray. Let stand until set. Drizzle with 3 Tbsp. warmed strawberry jam. Serve immediately. Makes 12 slices.

## *CHOCOLATE-DIPPED APRICOTS*

Gently loosen open edges of 24 dried apricot halves. Insert a shelled pistachio nut in the center of each. Press edges together to cover nuts. Dip half of each apricot into 6 oz. melted semisweet chocolate, letting excess drip off. Place on a waxed paper-lined tray. Let stand until set. Makes 24 apricots.

## *MARSHMALLOW DIP*

In a medium bowl beat one 8-oz. pkg. cream cheese, softened, with a mixer on low until smooth. Gradually beat in one 8-oz. carton sour cream until combined. Add one 7-oz. jar marshmallow creme and 1 tsp. vanilla; beat just until combined. Stir in 2 to 3 Tbsp. milk to reach dipping consistency. Cover; chill 1 hour before serving. Serve with assorted fresh fruit. Makes 2 cups.

## *FRUITY BAGELS*

Toast 2 bagel halves or frozen waffles; cool slightly. (Or use rice cakes.) Spread each with flavored cream cheese spread. Top with desired sliced fruit, such as kiwifruit, strawberries, and/or bananas, and/or mandarin orange sections. Makes 2 servings.

## *FRUITY MILK SHAKES*

In a blender combine 1 pt. vanilla ice cream; ½ to ¾ cup milk; and 2 cups sliced fresh or frozen fruit, such as peeled peaches, strawberries, peeled mango, and/or whole blueberries. Cover and blend until smooth. If desired, garnish with fruit. Makes 2 servings.

## *BAKED PARMESAN SNACK MIX*

Preheat oven to 300°F. In a roasting pan combine 5 cups bite-size wheat crackers and 4 cups small rye chips or bagel chips. Bake 5 minutes. Stir in 3 cups mini pretzel twists and 1 cup mixed nuts. Drizzle with ½ cup melted butter. Sprinkle with one 0.7-oz. any flavor dry salad dressing mix; stir to coat. Bake 10 minutes. Stir; sprinkle with ¼ cup grated Parmesan cheese. Bake 10 minutes more. Makes 12 cups.

## *CHOCOLATE-PB SNACK MIX*

In a bowl combine 8 cups bite-size square corn cereal and 2 cups pretzel sticks. In a bowl combine 1 cup dark chocolate chips, ½ cup peanut butter, and ¼ cup butter. Microwave 30 to 60 seconds or until melted, stirring every 20 seconds. Stir in 1 tsp. vanilla. Pour over cereal; stir to coat. In a 2-gallon resealable bag combine cereal mixture and 1⅓ cups powdered sugar. Shake to coat. Makes 9 cups.

## *PUFFED CEREAL GRANOLA*

Preheat oven to 350°F. In a bowl combine 1 cup each puffed rice cereal and rolled oats, ½ cup chopped walnuts, and 2 Tbsp. shredded coconut. In a bowl combine 3 Tbsp. maple syrup, 2 tsp. canola oil, 1½ tsp. orange zest, ½ tsp. cinnamon, and ¼ tsp. vanilla. Add to oats mixture; stir. Spread in a 15×10-inch baking pan. Bake 15 minutes or until golden, stirring once. Stir in 2 Tbsp. chopped dried cherries. Makes 3 cups.

## *CARAMEL MIX*

Butter a piece of foil. In a 4-qt. pot combine 1 cup packed brown sugar, ½ cup butter, 2 Tbsp. light corn syrup, and ½ tsp. salt. Cook and stir over medium-high to a gentle boil. Reduce heat to medium; cook 3 minutes, stirring occasionally. Remove from heat; stir in 1 tsp. vanilla and ½ tsp. baking soda. Stir in 6 cups assorted desired cereal, 2 cups pretzel twists, and 2 cups mixed nuts. Spread on foil; cool. Break apart. Makes 11 cups.

## *S'MORES MIX*

In a large airtight container combine 4 cups honey graham cereal, 2 cups each tiny marshmallows and peanuts, and 1 cup candy-coated chocolate pieces or semisweet chocolate chips. Stir to mix; cover. Makes 5 cups.

## *CHEESY SNACK MIX*

In a large airtight container combine 2 cups each bite-size fish-shape crackers, cheese-flavor bugle-shape corn snacks, small cheese-flavor crackers, and small cracker sandwiches with cheese. Add 1 cup roasted cashews. Stir to mix; cover. Makes 9 cups.

### YOGURT POPS

In a bowl combine 2 cups orange yogurt, one 12-oz. can orange juice concentrate, and ½ tsp. vanilla. In another bowl combine 2 cups cherry yogurt, one 12-oz. can cherry punch concentrate, and ½ tsp. vanilla. Alternately spoon mixtures into sixteen 5-oz. paper cups. Cover cups with foil. Cut slits in centers of foil; insert crafts sticks. Freeze until firm. Tear off cups. Makes 16 pops.

### FROZEN YOGURT BARK

In a bowl combine one 32-oz. carton plain whole milk Greek yogurt, ¼ cup honey, and 2 tsp. vanilla. Stir in 1 cup chopped dark chocolate and/or nuts. Spread mixture on two parchment-lined baking sheets. Sprinkle with cut-up berries or fruit. Freeze until firm. Break into pieces. Store in a freezer container in the freezer. Makes 24 servings.

### EASY FRUIT ICE CREAM

In a food processor combine 4 bananas, peeled, sliced, and frozen; ½ cup each sliced frozen strawberries and frozen raspberries; 2 Tbsp. refrigerated unsweetened coconut milk or milk; and 2 tsp. vanilla. Cover; process until smooth. Serve immediately for soft-serve or freeze at least 4 hours for firm ice cream. Store in a freezer container in the freezer. Makes 3 cups.

### BANANA POPS

Cut 2 peeled firm, ripe bananas in half crosswise; insert wooden crafts sticks into ends. Place about ¼ cup flavored Greek yogurt on a plate. Roll bananas in yogurt to coat. Sprinkle with toppers, such as crushed freeze-dried berries, toasted coconut, finely chopped nuts, and/or mini chocolate chips. Place on parchment-lined baking sheet. Freeze at least 8 hours. Store in a freezer container in the freezer. Makes 4 pops.

### ICE CREAM SANDWICHES

Open the top and ends of a brick-style container of ice cream. Cut off a ½-inch slab. Quickly cut slab into squares. Sandwich a square between 2 chocolate or honey graham cracker squares. Put on a parchment-lined baking sheet. Repeat for as many sandwiches as desired. Freeze 1 hour. Wrap each sandwich with plastic wrap. Store in a freezer container in the freezer.

### CHOCOLATE FUDGE POPS

In a blender combine 1½ cups milk; ½ cup hot fudge ice cream topping; 1 banana, cut up; and 2 Tbsp. almond or cashew butter. Cover; blend until smooth, scraping as needed. Spoon mixture into six 5-oz. paper cups. Cover cups with foil. Cut slits in centers of foil; insert crafts sticks. Freeze until firm. Remove the foil; peel off paper cups. Makes 6 pops.

### BERRY RED SMOOTHIES

In a saucepan cook 1½ cups small cauliflower florets in boiling water 10 minutes or until very tender. Drain; rinse with cold water. In a blender combine cauliflower; 2 cups frozen raspberries; 1½ cups frozen unsweetened whole strawberries; 1 red sweet pepper, seeded and chopped; one 6-oz. carton strawberry yogurt; and 2 Tbsp. strawberry jam. Cover; blend until smooth. Makes 4½ cups.

### SPICED KALE CHIPS

Preheat oven to 300°F. Arrange 4 cups torn curly kale leaves in a single layer on two parchment-lined baking sheets, allowing space between leaves. Brush with 2 Tbsp. olive oil; sprinkle with ½ tsp. sea salt and ½ tsp. chili powder and/or ground cumin. Bake 20 to 25 minutes or until crisp. Cool 30 minutes before serving. Makes 6 servings.

### BACON-CRANBERRY STUFFED CELERY

In a bowl beat one 8-oz. pkg. cream cheese, softened, and 2 Tbsp. milk until smooth. Stir in ⅓ cup chopped toasted walnuts, ⅓ cup dried cranberries, and 3 Tbsp. cooked bacon pieces. Season with salt and black pepper. Stuff into 24 three-inch pieces celery stalks. Top with blue cheese. Makes 24 pieces.

### GREEK PITA ROUNDS

Preheat oven to 400°F. Place 2 soft pita bread rounds on a parchment-lined baking sheet. Spread 2 Tbsp. bruschetta topping evenly on rounds. Sprinkle with ½ cup shredded mozzarella cheese. Top with halved grape tomatoes, halved Kalamata olives, and thinly sliced red onion. Bake about 10 minutes or until crust is golden and cheese is melted. Cut into wedges. Makes 4 servings.

### GARDEN VEGGIE BUNDLES

Spread two 10-inch tortillas with desired-flavor hummus. Cut each tortilla into six strips; cut four of the middle strips in half crosswise. Arrange desired veggies (carrot strips, cucumber strips, sweet pepper strips, and/or avocado slices) on one end of each tortilla strip. Roll up strips to make bundles. Makes 20 bundles.

### RICOTTA DIP

Remove 1 tsp. zest and squeeze 1 Tbsp. juice from 1 lemon. In a bowl whisk together zest and juice; 1 cup ricotta cheese; 2 Tbsp. plain whole milk yogurt; 2 tsp. chopped fresh dill; 1 small clove garlic, minced; and ¼ tsp. each salt and pepper. Wrap ½ cup shredded unpeeled seedless cucumber in paper towels; squeeze to remove excess moisture. Stir cucumber into ricotta mixture. Serve with veggie dippers. Makes 1½ cups.

# PROTEIN SNACKS

## PIZZA LETTUCE WRAPS

In a bowl combine 1 cup each cherry tomatoes, quartered, and canned cannellini (white kidney) beans, rinsed and drained; ¾ cup shredded mozzarella cheese; and ¼ cup each chopped thinly sliced pepperoni and chopped fresh basil. Divide tomato mixture among 8 large Bibb lettuce leaves. Roll up into wraps. Makes 8 wraps.

## TURKEY ROLL-UPS

In a bowl stir together ¼ cup sour cream, 2 tsp. chili powder, and 1 tsp. lime juice. Spread over 1 multigrain flatbread. Top with a thin layer fresh spinach to within 1 inch of one long edge. Sprinkle ¼ cup each red pepper strips and shredded carrot over spinach. Top with thin layer of deli-style turkey. Starting from the filled long edge, tightly roll up. Cut crosswise. Makes 4 roll-ups.

## ENERGY BITES

Combine 1¼ cups toasted rolled oats, ½ cup each toasted shredded coconut and flaxseed meal, ¼ cup each chopped golden raisins and sunflower kernels, and 1 Tbsp. chia seeds. In a bowl combine ⅔ cup almond butter, ⅓ cup honey, 1 tsp. orange zest, and ½ tsp. vanilla. Stir into oat mixture. Shape into 1-inch balls. Store in an airtight container in the refrigerator. Makes 30 bites.

## ROASTED BBQ CHICKPEAS

Preheat oven to 425°F. In a bowl combine ¼ cup olive oil, 1 Tbsp. chili powder, 1½ tsp. barbecue spice; 1 tsp. each dry mustard and paprika, and ¼ tsp. each garlic salt, celery salt, and onion powder. Add two 15-oz. cans chickpeas, rinsed and drained; toss. Spread in a 15×10-inch pan. Roast 40 minutes or until crisp, stirring every 10 minutes (chickpeas might burst); cool. Makes 2¼ cups.

## SPICY PEPITAS AND PECANS

Preheat oven to 350°F. Spread 1 cup each pepitas (pumpkin seeds) and pecan pieces in a parchment-lined 15×10-inch pan. In a bowl combine 1 Tbsp. each olive oil and honey; 1½ tsp. chili powder; 1 tsp. dried oregano; and ½ tsp. each salt, ground cumin, and ground coriander. Drizzle over nuts; toss. Bake 10 minutes or until light brown, stirring once; cool. Makes 2¾ cups.

## BLACK BEAN AND AVOCADO DIP

In a bowl combine one 15-oz. can black beans, rinsed and drained; ½ cup frozen corn, thawed; 1 avocado, seeded, peeled, and chopped; 2 Tbsp. chopped fresh cilantro; 1 to 2 Tbsp. lime juice; 2 tsp. olive oil; and ¼ tsp. each garlic salt and hot pepper sauce. Sprinkle with crumbled queso fresco. Serve with tortilla chips or crackers. Makes 2½ cups.

# GATHERINGS

APPETIZERS & DRINKS *p. 372* ▪ BRUNCH *p. 410*
MAIN DISHES *p. 428* ▪ SIDES *p. 448*

# [GATHERINGS]
# APPETIZERS & DRINKS

Better Homes & Gardens.
TEST KITCHEN

## BRUSCHETTA

**START TO FINISH** 30 minutes

| | |
|---|---|
| 3 | Tbsp. olive oil |
| 1 | Tbsp. chopped fresh chives |
| 1 | Tbsp. chopped fresh basil |
| 1 | Tbsp. lemon juice |
| 1 | clove garlic, minced |
| 2 | cups chopped, seeded roma, yellow, and/or cherry tomatoes |
| ½ | cup finely chopped red onion |
| | Salt and black pepper |
| 1 | 8-oz. loaf baguette-style French bread |

**1.** Preheat broiler. In a bowl stir together 1 Tbsp. of the olive oil and the next four ingredients (through garlic). Stir in tomatoes and onion. Season to taste with salt and pepper.

**2.** Cut the bread into 36 slices; arrange on two large baking sheets. Lightly brush tops of slices with the remaining 2 Tbsp. olive oil. Broil, one pan at a time, 3 to 4 inches from heat 2 to 3 minutes or until toasted, turning once.

**3.** Using a slotted spoon, spoon tomato mixture onto the oiled side of each toast. Serve within 30 minutes. **Makes 36 servings (1 toast each).**

**TO MAKE AHEAD** Bread slices may be toasted up to 24 hours ahead. Store in an airtight container at room temperature.

**EACH SERVING** *31 cal., 1 g fat (0 g sat. fat), 0 mg chol., 50 mg sodium, 4 g carb., 0 g fiber, 1 g sugars, 1 g pro.*

**WHITE BEAN BRUSCHETTA** Prepare Bruschetta as directed, except substitute chopped fresh thyme for the chives and chopped fresh oregano for basil. Decrease tomatoes to 1 cup. Add one 15-oz. can cannellini beans, rinsed and drained, to tomato mixture. Drizzle assembled toasts with an additional 2 Tbsp. olive oil.

# DEVILED EGGS

**START TO FINISH** 25 minutes

6   Hard-Boiled Eggs *(p. 46)*
¼   cup mayonnaise
1   tsp. yellow mustard
1   tsp. vinegar
    Paprika and/or fresh parsley
    (optional)

**1.** Halve Hard-Boiled Eggs lengthwise and remove yolks. Set whites aside. Place yolks in a small bowl; mash with a fork. Add mayonnaise, mustard, and vinegar; mix well. If desired, season with *salt* and *black pepper*. Spoon or pipe yolk mixture into egg white halves. Cover and chill until ready to serve. If desired, garnish with paprika and/or parsley. **Makes 12 servings (1 egg half each).**

**TO MAKE AHEAD** Cover and chill deviled eggs up to 24 hours.

**EACH SERVING** *72 cal., 6 g fat (1 g sat. fat), 109 mg chol., 62 mg sodium, 0 g carb., 0 g fiber, 0 g sugars, 3 g pro.*

**QUICK TIP**
Place yolks and other filling ingredients in a resealable plastic bag. Seal bag; mash contents to mix. Snip off a corner of the bag; squeeze bag to pipe yolk mixture into egg white halves.

**BACON AND CHIVE** —»
Prepare as directed, except stir in 2 slices bacon, crisp-cooked and crumbled; 2 Tbsp. chopped fresh tomato; and 1 Tbsp. chopped fresh chives. Top with crumbled bacon pieces.

«— **SRIRACHA** Prepare as directed, except omit mustard and vinegar. Stir in 2 tsp. each sriracha and lime juice and ⅛ tsp. each salt and ground ginger. Top with sriracha and/or fresh cilantro leaves.

**ITALIAN** Prepare —»
as directed, except substitute Dijon mustard for yellow; omit vinegar. Stir in 2 Tbsp. each finely chopped prosciutto and grated Parmesan cheese. Top with basil pesto and/or additional prosciutto and Parmesan.

«— **CONFETTI** Prepare as directed, except substitute ranch dressing for mayonnaise and stir in ¼ cup finely chopped red and green sweet peppers.

APPETIZERS & DRINKS

CHOCOLATE-ALMOND BUTTER FRUIT DIP

## CHOCOLATE-ALMOND BUTTER FRUIT DIP

**START TO FINISH** 15 minutes

1    cup plain Greek yogurt
½    cup almond butter
⅓    cup chocolate-hazelnut spread
1    Tbsp. honey
1    tsp. vanilla
     Sliced fresh fruit such as pears, apples, apricots, pineapple, bananas, and/or strawberries

**1.** In a bowl whisk together the first five ingredients (through vanilla). (For a smoother dip, place in a food processor or blender; cover and pulse until smooth). Serve with fruit.
**Makes 14 servings (2 Tbsp. each).**
**EACH SERVING** *115 cal., 8 g fat (2 g sat. fat), 2 mg chol., 29 mg sodium, 8 g carb., 1 g fiber, 6 g sugars, 4 g pro.*

## TANGY SOUR CREAM AND ONION DIP

**HANDS-ON TIME** 30 minutes
**CHILL** 2 hours

2    Tbsp. olive oil
1    cup chopped onions
     Pinch salt
     Pinch sugar
1    clove garlic, minced
½    cup sour cream
½    cup mayonnaise
½    cup plain Greek yogurt

**1.** In an 8-inch skillet heat olive oil over medium-low heat. Add onions, salt, and sugar. Cook about 15 minutes or until lightly browned, stirring occasionally. Add garlic; cook mixture 3 to 5 minutes more or until onions are golden and caramelized.
**2.** Transfer onion mixture to a bowl; let cool 5 minutes. Stir in sour cream, mayonnaise, and yogurt. Season to taste with additional salt and *black pepper*. Chill at least

CRAB DIP

» **CRAB TARTLETS** Prepare dip as directed through Step 1. Spoon dip into 30 miniature phyllo dough shells (two 2.1-oz. pkg.). For a hot appetizer, place the filled shells on a large baking sheet. Bake in a 350°F oven 5 to 8 minutes or until heated through. If desired, garnish with lemon zest and fresh dill.

2 hours before serving. Serve with *potato chips*. **Makes 12 servings (2 Tbsp. each).**
**TO MAKE AHEAD** Cover and chill dip up to 24 hours.
**EACH SERVING** *113 cal., 11 g fat (3 g sat. fat), 10 mg chol., 113 mg sodium, 2 g carb., 0 g fiber, 1 g sugars, 1 g pro.*

## CRAB DIP

**HANDS-ON TIME** 20 minutes
**CHILL** 2 hours

1    lemon or lime
1    cup cooked crabmeat or one 6-oz. can crabmeat, drained, flaked, and cartilage removed
½    cup mayonnaise
½    cup sour cream
2    Tbsp. finely chopped red onion or green onion
1    Tbsp. chopped fresh dill or 1 tsp. dried dill
     Several dashes hot pepper sauce
     Salt and black pepper
     Assorted crackers and/or vegetable dippers

**1.** Remove 1 tsp. zest and squeeze 1 tsp. juice from lemon. In a bowl stir together zest and juice and the next six ingredients (through hot pepper sauce). Season to taste with salt and black pepper.

**2.** Transfer dip to a dish. Cover and chill at least 2 hours. If desired, sprinkle with additional fresh dill. Serve with crackers and/or vegetable dippers. **Makes 11 servings (2 Tbsp. each).**
**TO MAKE AHEAD** Cover and chill crab dip up to 24 hours.
**EACH SERVING** *117 cal., 11 g fat (3 g sat. fat), 26 mg chol., 145 mg sodium, 1 g carb., 0 g fiber, 0 g sugars, 4 g pro.*

**BABA GANOUSH**
This spread—which originated in the Far East region of the Mediterranean—is a rich and flavorful mixture based on the pureed pulp of eggplants.

## BABA GANOUSH

**HANDS-ON TIME** 25 minutes
**ROAST** 30 minutes at 425°F

3   medium eggplants (about
    1 lb. each)
½   cup tahini (tip, *opposite*)
¼   cup fresh Italian parsley leaves
¼   cup lemon juice
2   cloves garlic, peeled
1   tsp. kosher salt
1   Tbsp. olive oil
    Crushed red pepper (optional)
    Toasted baguette slices

**1.** Preheat oven to 425°F. Line a 15×10-inch baking pan with foil. Prick eggplants all over with a fork. Place in the prepared pan. Bake 30 to 40 minutes or until very soft and skin is charred. Let cool until easy to handle.
**2.** Remove and discard skins from eggplant. Place eggplant in a food processor or blender. Add the next five ingredients (through salt). Cover and pulse until nearly smooth, leaving some pieces of eggplant. Season to

taste with additional salt. Transfer dip to a bowl. Drizzle with olive oil and, if desired, sprinkle with crushed red pepper. Serve with baguette slices. **Makes 18 servings (¼ cup each).**
**TO MAKE AHEAD** Transfer dip to an airtight storage container. Cover and chill up to 3 days. Let stand at room temperature before serving.
**EACH SERVING** *67 cal., 4 g fat (1 g sat. fat), 0 mg chol., 114 mg sodium, 6 g carb., 3 g fiber, 3 g sugars, 2 g pro.*

# HUMMUS

**START TO FINISH** 15 minutes

- 1    15- to 16-oz. can chickpeas (garbanzo beans), rinsed and drained
- ¼    cup tahini
- ¼    cup lemon juice
- ¼    cup olive oil
- ½    tsp. salt
- ¼    tsp. paprika
- 1    clove garlic, halved
- 2    to 3 tsp. olive oil (optional)

- 1    Tbsp. chopped fresh parsley Toasted pita wedges and/or assorted vegetable dippers

**1.** In a food processor or blender combine the first seven ingredients (through garlic). Cover and process or blend about 4 minutes or until very smooth, stopping and scraping sides as necessary.
**2.** Transfer hummus to a small bowl. If desired, drizzle with the 2 to 3 tsp. olive oil and sprinkle with additional paprika. Sprinkle with parsley. Serve with pita wedges and/or vegetable dippers. **Makes 14 servings (2 Tbsp. each).**
**TO MAKE AHEAD** Hummus can be made up to 24 hours ahead. Place it in an airtight container and store in the refrigerator.
**EACH SERVING** *83 cal., 7 g fat (1 g sat. fat), 0 mg chol., 119 mg sodium, 5 g carb., 0 g fiber, 0 g sugars, 2 g pro.*

## LAYERED GREEK DIP

Give classic layered dip a Mediterranean twist. Beat one 8-oz. pkg. softened cream cheese with 1 Tbsp. lemon juice, 1 tsp. dried Italian seasoning, and 3 cloves garlic, minced, until smooth. Spread the cream cheese in a 9-inch pie plate or dish. Spread a layer of any flavor hummus over cream cheese; sprinkle with chopped cucumber, chopped tomato, sliced pitted Kalamata olives, crumbled feta cheese, and sliced green onions. Serve with pita chips.

**ARTICHOKE-GREEN ONION HUMMUS** Drain one 7.5-oz. jar marinated artichoke hearts. Chop two artichoke heart quarters. Prepare as directed, except substitute one 15-oz. can cannellini (white kidney) beans for chickpeas, reduce lemon juice and olive oil to 3 Tbsp. each, and omit parsley. Add drained artichoke hearts and ½ cup chopped green onions to food processor with beans. Top Hummus with reserved chopped artichoke hearts, sliced green onions, and shaved Parmesan cheese.

**CAULIFLOWER-HARISSA HUMMUS** In a covered 2-qt. saucepan cook 2 cups cauliflower florets in a small amount of boiling water about 10 minutes or until tender; drain. Transfer cauliflower to a bowl of ice water until cool; drain very well. Prepare as directed, adding cauliflower and 2 Tbsp. harissa paste to food processor with chickpeas. If desired, swirl additional harissa paste on top of Hummus just before serving.

// APPETIZERS & DRINKS //

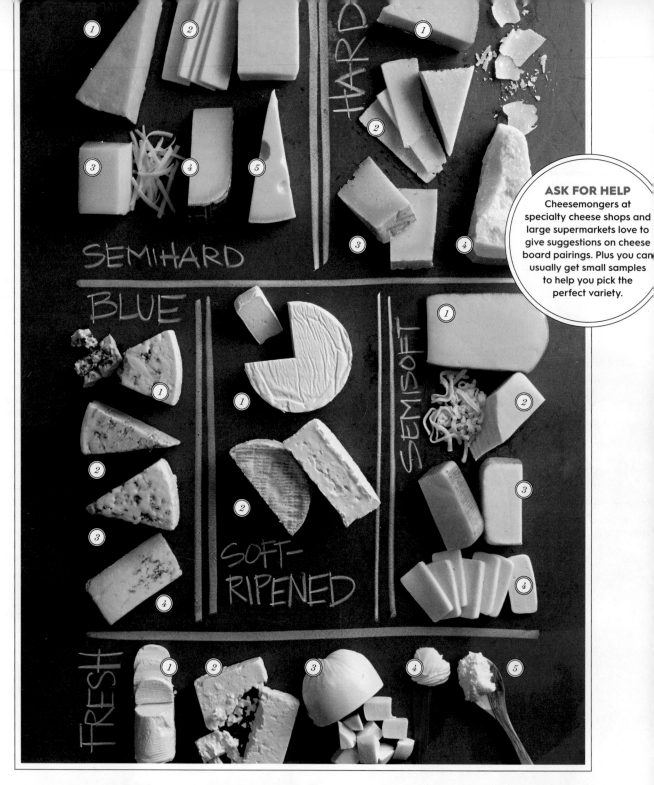

ASK FOR HELP
Cheesemongers at specialty cheese shops and large supermarkets love to give suggestions on cheese board pairings. Plus you can usually get small samples to help you pick the perfect variety.

**SEMIHARD CHEESE 1.** Cheddar **2.** White cheddar **3.** Gruyère **4.** Gouda **5.** Swiss ■ **HARD CHEESE 1.** Asiago
**2.** Manchego **3.** Pecorino Romano **4.** Parmigiano-Reggiano ■ **BLUE CHEESE 1.** Blue cheese **2.** Gorgonzola **3.** Roquefort
**4.** Stilton ■ **SOFT-RIPENED CHEESE 1.** Brie **2.** Camembert ■ **SEMISOFT CHEESE 1.** Fontina **2.** Monterey Jack
**3.** Muenster **4.** Havarti ■ **FRESH CHEESE 1.** Chèvre **2.** Feta **3.** Fresh mozzarella **4.** Mascarpone **5.** Ricotta

## BRIE AND CAMEMBERT WITH BRANDIED FRUIT

**HANDS-ON TIME** 10 minutes
**SLOW COOK** 2 to 3 hours (low)

Nonstick cooking spray
1    4- to 4½-oz. Brie cheese, rind removed, cut into ½- to ¾-inch cubes
2    oz. Camembert cheese, rind removed, cut into ½- to ¾-inch cubes
½    cup chopped assorted dried fruits, such as cranberries, cherries, golden raisins, and/or apricots
1    Tbsp. butter
¼    cup packed brown sugar
2    Tbsp. brandy

**BRANDY** is classically used to plump up dried fruit. You can also use rum—or use apple cider for an alcohol-free version.

»

½    cup chopped walnuts, toasted
Crostini, crackers, and/or apple slices

**1.** Lightly coat a 1½-qt. slow cooker with cooking spray. Add cheeses and dried fruits. In a 1- or 1½-qt. saucepan combine butter, brown sugar, and brandy. Bring to boiling; reduce heat. Simmer, uncovered, 1 minute. Pour mixture over cheese and dried fruit. Cover and cook on low 2 to 3 hours. Sprinkle with walnuts. Serve warm with crostini, crackers, and/or apple slices.
**Makes 6 servings.**
**EACH SERVING** *252 cal., 16 g fat, (7 g sat. fat), 31 mg chol., 217 mg sodium, 19 g carb., 1 g fiber, 17 g sugars, 7 g pro.*

## *TAKE A DIP*

When picking dippers to match up to your dip, consider the flavors, textures, and thickness of the dip.

### CRUNCHY DIPPERS
For thicker dips, set out pretzel rods, breadsticks, crackers, toasted baguette slices, herbed croutons, bagel chips, potato chips, tortilla chips, and multigrain chips.

### SWEET DIPPERS
Scoop up sweet dips with slices of fresh apple or pear, fresh orange sections, pieces of hard cheese *(opposite)*, cinnamon pita chips, biscotti, graham cracker sticks, honey-wheat pretzel braids, dried apricots, and banana chips.

### VEGGIE DIPPERS
Use crisp veggie dippers for both hot and cold dips. Good choices include sweet pepper strips in assorted colors, carrot sticks or baby carrots, broccoli and cauliflower florets, celery sticks, cucumber slices, and small roasted new or fingerling potatoes.

CUSTOMIZE IT

PICK THE INGREDIENTS
TO CREATE A RECIPE
THAT'S ALL YOUR OWN.

## HOW MUCH IS ENOUGH? FOR A PARTY BOARD, PLAN ON ABOUT 3 TO 4 OZ. CHEESE, 1 OZ. MEAT, AND 3 TO 4 CRACKERS PER GUEST.

### CHEESE AND MEAT BOARD

2    to 3 SEMIHARD or HARD
     CHEESES (p. 380)
1    to 2 SOFT CHEESES (p. 380)
     HARD SAUSAGES
     DELI-SLICED MEATS
     BREADS/CRACKERS
     FRUITS
     EXTRAS

**1.** On a large platter arrange desired assortment of CHEESES, HARD SAUSAGES, and DELI-SLICED MEATS. Cheeses can be sliced or served whole with a cheese knife or spreader. Thin meats should be rolled or piled attractively. Include BREADS/CRACKERS on the platter or in baskets alongside. FRUITS and EXTRAS can be used to fill in spaces on platter. Put wet ingredients, such as olives and mustard, in small bowls. Include serving utensils.

## MIX & MATCH INGREDIENTS

### HARD SAUSAGES
(Pick 1 or 2)
- Chorizo
- Peppered salami
- Soppressata

### DELI-SLICED MEATS
(Pick 1-3)
- Black Forest ham
- Capocollo
- Pancetta or prosciutto
- Roast beef
- Salami
- Herbed turkey

### BREADS/CRACKERS
(Pick 1-3)
- Artisanal crisps
- Baguette slices
- Breadsticks
- Whole grain crackers

### FRUITS
(Pick 1-3)
- Dried fruits (apricots, cherries, cranberries, figs)
- Fresh fruits (apple and pear slices, berries, clementine sections, grapes, pomegranate seeds)

### EXTRAS
(Pick 1-3)
- Cornichons
- Fig jam
- Grainy mustard
- Honey
- Nuts (Marcona almonds, smoked almonds, cashews, pistachios)
- Olives
- Onion chutney
- Pepper jelly
- Pepperoncini peppers

// APPETIZERS & DRINKS //

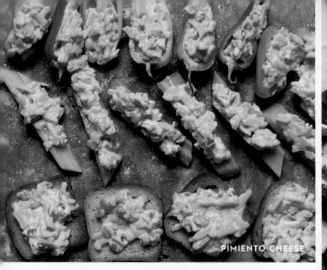
PIMIENTO CHEESE

BEER-CHEESE FONDUE

## PIMIENTO CHEESE

**HANDS-ON TIME** 10 minutes
**CHILL** 4 hours

**PIMIENTO CHEESE** is a vintage Southern spread made from a mix of cheddar cheese, pimientos (jarred pieces of red sweet pepper), mayo, and seasonings. It's been popping up at potlucks and picnics since the post-World War II era.

3   cups shredded cheddar cheese (12 oz.)
⅔  cup mayonnaise
1   4-oz. jar sliced pimientos, drained and chopped
1   tsp. Worcestershire sauce
1   tsp. yellow mustard
¼  tsp. garlic powder
     Assorted crackers, celery, and/or mini sweet peppers

**1.** In a bowl stir together the first six ingredients (through garlic powder), mashing with the back of a spoon as you mix (mixture will be chunky). Cover; chill 4 to 24 hours. Serve with crackers, celery, and/or sweet peppers. **Makes 18 servings (2 Tbsp. each).**

**EACH SERVING** 137 cal., 13 g fat (5 g sat. fat), 23 mg chol., 169 mg sodium, 1 g carb., 0 g fiber, 0 g sugars, 5 g pro.

**BEEF AND PICKLE CHEESE**
Prepare as directed, except omit pimientos, Worcestershire sauce, and mustard. Substitute Monterey Jack cheese for the cheddar. Add 3 oz. cream cheese, softened, and ½ cup each chopped dill pickle and chopped dried beef or boiled ham to cheese mixture. Serve on melba toasts or rye crackers.

## BEER-CHEESE FONDUE

**HANDS-ON TIME** 20 minutes
**SLOW COOK** 4 to 5 hours (low) + 30 minutes (high)

1½  cups reduced-sodium chicken broth
1¼  cups heavy cream
½   cup lager beer
2    cloves garlic, minced
½   cup butter, softened
½   cup all-purpose flour
1½  tsp. spicy brown mustard
2    cups shredded mild cheddar cheese (8 oz.)
1    cup shredded sharp cheddar cheese (4 oz.)
      Assorted dippers, such as French bread cubes, soft pretzels, smoked link sausage, fresh or steamed vegetables, and/or boiled potatoes

**1.** In a 1½- or 2-qt. slow cooker combine the first four ingredients (through garlic). Cover and cook on low 4 to 5 hours. Stir together butter and flour until a paste forms.
**2.** Turn cooker to high. Whisk paste into broth mixture until smooth (mixture will thicken immediately). Cover and cook 30 minutes more.

**3.** Whisk mustard into broth mixture in cooker. Slowly whisk in cheeses until smooth. Serve with dippers. **Makes 22 servings (¼ cup each).**
**STOVE-TOP DIRECTIONS** In a 2-qt. saucepan melt butter over medium heat. Add garlic; cook and stir 2 minutes. Whisk in flour; cook and stir 1 minute. Gradually whisk in broth, cream, and beer. Cook and stir until thickened and bubbly. Whisk in the mustard until smooth; gradually whisk in cheeses until melted and smooth. If desired for serving with dippers, transfer fondue to a slow cooker set to warm.

**EACH SERVING** 161 cal., 14 g fat (9 g sat. fat), 46 mg chol., 182 mg sodium, 3 g carb., 0 g fiber, 0 g sugars, 5 g pro.

## CHEESEBURGER DIP

**HANDS-ON TIME** 20 minutes
**SLOW COOK** 3 to 4 hours (low) or 1½ to 2 hours (high)

1    lb. lean ground beef
1    cup chopped onion
1    clove garlic, minced

**CHEESEBURGER DIP**

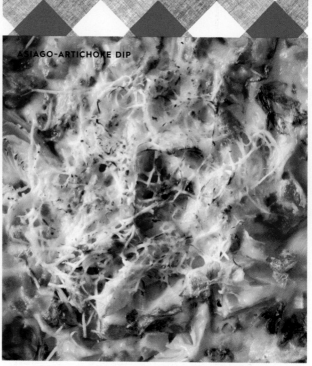

**ASIAGO-ARTICHOKE DIP**

12 oz. pasteurized prepared cheese product (Velveeta), cubed

⅔ cup chopped tomato

3 Tbsp. tomato paste

3 Tbsp. yellow mustard

2 tsp. Worcestershire sauce

2 to 3 Tbsp. milk (optional)
Pickle slices and/or chopped tomatoes (optional)
Assorted dippers, such as oven-fried potato wedges and/or crinkle-cut potatoes

**1.** In a 10-inch skillet cook beef, onion, and garlic over medium heat until meat is browned; drain. **2.** In a 1½- or 2-qt. slow cooker combine the meat mixture and next five ingredients (through Worcestershire sauce). Cover and cook on low 3 to 4 hours or on high 1½ to 2 hours. If needed, stir in milk to reach desired consistency. **3.** Serve immediately or hold on warm setting up to 2 hours, stirring twice. If desired, top with pickles and/or tomatoes. Serve with dippers. **Makes 16 servings (¼ cup each).**

EACH SERVING *125 cal., 8 g fat (4 g sat. fat), 35 mg chol., 401 mg sodium, 4 g carb., 1 g fiber, 3 g sugars, 10 g pro.*

# ASIAGO-ARTICHOKE DIP

**HANDS-ON TIME** 20 minutes
**BAKE** 30 minutes at 350°F
**STAND** 15 minutes

1 14-oz. can artichoke hearts, rinsed and drained

2 oz. thinly sliced prosciutto or 2 slices bacon

1 cup arugula or fresh spinach, chopped

1 8-oz. carton sour cream

3 Tbsp. all-purpose flour

½ cup mayonnaise

½ cup roasted red sweet peppers, drained and finely chopped

¾ cup finely shredded Asiago cheese or Parmesan cheese (3 oz.)

¼ cup thinly sliced green onions
Assorted crackers, pita chips, flatbread, and/or toasted baguette slices (optional)

**1.** Preheat oven to 350°F. Place artichoke hearts in a fine-mesh sieve; press firmly with paper towels to remove excess liquid. Chop artichoke hearts. **2.** Stack prosciutto slices; cut crosswise into thin strips. Separate strips as much as possible. In an 8-inch skillet cook and stir prosciutto over medium heat about 2 minutes or until slightly crisp. Add arugula; cook and stir 1 minute more. **3.** In a large bowl stir together sour cream and flour until combined. Stir in mayonnaise and roasted peppers. Stir in ½ cup of the cheese, the green onions, artichokes, and arugula mixture. Transfer to an ungreased 9-inch pie plate. Sprinkle with the remaining ¼ cup cheese (if desired, set aside 1 Tbsp. of the cheese to sprinkle on just before serving). **4.** Bake, uncovered, about 30 minutes or until edges are lightly browned and mixture is hot in center. Let stand 15 minutes before serving. If desired, sprinkle with additional crisp-cooked cut-up prosciutto and any reserved cheese. If desired, serve with crackers and/or baguette slices. **Makes 12 servings (¼ cup each).**

EACH SERVING *157 cal., 14 g fat (5 g sat. fat), 26 mg chol., 324 mg sodium, 4 g carb., 1 g fiber, 1 g sugars, 4 g pro.*

POTATO SKINS

## POTATO SKINS

**HANDS-ON TIME** 20 minutes
**BAKE** 50 minutes at 425°F
**COOL** 1 hour

| | |
|---|---|
| 6 | large baking potatoes (such as russet), scrubbed |
| 1 | Tbsp. vegetable oil |
| 1 | to 1½ tsp. chili powder |
| | Several drops hot pepper sauce |
| | Salt |
| 8 | slices crisp-cooked bacon, crumbled |
| ⅔ | cup finely chopped tomato |
| 2 | Tbsp. finely chopped green onion |
| 1 | cup shredded cheddar cheese (4 oz.) |
| ½ | cup sour cream |

**1.** Preheat oven to 425°F. Scrub potatoes; prick a few times with a fork. Bake 40 to 45 minutes or until tender; cool.

**2.** Cut each potato lengthwise into four wedges. Carefully scoop out the inside of each potato wedge, leaving a ¼-inch shell. Cover and chill leftover white portion of potato for another use.

**3.** Line a large baking sheet with foil. In a bowl stir together oil, chili powder, and hot pepper sauce. Using a pastry brush, brush the insides of potato wedges with oil mixture. Sprinkle with salt. Place potato wedges in a single layer on prepared baking sheet. Sprinkle with bacon, tomato, and green onion; top with cheese.

**4.** Bake about 10 minutes or until cheese is melted. Serve with sour cream. **Makes 24 servings (2 wedges each).**

**TO MAKE AHEAD** Prepare as directed through Step 3. Cover and chill potato wedges up to 24 hours. Uncover and bake as directed.

**EACH SERVING** *64 cal., 4 g fat (2 g sat. fat), 10 mg chol., 146 mg sodium, 4 g carb., 1 g fiber, 0 g sugars, 3 g pro.*

CHILE CON QUESO

GUACAMOLE

# CHILE CON QUESO

**START TO FINISH** 20 minutes

½ cup finely chopped onion
1 Tbsp. butter
1⅓ cups chopped, seeded
   tomatoes
1 4-oz. can diced green chiles,
   undrained
½ tsp. ground cumin
½ cup shredded Monterey Jack
   cheese with jalapeño peppers,
   shredded (2 oz.)
1 tsp. cornstarch
1 8-oz. pkg. cream cheese, cubed
   Corn chips or tortilla chips

**1.** In a 2-qt. saucepan cook onion in
butter until tender. Stir in tomatoes,
chiles, and cumin. Bring to boiling;
reduce heat. Simmer, uncovered,
10 minutes, stirring often.
**2.** Toss shredded cheese with
cornstarch. Gradually add cheese
mixture to saucepan, stirring until
cheese is melted. Gradually add
cream cheese, stirring until
melted and smooth. Serve
with chips. **Makes 21 servings
(2 Tbsp. each).**
**TO MAKE AHEAD** Transfer dip to
a 1½- or 2-qt. slow cooker. Keep on
warm or low setting up to 2 hours,
stirring occasionally.
**EACH SERVING** *58 cal., 5 g fat (3 g
sat. fat), 16 mg chol., 79 mg sodium,
5 g carb., 0 g fiber, 1 g sugars, 2 g pro.*

# GUACAMOLE

**START TO FINISH** 20 minutes

⅔ cup finely chopped, seeded
   roma tomatoes
1 to 2 Tbsp. finely chopped
   red onion
1 to 2 cloves garlic, minced
2 Tbsp. lime juice
1 Tbsp. olive oil
¼ tsp. salt
⅛ tsp. black pepper
2 ripe avocados, halved, seeded,
   peeled, and coarsely mashed

**1.** In a bowl combine the first seven
ingredients (through pepper).
Gently stir in avocados. If desired,
cover surface with plastic wrap and
chill up to 1 hour. Serve with *tortilla
chips* and *lime wedges.* **Makes
16 servings (2 Tbsp. each).**
**EACH SERVING** *48 cal., 5 g fat
(1 g sat. fat), 0 mg chol., 39 mg sodium,
3 g carb., 1 g fiber, 0 g sugars, 1 g pro.*

**SPICY GUACAMOLE** Prepare
as directed, except stir in one
or more of the following: 1 fresh
jalapeño chile pepper, seeded
and finely chopped (tip, p. 22);
1 canned chipotle chile pepper
in adobo sauce, finely chopped;
¼ tsp. ground ancho chile pepper;
⅛ tsp. cayenne pepper.

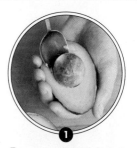

To remove the pit, halve
the avocado, then slide a
spoon under the seed. Twist
the spoon and lift the seed
out. Or cut the avocado into
quarters and use your fingers
to pull the seed out.

To keep the mess contained,
put all ingredients into a
resealable plastic bag.
Seal bag and squeeze to
mash the avocados and mix
ingredients together.

// **APPETIZERS & DRINKS** //

**BEYOND CHIPS**
Instead of tortilla chips, spoon nacho toppings over hot French fries, potato tots, baked potato skins, roasted sweet potato slices, pita rounds, shredded lettuce, or pizza crust.

CUSTOMIZE IT

PICK THE INGREDIENTS TO CREATE A RECIPE THAT'S ALL YOUR OWN.

## NACHOS

**HANDS-ON TIME** 15 minutes
**BAKE** 20 minutes at 350°F

5   cups bite-size tortilla chips
    (6 oz.)
    **MEAT**
1   15-oz. can BEANS, rinsed and
    drained
1   cup chunky salsa
2   to 3 cups shredded CHEESE
    (8 to 12 oz.)
    **TOPPINGS**

**1.** Preheat oven to 350°F. Spread half of the chips in a 13×9-inch baking pan. In a bowl combine MEAT, BEANS, and the salsa.

Spoon half of the meat mixture over chips. Sprinkle with half of the CHEESE.
**2.** Bake about 10 minutes or until cheese is melted. Top with the remaining chips, meat mixture, and cheese. Bake about 10 minutes more or until cheese is melted. Top with desired TOPPINGS. **Makes 8 servings (1 cup each).**
**NOTE** For restaurant-style loaded nachos, omit shredded cheese. Fully assemble the nachos and bake about 15 minutes. Spoon warmed purchased queso dip or Chile con Queso (p. 387) over baked nachos.

## FRESH TOMATO SALSA

**START TO FINISH** 30 minutes

3   cups coarsely chopped
    roma tomatoes
½   cup coarsely chopped
    red onion
1   large fresh poblano chile
    pepper, seeded and coarsely
    chopped (tip, p. 22)
1   to 2 large fresh jalapeño chile
    peppers, seeded and coarsely
    chopped (tip, p. 22)
2   Tbsp. lime juice
1   Tbsp. canola oil
1   tsp. cumin seeds, toasted* and
    ground, or ½ tsp. ground cumin
1   tsp. coriander seeds, toasted*
    and ground, or ½ tsp. ground
    coriander
½   tsp. kosher salt
¼   tsp. black pepper

**1.** In a food processor combine all ingredients. Cover; pulse until finely chopped. Cover and chill up to 3 days. **Makes 12 servings (¼ cup each).**
***NOTE** To toast seeds, in a dry 6-inch skillet heat the cumin and coriander seeds over medium-low heat 1 to 2 minutes or until lightly toasted, shaking skillet occasionally. Remove from heat; allow to cool before grinding with a spice grinder or mortar and pestle.
**EACH SERVING** *28 cal., 1 g fat (0 g sat. fat), 0 mg chol., 84 mg sodium, 4 g carb., 1 g fiber, 1 g sugars, 1 g pro.*

// **APPETIZERS & DRINKS** //

## MIX & MATCH INGREDIENTS

**MEAT** *(Pick 1)*
- 12 oz. ground beef, browned and drained
- 2 cups shredded cooked beef
- 2 cups chopped cooked chicken breast
- 2 cups shredded cooked pork

**BEANS** *(Pick 1)*
- Black beans
- Pinto beans
- Small red beans
- White beans (Great Northern or cannellini)

**CHEESE** *(Pick 1)*
- Cheddar cheese
- Colby and Monterey Jack cheese
- Mexican-style four-cheese blend
- Monterey Jack cheese with jalapeños

**TOPPINGS**
*(Pick 1 or more)*
- Chunky salsa
- Guacamole (p. 387)
- Pickled jalapeño chile peppers
- Sliced green onions
- Sliced pitted ripe olives
- Chopped fresh cilantro
- Sour cream

**COATINGS**
Use the same coating for all cheese balls or make a variety. Choose from coatings such as:

• crushed potato chips

• crushed cheese-flavored crackers

• finely chopped dried fruit

• crushed wasabi peas

• poppy seeds

• cooked crumbled bacon

• finely chopped fresh herbs

• finely chopped toasted almonds or other nuts

# DILLED ONION CHEESE BALLS

**HANDS-ON TIME** 35 minutes
**STAND** 45 minutes
**CHILL** 4 hours

| | |
|---|---|
| 1 | 8-oz. pkg. cream cheese |
| 1 | cup finely shredded Gouda cheese (4 oz.) |
| ¼ | cup butter |
| 1 | Tbsp. milk |
| 2 | Tbsp. thinly sliced green onion |
| 2 | Tbsp. chopped fresh dill or 2 tsp. dried dill |
| ½ | cup desired coating *(left)* Assorted crackers and/or flatbread |

**1.** Place cream cheese, Gouda cheese, and butter in a large bowl; let stand at room temperature 30 minutes. Add milk. Beat with a mixer on medium until light and fluffy. Stir in green onion and dill. Cover and chill 4 to 24 hours.

**2.** Form 2 Tbsp. cheese mixture into a ball; repeat to make 12 balls. Roll cheese balls in desired coating; let stand 15 minutes. Serve with crackers and/or flatbread. **Makes 12 servings (1 cheese ball each).**

**TO MAKE AHEAD** Prepare as directed; do not coat balls. Place balls in a single layer in a freezer container. Freeze up to 1 month. Thaw in the refrigerator overnight. Before serving, roll in coating.

**EACH SERVING** *63 cal., 6 g fat (3 g sat. fat), 16 mg chol., 62 mg sodium, 1 g carb., 0 g fiber, 0 g sugars, 2 g pro.*

## *GO BIG*

For a retro spin, form cheese mixture into one large cheese ball and serve it in on a plate surrounded by crackers.

# BACON-STUFFED MUSHROOMS

**HANDS-ON TIME** 20 minutes
**BAKE** 17 minutes at 425°F

- 8   slices bacon
- 1   5.2-oz. pkg. semisoft cheese with fines herbes (such as Boursin)
- 20  large cremini or button mushrooms (about 24 oz.)
     Chopped fresh parsley (optional)

**1.** Cook bacon until crisp; drain on paper towels and crumble. Stir together the semisoft cheese and crumbled bacon.

**2.** Lightly grease a 15×10-inch baking pan. Rinse mushrooms; wipe with paper towels. Remove stems from mushrooms; discard or reserve for another use. Place caps, stem sides up, in prepared baking pan. Spoon cheese mixture into mushrooms. Bake immediately or cover and refrigerate up to 24 hours.

**3.** When ready to serve, preheat oven to 425°F. Bake mushrooms 17 to 20 minutes or until tender. Let stand 5 minutes before serving. If desired, sprinkle with parsley. **Makes 20 servings (1 stuffed mushroom each).**

**EACH SERVING** *44 cal., 3 g fat (2 g sat. fat), 10 mg chol., 103 mg sodium, 1 g carb., 0 g fiber, 1 g sugars, 3 g pro.*

**SALMON- AND CHEESE-STUFFED MUSHROOMS** Prepare as directed, except omit bacon. Use 4 oz. thinly sliced smoked salmon (lox-style), chopped. Divide smoked salmon among mushrooms, pressing down lightly. Top each with about 1½ tsp. semisoft cheese. Continue as directed.

**SAUSAGE-STUFFED MUSHROOMS** Prepare as directed, except substitute 4 oz. Italian sausage for bacon. Cook sausage in an 8-inch skillet over medium heat until browned; drain. Continue as directed.

// APPETIZERS & DRINKS //

# COCKTAIL MEATBALLS

**HANDS-ON TIME** 35 minutes
**BAKE** 20 minutes at 375°F
**SLOW COOK** 3 to 4 hours (low) or
1½ to 2 hours (high)

2     eggs, lightly beaten
½     cup fine dry bread crumbs
½     cup finely chopped onion
¼     cup milk
½     tsp. salt
½     tsp. black pepper
1     lb. bulk pork sausage
1     lb. ground beef
1½    to 2 cups Marinara Sauce
      (p. 220) or purchased
      marinara sauce

**1.** Preheat oven to 375°F. In a large bowl combine the first six ingredients (through pepper). Add sausage and beef; mix well. Shape mixture into 36 meatballs (tip, p. 221); place in a shallow baking pan. Bake 20 to 25 minutes or until meatballs are done (160°F).

**2.** Using tongs, transfer meatballs to a 3½- or 4-qt. slow cooker. Add Marinara Sauce; stir. Cover and cook on low 3 to 4 hours or on high 1½ to 2 hours. Serve immediately or keep warm in cooker on warm or low setting up to 2 hours. **Makes 36 servings (1 meatball each).**
**TO MAKE AHEAD** Cool baked meatballs. Place meatballs in a single layer on a baking sheet lined with waxed paper. Freeze 30 minutes or until firm. Transfer meatballs to resealable freezer bags. Seal and freeze up to 3 months. Thaw in the refrigerator before using.
**EACH SERVING** *82 cal., 6 g fat (2 g sat. fat), 28 mg chol., 173 mg sodium, 2 g carb., 0 g fiber, 1 g sugars, 5 g pro.*

**HAM BALLS WITH CHERRY GLAZE** Make Cocktail Meatballs using 1 lb. ground ham and 1 lb. ground pork. Transfer cooked meatballs to a 3½- or 4-qt. slow cooker. For sauce, stir together ¾ cup black cherry preserves, ¾ cup cherry-flavor cola, ¼ cup Dijon mustard, and ¼ cup finely chopped onion. Pour over meatballs. Continue as directed in Step 2.

**CHICKEN-CHORIZO MEATBALLS** Make Cocktail Meatballs using 1 lb. ground chicken and one 15-oz. pkg. uncooked chorizo sausage. Transfer cooked meatballs to a 3½- or 4-qt. slow cooker. Stir together 1 cup salsa verde; 1 fresh poblano pepper, finely chopped (tip, p. 22); ¼ cup chicken broth; 1 tsp. ground cumin; and 2 cloves garlic, minced. Pour over meatballs. Continue as directed in Step 2.

**SWEET-AND-SOUR MEATBALLS** Make Cocktail Meatballs using 1 lb. bulk pork sausage and 1 lb. ground beef. Transfer cooked meatballs to a 3½- or 4-qt. slow cooker. For sauce, stir together ¾ cup apple jelly, ⅓ cup spicy brown mustard, ⅓ cup apple juice, 1½ tsp. Worcestershire sauce, and a dash of hot pepper sauce. Pour over meatballs. Continue as directed in Step 2.

**APRICOT-CURRY MEATBALLS** Make Cocktail Meatballs using 1 lb. ground pork and 1 lb. ground beef. Transfer cooked meatballs to a 3½- or 4-qt. slow cooker. For sauce, stir together one 12-oz. jar apricot preserves, ⅓ cup soy sauce, ¼ cup cider vinegar, 4 tsp. grated fresh ginger, and 2 tsp. curry powder. Pour over meatballs. Continue as directed in Step 2.

## BUFFALO CHICKEN WINGS

**HANDS-ON TIME** 25 minutes
**BAKE** 35 minutes at 450°F

1   cup Frank's RedHot Sauce or Louisiana hot sauce
6   Tbsp. butter, melted
2   Tbsp. cider vinegar
24  chicken wings (about 7 lb.)
1   recipe Blue Cheese Sauce
    Celery and carrot sticks

**1.** Preheat oven to 450°F. Line a shallow baking pan with foil. Place a wire rack in pan.
**2.** In an extra-large bowl combine hot sauce, butter, and vinegar; reserve ¾ cup. Cut off chicken wing tips; discard. Cut wings at joints to make 48 pieces. Add pieces to sauce mixture in bowl; toss to coat.
**3.** Arrange wing pieces on rack in the prepared pan. Bake 15 minutes. Turn wings. Bake about 20 minutes more or until tender, golden, and crisp. Place baked wings in a clean extra-large bowl. Add reserved ¾ cup sauce; toss to coat. Serve with Blue Cheese Sauce and celery and carrot sticks. **Makes 12 servings (4 wing pieces + 2 Tbsp. sauce each).**
**EACH SERVING** *558 cal., 46 g fat (15 g sat. fat), 222 mg chol., 1,102 mg sodium, 2 g carb., 0 g fiber, 1 g sugars, 32 g pro.*

### *BLUE CHEESE SAUCE*

In a bowl stir together one 8-oz. container sour cream; 1 cup each mayonnaise and crumbled blue cheese (4 oz.); ¼ cup thinly sliced green onions; 2 cloves garlic, minced; and ¼ tsp. each salt and black pepper. If desired, stir in 3 to 4 Tbsp. milk to thin to desired consistency. Cover and chill until serving time.

### CUTTING PIECES
On a cutting board use a chef's knife to cut each wing at the joints to make three pieces. The wing tips have no meat and should be discarded. The other two portions will be used for this recipe.

**SRIRACHA HOT WINGS** Prepare as directed, except omit hot sauce and cider vinegar. In the bowl combine ½ cup sriracha sauce or Asian chile paste; the 6 Tbsp. butter, melted; 3 Tbsp. each soy sauce and rice vinegar; and 1 tsp. toasted sesame oil. Omit Blue Cheese Sauce.

// APPETIZERS & DRINKS //

SHRIMP COCKTAIL

12  round rice papers
8   oz. shredded cooked chicken
    (about 1½ cups)*
½   of a medium cucumber, seeded
    and cut into thin sticks
    Soy sauce or Asian sweet
    chili sauce

## SHRIMP COCKTAIL

**HANDS-ON TIME** 25 minutes
**CHILL** 2 hours

1½  lb. fresh or frozen large
    shrimp in shells
¾   cup chili sauce
2   Tbsp. lemon juice
2   Tbsp. thinly sliced
    green onion
1   Tbsp. prepared horseradish
2   tsp. Worcestershire sauce
    Several dashes hot pepper
    sauce

### COCKTAIL SAUCE

The sauce with this recipe is a traditional cocktail sauce. You can swap for bottled cocktail sauce if you are in a hurry. For a large gathering, double the amount of shrimp and add the White Shrimp Sauce and/or Herbed Shrimp Sauce.

**1.** Thaw shrimp if frozen. Peel and devein shrimp. Cook shrimp in lightly salted boiling water 1 to 3 minutes or until shrimp turn opaque, stirring occasionally. Rinse in a colander under cold running water; drain again. Chill 2 hours or overnight.
**2.** For sauce, in a bowl stir together the remaining ingredients. Cover and chill until serving time. Serve shrimp with sauce. **Makes 8 servings (about 6 shrimp + 2 Tbsp. sauce each).**
**TO MAKE AHEAD** Prepare sauce as directed in Step 2. Place in an airtight container and store in the refrigerator up to 2 weeks.
**EACH SERVING** *84 cal., 0 g fat, 103 mg chol., 383 mg sodium, 8 g carb., 0 g fiber, 6 g sugars, 13 g pro.*

## WHITE SHRIMP SAUCE

Omit chili sauce ingredients. In a bowl stir together one 8-oz. carton sour cream, ¼ cup prepared horseradish, 2 Tbsp. chopped fresh chives, and 1 Tbsp. lemon juice. Cover and chill until serving time.

## HERBED SHRIMP SAUCE

Omit chili sauce ingredients. In a blender combine ¼ cup each lemon juice and olive oil; 2 Tbsp. each prepared horseradish and water; 2 tsp. Dijon mustard; ½ cup each chopped fresh parsley and chopped fresh basil; 4 oil-packed dried tomatoes, drained and patted dry; and ½ tsp. crushed red pepper. Cover and blend until nearly smooth, scraping down sides of blender as needed. Cover and chill until serving time.

## SPRING ROLLS

**START TO FINISH** 45 minutes

2   oz. dried rice vermicelli noodles
    (rice sticks)
1   cup finely shredded napa
    cabbage
½   cup coarsely shredded carrots
½   cup chopped fresh cilantro
    or mint
2   Tbsp. chopped dry-roasted
    cashews
2   tsp. reduced-sodium soy sauce

**1.** In a 2-qt. saucepan cook noodles in boiling, lightly salted water 2 to 3 minutes or just until tender; drain. Rinse with cold water; drain again. Using kitchen scissors, snip noodles into small pieces.
**2.** For cabbage filling, in a bowl combine cooked noodles, cabbage, carrots, cilantro, and cashews. Add soy sauce; toss to coat.
**3.** Fill a large shallow dish with warm water. Slide one rice paper into the water for a few seconds or until it is moistened and just pliable.. Carefully transfer the rice paper to a work surface.
**4.** Arrange about 2 Tbsp. chicken across the lower third of the softened rice paper. Top with a layer of cucumber sticks. Top with ¼ cup cabbage filling. Fold bottom of rice paper over filling. Fold in sides; roll up tightly. Place, seam side down, on a plate. Repeat with the remaining rice papers, chicken, cucumber, and filling. Serve with soy sauce. **Makes 12 servings (1 roll each).**
**\*NOTE** You can substitute shrimp or tofu for the chicken.
**TO MAKE AHEAD** Prepare as directed. Place in a single layer between damp paper towels in an airtight container; chill 4 hours.
**EACH SERVING** *114 cal., 3 g fat (1 g sat. fat), 17 mg chol., 91 mg sodium, 16 g carb., 1 g fiber, 2 g sugars, 7 g pro.*

SPRING ROLLS

**DIP TO SOFTEN**
For dipping, choose a shallow dish larger than the rice paper. Remove the paper when it is just pliable—it will continue to soften as you make the roll.

# SUSHI ROLLS
**START TO FINISH** 30 minutes

»

NORI is the Japanese name for dried edible seaweed sheets that are used in making sushi. Find them in Asian markets or in the international foods aisle of the supermarket.

2   8-inch-square sheets nori (seaweed)

1   recipe Sushi Rice
Desired fillings (such as small peeled and deveined cooked shrimp; small carrot, zucchini, sweet pepper, and/or cucumber sticks; and/or thin avocado slices)

1   recipe Honey-Ginger Sauce
Wasabi paste and/or pickled ginger (optional)

**1.** Lay nori on a sushi mat lined with plastic wrap; with damp fingers, spread half of the Sushi Rice over each sheet to within 1 inch of one edge. Arrange desired fillings crosswise just off the center of rice.

**2.** Roll nori toward the unfilled edge. (For a tight, even roll, place your hand under the edge of the mat, then carefully lift the edge of the nori and roll it over filling.) Brush unfilled edge with water and press against roll to seal.

**3.** Cut each roll into six pieces; arrange on a platter. If desired, cover and chill up to 4 hours. Serve with Honey-Ginger Sauce for dipping and/or wasabi paste and/or ginger. **Makes 12 servings (1 piece each).**

**SUSHI RICE** In a fine-mesh sieve wash ½ cup short grain rice under cold running water, rubbing grains together with your fingers. In a 1- or 1½-qt. saucepan combine rinsed rice and ¾ cup cold water. Bring to boiling; reduce heat. Simmer, covered, 15 minutes (rice should be sticky). Remove from heat. In a small bowl stir together 2 tsp. rice vinegar, 1 tsp. sugar, and ½ tsp. salt. Stir vinegar mixture into rice in saucepan; cover and cool about 45 minutes or until room temperature. (Rice can be covered and chilled up to 3 days.)

**HONEY-GINGER SAUCE** In a 1-qt. saucepan combine ⅓ cup honey; ¼ cup water; 2 Tbsp. each plum sauce and soy sauce; and a 1-inch piece fresh ginger, peeled and sliced. Bring to boiling while stirring; reduce heat. Simmer, uncovered, 15 minutes or until slightly thickened, stirring occasionally. Strain into a bowl; cool. Cover; chill.

**EACH SERVING** 73 cal., 0 g fat, 1 mg chol., 293 mg sodium, 17 g carb., 1 g fiber, 8 g sugars, 1 g pro.

**CALIFORNIA ROLLS** For fillings, use canned lump or imitation crabmeat, avocado slices, and cucumber sticks.

**SALMON ROLLS** For fillings, use smoked salmon and cucumber and red sweet pepper sticks.

**1** Press small handfuls of the sticky rice over the nori, leaving a 1-inch border along one edge. Arrange filling ingredients crosswise just off-center and opposite the unfilled edge. Distribute filling ingredients evenly.

**2** Use the sushi mat to lift and roll the nori toward the unfilled edge. Roll as tightly as you can. Wet the edge of the nori with water for a good seal.

**THE SUSHI MAT** Sushi mats are made by stitching thin round strips of bamboo together, making them flexible but supportive enough to lift and roll nori into sushi rolls. Cover the mats with plastic wrap before using for easy cleanup. You can find the mats in Asian markets and the kitchenware section of many stores.

## CUSTOMIZE IT

PICK THE INGREDIENTS TO CREATE A RECIPE THAT'S ALL YOUR OWN.

## PARTY MIX

**HANDS-ON TIME** 20 minutes
**BAKE** 45 minutes at 250°F

| | |
|---|---|
| 8 | cups CEREAL |
| 5 | cups CRUNCHY TREATS |
| 4 | cups round toasted oat cereal |
| 3 | cups WHOLE NUTS |
| 1 | cup butter |
| ¼ | cup Worcestershire sauce SEASONING |
| | Several drops hot pepper sauce (optional) |

**1.** Preheat oven to 250°F. In a roasting pan combine desired CEREAL, CRUNCHY TREATS, round cereal, and WHOLE NUTS.
**2.** In a 1- or 1½-qt. saucepan heat and stir butter, Worcestershire sauce, SEASONING, and hot pepper sauce (if desired) until butter melts. Drizzle butter mixture over cereal mixture; stir gently to coat.
**3.** Bake 45 minutes, stirring every 15 minutes. Spread on a large piece of foil to cool. Store in an airtight container at room temperature up to 2 weeks or in the freezer up to 3 months. **Makes 18 to 20 cups.**

## MIX & MATCH INGREDIENTS

**CEREAL** *(Pick 1–3)*
- Bite-size corn square cereal
- Bite-size rice square cereal
- Bite-size wheat square cereal
- Crispy corn and rice cereal
- Puffed corn cereal
- Sweetened oat square cereal

**CRUNCHY TREATS** *(Pick 1–3)*
- Bagel crisps
- Cheese crackers
- Corn chips
- Fish-shape crackers
- Oyster crackers
- Pretzel sticks
- Sesame sticks
- Small pretzel twists or squares
- Thin wheat crackers

**WHOLE NUTS** *(Pick 1)*
- Almonds
- Cashews
- Hazelnuts
- Mixed nuts
- Peanuts
- Pecan halves
- Soy nuts
- Walnuts

**SEASONING** *(Pick 1)*
- **BARBECUE** 1 tsp. each garlic powder and onion powder; substitute ½ cup barbecue sauce for Worcestershire sauce
- **CAJUN** 1 Tbsp. Cajun seasoning + 1 tsp. garlic powder
- **RANCH** One 1-oz. pkg. ranch dry salad dressing mix
- **ITALIAN** ½ cup grated Parmesan cheese + 1 tsp. garlic powder; substitute Italian vinaigrette for Worcestershire sauce
- **TACO** One 1-oz. pkg. taco seasoning mix + 1 tsp. ground cumin

## *PICKLE POPPERS*

Cut 12 whole baby dill pickles in half lengthwise. Scoop out centers; pat dry. Stir together 8 oz. cream cheese, softened; 2 Tbsp. finely shredded cheddar cheese; 1 jalapeño chile pepper, seeded and finely chopped (tip, *p. 22*); ¼ tsp. garlic powder; and salt and pepper to taste. Pipe into pickle halves. Wrap pickles with strips of deli-sliced ham; secure with toothpicks. Brush with hot pepper jelly. Bake in a 350°F oven 15 minutes.

## *SPICY MARINATED MOZZARELLA*

Combine 1 cup tiny fresh mozzarella balls; 1 cup halved cherry tomatoes; and 1 clove garlic, minced. Drizzle with olive oil; sprinkle with crushed red pepper and snipped fresh basil.

## *MELTY HERB PUFFS*

Roll 1 sheet thawed frozen puff pastry into an 11-inch square. Cut into sixteen 2½-inch rounds. Place eight rounds on a parchment-lined baking sheet. Top each with 2 tsp. semisoft cheese with fines herbes; brush edges with lightly beaten egg. Top with remaining rounds; seal edges with a fork. Brush with beaten egg. Bake in a 400°F oven 20 minutes or until golden.

## *PROSCIUTTO WRAPS*

Lightly brush thin slices of pear and/or apple with lemon juice. Place a pear or apple slice and one slice of Havarti cheese on the edge of slices of thinly sliced prosciutto; roll up.

## *OOZY BAKED BRIE*

If desired, slice the rind from the top of a Brie round. Place in a shallow baking dish. Bake in a 350°F oven 10 to 15 minutes or until softened. After baking, sprinkle with dried cranberries and chopped pecans; drizzle with honey. Serve with baguette slices. (Or top baked Brie with bruschetta topper, marmalade, tapenade, or fruit preserves.)

## *SALMON-WRAPPED ASPARAGUS*

Steam thin asparagus spears until crisp-tender. Rinse under cold water; drain and pat dry. Wrap each spear with a piece of lox-style smoked salmon. Thin sour cream with a little milk; stir in chopped fresh dill and cracked black pepper. Spoon over salmon or serve on the side.

# 6 CLASSIC COCKTAILS

### *NEGRONI*

In a cocktail shaker combine 2 Tbsp. (1 oz.) each dry gin, sweet vermouth, and bitter liqueur, such as Campari. Add ice cubes; cover and shake until very cold. Strain liquid into a martini or rocks glass. If desired, add ice. Garnish with an orange twist. Makes 1 serving.

### *WHISKEY SOUR*

In a rocks glass combine ¼ cup (2 oz.) bourbon, 2 Tbsp. (1 oz.) each lime juice and lemon juice, and 1 Tbsp. sugar. Using a spoon, stir until sugar dissolves. Add ice cubes. If desired, garnish with an orange slice and a maraschino cherry. Makes 1 serving.

### *APEROL SPRITZ*

Fill a Collins glass or wineglass with ice cubes. Add ⅓ cup Prosecco or other sparkling wine; ¼ cup (2 oz.) bitter orange aperitif, such as Aperol; and a splash chilled club soda. Stir gently. Add an orange slice to glass. Makes 1 serving.

### *MARTINI*

Thread 2 olives on a cocktail pick. In a cocktail shaker combine ¼ cup (2 oz.) gin or vodka and 1½ tsp. (¼ oz.) dry vermouth. Add ice cubes; cover and shake until very cold. Strain liquid into a martini glass. Garnish with olives and/or a lemon twist. Makes 1 serving.

### *MANHATTAN*

In a cocktail shaker combine ¼ cup (2 oz.) bourbon, 1 Tbsp. (½ oz.) vermouth, and a dash bitters. Add ice cubes; cover and shake until very cold. Strain liquid into a chilled glass or an ice-filled glass. Garnish with a maraschino cherry. Makes 1 serving.

### *COSMOPOLITAN*

In a cocktail shaker combine ¼ cup (2 oz.) vodka, 2 Tbsp. (1 oz.) each orange liqueur and cranberry juice, and 1 Tbsp. (½ oz.) lime juice. Add ice cubes; cover and shake until very cold. Strain liquid into a chilled glass. If desired, garnish with lime peel twist and/or fresh cranberries. Makes 1 serving.

## RED SANGRIA

**HANDS-ON TIME** 5 minutes
**CHILL** 3 hours

1    750-ml bottle dry red wine,
     such as Pinot Noir or Zinfandel
1    cup orange juice
¼    cup brandy
6    orange slices, halved
1    lime, sliced
1    cup halved strawberries
1    mango, seeded, peeled,
     and sliced
1    12-oz. can lemon-lime
     carbonated beverage
     Ice cubes

**1.** In a large pitcher stir together wine, orange juice, and brandy. Add orange slices, lime slices, strawberries, and mango slices. Cover and chill until ready to serve.
**2.** Just before serving, add carbonated beverage; stir gently. Serve over ice. **Makes 8 servings (about 1 cup each).**
**EACH SERVING** *161 cal., 0 g fat, 0 mg chol., 13 mg sodium, 19 g carb., 2 g fiber, 14 g sugars, 1 g pro.*

**WHITE SANGRIA** Prepare as directed, except substitute a dry white wine, such as Sauvignon Blanc or Pinot Grigio, for the red wine and gold rum for the brandy.

**GET-TOGETHER**
To serve a crowd, multiply the tequila, lime juice, and orange liqueur to make desired amount and stir them together in a large pitcher. Pour over ice in the prepared glasses.

## MARGARITAS

**START TO FINISH** 5 minutes

Lime wedge
Coarse salt
½   cup (4 oz.) silver or gold tequila
¼   cup (2 oz.) lime juice
¼   cup (2 oz.) orange liqueur
Ice cubes and lime slices

**1.** Rub lime wedge around rims of two 6- to 8-oz. rocks glasses. Dip the rims into a dish of coarse salt to coat. In a cocktail shaker combine tequila, lime juice, and orange liqueur. Add ice; cover and shake until very cold. Strain liquid into prepared glasses. Add additional ice. Garnish with lime slices. **Makes 2 servings (½ cup each).**

**EACH SERVING** *219 cal., 0 g fat, 0 mg chol., 281 mg sodium, 13 g carb., 0 g fiber, 1 g sugars, 0 g pro.*

**FROZEN MARGARITAS** Prepare 8 glasses as directed. In a blender combine one 12-oz. can frozen limeade concentrate, ⅔ cup silver or gold tequila, and ½ cup orange liqueur. Cover and blend until combined. With blender running, add 4 cups ice cubes, 1 cup at a time, blending until mixture becomes slushy. Pour into prepared glasses. **Makes 8 servings (about ¾ cup each).**

## MOSCOW MULE

**START TO FINISH** 5 minutes

Crushed ice
¼ cup (2 oz.) vodka
2 Tbsp. (1 oz.) lime juice
¾ cup ginger beer
Lime slices or wedge

**1.** Fill a Moscow mule mug or Collins glass with crushed ice. Add vodka and lime juice. Top with ginger beer; stir gently. Serve with lime slices. **Makes 1 serving (about 1 cup).**

**EACH SERVING** *234 cal., 0 g fat, 0 mg chol., 6 mg sodium, 27 g carb., 0 g fiber, 25 g sugars, 0 g pro.*

## MOJITO

**START TO FINISH** 10 minutes

8 large or 10 to 12 small fresh mint leaves
1 Tbsp. fresh lime juice
2 to 3 tsp. superfine sugar
Ice cubes
3 Tbsp. light rum
½ cup club soda, chilled
Lime wedges
Fresh mint sprigs (optional)

**1.** In a tall glass combine mint leaves, lime juice, and sugar. Use a muddler or the back of a spoon to crush mint against the side of the glass until mint is pulverized and sugar dissolves.
**2.** Fill glass three-quarters full with ice. Add rum and top with club soda. Squeeze and drop in lime wedges; stir again. If desired, garnish with mint sprigs. **Makes 1 serving (¾ cup).**

**EACH SERVING** *140 cal., 0 g fat, 0 mg chol., 29 mg sodium, 1 g carb., 1 g fiber, 9 g sugars, 0 g pro.*

## RASPBERRY FROSÉ POPS

**HANDS-ON TIME** 15 minutes
**STAND** 10 minutes
**FREEZE** overnight

8 5-oz. paper drink cups
6 raspberry herb tea bags or hibiscus tea bags
3 Tbsp. sugar
1 1-inch piece fresh ginger, peeled
3 cups fresh or frozen raspberries
¾ cup rosé wine
Wooden crafts sticks

**1.** Place paper cups in a shallow baking pan. In a medium bowl combine tea bags, sugar, and ginger. Add 2 cups boiling *water*. Let stand 5 minutes. Remove and discard tea bags and ginger.
**2.** In a blender combine tea mixture and raspberries. Cover; blend to combine. Strain mixture through a fine-mesh sieve; discard seeds. Let mixture stand 5 minutes. Use a spoon to remove any foam that forms on top of the tea mixture. Stir the wine into the mixture; pour the mixture into prepared paper cups. Cover each cup with a square of foil. Using a knife, make a small hole in center of each foil square. Slide a wooden crafts stick through each hole and into the mixture. Freeze overnight.
**3.** To serve, peel paper cups off of pops. Serve immediately or place on a parchment-lined baking pan and freeze until ready to serve. **Makes 8 servings (1 pop each).**
**EACH SERVING** *62 cal., 0 g fat, 0 mg chol., 2 mg sodium, 12 g carb., 3 g fiber, 7 g sugars, 1 g pro.*

MOSCOW MULE

MOJITO

RASPBERRY FROSÉ POPS

## BLOODY MARY MIX

**START TO FINISH** 10 minutes

| | |
|---|---|
| 1 | 46-oz. bottle hot-style or regular vegetable juice |
| ½ | cup lemon juice |
| 1 | Tbsp. prepared horseradish |
| 1 | Tbsp. Worcestershire sauce |
| 1 | tsp. celery salt |
| | Ice cubes |
| | Vodka |
| | Black pepper (optional) |

**1.** For mix, in a large pitcher combine the first five ingredients (through celery salt). Cover and chill until ready to serve.

**2.** For each drink, pour ½ cup drink mix into a glass filled with ice cubes. Add desired amount of vodka (1 to 2 oz.). If desired, sprinkle with pepper and add a garnish *(tip, right)*. **Makes 12 servings (½ cup mix each).**

**EACH SERVING** *91 cal., 0 g fat, 0 mg chol., 366 mg sodium, 6 g carb., 1 g fiber, 4 g sugars, 1 g pro.*

## *SNACKS IN A GLASS*

The best bloody mary is filled with tangy, zesty, crunchy, and pickled snacks. Do it right, and no extra appetizers are needed.

**TRADITIONAL TOPPERS** The classic bloody mary garnish is a celery stick with the leaves sticking out the top or a long dill pickle spear. Pickled green beans and asparagus spears are also good stand-ins when you want to keep it basic and classy.

**THE SKY'S THE LIMIT** Don't hold back when threading goodies on a long skewer for your glass. Mix sweet pickles, olives, cooked bacon strips, pickled pepperoncini peppers, cooked shrimp, cheese cubes, baby corn, beef jerky, cherry tomatoes, cocktail onions, rolled pepperoni, roasted garlic, smoked oysters, and green onions (just to name a few options).

**MORE FLAVOR** Add a little sass around the glass rim. You can find premixed rim salts in the liquor store and online. Or use lemon-pepper, BBQ rub, seafood seasoning, kosher salt, or celery salt. Rub the glass rim with a lemon wedge and dip in seasoning.

# SPARKLING PEACH PUNCH

**HANDS-ON TIME** 20 minutes
**FREEZE** 8 hours
**STAND** 1 hour

3   cups water
1½  cups sugar
1   3-oz. pkg. peach-flavor gelatin
1   29-oz. can peach slices in light syrup, undrained
5   cups peach juice blend
½   cup lemon juice
8   10-oz. bottles ginger ale or club soda, chilled

**1.** In a 4-qt. saucepan combine the water, sugar, and gelatin. Bring to boiling, stirring to dissolve sugar and gelatin. Remove from heat.
**2.** Place peaches in a blender; cover and blend until smooth. In an extra-large bowl combine gelatin mixture, pureed peaches, peach juice blend, and lemon juice. Divide peach mixture among four 1-qt. containers. Cover and freeze at least 8 hours or until firm.
**3.** To serve, let one or more containers of frozen peach mixture stand at room temperature 1 hour (each quart makes 6 servings). Break into chunks with a fork. Place in a punch bowl. Gently stir in 2 bottles ginger ale per quart peach mixture until slushy. Serve immediately.
**Makes 24 servings (1 cup each).**
**TO MAKE AHEAD** Peach mixture can be frozen up to 3 months.
**EACH SERVING** *143 cal., 0 g fat, 0 mg chol., 26 mg sodium, 37 g carb., 1 g fiber, 36 g sugars, 1 g pro.*

# LEMONADE

**START TO FINISH** 20 minutes

3   cups cold water
1   cup lemon juice (5 to 6 lemons)
¾   cup sugar
    Ice cubes and lemon wedges

**1.** In a 1½-qt. pitcher stir together the water, lemon juice, and sugar until sugar dissolves. If desired, chill in the refrigerator. Serve over ice with lemon wedges. **Makes 4 servings (1 cup each).**
**EACH SERVING** *163 cal., 0 g fat, 0 mg chol., 6 mg sodium, 44 g carb., 1 g fiber, 39 g sugars, 0 g pro.*

## GREEN TEA LEMONADE

Bring 1 cup of the water to boiling; add 2 green tea bags. Steep 5 minutes. Remove bags; cool. Prepare as directed, stirring tea with remaining 2 cups water and remaining ingredients. Garnish with lemon peel strips.

## RASPBERRY LEMONADE

Prepare as directed, except place 1 cup fresh raspberries in a blender; cover and blend until pureed. Press through a fine-mesh sieve; discard seeds. Add puree to pitcher. Stir in sugar to taste. Garnish with fresh raspberries.

## CUSTOMIZE IT

PICK THE INGREDIENTS
TO CREATE A RECIPE
THAT'S ALL YOUR OWN.

## PARTY PUNCH

**HANDS-ON TIME** 15 minutes
**CHILL** 4 hours

- 1    qt. water
- 1    12-oz. can FROZEN JUICE CONCENTRATE, thawed
- 1    cup sugar
- 2½  cups JUICE BLEND, chilled
- 1    2-liter bottle CARBONATED BEVERAGE, chilled
- 1    recipe Ice Ring or ice cubes
- 1    cup STIR-IN (optional)

**1.** In a large pitcher or bowl combine the water and FROZEN JUICE CONCENTRATE. Add sugar; stir until dissolved. Cover and chill at least 4 hours.

**2.** To serve, pour juice mixture into an extra-large punch bowl. Stir in JUICE BLEND. Slowly stir in CARBONATED BEVERAGE. Add Ice Ring and, if desired, STIR-IN. **Makes 16 servings (1 cup each).**

**ICE RING** In the bottom of a fluted tube pan or ice ring mold place 2 to 3 cups of whole or sliced fruit, fresh mint leaves, and citrus peel curls. Fill with enough club soda or lemon-lime carbonated beverage to cover the fruit mixture. Freeze several hours or until firm. Add 2 to 3 cups additional club soda. Freeze several hours more or until firm. To unmold, dip the bottom of the pan in warm water for a few seconds to loosen the ice ring. Invert over a large plate, tapping on bottom of pan to release the ice ring. Transfer ice ring to the punch bowl.

**ICY SECRET**
Adding a decorative ice ring to the punch bowl is a vintage trick for chilling punch. Or keep an ice pail nearby for guests to scoop cubes into glasses.

*// APPETIZERS & DRINKS //*

## MIX & MATCH INGREDIENTS

**FROZEN JUICE CONCENTRATE**
- Cranberry juice
- Lemonade
- Limeade
- Orange juice
- Pineapple juice

**JUICE BLEND** *(Pick 1)*
- Cranberry-apple juice
- Pineapple-orange-banana juice blend
- Pink grapefruit juice
- Pomegranate juice
- Raspberry juice blend
- Strawberry juice blend

**CARBONATED BEVERAGE**
- Cream soda
- Ginger ale
- Lemon-lime carbonated beverage
- Orange carbonated beverage
- Strawberry carbonated beverage

**STIR-IN** *(Pick 1 or 2)*
- Citrus fruit slices
- Fresh blackberries, blueberries, and/or raspberries
- Kiwifruit slices
- Rum, vodka, gin, bourbon, or tequila
- Sherbet or sorbet
- Sliced fresh strawberries

EGGNOG

HOT SPICED CIDER

HAZELNUT-PUMPKIN
SPICED LATTES

## EGGNOG

**HANDS-ON TIME** 15 minutes
**CHILL** 4 hours

| | |
|---|---|
| 4 | egg yolks, beaten |
| 2 | cups milk |
| ⅓ | cup sugar |
| 1 | cup heavy cream* |
| 2 | Tbsp. (1 oz.) light rum |
| 2 | Tbsp. (1 oz.) bourbon |
| 1 | tsp. vanilla |
| | Ground nutmeg |

**»**

RUM AND
BOURBON are
completely
optional.
For a
nonalcoholic
version, omit
them and
increase milk
to 2⅓ cups.

**1.** In a 3-qt. heavy saucepan stir together yolks, milk, and sugar. Cook and stir over medium heat until mixture just coats a metal spoon; do not boil. Place pan in a sink of ice water; stir 2 minutes. Stir in cream, rum, bourbon, and vanilla. Cover; chill 4 to 24 hours. Top each serving with nutmeg.
**Makes 7 servings (½ cup each).**
**\*NOTE** To cut fat and calories, omit heavy cream and increase milk to 3 cups.
**EACH SERVING** *240 cal., 16 g fat (10 g sat. fat), 150 mg chol., 47 mg sodium, 14 g carb., 0 g fiber, 14 g sugars, 5 g pro.*

## HOT SPICED CIDER

**START TO FINISH** 20 minutes

| | |
|---|---|
| 8 | cups apple cider or apple juice |
| ¼ | cup packed brown sugar |
| 6 | inches stick cinnamon |
| 1 | tsp. whole allspice |
| 1 | tsp. whole cloves |
| 2 | 3×¾-inch strips orange peel |
| | Apple slices (optional) |

**1.** In a 3-qt. saucepan stir together cider and brown sugar. For spice bag, place cinnamon, allspice, cloves, and orange peel in the center of a double-thick, 6-inch square of 100%-cotton cheesecloth. Tie closed with clean cotton kitchen string. Add bag to the saucepan. Bring to boiling; reduce heat. Simmer, covered, 10 minutes. Remove and discard spice bag. Serve cider in mugs. If desired, garnish with apple slices.
**Makes 8 servings (1 cup each).**
**EACH SERVING** *143 cal., 0 g fat, 0 mg chol., 13 mg sodium, 35 g carb., 1 g fiber, 31 g sugars, 0 g pro.*

## HAZELNUT-PUMPKIN SPICED LATTES

**HANDS-ON TIME** 10 minutes
**SLOW COOK** 3 to 4 hours (low)

| | |
|---|---|
| 4 | cups whole milk |
| 4 | cups strong brewed coffee |
| ⅓ | cup sugar |
| 1½ | to 2 tsp. pumpkin pie spice |
| ½ | cup hazelnut liqueur (optional) |
| 1 | cup heavy cream |
| 2 | Tbsp. caramel-flavor ice cream topping |

**1.** In a 3½- or 4-qt. slow cooker combine milk, coffee, sugar, and pie spice. Cover; cook on low 3 to 4 hours. If desired, stir in liqueur. Serve immediately or keep warm, covered, on warm up to 2 hours.
**2.** In a bowl beat cream and caramel topping with a mixer on medium until soft peaks form (tips curl). Top servings with caramel whipped topping and additional caramel topping and/or pumpkin pie spice.
**Makes 11 servings (¾ cup each).**
**EACH SERVING** *166 cal., 11 g fat (7 g sat. fat), 39 mg chol., 58 mg sodium, 14 g carb., 0 g fiber, 13 g sugars, 3 g pro.*

**ESPRESSO HOT CHOCOLATE** Prepare as directed, except stir in 1 to 2 Tbsp. instant espresso coffee powder with the vanilla. If desired, top with whipped cream and chopped chocolate-covered coffee beans.

**PEANUT BUTTER HOT CHOCOLATE** Microwave 3 Tbsp. creamy peanut butter in 10-second intervals until melted and smooth, stirring after each interval. Prepare as directed, except whisk in melted peanut butter with the vanilla. If desired, top with whipped cream, chopped peanuts, and cut-up chocolate-covered peanut butter cups.

# HOT CHOCOLATE

**START TO FINISH** 15 minutes

- 6 cups half-and-half
- 12 oz. bittersweet or semisweet chocolate, chopped
- 2 cups heavy cream
- 1 Tbsp. vanilla
  Marshmallows or Sweetened Whipped Cream (p. 474) (optional)

**1.** In a 4-qt. saucepan or Dutch oven combine half-and-half and chocolate. Cook and stir over medium heat until chocolate is melted and mixture is steaming. Add heavy cream; heat through, but do not boil.

**2.** Whisk well. Stir in vanilla. Serve immediately. If desired, top servings with marshmallows.
**Makes 12 servings (¾ cup each).**
**SLOW COOKER DIRECTIONS** In a 3½- or 4-qt. slow cooker combine half-and-half, chocolate, and heavy cream. Cover and cook on low 4 hours or high 2 hours, vigorously whisking once halfway through. Continue as directed in Step 2. If desired, keep warm, covered, on warm or low up to 2 hours.

**EACH SERVING** *430 cal., 38 g fat (24 g sat. fat), 88 mg chol., 85 mg sodium, 22 g carb., 2 g fiber, 17 g sugars, 7 g pro.*

**JOYFUL ALMOND HOT CHOCOLATE** Prepare as directed, except substitute one 14-oz. can unsweetened coconut milk (not light) for 2 cups half-and-half. Stir in 1 tsp. almond extract. Garnish with chocolate syrup, toasted coconut, and whipped cream.

**RASPBERRY HOT CHOCOLATE** Prepare as directed, except stir in ½ cup raspberry beverage-flavoring syrup or ¼ cup raspberry liqueur with the vanilla. If desired, top with whipped cream, raspberries, and chocolate curls.

# SPICED CITRUS TEA

**START TO FINISH** 25 minutes

| | |
|---|---|
| 3 | qt. water |
| 4 | family-size tea bags |
| 2 | cups sugar |
| 2 | cinnamon sticks |
| 1 | cup orange juice |
| 2 | cups pineapple juice |
| 2 | tsp. lemon juice |
| | Orange and lemon slices |

**1.** For tea, bring 2 qt. of the water to boiling in a 4-qt. saucepan. Remove from heat. Add the tea bags; let steep 10 minutes.

**2.** Meanwhile, for simple syrup, in a 2-qt. saucepan combine the remaining 1 qt. water, the sugar, and cinnamon. Cook and stir over medium heat until sugar is dissolved. Cool slightly.

**3.** Discard tea bags. In a pitcher combine tea, simple syrup, and juices. Add orange and lemon slices. Serve warm. **Makes 16 servings (½ cup each).**

EACH SERVING *122 cal., 0 g fat, 0 mg chol., 5 mg sodium, 31 g carb., 0 g fiber, 30 g sugars, 0 g pro.*

### TEA YOUR WAY
This hot spiced tea is a cozy treat in winter, but it does double duty as iced tea in summer. Prepare as directed and chill it to serve over ice.

# BLACKBERRY-GINGER ARNOLD PALMER

**HANDS-ON TIME** 20 minutes
**COOK** 10 minutes
**COOL** 1 hour

- 1 recipe Blackberry-Ginger Simple Syrup
- 4 cups Iced Tea
- 1⅓ cups club soda or water
- ½ cup lemon juice
  Ice cubes
- 24 fresh blackberries
  Lemon slices and/or fresh thyme sprigs

**1.** Prepare Blackberry-Ginger Simple Syrup. In a large pitcher combine syrup, Iced Tea, club soda, and lemon juice. Stir to combine. Serve in glasses filled with ice cubes. Garnish with fresh blackberries and lemon slices and/or thyme sprigs. **Makes 8 servings (1 cup each).**
**BLACKBERRY-GINGER SIMPLE SYRUP** In a 1- or 1½-qt. saucepan combine 1½ cups water, 1 cup sugar, ½ cup fresh blackberries, and 1 Tbsp. grated fresh ginger. Bring to boiling, stirring to dissolve sugar and to slightly mash berries; reduce heat. Simmer, uncovered, about 10 minutes or until slightly syrupy. Let cool; strain. Store in a covered container in the refrigerator up to 1 month.
**EACH SERVING** *119 cal., 0 g fat, 0 mg chol., 25 mg sodium, 30 g carb., 2 g fiber, 27 g sugars, 1 g pro.*

## *ICED TEA*

Using 1 qt. water and 4 to 8 tea bags or 4 to 8 tsp. loose tea, prepare tea as for Hot Tea. Steep as directed; remove bags and let tea cool 2 hours at room temperature (this prevents cloudy tea). Serve over ice.

## *HOT TEA*

Use 1 tea bag or about 1 tsp. loose-leaf tea per cup. Bring fresh, cool water to boiling. If using loose-leaf tea, place it in an infuser. Warm a teapot by filling it with boiling water; let it stand a minute or until pot is warmed. Empty the pot. Place the tea bag(s) or infuser into the pot. (If not using an infuser or bag(s), place loose tea directly into pot.) Add more boiling water; cover pot and let steep 3 to 5 minutes. Remove bag(s) or infuser and pour into teacup(s) or pour through a strainer to catch loose tea.

## *REFRIGERATOR-BREWED TEA*

Place 6 to 8 tea bags in 1½ qt. cold water; cover. Let tea "brew" in the refrigerator about 24 hours. Remove tea bags and serve tea over ice. In a hurry? Use instant tea or "cold brew" tea bags according to package directions.

**TEA CHOICES**
Tea is available in bags or loose-leaf form.

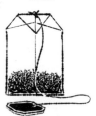

Unlike tea bags, loose-leaf tea requires an infuser such as a tea ball, spoon, or strainer.

// APPETIZERS & DRINKS //

# [GATHERINGS]
# BRUNCH

Better Homes &Gardens.

TEST KITCHEN

**MAKE-AHEAD RECIPE**

# EGG AND SAUSAGE BREAD BAKES

**HANDS-ON TIME** 30 minutes
**BAKE** 35 minutes at 350°F
**STAND** 5 minutes

2   14×4-inch unsliced loaves Italian or French bread
8   oz. uncooked sweet or mild Italian sausage, casings removed if present
¾   cup chopped red or yellow sweet pepper
½   cup sliced green onions
10  eggs, lightly beaten
⅔   cup heavy cream or half-and-half
¼   cup chopped fresh basil
½   tsp. salt
1½  cups shredded Fontina, mozzarella, or provolone cheese (6 oz.)

**1.** Preheat oven to 350°F. Line a 15×10-inch baking pan with parchment paper. Using a serrated knife, cut a wedge into the top of each loaf, cutting to about 1 inch from long sides. Using a spoon or your fingers, remove insides, leaving ¾-inch shells. Arrange in prepared baking pan.
**2.** In a 10-inch skillet cook sausage and sweet pepper 8 minutes or until sausage is browned and pepper is just tender, stirring in green onions the last 1 minute. Drain fat.
**3.** In a large bowl combine eggs, cream, basil, and salt. Stir in sausage mixture and 1 cup of the cheese.
**4.** Pour egg mixture into bread shells. Sprinkle with remaining ½ cup cheese. Bake 35 to 40 minutes or until eggs are set (160°F). Let stand 5 minutes before slicing. If desired, sprinkle with additional basil. **Makes 10 servings (two 1¼-inch slices each).**
**EACH SERVING** *490 cal., 23 g fat (11 g sat. fat), 245 mg chol., 977 mg sodium, 45 g carb., 0 g fiber, 1 g sugars, 20 g pro.*

### INSIDE SCOOP
Save the insides of the bread to make bread crumbs. Bake the pieces at 250°F for 8 to 10 minutes or until golden. Pulse into bread crumbs in a food processor. Place in freezer bags and store in the freezer up to 3 months.

// BRUNCH //

## SUGARED BACON-WRAPPED SAUSAGES

Preheat oven to 350°F. Line a 15×10-inch baking pan with foil; lightly coat with cooking spray. Cut 15 bacon slices into thirds and wrap pieces around 16 oz. small cooked smoked sausage links, securing ends with wooden toothpicks. Place ¾ cup brown sugar in a large plastic bag. Add bacon-wrapped sausages in batches to bag, seal, and gently shake. Place coated sausages in the prepared pan and bake, uncovered, about 30 minutes. Makes about 45 sausages.

## BACON-AND-EGG MUFFINS

**HANDS-ON TIME** 30 minutes
**BAKE** 15 minutes at 400°F
**COOL** 5 minutes

| | |
|---|---|
| 4 | slices bacon, cut into thirds |
| 5 | eggs |
| 2 | Tbsp. water |
| | Dash salt |
| | Dash black pepper |
| 1 | cup all-purpose flour |
| ½ | cup yellow cornmeal |
| 2 | Tbsp. sugar |
| 2½ | tsp. baking powder |
| ½ | tsp. salt |
| 1 | cup milk |
| ¼ | cup vegetable oil or melted butter |
| ½ | cup shredded cheddar cheese (2 oz.) |
| | Maple syrup (optional) |

**1.** Preheat oven to 400°F. In a 10-inch skillet cook bacon over medium heat just until it begins to crisp. Drain, reserving drippings. Return 2 tsp. drippings to skillet. For scrambled eggs, in a small bowl whisk together three of the eggs, the water, salt, and pepper; pour into hot skillet. Cook over medium heat, without stirring, until mixture begins to set on bottom and around edges. Using a spatula or large spoon, lift and turn partially cooked egg mixture so that uncooked portion flows underneath. Continue cooking 2 to 3 minutes or until egg mixture is cooked through but is still glossy and moist. Immediately remove from heat.

**2.** Brush twelve 2½-inch muffin cups with some of the remaining bacon drippings. In a medium bowl stir together flour, cornmeal, sugar, baking powder, and ½ tsp. salt. Make a well in center of flour mixture. In a small bowl combine remaining two eggs, milk, and oil. Add egg mixture all at once to flour mixture. Stir just until moistened (batter should be lumpy). Fold in scrambled eggs and cheese. Spoon batter into muffin cups (cups will be full); top with bacon pieces.

**3.** Bake 15 to 17 minutes or until light brown and a toothpick comes out clean. Cool in muffin cups on a wire rack 5 minutes. Remove from muffin cups. Serve warm. If desired, serve with syrup. **Makes 12 muffins.**

**EACH MUFFIN** *202 cal., 12 g fat (3 g sat. fat), 89 mg chol., 356 mg sodium, 16 g carb., 1 g fiber, 3 g sugars, 7 g pro.*

## EGGS BENEDICT

**START TO FINISH** 25 minutes

| | |
|---|---|
| 4 | Poached Eggs (p. 48) |
| 1 | recipe Hollandaise Sauce or Mock Hollandaise Sauce |
| 2 | English muffins, split |
| 4 | slices Canadian-style bacon Cracked black pepper |

**1.** Prepare Poached Eggs. Remove eggs from skillet with a slotted spoon and place in a large pan of warm (but not hot) water to keep warm. Prepare Hollandaise Sauce.
**2.** Preheat broiler. Place muffin halves, cut sides up, on a baking sheet. Broil 3 to 4 inches from heat 2 minutes or until toasted. Top with Canadian-style bacon; broil 1 minute more or until bacon is heated through.
**3.** To serve, top each bacon-topped muffin half with an egg. Spoon sauce over eggs and sprinkle with pepper. **Makes 4 servings (1 topped muffin half each).**

EACH SERVING  399 cal., 32 g fat (18 g sat. fat), 391 mg chol., 688 mg sodium, 15 g carb., 0 g fiber, 0 g sugars, 14 g pro.

## HOLLANDAISE SAUCE

**START TO FINISH** 15 minutes

| | |
|---|---|
| 3 | egg yolks, lightly beaten |
| 1 | Tbsp. lemon juice |
| 1 | Tbsp. water |
| ½ | cup butter, cut into thirds and softened |

No double boiler for making the sauce? Use a heat-safe bowl large enough to nestle in the top of a saucepan but not touch the simmering water below. Add the butter gradually to create a smooth sauce.

**1.** In top of a double boiler combine yolks, lemon juice, and the water. Add one-third of the butter. Place over gently boiling water (upper pan should not touch water). Cook, whisking rapidly, until butter melts and sauce begins to thicken. (Sauce may appear to curdle but will get smooth when remaining butter is added.) Add remaining butter, one-third at a time, whisking constantly until melted. Cook and stir 2 to 2½ minutes more or until thickened. Immediately remove from heat. If sauce is too thick or curdles, quickly whisk in 1 to 2 Tbsp. *hot water.* Season with *salt* and *black pepper.* **Makes ¾ cup (2 Tbsp. each).**

EACH SERVING  163 cal., 18 g fat (11 g sat. fat), 146 mg chol., 210 mg sodium, 1 g carb., 0 g fiber, 0 g sugars, 2 g pro.

## MOCK HOLLANDAISE

In a 1-qt. saucepan combine ⅓ cup each sour cream and mayonnaise, 2 tsp. lemon juice, and 1 tsp. yellow mustard. Heat and stir over medium-low heat until warm. Thin with a little milk. Makes ⅔ cup.

# EGG CASSEROLE

**HANDS-ON TIME** 20 minutes
**BAKE** 45 minutes at 325°F
**STAND** 10 minutes

8   cups BREAD CUBES (tip, *p. 18*)
    MEAT
    VEGETABLES
2   cups SHREDDED CHEESE (8 oz.)
8   eggs, lightly beaten
3   cups DAIRY
    SEASONING

**1.** Preheat oven to 325°F. Grease a 3-qt. rectangular baking dish. Spread half of the BREAD CUBES in prepared baking dish. Add MEAT, VEGETABLES, and SHREDDED CHEESE. Top with remaining BREAD CUBES.
**2.** In a medium bowl whisk together eggs, DAIRY, and SEASONING. Pour over layers in baking dish.
**3.** Bake 45 to 55 minutes or until a knife comes out clean. Let stand 10 minutes before serving. **Makes 12 servings.**

**EASY EVERYDAY**

*For a smaller crowd, prepare as directed, except cut ingredients in half and use a 2-qt. baking dish. Bake about 45 minutes or until a knife comes out clean. Let stand 10 minutes before serving.*

## CUSTOMIZE IT
PICK THE INGREDIENTS TO CREATE A RECIPE THAT'S ALL YOUR OWN.

≪

EGGS can be partially or completely replaced with refrigerated egg product (¼ cup per egg) to cut cholesterol.

**MAKE IT AHEAD**
Prepare as directed through Step 2. Cover and chill 2 to 24 hours. To serve, preheat oven to 350°F. Bake, uncovered, 60 to 65 minutes or until a knife comes out clean. Let stand 10 minutes.

# MIX & MATCH INGREDIENTS

**BREAD CUBES** (*Pick 1*)
- Baguette-style French bread
- English muffins
- Hawaiian sweet bread
- Pumpernickel bread
- Rye bread
- Texas toast
- White or whole wheat bread

**MEAT** (*Pick 1*)
- 12 slices bacon, crisp-cooked and crumbled
- 10 oz. chopped Canadian-style bacon
- Two 6-oz. cans lump crabmeat, drained and flaked
- 4 cups cubed cooked ham, smoked sausage, or smoked turkey
- 1 lb. cooked bulk sausage

**VEGETABLES**
(*Pick 1 or 2*)
- 3 cups blanched cut-up asparagus or broccoli florets
- 2 cups frozen hash brown potatoes
- 1 cup canned sliced mushrooms
- 2 cups fresh or frozen chopped spinach (thawed and squeezed dry if frozen)
- 1½ cups chopped sweet pepper

**SHREDDED CHEESE**
(*Pick 1*)
- Cheddar
- Italian blend
- Monterey Jack
- Swiss

**DAIRY** (*Pick 1*)
- Half-and-half
- Milk
- 2 cups milk + 1 cup sour cream

**SEASONING** (*Pick 1*)
- 2 Tbsp. chopped fresh basil or Italian parsley
- 2 tsp. dried dill
- 4 cloves garlic, minced
- ½ cup sliced green onions
- 2 Tbsp. Dijon or coarse-ground mustard

// BRUNCH //

QUICHE LORRAINE

»

**ROASTED TOMATOES** are easy to make. Preheat broiler; spread cherry tomatoes in a shallow baking pan. Broil 4 inches from heat about 4 minutes or until skins begin to brown lightly.

## QUICHE LORRAINE

**HANDS-ON TIME** 40 minutes
**BAKE** 13 minutes at 450°F +
45 minutes at 325°F
**STAND** 10 minutes

1   recipe Pastry for Single-Crust Pie *(p. 609)*
8   slices bacon
1½  cups halved and thinly sliced onion
4   eggs
1   cup half-and-half
¾   cup milk
¼   tsp. salt
    Dash grated whole or ground nutmeg
1½  cups shredded Swiss cheese (6 oz.)
1   Tbsp. all-purpose flour
    Roasted cherry tomatoes and/or fresh thyme (optional)

**1.** Preheat oven to 450°F. Prepare Pastry for Single-Crust Pie, crimping edge high to contain filling. Line unpricked pastry with a double thickness of heavy foil. Bake 8 minutes on a baking sheet; remove foil. Bake 5 to 6 minutes more or until light brown. Remove from oven. Reduce oven temperature to 325°F. (Pastry shell should still be hot when filling is added; do not partially bake pastry shell ahead of time.)

**2.** Meanwhile, in a 10-inch skillet cook bacon over medium heat until crisp. Drain, reserving 2 Tbsp. drippings in skillet. Finely crumble bacon. Add onion to reserved drippings; cook over medium heat 8 to 10 minutes or until tender and starting to brown.

**3.** In a medium bowl or extra-large measuring cup whisk together eggs, half-and-half, milk, salt, and nutmeg. Stir in bacon and onion. In another medium bowl combine cheese and flour; toss to coat. Add to egg mixture; mix well.

**4.** Place hot baked pastry shell on oven rack; pour in egg mixture. Bake 45 to 55 minutes or until edges are puffed and center is set. Let stand 10 minutes before serving. If desired, top with tomatoes and/or thyme.
**Makes 6 servings (1 slice each).**
**EACH SERVING** *590 cal., 41 g fat (19 g sat. fat), 202 mg chol., 678 mg sodium, 33 g carb., 2 g fiber, 5 g sugars, 22 g pro.*

» **ITALIAN QUICHE** Prepare as directed, except substitute 6 oz. pancetta, cut into strips, for the bacon and omit the nutmeg. Cook pancetta until crisp; drain on paper towels. Stir pancetta, ½ cup chopped roasted red sweet pepper, and ¼ cup chopped Italian parsley into egg mixture. Continue as directed, using shredded mozzarella cheese in place of the Swiss cheese.

» **MUSHROOM QUICHE** Prepare as directed, except omit bacon. Use 2 Tbsp. vegetable oil in place of the bacon drippings. Cook 1½ cups sliced fresh cremini mushrooms and 2 cloves garlic, minced, with the onion. Stir ½ cup diced cooked ham into filling with onion mixture. If desired, top with additional sautéed mushrooms.

# MINI QUICHES

**HANDS-ON TIME** 20 minutes
**BAKE** 13 minutes at 425°F

1   14.1-oz. pkg. (2 crusts) rolled refrigerated unbaked piecrusts
2   eggs, lightly beaten
⅔   cup milk
¼   cup finely chopped green onions (optional)
¼   tsp. salt
¼   tsp. freshly ground black pepper
½   to 1 cup desired finely chopped or crumbled cooked meat and/or vegetable, such as bacon, ham, sausage, spinach, broccoli, or red sweet pepper
¼   to ½ cup desired finely shredded or crumbled cheese

**1.** Preheat oven to 425°F. Let piecrusts stand according to package directions.
**2.** Meanwhile, in a large glass measuring cup or medium bowl combine next five ingredients (through black pepper).
**3.** Unroll piecrusts. Using a 2½- or 3-inch round cutter, cut out pastry. Press pastry circles onto bottoms and up sides of 24 muffin cups. Place a pinch of meat and/or vegetable and cheese into each pastry shell. Pour egg mixture over filling.
**4.** Bake 13 to 15 minutes or until filling is puffed and pastry is golden. Cool in muffin cups 2 minutes. Carefully remove from muffin cups. If desired, sprinkle with additional black pepper and cheese. Serve warm. **Makes 12 servings (2 mini quiches each).**
**TO FREEZE** Cool quiches. Place in a single layer in a freezer container; seal and freeze up to 1 month. To serve, let quiches stand at room temperature 30 minutes. Preheat oven to 350°F. Transfer quiches to a baking sheet. Bake 15 to 18 minutes.

**EACH SERVING** *168 cal., 10 g fat (4 g sat. fat), 40 mg chol., 295 mg sodium, 17 g carb., 0 g fiber, 1 g sugars, 4 g pro.*

ANY-FLAVOR MINI QUICHES

**MAKE IT AHEAD**
Prepare egg mixture and press pastry circles into muffin cups as directed. Cover tightly with plastic wrap and chill 2 to 24 hours. To serve, assemble quiches and bake as directed.

// **BRUNCH** //

## HAM AND CHEESE SLAB PIES

**HANDS-ON TIME** 30 minutes
**BAKE** 25 minutes at 400°F

6    oz. cream cheese, softened
2    Tbsp. honey mustard
1    17.3-oz. pkg. (2 sheets) frozen puff pastry sheets, thawed
6    oz. thinly sliced Black Forest ham
½    cup thinly sliced red onion
6    oz. thinly sliced Gruyère, Swiss, or cheddar cheese
1    egg

**1.** Preheat oven to 400°F. Line two large baking sheets with parchment paper. In a small bowl combine cream cheese and mustard. On a lightly floured surface roll each pastry sheet into a 15×12-inch rectangle. Transfer to prepared baking sheets.
**2.** Spread half of each pastry sheet lengthwise with cream cheese mixture, leaving ½ inch unfilled along outside edges. Layer with ham and onion; top with sliced cheese. Combine egg and 1 Tbsp. *water*. Brush edges of pastry with some of the egg mixture. Fold unfilled pastry over filling; seal edges with a fork. Brush tops with egg mixture. Using a sharp knife, cut slits in tops.
**3.** Bake 25 minutes or until tops and bottoms are golden. If tops brown too quickly, cover with foil. Slide pies and parchment paper onto wire racks; cool slightly. Cut into strips.
**Makes 12 servings (1 strip each).**
**TO MAKE AHEAD** Prepare as directed through Step 2, except do not brush tops with egg mixture. Freeze pies on parchment paper-lined baking sheets. Wrap tightly with plastic wrap, then with foil. Freeze up to 2 months. To serve, thaw in refrigerator overnight. Place on lined baking sheets; brush with egg mixture. Bake as directed.
**EACH SERVING** *360 cal., 26 g fat (9 g sat. fat), 56 mg chol., 361 mg sodium, 21 g carb., 1 g fiber, 2 g sugars, 11 g pro.*

» **PARCHMENT PAPER** is a disposable, grease- and moisture-resistant paper that is nonstick and can be used in the oven (up to approximately 425°F). Use it to line baking sheets and roasting pans for easy cleanup.

CAKE DONUTS

## CAKE DONUTS

**HANDS-ON TIME** 45 minutes
**CHILL** 1 hour

4    cups all-purpose flour
2    tsp. baking powder
¼    tsp. salt
2    eggs
1¼   cups granulated sugar
1    tsp. vanilla
⅔    cup milk
¼    cup butter, melted
     Vegetable oil for deep-fat frying (tip, p. 21)
     Granulated sugar, powdered sugar, Powdered Sugar Icing (p. 538), and/or Chocolate Powdered Sugar Icing (p. 538)

**1.** In a medium mixing bowl combine flour, baking powder, and salt. In a large mixing bowl combine eggs, granulated sugar, and vanilla; beat with a mixer on medium 3 minutes or until thick. In a small bowl combine milk and melted butter.
**2.** Add flour mixture and milk mixture alternately to egg mixture, beating on low speed after each addition until just combined. (Stir in the last of the flour mixture if needed.) Cover and chill dough 1 hour or until easy to handle.
**3.** On a lightly floured surface roll dough to ½-inch thickness. Cut dough with a floured 2½-inch donut cutter, dipping cutter into flour between cuts. Reroll dough as necessary.
**4.** Fry two or three donuts at a time in deep hot oil (365°F) about 2 minutes or until donuts are golden brown, turning once. Remove with a slotted spoon and drain on paper towels. Repeat with remaining dough. Cool donuts slightly and coat with additional granulated sugar (cool completely to coat with powdered sugar) or dip tops in Powdered Sugar Icing and/or Chocolate Powdered Sugar Icing.
**Makes 16 donuts.**
**EACH DONUT** *488 cal., 31 g fat (5 g sat. fat), 32 mg chol., 135 mg sodium, 49 g carb., 1 g fiber, 25 g sugars, 4 g pro.*

# FRUIT COFFEE CAKE

**HANDS-ON TIME** 30 minutes
**BAKE** 40 minutes at 350°F
**COOL** 30 minutes

MIXING SUGAR and cornstarch before adding to the fruit prevents cornstarch lumps from forming.

- 1 recipe Streusel
- 2 cups fresh red raspberries or blueberries; sliced, peeled apricots or peaches; and/or chopped, peeled apples
- ⅓ cup water
- ⅓ cup granulated sugar
- 2 Tbsp. cornstarch
- 1¾ cups all-purpose flour
- ¾ cup granulated sugar
- ¾ tsp. baking powder
- ¼ tsp. baking soda
- 5 Tbsp. butter, cut up
- 1 egg, lightly beaten
- ¾ cup buttermilk or sour milk (tip, *p. 474*)
- 1 tsp. vanilla
- 1 recipe Powdered Sugar Icing (*p. 538*) (optional)

**1.** Prepare Streusel. In a 2-qt. saucepan combine fruit and the water. Bring to boiling; reduce heat. Simmer (do not simmer if using all raspberries), covered, 5 minutes or until fruit is tender. Stir together ⅓ cup sugar and cornstarch; stir into fruit. Cook and stir over medium heat until thickened and bubbly.

**2.** Preheat oven to 350°F. Lightly grease a 9-inch square baking pan. In a large bowl stir together next four ingredients (through baking soda). Using a pastry blender, cut in butter until mixture resembles coarse crumbs. Make a well in center of flour mixture.

**3.** In a medium bowl combine egg, buttermilk, and vanilla. Add egg mixture all at once to flour mixture. Stir just until moistened (batter should be lumpy). Spread half of the batter into prepared baking pan. Spread with filling and sprinkle with ⅔ cup of the streusel. Drop remaining batter in small mounds onto layers in pan; sprinkle with remaining streusel.

**4.** Bake 40 to 45 minutes or until golden and a toothpick comes out clean. Cool in pan on a wire rack 30 minutes. Serve warm. If desired, sprinkle with additional raspberries. Or if desired, cool completely; drizzle with Powdered Sugar Icing and sprinkle with additional raspberries. **Makes 9 servings.**

**EACH SERVING** *520 cal., 18 g fat (11 g sat. fat), 66 mg chol., 308 mg sodium, 84 g carb., 2 g fiber, 47 g sugars, 7 g pro.*

## *STREUSEL*

In a medium bowl stir together 1½ cups all-purpose flour, ¾ cup packed brown sugar, ½ tsp. ground cinnamon, and ¼ tsp. salt. Drizzle with ½ cup melted butter and ½ tsp. vanilla; toss with a fork to combine.

**GET-TOGETHER**

*For a larger coffee cake, prepare as directed, except double ingredients and pour into a 13×9-inch baking pan. Bake 45 to 50 minutes or until a toothpick comes out clean. Makes 16 servings.*

## CHOCOLATE-PECAN COFFEE CAKE

**HANDS-ON TIME** 30 minutes
**BAKE** 55 minutes at 325°F
**COOL** 20 minutes

½   cup butter, softened
1    cup granulated sugar
2    tsp. baking powder
½   tsp. baking soda
¼   tsp. salt
2    eggs
1    tsp. vanilla
2¼  cups all-purpose flour
1    8-oz. carton sour cream
1    recipe Chocolate-Pecan
     Filling

**1.** Preheat oven to 325°F. Grease and flour a 10-inch fluted tube pan. In a large bowl beat butter with a mixer on medium to high 30 seconds. Add granulated sugar, baking powder, baking soda, and salt. Beat until combined, scraping bowl as needed. Add eggs, one at a time, beating after each addition. Beat in vanilla. Add flour and sour cream alternately, beating on low after each addition just until combined.

**2.** Sprinkle half of the Chocolate-Pecan Filling into prepared tube pan. Spread half of the batter over topping in pan. Sprinkle with remaining filling and spread with remaining batter.

**3.** Bake 55 to 65 minutes or until a long wooden skewer comes out clean. Cool in pan on a wire rack 20 minutes. Invert cake and remove pan. Serve warm. **Makes 12 servings (1 slice each).**

**EACH SERVING** *550 cal., 28 g fat (16 g sat. fat), 86 mg chol., 297 mg sodium, 71 g carb., 2 g fiber, 43 g sugars, 6 g pro.*

### CHOCOLATE-PECAN FILLING

In a large bowl stir together 1 cup each all-purpose flour and packed brown sugar and 1 tsp. ground cinnamon. Cut in ½ cup cold butter until mixture resembles coarse crumbs. Stir in ¾ cup semisweet chocolate chips and ½ cup each flaked coconut and chopped pecans.

### MIMOSAS

A classic mimosa ratio is one part fruit juice to three parts Champagne, Prosecco, or sparkling wine. Think outside the orange juice box, combining flavors and adding herbs or aromatics—mango-lime, grapefruit-rosemary, berry-ginger, strawberry-thyme—before topping off with bubbles.

**SWEET RICOTTA AND STRAWBERRY BOWLS**

# SWEET RICOTTA AND STRAWBERRY BOWLS

**START TO FINISH** 35 minutes

- 1   lb. fresh strawberries, halved or quartered
- 1   Tbsp. chopped fresh mint
- 1   tsp. sugar
- 1   15-oz. carton part-skim ricotta cheese
- 3   Tbsp. honey or agave syrup
- ½   tsp. vanilla
- ¼   tsp. lemon zest

**1.** In a medium bowl gently stir together strawberries, mint, and sugar. Let stand 15 minutes or until berries are softened and starting to release their juices.
**2.** Meanwhile, in a medium bowl beat remaining ingredients with a mixer on medium 2 minutes.
**3.** Divide ricotta mixture among bowls. Top each with strawberry mixture. Serve immediately or cover and chill up to 4 hours. Top with additional mint. **Makes 6 servings (1 bowl each).**

**EACH SERVING** *159 cal., 6 g fat (4 g sat. fat), 22 mg chol., 90 mg sodium, 18 g carb., 2 g fiber, 12 g sugars, 9 g pro.*

## *FRESH FRUIT COMPOTE*

For dressing, remove 1 tsp. zest and squeeze ¼ cup juice from 1 orange. In a small bowl combine orange zest and juice and, if desired, 1 Tbsp. finely snipped crystallized ginger. In a large bowl combine 2 cups each sliced strawberries and seedless green and/or red grapes, halved; 1 large banana, cut into bite-size pieces; 1 cup blueberries; ¾ cup chopped fresh pineapple; and ½ cup finely snipped pitted whole dates. Drizzle with dressing; toss gently to coat. Divide fruit mixture and 1 cup plain Greek yogurt among small bowls. Makes 8 servings.

PURE MAPLE SYRUP is maple sap that's been boiled down to reduce water and concentrate flavors. It has no added sugar, thickeners, artificial colors, or flavors. Maple-flavor syrup (aka pancake syrup or table syrup) is mostly corn and/or high-fructose syrup with added maple flavoring.

# PUFFED OVEN PANCAKE

**HANDS-ON TIME** 15 minutes
**BAKE** 20 minutes at 400°F

- 2   Tbsp. butter
- 4   eggs, lightly beaten
- ⅔   cup all-purpose flour
- ⅔   cup milk
- ¼   tsp. salt
     Maple syrup (optional)
     Powdered sugar (optional)

**1.** Preheat oven to 400°F. Place butter in a 12-inch oven-going skillet.* Heat skillet in oven 3 to 5 minutes or until butter is melted.
**2.** Meanwhile, in a medium bowl whisk together eggs, flour, milk, and salt until smooth. Immediately pour batter into hot skillet. Bake 20 to 25 minutes or until puffed and brown.
**3.** If desired, top pancake with syrup and sprinkle lightly with powdered sugar. Serve warm.
**Makes 8 servings (1 slice each).**
***NOTE** If you don't have a 12-inch oven-going skillet, use a 13×9-inch metal baking pan.

**EACH SERVING** *278 cal., 17 g fat (10 g sat. fat), 133 mg chol., 235 mg sodium, 24 g carb., 1 g fiber, 15 g sugars, 5 g pro.*

**CHANGE IT UP**

*This airy, eggy pancake (aka Dutch baby or German pancake) tastes delicious with berries or sliced fruit; a drizzle of honey, fudge sauce, or caramel sauce; and/or whipped cream or jam.*

PUFFED OVEN PANCAKE

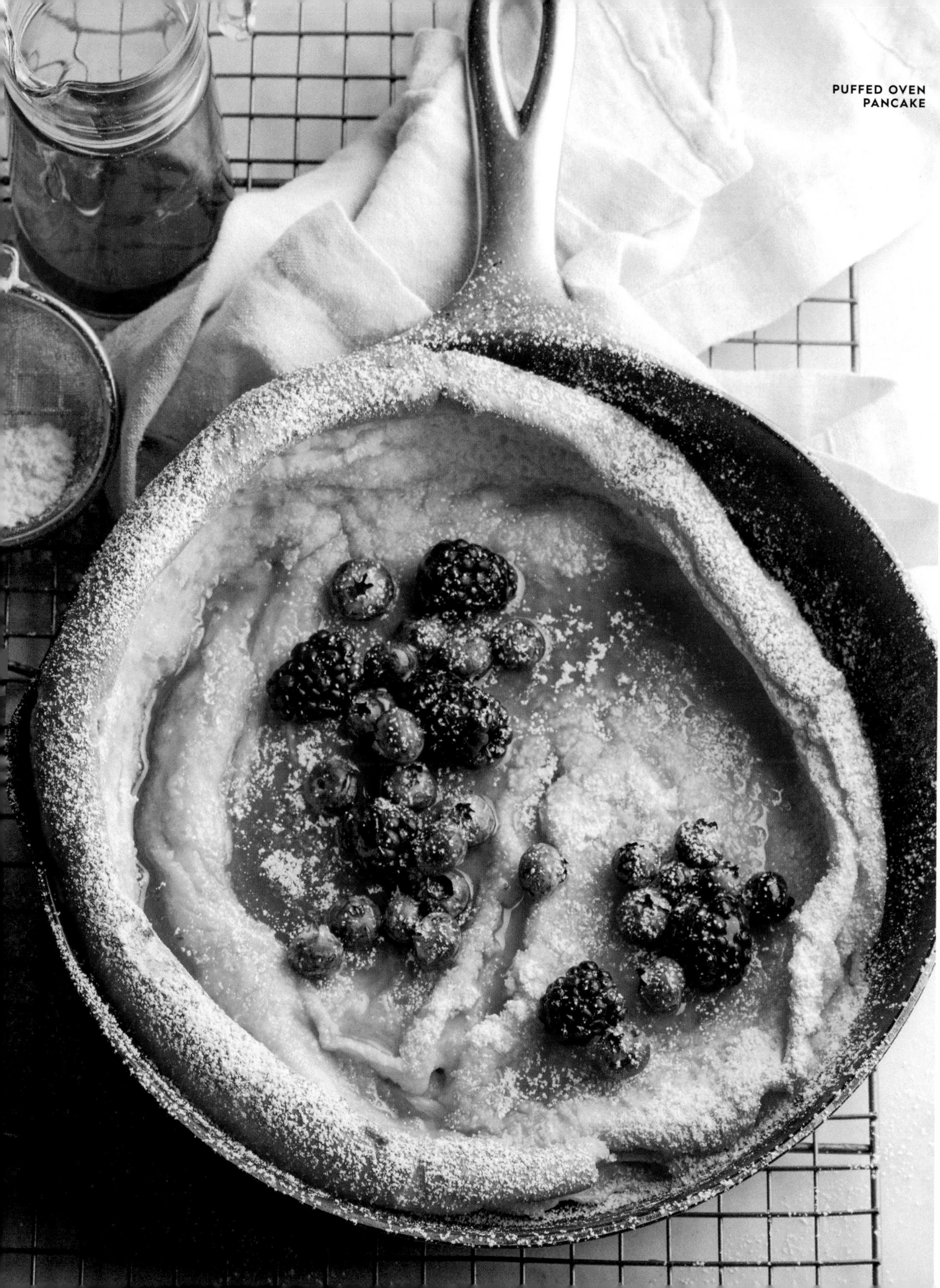

# CREPES

**START TO FINISH** 25 minutes

2      eggs, lightly beaten
1½    cups milk
1      cup all-purpose flour
1      Tbsp. vegetable oil
¼      tsp. salt

**1.** In a medium bowl whisk together all of the ingredients until smooth.
**2.** Heat a lightly greased 8- to 10-inch crepe pan or 8- or 10-inch flared-side skillet* over medium-high heat; remove from heat. Spoon 2 to 4 Tbsp. batter into pan or skillet; lift and tilt skillet to spread batter evenly. Cook about 1 minute or until brown on one side only. Invert over paper towels; remove crepe. Repeat with remaining batter, greasing skillet occasionally. If crepes are browning too quickly, reduce heat to medium. **Makes 9 servings (1 crepe each).**
**\*NOTE** Determine the amount of batter needed per crepe by measuring the bottom of the crepe pan or skillet. For a pan or skillet with a 6-inch bottom, use 2 Tbsp. batter. If it has an 8- to 10-inch bottom, use ¼ cup batter.
**EACH SERVING** *100 cal., 4 g fat (1 g sat. fat), 45 mg chol., 100 mg sodium, 13 g carb., 0 g fiber, 2 g sugars, 4 g pro.*

>> **CHOCOLATE-HAZELNUT CREPES** Prepare as directed, except for each crepe, spread unbrowned side with 1 to 2 Tbsp. chocolate-hazelnut spread. Sprinkle 1 to 2 Tbsp. chopped toasted hazelnuts along one edge of crepe; roll up from the filled edge.

>> **STRAWBERRY-CREAM CHEESE CREPES** Prepare as directed, except cool crepes. For each crepe, spread unbrowned side with 2 to 3 Tbsp. whipped cream cheese. Arrange ¼ to ⅓ cup sliced fresh strawberries along one edge of crepe. Drizzle with 1 to 2 tsp. honey; roll up from the filled edge.

**WARM AND TOASTY**
To keep crepes warm, arrange unfilled crepes on a baking sheet, overlapping slightly and using parchment paper between layers. Keep warm in a 200°F oven up to 30 minutes.

STRAWBERRY-CREAM CHEESE CREPES

STUFFED FRENCH TOAST

Use a bread knife to slice the bread pieces from the top, avoiding cutting all the way through. A gentle back-and-forth motion with a serrated blade cuts through without squishing the bread.

## STUFFED FRENCH TOAST

**HANDS-ON TIME** 25 minutes
**CHILL** 2 hours

| | |
|---|---|
| 4 | 1½-inch slices French bread or challah bread |
| ½ | of an 8-oz. pkg. cream cheese, softened |
| 2 | Tbsp. granulated sugar |
| ½ | tsp. vanilla |
| 4 | eggs |
| 1 | cup milk |
| 2 | Tbsp. honey or granulated sugar |
| 1 | tsp. vanilla |
| | Maple syrup or 1 recipe Caramel Sauce (p. 604) |
| | Powdered sugar (optional) |

**1.** Make a pocket in each bread slice by starting from top-crust edge and cutting almost to bottom edge. For filling, in a medium bowl beat cream cheese with a mixer on medium to high 30 seconds. Beat in 2 Tbsp. granulated sugar and ½ tsp. vanilla until smooth. Spoon filling into pockets. Place bread slices in a 2-qt. rectangular baking dish.

**2.** In a medium bowl whisk together eggs, milk, honey, and 1 tsp. vanilla. Pour egg mixture over bread slices. Press bread down lightly to moisten. Cover and chill 2 to 24 hours, turning bread slices once or twice.

**3.** Heat a lightly greased griddle over medium heat. Add bread slices; cook 4 to 6 minutes or until golden, turning once. Serve with syrup and, if desired, sprinkle lightly with powdered sugar. **Makes 4 servings (1 slice each).**

**EACH SERVING** *403 cal., 16 g fat (8 g sat. fat), 222 mg chol., 358 mg sodium, 51 g carb., 1 g fiber, 32 g sugars, 14 g pro.*

**BACON-STUFFED FRENCH TOAST** Prepare as directed, except stir 3 slices crisp-cooked and crumbled bacon into cream cheese mixture.

**STRAWBERRY-STUFFED FRENCH TOAST** Prepare as directed, except stir ½ cup chopped fresh strawberries into cream cheese mixture.

**BANANA-STUFFED FRENCH TOAST** Prepare as directed, except in a 6-inch skillet melt 1 Tbsp. butter over medium heat. Add ½ cup sliced banana and 2 tsp. granulated sugar; cook and stir 30 to 60 seconds or until banana is softened. Remove from heat. Stir in ¼ cup chopped toasted pecans; cool slightly. Stir into cream cheese mixture.

**MASCARPONE-STUFFED FRENCH TOAST** Prepare as directed, except in filling substitute ½ cup mascarpone cheese for the cream cheese, reduce granulated sugar to 1 Tbsp., and add ¼ cup chopped toasted pecans. In egg mixture substitute 2 Tbsp. packed brown sugar for the honey or granulated sugar and add ½ tsp. ground cinnamon.

**MASCARPONE** is a soft, rich Italian cheese that tastes like a cross between whipped butter and cream cheese. It can be used in place of cream cheese in any variation of this stuffed French toast.

// BRUNCH //

## WAYS TO BREW HOT COFFEE

**AUTOMATIC DRIP**
Automatic drip coffeemakers and single-cup brewers are convenient, make reliably good coffee, and offer a variety of options.

**MANUAL COFFEE CONE DRIPPER** A manual drip lets you control the temperature of the water used to brew the coffee. For a good cup of coffee, bring water to a full boil. Take the kettle off the heat and pause for a moment before pouring the water over the ground coffee. Water just under boiling (195°F to 205°F) best releases coffee's flavorful compounds.

**FRENCH PRESS** The French press produces a richly textured coffee filled with natural oils. Some sediment remains in the coffee, which adds character to the brew. To use a French press, measure coffee into the carafe. Heat water as for a manual coffee cone dripper. Pour water over coffee; place lid on carafe. Wait 4 minutes; slowly press plunger to bottom of carafe to trap the grounds; serve.

## COFFEE BASICS

Consider these points before you buy or make coffee.

**ROAST** The longer the beans are roasted, the darker they get. Choose light beans for lighter flavor and darker beans for a stronger, bolder flavor.

**GRIND** Once ground, coffee loses its freshness relatively quickly. Store ground coffee in a cool, dark place up to 3 months. Or purchase whole beans and grind them fresh each time you make coffee. Follow manufacturer's guidelines for your coffeemaker for fine or coarse grind. Coffee too coarsely ground can result in weak flavor; if it's too finely ground, it can taste bitter and clog the filter.

**MEASURE** For each 6-oz. cup, use ¾ cup fresh, cold water and 1 to 2 Tbsp. ground coffee, depending on how strong you like your brew.

**STORAGE** Whole beans stay fresh about a week, so buy in small amounts. Store at room temperature in an airtight container.

COLD BREW COFFEE

>> GROUND COFFEE can be added in any ratio you like for Cold Brew Coffee, but we like to use 1 to 2 Tbsp. coffee per ½ cup water.

## COLD BREW COFFEE

**HANDS-ON TIME** 5 minutes
**STAND** 12 hours

- 6 cups cold water
- 1½ cups coarse-ground coffee
  Ice cubes
  Coffee creamer or milk (optional)

**1.** In a 2-qt. pitcher or glass jar stir the water into ground coffee. Cover with plastic wrap and let stand at room temperature 12 to 24 hours.
**2.** Line a fine-mesh sieve with 100%-cotton cheesecloth or a coffee filter; pour coffee through sieve into a large bowl or another 2-qt. container. To serve, pour coffee over ice and, if desired, stir in coffee creamer. Store remaining coffee in refrigerator up to 2 weeks.
**Makes 6 servings (6 oz. each).**
**EACH SERVING** *2 cal., 0 fat, 0 mg chol., 4 mg sodium, 0 g carb., 0 g fiber, 0 g sugars, 0 g pro.*

## VANILLA COFFEE CREAMER

In a 1-qt. canning jar combine 2 cups heavy cream, half-and-half, or milk; one 14-oz. can sweetened condensed milk; and 2 tsp. vanilla. Seal and store in the refrigerator up to 2 weeks. Shake before serving.

## AMARETTO COFFEE CREAMER

In a 1-qt. canning jar combine 2 cups heavy cream, half-and-half, or milk; one 14-oz. can sweetened condensed milk; 1 tsp. almond extract; and ½ tsp. ground cinnamon. Seal and store in refrigerator up to 2 weeks. Shake before serving.

# BE YOUR OWN BARISTA

Espresso—brewed by forcing hot water through finely ground coffee at high pressure—is the base for many caffeinated coffee-shop drinks. Here are ratios for the classics, but adjust strength to your liking.

### CAFÉ AU LAIT
Foamed milk
Steamed milk 10 oz.
Espresso 2 oz.

### MOCHA
Steamed milk 1 oz.
Chocolate 2 oz.
Espresso 2 oz.

### FLAT WHITE
Steamed milk 4 oz.
Espresso 2 oz.

### CAPPUCCINO
Foamed milk 2 oz.
Steamed milk 2 oz.
Espresso 2 oz.

### LATTE
Steamed milk 10 oz.
Espresso 2 oz.

### CAFÉ BOMBON
Foamed milk 4 oz.
Espresso 2 oz.

### AMERICANO
Hot water 3 oz.
Espresso 2 oz.

### CON PANNA
Whipped cream 3 oz.
Espresso 2 oz.

### AFFOGATO
Vanilla ice cream 3 oz.
Espresso 2 oz.

[GATHERINGS]

# MAIN DISHES

**MAKE-AHEAD RECIPE.** See also cooking charts, *pp. 52–67.*

## STANDING RIB ROAST

**HANDS-ON TIME** 10 minutes
**ROAST** 1 hour 45 minutes at 350°F
**STAND** 15 minutes

»

BEEF RIB ROASTS include attached rib bones—which contribute flavor and act as a natural rack for the meat to roast on. To make carving easier, you can ask the butcher to cut the rack from the roast. Save the rack and use kitchen string to tie the roast to the ribs. After roasting, just untie bones and slice.

1   4- to 6-lb. beef rib roast
    Kosher salt and freshly ground black pepper
2   to 3 cloves garlic, slivered
1   recipe Peppercorn-Horseradish Sauce (optional)
    Roasted potatoes and onions (optional) (chart, p. 314)

**1.** Preheat oven to 350°F. Sprinkle meat with salt and pepper. Cut shallow slits all over meat and insert garlic slivers into slits. Place meat, fat side up, in a 15½×10½-inch roasting pan. Insert an oven-going meat thermometer into center of roast. The thermometer should not touch bone.

**2.** Roast, uncovered, 1¾ to 2¼ hours or until meat thermometer registers 135°F for medium rare. Cover roast with foil; let stand 15 minutes. (For medium, roast 2¼ to 2¾ hours or until meat thermometer registers 150°F.) Slice meat.
**3.** If desired, serve meat with Peppercorn-Horseradish Sauce and roasted potatoes and onions.
**Makes 8 servings (7 oz. beef each).**
EACH SERVING *541 cal., 40 g fat (16 g sat. fat), 169 mg chol., 211 mg sodium, 0 g carb., 0 g fiber, 0 g sugars, 41 g pro.*

### *BONELESS RIBEYE ROAST*

To roast a 3- to 4-lb. boneless ribeye roast instead, prepare as directed, except place roast on a rack in roasting pan. Roast 1½ to 1¾ hours or until 135°F for medium rare. (For medium, roast 1¾ to 2 hours or until 150°F.)

## PEPPERCORN-HORSERADISH SAUCE

**HANDS-ON TIME** 5 minutes
**CHILL** 1 hour

1   8-oz. carton sour cream
3   Tbsp. prepared horseradish
1   Tbsp. chopped fresh chives
2   tsp. white wine vinegar
1   tsp. coarsely ground black peppercorns

**1.** In a bowl stir together all ingredients. Cover and chill at least 1 hour before serving.
**Makes 1½ cups (2 Tbsp. each).**
EACH SERVING *40 cal., 4 g fat (2 g sat. fat), 11 mg chol., 22 mg sodium, 1 g carb., 0 g fiber, 1 g sugars, 1 g pro.*

## OVEN-ROASTED BEEF TENDERLOIN

**HANDS-ON TIME** 15 minutes
**ROAST** 35 minutes at 425°F
**STAND** 15 minutes

1    Tbsp. olive oil
1    3-lb. beef tenderloin roast, trimmed
1½   tsp. kosher salt
1    tsp. black pepper
1    recipe Bordelaise Sauce and/ or Peppercorn-Horseradish Sauce (opposite) (optional) Garnishes, such as fresh parsley and/or roasted garlic cloves (p. 24) (optional)

**1.** Preheat oven to 425°F. Brush oil over meat. Sprinkle salt and pepper over meat; rub in with your fingers.
**2.** Place roast on a rack set in a shallow roasting pan. Insert an oven-going meat thermometer into center of roast. Roast, uncovered, 35 to 40 minutes or until meat thermometer registers 135°F for medium rare. (For medium, roast 45 to 50 minutes or until meat thermometer registers 150°F.)
**3.** Transfer meat to a cutting board. Cover with foil; let stand 15 minutes. Slice meat across grain and arrange on a platter. If desired, serve with Bordelaise Sauce and/or Peppercorn-Horseradish Sauce. If desired, garnish with parsley and/or garlic. **Makes 12 servings (3 oz. beef each).**
**EACH SERVING** *168 cal., 7 g fat (2 g sat. fat), 69 mg chol., 190 mg sodium, 0 g carb., 0 g fiber, 0 g sugars, 25 g pro.*

## BORDELAISE SAUCE

**START TO FINISH** 40 minutes

1¼   cups reduced-sodium beef broth
¾    cup dry red wine
2    Tbsp. finely chopped shallot or onion
3    Tbsp. butter, softened
1    Tbsp. all-purpose flour

**1.** In a 2-qt. saucepan combine broth, wine, and shallot. Bring just to boiling; reduce heat. Simmer, uncovered, skimming the surface often with a spoon, 25 to 30 minutes or until reduced to 1 cup.
**2.** Using a fork, in a bowl stir together butter and flour. Whisk butter mixture into wine mixture, 1 tsp. at a time, whisking constantly (mixture will thicken). Cook and stir 1 minute more. Stir in ¼ tsp. *salt.*
**Makes about 1 cup (2 Tbsp. each).**
**EACH SERVING** *64 cal., 4 g fat (3 g sat. fat), 11 mg chol., 173 mg sodium, 2 g carb., 0 g fiber, 0 g sugars, 1 g pro.*

### ≫

TENDERLOIN—as the name implies— is the most tender cut of beef (and also one of the most expensive). Look for a roast that has been "peeled" (outside fat and connective tissue removed) for easy prep. It's a very lean cut, so do not overcook it.

### SECOND CHOICE

If beef tenderloin is out of your price range, try a 4-lb. beef top round roast. Roast it in a 350°F oven 1½ to 1¾ hours or until 135°F for medium rare. (For maximum tenderness, avoid roasting this cut past medium rare.)

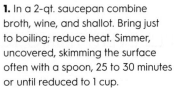
### MAKE IT A MENU

**OVEN-ROASTED BEEF TENDERLOIN**

**BRUSSELS SPROUTS GRATIN**
(P. 459)

**SAUTÉED MUSHROOMS**
(P. 462)

CRISP SPINACH SALAD WITH BALSAMIC VINAIGRETTE

SOFT DINNER ROLLS

OVEN-ROASTED BEEF TENDERLOIN

# BOARD-CERTIFIED A PARTY BOARD KEEPS THE WHOLE MEAL—BEEF, SHRIMP, SALAD, AND POTATOES—IN ONE SPOT FOR EASY SERVING AND EASY CLEANUP. DOUBLE EVERYTHING TO SERVE MORE.

## PEPPERED SHOULDER TENDERS

**HANDS-ON TIME** 30 minutes
**STAND** 20 minutes
**ROAST** 8 minutes at 400°F

SHOULDER PETITE TENDERS are juicy and tender. If you can't find, use a 1½ lb. center-cut tenderloin roast, trimmed. Roast about 35 minutes for medium rare (135°F).

2   to 3 beef shoulder petite tenders (about 1½ lb. total)
2   Tbsp. cracked black pepper
1½  tsp. kosher salt
2   Tbsp. vegetable oil
3   Tbsp. butter
¼   cup finely chopped shallots
⅓   cup Cognac or other brandy
1   cup heavy cream

**1.** Preheat oven to 400°F. Sprinkle meat with pepper and salt, pressing gently to adhere. Let stand at room temperature 20 minutes.
**2.** In a 12-inch oven-going skillet heat oil over medium-high heat. Add meat; cook about 8 minutes or until well browned on all sides. Transfer skillet to oven. Roast 8 to 10 minutes for medium rare (135°F). Remove meat from skillet and cover loosely with foil. Drain fat.
**3.** For pan sauce, in skillet melt butter over medium heat. Add shallots; cook 3 minutes, stirring occasionally. Remove skillet from heat. Carefully add Cognac, stirring to loosen any browned bits from skillet. Return to heat. Bring to boiling; reduce heat. Simmer, uncovered, until reduced by about half. Add cream. Return to boiling; reduce heat. Boil gently 3 to 5 minutes or until slightly thickened, stirring frequently. Slice meat and serve with pan sauce. **Makes 4 servings (5 oz. beef + about ⅓ cup sauce each).**
**EACH SERVING** 643 cal., 48 g fat (24 g sat. fat), 188 mg chol., 605 mg sodium, 5 g carb., 1 g fiber, 3 g sugars, 37 g pro.

## SHRIMP & SAUCE

Prepare Shrimp Cocktail (p. 394) or purchase chilled cooked shrimp at the meat and seafood counter of your supermarket. Then serve the shrimp with any of the sauces on p. 394. Other options are Romesco Sauce (p. 30) and Chimichurri (p. 30). Or use purchased cocktail sauce, sweet-and-sour sauce, or dried tomato pesto.

## ICEBERG WEDGE SALAD

Cut a head of iceberg lettuce into desired-size wedges, leaving core intact. Drizzle wedges with Blue Cheese Dressing (p. 301) and top with thinly sliced red onion, halved cherry tomatoes, crumbled blue cheese, and black pepper.

## ROASTED POTATOES

Toss tiny new potatoes with olive oil, salt, and black pepper; place in a single layer in a large baking pan. Roast in a 425°F oven about 30 minutes or until browned.

## TEXAS-STYLE BEEF BRISKET

**HANDS-ON TIME** 30 minutes
**SOAK** 1 hour  **GRILL** 4 hours
**STAND** 20 minutes

4   cups mesquite or hickory wood chips
½   cup Dry Rub
1   5-lb. fresh beef brisket
1   recipe Brisket Barbecue Sauce
12  kaiser rolls or ciabatta buns, split

**1.** At least 1 hour before grilling, soak wood chips in enough water to cover; drain. Sprinkle Dry Rub over both sides of brisket; rub in with your fingers.

**2.** Prepare grill for indirect heat using a drip pan (info, *pp. 16–17*). Fill drip pan with hot water. Sprinkle half of the wood chips over coals. Place brisket over drip pan. Grill, covered, 2½ hours; turn brisket. Grill, covered, 1½ to 2 hours more or until brisket is tender. Add coals and wood chips as needed to maintain temperature and smoke. (For a gas grill, add wood chips according to manufacturer's directions. Fill a small disposable foil pan with hot water and place on grill rack over a lit burner. Place brisket on a rack in a roasting pan; place pan on grill rack over burner that is off. Grill as directed.) Remove brisket from grill. Wrap in heavy foil and let stand 20 minutes.

**3.** Meanwhile, prepare Brisket Barbecue Sauce. Thinly slice brisket across the grain. Serve brisket on rolls with sauce. **Makes 12 sandwiches.**

**TO MAKE AHEAD** Prepare as directed. Refrigerate foil-wrapped brisket up to 2 days. Transfer sauce to a covered airtight container; refrigerate up to 1 week. To reheat, prepare grill for indirect heat. Grill foil-wrapped brisket over indirect medium heat, covered, 30 to 45 minutes or until heated through. Warm sauce in saucepan over medium-low heat or in a disposable foil pan on grill, stirring occasionally. **EACH SANDWICH** *721 cal., 44 g fat (16 g sat. fat), 127 mg chol., 1,516 mg sodium, 40 g carb., 3 g fiber, 8 g sugars, 38 g pro.*

## BRISKET BARBECUE SAUCE

**HANDS-ON TIME** 10 minutes
**COOK** 40 minutes

1   cup chopped onion
1   Tbsp. canola oil
1   14.5-oz. can whole tomatoes, undrained and cut up
⅔   cup white vinegar
¼   cup orange juice
2   Tbsp. Dijon mustard
1   Tbsp. granulated sugar
1   Tbsp. packed brown sugar
1   Tbsp. molasses
2   tsp. salt
1   tsp. liquid smoke
½   tsp. paprika
½   tsp. black pepper
¼   tsp. crushed red pepper

**1.** In a 3- to 4-qt. saucepan cook onion in hot oil over medium heat about 8 minutes or until golden brown, stirring frequently. Stir in the remaining ingredients. Bring to boiling; reduce heat. Simmer, uncovered, 30 to 40 minutes or until sauce is slightly thickened, stirring occasionally; cool slightly. Transfer sauce, half at a time, to a blender. Cover and blend until smooth. **Makes 2¼ cups (3 Tbsp. each).**
**EACH SERVING** *42 cal., 1 g fat (0 g sat. fat), 0 mg chol., 486 mg sodium, 7 g carb., 1 g fiber, 5 g sugars, 0 g pro.*

### *DRY RUB*

In a bowl stir together ½ cup paprika; ⅓ cup black pepper; ¼ cup each salt, chili powder, ground cumin, and packed brown sugar; 3 Tbsp. granulated sugar; and 2 Tbsp. cayenne pepper. Store in an airtight container up to 1 month. Makes about 2 cups.

### *FOR A SMOKER*

Rub brisket as directed. In a smoker arrange preheated coals, half of the wood chunks, and water pan according to manufacturer's directions. Pour water into pan. Place brisket, fat side up, on a rack over water pan. Cover; smoke 4 to 5 hours or until brisket is tender. Add coals and water as needed to maintain temperature and moisture. Add wood chunks as needed during the first 3 hours. Continue as directed in Step 3.

## MAKE IT A MENU

ROASTED LEG OF LAMB

MINTED PEA COUSCOUS (P. 462)

SAUTÉED ZUCCHINI AND SUMMER SQUASH

TZATZIKI SAUCE (P. 197)

WARM SOFT PITA BREAD

ROASTED LEG OF LAMB

## ROASTED LEG OF LAMB

**HANDS-ON TIME** 30 minutes
**ROAST** 2 hours at 325°F
**STAND** 15 minutes

| | |
|---|---|
| 1 | 5- to 6-lb. boneless whole leg of lamb, trimmed of fat |
| | Lemon juice |
| 2 | Tbsp. chopped fresh parsley |
| 1 | Tbsp. chopped fresh mint or basil or 1 tsp. dried mint or basil, crushed |
| 1 | Tbsp. chopped fresh rosemary or ½ tsp. dried rosemary, crushed |
| ½ | tsp. onion salt |
| ¼ | tsp. black pepper |
| 1 | to 2 cloves garlic, slivered |

**1.** Preheat oven to 325°F. Cut ½-inch-wide slits about 1 inch deep into meat. Drizzle lemon juice over meat and into slits. In a bowl combine next five ingredients (through pepper). Sprinkle mixture over meat and into slits; rub in with your fingers. Insert garlic into slits.
**2.** Place meat on a rack in a shallow roasting pan. Roast 2 to 2½ hours for medium rare (135°F) or 2½ to 3 hours for medium (150°F). Remove from oven. Cover with foil; let stand 15 minutes. **Makes 12 servings (4 to 5 oz. lamb each).**
**EACH SERVING** *311 cal., 21 g fat (9 g sat. fat), 100 mg chol., 151 mg sodium, 1 g carb., 0 g fiber, 0 g sugars, 27 g pro.*

## LEMON-ROSEMARY ROASTED PORK LOIN

**HANDS-ON TIME** 25 minutes
**ROAST** 1 hour at 375°F
**STAND** 10 minutes

| | |
|---|---|
| 1 | lemon |
| 6 | to 8 cloves garlic, minced |
| 2 | Tbsp. olive oil |
| 2 | Tbsp. coarse-ground Dijon mustard |
| 2 | Tbsp. chopped fresh rosemary |
| 1 | tsp. salt |
| ¼ | tsp. black pepper |
| 1 | 2- to 2½-lb. boneless pork top loin roast (single loin) |

**1.** Preheat oven to 375°F. Remove 2 tsp. zest and squeeze 2 Tbsp. juice from lemon. In a bowl combine zest, juice, and the next six ingredients (through pepper). Spread pork roast with lemon-rosemary mixture and place roast on a rack in a shallow roasting pan.
**2.** Roast, uncovered, 1 to 1¼ hours or until a thermometer inserted in thickest part of the roast registers 145°F. Transfer roast to a platter. Cover loosely with foil. Let stand 10 minutes before carving. **Makes 8 servings (4 oz. pork each).**
**EACH SERVING** *335 cal., 12 g fat (3 g sat. fat), 80 mg chol., 464 mg sodium, 28 g carb., 1 g fiber, 20 g sugars, 27 g pro.*

## SPANISH STUFFED PORK LOIN

**HANDS-ON TIME** 50 minutes
**ROAST** 20 minutes at 450°F + 1 hour at 325°F
**STAND** 15 minutes

| | |
|---|---|
| 15 | oz. uncooked chorizo sausage |
| ¾ | cup chopped onion |
| ½ | cup roasted piquillo peppers or sweet peppers, chopped |
| 2 | cloves garlic, minced |
| 1 | tsp. fresh thyme leaves |
| ½ | cup Marcona almonds, coarsely chopped |
| ¼ | cup chopped pitted dates |
| 1 | 4- to 5-lb. boneless pork top loin roast (single loin) |
| ½ | tsp. salt |
| ½ | tsp. black pepper |
| ¼ | tsp. smoked paprika |
| 1 | cup coarsely shredded Manchego cheese (4 oz.) |
| 10 | slices bacon |

**1.** Preheat oven to 450°F. If sausage is in links, remove casings. In a

LEMON-ROSEMARY
ROASTED PORK LOIN

SPANISH STUFFED
PORK LOIN

10-inch skillet cook sausage over medium heat 3 minutes. Add onion, roasted peppers, garlic, and thyme; cook and stir 10 minutes more. Drain fat. Stir in almonds and dates.

**2.** Trim fat from pork. Butterfly pork by making a lengthwise cut down the center of the meat, cutting to within ½ inch of the other side (tip, *far right*). Spread open. Place knife in the "V" of the cut. Cut horizontally into the meat and away from the center to within ½ inch of the other side of the meat. Repeat on opposite side of the "V." Spread meat open. Cover meat with plastic wrap. Using the flat side of a meat mallet, work from center (thicker part) to edges to flatten to ½ to ¾ inch thick.

**3.** Sprinkle pork with salt, black pepper, and smoked paprika. Spread sausage mixture over one side of pork; sprinkle sausage mixture with cheese. Starting with the filled side, roll pork into a spiral.

**4.** On a sheet of waxed paper arrange bacon slices with long sides touching. Place pork crosswise in center of the bacon. Use the waxed paper to lift the bacon and wrap it around the pork. Tie at 2-inch intervals with 100%-cotton kitchen string. Place pork on a rack in a shallow roasting pan. Insert an oven-going meat thermometer into center of meat.

**5.** Roast, uncovered, 20 minutes. Reduce oven temperature to 325°F and roast 1 to 1¼ hours or until thermometer registers 155°F.

**6.** Transfer roast to a cutting board. Cover loosely with foil; let stand 15 minutes. (Temperature of meat after standing should be 160°F.) Cut pork into 1½-inch-thick slices.
**Makes 10 servings (1 slice each).**
**EACH SERVING** *750 cal., 53 g fat (19 g sat. fat), 187 mg chol., 1,202 mg sodium, 8 g carb., 1 g fiber, 4 g sugars, 57 g pro.*

To butterfly a loin, make a lengthwise cut down the center of the roast, stopping ½ inch from the other side. Place the knife in the "V" you just made and lay it open on its side. Cut horizontally into the meat, away from center, to within ½ inch of other side.

Repeat on the opposite side of the "V," cutting the meat as evenly as possible. Spread the roast out, cover it with plastic wrap, and pound with a meat mallet to an even ½- to ¾-inch thickness.

HOLIDAY HAM
WITH CRANBERRY-
ORANGE GLAZE

# HOLIDAY HAM

**HANDS-ON TIME** 15 minutes
**BAKE** 1 hour 30 minutes at 325°F

1   6- to 8-lb. bone-in cooked ham, rump half
1   recipe Cranberry-Orange Glaze or Mustard-Bourbon Glaze

**1.** Preheat oven to 325°F. Score ham (*below left*). Place ham on a rack in a shallow roasting pan. Insert an oven-going thermometer into center of ham (thermometer should not touch bone). Cover with foil.
**2.** Bake 1¼ hours. Uncover; bake 15 to 60 minutes more or until thermometer registers 140°F. Meanwhile, prepare desired glaze. Brush ham with some of the glaze the last 15 minutes of baking. Carve ham. Serve with remaining glaze.
**Makes 20 servings (3 oz. ham + about 1 Tbsp. glaze each).**
**EACH SERVING** *164 cal., 3 fat (1 g sat. fat), 74 mg chol., 891 mg sodium, 7 g carb., 0 g fiber, 1 g sugars, 27 g pro.*

## *CRANBERRY-ORANGE GLAZE*

In a 1- or 1½-qt. saucepan combine 1 cup cranberry relish or orange-cranberry marmalade, ¼ cup orange juice, and 1 tsp. chopped fresh sage or thyme. Bring to boiling; reduce heat. Simmer, uncovered, 5 to 10 minutes or until mixture is thickened to glazing consistency.

## *MUSTARD-BOURBON GLAZE*

In a 1-qt. saucepan whisk together ⅓ cup each brown mustard and bourbon or orange juice; 2 Tbsp. each mild-flavor molasses and soy sauce; and 1 to 2 Tbsp. packed brown sugar. Cook and stir until mixture comes to boiling; reduce heat. Simmer, uncovered, about 10 minutes or until mixture is thickened to glazing consistency.

## *MAKE IT A MENU*

HOLIDAY HAM

POTATO-APPLE GRATIN
(P. 451)
(TO BAKE WITH HAM,
BAKE 1¾ HOURS; UNCOVER.
BAKE 15 MINUTES
MORE WHILE CARVING HAM.)

ORANGE- AND BALSAMIC-
GLAZED TRICOLOR CARROTS
(P. 461) OR STEAMED GREEN
BEANS OR ASPARAGUS

BUTTERMILK BISCUITS (P. 512)

Here's how to score your ham to get the flavor down deep. Using a sharp knife, cut the rind of the ham into a diamond pattern, making shallow diagonal cuts 1 inch apart and ¼ inch deep. Score top and sides.

# PICKLE-BRINED CHICKEN

**HANDS-ON TIME** 25 minutes
**MARINATE** 8 hours
**BAKE** 15 minutes at 475°F

- 1 64-oz. jar dill pickles
- 6 bone-in chicken thighs, skinned if desired (2½ to 2¾ lb. total)
- ¼ cup all-purpose flour
- ½ tsp. black pepper
- 1 Tbsp. vegetable oil
- ¼ cup dry white wine or reduced-sodium chicken broth
- ¾ cup reduced-sodium chicken broth
- 1 Tbsp. butter
- 1 Tbsp. chopped fresh dill
  Coarsely chopped dill pickles
  Chopped red, yellow, and/or orange sweet pepper

**1.** Drain pickles, reserving brine (about 4 cups). (Place pickles in an airtight container. Store, covered, in the refrigerator up to 2 weeks.) Add chicken to brine in the pickle jar or place in a large resealable plastic bag set in a bowl; seal jar or bag. Chill 8 to 24 hours.

**2.** Preheat oven to 475°F. Remove chicken from brine; pat dry. Discard brine. In a shallow dish combine flour and pepper. Coat chicken with flour mixture; shake off any excess.

**3.** In a 10-inch oven-going skillet heat oil over medium-high heat. Add chicken, skin sides down. Cook about 8 minutes or until golden; turn chicken. Place skillet in oven. Bake about 15 minutes or until done (at least 175°F). Transfer chicken to platter; let rest 5 minutes.

**4.** Drain all but 1 Tbsp. drippings from skillet. Return skillet to heat. Add wine; bring to boiling over medium-high heat, stirring to scrape any browned bits from bottom of pan. Boil about 2 minutes or until wine nearly evaporates. Add broth; bring to boiling. Boil about 2 minutes or until reduced to about ½ cup. Stir in butter until melted. Season to taste with additional black pepper. Remove from heat; stir in dill. Pour sauce over chicken. Top with chopped pickles, sweet pepper, and additional dill. **Makes 6 servings (1 thigh + about 1 Tbsp. sauce each).**
**EACH SERVING** *409 cal., 30 g fat (8 g sat. fat), 161 mg chol., 498 mg sodium, 5 g carb., 0 g fiber, 1 g sugars, 27 g pro.*

PICKLE-BRINED CHICKEN

## WHY PICKLE JUICE?
The long marinating soak in pickle brine keeps the meat moist and infuses it with a savory salty-vinegary flavor. Use the drained pickles to make Pickle Poppers (p. 398).

ROAST TURKEY THAT'S GOLDEN BROWN ON THE OUTSIDE,
JUICY ON THE INSIDE—YOU CAN DO IT! GET THE TRICKS FOR
GLAZING, STUFFING, CARVING, GRAVY, AND MORE.

## CLASSIC ROAST TURKEY

**HANDS-ON TIME** 15 minutes
**ROAST** 2 hours 45 minutes at 325°F
**STAND** 15 minutes

>> RAW TURKEY and other cuts of poultry don't need to be rinsed before cooking. See p. 155 for details.

1   **10- to 12-lb. turkey**
1   **recipe Orange and Herb Butter Rub and Glaze (optional)**
    **Salt and black pepper (optional)**
1   **recipe Stuffing** *(p. 465)* **or Turkey Aromatics (optional)**
    **Vegetable oil**
1   **recipe Perfect Turkey Gravy** *(p. 441)*

**1.** Preheat oven to 325°F. Remove neck and giblets from turkey; reserve for another use or discard. Pat turkey skin dry with paper towels; if stuffing turkey, wipe out cavity. If desired, use Orange and Herb Butter Rub as directed and sprinkle body cavity with salt and pepper. If desired, spoon desired stuffing loosely into cavity. Skewer neck skin to back. Tuck drumstick ends under band of skin across the tail if present or tie drumsticks securely to the tail using 100%-cotton kitchen string. Twist wing tips under back.
**2.** Place turkey, breast side up, on a rack in a shallow roasting pan. Brush with oil; sprinkle with additional salt and pepper. Insert an oven-going meat thermometer into the center of an inside thigh muscle (thermometer should not touch bone). Cover turkey loosely with foil.
**3.** Roast turkey 2¼ hours. Remove foil; cut string between drumsticks. Roast 30 to 45 minutes more

(1 to 1¼ hours if stuffed) or until thermometer registers at least 175°F; if stuffed, the center of stuffing must register 165°F. (Juices should run clear, and drumsticks should move easily in their sockets.) If desired, during the last 15 minutes of roasting, brush turkey twice with Orange and Herb Butter Glaze. Remove turkey from oven. Cover with foil; let stand 15 to 20 minutes before carving. Transfer turkey to a cutting board and carve (tip, *p. 440*). If desired, garnish with *fresh fruit* and *herbs*. Serve with Perfect Turkey Gravy. **Makes 10 servings (7 oz. turkey each).**
**EACH SERVING** *517 cal., 24 g fat (6 g sat. fat), 236 mg chol., 440 mg sodium, 3 g carb., 0 g fiber, 0 g sugars, 71 g pro.*

━━━

## ORANGE AND HERB BUTTER RUB AND GLAZE

**START TO FINISH** 10 minutes

½   **cup softened butter**
2   **tsp. chopped fresh sage**
2   **tsp. chopped fresh thyme**
2   **tsp. chopped fresh rosemary**
1   **tsp. orange zest**
½   **tsp. kosher salt**
¼   **tsp. black pepper**
⅓   **cup honey**

**1.** In a medium bowl combine the first seven ingredients (through pepper).
**2.** For rub, after the turkey has been dried with paper towels, use your fingers to loosen the skin over breast meat. Lift skin; spread half of the butter mixture under the skin

from front to back of turkey. Pull skin back over breast meat. Continue preparing turkey as directed in Step 1.
**3.** For glaze, microwave the remaining half of the butter mixture about 30 seconds or until melted. Stir in honey. Use to baste turkey the last 15 minutes of roasting. **Makes 10 servings (1 Tbsp. each).**

## *TURKEY AROMATICS*

If you aren't stuffing the turkey, fill the cavity with aromatics. As they heat, these fruits, vegetables, and herbs release scented steam into the turkey cavity, flavoring the meat from within. Aromatics are not eaten, so no need to remove peels and stems. After sprinkling the cavity with salt and pepper, insert 1 medium orange, cut into wedges; 1 medium apple, cored and cut into wedges; 1 medium onion, cut into wedges; 1 small bulb garlic, top and bottom cut off to expose cloves; and 3 sprigs fresh sage, thyme, and/or rosemary into the cavity. Continue as directed in Step 1. Discard aromatics after roasting.

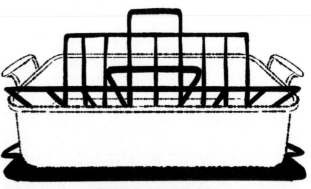

## PREP & COOK

**1**

If you plan to stuff the turkey, first wipe out the cavity with paper towels. Spoon stuffing loosely into body cavity of the turkey. Do not pack the stuffing. Leaving it a little loose allows air circulation so the stuffing cooks evenly and reaches a safe temperature at the same time as the turkey. (Bake any extra stuffing in a dish.)

**2**

Use kitchen string to tie the legs together. If the tail is still on the turkey, secure legs to the tail. Wrap the string around the legs and tail, pull it tight, and tie a knot. Tuck the wing tips behind the back. Tucking the wings and tying the legs keep them tight against the body of the turkey, creating a uniform shape. This also helps the turkey roast at an even rate and prevents burning.

**3**

According to the U.S. Department of Agriculture, turkey meat is safe to eat at 165°F. In our Test Kitchen, we think turkeys look and taste better when the temperature reaches 175°F in the dark meat. Insert an oven-going thermometer into the thigh muscle, making sure the probe does not touch bone.

**4**

Dry turkey happens because lean white breast meat cooks faster than fattier dark meat thighs. By the time the thighs are done, breast meat may be overcooked. Tenting with foil deflects heat from the breast so it cooks more evenly with the thighs. To tent, form a large piece of foil loosely over the breast, allowing for some air circulation.

## THE PAN PLAN

A large roasting pan with a rack is ideal for turkeys because it is sturdy and has strong handles for easy lifting and shifting of the pan. If you don't have one, use a 13×9-inch baking pan and place vegetables under the turkey to serve as a rack. Or purchase a large foil roasting pan at the supermarket and put a strong shallow baking pan under it for stability when transferring it in and out of the oven.

## CARVING

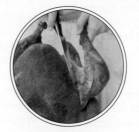

Pull the legs away from the body of the turkey and cut the joints that attach the thighs to the body. On the cutting board cut the joints connecting the drumsticks and thighs. Slice meat from the thighs.

Holding a breast half with one hand or a meat fork, gently cut the meat from the bone, following as close to the rib cage as possible. On the cutting board cut the breast halves crosswise into slices.

**TURKEY MATH** AS A GENERAL RULE WHEN BUYING TURKEY, PLAN ON 1 LB. PER PERSON. IF YOU LIKE LEFTOVER TURKEY, MAKE IT 1½ LB. PER PERSON.

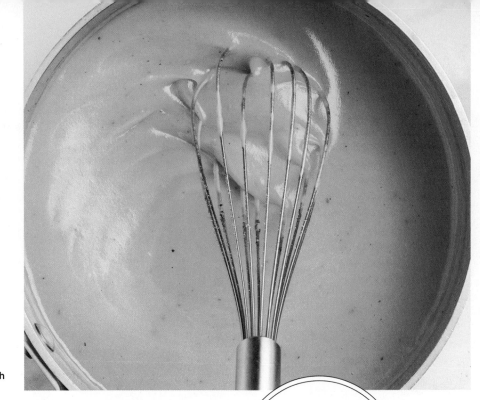

# PERFECT TURKEY GRAVY

**START TO FINISH** 15 minutes

Reduced-sodium chicken broth
or turkey broth
Pan drippings from Classic
Roast Turkey (*p. 439*)
Melted butter (optional)
¼ cup all-purpose flour
Salt and black pepper

**1.** Stir 1 cup chicken broth into pan drippings from roasted turkey in roasting pan, scraping any browned bits from bottom of pan. Pour drippings into a 2-cup glass measuring cup. Skim and reserve fat from drippings. If necessary, add enough melted butter to the reserved fat to make ¼ cup. Add enough additional broth to the drippings in the measuring cup to make 2 cups total liquid.
**2.** Pour the ¼ cup fat into a 2-qt. saucepan (discard any remaining fat). Whisk in flour until smooth.
**3.** Add broth mixture all at once to saucepan, stirring until smooth. Cook and stir over medium heat until thickened and bubbly. Cook and stir 1 minute more. Season to taste with salt and pepper. Before serving, strain gravy into a serving bowl. **Makes 2 cups (¼ cup each).**
EACH SERVING *76 cal., 6 g fat (2 g sat. fat), 7 mg chol., 211 mg sodium, 3 g carb., 0 g fiber, 0 g sugars, 1 g pro.*

## GRAVY FOR A CROWD

If 2 cups of gravy isn't enough, the recipe is easily doubled. Use drippings as directed in Step 1 and add enough broth to make 4 cups total liquid. If there isn't ½ cup fat from the drippings, add enough melted butter to reach ½ cup. Stir ½ cup flour into fat in Step 2; continue as directed.

### DRIPPINGS-FREE GRAVY

If you'd rather skip the drippings, just use all broth and substitute butter for the fat. Boost the flavor by adding 1 to 2 tsp. chicken broth base.

## MAKING GRAVY

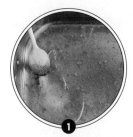

**1** The drippings are loaded with flavor—as are the browned bits stuck to the bottom of the pan. You definitely want that flavor in your gravy. Scrape the bottom of the roasting pan to loosen bits after adding the broth.

**2** Pour broth mixture into a measuring cup. The fat will rise to the top; skim with a shallow spoon. For a smooth roux (and smooth gravy), you'll need equal parts fat and flour. If the turkey didn't yield enough fat, add melted butter.

**3** A whisk works best to combine fat and flour. You want all the starch particles in the flour to be coated with fat. Whisk the roux while adding broth. Heat until bubbly to cook away raw flour flavor and thicken the gravy.

**BOILED LOBSTER WITH LEMON-CHIVE CLARIFIED BUTTER AND BEURRE BLANC**

# BOILED LOBSTER
**START TO FINISH** 30 minutes

| | |
|---|---|
| 8 | qt. water |
| ½ | cup coarse kosher salt or salt |
| 2 | 1- to 1½-lb. live lobsters |
| 1 | recipe Basic Clarified Butter (p. 445) or Beurre Blanc (opposite) |

**1.** In a 20-qt. or larger kettle bring water and salt t8o boiling. Grasp lobsters just behind the head and rinse under cold running water. Quickly put lobsters headfirst into the boiling water. Cover and return to boiling. Boil 15 minutes, adjusting heat as necessary to maintain a steady boil. Drain lobsters; remove any bands on large claws.

**2.** When cool enough to handle, place each lobster on its back. Separate the lobster tail from the body (*below left*). Cut through tail membrane to expose meat. Remove and discard the black vein running through the tail. Remove meat from tail. Twist the large claws away from the body. Using a nutcracker, break open the claws. Remove meat from claws. Crack the shell on remaining part of the body; remove meat with a small fork. Discard the green tomalley (liver) and the coral roe (found in female lobsters). Serve lobster meat with Basic Clarified Butter. **Makes 2 servings (1 lobster + 2 Tbsp. butter each).**

**EACH SERVING** *344 cal., 24 g fat (15 g sat. fat), 209 mg chol., 1,894 mg sodium, 1 g carb., 0 g fiber, 0 g sugars, 30 g pro.*

**CHANGE IT UP**
*Use any leftover lobster meat to make lobster rolls. Stir lobster meat together with a little mayonnaise, lemon juice, salt, and black pepper. Spoon the lobster salad into a toasted hoagie roll and sprinkle with chives.*

**1**

Remove tail by twisting the tail and body in opposite directions. Cut the membrane from the tail to expose the meat.

**2**

Twist the large claws where they join the body to remove them.

**3**

Break the large claws open with a nutcracker.

## BEURRE BLANC
**START TO FINISH** 20 minutes

¼ cup dry white wine
2 Tbsp. finely chopped shallot
1 Tbsp. white wine vinegar
2 Tbsp. heavy cream
¾ cup cold unsalted butter
(1½ sticks), cut into 2-Tbsp.
pieces
Salt and white pepper

**1.** In a 1- or 1½-qt. nonreactive saucepan (stainless-steel, enamel, or nonstick) combine the wine, shallot, and vinegar. Bring to boiling; reduce heat to medium. Boil gently, uncovered, 7 to 9 minutes or until almost all of the liquid has evaporated. Stir in the cream. Bring to boiling; boil about 1 minute to reduce the cream slightly. Reduce heat to medium-low.
**2.** Using a wire whisk, stir in the butter, one piece at a time, allowing each piece to melt before adding the next. Allow about 8 minutes. If desired, strain sauce. Season to taste with salt and white pepper. Serve with seafood or vegetables. **Makes 1 cup (2 Tbsp. each).**
**LEMONY BEURRE BLANC** Prepare as directed, except substitute lemon juice for the vinegar. If desired, garnish with lemon zest.
**CREAMY MUSTARD SAUCE** Prepare as directed, except whisk in 2 tsp. Dijon mustard before serving.
**EACH SERVING PLAIN, LEMONY, OR CREAMY MUSTARD VARIATION** *174 cal., 19 g fat (12 g sat. fat), 51 mg chol., 41 mg sodium, 1 g carb., 0 g fiber, 0 g sugars, 0 g pro.*

## STEAMED CRAB LEGS
**START TO FINISH** 15 minutes

4 4- to 8-oz. fresh or frozen crab legs
1 lemon

¼ cup butter, melted
1 Tbsp. chopped fresh basil or fresh Italian parsley

**1.** Thaw crab legs if frozen. Place crab legs in a steamer basket in a 12-inch skillet. If necessary, bend crab legs at joints to fit in steamer basket. Add water to skillet to just below the basket. Bring to boiling. Cover; steam 5 to 6 minutes or until heated through.
**2.** For butter sauce, remove ½ tsp. zest and squeeze 1 Tbsp. juice from lemon. Stir together butter, basil, lemon zest, and lemon juice.
**3.** To remove crabmeat, twist legs at joints or split shells using kitchen scissors. Peel back shells; remove meat. Serve with butter sauce. **Makes 4 servings (4 oz. crab each).**
**BOILED CRAB LEGS** Thaw crab legs if frozen. Place crab legs in a large pot of boiling salted water. Return to boiling. Cook, uncovered, 4 to 5 minutes or until heated through.
**EACH SERVING** *157 cal., 12 g fat (7 g sat. fat), 58 mg chol., 622 mg sodium, 0 g carb., 0 g fiber, 0 g sugars, 12 g pro.*

### MAKE IT A MENU
**STEAMED CRAB LEGS**

**BROCCOLINI WITH PEAS AND LEMONS** (P. 461) OR A GREEN SALAD WITH **FRESH HERB VINAIGRETTE** (P. 299)

ROASTED FINGERLING POTATOES SPRINKLED WITH COARSE SALT

CRUSTY ITALIAN BREAD

STEAMED CRAB LEGS

**FINGER FOOD**
Known as Low Country shrimp boil in the southeastern United States, this summery one-pot meal is traditionally served on a table lined with newspapers.

SHRIMP AND SAUSAGE BOIL

## SHRIMP AND SAUSAGE BOIL

**HANDS-ON TIME** 1 hour
**COOK** 25 minutes

1    3-oz. bag shrimp and
     crab boil
3    Tbsp. seafood seasoning,
     such as Old Bay
2¼ to 3 lb. small new potatoes
4    to 5 ears corn, husked and cut
     in 1½- to 3-inch pieces
1    to 2 lb. spicy smoked link
     sausage (kielbasa or
     andouille), diagonally sliced
     into 1-inch pieces
3    to 4 lb. medium to large
     unpeeled shrimp (preferably
     heads on)
3    to 4 lemons, halved
     Snipped fresh Italian parsley

**1.** In a 12- to 16-qt. pot bring
2 gallons *water* to boiling.
Add shrimp and crab boil and
seafood seasoning; reduce heat.
Simmer, uncovered, 10 minutes.
Add potatoes, a few at a time,
allowing water to continue
simmering. Simmer 7 to
10 minutes until nearly tender.
Add corn; simmer, uncovered,
5 minutes. Add sausage and
shrimp. Simmer 3 to 5 minutes or
until shrimp are opaque (do not
overcook shrimp) and sausage is
heated through; drain.
**2.** Transfer to large platter.
Add lemon halves and sprinkle
parsley over top. Serve hot or
within 1 hour of cooking. **Makes
6 servings.**
**EACH SERVING** *678 cal., 34 g fat
(11 g sat. fat), 339 mg chol., 1,356 mg
sodium, 41 g carb., 5 g fiber, 5 g
sugars, 53 g pro.*

BROILED LOBSTER TAILS

## BROILED LOBSTER TAILS

**START TO FINISH** 30 minutes

4    8-oz. fresh or frozen
     lobster tails
¼    cup butter
1    tsp. orange zest
½    tsp. chili powder
1    clove garlic, minced
     Snipped fresh parsley
     (optional)
2    recipes Basic Clarified Butter
     (optional)

**1.** Thaw lobster tails if frozen.
Preheat broiler. Butterfly the
lobster tails by using kitchen
scissors to cut lengthwise through
centers of hard top shells and
meat, cutting to but not through
bottoms of shells. Spread the
halves of tails apart. Place tails,
meat sides up, on unheated rack
of a broiler pan.
**2.** In saucepan melt butter. Add
orange zest, chili powder, and
garlic; heat about 30 seconds or
until garlic is tender. Brush mixture
over lobster meat. Broil 4 inches
from heat 12 to 14 minutes or until
lobster meat is opaque. If desired,
sprinkle with parsley and serve
with Basic Clarified Butter. **Makes
4 servings (1 tail each).**
**EACH SERVING** *149 cal., 12 g fat
(7 g sat. fat), 78 mg chol., 211 mg
sodium, 1 g carb., 0 g fiber, 0 g
sugars, 10 g pro.*

## CLARIFIED BUTTER

Clarified butter,
also called ghee, is
butter that has been
melted and the milk
solids removed. The
remaining butter fat
is clear when melted,
making it attractive
for serving with
lobster and crab.
Because the milk
solids are removed, it
can also be used for
sautéeing at higher
temperatures than
whole butter.

**BASIC CLARIFIED
BUTTER** Melt ¼ cup
butter over very low
heat without stirring;
cool slightly. Strain
through a sieve lined
with 100%-cotton
cheesecloth into a
glass measure. Pour
off clear top layer;
discard milky bottom
layer. Chill and remelt
to serve.

**LEMON-CHIVE
CLARIFIED BUTTER**
Prepare Basic
Clarified Butter as
directed. Stir in 2 Tbsp.
chopped fresh chives
and 1 tsp. lemon zest.

**BASIL CLARIFIED
BUTTER** Prepare
Basic Clarified Butter
as directed. Stir in
2 Tbsp. chopped
fresh basil.

CHICKEN, SHRIMP,
AND CHORIZO PAELLA

# CHICKEN, SHRIMP, AND CHORIZO PAELLA

**HANDS-ON TIME** 50 minutes
**STAND** 10 minutes

½ tsp. saffron threads, crushed
2 Tbsp. olive oil
1 lb. skinless, boneless chicken thighs, cut into 2-inch pieces
4 oz. smoked Spanish-style chorizo sausage, sliced
1 cup chopped onion
4 cloves garlic, minced
1 cup coarsely grated tomatoes (about 1 lb.)
1 Tbsp. smoked sweet paprika
6 cups reduced-sodium chicken broth
2 cups short grain rice
12 large shrimp, peeled and deveined
8 oz. frozen peas, thawed
Chopped green olives (optional)
Chopped Italian parsley

GRATING TOMATOES makes it easier to remove the skins (and makes them blend into the mixture better). Core and cut tomatoes in half. Grate on the coarse holes of a box grater into a shallow dish. Discard skins.

PAELLA PANS are wide and shallow so rice cooks in a thin layer. If you don't have one, use a 12-inch skillet. Prepare as directed, except reduce rice to 1½ cups and reduce chicken broth to 4 cups.

**1.** In a bowl combine saffron and ¼ cup *hot water*; let stand 10 minutes.

**2.** Meanwhile, in a 15-inch paella pan heat oil over medium-high heat. Add chicken; cook about 5 minutes or until chicken is browned, turning occasionally. Add chorizo; cook 1 minute more. Transfer chicken and chorizo to a plate. Add onion and garlic to pan; cook and stir 2 minutes. Add tomatoes and paprika; cook and stir 5 minutes more or until tomatoes are thickened and almost pastelike.

**3.** Return chicken and chorizo to pan. Add chicken broth, saffron mixture, and ½ tsp. *salt*; bring to boiling over high heat. Add rice to pan, stirring once to evenly distribute. Cook, without stirring, until rice has absorbed most of the liquid, about 12 minutes. (If your pan is bigger than your burner, rotate every few minutes to ensure the rice cooks evenly.) Reduce heat

**SAFFRON** Bright yellow saffron—the hand-harvested stigma of a special crocus flower—is paella's secret ingredient, giving it that trademark golden hue and deep flavor. It's pricey, but you need just a pinch. Steeping the threads in water releases all that color and flavor.

to low. Cook, without stirring, 5 to 10 minutes more until all the liquid is absorbed and rice is al dente. Top with shrimp and peas. Turn heat to high. Cook, without stirring, 1 to 2 minutes more (edges should look dry and a crust should form on the bottom). Remove from heat. Cover pan with foil. Let stand 10 minutes before serving. Sprinkle with olives (if desired) and parsley. **Makes 6 servings (1⅓ cups each).**

EACH SERVING *577 cal., 17 g fat (4 g sat. fat), 322 mg chol., 927 mg sodium, 63 g carb., 5 g fiber, 5 g sugars, 41 g pro.*

## MILE-HIGH LASAGNA PIE

**HANDS-ON TIME** 50 minutes
**BAKE** 1 hour at 375°F
**STAND** 15 minutes

| | |
|---|---|
| 16 | dried whole wheat or whole grain lasagna noodles |
| 2 | Tbsp. olive oil |
| 2 | cups finely chopped zucchini |
| 1½ | cups finely chopped carrots |
| 4 | cloves garlic, minced |
| 3 | cups sliced fresh mushrooms |
| 2 | 6-oz. pkg. fresh baby spinach |
| 2 | Tbsp. chopped fresh basil |
| 1 | egg, beaten |
| 1 | 15-oz. container ricotta cheese |
| ⅓ | cup finely shredded Parmesan cheese |
| ½ | tsp. salt |
| ¼ | tsp. black pepper |
| 1 | 26-oz. jar tomato and basil pasta sauce (2½ cups) |
| 2 | cups shredded Fontina or mozzarella cheese (8 oz.) Quartered cherry tomatoes (optional) |

**1.** Preheat oven to 375°F. In a 4- to 5-qt. pot cook noodles according to package directions. Drain noodles; rinse with cold water. Drain well.
**2.** Meanwhile, in a 10-inch skillet heat 1 Tbsp. of the olive oil over medium-high heat. Add zucchini, carrots, and half of the garlic. Cook and stir

about 5 minutes or until crisp-tender. Transfer vegetables to a bowl. Add the remaining oil to the same skillet and heat over medium-high heat. Add mushrooms and remaining garlic. Cook and stir about 5 minutes or until tender. Gradually add spinach. Cook and stir 1 to 2 minutes or until spinach is wilted. Remove from skillet with a slotted spoon; stir in basil.
**3.** In a bowl stir together the next five ingredients (through pepper).
**4.** To assemble, in the bottom of a 9×3-inch springform pan spread ½ cup of the pasta sauce. Arrange three to four of the cooked noodles over the sauce, trimming and overlapping as necessary to cover sauce with one layer. Top with half of the mushroom mixture. Spoon half of the ricotta cheese mixture over mushroom mixture. Top with another layer of noodles. Spread with 1 cup of the remaining sauce. Top with all of the carrot mixture. Sprinkle with half the Fontina cheese. Top with another layer of noodles. Layer with remaining

mushroom mixture and remaining ricotta cheese mixture. Top with another layer of noodles (you might have extra noodles) and remaining sauce. Gently press down pie with the back of a spatula.
**5.** Place springform pan on a foil-lined baking sheet. Bake about 60 minutes or until heated through, topping with remaining Fontina cheese the last 15 minutes. Cover and let stand 15 minutes before serving. Loosen outside edges of pie and carefully remove pan ring. To serve, cut lasagna into wedges. If desired, garnish with cherry tomatoes and additional fresh basil. **Makes 10 servings (1 wedge each).**

EACH SERVING *463 cal., 23 g fat (12 g sat. fat), 82 mg chol., 965 mg sodium, 38 g carb., 8 g fiber, 10 g sugars, 28 g pro.*

**EASY EVERYDAY**

*For oven-to-table dining, make this lasagna in a 13×9-inch pan instead. Use 4 noodles per layer and bake about 45 minutes or until heated.*

MILE-HIGH LASAGNA PIE

[GATHERINGS]
# SIDES

**MAKE-AHEAD RECIPE.** See also "Everyday Sides," *pp. 304–323;* cooking charts, *pp. 70–83.*

**FINISHING TOUCH**
Pretty-up your party potatoes! After baking, sprinkle the potatoes with grated Asiago cheese, cracked black pepper, and/or snipped fresh herbs.

SCALLOPED POTATOES

POTATO-APPLE GRATIN

## POTATO-APPLE GRATIN

**HANDS-ON TIME** 45 minutes
**BAKE** 1 hour 45 minutes at 350°F
**STAND** 10 minutes

**»**

**GRANNY SMITH** is our first choice of apple here because their tartness complements the richness of the cheese and cream.

- 8 cups thinly sliced Yukon gold or other yellow-flesh potatoes, (about 2½ lb.)
- 2 cups cored and thinly sliced Granny Smith apples
- ⅔ cup sliced green onions or thinly sliced leek
- 6 slices bacon, crisp-cooked and crumbled
- 3 cups shredded Gruyère, Swiss, or Jarlsberg cheese (12 oz.)
- 1⅔ cups heavy cream
- 3 cloves garlic, minced
- ½ tsp. freshly grated nutmeg or ⅛ tsp. ground nutmeg (optional)

**EASY SLICING** For thinly sliced potatoes, we often use a mandoline in the Test Kitchen. This special utensil was designed to create perfect slices so the potatoes bake evenly. For both of these recipes, aim for slices about ⅛ inch thick.

**1.** Preheat oven to 350°F. Grease a 3-qt. rectangular baking dish. Layer half of the potatoes, half of the apples, half of the sliced green onions, and two slices of the bacon in prepared dish. Sprinkle with ¾ tsp. *salt* and ¼ tsp. *black pepper*. Sprinkle with half of the cheese. Repeat layers. In a medium bowl combine the cream, garlic, and, if desired, nutmeg; pour over layers in baking dish. Cover with foil.
**2.** Bake 1½ hours. Uncover and bake 15 minutes more or until potatoes are tender and top is golden. Let stand 10 minutes. Sprinkle with remaining bacon and additional sliced green onions. **Makes 12 servings (about 1 cup each).**
**TO MAKE AHEAD** Cook the potatoes and apples in separate pots of lightly salted boiling water 5 minutes. Drain; pat dry. Assemble as directed in Step 1. Chill up to 24 hours. To serve, let stand at room temperature 30 minutes. Bake as directed in Step 2.
**EACH SERVING** *342 cal., 23 g fat (14 g sat. fat), 81 mg chol., 475 mg sodium, 22 g carb., 3 g fiber, 5 g sugars, 13 g pro.*

## SCALLOPED POTATOES

**HANDS-ON TIME** 30 minutes
**BAKE** 1 hour 25 minutes at 350°F
**STAND** 10 minutes

- 1 cup chopped onion
- 2 cloves garlic, minced
- ¼ cup butter
- ¼ cup all-purpose flour
- ½ tsp. salt
- ¼ tsp. black pepper
- 2½ cups milk
- 8 cups thinly sliced red, white, or yellow potatoes (about 2½ lb.)

**1.** Preheat oven to 350°F. Grease a 3-qt. rectangular baking dish. For sauce, in a 2-qt. saucepan cook onion and garlic in hot butter over medium heat until tender. Stir in flour, salt, and pepper. Add milk. Cook and stir until thickened and bubbly. Remove from heat.

**2.** Place half of the potatoes in the prepared baking dish. Top with half of the sauce. Repeat layers. Cover with foil.
**3.** Bake 45 minutes. Uncover and bake 40 to 50 minutes more or until potatoes are tender. Let stand 10 minutes before serving.
**Makes 10 servings (1 cup each).**
**EACH SERVING** *182 cal., 6 g fat (4 g sat. fat), 17 mg chol., 182 mg sodium, 28 g carb., 3 g fiber, 5 g sugars, 5 g pro.*

**CHANGE IT UP**
*Make your Scalloped Potatoes cheesy. Gradually add 1½ cups shredded cheddar or Gruyère cheese (6 oz.) to the thickened sauce at the end of Step 1, stirring until cheese melts.*

# HASSELBACK POTATOES

**HANDS-ON TIME** 35 minutes
**BAKE** 55 minutes at 375°F

| | |
|---|---|
| 8 | medium russet potatoes (6 to 8 oz. each) |
| 5 | Tbsp. butter, melted |
| 1 | tsp. salt |
| 3 | Tbsp. seasoned fine dry bread crumbs |
| 2 | Tbsp. grated Parmesan cheese |
| 1 | Tbsp. chopped fresh chives |
| 1 | tsp. chopped fresh thyme |

**CALL IT HASSELBACK** Originating in Sweden, these special-occasion potatoes are thinly sliced but remain connected at the base to hold their shape. When they bake, the slices fan out slightly to maximize the surface area that gets deliciously crispy.

**1.** Preheat oven to 375°F. Fill a large bowl with water. Add potatoes. Gather two ½-inch-thick chopsticks or dowel rods (or use the handles of wooden spoons).

**2.** For potatoes, slice a thin lengthwise slice from the bottoms of the potatoes so they stand without rolling on the cutting board. Arrange chopsticks lengthwise on opposite sides of one potato on a cutting board. Slice potato crosswise into ⅛-inch-thick slices, stopping the knife when it reaches the chopsticks to prevent slicing all the way through. Return sliced potato to water bowl. Repeat with remaining potatoes.

**3.** Line a 15×10-inch baking pan with foil; grease foil. Drain potatoes well and pat dry. Arrange potatoes in the prepared baking pan. Brush evenly with 2 Tbsp. of the melted butter and sprinkle with ½ tsp. of the salt. Cover with foil. Bake 45 minutes. Uncover and bake 10 to 15 minutes more or until tender.

**4.** Remove from oven. Preheat broiler. For crumb topping, in a small bowl stir together bread crumbs, cheese, chives, thyme, and the remaining ½ tsp. salt. Sprinkle potatoes evenly with crumb mixture. Slowly spoon on remaining 3 Tbsp. melted butter, being sure to cover all of the crumb mixture.

**5.** Broil potatoes 4 to 5 inches from the heat 2 to 3 minutes or

**CHEESY PROSCIUTTO AND PESTO HASSELBACK POTATOES**
Prepare as directed through Step 3. Omit crumb topping ingredients and broiling. In a small bowl combine 2 Tbsp. melted butter and 2 Tbsp. refrigerated basil pesto. Brush baked potatoes evenly with pesto mixture. Sprinkle with 1 tsp. dried oregano, crushed. Cut 3 to 4 oz. very thinly sliced prosciutto into 1½-inch pieces; stuff between every three to five potato slices. Bake 10 minutes more. Top with 1½ cups shredded mozzarella cheese. Return to oven; bake 5 to 10 minutes or until cheese is bubbly. If desired, top with additional pesto.

until topping is golden. Serve immediately. **Makes 8 servings (1 potato each).**

**TO MAKE AHEAD** Prepare potatoes as directed through Step 2. Cover bowl and refrigerate up to 24 hours. Drain potatoes well. Continue as directed.

**EACH SERVING** *210 cal., 8 g fat (5 g sat. fat), 20 mg chol., 425 mg sodium, 32 g carb., 4 g fiber, 2 g sugars, 4 g pro.*

## CREAMY POTLUCK POTATOES

**HANDS-ON TIME** 10 minutes
**BAKE** 1 hour 15 minutes at 350°F
**STAND** 5 minutes

1   32-oz. pkg. frozen diced hash brown potatoes, thawed (7½ cups)
1   10.75-oz. can reduced-fat and reduced-sodium condensed cream of chicken soup
1   8-oz. container sour cream
2   Tbsp. butter, melted
1   cup shredded cheddar cheese (4 oz.)
¼   cup sliced green onions
¼   cup milk
½   tsp. garlic salt
¼   tsp. black pepper

**1.** Preheat oven to 350°F. In a large bowl stir together potatoes, soup, sour cream, and butter. Stir in ½ cup of the shredded cheese, 3 Tbsp. of the green onions, the milk, garlic salt, and pepper. Transfer potato mixture to a 2-qt. rectangular baking dish. Cover with foil.

**2.** Bake 1¼ hours or until potatoes are tender. Sprinkle with the remaining cheese. Let stand 5 minutes. Sprinkle with the remaining green onions. **Makes 12 servings (¾ cup each).**

**EACH SERVING** *173 cal., 10 g fat (6 g sat. fat), 26 mg chol., 241 mg sodium, 17 g carb., 1 g fiber, 1 g sugars, 5 g pro.*

SWEET
POTATOES
WITH BLUE
CHEESE

## SWEET POTATOES WITH BLUE CHEESE

**HANDS-ON TIME** 30 minutes
**BAKE** 30 minutes at 375°F

2   large sweet potatoes (about 1½ lb.), peeled and cut lengthwise into thin wedges
1   small sweet onion, cut into 1-inch pieces
4   Tbsp. olive oil
1   Tbsp. butter
⅓   cup broken pecans
1   Tbsp. packed light brown sugar
4   tsp. cider vinegar
1½   tsp. honey
1   clove garlic, minced
2   Tbsp. crumbled blue cheese or finely shredded white cheddar cheese

**1.** Preheat oven to 375°F. In a 15×10-inch baking pan combine sweet potatoes and onion. Drizzle with 2 Tbsp. of the oil; sprinkle with ½ tsp. *salt* and ¼ tsp. *black pepper*. Toss to combine; spread in a single layer. Bake 30 to 35 minutes or until vegetables are tender, stirring once.
**2.** Meanwhile, in a 6-inch skillet melt butter over medium heat. Stir in pecans, brown sugar, and ¼ tsp. *salt*. Cook and stir 2 to 3 minutes or until pecans are coated in the brown sugar mixture. Spread pecans on a sheet of foil; cool completely.
**3.** For dressing, in a small bowl whisk together vinegar, honey, garlic, ¼ tsp. *salt*, and ¼ tsp. *black pepper*. Slowly whisk in the remaining 2 Tbsp. oil until combined. Stir in 1 Tbsp. of the cheese.
**4.** Transfer sweet potatoes and onion to a platter. Drizzle with dressing. Sprinkle with pecans and remaining 1 Tbsp. cheese. **Makes 6 servings (3 or 4 wedges each).**
**EACH SERVING** *273 cal., 16 g fat (3 g sat. fat), 7 mg chol., 500 mg sodium, 30 g carb., 4 g fiber, 10 g sugars, 3 g pro.*

## MERINGUE-TOPPED SWEET POTATO CASSEROLE

**HANDS-ON TIME** 30 minutes
**STAND** 30 minutes
**COOK** 25 minutes
**BAKE** 30 minutes at 350°F

4   eggs, separated
4   lb. sweet potatoes, peeled and cut into quarters
1   orange
½   cup packed brown sugar
½   cup half-and-half
¼   cup butter, melted
½   tsp. salt
1   tsp. vanilla
½   tsp. cream of tartar
½   cup granulated sugar
¾   cup pecan pieces, toasted

**1.** Allow the eggs to stand at room temperature 30 minutes. Grease a 2-qt. square baking dish. In a 4-qt. Dutch oven cook sweet potatoes, covered, in enough boiling salted water to cover 25 to 30 minutes or until tender; drain. Return the potatoes to the pan.
**2.** Preheat oven to 350°F. Remove ½ tsp. zest and squeeze 2 Tbsp. juice from the orange. Lightly mash potatoes; stir in brown sugar, half-and-half, melted butter, orange zest, orange juice, and salt. Cool 5 minutes. In a small bowl lightly beat the egg yolks with a fork. Stir the egg yolks into the sweet potato mixture. Transfer sweet potato mixture to prepared baking dish.
**3.** Bake, uncovered, 15 minutes. Meanwhile, for meringue, in a large mixing bowl combine egg whites, vanilla, and cream of tartar. Beat with a mixer on medium about 1 minute or until soft peaks form (tips curl). Gradually add the granulated sugar, 1 Tbsp. at a time, beating on high about 4 minutes more or until mixture forms stiff, glossy peaks and sugar dissolves.
**4.** Sprinkle pecans evenly over hot potatoes. Immediately spread meringue over top. Bake about 15 minutes or until browned and a thermometer registers 160°F. **Makes 10 servings (¾ cup each).**
**MARSHMALLOW-TOPPED SWEET POTATO CASSEROLE** Prepare as directed, except save egg whites for another use and omit vanilla, cream of tartar, and granulated sugar. Bake the potato mixture 15 minutes as directed in Step 3. Using one 13-oz. jar marshmallow creme, spoon small spoonfuls onto potato mixture, spreading evenly to cover surface. Bake 15 to 20 minutes more or until marshmallow creme is puffed and light brown.
**EACH SERVING PLAIN OR MARSHMALLOW-TOPPED VARIATION** *338 cal., 14 g fat (5 g sat. fat), 91 mg chol., 262 mg sodium, 49 g carb., 5 g fiber, 27 g sugars, 6 g pro.*

MERINGUE-TOPPED
SWEET POTATO CASSEROLE

OUR FROM-SCRATCH CREAMY SAUCE—WHICH IS SURPRISINGLY EASY—REPLACES CANNED SOUP, AND QUICK-FRIED SHALLOTS STAND IN FOR PURCHASED FRIED ONIONS. LITTLE STEPS MAKE A HUGE FLAVOR DIFFERENCE.

**»**

**HARICOTS VERTS** are a French variety of green beans. They are small, slender, and exceptionally tender even when mature. They're available in most large supermarkets. You can substitute regular green beans, but you may need to parcook them longer in Step 1 to get them crisp-tender.

**»**

Parcooking (or partially cooking) the green beans, then plunging them into ice water does two things: It starts them cooking so they get evenly tender when baked, and it keeps their color bright.

## HOMEMADE GREEN BEAN CASSEROLE

**HANDS-ON TIME** 40 minutes
**BAKE** 25 minutes at 375°F
**STAND** 10 minutes

1½   lb. haricots verts, trimmed
4     oz. pancetta or bacon
9     cups sliced, stemmed shiitake mushrooms and/or sliced cremini or button mushrooms (1½ lb.)
6     cloves garlic, minced
½     tsp. dried thyme, crushed
½     tsp. salt
½     tsp. black pepper
2     Tbsp. butter
2     Tbsp. all-purpose flour
1½   cups half-and-half
1     5.2-oz. pkg. semisoft cheese with garlic and fine herbs, broken into pieces
⅛     tsp. salt
⅛     tsp. black pepper
¼     cup dry white wine
1     recipe Crispy Shallots

**1.** Preheat oven to 375°F. Grease a 2½- to 3-qt. gratin or baking dish. In a 10-inch skillet parcook beans in enough lightly salted boiling water to cover 3 to 5 minutes or until crisp-tender; drain. Transfer beans to a large bowl of ice water to stop cooking them; drain.
**2.** In the same skillet cook pancetta over medium heat until crisp. Using a slotted spoon, transfer pancetta to paper towels to drain, reserving the drippings. Finely crumble or chop pancetta.

**3.** Meanwhile, add mushrooms, garlic, and thyme to drippings in skillet (if there aren't many drippings, you may need to add up to 1 Tbsp. vegetable oil); cook and stir 5 to 6 minutes or until mushrooms are tender and liquid has evaporated. Stir in pancetta, the ½ tsp. salt, and the ½ tsp. pepper. Add mushroom mixture to beans, tossing gently to combine.
**4.** For sauce, in a 1-qt. saucepan melt butter over medium heat. Stir in flour; cook and stir 1 minute. Add half-and-half all at once. Cook and stir over medium heat until thickened and bubbly. Whisk in the cheese, the ⅛ tsp. salt, and the ⅛ tsp. pepper. Remove from heat; stir in wine. Pour sauce over green bean mixture, stirring gently just until combined. Transfer green bean mixture to the prepared baking dish.
**5.** Bake, uncovered, 25 to 30 minutes or until bubbly and beans are tender. Let stand 10 minutes. Sprinkle with Crispy Shallots. **Makes 8 servings (1 cup each).**
**EACH SERVING** *370 cal., 27 g fat (13 g sat. fat), 49 mg chol., 436 mg sodium, 22 g carb., 4 g fiber, 6 g sugars, 12 g pro.*

**EASY EVERYDAY**

*Cut a step and replace the Crispy Shallots with 1 cup purchased french-fried onions. Sprinkle them on the bean mixture for the last 5 minutes of baking.*

## CRISPY SHALLOTS

In a 1- or 1½-qt. saucepan heat ¾ cup vegetable oil over medium-high heat. Thinly slice 4 large shallots (1 cup). Dip a small handful of sliced shallots in ½ cup milk, letting excess drip off. Toss shallots in 1 cup all-purpose flour; shake off excess flour. Place coated shallots in hot oil. Cook about 2 minutes or until golden and slightly crisp. Using a slotted spoon, transfer shallots to paper towels to drain; sprinkle lightly with salt. Repeat with remaining shallots, milk, and flour. If necessary, reheat Crispy Shallots on a foil-lined baking sheet in a 350°F oven 10 minutes before topping the casserole.

The roux (a thickener made of equal parts flour and butter) is the key to this creamy sauce. Flour is whisked into melted butter, which coats the flour particles with fat. This keeps the particles separated to prevent flour lumps in the sauce. The roux is cooked and stirred 1 minute, which removes the raw flour flavor. After the half-and-half is added, keep whisking the sauce slowly while cooking to distribute thickener evenly.

**»**

ASPARAGUS SPEARS of similar thicknesses will cook more evenly. If some stalks are thicker than others, cut the large ones in half lengthwise. If all the spears are super thin, reduce cooking time slightly.

**TRIMMED DOWN**

To remove the woody ends of asparagus, start at the base of each asparagus spear and bend the spear until you find a place where it is flexible. Snap off the base at that point (the inflexible portion is tough, so just throw it out).

## ASPARAGUS WITH TARRAGON SAUCE

**START TO FINISH** 30 minutes

| | |
|---|---|
| 1¼ | lb. asparagus spears |
| 2 | Tbsp. butter |
| 2 | Tbsp. finely chopped shallot |
| ¼ | cup mayonnaise |
| 2 | Tbsp. chopped fresh tarragon |
| 2 | Tbsp. Dijon mustard |
| 2 | Tbsp. cider vinegar |
| 1 | tsp. lemon juice |
| ½ | tsp. kosher salt |
| ¼ | tsp. cracked black pepper |
| 2 | oz. prosciutto, torn or cut into 2×1-inch pieces |
| 2 | Hard-Boiled Eggs (*p. 46*), finely chopped |

**1.** Snap off and discard woody bases from asparagus. If desired, scrape off scales.

**2.** For tarragon sauce, in a 1- or 1½-qt. saucepan melt 1 Tbsp. of the butter over medium heat. Add shallot; cook and stir about 2 minutes or until softened. Stir in the next seven ingredients (through pepper). Heat through, stirring frequently. Cover; keep warm.

**3.** In an 8-inch skillet heat the remaining 1 Tbsp. butter over medium-high heat; add prosciutto. Cook 2 to 4 minutes or until just crisp, turning once. Transfer to paper towels to drain.

**4.** Bring a 4-qt. saucepan of salted water to boiling. Add asparagus. Cook about 3 minutes or until crisp-tender; drain.

**5.** Transfer asparagus to a platter. Drizzle with the tarragon sauce. Sprinkle with prosciutto and chopped eggs. Sprinkle with additional chopped fresh tarragon, salt, and pepper. **Makes 6 servings (about 5 asparagus spears each).**

**EACH SERVING** *158 cal., 14 g fat (4 g sat. fat), 86 mg chol., 697 mg sodium, 3 g carb., 0 g fiber, 2 g sugars, 6 g pro.*

# BRUSSELS SPROUTS GRATIN

**HANDS-ON TIME** 30 minutes
**BAKE** 15 minutes at 400°F

- 1¼ lb. Brussels sprouts, trimmed and coarsely chopped*
- 1 cup chopped carrots*
- 3 oz. pancetta or 8 slices bacon, chopped
- ¼ cup finely chopped shallots or ½ cup chopped onion
- 1 Tbsp. butter
- 3 cloves garlic, minced
- 1 Tbsp. all-purpose flour
- 1 cup finely shredded Asiago or Parmesan cheese (4 oz.)
- ½ tsp. salt
- ½ tsp. black pepper
- 1 cup heavy cream
- 1 Tbsp. coarse-ground mustard Dash crushed red pepper
- ½ cup panko bread crumbs (tip, *p. 108*) or coarse bread crumbs

**1.** Preheat oven to 400°F. Lightly grease a 1½-qt. oval baking or rectangular dish. In a 3-qt. saucepan cook Brussels sprouts and carrots in lightly salted boiling water 5 to 6 minutes or until tender; drain. Return vegetables to saucepan.

**2.** Meanwhile, in a 10-inch skillet cook pancetta over medium heat until crisp. Using a slotted spoon, transfer pancetta to paper towels to drain, reserving drippings in skillet. Add shallots, butter, and garlic to drippings in skillet; cook and stir 30 seconds. Stir in flour. Stir shallot mixture into the vegetables in saucepan. Stir in pancetta, ½ cup of the cheese, the salt, and black pepper. Spoon Brussels sprouts mixture into the prepared dish.

**3.** In a small bowl stir together cream, mustard, and crushed red pepper; pour over Brussels sprouts mixture.

In another bowl combine remaining ½ cup cheese and the panko. Sprinkle over Brussels sprouts mixture.

**4.** Bake 15 to 20 minutes or until mixture is bubbly and topping is golden. **Makes 8 servings (¾ cup each).**

**TO MAKE AHEAD** Chop the Brussels sprouts and carrots. Place in an airtight container; cover. Chill up to 24 hours. Prepare as directed.

**EACH SERVING** *274 cal., 21 g fat (12 g sat. fat), 69 mg chol., 603 mg sodium, 13 g carb., 3 g fiber, 3 g sugars, 9 g pro.*

Trim the ends of Brussels sprouts close to the bases. Remove wilted outer leaves and coarsely chop sprouts.

CORN CASSEROLE

WHOLE ROASTED
CAULIFLOWER WITH
PICKLED ONIONS

## CORN CASSEROLE

**HANDS-ON TIME** 25 minutes
**BAKE** 50 minutes at 350°F

**ADD-INS**
If desired,
stir in any of
the following
ingredients
with the corn
in Step 1:

• ½ cup
drained,
chopped
roasted red
peppers

• One 4-oz.
can green
chile peppers,
drained

• 4 oz. bulk
sausage,
cooked and
crumbled

• Swap 1 cup
of the corn for
1 cup frozen
shelled
edamame or
lima beans

| | |
|---|---|
| 6 | slices bacon, chopped |
| ¾ | cup chopped onion |
| 2 | cloves garlic, minced |
| 3 | Tbsp. all-purpose flour |
| ½ | tsp. salt |
| ¼ | tsp. black pepper |
| 2 | cups half-and-half or whole milk |
| 2 | 16-oz. pkg. frozen whole kernel corn |
| ¼ | cup chopped fresh Italian parsley (optional) |
| 1 | Tbsp. chopped fresh thyme leaves or 1 tsp. dried thyme, crushed |
| 1 | sleeve saltine crackers (about 40 crackers) |
| 2 | eggs, lightly beaten |
| ¼ | cup butter, melted |
| | Paprika (optional) |

**1.** Preheat oven to 350°F. In a 3-qt. saucepan cook and stir bacon over medium heat until browned; with a slotted spoon, transfer bacon to paper towels to drain. Reserve drippings in pan. Add onion and garlic to saucepan; cook and stir 2 to 3 minutes or until softened.

Stir in flour, salt, and pepper. Whisk in half-and-half. Cook and stir over medium heat until thickened and bubbly. Stir in corn, parsley (if desired), and thyme.

**2.** Finely crush half of the crackers. Stir into corn mixture along with eggs. Spoon the mixture into a 2-qt. baking dish; cover with foil. Bake 15 minutes.

**3.** Meanwhile, coarsely crush remaining crackers. In a bowl combine crackers and melted butter; toss to coat.

**4.** Uncover casserole; top with crackers. If desired, sprinkle with paprika. Bake, uncovered, 35 to 40 minutes or until heated through. Sprinkle with bacon the last 5 minutes of baking. **Makes 12 servings (½ cup each).**

**EACH SERVING** 295 cal, 18 g fat (8 g sat. fat), 68 mg chol, 386 mg sodium, 28 g carb, 2 g fiber, 4 g sugars, 8 g pro.

**CHANGE IT UP**

*For a cheesy corn bake, stir in 1 cup shredded cheddar cheese with the corn in Step 1. Top with ½ cup shredded cheese when you add the bacon in Step 4.*

## WHOLE ROASTED CAULIFLOWER WITH PICKLED ONIONS

**HANDS-ON TIME** 30 minutes
**ROAST** 30 minutes at 425°F + 30 minutes at 450°F

| | |
|---|---|
| 2 | Tbsp. olive oil |
| 1 | Tbsp. coarse-ground mustard |
| 2 | tsp. caraway seeds, toasted and crushed |
| 1 | tsp. kosher salt |
| 1 | 2- to 2½-lb. cauliflower head, trimmed |
| ¼ | cup water |
| ½ | cup sliced red onion |
| ⅓ | cup red wine vinegar |
| 1 | tsp. sugar |
| ½ | tsp. kosher salt |
| ¼ | cup dried apricots |

**1.** Preheat oven to 425°F. In a bowl whisk together olive oil, mustard, caraway seeds, and the 1 tsp. salt. Spread caraway mixture over the cauliflower. Pour ¼ cup water into an 8- to 10-inch cast-iron or other oven-going skillet. Place cauliflower in skillet; cover with foil and roast 30 minutes.

**2.** Meanwhile, for pickled red onions, in a small bowl combine

ORANGE- AND
BALSAMIC-GLAZED
TRICOLOR CARROTS

BROCCOLINI WITH
PEAS AND LEMONS

the onion, vinegar, sugar, and the ½ tsp. salt; stir mixture occasionally.
**3.** Uncover cauliflower; increase oven temperature to 450°F. Roast about 30 minutes more or until golden brown and tender. Serve with pickled red onions, apricots, and, if desired, additional mustard.
**Makes 4 servings (¼ head cauliflower each).**
**EACH SERVING** *115 cal., 7 g fat (1 g sat. fat), 0 mg chol., 390 mg sodium, 12 g carb., 3 g fiber, 7 g sugars, 2 g pro.*

## ORANGE- AND BALSAMIC- GLAZED TRICOLOR CARROTS

**HANDS-ON TIME** 25 minutes
**COOK** 15 minutes

2 lb. medium red, yellow, and/or orange carrots, trimmed and peeled
½ cup orange juice
¼ cup balsamic vinegar
4 tsp. sugar
¾ tsp. salt
¼ tsp. black pepper
2 Tbsp. butter, cut up
1 Tbsp. chopped fresh chives

**1.** Place a steamer basket in a 4-qt. saucepan. Add water to just below the bottom of the basket; bring to boiling. Add carrots to basket. Cover; reduce heat. Steam 15 to 20 minutes or just until tender. Transfer the carrots to a platter; cover and keep warm.
**2.** Meanwhile, for glaze, in a 1- or 1½-qt. saucepan combine orange juice, vinegar, sugar, salt, and pepper. Bring to boiling; reduce heat. Simmer, uncovered, about 12 minutes or until thick and syrupy (about ⅓ cup). Stir in butter. Drizzle glaze over carrots and sprinkle with chives. **Makes 6 servings.**
**TO MAKE AHEAD** Trim and peel carrots. Prepare glaze as directed in Step 2. Cover and chill carrots and glaze separately up to 24 hours. Cook carrots as directed in Step 1. Reheat glaze in a 1- or 1½-qt. saucepan. Continue as directed.
**EACH SERVING** *126 cal., 4 g fat (2 g sat. fat), 10 mg chol., 432 mg sodium, 21 g carb., 4 g fiber, 13 g sugars, 2 g pro.*

## BROCCOLINI WITH PEAS AND LEMONS

**START TO FINISH** 30 minutes

2 lb. Broccolini, trimmed
8 oz. Swiss chard, trimmed and cut into 2- to 3-inch lengths
1 cup frozen peas
2 Tbsp. butter
1 lemon, thinly sliced
¼ cup chicken broth
¼ tsp. crushed red pepper
¼ cup chopped fresh chives
½ tsp. coarse salt

**1.** Cook Broccolini in a 4-qt. pot of salted boiling water 2 minutes. Add Swiss chard and peas. Cover and simmer 4 minutes; drain.
**2.** Meanwhile, melt butter in a 10-inch skillet. Add lemon slices; cook over medium-high heat about 3 minutes per side or until lemon slices and butter are browned.
**3.** Return vegetables to pot. Stir in broth and crushed red pepper. Transfer to a serving dish. Top with the lemon slices, chives, and salt.
**Makes 12 servings (½ cup each).**
**EACH SERVING** *48 cal., 2 g fat (1 g sat. fat), 5 mg chol., 185 mg sodium, 6 g carb., 2 g fiber, 2 g sugars, 2 g pro.*

**BROCCOLINI** looks like broccoli for good reason— it's a hybrid cross between Chinese broccoli and regular broccoli. With long, tender stalks and a topping of small florets, it cooks quickly because of the thin stems. Broccolini is widely available, but you can substitute regular broccoli (with stems) cut into thin spears.

# 12 EASY SIDES

## ROASTED CABBAGE WITH PEARS

Cut one 1½-lb. cabbage head into eight wedges. Place in a shallow baking pan. Drizzle with olive oil; sprinkle with salt and pepper. Roast in a 425°F oven 35 to 40 minutes or until tender, turning cabbage once and adding 3 pears, halved and cored, the last 10 minutes. Drizzle with 2 Tbsp. lemon juice; sprinkle with ¾ cup chopped toasted walnuts and ½ cup crumbled blue cheese. Makes 4 servings.

## JEWELED WILD RICE

In a 12-inch skillet cook 1½ cups shredded sweet potato and 1 cup sliced leek in 2 Tbsp. butter over medium heat about 5 minutes or until tender. Stir in 3 cups hot cooked long grain and wild rice blend (without spice packet), 1 cup chopped dried cherries, and ½ cup chicken broth. Bring to boiling; simmer, uncovered, until liquid is absorbed. Stir in 2 Tbsp. chopped fresh parsley and ¼ cup toasted pecans. Season with salt and pepper. Makes 8 servings.

## ROASTED ROSEMARY DELICATA SQUASH

Line a 15×10-inch baking pan with foil; grease foil. Halve, seed, and cut two 1-lb. delicata squash into ½-inch slices. Toss with 2 shallots, cut into wedges; 2 Tbsp. olive oil; and 2 tsp. chopped fresh rosemary. Spread in prepared pan. Roast in a 425°F oven about 30 minutes or until squash is tender, stirring once. Sprinkle with shredded Parmesan cheese and chopped toasted walnuts. Season with salt and pepper. Makes 8 servings.

## SAUTÉED MUSHROOMS

Slice 1 lb. fresh mushrooms, such as button, cremini, and/or stemmed shiitake. In a 12-inch skillet cook mushrooms in 2 Tbsp. each butter and olive oil over medium heat 20 minutes or until tender, stirring occasionally. Stir in 3 Tbsp. chopped fresh thyme and 2 Tbsp. heavy cream. Season with salt and pepper. Makes 4 servings.

## MINTED PEA COUSCOUS

In a 2-qt. saucepan stir 1½ cups Israeli (large pearl) couscous into 2 cups boiling water. Simmer, covered, 5 minutes. Stir in 2 cups fresh or frozen peas. Cook, covered, 5 minutes more. Add 2 Tbsp. each butter and chopped fresh mint, 1 tsp. lemon zest, and ¼ tsp. each salt and pepper; stir until butter is melted. Sprinkle with crumbled feta cheese. Makes 6 servings.

## HERB-GLAZED CARROTS

In a 3-qt. saucepan cook 5 cups sliced carrots in boiling salted water about 7 minutes or until crisp-tender; drain in a colander. In the same pan combine 2 Tbsp. each butter and maple syrup and 1 Tbsp. chopped fresh thyme. Cook and stir over medium heat until smooth. Add hot carrots. Season with salt and pepper. Makes 8 servings.

### GREMOLATA CAULIFLOWER STEAKS

Cut three 1-inch-thick slices from center of each of 2 medium heads cauliflower. Brush both sides of slices with olive oil; sprinkle with salt and pepper. Roast on a foil-lined baking sheet in a 450°F oven 15 minutes; turn. Roast 10 minutes or until tender. Drizzle with additional olive oil; top with ¼ cup chopped fresh parsley, 2 Tbsp. each chopped hazelnuts and snipped golden raisins, and ½ tsp. orange zest. Makes 6 servings.

### ROASTED ONIONS AND FENNEL

In a foil-lined baking pan combine 3 medium fennel bulbs, trimmed and cut into 1-inch wedges; 2 medium red onions, cut into 1-inch wedges; and 2 Tbsp. olive oil. Toss to coat. Sprinkle with salt and pepper. Roast in a 400°F oven 35 to 40 minutes or until tender and light brown, stirring occasionally. Top with 2 oz. prosciutto strips; 2 Tbsp. shredded Asiago cheese; 1 tsp. chopped fresh thyme; and chopped fennel fronds. Makes 6 servings.

### VEGGIE AND BREAD SKEWERS

Cut 1 medium zucchini lengthwise into thin ribbons; combine with 12 fresh mushrooms, halved, and 1 cup cherry tomatoes. Toss with ¼ cup Italian vinaigrette; let stand 30 minutes. Stir in 1½ cups 1-inch bread cubes. Thread onto 8 skewers, threading zucchini accordion-style. Grill, covered, over medium heat 10 minutes, turning once Makes 8 servings.

### DOUBLE-CRANBERRY SAUCE

In a 2-qt. saucepan combine one 12-oz. bag fresh or frozen cranberries, 1 cup dried cranberries, 1 cup pomegranate juice, ⅓ cup mild-flavor molasses, 1 Tbsp. orange zest, and ¼ tsp. ground cinnamon. Bring to a simmer. Cook until cranberry skins begin to burst. Taste and, if desired, add more molasses. Serve warm or at room temperature. Makes 10 servings.

### CRANBERRY-ORANGE RELISH

Cut the peel and white pith from 1 orange; cut orange segments from the membrane. In a food processor pulse orange segments; one 12-oz. bag fresh cranberries; 1 apple, cored, peeled, and chopped; ¼ cup sugar; and ¼ tsp. ground allspice until coarsely chopped. If desired, stir in 1 to 2 Tbsp. sugar to taste. Refrigerate in an airtight container up to 1 week. Makes 10 servings.

### ASPARAGUS WITH PINE NUTS

In a 10-inch skillet bring 1 inch water to boiling. Add 1¼ lb. asparagus spears, trimmed. Cook about 3 minutes or until crisp-tender; drain. Add 1 Tbsp. butter and shake pan until melted and asparagus is coated. Top with 2 Tbsp. coarsely chopped toasted pine nuts and 2 Tbsp. chopped fresh basil. Season with salt and pepper. Makes 4 servings.

## COOKED FARRO

In a saucepan combine 3 cups water and 1¼ cups pearled or semipearled farro. Bring to boiling; reduce heat. Simmer, covered, about 25 minutes or until farro is tender. Drain if necessary.

SHAVED BRUSSELS SPROUTS are often available in packages. If you can't find them, cut 10 oz. fresh Brussels sprouts into thin slices.

# ITALIAN-STYLE FRIED FARRO

**START TO FINISH** 20 minutes

- 2    Tbsp. olive oil
- 1    10-oz. pkg. shaved Brussels sprouts
- ½    cup coarsely chopped red onion
- 2    oz. very thinly sliced prosciutto, cut into thin strips
- ½    cup chopped walnuts
- 2    cloves garlic, minced
- 3    cups cooked farro, chilled
- 2    Tbsp. balsamic glaze
- 2    Tbsp. shredded Parmesan cheese
- 2    Tbsp. chopped fresh basil
      Cracked black pepper

**1.** In an extra-large wok or 12-inch nonstick skillet heat 1 Tbsp. of the olive oil over medium-high heat. Add Brussels sprouts and onion; cook and stir about 4 minutes or until just crisp-tender. Add prosciutto, walnuts, and garlic; cook and stir 2 minutes.

**2.** Add farro and the remaining 1 Tbsp. olive oil. Cook and stir 3 to 4 minutes or until heated.

**3.** To serve, drizzle balsamic glaze over mixture. Sprinkle with Parmesan, basil, and pepper.

**Makes 4 servings (1½ cups each).**

EACH SERVING  461 cal., 20 g fat (3 g sat. fat), 17 mg chol, 393 mg sodium, 56 g carb., 10 g fiber, 4 g sugars, 17 g pro.

## STUFFING

**HANDS-ON TIME** 35 minutes
**BAKE** 35 minutes at 325°F

½   cup butter
1½  cups VEGETABLES
    HERB
¼   tsp. black pepper
⅛   tsp. salt
8   cups dry BREAD cubes
    MEAT (optional)
1   cup FRUIT (optional)
¼   cup NUTS (optional)
1½  to 2 cups LIQUID

**1.** Preheat oven to 325°F. In a
10-inch skillet melt butter over
medium heat. Add VEGETABLES;
cook until tender but not brown.
Remove from heat. Stir in HERB,
pepper, and salt. Place the BREAD
cubes and, if desired, MEAT, FRUIT,
and NUTS in an extra-large bowl;
add vegetable mixture. Drizzle with
enough LIQUID to moisten, tossing
lightly to combine. Transfer bread
mixture to a 2-qt. baking dish.
**2.** Bake, covered, 35 to 40 minutes
or until heated through. **Makes
10 servings (about ¾ cup each).**

## CUSTOMIZE IT
PICK THE INGREDIENTS
TO CREATE A RECIPE
THAT'S ALL YOUR OWN.

### STUFF IT
If you like your stuffing in
the turkey, spoon it loosely
(don't pack it) into the cavity
of an 8- to 10-lb. turkey. This
will add about 45 minutes to
roasting time. The stuffing
must reach 165°F if it's
baked in the cavity.

// SIDES //

# MIX & MATCH INGREDIENTS

**VEGETABLES**
*(Pick 1–3)*

- Butternut squash, peeled and cubed
- Celery, chopped
- Fennel bulb, cored and chopped
- Mushrooms, sliced
- Onions, chopped
- Sweet peppers, chopped
- Sweet potatoes, peeled and cubed

**HERB** *(Pick 1)*

- 1 Tbsp. chopped fresh sage or 1 tsp. ground sage
- 1 tsp. poultry seasoning

**BREAD** *(Pick 1)*

- Ciabatta bread
- Corn bread
- Focaccia bread
- Italian bread
- Multigrain bread
- Sourdough bread
- Wheat bread
- White bread

**MEAT** *(Pick 1)*

- 1 lb. chorizo, cooked and drained
- 1 lb. Italian sausage, cooked and drained
- 1 lb. pork sausage, cooked and drained
- 1 pt. shucked oysters, drained, chopped, and cooked with VEGETABLES
- Turkey giblets, cooked, drained, and chopped

**FRUIT** *(Pick 1 or 2)*

- Apples, cored and chopped
- Dried apricots, snipped
- Dried cherries
- Golden raisins
- Pears, cored and chopped

**NUTS** *(Pick 1)*

- Almonds, toasted and chopped
- Hazelnuts, toasted and chopped
- Pecans, toasted and chopped
- Walnuts, toasted and chopped

**LIQUID** *(Pick 1)*

- 1 cup apple juice or apple cider + 1 cup chicken broth or water
- 1½ cups chicken broth + ½ cup dry white wine
- Turkey broth, chicken broth, or vegetable broth

## SLOW COOKER RISOTTO

**HANDS-ON TIME** 25 minutes
**SLOW COOK** 1 hour 15 minutes (high)
**STAND** 15 minutes

⅔ cup sliced leeks
2  cloves garlic, minced
1  Tbsp. butter
1¾ cups uncooked Arborio rice
4  cups chicken broth
⅔ cup dry white wine
½  tsp. cracked black pepper
2  oz. Gruyère or Swiss cheese, shredded
1  recipe Arugula Gremolata (optional)

**1.** In a 12-inch skillet cook and stir leeks and garlic in hot butter over medium heat 3 to 5 minutes or until leeks are tender. Stir in rice; cook and stir 1 minute more. Transfer rice mixture into a 3½- or 4-qt. slow cooker. Stir in broth, wine, and pepper.
**2.** Cover; cook on high about 1¼ hours or until rice is tender. Remove crockery liner from cooker, if possible, or turn off cooker. Let risotto stand, uncovered, 15 minutes before serving. Top with cheese and, if desired, Arugula Gremolata. **Makes 8 to 10 servings (⅔ cup each).**

**EACH SERVING** *224 cal., 6 g fat (3 g sat. fat), 18 mg chol., 553 mg sodium, 34 g carb., 1 g fiber, 1 g sugars, 7 g pro.*

### *ARUGULA GREMOLATA*

In a bowl stir together 1 cup chopped fresh arugula; 1 oz. prosciutto, crisp-cooked and crumbled; 2 Tbsp. chopped toasted pine nuts; 1 Tbsp. lemon zest; and 1 clove garlic, minced.

CORN AND BACON MACARONI

## CORN AND BACON MACARONI

**HANDS-ON TIME** 35 minutes
**BAKE** 25 minutes at 350°F

8  oz. dried elbow macaroni (2 cups)
¼  cup butter
¼  cup all-purpose flour
1  tsp. dry mustard
⅛  tsp. black pepper
2  cups milk
1  tsp. Worcestershire sauce
2  cups shredded white cheddar cheese (8 oz.)
6  slices bacon or 4 oz. pancetta, crisp-cooked and chopped
2  cups frozen whole kernel corn, thawed
¼  cup sliced green onions
1  recipe Crumb Topping (optional)

**1.** Preheat oven to 350°F. Cook macaroni according to package directions; drain. Return macaroni to hot pan.
**2.** Meanwhile, in a 12-inch skillet melt butter over medium heat. Whisk in flour, mustard, and pepper; cook and stir 2 minutes. Whisk in milk and Worcestershire sauce; cook and stir until thickened and bubbly. Reduce heat to low. Gradually add cheddar cheese, stirring until cheese is melted. Remove from heat.
**3.** Stir macaroni, bacon, corn, and green onions into the cheese mixture. Spoon macaroni mixture into a lightly greased 2-qt. round baking dish. If desired, sprinkle Crumb Topping evenly over macaroni mixture.
**4.** Bake, uncovered, 25 to 30 minutes or until heated through (160°F). If desired, sprinkle with additional sliced green onions.
**Makes 10 servings (⅔ cup each).**
**CRUMB TOPPING** In a bowl combine ½ cup each panko bread crumbs (tip, *p. 108*) and shredded Parmesan cheese and 2 Tbsp. each melted butter and chopped fresh parsley.

**EACH SERVING** *306 cal., 15 g fat (8 g sat. fat), 43 mg chol., 296 mg sodium, 30 g carb., 2 g fiber, 4 g sugars, 13 g pro.*

SUMMER SPAGHETTI SALAD

## SUMMER SPAGHETTI SALAD

**START TO FINISH** 50 minutes

½   cup olive oil
3   cloves garlic, sliced
12  oz. dried spaghetti, broken in half
3   cups reduced-sodium chicken broth
1   medium zucchini, ends trimmed
1   medium yellow summer squash, ends trimmed
6   sticks string cheese, pulled into thin strands
4   cups red and yellow cherry tomatoes, chopped
1   cup finely chopped onion
1   cup chopped fresh Italian parsley
1   tsp. kosher salt
½   tsp. black pepper
¼   cup red wine vinegar
    Toasted walnuts (tip, p. 18) (optional)

**1.** In a 10-inch skillet heat 2 Tbsp. of the oil over medium heat. Add garlic; cook and stir 1 minute. Stir in uncooked pasta. Add broth. Bring to boiling. Cook, uncovered, about 10 minutes or until liquid is nearly absorbed, stirring occasionally.

Remove from heat; cool 10 minutes. Transfer to a large serving dish. Meanwhile, use a spiral vegetable slicer (tip, p. 209) to cut zucchini and yellow squash into long strands. Add to spaghetti; toss to combine. Cool completely.
**2.** Stir cheese into spaghetti mixture. In a bowl combine tomatoes, onion, parsley, salt, pepper, remaining oil, and vinegar. Top with tomato mixture and, if desired, toasted walnuts. **Makes 10 servings (1½ cups each).**

**EACH SERVING** *298 cal., 15 g fat (4 g sat. fat), 9 mg chol., 415 mg sodium, 32 g carb., 2 g fiber, 5 g sugars, 11 g pro.*

## BAKED BEANS WITH BACON

**HANDS-ON TIME** 30 minutes
**STAND** 1 hour
**COOK** 1 hour
**BAKE** 1 hour 30 minutes at 300°F

1   lb. dried navy beans or Great Northern beans (2⅓ cups)
4   oz. bacon, chopped
1   cup chopped onion
¼   cup packed brown sugar
⅓   cup molasses or maple syrup
¼   cup Worcestershire sauce
1½  tsp. dry mustard
½   tsp. salt
¼   tsp. black pepper
    Crisp-cooked bacon, crumbled (optional)

**1.** Rinse beans. In a 4- to 5-qt. Dutch oven combine beans and 8 cups *water*. Bring to boiling; reduce heat. Simmer, uncovered, 2 minutes. Remove from heat. Cover and let stand 1 hour. (Or place beans in water in Dutch oven. Cover and let soak in a cool place overnight.) Drain and rinse beans.
**2.** Return beans to Dutch oven. Stir in 8 cups fresh *water*. Bring to boiling; reduce heat. Cover and simmer 1 to 1½ hours or until beans are tender, stirring occasionally. Drain beans, reserving liquid.
**3.** Preheat oven to 300°F. In the same Dutch oven cook bacon and onion over medium heat until bacon is slightly crisp and onion is tender, stirring occasionally. Add brown sugar; cook and stir until sugar is dissolved. Stir in molasses, Worcestershire sauce, dry mustard, salt, and pepper. Stir in drained beans and 1¼ cups of the reserved bean liquid. If desired, transfer to a 2-qt. casserole.
**4.** Bake, covered, 1 hour. Uncover and bake 30 to 45 minutes or until desired consistency, stirring occasionally. Beans will thicken slightly as they cool. If beans are too thick, stir in additional reserved bean liquid. If desired, sprinkle with additional cooked bacon. **Makes 10 servings (½ cup each).**

**EACH SERVING** *266 cal., 5 g fat (2 g sat. fat), 7 mg chol., 266 mg sodium, 44 g carb., 7 g fiber, 17 g sugars, 12 g pro.*

# BAKING & sweets

# HOW TO BAKE

## SUCCESSFUL BAKING REQUIRES ATTENTION TO DETAIL. REMEMBER THESE KEY POINTS EVERY TIME YOU BAKE.

## FLOURS

Flour is the foundation of baked recipes because it provides structure. When combined with liquid and after mixing and kneading, flour's protein (gluten) begins to develop. This tough, elastic substance traps and holds air produced by yeast and other leaveners, enabling baked goods to rise. For yeast breads, gluten development is key to texture. For tender cakes and crusts, avoid overworking mixtures once liquid is added to prevent overdevelopment of gluten.

## MEASURING FLOUR

To measure flour properly, start by stirring it in the bag or canister to aerate it. Sifting is not necessary (except for cake flour). Gently spoon flour into a dry measuring cup and fill it to overflowing. Level off the top with the edge of a knife. (Never pack flour into a measuring cup; it will increase the amount of flour added to the recipe and cause dryness.)

### GLUTEN-FREE FLOUR MIX

Whisk together 3 cups white rice flour, 3 cups potato starch, 2 cups sorghum flour, and 4 tsp. xanthan gum. Use as directed (right). Makes 8 cups.

### ALL-PURPOSE FLOUR

This is the most common flour used in recipes. It is made from both "soft" (low-protein) and "hard" (high–protein) wheats. Bleached flour (chemically whitened) and unbleached flour are used interchangeably.

### GLUTEN-FREE FLOUR MIX

We developed this wheat-free mixture (recipe, left) to use as a flour substitute in almost all of our baked goods. Swap at a 1 to 1 ratio in cookies, bars, and cakes. (Avoid using for yeast breads.) Cover and store mix at room temp up to 6 months.

### BREAD FLOUR

This flour is ground from "hard" wheat varieties with high protein (gluten) content. This flour is ideal for yeast breads and pizza crusts because the higher protein content creates a tuggy, chewy texture.

### CAKE FLOUR

Made from "soft" wheat varieties with low protein (gluten), cake flour is high in starch and creates a tender, delicate texture. We use it in our Angel Food Cake (p. 530).

### WHOLE WHEAT FLOUR

This coarse flour contains nutritious wheat germ. It creates a denser texture, so only replace a portion of the all-purpose flour in a recipe. White whole wheat flour (a lighter-color wheat variety) is also available.

## SUGARS & SWEETENERS

Sweeteners like sugar are the key to the luscious flavor in baked goods, but they also contribute to overall tenderness and moistness. In addition, sweeteners feed yeast in bread dough, stabilize whipped egg whites in meringues, and create a caramel color on crusts.

### POWDERED SUGAR

Also known as confectioners' sugar, powdered sugar is a mixture of crushed (powderized) granulated sugar and cornstarch (to help prevent clumping). Sifting removes lumps that may have developed.

### HONEY

This natural sweetener is made when bees extract the syrupy nectar from flowers. Its flavor and color—from off-white to dark brown—depend on the source of the nectar.

### BROWN SUGAR

Brown sugar is a mixture of white sugar and molasses. Molasses gives it the trademark color and makes it moister and richer with a caramel flavor. It's available in light and dark varieties; dark brown sugar has more molasses and a stronger flavor.

### CORN SYRUP

Corn syrup is the thick, sweet product processed from cornstarch. Dark and light corn syrups perform similarly in baked recipes and are interchangeable. Use light corn syrup when a delicately sweet flavor is desired. Dark corn syrup has a more robust flavor and color.

### GRANULATED SUGAR

Also known as white or table sugar, granulated sugar is the most common sugar used in baking. It is a refined product from sugar cane and sugar beets.

### MOLASSES

During refining, the juice drained from sugar beets or sugar cane is boiled down. Then the sugar crystals are removed. The remaining syrup is called molasses. Purchase either light or dark molasses (dark is less sweet and more robust).

### MEASURING SWEETENERS

Pack brown sugar firmly into a dry measuring cup with the back of a spoon. Liquid sweeteners (like molasses) should be measured in a liquid measuring cup (more info, p. 10).

## HIGH ALTITUDE FOR TIPS ON BAKING AT HIGH ALTITUDES, SEE *P. 703.*

### *LEAVENERS*

Breads, cakes, cookies, and bars typically contain a leavening agent. There are two categories of leaveners: chemical (baking soda and baking powder) and biological (yeast). Start by checking expiration dates on all leaveners. Here's the science behind how they work.

**BAKING SODA** Baking soda, or sodium bicarbonate, is used in batters that contain acidic ingredients—such as buttermilk, yogurt, sour cream, molasses, honey, or fruit juices—because it requires activation by an acid to produce carbon dioxide.

**BAKING POWDER** Baking powder is a mixture of baking soda and a powdered acidic ingredient (such as cream of tartar), so no other acidic ingredients are needed in the recipe. It also contains cornstarch to absorb moisture. Most baking powders are "double-acting." They produce gases in two stages—once when liquids are added and again during baking. Be sure to thoroughly stir baking powder into a flour or dry ingredient mixture to prevent oversize gas bubbles from forming (which may cause tunnels or large air pockets to form). Although recipes call for small amounts of baking powder and baking soda, they are not optional ingredients and are necessary for proper rising. Don't be tempted to substitute one for another (see *inside front cover* for emergency substitution of baking powder). If a recipe calls for both baking powder and soda, the baking soda is included to neutralize an added acid (such as brown sugar).

**YEAST** Active dry yeast is a dehydrated single-cell organism. It is activated by warm liquid, then converts sugar into carbon dioxide gas that makes dough rise.

**EGGS** Although not a chemical or biological leavener, beaten egg whites work as leaveners in certain recipes. They trap and hold air and, when other ingredients are folded in, add lift. See Chocolate Soufflé (*p. 595*) and Angel Food Cake (*p. 530*).

## MEASURING LIQUIDS

Always measure milk and liquid ingredients (including oils) in a clear glass or plastic measuring cup. Place the cup on a flat work surface and pour the liquid in the cup to the measurement marking on the cup. Check at eye level to make sure it lines up exactly.

### ↑↑
### MAKING SOUR MILK

For each 1 cup sour milk, add 1 Tbsp. lemon juice or vinegar to a liquid measuring cup. Add enough milk to make 1 cup total liquid. Stir; let stand 5 minutes before using.

## DAIRY

Before you hit the dairy case for your baking needs, consider your options.

**WHOLE, REDUCED-FAT, LOW-FAT, AND SKIM MILKS**

We test our recipes with reduced-fat milk (2%). But unless a recipe specifies, these types can be used interchangeably. They differ in amounts of fat, so this will directly affect the richness and flavor in foods.

**ALTERNATIVE MILKS**

Dairy milk can be replaced with a nondairy option—such as almond milk, soymilk, or coconut milk—in a 1 to 1 ratio for most baked goods. They may impart a slight nutty flavor to your recipe. (When using coconut milk, use the refrigerated variety, not the canned option.)

**BUTTERMILK**

Buttermilk is low-fat or fat-free milk with added bacterial cultures. It is thick and creamy with a mildly acidic taste. Do not substitute with regular milk (buttermilk's acidity works with the baking soda in a recipe to leaven). Instead, make sour milk (above) to replace buttermilk.

**EVAPORATED MILK VS. SWEETENED CONDENSED MILK**

Sweetened condensed milk contains 40% sugar and has 60% of the water removed. Canned evaporated milk is essentially condensed milk without the sugar. Don't substitute one for the other in recipes. (They look similar, so check the can before you buy.)

## SWEETENED WHIPPED CREAM

**1**

In a large chilled bowl combine 1 cup heavy cream, 2 Tbsp. sugar, and ½ tsp. vanilla. Beat with a mixer on medium until soft peaks form (tips curl). Serve like this or continue beating.

**2**

If you prefer, continue beating until stiff peaks form (tips stand straight). (Do not overbeat or the cream will turn to butter.)

## FATS

Fats and oils add flavor and contribute to the texture of baked goods. Here are the fat facts you need to know before you start baking.

### BUTTER

We love butter! Nothing beats the flavor of it, especially in butter-specific recipes like pound cake and shortbread. But it goes deeper than that. Margarines and buttery spreads contain water, which reduces the fat in your recipe and affects the final outcome. If a recipe calls for butter, use butter. We can't guarantee success if margarine is used as a substitute.

### SOFTENED BUTTER

Let cold butter stand at room temperature 30 minutes or until it is soft and easy to spread and blend. To quickly soften butter, microwave on defrost 15 seconds. Check and repeat.

### MELTED BUTTER

Heat butter in the microwave or on the stove until it liquefies.

### SHORTENING

Shortening is a solid fat made from vegetable oils. We use a combination of shortening with butter for tender piecrusts and biscuits and to get the right texture and spread in our Chocolate Chip Cookies (p. 554).

Shortening spreads less than butter because it melts at a higher temperature. To measure shortening, see photos, p. 10.

### VEGETABLE OIL

Oil adds tenderness and moisture to baked goods and coats flour proteins better than shortening. This prevents the proteins from absorbing liquid and forming gluten. We use oil in recipes where the flavor of butter won't be missed, such as Pumpkin Bread (p. 505). For more info on oils to use, see p. 21.

## EGGS

We always use large eggs when we test recipes. When it comes to baking, eggs are magical.

### EGG SCIENCE

An egg is a simple ingredient that plays a complex role in baking and cooking. Eggs are the glue that holds ingredients together (especially in custards and puddings); they act as a leavener in recipes such as Angel Food Cake (p. 530); and they add structure, richness, and moisture to baked goods. Egg yolks are high in fat and flavor; egg whites (a mixture of protein and water) add moisture and contribute to structure in baked products.

### STORAGE

Store eggs in the original carton in the coldest part of the refrigerator up to 5 weeks.

### EGG TEMPERATURE

In order for eggs to reach their maximum volume, we suggest letting your eggs stand at room temperature about 30 minutes (take them out of the fridge when you set the butter out). If you need to separate yolks and whites, do it as soon as you take the eggs out of the fridge. If you try to separate a room-temperature egg, the yolk is more likely to break.

### BEATING

For meringue, the first step is to beat egg whites on medium speed until soft peaks (below left) form with tips that curl when beaters are lifted. At this point, the sugar is beaten in gradually until stiff peaks form (tips stand straight; below right). The sugar adds stability to the egg whites so they are able to hold their shape.

### SALTED OR UNSALTED BUTTER WE TEST ALL OUR RECIPES WITH SALTED BUTTER. IF YOU USE UNSALTED, ADD ¼ TSP. SALT TO YOUR RECIPE.

### BUTTER MATH

**4 STICKS =**

# 1 LB.

**½ CUP = 8 TBSP. =**

# 1 STICK

**¼ CUP = 4 TBSP. =**

# ½ STICK

**SOFT PEAKS**

**STIFF PEAKS**

## VANILLA BEANS

There's nothing boring about the big flavor of vanilla. Vanilla beans are the dried pods of a tropical orchid; they are used to make extract and paste. Find all these forms in the spice aisle and spice stores.

**1 vanilla bean = 1 Tbsp. paste = 1 Tbsp. extract**

### VANILLA BEANS
To seed a vanilla bean, use a paring knife to cut the bean in half lengthwise and scrape seeds out of the pod.

### VANILLA BEAN PASTE
This thick, viscous liquid is the next best thing to the whole bean and contains actual seeds from the bean.

### PURE VANILLA EXTRACT
Extract is made by combining chopped vanilla beans with a mixture of alcohol and water. Avoid imitation vanilla.

## COCONUT

Coconut is available in a few different forms (brands aren't always consistent in their terminology). In this book, unless otherwise specified, we tested with sweetened flaked (often called "shredded"). Large coconut chips (sometimes called "flakes") are typically used for garnishing. To toast coconut, see *p. 18*.

## GRATED NUTMEG

When a recipe calls for ground nutmeg, our vote is to always use freshly grated. The texture is light and fluffy and the flavor is deliciously sweet and aromatic (1 tsp. freshly grated replaces ½ tsp. preground nutmeg). Use a Microplane (rasp) grater to quickly create mounds of grated nutmeg.

## CHOCOLATE

All chocolate starts from the beans of the cacao (*kay-KAY-oh*) tree. The beans are fermented, dried, roasted, and cracked. The extraction process produces cocoa butter and an intense brown paste called chocolate liquor. The percentage number on the chocolate package represents the amount of chocolate liquor contained in the bar. The rest is sugar. The greater the percentage of chocolate liquor in proportion to sugar, the more pronounced and complex the chocolate flavor.

### COCOA POWDER
Unsweetened cocoa results from a final extraction of cocoa butter from chocolate liquor, resulting in a solid product that is ground into a powder.

### UNSWEETENED CHOCOLATE
Also called baking chocolate, this variety is pure chocolate and cocoa butter with no added sugar. Recipes that call for it also require plenty of sugar. Don't substitute other types of chocolate; the sugar ratio will be off.

### SWEET, SEMISWEET, AND BITTERSWEET CHOCOLATES
These three chocolates contain varying amounts of chocolate liquor and sugar. Sweet and semisweet contain 15% to 35% chocolate liquor and have more sugar than bittersweet, which contains 35% chocolate liquor or higher. Use these interchangeably.

### MILK CHOCOLATE
Dry milk gives this sweetened chocolate a creamy texture. Because of this added ingredient, milk chocolate can't always be substituted for other chocolate in recipes.

### WHITE CHOCOLATE
This chocolate contains no chocolate liquor. Instead, it's a mixture of cocoa butter (extracted from cacao beans), milk solids, and sugar. The recipes in this book call for white chocolate with cocoa butter (available with baking chocolate in the baking aisle). White baking pieces do not contain cocoa butter and won't work correctly.

# BAKEWARE

These are the most common pans we call for in our baking recipes. If you're just starting out, buy pans as you need them. You may find the recipes you love to make don't require special pans.

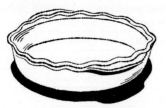

### PIE PLATE

Recipes in this book call for a standard 9-inch plate with 1½-inch-deep sides. These are typically made of glass. Deep-dish pie plates (above) are up to 2 inches deep (more info, p. 613). Use the size called for in each recipe.

### RAMEKINS AND CUSTARD CUPS

Use these small dishes for baking desserts and custards. Each recipe will specify the size to use.

### SPRINGFORM PAN

A latch on this pan opens to release the sides from a baked dessert, such as cheesecake, for easy serving.

### COOKIE SHEETS

Look for sturdy cookie sheets, with one or two raised sides, that are light to medium in color (dark-color pans tend to brown cookies faster).

### ROUND CAKE PANS

Buy two of these for baking standard layer cakes, although one will do (just bake layers one at a time). Pans come in an 8- or 9-inch diameter. If you use 9-inch rounds, your layers will be wider and thinner.

### 15×10×1-INCH PAN

Also commonly called a jelly-roll pan, this pan is used for a variety of recipes, including sponge cakes for jelly rolls and certain bar cookies and brownies. (You can also use it for roasting veggies.)

### WIRE COOLING RACK

Most recipes call for a rack to completely cool recipes after removing them from the oven.

### RECTANGULAR AND SQUARE PANS AND DISHES

Stock up on rectangular (13×9-inch) and square (8×8-inch or 9×9-inch) baking pans for brownies, cakes, bars, and more.

### LOAF PANS

These are used for yeast breads, quick breads, and pound cakes. They come in 8×4×2-inch and 9×5×3-inch—both of which are called for in this book (we recommend metal pans over glass).

## BAKING PANS OR BAKING DISHES

In this book, a baking dish means an oven-safe glass or ceramic vessel. A baking pan refers to a metal vessel.

**BAKING DISHES (GLASS OR CERAMIC)** Use these when a 2- or 3-qt. baking dish is called for—specifically when baking egg dishes and acidic foods, including citrus- and other fruit-based desserts. Use dishes for crisps, cobblers, and other crustless fruit desserts.

**BAKING PANS (METAL)** Aluminum—nonstick or not—is a great choice for baking pans. They are lightweight and conduct heat well for even baking. Pale or shiny metal pans, such as heavy-gauge aluminum, deliver a tender, delicate crust for breads and cookies. Dark metal pans, which conduct, retain, and distribute heat well, are for items that require more crispness or browning.

// HOW TO BAKE //

## LINING A PAN WITH FOIL

Lining the inside of pans with foil before baking makes removal and cleanup easy.

### 1
*Tear off a piece of foil that is longer than the pan (allow for overhang on either end) and shape over the outside of the pan bottom, folding foil at corners.*

### 2
*Gently lift the shaped foil off the pan and turn pan over. Fit shaped foil into inside of the pan, leaving the overhang to use as "handles" to lift the recipe out of the pan.*

## LINING A PAN WITH PARCHMENT PAPER OR WAXED PAPER

This technique is commonly used for cakes that are likely to stick, such as Carrot Cake (p. 522).

### 1
*Grease bottom and sides of pan as directed in recipe. Set pan on a large sheet of waxed paper or parchment paper; trace around the pan with a pencil.*

### 2
*Cut around the traced line on the paper. Fit the paper cutout to the bottom of the pan, pressing corners and smoothing out wrinkles or bubbles. Grease paper if directed in recipe.*

## BAKING PAN CAPACITIES

| PAN SHAPE | PAN DIMENSION | TOTAL VOLUME | BATTER AMOUNT |
|---|---|---|---|
| Angel food cake pan | 10-inch | 16 cups | 8 to 10 cups |
| Fluted tube pan | 10-inch | 12 cups | 6 to 8 cups |
| Jelly-roll pan | 15×10×1-inch | 10 cups | 5 to 6½ cups |
| Loaf pan | 8×4×2-inch | 4 cups | 2 to 2½ cups |
| Loaf pan | 9×5×3-inch | 8 cups | 4 to 5 cups |
| Mini muffin pan | 1¾-inch cups | 2 Tbsp. | 1 to 1½ Tbsp. |
| Muffin pan | 2½-inch cups | ½ cup | ¼ to ⅓ cup |
| Pie pan or plate | 9×1½-inch | 6 cups | 3 to 4 cups |
| Pie pan or plate (deep-dish) | 9×2-inch | 8 cups | 4 to 5½ cups |
| Rectangular pan | 11×7-inch | 6 cups | 3 to 4 cups |
| Rectangular pan | 13×9-inch | 14 cups | 7 to 8 cups |
| Round pan | 8-inch | 4 to 5 cups | 2 to 2½ cups |
| Round pan | 9-inch | 6 to 7 cups | 3 to 3½ cups |
| Springform pan | 8-inch | 11 cups | 6 to 7 cups |
| Springform pan | 9-inch | 12 cups | 6 to 7 cups |

## GREASING AND FLOURING A PAN

Cakes that will be removed from the pan call for a greased and floured pan; recipes that are served in the pan simply call for greasing.

### 1
*With a pastry brush or paper towel, apply shortening evenly on the bottom and sides of the pan.*

### 2
*Sprinkle a few spoonfuls of all-purpose flour into the bottom of the pan.*

### 3
*Hold one edge of pan; tap the other with free hand to distribute flour. Tilt pan to coat sides. Tap any extra flour into the garbage.*

## QUICK NONSTICK BRUSH-ON STIR TOGETHER ¼ CUP EACH VEGETABLE OIL, SHORTENING, AND FLOUR. BRUSH ON PANS INSTEAD OF GREASING/FLOURING.

# TROUBLESHOOTING GUIDE

If something seems a little off with a baked item, take a look at this chart to see what might have gone wrong and what you can do to prevent it from happening again.

## CAKES

| PROBLEM | POSSIBLE CAUSES |
|---------|-----------------|
| Cake has coarse texture. | • Excess baking soda<br>• Too little liquid<br>• Butter and sugar not thoroughly blended |
| Cake sticks to pan. | • Insufficient greasing<br>• Cake removed from pan too quickly<br>• Cake cooled in pan too long |
| Cake is dry. | • Excess flour or baking powder<br>• Too little shortening, butter, or sugar<br>• Oven too hot or cake baked too long |
| Cake is heavy/dense. | • Too little baking powder<br>• Too many eggs<br>• Batter overmixed |
| Cake sinks in middle. | • Pan is too small<br>• Too much liquid<br>• Opening oven or moving pans during baking<br>• Oven temperature too low or cake not baked long enough |

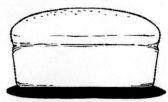

## YEAST BREADS

| PROBLEM | POSSIBLE CAUSES |
|---------|-----------------|
| Loaf did not rise enough before baking. | • Expired yeast<br>• Liquid too hot<br>• Not enough sugar<br>• Environment too cool or drafty<br>• Dough not kneaded enough |
| Loaf did not rise enough during baking. | • Oven temperature too low<br>• Dough raised too much before baking |
| Crust did not brown. | • Oven temperature too low<br>• Not enough sugar in dough |
| Bread is dense on bottom. | • Oven temperature too high |
| Bread collapsed in oven. | • Dough raised too much before baking |

## COOKIES

| PROBLEM | POSSIBLE CAUSES |
|---------|-----------------|
| Cookies are tough and hard. | • Too much flour<br>• Overmixed dough |
| Cookies are baked unevenly. | • Misshapen dough balls<br>• Cookie sheet with raised/high edges used |
| Cookies are too brown on the bottom. | • Dark-color cookie sheet |
| Cookies spread too much. | • Unnecessary greasing of cookie sheet<br>• Dough placed on warm cookie sheet<br>• Oven temperature too low<br>• Too much sugar<br>• Wrong fat used |
| Cookies are burned. | • Baked too long<br>• Left on baking sheet too long |

## QUICK BREADS

| PROBLEM | POSSIBLE CAUSES |
|---------|-----------------|
| Bread is dense. | • Not baked long enough<br>• Not enough liquid<br>• Leavener expired |
| Bread is tough. | • Too much liquid<br>• Not enough liquid<br>• Too much flour |
| Muffins have tunnels. | • Batter overmixed<br>• Not enough liquid<br>• Too much flour<br>• Overbaked |

# BREADS

**MAKE-AHEAD RECIPE.** See also make-ahead tip, *p. 494.*

**KNOW YOUR DOUGH**

In each bread recipe in this chapter, we specify what the dough should feel like after kneading. For the right texture, structure, and density, follow these specifications as closely as you can. Here's what the terms mean.

**SOFT DOUGH**
Extremely sticky; used for breads that don't require kneading.

**MODERATELY SOFT DOUGH**
Slightly sticky but smooth; used for rich, sweet breads.

**MODERATELY STIFF DOUGH**
Slightly firm to the touch but not sticky; for nonsweet breads.

**STIFF DOUGH**
Firm to the touch; holds shape after 8 to 10 minutes of kneading.

## WHITE BREAD

**HANDS-ON TIME** 40 minutes
**RISE** 1 hour 15 minutes
**BAKE** 35 minutes at 375°F

5¾ to 6¼ cups all-purpose
    flour
1   pkg. active dry yeast
2¼ cups milk or buttermilk
2   Tbsp. sugar
1   Tbsp. butter
1½ tsp. salt

>>

YEAST needs a warm liquid to get it going to make the bread rise. But be careful! If the liquid is too hot, the yeast will die; too cool and the yeast won't activate. Use an instant-read thermometer to check that the liquid is between 120°F and 130°F.

**1.** In a large bowl stir together 2½ cups of the flour and the yeast. In a 2-qt. saucepan heat and stir milk, sugar, butter, and salt just until warm (120°F to 130°F) and butter almost melts; add to flour mixture. Beat with a mixer on low 30 seconds, scraping bowl constantly. Beat on high 3 minutes. Stir in as much of the remaining flour as you can.

**2.** Turn dough out onto a lightly floured surface. Knead in enough of the remaining flour to make a moderately stiff dough that is smooth and elastic (6 to 8 minutes total). Shape dough into a ball. Place in a lightly greased bowl, turning to grease surface of dough. Cover; let rise in a warm place until double in size (45 to 60 minutes).
**3.** Punch dough down. Turn out onto a lightly floured surface; divide in half. Cover and let rest 10 minutes. Meanwhile, lightly grease two 8×4-inch loaf pans.
**4.** Shape each dough half into a loaf by patting or rolling (tip, *below right*).
**5.** Place shaped dough halves, seam sides down, in prepared loaf pans. Cover and let rise in a warm place until nearly double in size (30 minutes).

**6.** Preheat oven to 375°F. Bake 35 to 40 minutes or until bread sounds hollow when lightly tapped (if necessary to prevent overbrowning, cover loosely with foil the last 5 to 10 minutes). Immediately remove from pans; cool on wire racks. **Makes 2 loaves (12 slices each).**
**WHOLE WHEAT BREAD** Prepare as directed, except reduce all-purpose flour to 3¾ to 4¼ cups and stir in 2 cups whole wheat flour after beating 3 minutes in Step 1.
**EACH SLICE WHITE OR WHOLE WHEAT VARIATION** 130 cal., 1 g fat (1 g sat. fat), 3 mg chol., 159 mg sodium, 25 g carb., 1 g fiber, 2 g sugars, 4 g pro.

**1**

The dough gets too stiff for a mixer, so you'll need to stir in as much of the remaining flour as you can with a wooden spoon. Stir until dough looks ropy and pulls away from the sides of the bowl.

**2**

To knead dough, fold it over and push with the heel of your hand. Turn the dough a quarter turn and repeat until the dough is smooth but elastic.

**3**

The dough is ready to shape when it has risen, or proofed, sufficiently. It is ready when indentations stay after two fingers are pressed ½ inch into the center of the dough.

**4**

Punch the dough in the center with your fist. Pull the edges in and away from the sides of the bowl.

## *SHAPING DOUGH*

**PAT INTO A LOAF**
Use your hands to gently pull, pat, and pinch dough. Place, seam side down, into prepared pan.

**OR**

**SHAPE BY ROLLING**
Roll dough into a 12×8-inch rectangle. Tightly roll up rectangle, starting from short side. Pinch seam with fingertips to seal.

POTATO BREAD

# POTATO BREAD

**HANDS-ON TIME** 1 hour
**COOL** 15 minutes
**RISE** 1 hour 30 minutes
**BAKE** 35 minutes at 375°F

| | |
|---|---|
| 2 | cups water |
| 1¾ | cups cubed, peeled russet potato |
| ¼ | cup butter, cut up |
| 1½ | tsp. salt |
| 4½ to 4¾ | cups all-purpose flour |
| 2 | pkg. active dry yeast |
| 2 | eggs |

**1.** In a 2-qt. saucepan bring the water and potato to boiling; reduce heat. Simmer, covered, 12 to 15 minutes or until very tender. Drain, reserving 1 cup of the hot cooking water. Mash potato (should have 1 cup).
**2.** In a small bowl combine reserved 1 cup cooking water, butter, and salt. Cool to 120°F to 130°F.
**3.** In a large bowl stir together 2 cups of the flour and the yeast. Add butter mixture and eggs. Beat with a mixer on low 30 seconds, scraping bowl constantly. Beat on high 3 minutes. Stir in mashed potato and as much of the remaining flour as you can (photos, p. 483).
**4.** Turn dough out onto a lightly floured surface. Knead in enough of the remaining flour to make a moderately stiff dough that is smooth and elastic (6 to 8 minutes total). Shape dough into a ball. Place in a lightly greased bowl, turning to grease surface of dough. Cover and let rise in a warm place until double in size (1 to 1½ hours).
**5.** Punch dough down. Turn out onto a lightly floured surface; divide in half. Cover; let rest 10 minutes. Meanwhile, lightly grease two 8×4-inch loaf pans.
**6.** Shape each dough half into a loaf by patting or rolling (tip, p. 483). Place shaped dough halves, seam sides down, in prepared loaf pans. Lightly sprinkle tops with additional flour. Cover and let rise in a warm place until nearly double in size (30 to 40 minutes).
**7.** Preheat oven to 375°F. Bake 35 to 40 minutes or until bread sounds hollow when lightly tapped (if necessary to prevent overbrowning, cover loosely with foil the last 15 minutes). Immediately remove from pans; cool on wire racks. **Makes 2 loaves (12 slices each).**
**EACH SLICE** *119 cal., 3 g fat (1 g sat. fat), 23 mg chol., 167 mg sodium, 20 g carb., 1 g fiber, 0 g sugars, 3 g pro.*

# MIXED-GRAIN BREAD

**HANDS-ON TIME** 40 minutes
**RISE** 1 hour 30 minutes
**BAKE** 30 minutes at 375°F

| | |
|---|---|
| 3½ to 4 | cups all-purpose flour |
| 2 | pkg. active dry yeast |
| 1½ | cups milk |
| ¾ | cup water |
| ½ | cup cracked wheat |
| ¼ | cup cornmeal |
| ¼ | cup packed brown sugar |
| 3 | Tbsp. vegetable oil or canola oil |
| 2 | tsp. salt |
| 1½ | cups whole wheat flour |
| ½ | cup regular rolled oats |

**1.** In a large bowl stir together 2 cups of the all-purpose flour and the yeast. In a 2-qt. saucepan heat and stir next seven ingredients (through salt) just until warm (120°F to 130°F). Add milk mixture to flour mixture. Beat with a mixer on low 30 seconds, scraping bowl constantly. Beat on high 3 minutes. Stir in whole wheat flour, oats, and as much remaining all-purpose flour as you can (photos, p. 483).
**2.** Turn dough out onto a lightly floured surface. Knead in enough of the remaining all-purpose flour to make a moderately stiff dough that is nearly smooth and elastic (6 to 8 minutes total). Shape dough

**POTATO ROLLS** Prepare as directed through Step 5, except use baking sheets. Divide each dough half into 12 pieces. Shape into balls; dip tops in flour. Arrange balls 1½ inches apart on greased baking sheets. Bake 20 to 25 minutes or until golden. Remove; cool on wire racks. **Makes 24 rolls.**

MIXED-GRAIN BREAD

GOLDEN WHEAT BREAD

into a ball. Place in a lightly greased bowl, turning to grease surface of dough. Cover and let rise in a warm place until double in size (1 hour).

**3.** Punch dough down. Turn out onto a lightly floured surface; divide in half. Cover and let rest 10 minutes. Meanwhile, lightly grease two 8×4-inch loaf pans.

**4.** Shape each dough half into a loaf by patting or rolling (tip, *p. 483*). Place shaped dough halves, seam sides down, in prepared loaf pans. Cover and let rise in a warm place until nearly double in size (30 minutes).

**5.** Preheat oven to 375°F. Brush tops of loaves with additional water; sprinkle with additional oats. Bake 30 to 35 minutes or until bread sounds hollow when lightly tapped (if necessary to prevent overbrowning, cover loosely with foil last 10 minutes). Immediately remove from pans; cool on wire racks. **Makes 2 loaves (12 slices each).**

**MIXED-GRAIN SEED BREAD**
Prepare as directed, except stir in ¼ cup each sunflower kernels and millet or sesame seeds and 2 Tbsp. poppy seeds with the oats.

**EACH SLICE** *148 cal., 3 g fat (0 g sat. fat), 1 mg chol., 203 mg sodium, 27 g carb., 2 g fiber, 3 g sugars, 4 g pro.*

# GOLDEN WHEAT BREAD

**HANDS-ON TIME** 50 minutes
**RISE** 1 hour 45 minutes
**BAKE** 55 minutes at 350°F

| | |
|---|---|
| 2 | pkg. active dry yeast |
| ½ | cup warm water (105°F to 115°F) |
| 2 | cups milk |
| ¾ | cup packed brown sugar |
| ½ | cup shortening |
| 2 | cups whole wheat flour |
| 1 | egg, lightly beaten |
| 1½ | tsp. salt |
| 4¾ to 5¼ | cups bread flour (tip, *right*) |

**1.** In a small bowl dissolve yeast in the warm water. In a 2-qt. saucepan bring milk just to simmering; remove from heat. Pour milk into a large bowl. Whisk in brown sugar and shortening until shortening melts. Whisk in whole wheat flour. Cool to lukewarm (105°F to 115°F). Stir in yeast mixture, egg, and salt. Stir in as much of the bread flour as you can (photos, *p. 483*).

**2.** Turn dough out onto a lightly floured surface. Knead in enough of the remaining bread flour to make a moderately stiff dough that is smooth and elastic (6 to 8 minutes total). Shape dough into a ball. Place in a lightly greased bowl, turning to grease surface of dough. Cover and let rise in a warm place until double in size (1¼ to 1½ hours).

**3.** Punch dough down. Turn out onto a lightly floured surface; divide in half. Cover and let rest 10 minutes. Meanwhile, lightly grease two 9×5-inch loaf pans.

**4.** Shape each dough half into a loaf by patting or rolling (tip, *p. 483*). Place shaped dough halves, seam sides down, in prepared loaf pans. Cover and let rise in a warm place until nearly double in size (30 minutes).

**5.** Preheat oven to 350°F. Bake 55 minutes or until a thermometer registers 210°F* (if necessary to prevent overbrowning, cover loosely with foil the last 25 minutes). Immediately remove from pans; cool on wire racks. **Makes 2 loaves (12 slices each).**

***NOTE** This bread will not sound hollow when tapped, so it is necessary to take an internal temperature reading in the center of bread to ensure that it is done.

**EACH SLICE** *210 cal., 5 g fat (1 g sat. fat), 10 mg chol., 160 mg sodium, 35 g carb., 2 g fiber, 8 g sugars, 6 g pro.*

**BREAD FLOUR**
Bread flour has a higher protein content than other flours, which contributes to the texture of the baked bread. How? When combined with liquid, the proteins bind together to develop gluten (the compound that makes bread dough stretchy and elastic). For the best texture, don't substitute all-purpose when a recipe calls for bread flour.

// BREADS //

## KNOW YOUR STARTER

Sourdough Starter uses natural yeasts and lactobacilli from the air to grow—they settle into the flour-water mixture and feed on the sugars in the flour. The "sour" flavor is from fermentation by the lactobacilli, which produces sour-tasting lactic acid.

Use only utensils that are plastic, silicone, or wooden and a container that is glass or plastic. It must be very clean.

The container needs to be at least 2 to 3 qt. to allow for growth (mixture will bubble and expand as the yeasts feed).

Feed the starter (i.e., add fresh flour and water) daily until mixture is vigorous.

Loosely cover the starter at first. Once it gets going and is refrigerated, you can put a lid on the container.

Let chilled starter come to room temperature before you begin making bread dough.

---

### BREAD-BAKING OPTIONS

### 1

**PROOFING BASKET**
Proofing baskets, also known as brotforms and bannetons, are used to support dough in a certain shape as it proofs (rises). They're optional but give the loaf a floured artisanal pattern (below).

### 2

**DUTCH OVEN**
Baking the loaf in a preheated Dutch oven gives the loaf a darker, crispier crust than one baked on a baking sheet.

### 3

**BAKING SHEET**
A loaf baked on a baking sheet spreads out, giving it a more irregular shape. The bread's crust will have a light golden appearance.

---

## CLASSIC SOURDOUGH BREAD

**HANDS-ON TIME** 20 minutes
**RISE** 8 hours
**CHILL** overnight
**BAKE** 25 minutes at 425°F

3½ to 3¾ cups all-purpose flour
1½ cups warm water (105°F to 115°F)
1 cup Sourdough Starter, room temperature
1 Tbsp. salt

**1.** In a large bowl stir together 3 cups of the flour, the water, and Sourdough Starter until smooth. Cover bowl with waxed paper or plastic wrap. Let rise at room temperature 4 hours. Place bowl in refrigerator; chill overnight.
**2.** Stir in salt and as much of the remaining flour as you can (photos, p. 483). Turn dough out onto a floured surface. Knead in enough of the remaining flour to make a smooth dough (2 to 3 minutes). Place in a greased bowl, turning to grease surface of dough. Cover and let rise at room temperature about 2 hours or until slightly increased in size (you may see a few bubbles).
**3.** Line a large baking sheet with parchment paper. Turn dough out onto a floured surface; gently divide in half. Shape each dough half into an oval loaf. Place loaves on prepared baking sheet and cover with greased plastic wrap. Let rise at room temperature about 2 hours or until nearly double in size.
**4.** Preheat oven to 425°F. Using a sharp knife, make three or four diagonal cuts across top of each loaf. Bake 25 to 30 minutes or until bread is golden and sounds hollow when lightly tapped. Remove from baking sheet; cool on wire racks.
**Makes 2 loaves (10 slices each).**

---

**DUTCH OVEN METHOD** Prepare as directed through Step 2. Line two large bowls with floured towels or flour two proofing baskets. After dividing dough in half, place each half in prepared bowl. Let rise as directed in Step 3. Place a greased 4-qt. Dutch oven in oven as it preheats. Carefully turn one of the dough halves onto a floured surface. Make cuts in top of bread. Carefully lift and place dough into hot Dutch oven. Bake, covered, 15 minutes. Bake, uncovered, about 10 minutes more or until golden. Remove; cool on a wire rack. Repeat with remaining dough half.
**EACH SLICE** 102 cal., 0 g fat, 0 mg chol., 350 mg sodium, 21 g carb., 1 g fiber, 0 g sugars, 3 g pro.

---

## SOURDOUGH STARTER

All-purpose flour
Water

**1.** In a large clean container stir together 1 cup flour and ½ cup water. Cover loosely with plastic wrap. Set in a warm place (about 70°F); let stand 24 hours.
**2.** Stir in another 1 cup flour and ½ cup water. Cover loosely; let stand in a warm place 24 hours more. Repeat every day 5 to 7 days or until very bubbly and aromatic. Starter is ready to use at this point.
**3.** If not using, to keep at room temperature, feed starter by stirring in 1 cup flour and ½ cup water. Let stand in a warm place overnight. Repeat daily. To slow down fermenting, store in refrigerator; feed once a week. Let starter come to room temperature before measuring. Remove desired amount. Feed remaining starter; let stand at room temp 24 hours before chilling. When starter gets to be too much, discard half before feeding.

## WHAT IS BABKA?

THIS EASTERN EUROPEAN YEAST BREAD IS RICH AND TENDER WITH A SWIRL OF CHOCOLATY FILLING. IT DOES DOUBLE DUTY AS BOTH A BREAKFAST BREAD AND DESSERT (CUPS OF COFFEE RECOMMENDED).

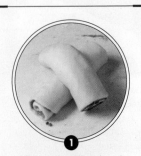

**1**

After cutting the dough log in half crosswise to make two shorter logs, place one log on top of the other to make an "X."

**2**

Twist logs at each end. Carefully transfer to the prepared pan.

# BABKA

**HANDS-ON TIME** 40 minutes
**RISE** 2 hours 15 minutes
**BAKE** 1 hour 10 minutes at 325°F

| | |
|---|---|
| 3 | cups all-purpose flour |
| 1 | pkg. active dry yeast |
| ¾ | cup milk |
| ½ | cup butter, cut up |
| ¼ | cup sugar |
| 1 | tsp. salt |
| 2 | eggs |
| ⅓ | cup sugar |
| 3 | Tbsp. unsweetened cocoa powder |
| 2 | Tbsp. butter, melted |
| ¾ | cup miniature semisweet chocolate chips |
| 1 | Tbsp. heavy cream |

**1.** In a large bowl stir together 2 cups of the flour and the yeast. In a saucepan heat and stir milk, ½ cup butter, ¼ cup sugar, and salt until warm (120°F to 130°F). Stir milk mixture and 1 egg into flour mixture. Stir in as much remaining flour as you can (photos, p. 483).

**2.** Turn dough out onto a lightly floured surface. Knead in enough of the remaining flour to make a moderately soft dough that is smooth and elastic (3 to 5 minutes total).* Shape dough into a ball. Place in a lightly greased bowl, turning to grease surface of dough. Cover and let rise in a warm place until nearly double in size (1½ to 2 hours).

**3.** Punch dough down. Turn out onto a lightly floured surface. Cover and let rest 10 minutes. Meanwhile, grease an 8×4-inch loaf pan. In a bowl stir together ⅓ cup sugar and cocoa powder.

**4.** Roll dough into a 16×12-inch rectangle. Brush with melted butter and sprinkle with cocoa mixture and chocolate chips. Roll up rectangle, starting from a long side, and seal seam with fingertips. Cut in half crosswise. Form an "X" with the pieces and make a twist at each end. Place dough twist in prepared loaf pan. Cover and let rise in a warm place until nearly double in size (45 to 60 minutes).

**5.** Preheat oven to 325°F. Combine the remaining egg and cream; brush over top of loaf. Bake 70 to 75 minutes or until golden and a thermometer registers 180°F to 190°F (if necessary to prevent overbrowning, cover loosely with foil the last 20 to 25 minutes). Remove from pan; cool on a wire rack. **Makes 1 loaf (12 slices each).**

**\*NOTE** If you have a mixer with a dough hook, use it to mix the dough and work in the last 1 cup of flour. If necessary, turn dough out on a lightly floured surface and knead until a moderately soft dough forms.

**EACH SLICE** *345 cal., 16 g fat (9 g sat. fat), 59 mg chol., 291 mg sodium, 46 g carb., 1 g fiber, 19 g sugars, 6 g pro.*

BABKA

FRENCH BREAD   CARAWAY-RYE BREAD

¼ cup packed brown sugar
2 Tbsp. vegetable oil
1½ tsp. salt
1½ cups rye flour
1 Tbsp. caraway seeds
   Cornmeal
2 tsp. milk

**1.** In a large bowl stir together 2¾ cups of the bread flour and the yeast. Add the warm water, brown sugar, oil, and salt. Beat with a mixer on low 30 seconds, scraping bowl constantly. Beat on high 3 minutes. Stir in rye flour, caraway seeds, and as much of the remaining bread flour as you can (photos, p. 483).
**2.** Turn dough out onto a lightly floured surface. Knead in enough of the remaining bread flour to make a moderately stiff dough that is smooth and elastic (6 to 8 minutes total). Shape dough into a ball. Place in a lightly greased bowl, turning to grease surface of dough. Cover; let rise in a warm place until double in size (1 hour).
**3.** Punch dough down. Turn dough out onto a lightly floured surface; divide in half. Cover; let rest 10 minutes. Grease a baking sheet; sprinkle with cornmeal.
**4.** Shape each dough half into a ball, tucking edges under. Place on prepared baking sheet. Flatten to 6 inches in diameter. If desired, lightly score tops with a knife. Cover; let rise in a warm place until nearly double in size (30 to 45 minutes).
**5.** Preheat oven to 375°F. Brush tops of loaves with milk. Bake 30 to 35 minutes or until tops and sides are deep golden brown and bread sounds hollow when lightly tapped. Immediately remove from baking sheet; cool on wire racks. **Makes 2 loaves (12 slices each).**
EACH SLICE *126 cal., 2 g fat (0 g sat fat), 0 mg chol., 148 mg sodium, 24 g carb., 2 g fiber, 2 g sugars, 4 g pro.*

FRENCH BREAD'S classic crisp crust comes from a moist baking environment. Get the same results at home by placing a pan of hot water on the oven rack below the bread while it bakes.

# FRENCH BREAD

**HANDS-ON TIME** 55 minutes
**RISE** 1 hour 35 minutes
**BAKE** 20 minutes at 450°F

5½ to 6 cups all-purpose flour
2 pkg. active dry yeast
2 tsp. salt
2 cups warm water (120°F to 130°F)
   Cornmeal
1 egg white
1 Tbsp. water

**1.** In a large bowl stir together 2 cups of the flour, the yeast, and salt; add the 2 cups warm water. Beat with a mixer on low 30 seconds, scraping bowl constantly. Beat on high 3 minutes. Stir in as much of the remaining flour as you can (photos, p. 483).
**2.** Turn dough out onto a lightly floured surface. Knead in enough of the remaining flour to make a stiff dough that is smooth and elastic (8 to 10 minutes total). Shape dough into a ball. Place in a lightly greased bowl, turning to grease surface of dough. Cover and let rise in a warm place until double in size (1 hour).
**3.** Punch dough down. Turn dough out onto a lightly floured surface; divide in half. Cover and let rest 10 minutes. Meanwhile, lightly grease a large baking sheet; sprinkle with cornmeal.

**4.** Roll each dough half into a 10×8-inch rectangle. Tightly roll up, starting from a long side, and seal seam with fingertips. If desired, pinch and slightly pull to taper loaves. Place, seam sides down, on prepared baking sheet. Combine egg white and the 1 Tbsp. water; brush some of the mixture over tops of loaves. Let rise until nearly double in size (35 to 45 minutes). Brush again with egg white mixture.
**5.** Preheat oven to 450°F. Make four ¼-inch-deep cuts on each loaf top. Place on middle oven rack; place a shallow roasting pan with 2 cups hot water on the rack below. Bake 20 to 25 minutes or until bread is golden brown and sounds hollow when lightly tapped. Remove from baking sheet; cool on a wire rack. **Makes 2 loaves (14 slices each).**
EACH SLICE *93 cal., 0 g fat, 0 mg chol., 169 mg sodium, 19 g carb., 1 g fiber, 0 g sugars, 3 g pro.*

# CARAWAY-RYE BREAD

**HANDS-ON TIME** 50 minutes
**RISE** 1 hour 30 minutes
**BAKE** 30 minutes at 375°F

4 to 4½ cups bread flour
1 pkg. active dry yeast
2 cups warm water (120°F to 130°F)

## HERBED FOCACCIA

**HANDS-ON TIME** 20 minutes
**STAND** 2 hours
**RISE** 1 hour 30 minutes
**BAKE** 30 minutes at 400°F

4   cups all-purpose flour
½   cup chopped fresh herbs, such
    as basil, thyme, oregano,
    and/or Italian parsley
1¾  tsp. kosher salt
½   tsp. active dry yeast
1⅔  cups warm water (120°F to
    130°F)
    Nonstick cooking spray
3   Tbsp. olive oil
4   cloves garlic, minced

**1.** In a large bowl combine 3 cups
of the flour, ¼ cup of the herbs,
1½ tsp. of the salt, and the yeast.
Stir in the warm water until mixture
is moistened (dough will be sticky

and soft). Cover bowl loosely with
plastic wrap. Let stand at room
temperature 2 hours.
**2.** Grease a 15×10-inch baking pan.
Stir remaining 1 cup flour into dough
with a fork. Using a rubber spatula
coated with cooking spray, gently
spread dough in prepared baking
pan (dough will be sticky). Cover
with greased plastic wrap. Let rise
at room temperature until puffy
(1½ to 2 hours).
**3.** Preheat oven to 400°F. In a small
bowl combine remaining ¼ cup
herbs, oil, and garlic; drizzle over
dough. Sprinkle with remaining
¼ tsp. salt. Bake 30 minutes or until
golden. Cool slightly; serve warm.
**Makes 12 pieces.**

**EACH PIECE** *184 cal., 4 g fat (1 g sat.
fat), 0 mg chol., 167 mg sodium, 32 g
carb., 1 g fiber, 0 g sugars, 5 g pro.*

## EVERYDAY ARTISAN BREAD

**HANDS-ON TIME** 15 minutes
**STAND** 2 hours
**RISE** 20 minutes
**BAKE** 25 minutes per loaf at 450°F

6   cups all-purpose flour
1   cup Add-In (optional)
    *(opposite, below)*
4   tsp. kosher salt
1   pkg. active dry yeast
3   cups warm water (120°F to
    130°F)
    Cornmeal

**1.** In an extra-large bowl combine
flour, Add-In (if desired), salt, and
yeast. Stir in the warm water until
mixture is moistened (dough will be
very sticky and soft). Cover bowl
loosely with plastic wrap. Let stand
at room temperature 2 hours. If
desired, refrigerate up to 7 days.
**2.** For each loaf, grease a 10- to
12-inch cast-iron skillet or a baking
sheet; sprinkle generously with
cornmeal. Using a sharp knife,
cut off a third of the dough (place
remaining dough in refrigerator).
Do not punch dough down. Place
dough portion on a well-floured
surface; sprinkle lightly with flour.
Shape dough by gently pulling
it into a ball, tucking edges
underneath and adding flour
as needed to keep dough from
sticking to hands. Place in prepared
skillet; sprinkle with flour. Cover
loosely with plastic wrap. Let rise in
a warm place 20 minutes.*
**3.** Preheat oven to 450°F.** Score
top of loaf with sharp knife. Place
on middle oven rack; place a
shallow roasting pan with 2 cups
hot water on the rack below. Bake
25 to 30 minutes or until bread is
deep golden brown. Remove from
skillet; cool on a wire rack. **Makes
3 loaves (10 slices each).**
***NOTE** If using chilled dough,
increase rising time to 45 minutes.

HERBED FOCACCIA

EVERYDAY ARTISAN BREAD

**MAKE AHEAD**
Make a batch of this artisan bread dough and refrigerate it up to a week (it's ready when you are). When you want a loaf of fresh-baked bread, cut a third of the dough off, shape, and bake.

The dough becomes stickier the longer it stands in the refrigerator. Take care not to overwork the sticky dough; overworking can destroy the air pockets that have formed in the dough.
**\*\*NOTE** If desired, place a baking stone on the middle oven rack

before preheating. After dough has risen, carefully transfer to the hot baking stone. Bake as directed.
**EACH SLICE** *93 cal., 0 g fat, 0 mg chol., 151 mg sodium, 19 g carb., 1 g fiber, 0 g sugars, 3 g pro.*

**ADD-IN (PICK ONE)**
• Shredded cheese
• Snipped dried fruit
• Sliced green onions
• Chopped toasted nuts
• Chopped pitted Kalamata olives
• Snipped dried tomatoes

## CHEESE BOMBS

**HANDS-ON TIME** 15 minutes
**BAKE** 26 minutes at 375°F

Nonstick cooking spray
1   16.3-oz. pkg. (8 biscuits) refrigerated large buttermilk biscuits
6   oz. cheese, such as Monterey Jack with jalapeño peppers, cheddar, or American, cut into 16 cubes
3   Tbsp. butter, melted
1   tsp. sesame seeds

**1.** Preheat oven to 375°F. Lightly coat a 9×5-inch loaf pan with cooking spray.
**2.** Separate biscuits and place on a lightly floured surface. Split each biscuit in half horizontally, making 16 dough rounds. Press rounds into 4-inch circles. Top with cheese cubes. Stretch dough up around cheese to enclose; pinch edges together tightly to seal. Place, sealed sides down, in prepared loaf pan.
**3.** Drizzle dough with melted butter and sprinkle with sesame seeds. Bake 26 to 30 minutes or until golden. Remove rolls from pan; serve hot. **Makes 16 rolls.**
**EACH ROLL** *153 cal., 9 g fat (4 g sat. fat), 17 mg chol., 374 mg sodium, 13 g carb., 0 g fiber, 2 g sugars, 4 g pro.*

**CHANGE IT UP**
*If you have access to fresh cheese curds, substitute regular or flavored cheese curds for the cubed cheese.*

>> CHEDDAR-BACON LOAF
In a small bowl combine 1 cup shredded sharp cheddar cheese; ½ cup softened butter; 6 slices bacon, crisp-cooked and crumbled; ¼ cup sliced green onions; 2 tsp. yellow mustard; and 1 tsp. lemon juice. Spread mixture on cut sides of bread halves. Bake or broil as directed.

>> ROASTED GARLIC BREAD
Prepare Roasted Garlic (p. 24), except use 2 garlic bulbs. In a small bowl combine ½ cup softened butter, 2 Tbsp. finely chopped fresh Italian parsley, and the roasted garlic. Spread mixture on cut sides of bread halves. Bake or broil as directed.

## GARLIC BREAD

**HANDS-ON TIME** 15 minutes
**BAKE** 12 minutes at 400°F

- 1    16-oz. loaf baguette-style French bread
- ½    cup butter, softened
- ½    tsp. garlic salt

>>

**BUTTER** straight from the fridge is too firm to spread. Microwave it on the defrost setting 15 seconds at a time until spreadable.

**1.** Preheat oven to 400°F. Using a serrated knife, cut bread in half horizontally. In a small bowl combine butter and garlic salt. Spread mixture on cut sides of bread halves.

**2.** Reassemble loaf and wrap tightly in heavy foil. Bake 12 to 15 minutes or until heated through. **Makes 12 pieces.**

**TO BROIL** Preheat broiler. Prepare as directed in Step 1. Place bread halves, spread sides up, on a baking sheet. Broil 4 to 5 inches from heat 3 to 4 minutes or until toasted.

**EACH PIECE** *177 cal., 8 g fat (5 g sat. fat), 20 mg chol., 340 mg sodium, 21 g carb., 1 g fiber, 1 g sugars, 5 g pro.*

// BREADS //

# MULTIGRAIN ROLLS

**HANDS-ON TIME** 45 minutes
**RISE** 1 hour 30 minutes
**BAKE** 12 minutes at 375°F

3¾ to 4¼ cups all-purpose flour
2   pkg. active dry yeast
1½  cups milk
⅓   cup honey
¼   cup butter, cut up
2   tsp. salt
2   eggs
⅔   cup whole wheat flour
½   cup rye flour
½   cup quick-cooking rolled oats
⅓   cup toasted wheat germ
1   Tbsp. cornmeal
1   egg, lightly beaten
1   Tbsp. water
    Sesame or poppy seeds

**1.** In a large bowl stir together 2 cups of the all-purpose flour and the yeast. In a 2-qt. saucepan heat and stir milk, honey, butter, and salt just until warm (120°F to 130°F) and butter almost melts. Add milk mixture and 2 eggs to flour mixture. Beat with a mixer on low 30 seconds, scraping bowl constantly. Beat on high 3 minutes. Stir in whole wheat and rye flours, oats, wheat germ, and cornmeal. Stir in as much of the remaining all-purpose flour as you can (photos, *p. 483*).

**2.** Turn dough out onto a lightly floured surface. Knead in enough of the remaining all-purpose flour to make a moderately stiff dough that is smooth and elastic (6 to 8 minutes total). Shape dough into a ball. Place in a lightly greased bowl, turning to grease surface of dough. Cover and let rise in a warm place until double in size (1 to 1½ hours).

**3.** Punch dough down. Turn out onto a lightly floured surface; divide into six portions. Cover; let rest 10 minutes. Line two large baking sheets with parchment paper.

**4.** Divide each dough portion into thirds. Shape each third into a ball, tucking edges underneath. Flatten and pull each ball to form a 4×2-inch oval. Place on prepared baking sheets. Using kitchen scissors, make three diagonal cuts ¾ inch deep on both long sides of each oval, creating a feathered look. Cover and let rise in a warm place until nearly double in size (30 to 45 minutes).

**5.** Preheat oven to 375°F. Combine 1 egg and the water; brush over tops of rolls. Sprinkle with sesame or poppy seeds and/or additional cornmeal. Bake 12 to 15 minutes or until golden. Remove from baking sheets; cool on wire racks. **Makes 18 rolls.**

**EACH ROLL** *211 cal., 5 g fat (2 g sat. fat), 44 mg chol., 298 mg sodium, 36 g carb., 2 g fiber, 7 g sugars, 7 g pro.*

**MAKE-AHEAD FRESH BREAD** Make and bake your bread or rolls and freeze to keep them fresh until you're ready to serve (this works great for the holidays). Wrap cooled bread or rolls in foil; place in resealable plastic freezer bags or freezer containers. Freeze up to 3 months. Unwrap and thaw at room temperature.

# OVERNIGHT REFRIGERATOR ROLLS

**HANDS-ON TIME** 45 minutes
**CHILL** overnight
**RISE** 45 minutes
**BAKE** 20 minutes at 375°F

1   pkg. active dry yeast
1¼  cups warm water (105°F to 115°F)
4   to 4¼ cups all-purpose flour
⅓   cup sugar
⅓   cup butter, melted
1   egg
1   tsp. salt
2   Tbsp. butter, melted (optional)

**1.** In a large bowl dissolve yeast in the warm water. Add 1½ cups of the flour, the sugar, ⅓ cup melted butter, egg, and salt. Beat with a mixer on low 1 minute, scraping constantly.

**2.** Stir in enough of the remaining flour to make a soft dough that just starts to pull away from sides of bowl (dough will be slightly sticky). Place dough in a greased 3-qt. container, turning to grease surface of dough. Cover and refrigerate overnight.

**3.** Punch dough down. Turn out onto a lightly floured surface; divide in half. Cover and let rest 10 minutes. Meanwhile, lightly grease a 13×9-inch baking pan or two large baking sheets.

**4.** Shape dough into 24 balls or desired rolls. Place rolls in prepared baking pan or 2 to 3 inches apart on prepared baking sheets. Cover and let rise in a warm place until nearly double in size (45 minutes).

**5.** Preheat oven to 375°F. Bake 20 minutes for pan rolls, 12 to 15 minutes for sheet rolls, or until golden. Immediately remove from pan or baking sheets. If desired, brush tops of rolls with 2 Tbsp. melted butter. Serve warm. **Makes 24 rolls.**

**EACH ROLL** *113 cal., 3 g fat (2 g sat. fat), 16 mg chol., 119 mg sodium, 19 g carb., 1 g fiber, 3 g sugars, 23 g pro.*

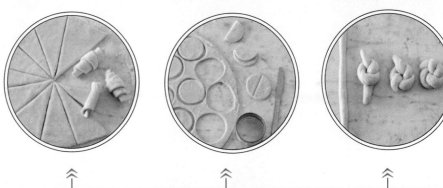

**BUTTERHORN ROLLS**
Prepare as directed through Step 3 (use baking sheets). On a lightly floured surface roll each dough half into a 10-inch circle. If desired, brush with melted butter. Cut each circle into 12 wedges. To shape, begin at wide end of each wedge and loosely roll toward the point. Place, point sides down, 2 to 3 inches apart on prepared baking sheets. **Makes 24 rolls.**

**PARKER HOUSE ROLLS**
Prepare as directed through Step 3 (use baking sheets). On a lightly floured surface roll each dough half until ¼ inch thick. Using a floured 2½-inch round cutter, cut out dough. Brush with melted butter. Make an off-center crease in each with dull edge of knife. Fold along crease and press firmly. Place, large sides up, 2 to 3 inches apart on prepared sheets. **Makes 24 rolls.**

**ROSETTES** Prepare as directed through Step 3 (use baking sheets). Divide each dough half into 16 pieces. On a lightly floured surface roll each piece into a 12-inch rope. Tie rope in a loose knot, leaving two long ends. Tuck top end under knot and bottom end into top center. Place 2 to 3 inches apart on prepared baking sheets. **Makes 32 rolls.**

# FEATHER ROLLS

**HANDS-ON TIME** 50 minutes
**RISE** 2 hours 50 minutes
**BAKE** 20 minutes at 400°F

4¼ to 4¾ cups all-purpose flour
1    pkg. active dry yeast
1½  cups warm water (120°F to 130°F)
½   cup mashed potato
⅓   cup butter, melted
¼   cup sugar
1¼  tsp. salt

**MASHED POTATO** For quick mashed potato, prick a small unpeeled russet potato with a fork. Microwave about 5 minutes or until tender. Scoop pulp out; discard skin. Mash pulp. Measure ½ cup mashed potato (for 1 cup mashed potato, use a 10-oz. potato).

3    Tbsp. sesame seeds
3    Tbsp. poppy seeds
1    Tbsp. dried minced onion
3    Tbsp. yellow cornmeal
3    Tbsp. grated Parmesan cheese
¼   cup butter, melted

**1.** In a large bowl stir together 2 cups of the flour and the yeast. In a medium bowl combine next five ingredients (through salt). Add potato mixture to flour mixture. Beat with a mixer on low 30 seconds, scraping bowl constantly. Beat on high 3 minutes. Stir in as much of the remaining flour as you can (photos, *p. 483*).
**2.** Turn dough onto a lightly floured surface. Knead in enough remaining flour to make a moderately soft dough that is smooth and elastic (3 to 5 minutes total). Shape dough into a ball. Place in a greased bowl, turning to grease surface of dough. Cover; let rise in a warm place until double in size (2 hours).
**3.** Punch dough down. Turn out onto a lightly floured surface. Cover and let rest 10 minutes. Meanwhile, grease a 13×9-inch baking pan.
**4.** In a shallow dish stir together sesame and poppy seeds and dried onion. In a second shallow dish stir together cornmeal and cheese. Pour ¼ cup melted butter into a third shallow dish. Using lightly floured hands, shape dough into 15 balls. Working quickly, roll balls in butter, then in one of the seasoning mixtures to lightly coat. (Coat half of the rolls with seed mixture and half with cornmeal mixture.) Alternate rolls in prepared baking pan. Cover lightly with greased plastic wrap and let rise in a warm place until nearly double in size (50 minutes).
**5.** Preheat oven to 400°F. Bake 20 to 25 minutes or until rolls are golden and sound hollow when lightly tapped. Immediately remove from pan. Serve warm.
**Makes 15 rolls.**

**EACH ROLL** *240 cal., 9 g fat (5 g sat. fat), 20 mg chol., 268 mg sodium, 34 g carb., 2 g fiber, 4 g sugars, 5 g pro.*

**BE QUICK**
Pop these fluffy rolls out of the pan immediately after baking. If they start to cool in the pan, condensation will form and make the roll bottoms soggy.

**CHANGE IT UP**

*To make simple buttery rolls, omit the last six ingredients (starting with sesame seeds). Instead, immediately after baking in Step 5, brush tops of rolls with 2 Tbsp. melted butter.*

## ORANGE BOWKNOTS

**HANDS-ON TIME** 55 minutes
**RISE** 1 hour 30 minutes
**BAKE** 12 minutes at 375°F

| | |
|---|---|
| 2 | oranges |
| 5½ to 6 | cups all-purpose flour |
| 1 | pkg. active dry yeast |
| 1¼ | cups milk |
| ½ | cup butter or shortening |
| ⅓ | cup granulated sugar |
| ½ | tsp. salt |
| 2 | eggs |
| 1 | recipe Orange Icing |

**1.** Remove 2 Tbsp. zest and squeeze ¼ cup juice from oranges. In a large bowl stir together 2 cups of the flour and the yeast. In a 2-qt. saucepan heat and stir milk, butter, granulated sugar, and salt just until warm (120°F to 130°F) and butter almost melts. Add milk mixture and eggs to flour mixture. Beat with a mixer on low 30 seconds, scraping bowl constantly. Beat on high 3 minutes. Stir in orange zest and juice and as much of the remaining flour as you can (photos, p. 483).
**2.** Turn dough out onto a lightly floured surface. Knead in enough of the remaining flour to make a moderately soft dough that is smooth and elastic, using a dough scraper as needed (dough will be slightly sticky). Shape dough into a ball. Place in a lightly greased bowl, turning to grease surface of dough. Cover and let rise in a warm place until double in size (1 hour).
**3.** Punch dough down. Turn out onto a lightly floured surface; divide in half. Cover and let rest 10 minutes. Meanwhile, lightly grease two large baking sheets.
**4.** Roll each dough half into a 12×7-inch rectangle. Cut each rectangle crosswise into twelve 7-inch strips. Tie each strip in a loose knot (tip, *right*). Place 2 inches apart on prepared baking sheets. Cover and let rise in a warm

place until nearly double in size (30 minutes).
**5.** Preheat oven to 375°F. Bake 12 to 14 minutes or until golden. Remove from baking sheets; cool on wire racks. Drizzle with Orange Icing.
**Makes 24 rolls.**
**EACH ROLL** *194 cal., 5 g fat (3 g sat. fat), 27 mg chol., 92 mg sodium, 33 g carb., 1 g fiber, 11 g sugars, 4 g pro.*

### ORANGE ICING

Remove 1½ tsp. zest and squeeze 2 to 3 Tbsp. juice from 1 orange. In a medium bowl stir together 1½ cups powdered sugar and orange zest. Stir in enough of the orange juice to reach drizzling consistency.

To make the bowknots, start by folding each strip into a loose loop. Tuck one end under the loop and ease it up through the hole of the loop. Readjust dough to make an even knot.

## CINNAMON ROLLS

**HANDS-ON TIME** 55 minutes
**RISE** 1 hour 15 minutes
**BAKE** 25 minutes at 375°F
**COOL** 10 minutes

4¼ to 4¾ cups all-purpose flour
1    pkg. active dry yeast
1    cup milk
1    cup mashed potato (tip, p. 496)
⅓    cup butter
⅓    cup granulated sugar
1    tsp. salt
2    eggs
½    cup packed brown sugar
1    Tbsp. ground cinnamon
¼    cup butter, softened
1    recipe Powdered Sugar
      Icing (p. 538), Browned Butter
      Frosting (p. 500), or Cream
      Cheese Icing (p. 500)

**1.** In a large bowl stir together 1½ cups of the flour and the yeast. In a 2-qt. saucepan heat and stir next five ingredients (through salt) just until warm (120°F to 130°F) and butter almost melts. Add milk mixture and eggs to flour mixture. Beat with a mixer on low 30 seconds, scraping bowl constantly. Beat on high 3 minutes. Stir in as much of the remaining flour as you can (photos, p. 483).

**2.** Turn dough out onto a lightly floured surface. Knead in enough of the remaining flour to make a moderately soft dough that is smooth and elastic (3 to 5 minutes total). Shape dough into a ball. Place in a lightly greased bowl, turning to grease surface of dough. Cover and let rise in a warm place until double in size (45 to 60 minutes).

**3.** Punch dough down. Turn out onto a lightly floured surface. Cover and let rest 10 minutes. Meanwhile, lightly grease a 13×9-inch baking pan. For filling, in a small bowl stir together brown sugar and cinnamon.

**4.** Roll dough into an 18×12-inch rectangle. Spread with softened butter and sprinkle with filling, leaving 1 inch unfilled along one of the long sides. Tightly roll up, starting from filled long side, and seal seam with fingertips. Cut into 12 slices; arrange in prepared baking pan. Cover and let rise in a warm place until nearly double in size (30 minutes).

**5.** Preheat oven to 375°F. Bake 25 to 30 minutes or until golden. Cool in pan on a wire rack 10 minutes; remove from pan. Drizzle or spread with icing. Serve warm. **Makes 12 rolls.**

**EACH ROLL** *394 cal., 11 g fat (6 g sat fat), 57 mg chol., 294 mg sodium, 68 g carb., 2 g fiber, 31 g sugars, 7 g pro.*

**MORE OPTIONS** This tender, soft dough lends itself to many more options. Vary the filling, frosting, topping, or the shape of your Cinnamon Rolls with the additional ideas on p. 500.

**YEAST** Yeast has a reputation for being temperamental, but it's actually easy to use. Put simply, yeast is a living organism that feeds on sugars to create carbon dioxide (which causes dough to rise). There are two main types: Active dry yeast comes in packets and jars; it's mixed with flour or dissolved in warm liquid before use. Quick-rising yeast, also called instant or rapid-rise yeast, cuts the rising time by about one-third; it can be substituted for active dry yeast, except in doughs that rise in the refrigerator. Check the expiration date on the package and store any opened yeast in the refrigerator.

**1**

This is the most important step: If you heat the milk mixture beyond 130°F, you might kill the yeast. If it's not warm enough, the yeast won't activate. Use a thermometer to make sure the temp is just right.

**2**

Kneading dough is important to developing the structure of the rolls. Fold dough in half; push down and away with the heels of your hands. Turn the dough; repeat until dough is smooth.

**3**

Boil water in a 2-cup glass measure. Cover dough; place in a cold microwave with the steaming water. Shut the door and let dough rise for amount of time specified in recipe.

**4**

After rising 45 minutes, look to see if it is nearly double in size. Gently press two fingers into the surface of the dough. If the indentations remain, the dough has risen adequately.

**5**

Punch your fist into the center of the dough to deflate it. This is important so your dough does not have big pockets of air.

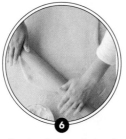

**6**

The hardest part about rolling an 18×12-inch rectangle is making four good corners. Alternate rolling dough from the center to the sides with rolling from the center to the corners diagonally.

**7**

Gently push and pull the corners so they're square and even. This makes it easier to use the entire roll of dough without trimming.

**8**

Gently lift dough into a spiral, starting with a long side. You may have to guide the roll along, moving your hands from one end of the dough to another, to make it even.

**9**

Using your index finger and thumb, pinch the seam to seal the edges.

**10**

Use a ruler so you cut equal-size rolls. Put a loop of unwaxed dental floss around the log and pull the ends of the string in opposite directions to cut through the dough.

**TO MAKE AHEAD** Prepare as directed through Step 4, except do not let rise after shaping. Cover loosely with oiled waxed paper, then with plastic wrap. Chill 2 to 24 hours. Before baking, let chilled rolls stand, covered, at room temperature about 1 hour or until nearly double. Uncover; bake as directed.

// BREADS //

# MORE OPTIONS! GO BEYOND BASIC CINNAMON ROLLS WITH THESE FILLING, FROSTING, AND SHAPING IDEAS.

## CRANBERRY-PISTACHIO ROLLS

Prepare Cinnamon Rolls (p. 498) as directed, except reduce brown sugar in filling to ⅓ cup. Stir in ⅓ cup chopped dried cranberries and ¼ cup chopped pistachio nuts.

## APPLE-RAISIN ROLLS

Prepare Cinnamon Rolls (p. 498) as directed through Step 4, except instead of using brown sugar and cinnamon for the filling, stir together ⅓ cup each granulated sugar and chopped dried apples, ¼ cup raisins, and 2 tsp. apple pie spice. If desired, omit icing.

## CARAMEL-PECAN ROLLS

Prepare Cinnamon Rolls (p. 498) as directed through Step 3. In a bowl combine ¾ cup packed brown sugar, ½ cup melted butter, and ¼ cup light-color corn syrup. Stir in ¾ cup chopped pecans. Spread in prepared baking pan. Continue as directed in Step 4, placing rolls on top of mixture in pan. After baking, immediately invert rolls onto a platter (spoon any nut mixture remaining in pan onto rolls). Omit icing.

## CINNAMON ROLL COFFEE CAKE

Prepare Cinnamon Rolls (p. 498) as directed in Step 4 through sealing dough seam. Slice the dough spiral in half lengthwise. Line two baking sheets with parchment paper. In center of each prepared sheet coil one dough half, cut side up, to form a snail shape; tuck end under. Let rise as directed in Step 4. Preheat oven to 350°F. Bake about 30 minutes or until golden brown, covering edges with foil if necessary to prevent overbrowning.

## BROWNED BUTTER FROSTING

In a 1- or 1½-qt. saucepan melt ¾ cup butter over low heat. Continue heating until butter turns a delicate light brown, stirring occasionally. Remove from heat. In a large bowl combine 3 cups powdered sugar, 2 Tbsp. milk, and 1 tsp. vanilla. Add the browned butter. Beat with a mixer on low speed until combined. Beat on medium speed, adding additional milk, 1 tsp. at a time, to reach spreading consistency.

## CREAM CHEESE ICING

In a medium bowl beat 3 oz. softened cream cheese, 2 Tbsp. softened butter, and 1 tsp. vanilla with a mixer on medium until combined. Gradually beat in 2½ cups powdered sugar until smooth. Beat in enough milk, 1 tsp. at a time, to reach spreading consistency.

## APPLE PIE PULL-APART LOAF

**HANDS-ON TIME** 30 minutes
**RISE** 1 hour 25 minutes
**BAKE** 45 minutes at 350°F
**COOL** 10 minutes

¾ cup milk
1 pkg. active dry yeast
1 egg
¼ cup butter, melted
2 Tbsp. granulated sugar
½ tsp. salt
3 cups all-purpose flour
¼ cup butter, melted
1½ cups finely chopped, peeled
 apples
¾ cup packed brown sugar
2 tsp. apple pie spice
1 recipe Powdered Sugar Icing
 (p. 538)

**1.** In a saucepan heat milk just until warm (105°F to 115°F). In a large bowl combine warm milk and yeast; stir to dissolve. Let stand 5 minutes. **2.** Add egg, ¼ cup melted butter, granulated sugar, and salt to yeast mixture. Beat with a mixer on medium until combined. Add half of the flour; beat on low 30 seconds, scraping bowl constantly. Beat on medium 3 minutes. Stir in remaining flour. Shape dough into a ball (dough will not be smooth). Place in a lightly greased bowl, turning to grease surface of dough. Cover and let rise in a warm place until nearly double in size (45 to 60 minutes). **3.** Grease a 9×5-inch loaf pan. Turn dough out onto a lightly floured surface. Roll dough into a 20×12-inch rectangle. Brush with ¼ cup melted butter. Sprinkle with apples, brown sugar, and apple pie spice. Cut rectangle lengthwise into two 20×6-inch strips. Cut each strip crosswise into five 6×4-inch strips. Make two stacks of five strips each; cut each stack into 4×2-inch pieces. Loosely stagger pieces, cut sides up, in prepared loaf pan. Cover; let rise in a warm place until nearly double in size (40 to 45 minutes). **4.** Preheat oven to 350°F. Bake about 45 minutes or until golden and a thermometer registers 200°F. Cool in pan on a wire rack 10 minutes. Remove from pan. Drizzle with Powdered Sugar Icing. Serve warm. **Makes 10 servings (1 piece each).**
**TO MAKE AHEAD** Prepare as directed through Step 2, except do not let dough rise. Cover bowl and chill up to 24 hours. Let dough stand at room temperature 30 minutes before continuing with Step 3.
**EACH SERVING** *386 cal., 13 g fat (7 g sat. fat), 51 mg chol., 233 mg sodium, 63 g carb., 2 g fiber, 33 g sugars, 6 g pro.*

Cut dough rectangle in half lengthwise and make five cuts crosswise in each half to create ten 6×4-inch strips.

Layer the strips into two stacks of five strips each. Cut each stack into 4×2-inch portions.

Place 4×2-inch stacks on their sides (cut sides up) in prepared loaf pan, staggering them loosely in the pan.

EASY SAUSAGE-
PESTO RING

CORN BREAD

# EASY SAUSAGE-PESTO RING

**HANDS-ON TIME** 20 minutes
**BAKE** 35 minutes at 350°F
**COOL** 10 minutes

5   Tbsp. butter, melted
2   16.3-oz. pkg. (16 biscuits) refrigerated biscuits
⅓   cup basil pesto
⅓   cup cooked bulk Italian sausage
1¼  cups shredded Italian cheese blend (5 oz.)

**1.** Preheat oven to 350°F. Grease a 10-inch fluted tube pan with 3 Tbsp. of the melted butter.
**2.** Top each biscuit with 1 tsp. pesto and 1 tsp. sausage; sprinkle with 1 Tbsp. cheese. Stack four biscuits; press down gently. Turn stack on its side and place in prepared tube pan. Repeat with remaining biscuits, arranging biscuit stacks in pan to create a ring. Drizzle with remaining 2 Tbsp. melted butter.
**3.** Bake 30 minutes. Sprinkle with remaining ¼ cup cheese. Cover with foil and bake 5 minutes more or until a toothpick comes out clean, top is golden, and cheese is melted. Cool in pan 10 minutes. Remove bread ring from pan. Serve warm. **Makes 1 ring (16 pieces).**
**EACH PIECE** *273 cal., 16 g fat (6 g sat. fat), 20 mg chol., 784 mg sodium, 26 g carb., 1 g fiber, 4 g sugars, 7 g pro.*

**YELLOW CORNMEAL** is the traditional choice for this bread. If you prefer a coarser corn bread, prepare as directed, except substitute ½ cup stone-ground whole grain cornmeal for ½ cup of the yellow cornmeal. Store whole grain cornmeal in the freezer for freshness.

# CORN BREAD

**HANDS-ON TIME** 15 minutes
**BAKE** 20 minutes at 400°F

1   cup cornmeal
¾   cup all-purpose flour
2   to 4 Tbsp. sugar
2½  tsp. baking powder
½   tsp. salt
1   cup milk
2   eggs
¼   cup butter, melted

**1.** Preheat oven to 400°F. Grease an 8-inch square or 9-inch round baking pan. In a medium bowl stir together first five ingredients (through salt).
**2.** In a small bowl whisk together milk, eggs, and melted butter. Add egg mixture all at once to cornmeal mixture. Stir just until moistened. Pour batter into prepared pan.
**3.** Bake 20 minutes or until edges of bread are golden. Cool slightly; serve warm. **Makes 9 pieces.**
**EACH PIECE** *173 cal., 7 g fat (4 g sat. fat), 63 mg chol., 298 mg sodium, 23 g carb., 1 g fiber, 4 g sugars, 5 g pro.*

>> **SKILLET CORN BREAD** Prepare as directed, except place a 9-inch cast-iron skillet in oven with butter; when butter melts, swirl to coat pan. Pour butter into egg mixture. Continue as directed, working quickly so batter goes into hot skillet. Bake as directed. **Makes 12 wedges.**

>> **CORN MUFFINS** Prepare as directed, except spoon batter into 12 greased 2½-inch muffin cups, filling cups two-thirds full. Bake 15 minutes or until edges are golden. **Makes 12 muffins.**

# ZUCCHINI BREAD

**HANDS-ON TIME** 25 minutes
**BAKE** 55 minutes at 350°F
**COOL** 10 minutes
**STAND** overnight

- 3 cups all-purpose flour
- 1 Tbsp. baking powder
- 1½ tsp. ground cinnamon
- 1 tsp. salt
- 2 eggs, lightly beaten
- 2½ cups coarsely shredded, unpeeled zucchini
- 2 cups sugar
- 1 cup vegetable oil
- 2 tsp. vanilla
- 1 cup chopped walnuts or pecans (optional)
- ⅔ cup raisins (optional)

>>

**BRUSH SHORTENING** just over the bottom and slightly up sides of pan. The ungreased portion of the pan sides allows the bread to maintain its height as it rises.

**1.** Preheat oven to 350°F. Grease bottom and ½ inch up sides of two 8×4-inch loaf pans. In a large bowl stir together flour, baking powder, cinnamon, and salt. Make a well in center of flour mixture.

**2.** In a medium bowl combine next five ingredients (through vanilla). Add zucchini mixture all at once to flour mixture. Stir just until moistened (batter should be lumpy). If desired, fold in nuts and raisins. Spoon batter into prepared loaf pans.

**3.** Bake 55 minutes or until a toothpick comes out clean. Cool in pans on a wire rack 10 minutes. Remove from pans; cool completely on wire rack. Wrap and store overnight before slicing. **Makes 2 loaves (14 slices each).**
**EACH SLICE** *181 cal., 8 g fat (1 g sat. fat), 15 mg chol., 115 mg sodium, 25 g carb., 1 g fiber, 15 g sugars, 2 g pro.*

### CHANGE IT UP

*Give your Zucchini Bread
a chocolate boost.
You can fold ⅔ cup mini
chocolate chips into the batter.
Or just before serving,
drizzle it with melted semisweet
or dark chocolate.*

PUMPKIN BREAD

# PUMPKIN BREAD

**HANDS-ON TIME** 20 minutes
**BAKE** 55 minutes at 350°F
**COOL** 10 minutes
**STAND** overnight

| | |
|---|---|
| 3 | cups sugar |
| 1 | cup vegetable oil |
| 4 | eggs |
| 3⅓ | cups all-purpose flour |
| 2 | tsp. baking soda |
| 1½ | tsp. salt |
| 1 | tsp. ground cinnamon |
| 1 | tsp. ground nutmeg |
| ⅔ | cup water |
| 1 | 15-oz. can pumpkin |

**1.** Preheat oven to 350°F. Grease bottom and ½ inch up sides of two 9×5-inch or three 8×4-inch loaf pans (photo, *p. 504*). In an extra-large bowl beat sugar and oil with a mixer on medium until combined. Beat in eggs.
**2.** In a large bowl stir together next five ingredients (through nutmeg). Add flour mixture and the water alternately to sugar mixture, beating on low after each addition just until combined. Beat in pumpkin. Spoon batter into prepared loaf pans.
**3.** Bake 55 to 60 minutes for 9-inch loaves, 45 to 50 minutes for 8-inch loaves, or until a toothpick comes out clean. Cool in pans on a wire rack 10 minutes. Remove from pans; cool completely on wire rack. Wrap and store overnight before slicing. **Makes 2 loaves (16 slices each).**
**EACH SLICE** *195 cal., 8 g fat (1 g sat. fat), 23 mg chol., 198 mg sodium, 30 g carb., 1 g fiber, 19 g sugars, 2 g pro.*

**PUMPKIN-RAISIN-CINNAMON BREAD** Prepare two 9×5-inch loaf pans as directed. Stir together ⅔ cup sugar and 1½ tsp. ground cinnamon; stir in 1 cup finely chopped pecans. Prepare batter as directed, except stir in ¼ cup raisins. Spoon half of the batter into prepared loaf pans; sprinkle with half of the nut mixture. Repeat with remaining batter and nut mixture. Bake as directed (cover loosely with foil the last 15 to 20 minutes). Remove; continue as directed. **Makes 2 loaves (16 slices each).**

**CREAM CHEESE RIBBON PUMPKIN BREAD** Prepare three 8×4-inch loaf pans as directed. In a medium bowl beat together 4 oz. softened cream cheese and ¼ cup sugar with a mixer on medium until combined. Beat in ½ cup sour cream, 1 egg, and 1 Tbsp. milk. Stir in 3 Tbsp. finely snipped crystallized ginger. Prepare batter as directed. Spoon 1½ cups of the batter into each prepared loaf pan. Divide cream cheese mixture among pans; spread remaining batter over cream cheese mixture. Bake 60 to 65 minutes or until cracks on tops of loaves appear dry. Remove; cool. Wrap; store in refrigerator overnight. Let stand at room temperature 1 hour before serving. **Makes 3 loaves (16 slices each).**

# POPPY SEED BREAD

**HANDS-ON TIME** 15 minutes
**BAKE** 50 minutes at 325°F
**COOL** 10 minutes
**STAND** overnight

- 3 cups all-purpose flour
- 2¼ cups sugar
- 1½ tsp. baking powder
- 1½ tsp. salt
- 3 eggs, lightly beaten
- 1½ cups milk
- 1 cup butter, melted and cooled
- 4 tsp. poppy seeds
- 1½ tsp. almond extract
- 1½ tsp. vanilla
- 1 recipe Orange Glaze

»

**WHEN GREASING** pans for quick bread, always use shortening unless the recipe specifies butter. Shortening is all fat, but butter has some water in it, which might cause sticking.

**1.** Preheat oven to 325°F. Grease and flour bottom and ½ inch up sides of two 9×5-inch loaf pans (*p. 504*). In a bowl stir together flour, sugar, baking powder, and salt.
**2.** In a medium bowl combine next six ingredients (through vanilla). Add egg mixture to flour mixture. Beat with a mixer on medium to high 2 minutes. Spoon batter into prepared loaf pans.
**3.** Bake 50 to 55 minutes or until a toothpick comes out clean. Cool in pans on a wire rack 10 minutes. Remove from pans. Brush loaves with Orange Glaze. Cool completely on wire rack. Store in an airtight container overnight before slicing. **Makes 2 loaves (8 slices each).**

**EACH SLICE** *369 cal., 13 g fat (8 g sat. fat), 67 mg chol., 380 mg sodium, 58 g carb., 1 g fiber, 39 g sugars, 5 g pro.*

## *ORANGE GLAZE*

In a 1- or 1½-qt. saucepan combine ¾ cup sugar and ¼ cup orange juice. Cook and stir over medium-high heat just until sugar is dissolved. Remove from heat. Stir in ½ tsp. each almond extract and vanilla.

## ROAST FOR FLAVOR

The flavor of bananas gets even deeper when you roast them first. Arrange the bananas, unpeeled, on a foil-lined 15×10-inch baking pan. Prick banana skins with a fork at 1-inch intervals. Bake in a 350°F oven 15 minutes (banana skins will get very dark); cool bananas in pan. Split banana peels. Measure 1½ cups of the roasted bananas, pressing gently into measuring cup.

# BANANA BREAD

**HANDS-ON TIME** 25 minutes
**BAKE** 50 minutes at 350°F
**COOL** 10 minutes
**STAND** overnight

| | |
|---|---|
| 2 | cups all-purpose flour |
| 1½ | tsp. baking powder |
| 1 | tsp. ground cinnamon |
| ½ | tsp. baking soda |
| ¼ | tsp. salt |
| ¼ | tsp. ground ginger |
| ¼ | tsp. ground nutmeg |
| 2 | eggs, lightly beaten |
| 1 | cup granulated sugar |
| ½ | cup vegetable oil or melted butter |
| 1½ | cups mashed ripe bananas |
| ¼ | cup chopped walnuts |
| 1 | recipe Streusel-Nut Topping (optional) |

**1.** Preheat oven to 350°F. Grease bottom and ½ inch up sides of one 9×5-inch loaf pan (photo, p. 504). In a large bowl stir together first seven ingredients (through nutmeg). Make a well in center of flour mixture.

**2.** In a medium bowl combine eggs, granulated sugar, and oil; stir in mashed bananas. Add egg mixture all at once to flour mixture. Stir just until moistened (batter should be lumpy). Fold in walnuts. Spoon batter into prepared loaf pan. If desired, sprinkle with Streusel-Nut Topping.

**3.** Bake 50 to 55 minutes or until a toothpick comes out clean (if necessary to prevent overbrowning, cover loosely with foil the last 15 minutes). Cool in pan on a wire rack 10 minutes. Remove from pan; cool completely on wire rack. Wrap and store overnight before slicing. **Makes 1 loaf (16 slices).**

**EACH SLICE** *220 cal., 9 g fat (1 g sat. fat), 23 mg chol., 131 mg sodium, 34 g carb., 2 g fiber, 17 g sugars, 3 g pro.*

## *STREUSEL-NUT TOPPING*

In a small bowl stir together 3 Tbsp. packed brown sugar and 2 Tbsp. all-purpose flour. Using a pastry blender, cut in 4 tsp. butter until mixture resembles coarse crumbs. Stir in ¼ cup chopped walnuts.

### LET IT STAND

We recommend wrapping cooled quick bread in plastic wrap and letting it stand at room temperature overnight before serving. The loaf's texture will be more evenly moist and less crumbly.

**》 BLUEBERRY-COCONUT BANANA BREAD** Prepare as directed, except toss ½ cup fresh or frozen blueberries with 1 Tbsp. all-purpose flour; fold into batter with the walnuts. Sprinkle an additional ¼ cup fresh or frozen blueberries on top of batter in pan. If using the Streusel-Nut Topping, add ¼ cup flaked coconut with the walnuts.

**RIPE FOR BAKING** Ripe bananas—with speckled brown peels—are what you want for banana bread. During ripening, the starches in the banana turn to sugar, making the bread sweeter and richer. If you don't have time to wait for your bananas to ripen, roast them (tip, *above left*). This turns the natural sugars in less-ripe bananas into a caramel-like syrup.

BRAN CEREAL
MUFFINS

DOUBLE-CHOCOLATE
MUFFINS

## BRAN CEREAL MUFFINS

**HANDS-ON TIME** 20 minutes
**BAKE** 20 minutes at 400°F

3 cups whole bran cereal (not flakes)
1 cup boiling water
2½ cups all-purpose flour
½ cup granulated sugar
½ cup packed brown sugar
2 tsp. baking powder
1 tsp. ground cinnamon
½ tsp. baking soda
½ tsp. salt
2 eggs, lightly beaten
2 cups buttermilk
½ cup vegetable oil

**1.** Preheat oven to 400°F. Grease twenty-four 2½-inch muffin cups or line with paper bake cups. In a medium bowl stir together cereal and boiling water until moistened.
**2.** In another medium bowl stir together next seven ingredients (through salt). In a large bowl combine eggs, buttermilk, and oil. Stir cereal and flour mixture into egg mixture just until moistened.
**3.** Spoon batter into prepared muffin cups, filling each three-fourths full. Bake 20 minutes or until a toothpick comes out clean. Cool in pan on a wire rack 5 minutes. Remove from cups; serve warm.
**Makes 24 muffins.**

**TO MAKE AHEAD** This batter can refrigerated up to 3 days. Bake chilled batter 20 to 22 minutes.
**EACH MUFFIN** *162 cal., 5 g fat (1 g sat. fat), 18 mg chol., 201 mg sodium, 29 g carb., 5 g fiber, 13 g sugars, 3 g pro.*

## DOUBLE-CHOCOLATE MUFFINS

**HANDS-ON TIME** 20 minutes
**BAKE** 18 minutes at 375°F

1¼ cups all-purpose flour
½ cup granulated sugar
⅓ cup packed brown sugar
¼ cup unsweetened cocoa powder

**BUTTERMILK MUFFINS WITH BLUEBERRIES**

2    tsp. baking powder
¼    tsp. baking soda
¼    tsp. salt
1    cup miniature semisweet chocolate chips
½    cup vegetable oil
½    cup milk
1    egg

**1.** Preheat oven to 375°F. Grease twelve 2½-inch muffin cups or line with paper bake cups. In a medium bowl combine the first seven ingredients (through salt). Stir in chocolate chips. Make a well in the center of the flour mixture.
**2.** In a bowl whisk oil, milk, and egg. Add oil mixture to the flour mixture. Stir just until moistened.
**3.** Spoon batter into prepared muffin cups, filling each two-thirds full. Bake 18 to 20 minutes or until edges are firm (tops will be slightly rounded). Cool in muffin cups on a wire rack 5 minutes. Remove from muffin cups; serve warm. **Makes 12 muffins.**
EACH MUFFIN *295 cal., 15 g fat (4 g sat. fat), 19 mg chol., 148 mg sodium, 38 g carb., 2 g fiber, 25 g sugars, 3 g pro.*

**NO BUTTERMILK?** Use ¾ cup milk and omit baking soda.

**FRUIT options** include blueberries, sweet cherries, raspberries, or chopped peaches or strawberries.

# BUTTERMILK MUFFINS

**HANDS-ON TIME** 20 minutes
**BAKE** 18 minutes at 375°F

2    cups all-purpose flour
¾    cup sugar
2½   tsp. baking powder
¼    tsp. baking soda
¼    tsp. salt
2    eggs, lightly beaten
1    cup buttermilk
6    Tbsp. butter, melted
1    cup fresh or frozen fruit
1    recipe Cinnamon-Sugar Topping or Citrus-Sugar Topping

**1.** Preheat oven to 375°F. Grease twelve 2½-inch muffin cups or line with paper bake cups.
**2.** In a medium bowl stir together first five ingredients (through salt). Make a well in center of flour mixture.
**3.** In a small bowl combine eggs, buttermilk, and melted butter. Add egg mixture all at once to flour mixture. Stir just until moistened (batter should be lumpy). Fold in fruit.
**4.** Spoon batter into prepared muffin cups, filling each nearly full. Sprinkle with desired topping. Bake 18 to 20 minutes or until golden. Cool in cups on a wire rack 5 minutes. Remove from cups; serve warm.
**Makes 12 muffins.**
EACH MUFFIN *209 cal., 7 g fat (4 g sat. fat), 48 mg chol., 255 mg sodium, 33 g carb., 1 g fiber, 16 g sugars, 4 g pro.*

## *CINNAMON-SUGAR TOPPING*

In a small bowl stir together 1 Tbsp. sugar and 1 tsp. ground cinnamon.

## *CITRUS-SUGAR TOPPING*

In a small bowl stir together 2 Tbsp. sugar and 1 tsp. each orange zest and lemon zest.

## SCONES

**HANDS-ON TIME** 25 minutes
**BAKE** 12 minutes at 400°F

2½ cups all-purpose flour
¼ cup granulated sugar
1 Tbsp. baking powder
¼ tsp. salt
½ cup butter, cut up
1 egg, lightly beaten
⅓ cup heavy cream
⅓ cup sour cream
Coarse sugar

>>

**COLD BUTTER is** easier to cut into the flour when it's cut into small pieces. After blending, you're aiming for pieces the size of coarse crumbs. These small pieces melt during baking and create tiny pockets of steam that make tender layers in your scones.

**1.** Preheat oven to 400°F. Line a baking sheet with parchment paper. In a large bowl stir together first four ingredients (through salt). Using a pastry blender, cut in butter until mixture resembles coarse crumbs. Make a well in center of flour mixture.

**2.** In a medium bowl combine egg, heavy cream, and sour cream. Add egg mixture all at once to flour mixture. Using a fork, stir just until moistened.

**3.** Turn dough out onto a lightly floured surface. Knead dough by folding and gently pressing it 10 to 12 strokes or until nearly smooth. Divide in half. Pat or lightly roll each dough half into a 6-inch circle. Using a pizza cutter or sharp knife, cut each circle into six wedges.

**4.** Place dough wedges 2 inches apart on prepared baking sheet. Brush with additional heavy cream and sprinkle with coarse sugar. Bake 12 to 14 minutes or until bottoms are golden. Remove from baking sheet; cool on a wire rack.

**Makes 12 scones.**

**EACH SCONE** *223 cal., 12 g fat (7 g sat. fat), 49 mg chol., 243 mg sodium, 25 g carb., 1 g fiber, 5 g sugars, 4 g pro.*

## MAKE AHEAD

These scones can be made ahead by either freezing the dough or the baked scones.

**TO FREEZE THE DOUGH,** place unbaked scones in a single layer in a freezer container lined with parchment paper. Freeze up to 1 month and bake as directed; do not thaw before baking.

**TO FREEZE BAKED SCONES,** place in a freezer bag or container; seal and freeze up to 2 months. To serve, thaw in the refrigerator overnight. Preheat oven to 350°F. Place scones on a baking sheet. Bake 5 to 6 minutes or until warm.

**STRAWBERRY-BASIL SCONES** Prepare as directed, except stir ¾ cup chopped strawberries, 1 to 2 Tbsp. chopped fresh basil (if desired), and 1 tsp. cracked black pepper into flour mixture in Step 1.

**MOCHA CHIP SCONES** Prepare as directed, except reduce flour to 2 cups, increase granulated sugar to ⅓ cup, and stir ¼ cup unsweetened cocoa powder into flour mixture. Stir 1 tsp. instant espresso coffee powder or instant coffee crystals into egg mixture. After stirring egg mixture into flour mixture, stir in ½ cup semisweet chocolate chips.

**LEMON-RICOTTA SCONES** Prepare as directed, except stir 2 tsp. lemon zest into flour mixture in Step 1. Substitute ricotta cheese for the sour cream and stir 1 Tbsp. lemon juice into egg mixture in Step 2.

**HOT CROSS BUN SCONES** Prepare as directed, except stir ⅓ cup each dried currants and golden raisins and ½ tsp. each ground allspice, lemon zest, and orange zest into flour mixture in Step 1.

# FLAKY BISCUITS

**HANDS-ON TIME** 15 minutes
**BAKE** 10 minutes at 450°F

3   cups all-purpose flour
1   Tbsp. sugar
1   Tbsp. baking powder*
1   tsp. salt
¾   tsp. cream of tartar*
½   cup butter, cut up
¼   cup shortening
1   cup milk

**DOUBLE-ACTING BAKING POWDER** creates carbon dioxide bubbles that "lift" baked goods in two ways: once when baking powder is combined with a liquid and again when it is exposed to heat.

**1.** Preheat oven to 450°F. In a large bowl stir together flour, sugar, baking powder, salt, and cream of tartar. Using a pastry blender, cut in butter and shortening until mixture resembles coarse crumbs. Make a well in center of flour mixture. Add milk all at once. Using a fork, stir just until moistened.

**2.** Turn dough out onto a lightly floured surface. Knead dough by folding and gently pressing it just until dough holds together. Pat or lightly roll dough until ¾ inch thick. Cut with a floured 2½-inch biscuit cutter; reroll scraps as necessary and dip cutter into flour between cuts.

**3.** Place dough cutouts 1 inch apart on an ungreased baking sheet. If desired, brush with additional milk. Bake 10 to 14 minutes or until golden. Remove from baking sheet; serve warm. **Makes 12 biscuits.**

**\*NOTE** If baking powder or cream of tartar appears lumpy, sift through a fine-mesh sieve.

**EACH BISCUIT** *231 cal., 12 g fat (7 g sat. fat), 32 mg chol., 427 mg sodium, 26 g carb., 1 g fiber, 2 g sugars, 4 g pro.*

### THINK OUTSIDE THE CIRCLE
Biscuits don't have to be round. You can also roll the dough into a rectangle and cut it into strips or squares. Or roll dough into a circle and cut into wedges.

**EASY EVERYDAY**

*Skip the rolling or cutting and simply drop dough from a spoon. Prepare as directed through Step 1, except increase the milk to 1¼ cups. Using a large spoon, drop dough in 12 mounds onto a greased baking sheet. Bake as directed.*

**BUTTERMILK BISCUITS**
Prepare as directed, except for rolled-dough biscuits substitute 1¼ cups buttermilk or sour milk (tip, *p. 474*) for the 1 cup milk. For drop biscuits, increase buttermilk or sour milk to 1½ cups.

**FAT = FLAKINESS** Fat creates a tender texture in biscuits and helps form the flaky layers. Butter delivers rich flavor. But because there is no water in shortening, it creates more-distinct layers. We like to use a combination of the two to get the benefits from both. If you choose to just use one, use ¾ cup butter total.

# POPOVERS

**HANDS-ON TIME** 10 minutes
**BAKE** 35 minutes at 400°F

| | |
|---|---|
| 1 | Tbsp. shortening |
| 2 | eggs, lightly beaten |
| 1 | cup milk |
| 1 | Tbsp. vegetable oil |
| 1 | cup all-purpose flour |
| ½ | tsp. salt |

**1.** Preheat oven to 400°F. Using ½ tsp. shortening for each cup, grease bottom and sides of six popover pan cups.
**2.** In a medium bowl combine eggs, milk, and oil. Add flour and salt; stir until smooth. Pour batter into prepared cups, filling each half full. Bake 35 minutes or until very firm.
**3.** Immediately after removing from oven, prick popovers to let steam escape. Turn off oven. For crisper popovers, return popovers to oven 5 to 10 minutes or until desired crispness. Remove popovers from cups; serve immediately. **Makes 6 popovers.**

**CHEESY HERB POPOVERS**
Prepare as directed, except add 2 Tbsp. grated Parmesan cheese and 1 Tbsp. chopped fresh dill or basil with the flour.

*EACH POPOVER 158 cal., 7 g fat (2 g sat. fat), 74 mg chol., 234 mg sodium, 18 g carb., 1 g fiber, 2 g sugars, 6 g pro.*

**PAN SWAP**
You can still make Popovers even if you don't have the specialty pan. Substitute six 6-oz. custard cups and place them in a 15×10-inch baking pan. Bake as directed.

# CAKES

**MAKE-AHEAD RECIPE.** See also storage/freezing tip, p. 535.

## WHITE CAKE

**HANDS-ON TIME** 30 minutes
**BAKE** 30 minutes at 350°F
**COOL** 1 hour

- 2 cups all-purpose flour
- 1 tsp. baking powder
- ½ tsp. baking soda
- ½ tsp. salt
- ½ cup butter, softened, or shortening
- 1¾ cups sugar
- 1 tsp. vanilla
- 4 egg whites, room temperature
- 1⅓ cups buttermilk or sour milk (tip, p. 474)

**1.** Preheat oven to 350°F. Grease and lightly flour two 9-inch or 8-inch round cake pans or grease one 13×9-inch baking pan (tips, *opposite; p. 531*). In a bowl stir together first four ingredients (through salt).
**2.** In a large bowl beat butter with a mixer on medium 30 seconds. Add sugar and vanilla; beat on medium 3 to 5 minutes or until light. Add egg whites, one at a time, beating after each. Add flour mixture and buttermilk alternately, beating on low after each addition just until combined. Spread batter into prepared pan(s).
**3.** Bake 30 to 35 minutes or until a toothpick comes out clean. Cool cake layers in pans 10 minutes. Remove layers from pans; cool on wire racks. Or place 13×9-inch cake in pan on a wire rack; cool. Frost with *desired frosting (pp. 538–539)*.
**Makes 12 servings (1 slice each).**
**NOTE** To create a naked cake (info, *opposite*), prepare as directed, except use three 8-inch round cake pans and bake 20 to 25 minutes. Frost cooled layers with Buttercream Frosting *(p. 538)*. Before serving, top with mixed fresh berries and sprinkle with powdered sugar.
**EACH SERVING** *275 cal., 8 g fat (5 g sat. fat), 21 mg chol., 271 mg sodium, 47 g carb., 1 g fiber, 31 g sugars, 4 g pro.*

## NAKED CAKE

Trendy naked cakes can be made from virtually any flavor of cake and feature lightly frosted (or unfrosted) layers that highlight a cake's natural texture.

### ADD A DRIZZLE

If desired, drizzle the top with Ganache (p. 539), tinted Powdered Sugar Icing (p. 538), or Caramel Sauce (p. 604).

**TOP IT OFF** Get creative with the toppers. Here are a few to try:

- Fresh berries or fruit
- Fresh edible organic flowers (grown without pesticides)
- Fresh herbs
- Lemon, lime, or orange zest
- Dried fruit
- Chopped toasted nuts
- Toasted flaked coconut
- Chocolate candies, chips, or curls
- Sifted powdered sugar or cocoa powder
- Crushed or chopped candy bars
- Sprinkles or coarse sugar

### MAKE IT PRETTY

We love the simplicity of "naked cakes." To get this look, first spread frosting around the filled and stacked layers. Angle a long, clean spatula vertically against the cake to scrape excess frosting off the outside edges.

## FROM SCRATCH
### LEARN WHAT IT TAKES TO MAKE THE BEST CAKES.

### PREPPING CAKE PANS

With the exception of angel food and chiffon cakes, most cakes require pans to be greased and floured. For a quick brush-on, stir together ¼ cup each vegetable oil, shortening, and all-purpose flour. Use this for recipes that call for greased and floured pans. The mixture may be stored in the refrigerator up to 1 month. If you're still leery about getting your cake out of the pan in one piece, line the bottom of the pan with waxed or parchment paper (info, p. 531). Grease the paper with the brush-on mixture and flour.

**1** This is the most important step when making creamed cakes: Beat fat and sugar 3 to 5 minutes (DON'T cut this short). Tiny bubbles will be created, giving the cake a light, fluffy texture.

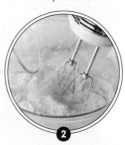

**2** Add eggs (or egg whites), one at a time, beating well after each. Their protein creates structure around air bubbles to maintain texture.

**3** When liquid is mixed into flour, gluten begins to form—too much gluten makes a tough cake. To prevent this, add more of the flour mixture first to coat the flour with butter. As soon as you add liquid, do not overmix.

**4** Pour batter evenly into prepared pans. Use a metal spatula to smooth tops before baking.

**5** When the cake layers have cooled ONLY 10 minutes, run a thin metal spatula or table knife around the edges of the cake pan. Place a cooling rack over the top. Invert the pan with the rack so the pan is on top. Shake gently to loosen cake layer from pan.

**6** If you lined the bottom of the cake pan with waxed paper, carefully peel off the paper.

**BAKERY-STYLE**
Bakeries never skimp on frosting. For an extra-thick coating (especially if you're piping the frosting, *opposite*), multiply the frosting recipe 1½ to 2 times. This helps make dramatic swoops and swirls.

**FROSTING TOOLS** Two of the best tools to have are a thin straight or offset metal spatula and a long serrated knife. The thin metal spatula comes in many sizes. If you're a rookie cake decorator, choose a smaller spatula. Find the spatula in cooking shops and the cake-decorating section of hobby stores. A long serrated knife is best for making the tops of cake layers even and trimming when necessary.

# YELLOW CAKE

**HANDS-ON TIME** 25 minutes
**BAKE** 20 minutes at 375°F
**COOL** 1 hour

2½ cups all-purpose flour
2½ tsp. baking powder
½ tsp. salt
¾ cup butter, softened
1¾ cups sugar
3 eggs, room temperature
1½ tsp. vanilla
1¼ cups milk

**1.** Preheat oven to 375°F. Grease and lightly flour two 9-inch or 8-inch round cake pans or grease one 13×9-inch baking pan (tips, *p. 517; p. 531*). In a bowl stir together flour, baking powder, and salt.
**2.** In a large bowl beat butter with a mixer on medium 30 seconds. Gradually add sugar, ¼ cup at a time, beating on medium until combined. Scrape bowl; beat 2 minutes more. Add eggs, one at a time, beating after each. Beat in vanilla. Add flour mixture and milk alternately, beating on low after each addition just until combined. Spread batter into prepared pan(s).

**3.** Bake 20 to 25 minutes for 9-inch pans, 30 to 35 minutes for 8-inch pans, 25 to 30 minutes for 13×9-inch pan, or until a toothpick comes out clean. Cool cake layers in pans 10 minutes. Remove layers from pans; cool on wire racks. Or place 13×9-inch cake in pan on a wire rack; cool. Frost with *desired frosting (pp. 538–539).* **Makes 12 servings (1 slice each).**
**EACH SERVING** *342 cal., 14 g fat (8 g sat. fat), 885 mg chol., 257 mg sodium, 51 g carb., 1 g fiber, 31 g sugars, 5 g pro.*

### CHANGE IT UP
*Give your cake a bright lemony flavor. Prepare as directed, except stir 2 tsp. lemon zest into batter. Use a white frosting, such as Meringue Frosting (p. 538) and spread lemon curd between the layers.*

**EGGS** that stand at room temp for 30 minutes before beating allow more air to be incorporated in batter for a lighter cake.

---

## BAKING CLASS

THE SECRET TO THE PRETTIEST FROSTED CAKES IS A CRUMB COAT. THIS THIN LAYER OF ICING—WHICH IS APPLIED, THEN ALLOWED TO STAND UNTIL SET—WILL KEEP CRUMBS OUT OF YOUR TOP LAYER OF FROSTING AND PREVENT TEARS IN TENDER CAKES.

**1** For quick cleanup, tuck small pieces of waxed paper around and under the first cake layer on a pedestal or cake plate. Spread ½ cup frosting evenly over the surface to ¼ inch of the edge. If necessary, use a serrated knife to trim the rounded surface off the cake layer. Place the second cake layer on top of the frosting. Center the cake, aligning the edges of the cakes.

**2** A thin, light layer of frosting (crumb coat) spread over the entire cake seals in crumbs and fills in any imperfections. Allow the crumb coat to dry before applying final layer of frosting to the cake. Using a thin metal spatula, frost cake with the remaining frosting. For a smooth surface, push the frosting onto sides of the cake without moving the spatula back and forth.

---

### STRIPES

Using a straight metal spatula and starting at the base of the cake, pull the spatula straight up toward the top of the cake. Repeat until you've covered the entire cake.

### PETALS

Prepare extra frosting; place in a pastry bag with an open tip or transfer frosting to a gallon resealable plastic bag and cut off a corner. Pipe three dots of frosting of similar size in a row from top to bottom. Using a thin metal spatula, place the tip in the center of the frosting dot and pull the frosting horizontally to one side; repeat.

### ROSES

Prepare extra frosting; place the frosting (tip, *opposite*) in a pastry bag fitted with a large star tip; pipe rose circles around the cake. You can decide how large or small they are.

# RED VELVET CAKE

**HANDS-ON TIME** 45 minutes
**BAKE** 35 minutes at 350°F
**COOL** 2 hours 30 minutes

| | |
|---|---|
| 3 | cups all-purpose flour |
| 1 | Tbsp. unsweetened cocoa powder |
| ¾ | tsp. salt |
| ¾ | cup butter, softened |
| 2¼ | cups sugar |
| 3 | eggs, room temperature |
| 1 | 1-oz. bottle (2 Tbsp.) red food coloring |
| 1½ | tsp. vanilla |
| 1½ | cups buttermilk or sour milk (tip, *p. 474*) |
| 1½ | tsp. baking soda |
| 1½ | tsp. vinegar |
| 1 | recipe Cooked White Frosting |

**1.** Preheat oven to 350°F. Grease and lightly flour two 9×2-inch or three 9×1½-inch round cake pans (tips, *p. 517; p. 531*). In a medium bowl stir together flour, cocoa powder, and salt.
**2.** In an extra-large bowl beat butter with a mixer on medium 30 seconds. Gradually add sugar, ¼ cup at a time, beating on medium until combined. Scrape bowl; beat 2 minutes more. Add eggs, one at a time, beating after each. Beat in food coloring and vanilla. Add flour mixture and buttermilk alternately, beating on low after each addition just until combined. In a small bowl combine baking soda and vinegar; fold into batter. Spread batter into prepared pans.
**3.** Bake 35 minutes for 9×2-inch pans, 22 to 25 minutes for 9×1½-inch pans, or until a toothpick comes out clean. Cool cake layers in pans 10 minutes. Remove layers from pans; cool on wire racks.
**4.** Meanwhile, prepare Cooked White Frosting. To assemble two 9×2-inch cake layers,* place one layer, bottom side up, on a plate.

Spread with 1½ cups frosting. Top with second layer, bottom side up; spread top and sides of cake with remaining frosting. Store in refrigerator up to 3 days. (Before serving, let stand at room temperature 30 to 60 minutes or until frosting is softened.) **Makes 16 servings (1 slice each).**
**\*NOTE** To assemble three 9×1½-inch cake layers, spread one layer with ¾ cup frosting; add second layer and spread with ¾ cup frosting. Add remaining layer; spread top and sides with remaining frosting.
**EACH SERVING** *544 cal., 28 g fat (17 g sat. fat), 106 mg chol., 514 mg sodium, 70 g carb., 1 g fiber, 50 g sugars, 6 g pro.*

## COOKED WHITE FROSTING

In a 2-qt. saucepan whisk together 1½ cups each sugar and milk, ⅓ cup all-purpose flour, and dash salt. Cook and stir over medium heat until thickened and bubbly. Reduce heat; cook and stir 1 minute more. Remove from heat; stir in 2 tsp. vanilla. Transfer to a large bowl. Cover surface with plastic wrap and cool completely (2½ to 3 hours). Cut 1½ cups softened butter into 1 Tbsp. pieces. Beat in butter, one piece at time, with a mixer on medium until smooth, scraping bowl as needed. Make sure each piece of butter is incorporated before adding the next. Frosting may look curdled until all the butter is added.

**RED VELVET CUPCAKES** Grease and flour twenty-eight 2½-inch muffin cups or line with paper bake cups. Prepare as directed through Step 2, except divide batter among prepared muffin cups. Bake 15 to 17 minutes or until a toothpick comes out clean. Cool in cups on wire racks 5 minutes. Remove from cups; cool on wire racks. Frost with Cooked White Frosting. **Makes 28 cupcakes.**

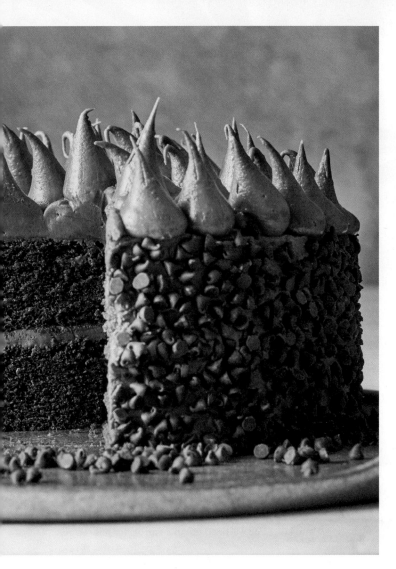

## PICK A PAN

If you want to make your cake a different size or shape than the one specified in the recipe, here's an easy guide. Start with a two-layer-size cake. Then pick your pan, add the approximate amount of batter recommended, and follow the general baking times. (Baking times vary slightly between cake batters.) Always test cake at minimum baking time.

**13×9-IN. BAKING PAN
7 CUPS BATTER
30 TO 35 MINUTES**

**FLUTED TUBE PAN
5 TO 6 CUPS BATTER
40 TO 45 MINUTES**

**2½-INCH CUPCAKES
¼ CUP BATTER EACH
15 TO 20 MINUTES**

**9-INCH ROUND PAN
3 TO 3½ CUPS BATTER
30 TO 35 MINUTES**

OUR CHOCOLATE CAKE recipe can easily be turned into Devil's Food Cake. To do this, omit baking powder and increase baking soda to 1¼ tsp. The extra boost of baking soda, when combined with the cocoa powder, gives the cake its distinctively richer chocolate flavor; lighter, fluffier texture; and reddish tinge.

## CHOCOLATE CAKE

**HANDS-ON TIME** 30 minutes
**BAKE** 30 minutes at 350°F
**COOL** 1 hour

2   cups all-purpose flour
¾   cup unsweetened cocoa powder
1   tsp. baking soda
¾   tsp. baking powder
½   tsp. salt
¾   cup butter, softened
2   cups sugar
3   eggs, room temperature
2   tsp. vanilla
1½  cups milk

**1.** Preheat oven to 350°F. Lightly grease bottoms of two 9-inch round or 8-inch square cake pans. Line bottoms with waxed paper; grease and lightly flour pans (tips, *p. 517; p. 531*). Or grease one 13×9-inch baking pan. In a bowl stir together first five ingredients (through salt).
**2.** In a large bowl beat butter with a mixer on medium 30 seconds. Gradually add sugar, ¼ cup at a time, beating on medium until combined. Scrape bowl; beat 2 minutes more. Add eggs, one at a time, beating after each. Beat in vanilla. Add flour mixture and milk alternately, beating on low after each addition just until combined. Beat on medium to high 20 seconds more. Spread batter into prepared pan(s).

**3.** Bake 30 to 35 minutes for 9-inch pans, 35 to 40 minutes for 8-inch pans, about 40 minutes for 13×9-inch pan, or until a toothpick comes out clean. Cool cake layers in pans 10 minutes. Remove layers from pans; peel off waxed paper. Cool on wire racks. Or place 13×9-inch cake in pan on a wire rack; cool. Frost with *desired frosting (pp. 538–539)*. **Makes 12 servings (1 slice each).**

**EACH SERVING** *354 cal., 14 g fat (9 g sat. fat), 86 mg chol., 330 mg sodium, 54 g carb., 2 g fiber, 35 g sugars, 6 g pro.*

// CAKES //

# CARROT CAKE

**HANDS-ON TIME** 30 minutes
**BAKE** 35 minutes at 350°F
**COOL** 2 hours

| | |
|---|---|
| 2 | cups all-purpose flour |
| 2 | cups sugar |
| 2 | tsp. baking powder |
| 1 | tsp. ground cinnamon (optional) |
| ½ | tsp. baking soda |
| ½ | tsp. salt |
| 4 | eggs, room temperature |
| 3 | cups finely shredded carrots (lightly packed) |
| ¾ | cup vegetable oil |
| 1 | recipe Cream Cheese Frosting (p. 539) |
| ½ | cup chopped pecans, toasted (tip, p. 18) (optional) |

**1.** Preheat oven to 350°F. Lightly grease bottom of two 8-inch round cake pans (tips, *p. 517; p. 531*). Line bottoms with waxed paper; grease pans. In a large bowl stir together first six ingredients (through salt).
**2.** In a medium bowl lightly beat eggs; stir in carrots and oil. Add egg mixture to flour mixture; stir until combined. Spread batter into prepared pans.
**3.** Bake 35 to 40 minutes or until a toothpick comes out clean. Cool cake layers in pans 10 minutes. Remove layers from pans; peel off waxed paper. Cool on wire racks.
**4.** Frost cake with Cream Cheese Frosting. If desired, lightly press pecans onto sides of cake. Store in refrigerator up to 3 days. **Makes 12 servings (1 slice each).**
**GINGER-CARROT CAKE** Prepare as directed, except do not add the cinnamon; stir 2 tsp. grated fresh ginger or ¾ tsp. ground ginger into egg mixture.

**EACH SERVING** *711 cal., 30 g fat (10 g sat. fat), 112 mg chol., 350 mg sodium, 108 g carb., 1 g fiber, 90 g sugars, 6 g pro.*

**CARROT MATH**
1 carrot = ½ cup finely shredded
You will need about 6 carrots for this recipe.

Use the fine shredding surface of a box grater to shred your carrots. They will stay evenly distributed in the cake and won't sink.

Oil-based cakes are usually moist with a dense crumb. These easy cakes use baking powder and baking soda to get their lift, and you can mix them by hand.

The tops of baked cakes are never flat and even. So they stack better, use a long serrated bread knife to carefully saw the uneven portion off horizontally. Turn the cut top upside down so you can frost the less crumbly side.

# GERMAN CHOCOLATE CAKE

**HANDS-ON TIME** 30 minutes
**BAKE** 35 minutes at 350°F
**COOL** 1 hour

»

**SWEET BAKING CHOCOLATE** has more sugar than semisweet chocolate, so don't swap one for the other. For a substitute, use ¼ cup unsweetened cocoa powder, ⅓ cup sugar, and 3 Tbsp. shortening for 4 oz. sweet baking chocolate.

1   4-oz. pkg. sweet baking chocolate, chopped
1½  cups milk
2   cups all-purpose flour
1   tsp. baking soda
¾   tsp. baking powder
½   tsp. salt
¾   cup butter, softened
1¾  cups sugar
3   eggs, room temperature
2   tsp. vanilla
1   recipe Coconut-Pecan Frosting

**1.** In a 1- or 1½-qt. saucepan cook and stir chocolate and milk over low heat until chocolate melts; cool.
**2.** Preheat oven to 350°F. Lightly grease bottoms of two 8-inch square or 9-inch round cake pans. Line bottoms with waxed paper; grease and lightly flour pans (tips, *p. 517; p. 531*). Or grease one 13×9-inch baking pan. In a medium bowl stir together flour, baking soda, baking powder; and salt.
**3.** In a large bowl beat butter with a mixer on medium 30 seconds. Gradually add sugar, ¼ cup at a time, beating on medium until combined. Scrape bowl; beat 2 minutes more. Add eggs, one at a time, beating after each. Beat in vanilla. Add flour mixture and chocolate mixture alternately, beating on low after each addition just until combined. Beat on medium to high 20 seconds more. Spread batter into the prepared pan(s).
**4.** Bake 35 to 40 minutes for 8-inch pans, 30 to 35 minutes for 9-inch pans, 45 minutes for 13×9-inch pan, or until a toothpick comes out clean. Cool cake layers in pans 10 minutes. Remove layers from pans; peel off waxed paper. Cool on wire racks. Or place 13×9-inch cake in pan on a wire rack; cool.
**5.** Spread Coconut-Pecan Frosting over top of each layer; stack layers on a plate. Or spread frosting over top of 13×9-inch cake. **Makes 12 servings (1 slice each).**

**EACH SERVING** *730 cal., 39 g fat (21 g sat. fat), 170 mg chol., 514 mg sodium, 91 g carb., 4 g fiber, 71 g sugars, 10 g pro.*

## GET FANCY
For an impressive finish, prepare a half-recipe of Chocolate Buttercream Frosting (*p. 538*). Assemble cake layers. Frost sides with chocolate frosting and pipe remaining around the cake top.

# COCONUT-PECAN FROSTING

In a 2-qt. saucepan combine 4 egg yolks, one 12-oz. can evaporated milk, 1½ cups sugar, and ½ cup butter. Cook and stir over medium heat 20 to 25 minutes or until thickened and mixture coats the back of a metal spoon. Remove from heat. Stir in one 7-oz. pkg. (2⅔ cups) flaked coconut and 1 cup chopped pecans. Cover and cool before using.

# ITALIAN CREAM CAKE

**HANDS-ON TIME** 40 minutes
**BAKE** 35 minutes at 350°F
**COOL** 1 hour

5   eggs, room temperature
2   cups all-purpose flour
1   tsp. baking soda
½   cup butter, softened
½   cup shortening
2   cups sugar
1   tsp. vanilla
1   cup buttermilk or sour milk
    (tip, *p. 474*)
1   cup flaked coconut
½   cup finely chopped toasted
    pecans (tip, *p. 18*)
1   recipe Cream Cheese Frosting
    (*p. 539*)
1   cup chopped toasted pecans
    (tip, *p. 18*)

**1.** Preheat oven to 350°F. Grease and flour three 8-inch or 9-inch round cake pans (tips, *p. 517; p. 531*). Separate eggs. In a medium bowl stir together flour and baking soda.
**2.** In an extra-large bowl beat butter and shortening with a mixer on medium 30 seconds. Add sugar; beat until combined. Add egg yolks and vanilla; beat on medium until combined. Add flour mixture and buttermilk alternately, beating on low after each addition just until combined. Fold in coconut and finely chopped pecans.
**3.** Thoroughly wash beaters. In a medium bowl beat egg whites on medium until stiff peaks form (tips stand straight) (photo, *p. 475*). Fold one-third of the egg whites into batter to lighten; fold in remaining egg whites. Spread batter into prepared pans.
**4.** Bake 35 minutes for 8-inch pans, 25 minutes for 9-inch pans, or until a toothpick comes out clean. Cool cake layers in pans 10 minutes. Remove layers from pans; cool on wire racks.
**5.** Place one cake layer, bottom side up, on a plate. Spread with ½ cup of the Cream Cheese Frosting; sprinkle with ¼ cup of the chopped pecans. Top with second layer, bottom side down. Spread with ½ cup frosting; sprinkle with ¼ cup chopped pecans. Top with remaining layer, bottom side up; spread top and sides of cake with remaining frosting and sprinkle with remaining ½ cup chopped pecans. Store in refrigerator up to 2 days. **Makes 16 servings (1 slice each).**

**EACH SERVING** *646 cal., 33 g fat (14 g sat. fat), 104 mg chol., 267 mg sodium, 84 g carb., 2 g fiber, 69 g sugars, 6 g pro.*

**CLEAN CUTS**
Cakes that are full of goodies like nuts and coconut cut best with a long serrated knife, such as a bread knife. If necessary, wipe the knife off between cuts (tip, *p. 535*).

## UPSIDE-DOWN APPLE-HONEY CAKE

**HANDS-ON TIME** 25 minutes
**BAKE** 40 minutes at 350°F
**COOL** 35 minutes

1½   cups all-purpose flour
2    tsp. baking powder
¼    tsp. salt
¾    cup milk
½    cup honey
1    tsp. vanilla
½    cup butter, softened
1    cup packed brown sugar
2    medium baking apples, cored and cut into ½-inch rounds
½    cup pecan halves
2    eggs, room temperature

**1.** Preheat oven to 350°F. In a bowl stir together flour, baking powder, and salt. In another bowl combine milk, honey, and vanilla.
**2.** Place ¼ cup of the butter in a 9-inch square baking pan. Place pan in oven until butter melts. Stir in ½ cup of the brown sugar. Arrange nine apple rounds and the pecans in pan, overlapping as needed (you may have extra apple rounds).
**3.** In a large bowl beat remaining ¼ cup butter with a mixer on medium 30 seconds. Gradually beat in the remaining ½ cup brown sugar until light and fluffy. Add eggs; beat 1 minute. Alternately add flour and milk mixtures, beating on low after each addition just until combined. Spread batter over apples in pan.
**4.** Bake 40 to 45 minutes or until a toothpick comes out clean. Cool in pan on wire rack 5 minutes. Loosen cake from pan and invert onto a plate. Cool 30 minutes; serve warm.
**Makes 9 servings (1 piece each).**
**EACH SERVING** *403 cal., 16 g fat (7 g sat. fat), 70 mg chol., 288 mg sodium, 63 g carb., 2 g fiber, 45 g sugars, 5 g pro.*

**» UPSIDE-DOWN PINEAPPLE-HONEY CAKE** Prepare as directed, except substitute six ¼-inch slices peeled, cored, and halved fresh pineapple for the apples. Arrange pineapple slices and pecans in pan, overlapping and cutting pineapple as needed. Continue as directed.

// CAKES //

GINGERBREAD

## GINGERBREAD

**HANDS-ON TIME** 20 minutes
**BAKE** 25 minutes at 325°F
**COOL** 30 minutes

1¼   cups all-purpose flour
1     tsp. ground ginger
½     tsp. baking powder
½     tsp. ground cinnamon
¼     tsp. baking soda
¼     tsp. salt
¼     tsp. ground cloves
¼     cup sour cream
3     Tbsp. strong brewed coffee,
       cooled, or milk
⅓     cup butter, softened
¼     cup packed brown sugar
1     egg
½     cup molasses
1     recipe Sweetened Whipped
       Cream (p. 474) (optional)

**1.** Preheat oven to 325°F. Grease
an 8-inch square baking pan (tip,
*p. 531*). In a bowl combine first
seven ingredients (through cloves).
In another bowl combine sour
cream and coffee.
**2.** In a medium bowl beat butter
and brown sugar with a mixer
on medium until light and fluffy.
Add egg, beating on medium
until combined. Gradually beat in
molasses. Add flour mixture and
sour cream mixture alternately,
beating on low after each addition
just until combined. Beat on high
20 seconds more. Spread batter
into prepared pan.
**3.** Bake 25 minutes or until a
toothpick comes out clean (cake
may dip in center). Cool in pan on
a wire rack 30 minutes. If desired,

top warm cake with Sweetened
Whipped Cream and cinnamon.
**Makes 9 servings (1 piece each).**
**EACH SERVING** *222 cal., 9 g fat (5 g
sat. fat), 42 mg chol., 199 mg sodium,
34 g carb., 1 g fiber, 20 g sugars,
3 g pro.*

## OATMEAL CAKE

**HANDS-ON TIME** 35 minutes
**BAKE** 30 minutes at 350°F
**COOL** 30 minutes

2¼   cups water
1½   cups regular rolled oats
½     cup butter, cut up
3     eggs, lightly beaten
1½   cups packed brown sugar
1¼   cups whole wheat flour
1     cup all-purpose flour
1½   tsp. baking soda
1½   tsp. ground cinnamon
¾     tsp. salt
¾     tsp. ground nutmeg
½     cup butter
1⅓   cups packed brown sugar
½     cup half-and-half or
       evaporated milk
2     cups flaked coconut
1     cup chopped pecans
1     tsp. vanilla

**1.** Preheat oven to 350°F. Lightly
grease bottom of a 13×9-inch
baking pan (tip, *p. 531*). In a 3- or
4-qt. saucepan bring the water
to boiling. Stir in oats and ½ cup
butter; reduce heat to low. Cook
5 minutes or until oats are softened,
stirring occasionally.
**2.** In a large bowl combine eggs and
the 1½ cups brown sugar. In another
bowl combine next six ingredients
(through nutmeg). Stir oats into egg
mixture. Fold in flour mixture just
until moistened (batter will be thick).
Spread batter into prepared pan.
**3.** Bake 30 to 35 minutes or until a
toothpick comes out clean. Transfer
to a wire rack. Preheat broiler.

### GET-TOGETHER

*For extra-special occasions,
serve Gingerbread with
Bourbon Sauce (p. 604) or
Custard Sauce (p. 605).*

OATMEAL CAKE

**4.** Meanwhile, in a 2-qt. saucepan melt ½ cup butter. Stir in 1⅓ cups brown sugar and half-and-half until combined. Remove from heat. Stir in coconut, pecans, and vanilla. Spoon coconut mixture over hot cake.

**5.** Broil 4 to 5 inches from heat 3 to 4 minutes or until topping is bubbly and begins to brown, watching closely. Cool in pan on a wire rack at least 30 minutes. Serve warm or at room temperature. **Makes 16 servings (1 piece each).**

**EACH SERVING** *481 cal., 24 g fat (13 g sat. fat), 73 mg chol., 378 mg sodium, 64 g carb., 4 g fiber, 44 g sugars, 6 g pro.*

## ONE-BOWL BUTTER CAKE

**HANDS-ON TIME** 20 minutes
**BAKE** 30 minutes at 350°F
**COOL** 40 minutes

| | |
|---|---|
| 1⅓ | cups all-purpose flour |
| ⅔ | cup sugar |
| 2 | tsp. baking powder |
| ½ | tsp. salt |
| ⅔ | cup milk |
| ¼ | cup butter, softened |
| 1 | egg |
| 1 | Tbsp. vanilla |
| 3 | cups assorted fresh berries |
| 1 | recipe Sweetened Whipped Cream (*p. 474*) (optional) Honey (optional) |

**1.** Preheat oven to 350°F. Grease and lightly flour an 8-inch round cake pan (tips, *p. 517; p. 531*).

**2.** In a medium bowl combine flour, sugar, baking powder, and salt. Add milk, butter, egg, and vanilla. Beat with a mixer on low until combined. Beat on medium 1 minute more. Spread batter into prepared pan.

**3.** Bake 30 minutes or until a toothpick comes out clean. Cool cake in pan 10 minutes. Loosen sides of cake; invert onto a plate.

ONE-BOWL BUTTER CAKE

Cool 30 minutes. Serve warm with berries and, if desired, Sweetened Whipped Cream and honey. **Makes 8 servings (1 slice each).**

**EACH SERVING** *233 cal., 7 g fat (4 g sat. fat), 40 mg chol., 333 mg sodium, 38 g carb., 2 g fiber, 21 g sugars, 4 g pro.*

## *FLAVOR CHANGE-UPS*

This cake is your easiest pathway to weeknight dessert. The quick mix-and-pour method and common pantry ingredients create a moist, tender everyday cake. Customize it with any of these toppings.

### SAUCES
Fudge, caramel, or butterscotch ice cream topping, or honey

### BERRIES
Sugared strawberries, raspberries, blueberries, or blackberries

### NUTS
Chopped toasted pecans, walnuts, hazelnuts, almonds, or macadamia nuts

### JAM OR PRESERVES
Any flavor

### CHOCOLATE CHIPS
Melted semisweet, milk chocolate, dark chocolate, or peanut butter-flavor chips

### GRILLED FRUIT
Peaches, nectarines, pineapple slices, or bananas

### ICE CREAM OR FROZEN YOGURT
Any flavor

### CITRUS CURD (*P. 603*)
Lemon or orange

// CAKES //

For cake rolls, the cake needs to be rolled up immediately while still hot so the cake cools in the rolled shape (a cooled cake would crack if rolled). To do this, once you pull the cake out of the oven, loosen the edges and immediately invert cake onto a clean kitchen towel sprinkled lightly with powdered sugar. Gently peel the waxed paper off the cake. Fold the towel slightly over the end of one short side of the hot cake and immediately roll up the cake and towel together as tightly as possible to create a spiral (rolling the towel into the cake will prevent the cake from sticking to itself when you unroll it).

Carefully and slowly unroll the cooled cake and remove the towel. Evenly spread with the Strawberry Cream Filling, leaving a 1-inch border around the edge. The border will fill as you roll the cake. Reroll the filled cake into a tight spiral.

BANANA SPLIT CAKE ROLL

**THE RIGHT PAN** A 15×10-inch baking pan—also known as a jelly-roll pan—has a small rim on the edge, making it ideal for baking shallow sponge cakes like this one. Its large size also makes it perfect for roasting vegetables and toasting large amounts of nuts, coconut, bread slices, and croutons.

## BANANA SPLIT CAKE ROLL

**HANDS-ON TIME** 50 minutes
**BAKE** 15 minutes at 375°F
**COOL** 1 hour
**CHILL** 2 hours

¾  cup all-purpose flour
1   tsp. baking powder
¼   tsp. salt
¼   tsp. ground nutmeg
¼   tsp. ground cinnamon
3   eggs, room temperature
¾   cup granulated sugar
⅔   cup mashed ripe banana
1   tsp. lemon juice
    Powdered sugar
1   recipe Strawberry Cream
    Filling
    Chocolate-flavor syrup
    (optional)
    Sweetened Whipped Cream
    (p. 474) (optional)
    Maraschino cherries (optional)

**1.** Grease a 15×10-inch baking pan (tip, *p. 531*). Line bottom with waxed paper or parchment paper; grease and lightly flour pan. In a small bowl stir together flour, baking powder, salt, nutmeg, and cinnamon.
**2.** Preheat oven to 375°F. In a large bowl beat eggs with a mixer on high 5 minutes. Gradually add granulated sugar, beating until combined. Stir in mashed banana and lemon juice. Fold flour mixture into banana mixture. Spread batter into prepared pan.
**3.** Bake 15 minutes or until top springs back when lightly touched. Immediately loosen cake from pan and turn out onto a towel sprinkled with powdered sugar. Remove waxed paper. Starting from a short side, roll towel and cake into a spiral. Cool on a wire rack 1 hour. Meanwhile, prepare Strawberry Cream Filling.
**4.** Unroll cake; remove towel. Spread cake with filling to within 1 inch of the edges. Roll up cake; trim ends. Cover and chill 2 to 24 hours. If desired, before serving, drizzle cake roll with chocolate syrup and/or top with Sweetened Whipped Cream. If desired, serve with maraschino cherries. **Makes 12 servings (1 slice each).**
**EACH SERVING** *200 cal., 9 g fat (5 g sat. fat), 71 mg chol., 141 mg sodium, 26 g carb., 1 g fiber, 19 g sugars, 4 g pro.*

### *STRAWBERRY CREAM FILLING*

In a medium bowl beat ⅔ cup heavy cream, 1 Tbsp. granulated sugar, and ½ tsp. vanilla with a mixer on medium until soft peaks form (tips curl). Beat in 4 oz. cream cheese, cut up and softened, until combined. Fold in 1 cup chopped fresh strawberries. If desired, cover and chill up to 8 hours before using.

## BLUEBERRY-LEMONADE POKE CAKE

**HANDS-ON TIME** 20 minutes
**BAKE** 25 minutes at 350°F
**COOL** 2 hours

1   pkg. two-layer-size white
    cake mix
1   cup buttermilk
4   eggs
⅓   cup canola oil
1   Tbsp. lemon zest
½   tsp. almond extract
1   recipe Blueberry Sauce
½   cup frozen lemonade
    concentrate, thawed
½   cup lemon curd
3   Tbsp. milk
1   8-oz. container frozen whipped
    dessert topping, thawed

**1.** Preheat oven to 350°F. Grease a 13×9-inch baking pan (tip, *p. 531*).
**2.** In a large bowl combine first six ingredients (through almond extract). Beat with a mixer on low just until combined. Beat on medium 2 minutes, scraping sides of bowl occasionally. Spread batter into prepared pan.
**3.** Bake 25 to 30 minutes or until a toothpick comes out clean. Cool cake in pan on a wire rack 5 minutes. Meanwhile, prepare Blueberry Sauce.
**4.** Using the handle of a wooden spoon, poke holes 1 inch apart in cake. Brush with lemonade concentrate and spread with sauce. Cool on wire rack.
**5.** In a medium bowl combine lemon curd and milk; stir in whipped topping. Spread over cake. If desired, top with additional blueberries and lemon zest. Store leftovers in refrigerator up to 24 hours. **Makes 24 servings (1 piece each).**
**EACH SERVING** *208 cal., 7 g fat (3 g sat. fat), 37 mg chol., 174 mg sodium, 33 g carb., 1 g fiber, 22 g sugars, 3 g pro.*

### *BLUEBERRY SAUCE*

In a 2-qt. saucepan stir together ⅓ cup sugar and 1 tsp. cornstarch; stir in ¼ cup water. Add 2 cups fresh or frozen blueberries. Cook and stir over medium heat until slightly thickened and bubbly. Cook and stir 2 minutes more. Remove from heat; mash until nearly smooth.

**BLUEBERRY-LEMONADE POKE CAKE**

**ANGEL FOOD CAKE**

# ANGEL FOOD CAKE

**HANDS-ON TIME** 50 minutes
**BAKE** 40 minutes at 350°F
**COOL** 2 hours

| | |
|---|---|
| 1½ | cups powdered sugar, sifted |
| 1 | cup cake flour or all-purpose flour, sifted |
| 1½ | cups egg whites (10 to 12 large), room temperature |
| 1½ | tsp. cream of tartar |
| 1 | tsp. vanilla |
| 1 | cup granulated sugar |
| 1 | recipe Powdered Sugar Icing (p. 538) (optional) |

**1.** Sift powdered sugar and flour together three times.
**2.** Adjust baking rack to lowest position in oven. Preheat oven to 350°F. In an extra-large bowl combine egg whites, cream of tartar, and vanilla. Beat with a mixer on medium until soft peaks form (tips curl). Gradually add granulated sugar, 2 Tbsp. at a time, beating until stiff peaks form (tips stand straight) (photo, *below*).
**3.** Sift one-fourth of the flour mixture over beaten egg whites; fold in gently. Repeat, folding in remaining flour mixture by fourths. Gently transfer to an ungreased angel food cake pan. Gently cut

**NOT A SPECK OF FAT**
When making angel food cake, beating air into egg whites is crucial for volume and texture. Even a tiny bit of egg yolk in the whites or greasy residue on your beaters will prevent the egg whites from performing. Wash your equipment well.

**ANGEL FOOD CAKE PAN**
This special pan is also called a 10-inch tube pan. It may have a removable bottom. Many have small "feet" on the pan top to allow for airflow to cool the cake when inverted. No feet? Invert the pan onto a sturdy narrow-neck bottle or a wire rack.

**1**
Once egg white mixture reaches soft peaks, continue beating while adding sugar a little at a time. Beat until stiff peaks form. Do not overbeat.

**2**
To eliminate large air pockets or bubbles, gently cut through the batter in the pan with a thin metal spatula or table knife.

through batter with a thin metal spatula or table knife to remove any large air pockets.

**4.** Bake on lowest rack 40 to 45 minutes or until top springs back when lightly touched. Immediately invert cake; cool in pan. Loosen cake from pan; remove cake and place on a plate. If desired, spoon Powdered Sugar Icing over top. **Makes 12 servings (1 slice each).**
EACH SERVING *172 cal., 0 g fat, 0 mg chol., 51 mg sodium, 39 g carb., 0 g fiber, 29 g sugars, 4 g pro.*

# CHOCOLATE FLOURLESS TORTE

**HANDS-ON TIME** 20 minutes
**BAKE** 20 minutes at 350°F
**COOL** 1 hour
**CHILL** 3 hours

8  oz. semisweet chocolate, chopped
1  cup butter, cut up
½  cup sugar
½  cup heavy cream
4  eggs
2  tsp. vanilla
   Unsweetened cocoa powder

**1.** Preheat oven to 350°F. Grease bottom and sides of an 8- to 9-inch springform pan *(right)*. Line a baking sheet with foil; place springform pan on prepared baking sheet.
**2.** In a 3-qt. heavy saucepan combine chocolate, butter, sugar, and cream. Cook over medium-low heat until chocolate and butter are melted, stirring frequently. Remove from heat.
**3.** In a medium bowl whisk together eggs and vanilla. Gradually stir about half of the hot chocolate mixture into egg mixture; return to remaining hot mixture in saucepan. Spread batter into prepared pan.

**4.** Bake 20 to 25 minutes or until a 2½-inch area around outside edge appears set when gently shaken (180°F). Cool in pan on a wire rack 1 hour. Cover and chill 3 hours or until firm. Loosen torte from pan; remove sides of

**CHOCOLATE FLOURLESS TORTE**

pan. Sprinkle torte with cocoa powder. **Makes 16 servings (1 slice each).**
EACH SERVING *239 cal., 20 g fat (12 g sat. fat), 87 mg chol., 111 mg sodium, 16 g carb., 1 g fiber, 13 g sugars, 3 g pro.*

*DON'T GET STUCK*

## DON'T GET STUCK

Removing a cake from the pan is a make-or-break moment. Follow these tips so your cakes slip out easily.

### GREASE AND LIGHTLY FLOUR

Unless a recipe says otherwise, use a paper towel or pastry brush to evenly spread shortening or butter on bottom, sides, and corners of a pan. (See p. 517 for a quick brush-on.) Sprinkle a little flour into the pan; tap so flour covers all greased surfaces. Invert and tap out any extra flour. For chocolate cakes, you can use unsweetened cocoa powder instead of flour.

### USE NONSTICK COOKING SPRAY

As an alternative to shortening or butter, coat pan with nonstick cooking spray; flour as directed.

### LINE THE PAN

If a recipe calls for waxed paper or parchment paper, place the pan on the paper and trace around its base with a pencil. Cut just inside the traced line and line the bottom of a lightly greased pan with the paper, smoothing out any wrinkles or bubbles. Unless otherwise specified, grease and flour pan with paper liner as directed.

// CAKES //

1. Preheat oven to 350°F. Line twenty to twenty-two 2½-inch muffin cups with paper bake cups. In a small bowl stir together first four ingredients (through salt).

2. In a large bowl beat butter and peanut butter with a mixer on medium 30 seconds. Add brown sugar, ¼ cup at a time, beating on medium until combined. Scrape bowl; beat 2 minutes more. Add eggs, one at a time, beating after each. Beat in vanilla. Alternately add flour mixture and buttermilk, beating on low after each addition until combined. Stir in chopped candy bars. Spoon batter into prepared muffin cups, filling each two-thirds full.

3. Bake 18 to 20 minutes or until a toothpick comes out clean. Cool in muffin cups on a wire rack 5 minutes. Remove from muffin cups; cool on wire rack.

4. Spoon Caramel Frosting into a decorating bag fitted with a large star tip. Pipe frosting onto tops. If desired, top with additional chopped candy bars. **Makes 20 to 22 cupcakes.**

EACH CUPCAKE *465 cal., 15 g fat (8 g sat. fat), 47 mg chol., 336 mg sodium, 80 g carb., 1 g fiber, 69 g sugars, 4 g pro.*

## CARAMEL FROSTING

In a large bowl beat ¾ cup softened butter with a mixer on medium 30 seconds. Gradually add 2 cups powdered sugar, beating well. Beat in ½ cup caramel-flavor ice cream topping and ¼ tsp. salt. Gradually beat in 6 cups additional powdered sugar. Beat in enough milk (4 to 5 Tbsp.) to reach piping consistency.

## CANDY BAR CUPCAKES

**HANDS-ON TIME** 40 minutes
**BAKE** 18 minutes at 350°F
**COOL** 45 minutes

| | |
|---|---|
| 1½ | cups all-purpose flour |
| 2 | tsp. baking powder |
| ½ | tsp. baking soda |
| ½ | tsp. salt |
| ⅓ | cup butter, softened |
| ⅓ | cup peanut butter |
| 1 | cup packed brown sugar |
| 2 | eggs |
| 1 | tsp. vanilla |
| 1 | cup buttermilk or sour milk (tip, *p. 474*) |
| 1 | cup chopped chocolate-coated caramel-topped nougat bars with peanuts |
| 1 | recipe Caramel Frosting |

# S'MORES CUPCAKES

**HANDS-ON TIME** 45 minutes
**BAKE** according to package
**COOL** 45 minutes

   Nonstick cooking spray
2   cups graham cracker crumbs
¼   cup sugar
½   cup butter, melted
1   pkg. two-layer-size chocolate cake mix
1   recipe Marshmallow Frosting
   Kisses milk chocolates

**1.** Line thirty-two 2½-inch muffin cups with paper bake cups; coat bake cups with cooking spray.

**2.** In a medium bowl stir together graham cracker crumbs and sugar; stir in melted butter. Spoon 1 Tbsp. of the mixture into each prepared muffin cup; press onto bottoms with back of a spoon.

**3.** Prepare cake mix according to package directions. Spoon batter into muffin cups, filling each half full. Bake according to package. Cool in muffin cups on wire racks 5 minutes. Remove from muffin cups; cool on wire racks.

**4.** Frost tops of cupcakes with Marshmallow Frosting. Sprinkle with additional graham cracker crumbs and top each with a chocolate. **Makes 32 cupcakes.**

**EACH CUPCAKE** *274 cal., 12 g fat (7 g sat. fat), 24 mg chol., 257 mg sodium, 41 g carb., 0 g fiber, 27 g sugars, 2 g pro.*

## MARSHMALLOW FROSTING

In a large bowl beat 1 cup softened butter with a mixer on medium 30 seconds. Beat in one 13-oz. jar marshmallow creme and 1 Tbsp. clear vanilla just until combined. Gradually add 2½ cups powdered sugar, beating just until combined.

### GRAHAM CRACKERS
You'll need about 28 squares of graham crackers to make 2 cups crushed. To crush, place graham crackers in a resealable plastic bag and roll with a rolling pin to create fine crumbs.

## MEYER LEMON CAKE

**HANDS-ON TIME** 15 minutes
**BAKE** 1 hour at 325°F
**COOL** 1 hour

»

MEYER LEMONS are a cross between lemons and mandarin oranges; they're smaller than regular lemons. They are usually only available in winter. Regular lemons are fine to use in a pinch.

| 2 | Meyer lemons or lemons |
| 3 | eggs |
| 1½ | cups milk |
| ½ | cup vegetable oil |
| ½ | cup butter, melted and cooled |
| 1 | Tbsp. lemon extract |
| 3 | cups all-purpose flour |
| 2 | cups granulated sugar |
| 1½ | tsp. baking powder |
| 1 | tsp. salt |
| 1 | recipe Meyer Lemon Glaze |

**1.** Preheat oven to 325°F. Grease and flour a 10-inch fluted tube pan (tips, *p. 517; p. 531*). Remove 2 tsp. zest from lemons. In an extra-large bowl whisk together eggs, milk, oil, melted butter, lemon extract, and lemon zest. Whisk in next four ingredients (through salt) until smooth. Spread batter into prepared pan.

**2.** Bake about 1 hour or until a toothpick comes out clean. Cool cake in pan on a wire rack 10 minutes. Remove from pan; cool on wire rack. Drizzle with Meyer Lemon Glaze. **Makes 16 servings (1 slice each).**

**MINI CAKES** Prepare as directed through Step 1, except spoon batter into sixteen 3½-inch fluted individual tube pans, using ⅓ cup for each cake. (If you don't have enough pans, bake cakes in batches, chilling batter and cooling pans between each batch.) Bake about 30 minutes or until a toothpick comes out clean. Cool in pans on wire racks 10 minutes. Remove from pans; cool on wire racks. Drizzle with Meyer Lemon Glaze. **Makes 16 servings (1 mini cake each).**
**EACH SERVING** *351 cal., 14 g fat (5 g sat. fat), 52 mg chol., 262 mg sodium, 52 g carb., 1 g fiber, 34 g sugars, 4 g pro.*

### *MEYER LEMON GLAZE*

In a small bowl stir together 1 cup powdered sugar and enough Meyer lemon juice or lemon juice (1½ to 2 Tbsp.) to reach drizzling consistency.

**LET CAKES STAND** at least an hour before slicing to let the frosting set (if they are frosted with buttery frosting).

**ASSEMBLE CAKES** that are filled or frosted with whipped cream no more than 2 hours before serving to prevent them from becoming soggy.

**CUT CAKES** with a thin-bladed knife. Run knife under hot water and wipe dry before the first cut and between subsequent cuts.

**STORE CAKES,** covered, at room temperature 1 day or refrigerate up to 3 days. If you don't have a cake cover, invert a large bowl over cake. Directly covering a cake with plastic wrap will mar the frosting.

**CAKE FILLINGS AND FROSTINGS** that contain whipped cream, cream cheese, sour cream, or eggs need to be stored in fridge.

**TO FREEZE,** place cooled, unfrosted layers on a baking sheet; freeze until firm. Transfer layers to large freezer bags or wrap and seal in freezer wrap. Freeze up to 4 months. Thaw at room temperature before frosting.

**CAKES SERVED FROM PANS** can be covered and frozen in pans. Frost after thawing.

**2.** In an extra-large bowl beat butter with a mixer on medium 30 seconds. Gradually add granulated sugar, beating on medium until combined. Add eggs, one at a time, beating 1 minute after each. Beat in sour cream and vanilla. Alternately add flour mixture and milk, beating on low after each addition just until combined.
**3.** Transfer half (3½ cups) of the batter to a medium bowl; stir in melted chocolate. Stir peanut butter into remaining batter.
**4.** Using a separate large spoon for each batter, alternately drop spoonfuls of chocolate batter and peanut butter batter into prepared pan. Using a thin metal spatula or table knife, gently cut through batters to swirl them together (do not overmix).
**5.** Bake 1 hour or until a toothpick comes out clean. Cool cake in pan on a wire rack 15 minutes. Remove from pan; cool on wire rack. Drizzle with Peanut Butter Glaze. **Makes 12 to 16 servings (1 slice each).**

EACH SERVING  *716 cal., 36 g fat (17 g sat. fat), 100 mg chol., 602 mg sodium, 91 g carb., 3 g fiber, 62 g sugars, 13 g pro.*

## PEANUT BUTTER GLAZE

In a small bowl stir together 1¼ cups powdered sugar, ⅓ cup creamy peanut butter, and enough milk (4 to 5 Tbsp.) to reach drizzling consistency.

# CHOCOLATE-PEANUT BUTTER MARBLE CAKE

**HANDS-ON TIME** 30 minutes
**BAKE** 1 hour at 350°F
**COOL** 1 hour

| | |
|---|---|
| 3 | cups all-purpose flour |
| 4 | tsp. baking powder |
| ½ | tsp. baking soda |
| ½ | tsp. salt |
| 1 | cup butter, softened |
| 2½ | cups granulated sugar |
| 3 | eggs |
| 1 | 8-oz. carton sour cream |
| 2 | tsp. vanilla |
| 1¼ | cups milk |
| 4 | oz. bittersweet chocolate, melted and cooled |
| ¾ | cup creamy peanut butter |
| 1 | recipe Peanut Butter Glaze |

**1.** Preheat oven to 350°F. Grease and flour a 10-inch fluted tube pan (tips, p. 517; p. 531). In a bowl stir together flour, baking powder, baking soda, and salt.

# WHY IS IT CALLED A POUND CAKE? THE ORIGINAL POUND CAKES WERE MADE FROM A POUND EACH OF BUTTER, SUGAR, FLOUR, AND EGGS. OUR RECIPE DEVIATES FROM THIS RATIO SLIGHTLY FOR THE PERFECT RICHNESS.

## POUND CAKE

**HANDS-ON TIME** 25 minutes
**BAKE** 1 hour at 325°F
**COOL** 2 hours

| | |
|---|---|
| 1⅔ | cups all-purpose flour |
| ½ | tsp. salt |
| 1 | cup butter, softened |
| 1 | cup sugar |
| 1 | tsp. vanilla |
| 4 | eggs, room temperature |
| 1 | recipe Sweetened Whipped Cream (p. 474) (optional) |
| | Fresh berries (optional) |

**1.** Preheat oven to 325°F. Grease and lightly flour a 9×5-inch loaf pan (tips, p. 517; p. 531). In a medium bowl stir together flour and salt.
**2.** In a large bowl beat butter with a mixer on medium 30 seconds. Gradually add sugar, beating 6 to 8 minutes or until mixture is pale and fluffy. Beat in vanilla. Add eggs, one at a time, beating 1 minute after each. Add flour mixture, one-third at a time, beating on low to medium after each addition just until combined. Spread batter into prepared pan. Tap pan gently on counter.
**3.** Bake about 1 hour or until a toothpick comes out clean. Cool cake in pan on wire rack 10 minutes. Remove from pan; cool on rack. If desired, serve with Sweetened Whipped Cream and berries.
**Makes 10 servings (1 slice each).**
**EACH SERVING** *347 cal., 21 g fat (12 g sat. fat), 123 mg chol., 291 mg sodium, 36 g carb., 1 g fiber, 20 g sugars, 5 g pro.*

## LAYERED ICE CREAM CAKE

**HANDS-ON TIME** 30 minutes
**BAKE** 15 minutes at 350°F
**COOL** 1 hour
**FREEZE** 4 hours
**STAND** 10 minutes

- 1    pkg. two-layer-size chocolate or white cake mix
- ½    gal. vanilla bean or other desired-flavor ice cream, softened
- 1    8-oz. pkg. cream cheese, softened
- ½    cup powdered sugar
- ¼    cup milk
- 1    tsp. vanilla
- 1    16-oz. container frozen whipped dessert topping, thawed

**1.** Preheat oven to 350°F. Grease and flour three 9-inch round cake pans (tips, *p. 517; p. 531*). Prepare cake mix according to package directions. Spread batter into prepared pans. Bake 15 to 18 minutes or until tops spring back when lightly touched. Cool cake layers in pans 10 minutes. Remove from pans; cool on wire racks.
**2.** To assemble, place one cake layer in a 9-inch springform pan, trimming to fit if needed. Spread half of the ice cream over cake in pan. Top with second cake layer; spread with remaining ice cream. Top with remaining cake layer. Cover with plastic wrap and freeze 3 to 4 hours or until firm.
**3.** For frosting, in a large bowl beat cream cheese, powdered sugar, milk, and vanilla with a mixer on medium to high until light and fluffy. Stir in a small amount of whipped topping to lighten; stir in remaining topping.

### SOFTENING ICE CREAM
Let ice cream stand at room temperature 10 to 15 minutes. Spoon ice cream into a large bowl and use a wooden spoon to stir just enough to soften.

**4.** Remove sides of springform pan. Using a wide spatula, transfer cake to a plate. Spread top and sides with frosting. If desired, pipe additional frosting around top edge of cake. Freeze, uncovered, 1 to 2 hours or until firm. Store, covered with plastic wrap, in freezer up to 1 month. Let stand at room temperature 10 to 15 minutes before serving. **Makes 16 servings (1 slice each).**

**EACH SERVING** *481 cal., 26 g fat (14 g sat. fat), 88 mg chol., 321 mg sodium, 55 g carb., 1 g fiber, 38 g sugars, 6 g pro.*

## CUSTOMIZE YOUR CAKE

**STIR** chopped cookies or brownies, chocolate candies, toasted flaked coconut, chocolate chips, chopped toasted nuts, or chopped fresh fruit or berries into softened ice cream.

**ADD A LAYER** of fudge, caramel, marshmallow, or butterscotch-flavor ice cream topping or jam on the top or between layers. Decorate the outside of the cake with sprinkles or cookies.

## FROSTING FLAVORS

Add flavor twists to Buttercream Frosting recipe.

**ALMOND** Add ¼ tsp. almond extract with the vanilla. Top frosted cake with toasted sliced almonds.

**CITRUS**
Beat in 1 to 2 tsp. lemon, lime, or orange zest with the butter. Top frosted cake with additional zest or quartered citrus slices.

**ESPRESSO**
Beat in 1 to 1½ tsp. instant espresso powder or instant coffee crystals with the vanilla. Top frosted cake with chocolate-covered coffee beans.

**STRAWBERRY JAM**
Beat 3 Tbsp. strawberry jam (large pieces snipped) into butter before adding powdered sugar. Top frosted cake with fresh strawberries.

**PEPPERMINT**
Substitute ¼ tsp. peppermint extract for the vanilla. If desired, tint pink with red food coloring. Top frosted cake with crushed peppermint candies; press additional candies onto sides of cake.

**PEANUT BUTTER**
Substitute ¼ cup peanut butter for ¼ cup of the butter. Sprinkle cake with chopped peanuts.

## BUTTERCREAM FROSTING

**START TO FINISH**
15 minutes

In an extra-large bowl beat 1 cup softened butter with a mixer on medium 1 to 2 minutes or until creamy. Beat in 1 cup powdered sugar. Add 2 Tbsp. heavy cream, 1 tsp. clear vanilla, and dash salt; beat on low until combined. Gradually beat in 3 additional cups powdered sugar just until combined. Beat on medium 5 minutes or until fluffy, scraping bowl occasionally. Add 1 Tbsp. heavy cream; beat on high 1 minute more. (This frosts tops and sides of two 8- or 9-inch cake layers.)
**Makes 3½ cups.**
**CHOCOLATE BUTTERCREAM FROSTING** Prepare as directed, except add 3 Tbsp. heavy cream with the vanilla, ½ cup unsweetened cocoa powder with the 3 cups powdered sugar, and 2 Tbsp. heavy cream before beating on high 1 minute more.
**Makes 4 cups.**

## POWDERED SUGAR ICING

**START TO FINISH**
15 minutes

In a small bowl combine 1 cup powdered sugar, 1 Tbsp. milk or orange juice, and ¼ tsp. vanilla. Stir in additional milk, 1 tsp. at a time, to reach desired consistency. (This makes enough to drizzle over one angel food cake.) **Makes ½ cup.**
**CHOCOLATE POWDERED SUGAR ICING** Prepare as directed, except add 2 Tbsp. unsweetened cocoa powder and use milk, not orange juice.
**Makes ½ cup.**

## CREAMY WHITE FROSTING

**START TO FINISH**
15 minutes

In a large mixing bowl beat 1 cup shortening, 1½ tsp. vanilla, and ½ tsp. almond extract with a mixer on medium 30 seconds. Slowly add 2 cups powdered sugar, beating well. Add 2 Tbsp. milk. Gradually beat in 2 additional cups powdered sugar and 1 to 2 Tbsp. milk to reach spreading consistency. (This frosts tops and sides of two 8- or 9-inch cake layers. Halve the recipe to frost a 13×9-inch cake.)
**Makes about 3 cups.**

## MERINGUE FROSTING

**START TO FINISH**
15 minutes

In the 3-qt. top of a double boiler combine 1½ cups sugar, ⅓ cup cold water, 2 egg whites, and ¼ tsp. cream of tartar. Beat with a mixer on low 30 seconds. Place the pan over boiling water (upper pan should not touch the water). Cook, beating constantly with the mixer on high, 10 to 13 minutes or until an instant-read thermometer registers 160°F when inserted in the mixture, stopping and quickly scraping bottom and sides of pan every 5 minutes to prevent sticking. Remove pan from heat. Add 1 tsp. vanilla; beat about 1 minute more or until frosting is fluffy and holds soft peaks. (This frosts tops and sides of two 8- or 9-inch cake layers or one angel food cake.) Store frosted cake in the refrigerator and serve the day it is made.
**Makes 5 cups.**

## CREAM CHEESE FROSTING

**START TO FINISH**
15 minutes

In a large mixing bowl beat one 8-oz. pkg. softened cream cheese, ½ cup softened butter, and 2 tsp. vanilla with a mixer on medium until light and fluffy. Gradually beat in 5½ to 6 cups powdered sugar to reach spreading consistency. (This frosts tops and sides of two 8- or 9-inch cake layers. Halve the recipe to frost a 13×9-inch cake.) Cover and store frosted cake in the refrigerator. **Makes about 3½ cups.**
**COCOA CREAM CHEESE FROSTING**
Prepare as directed, except beat ½ cup unsweetened cocoa powder into the cream cheese mixture and reduce powdered sugar to 5 to 5½ cups. **Makes about 3½ cups.**

## BROWNED BUTTER FROSTING

**START TO FINISH**
15 minutes

In a 1- or 1½-qt. saucepan heat ¾ cup cut-up butter over low heat until melted. Continue heating until butter turns a light golden brown. Remove from heat. In a large mixing bowl combine 6 cups powdered sugar, ¼ cup milk, and 2 tsp. vanilla. Add browned butter. Beat with a mixer on low until combined. Beat on medium to high, adding an additional 1 Tbsp. milk if necessary to reach spreading consistency. (This frosts the tops and sides of two 8- or 9-inch cake layers.) **Makes about 3 cups.**

## NO-COOK FUDGE FROSTING

**START TO FINISH**
15 minutes

In a large bowl combine 8 cups powdered sugar and 1 cup unsweetened cocoa powder. Add 1 cup softened butter, ⅔ cup boiling water, and 2 tsp. vanilla. Beat with a mixer on low until combined. Beat 1 minute on medium speed. If necessary, cool about 20 minutes or until frosting is spreading consistency. If frosting is too thick, add boiling water, 1 Tbsp. at a time, to reach spreading consistency. (This frosts tops and sides of two 8- or 9-inch cake layers. Halve the recipe to frost a 13×9-inch cake.) **Makes 4½ cups.**

## CHOCOLATE-SOUR CREAM FROSTING

**START TO FINISH**
15 minutes

In a 3- or 4-qt. saucepan melt 2 cups semisweet chocolate chips and ½ cup butter over low heat until melted, stirring frequently. Cool 5 minutes. Stir in one 8-oz. carton sour cream. Gradually add 4½ cups powdered sugar, beating with a wooden spoon until smooth. (This frosts tops and sides of two 8- or 9-inch cake layers. Halve the recipe to frost a 13×9-inch cake.) Cover and store frosted cake in the refrigerator. **Makes 4½ cups.**
**CHOCOLATE-MINT SOUR CREAM FROSTING** Prepare as directed, except stir in ½ tsp. mint extract with the sour cream. **Makes 4½ cups.**

## GANACHE

**START TO FINISH**
15 minutes

In a 2-qt. saucepan bring 1 cup heavy cream just to boiling over medium-high heat. Remove from heat. Add 12 oz. chopped milk chocolate, semisweet chocolate, or bittersweet chocolate (do not stir). Let stand 5 minutes. Stir until smooth. Cool 15 minutes. (This frosts tops and sides of one 8- or 9-inch cake layer.) **Makes about 2 cups.**

**MAKE AHEAD** Most of these frostings (except the Powdered Sugar Icing, Meringue Frosting, and Ganache) can be prepped ahead of time and refrigerated in an airtight container up to 3 days. When ready to frost your cake, let frosting stand at room temperature until soft and spreadable.

// CAKES //

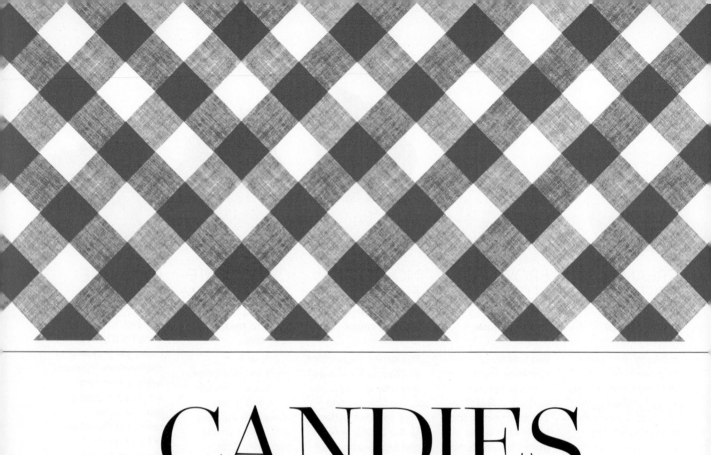

# CANDIES

**MAKE-AHEAD RECIPE**

# EASY FUDGE

**HANDS-ON TIME** 45 minutes
**CHILL** 2 hours

4½ cups sugar
1    12-oz. can (1½ cups)
     evaporated milk
½    tsp. salt
1    lb. milk chocolate bar, chopped
1    12-oz. pkg. semisweet chocolate
     chips (2 cups)
1    7-oz. jar marshmallow creme
1    tsp. vanilla
1    cup chopped walnuts or
     pecans (optional)

**1.** Line a 13×9-inch baking pan with foil, extending foil over edges of the pan (tip, *p. 478*). Butter the foil.
**2.** Butter the sides of a 3-qt. heavy saucepan. In the saucepan combine the sugar, evaporated milk, and salt. Cook and stir over medium-high heat until boiling. Reduce heat to medium; cook and stir 10 minutes more; remove from heat.

**3.** Add the next four ingredients (through vanilla) and, if desired, the walnuts. Stir until melted. Beat by hand 3 to 5 minutes or until thickened.
**4.** Pour mixture into prepared pan, turning pan to spread evenly. Cover; chill 2 to 3 hours or until firm. Use foil to lift uncut fudge out of pan; cut into squares (tip, *opposite*).
**Makes 5 lb. (96 pieces).**

**TO STORE** Layer fudge pieces between waxed paper in an airtight container; cover. Store at room temperature up to 2 days or in the refrigerator up to 1 month.
**EACH PIECE** *90 cal., 3 g fat (2 g sat. fat), 2 mg chol., 21 mg sodium, 17 g carb., 0 g fiber, 16 g sugars, 1 g pro.*

**EASY CHOCOLATE-PEANUT BUTTER FUDGE** Prepare as directed, except stir ½ cup creamy peanut butter into the mixture in saucepan before bringing to boiling and substitute 1 cup chopped peanuts for the walnuts.

**EASY ROCKY ROAD FUDGE** Prepare as directed, except after spreading fudge in pan, sprinkle top with a mixture of 1 cup semisweet chocolate chips, 1 cup tiny marshmallows, and ½ cup chopped toasted walnuts. Press mixture lightly into fudge. Chill as directed.

**EASY MOCHA FUDGE** Prepare as directed, except stir 2 Tbsp. instant espresso coffee powder or instant coffee crystals into the mixture with the vanilla.

**GET IT RIGHT**
When buying evaporated milk, double-check the label to make sure you have the right product. Sweetened condensed milk—sold near the evaporated milk—contains more sugar and will affect your success.

**CLEAN CUT**
For easiest cutting, run a long chef's knife under very hot tap water. Wipe dry with a kitchen towel and quickly make the cut. Repeat for additional cuts. The hot knife will cut through the fudge like butter.

## EASY FUDGE OR OLD-FASHIONED FUDGE?

Old-fashioned fudge is tricky and requires perfection on three key levels: reaching the exact temperature on the candy thermometer, aggressive by-hand stirring, and a trained eye for the correct texture. One misstep, and the fudge will take on an unappealing graininess. Even among our Test Kitchen staff, we prefer the Easy Fudge (*opposite*), which requires no candy thermometer. The key to success is to use the exact size of saucepan called for in the recipe. Any variation on the size of pan (too big or too small) will affect the formation of the sugar crystals.

»

MARSHMALLOW CREME deflates if you work with it too much, so measuring it with a cup measure is difficult. Just eyeball it when scooping out half of the jar. If you're off slightly, it won't affect the results.

# PEANUT BUTTER FUDGE

**HANDS-ON TIME** 30 minutes
**STAND** 1 hour

2    cups sugar
1    5-oz. can (⅔ cup) evaporated milk
½    cup butter
¾    cup peanut butter
½    of a 7-oz. jar marshmallow creme or 2 cups tiny marshmallows
½    tsp. vanilla
½    cup finely chopped peanuts (optional)

**1.** Line a 9-inch square baking pan with foil, extending foil over edges of the pan (tip, *p. 478*). Butter foil.
**2.** Butter the sides of a 1½- or 2-qt. heavy saucepan. In saucepan combine sugar, milk, and butter. Cook and stir over medium-high heat until mixture boils. Reduce heat to medium; continue boiling 12 minutes, stirring occasionally.
**3.** Remove saucepan from heat. Add peanut butter, marshmallow creme, vanilla, and, if desired, peanuts; stir until combined. Spread fudge evenly in the prepared pan. Let stand 1 to 2 hours or until firm. Use foil to lift uncut fudge out of pan; cut into squares.
**Makes 1½ lb. (64 pieces).**
**TO STORE** Layer fudge pieces between waxed paper in an airtight container; cover. Store at room temperature up to 2 days or in the refrigerator up to 1 month.
**EACH PIECE** 63 cal, 3 g fat (1 g sat. fat), 4 mg chol, 28 mg sodium, 9 g carb., 0 g fiber, 8 g sugars, 1 g pro.

PEANUT BUTTER BALLS

CHOCOLATE-COVERED CHERRIES

## PEANUT BUTTER BALLS

**HANDS-ON TIME** 45 minutes
**STAND** 10 minutes

| 1 | cup peanut butter |
| 6 | Tbsp. butter, softened |
| 2 | cups powdered sugar |
| 12 | oz. chocolate-flavor candy coating (almond bark), cut up |

**DIP IT**
Place one ball on the tines of a fork. Lower the fork into the candy coating; turn as necessary (or use a spoon to drizzle candy coating over the ball). Lift the ball out, letting coating drip off so you don't end up with a pool of coating on the waxed paper. Repeat for all.

**1.** Line a tray or baking sheet with waxed paper. In a large bowl stir together peanut butter and butter. Gradually add powdered sugar, stirring until combined. If necessary, knead with hands until smooth. Shape peanut butter mixture into 1-inch balls; place on prepared tray.
**2.** In a 2-qt. heavy saucepan melt candy coating over low heat, stirring constantly, until smooth. Remove from heat; let cool 5 minutes. Using a fork, dip balls, one at a time, into coating, allowing excess coating to drip off. Return to waxed paper; let stand 10 minutes or until set. If desired, after coating has set, drizzle with additional melted candy coating to decorate.
**Makes 40 balls.**

**CRISPY PEANUT BUTTER BALLS**
Prepare as directed, except stir 1 cup crisp rice cereal into peanut butter mixture before shaping into balls.
**TO STORE** Place balls in a single layer in an airtight container; cover. Store in the refrigerator up to 1 month or freeze up to 3 months. If frozen, thaw at room temperature before serving.
**EACH BALL** 105 cal., 7 fat (3 g sat. fat), 5 mg chol., 46 mg sodium, 11 g carb., 0 g fiber, 9 g sugars, 1 g pro.

## CHOCOLATE-COVERED CHERRIES

**HANDS-ON TIME** 1 hour 15 minutes
**STAND** 3 hours
**CHILL** 1 hour

| 2 | 10-oz. jars maraschino cherries with stems (40 cherries) |
| 3 | Tbsp. butter, softened |
| 3 | Tbsp. light-color corn syrup |
| 2 | cups powdered sugar |
| 8 | oz. chocolate-flavor candy coating (almond bark), cut up |
| 8 | oz. bittersweet or semisweet chocolate, cut up |

**1.** Let cherries stand on paper towels 2 hours to drain. Line a baking sheet with waxed paper.
**2.** In a medium bowl combine butter and corn syrup; stir in powdered sugar. Knead until smooth (chill if mixture is too soft to handle). Shape about ¾ tsp. mixture around each cherry. Place coated cherries, stem sides up, on the prepared baking sheet. Chill 1 to 4 hours or until firm.
**3.** In a 2-qt. heavy saucepan melt candy coating and chocolate over low heat, stirring constantly, until smooth. Line another baking sheet with waxed paper. Holding cherries by stems, dip one at a time into melted mixture. If necessary, spoon mixture over cherries to cover completely (prevents juice from leaking). Let excess mixture drip off. Place coated cherries, stem sides up, on prepared baking sheet. Let cherries stand until coating is set (1 to 2 hours). **Makes 40 cherries.**
**TO STORE** Place cherries in single layer in an airtight container; cover. Store in refrigerator up to 1 month.
**EACH CHERRY** 93 cal., 4 g fat (3 g sat. fat), 2 mg chol., 12 mg sodium, 15 g carb., 1 g fiber, 13 g sugars, 0 g pro.

## CLASSIC TRUFFLES

**HANDS-ON TIME** 30 minutes
**CHILL** 1 hour 30 minutes
**STAND** 30 minutes

1 12-oz. pkg. semisweet chocolate chips or one 11.5-oz. pkg. milk chocolate chips
⅓ cup heavy cream
4 tsp. cherry brandy, hazelnut or orange liqueur, or milk
3 Tbsp. finely chopped candied cherries or candied orange peel (optional)
Toppings such as unsweetened cocoa powder, finely chopped toasted nuts, chocolate sprinkles, crushed candies or cookie, and/or powdered sugar

**1.** In a 2-qt. heavy saucepan combine chocolate chips and cream. Cook and stir constantly over low heat until melted. Remove from heat; cool slightly. Stir in cherry brandy. Beat the truffle mixture with a mixer on low until mixture is smooth. If desired, stir in candied cherries. Chill 1½ to 2 hours or until firm.

**2.** Line a tray or baking sheet with waxed paper. Shape the chocolate mixture into ¾- to 1-inch balls. Roll balls in desired toppings; place on prepared tray. Let stand at room temperature about 30 minutes before serving. **Makes 25 truffles.**

**TO STORE** Place truffles in a single layer in an airtight container; cover. Store in the refrigerator up to 2 weeks.

**EACH TRUFFLE** *90 cal., 6 g fat (3 g sat. fat), 4 mg chol., 2 mg sodium, 10 g carb., 1 g fiber, 9 g sugars, 1 g pro.*

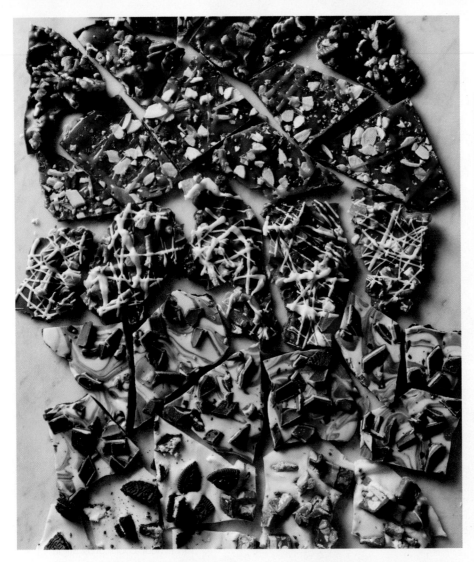

## CANDY BARK

**HANDS-ON TIME** 20 minutes
**CHILL** 30 minutes

>> **CANDY COATING AND CHOCOLATE** are both used here for a smooth, rich texture. (We've found that using only chocolate results in a finished bark with a tacky texture.)

6 oz. chocolate- or vanilla-flavor candy coating (almond bark), cut up (1 cup)

6 oz. milk, semisweet, or dark chocolate, chopped, or white baking chips (1 cup)

1 Tbsp. shortening

1½ cups chopped toasted pecans, walnuts, or almonds

**1.** Line a large baking sheet with heavy foil; grease foil.

**2.** In a large microwave-safe bowl combine candy coating, chocolate, and shortening. Microwave, uncovered, 1½ to 2 minutes or until chocolate melts, stirring every 30 seconds. Add ¾ cup of the nuts; mix well.

**3.** Pour mixture onto prepared baking sheet. Spread to ¼ inch thick. Sprinkle on remaining ¾ cup nuts.

**4.** Chill 30 minutes or until firm. Use foil to lift candy; carefully break into pieces. **Makes 36 pieces.**

**TO STORE** Layer pieces between waxed paper in an airtight container; cover. Store in the refrigerator up to 2 weeks.

**EACH PIECE** *75 cal., 6 g fat (2 g sat. fat), 1 mg chol., 6 mg sodium, 5 g carb., 1 g fiber, 4 g sugars, 1 g pro.*

>> **SALTED CARAMEL** Prepare and spread mixture as directed, using sliced almonds. Don't sprinkle nuts as in Step 3. In a bowl combine half of a 14-oz. pkg. vanilla caramels, unwrapped, and 1 Tbsp. milk. Microwave, uncovered, 1 to 2 minutes or until melted, stirring every 30 seconds. Drizzle caramel over chocolate mixture. Sprinkle with ¾ cup toasted sliced almonds; sprinkle with sea salt. Continue as directed.

>> **DRIED FRUIT AND PRETZEL** Prepare as directed, except use broken pretzels and dried cherries, raisins, cranberries, and/or snipped dried apricots in place of the nuts. Drizzle with 2 oz. melted white chocolate after the mixture sets. Continue as directed.

>> **MINT-CHOCOLATE** Prepare as directed, except omit nuts. Arrange 9 chocolate wafer cookies in a single layer on the greased foil. Use vanilla coating; melt half of the coating with 3 oz. milk chocolate chips and half of the shortening. Melt remaining coating with 3 oz. green mint-flavor baking chips. Drop alternating spoonfuls of milk chocolate and mint mixtures over the cookies; swirl. Sprinkle with chopped chocolate-mint layered candies. Chill as directed.

>> **CANDY BAR OR COOKIE** Prepare as directed, except omit nuts. Sprinkle with assorted chopped chocolate-covered candy bars or crushed cream-filled chocolate sandwich cookies.

# 6 EASY CANDIES

## CANDY CLUSTERS

In a 2-qt. heavy saucepan stir one 12-oz. pkg. vanilla-flavor candy coating, chopped, over low heat until melted (do not overheat). Remove from heat. Stir in ⅓ cup peanut butter until smooth (do not overstir). Stir in 5 cups assorted desired ingredients (such as cereal, pretzels, nuts, and/or candies). Drop spoonfuls onto waxed paper. Chill 15 minutes. Makes 48 clusters.

## SPICED NUTS

Preheat oven to 325°F. Line a 15×10-inch baking pan with foil; spray with cooking spray. Stir together ¾ cup sugar, ½ tsp. kosher salt, and 1 tsp. cinnamon. In a bowl beat 1 egg white and 1 Tbsp. water with a mixer on high until stiff peaks form. Add 4 cups pecan halves; toss. Toss with sugar mixture. Spread in the pan. Bake 10 minutes; stir nuts. Bake 10 minutes more. Cool; break into pieces. Makes 5 cups.

## DIPPED PRETZELS

Microwave 12 oz. chopped vanilla- or chocolate-flavor candy coating 1 minute or until melted, stirring every 30 seconds. (Or melt one 14-oz. bag vanilla caramels with 2 Tbsp. heavy cream.) Dip 20 large pretzel rods halfway in coating. Sprinkle with sprinkles or drizzle with melted coating. Let stand on waxed paper until set. Makes 20 pretzels.

## STUFFED MARSHMALLOWS

Make a slit in one flat side of each of 24 large marshmallows. Press desired-flavor small candy into each slit. Microwave 12 oz. chopped vanilla-flavor candy coating 1 minute or until melted, stirring every 30 seconds. Dip the cut ends of marshmallows into coating. Sprinkle with sprinkles. Let stand, uncoated ends up, on waxed paper. Makes 24 marshmallows.

## CREAM CHEESE MINTS

In a bowl stir together 3 oz. softened cream cheese and ½ tsp. peppermint extract. Gradually add 3 cups powdered sugar, stirring until smooth. Tint with food coloring, kneading to distribute it. Form into ¾-inch balls. Roll balls in granulated sugar; flatten with the tines of a fork. Store, tightly covered, in refrigerator. Makes 50 mints.

## CANDY BOX CARAMELS

Microwave 12 oz. chopped vanilla- or chocolate-flavor candy coating 1 minute or until melted, stirring every 30 seconds. Unwrap a 14-oz. pkg. of caramels; insert a toothpick in each caramel. Dip in melted candy coating, letting excess drip off. Sprinkle with finely chopped pistachio nuts, toffee bits, or sprinkles. Let stand on waxed paper until set. Makes 44 caramels.

TRUE CANDY MAKING—WHICH INVOLVES COOKING SUGARY MIXTURES TO EXTREMELY HIGH TEMPERATURES— IS PART ART AND PART SCIENCE. IT MIGHT TAKE SOME PRACTICE TO GET THE HANG OF THE DIFFERENT TECHNIQUES.

# AT EACH STAGE OF THE CANDY-MAKING PROCESS, THE MIXTURE WILL BEHAVE IN A DIFFERENT WAY WHEN A FEW DROPS ARE SPOONED INTO COLD WATER. HERE'S WHAT THE MIXTURE LOOKS LIKE AT EACH STAGE.

**THREAD STAGE**
*(230°F to 233°F)*
The candy mixture falls off a spoon in a 2-inch-long fine, thin thread.

**SOFT-BALL STAGE**
*(234°F to 240°F)*
When the ball of candy is removed from water, it instantly flattens and runs over your finger.

**FIRM-BALL STAGE**
*(244°F to 248°F)*
When the ball of candy is removed from water, it is firm enough to hold its shape but quickly flattens.

**HARD-BALL STAGE**
*(250°F to 266°F)*
When the ball of candy is removed from water, it can be deformed by pressure, but it doesn't flatten until pressed.

**SOFT-CRACK STAGE**
*(270°F to 290°F)*
When the ball of candy is removed from water, the candy separates into hard but pliable threads.

**HARD-CRACK STAGE**
*(295°F to 310°F)*
When the ball of candy is removed from water, it separates into hard, brittle threads that snap easily and cannot be shaped into a ball.

# PEANUT BRITTLE

**HANDS-ON TIME** 10 minutes
**COOK** 45 minutes

2   cups sugar
1   cup light-color corn syrup
½   cup water
¼   cup butter
2½  cups raw Spanish peanuts or cashews
1½  tsp. baking soda, sifted

**1.** Calibrate your candy thermometer (tip, *opposite*). Butter two large baking sheets. Butter the sides of a 3-qt. heavy saucepan.
**2.** In the saucepan combine sugar, corn syrup, water, and ¼ cup butter. Cook and stir until butter melts and sugar is dissolved. Continue cooking until mixture boils, stirring occasionally. Clip a candy thermometer to side of pan. Reduce heat to medium-low;

continue boiling 30 minutes or until the thermometer registers 275°F (soft-crack stage) *(opposite)*, stirring occasionally. Adjust heat as necessary to maintain a steady boil.
**3.** Stir in nuts. Cook over medium-low heat 15 to 20 minutes more or until thermometer registers 295°F (hard-crack stage), stirring often.
**4.** Remove saucepan from heat; remove thermometer. Sprinkle baking soda over corn syrup mixture, stirring constantly. Pour onto prepared sheets. Let cool 2 minutes. Using two forks, lift and pull candy into an even layer. Cool completely; break into pieces.
**Makes 72 pieces.**
**TO STORE**  Place pieces in an airtight container; cover. Store at room temperature up to 1 week.
**EACH PIECE**  *70 cal., 3 g fat (1 g sat. fat), 2 mg chol., 36 mg sodium, 10 g carb., 0 g fiber, 10 g sugars, 1 g pro.*

**TROUBLE-SHOOTING**
**If your brittle pulls apart when pulling it with forks, leaving holes in the sheet, it might have cooled too much before you started working with it.**

**If candy is too sticky (i.e., it sticks in your teeth), the final temperature reached during cooking might have been off slightly. Calibrate your candy thermometer *every time* you make candy (tip, *opposite*).**

After the mixture comes to a boil, carefully clip the candy thermometer to the side of the pan. It will take a while to get the mixture to 275°F, but keep a close eye on the mixture and adjust heat up or down to maintain a steady, controlled boil.

Carefully stir in the peanuts. Brittle calls for *raw Spanish peanuts* because they are cooked in the mixture. If you use roasted peanuts, they will get overcooked by the time the mixture makes it to 295°F

The baking soda will change the consistency and appearance of the candy mixture. After stirring it in, immediately pour the mixture out onto buttered sheets to cool slightly. Begin pulling the candy gently using two forks.

CARAMELS

CARAMEL APPLES

## CARAMELS

**HANDS-ON TIME** 20 minutes
**COOK** 45 minutes
**STAND** 2 hours

**SHORTCUT CARAMELS**
Prepare as directed, except substitute one 14-oz. can (1¼ cups) sweetened condensed milk for the half-and-half. Bring mixture to boiling over medium heat instead of medium-high heat. This mixture will take less time to reach 248°F (about 20 to 25 minutes instead of 45 to 60 minutes).

1   cup chopped walnuts, toasted
1   cup butter, cut up
2¼  cups packed brown sugar
2   cups half-and-half
1   cup light-color corn syrup
1   tsp. vanilla
    Flaked sea salt (optional)

**1.** Calibrate your candy thermometer (tip, p. 548). Line an 8-inch or 9-inch square baking pan with foil, extending foil over edges of pan (tip, p. 478). Butter the foil. Sprinkle walnuts in pan.
**2.** In a 3-qt. heavy saucepan melt butter over low heat. Add brown sugar, half-and-half, and corn syrup; mix well. Cook and stir over medium-high heat until mixture boils. Clip a candy thermometer to the side of the pan. Reduce heat to medium; continue boiling at a moderate, steady rate, stirring frequently, until the thermometer registers 248°F (firm-ball stage, p. 548) (45 to 60 minutes). Adjust heat as necessary

to maintain a steady boil and watch temperature carefully during the last 10 to 15 minutes of cooking; the temperature can increase quickly at the end.
**3.** Remove saucepan from heat; remove thermometer. Stir in vanilla. Quickly pour mixture into prepared pan. Let stand 2 hours or until firm. When firm, use foil to lift uncut caramel out of pan. Use a buttered knife to cut into 1-inch squares. If desired, sprinkle with sea salt. Wrap each piece in waxed paper. **Makes 64 caramels.**
**TO STORE** Place caramels in an airtight container; cover. Store at room temperature up to 2 weeks.
**EACH CARAMEL** *80 cal., 4 g fat (2 g sat. fat), 10 mg chol., 33 mg sodium, 12 g carb., 0 g fiber, 12 g sugars, 0 g pro.*

---

## CARAMEL APPLES

**START TO FINISH** 25 minutes

6   small tart apples
6   crafts sticks or wooden skewers
1   14-oz. pkg. vanilla caramels, unwrapped

2   Tbsp. heavy cream or half-and-half
    Toppers, such as toasted coconut, jimmies, melted chocolate, crushed candies, and/or chopped nuts (optional)

**1.** Wash and dry apples; remove stems. Insert a crafts stick into the stem end of each apple. Place apples on a buttered baking sheet.
**2.** In a 2-qt. heavy saucepan combine caramels and cream. Cook and stir over medium-low heat until caramels are completely melted, stirring constantly. Working quickly, dip each apple into hot caramel mixture; turn to coat (heat caramel again over low heat if it becomes too thick to easily coat apples). If desired, drizzle, dip, or sprinkle with desired toppers. Let stand on prepared baking sheet until set. Serve the same day. **Makes 6 apples.**
**EACH APPLE** *351 cal., 10 g fat (7 g sat. fat), 6 mg chol., 164 mg sodium, 63 g carb., 3 g fiber, 40 g sugars, 4 g pro.*

CARAMEL CORN

POPCORN AND
CANDY BALLS

## BUTTER UP

Buttering your hands
makes it easier to shape
the popcorn into balls.
Rub a dab of softened
butter into the palms of
your hands and on your
fingers. Repeat
as necessary.

# CARAMEL CORN

**HANDS-ON TIME** 20 minutes
**BAKE** 20 minutes at 300°F

14  cups popped popcorn
2   cups whole almonds (optional)
1½  cups packed brown sugar
¾   cup butter, cut up
⅓   cup light-color corn syrup
½   tsp. baking soda
½   tsp. vanilla

**1.** Preheat oven to 300°F. Remove
all unpopped kernels from popped
popcorn. Put popcorn and, if
desired, nuts into a 17×12-inch
roasting pan. Keep warm in oven
while preparing caramel.
**2.** Butter a large piece of foil. For
caramel, in a 2-qt. heavy saucepan
combine brown sugar, butter, and
corn syrup. Cook and stir over
medium heat until mixture boils.
Continue boiling at a moderate,
steady rate, without stirring,
5 minutes more.
**3.** Remove saucepan from heat.
Stir in baking soda and vanilla.
Pour caramel over popcorn; stir
gently to coat. Bake 15 minutes.
Stir mixture; bake 5 minutes more.
Spread caramel corn on prepared
foil; cool. **Makes 18 servings (1 cup
each).**
**TO STORE**  Place popcorn in an
airtight container; cover. Store at
room temperature up to 1 week.
**EACH SERVING** *181 cal., 8 g fat (5 g
sat. fat), 20 mg chol., 106 mg sodium,
28 g carb., 1 g fiber, 23 g sugars,
1 g pro.*

# POPCORN AND CANDY BALLS

**START TO FINISH** 45 minutes

20   cups popped popcorn
1½   cups light-color corn syrup
1½   cups sugar
1    7-oz. jar marshmallow creme
2    Tbsp. butter
1    tsp. vanilla
1½   cups candy-coated milk
     chocolate pieces

**1.** Preheat oven to 300°F. Remove
all unpopped kernels from popped
popcorn. Place popcorn in a
buttered 17×12-inch baking pan
or roasting pan. Keep popcorn
warm in oven while preparing
marshmallow mixture.
**2.** In a 3-qt. heavy saucepan bring
corn syrup and sugar to boiling
over medium-high heat, stirring
constantly. Remove from heat. Stir
in marshmallow creme, butter, and
vanilla until combined.
**3.** Pour marshmallow mixture over
hot popcorn; stir gently to coat.
Cool until popcorn mixture can be
handled easily. Stir in chocolate
pieces. With buttered hands, quickly
shape mixture into 3-inch-diameter
balls. Wrap each ball in plastic wrap.
**Makes 16 balls.**
**TO STORE**  Place balls in a single
layer in an airtight container;
cover. Store at room temperature
up to 1 week.
**EACH BALL** *340 cal., 5 g fat (3 g sat.
fat), 6 mg chol., 52 mg sodium, 74 g
carb., 2 g fiber, 62 g sugars, 2 g pro.*

# COOKIES
# & BARS

Cookie storing info and tips, p. 564

CHOCOLATE CHIP COOKIES

OUR CLASSIC CHOCOLATE CHIP COOKIE HOLDS ITS SHAPE AND HAS A SLIGHT CHEWINESS FROM THE COMBO OF BUTTER AND SHORTENING. BUTTER ADDS THE EXCEPTIONAL FLAVOR, AND SHORTENING KEEPS COOKIES FROM SPREADING TOO MUCH WHILE BAKING.

## CHOCOLATE CHIP COOKIES

**HANDS-ON TIME** 30 minutes
**BAKE** 6 minutes per batch at 375°F
**COOL** 2 minutes

½    cup butter, softened
½    cup shortening
1    cup packed brown sugar
½    cup granulated sugar
1    tsp. baking soda
¾    tsp. salt
2    eggs
1    Tbsp. vanilla
2¾   cups all-purpose flour
1    12-oz. pkg. semisweet chocolate chips (2 cups)

**1.** Preheat oven to 375°F. In a large bowl beat butter and shortening on medium to high 30 seconds. Add both sugars, baking soda, and salt. Beat on medium 2 minutes, scraping bowl occasionally. Beat in eggs and vanilla until combined. Beat in as much of the flour as you can. Stir in any remaining flour. Stir in chocolate chips.

**2.** Drop dough by small spoonfuls 2 inches apart onto ungreased cookie sheets. Bake 6 to 8 minutes or just until edges are light brown (cookies may not appear set). Cool on cookie sheets 2 minutes. Remove; cool on wire racks. **Makes about 48 cookies.**

**EACH COOKIE** *125 cal., 6 g fat (3 g sat. fat), 13 mg chol., 83 mg sodium, 17 g carb., 1 g fiber, 10 g sugars, 1 g pro.*

**BAKERY-STYLE COOKIES** Prepare Chocolate Chip Cookies as directed, except preheat oven to 350°F; use 1 cup butter, omit shortening, and reduce flour to 2¼ cups. Substitute 12 oz. bittersweet chocolate, chopped (2 cups), for the chocolate chips. Drop dough by ¼-cup portions 3 inches apart onto ungreased cookie sheets. Bake 7 minutes. Remove cookie sheet and firmly tap three times on the counter.* Return to oven and bake 2 minutes more. Repeat tapping. Bake 2 minutes more or until evenly golden brown. Repeat tapping. Remove; cool on wire rack. **Makes about 20 cookies.**

**\*NOTE** Occasionally tapping the pan firmly on the counter during baking flattens these all-butter cookies, giving them extra-crispy wrinkles and soft and gooey insides.

**CHANGE IT UP**

*Add one of these stir-ins: 2 cups chopped peanut butter cups, 1½ cups chopped nuts, or 1 cup snipped dried fruit.*

BROWN SUGAR is available in both light and dark varieties. Either works fine here. Light brown sugar is more subtle because it has less molasses. Dark brown sugar has a slightly more pronounced and complex flavor similar to caramel or toffee.

GLUTEN-FREE CHOCOLATE CHIP COOKIES

## GLUTEN-FREE CHOCOLATE CHIP COOKIES

**HANDS-ON TIME** 30 minutes
**BAKE** 6 minutes per batch at 375°F

⅓    cup butter, softened
⅓    cup shortening
1    cup packed brown sugar
½    cup granulated sugar
1    tsp. baking soda
1    tsp. salt
1    egg
1    Tbsp. vanilla
2¾   cups almond flour
1    12-oz. pkg. semisweet chocolate chips (2 cups)

**IS IT DONE YET?** Chocolate chip cookies are done when they have a firm golden edge or bottom and appear slightly set on top. If the edges become dark brown, they are overbaked. If edges aren't golden and tops are soft and shiny, bake a little longer.

## PICK PARCHMENT

Lining your cookie sheet with parchment paper is always a good idea. It's nonstick and makes cookie removal so easy. Plus, you can scoop extra batches onto other parchment pieces while the pan is still in the oven.

## KNOW YOUR COOKIE SHEET

Baking sheets come in all colors, textures, and sizes. We found that sheets—even inexpensive ones—with these characteristics yielded the most evenly baked cookies.

**ONE RAISED SIDE ONLY**
The pan can have two raised sides at most; more than two prevents good air circulation. You can use four-sided baking sheets, but know that your baking times and results may be slightly different.

**LIGHT TO MEDIUM COLOR**
These are better than dark-color pans, which result in darker cookies. Shiny and nonstick surfaces don't influence results.

**1.** Preheat oven to 375°F. In a large bowl beat butter and shortening with a mixer on medium to high 30 seconds. Add both sugars, baking soda, and salt. Beat on medium 2 minutes, scraping bowl as needed. Beat in egg and vanilla. Beat in almond flour. Stir in chocolate chips.
**2.** Drop dough by small spoonfuls 2 inches apart onto ungreased cookie sheets. Bake 6 to 8 minutes or just until edges are light brown (cookies may not appear set). Remove; cool on wire racks layered with parchment paper. **Makes about 48 cookies.**

**EACH COOKIE** *122 cal., 8 g fat (3 g sat. fat), 7 mg chol., 91 mg sodium, 13 g carb., 1 g fiber, 11 g sugars, 2 g pro.*

**STURDY AND HEAVY-DUTY**
Avoid flimsy, lightweight pans, which may warp in the oven.

**NONINSULATED**
Insulation increases baking time and causes cookies to spread.

**NONPERFORATED**
Crumbs stick in the holes of perforated pans. (You can line perforated pans with parchment paper.)

**1** Softened butter creams smoothly with sugar. To soften, let butter sit on the counter at room temperature 30 minutes or microwave at 5- to 10-second intervals until you can press into it easily. Don't let the butter melt.

**2** Creaming the butter and sugar together traps tiny air bubbles, which help leaven the cookies along with the baking soda. Beat the butter and sugar together until the mixture is light in color and resembles whipped butter.

**3** Use a small cookie scoop for perfectly portioned cookies. Or scoop dough with two small silverware spoons. Scoop dough with one spoon and use the other to push it onto a cookie sheet. Each dough portion should roll into a 1-inch ball.

## COOKIE SANDWICH

Spread marshmallow creme,
dulce de leche, chocolate-hazelnut
spread, peanut butter, frosting,
and/or softened ice cream on the
bottom of a cookie, then top with
another cookie, bottom side down.
If desired, roll in sprinkles.

## CUSTOMIZE IT

PICK THE INGREDIENTS
TO CREATE A RECIPE
THAT'S ALL YOUR OWN.

## OATMEAL COOKIES

**HANDS-ON TIME** 30 minutes
**BAKE** 8 minutes per batch at 350°F
**COOL** 2 minutes

|   | |
|---|---|
|   | FAT |
|   | SUGAR |
| 1 | tsp. baking soda |
|   | SPICE |
| ½ | tsp. salt |
| 2 | eggs |
|   | FLAVORING |
|   | FLOUR |
| 3 | cups regular or quick-cooking rolled oats |
| 1 | cup STIR-INS total (optional) |

**1.** Preheat oven to 350°F. In a large bowl beat FAT with a mixer on medium to high 30 seconds. Add SUGAR, baking soda, SPICE, and salt. Beat until combined, scraping sides of bowl. Beat in eggs and FLAVORING. Beat in as much of the FLOUR as you can with the mixer. Stir in any remaining FLOUR and the oats. If desired, add STIR-INS. **2.** Drop dough by small spoonfuls, a small cookie scoop, or a ¼-cup measure 2 to 3 inches apart onto ungreased cookie sheets. Bake 8 to 10 minutes for small spoonfuls, 12 to 14 minutes for ¼-cup portions, or until light brown and centers appear set. Cool on cookie sheets 2 minutes. Remove; cool on wire racks. **Makes about 36 small or 24 large cookies.**

## MIX & MATCH INGREDIENTS

**FAT** (Pick 1)

- 1 cup butter
- ½ cup butter + ½ cup shortening
- ½ cup butter + ½ cup peanut butter

**SUGAR** (Pick 1)

- 1 cup packed brown sugar + ½ cup granulated sugar
- 1½ cups packed brown sugar
- 1 cup granulated sugar + ½ cup molasses (add ¼ cup additional all-purpose flour)
- 1 cup granulated sugar + ½ cup honey

**SPICE** (Pick 1)

- 1 tsp. ground cinnamon, pumpkin pie spice, or apple pie spice
- ½ tsp. ground allspice

**FLAVORING** (Pick 1)

- 1 tsp. vanilla
- ½ tsp. coconut flavoring
- ½ tsp. maple flavoring

**FLOUR** (Pick 1)

- 1½ cups all-purpose flour
- ¾ cup all-purpose flour + ¾ cup whole wheat flour
- 1¼ cups all-purpose flour + ¼ cup toasted wheat germ

**STIR-INS** (Pick 1 or 2)

- Raisins, dried fruit bits, or dried tart red cherries
- Semisweet or milk chocolate chips
- White baking chips
- Butterscotch-flavor chips
- Flaked coconut
- Candy-coated milk chocolate pieces

TRIPLE-CHOCOLATE COOKIES

**COOKIE CONSISTENCY** Using a wooden spoon, gently stir in the chopped pecans. Before standing, the dough has a batterlike consistency. After standing, the dough is thick enough to scoop.

## TRIPLE-CHOCOLATE COOKIES

**HANDS-ON TIME** 40 minutes
**STAND** 20 minutes
**BAKE** 9 minutes per batch at 350°F
**COOL** 1 minute

| | |
|---|---|
| 7 | oz. bittersweet chocolate, chopped |
| 5 | oz. unsweetened chocolate, chopped |
| ½ | cup butter |
| ⅓ | cup all-purpose flour |
| ¼ | tsp. baking powder |
| ¼ | tsp. salt |
| 1 | cup granulated sugar |
| ¾ | cup packed brown sugar |
| 4 | eggs |
| ¼ | cup finely chopped pecans, toasted (tip, *p. 18*) |
| 1 | recipe Chocolate Drizzle |

**1.** In a 2-qt. saucepan combine chocolates and butter. Heat and stir over low heat until chocolate melts and is smooth. Remove from heat. Cool 10 minutes. In a bowl combine flour, baking powder, and salt.

**2.** Meanwhile, in a large bowl combine both sugars and eggs. Beat with a mixer on medium to high 2 to 3 minutes or until color lightens slightly, scraping bowl as needed. Beat in melted chocolate mixture. Add flour mixture to chocolate mixture; beat until combined. Stir in pecans. Cover surface of cookie dough with plastic wrap. Let stand 20 minutes (dough thickens as it stands).

**3.** Preheat oven to 350°F. Line cookie sheets with parchment paper or foil. Drop dough by small spoonfuls 2 inches apart on prepared cookie sheets. Bake 9 minutes or just until tops are set. Cool on cookie sheet 1 minute. Remove; cool on wire rack. Spoon Chocolate Drizzle over cookies.

**Makes about 60 cookies.**

**EACH COOKIE** *92 cal., 6 g fat (3 g sat. fat), 18 mg chol., 19 mg sodium, 11 g carb., 1 g fiber, 9 g sugars, 1 g pro.*

## *CHOCOLATE DRIZZLE*

In a 1- or 1½-qt. saucepan heat and stir 1 cup semisweet chocolate chips and 4 tsp. shortening over low heat until chocolate melts and mixture is smooth. Remove from heat.

## COCONUT MACAROONS

**HANDS-ON TIME** 30 minutes
**BAKE** 20 minutes per batch at 325°F

| | |
|---|---|
| 4 | egg whites |
| 1 | tsp. vanilla |
| ¼ | tsp. cream of tartar |
| ⅛ | tsp. salt |
| 1⅓ | cups sugar |
| 1 | 14-oz. pkg. flaked coconut (5⅓ cups) |

**1.** Preheat oven to 325°F. Line cookie sheets with parchment paper. In an extra-large bowl beat egg whites, vanilla, cream of

COCONUT MACAROONS

PUMPKIN COOKIES

tartar, and salt with a mixer on high until soft peaks form (tips curl) (tip, p. 475). Gradually add sugar, about 1 Tbsp. at a time, beating until stiff peaks form (tips stand straight) (tip, p. 475). Fold in coconut, half at a time.

**2.** Drop mixture by small spoonfuls 1 inch apart onto prepared cookie sheets.* Bake 20 to 25 minutes or until bottoms are light brown. Remove; cool on wire racks.

**Makes 60 cookies.**

**\*NOTE** Cover and chill remaining cookie mixture while the first batch bakes.

**EACH COOKIE** *49 cal., 2 g fat (2 g sat. fat), 0 mg chol, 27 mg sodium, 7 g carb., 0 g fiber, 8 g sugars, 0 g pro.*

### CHANGE IT UP

*Dip cooled macaroons halfway into melted chocolate. Let stand on a wire rack set over waxed paper until set. Or drizzle melted chocolate over macaroons.*

## PUMPKIN COOKIES

**HANDS-ON TIME** 30 minutes
**BAKE** 9 minutes per batch at 350°F

2   cups butter, softened
2   cups granulated sugar
2   tsp. baking powder
2   tsp. baking soda
2   tsp. pumpkin pie spice
1   tsp. salt
1   15-oz. can pumpkin
2   eggs
2   tsp. vanilla
4   cups all-purpose flour
1   recipe Penuche Icing

**1.** Preheat oven to 350°F. In a large bowl beat butter with a mixer on medium 30 seconds. Add the next five ingredients (through salt). Beat on medium 2 minutes, scraping bowl as needed. Beat in pumpkin, eggs, and vanilla. Beat in flour.

**2.** Drop dough by small spoonfuls 2 inches apart onto ungreased cookie sheets. Bake 9 to 11 minutes

or until edges are firm and golden. Remove; cool on wire racks.

**3.** Spread cooled cookies with Penuche Icing. If desired, sprinkle with additional pumpkin pie spice.

**Makes about 64 cookies.**

**EACH COOKIE** *149 cal., 7 g fat (5 g sat. fat), 25 mg chol, 152 mg sodium, 20 g carb., 0 g fiber, 13 g sugars, 1 g pro.*

### *PENUCHE ICING*

In a 2-qt. saucepan cook and stir ½ cup butter and ½ cup packed brown sugar over medium heat until brown sugar is dissolved. Stir in 1 tsp. vanilla, 2¾ cups powdered sugar, and enough milk (3 to 4 Tbsp.) to make smooth. Use immediately. (Icing will stiffen as it cools; if necessary, stir in a few drops very hot water at a time until icing returns to spreading consistency.)

# SNICKERDOODLES

**HANDS-ON TIME** 35 minutes
**CHILL** 1 hour
**BAKE** 10 minutes per batch at 375°F

1     cup butter, softened
1½   cups sugar
1     tsp. baking soda
1     tsp. cream of tartar
¼    tsp. salt
2     eggs
1     tsp. vanilla
3     cups all-purpose flour
¼    cup sugar
2     tsp. ground cinnamon

**1.** In a large bowl beat butter with a mixer on medium to high 30 seconds. Add the 1½ cups sugar, the baking soda, cream of tartar, and salt. Beat until combined, scraping sides of bowl occasionally. Beat in eggs and vanilla until combined. Beat in as much of the flour as you can with the mixer. Stir in any remaining flour. Cover and chill dough about 1 hour or until easy to handle.
**2.** Preheat oven to 375°F. In a small bowl combine the ¼ cup sugar and the cinnamon. Shape dough into 1¼-inch balls. Roll balls in sugar mixture to coat. Place 2 inches apart on ungreased cookie sheets.
**3.** Bake 10 to 12 minutes or until bottoms are light brown. Remove; cool on wire racks.
**Makes about 48 cookies.**
**EACH COOKIE** *94 cal., 4 g fat (3 g sat. fat), 19 mg chol., 69 mg sodium, 13 g carb., 0 g fiber, 7 g sugars, 1 g pro.*

# SPRITZ

**HANDS-ON TIME** 25 minutes
**BAKE** 8 minutes per batch at 375°F

1½   cups butter, softened
1     cup granulated sugar
1     tsp. baking powder
1     egg
1     tsp. vanilla
¼    tsp. almond extract (optional)
3½   cups all-purpose flour
      Colored sugar (optional)
1     recipe Powdered Sugar Icing (*p. 571*) (optional)
      Small candies and/or sprinkles (optional)

**1.** Preheat oven to 375°F. In a large bowl beat butter with a mixer on medium to high 30 seconds. Add granulated sugar and baking powder. Beat until combined, scraping sides of bowl occasionally. Beat in egg, vanilla, and, if desired, almond extract until combined. Beat in as much of the flour as you can with the mixer. Stir in any remaining flour.
**2.** Force unchilled dough through a cookie press onto ungreased cookie sheets. If desired, sprinkle cookies with colored sugar. Bake 8 to 10 minutes or until edges are firm but not brown. Remove; cool on wire rack. If desired, drizzle cookies with Powdered Sugar Icing and decorate with small candies.
**Makes about 84 cookies.**
**EACH COOKIE** *58 cal., 3 g fat (2 g sat. fat), 11 mg chol., 27 mg sodium, 6 g carb., 0 g fiber, 2 g sugars, 1 g pro.*

SPRITZ

**PEPPERMINT SPRITZ** Prepare as directed, except substitute 1 tsp. peppermint extract or 14 drops peppermint oil for the vanilla and almond extract. If desired, drizzle cookies with Powdered Sugar Icing and immediately sprinkle with finely crushed striped round peppermint candies.

# SUGAR COOKIES

**HANDS-ON TIME** 35 minutes
**BAKE** 12 minutes per batch at 300°F
**COOL** 2 minutes

½   cup butter, softened
½   cup shortening
2   cups sugar
1   tsp. baking soda
1   tsp. cream of tartar
⅛   tsp. salt
3   egg yolks
½   tsp. vanilla
1¾   cups all-purpose flour

**1.** Preheat oven to 300°F. In a large bowl beat butter and shortening with a mixer on medium to high 30 seconds. Add sugar, baking soda, cream of tartar, and salt. Beat mixture until combined, scraping sides of bowl occasionally. Beat in egg yolks and vanilla. Beat in as much of the flour as you can with the mixer. Stir in any remaining flour.
**2.** Shape dough into 1-inch balls. Place balls 2 inches apart on ungreased cookie sheets.
**3.** Bake 12 to 14 minutes or until edges are set; do not let edges brown. Cool cookies 2 minutes on cookie sheet. Remove; cool on wire racks. **Makes about 48 cookies.**
**EACH COOKIE** *88 cal., 4 g fat (2 g sat. fat), 18 mg chol., 47 mg sodium, 12 g carb., 0 g fiber, 8 g sugars, 1 g pro.*

# PEANUT BUTTER COOKIES

**HANDS-ON TIME** 35 minutes
**BAKE** 7 minutes per batch at 375°F
**COOL** 1 minute

| | |
|---|---|
| 1 | cup peanut butter |
| ½ | cup butter, softened |
| ½ | cup shortening |
| 1 | cup packed brown sugar |
| ½ | cup granulated sugar |
| 1 | tsp. baking soda |
| 1 | tsp. baking powder |
| 2 | eggs |
| 1 | tsp. vanilla |
| 2¼ | cups all-purpose flour |

**1.** Preheat oven to 375°F. In a large bowl beat peanut butter, butter, and shortening with a mixer on medium to high 30 seconds. Add the sugars, baking soda, and baking powder. Beat until combined, scraping sides of bowl occasionally. Beat in eggs and vanilla until combined. Beat in as much of the flour as you can with the mixer. Stir in any remaining flour.
**2.** Shape dough into 1¼-inch balls. Roll in additional granulated sugar to coat. Place 2 inches apart on ungreased cookie sheets. Flatten by pressing crisscross marks with the tines of a fork. Bake 7 to 9 minutes or until edges are light brown. Let cool on cookie sheets 1 minute. Remove; cool on wire racks. **Makes about 75 cookies.**
**EACH COOKIE** *79 cal., 5 g fat (2 g sat. fat), 8 mg chol., 50 mg sodium, 9 g carb., 0 g fiber, 5 g sugars, 1 g pro.*

### GLUTEN-FREE PEANUT BUTTER COOKIES
Preheat oven to 375°F. Grease cookie sheets or line with parchment paper. In a medium bowl stir together 1 cup each sugar and peanut butter and 1 egg until well mixed. Shape and bake as directed in Step 2. **Makes 32 cookies.**

SANDIES

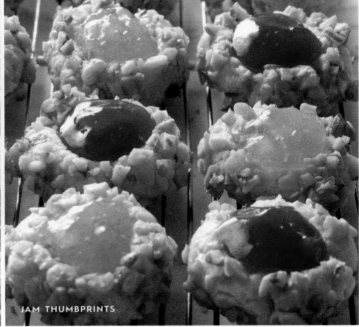

JAM THUMBPRINTS

## SANDIES

**HANDS-ON TIME** 35 minutes
**CHILL** 30 minutes
**BAKE** 15 minutes per batch at 325°F

1    cup butter, softened
½    cup powdered sugar
1    Tbsp. water
1    tsp. vanilla
2    cups all-purpose flour
1½   cups finely chopped pecans, toasted (tip, *p. 18*)
1    cup powdered sugar

**1.** In a large bowl beat butter with a mixer on medium to high 30 seconds. Add the ½ cup powdered sugar. Beat until combined, scraping sides of bowl occasionally. Beat in the water and vanilla until combined. Beat in as much of the flour as you can with the mixer. Stir in any remaining flour and the pecans. Cover and chill dough 30 to 60 minutes or until easy to handle.
**2.** Preheat oven to 325°F. Shape dough into 1-inch balls or 2½-inch logs. Place 1 inch apart on ungreased cookie sheets. Bake about 15 minutes or until bottoms are light brown.

Remove; cool on wire racks. Place the 1 cup powdered sugar in a large plastic bag. Add cooled cookies in batches to bag. Gently shake to coat. **Makes about 55 (1-inch) ball cookies.**

**EACH COOKIE** *80 cal., 6 g fat (2 g sat. fat), 9 mg chol., 24 mg sodium, 7 g carb., 0 g fiber, 3 g sugars, 1 g pro.*

## JAM THUMBPRINTS

**HANDS-ON TIME** 25 minutes
**CHILL** 1 hour
**BAKE** 10 minutes per batch at 375°F

⅔    cup butter, softened
½    cup sugar
2    egg yolks
1    tsp. vanilla
1½   cups all-purpose flour
2    egg whites, lightly beaten
1    cup finely chopped walnuts or pecans
⅓    to ½ cup jam or preserves

**1.** In a large bowl beat butter with a mixer on medium to high 30 seconds. Add sugar. Beat until combined, scraping sides of bowl occasionally. Beat in egg yolks and vanilla until combined. Beat in as much of the flour as you can with

the mixer. Stir in any remaining flour. Cover and chill dough about 1 hour or until easy to handle.
**2.** Preheat oven to 375°F. Grease cookie sheets or line with parchment paper. Shape dough into 1-inch balls. Roll balls in egg whites, then in walnuts. Place 1 inch apart on the prepared cookie sheets. Press your thumb into the center of each ball. Bake 10 to 12 minutes or until bottoms are light brown. If the cookie centers have puffed up during baking, press again with the back of a small spoon. Remove; cool on a wire rack. Just before serving, fill centers with jam. **Makes about 30 cookies.**
**EACH COOKIE** *112 cal., 7 g fat (3 g sat. fat), 25 mg chol., 35 mg sodium, 11 g carb., 0 g fiber, 5 g sugars, 2 g pro.*

**CHANGE IT UP**

*For the nuts, use finely chopped peanuts, almonds, hazelnuts, pistachios, or cashews. Instead of jam, fill cookies with chocolate-hazelnut spread, Lemon Curd (p. 603), dulce de leche, or desired frosting (pp. 538–539).*

CHOCOLATE CRINKLES

GINGER COOKIES

# CHOCOLATE CRINKLES

**HANDS-ON TIME** 1 hour
**BAKE** 8 minutes per batch at 350°F
**COOL** 2 minutes

- 4 oz. unsweetened chocolate, chopped
- ½ cup shortening
- ¼ cup butter
- 3 eggs, lightly beaten
- 1¾ cups granulated sugar
- 2 tsp. baking powder
- ¼ tsp. baking soda
- ¼ tsp. salt
- 2 tsp. vanilla
- 1⅓ cups all-purpose flour
- ⅓ cup unsweetened cocoa powder
- ¼ cup granulated sugar
- ⅔ cup powdered sugar

**1.** In a 1-qt. saucepan cook and stir chocolate, shortening, and butter over low heat until melted. Cool.
**2.** Preheat oven to 350°F. Lightly grease cookie sheets. In a bowl combine the next five ingredients (through salt). Stir in melted chocolate mixture and vanilla. Stir in flour and cocoa powder.
**3.** Shape dough into 1½-inch balls. Roll balls in the ¼ cup granulated sugar, then in powdered sugar to coat. Place balls 2 inches apart on prepared cookie sheets. Bake 8 to 10 minutes or just until edges are firm and cracks appear slightly moist. Cool on cookie sheets 2 minutes. Remove; cool on wire racks. **Makes about 36 cookies.**
**EACH COOKIE** *134 cal., 6 g fat (3 g sat. fat), 19 mg chol., 69 mg sodium, 18 g carb., 1 g fiber, 13 g sugars, 2 g pro.*

# GINGER COOKIES

**HANDS-ON TIME** 40 minutes
**BAKE** 8 minutes per batch at 350°F
**COOL** 2 minutes

- 4½ cups all-purpose flour
- 4 tsp. ground ginger
- 2 tsp. baking soda
- 1½ tsp. ground cinnamon
- 1 tsp. ground cloves
- ¼ tsp. salt
- 1½ cups shortening
- 2 cups granulated sugar
- 2 eggs
- ½ cup molasses
- ¾ cup granulated sugar or coarse sugar

**1.** Preheat oven to 350°F. In a medium bowl stir together flour, ginger, baking soda, cinnamon, cloves, and salt. In a large bowl beat shortening with a mixer on low 30 seconds. Add 2 cups granulated sugar. Beat until combined, scraping sides of bowl occasionally. Beat in eggs and molasses until combined. Beat in as much of the flour mixture as you can with the mixer. Stir in any remaining flour mixture.
**2.** Shape dough into 1- or 2-inch balls. Roll balls in ¾ cup granulated sugar. Place 2 to 3 inches apart on ungreased cookie sheets. Bake 8 to 9 minutes for small cookies, 11 to 13 minutes for big cookies, or until bottoms are light brown and tops are puffed (do not overbake). Cool on sheet 2 minutes. Remove; cool on a wire rack. **Makes about 120 small cookies or 24 large cookies.**
**EACH SMALL COOKIE** *62 cal., 3 g fat (1 g sat. fat), 4 mg chol., 28 mg sodium, 9 g carb., 0 g fiber, 5 g sugars, 1 g pro.*

## *STORING COOKIES*

- Cool cookies completely before storing. Layer unfrosted or unfilled cookies between sheets of waxed paper in airtight containers or freezer containers.
- Store cookies or bars that have creamy or delicate toppings in a single layer.
- Don't store crisp and soft cookies in the same container.
- Store cookies and bars at room temperature up to 3 days or freeze up to 3 months. Thaw, if necessary, and frost or fill before serving.

# PEANUT BUTTER BLOSSOMS

**HANDS-ON TIME** 25 minutes
**BAKE** 10 minutes per batch at 350°F

½  cup shortening
½  cup peanut butter
½  cup granulated sugar
½  cup packed brown sugar
1  tsp. baking powder
⅛  tsp. baking soda
1  egg
2  Tbsp. milk
1  tsp. vanilla
1¾ cups all-purpose flour
¼  cup granulated sugar
   Milk chocolate stars

**1.** Preheat oven to 350°F. In a large bowl beat shortening and peanut butter with a mixer on medium to high 30 seconds. Add the ½ cup granulated sugar, the brown sugar, baking powder, and baking soda. Beat until combined, scraping sides of bowl. Beat in egg, milk, and vanilla until combined. Beat in as much of the flour as you can with the mixer. Stir in any remaining flour.
**2.** Shape dough into 1-inch balls. Roll balls in the ¼ cup granulated sugar. Place 2 inches apart on an ungreased cookie sheet. Bake 10 to 12 minutes or until edges are firm and bottoms are light brown. Immediately press chocolate stars into cookie centers. Remove; cool on a wire rack. **Makes about 54 cookies.**
**EACH COOKIE** *96 cal., 5 g fat (2 g sat. fat), 5 mg chol., 27 mg sodium, 11 g carb., 0 g fiber, 8 g sugars, 2 g pro.*

PECAN TASSIES

## PECAN TASSIES

**HANDS-ON TIME** 30 minutes
**BAKE** 25 minutes at 325°F
**COOL** 5 minutes

½ cup butter, softened
3 oz. cream cheese, softened
1 cup all-purpose flour
1 egg, lightly beaten
¾ cup packed brown sugar
1 Tbsp. butter, melted
⅔ cup coarsely chopped pecans

**1.** Preheat oven to 325°F. In a bowl beat the ½ cup butter and cream cheese until combined. Stir in flour. Shape dough into 24 balls. Press balls into bottoms and up sides of 24 ungreased 1¾-inch muffin cups.
**2.** For filling, in a bowl stir together egg, brown sugar, and butter. Stir in pecans. Add a small spoonful of filling to each pastry-lined cup.
**3.** Bake 25 to 30 minutes or until pastry is light brown. Cool in pan on a wire rack 5 minutes. Remove; cool on rack. **Makes 24 tassies.**

**EACH TASSIE** *119 cal., 8 g fat (4 g sat. fat), 24 mg chol., 47 mg sodium, 11 g carb., 0 g fiber, 7 g sugars, 1 g pro.*

## CHERRY PIE BITES

**HANDS-ON TIME** 30 minutes
**BAKE** 25 minutes at 325°F
**COOL** 5 minutes

½ cup butter, softened
3 oz. cream cheese, softened
1 cup + 2 Tbsp. all-purpose flour
2 Tbsp. chopped toasted walnuts or pecans (tip, p. 18)
2 Tbsp. packed brown sugar
⅛ tsp. ground nutmeg
1½ Tbsp. butter
2 cups fresh or frozen unsweetened pitted tart red cherries, thawed
⅓ cup granulated sugar
2 tsp. cornstarch

**1.** Preheat oven to 325°F. In a medium bowl beat the ½ cup butter and the cream cheese with a mixer on medium to high until combined. Stir in the 1 cup flour. Shape dough into 24 balls. Press the balls into the bottoms and up the sides of 24 ungreased 1¾-inch muffin cups.
**2.** For streusel, in a small bowl stir together the 2 Tbsp. flour, the walnuts, brown sugar, and nutmeg.

Using a pastry blender, cut in the 1½ Tbsp. butter until mixture is crumbly.
**3.** For filling, in a 1- or 1½-qt. saucepan combine cherries, granulated sugar, and cornstarch. Cook over medium heat until cherries release juices, stirring occasionally. Continue to cook, stirring constantly, over medium heat until thick and bubbly. Spoon about 1 heaping tsp. of the filling into each pastry-lined cup. Sprinkle filled cups evenly with streusel.
**4.** Bake 25 to 30 minutes or until edges are light brown. Cool bites in pan on a wire rack 5 minutes. Carefully remove; cool on wire rack.
**Makes 24 tassies.**

**EACH TASSIE** *100 cal., 6 g fat (4 g sat. fat), 16 mg chol., 52 mg sodium, 10 g carb., 0 g fiber, 5 g sugars, 1 g pro.*

CHERRY PIE BITES

Use a tassie tamper or your fingers to press the pastry dough balls into the bottom and up the sides of each muffin cup.

Carefully spoon a heaping teaspoon of the filling into each of the pastry dough-lined cups, being sure to get some cherries into each cup. Clean up any drips on the pan; the filling could burn during baking.

# GINGERBREAD CUTOUTS

**HANDS-ON TIME** 50 minutes
**CHILL** 1 hour
**BAKE** 6 minutes per batch at 375°F
**COOL** 1 minute

½  cup shortening
¼  cup butter, softened
½  cup granulated sugar
1  tsp. baking powder
1  tsp. ground ginger
½  tsp. baking soda
½  tsp. ground cinnamon
½  tsp. ground cloves
¼  tsp. salt
1  egg
½  cup molasses
1  Tbsp. cider vinegar
3  cups all-purpose flour
1  recipe Royal Icing (*p. 571*) or
   Powdered Sugar Icing (*p. 571*)
   (optional)

**1.** In a large bowl beat shortening and butter with a mixer on medium to high 30 seconds. Add the next seven ingredients (through salt). Beat until combined, scraping bowl occasionally. Beat in egg, molasses, and vinegar. Beat in as much flour as you can with the mixer. Stir in any remaining flour. Divide dough in half. Cover and chill 1 hour or until dough is easy to handle.

**2.** Preheat oven to 375°F. On a lightly floured surface roll a dough portion to ¼ inch thick. Cut with 3- to 4-inch cutters; reroll scraps as needed. Place cutouts 1 inch apart on ungreased cookie sheets. Repeat with remaining dough.

**3.** Bake 6 to 8 minutes or until edges are firm. Cool on cookie sheets 1 minute. Remove; cool on a wire rack. If desired, decorate with Royal Icing. **Makes about 24 cookies.**

**EACH COOKIE** *151 cal., 7 g fat (2 g sat. fat), 13 mg chol., 92 mg sodium, 21 g carb., 0 g fiber, 9 g sugars, 2 g pro.*

**SHAPE SWAPS**
You can make different shortbread shapes. On a lightly floured surface roll or pat dough until ½ inch thick. Use cookie cutters or a knife to cut desired shapes. Place 1 inch apart on ungreased cookie sheets. Bake 20 to 25 minutes.

**BUTTER-PECAN** Prepare as directed, except substitute brown sugar for granulated sugar. After cutting in butter, stir in 2 Tbsp. finely chopped pecans. Sprinkle mixture with ½ tsp. vanilla before kneading. Press pecan halves into wide ends of wedges before baking.

**LEMON-POPPY SEED** Prepare as directed, except stir in 1 Tbsp. poppy seeds with the flour mixture and add 1 tsp. lemon zest with the butter. Before serving, sprinkle with powdered sugar.

**CHOCOLATE-ORANGE** Prepare as directed, except add 1½ tsp. orange zest with the butter. After cutting in butter, stir in ⅓ cup miniature semisweet chocolate chips.

**CHERRY-PISTACHIO** Prepare as directed, except after cutting in butter, stir in 2 Tbsp. each snipped dried cherries and finely chopped pistachio nuts. Drizzle cooled cookies with melted white chocolate. Sprinkle with additional pistachios.

# SHORTBREAD

**HANDS-ON TIME** 15 minutes
**BAKE** 25 minutes at 325°F
**COOL** 5 minutes

1¼ cups all-purpose flour
3 Tbsp. sugar
½ cup butter

**1.** Preheat oven to 325°F. In a medium bowl combine flour and sugar. Use a pastry blender to cut in butter until mixture resembles fine crumbs and starts to cling. Form the mixture into a ball and knead until smooth.

**2.** To make shortbread wedges, on an ungreased cookie sheet pat or roll the dough into an 8-inch circle. Make a scalloped edge. Cut circle into 16 wedges. Prick wedges with tines of a fork. Leave wedges in the circle. Bake 25 to 30 minutes or until bottom just starts to brown and center is set. Cut circle into the wedges again while warm. Cool on cookie sheet 5 minutes. Remove; cool on a wire rack.
**Makes 16 cookies.**
**EACH COOKIE** 96 cal., 6 g fat (4 g sat. fat), 15 mg chol., 41 mg sodium, 10 g carb., 0 g fiber, 2 g sugars, 1 g pro.

IT'S SIMPLE—IF A COOKIE RECIPE CALLS FOR BUTTER, USE REAL BUTTER. STEER CLEAR OF MARGARINE AND BUTTERY SPREADS. THE WATER-TO-FAT RATIO VARIES TOO MUCH AND WILL AFFECT THE TEXTURE AND SPREAD OF THE COOKIE.

## SUGAR COOKIE CUTOUTS

**HANDS-ON TIME** 40 minutes
**CHILL** 30 minutes
**BAKE** 7 minutes per batch at 375°F

| | |
|---|---|
| 1 | cup butter, softened |
| 1¼ | cups granulated sugar |
| 1½ | tsp. baking powder |
| ½ | tsp. salt |
| 2 | eggs |
| 2 | tsp. vanilla |
| 3 | cups all-purpose flour |
| 1 | recipe Powdered Sugar Icing, Royal Icing, or Creamy White Frosting *(opposite)* (optional) |

**1.** In a large bowl beat butter with a mixer on medium to high 30 seconds. Add granulated sugar, baking powder, and salt. Beat until combined, scraping bowl occasionally. Add eggs and vanilla; beat until combined. Beat in as much of the flour as you can. Stir in any remaining flour. Divide dough in half. Cover; chill about 30 minutes or until dough is easy to handle.
**2.** Preheat oven to 375°F. On a lightly floured surface roll a dough portion to ⅛ to ¼ inch thick. Using 2½-inch cookie cutters, cut dough into desired shapes (dip cutters in flour to prevent sticking). Place cutouts 1 inch apart on ungreased cookie sheets. Repeat with the remaining dough.
**3.** Bake about 7 minutes or until edges are firm and bottoms are very light brown. Remove; cool on a wire rack. If desired, frost with desired icing and, if desired, top with *sprinkles* Let stand until icing is set. **Makes about 52 cookies.**
**EACH COOKIE** *80 cal., 4 g fat (2 g sat. fat), 17 mg chol., 63 mg sodium, 10 g carb., 0 g fiber, 5 g sugars, 1 g pro.*

**SUGAR ON TOP**

For a subtle sparkly touch, sprinkle colored sugar over cookie cutouts before baking. The sugar will bake into the dough for decoration, so the cookies need no icing.

## POWDERED SUGAR ICING

In a small bowl combine 1½ cups powdered sugar, ¼ tsp. vanilla or almond extract, and 2 Tbsp. milk. If necessary, add additional milk, 1 tsp. at a time, to make icing drizzling consistency.

## CREAMY WHITE FROSTING

In a large bowl beat 1 cup shortening, 1½ tsp. vanilla, and, if desired, ½ tsp. almond extract on medium 30 seconds. Gradually add about 2 cups powdered sugar, beating well. Beat in 2 Tbsp. milk. Gradually beat in 2 cups powdered sugar and 1 to 2 Tbsp. milk to reach spreading consistency.

## ROYAL ICING

In a large bowl stir together one 16-oz. pkg. powdered sugar (4 cups), 3 Tbsp. meringue powder, and ½ tsp. cream of tartar. Add ½ cup warm water and 1 tsp. vanilla. Beat on low until combined; beat on high 7 to 10 minutes or until icing is very stiff. Beat in additional water to reach desired consistency for piping or "flooding" (photo, *right*). Cover bowl with a damp paper towel to prevent icing from drying out.

**MERINGUE POWDER**
Look for meringue powder in hobby stores where cake-decorating supplies are sold.

# ROLL IT OUT DUST THE WORK SURFACE WITH FLOUR, USING JUST ENOUGH FLOUR TO PREVENT STICKING, OR USE A PASTRY CLOTH.

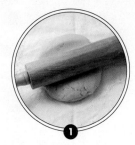

To roll out dough, place a rolling pin in the middle of the dough portion and roll to the edge. Continue rolling from middle to edge, giving the rolling pin a quarter turn with each stroke. This creates an even thickness across the dough.

It's up to you whether you want thin (⅛-inch) or thicker (¼-inch) cookies. Thinner cookies will be crispier; thicker cookies will be softer. (Keep a close eye on thinner cookies when baking because they can overbake quickly.)

Cut out cookie shapes as close to each other as possible to avoid excess dough scraps. You can reroll scraps, but do not overwork the dough. Usually, one or two rerolls is all you should do for tender cookies.

# DECORATE USE ROYAL ICING IF YOU WANT TO MAKE ELABORATELY DECORATED COOKIES. IT DRIES FIRM FOR EASY STORING.

Food coloring in paste and gel forms creates bright colors and doesn't thin icing like liquid coloring. Use a clean toothpick to add paste coloring to icing a little at a time until you reach the desired depth of color. (If you use liquid coloring, adjust icing consistency *after* adding coloring.)

Decorating can be as easy as piping icing from a heavy resealable plastic bag with a tiny hole cut in one corner. Or look in the cake decorating aisle of hobby stores for disposable plastic pastry bags and assorted decorating tips—small round and small star tips are good to start with.

To apply Royal Icing, pipe a thin line around cookie edges. "Flood" the rest of the cookie with a layer of glaze-consistency icing. Spread icing to edges with a thin spatula. If desired, while icing is still wet, pipe a second color of icing in designs on cookies.

# COOKIES AND CREAM ICEBOX COOKIES

**HANDS-ON TIME** 30 minutes
**CHILL** 1 hour
**BAKE** 7 minutes per batch at 375°F

⅔ cup butter, softened
¾ cup sugar
1 tsp. baking powder
¼ tsp. salt
1 egg
1 tsp. vanilla
2 cups all-purpose flour
1 cup crushed chocolate
   sandwich cookies with white
   filling (about 10 cookies)

**1.** In a large bowl beat butter with a mixer on medium to high 30 seconds. Add sugar, baking powder, and salt. Beat until combined, scraping as needed. Beat in egg and vanilla. Beat in as much of the flour as you can with the mixer. Stir in any remaining flour. Stir in ¾ cup of the crushed cookies. If necessary, cover and chill dough until easy to handle.
**2.** Shape dough into a 2-inch-diameter roll. Coat roll with the remaining ¼ cup crushed cookies. Wrap in plastic wrap or waxed paper; chill until firm enough to slice (1 to 2 hours in refrigerator or 30 minutes in freezer).
**3.** Preheat oven to 375°F. Use a serrated knife to cut roll into ¼-inch slices; place 2 inches apart on an ungreased cookie sheet.
**4.** Bake 7 to 9 minutes or until bottoms are light brown. Cool on cookie sheet 2 minutes. Remove; cool on wire rack. **Makes about 24 cookies.**

**EACH COOKIE** 133 cal., 6 g fat (4 g sat. fat), 21 mg chol., 108 mg sodium, 18 g carb., 0 g fiber, 8 g sugars, 2 g pro.

## READY TO BAKE
Icebox cookies are the original make-ahead treat. Wrap the dough log in plastic wrap and foil; freeze up to 3 months until you're ready to bake. Let dough stand at room temp 20 minutes; slice and bake as directed.

CINNAMON ROLL COOKIES

ALMOND BISCOTTI

## CINNAMON ROLL COOKIES

**HANDS-ON TIME** 30 minutes
**CHILL** 30 minutes
**FREEZE** 30 minutes
**BAKE** 8 minutes per batch at 375°F
**COOL** 1 minute

1    cup butter, softened
⅔    cup granulated sugar
½    tsp. salt
1    egg
1    Tbsp. vanilla
2    cups all-purpose flour
1    egg, lightly beaten
½    cup packed brown sugar
2    tsp. ground cinnamon, pumpkin pie spice, or apple pie spice
1    recipe Cream Cheese Icing

**1.** In a large bowl beat butter with a mixer on medium to high 30 seconds. Add granulated sugar and salt. Beat on medium 2 minutes, scraping sides of bowl. Beat in 1 egg and the vanilla. Beat in flour.
**2.** Wrap dough in plastic wrap; chill until easy to handle (30 to 60 minutes). On a floured surface roll dough to a 15×10-inch rectangle. Brush the lightly beaten egg evenly over rectangle. Stir together brown sugar and cinnamon; sprinkle over dough. Cut rectangle in half crosswise. Starting from short sides of dough halves, roll up dough. Place rolls on a baking sheet or tray, cover, and freeze about 30 minutes or until firm enough to slice.

**3.** Preheat oven to 375°F. Line a cookie sheet with parchment paper. Use a serrated knife to cut rolls into ¼-inch-thick slices; place 2 inches apart on cookie sheet.
**4.** Bake 8 to 10 minutes or until edges are light brown. Cool on cookie sheet 1 minute. Remove; cool on a wire rack. Spread Cream Cheese Icing over cookies. **Makes about 40 cookies.**

**EACH COOKIE** *108 cal., 6 g fat (3 g sat. fat), 24 mg chol., 77 mg sodium, 13 g carb., 0 g fiber, 8 g sugars, 1 g pro.*

### *CREAM CHEESE ICING*

In a medium bowl beat 2 oz. softened cream cheese and 1 Tbsp. softened butter with a mixer on medium until smooth. Beat in ¾ cup powdered sugar and enough milk (2 to 3 Tbsp.) to make desired consistency.

## ALMOND BISCOTTI

**HANDS-ON TIME** 25 minutes
**BAKE** 41 minutes at 325°F
**COOL** 15 minutes

2¾   cups all-purpose flour
1½   cups sugar
1½   tsp. baking powder
1    tsp. salt
2    eggs
2    egg yolks
6    Tbsp. butter, melted

1½   cups coarsely chopped almonds
1    Tbsp. sugar
     Melted semisweet or white baking chocolate (optional)

**1.** Preheat oven to 325°F. Line two large cookie sheets with parchment paper.
**2.** In a large bowl combine flour, the 1½ cups sugar, the baking powder, and salt. Make a well in the center of the flour mixture. In a small bowl lightly beat eggs and egg yolks. Stir the melted butter into beaten eggs. Place egg mixture in the well in flour mixture; stir flour mixture until the dough starts to form a ball. Stir in almonds (dough will be crumbly). Use your hands to knead the dough until it comes together.
**3.** Turn the dough out onto a lightly floured surface. Divide dough into three equal portions. Shape each portion into a 14-inch roll. Place two rolls about 3 inches apart on one of the prepared cookie sheets. Place remaining roll on remaining cookie sheet; flatten rolls slightly to about 1½ inches wide. Sprinkle rolls with the 1 Tbsp. sugar.
**4.** Bake on separate oven racks 25 to 30 minutes or until rolls are firm and light brown, rotating sheets halfway through. Cool cookie sheets on wire racks 15 minutes.
**5.** Transfer rolls to a cutting board. Use a serrated knife to diagonally cut rolls into ½-inch slices. Put slices, cut sides down, on cookie sheets.
**6.** Bake 8 to 10 minutes. Turn slices over; bake 8 to 10 minutes more or until light golden brown. Remove; cool on wire racks. Biscotti will continue to crisp as they cool. If desired, drizzle melted chocolate over cookies. Let stand until set. **Makes about 60 cookies.**

**EACH COOKIE** *71 cal., 3 g fat (1 g sat. fat), 15 mg chol., 63 mg sodium, 10 g carb., 0 g fiber, 5 g sugars, 1 g pro.*

## BLONDIES

**HANDS-ON TIME** 20 minutes
**COOL** 10 minutes
**BAKE** 45 minutes at 350°F

| | |
|---|---|
| 4 | cups packed brown sugar |
| 1⅓ | cups butter |
| 4 | cups all-purpose flour |
| 2 | tsp. baking powder |
| ½ | tsp. baking soda |
| 4 | eggs |
| 1 | Tbsp. vanilla |

**1.** Preheat oven to 350°F. In a 4-qt. saucepan cook and stir brown sugar and butter over medium heat about 6 minutes or until melted and smooth. Cool 10 minutes.
**2.** Meanwhile, line a 13×9-inch baking pan with foil, extending the foil over edges (tip, p. 478). Grease foil. In a medium bowl stir together flour, baking powder, and baking soda. Stir eggs and vanilla into brown sugar mixture. Stir in flour mixture. Spread in prepared pan.
**3.** Bake 45 minutes. Cool slightly in pan on a wire rack. Cool completely. Use foil to lift uncut bars out of pan; cut into bars. **Makes 36 bars.**

**EACH BAR** *231 cal., 8 g fat (5 g sat. fat), 40 mg chol., 119 mg sodium, 38 g carb., 1 g fiber, 27 g sugars, 2 g pro.*

**CHOCOLATE-PECAN BLONDIES**
Prepare as directed, except after spreading batter in pan, sprinkle evenly with ¾ cup chopped pecans and ¾ cup semisweet chocolate or white baking chips. Bake as directed.

**CINNAMON BLONDIES** Prepare as directed, except stir in 1 Tbsp. ground cinnamon with flour. Bake bars. Combine ½ cup granulated sugar and 2 tsp. ground cinnamon. Brush 2 Tbsp. melted butter over warm bars. Sprinkle with mixture.

**PEANUT BUTTER BROWNIES** Prepare as directed, except fold ¾ cup chopped chocolate-covered peanut butter cups into batter. Sprinkle frosted brownies with additional peanut butter cups.

**CHOCOLATE BAR BROWNIES** Prepare as directed, except after baking, immediately sprinkle with one 4.63-oz. pkg. milk chocolate squares (such as Ghirardelli—10 squares total), broken into pieces. Omit the frosting.

**MOCHA BROWNIES** Prepare as directed, except stir 1 tsp. instant espresso coffee powder into flour mixture. Frost as directed; sprinkle with chopped chocolate-covered coffee beans.

# FUDGY BROWNIES

**HANDS-ON TIME** 20 minutes
**BAKE** 30 minutes at 350°F

½   cup butter, cut up
3   oz. unsweetened chocolate, coarsely chopped
⅔   cup all-purpose flour
¼   tsp. baking soda
1   cup granulated sugar
2   eggs
1   tsp. vanilla
½   cup chopped nuts (optional)
1   recipe Chocolate Cream Cheese Frosting (optional)

**1.** In a 2-qt. saucepan cook and stir butter and chocolate over low heat until melted; cool about 10 minutes.
**2.** Meanwhile, preheat oven to 350°F. Line an 8-inch square baking pan with foil, extending foil over edges (tip, *p. 478*). Grease foil. In a bowl combine flour and baking soda.
**3.** Stir granulated sugar into cooled chocolate mixture. Add eggs, one at a time, beating with a spoon until combined. Stir in vanilla. Stir in flour mixture just until combined. If desired, stir in nuts. Spread batter in prepared pan.
**4.** Bake 30 minutes. Cool in pan on a wire rack. If desired, spread with Chocolate Cream Cheese Frosting. Use foil to lift uncut brownies out of pan; cut into bars. Cover and store frosted brownies in the refrigerator.
**Makes 16 brownies.**

**EACH BROWNIE** *162 cal., 9 g fat (6 g sat. fat), 39 mg chol., 76 mg sodium, 18 g carb., 1 g fiber, 13 g sugars, 2 g pro.*

## CHOCOLATE CREAM CHEESE FROSTING

In a 1- or 1½-qt. saucepan cook and stir 1 cup semisweet chocolate pieces over low heat until melted; cool. In a medium bowl stir together 6 oz. softened cream cheese and ½ cup powdered sugar. Stir in melted chocolate.

**DONENESS TEST**
Since Fudgy Brownies are so moist, a toothpick test doesn't work. Use an oven thermometer to make sure your oven temp is accurate (adjust the temperature as necessary if it's not). Bake these brownies no longer than 30 minutes.

LEMON BARS

APPLE PIE BARS

## LEMON BARS

**HANDS-ON TIME** 10 minutes
**BAKE** 33 minutes at 350°F

2    cups all-purpose flour
½    cup powdered sugar
2    Tbsp. cornstarch
¼    tsp. salt
¾    cup butter, cut up
4    eggs, lightly beaten
1½   cups granulated sugar
3    Tbsp. all-purpose flour
1    tsp. lemon zest
¾    cup lemon juice
¼    cup half-and-half or milk
     Powdered sugar

**LEMON ZEST** is easiest to remove with a Microplane (rasp) grater. It's worth the investment (and you can use it to grate fresh nutmeg, too) (info, p. 476).

**1.** Preheat oven to 350°F. Line a 13×9-inch baking pan with foil, extending foil over edges of the pan (tip, *p. 478*). Grease foil.
**2.** In a large bowl combine the first four ingredients (through salt). Use a pastry blender to cut in butter until mixture resembles coarse crumbs. Press mixture into bottom of the prepared pan. Bake 18 to 20 minutes or until edges are light brown.
**3.** Meanwhile, for filling, in a medium bowl stir together the next six ingredients (through half-and-half). Pour filling over hot crust.
**4.** Bake 15 to 20 minutes more or until center is set. Cool completely in pan on a wire rack. Use foil to lift uncut bars out of pan; cut into bars. Just before serving, sift powdered sugar over tops. Cover and store in the refrigerator. **Makes 36 bars.**
**EACH BAR** *115 cal., 5 g fat (3 g sat. fat), 34 mg chol., 52 mg sodium, 17 g carb., 0 g fiber, 10 g sugars, 2 g pro.*

## APPLE PIE BARS

**HANDS-ON TIME** 40 minutes
**BAKE** 45 minutes at 350°F

3¾   cups all-purpose flour
2    Tbsp. sugar
1½   tsp. salt
¾    cup shortening
⅓    cup butter, chilled and cut up
⅔    to 1 cup ice water
8    cups thinly sliced, peeled tart cooking apples (8 to 10)
1¼   cups sugar
2    tsp. ground cinnamon
1    egg white
1    Tbsp. cold water

**1.** Preheat oven to 350°F. In a large bowl combine flour, the 2 Tbsp. sugar, and the salt. Using a pastry blender, cut in shortening and butter until pea size. Sprinkle 1 Tbsp. of the ice water over part of the flour mixture; toss with a fork. Push moistened dough to one side of bowl. Repeat moistening flour mixture, 1 Tbsp. ice water at a time, until flour mixture is moistened. Shape two-thirds of the dough into a ball. Shape remaining dough into a ball.
**2.** Place large ball of dough between two pieces of lightly floured waxed paper. Roll dough to a 17×12-inch rectangle. Remove top piece of waxed paper. Carefully invert pastry into a 15×10-inch baking pan. Peel off waxed paper. Press dough up sides of pan; trim edges (if needed, use trimmed pieces to patch any holes). Top with apples. In a bowl combine the 1¼ cups sugar and the cinnamon, reserving ⅓ cup mixture. Sprinkle the remaining cinnamon-sugar mixture over apples.
**3.** Place the small ball of dough between two pieces of lightly floured waxed paper. Roll dough into a 16×11-inch rectangle. Remove top piece of waxed paper. If desired, cut shapes from center of pastry. Carefully invert pastry over apple layer. Peel off waxed paper. Pinch edges of pastry together to seal. If you didn't cut out shapes, cut slits in top pastry. In a bowl whisk together egg white and the 1 Tbsp. cold water; brush over pastry. Sprinkle reserved cinnamon-sugar mixture over pastry.
**4.** Bake about 45 minutes or until golden brown and apples are tender. Cool in pan on a wire rack.
**Makes 32 bars**
**EACH BAR** *171 cal., 7 g fat (2 g sat. fat), 5 mg chol., 127 mg sodium, 26 g carb., 2 g fiber, 13 g sugars, 2 g pro.*

CHOCOLATE REVEL BARS

BUTTERMILK BROWNIES

## CHOCOLATE REVEL BARS

**HANDS-ON TIME** 30 minutes
**BAKE** 25 minutes at 350°F

**TOP IT OFF**
You want to distribute the oats mixture evenly over the filling in Step 4. Use your fingers to grab bits of dough—slightly flatten some of them—and place them randomly over the filling. Leave small gaps so a little of the filling peeks through.

1    cup butter, softened
2    cups packed brown sugar
1    tsp. baking soda
2    eggs
4    tsp. vanilla
2½   cups all-purpose flour
3    cups quick-cooking rolled oats
1½   cups semisweet chocolate chips
1    14-oz. can (1¼ cups) sweetened condensed milk
½    cup chopped walnuts or pecans

**1.** Preheat oven to 350°F. Line a 15×10-inch baking pan with foil, extending foil over edges of pan (tip, p. 478). Set aside 2 Tbsp. butter.
**2.** In a large bowl beat the remaining butter with a mixer on medium to high 30 seconds. Add brown sugar and baking soda. Beat until combined, scraping sides of bowl. Beat in eggs and 2 tsp. of the vanilla. Beat in as much of the flour as you can with mixer. Stir in any remaining flour. Stir in oats.
**3.** For filling, in a 2-qt. saucepan combine the reserved 2 Tbsp. butter, the chocolate chips, and sweetened condensed milk. Cook over low heat until chocolate melts and mixture is smooth, stirring occasionally.

Remove from heat. Stir in the nuts and the remaining 2 tsp. vanilla.
**4.** Press two-thirds (about 3⅓ cups) of the oats mixture into the bottom of the prepared pan. Spread filling evenly over the oats mixture. Drop the remaining oats mixture in small pieces on top of filling (tip, *left*).
**5.** Bake about 25 minutes or until top is light brown (chocolate filling will still look moist). Cool in pan on wire rack. Use foil to lift uncut bars out of pan; cut into bars. **Makes 60 bars.**
**EACH BAR** *145 cal., 6 g fat (3 g sat. fat), 17 mg chol., 56 mg sodium, 21 g carb., 1 g fiber, 13 g sugars, 2 g pro.*

## BUTTERMILK BROWNIES

**HANDS-ON TIME** 30 minutes
**BAKE** 25 minutes at 350°F

2    cups all-purpose flour
2    cups sugar
1    tsp. baking soda
¼    tsp. salt
1    cup butter, cut up
⅓    cup unsweetened cocoa powder
1    cup water
2    eggs
½    cup buttermilk or sour milk (tip, p. 474)
1½   tsp. vanilla
1    recipe Chocolate Buttermilk Frosting
     Chocolate sprinkles (optional)

**1.** Preheat oven to 350°F. Grease a 15×10-inch or 13×9-inch baking pan. In a bowl stir together flour, sugar, baking soda, and salt.
**2.** In a 2-qt. saucepan combine butter, cocoa powder, and the water. Bring mixture just to boiling, stirring constantly. Remove from heat. Add cocoa mixture to flour mixture; beat with a mixer on medium to high until combined. Add eggs, buttermilk, and vanilla; beat 1 minute (batter will be thin). Pour batter into prepared pan.
**3.** Bake about 25 minutes for 15×10-inch pan, 35 minutes for 13×9-inch pan, or until a toothpick inserted in center comes out clean.
**4.** Pour warm Chocolate Buttermilk Frosting over warm brownies, spreading evenly. If desired, add sprinkles. Cool in pan on wire rack.
**Makes 24 brownies.**
**EACH BROWNIE** *245 cal., 10 g fat (6 g sat. fat), 43 mg chol., 158 mg sodium, 37 g carb., 1 g fiber, 28 g sugars, 2 g pro.*

### *CHOCOLATE BUTTERMILK FROSTING*

In a 2-qt. saucepan combine ¼ cup butter and 3 Tbsp. each unsweetened cocoa powder and buttermilk or milk. Bring to boiling. Remove from heat. Add 2¼ cups powdered sugar and ½ tsp. vanilla. Beat until smooth.

## CUTTING BARS

The number of bars a recipe makes is only a suggestion. The size of the bars you cut is up to you. To go up or down on the yield, make more or fewer horizontal and crosswise cuts using the guide *below*. Note that smaller is better when bars are especially rich.

### 13×9-INCH PAN

2 lengthwise & 7 crosswise =
**24** (3×1⅝-inch) bars

___

3 lengthwise & 7 crosswise =
**32** (2¼×1⅝-inch) bars

___

5 lengthwise & 5 crosswise =
**36** (1½×2⅛-inch) bars

___

7 lengthwise & 4 crosswise =
**40** (1⅛×2⅝-inch) bars

___

7 lengthwise & 5 crosswise =
**48** (1⅛×2⅛-inch) bars

### 15×10-INCH PAN

3 lengthwise & 8 crosswise =
**36** (2½×1¾-inch) bars

___

3 lengthwise & 11 crosswise =
**48** (2½×1¼-inch) bars

___

3 lengthwise & 14 crosswise =
**60** (2½×1-inch) bars

___

7 lengthwise & 7 crosswise =
**64** (1¼×1⅞-inch) bars

___

7 lengthwise & 8 crosswise =
**72** (1¼×1¾-inch) bars

COCONUT JOY CANDY BARS

OATMEAL-JAM BARS

PUMPKIN BARS

## COCONUT JOY CANDY BARS

**HANDS-ON TIME** 20 minutes
**BAKE** 32 minutes at 350°F
**COOL** 1 hour 30 minutes
**CHILL** 1 hour

¾   cup butter, melted
2    cups sugar
2    tsp. vanilla
3    eggs, lightly beaten
1¼  cups all-purpose flour
½   cup unsweetened cocoa powder
1    tsp. baking powder
½   tsp. salt
4    cups flaked coconut
1    14-oz. can sweetened condensed milk
½   tsp. almond extract
½   cup chopped almonds, toasted
1    recipe Milk Chocolate Ganache

» **TOASTING NUTS** adds depth to the nuts' flavor. Preheat oven to 300°F. Spread nuts in a shallow baking pan. Bake 10 to 15 minutes or just until nuts are golden, stirring once or twice; let cool.

**1.** Preheat oven to 350°F. Line a 13×9-inch baking pan with foil, extending foil over edges of pan (tip, p. 478). Lightly coat foil with *nonstick cooking spray.* In a large bowl stir together melted butter, sugar, and 1 tsp. of the vanilla. Stir in eggs until combined.
**2.** In another bowl combine the next four ingredients (through salt). Add flour mixture to butter mixture and stir until combined. Spread half of the batter into the prepared pan. Bake 12 minutes or just until set. Cool in pan on a wire rack 30 minutes.
**3.** Meanwhile, for filling, in a large bowl combine coconut, condensed milk, almond extract, and the remaining 1 tsp. vanilla.
**4.** Spread filling over baked chocolate layer; sprinkle with almonds. Carefully spread the remaining chocolate batter over filling. Bake 20 to 25 minutes or until chocolate layer is set. Cool in pan on a wire rack 1 hour.
**5.** Spoon Milk Chocolate Ganache over cooled bars, spreading evenly. Chill about 1 hour or until ganache

is firm. Use foil to lift uncut bars out of pan; cut into bars. **Makes 48 bars.**
**TO STORE** Place bars in a single layer in an airtight container; cover. Store in the refrigerator up to 3 days or freeze up to 3 months.
**EACH BAR** *187 cal., 10 g fat (6 g sat. fat), 28 mg chol., 96 mg sodium, 24 g carb., 1 g fiber, 19 g sugars, 3 g pro.*

## MILK CHOCOLATE GANACHE

Pour one 11.5-oz. pkg. milk chocolate chips into a medium bowl. In a 1- or 1½-qt. saucepan bring ¾ cup heavy cream just to boiling. Immediately pour cream over chocolate in bowl. Let stand 5 minutes, without stirring. Stir until smooth.

## OATMEAL-JAM BARS

**HANDS-ON TIME** 15 minutes
**BAKE** 35 minutes at 350°F

1    lemon
1⅓  cups all-purpose flour
¼   tsp. baking soda
¼   tsp. salt
¾   cup quick-cooking rolled oats
⅓   cup packed brown sugar
6    oz. cream cheese, softened
¼   cup butter, softened
¾   cup seedless raspberry jam

**1.** Preheat oven to 350°F. Line a 9-inch square baking pan with foil, extending foil over edges of pan (tip, p. 478). Lightly coat foil with *nonstick cooking spray.* Remove 1 tsp. zest and squeeze 1 tsp. juice from the lemon. In a medium bowl stir together flour, baking soda, and salt. Stir in oats, brown sugar, and the lemon zest.
**2.** In a large bowl beat cream cheese and butter with a mixer on medium 30 seconds. Add flour mixture; beat on low until crumbly. Remove 1 cup of the crumb mixture. Press the remaining crumb mixture

into the bottom of the prepared baking pan. Bake 20 minutes.
**3.** Meanwhile, in a small bowl combine jam and the lemon juice. Carefully spread jam mixture over hot crust. Sprinkle with the reserved 1 cup crumb mixture.
**4.** Bake about 15 minutes more or until top is golden. Cool in pan on a wire rack. Use foil to lift uncut bars out of pan; cut into bars. **Makes 16 bars.**
**EACH BAR** *173 cal., 7 g fat (5 g sat. fat), 20 mg chol., 121 mg sodium, 25 g carb., 0 g fiber, 11 g sugars, 2 g pro.*

## PUMPKIN BARS

**HANDS-ON TIME** 25 minutes
**BAKE** 25 minutes at 350°F
**COOL** 2 hours

2    cups all-purpose flour
1½  cups sugar
2    tsp. baking powder
2    tsp. ground cinnamon
1    tsp. baking soda
½   tsp. salt
¼   tsp. ground cloves
4    eggs, lightly beaten
1    15-oz. can pumpkin
1    cup vegetable oil
2½  cups Cream Cheese Frosting (p. 539)

**1.** Preheat oven to 350°F. In a large bowl stir together the first seven ingredients (through cloves). Stir in the eggs, pumpkin, and oil until combined. Pour batter into an ungreased 15×10-inch baking pan, spreading evenly.
**2.** Bake 25 to 30 minutes or until a toothpick inserted near the center comes out clean. Cool in pan on a wire rack 2 hours. Spread with Cream Cheese Frosting. If desired, sprinkle with additional sugar and cinnamon. Cut into bars. Cover and store bars in the refrigerator up to 3 days. **Makes 36 bars.**
**EACH BAR** *243 cal., 11 g fat (3 g sat. fat), 37 mg chol., 135 mg sodium, 34 g carb., 1 g fiber, 28 g sugars, 2 g pro.*

# DESSERTS

585

586

589

592

594

596

599

605

**MAKE-AHEAD RECIPE**

TENDER SHORTCAKES THAT ARE LIGHT AND FLUFFY INSIDE REQUIRE A HIGH OVEN TEMP. IT TURNS THE LIQUID AND BUTTER IN THE BATTER TO STEAM, WHICH LIGHTENS THE TEXTURE.

**BAKING SODA** is added along with the baking powder to neutralize the acidity from the sour cream. They work differently, so be sure to get them both in.

## STRAWBERRY SHORTCAKES

**HANDS-ON TIME** 25 minutes
**BAKE** 12 minutes at 400°F
**COOL** 30 minutes

1½  cups all-purpose flour
¼   cup sugar
1   tsp. baking powder
½   tsp. salt
¼   tsp. baking soda
⅓   cup cold butter, cut up
1   egg, lightly beaten
½   cup sour cream or plain yogurt
3   Tbsp. milk

5   cups sliced fresh strawberries
3   Tbsp. sugar
1   recipe Sweetened Whipped Cream (p. 474)

**1.** Preheat oven to 400°F. Line a large baking sheet with parchment paper. In a medium bowl stir together flour, ¼ cup sugar, baking powder, salt, and baking soda. Using a pastry blender, cut in butter until mixture resembles coarse crumbs. Make a well in the center of flour mixture. In a small bowl combine egg, sour cream, and milk; add all at once to flour mixture, stirring with a fork just until moistened.
**2.** Drop dough in eight mounds onto the prepared baking sheet. Bake 12 to 15 minutes or until golden. Remove; cool on a wire rack 30 minutes.
**3.** Meanwhile, in a medium bowl toss together 4 cups of the strawberries and the 3 Tbsp. sugar. If desired, mash berries slightly.
**4.** To serve, cut shortcakes in half horizontally. Spoon half of the strawberry mixture over shortcake bottoms. Replace tops. Top with remaining strawberry mixture and 1 cup sliced strawberries. Serve with Sweetened Whipped Cream. **Makes 8 servings (1 shortcake each).**

**EACH SERVING** *376 cal., 22 g fat (13 g sat. fat), 85 mg chol., 332 mg sodium, 41 g carb., 2 g fiber, 20 g sugars, 5 g pro.*

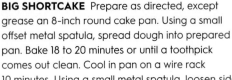

**BIG SHORTCAKE** Prepare as directed, except grease an 8-inch round cake pan. Using a small offset metal spatula, spread dough into prepared pan. Bake 18 to 20 minutes or until a toothpick comes out clean. Cool in pan on a wire rack 10 minutes. Using a small metal spatula, loosen sides of shortcake. Place a wire rack on top of pan; place one hand on top of rack and other hand under pan with a hot pad and invert pan with rack; cool shortcake. Split and fill with Sweetened Whipped Cream and half of the strawberry mixture. Top with remaining strawberry mixture.

**PEACH-HONEY SHORTCAKES**
Prepare as directed, except substitute 4 cups thinly sliced fresh peaches or nectarines for the 5 cups sliced strawberries and toss with 3 Tbsp. honey instead of the 3 Tbsp. sugar. Do not mash fruit. Fill shortcakes with Sweetened Whipped Cream, peach mixture, and additional honey.

**LEMON-POPPY SEED SHORTCAKES WITH BERRIES**
Prepare as directed, except stir 1 Tbsp. each poppy seeds and lemon zest into flour mixture after cutting in butter. Bake as directed. For filling, substitute 5 cups desired mixed fresh berries for the sliced strawberries. Stir 2 tsp. lemon zest into Sweetened Whipped Cream. Fill shortcakes with whipped cream and fruit mixture.

### MAKE IT YOUR OWN
Mix and match your favorite fruits to customize the flavor of your shortcakes. You can also add a drizzle of melted chocolate or a dusting of powdered sugar over the shortcakes.

Add the egg mixture to the flour mixture all at once and stir just until moistened (until wet and dry ingredients are just combined and the batter starts to pull away from the sides of the bowl). Stirring too much will overdevelop the gluten in the flour and result in a tough shortcake.

# APPLE CRISP

**HANDS-ON TIME** 20 minutes
**BAKE** 35 minutes at 375°F

| | |
|---|---|
| 6 | cups sliced, peeled cooking apples |
| 2 | Tbsp. packed brown sugar |
| 1 | Tbsp. lemon juice |
| 1 | cup regular rolled oats |
| ¾ | cup packed brown sugar |
| ¼ | cup all-purpose flour |
| ½ | tsp. ground cinnamon or ¼ tsp. ground ginger or nutmeg |
| ½ | cup butter, cut up |
| ½ | cup chopped nuts or flaked coconut |

**1.** Preheat oven to 375°F. In a large bowl combine apples and 2 Tbsp. brown sugar. Transfer to a 2-qt. baking dish. Drizzle with lemon juice.
**2.** For topping, in a large bowl combine oats, ¾ cup brown sugar, flour, and cinnamon. Using a pastry blender, cut in butter until the mixture resembles coarse crumbs. Stir in nuts. Sprinkle topping over apple mixture.
**3.** Bake 35 to 40 minutes or until apples are tender and topping is golden. Serve warm. If desired, serve with *ice cream* and sprinkle with additional cinnamon. **Makes 9 servings (½ cup each).**
**EACH SERVING** *298 cal., 15 g fat (7 g sat. fat), 27 mg chol., 88 mg sodium, 41 g carb., 3 g fiber, 29 g sugars, 2 g pro.*

**PEACH CRISP** Prepare filling as directed, except substitute 6 cups sliced, peeled ripe peaches or two 16-oz. pkg. frozen unsweetened sliced peaches for the apples. Thaw peaches if frozen (do not drain). Increase the 2 Tbsp. brown sugar to ⅓ cup, add 1 Tbsp. all-purpose flour, and omit lemon juice. Sprinkle with topping. Bake 55 minutes or until bubbly. Cover loosely with foil the last 15 minutes. Cool 30 minutes.

**RHUBARB CRISP** Prepare filling as directed, except substitute 6 cups sliced fresh rhubarb or two 16-oz. pkg. frozen unsweetened sliced rhubarb, thawed and drained, for the apples. Increase 2 Tbsp. brown sugar to ⅓ cup; omit lemon juice. Sprinkle with topping. Bake 45 minutes or until filling is bubbly. If needed, cover loosely with foil the last 10 minutes. Cool at least 30 minutes before serving.

# CHERRY COBBLER

**HANDS-ON TIME** 30 minutes
**BAKE** 20 minutes at 400°F
**COOL** 30 minutes

1½ cups all-purpose flour
3   Tbsp. sugar
2   tsp. baking powder
½   tsp. salt
½   tsp. ground cinnamon
6   Tbsp. butter, cut up
6   cups fresh or frozen
    unsweetened pitted
    tart red cherries (2 lb.)
1   cup sugar
3   Tbsp. cornstarch
1   egg, lightly beaten
⅓   cup milk

**1.** Preheat oven to 400°F. For topper, in a medium bowl stir together first five ingredients (through cinnamon). Cut in butter until mixture resembles coarse crumbs; set aside.

**2.** For filling, in a 3-qt. saucepan combine cherries, 1 cup sugar, and cornstarch. Cook over medium heat until cherries release juices, stirring occasionally. Continue to cook until thickened and bubbly, stirring constantly. Keep filling hot.

**3.** To finish the topper, in a small bowl combine egg and milk. Stir egg mixture into flour mixture just until moistened. Transfer hot filling to a 2-qt. baking dish. Immediately drop biscuit topper into mounds on top of filling. If desired, sprinkle with additional sugar.

**4.** Bake 20 to 25 minutes or until biscuits are golden. Cool on a wire rack 30 minutes. **Makes 6 servings (1 cup each).**

**EACH SERVING** *482 cal., 13 g fat (8 g sat. fat), 63 mg chol., 472 mg sodium, 87 g carb., 3 g fiber, 54 g sugars, 6 g pro.*

>> **RHUBARB COBBLER**
Prepare as directed, except substitute 6 cups fresh or frozen unsweetened sliced rhubarb for the cherries and reduce cornstarch to 2 Tbsp.

>> **PEACH COBBLER** Prepare as directed, except substitute 6 cups fresh or frozen unsweetened sliced peaches for the cherries and reduce cornstarch to 2 Tbsp.

>> **BLUEBERRY COBBLER**
Prepare as directed, except substitute 6 cups fresh or frozen blueberries for the cherries, reduce the 1 cup sugar to ¾ cup, and reduce cornstarch to 2 Tbsp.

## PEACHY BLUEBERRY TURNOVERS

**HANDS-ON TIME** 25 minutes
**BAKE** 15 minutes at 400°F

| | |
|---|---|
| 2 | Tbsp. granulated sugar |
| 1 | Tbsp. all-purpose flour |
| ⅛ | tsp. ground cinnamon |
| 1 | cup chopped peaches or apples |
| ⅓ | cup fresh or frozen blueberries |
| ½ | of a 17.3-oz. pkg. (1 sheet) frozen puff pastry sheets, thawed |
| 1 | Tbsp. milk |
| | Coarse sugar (optional) |

**1.** Preheat oven to 400°F. Line a large baking sheet with parchment paper. In a small bowl stir together granulated sugar, flour, and cinnamon. Add peaches and blueberries; toss to coat.

**2.** Unfold pastry. Cut pastry into four squares; brush edges with some of the 1 Tbsp. milk. Spoon fruit mixture onto centers of squares. Fold one corner of each square over filling to opposite corner; press edges with a fork to seal. Place turnovers on prepared baking sheet. Prick tops several times with fork. Brush with remaining milk and, if desired, sprinkle with coarse sugar.

**3.** Bake 15 to 18 minutes or until puffed and golden. Cool slightly on baking sheet on a wire rack. Serve warm. **Makes 4 turnovers.**

**EACH TURNOVER** 413 cal, 18 g fat (9 g sat. fat), 9 mg chol., 287 mg sodium, 60 g carb., 2 g fiber, 35 g sugars, 6 g pro.

**PUFF PASTRY** Puff pastry—made from folding and rolling layers of butter or other fat between dough—is extremely flaky. The fat between the layers creates steam, which "puffs" the dough up during baking, forming clearly defined flaky layers. Sheets of puff pastry are sold in the supermarket frozen food aisle and should be stored in the freezer. Thaw overnight in the fridge or at room temperature for 30 minutes. (Thaw only what you need; this pastry does not refreeze well.)

**1**

To fill the apples easily, place filling in a disposable decorating bag or heavy resealable plastic bag; snip tip or a corner. Squeeze filling into the cored apple. The filling will expand slightly when baked, popping out of the apple core, so don't overfill.

**2**

Place the pastry circle over the top of the filled apple. Pleat the pastry around the bottom of the apple, pressing lightly to hold. (It's not necessary to fully enclose the pastry around the bottom.)

**APPLE VARIETIES** that work well for baking (i.e., in dumplings and pies) include Jazz, Braeburn Jonagold, Fuji, Cortland, Pink Lady, Honeycrisp, Golden Delicious, Idared, and/or Granny Smith (use these if you like tartness).

## APPLE DUMPLINGS WITH CARAMEL-NUT FILLING

**HANDS-ON TIME** 45 minutes
**BAKE** 30 minutes at 425°F
**STAND** 30 minutes

| | |
|---|---|
| 1½ | cups sugar |
| 1½ | cups water |
| ½ | tsp. ground cinnamon |
| 3 | Tbsp. butter, cut up |
| 1 | recipe Pastry for Double-Crust Pie (p. 610) |
| 6 | small apples |
| ¼ | cup chunky peanut butter |
| 3 | Tbsp. caramel-flavor ice cream topping |
| 3 | Tbsp. finely snipped dried fruit, such as cranberries or apricots |
| 1 | egg, lightly beaten |
| 1 | Tbsp. water |

**1.** Preheat oven to 425°F. For sauce, in a 1- or 1½-qt. saucepan combine sugar, the 1½ cups water, and cinnamon. Bring to boiling; reduce heat. Simmer, uncovered, 8 minutes. Stir in butter until melted. Pour sauce into a 3-qt. rectangular baking dish.

**2.** Prepare Pastry for Double-Crust Pie as directed through Step 2. On a lightly floured surface slightly flatten one pastry ball. Roll pastry from center to edges into a 15-inch circle. Cut out three 7-inch circles. If desired, use a small cookie cutter to cut shapes from scraps. Repeat with remaining pastry ball to make three more 7-inch circles.

**3.** Core and peel apples. Cut a thin slice from bottoms of apples. In a bowl combine peanut butter, caramel topping, and dried fruit. Fill apples with peanut butter mixture. Top with pastry circles; fold pastry around apples, pleating at bottoms. Place dumplings in sauce in dish. Combine egg and the 1 Tbsp. water; brush over dumplings. If using, add pastry cutouts.

**4.** Bake 30 to 35 minutes or just until apples are tender and pastry is golden. Let stand 30 minutes. Spoon sauce over dumplings; serve warm. **Makes 6 dumplings.**

**EACH DUMPLING** *708 cal., 29 g fat (11 g sat. fat), 44 mg chol., 422 mg sodium, 109 g carb., 5 g fiber, 74 g sugars, 7 g pro.*

**EASY EVERYDAY**

*For a quick shortcut, sub one 14.1-oz. pkg. (2 crusts) rolled refrigerated unbaked piecrusts for Pastry for Double-Crust Pie. Roll crusts into 15-inch circles.*

PHYLLO (also called filo) dough is in the freezer section of the supermarket. A box of phyllo dough contains a roll of tissue-thin pastry layers that are removed one at a time for buttering. Cover the phyllo dough sheets with plastic wrap while you work to keep them from drying out.

# PISTACHIO-CRANBERRY BAKLAVA

**HANDS-ON TIME** 45 minutes
**BAKE** 35 minutes at 325°F

1½  cups pistachio nuts, finely chopped
1½  cups dried cranberries
1⅓  cups sugar
½  tsp. ground cardamom
¾  cup butter, melted
½  of a 16-oz. pkg. (20 to 24 sheets) frozen phyllo dough (14×9-inch rectangles), thawed
¾  cup water
3  Tbsp. honey
1  tsp. vanilla

**1.** Preheat oven to 325°F. For filling, in a large bowl combine pistachios, cranberries, ⅓ cup of the sugar, and the cardamom.
**2.** Brush the bottom of a 13×9-inch baking pan with some of the melted butter. Unroll phyllo. Layer five or six phyllo sheets in prepared baking pan, brushing each sheet generously with some of the melted butter. Sprinkle with 1 cup of the filling. Repeat layering phyllo sheets and filling two more times, brushing each sheet with melted butter.
**3.** Layer remaining phyllo sheets on top of filling, brushing each sheet with more butter. Drizzle with any remaining butter. Using a sharp knife, cut stacked layers into 24 to 48 diamond-, rectangle-, or square-shape pieces.
**4.** Bake 35 to 45 minutes or until golden. Cool slightly in pan on a wire rack.
**5.** Meanwhile, for syrup, in a 2-qt. saucepan combine remaining 1 cup sugar, the water, honey, and vanilla. Bring to boiling; reduce heat. Simmer, uncovered, 20 minutes. Pour syrup over warm baklava in pan; cool completely.
**Makes 24 servings (1 piece each).**
**TO STORE** Layer pieces between waxed paper in an airtight container; cover. Store in refrigerator up to 3 days or freeze up to 3 months. If frozen, thaw pieces at room temperature 1 hour before serving.
**EACH SERVING** *202 cal., 10 g fat (4 g sat. fat), 15 mg chol., 117 mg sodium, 28 g carb., 1 g fiber, 20 g sugars, 3 g pro.*

**❶** Brush baking pan bottom with butter; add the first sheet of phyllo. (The pastry sheets will be a little longer than the pan; press phyllo into the pan, allowing excess to go up the pan sides.) Brush the phyllo evenly with butter; repeat.

**❷** Use a sharp knife to cut baklava into pieces before popping the pan into the oven. Cutting is easier to do at this point before phyllo is crispy and fragile.

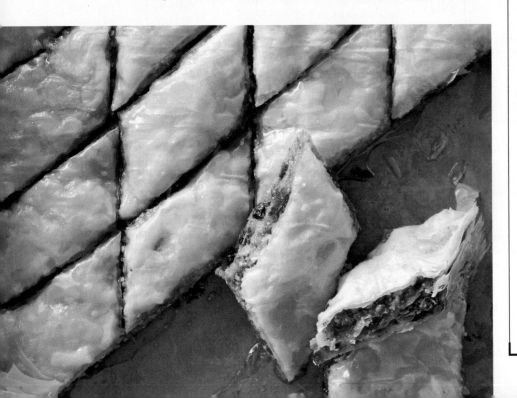

Fresh raspberries
Finely chopped pistachio nuts
(optional)

**1.** In an extra-large bowl allow egg whites to stand at room temperature 30 minutes. Meanwhile, line a baking sheet with parchment paper. Draw a 9-inch circle on paper; turn paper over.
**2.** Position baking rack in center of oven. Preheat oven to 250°F. For meringue, add cream of tartar to egg whites. Beat with a mixer on medium until soft peaks form (tips curl). Add 1½ cups sugar, 1 Tbsp. at a time, beating on high until stiff peaks form (tips stand straight). Beat in 2 tsp. of the vanilla. Sift cornstarch over beaten egg whites; fold in gently.
**3.** Using a large spoon, spread meringue over circle on paper, building up edges slightly to form a shell. Bake 1½ hours (do not open door). Turn off oven; let meringue stand in oven with door closed 1 hour.
**4.** Meanwhile, for topping, in a chilled large bowl beat cream, 1 Tbsp. sugar, and remaining 1 tsp. vanilla with chilled clean beaters on medium until stiff peaks form (tips stand straight). Fold in Lemon Curd.
**5.** Lift meringue shell off paper and transfer to a plate. Spread with topping and sprinkle with raspberries and, if desired, pistachios and *fresh mint*. **Makes 12 servings (1 piece each).**
EACH SERVING *273 cal., 12 g fat (7 g sat. fat), 79 mg chol., 66 mg sodium, 38 g carb., 1 g fiber, 36 g sugars, 3 g pro.*

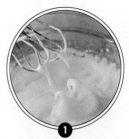

Beating the egg whites whips in air, creating a foamy texture. To check for soft peaks, stop the mixer and lift up the beaters slightly. The peaks in the bowl will curl slightly at the tips.

Beating the sugar into the egg whites stiffens the egg white foam and turns it into a glossy meringue. How? The moisture from the egg foam dissolves the sugar, turning it into a syrupy coating that blankets the proteins in the mixture.

Draw a circle on the backside of the parchment paper to create an outline for the shell. Spread the meringue mixture to the edges of the outline and create a shallow center well.

**CORNSTARCH** works as a stabilizer for the egg white mixture during baking. We found that it helped reduce cracks and increase volume; it also contributes to a smoother, shinier surface.

## LEMON-CREAM PAVLOVA WITH BERRIES

**HANDS-ON TIME** 45 minutes
**BAKE** 1 hour 30 minutes at 250°F
**STAND** 1 hour

| | |
|---|---|
| 6 | egg whites |
| ¼ | tsp. cream of tartar |
| 1½ | cups sugar |
| 3 | tsp. vanilla |
| 1 | Tbsp. cornstarch |
| 1 | cup heavy cream |
| 1 | Tbsp. sugar |
| 1 | cup Lemon Curd (*p. 603*) or one 10-oz. jar lemon curd |

**MERINGUE KNOW-HOW** Any amount of grease or egg yolk will keep your meringue from beating up properly. Before you begin, wash all your equipment with hot, soapy water. Break each egg into a small bowl, using clean fingers to carefully lift yolk from white (prevents the sharp shell edges from puncturing the yolk). Transfer each white to a larger bowl; repeat breaking each egg separately into the small bowl. This keeps the rest of the batch uncontaminated if a yolk breaks. (If you like, save yolks for Lemon Curd, *p. 603*.)

MOLTEN
CHOCOLATE
CAKES

# MOLTEN CHOCOLATE CAKES

**HANDS-ON TIME** 30 minutes
**COOL** 15 minutes
**CHILL** 2 hours
**BAKE** 15 minutes at 375°F
**STAND** 10 minutes

2   cups semisweet chocolate chips
½   cup heavy cream
1   Tbsp. butter
½   cup butter, cut up
4   eggs
½   cup sugar
½   cup all-purpose flour
    Vanilla ice cream (optional)

**1.** In a 1-qt. saucepan combine 1¼ cups of the chocolate chips, the cream, and 1 Tbsp. butter. Cook and stir over low heat until chocolate is melted and mixture is smooth. Cool 15 minutes, stirring occasionally. Cover and chill 2 hours or until mixture reaches a fudgelike consistency.

**2.** Preheat oven to 375°F. Generously butter eight 6-oz. ramekins or custard cups. In another 1-qt. saucepan combine remaining ¾ cup chocolate chips and the ½ cup butter. Cook and stir over low heat until chocolate is melted and mixture is smooth; cool slightly.

**3.** In a large bowl beat eggs and sugar with a mixer on medium to high 5 minutes. Beat in flour and slightly cooled chocolate mixture. Spoon enough batter into prepared ramekins to measure 1 inch in depth.

**4.** Form chilled chocolate mixture into eight portions. Working quickly, roll each portion into a ball. Place balls on top of batter in ramekins without touching sides of dishes. Cover balls with remaining batter.

**5.** Bake 15 minutes. Remove from oven; let stand 10 minutes. Using a knife, loosen cakes from sides of ramekins. Invert onto plates. Serve immediately. If desired, serve with ice cream. **Makes 8 cakes.**

**TO MAKE AHEAD** Prepare as directed through Step 4. Cover and chill up to 4 hours. Let stand at room temperature 30 minutes before baking as directed.

**EACH CAKE** *490 cal., 34 g fat (20 g sat. fat), 161 mg chol., 138 mg sodium, 47 g carb., 3 g fiber, 37 g sugars, 6 g pro.*

## BREAD PUDDING

**HANDS-ON TIME** 20 minutes
**BAKE** 50 minutes at 350°F

- 4 cups dried **BREAD CUBES**
- ½ cup **DRIED FRUIT**
- ¼ cup chopped **NUTS** (optional)
- 2 eggs, lightly beaten
- 1¾ cups **MILK**
- ½ cup granulated or packed brown sugar
- ¼ cup butter, melted
- 1 tsp. **SPICE**
- 1 tsp. vanilla
  **TOPPING**

**1.** Preheat oven to 350°F. Grease a 2-qt. square baking dish. Place BREAD CUBES, DRIED FRUIT, and, if desired, NUTS in prepared baking dish. In a medium bowl combine eggs, MILK, sugar, butter, SPICE, and vanilla. Pour over bread mixture in dish. Use the back of a spoon to press bread down lightly to moisten.
**2.** Bake, uncovered, about 50 minutes or until puffed and a knife comes out clean. Cool slightly. Serve warm with TOPPING. **Makes 8 servings.**

**DRY AND TOASTY**
To dry bread cubes, preheat oven to 300°F. Arrange cubes in a single layer on a baking sheet. Bake 10 to 15 minutes or until golden, stirring once or twice.

## MIX & MATCH INGREDIENTS

**BREAD CUBES** (Pick 1)
- Baguette
- Challah
- Cinnamon-swirl
- Sourdough
- White or wheat

**DRIED FRUIT** (Pick 1)
- Snipped apricots
- Tart cherries
- Cranberries
- Snipped figs
- Raisins (dark or golden)

**NUTS** (Pick 1)
- Almonds
- Toasted hazelnuts
- Macadamia nuts
- Pecans
- Pistachio nuts
- Walnuts

**MILK** (Pick 1)
- Unsweetened almond or chocolate-almond milk
- Refrigerated unsweetened coconut milk
- Refrigerated eggnog
- Fat-free milk
- Reduced-fat (2%) milk

**SPICE** (Pick 1)
- Ground cinnamon
- Ground ginger (or 1 Tbsp. grated fresh ginger)
- Pumpkin pie spice or apple pie spice

**TOPPING** (Pick 1)
- Bourbon Sauce (p. 604)
- Caramel Sauce (p. 604)
- Custard Sauce (p. 605)
- Fudge Sauce (p. 604) or fudge ice cream topping, warmed
- Raspberry Sauce (p. 605) or raspberry preserves, warmed
- Ice cream
- Sweetened Whipped Cream (p. 474)

**MANDARIN CREAM BARS**

# CLASSIC NEW YORK-STYLE CHEESECAKE

**HANDS-ON TIME** 40 minutes
**BAKE** 45 minutes at 350°F
**COOL** 45 minutes
**CHILL** 4 hours **STAND** 15 minutes

- 2¼ cups finely crushed graham crackers
- 1 Tbsp. sugar
- ½ tsp. ground cinnamon
- ⅔ cup butter, melted
- 4 8-oz. pkg. cream cheese, softened
- 1½ cups sugar
- ¼ cup all-purpose flour
- 3 eggs, lightly beaten
- 4 tsp. vanilla
- 2 8-oz. cartons sour cream

A springform pan is a round pan with straight sides that are removable by releasing a clamp (making serving super easy). Springform pans are ideal for the soft texture of cheesecake—removing a cheesecake intact from any other type of pan is nearly impossible.

**1.** Preheat oven to 350°F. For crust, in a bowl combine first three ingredients (through cinnamon). Stir in melted butter. Press mixture onto bottom and 2 inches up sides of a 10-inch springform pan.
**2.** In a large bowl beat cream cheese and 1¼ cups of the sugar with a mixer on medium until fluffy, scraping bowl. Beat in flour on low until smooth. Stir in eggs and 3 tsp. of the vanilla. Stir in ½ cup of the sour cream; pour into crust in pan. Set in a shallow baking pan.
**3.** Bake 40 minutes or until a 2½-inch area around edge is set when gently shaken. Remove from oven. For topping, combine the remaining ¼ cup sugar, 1 tsp. vanilla, and sour cream; spread over cheesecake. Bake 5 minutes more.
**4.** Cool in pan on a wire rack 15 minutes. Using a knife, loosen crust from sides of pan; cool 30 minutes. Remove sides of pan; cool on wire rack. Cover; chill 4 to 12 hours. Let stand at room temperature 15 minutes before serving. **Makes 16 servings (1 slice each).**
**EACH SERVING** *466 cal., 35 g fat (20 g sat. fat), 132 mg chol., 342 mg sodium, 34 g carb., 0 g fiber, 26 g sugars, 6 g pro.*

# MANDARIN CREAM BARS

**HANDS-ON TIME** 30 minutes
**BAKE** 12 minutes at 375°F
**CHILL** 3 hours 30 minutes

- 2 cups finely crushed shortbread cookies
- ⅔ cup flaked coconut
- ½ cup butter, melted
- 1 tsp. orange zest
- 2 cups boiling water
- 2 3-oz. pkg. orange-flavor gelatin
- 1 8-oz. pkg. cream cheese, softened
- ¾ cup sugar
- 1 8-oz. container frozen whipped dessert topping, thawed
- 2 11-oz. cans mandarin orange sections, drained

**1.** Preheat oven to 375°F. In a bowl combine crushed cookies, coconut, melted butter, and orange zest. Press mixture onto bottom of a 3-qt. rectangular baking dish. Bake 12 to 14 minutes or until crust is light brown. Cool on a wire rack.
**2.** In a bowl stir boiling water into gelatin until dissolved; cool.
**3.** Meanwhile, in a large bowl beat cream cheese and sugar with a mixer on medium 1 to 2 minutes or until light and fluffy. Fold in whipped topping. Spread cream cheese mixture over crust. Chill at least 30 minutes.
**4.** Stir orange sections into gelatin mixture. Carefully pour orange mixture over chilled cream cheese layer. Cover and chill 3 to 24 hours or until firm. **Makes 18 servings (1 piece each).**
**EACH SERVING** *283 cal., 16 g fat (9 g sat. fat), 27 mg chol., 204 mg sodium, 34 g carb., 1 g fiber, 25 g sugars, 2 g pro.*

**HEALTHY TWIST**

*You can cut the fat in this recipe by substituting reduced-fat versions of the cream cheese and whipped dessert topping.*

WOBBLY ZONE

Add the topping to your cheesecake when the center is still wobbly when gently shaken (outside edge will be set). Baking any longer than this before adding the topping will result in an overbaked cheesecake (see *opposite, above left*).

OVERBAKING makes the filling dry and crumbly—nothing like the delicate, creamy texture characteristic of cheesecakes.

OVERBEATING the eggs or filling incorporates excess air, which causes the filling to puff too much in the oven, then fall and crack as it cools.

Although it's not a necessary step, a water bath lets the cheesecake bake more slowly and evenly, protecting and insulating the delicate filling so the outer edge of the cake won't bake faster than the center. To do this, place your crust-lined springform pan on a double layer of heavy-duty foil. Bring edges of foil up and mold them around sides of pan to form a watertight seal. Place springform pan into a roasting pan. After adding the filling, pour enough boiling water into the roasting pan to reach halfway up the sides of the pan (keep water level below the foil). Bake 1 hour. Turn off oven; let stand in oven 1 hour. Promptly remove from water bath; cool as directed.

CLASSIC
NEW YORK-STYLE
CHEESECAKE

**PIECE BY PIECE**
Cheesecake can be stored in an airtight container in the refrigerator up to 5 days or in the freezer up to 1 month. To make serving a piece or two at a time easy, cut the entire dessert before storing.

## CRÈME BRÛLÉE

**HANDS-ON TIME** 10 minutes
**BAKE** 30 minutes at 325°F
**CHILL** 1 hour
**STAND** 20 minutes

1¾  cups half-and-half
5    egg yolks, lightly beaten
⅓    cup sugar
1    tsp. vanilla
⅛    tsp. salt
¼    cup sugar

**1.** Preheat oven to 325°F. In a 1-qt. heavy saucepan heat half-and-half over medium-low heat just until bubbly. Remove from heat.
**2.** Meanwhile, in a medium bowl combine egg yolks, ⅓ cup sugar, vanilla, and salt. Beat with a whisk just until combined. Slowly whisk hot half-and-half into egg mixture (tip, *opposite, below*).
**3.** Place six 4-oz. ramekins or 6-oz. custard cups in a 3-qt. rectangular baking dish. Divide egg mixture among ramekins. Place baking dish on oven rack. Pour enough boiling water into baking dish to reach halfway up sides of ramekins.
**4.** Bake 30 to 40 minutes or until a knife comes out clean (centers will still shake slightly). Remove ramekins from water; cool on a wire rack. Cover and chill 1 to 8 hours.
**5.** Before serving, let custards stand at room temperature 20 minutes. Sprinkle tops of custards with ¼ cup sugar. Using a kitchen torch, melt the sugar by moving tip of flame across custards to form a crispy layer. Serve immediately. **Makes 6 servings (1 ramekin each).**
**EACH SERVING** *210 cal., 11 g fat (6 g sat. fat), 178 mg chol., 99 mg sodium, 24 g carb., 0 g fiber, 23 g sugars, 4 g pro.*

**A SMALL TORCH** is traditionally used to melt and caramelize the sugar on the top of Crème Brûlée. You can buy culinary torches at most kitchen supply stores and online. Use caution.

**WHITE CHOCOLATE CRÈME BRÛLÉE** Prepare as directed, except in Step 1 cook and stir ½ cup of the half-and-half with 4 oz. chopped white baking chocolate with cocoa butter (tip, *p. 476*) over low heat just until chocolate is melted. Gradually whisk in remaining 1¼ cups half-and-half. Bring to simmering; remove from heat. Continue as directed.

## *CARAMELIZED SUGAR*

If you don't have a culinary torch, do this: In an 8-inch heavy skillet cook ¼ cup sugar over medium-high heat until sugar starts to melt, shaking skillet occasionally. Do not stir. Once sugar starts to melt, reduce heat to low and cook 5 minutes or until all of the sugar is melted and golden, stirring as needed with a wooden spoon. Quickly drizzle caramelized sugar over custards. (If sugar hardens in skillet, heat and stir until melted.)

### TEMPERING EGGS
Go slowly when gradually whisking the hot half-and-half mixture into the beaten egg yolks for Crème Brûlée (*opposite*). This process is called tempering, which slowly heats the yolks through to avoid a sudden temperature shock. If eggs are exposed to a high temp too quickly, the egg proteins will cook and coagulate, which will leave what looks like chunks of scrambled eggs in the custard mixture.

A 2-qt. soufflé dish (photo, *below*) has straight, tall sides that allow the delicate soufflé mixture to rise high while baking. A regular casserole dish just won't cut it here. Think ahead and invest in the right dish before you begin—you can get one for $10–$20 in shops and online.

# CHOCOLATE SOUFFLÉ

**HANDS-ON TIME** 25 minutes
**BAKE** 40 minutes at 350°F

4  oz. bittersweet or semisweet chocolate, chopped
3  Tbsp. all-purpose flour
1  Tbsp. unsweetened cocoa powder
3  Tbsp. butter
1¼  cups half-and-half or milk
1  tsp. vanilla
4  egg yolks
6  egg whites
⅓  cup sugar

**1.** Preheat oven to 350°F. Butter sides of a 2-qt. soufflé dish; sprinkle with sugar. In a pan stir chocolate over low heat until melted.
**2.** In a bowl stir together flour and cocoa powder. In a 2-qt. saucepan melt 3 Tbsp. butter over medium heat. Stir in flour mixture; gradually stir in half-and-half. Cook and stir over medium heat until thickened and bubbly; remove. Stir in vanilla. Stir in melted chocolate. In a bowl beat egg yolks with a fork just until combined. Gradually stir chocolate mixture into egg yolks.
**3.** In a large bowl beat egg whites with a mixer on medium until soft peaks form (tips curl) (photos, *p. 589*). Add ⅓ cup sugar, 1 Tbsp. at a time, beating on high until stiff peaks form (tips stand straight). Fold one-fourth of the beaten egg whites into chocolate mixture to lighten. Gently fold chocolate mixture into remaining beaten egg whites. Pour into prepared soufflé dish.
**4.** Bake 40 to 45 minutes or until a wooden skewer comes out clean. If desired, sift with *powdered sugar*. Serve soufflé immediately by inserting two forks back to back to separate into six wedges. Spoon onto plates. **Makes 6 servings.**
**EACH SERVING** *333 cal, 23 g fat (13 g sat. fat), 159 mg chol, 138 mg sodium, 28 g carb., 2 g fiber, 19 g sugars, 9 g pro.*

CREAMY FLAN

VANILLA BEAN
PANNA COTTA

# WHAT IS FLAN? TRADITIONAL FLAN IS ALMOST SPONGY IN TEXTURE. THIS VERSION IS RICH AND CREAMY— LIKE A CRUSTLESS CHEESECAKE.

## CREAMY FLAN

**HANDS-ON TIME** 30 minutes
**BAKE** 1 hour at 325°F
**COOL** 30 minutes
**CHILL** 24 hours

⅔ cup sugar
1   8-oz. pkg. cream cheese, softened
½   cup sugar
1   14-oz. can sweetened condensed milk
6   eggs, lightly beaten
1¼  cups half-and-half
1   tsp. vanilla

**1.** To caramelize sugar, in an 8-inch heavy skillet cook the ⅔ cup sugar over medium heat until sugar starts to melt, shaking skillet occasionally. Do not stir. Once sugar starts to melt, cook 5 minutes more or until all the sugar is melted and golden, stirring as needed with a wooden spoon. Pour caramelized sugar into a 9-inch deep-dish pie plate; tilt pie plate to coat bottom. Let stand 10 minutes.

**2.** Meanwhile, preheat oven to 325°F. In a large bowl beat cream cheese with a mixer on medium 30 seconds. Beat in the ½ cup sugar until combined. Beat in sweetened condensed milk. Beat in eggs, half-and-half, and vanilla until smooth.
**3.** Place pie plate in a roasting pan on oven rack. Pour egg mixture into pie plate. Pour boiling water into roasting pan around pie plate to a depth of 1 inch. Bake 60 to 70 minutes or until top is light brown and a knife comes out clean.
**4.** Remove pie plate from water. Cool on a wire rack 30 minutes. Cover and chill 24 hours.
**5.** To unmold, loosen flan from sides of pie plate with a knife. Invert a rimmed plate over pie plate; turn both over together. Remove pie plate. Spoon any caramelized sugar remaining in pie plate onto flan.
**Makes 12 servings (1 slice each).**
**EACH SERVING** 316 cal., 14 g fat (8 g sat. fat), 132 mg chol., 152 mg sodium, 40 g carb., 0 g fiber, 39 g sugars, 8 g pro.

**UNFLAVORED GELATIN** thickens this sweet cream mixture (other similar custards use egg yolks for thickening).

**THE CARAMEL LAYER** at the bottom of the dish will soften as the flan chills. When you invert the flan to remove the pan, the caramel will release from the pan to coat the flan. Don't worry if there is extra hardened caramel left in the pan.

## VANILLA BEAN PANNA COTTA

**HANDS-ON TIME** 20 minutes
**CHILL** 4 hours

1    envelope unflavored gelatin
1½   cups heavy cream
1    cup sugar
1    vanilla bean, split lengthwise and seeds scraped, or 2 tsp. vanilla (tip, p. 476)
2    cups buttermilk
     Fresh blackberries (optional)

**1.** Place eight 4-oz. canning jars or 4- to 6-oz. ramekins in a shallow baking pan. In a small bowl sprinkle gelatin over ¼ cup water (do not stir). Let stand 5 minutes.
**2.** Meanwhile, in a 1- or 1½-qt. saucepan combine cream, sugar, and, if using, vanilla bean and seeds. Cook over medium heat until hot but not boiling. Add gelatin mixture; stir until gelatin is dissolved. Remove from heat. Remove and discard vanilla bean. Stir in buttermilk and vanilla (if using).
**3.** Pour mixture into jars. Cover and chill 4 to 24 hours. If desired, serve with berries. **Makes 8 servings (1 jar each).**
**EACH SERVING** 294 cal., 17 g fat (11 g sat. fat), 64 mg chol., 82 mg sodium, 32 g carb., 1 g fiber, 30 g sugars, 4 g pro.

**VANILLA PUDDING IN TRIFLES**

# VANILLA PUDDING
**START TO FINISH** 30 minutes

¾   cup sugar
3   Tbsp. cornstarch
3   cups milk
4   egg yolks, lightly beaten
1   Tbsp. butter
1½  tsp. vanilla

**1.** In a 2-qt. heavy saucepan stir together sugar and cornstarch; stir in milk. Cook and stir over medium heat until thickened and bubbly. Cook and stir 2 minutes more. Remove from heat.
**2.** Gradually stir 1 cup of the hot mixture into egg yolks (tip, p. 595); return to hot mixture in saucepan. Bring to a gentle boil; reduce heat. Cook and stir 2 minutes. Remove from heat. Stir in butter and vanilla.
**3.** Pour pudding into a bowl; cover surface with plastic wrap. Cool slightly and serve warm. Or chill; do not stir during chilling.
**Makes 4 servings (¾ cup each).**
**EACH SERVING** *345 cal., 11 g fat (6 g sat. fat), 207 mg chol., 118 mg sodium, 53 g carb., 0 g fiber, 47 g sugars, 9 g pro.*

**CHOCOLATE PUDDING** Prepare as directed, except add ⅓ cup unsweetened cocoa powder with the sugar. (For a more-intense chocolate flavor, use Dutch-process cocoa powder.) Reduce cornstarch to 2 Tbsp. and milk to 2⅔ cups.

**GET-TOGETHER**

*Homemade pudding makes the best trifles. Layer cubes of pound cake or angel food cake with spoonfuls of pudding and fresh berries or other fruit.*

# CREAM PUFFS

**HANDS-ON TIME** 25 minutes
**COOL** 10 minutes
**BAKE** 30 minutes at 400°F

| 1 | cup water |
| ½ | cup butter |
| ⅛ | tsp. salt |
| 1 | cup all-purpose flour |
| 4 | eggs |
| 1½ | recipes Sweetened Whipped Cream (p. 474) |

**1.** Preheat oven to 400°F. Grease a large baking sheet. In a 2-qt. saucepan combine the water, butter, and salt. Bring to boiling. Add flour all at once, stirring vigorously. Cook and stir until mixture forms a ball. Remove from heat; cool 10 minutes. Add eggs, one at a time, stirring well after each addition.

**2.** Drop 12 heaping tablespoons dough onto prepared sheet. Bake 30 to 35 minutes or until golden and firm. Transfer to a wire rack; cool.

**3.** To serve, cut tops from cream puffs; remove soft dough from inside. Fill with Sweetened Whipped Cream. **Makes 12 cream puffs.**

**EACH CREAM PUFF** *245 cal., 20 g fat (12 g sat. fat), 116 mg chol, 118 mg sodium, 12 g carb., 0 g fiber, 4 g sugars, 4 g pro.*

**MINI PUFFS** Prepare as directed, except drop 30 rounded teaspoons dough 2 inches apart onto greased baking sheets. Bake, one sheet at a time, 25 minutes (keep remaining dough covered while first batch bakes). Cool, split, and fill as directed. **Makes 30 mini puffs.**

---

**CHANGE IT UP**

*Customize your puffs with other fillings—ice cream, chocolate-hazelnut spread, lemon curd, pudding, or chocolate whipped cream. If you wish, sift powdered sugar over the tops.*

After adding the flour, vigorously stir the dough until it pulls away from the pan sides and comes together. Once the dough ball forms, remove pan from heat and let dough stand to cool. Slight cooling will prevent pieces of the eggs from cooking when you start stirring them in.

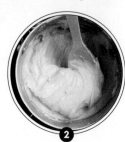

Add 1 egg to the warm dough and stir well until egg is mixed in and dough is smooth. Continue stirring in 1 egg at a time. After adding eggs, dough will be shiny smooth (but also sticky and pasty).

## TIRAMISU

**HANDS-ON TIME** 30 minutes
**CHILL** 4 hours

**LADYFINGERS** are an egg-based, spongy dessert that are a cross between biscuits, cookies, and small cakes. They are available in soft and crisp varieties. Look for them by cookies in large supermarkets and Italian markets.

½ cup granulated sugar
½ cup water
2 Tbsp. instant espresso coffee powder
2 Tbsp. hazelnut-, coffee-, or almond liqueur (optional)
1⅓ cups heavy cream
2 8-oz. cartons mascarpone cheese, room temperature
½ cup powdered sugar
2 3-oz. pkg. (48) soft ladyfingers or one 7-oz. pkg. (24) crisp ladyfingers
2 Tbsp. unsweetened cocoa powder

**1.** For syrup, in a 1-qt. saucepan combine granulated sugar, the water, and espresso powder. Bring to boiling over medium heat, stirring to dissolve sugar. Boil gently, uncovered, 1 minute. Remove from heat. If desired, stir in liqueur.

**2.** In a chilled large bowl beat cream with chilled beaters of a mixer on medium until soft peaks form (tips curl). In a medium bowl stir together mascarpone cheese and powdered sugar. Fold ½ cup of the whipped cream into mascarpone mixture to lighten. Gently fold the mascarpone mixture into the remaining whipped cream.

**3.** To assemble, arrange half of the ladyfingers in the bottom of a 9-inch square baking pan, cutting to fit as needed. Brush with half of the syrup. Spread with half of the mascarpone mixture and sprinkle with 1 Tbsp. of the cocoa powder. Repeat ladyfinger, syrup, and mascarpone layers.

**4.** Cover and chill 4 to 24 hours. Before serving, sift remaining 1 Tbsp. cocoa powder over top.
**Makes 9 servings (1 piece each).**
**EACH SERVING** *482 cal., 36 g fat (21 g sat. fat), 154 mg chol., 57 mg sodium, 32 g carb., 1 g fiber, 24 g sugars, 5 g pro.*

BUTTERSCOTCH
CRUNCH SQUARES

## BUTTERSCOTCH CRUNCH SQUARES

**HANDS-ON TIME** 40 minutes
**BAKE** 10 minutes at 400°F
**FREEZE** 6 hours **STAND** 5 minutes

1   cup all-purpose flour
¼   cup quick-cooking rolled oats
¼   cup packed brown sugar
½   cup butter, cut up
½   cup chopped pecans
½   cup butterscotch-flavor
    ice cream topping
½   gal. butter brickle or vanilla
    ice cream

**1.** Preheat oven to 400°F. In a bowl stir together flour, oats, and brown sugar. Cut in butter until mixture resembles coarse crumbs. Stir in nuts. Press mixture onto bottom of a 13×9-inch baking pan. Bake 10 to 15 minutes or until golden. While warm, stir until crumbled; cool.
**2.** Spread half of the oat mixture in a 9-inch square pan; drizzle with half of the butterscotch topping. Place ice cream in a chilled bowl; stir to soften. Spread ice cream over mixture in pan. Top with remaining butterscotch topping and oat mixture. Cover and freeze about 6 hours or until firm. Let stand at room temperature 5 to 10 minutes before serving. **Makes 12 servings (1 square each).**
**EACH SERVING** *404 cal., 25 g fat (11 g sat. fat), 47 mg chol., 239 mg sodium, 43 g carb., 1 g fiber, 31 g sugars, 4 g pro.*

## VANILLA ICE CREAM

**HANDS-ON TIME** 50 minutes
**CHILL** 4 hours
**FREEZE** according to manufacturer

8   egg yolks
2   cups whole milk
¾   cup sugar
2   cups heavy cream
2   Tbsp. vanilla
½   tsp. kosher salt or ¼ tsp. salt
    Kosher or rock salt and crushed
    ice (for hand-crank and electric
    ice cream freezers)

**1.** In a 2-qt. heavy saucepan combine egg yolks, milk, and sugar. Cook over medium heat, stirring constantly with a heatproof spatula, until mixture coats the back of spatula or a clean metal spoon.
**2.** Strain mixture through a fine-mesh sieve into a bowl placed in a larger bowl of ice water. Stir mixture until cooled. Stir in cream, vanilla, and ½ tsp. kosher salt. Cover and chill 4 to 24 hours.
**3.** Freeze chilled mixture in a 4- to 5-qt. ice cream freezer according to manufacturer's directions. If desired, ripen at least 4 hours.*
**Makes 12 servings (½ cup each).**
***NOTE** To ripen, for a traditional ice cream freezer, after churning, remove lid and dasher. Cover top with foil. Plug lid hole with a cloth; replace lid on can and fill outer freezer bucket with ice and rock salt (enough to cover top of freezer can) in a ratio of 4 cups ice to 1 cup rock salt. Let stand at room temperature 4 hours.
**EACH SERVING** *252 cal., 19 g fat (11 g sat. fat), 172 mg chol., 81 mg sodium, 16 g carb., 0 g fiber, 16 g sugars, 4 g pro.*

CHOCOLATE
ICE CREAM

## 1½- OR 2-QT. FREEZER VARIATION

Prepare as directed, except in a 1-qt. heavy saucepan combine 4 egg yolks, 1 cup milk, and ⅓ cup sugar. Cook over medium heat, stirring constantly with a heatproof spatula, until mixture coats the back of spatula. Strain and cool as directed in Step 2. Stir in 1 cup heavy cream, 1 Tbsp. vanilla, and ¼ tsp. kosher salt. Cover; chill 4 to 24 hours. Freeze chilled mixture in a 1½- or 2-qt. ice cream freezer according to manufacturer's directions. Transfer to a freezer container and freeze until firm. Makes 6 servings.

STRAWBERRY
ICE CREAM

VANILLA
ICE CREAM

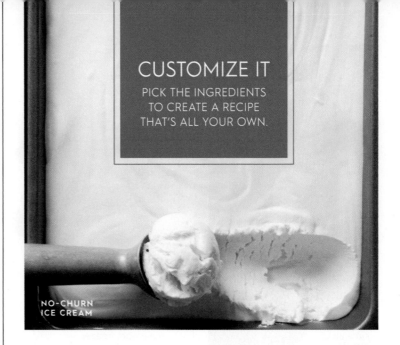

# CUSTOMIZE IT

PICK THE INGREDIENTS
TO CREATE A RECIPE
THAT'S ALL YOUR OWN.

NO-CHURN
ICE CREAM

## NO-CHURN ICE CREAM

**HANDS-ON TIME** 20 minutes
**FREEZE** 8 hours

2   **14-oz. cans sweetened condensed milk**
¾   **cup unsweetened cocoa powder (optional)**
1   **qt. heavy cream**
1   **Tbsp. vanilla**
2   **cups coarsely chopped STIR-IN total**
1   **cup RIBBON**

**1.** Pour sweetened condensed milk into an extra-large bowl. If desired, stir in cocoa powder. In a large bowl beat cream and vanilla with a mixer on medium-high until soft peaks form (tips curl). Fold whipped cream into milk mixture. Fold in STIR-IN. Spread half of the cream mixture into a 3-qt. rectangular baking dish. Drizzle with RIBBON and top with remaining cream mixture. Cover and freeze at least 8 hours or until firm. **Makes 24 servings (½ cup each).**

>> **STRAWBERRY ICE CREAM**
Prepare as directed, except stir 4 cups strawberries, coarsely mashed, into chilled mixture before freezing in ice cream freezer. (Use 2 cups strawberries for the 1½- or 2-qt. freezer.) **Makes 20 servings (½ cup each).**

>> **CHOCOLATE ICE CREAM**
Prepare as directed, except increase sugar to 1 cup and stir together sugar and ½ cup unsweetened cocoa powder in the saucepan before adding egg yolks and milk in Step 1. Continue cooking as directed. (Use ½ cup sugar and ¼ cup unsweetened cocoa powder for the 1½- or 2-qt. freezer.) **Makes 13 servings (½ cup each).**

## MIX & MATCH INGREDIENTS

**STIR-IN** (*Pick 1 or 2*)
- Chopped cookies (peanut butter sandwich cookies with peanut butter filling, chocolate sandwich cookies with white filling, gingersnaps, vanilla wafers, or shortbread cookies)
- Chopped candies (chocolate-covered peanut butter cups, malted milk balls, chocolate-covered peanuts, peanut brittle, chocolate-covered English toffee bars, candy-coated milk chocolate pieces, chocolate-coated caramel-topped nougat bars with peanuts, or chocolate-covered crisp peanut butter candy)
- Fruit (coarsely chopped bananas, peaches, strawberries, or sweet cherries; or whole raspberries)

**RIBBON** (*Pick 1*)
- Caramel or salted caramel ice cream topping
- Fudge ice cream topping
- Fruit preserves (strawberry, apricot, or raspberry)
- Lemon, lime, or raspberry curd
- Marshmallow creme

**GREEK FROZEN YOGURT**

# GREEK FROZEN YOGURT

**HANDS-ON TIME** 15 minutes
**FREEZE** according to manufacturer + 2 hours
**STAND** 5 minutes

3  cups plain low-fat (2%) Greek yogurt
1  cup sugar
¼  cup lemon juice
2  tsp. vanilla
⅛  tsp. salt
   Fresh strawberries (optional)

**1.** In a medium bowl stir together all ingredients until smooth.
**2.** Freeze yogurt mixture in a 1½- or 2-qt. ice cream freezer according to manufacturer's directions. Transfer to a freezer container and freeze 2 to 4 hours to ripen. Let stand at room temperature 5 to 15 minutes before serving. If desired, serve with strawberries. **Makes 16 servings (¼ cup each).**
**EACH SERVING** *84 cal., 1 g fat (1 g sat. fat), 3 mg chol., 35 mg sodium, 15 g carb., 0 g fiber, 15 g sugars, 4 g pro.*

>> **BERRY** Prepare as directed, except add 1 cup blueberries, blackberries, and/or raspberries during last 1 minute of freezing in ice cream freezer.

>> **ALMOND CHOCOLATE CHUNK** Prepare as directed, except omit lemon juice and increase vanilla to 1 Tbsp. Stir 1 cup chocolate chunks and ½ cup chopped toasted almonds into yogurt before placing in freezer container and ripening.

>> **PEACH** Prepare as directed, except puree 2 cups fresh or thawed frozen sliced peaches; swirl into yogurt before placing in freezer container and ripening.

**FREEZING YOGURT**
Use the right ice cream maker. Most countertop ice cream freezers are small-batch appliances. If you want to use a larger freezer, double the recipe.

It should take 20 to 30 minutes for the yogurt to be frozen. The mixture should be thickened like soft-serve ice cream and be rich and creamy.

Transfer the frozen yogurt to a freezer container with a tight-fitting lid. Freeze 2 to 4 hours to ripen before serving for improved consistency and flavor.

# RASPBERRY SORBET

**HANDS-ON TIME** 20 minutes
**CHILL** 1 hour
**FREEZE** 10 hours
**STAND** 5 minutes

1  cup sugar
1  cup water
2  Tbsp. lemon juice
3  cups fresh raspberries
2  Tbsp. orange juice

**1.** In a 1-qt. saucepan bring sugar and the water just to simmering over medium heat, stirring to dissolve sugar. Remove from heat; stir in lemon juice. Transfer to a bowl. Cover; chill 1 hour.
**2.** In a food processor combine raspberries and orange juice. Cover; process until smooth. Press mixture through a fine-mesh sieve; discard seeds. Stir into chilled syrup.
**3.** Spread raspberry mixture into a 2-qt. square baking dish. Cover; freeze 4 hours or until firm. Break up mixture with a fork; place in food processor, half at a time. Cover; process 30 seconds or until smooth. Return to baking dish; cover and freeze 6 to 8 hours or until firm. Let stand at room temperature 5 minutes before serving. **Makes 9 servings (⅓ cup each).**
**EACH SERVING** *110 cal., 0 g fat, 0 mg chol., 1 mg sodium, 28 g carb., 3 g fiber, 25 g sugars, 1 g pro.*

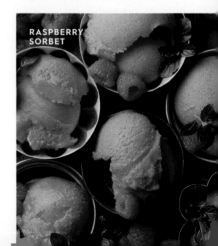

**RASPBERRY SORBET**

CHOCOLATE FONDUE

LEMON CURD

## LOVE FOR LEMON
Swirl lemon curd into yogurt or vanilla ice cream, smear on pound cake or shortbread cookies, use in a no-bake tart, roll into crepes, or use as a pancake topper.

## CHOCOLATE FONDUE

**START TO FINISH** 15 minutes

- 8 oz. semisweet chocolate, chopped
- 1 14-oz. can sweetened condensed milk
- ⅓ cup milk
  Assorted dippers, such as pretzel rods, pound cake sticks, cut-up fruit, cookies, brownie squares, and/or marshmallows

**1.** In a 1-qt. heavy saucepan stir chocolate over low heat until melted. Stir in sweetened condensed milk and milk; heat through. Transfer to a fondue pot; keep warm.
**2.** Serve fondue with dippers. Swirl pieces as you dip. If the fondue mixture thickens, stir in more milk. **Makes 8 servings (¼ cup each).**
**EACH SERVING** 300 cal., 13 g fat (8 g sat. fat), 18 mg chol., 71 mg sodium, 46 g carb., 2 g fiber, 43 g sugars, 5 g pro.

》》
**FOR GROWN-UP FONDUE,** stir 2 to 4 Tbsp. amaretto or orange, hazelnut, or cherry liqueur into mixture after heating.

## LEMON CURD

**HANDS-ON TIME** 15 minutes
**CHILL** 1 hour

- 2 extra-large lemons
- 1 cup sugar
- 2 Tbsp. cornstarch
- 6 Tbsp. water
- 6 egg yolks, lightly beaten
- ½ cup butter, cut up

**1.** Remove 1 Tbsp. zest and squeeze 6 Tbsp. juice from lemons. In a 2-qt. saucepan stir together sugar and cornstarch. Stir in zest, juice, and the water. Cook and stir over medium heat until thickened and bubbly.
**2.** Gradually stir half of the hot mixture into yolks; return to mixture in saucepan. Bring to a gentle boil over medium heat, stirring constantly. Cook and stir 2 minutes. Remove from heat. Stir in butter. Transfer to bowl; cover surface with plastic wrap. Chill 1 hour. **Makes 16 servings (2 Tbsp. each).**

**TO STORE** Place curd in an airtight container; cover. Store in refrigerator up to 1 week or freeze up to 2 months. If frozen, thaw in refrigerator before serving.
**EACH SERVING** 125 cal., 7 g fat (4 g sat. fat), 84 mg chol., 49 mg sodium, 14 g carb., 0 g fiber, 13 g sugars, 1 g pro.

⌄

**ORANGE CURD** Prepare as directed, except reduce sugar to ¾ cup; substitute orange zest for the lemon zest and ¾ cup orange juice for the lemon juice and water. **Makes 12 servings (2 Tbsp. each).**

FUDGE SAUCE

CARAMEL SAUCE

BOURBON SAUCE

## FUDGE SAUCE

**START TO FINISH** 15 minutes

1   cup heavy cream
¼   cup light-color corn syrup
1   Tbsp. coffee liqueur or
    1 tsp. vanilla
    Dash salt
8   oz. semisweet or bittersweet
    chocolate, chopped

**MAKE AHEAD**
Unless
specified,
these dessert
sauces can be
made ahead
and stored
in an airtight
container in
the refrigerator
up to 1 week.
Warm sauces
before serving.

**1.** In a 1-qt. heavy saucepan combine cream, corn syrup, coffee liqueur (if using), and salt. Cook over medium heat just until simmering, stirring occasionally. Remove from heat. Add chocolate (do not stir); let stand 5 minutes. Stir until smooth. If using, stir in vanilla. **Makes 16 servings (2 Tbsp. each).**
**EACH SERVING** *142 cal., 10 g fat (6 g sat. fat), 21 mg chol., 18 mg sodium, 13 g carb., 1 g fiber, 11 g sugars, 1 g pro.*

## CARAMEL SAUCE

**HANDS-ON TIME** 15 minutes
**COOL** 2 hours

¾   cup packed brown sugar
½   cup butter, cut up
½   cup heavy cream
3   Tbsp. light-color corn syrup
1   tsp. vanilla

**1.** In a 2-qt. heavy saucepan combine brown sugar, butter, cream, and corn syrup. Bring to boiling over medium-high heat, stirring to dissolve sugar and melt butter. Reduce heat to medium. Boil, uncovered, at a moderate, steady rate 5 minutes (do not stir). Remove from heat; stir in vanilla.
**2.** Transfer to a heatproof bowl. Cover; cool 2 hours. If desired, before serving, sprinkle with ½ tsp. *sea salt or kosher salt.* **Makes 12 servings (2 Tbsp. each).**
**EACH SERVING** *171 cal., 11 g fat (7 g sat. fat), 34 mg chol., 170 mg sodium, 18 g carb., 0 g fiber, 18 g sugars, 0 g pro.*

## BOURBON SAUCE

**START TO FINISH** 15 minutes

¼   cup butter, cut up
½   cup sugar
1   egg yolk
2   Tbsp. water
2   Tbsp. bourbon

**1.** In a 1-qt. heavy saucepan melt butter over medium heat. Stir in sugar, egg yolk, and the water. Cook and stir 6 to 8 minutes or just until boiling. Remove from heat; stir in bourbon. Cool slightly. Serve warm over bread pudding or ice cream. **Makes 6 servings (2 Tbsp. each).**
**EACH SERVING** *153 cal., 8 g fat (5 g sat. fat), 55 mg chol., 56 mg sodium, 17 g carb., 0 g fiber, 17 g sugars, 1 g pro.*

## RASPBERRY SAUCE

**HANDS-ON TIME** 20 minutes
**CHILL** 1 hour

»

**RASPBERRIES** can be replaced with 3 cups fresh strawberries or one 16-oz. pkg. frozen unsweetened whole strawberries, thawed. Do not use sieve; reduce sugar to ¼ cup.

3 cups fresh or frozen raspberries
⅓ cup sugar
1 tsp. cornstarch

**1.** Thaw raspberries if frozen (do not drain). Place berries in a food processor or blender. Cover and process or blend until smooth. Press berries through a fine-mesh sieve; discard seeds.
**2.** In a 1- or 1½-qt. saucepan stir together sugar and cornstarch; add raspberry puree. Cook and stir over medium heat until thickened and bubbly. Cook and stir 2 minutes more. Transfer to a small bowl. Cover and chill at least 1 hour.

**Makes 10 servings (2 Tbsp. each).**
**EACH SERVING** *46 cal., 0 g fat, 0 mg chol., 0 mg sodium, 11 g carb., 2 g fiber, 8 g sugars, 0 g pro.*

## CUSTARD SAUCE

**HANDS-ON TIME** 15 minutes
**CHILL** 2 hours

5 egg yolks, lightly beaten
1½ cups whole milk
¼ cup sugar
1½ tsp. vanilla

**1.** In a 2-qt. heavy saucepan combine egg yolks, milk, and sugar. Cook over medium heat, stirring constantly with a wooden spoon or heatproof spatula, just until mixture coats the back of spatula or a clean metal spoon. Remove from heat. Stir in vanilla. Quickly cool mixture by placing the saucepan in a large bowl of ice water 1 to 2 minutes, stirring constantly.
**2.** Pour custard mixture into a bowl. Cover surface with plastic wrap; chill at least 2 hours (do not stir). Store in airtight container in the refrigerator up to 3 days.
**Makes 16 servings (2 Tbsp. each).**
**EACH SERVING** *44 cal., 2 g fat (1 g sat. fat), 68 mg chol., 12 mg sodium, 4 g carb., 0 g fiber, 4 g sugars, 2 g pro.*

**CHANGE IT UP**
*To give this classic sauce a flavor twist, prepare as directed, except add 1 to 2 Tbsp. brandy or desired liqueur (such as cinnamon, orange, amaretto, or raspberry) with the vanilla.*

RASPBERRY SAUCE

CUSTARD SAUCE

# PIES & TARTS

**MAKE-AHEAD RECIPE**

## PRESSED FLUTE

Crimp pastry; flatten flutes slightly. Press inside flutes with tines of fork.

## CRISSCROSS

Trim pastry even with edge of plate. Use tines of fork to make crisscross pattern.

## THE WEAVE

Trim pastry even with edge of plate. Cut at ½-inch intervals. Fold every other section in.

## SPOON FINISH

Trim pastry even with edge of the plate. Use a spoon to press design into edge.

## BUTTER OR SHORTENING?

All types of fat coat flour proteins so gluten doesn't form. This prevents a tough pastry. Because shortening has a higher melting point, it stays in pockets in the pastry dough longer than butter while baking. When the shortening finally melts, steam forms in the pockets and the layers puff apart. This makes a flaky pastry. Butter, however, adds rich flavor to pastry. For the best results, this recipe uses both types of fat.

## BRAID

Cut rolled pastry into long narrow strips. Lay three strips next to each other and braid. Attach braid to edge of pie with water or milk.

## CIRCLES

Cut small circles out of rolled pastry. Brush edge of crust with water or milk and attach cutouts, slightly overlapping.

## LEAVES

Use a knife or small leaf cutter to cut out rolled pastry. Use a table knife to make veins in leaves. Attach leaves as for CIRCLES.

## RECTANGLES

Cut rolled pastry into narrow strips, then cut strips into rectangles. Prick with a fork. Attach as for CIRCLES.

**DECORATE** If you're making a fancy finish (like Braids, Leaves, Rectangles, or Circles), make an extra half batch of pastry dough to use for the cutouts.

**FREEZING PASTRY SHELLS** Have a pastry shell ready whenever you want to bake pie. Fit the pastry dough into a freezer-to-oven pie pan or tart pan. Place the whole thing in a resealable freezer bag; seal. Freeze up to 3 months. Fill frozen pie shell as desired and bake. You may need to add 5 to 10 minutes to the baking time.

## PASTRY FOR SINGLE-CRUST PIE

**START TO FINISH** 15 minutes

1½ cups all-purpose flour
½ tsp. salt
¼ cup shortening
¼ cup butter, cut up, or shortening
¼ to ⅓ cup ice-cold water

**1.** In a medium bowl stir together flour and salt. Using a pastry blender, cut in shortening and butter until pea size.

**2.** Sprinkle 1 Tbsp. of the water over part of the flour mixture; toss with a fork. Push moistened pastry to side of bowl. Repeat moistening flour mixture, gradually adding water until mixture begins to come together. Gather pastry into a ball, kneading gently just until it holds together.

**3.** On a lightly floured surface use your hands to slightly flatten pastry. Roll pastry into a 12-inch circle.

**4.** Fold pastry circle into fourths and transfer to a 9-inch pie plate. Unfold and ease pastry into pie plate without stretching it.

**5.** Trim pastry to ½ inch beyond edge of pie plate. Fold under extra pastry even with the plate's edge; crimp edge as desired. Do not prick pastry. Fill and bake as directed in recipes. **Makes 8 servings (1 slice each).**

**BAKED PASTRY SHELL** Preheat oven to 450°F. Prepare as directed, except prick bottom and sides of pastry with a fork. Line pastry with a double thickness of foil. Bake 8 minutes. Remove foil. Bake 6 to 8 minutes more or until golden. Cool on a wire rack.

**EACH SERVING** *191 cal., 12 g fat (5 g sat. fat), 15 mg chol., 187 mg sodium, 18 g carb., 1 g fiber, 0 g sugars, 2 g pro.*

## THE SECRET TO FLAKY PIECRUST IS TO WORK THE DOUGH AS LITTLE AS POSSIBLE AFTER ADDING THE WATER.

Fat tenderizes and creates flakiness. When cutting shortening and butter into the flour, stop when fat pieces are the size of peas.

Ice-cold water keeps the fat pieces cold so they don't melt during mixing. Add water, 1 Tbsp. at a time, tossing with a fork. Push moistened dough to side of bowl.

Once the dough is just moistened, gather it into a ball and knead gently until it holds together. At this point you can wrap dough in plastic wrap and refrigerate up to 3 days or freeze up to 3 months. Thaw at room temperature before using.

When rolling out pastry, add just enough flour to keep it from sticking. Adding too much flour or overworking the dough will make it tough. A floured pastry cloth and a cotton stockinette rolling pin cover are also designed to help prevent sticking.

Once the pastry is rolled into a circle, carefully fold it in half, then in half again to make fourths. Place folded pastry on top of the pie plate with the folded tip in the center. Unfold pastry and ease it into the plate, being careful not to stretch or tear the pastry.

Use a small sharp knife or kitchen scissors to trim the pastry to ½ inch beyond the edge of the pie plate. After trimming, use your fingers to fold the pastry under so it's even with the edge of the pie plate.

Crimping keeps the filling from overflowing. Crimp edges high for pies with a lot of filling. For a basic crimp, place an index finger against the inside edge of the pastry. Using the thumb and index finger of your other hand, press the pastry from the outside onto your finger.

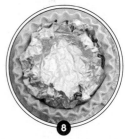

Blind baking means baking a pastry shell before it is filled to create a stronger crust that can better hold moist filling. Before baking, line the inside of the shell with a double thickness of heavy-duty foil. The foil weights down the crust, which prevents it from bubbling up or blistering.

BLUEBERRY PIE

## PASTRY FOR DOUBLE-CRUST PIE

**START TO FINISH** 15 minutes

2½ cups all-purpose flour
1 tsp. salt
½ cup shortening
¼ cup butter, cut up, or shortening
½ to ⅔ cup ice-cold water

**1.** In a large bowl stir together flour and salt. Using a pastry blender, cut in shortening and butter until pea size (photos, *p. 609*).
**2.** Sprinkle 1 Tbsp. of the water over part of the flour mixture; toss with a fork. Push moistened pastry to side of bowl. Repeat moistening flour mixture, gradually adding water until mixture begins to come together. Gather pastry into a ball, kneading gently just until it holds together. Divide pastry in half; form two balls.
**3.** On a lightly floured surface use your hands to slightly flatten one pastry ball. Roll pastry into a 12-inch circle.
**4.** Fold pastry circle into fourths and transfer to a 9-inch pie plate. Unfold and ease pastry into pie plate without stretching it. Transfer desired filling to pastry-lined pie plate. Trim pastry even with the plate's edge (photos, *opposite*).
**5.** Roll remaining pastry ball into a 12-inch circle. Using a sharp knife, cut slits in pastry. Place pastry circle on filling; trim to ½ inch beyond edge of pie plate. Fold top pastry under bottom pastry; crimp edge as desired (*pp. 608–609*). Bake as directed in recipes. **Makes 8 servings (1 slice each).**
**NUT PASTRY** Prepare as directed, except substitute ¼ cup ground toasted pecans or almonds for ¼ cup of the flour.

**GO EASY ON THE FLOUR**—a little goes a long way, and working too much into the dough will make it tough. To minimize the need for flour, roll out dough on a pastry cloth or a smooth lint-free flour-sack towel. You can also cover the rolling pin with a cotton stockinette designed for pastry; lightly flour both the cloth and stockinette.

**LATTICE-TOP METHOD** Prepare as directed through Step 4. Roll out remaining pastry and cut into ½-inch strips (or cut varying widths of strips for extra interest) (photos, *opposite*). Transfer desired filling to pastry-lined pie plate. Weave strips over filling in a lattice pattern, twisting strips if desired. Trim any excess dough from strips. Press strip ends into bottom pastry edge. If desired, press edges with tines of fork. Bake as directed in recipes.
**EACH SERVING** *306 cal., 19 g fat (7 g sat. fat), 15 mg chol., 338 mg sodium, 30 g carb., 1 g fiber, 0 g sugars, 4 g pro.*

## BLUEBERRY PIE

**HANDS-ON TIME** 25 minutes
**BAKE** 15 minutes at 450°F + 1 hour at 375°F

6 cups fresh blueberries or three 12-oz. pkg. frozen unsweetened blueberries
¾ to 1 cup sugar
3 Tbsp. cornstarch
1 recipe Pastry for Double-Crust Pie *(left)*

**1.** For filling, thaw blueberries if using frozen (do not drain). In a large bowl stir together sugar and cornstarch. Add berries; toss to coat.
**2.** Preheat oven to 450°F. Prepare and roll out Pastry for Double-Crust Pie through Step 4, lining a 9-inch pie plate with a pastry circle.
**3.** Stir berry mixture; transfer to pastry-lined pie plate. Trim bottom pastry even with the plate's edge (photos, *opposite*). Roll out remaining pastry and cut slits in circle; place on filling and seal. (If desired, use Lattice-Top Method; photos, *opposite*.) Crimp edge as desired (*pp. 608–609*). If desired, brush with *milk* and sprinkle with additional sugar.
**4.** Place a foil-lined baking sheet on rack below pie in oven. Bake 15 minutes. Reduce oven temperature to 375°F. Bake 1 hour more or until filling is bubbly. If needed to prevent overbrowning, cover pie loosely with foil the last 5 to 10 minutes. Cool on a wire rack.
**Makes 8 servings (1 slice each).**
**EACH SERVING** *453 cal., 19 g fat (7 g sat. fat), 15 mg chol., 340 mg sodium, 67 g carb., 4 g fiber, 30 g sugars, 5 g pro.*

## BERRY PIE CHANGE-UPS

Swap the blueberries in Blueberry Pie for a different flavor.

### RED RASPBERRY PIE
Prepare as directed, except substitute 6 cups fresh red raspberries or three 12-oz. pkg. frozen unsweetened red raspberries for the blueberries.

### BLACKBERRY PIE
Prepare as directed, except substitute 6 cups fresh blackberries or three 12-oz. pkg. frozen unsweetened blackberries for the blueberries.

### TRI-BERRY PIE
Prepare as directed, except use a combination of 2 cups each fresh blueberries, red raspberries, and blackberries or one 12-oz. pkg. each frozen unsweetened blueberries, red raspberries, and blackberries for the blueberries.

---

## DOUBLE-CRUST METHOD

### CLASSIC DOUBLE-CRUST PIES ARE BOTH RUSTIC AND BEAUTIFUL (EASY, TOO).

**1** After filling the pastry-lined pie plate with the desired filling, use kitchen scissors or a sharp knife to trim the bottom pastry even with the plate's edge.

**2** Roll out the remaining pie pastry. Use a sharp knife to cut slits in the pastry. You can also use small cutters for a decorative look. This allows steam to escape from the filling while the pie bakes.

**3** Gently fold the pastry in half and carefully place it on top of the filling, making sure to cover half of filling. Unfold pastry to cover other half of filling.

**4** Using kitchen scissors, trim the top pastry ½ inch beyond the edge of the plate. Fold the top pastry under the edge of the bottom pastry.

**5** Use the tines of a fork to press the edge of the pastry or crimp as desired (pp. 608–609).

---

## LATTICE-TOP METHOD

**1** For a lattice top, roll top pastry out and cut into strips. Strips can be the same width or varying. Place half of the pastry strips on the filling about 1 inch apart.

**2** Fold every other strip back halfway. Place a strip in the center of the pie across the unfolded strips already in place.

**3** Unfold the folded strips and fold back other strips. Place another strip across unfolded strips parallel to the first strip in the center.

**4** Continue folding, unfolding, and adding strips of pastry until lattice covers filling. Trim excess dough. Press strip ends into bottom pastry edge.

// PIES & TARTS //

## PEACH PIE

**HANDS-ON TIME** 40 minutes
**BAKE** 15 minutes at 450°F +
50 minutes at 375°F

PEACH PIE

>>

**FRESH PEACHES** should be peeled before making the pie filling. Here's the easiest peeling method: Dunk peaches in a large pot of boiling water for 30 to 60 seconds or until skins start to split. Use a slotted spoon to transfer peaches to a large bowl of ice water. When cool enough to handle, take them out of the water and use a paring knife to pull off the skin.

6   cups sliced, peeled fresh peaches or two 16-oz. pkg. frozen unsweetened sliced peaches
½   to ¾ cup sugar
3   Tbsp. cornstarch
½   tsp. ground cinnamon or ground ginger (optional)
1   recipe Pastry for Double-Crust Pie (p. 610)

**1.** Thaw peaches if using frozen (do not drain). In an extra-large bowl stir together sugar, cornstarch, and, if desired, cinnamon. Add peaches; toss to coat.
**2.** Preheat oven to 450°F. Prepare and roll out Pastry for Double-Crust Pie through Step 4, lining a 9-inch pie plate with a pastry circle.
**3.** Transfer filling to pastry-lined pie plate. Trim bottom pastry even with plate's edge. Roll out remaining pastry and cut slits in circle; place on filling and seal. Crimp edge as desired (pp. 608–609). If desired, brush top pastry with *milk* and sprinkle with sugar.
**4.** Place a foil-lined baking sheet on rack below pie in oven. Bake 15 minutes. Reduce oven temperature to 375°F. Bake 50 to 60 minutes more or until filling is bubbly in center. If needed to prevent overbrowning, cover pie loosely with foil the last 5 to 10 minutes. Cool on a wire rack.
**Makes 8 servings (1 slice each).**
**EACH SERVING** 411 cal, 19 g fat (7 g sat. fat), 15 mg chol, 338 mg sodium, 56 g carb., 3 g fiber, 22 g sugars, 5 g pro.

---

**CHANGE IT UP**

*Make your top crust a work of art. After rolling out pastry, cut into desired-size squares or shapes. Overlap on filling; continue as directed.*

## CHERRY PIE

**HANDS-ON TIME** 55 minutes
**BAKE** 15 minutes at 450°F + 1 hour at 375°F

6   cups fresh tart red cherries, pitted, or two 12-oz. pkg. frozen unsweetened pitted tart red cherries
1   to 1¼ cups sugar
3   Tbsp. cornstarch
1   recipe Pastry for Double-Crust Pie (p. 610)

**1.** Thaw cherries if using frozen (drain, reserving ¼ cup juice). In an extra-large bowl stir together sugar and cornstarch. Add cherries and reserved juice if using frozen cherries; toss to coat.
**2.** Preheat oven to 450°F. Prepare and roll out Pastry for Double-Crust Pie through Step 4, lining a 9-inch pie plate with a pastry circle.
**3.** Stir cherry mixture; transfer to pastry-lined pie plate. Trim bottom pastry even with plate's edge. Roll out remaining pastry and cut slits in circle; place on filling and seal. Crimp edge as desired (pp. 608–609). If desired, brush top with *milk* and sprinkle with sugar.
**4.** Place a foil-lined baking sheet on rack below pie in oven. Bake 15 minutes. Reduce oven temperature to 375°F. Bake about 1 hour more or until filling is bubbly. If needed to prevent overbrowning, cover pie loosely with foil the last 5 to 10 minutes. Cool on a wire rack.
**Makes 8 servings (1 slice each).**
**EACH SERVING** 473 cal, 19 g fat (7 g sat. fat), 15 mg chol, 342 mg sodium, 72 g carb., 3 g fiber, 35 g sugars, 5 g pro.

**FRESH OR FROZEN** If you have fresh cherries for pie, measure them before pitting. Put on an apron and work over a shallow dish to catch the juices. Invest in a cherry pitter or use a paper clip to pluck the pit out. Frozen cherries release a lot of juice when thawed, so drain the excess juice. Measure ¼ cup juice to return to cherries (this is the exact amount of liquid you need to work with the thickener perfectly).

APPLE PIE

CHERRY PIE

## APPLE PIE

**HANDS-ON TIME** 30 minutes
**BAKE** 15 minutes at 450°F +
50 minutes at 375°F

1    recipe Pastry for Double-Crust Pie *(p. 610)*
½ to ¾ cup sugar
2    Tbsp. all-purpose flour
½ tsp. ground cinnamon
6    cups thinly sliced, peeled apples

**1.** Preheat oven to 450°F. Prepare and roll out Pastry for Double-Crust Pie through Step 4, lining a 9-inch pie plate with a pastry circle.
**2.** For filling, in an extra-large bowl combine sugar, flour, and cinnamon. Add apples; toss. Transfer to pastry-lined pie plate. Trim bottom pastry even with plate's edge. Roll out remaining pastry and cut slits in circle; place on filling and seal. (If desired, use Lattice-Top Method; photos, *p. 611*.) Crimp edge as desired *(pp. 608–609)*. If desired, brush with *milk*; sprinkle with sugar.
**3.** Place a foil-lined baking sheet on rack below pie. Bake 15 minutes. Reduce oven temperature to 375°F. Bake 50 to 60 minutes more or until bubbly in center. If needed to prevent overbrowning, cover pie loosely with foil the last 10 to 15 minutes. Cool on a wire rack.
**Makes 8 servings (1 slice each).**
**EACH SERVING** *405 cal., 19 g fat (7 g sat. fat), 15 mg chol., 339 mg sodium, 55 g carb., 3 g fiber, 21 g sugars, 5 g pro.*
**DEEP-DISH APPLE PIE** Prepare as directed, except use a 9-inch deep-dish pie plate. Roll pastry into 14-inch circles. Use ¾ cup sugar, increase flour to 3 Tbsp., and increase apples to 8 cups in filling. Continue as directed.

**CHANGE IT UP**

*Omit cinnamon. Stir 1 tsp. apple pie spice into the sugar and flour.*

## ABOUT PIE PLATES

The depth and size of your pie plate do matter for these recipes.

**STANDARD PIE PLATES** are what we used for testing all the recipes in this book. The standard is a 9-inch glass pie plate (with 1½-inch-high sides). It's important to make sure you aren't using a deep-dish pie plate.

**DEEP-DISH PIE PLATES** have tall sides up to 2 inches high. They may be ceramic, glass, or stoneware and are beautiful for presentation (which is why there are so many on the market). But they are too deep for the pies in this chapter (the filling will be too shallow in the plate after baking). If you have a deep-dish plate you would like to use, make the Deep-Dish Apple Pie *(below left)*.

## STREUSEL TOPPING

Use any fruit filling from pies on *pp. 610–614* and substitute Pastry for Single-Crust Pie *(p. 609)* for the Pastry for Double-Crust Pie. Combine ⅔ cup each rolled oats and all-purpose flour, ½ cup packed brown sugar, and ¼ tsp. each salt and ground cinnamon. Cut in 6 Tbsp. butter, cut up, until mixture resembles coarse crumbs. Stir in ¼ cup chopped toasted walnuts or pecans. Sprinkle over filling before baking. Loosely cover top of pie with foil the last 10 to 15 minutes of baking.

// PIES & TARTS //

# STRAWBERRY-RHUBARB PIE

**HANDS-ON TIME** 40 minutes
**BAKE** 15 minutes at 450°F +
50 minutes at 375°F

3   cups 1-inch pieces fresh
    rhubarb or one 16-oz. pkg.
    frozen unsweetened sliced
    rhubarb
1¼  cups sugar
3   Tbsp. quick-cooking tapioca,
    crushed, or cornstarch
¼   tsp. salt
¼   tsp. ground nutmeg
3   cups sliced fresh strawberries
1   recipe Pastry for Double-Crust
    Pie (p. 610)

**1.** Thaw rhubarb if using frozen (do
not drain). In a bowl combine sugar,
tapioca, salt, and nutmeg. Add
rhubarb and strawberries; toss to
coat. Let mixture stand 15 minutes,
stirring occasionally.
**2.** Preheat oven to 450°F. Prepare
and roll out Pastry for Double-
Crust Pie through Step 4, lining a
9-inch pie plate with pastry circle.
**3.** Transfer rhubarb mixture to pastry.
Trim bottom pastry even with plate's
edge. Roll out remaining pastry;
place on filling and seal. Crimp edge
as desired (pp. 608–609).
**4.** Place a foil-lined baking
sheet on rack below pie in oven.
Bake 15 minutes. Reduce oven
temperature to 375°F. Bake 50 to
55 minutes more or until bubbly in
center. If needed, cover pie loosely
with foil the last 5 to 10 minutes.
Cool on a wire rack. **Makes
8 servings (1 slice each).**

**EACH SERVING** *473 cal., 19 g fat (7 g sat.
fat), 15 mg chol., 414 mg sodium, 72 g
carb., 3 g fiber, 35 g sugars, 5 g pro.*

**CHANGE IT UP**

*Instead of cutting slits in top
crust, cut out shapes. Attach
cutouts to top crust by brushing
lightly with milk. If desired,
sprinkle with coarse sugar.*

TAPIOCA is a
granular, starchy
substance used
to thicken fruit
pies and sauces.
Before using,
crush the tapioca
with a mortar and
pestle to avoid
gelatinous pearls
forming in the
filling. Look for
quick-cooking
(also called
"instant" or
"minute") tapioca
in the aisle with
pudding mixes.

**KEY LIMES**
are smaller
than regular
(Persian) limes
and are at peak
season in the
summer. They
have leathery
skin and more
acidic juice than
Persian limes. If
key limes aren't
available, use
regular ones.

# KEY LIME PIE

**HANDS-ON TIME** 30 minutes
**BAKE** 35 minutes at 325°F
**COOL** 1 hour
**CHILL** 2 hours

1   recipe Graham Cracker Crust
    (p. 623)
36  Key limes or 4 medium Persian
    limes
3   egg yolks, lightly beaten
1   14-oz. can sweetened
    condensed milk
½   cup heavy cream
2   drops green food coloring
    (optional)
1   recipe Sweetened Whipped
    Cream (p. 474)
    Lime slices (optional)

**1.** Prepare Graham Cracker Crust.
Reduce oven temperature to 325°F.
Remove ½ tsp. zest and squeeze
½ cup juice from limes.
**2.** For filling, in a bowl combine
egg yolks, sweetened condensed
milk, and lime zest. Whisk in lime
juice until combined (mixture will
thicken). Whisk in cream and, if
desired, the food coloring. Transfer
filling to crust.
**3.** Bake 35 minutes or until filling
reaches 160°F. Cool on a wire rack
1 hour. Cover and chill 2 to 24 hours.
**4.** Before serving, spoon or pipe
Sweetened Whipped Cream onto
pie. If desired, top with lime slices.
**Makes 8 servings (1 slice each).**

**EACH SERVING** *505 cal., 32 g fat
(19 g sat. fat), 157 mg chol., 205 mg
sodium, 50 g carb., 1 g fiber,
42 g sugars, 7 g pro.*

**GET-TOGETHER**

*Use a pastry bag fitted with a
star tip to pipe whipped cream
in large and small stars or other
designs. Add thin slices of lime.*

# FRESH STRAWBERRY PIE

**HANDS-ON TIME** 35 minutes
**COOL** 10 minutes
**CHILL** 1 hour

1   recipe Baked Pastry Shell
    (p. 609)
9   cups fresh strawberries, halved
½   cup water
⅔   cup sugar
2   Tbsp. cornstarch
    Several drops red food
    coloring (optional)
    Lemon zest and/or fresh mint
    (optional)

**1.** Prepare Baked Pastry Shell and
decorate edge (photo, p. 608).
**2.** For glaze, in a blender or food
processor combine 1½ cups of
the strawberries and the water.
Cover and blend or process until
smooth. In a 2-qt. saucepan stir
together sugar and cornstarch; stir
in strawberry puree. Cook and stir
over medium heat until thickened
and bubbly. Cook and stir 2 minutes
more. If desired, stir in food coloring.
Cool 10 minutes without stirring.
**3.** In a large bowl combine
remaining strawberries and glaze;
toss to coat. Transfer strawberry
mixture to baked shell. Chill 1 to
3 hours before serving (after
3 hours, bottom of crust starts to
soften). If desired, top with lemon
zest and/or mint. **Makes 8 servings
(1 slice each).**

**EACH SERVING** *316 cal., 12 g fat (5 g
sat. fat), 15 mg chol., 189 mg sodium,
49 g carb., 4 g fiber, 25 g sugars,
4 g pro.*

STRAWBERRY-RHUBARB PIE

FRESH STRAWBERRY PIE

KEY LIME PIE

PECAN PIE

BUTTERMILK PIE

## PECAN PIE

**HANDS-ON TIME** 25 minutes
**BAKE** 45 minutes at 350°F

1    recipe Pastry for Single-Crust Pie (p. 609)
3    eggs, lightly beaten
1    cup light-color corn syrup
⅔    cup sugar
⅓    cup butter, melted
1    tsp. vanilla
1¼   cups pecan halves or chopped macadamia nuts

**PECAN HALVES** give this pie its classic look, but you can use less-expensive pecan pieces, which make it easier to cut the pie cleanly.

**FOR A CHOCOLATE VERSION,** before adding filling to the pastry-lined pie plate, sprinkle pastry with ¾ cup semisweet chocolate chips.

**1.** Preheat oven to 350°F. Prepare and roll out Pastry for Single-Crust Pie. Line a 9-inch pie plate with pastry circle and trim. Crimp edge as desired (pp. 608–609).
**2.** For filling, in a medium bowl combine next five ingredients (through vanilla). Stir in nuts.
**3.** Transfer filling to pastry-lined pie plate. To prevent overbrowning, cover edge of pie loosely with foil. Bake 25 minutes. Remove foil. Bake 20 to 25 minutes more or until filling is puffed and appears set. Cool on a wire rack. Cover; chill within 2 hours. **Makes 8 servings (1 slice each).**

**EACH SERVING** 586 cal., 33 g fat (12 g sat. fat), 105 mg chol., 307 mg sodium, 71 g carb., 2 g fiber, 51 g sugars, 6 g pro.

## BUTTERMILK PIE

**HANDS-ON TIME** 30 minutes
**BAKE** 12 minutes at 450°F + 45 minutes at 350°F
**COOL** 1 hour
**CHILL** 4 hours

1    recipe Pastry for Single-Crust Pie (p. 609)
½    cup butter, cut up
1    cup sugar
3    Tbsp. all-purpose flour
3    eggs
1    cup buttermilk
1    tsp. vanilla
     Powdered sugar (optional)

**1.** Preheat oven to 450°F. Prepare and roll out Pastry for Single-Crust Pie. Line a 9-inch pie plate with pastry circle and trim. Crimp edge as desired (pp. 608–609). Do not prick pastry. Line pastry with a double thickness of foil. Bake 8 minutes. Remove foil. Bake 4 to 5 minutes more or until pastry is set and dry. Remove from oven; reduce oven temperature to 350°F.
**2.** Meanwhile, for filling, in a 2-qt. saucepan melt butter over medium-low heat. Stir in sugar and flour. Remove from heat. In a medium bowl beat eggs with a mixer on medium to high 1 minute.

Stir in buttermilk and vanilla. Gradually whisk egg mixture into butter mixture until smooth.
**3.** Place partially baked pastry shell on oven rack; pour filling into pastry shell. Cover edge of pie loosely with foil. Bake 45 to 50 minutes or until center appears set when gently shaken. Cool on a wire rack 1 hour. Cover and chill at least 4 hours before serving. If desired, sprinkle with powdered sugar. Store leftovers in the refrigerator up to 2 days. **Makes 8 servings (1 slice each).**

**EACH SERVING** 394 cal., 22 g fat (10 g sat. fat), 111 mg chol., 214 mg sodium, 44 g carb., 1 g fiber, 27 g sugars, 6 g pro.

## SNICKERDOODLE PIE

**HANDS-ON TIME** 40 minutes
**BAKE** 45 minutes at 350°F
**COOL** 30 minutes

1    recipe Pastry for Single-Crust Pie (p. 609)
1    Tbsp. granulated sugar
¾    tsp. ground cinnamon
2    tsp. butter, melted
½    cup packed brown sugar
¼    cup butter
3    Tbsp. water

SNICKERDOODLE PIE

PUMPKIN PIE

2 Tbsp. light-color corn syrup
1½ tsp. vanilla
¼ cup butter, softened
½ cup granulated sugar
¼ cup powdered sugar
1 tsp. baking powder
½ tsp. salt
¼ tsp. cream of tartar
1 egg
½ cup milk
1¼ cups all-purpose flour
Vanilla ice cream (optional)

**1.** Preheat oven to 350°F. Prepare and roll out Pastry for Single-Crust Pie. Line a 9-inch pie plate with pastry circle; trim. Crimp edge as desired (pp. 608–609). In a small bowl combine 1 Tbsp. granulated sugar and ½ tsp. of the cinnamon. Brush pastry with 2 tsp. melted butter and sprinkle with 1 tsp. cinnamon-sugar.

**2.** For syrup, in a 1-qt. saucepan combine brown sugar, ¼ cup butter, the water, corn syrup, and remaining ¼ tsp. cinnamon. Bring to boiling over medium heat, stirring to dissolve brown sugar. Boil gently, uncovered, 2 minutes. Remove from heat. Stir in ½ tsp. of the vanilla.

**3.** For filling, in a large bowl beat ¼ cup softened butter with a mixer on medium 30 seconds. Beat in the next five ingredients (through cream of tartar) until combined. Beat in egg and remaining 1 tsp. vanilla. Gradually beat in milk until combined. Beat in flour. Spread filling into pastry. Slowly pour syrup over filling; sprinkle with remaining cinnamon-sugar.

**4.** Cover edge of pie loosely with foil. Bake 25 minutes. Remove foil. Bake 20 minutes more or until top is puffed and golden and a toothpick comes out clean. Cool on a wire rack at least 30 minutes. If desired, serve with ice cream. **Makes 10 servings (1 slice each).**

**EACH SERVING** *423 cal., 20 g fat (11 g sat. fat), 61 mg chol., 380 mg sodium, 55 g carb., 1 g fiber, 27 g sugars, 5 g pro.*

## PUMPKIN PIE

**HANDS-ON TIME** 30 minutes
**BAKE** 1 hour at 400°F
**COOL** 1 hour

1 recipe Pastry for Single-Crust Pie (p. 609)
1 15-oz. can pumpkin
¾ cup packed brown sugar
1¼ tsp. ground cinnamon
1 tsp. ground ginger
½ tsp. salt
¼ tsp. ground cloves
4 eggs, lightly beaten
1½ cups half-and-half
1 recipe Sweetened Whipped Cream (p. 474) (optional)

**1.** Preheat oven to 400°F. Prepare and roll out Pastry for Single-Crust Pie. Line a 9-inch pie plate with pastry circle and trim. Crimp edge as desired (pp. 608–609). Do not prick pastry. Line pastry with a double thickness of foil. Bake 15 minutes. Remove foil.

**2.** Meanwhile, for filling, in a large bowl combine next six ingredients (through cloves). Stir in eggs. Gradually stir in half-and-half just until combined.

**3.** Place baked pastry shell on oven rack; pour filling into pastry shell. Cover edge of pie loosely with foil. Bake 20 minutes. Remove foil. Bake 25 to 30 minutes more or until a knife comes out clean. Cool on a wire rack 1 hour. Cover and chill within 2 hours. If desired, serve with Sweetened Whipped Cream. **Makes 8 servings (1 slice each).**

**EACH SERVING** *449 cal., 25 g fat (13 g sat. fat), 158 mg chol., 400 mg sodium, 49 g carb., 3 g fiber, 25 g sugars, 8 g pro.*

After spreading with butter and cinnamon-sugar, roll pastry up tightly. (Keep the roll snug.) Brush seam with a little water; press to seal the seam and the ends. Use a sharp knife to cut the pastry roll into ¼-inch slices.

# CINNAMON ROLL-SWEET POTATO PIE

**HANDS-ON TIME** 35 minutes
**BAKE** 12 minutes at 450°F + 55 minutes at 350°F

| | |
|---|---|
| 1 | 14.1-oz. pkg. (2 crusts) rolled refrigerated unbaked piecrust |
| 1¼ | lb. sweet potatoes, peeled and cut into 1-inch pieces |
| 3 | Tbsp. butter, melted |
| ¼ | cup granulated sugar |
| 1½ | tsp. ground cinnamon |
| 2 | eggs, lightly beaten |
| ⅓ | cup milk |
| ⅓ | cup sour cream |
| 2 | Tbsp. bourbon |
| 1 | tsp. vanilla |
| ¾ | cup packed brown sugar |
| 2 | Tbsp. all-purpose flour |
| ¼ | tsp. salt |
| ¼ | tsp. ground nutmeg |

**1.** Let piecrusts stand at room temperature according to package directions. Meanwhile, in a 3-qt. saucepan cook sweet potatoes in enough boiling lightly salted water

to cover 15 minutes or until tender. Drain and return to saucepan. Mash sweet potatoes; measure 1½ cups potatoes.

**2.** On a lightly floured surface roll one piecrust into a 14-inch circle. Brush with 1 Tbsp. of the melted butter. In a small bowl combine granulated sugar and 1 tsp. of the cinnamon. Sprinkle cinnamon-sugar over pastry; press lightly. Roll pastry into a cylinder; seal seam and ends. Cover and chill until needed.

**3.** Preheat oven to 450°F. Unroll remaining piecrust into a 9-inch pie plate. Fold under extra pastry even with the plate's edge; crimp edge as desired *(pp. 608–609)*. Do not prick pastry. Line pastry with a double thickness of foil. Bake 8 minutes. Remove foil. Bake 4 to 5 minutes more or until set and dry. Remove from oven. Reduce oven temperature to 350°F.

**4.** Meanwhile, for filling, in a large bowl whisk together eggs, milk, sour cream, bourbon, and vanilla. Stir in mashed sweet potatoes and remaining 2 Tbsp. melted butter. Stir in brown sugar, flour, salt, nutmeg, and remaining ½ tsp. cinnamon until combined.

**5.** Pour filling into partially baked pastry shell. To prevent overbrowning, cover edge of pie loosely with foil. Bake 30 minutes. Cut pastry cylinder into ¼-inch slices. Remove pie from oven. Remove foil. Arrange pastry slices on filling close together without overlapping. Bake 25 minutes more or until filling is puffed and set and pastry circles are light brown. Cool on a wire rack. Cover and chill within 2 hours. **Makes 8 servings (1 slice each).**

**EACH SERVING** *442 cal., 19 g fat (9 g sat. fat), 68 mg chol., 424 mg sodium, 64 g carb., 2 g fiber, 29 g sugars, 4 g pro.*

>> 

DARK CHOCOLATE CREAM PIE Prepare as directed, except increase sugar to 1 cup and stir in 3 oz. chopped unsweetened chocolate with the half-and-half. If desired, lightly sprinkle the finished pie with unsweetened cocoa powder.

## VANILLA CREAM PIE

**HANDS-ON TIME** 50 minutes
**BAKE** 20 minutes at 325°F
**COOL** 1 hour 30 minutes
**CHILL** 3 hours

>>

MERINGUE is a little finicky and needs some TLC. Learn all about it on pp. 620–621.

| | |
|---|---|
| 1 | recipe Baked Pastry Shell (p. 609) |
| 4 | eggs |
| 1 | recipe Meringue for Pie (p. 620) |
| ¾ | cup sugar |
| 3 | Tbsp. cornstarch |
| 2½ | cups half-and-half or milk |
| 1 | Tbsp. butter |
| 1½ | tsp. vanilla or vanilla bean paste |

**1.** Prepare Baked Pastry Shell. Separate egg yolks from egg whites. Set aside yolks for filling and whites for meringue.

**2.** Preheat oven to 325°F. Prepare Meringue for Pie.

**3.** For filling, in a 2-qt. saucepan stir together sugar and cornstarch. Gradually whisk in half-and-half. Cook and whisk over medium-high heat until thickened and bubbly; reduce heat. Cook and stir 2 minutes more. Remove from heat.

**4.** Gradually whisk about 1 cup of the hot mixture into egg yolks (photos, p. 620); return to remaining hot mixture in saucepan. Bring to a gentle boil, whisking constantly; reduce heat. Cook and whisk 2 minutes more. Remove from heat. Stir in butter and vanilla.

**5.** Pour hot filling into baked shell. Immediately spread meringue over hot filling, sealing to edge of pastry. Using the back of a spoon, swirl meringue to form high, decorative peaks. Bake 20 to 25 minutes or until golden and a thermometer registers 160°F (tip, p. 620). Cool on a wire rack 1½ hours. Chill 3 to 6 hours before serving; cover pie for longer storage in refrigerator.

**Makes 8 servings (1 slice each).**

**EACH SERVING** 483 cal., 24 g fat (12 g sat. fat), 139 mg chol., 314 mg sodium, 57 g carb., 1 g fiber, 35 g sugars, 10 g pro.

**CHANGE IT UP**

*If you're not a fan of meringue, top with whipped cream instead. Pour filling into the baked pastry shell and cover surface with plastic wrap; chill 3 to 6 hours. To serve, prepare Sweetened Whipped Cream (p. 474) and spread or pipe onto pie.*

>>

COCONUT CREAM PIE Prepare as directed, except stir in 1 cup toasted flaked coconut with the butter and vanilla. If desired, sprinkle the finished pie with ⅓ cup toasted flaked coconut.

>>

BANANA CREAM PIE Prepare as directed, except before adding filling to the baked pastry shell, arrange 3 medium bananas, sliced, in bottom of pastry. If desired, drizzle the finished pie with caramel ice cream topping.

// PIES & TARTS //

THE MOMENT OF TRUTH IS IN THAT FIRST CUT—DOES YOUR PIE FILLING HOLD A STRAIGHT EDGE? TWO THINGS WILL GET YOU THERE: SLOWLY WHISK THE YOLKS INTO THE HOT LIQUID TO SMOOTHLY DISTRIBUTE. AND COOK FILLING FOR THE FULL 2 MINUTES SO CORNSTARCH REACHES ITS FULL THICKENING POTENTIAL.

**FRESHLY SQUEEZED LEMON JUICE is a must here** (bottled just won't cut it). To get the most juice from a lemon, microwave it for 10 to 20 seconds, then roll it on the countertop under your palm to break up the pulp inside. Cut it in half and use a juicer for best results.

**CORNSTARCH molecules swell and absorb water when they are heated.** But continue cooking and whisking the filling the full 2 minutes after simmering starts. Undercooked starch-thickened fillings don't have the strength to hold a cut edge and are more likely to weep during storage.

## LEMON MERINGUE PIE

**HANDS-ON TIME** 50 minutes
**BAKE** 20 minutes at 325°F
**COOL** 1 hour 30 minutes
**CHILL** 3 hours

1   recipe Baked Pastry Shell (p. 609)
5   eggs
3   large lemons
1   recipe Meringue for Pie
2   cups sugar
⅓   cup cornstarch
1   cup water
⅓   cup butter, cut up

**1.** Prepare Baked Pastry Shell. Separate egg yolks from egg whites. Set aside five yolks for filling and four whites for meringue. (Discard remaining white.) Remove 2 tsp. zest and squeeze ¾ cup juice from lemons.
**2.** Preheat oven to 325°F. Prepare Meringue for Pie.
**3.** For filling, in a 2-qt. saucepan stir together sugar and cornstarch. Whisk in lemon zest, lemon juice, and the water. Cook and stir over medium heat until thickened and bubbly. Remove from heat.
**4.** Gradually whisk about half of the hot mixture into egg yolks; return to remaining hot mixture in saucepan. Bring to a gentle boil, whisking constantly; reduce heat. Cook and whisk 2 minutes more. Remove from heat. Add butter; stir until melted.
**5.** Pour hot filling into pastry shell. Spread meringue over filling; seal to pastry edge. Swirl meringue to make peaks. Bake 20 to 25 minutes

or until golden and a thermometer registers 160°F (tip, *right*). Cool on a wire rack 1½ hours. Chill 3 to 6 hours before serving; cover pie for longer storage in refrigerator. **Makes 8 servings (1 slice each).**
**EACH SERVING** *577 cal., 23 g fat (11 g sat. fat), 151 mg chol., 288 mg sodium, 89 g carb., 1 g fiber, 64 g sugars, 6 g pro.*

## MERINGUE FOR PIE

**HANDS-ON TIME** 15 minutes
**STAND** 30 minutes

4   egg whites
½   cup water
2   tsp. cornstarch
1   tsp. vanilla
½   tsp. cream of tartar
½   cup sugar

**1.** In a large bowl allow egg whites to stand at room temperature 30 minutes.
**2.** In a 1-cup liquid measure whisk to combine the water and cornstarch. Microwave 45 to 60 seconds or until boiling, stirring once.
**3.** Add vanilla and cream of tartar to egg whites. Beat with a mixer on medium 1 minute or until soft peaks form (tips curl). Add sugar, 1 Tbsp. at a time, beating on high. Gradually beat in warm cornstarch mixture until stiff, glossy peaks form (tips stand straight) (photos, *opposite*).
**4.** Prepare desired pie filling. Quickly beat meringue with mixer and spread meringue over hot filling, sealing to edge of pastry to prevent shrinkage. Bake as directed in recipes.

### IS IT DONE?
To determine the doneness of the meringue, insert an instant-read thermometer into the center of the meringue, holding the thermometer at an angle.

❶ Tempering your yolks— whisking half the hot mixture into yolks, then slowly adding it all back into the pan—heats the yolks slowly and evenly to prevent bits of cooked eggs in your filling. Don't stop whisking.

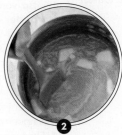

❷ After cooking filling, remove pan from heat and use a spatula to stir in the pieces of butter, which add richness and help thicken the filling. You'll want your filling to be HOT when you pour it into the pastry shell and spread the meringue over top.

## WHY THE WEEPING?

Weeping—a layer of moisture that forms between the meringue and filling after chilling—is the top complaint about homemade meringue pies. Three steps will help prevent this.

**FIRST,** beat the mixture of thickened cornstarch and water into the egg whites to bind and stabilize the liquid in the meringue (and keep it from seeping out).

**SECOND,** cook the filling for the full 2 minutes on the stove top so the cornstarch thickens completely—and doesn't start breaking down and "leaking" during chilling.

**THIRD,** spread the meringue on the filling while the filling is HOT. This heats (and seals) the underside of the meringue so it cooks as thoroughly as the top (which is exposed to the heat of the oven).

**1** Wash your bowl and beaters with hot, soapy water (any oily residue will hinder your meringue). Beat room-temperature egg whites, vanilla, and cream of tartar just until the tips of the whites curl over when you pull out the beaters.

**2** Add the sugar to the egg white mixture, 1 Tbsp. at a time, beating constantly. You want each addition of sugar to be fully incorporated before adding the next spoonful.

**3** Gradually beat in the thickened cornstarch mixture and keep beating until the mixture forms stiff, glossy peaks (the tips will stand straight).

COOKIE-LAYERED FRENCH SILK PIE

ICE CREAM PIE

## FRENCH SILK PIE

**HANDS-ON TIME** 1 hour
**CHILL** 5 hours

| | |
|---|---|
| 1 | recipe Baked Pastry Shell (p. 609) |
| 1 | cup heavy cream |
| 1 | cup semisweet chocolate chips |
| ⅓ | cup butter, cut up |
| ⅓ | cup sugar |
| 2 | egg yolks, lightly beaten |
| 3 | Tbsp. crème de cacao or heavy cream |
| 1 | recipe Sweetened Whipped Cream (p. 474) |
| 1 | recipe Giant Chocolate Curls (optional) |

**1.** Prepare Baked Pastry Shell. In a 2-qt. heavy saucepan combine 1 cup cream, chocolate chips, butter, and sugar. Cook over low heat until chocolate is melted (about 10 minutes), stirring frequently. Remove from heat.
**2.** Gradually stir about half of the hot mixture into egg yolks; return to remaining hot mixture in saucepan. Cook and stir over medium-low heat until mixture is slightly thickened and begins to bubble (about 5 minutes). Remove from heat (mixture may appear slightly curdled). Stir in crème de cacao. Place saucepan in a bowl of ice water, stirring occasionally, until mixture stiffens and becomes hard to stir (about 20 minutes).
**3.** Transfer chocolate mixture to a medium bowl. Beat with a mixer on medium to high 2 to 3 minutes or until light and fluffy. Spread filling into baked shell. Cover and chill 5 to 24 hours. Before serving, top with Sweetened Whipped Cream and, if desired, Giant Chocolate Curls. Cover and chill any leftovers.
**Makes 8 servings (1 slice each).**
**COOKIE-LAYERED FRENCH SILK PIE** Prepare as directed, except in Step 3, spread about half of the filling into baked shell. Sprinkle with ½ cup crushed chocolate sandwich cookies with white filling and spread with remaining filling. Chill and serve as directed.
**EACH SERVING** *647 cal., 49 g fat (28 g sat. fat), 150 mg chol., 274 mg sodium, 47 g carb., 2 g fiber, 27 g sugars, 6 g pro.*

## GIANT CHOCOLATE CURLS

Turn a 3-qt. rectangular glass baking dish upside down. In a small bowl microwave 2 oz. chopped bittersweet chocolate 45 seconds or until melted and smooth, stirring every 15 seconds. Using an offset spatula, spread chocolate over bottom of dish. Let stand 30 minutes or until set. (If needed, place dish in freezer 1 to 3 minutes to help set the chocolate; let stand at room temperature 5 to 10 minutes.) Hold a straight-edge metal spatula at an angle at one edge of the chocolate. Applying gentle, steady pressure, push the spatula forward to create curls. (You may need to repeat freezing and standing to get chocolate to the right consistency to do this.)

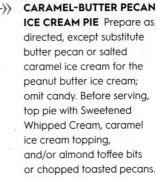

**PICK A FLAVOR**
The possibilities are endless. Mix and match any flavor of ice cream with sauces, toppings, candies, cookies, and/or sprinkles.

## ICE CREAM PIE

**HANDS-ON TIME** 20 minutes
**FREEZE** 4 hours
**STAND** 10 minutes

1   recipe Graham Cracker Crust
2   pt. (4 cups) peanut butter-swirl
    ice cream
    Chopped or crushed
    chocolate-covered crisp
    peanut butter candy bars
1   recipe Sweetened Whipped
    Cream (p. 474) and/or hot
    fudge ice cream topping
    (optional)

**1.** Prepare Graham Cracker Crust. In a chilled large bowl stir ice cream until softened but not melted. Spread ice cream into cooled crust. Sprinkle with candy bars. Cover and freeze 4 hours or until firm.
**2.** Let pie stand at room temperature 10 to 15 minutes before serving. If desired, top with Sweetened Whipped Cream and/or hot fudge topping. **Makes 8 servings (1 slice each).**
**EACH SERVING** *403 cal., 23 g fat (12 g sat. fat), 45 mg chol., 251 mg sodium, 44 g carb., 1 g fiber, 31 g sugars, 6 g pro.*

« **PURCHASED GRAHAM CRACKER CRUST** can be used instead of the homemade version. The crust can be crumbly. To make it easy to cut, preheat oven to 375°F. Brush crust with 1 lightly beaten egg white and bake 5 minutes. Cool on a wire rack before filling.

» **CARAMEL-BUTTER PECAN ICE CREAM PIE** Prepare as directed, except substitute butter pecan or salted caramel ice cream for the peanut butter ice cream; omit candy. Before serving, top pie with Sweetened Whipped Cream, caramel ice cream topping, and/or almond toffee bits or chopped toasted pecans.

» **LAYERED COFFEE ICE CREAM PIE** Prepare Chocolate Wafer Crust (*right*); omit peanut butter ice cream and candy. Soften 1 pt. (2 cups) vanilla bean or chocolate chunk ice cream and spread into chilled crust. Freeze 1 hour. Soften 1 pt. (2 cups) coffee ice cream; spread over ice cream in crust. Cover and freeze 4 hours or until firm. Top pie with Sweetened Whipped Cream and crushed chocolate-covered coffee beans before serving.

## GRAHAM CRACKER CRUST

**HANDS-ON TIME** 10 minutes
**BAKE** 5 minutes at 375°F

⅓   cup butter, melted
¼   cup sugar
1¼  cups finely crushed graham
    crackers (about 10 full
    cracker sheets)

**1.** Preheat oven to 375°F. Lightly coat a 9-inch pie plate with *nonstick cooking spray*. In a medium bowl combine melted butter and sugar. Add crushed graham crackers; toss to mix well. Spread in prepared pie plate; press onto bottom and sides.
**2.** Bake 5 minutes or until edges are light brown. Cool on a wire rack. **Makes 8 servings (1 slice each).**
**VANILLA WAFER CRUST** Prepare as directed, except omit sugar and substitute 1½ cups finely crushed vanilla wafers (about forty-two 1½-inch-diameter cookies) for the graham crackers.
**CHOCOLATE WAFER CRUST** Prepare as directed, except omit sugar and substitute 1½ cups finely crushed chocolate wafer cookies (about 25) for the graham crackers. Do not bake; chill 1 hour or until firm.
**DEEP-DISH VERSION** Prepare as directed, except use ½ cup melted butter, ⅓ cup sugar, and 1½ cups crushed graham crackers. Spread in a 9-inch deep-dish pie plate; press onto bottom and sides.
**EACH SERVING** *154 cal., 9 g fat (5 g sat. fat), 20 mg chol., 126 mg sodium, 17 g carb., 0 g fiber, 10 g sugars, 1 g pro.*

// **PIES & TARTS** //

MAPLE-NUT PAN PIE

## MAPLE-NUT PAN PIE

**HANDS-ON TIME** 25 minutes
**BAKE** 40 minutes at 350°F

| | |
|---|---|
| 1½ | cups all-purpose flour |
| ⅔ | cup powdered sugar |
| ¼ | tsp. salt |
| ⅔ | cup butter, cut up |
| 3 | eggs, lightly beaten |
| 1¼ | cups chopped mixed nuts |
| ¾ | cup packed brown sugar |
| ¾ | cup pure maple syrup |
| 3 | Tbsp. butter, melted |
| ½ | tsp. maple flavoring or 1 tsp. vanilla |
| | Sweetened Whipped Cream (p. 474) (optional) |

**1.** Preheat oven to 350°F. Line a 13×9-inch baking pan with foil, extending foil over edges. Lightly coat foil with *nonstick cooking spray*.

**2.** In a medium bowl stir together flour, powdered sugar, and salt. Using a pastry blender, cut in ⅔ cup butter until mixture resembles coarse crumbs. Press onto bottom of prepared pan. Bake about 20 minutes or until light brown.

**3.** Meanwhile, for filling, in another medium bowl combine next six ingredients (through maple flavoring). Spread filling into hot crust.

**4.** Bake 20 minutes more or until filling is set. Cool on a wire rack. Use foil to lift out uncut pie. Cut into bars. If desired, top with Sweetened Whipped Cream. **Makes 24 bars.**
**TO STORE** Place bars in a single layer in an airtight container; cover. Store in refrigerator up to 3 days.
**EACH BAR** *203 cal., 11 g fat (5 g sat fat), 41 mg chol., 113 mg sodium, 25 g carb., 1 g fiber, 16 g sugars, 3 g pro.*

**GET-TOGETHER**

*Slab or pan pies are great for serving crowds. Cut them smaller if serving more than one dessert. A little whipped cream is all the garnish they need.*

---

**PUFF PASTRY** is our secret weapon for making effortless fancy desserts. Scoring the edges of the squares and pricking the centers allow the edges to puff up to create a pastry "bowl."

---

## ROASTED APPLE AND PEAR TARTS

**HANDS-ON TIME** 20 minutes
**BAKE** 32 minutes at 425°F

| | |
|---|---|
| ½ | cup packed brown sugar |
| ¼ | cup butter, melted |
| ½ | tsp. ground cinnamon |
| 2 | cups sliced apples and/or pears |
| 1 | Tbsp. bourbon (optional) |
| ½ | of a 17.3-oz. pkg. (1 sheet) frozen puff pastry sheets, thawed |
| ¼ | cup chopped toasted pecans or walnuts |
| | Sea salt flakes (optional) |

**1.** Preheat oven to 425°F. In a bowl combine brown sugar, melted butter, and cinnamon. Spread in a 13×9-inch baking pan. Top with apples and/or pears. Roast 15 minutes. Remove fruit. If desired, stir bourbon into sugar mixture in pan.

**2.** Line a baking sheet with foil. On a lightly floured surface unfold puff pastry and cut into nine 3-inch squares. Using a paring knife, make a shallow cut around each square ½ inch from the edges. Generously prick centers with a fork. Place 1 inch apart on prepared baking sheet. Bake 10 minutes. Press down centers with the back of a spoon.

**3.** Spoon apples and/or pears into centers of tarts. Drizzle 2 tsp. of the sugar mixture from baking pan over fruit in each tart. Sprinkle with nuts. Bake 7 to 10 minutes more or until pastry is light brown. Drizzle tarts with remaining sugar mixture and, if desired, sprinkle with salt.

**Makes 9 tarts.**
**EACH TART** *284 cal., 18 g fat (6 g sat. fat), 14 mg chol., 112 mg sodium, 30 g carb., 2 g fiber, 16 g sugars, 2 g pro.*

**ROASTED APPLE AND PEAR TARTS**

# CHERRY HAND PIES

**HANDS-ON TIME** 45 minutes
**BAKE** 20 minutes at 375°F

- 3 cups fresh or frozen unsweetened pitted tart red cherries
- ⅔ cup granulated sugar
- 3 Tbsp. cornstarch
- 1 tsp. orange zest
- 1 Tbsp. orange juice
- 3½ cups all-purpose flour
- 2 Tbsp. granulated sugar
- 1 tsp. salt
- 1½ cups butter, cut up
- 2 eggs, lightly beaten
- ¼ to ½ cup milk

**1.** For filling, in a 2-qt. saucepan combine first five ingredients (through orange juice). Cook and stir over medium heat until thickened and bubbly; cool. (Or transfer to an airtight container, cover, and chill overnight; stir before using.)

**2.** For pastry, in an extra-large bowl stir together flour, 2 Tbsp. granulated sugar, and salt. Using a pastry blender, cut in butter until mixture resembles fine crumbs. Stir in eggs. Sprinkle 1 Tbsp. of the milk over part of the flour mixture; toss with a fork. Push moistened pastry to side of bowl. Repeat moistening flour mixture, gradually adding milk until mixture begins to come together.

**3.** Gather pastry into a ball, kneading gently just until it holds together. Divide pastry into fourths; form four balls. If needed, cover with plastic wrap and chill until easy to handle (up to 1 hour).

**4.** Preheat oven to 375°F. Line two large baking sheets with parchment paper. On a lightly floured surface roll each pastry ball into a 9×8-inch rectangle; cut into four 4½×4-inch rectangles. Brush edges with additional milk. Spoon 1 well-rounded Tbsp. filling onto half of each rectangle; fold remaining rectangle half over filling. Seal edges and prick tops with a fork. Place on baking sheets. Brush pies with additional milk and, if desired, sprinkle with *coarse sugar*.

**5.** Bake 20 to 25 minutes or until light brown. Remove; cool slightly on wire racks. Serve warm or at room temperature. **Makes 16 pies.**

**EACH PIE** *327 cal., 18 g fat (11 g sat. fat), 69 mg chol., 295 mg sodium, 37 g carb., 1 g fiber, 14 g sugars, 4 g pro.*

### CHANGE IT UP
*Sweeten these pick-up-and-eat pies even more. Stir together Powdered Sugar Icing (p. 538) and drizzle over warm or cooled pies.*

**BLUEBERRY HAND PIES** Prepare as directed, except for filling, use 3 cups fresh or frozen blueberries, ⅔ cup granulated sugar, ¼ cup all-purpose flour, 1 tsp. lemon zest, and 2 Tbsp. lemon juice.

**PLUM HAND PIES** Prepare as directed, except for filling, use 3 cups chopped fresh plums, ½ cup granulated sugar, 3 Tbsp. cornstarch, 1 Tbsp. each butter and lemon juice, and ⅛ tsp. ground cloves.

# COUNTRY PEACH TART

**HANDS-ON TIME** 30 minutes
**BAKE** 50 minutes at 375°F
**COOL** 30 minutes

1   recipe Pastry for Single-Crust Pie *(p. 609)*
¼   cup sugar
4   tsp. all-purpose flour
¼   tsp. ground nutmeg, cinnamon, or ginger
3   cups sliced, peeled peaches or nectarines or 3 cups frozen sliced peaches, thawed (do not drain)
1   Tbsp. lemon juice
1   Tbsp. sliced almonds
    Milk

**1.** Preheat oven to 375°F. Prepare Pastry for Single-Crust Pie through Step 2. On a large piece of lightly floured parchment paper roll pastry into a 13-inch circle. Slide paper with pastry onto a baking sheet.

**2.** For filling, in a large bowl stir together sugar, flour, and nutmeg. Add peaches and lemon juice; toss to coat. Mound filling in center of pastry, leaving outer 2 inches uncovered. Using paper to lift pastry border, fold unfilled edge of pastry over filling, pleating as needed. Sprinkle filling with almonds. Lightly brush pastry top and sides with milk and sprinkle with additional sugar.

**3.** Bake 50 to 55 minutes or until filling is bubbly and pastry is golden. If needed to prevent overbrowning, cover tart loosely with foil the last 5 to 10 minutes. Cool on baking sheet on a wire rack 30 minutes. **Makes 8 servings (1 slice each).**

**EACH SERVING** *250 cal., 13 g fat (5 g sat. fat), 15 mg chol., 193 mg sodium, 31 g carb., 2 g fiber, 11 g sugars, 3 g pro.*

**COUNTRY APPLE OR PEAR TART** Prepare as directed, except increase sugar to ⅓ cup and substitute 1 Tbsp. finely snipped crystallized ginger and ¼ tsp. ground cinnamon for the nutmeg; substitute 4 cups sliced, peeled apples or pears for the peaches. Assemble tart as directed, except dot filling with 1 Tbsp. butter and substitute chopped walnuts or pecans for the almonds.

**COUNTRY PEACH-BERRY TART** Prepare as directed, except add 1 cup fresh red raspberries or blueberries with the peaches; substitute chopped dry-roasted pistachio nuts for the almonds. Increase baking time to 55 to 65 minutes or until filling is bubbly.

BERRIES AND CREAM TART

SALTED TRUFFLE TART

## BERRIES AND CREAM TART

**HANDS-ON TIME** 30 minutes
**CHILL** 4 hours 30 minutes
**BAKE** 14 minutes at 450°F

**TART PANS**
A tart is baked in a fluted pan with a removable bottom so it can be easily removed from the pan. Just press on the bottom to lift the removable round from the pan, slowly easing the tart out so the crust doesn't crumble.

1   recipe Rich Tart Pastry
1   8-oz. pkg. cream cheese, softened
⅓  cup orange marmalade
1   cup heavy cream
    Assorted fresh berries, such as blueberries, raspberries, blackberries, and/or quartered strawberries

**1.** Prepare and chill Rich Tart Pastry. Preheat oven to 450°F. On a lightly floured surface roll pastry to a 12-inch circle. Fold pastry circle into fourths and transfer to a 10-inch round tart pan with a removable bottom. Unfold pastry and ease into tart pan. Press pastry into fluted sides; trim edge. Prick bottom and sides of pastry with a fork. Line pastry with a double thickness of foil. Bake 8 minutes. Remove foil. Bake 6 to 8 minutes more or until golden. Cool on a wire rack.

**2.** Meanwhile, for filling, in a bowl beat cream cheese and marmalade with a mixer on medium until combined. Gradually beat in cream until mixture is light and fluffy.

**3.** Spread filling in baked shell. Cover; chill 4 to 24 hours. Remove sides of tart pan. Top with berries.

**Makes 12 servings (1 slice each).**

**INDIVIDUAL TARTS** Prepare, chill, and roll out Rich Tart Pastry. Cut into six 4½-inch circles, rerolling scraps as needed. Transfer pastry circles to six 3½-inch individual tart pans with removable bottoms; press into sides and trim edges. Prick pastries; line with foil. Bake 6 minutes. Remove foil. Bake 4 to 5 minutes more or until pastries are golden. Cool on a wire rack.

Spread filling in tart shells. Cover and chill 4 to 24 hours. Remove sides of tart pans. Top with berries.

**Makes 12 servings (½ tart each).**

**EACH SERVING** 307 cal., 22 g fat (14 g sat. fat), 93 mg chol., 133 mg sodium, 24 g carb., 1 g fiber, 13 g sugars, 4 g pro.

## RICH TART PASTRY

In a medium bowl stir together 1¼ cups all-purpose flour and ¼ cup sugar. Using a pastry blender, cut in ½ cup butter, cut up, until pea size. In a small bowl combine 2 lightly beaten egg yolks and 1 Tbsp. cold water. Gradually stir egg yolk mixture into flour mixture just until moistened. Gather pastry into a ball, kneading gently just until it holds together. Cover and chill until easy to handle (30 to 60 minutes).

## SALTED TRUFFLE TART

**HANDS-ON TIME** 30 minutes
**FREEZE** 45 minutes
**BAKE** 18 minutes at 400°F
**CHILL** 4 hour
**STAND** 30 minutes

½   cup almonds or hazelnuts, coarsely chopped
⅓   cup packed brown sugar
⅓   cup regular rolled oats
¾   cup all-purpose flour
½   cup chilled butter, cut up
1   egg yolk
12  oz. bittersweet chocolate, chopped
2   Tbsp. butter, cut up
1   Tbsp. packed brown sugar
1¼  cups heavy cream
½   tsp. vanilla
¼   tsp. sea salt
    Sea salt flakes (optional)

»

SEA SALT FLAKES have a clean flavor and crunchy texture. Maldon is a well-known brand, but many are available at large supermarkets and specialty stores.

**1.** Lightly butter a 9-inch square or round tart pan with a removable bottom; place in freezer. In a food processor combine nuts, ⅓ cup brown sugar, and oats. Cover and process until nuts are finely ground. Add flour; cover and pulse until combined. Add ½ cup butter; cover and pulse until mixture resembles coarse meal. Add egg yolk; cover and pulse 30 seconds or until mixture begins to come together. Remove from bowl; knead gently until pastry just holds together. Press onto bottom and sides of prepared tart pan; prick bottom. Line crust with foil. Freeze at least 45 minutes or overnight.
**2.** Preheat oven to 400°F. Fill foil-lined crust with dried beans or pie weights, spreading to edges. Bake 12 minutes. Remove foil and beans. Bake 6 to 8 minutes more or until deep golden. Cool on a wire rack.
**3.** Meanwhile, for filling, in a medium heatproof bowl combine chocolate, 2 Tbsp. butter, and 1 Tbsp. brown sugar. Bring cream just to boiling. Pour through a fine-mesh sieve into chocolate mixture (do not stir). Let

stand 5 minutes. Stir in vanilla and ¼ tsp. salt until smooth. Spread filling into crust. Chill 4 to 24 hours; cover after 3 hours.
**4.** Let stand at room temperature 30 minutes before serving. If desired, sprinkle with sea salt flakes.
**Makes 16 servings (1 piece each).**
**EACH SERVING** *313 cal., 25 g fat (14 g sat. fat), 52 mg chol., 99 mg sodium, 24 g carb., 2 g fiber, 15 g sugars, 4 g pro.*

---

## CHOCOLATE GANACHE-PEANUT BUTTER TART

**HANDS-ON TIME** 30 minutes
**BAKE** 10 minutes at 350°F
**CHILL** 4 hours
**STAND** 10 minutes

2   Tbsp. sugar
2   Tbsp. butter, melted
1   cup finely crushed chocolate sandwich cookies with white filling
1½  cups half-and-half
2   Tbsp. all-purpose flour
¼   tsp. salt
3   egg yolks
⅓   cup sugar
½   cup creamy peanut butter
1   tsp. vanilla
4   oz. bittersweet chocolate, chopped
⅓   cup heavy cream

**1.** Preheat oven to 350°F. For crust, in a medium bowl combine 2 Tbsp. sugar and melted butter. Add crushed cookies; toss to mix well. Press onto bottom of a 9-inch tart pan with a removable bottom. Bake 10 minutes or until set. Cool on a wire rack.
**2.** Meanwhile, for filling, in a 2-qt. saucepan combine half-and-half, flour, and salt. Cook and stir over medium heat until thickened and bubbly. In a bowl combine egg yolks and ⅓ cup sugar. Gradually stir about half of the hot mixture into egg yolk mixture; return to

**PERFECT CUTS**
To get perfect cuts on chocolate tarts, first hold a long sharp knife under hot tap water to heat. Wipe knife dry and make a cut. Repeat between cuts.

remaining hot mixture in saucepan. Cook and stir over medium heat until thickened and bubbly. Reduce heat to medium-low; cook and stir 2 minutes more. Remove from heat. Whisk in peanut butter and vanilla. Spread filling into crust. Cover and chill 3 hours.
**3.** For ganache, place chocolate in a small heatproof bowl. In another small bowl microwave cream 30 to 40 seconds or just until boiling. Pour over chocolate (do not stir). Let stand 5 minutes. Stir until smooth; spread over filling. Cover and chill 1 to 24 hours.
**4.** Let stand at room temperature 10 minutes before removing sides of tart pan and serving. **Makes 16 servings (1 slice each).**
**EACH SERVING** *220 cal., 15 g fat (7 g sat. fat), 52 mg chol., 134 mg sodium, 20 g carb., 1 g fiber, 14 g sugars, 4 g pro.*

**CHOCOLATE GANACHE-PEANUT BUTTER TART**

# PRESERVING

Better Homes
& Gardens.

TEST KITCHEN

**ALL RECIPES ARE MAKE-AHEAD RECIPES**

# CANNING

THIS CLASSIC PRESERVATION TECHNIQUE USES BOILING WATER TO PROCESS JARS OF FOOD SO THEY ARE SHELF-STABLE UP TO A YEAR. THE BOILING WATER DESTROYS HARMFUL MICROORGANISMS, INACTIVATES THE FOOD'S ENZYMES, AND VACUUM-SEALS THE JARS SO THEY ARE AIRTIGHT.

## JAR BASICS

The type of jars you use for canning is important. Look for canning-specific jars with the canning supplies in hardware stores and supermarkets.

**SCREW BANDS** may be reused; they secure lids to the jars during processing. They can be removed before storage or left on to provide cushioning between stacked jars. Wipe the threads of the jars and screw bands after processing to remove food particles before storing.

**LIDS** (the flat round discs) are for one canning session only (purchase lids separately for each canning session). The red substance on the lid helps seal the lid onto the jar for an airtight seal. (For visual purposes, the lid is shown upside-down, *left*; the red substance seals onto the glass.) The compound only seals once, so discard the lid when the contents of the jar are gone.

**JARS** are molded from thick glass designed to withstand processing. They are available in many sizes; the jar tops are either regular-mouth or wide-mouth. As long as they are free of chips and cracks, canning jars can be reused year after year.

## USING LIDS AND SCREW BANDS

**1 ALWAYS USE NEW LIDS** (the flat round piece, *opposite*). The sealing compound is effective only one time. Check the undersides to be sure the lids are free of scratches and the sealing compound is intact and covers the circumference of the lid.

**2 BE SURE THE SCREW BANDS** will fit the jars and are free of rust. Wash with soap and hot water before and after each use.

**3 WASH LIDS IN SOAPY WATER** and place them in a bowl, ladling some of the simmering water from your sterilizing pot over them; let stand until ready to use. Don't boil the lids; this will affect the sticky compound and might prevent proper sealing (check the manufacturer's directions for preparing lids).

**4 EACH LID HAS A RAISED CIRCLE** in the center. After canning, if a proper vacuum seal has been created, that raised circle is sucked down tight (while the jars are cooling, you will hear a loud pop from each jar as the vacuum is formed and the lid is sealed tight). Check the seals after the jars have cooled (tip, *far right*).

---

## STERILIZING

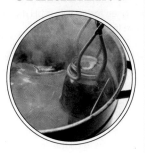

### 1
#### WASHING

Wash empty canning jars in hot, soapy water. Rinse thoroughly. Place jars right side up in the boiling-water canner on a rack. Cover jars with hot water 1 inch over tops of jars. Bring to boiling; boil 10 minutes to sterilize.

### 2
#### HEATING

Keep jars in the simmering water until needed. Wash any equipment that will also touch the food. Heat extra water in another large pot (to top off water in canner after jars are added).

### 3
#### ONE JAR AT A TIME

Take out just one jar at a time, fill it, put on the lid and screw band, and return it to the simmering water in the canner. We recommend doing one jar at a time rather than doing them all at one time (photos, *p. 635*).

---

## BOILING-WATER CANNING

**PROCESS HIGH-ACID FOODS ONLY** Boiling-water canners are safe only for high-acid foods, such as most jams, jellies, pickles, relishes, and tomatoes (with added bottled lemon juice). These foods have a pH of 4.6 or lower (info, *p. 634*), which allows them to naturally resist bacterial growth. Pressure canners (info, *p. 634*) must be used for low-acid foods—such as veggies—that are prone to bacterial growth.

**THE RIGHT JARS** Use only modern jars made specifically for canning. Vintage jars are pretty, but they are not safe for canning. Do not reuse glass jars that contained purchased foods such as pasta sauce, even if they look like canning jars. Check jars carefully before each canning session, making sure they are free of chips or cracks. And always use the size jar specified in your recipe—the timings provided are crucial for that size to reach the internal temperature needed to kill microorganisms.

**USE LIDS PROPERLY** Always use the lids made specifically for canning. The screw bands are reusable, but the flat lids are one-time-use only.

Avoid screwing bands on too tightly—doing so might prevent a proper vacuum seal.

**CHOOSE THE RIGHT RECIPE** Modern canning recipes based on USDA recommendations—like the ones in this book—are safer than those used years ago. Always use tested recipes from reliable, current sources and follow the recipes exactly. Do not substitute or add ingredients; this could compromise the food's safety.

**KEEP IT CLEAN AND HOT** When canning, keep everything scrupulously clean. Make sure that fruits and vegetables are scrubbed free of dirt and chemical residue. Wash and sterilize jars and lids. Pack hot food into jars one at a time and return to the simmering water in the boiling-water canner to avoid the contents of the jars cooling between steps.

**TEST SEALS** Once jars are completely cooled (4 to 5 hours), test each seal by pressing the center of the lid. If it is firm and slightly concave, the jar is properly sealed. If the lid appears flat and you are able to make it bounce up and down, the jar is not properly sealed. (In that case, refrigerate and eat the food within 3 days.)

## ALTITUDE ADJUSTMENTS

The timings listed in recipes in this book are for altitudes up to 1,000 feet above sea level. Water boils at a lower temperature at higher altitudes, so follow these adjustments for your location.

**BLANCHING** Add 1 minute if you live 5,000 feet or more above sea level.

**BOILING-WATER CANNING** Call your county extension office for detailed instructions.

**JELLIES AND JAMS** Add 1 minute processing time for each additional 1,000 feet above sea level.

**STERILIZING JARS** Boil jars an additional 1 minute for each additional 1,000 feet above sea level.

## THE SCIENCE OF CANNING: pH LEVELS

Essential to proper canning, pH is a scale from 1 to 14 that measures the chemical properties of foods. Foods with a pH of less than 7 are acidic. Foods with a pH of more than 7 are alkaline, or basic. To safely can foods with a boiling-water canner, they must be acidic. (Our Test Kitchen follows the USDA guidelines for a safe pH level of 4.6 or lower.) This is why you will find bottled lemon juice—an acid—added to so many recipes. Professionally developed recipes, such as the ones on these pages, have been tested with a pH meter to ensure their safety.

## PRESSURE CANNERS

All of our canning recipes are appropriate for water-bath canning only (instead of pressure canning). What's the difference? A pressure canner has a tight-locking lid that seals in all the steam as the canner gets hot; this creates intense pressure and raises the temperature past 212°F. It is safe to preserve meats and vegetables using this canner (without adding acidic ingredients). The water-bath canner is easier to work with and a good place to start if you're new to canning or primarily can fruits, tomatoes, pickles, or pickled vegetables. If you want to dive into canning meat and/or unpickled vegetables, take the next step to the pressure canner.

## *MEASURING HEADSPACE*

The amount of headspace, or the space between the top of the jar and the top of the contents, is specified by a recipe to ensure jars seal properly.

### 1

#### MEASURING

Measure headspace with a ruler or canning tool from the top of the jar to the top of the contents.

### 2

#### PROCESSING

Process only jars that are filled to the recommended headspace. If you have any remaining mixture that doesn't fill the jar, cover and refrigerate the leftovers (eat within 3 days). Partially full jars may not seal properly and are not considered safe.

## *CANNING TOOLBOX*

**JAR LIFTER** This tool lifts jars firmly and securely in and out of hot water. Use two hands and squeeze firmly.

**MAGNETIC WAND** This magic wand enables you to grab and lift lids and bands from hot water so you don't burn your fingers.

**JAR FUNNELS** Wider and shorter than other funnels, jar funnels come in both wide-mouth and regular-mouth versions. They're invaluable for preventing spills when filling jars.

**RULER-SPATULA** Use the tapered end to release air bubbles along the jar sides. The calibrated, notched end measures the headspace.

**ABOUT LEMON JUICE**
When a canning recipe calls for lemon juice, it's best to use bottled lemon juice. The pH of bottled is always spot-on; the pH in fresh lemons may vary too much.

**STICK TO THE RECIPE**
Do not alter the amounts of the main components of a recipe, such as the amount of produce, vinegar, sugar, salt, or water. Changing these amounts could alter the pH and make the recipe unsafe to can.

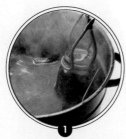

**1 STERILIZE** Wash canning jars in hot, soapy water; rinse well. To sterilize jars, place jars in a boiling-water canner with a rack. Cover with hot tap water. Bring to boiling; sterilize jars 10 minutes at a steady boil. (For jars that are processed for more than 10 minutes with food in them, you do not need to sterilize first; but do keep jars hot in simmering water until ready to fill.)

**2 PACK JARS** Prepare only as much food as needed to fill your canner at one time (most canning racks hold, at most, seven pint or quart jars). Remove the first jar from the hot water; pack food and liquid into the hot jar using a jar funnel. Remove air bubbles.

**3 WIPE RIM** Check headspace with a ruler or the measuring notches on a canning spatula. Using a clean, damp cloth, wipe the rim and threads of the jar to remove any residue. Food particles or liquid left on the jar rim might interfere with the seal.

**4 PUT LID ON IT** Remove lid from hot water with a magnetic wand or tongs. Place lid on jar and screw on band no more than fingertip-tight (just tight enough that you could turn the band another ¼ to ½ inch tighter with your fingertips). If applied too tightly, the lids might not seal.

**5 IN THE POT** When all jars are filled and in the canner, if necessary, add additional boiling water to the canner to cover the jars by 1 inch. Cover canner; bring to a full rolling boil. Start processing time from the moment the water starts to boil. Keep at a steady, gentle boil. If the water stops boiling at anytime, turn the burner up and stop the timing until water returns to boiling.

**6 REMOVE JARS** When the processing time is up, turn off heat. Using pot holders, lift up the canner rack and rest the handles on the side of the canner. Allow jars to cool in place for a few minutes.

**7 COOL** Use a jar lifter to remove jars from canner and set on a wire rack or a towel placed on the countertop (cold countertops can crack jars). Do not tighten bands. Let cool 4 to 5 hours.

**8 SEAL TEST** After that time, test the seal by pressing your finger on the center of the lid. It should not bounce up and down. If it does give (and makes a clicking sound), it is not properly sealed. (If a jar fails to seal, refrigerate immediately and eat the food within 3 days.) Remove screw bands. Wipe the jar rims to remove any food particles. Store canned foods in a cool, dry place up to 1 year.

// CANNING //

PICKLED
THREE-BEAN
SALAD

GARLICKY PICKLED
MIXED VEGGIES

## PICKLED THREE-BEAN SALAD

**HANDS-ON TIME** 30 minutes
**COOK** 45 minutes
**PROCESS** 15 minutes

>>

DRIED
BLACK-EYED
PEAS can
be replaced
with two
15-oz. cans
black-eyed
peas, rinsed
and drained.
Omit Step 1.

8  oz. dried black-eyed peas
   (1¼ cups), rinsed
12 oz. fresh green beans, trimmed
   and cut into 2-inch pieces
   (3½ cups)
1¾ cups cider vinegar
1½ cups sugar
1½ cups water
¾  cup bottled lemon juice
½  cup olive oil
1  tsp. salt
1½ cups frozen shelled edamame
1  medium yellow sweet pepper,
   chopped (¾ cup)
1  medium red onion, thinly sliced
   (½ cup)
2  cloves garlic, minced

**1.** In a 4- to 5-qt. nonreactive pot (tip, *p. 643*) bring 4 cups water and black-eyed peas to boiling; reduce heat. Simmer, covered, 45 to 60 minutes or until tender. Drain; rinse with cold water and drain again.
**2.** Bring 4 cups fresh water to boiling. Add green beans. Boil gently, uncovered, 3 minutes. Drain; rinse with cold water and drain again.
**3.** In the pot stir together vinegar, sugar, the 1½ cups water, the lemon juice, oil, and salt. Bring to boiling, stirring to dissolve sugar. Stir in black-eyed peas, green beans, and remaining ingredients. Return to boiling; remove from heat.
**4.** Ladle solids into hot, clean half-pint or pint canning jars (tips and photos, *p. 635*), leaving a ½-inch headspace. Add hot liquid to jars, maintaining the ½-inch headspace. Wipe jar rims; adjust lids and bands.
**5.** Process in a boiling-water canner 15 minutes (start timing when water returns to boiling). Remove jars from canner; cool on wire racks. **Makes 10 half-pints.**
**EACH ¼ CUP** *35 cal., 1 g fat (0 g sat. fat), 0 mg chol., 34 mg sodium, 5 g carb., 1 g fiber, 3 g sugars, 1 g pro.*

## GARLICKY PICKLED MIXED VEGGIES

**HANDS-ON TIME** 45 minutes
**PROCESS** 10 minutes

2  ears of corn
3  cups cauliflower florets
3  medium red sweet peppers,
   cut into 1-inch pieces
12 oz. green beans, trimmed and
   cut into 1-inch pieces
3  medium carrots, cut into
   ½-inch slices
2  medium onions, cut into small
   wedges
3  cups water
3  cups white vinegar
1  cup sugar
1  Tbsp. kosher salt
18 cloves garlic, smashed and
   peeled
1½ tsp. crushed red pepper

**1.** Remove husks from ears of corn. Scrub to remove silks; rinse. Cut cobs into 1- to 1½-inch pieces. In an 8-qt. pot combine corn and next five ingredients (through onions). Add enough water to cover. Bring to boiling. Cook, uncovered, 3 minutes; drain. If desired, cut corn lengthwise into halves or quarters.
**2.** In a 4- to 5-qt. nonreactive pot (tip, *p. 643*) combine the 3 cups water, vinegar, sugar, and salt. Bring to boiling, stirring to dissolve sugar.
**3.** Pack vegetables into six hot, sterilized pint canning jars (photos, *p. 635*), leaving a ½-inch headspace. Add three cloves garlic and ¼ tsp. crushed red pepper to each jar. Pour hot vinegar mixture over vegetables, maintaining the ½-inch headspace. Wipe jar rims; adjust lids and bands.
**4.** Process filled jars in a boiling-water canner 10 minutes (start timing when water returns to boiling). Remove jars from canner; cool on a wire rack. **Makes 6 pints.**
**EACH ¼ CUP** *45 cal., 0 g fat, 0 mg chol., 164 mg sodium, 9 g carb., 1 g fiber, 7 g sugars, 1 g pro.*

# PICKLED BEETS

**HANDS-ON TIME** 20 minutes
**COOK** 30 minutes
**PROCESS** 30 minutes

BEETS are notorious for staining anything they touch—hands, clothes, and cutting boards. Wear plastic gloves and an apron when working with beets.

3 lb. small whole beets (about 2-inch diameter)
2 cups vinegar
1 cup water
½ cup sugar
3 inches stick cinnamon
1 tsp. whole allspice
6 whole cloves

**1.** Wash beets. Cut off beet tops, leaving 1 inch of stems; trim root ends. Do not peel. In a 4-qt. saucepan cook beets in enough boiling, lightly salted water to cover about 25 minutes or until tender; drain. Cool beets slightly; trim off roots and stems. Slip off and discard skins; quarter the beets.
**2.** In a 2-qt. nonreactive heavy saucepan (tip, p. 643) combine vinegar, the 1 cup water, and sugar. Place cinnamon, allspice, and cloves in center of a double-thick, 6-inch square of 100%-cotton cheesecloth. Bring up corners; tie with clean kitchen string. Add to saucepan. Bring to boiling, stirring to dissolve sugar; reduce heat. Simmer, uncovered, 5 minutes. Remove and discard bag.
**3.** Pack beets into six hot, clean half-pint canning jars (photos, p. 635), leaving a ½-inch headspace. Pour hot vinegar mixture over beets, maintaining the ½-inch headspace. Wipe jar rims; adjust lids and bands.
**4.** Process filled jars in a boiling-water canner 30 minutes (start timing when water returns to boiling). Remove jars from canner; cool on a wire rack. **Makes 6 half-pints.**
**EACH ⅓ CUP** *25 cal., 0 g fat, 0 mg chol., 38 mg sodium, 8 g carb., 1 g fiber, 4 g sugars, 1 g pro.*

PICKLED BEETS

**USE IT UP!**
Top a spinach salad with Pickled Beets, cut-up apple, blue cheese, and toasted pecans. Add your favorite dressing and, if you like, a poached or soft-boiled egg (pp. 46–48).

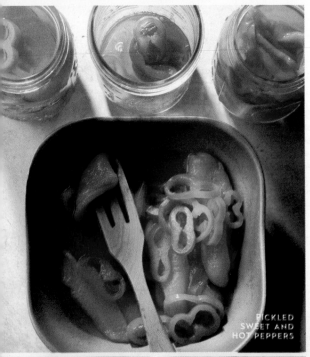

PICKLED
SWEET AND
HOT PEPPERS

## PICKLED SWEET AND HOT PEPPERS

**HANDS-ON TIME** 1 hour
**BAKE** 20 minutes at 450°F
**STAND** 10 minutes
**PROCESS** 15 minutes

4½ lb. green, red, yellow, and/or orange sweet peppers
1½ lb. hot chile peppers, such as Anaheim, jalapeño, yellow banana, and/or Hungarian
6½ cups white or cider vinegar
1⅓ cups water
⅔ cup sugar
4 tsp. pickling salt
3 cloves garlic, peeled

**1.** Preheat oven to 450°F. Cut sweet peppers into quarters, removing stems, seeds, and membranes. Line two extra-large baking sheets with foil. Place sweet pepper quarters, cut sides down, on prepared baking sheets. Bake about 20 minutes or until skins are bubbly and dark. Wrap peppers in the foil to steam. Let stand 10 minutes or until cool enough to handle. Using a paring knife, gently peel off skins; discard skins.
**2.** Wearing gloves, remove stems and seeds from hot chile peppers (tip, p. 22). Slice into rings.
**3.** In a large nonreactive saucepan (tip, p. 643) combine remaining ingredients. Bring to boiling; reduce heat. Simmer, uncovered, 10 minutes. Remove and discard garlic cloves.
**4.** Pack sweet and hot peppers into hot, clean (tip, p. 635) pint or half-pint canning jars, leaving a ½-inch headspace. Pour hot vinegar mixture over peppers, maintaining the ½-inch headspace. Wipe jar rims; adjust lids and screw bands.
**5.** Process filled jars in a boiling-water canner 15 minutes (start timing when water returns to

boiling). Remove jars from canner; cool on wire racks. **Makes 6 pints.**
**EACH 2 TBSP.** *12 cal., 0 g fat, 0 mg chol., 41 mg sodium, 3 g carb., 1 g fiber, 2 g sugars, 0 g pro.*

## BREAD AND BUTTER PICKLES

**HANDS-ON TIME** 40 minutes
**CHILL** 3 hours
**PROCESS** 10 minutes

4 qt. (16 cups) sliced medium cucumbers
8 medium white onions, sliced
⅓ cup pickling salt
3 cloves garlic, halved
Crushed ice
4 cups sugar
3 cups cider vinegar
2 Tbsp. mustard seeds
1½ tsp. ground turmeric
1½ tsp. celery seeds

**1.** In a 6- to 8-qt. nonreactive heavy pot (tip, p. 643) combine cucumbers, onions, pickling salt, and garlic. Add 2 inches crushed ice. Cover and chill 3 to 12 hours. Remove any remaining ice. Drain mixture well; remove and discard garlic.
**2.** In same pot combine remaining ingredients. Bring to boiling; add cucumber mixture. Return to boiling.
**3.** Pack hot cucumber mixture and liquid into seven hot, sterilized pint canning jars (photos, p. 635), leaving a ½-inch headspace. Wipe jar rims; adjust lids and screw bands. Process in a boiling-water canner 10 minutes (start timing when water returns to boiling). Remove jars from canner; cool on wire racks. **Makes 7 pints.**
**EACH ¼ CUP** *32 cal., 0 g fat, 0 mg chol., 278 mg sodium, 8 g carb., 0 g fiber, 7 g sugars, 0 g pro.*

BREAD AND
BUTTER PICKLES

> **GARDEN CUKES**
> If pickling cucumbers aren't available, use regular-size cucumbers from the garden. Do not use waxed cucumbers that are sold in the supermarket.

# BEST-EVER DILL PICKLES

**HANDS-ON TIME** 30 minutes
**PROCESS** 10 minutes
**STAND** 1 week

»

CUCUMBERS we prefer for pickling include Kirby, Persian, and gherkin varieties. Look for the best pickling cucumbers at your local farmers market in early to midsummer. Choose those that are firm and bright-colored with no soft spots.

| | |
|---|---|
| 3 | to 3¼ lb. 4-inch pickling cucumbers |
| 4 | cups water |
| 4 | cups white vinegar |
| ½ | cup sugar |
| ⅓ | cup pickling salt |
| 6 | Tbsp. dill seeds |

**1.** Thoroughly scrub cucumbers with a soft vegetable brush in plenty of cold running water. Remove stems and blossoms; slice off blossom ends. Cut cucumbers lengthwise into quarters.
**2.** In a 4- to 5-qt. nonreactive heavy pot (tip, *p. 643*) combine the water, vinegar, sugar, and pickling salt. Bring to boiling, stirring to dissolve sugar.
**3.** Pack cucumber spears loosely into six, hot sterilized pint canning jars (photos, *p. 635*), leaving a ½-inch headspace. Add 1 Tbsp. dill seeds to each jar. Pour hot vinegar mixture into jars, maintaining the ½-inch headspace. Discard any remaining vinegar mixture. Wipe jar rims; adjust lids and screw bands.
**4.** Process filled jars in a boiling-water canner 10 minutes (start timing when water returns to boiling). Remove jars from canner; cool on a wire rack. Let stand at room temperature 1 week before serving. **Makes 6 pints.**
**EACH SPEAR** *11 cal., 0 g fat, 0 mg chol., 358 mg sodium, 2 g carb., 0 g fiber, 1 g sugars, 0 g pro.*

» **HOT GARLIC PICKLES**
Prepare as directed, except substitute cider vinegar for the white vinegar. Before packing cucumbers in jars, add 1 to 2 fresh Thai chile peppers and 2 cloves garlic, halved, to each jar. **Makes 6 pints.**

» **CRUNCHY DILL AND ONION CHIPS** In an extra-large bowl combine 12 cups sliced pickling cucumbers, 2 cups thinly sliced onions, and ⅓ cup pickling salt. Set a large nonreactive colander in an extra-large nonreactive bowl. In the colander alternately layer cucumber mixture and crushed ice, ending with a layer of crushed ice. Weight down mixture with a heavy plate. Chill 8 to 24 hours. Remove any ice remaining in cucumber mixture; discard any liquid in bowl. In a 4- to 5-qt. nonreactive heavy pot combine 4 cups water, 4 cups white vinegar, and ½ cup sugar. Bring to boiling, stirring to dissolve sugar. Pack cucumbers and onions into jars as directed in Step 3 and continue as directed. **Makes 5 pints.**

» **SWEET DILL PICKLES**
Prepare as directed, except increase sugar to 3 cups. **Makes 6 pints.**

» **REFRIGERATOR PICKLES**
Prepare as directed through Step 3, except add 1 or 2 sprigs fresh dill to each jar. Store pickles in the refrigerator up to 1 month. **Makes 6 pints.**

**ZUCCHINI RELISH**

## ZUCCHINI RELISH

**HANDS-ON TIME** 55 minutes
**STAND** 3 hours
**PROCESS** 10 minutes

5   cups finely chopped zucchini
    (about 4 medium)
1½  cups finely chopped onions
¾   cup finely chopped green
    sweet pepper
¾   cup finely chopped red
    sweet pepper
¼   cup pickling salt
1¾  cups sugar
1½  cups white vinegar
¼   cup water

1   tsp. celery seeds
1   tsp. ground turmeric
½   tsp. mustard seeds
1   to 2 drops green food coloring
    (optional)

**1.** In a large bowl combine zucchini, onions, and sweet peppers. Sprinkle the pickling salt over vegetables. Pour enough water (about 4 cups) over vegetables to cover. Cover; let stand 3 hours. Drain vegetables in a colander; rinse and drain well.

**2.** In an 8- to 10-qt. nonreactive heavy pot (tip, p. 643) combine sugar, vinegar, the ¼ cup water, the celery seeds, turmeric, and mustard seeds. Bring to boiling; reduce heat. Simmer, uncovered, 3 minutes. Stir in drained vegetables and, if desired, green food coloring. Return to boiling; reduce heat. Simmer, uncovered, 10 minutes.

**3.** Ladle hot relish into five hot, sterilized half-pint canning jars (photos, p. 635), leaving a ½-inch headspace. Wipe jar rims; adjust lids and screw bands.

**4.** Process filled jars in a boiling-water canner 10 minutes (start timing when water returns to boiling). Remove jars from canner; cool on a wire rack. **Makes 5 half-pints.**

EACH 1 TBSP. *21 cal., 0 g fat, 0 mg chol., 350 mg sodium, 5 g carb., 0 g fiber, 5 g sugars, 0 g pro.*

**ABOUT THE VINEGAR** The acidity level in any pickled food (including relishes) is extremely important because it's directly related to the safety, taste, and texture of the final product. Play it safe by always using the type of vinegar called for in each recipe. When you purchase vinegar for pickling, be sure it has at least 5% acidity.

CORN RELISH

SWEET PICKLE RELISH

# CORN RELISH

**HANDS-ON TIME** 1 hour
**COOK** 25 minutes
**PROCESS** 15 minutes

| | |
|---|---|
| 16 | to 20 ears of corn |
| 2 | cups water |
| 3 | cups chopped celery |
| 1½ | cups chopped red sweet peppers |
| 1½ | cups chopped green sweet peppers |
| 1 | cup chopped onion |
| 2½ | cups vinegar |
| 1¾ | cups sugar |
| 4 | tsp. dry mustard |
| 2 | tsp. pickling salt |
| 2 | tsp. celery seeds |
| 1 | tsp. ground turmeric |

**1.** Remove husks from ears of corn. Scrub with a stiff brush to remove silks; rinse. Cut kernels from cobs; do not scrape. Measure 8 cups kernels.
**2.** In an 8- to 10-qt. nonreactive heavy pot (tip, p. 643) combine the 8 cups corn kernels and the 2 cups water. Bring to boiling; reduce heat. Simmer, covered, 4 to 5 minutes or until corn is nearly tender; drain.
**3.** In the same pot combine corn, celery, sweet peppers, and onion. Stir in remaining ingredients. Bring to boiling, stirring to dissolve sugar; reduce heat. Simmer, uncovered, 25 minutes, stirring occasionally.
**4.** Ladle hot relish into five hot, clean (tip, p. 635) pint canning jars, leaving a ½-inch headspace. Wipe jar rims; adjust lids and screw bands.
**5.** Process filled jars in a boiling-water canner 15 minutes (start timing when water returns to boiling). Remove jars from canner; cool on a wire rack. **Makes 5 pints.**
**EACH 2 TBSP.** *43 cal., 0 g fat, 0 mg chol., 75 mg sodium, 10 g carb., 1 g fiber, 7 g sugars, 1 g pro.*

# SWEET PICKLE RELISH

**HANDS-ON TIME** 1 hour
**STAND** 2 hours
**COOK** 10 minutes
**PROCESS** 10 minutes

| | |
|---|---|
| 6 | cups finely chopped cucumbers, seeded if desired* |
| 3 | cups finely chopped green and/or red sweet peppers* |
| 3 | cups finely chopped onions* |
| ¼ | cup pickling salt |
| 3 | cups sugar |
| 2 | cups cider vinegar |
| 1 | Tbsp. mustard seeds |
| 2 | tsp. celery seeds |
| ½ | tsp. ground turmeric |

**1.** In an extra-large bowl combine cucumbers, sweet peppers, and onions. Sprinkle with pickling salt; add cold water to cover. Let stand at room temperature 2 hours.
**2.** Drain vegetables through a colander. Rinse; drain well. In an 8-qt. nonreactive heavy pot (tip, p. 643) combine remaining ingredients. Bring to boiling. Add vegetables; return to boiling. Cook, uncovered, over medium-high heat 10 minutes, stirring occasionally.
**3.** Ladle hot relish into four hot, sterilized pint canning jars (photos, p. 635), leaving a ½-inch headspace. Wipe the jar rims; adjust lids and screw bands.
**4.** Process filled jars in a boiling-water canner 10 minutes. Remove jars; cool on a wire rack. **Makes 4 pints.**
**\*NOTE** For faster prep, use a food processor to chop vegetables.
**EACH 1 TBSP.** *22 cal., 0 g fat, 0 mg chol., 218 mg sodium, 5 g carb., 0 g fiber, 5 g sugars, 0 g pro.*

KNOW YOUR TOMATOES—ANY VARIETY CAN BE CANNED,
BUT YOUR RESULTS WILL VARY. ROMA TOMATOES HAVE MEATY
FLESH AND LESS JUICE; FRESH HEIRLOOMS ARE SO JUICY,
YOU'LL END UP WITH EXTRA LIQUID IN YOUR JARS. THE BEST
FOR CANNING ARE SOMEWHERE IN BETWEEN.

## CAN-YOUR-OWN TOMATOES

**HANDS-ON TIME** 15 minutes
**PROCESS** 1 hour 25 minutes

»

THE TOMATO
weights we give
here are for each
pint or quart jar.
For example,
you will need 5 to
6 lb. tomatoes to
fill 4 pint jars. Or
10 to 14 lb. to fill
4 quart jars. Only
fill as many jars as
your canner will
hold at one time.
After processing
the first batch,
you can prepare,
fill, and process
additional jars.

1¼ to 1½ lb. ripe tomatoes per
  *each* pint jar or 2½ to 3½ lb.
  per *each* quart jar
Bottled lemon juice
Salt (optional)

**1.** Peel skins off tomatoes (photos,
*opposite*). If desired, cut tomatoes
in half.
**2.** Pack tomatoes into hot, clean
(tip, *p. 635*) pint or quart canning
jars, pressing the tomatoes into jars
until spaces between tomatoes
are filled with juice. Leave a ½-inch
headspace. Add 1 Tbsp. lemon juice
to each pint or 2 Tbsp. lemon juice
to each quart. If desired, add ¼ to
½ tsp. salt to each pint or ½ to 1 tsp.
salt to each quart. Wipe rims; adjust
lids and bands (photos, *p. 635*).
**3.** Process filled pint or quart jars in
a boiling-water canner 85 minutes
(start timing when water returns to
boiling). Remove jars from canner;
cool on wire racks. (Yield varies.)
**EACH ¼ CUP** *13 cal., 0 g fat, 0 mg
chol., 4 mg sodium, 3 g carb., 1 g fiber,
2 g sugars, 1 g pro.*

**BOOST ACIDITY** Tomatoes are higher in acidity (lower
in pH) than many vegetables, but they still require the
addition of lemon juice to make them safe for water-
bath canning. This ups the acidity level enough to
create an environment in which harmful bacteria won't
grow. Always use bottled lemon juice (tip, *p. 635*).

» **HOT-PACK TOMATOES IN
WATER** Prepare tomatoes
as directed in Step 1; place
in a nonreactive heavy pot.
Add enough water to cover.
Bring to boiling; reduce
heat. Simmer, uncovered,
5 minutes. Pack jars with
tomatoes and cooking
liquid (photo, *opposite,
bottom right*), leaving a
½-inch headspace. Add
lemon juice and, if desired,
salt as directed in Step 2.
Wipe jar rims; adjust lids
and screw bands. Process
filled jars in a boiling-water
canner 40 minutes for pints,
45 minutes for quarts (start
timing when water returns to
boiling). Remove jars from
canner; cool on wire racks.

» **RAW-PACK TOMATOES
IN WATER** Prepare
tomatoes and fill jars as
directed in Steps 1 and 2,
except do not press on
tomatoes. Pour boiling water
into each jar, maintaining
the ½-inch headspace.
Wipe jar rims; adjust lids
and screw bands. Process
in a boiling-water canner
40 minutes for pints,
45 minutes for quarts
(start timing when water
returns to boiling). Remove
jars from canner; cool
on wire racks.

» **CRUSHED TOMATOES** Peel
tomatoes (photos, *opposite*);
cut into quarters. Add enough
tomatoes to a nonreactive
heavy pot (tip, *opposite*) to
cover the bottom. Crush with
a wooden spoon. Bring to
boiling, stirring constantly.
Slowly add the remaining
quartered tomatoes,
stirring constantly. Simmer,
uncovered, 5 minutes. Pack
jars with tomatoes, leaving
a ½-inch headspace. Add
lemon juice and, if desired,
salt as directed in Step 2.
Wipe jar rims; adjust lids and
screw bands (photos, *p. 635*).
Process in a boiling-water
canner 35 minutes for pints,
45 minutes for quarts (start
timing when water returns to
boiling). Remove jars from
canner; cool on wire racks.

**TRUE COLORS**
To avoid a muddy-colored mixture, use only one color of tomato in each jar (i.e., don't mix yellow, green, and red varieties).

**PICK A POT** When we call for a nonreactive pot, we are referring to the type of material the pot is made from—such as stainless steel or enamel. Other types of metal pots and pans, such as aluminum, might react with the acidity in certain recipes and produce off-flavors in the finished food. When a heavy pot is called for, choose one that feels heavy in the hand and has a thick bottom to it—this will prevent scorching and burning during simmering.

## CANNING TOMATOES
IS EASY. START WITH THIS QUICK PEELING TIP, THEN PICK YOUR CANNING METHOD—CRUSHED, HOT-PACK, OR RAW-PACK.

**1**

To peel tomatoes, use a sharp knife to cut a shallow "X" into the blossom end of each tomato.

**2**

Working in batches, immerse tomatoes in boiling water 1 to 2 minutes or until the skins begin to split open. Use a slotted spoon to transfer the tomatoes to a large bowl of ice water. When cool enough to handle, use your fingers or a knife to peel off skin.

**For Hot-Pack Tomatoes** (opposite), pack tomatoes into jars as tightly as you can without crushing them. Check headspace. Top with hot liquid as specified in the recipe; push out air bubbles with a thin nonmetal spatula. Recheck headspace. Process as directed.

**For Crushed Tomatoes** (opposite), cover the bottom of a large pot with a layer of tomato quarters. Use a wooden spoon to crush and break apart tomatoes. Stir in the remaining quartered tomatoes (these added tomatoes will break apart when simmering). Simmer, uncovered, 5 minutes.

ROASTED GARLIC
PASTA SAUCE

PIZZA SAUCE

## ROASTED GARLIC PASTA SAUCE

**HANDS-ON TIME** 2 hours 30 minutes
**ROAST** 40 minutes at 400°F
**COOK** 1 hour
**PROCESS** 35 minutes

| | |
|---|---|
| 6 | bulbs garlic |
| 3 | Tbsp. olive oil |
| 4 | medium red, yellow, and/or green sweet peppers, halved and seeded |
| 12 | lb. ripe tomatoes (about 25 tomatoes), peeled (photos, p. 643) |
| 3 | Tbsp. packed brown sugar |
| 2 | Tbsp. kosher salt or 4 tsp. salt |
| 1 | Tbsp. balsamic vinegar |
| 1 | tsp. black pepper |
| 2 | cups lightly packed fresh basil leaves, chopped |
| 1 | cup lightly packed assorted fresh herbs (such as oregano, thyme, parsley, Italian parsley, and basil), chopped |
| 6 | Tbsp. bottled lemon juice |

**1.** Preheat oven to 400° F. Peel away the dry outer layers of skin from garlic bulbs, leaving skins and cloves intact. Cut off the pointed top portions (about ½ inch), leaving bulbs intact but exposing the individual cloves. Place the garlic bulbs, cut sides up, in a 1- or 1½-qt. casserole. Drizzle with about 1 Tbsp. of the olive oil. Cover casserole. Arrange peppers, cut sides down, on a foil-lined baking sheet; brush with remaining olive oil. Roast garlic and peppers about 40 minutes or until cloves of garlic are soft and pepper skins are charred. Cool garlic on a wire rack until cool enough to handle. Pull up sides of foil to fully enclose peppers. Let peppers stand 15 to 20 minutes or until cool enough to handle. When peppers are cool enough to handle, peel off skins and discard; chop peppers.

**2.** Remove garlic cloves from papers by squeezing the bottoms of the bulbs. Place garlic cloves in a food processor. Cut peeled tomatoes into chunks and add some chunks to the food processor with garlic. Cover and process until chopped. Transfer chopped garlic and tomatoes to a 7- to 8-qt. nonreactive heavy pot (tip, p. 643). Repeat chopping remaining tomatoes, in batches, in the food processor. Add all tomatoes to the pot.

**3.** Add brown sugar, salt, vinegar, and black pepper to the tomato mixture. Bring to boiling. Boil steadily, uncovered, 50 minutes, stirring occasionally. Add chopped peppers to tomato mixture. Continue boiling 10 to 20 minutes more or until mixture is reduced to about 11 cups and reaches desired sauce consistency, stirring occasionally. Remove from heat; stir in basil and assorted herbs.

**4.** Spoon 1 Tbsp. lemon juice into each of six hot, clean pint canning jars (tips and photos, p. 635). Ladle sauce into jars with lemon juice, leaving a ½-inch headspace. Wipe jar rims; adjust lids and screw bands.

**5.** Process filled jars in a boiling-water canner 35 minutes (start timing when water returns to a full boil). Remove jars from canner; cool on a wire rack. **Makes 6 pints.**
**EACH ½ CUP** *95 cal., 3 g fat (0 g sat. fat), 0 mg chol., 542 mg sodium, 17 g carb., 4 g fiber, 10 g sugars, 3 g pro.*

# PIZZA SAUCE

**HANDS-ON TIME** 45 minutes
**ROAST** 30 minutes at 450°F
**COOK** 1 hour
**PROCESS** 35 minutes

| | |
|---|---|
| 10 | lb. ripe roma tomatoes |
| 1 | garlic bulb |
| | Olive oil |
| 1 | cup dry red wine |
| 2 | Tbsp. sugar |
| 4 | tsp. kosher salt |
| 1 | cup lightly packed fresh basil leaves, chopped |
| ½ | cup lightly packed fresh oregano leaves, chopped |
| ½ | tsp. black pepper |
| ¼ | tsp. crushed red pepper |
| ½ | cup bottled lemon juice |

**1.** Preheat oven to 450°F. Line two shallow roasting pans or 15×10-inch baking pans with foil. Cut one or two small slits in each tomato. Place tomatoes in a single layer in the prepared pans. Cut off the top ½ inch of garlic bulb to expose ends of individual cloves. Leaving garlic bulb whole, remove loose, papery outer layers. Place bulb, cut end up, in a custard cup. Drizzle bulb with a little oil; cover with foil. Roast tomatoes and garlic on separate oven racks 30 minutes or until tomato skins are blistered and garlic is soft; cool.

**2.** Coarsely chop tomatoes, discarding loose skins and excess juice. Squeeze roasted garlic from individual cloves. Transfer tomatoes and garlic to a 6- to 8-qt. nonreactive heavy pot (tip, p. 643). Stir in wine, sugar, and salt. Bring to boiling over medium-high heat, stirring occasionally; reduce heat. Simmer, uncovered, 15 minutes, stirring occasionally.

**3.** Press tomato mixture through a food mill fitted with a coarse disk. (Or working in batches, transfer tomato mixture to a food processor or blender. Cover and process or blend until smooth. Press pureed mixture through a sieve.) Discard seeds and skins.

**4.** Return the strained mixture to the pot. Stir in basil, oregano, black pepper, and crushed red pepper. Bring to boiling; reduce heat. Simmer, uncovered, 45 to 50 minutes or until reduced to 8 cups. Remove from heat. Stir in lemon juice.

**5.** Ladle hot sauce into hot, clean half-pint canning jars (tips and photos, p. 635), leaving a ½-inch headspace. Wipe jar rims; adjust lids and screw bands.

**6.** Process filled jars in a boiling-water canner 35 minutes (start timing when water returns to boiling). Remove jars from canner; cool on wire racks.

**Makes 8 half-pints.**

**EACH 2 TBSP.** *19 cal., 0 g fat, 0 mg chol., 127 mg sodium, 4 g carb., 1 g fiber, 2 g sugars, 1 g pro.*

---

# CHILI STARTER

**HANDS-ON TIME** 30 minutes
**COOK** 1 hour
**PROCESS** 40 minutes

| | |
|---|---|
| 12 | lb. ripe tomatoes |
| 1½ | cups chopped onions |
| 1½ | cups chopped green sweet peppers |
| 1 | large fresh jalapeño pepper, chopped (tip, p. 22) |
| 1 | 6-oz. can tomato paste |
| 6 | cloves garlic, minced |
| 2 | Tbsp. packed brown sugar |
| 3 | to 4 Tbsp. chili powder |
| 4 | tsp. ground cumin |
| 1 | Tbsp. salt |
| 1 | Tbsp. dried oregano, crushed |
| 1 | tsp. black pepper |
| ¼ | cup cider vinegar |
| ¼ | cup lime juice |

**1.** Peel skins off tomatoes (photos, p. 643). Cut peeled tomatoes into chunks; add some chunks to a food processor. Cover and process until almost smooth. Transfer tomato puree to a 7- to 8-qt. nonreactive heavy pot (tip, p. 643). Repeat with remaining tomatoes.

**2.** Add next 11 ingredients (through black pepper) to puree in pot. Bring to boiling, stirring frequently; reduce heat. Simmer, uncovered, about 60 minutes or until mixture is reduced to about 20 cups and is desired sauce consistency, stirring occasionally. Remove from heat; stir in vinegar and lime juice.

**3.** Ladle hot mixture into five hot, clean quart canning jars (tips and photos, p. 635), leaving a ½-inch headspace. Wipe jar rims; adjust lids and screw bands.

**4.** Process filled jars in a boiling-water canner 40 minutes (start timing when water returns to boiling). Remove jars from canner; cool on wire racks. **Makes 5 quarts.**

**EACH ⅔ CUP** *48 cal., 1 g fat (0 g sat. fat), 0 mg chol., 310 mg sodium, 11 g carb., 3 g fiber, 7 g sugars, 2 g pro.*

## *MAKE CHILI*

In a 3- to 4-qt. saucepan cook 8 oz. ground beef over medium-high heat until browned; drain off fat. Add one 15-oz. can kidney beans, rinsed and drained, and 1 jar Chili Starter. Cook and stir over medium-high heat until heated through, stirring occasionally. Makes 6 servings.

**USING THE FOOD PROCESSOR** and sieve instead of a food mill will result in a thinner pizza sauce because more solids will be removed. You won't have as much mixture to cook down to 8 cups, so adjust the cooking time in Step 4 to 15 to 20 minutes.

## SMOKY HONEY-PEACH ROASTED POBLANO SALSA

**HANDS-ON TIME** 45 minutes
**ROAST** 25 minutes at 450°F
**STAND** 10 minutes
**COOK** 20 minutes
**PROCESS** 20 minutes

**FILL IT UP**
If you have remaining salsa that won't fill a jar up to the recommended headspace, cover and refrigerate the leftovers.

3   lb. roma tomatoes, cored
3   medium sweet onions, cut into ¾-inch wedges
3   fresh poblano chile peppers, stemmed, halved, and seeded (tip, p. 22)
3   to 4 fresh jalapeño chile peppers, stemmed, halved, and seeded (tip, p.22)
9   cloves garlic, peeled
3   Tbsp. olive oil
6   large peaches (about 3½ lb.), peeled, pitted, and chopped (6¾ cups)
1   cup cider vinegar
⅓   cup honey
3   Tbsp. finely chopped canned chipotle peppers in adobo sauce
1   Tbsp. kosher salt
1½  tsp. ground cumin
1½  tsp. black pepper

**1.** Preheat oven to 450°F. Place tomatoes, onion wedges, poblano and jalapeño peppers, and garlic in two 15×10-inch baking pans. Drizzle with olive oil. Roast 15 minutes. Remove garlic; mince and set aside. Turn vegetables and roast 10 to 15 minutes more or until vegetables are charred. Cover pan with foil; let stand about 10 minutes. When peppers are cool enough to handle, use a sharp knife to gently remove skins; discard skins. Remove and discard tomato skins.
**2.** Transfer the garlic and the roasted vegetables and cooking juices to a food processor (in batches, if necessary); cover and pulse with several on/off turns until all ingredients are chopped.
**3.** Transfer tomato mixture to a 4- to 6-qt. nonreactive heavy pot (tip, p. 643). Add remaining ingredients. Bring to boiling; reduce heat. Simmer, uncovered, 20 minutes, stirring occasionally.
**4.** Ladle hot salsa into six hot, clean pint canning jars (tips and photos, p. 635), leaving a ½-inch headspace. Wipe jar rims; adjust lids and screw bands.

**5.** Process filled jars in a boiling-water canner 20 minutes (start timing when water returns to boiling). Remove jars from canner; cool on a wire rack. **Makes 6 pints.**
**EACH 2 TBSP.** *18 cal., 1 g fat (0 g sat. fat), 0 mg chol., 64 mg sodium, 3 g carb., 0 g fiber, 2 g sugars, 0 g pro.*

## CHERRY-ANCHO BARBECUE SAUCE

**HANDS-ON TIME** 1 hour 30 minutes
**COOK** 2 hours 45 minutes
**PROCESS** 20 minutes

10  lb. ripe tomatoes
2   lb. tart red cherries, stemmed and pitted, or 1¾ lb. frozen pitted tart red cherries
3   cups chopped red onions (3 large)
2¼  cups chopped celery
4   to 6 dried ancho chile peppers, stemmed, seeded, and chopped (tip, p. 22)
4   cloves garlic, quartered
2   cups cider vinegar
1½  cups honey
½   cup packed brown sugar
3   Tbsp. Worcestershire sauce
4   tsp. salt
2   tsp. ground coriander
½   tsp. black pepper

**1.** Remove stem ends and cores from tomatoes. Cut tomatoes into quarters. In a 10- to 12-qt. nonreactive heavy pot (tip, p. 643) combine tomatoes and cherries. Bring to boiling; reduce heat. Simmer, covered, over medium-low heat about 15 minutes or until tomatoes are soft, stirring occasionally. Stir in onions, celery, ancho peppers, and garlic. Bring to boiling; reduce heat. Simmer, uncovered, 30 minutes, stirring occasionally.
**2.** Press tomato mixture through a food mill (tip, p. 645). Discard seeds and skins. Measure 18 cups tomato mixture; return to pot. Measure the depth of the mixture with a

SMOKY HONEY-PEACH ROASTED POBLANO SALSA

CHERRY-ANCHO BARBECUE SAUCE

CLASSIC CHUNKY SALSA

ruler. Bring to boiling; reduce heat. Simmer, uncovered, 1 to 1¼ hours or until mixture is reduced by half, stirring occasionally. (Measure the depth again with a ruler; should be half of original depth.)

**3.** Stir in remaining ingredients. Simmer, uncovered, about 1 hour more or until sauce is desired consistency, stirring frequently.

**4.** Ladle hot sauce into eight hot, clean half-pint canning jars (tips and photos, p. 635), leaving a ½-inch headspace. Wipe jar rims; adjust lids and screw bands.

**5.** Process filled jars in a boiling-water canner 20 minutes (start timing when water returns to boiling). Remove jars from canner; cool on wire racks.

**6.** After opening a jar, store any remaining sauce in the jar in the refrigerator up to 2 weeks. **Makes 8 half-pints.**

**TO FREEZE** Prepare as directed through Step 3. Place pot of sauce in a sink filled with ice water; stir to cool. Ladle into clean wide-mouth half-pint freezer containers, leaving a ½-inch headspace. Seal and label. Freeze up to 10 months.

**EACH 1 TBSP.** *32 cal., 0 g fat, 0 mg chol., 92 mg sodium, 8 g carb., 1 g fiber, 7 g sugars, 1 g pro.*

## CLASSIC CHUNKY SALSA

**HANDS-ON TIME** 2 hours
**STAND** 30 minutes
**COOK** 1 hour 40 minutes
**PROCESS** 15 minutes

- 8  lb. ripe tomatoes (about 16 medium)
- 2  cups chopped, seeded fresh Anaheim or poblano chile peppers (tip, *p. 22*)
- ⅓  to ½ cup chopped, seeded fresh jalapeño chile peppers (tip, *p. 22*)
- 2  cups chopped onions
- ½  cup chopped fresh cilantro
- ½  cup lime juice
- ½  cup white vinegar
- ½  of a 6-oz. can tomato paste (⅓ cup)
- 5  cloves garlic, minced
- 1  tsp. cumin seeds, toasted and crushed*
- 1  tsp. salt
- 1  tsp. black pepper

**1.** If desired, peel tomatoes (tips, *p. 643*). Seed, core, and coarsely chop tomatoes (about 15 cups). Place tomatoes in a large nonreactive colander. Let drain 30 minutes.

**2.** Place drained tomatoes in a 7- to 8-qt. nonreactive heavy pot (tip, *p. 643*). Bring to boiling; reduce heat. Boil gently, uncovered, about 1½ hours or until desired consistency, stirring occasionally. Add remaining ingredients. Return to boiling; reduce heat. Simmer, uncovered, 10 minutes. Remove from heat.

**3.** Ladle hot salsa into hot, clean pint canning jars (tips and photos, *p. 635*), leaving a ½-inch headspace. Wipe jar rims; adjust lids and screw bands.

**4.** Process filled jars in a boiling-water canner 15 minutes (start timing when water returns to boiling). Remove jars from canner; cool on a wire rack. **Makes 5 pints.**

**\*NOTE** To toast cumin seeds, place seeds in a small dry skillet over medium heat 1 to 2 minutes or until lightly toasted, shaking skillet occasionally. Remove seeds from heat; allow to cool before crushing with a mortar and pestle.

**EACH 2 TBSP.** *13 cal., 0 g fat, 0 mg chol., 40 mg sodium, 3 g carb., 1 g fiber, 2 g sugars, 1 g pro.*

**WAIT FOR IT**
The flavors of condiments such as barbecue sauce will improve and intensify if the jars are allowed to stand for several weeks before opening. Once the jars are opened, refrigerate and use within 2 weeks.

// CANNING //

**APPLE-CHERRY CHUTNEY**

## APPLE-CHERRY CHUTNEY

**HANDS-ON TIME** 30 minutes
**COOK** 1 hour
**PROCESS** 10 minutes

| | |
|---|---|
| 3 | lb. apples, peeled, cored, and chopped (8 cups) |
| 1½ | cups dried tart red cherries |
| 2 | cups packed brown sugar |
| 2 | cups cider vinegar |
| 1 | cup chopped sweet onion |
| 1 | cup chopped red sweet pepper |
| 2 | tsp. ground cardamom |
| ½ | tsp. salt |

**1.** In a 6- to 8-qt. heavy pot stir together all ingredients. Bring to boiling; reduce heat. Simmer, uncovered, about 1 hour or until thickened, stirring occasionally.

**2.** Ladle hot chutney into seven hot, sterilized half-pint canning jars (photos, p. 635), leaving a ½-inch headspace. Wipe jar rims; adjust lids and screw bands.

**3.** Process filled jars in a boiling-water canner 10 minutes (start timing when water returns to boiling). Remove jars from canner; cool on wire racks.

**Makes 7 half-pints.**

**EACH 2 TBSP.** *76 cal., 0 g fat, 0 mg chol., 31 mg sodium, 19 g carb., 1 g fiber, 17 g sugars, 0 g pro.*

## BLUEBERRY-MAPLE-PECAN CONSERVE

**HANDS-ON TIME** 25 minutes
**COOK** 30 minutes
**PROCESS** 10 minutes

| | |
|---|---|
| 4 | cups blueberries |
| 1 | cup water |
| 1 | cup pure maple syrup |
| 2 | Tbsp. bottled lemon juice |
| 2 | cups packed brown sugar |
| 1 | cup dried currants |
| 1 | cup chopped pecans |
| 1 | tsp. ground cinnamon |

**1.** In a 4- to 6-qt. heavy pot combine blueberries, the water, maple syrup, and lemon juice. Using a potato masher, slightly crush the blueberries. Bring to boiling; reduce heat. Simmer, covered, about 5 minutes or until blueberries are tender, stirring occasionally.

**2.** Stir brown sugar and currants into blueberry mixture. Return to boiling, stirring until sugar dissolves; reduce heat. Simmer, uncovered, about 30 minutes or until mixture thickens, stirring occasionally. Remove from heat. Stir in pecans and cinnamon.

**3.** Ladle hot conserve into five hot, sterilized half-pint canning jars (photos, p. 635), leaving a ¼-inch headspace. Wipe jar rims; adjust lids and screw bands.

**4.** Process filled jars in a boiling-water canner 10 minutes (start timing when water returns to boiling). Remove jars from canner; cool on a wire rack. **Makes 5 half-pints.**

**EACH 2 TBSP.** *111 cal., 2 g fat (0 g sat. fat), 0 mg chol., 5 mg sodium, 24 g carb., 1 g fiber, 23 g sugars, 1 g pro.*

**CHUTNEY OR CONSERVE?** HAILING FROM INDIA, CHUTNEY IS A THICK MIXTURE OF FRUIT, VINEGAR, AND SUGAR. CONSERVE IS A THICK, SWEET SPREAD WITH ADDED DRIED FRUIT AND/OR NUTS.

**GET-TOGETHER**

*Feature any of these chutney, jam, and conserve recipes on a cheese board (p. 383). Add crackers or bread, several soft and hard cheeses, and in-season fresh fruit.*

# DOUBLE PEACH-PISTACHIO CONSERVE

**HANDS-ON TIME** 40 minutes
**COOK** 30 minutes
**PROCESS** 5 minutes

| | |
|---|---|
| 5 | lb. fresh medium peaches, peeled, pitted, and chopped |
| 1 | cup honey |
| ½ | cup water |
| ¼ | cup champagne vinegar or white wine vinegar |
| 2 | cups sugar |
| 1 | cup snipped dried peaches or apricots |
| 1 | cup chopped pistachio nuts |
| ½ | tsp. ground cardamom |

**1.** In a 6- to 8-qt. heavy pot combine the first four ingredients (through vinegar). Use a potato masher to slightly crush the peaches. Bring to boiling; reduce heat. Simmer, covered, about 5 minutes or until peaches are tender, stirring occasionally.

**2.** Stir sugar and dried peaches into peach mixture in pot. Return to boiling, stirring to dissolve sugar; reduce heat. Boil gently, uncovered, about 30 minutes or until mixture is syrupy, stirring occasionally. Remove from heat. Stir in pistachios and cardamom.

**3.** Ladle hot conserve into six hot, sterilized half-pint canning jars (photos, *p. 635*), leaving a ¼-inch headspace. Wipe jar rims; adjust lids and screw bands.

**4.** Process filled jars in a boiling-water canner 5 minutes (start timing when water returns to boiling). Remove jars from canner; cool on wire racks. **Makes 6 half-pints.**

**EACH 1 TBSP.** *46 cal., 1 g fat (0 g sat. fat), 0 mg chol., 7 mg sodium, 10 g carb., 0 g fiber, 9 g sugars, 0 g pro.*

DOUBLE PEACH-PISTACHIO CONSERVE

BLUEBERRY-MAPLE-PECAN CONSERVE

OUR TWO BEST TIPS FOR JAM-MAKING SUCCESS: FIRST, MAKE A SINGLE BATCH AT A TIME (DOUBLING THE RECIPE PREVENTS PROPER JELLING AND CAUSES SCORCHING). SECOND, ALWAYS USE THE EXACT AMOUNT OF SUGAR SPECIFIED (PECTIN REQUIRES A SPECIFIC RATIO OF SUGAR TO PECTIN FOR PERFECT JELLING).

Unless otherwise specified in the recipe, bring mixture to a full rolling boil (bubbles break the surface so rapidly that you can't stir them down).

# STRAWBERRY JAM

**HANDS-ON TIME** 35 minutes
**PROCESS** 5 minutes

PECTIN is a soluble fruit-derived fiber that gives jams and jellies thickness and body. Pectin comes in powdered and liquid forms and in a formulation suitable for low-sugar recipes. Always use the type of pectin and exact amount of sugar specified in the recipe; a specific ratio of sugar to pectin is needed for each type of pectin to work properly.

12   cups hulled fresh strawberries
1   1.75-oz. pkg. regular powdered fruit pectin or 6 Tbsp. classic powdered fruit pectin
½   tsp. butter
7   cups sugar

**1.** Place 1 cup of the strawberries in an 8-qt. heavy pot. Using a potato masher, crush berries. Continue adding and crushing berries. Measure 5 cups crushed berries. Stir in pectin and butter. Bring to a full rolling boil, stirring constantly. Quickly stir in sugar. Return to a full rolling boil over high heat, stirring constantly. Boil hard 1 minute, stirring constantly. Remove from heat. Skim off any foam with a metal spoon.
**2.** Ladle hot jam into seven hot, sterilized half-pint canning jars (photos, p. 635), leaving a ¼-inch headspace. Wipe jar rims; adjust lids and screw bands.
**3.** Process filled jars in a boiling-water canner 5 minutes (start timing when water returns to boiling). Remove jars from canner; cool on wire racks. **Makes 7 half-pints.**
**EACH 1 TBSP. JAM AND VARIATIONS**
*54 cal., 0 g fat, 0 mg chol., 0 mg sodium, 14 g carb., 0 g fiber, 13 g sugars, 0 g pro.*

**》 RASPBERRY JAM** Prepare as directed, except replace the 12 cups strawberries with 12 cups fresh raspberries. If desired, press half of the 5 cups crushed berries through a sieve before stirring in the pectin and butter. **Makes 7 half-pints.**

**》 STRAWBERRY AND GINGER ALE JAM** Prepare as directed, except add ½ cup ginger ale before skimming off the foam in Step 1. **Makes 8 half-pints.**

**》 STRAWBERRY-MARSALA-THYME JAM** Prepare as directed, except add ½ cup Marsala wine with the pectin and butter. Add ¼ cup chopped fresh thyme after skimming off the foam. **Makes 7 half-pints.**

**RIGHT SIDE UP**
Vintage recipes used to recommend cooling jars of jam upside down so chunks of fruit wouldn't float to the top. We found cooling this way disrupted the seal on the jar, so we recommend you cool and store your jam right side up. If the fruit pieces aren't distributed evenly when the gel sets, stir the jam before serving.

Boiling creates foam that you need to remove before filling jars. To skim foam, quickly glide a metal spoon over the surface, catching the foam; remove and discard the frothy bubbles.

Use a clean canning funnel and ladle for filling sterilized canning jars with jams and jellies. A funnel helps prevent sticky liquid from getting on the rim or running down the outsides of the jars.

**BREAKFAST TARTS**
To make these yummy strawberry jam-filled tarts, follow the Hand Pies recipe on *p. 626*, filling each tart with jam or jelly instead of fruit filling. Drizzle with icing and top with sprinkles.

# LEMON-LIME-ORANGE MARMALADE

**HANDS-ON TIME** 55 minutes
**PROCESS** 5 minutes
**STAND** 1 week

3 medium oranges
1 medium Meyer lemon
1 medium lime
1½ cups water
⅛ tsp. baking soda
5 cups sugar
½ of a 6-oz. pkg. (1 foil pouch) liquid fruit pectin

**1.** Use a paring knife to score the peels of the oranges, lemon, and lime into four lengthwise sections; remove peels. Scrape off white pith; discard. Cut peels into thin strips. In a 3-qt. saucepan bring peels, the water, and the baking soda to boiling; reduce heat. Simmer, covered, 20 minutes; do not drain.
**2.** Meanwhile, working over a bowl, remove fruit sections (cut between a section and the membrane) (photo, p. 12). Cut back between the section and the next membrane to release the section. Repeat until all fruits are sectioned. Add sections and juices to saucepan; return to boiling. Simmer, covered, 10 minutes (3 cups fruit mixture).
**3.** In an 8- to 10-qt. heavy pot combine fruit mixture and sugar. Bring to boiling, stirring constantly to dissolve sugar. Quickly stir in pectin. Bring to a full rolling boil (photos, p. 650), stirring constantly. Boil hard 1 minute, stirring constantly. Remove from heat. Quickly skim off foam with a metal spoon.
**4.** Ladle hot marmalade into five hot, sterilized half-pint canning jars (photos, p. 635), leaving a ¼-inch headspace. Wipe jar rims; adjust lids and screw bands.
**5.** Process filled jars in a boiling-water canner 5 minutes (start timing when water returns to boiling). Remove jars from canner; cool on a wire rack. Allow jars to stand at room temperature at least 1 week for marmalade to set. **Makes 5 half-pints.**
**EACH 1 TBSP.** *52 cal., 0 g fat, 0 mg chol., 2 mg sodium, 13 g carb., 0 g fiber, 13 g sugars, 0 g pro.*

---

# PEACH JAM

**HANDS-ON TIME** 30 minutes
**PROCESS** 5 minutes

7 cups sugar
4 cups finely chopped, peeled ripe peaches* (about 3 lb. fresh or 2 lb. frozen, thawed)
¼ cup fresh lemon juice
½ of a 6-oz. pkg. (1 foil pouch) liquid fruit pectin

**1.** In a 6- to 8-qt. heavy pot combine sugar, peaches, and lemon juice. Cook over high heat until mixture comes to a full rolling boil, stirring constantly. Quickly stir in pectin. Return to a full rolling boil (photos, p. 650), stirring constantly. Boil hard 1 minute, stirring constantly. Remove from heat. Quickly skim off foam with a metal spoon.
**2.** Ladle hot jam into seven hot, sterilized half-pint canning jars (photos, p. 635), leaving a ¼-inch headspace. Wipe jar rims; adjust lids and screw bands.
**3.** Process filled jars in a boiling-water canner 5 minutes (start timing when water returns to boiling). Remove jars from canner; cool on wire racks. **Makes 7 half-pints.**
**\*NOTE** If desired, place small batches of cut-up peeled peaches in a food processor. Cover and pulse until peaches are finely chopped.
**EACH 1 TBSP.** *51 cal., 0 g fat, 0 mg chol., 0 mg sodium, 13 g carb., 0 g fiber, 13 g sugars, 0 g pro.*

**CHANGE IT UP**
*Add a touch of savory flavor to Peach Jam. After skimming off the foam in Step 1, stir in ½ cup chopped fresh basil or ¾ tsp. freshly ground cardamom.*

---

THOMCORD GRAPES are available in supermarkets during late summer and early fall. This hybrid combines the deep, lush flavor and color of Concord grapes (which are more difficult to find) with the light, mellow sweetness of Thompson grapes. Another bonus is they're seedless. Don't use regular table grapes for this recipe.

---

# GRAPE JELLY

**HANDS-ON TIME** 30 minutes
**COOK** 10 minutes
**STAND** 30 minutes
**PROCESS** 5 minutes

3 lb. Thomcord grapes*
½ cup water
Bottled unsweetened grape juice (optional)
1 1.75-oz. pkg. regular powdered fruit pectin or 6 Tbsp. classic powdered fruit pectin
4½ cups sugar

**1.** Wash and stem grapes. In a 6- to 8-qt. heavy pot crush grapes with a potato masher. Add the water. Bring to boiling; reduce heat. Simmer, covered, about 10 minutes or until grapes are very soft.
**2.** Line a colander or sieve with several layers of 100%-cotton cheesecloth. Place colander over a large bowl. Pour grapes and cooking liquid into colander. Let stand at room temperature 30 minutes or until dripping has almost stopped (do not squeeze cheesecloth). Discard grapes in colander. Measure 3 cups juice (add unsweetened grape juice if necessary to equal 3 cups).
**3.** Place strained juice in same pot. Stir in pectin. Bring to a full rolling boil (photos, p. 650), stirring constantly. Quickly stir in sugar. Return to a full rolling boil over high heat, stirring constantly. Boil hard 1 minute, stirring constantly. Remove from heat. Quickly skim off foam with a metal spoon.
**4.** Ladle hot jelly into five hot, sterilized half-pint canning jars (photos, p. 635), leaving a ¼-inch headspace. Wipe jar rims; adjust lids and bands.
**5.** Process filled jars in a boiling-water canner 5 minutes (start timing when water returns to boiling). Remove jars from canner; cool on a wire rack.
**Makes 5 half-pints.**

**\*NOTE** The amount of juice you get from the grapes may vary depending on the freshness of the grapes. If you can't find these grapes, you may use 3 cups bottled unsweetened Concord grape juice and omit Steps 1 and 2.
**EACH 1 TBSP.** *55 cal., 0 g fat, 0 mg chol., 0 mg sodium, 14 g carb., 0 g fiber, 14 g sugars, 0 g pro.*

LEMON-LIME-ORANGE MARMALADE

### GIFT IT
Extra jars of jams and jellies make sweet holiday and hostess gifts. Tie a ribbon around the lid or secure a small square of fabric under the screw band for a vintage look.

PEACH JAM

GRAPE JELLY

JUICE JELLY

**HANDS-ON TIME** 30 minutes
**PROCESS** 5 minutes

3 cups bottled unsweetened
  grape juice (options, *right*)
1 1.75-oz. pkg. regular powdered
  fruit pectin or 6 Tbsp. classic
  powdered fruit pectin
4½ cups sugar

**1.** In a 6- to 8-qt. heavy pot
combine juice and pectin. Bring
to a full rolling boil (photos,
*p. 650*), stirring constantly. Quickly
stir in sugar. Return to a full
rolling boil over high heat, stirring
constantly. Boil hard 1 minute,
stirring constantly. Remove from
heat. Quickly skim off foam with a
metal spoon.
**2.** Ladle hot jelly into five hot,
sterilized half-pint canning jars
(photos, *p. 635*), leaving a ¼-inch
headspace. Wipe jar rims; adjust lids
and bands.
**3.** Process filled jars in a boiling-
water canner 5 minutes (start timing
when water returns to boiling).
Remove jars from canner; cool on
a wire rack. **Makes 5 half-pints.**
**EACH 1 TBSP.** *57 cal., 0 g fat, 0 mg
chol., 2 mg sodium, 14 g carb., 0 g fiber,
14 g sugars, 0 g pro.*

### MORE JUICE

These juices also
make excellent
Juice Jelly.

**FRUIT JUICES**
• Apple juice or
  apple cider
• Orange juice
• Cranberry juice

**VEGETABLE
JUICES**
• Purple carrot,
  beet, and
  green apple
  vegetable juice
  blend with fruit
• Yellow and
  orange carrot,
  sweet potato,
  and orange
  vegetable juice
  blend with fruit

**JUICE JELLY**

**IS IT READY?**
You'll know this fruit butter is ready to ladle into the jars when it has thickened enough to mound on a spoon. Be sure to stir it often to keep it from sticking.

## APPLE BUTTER

**HANDS-ON TIME** 45 minutes
**COOK** 2 hours
**PROCESS** 5 minutes

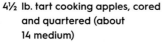

TART APPLE varieties that we recommend for this spiced butter include Granny Smith (the tartest of all!), Cortland, Jonathan, Jonagold, and McIntosh.

4½ lb. tart cooking apples, cored and quartered (about 14 medium)
3 cups apple cider or apple juice
2 cups granulated sugar
2 Tbsp. fresh lemon juice
½ tsp. ground cinnamon

**1.** In an 8- to 10-qt. heavy pot combine apples and cider. Bring to boiling; reduce heat. Simmer, covered, 30 minutes, stirring occasionally. Press apple mixture through a food mill or sieve until you have 7½ cups. Return pulp to pot.
**2.** Stir in granulated sugar, lemon juice, and cinnamon. Bring to boiling; reduce heat. Cook, uncovered, over very low heat 1½ to 1¾ hours or until very thick and mixture mounds on a spoon, stirring often.
**3.** Ladle hot apple butter into six hot, sterilized half-pint canning jars (photos, p. 635), leaving a ¼-inch headspace. Wipe jar rims; adjust lids and screw bands.
**4.** Process filled jars in a boiling-water canner 5 minutes (start timing when water returns to boiling). Remove jars from canner; cool on a wire rack. **Makes 6 half-pints.**
**TO FREEZE** Place pot of apple butter in a sink filled with ice water; stir to cool. Ladle into clean wide-mouth half-pint freezer containers, leaving a ½-inch headspace. Seal and label. Store in refrigerator up to 2 weeks or freeze up to 6 months. Apple butter may darken slightly on freezing.

**EACH 1 TBSP. PLAIN AND VARIATIONS**
*28 cal., 0 g fat, 0 mg chol., 0 mg sodium, 7 g carb., 0 g fiber, 7 g sugars, 0 g pro.*

**APPLE-PEAR BUTTER**
Prepare as directed, except substitute 2 lb. cored, quartered ripe pears for 2 lb. of the apples.

**CARAMEL APPLE BUTTER**
Prepare as directed, except decrease granulated sugar to ½ cup and add 1½ cups packed brown sugar.

## APPLESAUCE

**HANDS-ON TIME** 1 hour
**COOK** 25 minutes
**PROCESS** 15 minutes

8   lb. cooking apples, cored and quartered (24 cups)
2   cups water
¼   cup fresh lemon juice
¾   to 1¼ cups granulated sugar

**1.** In an 8- to 10-qt. heavy pot combine apples, the water, and lemon juice. Bring to boiling; reduce heat. Simmer, covered, 25 to 30 minutes or until apples are very tender, stirring often.
**2.** Press apples through a food mill or sieve. Return pulp to pot; discard skins. Stir in sugar to taste. If necessary, add ½ to 1 cup water for desired consistency. Bring to boiling.
**3.** Ladle hot applesauce into hot, clean pint or quart canning jars (tips and photos, *p. 635*), leaving a ½-inch headspace. Wipe jar rims; adjust lids and screw bands.
**4.** Process filled jars in a boiling-water canner 15 minutes for pints and 20 minutes for quarts (start timing when water returns to boiling). Remove jars from canner; cool on wire racks. **Makes 6 pints or 3 quarts.**

**TO FREEZE** Place pot of applesauce in a sink filled with ice water; stir to cool. Ladle into clean wide-mouth half-pint or quart freezer containers, leaving a ½-inch headspace. Seal and label. Store in refrigerator up to 2 weeks or freeze up to 8 months.
**EACH ½ CUP PLAIN AND VARIATIONS** *81 cal., 0 g fat, 0 mg chol., 1 mg sodium, 21 g carb., 2 g fiber, 18 g sugars, 0 g pro.*

>> **SPICED APPLESAUCE**
Prepare as directed, except add 10 inches stick cinnamon and 1½ tsp. apple pie spice in Step 1. Simmer as directed. Remove stick cinnamon and discard. Substitute ¾ cup packed brown sugar for the granulated sugar. Stir in enough additional brown sugar to taste (¼ to ¾ cup).

>> **VERY BERRY APPLESAUCE**
Prepare as directed, except replace 1 lb. (4 cups) of the apples with 1 lb. (4 cups) fresh or frozen thawed raspberries and/or strawberries and decrease water to 1½ cups in Step 1.

## CANNING FRUITS WITH SYRUPS

If you want to can fruits with syrup (chart, *opposite*), choose the syrup that best suits your tastes. Sour fruits are best with heavier syrups; mild fruits are best with lighter syrups.

**PREPARING SYRUP**
To prepare a syrup, place the recommended amounts (below) of sugar and water in a 3-qt. saucepan. Heat until sugar dissolves. Skim off any foam. Use the syrup hot for canned fruits and chilled for frozen fruits. Allow ½ to ⅔ cup syrup for each 2 cups fruit.

**VERY THIN SYRUP**
1 cup sugar and 4 cups water to yield about 4 cups syrup.

**THIN SYRUP**
1⅔ cups sugar and 4 cups water to yield about 4¼ cups syrup.

**MEDIUM SYRUP**
2⅔ cups sugar and 4 cups water to yield 4⅔ cups syrup.

**HEAVY SYRUP**
4 cups sugar and 4 cups water to yield about 5¾ cups syrup.

# CANNING FRUIT

Wash all fruits with cool tap water, but do not soak them. Drain well and follow the preparation directions *below*. Also see notes on canning fruits with syrup (*opposite*).

| FRUIT | PREP | RAW-PACK | HOT-PACK |
|---|---|---|---|
| **APPLES & PEARS** | Allow 2 to 3 lb. per quart. For apples, select varieties that are crisp, not mealy, in texture. Peel and core; halve, quarter, or slice; dip into absorbic-acid color-keeper solution (tip, p. 678); drain. | Not recommended. | Simmer fruit in syrup (syrups, *opposite*) 5 minutes, stirring occasionally. Fill jars with fruit and syrup, leaving a ½-inch headspace. For apples, process pints and quarts 20 minutes. For pears, process pints 20 minutes and quarts 25 minutes. |
| **APRICOTS, NECTARINES & PEACHES** | Allow 2 to 3 lb. per quart. To peel peaches (peeling nectarines and apricots is not necessary), immerse in boiling water 30 to 60 seconds or until skins start to split; remove and plunge into cold water. Halve and pit. If desired, slice. Treat with ascorbic-acid color-keeper solution (tip, p. 678); drain. | Fill jars, placing fruit cut sides down. Add boiling syrup or water, leaving a ½-inch headspace (tip, p. 634). Process pints 25 minutes and quarts 30 minutes. Do not raw-pack apricots. (Hot-packing generally results in a better product.) | Add fruit to hot syrup; bring to boiling. Fill jars with fruit (placing cut sides down) and syrup (syrups, *opposite*), leaving a ½-inch headspace (tip, p. 634). Process pints 20 minutes and quarts 25 minutes. |
| **BERRIES** | Allow 1 to 3 lb. per quart. Can or freeze blackberries, blueberries, currants, elderberries, gooseberries, huckleberries, loganberries, and mulberries. Freeze (chart, p. 678) boysenberries, raspberries, and strawberries (do not can). | Fill jars with berries. Shake down gently. Add boiling syrup, leaving a ½-inch headspace (tip, p. 634). Process pints 15 minutes and quarts 20 minutes. | Simmer berries in water 30 seconds; drain. Fill jars with berries and hot syrup (syrups, *opposite*), leaving a ½-inch headspace (tip, p. 634). Process pints and quarts 15 minutes. |
| **CHERRIES** | Allow 2 to 3 lb. per quart. If desired, treat with ascorbic-acid color-keeper solution (tip, p. 678); drain. If unpitted, prick skin on opposite sides to prevent splitting. | Fill jars, shaking down gently. Add boiling syrup or water, leaving a ½-inch headspace (tip, p. 634). Process pints and quarts 25 minutes. | Add cherries to hot syrup (syrups, *opposite*); bring to boiling. Fill jars with fruit and syrup, leaving a ½-inch headspace (tip, p. 634). Process pints 15 minutes and quarts 20 minutes. |
| **RHUBARB** | Allow 1½ lb. per quart. Discard leaves and woody ends. Cut into ½- to 1-inch pieces. Freeze for best quality. | Not recommended. | In a pot sprinkle ½ cup sugar over 4 cups fruit; mix. Let stand until juice forms. Bring slowly to boiling, stirring. Fill jars with hot fruit and juice, leaving a ½-inch headspace (tip, p. 634). Process pints and quarts 15 minutes. |

# DRYING

PRESERVING FOODS THROUGH DEHYDRATION SERVES TWO PURPOSES: IT CONCENTRATES FLAVOR AND PROLONGS SHELF LIFE BY EXTRACTING MOISTURE FROM FRUITS, VEGETABLES, AND MEATS.

## DRYING BASICS

### THE DEHYDRATOR

The best way to dry foods is in a dehydrator. The low temperatures and air circulation are specifically designed for this task. In some recipes (only where specified), you can dehydrate in your oven. If you're unsure about the accuracy of the oven's temperature, check it using an oven thermometer and adjust temperature accordingly before using oven to dehydrate foods. The temperature needs to be low enough to dry out foods evenly without burning them.

**VEGETABLES** must be dried until firm and crisp to prevent spoilage.

**FRUITS** can be softer than vegetables when dried because their sugar content helps preserve them.

**CERTAIN FRUITS,** such as apples and peaches, tend to brown, or oxidize, which does not affect flavor. Dipping fruits in an ascorbic-acid color-keeper solution (p. 678) before drying helps prevent oxidation.

**SOME FRUIT** pieces may be more moist than others after drying, which can promote mold growth. To prepare for storing, place cooled, dried fruit pieces in a plastic container, filling it about two-thirds full. Cover container and let stand 7 to 10 days, shaking contents daily. Any excess moisture will be absorbed by the drier pieces of fruit. (If moisture appears in the container, return fruit to dehydrator.)

## MAPLE-CRACKED PEPPER JERKY

**HANDS-ON TIME** 45 minutes
**STEAM** 10 minutes
**COOL** 10 minutes
**FREEZE** 45 minutes
**MARINATE** 1 hour
**DEHYDRATE** 5 hours

- 2 lb. boneless beef chuck roast and/or boneless beef sirloin roast, trimmed of excess fat
- 1 cup reduced-sodium soy sauce
- 2 Tbsp. pure maple syrup
- 2 Tbsp. olive oil
- 4 cloves garlic, minced
- 2 tsp. cracked assorted peppercorns or black peppercorns
- 2 tsp. sea salt
- 1 tsp. dried thyme, crushed

**1.** Place a steamer insert in a 12-inch skillet. Add enough water to the skillet to come just below the steamer insert. Bring water to boiling. Place roast in steamer insert. Cover; steam 10 to 15 minutes or until an instant-read thermometer inserted into the center of the roast registers 160°F. Let cool 10 minutes. Wrap meat in plastic wrap; freeze about 45 minutes or until firm.

**2.** Using a sharp knife, cut meat across the grain into ⅛- to ¼-inch slices that are 5 to 6 inches long.

**3.** For marinade, in a large bowl combine remaining ingredients. Add meat to marinade, stirring to coat the meat evenly. Cover and marinate in the refrigerator 1 to 2 hours. (The longer you marinate, the stronger the flavor.) Drain meat in a colander set in a sink; discard marinade.

**4.** Place meat slices in a single layer on mesh-lined dehydrator trays. Dehydrate at 160°F for 5 to 6 hours or until dry. To check doneness, remove one slice from dehydrator; cool. Slice should easily break when done. Store in a covered container at room temperature up to 3 weeks before using. **Makes 16 servings (about 1 oz. each).**

**OVEN DIRECTIONS** Prepare as directed through Step 3. Preheat oven to 200°F. Place meat on a wire rack placed in a shallow baking pan. Bake 3½ to 5 hours or until dry. To check doneness, remove one slice from oven; cool. Slice should easily break when done. Store as directed.

**EACH SERVING** *87 cal., 4 g fat (2 g sat. fat), 39 mg chol., 255 mg sodium, 1 g carb., 0 g fiber, 1 g sugars, 12 g pro.*

## SRIRACHA-HONEY BEEF JERKY

**HANDS-ON TIME** 20 minutes
**STEAM** 10 minutes
**COOL** 10 minutes
**FREEZE** 30 minutes
**MARINATE** overnight
**DEHYDRATE** 6 hours

| | |
|---|---|
| 2 | lb. top or bottom round steak, cut 1 to 1½ inches thick and trimmed of excess fat |
| ⅓ | cup reduced-sodium soy sauce |
| ⅓ | cup sriracha sauce |
| 3 | Tbsp. honey |
| 3 | Tbsp. olive oil |
| 2 | tsp. salt |
| 1 | tsp. chili powder |

**1.** Place a steamer insert in a 12-inch skillet. Add enough water to the skillet to come just below the steamer insert. Bring to boiling. Place steak in the steamer insert. Cover; steam 10 to 15 minutes or until an instant-read thermometer inserted into the center of the meat registers 160°F. Let cool 10 minutes. Wrap meat in plastic wrap or waxed paper; freeze about 30 minutes or until firm.

**2.** Using a sharp knife, cut meat across the grain into ⅛- to ¼-inch slices.

**3.** For marinade, in a large bowl combine remaining ingredients. Add meat to marinade, stirring to coat meat evenly. Cover; marinate in the refrigerator overnight. Drain meat slices in a colander set in sink; discard marinade.

**4.** Place meat slices in a single layer on mesh-lined dehydrator trays. Dehydrate at 160°F about 6 hours or until dry. To check doneness, remove one slice; cool. Slice should easily break when done. Store cooled jerky in a covered container at room temperature up to 3 weeks. **Makes 16 servings (about 1 oz. each).**

**EACH SERVING** *102 cal., 4 g fat (1 g sat. fat), 35 mg chol., 435 mg sodium, 4 g carb., 0 g fiber, 4 g sugars, 14 g pro.*

**≫**

**THE BEEF is** precooked since the low heat of the dehydrator can't get the meat up to a safe temperature fast enough. When cutting the beef, look for the "grain" of the meat—which refers to the long muscle fibers that run parallel to each other. Cutting across these fibers makes cuts more tender and less stringy.

**≫**

**OVEN-DRYING** is not recommended for this recipe.

SRIRACHA-HONEY BEEF JERKY

MAPLE-CRACKED PEPPER JERKY

## DRIED TOMATOES

**HANDS-ON TIME** 15 minutes
**DEHYDRATE** 11 hours

»

TOMATOES of
any kind can be
used here—try
halved cherry
tomatoes or
regular tomatoes
cut into ¼-inch
slices. Place
tomatoes, cut
sides up, on
mesh-lined
dehydrator
trays or in a
parchment-lined
baking pan. Dry
cherry tomatoes
in dehydrator
10 to 11 hours
or in oven 4 to
5 hours. Dry
sliced tomatoes in
dehydrator 7½ to
8½ hours or in
oven 3 to 4 hours.

3  lb. roma tomatoes, quartered
   lengthwise
2  Tbsp. fresh thyme leaves
1  Tbsp. packed brown sugar
1½ tsp. kosher salt
½  to ¾ tsp. cracked black pepper

**1.** Sprinkle tomatoes with thyme, brown sugar, salt, and pepper. Place tomatoes in a single layer on mesh-lined dehydrator trays. Dehydrate at 135°F for 11 to 12 hours or until leathery but not brittle. Remove tomatoes as they finish drying and allow remaining tomatoes to continue drying. Cool to room temperature.

**2.** Pack dried tomatoes in resealable plastic freezer bags. Freeze up to 9 months. Thaw before using.
**Makes 10 servings (¼ cup each).**
**OVEN DIRECTIONS** Preheat oven to 225°F. Line a 15×10-inch baking pan with parchment paper. Arrange tomatoes in a single layer on parchment paper. Sprinkle with thyme, brown sugar, salt, and pepper. Bake 5½ to 6½ hours or until leathery but not brittle, turning tomatoes after 2 hours. Remove tomatoes as they finish drying and allowing remaining tomatoes to continue drying. Continue as directed.

**EACH SERVING** *30 cal., 0 g fat, 0 mg chol., 302 mg sodium, 7 g carb., 2 g fiber, 5 g sugars, 1 g pro.*

## DRIED CRANBERRIES

**HANDS-ON TIME** 20 minutes
**DEHYDRATE** 11 hours

2  12-oz. pkg. fresh or frozen
   cranberries
2  cups water
¼  cup sugar
2  Tbsp. vegetable oil

A TASTE OF TOMATO

The bold, concentrated flavor of dried tomatoes makes them a savory addition to salad dressings, salads, sauces, soups, and antipasti.

DRIED TOMATOES

DRIED CRANBERRIES

**1.** In a 3- or 4-qt. saucepan combine cranberries and the water. Bring to boiling; remove from heat. Let stand, covered, 2 minutes; drain well. Spread drained cranberries on paper towel-lined trays, pressing gently to release juices. Transfer cranberries to a large bowl. Add sugar and oil; toss to coat.

**2.** Arrange cranberries in a single layer on mesh-lined dehydrator trays, separating the berries as much as possible.

**3.** Dehydrate at 135°F for 11 to 12 hours or until dry and chewy, rearranging trays once or twice during drying. Let cool completely. Store in a covered container at room temperature up to 6 months.
**Makes 8 servings (¼ cup each).**
**EACH SERVING** *94 cal., 4 g fat (0 g sat. fat), 0 mg chol., 2 mg sodium, 17 g carb., 4 g fiber, 10 g sugars, 0 g pro.*

# STRAWBERRY FRUIT LEATHER

**HANDS-ON TIME** 30 minutes
**COOK** 35 minutes
**DEHYDRATE** 12 hours

2  lb. ripe fresh strawberries, hulled and coarsely chopped
1  cup sugar
2  tsp. lemon zest
   Nonstick cooking spray

**1.** In a food processor combine strawberries and sugar. Cover and process until smooth. Press strawberry mixture through a fine-mesh sieve placed over a bowl; discard seeds remaining in sieve.
**2.** In a 4-qt. heavy saucepan combine the strawberry mixture and the lemon zest. Bring to boiling over medium-high heat, stirring occasionally; reduce heat. Simmer, uncovered, 35 to 40 minutes or until the mixture is thick enough to mound slightly on a spoon and is reduced to about 1½ cups, stirring frequently.

**3.** Lightly coat two fruit leather dehydrator sheets with nonstick spray. Divide strawberry mixture between the prepared leather sheets, spreading to an even ¼-inch thickness.
**4.** Dehydrate at 135°F for 12 to 13 hours. Turn leather over during last 1 hour of dehydrating to allow bottoms to dry.
**5.** Peel fruit leather from leather sheets. Roll into a spiral; wrap in plastic wrap. Store at room temperature up to 2 weeks. To serve, cut into pieces.
**Makes 16 servings.**

**OVEN DIRECTIONS** Preheat oven to 170°F. Line a 15×10-inch baking pan with parchment paper. Coat parchment with cooking spray. Pour strawberry mixture into the prepared pan, spreading to an even ¼-inch thickness. Bake 10 to 11 hours, rotating pan occasionally. Holding parchment paper, lift fruit leather out of pan; cool. Roll leather in a spiral; wrap in plastic wrap. Store as directed.
**EACH SERVING** *66 cal., 0 g fat, 0 mg chol., 1 mg sodium, 17 g carb., 1 g fiber, 15 g sugars, 0 g pro.*

>> **HERBED STRAWBERRY FRUIT LEATHER** Prepare as directed, except substitute 2 Tbsp. chopped fresh tarragon, basil, mint, and/or thyme for the lemon zest.

>> **STRAWBERRY-GINGER FRUIT LEATHER** Prepare as directed, except substitute 1 Tbsp. grated fresh ginger for the lemon zest.

>> **STRAWBERRY-KUMQUAT FRUIT LEATHER** Prepare as directed, except puree ½ cup quartered, seeded kumquats with the strawberries and sugar in Step 1. Omit the lemon zest.

STRAWBERRY FRUIT LEATHER

# HERB-DRYING OPTIONS

## HANG IN BUNCHES
Gather small amounts of herbs into bunches, tie stems with 100%-cotton kitchen string, and hang in a dry area with good air circulation until dry.

## LAY FLAT
Scatter herb sprigs on a sheet of waxed paper and let them dry, undisturbed, at room temperature.

## DEHYDRATOR
Dehydrators cut drying time significantly and dry herbs evenly. Prepare herbs and dehydrate as directed. Cool herbs completely before storing.

## MICROWAVE
This method works best with woody-stemmed herbs such as rosemary, thyme, and oregano. Do not microwave delicate herbs like basil and parsley. They will wither and turn brown and might cause the paper towels to catch fire.

## ARRANGE
Place herbs in a single layer between two paper towels. Microwave 1 minute, testing for dryness every 20 seconds. Remove the dried herb leaves from the stems.

## STORING
Place dried herbs in airtight containers and store in a cool, dark place up to 1 year. Before using, crush dried herbs with your fingers to release their oils and boost their flavor.

# DEHYDRATOR-DRIED HERBS

1 bunch (about ¾ oz.) fresh herbs

**1.** Wash herbs in cool water; drain. Use a salad spinner to dry herbs or pat dry with paper towels.
**2.** Prepare herbs for drying in a dehydrator, following guidelines *opposite*.
**3.** Place herb leaves in a single layer on a dehydrator tray. If herb leaves are very small, line the dehydrator tray with a mesh or leather dehydrator sheet. Dehydrate at 95°F until leaves are crisp enough to crumble. If leaves blow around during dehydrating, place another mesh dehydrator sheet on top of the herbs.
**4.** Cool herbs. Crumble larger leaves, but keep smaller leaves intact for best flavor (crush when you use them for cooking). Label and store herbs in airtight containers in a cool, dark place.

## ITALIAN SEASONING
Measure, crush lightly, and combine 1 Tbsp. each dried basil, dried oregano, dried rosemary, and dried thyme. Stir in ¼ tsp. crushed red pepper.

## POULTRY SEASONING
Measure, crush lightly, and combine 1 Tbsp. each dried sage, dried thyme, and dried marjoram and 1 tsp. dried rosemary. Stir in ½ tsp. black pepper and ¼ tsp. celery salt.

## GREEK SEASONING
Measure, crush lightly, and combine 1 Tbsp. dried oregano, 2 tsp. dried thyme, and 1 tsp. each dried basil and dried marjoram. Stir in 1 tsp. dried minced onion and ½ tsp. dried minced garlic.

## DRYING HERBS

Prepare herbs as directed (*opposite*). To determine if an herb is done drying, crush a little with your fingers. A completely dry herb crumbles easily. Each of these timings is for 1 bunch of the fresh herb. (Timings and amounts vary depending on the freshness of the herbs, size of the leaves, and air humidity and temperature.)

## DEHYDRATOR PREP

**SMALL-LEAF HERBS**
Pull leaves from stems and discard stems.

**BROAD-LEAF HERBS**
Remove leaves from stems. For quicker drying, cut each leaf in half lengthwise.

**CHIVES**
Cut into ¼- to ½-inch lengths.

## BASIL

**HANGING OR
ON WAXED PAPER**
6 days

**DEHYDRATOR**
18 hours

**DRIED AMOUNT**
4 Tbsp.

## CHIVES

**HANGING OR
ON WAXED PAPER**
24 hours

**DEHYDRATOR**
7 hours

**DRIED AMOUNT**
2 Tbsp.

## DILL

**HANGING OR
ON WAXED PAPER**
24 hours

**DEHYDRATOR**
12 hours

**DRIED AMOUNT**
2 Tbsp.

## MARJORAM

**HANGING OR
ON WAXED PAPER**
1½ days

**DEHYDRATOR**
5 hours

**DRIED AMOUNT**
5 Tbsp.

## MINT

**HANGING OR
ON WAXED PAPER**
4 days

**DEHYDRATOR**
8 hours

**DRIED AMOUNT**
3 Tbsp.

## OREGANO

**HANGING OR
ON WAXED PAPER**
4 days

**DEHYDRATOR**
12 hours

**DRIED AMOUNT**
3 Tbsp.

## ROSEMARY

**HANGING OR
ON WAXED PAPER**
4 days

**DEHYDRATOR**
12 hours

**DRIED AMOUNT**
5 Tbsp.

## SAGE

**HANGING OR
ON WAXED PAPER**
4 days

**DEHYDRATOR**
8 hours

**DRIED AMOUNT**
4 Tbsp.

## TARRAGON

**HANGING OR
ON WAXED PAPER**
2 days

**DEHYDRATOR**
17 hours

**DRIED AMOUNT**
3 Tbsp.

## THYME

**HANGING OR
ON WAXED PAPER**
2½ days

**DEHYDRATOR**
5 hours

**DRIED AMOUNT**
3 Tbsp.

# FERMENTING

THIS FORM OF FOOD PRESERVATION DEPENDS UPON NATURALLY OCCURRING "GOOD" GUT-FRIENDLY FLORA (ORGANISMS) TO CONVERT NATURAL SUGARS IN FOODS INTO ACIDS. THE PROCESS CREATES A LESS-FRIENDLY ENVIRONMENT FOR THE BACTERIA THAT CAUSE SPOILAGE.

## *FERMENTING BASICS*

Cultivating your own crop of good gut-friendly bacteria through fermenting is worth trying. Without getting too much into the science behind it, here's the bottom line: Research shows that probiotics—such as the Lactobacillus strain—from fermented foods help aid digestion and boost immune health. In addition, studies show that fermentation increases the vitamin content and digestibility of those foods. Start by eating small amounts of fermented foods so your digestive tract can get used to these new little friends.

**USE ONLY TESTED RECIPES** from a reliable source (such as this book and the United States Department of Agriculture [USDA]). Do not alter the vinegar, salt, food, or water proportions in your recipe.

**USE ADDITIVE-FREE SALT,** such as pickling salt or natural fine sea salt (tip, p. 666).

**SELECTING AND CLEANING PRODUCE** are important. Select only unblemished foods for fermenting. Bruises and cuts can breach the natural antimicrobial barriers of fruits and vegetables. Look for firm but ripe fruits and vegetables. Soft or overripe produce may contain undesirable yeasts and/or molds. Thoroughly rinse all produce that is to be used for fermentation.

Most microbial pathogens are found on the surfaces of fruits and vegetables. When applicable, peel and/or trim produce before washing to reduce the risk of surface contamination.

**FOOD MUST REMAIN FULLY SUBMERGED** (at least 1 to 2 inches) under the brine while fermenting. If you don't own fermenting weights that fit inside your container, use a dinner plate or glass pie plate weighted down to keep food submerged.

**COVER** the fermentation container with a clean towel or cloth that keeps dust and particles out but allows air into the crock. Don't use plastic wrap or any other airtight cover; this will disrupt the fermenting process.

**A TEMPERATURE RANGE** of 70°F to 75°F is ideal for fermentation to occur within the recipes' recommended timings. At 60°F to 65°F, fermentation will take considerably longer. Avoid fermenting foods at temperatures higher than 75°F due to the risk of spoilage. After fermenting the food at room temperature for the recommended times, store it in the refrigerator to halt the process.

**ABOUT CROCKS**
It's important to select the proper size and type of container for fermentation. A general rule is to use a 1-gal. vessel for every 5 lb. of fresh vegetables. Use only food-safe ceramic, glass, or plastic containers with straight edges. Avoid using metal containers that might react with the acids in the foods.

## HOMEMADE SAUERKRAUT

**HANDS-ON TIME** 45 minutes
**STAND** 2 hours + 10 minutes
**FERMENT** 3 weeks

3  to 4 lb. green or red cabbage
1½  Tbsp. pickling salt (tip, p. 666)
1  Tbsp. sugar
4  tsp. pickling salt

1. Remove outer leaves from cabbage. Quarter cabbage heads lengthwise; remove cores. Using a mandoline, food processor, or large chef's knife, finely shred cabbage. Measure 2½ lb. shredded cabbage.
2. Place the 2½ lb. shredded cabbage in a large ceramic crock, glass container, or plastic food container that holds at least 1 gallon. Add the 1½ Tbsp. pickling salt and the sugar. Using very clean hands or tongs, toss cabbage with pickling salt and sugar. Let stand 10 minutes. Using a clean, heavy plate that fits just inside the container, press plate down on cabbage. Let stand at room temperature 2 to 24 hours, tossing cabbage and pressing plate down on cabbage every hour or until enough liquid is released to cover cabbage by at least 1 inch. (If the cabbage does not release enough liquid, you will need to add additional brine to the cabbage. Make a brine by combining water and pickling salt in a ratio of 1 cup water to 1 tsp. pickling salt; add just enough of this brine to cover the cabbage.)
3. Place a large resealable plastic bag filled with 1 qt. water plus the 4 tsp. pickling salt (or a clean 1-gal. jug full of water) on the plate to weight it down. Cover container with a clean dishcloth or loose-fitting lid. Place container in a cool place out of direct sunlight to ferment. At temperatures between 70°F and 75°F, fermentation will take 3 to 4 weeks; at 60°F to 65°F, fermentation will take 5 to 6 weeks.
4. Every 2 or 3 days, replace dishcloth with a clean dishcloth, skim off any scum that forms on surface of cabbage, and clean and replace the plate. If any discolored cabbage appears at the top, remove and discard it. If the water level gets too low, add enough brine to cover. It must be submerged completely in brine to ferment safely. The sauerkraut is ready when it has a slightly crunchy texture and pleasantly tangy flavor.
5. Transfer undrained sauerkraut to canning jars or airtight containers; seal and label. Store in the refrigerator up to 2 months.
**Makes 8 cups.**

**EACH ¼ CUP** 10 cal., 0 g fat, 0 mg chol., 338 mg sodium, 2 g carb., 1 g fiber, 2 g sugars, 0 g pro.

**THE WHITE STUFF**
Did a white film or residue appear on the surface of your sauerkraut or hot sauce while it was fermenting? No worries. What you're seeing are wild yeasts that tend to form at the higher end of the fermenting temperature range—and they are completely safe. Skim off what you can and continue with the recipe as directed. However, if furry, colorful mold appears on the surface, or if you detect an unpleasant odor, throw out the food and start over.

Combine the shredded cabbage with pickling salt and sugar, tossing and squeezing the cabbage with your hands to help it release liquid.

Pack the cabbage, along with its liquid, into a container and cover with a plate.

Press the cabbage down with a weight, allowing the liquid to rise above the cabbage and around the edges of the weight on the plate.

## KIMCHI

**HANDS-ON TIME** 20 minutes
**STAND** 4 hours + 10 minutes
**FERMENT** 2 days

1   medium head napa cabbage
3   Tbsp. kosher salt
½   cup coarsely shredded daikon
    or carrots
½   cup coarsely shredded carrot
¼   cup chopped green onions
2   Tbsp. fish sauce
1   to 2 Tbsp. Korean chili powder
    or flakes (gochugaru) (tip,
    *opposite*)
1   Tbsp. grated fresh ginger
2   cloves garlic, minced
1   tsp. sugar

**1.** Remove any wilted outer leaves
from cabbage. Core and chop
cabbage into 2-inch pieces.
Measure 12 cups cabbage pieces.
Toss cabbage with the 3 Tbsp.
kosher salt; place in a large
colander set over a bowl. Let stand
2 to 3 hours or until wilted.
**2.** In a large clean bowl combine
the remaining ingredients. Rinse
cabbage; drain well. Add cabbage
to daikon mixture; toss to combine.
Let stand 10 minutes.
**3.** Transfer cabbage mixture
to a large ceramic crock, glass
container, or plastic food
container. Using a clean, heavy
plate that fits just inside the
container, press plate down on
cabbage mixture. Let stand at
room temperature 2 to 24 hours
(5 to 24 hours if fermenting in the
refrigerator), tossing cabbage and
pressing plate down on cabbage
every hour or until enough liquid is
released to cover cabbage by at
least 1 inch. (If the cabbage does
not release enough liquid, you
will need to add additional brine
to the cabbage. Make a brine by
combining water and kosher salt in
a ratio of 1 cup water to 1 tsp. kosher
salt; add just enough of this brine to
cover the cabbage.)

**FERMENTED
WHOLE GRAIN
MUSTARD**

## FERMENTED WHOLE GRAIN MUSTARD

**HANDS-ON TIME** 10 minutes
**STAND** 26 hours
**CHILL** 3 days

>>

SALT for
fermentation
needs to be free
of additives such
as potassium,
iodine, and
anticaking
agents, which
could impede
the fermentation
process.

¾   cup cider vinegar
⅓   cup yellow mustard seeds
⅓   cup brown mustard seeds
1   tsp. fine sea salt
3   Tbsp. honey
2   cloves garlic, peeled
1   Tbsp. liquid whey*

**1.** In a medium bowl combine
vinegar, yellow and brown mustard
seeds, and salt. Cover and let stand
at room temperature 24 hours (the
seeds will absorb some of the liquid).
**2.** Place mustard seed mixture,
honey, garlic, and whey in a food
processor. Cover and process 1 to
2 minutes until a thick, chunky paste
forms. Spoon into a clean 2-cup
crock; cover tightly. Let stand at room
temperature 2 hours. Refrigerate
3 days to blend flavors before
serving. Store in the refrigerator up to
2 months. **Makes 1⅓ cups.**
**\*NOTE** For liquid whey, place
6 oz. (¾ cup) plain yogurt (do not
use Greek yogurt or yogurt that
contains gelatin) in a fine-mesh
sieve lined with 100%-cotton
cheesecloth or a coffee filter. Place
the sieve over a small bowl. Cover
and chill 24 hours. The liquid that
collects in the bowl is whey. Save
the yogurt to serve as a dip or with
desserts. (Or purchase liquid whey
from a health food store.)
**EACH 1 TSP.** *12 cal., 1 g fat (0 g sat. fat),
0 mg chol., 35 mg sodium, 1 g carb.,
0 g fiber, 1 g sugars, 0 g pro.*

**WHAT IS KIMCHI?** THIS SPICY FERMENTED CABBAGE MIX IS A KOREAN CONDIMENT THAT'S SPOONED OVER RICE, NOODLES, EGGS, AND STIR-FRIES.

KIMCHI

**4.** Place a large resealable plastic bag filled with 1 qt. water plus 4 tsp. kosher salt over the plate to weight it down. Cover container with a clean dishcloth.

**5.** To ferment at room temperature, set container in a cool place out of direct sunlight; let stand 2 to 3 days. To ferment in the refrigerator, chill 3 to 6 days. The kimchi is ready when it is bubbling.

**6.** Transfer kimchi to jars or airtight containers; seal and label. Store in the refrigerator up to 3 weeks. **Makes 4 cups.**

EACH ¼ CUP *15 cal., 0 g fat, 0 mg chol., 561 mg sodium, 3 g carb., 1 g fiber, 1 g sugars, 1 g pro.*

---

## GOCHUGARU
Korean chili powder is a traditional ingredient in authentic kimchi and is available in mild or hot varieties. Look for it in Asian or specialty food stores and online. Store the opened bag in the freezer.

---

## SRIRACHA-STYLE ASIAN CHILI SAUCE

**HANDS-ON TIME** 25 minutes
**FERMENT** 8 days
**COOK** 5 minutes

1½  lb. hot red chile peppers, such as Thai, stemmed and chopped (tip, *p. 22*)
¼  cup packed brown sugar
¼  cup water
1  Tbsp. kosher salt
5  cloves garlic, smashed and peeled
½  cup rice vinegar
1  tsp. fish sauce (optional)

**1.** In a food processor or blender combine chile peppers, brown sugar, the water, salt, and garlic. Process 3 minutes or until smooth.

**2.** Transfer mixture to a 2-qt. food-safe ceramic, glass, or plastic bowl or container. Cover with a clean dish towel or 100%-cotton cheesecloth. Place in a dark, dry place at room temperature and let stand 8 days to ferment, stirring once every day. After 2 to 3 days, you should notice bubbling in the mixture, showing that fermentation is occurring.

**3.** Return mixture to food processor or blender. Add vinegar. Cover and process until very smooth. Strain mixture through a fine-mesh sieve into a 3-qt. saucepan; discard solids.

**4.** Bring to boiling; reduce heat. Simmer, uncovered, 5 to 10 minutes or until slightly thickened, stirring frequently (the sauce will thicken a bit more as it cools). Remove from heat. If desired, stir in fish sauce. Cool to room temperature.

**5.** Transfer chili sauce to canning jars or airtight storage containers. Seal and store in the refrigerator up to 6 months. **Makes 1¾ cups.**

EACH 1 TSP. *7 cal., 0 g fat, 0 mg chol., 71 mg sodium, 1 g carb., 0 g fiber, 1 g sugars, 0 g pro.*

SRIRACHA-STYLE ASIAN CHILI SAUCE

FIRST RULE OF MAKING KOMBUCHA—EMBRACE THE SCOBY (SYMBIOTIC CULTURE OF BACTERIA AND YEAST). THE SCOBY STARTS AS A RESIDUE ON THE SURFACE OF SWEETENED GREEN OR BLACK TEA. IT GETS THICKER, GROWING TO FILL THE DIAMETER OF THE JAR, ALL THE WHILE WORKING ITS (GOOD) BACTERIAL MAGIC AS IT FERMENTS.

## A LITTLE HISTORY

Kombucha tea is thought to have originated in East Asia more than 2,000 years ago. It was introduced to Europe in the early 20th century; its popularity spread to the United States in the 1990s. Look for purchased kombucha in supermarkets (it's widely available). You'll need it to start your batch.

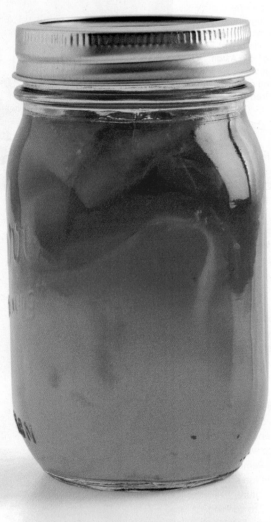

**SAFETY FIRST**
Altering ingredients, method, and/or timings of this tested recipe can compromise its safety.

**KEEP IT CLEAN**
Wash all containers and utensils that will be used to make Kombucha with hot, soapy water; rinse well. Scrub your hands and nails before handling the SCOBY.

**SCOBY DOS**
Cover the fermented mixture with clean cheesecloth or a paper towel to keep out dust, dirt, pests, and anything else that might disrupt fermentation.

**LOOK CLOSELY**
Fermenting involves a delicate balance of organisms. If your Kombucha or SCOBY looks moldy (furry) or has an off smell, discard the mixture and start over.

**TEMP TIP**
Kombucha fermenting works best in a temperature that is on the warmer side. Keep it between 70°F and 75°F.

**TO STORE SCOBY**
Place SCOBY in a clean jar in enough homemade or purchased kombucha to cover. Cover jar and store in the refrigerator up to 1 month.

## THE SCOBY

A SCOBY looks like a pancake and feels gelatinous. It can vary in texture and color but is usually creamy tan.

**TO MAKE SCOBY**
To make your own SCOBY, bring 4 cups water to boiling. In a large heatproof glass bowl or pitcher combine the boiling water and ½ cup sugar; stir to dissolve. Add 4 black tea bags. Let stand 1 hour. Remove tea bags. Stir in 3 cups water. Transfer to a clean 2- to 3-qt. jar. Stir in 1 cup purchased plain kombucha. Cover jar with 100%-cotton cheesecloth or paper towels and secure with a rubber band. Let stand in a dark place where the temperature is between 70°F and 75°F for 3 weeks. Remove SCOBY with clean hands; discard liquid. You can also purchase a SCOBY online (use reliable sources only).

**HEALTH CLAIMS** Kombucha tea drinkers claim its health benefits include promoting digestion, strengthening the immune system, and aiding in a variety of other ailments. Currently there are not enough scientific studies to support these claims, so the tea should not be used to treat any illness. Talk to a doctor if you are pregnant, nursing, or have any health concerns. As with many consumables, Kombucha should be enjoyed in moderation. Start by drinking small amounts and keep the total to about 8 oz. or less a day.

**PICK A BOTTLE**
Measure out and store prepared Kombucha in resealable glass bottles. The swing-top cap creates an airtight seal that ensures successful carbonation for maximum fizziness. Plus, they're reusable.

## KOMBUCHA

**HANDS-ON TIME** 20 minutes
**STAND** 1 hour
**FERMENT** 1 week

**THIS GLASS JAR is a USDA-approved 1-gallon container perfect for brewing Kombucha (without the lid).**

14  cups water
1   cup sugar
8   black tea bags
2   cups purchased plain kombucha
1   recipe SCOBY (opposite)

**1.** Bring 4 cups of the water to boiling. In an extra-large heatproof glass bowl or pitcher combine the boiling water and sugar; stir to dissolve. Add tea bags. Let stand 1 hour or until cool. Remove and discard tea bags. Add the remaining 10 cups water and the purchased kombucha. Transfer to a clean 1-gal. jar. Add SCOBY. Cover jar with paper towels and secure with a rubber band. Let stand in a dark place where temperature is between 70°F to 75°F for 1 week.
**2.** Remove SCOBY with clean hands and store (tip, *opposite*). If desired, reserve enough Kombucha (2 cups) to make another batch of Kombucha. If desired, strain remaining Kombucha through a sieve lined with 100%-cotton cheesecloth; transfer to clean bottles with swing-top seals, leaving a 2-inch headspace. Seal bottles. To carbonate, let stand in a dark place where temperature is between 70°F and 72°F for 2 to 3 days. Store in the refrigerator up to 1 month. **Makes 16 cups.**
**EACH 1 CUP** *53 cal., 0 g fat, 0 mg chol., 10 mg sodium, 14 g carb, 0 g fiber, 13 g sugars, 0 g pro.*

### GINGER KOMBUCHA
Prepare as directed through Step 1. Remove SCOBY. Add 1 oz. fresh ginger, peeled and thinly sliced, to the jar. Cover and chill 1 to 2 weeks. Remove and discard ginger. Continue with Step 2.

### ORANGE KOMBUCHA
Prepare as directed through Step 1. Remove SCOBY. Add 1 orange, peeled and thinly sliced, to the jar. Cover and chill 1 to 2 days. Remove and discard orange slices. Continue with Step 2.

# FREEZING

AS THE EASIEST OF ALL PRESERVING METHODS, FREEZING WORKS FOR A VARIETY OF FRUITS AND VEGETABLES FROM GARDENS AND FARMERS MARKETS. FOR BEST RESULTS, USE TOP-QUALITY, GARDEN-FRESH PRODUCE AND FOLLOW THESE GUIDELINES.

## FREEZING BASICS

**SELECT** fruits and vegetables that are at their peak of maturity. Hold produce in the refrigerator if it can't be frozen immediately. Rinse and drain small quantities through several changes of cold water. Take fruits and vegetables out of the water; do not let them soak. Prepare cleaned produce for freezing as specified *(opposite)*.

**BLANCH** vegetables (and fruits when directed) by partially cooking them in boiling water for specified time (tip, p. 673). This inactivates or slows enzymes that cause loss of flavor and color and toughen the food. Do not blanch in the microwave; it might not inactivate some enzymes. Timings on veggies vary.

**SPOON** cooled, drained food into freezer containers or bags, leaving the specified headspace (tip, p. 634). If using containers, wipe rims.

**SEAL** containers or bags according to the manufacturer's directions, pressing out as much air as possible. If necessary, use freezer tape around container lid edges for a tight seal.

**LABEL** each container or bag with its contents, amount, and date. Lay bags flat; add packages to the freezer in batches to make sure food freezes quickly. Leave space between packages so air can circulate around them. When frozen solid, the packages can be placed closer together.

## FREEZER CONTAINERS

**WHAT TO USE** When freezing foods, use containers and packing materials that are durable, easy to seal, resistant to cracking at low temperatures, and moisture- and vapor-resistant. Choose the right size container for your volume of food; wasted space can lead to oxidation and freezer burn. Remember that foods containing water expand when frozen, so leave enough headspace for expansion.

**PLASTIC CONTAINERS** Use rigid plastic containers with airtight lids designed for freezing.

**CANNING JARS** Select canning jars that are approved for freezing—this information is clearly noted on the jar packaging. Use only wide-mouth glass jars; jars with necks can crack more easily as contents expand. To allow for food expansion, do not fill jars above the 1-inch line.

**PLASTIC FREEZER BAG** Use bags designated for freezing, such as resealable bags and vacuum freezer bags. These are made of thicker material than regular plastic bags and are more resistant to moisture and oxygen. Remove as much air as possible from the bags.

# *FREEZING VEGETABLES*

Wash fresh vegetables with cool tap water. Scrub firm vegetables with a produce brush.

| VEGETABLE | PREP | FREEZING |
|---|---|---|
| **ASPARAGUS** | Allow 2½ to 4½ lb. per quart. Wash; scrape off scales. Break off woody bases where spears snap easily; wash again. Sort by thickness. Leave whole or cut into 1-inch lengths. | Blanch small spears 2 minutes, medium 3 minutes, and large 4 minutes (tip, p. 673). Cool quickly by plunging into ice water; drain. Fill containers, shaking to pack and leaving no headspace (tip, p. 634). |
| **BEANS** (GREEN, ITALIAN, SNAP, OR WAX) | Allow 1½ to 2½ lb. per quart. Wash; remove ends and strings. Leave whole or cut into 1-inch pieces. | Blanch 3 minutes (tip, p. 673). Cool by plunging into ice water; drain. Fill containers, leaving a ½-inch headspace (tip, p. 634). |
| **BEETS** | Allow 3 lb. (without tops) per quart. Trim off beet tops, leaving 1 inch of stem and roots, to reduce bleeding of color. Scrub well. | Cook unpeeled beets in boiling water until tender. (Allow 25 to 30 minutes for small beets; 45 to 50 minutes for medium beets.) Cool quickly in ice water; drain. Peel; remove stem and roots. Cut into slices or cubes. Fill containers, leaving a ½-inch headspace. |
| **CARROTS** | Use 1- to 1¼-inch-diameter carrots (larger carrots might be too fibrous). Allow 2 to 3 lb. per quart. Wash, trim, peel, and rinse. Leave tiny carrots whole; slice or dice the remainder. | Blanch tiny whole carrots 5 minutes and cut-up carrots 2 minutes (tip, p. 673). Cool quickly by plunging into ice water; drain. Pack tightly into containers, leaving a ½-inch headspace (tip, p. 634). |
| **CORN** | Allow 4 to 5 lb. per quart. Remove husks. Scrub with a vegetable brush to remove silks. Wash and drain. | Cover ears with boiling water. Boil 4 minutes. Cool quickly in ice water; drain. Cut corn from cobs at two-thirds depth of kernels; do not scrape. Fill containers, leaving a ½-inch headspace (tip, p. 634). |
| **PEAS** (ENGLISH OR GREEN) | Allow 2 to 2½ lb. per pt. Wash, shell, rinse, and drain. | Blanch 1½ minutes (tip, p. 673). Cool quickly in ice water; drain. Fill containers, shaking to pack and leaving a ½-inch headspace (tip, p. 634). |
| **PEPPERS** (CHILE) | Select firm chile peppers; wash. Halve large peppers. Remove stems, seeds, and membranes (tip, p. 22). Bake, cut sides down, on a foil-lined baking sheet in a 425°F oven 20 to 25 minutes or until skins are bubbly. Wrap in foil; let stand 15 minutes. Pull the skin off with a small knife. | Pack in freezer containers, leaving no headspace (tip, p. 634). |
| **PEPPERS** (SWEET) | Select firm sweet peppers (any color); wash. Remove stems, seeds, and membranes. Bake, cut sides down, on a foil-lined baking sheet in a 425°F oven 20 to 25 minutes or until skins are bubbly. Wrap in foil; let stand 15 minutes or until cool. Pull the skin off slowly using a small knife. | Quarter large pepper pieces or cut into strips. Fill containers, leaving a ½-inch headspace. Or spread peppers in a single layer on a baking sheet; freeze until firm. Fill container, shaking to pack and leaving no headspace (tip, p. 634). |

>>

**FROZEN VEGETABLES** are best used within 8 to 10 months. Cook vegetables from a frozen state, without thawing them first. Thaw fruits in their containers in the fridge.

# FREEZER CONFETTI CORN

**HANDS-ON TIME** 25 minutes
**FREEZE** 3 hours

½ cup butter, softened
2 Tbsp. chopped fresh chives
2 Tbsp. chopped fresh parsley
½ tsp. salt
½ tsp. black pepper
14 ears of corn, husks and silks removed
¾ cup finely chopped red sweet pepper
½ cup finely chopped sweet onion

**1.** In a small bowl combine the first five ingredients (through black pepper). Shape butter mixture into a 5-inch log. Wrap in waxed paper or plastic wrap. Freeze about 1 hour or until firm. Cut butter into eight slices. Place in a freezer container and freeze until needed.

**2.** Meanwhile, in an 8-qt. pot cook corn, covered, in enough boiling water to cover 3 minutes; drain. Plunge corn into two extra-large bowls of ice water. Let stand until chilled. Cut kernels from cobs; do not scrape (should have about 7 cups).

**3.** Line two 15×10-inch baking pans with parchment paper or foil. Spread corn kernels, sweet pepper, and onion in an even layer in the prepared pans. Freeze, loosely covered, about 2 hours or until nearly firm.

**4.** Divide vegetables evenly among four 1-qt. freezer bags. Add two slices frozen butter to each bag. Squeeze air from bags; seal and label. Freeze up to 6 months. **Makes 8 servings (½ cup each).**

**TO COOK** Transfer one portion frozen vegetables to a medium saucepan or skillet. Cook, covered, over medium heat 10 to 12 minutes or until butter is melted and vegetables are heated through, stirring occasionally.

**EACH SERVING** *114 cal., 7 g fat (4 g sat. fat), 15 mg chol., 134 mg sodium, 14 g carb., 2 g fiber, 5 g sugars, 2 g pro.*

Place corn, a few cobs at a time, in a large pot of boiling water; return to boiling. Boil 4 minutes. Remove and plunge into a bowl of ice water.

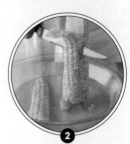

When corn is cool, remove from ice water and cut kernels from cob using a downward motion with a sharp knife.

Spoon corn into freezer-safe bags or containers. Squeeze air from bags and seal. Label each container with contents, amount, and date.

# FREEZE-YOUR-OWN VEGETABLE BLEND

**HANDS-ON TIME** 45 minutes
**FREEZE** 2 hours

½ cup butter, softened
Seasoning Mix
¼ tsp. salt
2 ears of corn, husks and silks removed
2 cups broccoli and/or cauliflower florets
3 medium carrots, bias-sliced ¼ inch thick
1½ cups yellow summer squash and/or zucchini, bias-sliced ½ inch thick
1 large sweet pepper, seeded and cut into bite-size strips
1 small sweet onion, cut into thin wedges

**1.** In a medium bowl stir together butter, Seasoning Mix, and salt. Shape butter mixture into a 5-inch log. Wrap in waxed paper or plastic wrap. Freeze about 1 hour or until firm. Cut butter into eight slices. Place in a freezer container and freeze until needed.

**2.** Meanwhile, in a 6-qt. pot cook corn, covered, in enough boiling water to cover 1 minute. Add broccoli, carrots, and squash. Cook, covered, 2 minutes; drain. Plunge vegetables into an extra-large bowl filled with ice water. Let stand until chilled. Remove corn cobs. Cut kernels from cobs; do not scrape. Using a slotted spoon, transfer the remaining vegetables to a paper towel-lined tray and pat dry.

**3.** Line a 15×10-inch baking pan with parchment paper or foil. Spread corn kernels, drained vegetables, sweet pepper, and onion in an even layer in the prepared pan. Freeze, loosely covered, about 1 hour or until nearly firm.

**4.** Divide vegetables evenly among four 1-qt. freezer bags. Add two slices frozen butter mixture to each bag. Squeeze air from bags. Seal and label. Freeze up to 6 months.

**Makes 12 servings (½ cup each).**
**TO COOK** Transfer one portion frozen vegetables to a 2-qt. saucepan or a 10-inch skillet. Cook, covered, over medium heat 5 to 10 minutes or until butter is melted and vegetables are heated through, stirring occasionally. Season to taste with salt and black pepper.

**EACH SERVING** *106 cal., 8 g fat (5 g sat. fat), 20 mg chol., 136 mg sodium, 8 g carb., 2 g fiber, 4 g sugars, 2 g pro.*

**FOR SAUCY VEGETABLES** Stir 2 Tbsp. all-purpose flour into a reheated portion of vegetable mixture. Stir in 1 cup reduced-sodium chicken broth. Cook and stir until thickened and bubbly. Cook and stir 1 minute more. If desired, stir in 2 cups bite-size strips of cooked chicken breast, beef sirloin steak, or pork loin chops; or 2 cups peeled, cooked shrimp. Season to taste with salt and black pepper.

## SEASONING MIX

**ASIAN** Stir together 1 Tbsp. grated fresh ginger; 2 cloves garlic, minced; and 3 drops toasted sesame oil.

**SOUTHWESTERN** Stir together 1 tsp. ground ancho chile pepper; ½ tsp. dried oregano, crushed; and ½ tsp. lime zest.

**ITALIAN** Stir together 2 cloves garlic, minced, and ½ tsp. dried Italian seasoning, crushed.

**HERB AND CITRUS** Stir together 1 Tbsp. lemon zest; ½ tsp. dried dill; ½ tsp. dried basil, crushed; and ¼ tsp. coarsely ground black pepper.

**WHAT IS BLANCHING?** Blanching is a heat-and-cool process. Fill a large pot with water, using 1 gal. of water per 1 lb. of prepared food. Heat to boiling. Add prepared food to the boiling water (or place it in a wire basket and lower it into the water); cover. Start timing immediately. Cook over high heat for the time specified in the chart (p. 671). Fill a large clean container with ice water. When blanching time is complete, use a slotted spoon to remove the food from the boiling water. Immediately plunge food into the ice water. Chill for the same amount of time it was boiled; drain. (For high-altitude adjustment, see p. 634.)

## FRESH TOMATO-MEAT SAUCE

**HANDS-ON TIME** 20 minutes
**COOK** 20 minutes

1   lb. lean ground beef or uncooked ground turkey
2   oz. pancetta, chopped
⅓   cup finely chopped onion
4   cloves garlic, minced
2   lb. fresh roma tomatoes, peeled (tip, p. 643), seeded, and chopped (about 3 cups)
½   cup dry red wine
1   to 2 tsp. balsamic vinegar
½   tsp. salt
½   tsp. black pepper
½   cup chopped fresh basil

**1.** In a 3-qt. saucepan cook ground meat and pancetta over medium heat until meat is browned. Drain fat. Stir in onion and garlic; cook 3 to 5 minutes more or until onion is tender, stirring occasionally.
**2.** Stir in next five ingredients (through pepper). Bring to boiling; reduce heat. Simmer, uncovered, 20 to 25 minutes or until sauce is slightly thickened, stirring occasionally. Stir in basil.
**3.** Cool slightly and transfer to freezer containers. Seal and freeze up to 3 months. (Or store in the refrigerator up to 3 days.) **Makes 7 servings (½ cup each).**
**TO COOK** Thaw sauce in the refrigerator overnight. Transfer to a 2-qt. saucepan. Cook over medium-low heat until simmering, stirring occasionally.

**EACH SERVING** *177 cal., 8 g fat (3 g sat. fat), 44 mg chol., 263 mg sodium, 7 g carb., 2 g fiber, 4 g sugars, 16 g pro.*

## *FREEZING TOMATOES*

Allow 2½ to 3½ lb. unblemished tomatoes per quart.

| CUT | PREP | FREEZING |
| --- | --- | --- |
| **CRUSHED** | Wash and peel tomatoes (tip, p. 643). Cut into quarters; add enough to a pan to cover bottom. Lightly crush with a spoon. Heat and stir until boiling. Slowly add remaining pieces, stirring constantly. Simmer 5 minutes. | Set pan of tomatoes in ice water to cool. Fill containers (tip, p. 670), leaving a 1-inch headspace. If desired, add ¼ to ½ tsp. salt for pints or ½ to 1 tsp. salt for quarts. |
| **WHOLE OR HALVED** (NO ADDED LIQUID) | Wash and peel tomatoes (tip, p. 643); halve if desired. | Fill freezer containers, pressing to fill spaces with juice, leaving a 1-inch headspace. If desired, add ¼ to ½ tsp. salt for pints or ½ to 1 tsp. salt for quarts. |
| **WHOLE OR HALVED** (WATER-PACK) | Wash and peel tomatoes (tip, p. 643); halve if desired. Heat all of the tomatoes in a saucepan with enough water to cover; simmer 5 minutes. | Set pan of tomatoes in cold water to cool. Fill containers with tomatoes and cooking liquid, leaving a 1-inch headspace. If desired, add ¼ to ½ tsp. salt for pints or ½ to 1 tsp. salt for quarts. |

## *FREEZING CRUSHED TOMATOES*

Peel tomatoes as directed on *p. 643.* Cut the peeled tomatoes into quarters. Place a single layer of tomatoes in a large pot. Using a wooden spoon, lightly crush the tomatoes.

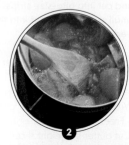

Add the remaining tomato pieces. Bring to boiling over medium heat, stirring constantly with the wooden spoon. Reduce heat to low and simmer 5 minutes.

Fill freezer containers with hot tomatoes, leaving a 1-inch headspace.

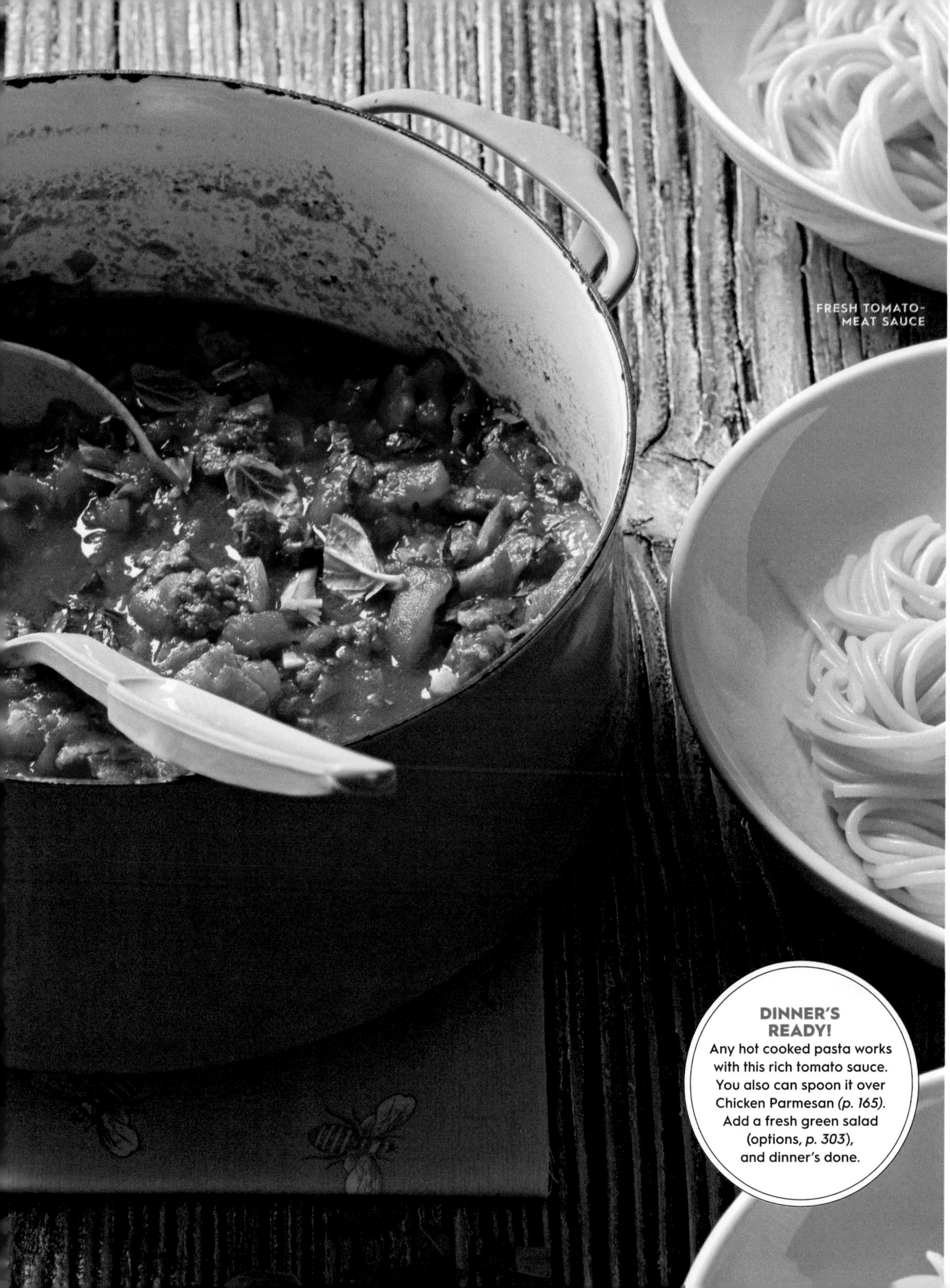

FRESH TOMATO-MEAT SAUCE

**DINNER'S READY!**

Any hot cooked pasta works with this rich tomato sauce. You also can spoon it over Chicken Parmesan *(p. 165)*. Add a fresh green salad (options, *p. 303*), and dinner's done.

## WAYS TO FREEZE FRUIT

**UNSWEETENED (DRY) PACK** does not require sugar or liquid to be added to the fruit; simply pack fruit in freezer jars or containers. This works well for small whole fruit, such as berries. (Or freeze berries in a single layer on a parchment-lined sheet pan; transfer to a resealable freezer bag.)

**WATER-PACK** has water covering the fruit. (Do not use glass jars for this method.) Maintain the recommended headspace. Unsweetened fruit juice also can be used.

**SUGAR-PACK** involves layering fruit with sugar. To do this, place a small amount of fruit in the container and sprinkle lightly with sugar; repeat layering. Cover; let stand about 15 minutes or until juicy. Seal container.

**SYRUP-PACK** has syrup (syrups, *p. 656*) covering the fruit. Select the syrup that best suits the fruit and your taste. Heavier syrups are used with sour fruits; lighter syrups are recommended for mild fruits.

**CHECK HEADSPACE** while filling containers. When using unsweetened pack, leave a ½-inch headspace (tip, *p. 634*) unless otherwise directed. When using water, sugar, or syrup, pack in freezer containers with wide tops; measure a ½-inch headspace for pints and a 1-inch for quarts.

## FREEZER BERRY PIE FILLING

**HANDS-ON TIME** 20 minutes

1   cup sugar
2   Tbsp. quick-cooking tapioca (info, *p. 614*)
1   Tbsp. cornstarch
4   cups fresh raspberries, blueberries, blackberries, and/or chopped strawberries
2   Tbsp. lemon juice

**1.** In a large bowl stir together sugar, tapioca, and cornstarch. Gently stir in berries and lemon juice.
**2.** Transfer berry mixture to a 1-gal. freezer bag. Squeeze air from bag; seal and label. Freeze up to 3 months. To use, thaw in the refrigerator overnight. **Makes 1 pie (8 servings).**
**EACH SERVING** *144 cal., 0 g fat, 0 mg chol., 1 mg sodium, 36 g carb., 3 g fiber, 29 g sugars, 1 g pro.*

## DOUBLE-CRUST BERRY PIE

Preheat oven to 375°F. Let one 14.1-oz. pkg. (2 crusts) rolled refrigerated unbaked piecrust stand according to package directions (or prepare Pastry for Double-Crust Pie, *p. 610*). Unroll one piecrust and fit into a 9-inch pie plate. Transfer thawed Freezer Berry Pie Filling to pastry-lined pie plate. Trim pastry even with pie plate rim. Place the remaining piecrust on filling; trim pastry to ½ inch beyond edge of plate. Fold top pastry edge under bottom pastry. Crimp edge. If desired, brush top pastry with milk and sprinkle with sugar. To prevent overbrowning, cover edge of pie with foil. Place a foil-lined baking sheet on the rack below pie in the oven. Bake 30 minutes. Remove foil. Bake 35 to 40 minutes more or until filling is bubbly. Cool completely on a wire rack. Makes 8 servings.

## BRANDIED STRAWBERRY FREEZER JAM

**HANDS-ON TIME** 25 minutes
**STAND** 30 minutes

8 cups strawberries
1⅔ cups sugar
5 Tbsp. instant powdered fruit pectin (not regular pectin)
3 Tbsp. brandy
½ tsp. lemon zest

**1.** In a large bowl crush 1 cup of the strawberries with a potato masher. Continue adding berries and crushing until you have 4 cups crushed berries. In a small bowl stir together sugar and pectin. Add to the strawberries; stir in brandy and zest. Stir 3 minutes.
**2.** Ladle jam into five clean half-pint freezer containers, leaving a ½-inch headspace. Seal and label. Let stand at room temperature 30 minutes. Store in the freezer up to 1 year or in the refrigerator up to 3 weeks. **Makes 5 half-pints.**
**EACH 1 TBSP.** *26 cal., 0 g fat, 0 mg chol., 8 mg sodium, 6 g carb., 0 g fiber, 5 g sugars, 0 g pro.*

»

**INSTANT PECTIN** gives freezer jams the best flavor because the formulation requires less sugar to gel than other pectin (don't substitute other pectin types here). Look for instant pectin where canning supplies are sold or online. Note that freezer jam has a softer set than canned jam.

## BLUEBERRY-RHUBARB FREEZER JAM

**HANDS-ON TIME** 15 minutes
**COOK** 10 minutes
**COOL** 2 hours
**STAND** 30 minutes

2 cups fresh blueberries
2 cups chopped fresh or frozen rhubarb
1 large Granny Smith or other tart apple, peeled, cored, and coarsely shredded (1 cup)
1 cup honey
1 Tbsp. lemon juice

**1.** In a 2-qt. saucepan combine first four ingredients (through honey). Bring to boiling over medium-high heat, stirring occasionally; reduce heat. Simmer, uncovered, 10 to 15 minutes or until slightly thickened (mixture will thicken as it cools); stir mixture occasionally while cooking, using a wooden spoon to gently crush the blueberries against the side of the saucepan.
**2.** Stir in lemon juice. Remove saucepan from heat; cool about 2 hours or until room temperature.
**3.** Ladle jam into three clean half-pint freezer containers, leaving a ½-inch headspace. Seal and label. Let stand at room temperature 30 minutes before storing. Store in the freezer up to 1 year or in the refrigerator up to 3 weeks. **Makes 3 half-pints.**
**EACH 1 TBSP.** *28 cal., 0 g fat, 0 mg chol., 1 mg sodium, 8 g carb., 0 g fiber, 7 g sugars, 0 g pro.*

### QUICK CHECK
To see if jam is cooked enough, remove it from heat. Drop 1 tsp. of jam onto a plate. Place it in the freezer 1 to 2 minutes. The jam should be slightly set with no running juices. If not set, continue cooking.

BRANDIED STRAWBERRY FREEZER JAM

BLUEBERRY-RHUBARB FREEZER JAM

## FREEZING APPLES, PEARS & STONE FRUIT

Wash fresh fruits with cool tap water, but do not soak them; drain.

| FRUIT | PREP | FREEZING |
|---|---|---|
| **APPLES & PEARS** | Allow 2 to 3 lb. per quart. For apples, select varieties that are crisp, not mealy, in texture. Peel and core; halve, quarter, or slice. Dip into ascorbic-acid color-keeper solution (tip, *below*); drain. | Use a syrup-, sugar-, or unsweetened pack (tip, p. 676), leaving the recommended headspace (tip, p. 634). |
| **PEACHES & NECTARINES** | Allow 2 to 3 lb. per quart. Dunk peaches in boiling water (as with tomatoes; photos, p. 643) to loosen skins to peel. Peeling nectarines is not necessary. Halve and pit. If desired, slice. Treat with ascorbic-acid color-keeper solution (tip, *below*); drain. | Use a syrup-, sugar-, or water-pack (tip, p. 676), leaving the recommended headspace (tip, p. 634). |

## FREEZING BERRIES, CHERRIES & RHUBARB

Wash fresh fruits with cool tap water, but do not soak them; drain.

| FRUIT | PREP | FREEZING |
|---|---|---|
| **BERRIES** | Allow 1 to 3 lb. per quart. Berries that freeze well include blackberries, blueberries, boysenberries, currants, elderberries, gooseberries, huckleberries, loganberries, mulberries, raspberries, and strawberries. | Slice strawberries if desired. Use a syrup-, sugar-, or unsweetened pack (tip, p. 676), leaving the recommended headspace (tip, p. 634). |
| **CHERRIES** | Allow 2 to 3 lb. per quart. If desired, treat with ascorbic-acid color-keeper solution (tip, *below*); drain. If unpitted, prick skin on opposite sides to prevent splitting. | Use a syrup-, sugar-, or unsweetened pack (tip, p. 676), leaving the recommended headspace (tip, p. 634). |
| **RHUBARB** | Allow 1½ lb. per quart. Discard leaves and woody ends. Cut into ½- to 1-inch pieces. | Blanch 1 minute (tip, p. 673); cool quickly and drain. Use a syrup- or unsweetened pack (tip, p. 676) or use a sugar-pack of ½ cup sugar to each 3 cups fruit, leaving the recommended headspace (tip, p. 634). |

**WHAT IS ASCORBIC-ACID COLOR-KEEPER?** The main ingredient of this product is vitamin C. It is marketed under different names (such as Fruit-Fresh). It prevents certain fruits—like apple slices—from oxidizing and turning brown during preserving. Look for it with canning supplies and online. Follow package directions for use.

# INDEX

# COOKING AT HIGH ALTITUDES

ALTHOUGH THERE IS NO SIMPLE FORMULA FOR CONVERTING ALL RECIPES FOR HIGH-ALTITUDE CONDITIONS, FOLLOW THESE ADJUSTMENTS IF YOU LIVE MORE THAN 1,000 FEET ABOVE SEA LEVEL.

## GENERAL HIGH-ALTITUDE ISSUES

Higher than 3,000 feet above sea level:

**WATER BOILS** at lower temperatures, causing moisture to evaporate more quickly. This can cause food to dry out during cooking and baking.

**BECAUSE OF A LOWER BOILING POINT,** foods cooked in steam or boiling liquids take longer to cook.

**LOWER AIR PRESSURE** may cause baked goods that use yeast, baking powder, baking soda, egg whites, or steam to rise excessively, then fall.

## COOKING ABOVE 6,000 FEET

Cooking at altitudes higher than 6,000 feet above sea level poses further challenges because the dry air found at such elevations influences cooking. Call your local United States Department of Agriculture Extension Service Office for advice.

## SUGGESTIONS FOR BAKING

**FOR CAKES LEAVENED BY AIR,** such as angel food, beat the egg whites only to soft peaks; otherwise, the batter may expand too much.

**FOR CAKES MADE WITH SHORTENING,** you may want to decrease the baking powder (start by decreasing it by 1/8 tsp. per tsp. called for); decrease the sugar (start by decreasing by about 1 Tbsp. for each cup called for); and increase the liquid (start by increasing it 1 to 2 tablespoons for each cup called for). These estimates are based on an altitude of 3,000 feet above sea level—at higher altitudes you may need to alter these measures proportionally. You can also try increasing the baking temperature by 15°F to 25°F to help set the batter.

**WHEN MAKING A RICH CAKE,** reduce the shortening by 1 to 2 Tbsp. per cup and add 1 egg (for a 2-layer cake) to prevent cake from falling.

**COOKIES** generally yield acceptable results, but if you're not satisfied, try slightly increasing baking temperature; slightly decreasing the baking powder or soda, fat, and/or sugar; and/or slightly increasing the liquid ingredients and flour.

**MUFFINLIKE QUICK BREADS AND BISCUITS** generally need little adjustment, but if you find that these goods develop a bitter flavor, decrease the baking soda or powder slightly. Because cakelike quick breads are more delicate, you may need to follow guidelines for cakes.

**YEAST BREADS** will rise more quickly at high altitudes. Allow unshaped dough to rise only until double in size, then punch the dough down. Repeat this rising step once more before shaping dough. Flour tends to be drier at high altitudes and sometimes absorbs more liquid. If your yeast dough seems dry, add more liquid and reduce the amount of flour the next time you make the recipe.

**LARGE CUTS OF MEAT** may take longer to cook. Be sure to use a meat thermometer to determine proper doneness.

## SUGGESTIONS FOR RANGE-TOP COOKING

**CANDY MAKING** Rapid evaporation caused by cooking at high altitudes can cause candies to cook down more quickly. Therefore, decrease the final cooking temperature by the difference in boiling-water temperature at your altitude and that of sea level (212°F). This is an approximate decrease of 2°F for every increase of 1,000 feet in elevation above sea level.

**CANNING & FREEZING FOODS** When canning at high altitudes, adjustments in processing time or pressure are needed to guard against contamination; when freezing, an adjustment in the blanching time is needed (tip, *p. 634*).

**DEEP-FAT FRYING** At high altitudes, deep-fried foods can overbrown but remain underdone inside. While foods vary, a rough guideline is to lower the temperature of the fat about 3°F for every 1,000 feet in elevation above sea level.

---

### MORE INFO

For more information on cooking at high altitudes, contact your county extension office or visit the Colorado State University extension services at *extension.colostate.edu* and search for "High Altitude Food Preparation."

# METRIC INFORMATION

## OVEN TEMPERATURE EQUIVALENTS

| FAHRENHEIT SETTING | CELSIUS SETTING |
|---|---|
| 300°F | 150°C |
| 325°F | 160°C |
| 350°F | 180°C |
| 375°F | 190°C |
| 400°F | 200°C |
| 425°F | 220°C |
| 450°F | 230°C |
| 475°F | 240°C |
| 500°F | 260°C |
| Broil | Broil |

*For convection or forced air ovens (gas or electric), lower the temperature setting 25°F/10°C when cooking at all heat levels.

## PRODUCT DIFFERENCES

Most of the ingredients called for in the recipes in this book are available in most countries. However, some are known by different names. Here are some common American ingredients and their possible counterparts:

**SUGAR** (white) is granulated,fine granulated, or castor sugar.

**POWDERED SUGAR** is icing sugar.

**ALL-PURPOSE FLOUR** is enriched, bleached or unbleached white household flour. When self-rising flour is used in place of all-purpose flour in a recipe that calls for leavening, omit the leavening agent (baking soda or baking powder) and salt.

**LIGHT-COLOR CORN SYRUP** is golden syrup.

**CORNSTARCH** is cornflour.

**BAKING SODA** is bicarbonate of soda.

**VANILLA OR VANILLA EXTRACT** is vanilla essence.

**GREEN, RED, OR YELLOW SWEET PEPPERS** are capsicums or bell peppers.

**GOLDEN RAISINS** are sultanas.

**SHORTENING** is solid vegetable oil (substitute Copha or lard).

## APPROXIMATE STANDARD METRIC EQUIVALENTS

| MEASUREMENT | OUNCES | METRIC |
|---|---|---|
| ⅛ tsp. | | 0.5 ml |
| ¼ tsp. | | 1 ml |
| ½ tsp. | | 2.5 ml |
| 1 tsp. | | 5 ml |
| 1 Tbsp. | | 15 ml |
| 2 Tbsp. | 1 fl. oz. | 30 ml |
| ¼ cup | 2 fl. oz. | 60 ml |
| ⅓ cup | 3 fl. oz. | 80 ml |
| ½ cup | 4 fl. oz. | 120 ml |
| ⅔ cup | 5 fl. oz. | 160 ml |
| ¾ cup | 6 fl. oz. | 180 ml |
| 1 cup | 8 fl. oz. | 240 ml |
| 2 cups | 16 fl. oz. (1 pt.) | 480 ml |
| 1 qt. | 64 fl. oz. (2 pt.) | 0.95 L |

## MEASUREMENT ABBREVIATIONS

| MEASUREMENT | ABBREVIATIONS |
|---|---|
| fluid ounce | fl. oz. |
| gallon | gal. |
| gram | g |
| liter | L |
| milliliter | ml |
| ounce | oz. |
| package | pkg. |
| pint | pt. |

## COMMON WEIGHT EQUIVALENTS

| IMPERIAL / U.S. | METRIC |
|---|---|
| ½ ounce | 14.18 g |
| 1 ounce | 28.35 g |
| 4 ounces (¼ pound) | 113.4 g |
| 8 ounces (½ pound) | 226.8 g |
| 16 ounces (1 pound) | 453.6 g |
| 1¼ pounds | 567 g |
| 1½ pounds | 680.4 g |
| 2 pounds | 907.2 g |

## CONVERTING TO METRIC

| | |
|---|---|
| centimeters to inches | divide centimeters by 2.54 |
| cups to liters | multiply cups by 0.236 |
| cups to milliliters | multiply cups by 236.59 |
| gallons to liters | multiply gallons by 3.785 |
| grams to ounces | divide grams by 28.35 |
| inches to centimeters | multiply inches by 2.54 |
| kilograms to pounds | divide kilograms by 0.454 |
| liters to cups | divide liters by 0.236 |
| liters to gallons | divide liters by 3.785 |
| liters to pints | divide liters by 0.473 |
| liters to quarts | divide liters by 0.946 |
| milliliters to cups | divide milliliters by 236.59 |
| milliliters to fluid ounces | divide milliliters by 29.57 |
| milliliters to tablespoons | divide milliliters by 14.79 |
| milliliters to teaspoons | divide milliliters by 4.93 |
| ounces to grams | multiply ounces by 28.35 |
| ounces to milliliters | multiply ounces by 29.57 |
| pints to liters | multiply pints by 0.473 |
| pounds to kilograms | multiply pounds by 0.454 |
| quarts to liters | multiply quarts by 0.946 |
| tablespoons to milliliters | multiply tablespoons by 14.79 |
| teaspoons to milliliters | multiply teaspoons by 4.93 |

# TROUBLESHOOTING GUIDE

If something seems a little off with a baked item, take a look at this chart to see what might have gone wrong and what you can do to prevent it from happening again.

## CAKES

| PROBLEM | POSSIBLE CAUSES |
|---|---|
| Cake has coarse texture. | • Excess baking soda<br>• Too little liquid<br>• Butter and sugar not thoroughly blended |
| Cake sticks to pan. | • Insufficient greasing<br>• Cake removed from pan too quickly<br>• Cake cooled in pan too long |
| Cake is dry. | • Excess flour or baking powder<br>• Too little shortening, butter, or sugar<br>• Oven too hot or cake baked too long |
| Cake is heavy/dense. | • Too little baking powder<br>• Too many eggs<br>• Batter overmixed |
| Cake sinks in middle. | • Pan is too small<br>• Too much liquid<br>• Opening oven or moving pans during baking<br>• Oven temperature too low or cake not baked long enough |

## YEAST BREADS

| PROBLEM | POSSIBLE CAUSES |
|---|---|
| Loaf did not rise enough before baking. | • Expired yeast<br>• Liquid too hot<br>• Not enough sugar<br>• Environment too cool or drafty<br>• Dough not kneaded enough |
| Loaf did not rise enough during baking. | • Oven temperature too low<br>• Dough raised too much before baking |
| Crust did not brown. | • Oven temperature too low<br>• Not enough sugar in dough |
| Bread is dense on bottom. | • Oven temperature too high |
| Bread collapsed in oven. | • Dough raised too much before baking |

## COOKIES

| PROBLEM | POSSIBLE CAUSES |
|---|---|
| Cookies are tough and hard. | • Too much flour<br>• Overmixed dough |
| Cookies are baked unevenly. | • Misshapen dough balls<br>• Cookie sheet with raised/high edges used |
| Cookies are too brown on the bottom. | • Dark-color cookie sheet |
| Cookies spread too much. | • Unnecessary greasing of cookie sheet<br>• Dough placed on warm cookie sheet<br>• Oven temperature too low<br>• Too much sugar<br>• Wrong fat used |
| Cookies are burned. | • Baked too long<br>• Left on baking sheet too long |

## QUICK BREADS

| PROBLEM | POSSIBLE CAUSES |
|---|---|
| Bread is dense. | • Not baked long enough<br>• Not enough liquid<br>• Leavener expired |
| Bread is tough. | • Too much liquid<br>• Not enough liquid<br>• Too much flour |
| Muffins have tunnels. | • Batter overmixed<br>• Not enough liquid<br>• Too much flour<br>• Overbaked |

# FRUIT & VEGETABLE MEASURING EQUIVALENTS

| FOOD | BEGINNING SIZE OR AMOUNT | YIELD AND CUT |
|---|---|---|
| Apple | 1 medium (6 oz.) | 1⅓ cups sliced or 1 cup chopped |
| Apricots | 1 lb. (8 to 12 medium) | 2½ cups sliced or chopped |
| Asparagus | 1 lb. (20 spears) | 2 cups 1-inch pieces |
| Avocado | 1 medium (7 oz.) | ¾ cup cubed or ½ cup mashed |
| Banana | 1 medium (6 oz.) | ½ cup mashed or ¾ cup sliced |
| Beans, green | 1 lb. | 3 to 3½ cups 1-inch pieces |
| Beet | 1 medium (6 oz.) | ¾ cup peeled and grated |
| Blueberries | 1 lb. | 3 cups |
| Broccoli | 1 lb. | 3½ cups florets |
| Cabbage | 1 medium head (2 lb.) | 10 cups shredded or chopped |
| Carrot | 1 medium (2 oz.) | ½ cup sliced, chopped, julienned, or finely shredded |
| Cauliflower | 1 head (1½ lb.) | 5 cups florets or 4 cups rice |
| Celery | 1 stalk (1 oz.) | ½ cup sliced or chopped |
| Cherries | 1 lb. | 3 cups whole or 2½ cups halved |
| Cranberries | 1 lb. | 4 cups |
| Cucumber | 1 medium (10 oz.). | 2½ cups sliced |
| Eggplant | 1 medium (1 lb.) | 6 cups cubed |
| Fennel | 1 medium (1 lb.) | 3 cups chopped |
| Garlic | 1 medium clove | 1 tsp. minced |
| Grapes | 1 lb. | 2½ cups |
| Greens, cooking | 12 oz. | 12 cups torn |
| Greens, salad (see p. 302) | | |
| Kale | 1 bunch (10 oz.) | 8 cups chopped |
| Leek | 1 medium (8 oz.) | 1 cup chopped |
| Lemon | 1 medium | 2 tsp. finely shredded zest (1 tsp. packed) or 3 Tbsp. juice |

| FOOD | BEGINNING SIZE OR AMOUNT | YIELD AND CUT |
|---|---|---|
| Lime | 1 medium | 1½ tsp. finely shredded zest (¾ tsp. packed) or 2 Tbsp. juice |
| Mango | 1 medium (12 oz.) | 1 cups cubed |
| Melon (cantaloupe, honeydew) | 1 medium (2½ lb.) | 6 cups cubed or 5½ cups balls |
| Mushrooms | 8 oz. | 3 cups sliced or chopped |
| Nectarine | 1 medium (6 oz.) | 1 cup sliced or chopped |
| Onion | 1 medium (6 oz.) | 1 cup chopped |
| Onion, green | 1 medium | 2 Tbsp. sliced |
| Orange | 1 large (10 oz.) | 1 Tbsp. finely shredded zest (1½ tsp. packed) or ⅓ cup juice or ⅓ cup sections |
| Papaya | 1 medium (1 lb.) | 1¼ cups sliced |
| Parsnip | 1 medium | ½ to ¾ cup sliced or chopped |
| Peach | 1 medium | 1 cup sliced or chopped |
| Pear | 1 medium (8 oz.) | 1½ cups chopped |
| Pepper, sweet | 1 medium | 1¼ cups strips or 1 cup chopped |
| Pineapple | 1 medium (4 lb.) | 4½ cups peeled and cubed |
| Plum | 1 medium (4 oz.) | ½ cup sliced |
| Potatoes | 1 lb. | 3 cups cubed (peeled) |
| Potatoes, sweet | 1 medium (8 oz.) | 1½ cups peeled and cubed |
| Raspberries | 1 lb. | 4½ cups |
| Rhubarb | 1 lb. | 4 cups sliced |
| Shallot | 1 medium | 2 Tbsp. finely chopped |
| Squash, summer (yellow, zucchini) | 1 medium (8 oz.) | 2 cups sliced or 3 cups zoodles |
| Squash, winter (acorn, butternut) | 2 lb. | 6 cups cubed |
| Strawberries | 1 pt. (about 1 lb.) | 3 cups whole or sliced |
| Tomato | 1 medium (6 oz.) | 1 cup chopped |

**1 GAL. =**
4 qt.
8 pt.
16 cups
128 fl. oz.
3.8 L

**1 QT. =**
2 pt.
4 cups
32 fl. oz.
0.95 L

**1 PT. =**
2 cups
16 fl. oz.
480 ml

**1 CUP =**
8 fl. oz.
240 ml
16 Tbsp.

**3/4 CUP =**
6 fl. oz.
180 ml
12 Tbsp.

**1/2 CUP =**
4 fl. oz.
120 ml
8 Tbsp.

**1/3 CUP =**
3 fl. oz.
80 ml
5 Tbsp.
+ 1 tsp.

**1/4 CUP =**
4 Tbsp.
12 tsp.
2 fl. oz.
60 ml

**1 TBSP. =**
3 tsp.
½ fl. oz.
15 ml

## *INFORMAL TABLE SETTING*

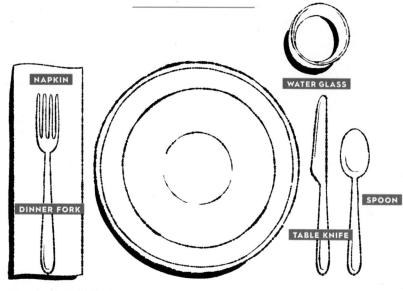

WATER GLASS

NAPKIN

DINNER FORK

TABLE KNIFE

SPOON

## *FORMAL TABLE SETTING*

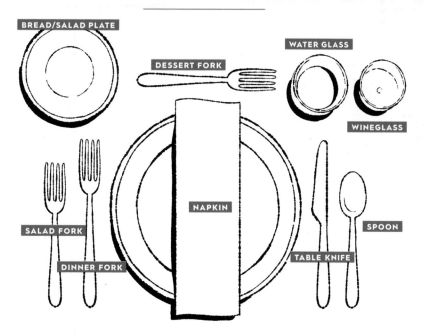

BREAD/SALAD PLATE

DESSERT FORK

WATER GLASS

WINEGLASS

NAPKIN

SALAD FORK

DINNER FORK

TABLE KNIFE

SPOON